OPPRESSION, PR...
AND RESISTANC...

THEORETICAL PERSPECTIVES ON RACISM, SEXISM, AND HETEROSEXISM

LISA HELDKE and PEG O'CONNOR

Mc
Graw
Hill

Boston Burr Ridge, IL Dubuque, IA Madison, WI New York
San Francisco St. Louis Bangkok Bogotá Caracas Kuala Lumpur
Lisbon London Madrid Mexico City Milan Montreal New Delhi
Santiago Seoul Singapore Sydney Taipei Toronto

Higher Education

OPPRESSION, PRIVILEGE, AND RESISTANCE

Published by McGraw-Hill, a business unit of The McGraw-Hill Companies, Inc., 1221 Avenue of the Americas, New York, NY 10020.

This book is printed on acid-free paper.

2 3 4 5 6 7 8 9 0 FGR/FGR 0 9 8 7 6 5 4

ISBN: 0-07-288243-3

Vice president and editor-in-chief: *Thalia Dorwick*
Publisher: *Chris Freitag*
Sponsoring editor: *Jon-David Hague*
Marketing manager: *Zina Craft*
Production supervisor: *Randy Hurst*
Project manager: *Christina Gimlin*
Cover designer: *Yvo Riezebos*
Interior designer: *Susan Breitbard*
Senior designer: *Violeta Diaz*
Photo research coordinator: *Natalia Peschiera*
Editorial assistant: *Allison Rona*
Compositor: *Thompson Type*
Printer: *Quebecor, Fairfield*

Cover images: © Photodisc Collection.

Library of Congress Cataloging-in-Publication Data
Oppression, privilege, and resistance: theoretical perspectives on racism, sexism, and heterosexism / [edited by] Lisa Heldke, Margaret O'Connor.
    p. cm.
Includes bibliographical references and index.
ISBN 0-07-288243-3
    1. Social stratification. 2. Oppression (Psychology) 3. Stereotype (Psychology)
4. Racism. 5. Sexism. 6. Heterosexism. 7. Social Ethics. I. Heldke, Lisa M.
(Lisa Maree), 1960–   II. O'Connor, Peg, 1965–

HM821.O67 2003
303.3—dc22
                                                                    2003066623

www.mhhe.com

Contents

Preface

OPPRESSION, PRIVILEGE, RESISTANCE, AND COMPLICATIONS: THE SUBJECTS OF THIS BOOK

This book employs the oppression model of racism, sexism, and heterosexism. Although other models for understanding these phenomena exist (the model that sees them as forms of discrimination, for example), we believe that this is the most powerful and useful model for explaining these interlocking systems. Therefore, Part I begins with several texts that analyze what oppression means at the level of greatest generality, and then proceeds to apply the term along three different axes: racism, sexism, and heterosexism. In this first section of the course, texts focus on just one form of oppression at a time, isolating it from all the others.

Part II considers what we might call the "flip side" of oppression—privilege. If oppression systematically and unfairly marginalizes some members of a society, then it must also grant other members of that society an unfair advantage—which we define as privilege. Part II uses the same structure as Part I; it begins with an analysis of privilege in general, and then proceeds to look, individually, at privilege along each of the three axes—white privilege, masculine privilege, and heterosexual privilege.

Part III complicates this rather neat and tidy picture of oppression and privilege by challenging some of the assumptions from Parts I and II and pointing out the weaknesses in their one-axis-at-a-time models of oppression. We sort these "complicating" articles into three categories. The first section comprises readings that challenge the neatly dichotomous way in which race, gender, and sexuality are often conceived—so that everyone is Black or white, a woman or a man, heterosexual or homosexual. These readings identify and theorize about those whose lives lie between the two poles—Latino/as, people of mixed races, bisexuals, and intersexuals. The second section explores what happens when we notice that, for instance, some people are, lo and behold, both women *and* black. Finally, the third section explores the complicating fact that our lives are often some tangled mix of privilege and oppression; theories must be able to address and account for that reality. Models of oppression that place people squarely on one side or the other are inadequate.

Part IV explores resistance to oppression. Resistance is a forceful word—and we use it intentionally. The readings in this section are aimed not at helping individuals to feel better about themselves or to become better (nicer, kinder, gentler) people but at encouraging people to understand that social change requires collective action working *against* existing *systems*. Readings are divided into six sections, some of which focus on a conceptual stance or position from which one might engage in resistance to systems of oppression and privilege, and others of which focus on conceptual strategies for resistance. The six include education, disloyalty, separatism and identity politics, revolution, coalition, and "neither/nor." Although these readings don't present anything like a blueprint for changing the world, they do take readers beyond the analysis of "what's wrong with the world" and provide some broad theoretical frameworks for thinking about how to bring about change, and for understanding the ways in which people are already actively engaged in doing just that. We know, from teaching this course, that students often feel an overwhelming hopelessness as they start to confront the enormity and strength of systems of oppression. It is very important for you to have the opportunity to think creatively and constructively about challenging those systems.

SOME THOUGHTS ABOUT REPRESENTATION

We believe that it is important for people's lives, their experiences, and their ways of understanding the world to be analyzed by theorists who are "like them" in important respects. It is crucial, for example, that Black writers figure prominently among those who are writing about the effects of racism on African Americans and that transgendered individuals are leading voices among those analyzing the nature of various forms of gender oppression. This claim about the need for representation is in part and in some cases an ethical or political claim. That is, one way to begin to address and redress some of the harm of oppression is for groups of people whose perspectives have historically been ignored or silenced—people of color, women, glbt persons—to speak, write, and otherwise communicate their perspectives on that oppression. Alongside that speaking and writing there must be listening, reading, and learning by groups of people whose perspectives have normally been at the center of history—whites, men, heterosexuals. So, in part, it is a form of resistance for marginalized people to speak and for dominant people (among others) to listen to them.

But there is also an important knowledge claim buried in this belief about the need for representation. It is this: Those who stand on the "oppressed" side of the oppression/privilege divide routinely have an opportunity to develop insights and understandings that are unavailable, or available only with difficulty, to those who stand on the side of privilege. To claim this means *neither* that people with privilege can never speak with insight about the nature of oppression—that whites can never write meaningfully about the effect of racism on Native Americans, for example—*nor* that oppressed people always automatically have the insight and authority to speak about their oppression—that being Native American automatically gives one a theoretical understanding of racism, for instance. (One's race, gender, and sexual orientation simply do not, cannot, automatically determine one's beliefs. To hold that they do is to subscribe to a naïve, cartoon version of identity politics. We will explore more sophisticated versions of this view in the last section of the anthology.)

Making this claim also does not mean that every Asian (or lesbian or working-class person) "thinks the same" on some particular issue; just because we present *a* Latina perspective on a given concept in this anthology doesn't mean that we have presented *the* Latina perspective.

But even after all those caveats have been taken into account, theories developed by people who are marginalized—by race, class, gender, sexuality, ability, or disability—regularly and routinely offer insights into the structure of our social reality that are simply not readily available to those who stand at the center of things. Thus, in the study of forms of oppression, it is absolutely vital that theories by marginalized people occupy positions of prominence.

We have attempted to represent a wide variety of contemporary U.S. identities in this book. (Most of the writers live or lived in the United States, and most of the readings were written after 1970.) We didn't employ a quota system, but we did count noses, and we did think long and hard when we noticed sharp imbalances—that virtually none of the theorists were Asian, for example, whereas a great many of them were white, and that although we had numerous articles by women and men, we had only one by someone identified as transgender. And so on. We worked to rectify those imbalances—it's not sufficient to shrug and say, "Well, I guess Those Kinds of People just don't do theory"—but in the end, we have still succeeded only partially in meeting our goals of representation.

THE ANTHOLOGY AS TEXTBOOK

This is an anthology that sees itself as a textbook. To understand what we mean by that, consider what most textbooks do. In a series of chapters, an author dissects a subject into its parts, which are then laid out, in some kind of order, for your examination. A textbook's organization usually illustrates the way that its author understands the structure of the subject—which aspects of it are important, which are less so, which concepts are most fundamental, which are more derivative. For example, a textbook on American philosophy might organize that topic by identifying a set of events in U.S. history—the revolution, the abolition movement, the industrial revolution—and explaining how various philosophers responded to each. A textbook author who organized a book that way would be saying, in effect, that American philosophy is best understood as a series of responses to different historical circumstances.

In sum, a textbook presents an internally coherent picture or schema, a map of a particular terrain that points out all the most important features of that terrain. It's not that everything has to fit neatly into a textbook (indeed, we tend to be suspicious of authors who "tidy things up" too much), but a good textbook does leave its readers with a usable conceptual map.

Anthologies are less like maps and more like the accumulated contents of file drawers. Articles in anthologies are still arranged by some organizing system—there is an organizing system at work in file drawers, after all—and anthology editors, like textbook authors, may have the goal of "covering" the material. But anthologies don't necessarily present a coherent, internally cohesive account of their subject matter the way textbooks do. Readers may create such an account for themselves as they read the articles in an anthology, but it isn't usually considered the obligation of an anthology creator to do so. An anthology asks, "Who are the important (or clear or available) writers on this topic? What do they have to say? Let's hear from them firsthand—and out of these writings, you may formulate a catalogue of the central concepts yourself."

Whatever other goals are differently served by anthologies as opposed to textbooks, it is probably safe to say this: One chief virtue of a textbook is that it gives its readers conceptual frameworks with which to understand a topic. One the other hand, one chief virtue of an anthology is that it presents a diversity of original accounts; readers encounter original texts and can draw their own conceptual maps on the basis of those texts.

This book attempts to do some of the work of a textbook while using the format of an anthology. We have designed a book that introduces its readers to the terrain of racism and sexism by providing them with an interlocking set of concepts—oppression, privilege, and resistance—and by explaining what those concepts mean and how they function to describe that terrain. In this regard, it works like a textbook. But whereas an actual textbook can achieve these goals very tidily and coherently—in the unitary voice of The Authors—we choose instead to try to *construct* that conceptual framework out of multiple authors' voices, using original texts. What the book lacks in tidiness we believe it recoups by presenting concepts from multiple perspectives. And in the end, we believe it is far more useful for students to develop an understanding of racism, sexism, and other forms of oppression by reading a diversity of perspectives than by reading two writers' *interpretations* of a diversity of perspectives.

It is obvious that the book is an anthology, but the features that make it a textbook may be less easy to spot. There are two important places you can go if you're looking for some textbook-style help. First, the Table of Contents outlines the central concepts that will be explored in the book; in fact, the Table of Contents is actually a mini-outline of the structure of our course. The Table of Contents can serve as your quick-reference road map should you ever become confused or disoriented about how concepts fit together. Second, the introduction to each section provides a brief explanation of the new concept being introduced and connects it to the concepts that precede and follow it. These introductions are extremely brief; our goal is not to explain the concept to you. That is the task of the articles themselves; the introductions are there only to serve as guideposts.

One other feature of this book also contributes to its function as a textbook. Many of the theorists included here are writing to and for one another; they develop and critique one another's ideas and use one another's concepts. We have intentionally chosen texts that interconnect in these ways, in order to increase the cohesiveness of this book. This "conversation" among authors also develops the nuances of concepts, making them more flexible and stronger—and also bringing out their inadequacies and weaknesses.

The overall coherence of the book emerges, then, not like a single thread spun out by a single author, but like a set of shorter fibers that twine, cross, and bind to one another in many ways to make a strong conceptual fabric. We hope that the weave is just tight enough to leave you with the confidence to employ and explore these ideas on your own, but that it also contains enough loose ends and ragged edges to prevent you from seeing these issues as settled, final, and beyond dispute.

A COUPLE OF NOTES TO STUDENTS ABOUT WHAT THIS BOOK IS NOT

A philosophy course on racism and sexism (or a course on racism and sexism in any theoretical discipline) is often mistaken for some other kind of course, a misconception that tends to leave students frustrated and angry when they realize their mistake. Since the target of their frustration and anger is often their instructor, we want to head off the confusion before it has a chance to form, by telling you what *not* to expect in this book.

First, this is not a work on current events. Daily life, whether the life of an individual or that of a nation, is of course filled with examples of oppression, privilege, and resistance. It wouldn't be hard to design a course on racism and sexism that used the front section of your local newspaper and discussed the race and gender implications of the various stories in it.

This philosophical anthology is something quite different from the newspaper; it is a collection of theoretical tools that can give you insights into the nature of systems of oppression. In all likelihood, you *will* find yourself using these tools to analyze particular events and conditions in the world around you, but this book is devoted to an examination of the analytical tools and concepts themselves.

There is another very important thing this book is not: It is not a "balanced" look at "both sides" of racism and sexism. (Indeed, there are far more than two "sides" to the structures of racism, sexism, and heterosexism.) It is not a book that begins by musing about whether sexism is real, whether black people are oppressed, whether there is any sense to the term *homophobia*. This book begins with the assumption that racism, sexism, and heterosexism exist, and that they shape the life of everyone living within their reach. They are systematic forms of oppression that require analysis and explanation.

If you disagree with this claim, this book will probably be quite a frustration to you—but that frustration needn't be disastrous or a waste of your time. We ask you, in the spirit of the academic endeavor, to suspend your disagreement long enough to understand the theses of the authors you are reading. If nothing else, you will acquire a more sophisticated understanding of positions with which you disagree. (Of course, we hope that you will find that the arguments you read here have merit and that you will be compelled by them to revise your thinking about the reality of racism and sexism. But we will let the weight of argument do its own work.)

If you are coming to this book fully convinced that racism and sexism *do* exist, you have another kind of challenge in reading it, however. It will not do for you, as a philosopher, simply to accept, unquestioningly, the claim of each author you encounter, on the assumption that she or he is on "the same side" as you and thus must be "right." (In point of fact, it would be impossible to agree with every author in this book and remain consistent; many of the writers represented here disagree sharply with one another about the best ways to think about systems of oppression.) We ask you to remember that one of the tasks of the philosopher is to develop a capacity for critical questioning. Your reward will be a more nuanced—and thus stronger—understanding of what you believe.

Acknowledgments

We would like to thank Kal Alston (University of Illinois at Urbana–Champaign), Diane Raymond (Simmons College), Marya Bower (Earlham College), Ari Santas (Valdosta State University), and Gail Weiss (The George Washington University), who evaluated the manuscript for McGraw-Hill. Their perspectives—representing a diversity of institutions—valuably informed our thinking about how this work might be used in the classroom.

We owe a debt of gratitude to the many students in our philosophy course "Racism and Sexism," who over the years engaged in our trial-and-error process of finding The Perfect Readings and Conceptual Structure. Their comments and suggestions played a very important role in shaping this book.

Thanks to Linda Elvee, Anna Marsh, Megan Nerison, and Nikki Briggs, who were the permissions mavens. By the end of that process, they were qualified to teach their own course on copyright and permissions.

It has been a wonderful experience working with Jon-David Hague, Allison Rona, and Christina Gimlin at McGraw-Hill. They have provided encouragement and guidance whenever we needed it. And we did need it when we were about to scale the permissions equivalent of Mount McKinley.

About the Authors

Lisa Heldke is Associate Professor of Philosophy at Gustavus Adolphus College, where she also teaches in the Women's Studies Program. She is the author of *Exotic Appetites: Ruminations of a Food Adventurer* (Routledge, 2003) and the co-editor of *Cooking, Eating, Thinking: Transformative Philosophies of Food* (Indiana University Press, 1992).

Peg O'Connor is Associate Professor of Women's Studies at Gustavus Adolphus College, where she also teaches in the Department of Philosophy. She is the author of *Oppression and Responsibility: A Wittgensteinian Approach to Social Practices and Moral Theory* (The Pennsylvania State University Press, 2003) and the co-editor of *Feminist Interpretations of Ludwig Wittgenstein* (The Pennsylvania State University Press, 2003).

Lisa Heldke and Peg O'Connor are co-editors of *Philosophers on Holiday,* a quarterly 'zine in the philosophical travel/leisure genre. They can be found on the web at http://www.gustavus.edu/~poconnor

Part I: Theorizing Oppression

INTRODUCTION

This anthology is organized around the concept of *oppression*. The theorists whose works you will read here use that concept as the foundation upon which to build their analyses of racism, sexism, and heterosexism, and also their analyses of privilege and resistance. We describe these particular "isms" as *axes of oppression,* to emphasize this common connection.

Part I begins by introducing you to the ways that some theorists have understood and analyzed oppression (Chapter 1). Their theories define the concept in terms that are sometimes compatible, sometimes in tension with one another. One theorist identifies the relationship of *domination* and *subordination* to be the defining characteristic of oppression, whereas another's analysis rests on the concept of *dehumanization*. Still another theorist argues that we should not understand all forms of oppression as having one characteristic in common, but should recognize that oppression has different "faces," or aspects.

In spite of their disagreements, all the theorists you will read agree that oppression is not just the sum total of the attitudes and deeds of individuals, acting alone. They understand that oppression is *structural* and *systemic;* it pervades social institutions and practices, and it shapes the very nature of our social world.

As you read the remaining sections of Part I, you will find that the theorists represented there employ these general definitions of oppression to analyze a specific axis of it—racism, sexism, or heterosexism.

The first axis of oppression the anthology takes up, in Chapter 2, is racism, which has been, and remains, one of the most pervasive forms of oppression in the United States—some theorists would say *the* most pervasive. Racism is remarkably adaptable, capable of changing its face and its nature over time, and capable of flourishing in both overt and subtle forms. An analysis of racism as oppression calls attention to the subtle, structural forms of it that often underlie the obvious, attention-grabbing racist acts that make it to the nightly news.

One of the theorists you will read argues that racism should be understood as *white supremacy,* defined in terms of the organization of social, economic, and political life. Another theorist introduces the concept of *genocide*—the intentional and systematic killing of a national or ethnic group—as the best way to explain whites' treatment of Native Americans in the United States. Another theorist compares the settlement of the Southwest to *colonialism,* which most often is understood as one country's taking over or occupying another to exploit it.

The second axis of oppression you will examine, in Chapter 3, is sexism. Although there is wide cultural variation in how this form of oppression manifests itself, it is true that women as a group are generally lower than, and dependent on, men—politically, economically, and socially. That subordination is sexism.

The theorists who address sexism examine the customs and practices that create, maintain, and reinforce oppressive gender relationships. One theorist explores the ways that those customs and practices create the expectations for masculinity and femininity and impose penalties for violating appropriate gender norms. Another uses the imagery of a caged bird to understand sexism. If someone looks at only one wire of the cage at a time, she will not understand why the bird does not fly away; it is only when she notices the systematic and structural nature of the cage that she will come to comprehend the nature of the bird's confinement.

The third axis of oppression is heterosexism and homophobia, explored in Chapter 4. Most people would define homophobia as the fear or hatred of gays, lesbians, and bisexuals. Heterosexism remains the harder concept to define. One way to understand the relation of heterosexism to homophobia is to conceive of heterosexism as the background system that presumes that all people are or can be heterosexual—attracted to members of the opposite sex. Heterosexism is the system that makes particular acts of homophobia possible. If the prevailing cultural expectation is that everyone is heterosexual, then it is not surprising that people react with fear or surprise or anger when confronted by people who don't conform to the expectation. This fear of "gender traitors" who desire same-sex partners serves as a link between sexism and heterosexism/homophobia. Indeed, as one theorist argues, homophobia may be best understood as a weapon enlisted to maintain sexism and the rigid gender dichotomy it creates; fear of being branded a "homo" encourages both women and men to adhere to gender-stereotypical behavior.

"Summing Up," the final chapter of Part I, addresses blame and responsibility. Members of a society shaped by the axes of oppression may attempt to alleviate the guilt they feel for their obvious advantages by blaming the victim. To the victim-blamer, it is obvious that "those people"—those who do not share in the advantages—are responsible for their disadvantaged state. They haven't worked hard enough, or they blew their chances, or they had mixed-up priorities.

Theorists in this section reject such an individualistic account of success and failure. They draw attention instead to analyses of the structures of oppression—structures that make it harder for some to succeed because they are members of the group "Black" or "gay" or "woman" or "Latina." They also point out that the shift away from blaming the victim raises different questions for those who are not members of oppressed groups. What responsibility do they have for maintaining systems that harm and oppress others? Here too, we must avoid the move of overindividualization, and focus on the ways in which members of privileged groups share responsibility, by virtue of their membership in those groups.

Part I equips you with a working understanding of the notion of oppression; you will continue to develop and refine that understanding throughout the course of this book. In Part II, you will examine *privilege,* a companion concept. Part III challenges the orderliness of these notions, by examining some of the real-world complexities they don't seem to address. Part IV introduces six strategies for resistance—strategies that take into account the systematic and structural nature of oppression.

Oppression: General Theories

1

■ ■ ■ ■

PEDAGOGY OF THE OPPRESSED

Paulo Freire

CHAPTER 1

While the problem of humanization has always, from an axiological point of view, been man's central problem, it now takes on the character of an inescapable concern.[1] Concern for humanization leads at once to the recognition of dehumanization, not only as an ontological possibility but as an historical reality. And as man perceives the extent of dehumanization, he asks himself if humanization is a viable possibility. Within history, in concrete, objective contexts, both humanization and dehumanization are possibilities for man as an uncompleted being conscious of his incompletion.

But while both humanization and dehumanization are real alternatives, only the first is man's vocation. This vocation is constantly negated, yet it is affirmed by that very negation. It is thwarted by injustice, exploitation, oppression, and the violence of the oppressors; it is affirmed by the yearning of

---

[1] The current movements of rebellion, especially those of youth, while they necessarily reflect the peculiarities of their respective settings, manifest in their essence this preoccupation with man and men as beings in the world and with the world—preoccupation with *what* and *how* they are "being." As they place consumer civilization in judgment, denounce bureaucracies of all types, demand the transformation of the universities (changing the rigid nature of the teacher–student relationship and placing that relationship within the context of reality), propose the transformation of reality itself so that universities can be renewed, attack old orders and established institutions in the attempt to affirm men as the Subjects of decision, all these movements reflect the style of our age, which is more anthropological than anthropocentric.

the oppressed for freedom and justice, and by their struggle to recover their lost humanity.

Dehumanization, which marks not only those whose humanity has been stolen, but also (though in a different way) those who have stolen it, is a *distortion* of the vocation of becoming more fully human. This distortion occurs within history; but it is not an historical vocation. Indeed, to admit of dehumanization as an historical vocation would lead either to cynicism or total despair. The struggle for humanization, for the emancipation of labor, for the overcoming of alienation, for the affirmation of men as persons would be meaningless. This struggle is possible only because dehumanization, although a concrete historical fact, is *not* a given destiny by the result of an unjust order that engenders violence in the oppressors, which in turn dehumanizes the oppressed.

Because it is a distortion of being more fully human, sooner or later being less human leads the oppressed to struggle against those who made them so. In order for this struggle to have meaning, the oppressed must not, in seeking to regain their humanity (which is a way to create it), become in turn oppressors of the oppressors, but rather restorers of the humanity of both.

5　　This, then, is the great humanistic and historical task of the oppressed: to liberate themselves and their oppressors as well. The oppressors, who oppress, exploit, and rape by virtue of their power, cannot find in this power the strength to liberate either the oppressed or themselves. Only power that springs from the weakness of the oppressed will be sufficiently strong to free both. Any attempt to "soften" the power of the oppressor in deference to the weakness of the oppressed almost always manifests itself in the form of false generosity; indeed, the attempt never goes beyond this. In order to have the continued opportunity to express their "generosity," the oppressors must perpetuate injustice as well. An unjust social order is the permanent fount of this "generosity," which is nourished by death, despair, and poverty. That is why the dispensers of false generosity become desperate at the slightest threat to its source.

True generosity consists precisely in fighting to destroy the causes which nourish false charity. False charity constrains the fearful and subdued, the "rejects of life," to extend their trembling hands. True generosity lies in striving so that these hands—whether of individuals or entire peoples—need be extended less and less in supplication, so that more and more they become human hands which work and, working, transform the world.

This lesson and this apprenticeship must come, however, from the oppressed themselves and from those who are truly solidary with them. As individuals or as peoples, by fighting for the restoration of their humanity they will be attempting the restoration of true generosity. Who are better prepared than the oppressed to understand the terrible significance of an oppressive society? Who suffer the effects of oppression more than the oppressed? Who can better understand the necessity of liberation? They will not gain this liberation by chance but through the praxis of their quest for it, through their recognition of the necessity to fight for it. And this fight, because of the purpose given it by the oppressed, will actually constitute an act of love opposing the lovelessness which lies at the heart of the oppressors' violence, lovelessness even when clothed in false generosity.

But almost always, during the initial stage of the struggle, the oppressed, instead of striving for liberation, tend themselves to become oppressors, or "sub-oppressors." The very structure of their thought has been conditioned by the contradictions of the concrete, existential situation by which they were shaped. Their ideal is to be men; but for them, to be men is to be oppressors. This is their model of humanity. This phenomenon derives from the fact that the oppressed, at a certain moment of their existential experience, adopt an attitude of "adhesion" to the oppressor. Under these circumstances they cannot "consider" him sufficiently clearly to objectivize him—to discover him "outside" themselves. This does not necessarily mean that the oppressed are unaware that they are downtrodden. But their perception of themselves as oppressed is impaired by their submersion in the reality of oppression. At this level, their perception of themselves as opposites of the oppressor does not yet signify engagement in a struggle to overcome the contradiction;[2] the one pole aspires not to liberation, but to identification with its opposite pole.

In this situation the oppressed do not see the "new man" as the man to be born from the resolution of this contradiction, as oppression gives way to liberation. For them, the new man is themselves become oppressors. Their vision of the new man is individualistic; because of their identification with the oppressor, they have no consciousness of themselves as persons or as members of an oppressed class. It is not to become free men that they want agrarian reform, but in order to acquire land and thus become landowners—or, more precisely, bosses over other workers. It is a rare peasant who, once "promoted" to overseer, does not become more of a tyrant towards his former comrades than the owner himself. This is because the context of the peasant's situation, that is, oppression, remains unchanged. In this example, the overseer, in order to make sure of his job, must be as tough as the owner—and more so. Thus is illustrated our previous assertion that during the initial stage of their struggle the oppressed find in the oppressor their model of "manhood."

Even revolution, which transforms a concrete situation of oppression by establishing the process of liberation, must confront this phenomenon. Many of the oppressed who directly or indirectly participate in revolution intend—conditioned by the myths of the old order—to make it their private revolution. The shadow of their former oppressor is still cast over them.

The "fear of freedom" which afflicts the oppressed,[3] a fear which may equally well lead them to desire the role of oppressor or bind them to the role of oppressed, should be examined. One of the basic elements of the relationship between oppressors and oppressed is *prescription*. Every prescription

---

[2]As used throughout this book, the term "contradiction" denotes the dialectical conflict between opposing social forces. —Translator's note.

[3]This fear of freedom is also to be found in the oppressors, though, obviously, in a different form. The oppressed are afraid to embrace freedom; the oppressors are afraid of losing the "freedom" to oppress.

represents the imposition of one man's choice upon another, transforming the consciousness of the man prescribed to into one that conforms with the prescriber's consciousness. Thus, the behavior of the oppressed is a prescribed behavior, following as it does the guidelines of the oppressor.

The oppressed, having internalized the image of the oppressor and adopted his guidelines, are fearful of freedom. Freedom would require them to eject this image and replace it with autonomy and responsibility. Freedom is acquired by conquest, not by gift. It must be pursued constantly and responsibly. Freedom is not an ideal located outside of man; nor is it an idea which becomes myth. It is rather the indispensable condition for the quest for human completion.

To surmount the situation of oppression, men must first critically recognize its causes, so that through transforming action they can create a new situation, one which makes possible the pursuit of a fuller humanity. But the struggle to be more fully human has already begun in the authentic struggle to transform the situation. Although the situation of oppression is a dehumanized and dehumanizing totality affecting both the oppressors and those whom they oppress, it is the latter who must, from their stifled humanity, wage for both the struggle for a fuller humanity; the oppressor, who is himself dehumanized because he dehumanizes others, is unable to lead this struggle.

However, the oppressed, who have adapted to the structure of domination in which they are immersed, and have become resigned to it, are inhibited from waging the struggle for freedom so long as they feel incapable of running the risks it requires. Moreover, their struggle for freedom threatens not only the oppressor, but also their own oppressed comrades who are fearful of still greater repression. When they discover within themselves the yearning to be free, they perceive that this yearning can be transformed into reality only when the same yearning is aroused in their comrades. But while dominated by the fear of freedom they refuse to appeal to others, or to listen to the appeals of others, or even to the appeals of their own conscience. They prefer gregariousness to authentic comradeship; they prefer the security of conformity with their state of unfreedom to the creative communion produced by freedom and even the very pursuit of freedom.

15   The oppressed suffer from the duality which has established itself in their innermost being. They discover that without freedom they cannot exist authentically. Yet, although they desire authentic existence, they fear it. They are at one and the same time themselves and the oppressor whose consciousness they have internalized. The conflict lies in the choice between being wholly themselves or being divided; between ejecting the oppressor within or not ejecting him; between human solidarity or alienation; between following prescriptions or having choices; between being spectators or actors; between acting or having the illusion of acting through the action of the oppressors; between speaking out or being silent, castrated in their power to create and re-create, in their power to transform the world. This is the tragic dilemma of the oppressed which their education must take into account.

This book will present some aspects of what the writer has termed the pedagogy of the oppressed, a pedagogy which must be forged *with,* not *for,* the oppressed (whether individuals or peoples) in the incessant struggle to regain their humanity. This pedagogy makes oppression and its causes objects of reflection by the oppressed, and from that reflection will come their necessary engagement in the struggle for their liberation. And in the struggle this pedagogy will be made and remade.

The central problem is this: How can the oppressed, as divided, unauthentic beings, participate in developing the pedagogy of their liberation? Only as they discover themselves to be "hosts" of the oppressor can they contribute to the midwifery of their liberating pedagogy. As long as they live in the duality in which *to be* is *to be like,* and *to be like* is *to be like the oppressor,* this contribution is impossible. The pedagogy of the oppressed is an instrument for their critical discovery that both they and their oppressors are manifestations of dehumanization.

Liberation is thus a childbirth, and a painful one. The man who emerges is a new man, viable only as the oppressor–oppressed contradiction is superseded by the humanization of all men. Or to put it another way, the solution of this contradiction is born in the labor which brings into the world this new man: no longer oppressor nor longer oppressed, but man in the process of achieving freedom.

This solution cannot be achieved in idealistic terms. In order for the oppressed to be able to wage the struggle for their liberation, they must perceive the reality of oppression not as a closed world from which there is no exit, but as a limiting situation which they can transform. This perception is a necessary but not a sufficient condition for liberation; it must become the motivating force for liberating action. Nor does the discovery by the oppressed that they exist in dialectical relationship to the oppressor, as his antithesis— that without them the oppressor could not exist[4]—in itself constitute liberation. The oppressed can overcome the contradiction in which they are caught only when this perception enlists them in the struggle to free themselves.

The same is true with respect to the individual oppressor as a person. *20* Discovering himself to be an oppressor may cause considerable anguish, but it does not necessarily lead to solidarity with the oppressed. Rationalizing his guilt through paternalistic treatment of the oppressed, all the while holding them fast in a position of dependence, will not do. Solidarity requires that one enter into the situation of those with whom one is solidary; it is a radical posture. If what characterizes the oppressed is their subordination to the consciousness of the master, as Hegel affirms,[5] true solidarity with the oppressed

---

[4] See Georg Hegel, *Phenomenology of Mind* (New York, 1967), pp. 236–237.

[5] Analyzing the dialectical relationship between the consciousness of the master and the consciousness of the oppressed, Hegel states: "The one is independent, and its essential nature is to be for itself; the other is dependent, and its essence is life or existence for another. The former is the Master, or Lord, the latter Bondsman." Ibid., p. 234.

means fighting at their side to transform the objective reality which has made them these "beings for another." The oppressor is solidary with the oppressed only when he stops regarding the oppressed as an abstract category and sees them as persons who have been unjustly dealt with, deprived of their voice, cheated in the sale of their labor—when he stops making pious, sentimental, and individualistic gestures and risks an act of love. True solidarity is found only in the plenitude of this act of love, in its existentiality, in its praxis. To affirm that men are persons and as persons should be free, and yet to do nothing tangible to make this affirmation a reality, is a farce.

Since it is in a concrete situation that the oppressor–oppressed contradiction is established, the resolution of this contradiction must be *objectively* verifiable. Hence, the radical requirement—both for the man who discovers himself to be an oppressor and for the oppressed—that the concrete situation which begets oppression must be transformed.

To present this radical demand for the objective transformation of reality, to combat subjectivist immobility which would divert the recognition of oppression into patient waiting for oppression to disappear by itself, is not to dismiss the role of subjectivity in the struggle to change structures. On the contrary, one cannot conceive of objectivity without subjectivity. Neither can exist without the other, nor can they be dichotomized. The separation of objectivity from subjectivity, the denial of the latter when analyzing reality or acting upon it, is objectivism. On the other hand, the denial of objectivity in analysis or action, resulting in a subjectivism which leads to solipsistic positions, denies action itself by denying objective reality. Neither objectivism nor subjectivism, nor yet psychologism is propounded here, but rather subjectivity and objectivity in constant dialectical relationship.

To deny the importance of subjectivity in the process of transforming the world and history is naïve and simplistic. It is to admit the impossible: a world without men. This objectivistic position is as ingenuous as that of subjectivism, which postulates men without a world. World and men do not exist apart from each other, they exist in constant interaction. Marx does not espouse such a dichotomy, nor does any other critical, realistic thinker. What Marx criticized and scientifically destroyed was not subjectivity, but subjectivism and psychologism. Just as objective social reality exists not by chance, but as the product of human action, so it is not transformed by chance. If men produce social reality (which in the "inversion of the praxis" turns back upon them and conditions them), then transforming that reality is an historical task, a task for men.

Reality which becomes oppressive results in the contradistinction of men as oppressors and oppressed. The latter, whose task it is to struggle for their liberation together with those who show true solidarity, must acquire a critical awareness of oppression through the praxis of this struggle. One of the gravest obstacles to the achievement of liberation is that oppressive reality absorbs those within it and thereby acts to submerge men's consciousness.[6] Functionally, oppression is domesticating. To no longer be prey to its force, one must emerge from it and turn upon it. This can be done only by means of the praxis: reflection and action upon the world in order to transform it.

> Hay que hacer al opresión real todavía mas opresiva añadiendo
> a aquella la *conciéncia* de la opresión haciendo la infamia todavía
> mas infamante, al pregonarla.[7]

Making "real oppression more oppressive still by adding to it the realiza- tion of oppression" corresponds to the dialectical relation between the subjective and the objective. Only in this interdependence is an authentic praxis possible, without which it is impossible to resolve the oppressor–oppressed contradiction. To achieve this goal, the oppressed must confront reality critically, simultaneously objectifying and acting upon that reality. A mere perception of reality not followed by this critical intervention will not lead to a transformation of objective reality—precisely because it is not a true perception. This is the case of a purely subjectivist perception by someone who forsakes objective reality and creates a false substitute.

A different type of false perception occurs, when a change in objective reality would threaten the individual or class interests of the perceiver. In the first instance, there is no critical intervention in reality because that reality is fictitious; there is none in the second instance because intervention would contradict the class interests of the perceiver. In the latter case the tendency of the perceiver is to behave "neurotically." The fact exists; but both the fact and what may result from it may be prejudicial to him. Thus it becomes necessary, not precisely to deny the fact, but to "see it differently." This rationalization as a defense mechanism coincides in the end with subjectivism. A fact which is not denied but whose truths are rationalized loses its objective base. It ceases to be concrete and becomes a myth created in defense of the class of the perceiver.

Herein lies one of the reasons for the prohibitions and the difficulties designed to dissuade the people from critical intervention in reality. The oppressor knows full well that this intervention would not be to his interest. What *is* to his interest is for the people to continue in a state of submersion, impotent in the face of oppressive reality. Of relevance here is Lukács' warning to the revolutionary party:

> ... il doit, pour employer les mots de Marx, expliquer aux
> masses leur propre action non seulement afin d'assurer la
> continuité des expériences révolutionnaires du prolétariat, mais

---

[6] "Liberating action necessarily involves a moment of perception and volition. This action both precedes and follows that moment, to which it first acts as a prologue and which it subsequently serves to effect and continue within history. The action of domination, however, does not necessarily imply this dimension; for the structure of domination is maintained by its own mechanical and unconscious functionality." From an unpublished work by José Luiz Fiori, who has kindly granted permission to quote him.

[7] Karl Marx and Friedrich Engels, *La Sagrada Familia y otros Escritos* (Mexico, 1962), p. 6. Emphasis added.

25

aussi d'activer consciemment le développement ultérieur de ces expériences.[8]

In affirming this necessity, Lukács is unquestionably posing the problem of critical intervention. "To explain to the masses their own action" is to clarify and illuminate that action, both regarding its relationship to the objective facts by which it was prompted, and regarding its purposes. The more the people unveil this challenging reality which is to be the object of their transforming action, the more critically they enter that reality. In this way they are "consciously activating the subsequent development of their experiences." There would be no human action if there were no objective reality, no world to be the "not I" of man and to challenge him; just as there would be no human action if man were not a "project," if he were not able to transcend himself, to perceive his reality and understand it in order to transform it.

In dialectical thought, world and action are intimately interdependent. But action is human only when it is not merely an occupation but also a preoccupation, that is, when it is not dichotomized from reflection. Reflection, which is essential to action, is implicit in Lukács' requirement of "explaining to the masses their own action," just as it is implicit in the purpose he attributes to this explanation: that of "consciously activating the subsequent development of experience."

For us, however, the requirement is seen not in terms of explaining to, but rather dialoguing with the people about their actions. In any event, no reality transforms itself,[9] and the duty which Lukács ascribes to the revolutionary party of "explaining to the masses their own action" coincides with our affirmation of the need for the critical intervention of the people in reality through the praxis. The pedagogy of the oppressed, which is the pedagogy of men engaged in the fight for their own liberation, has its roots here. And those who recognize, or begin to recognize, themselves as oppressed must be among the developers of this pedagogy. No pedagogy which is truly liberating can remain distant from the oppressed by treating them as unfortunates and by presenting for their emulation models from among the oppressors. The oppressed must be their own example in the struggle for their redemption.

30   The pedagogy of the oppressed, animated by authentic, humanist (not humanitarian) generosity, presents itself as a pedagogy of man. Pedagogy which begins with the egoistic interests of the oppressors (an egoism cloaked in the false generosity of paternalism) and makes of the oppressed the objects of its humanitarianism, itself maintains and embodies oppression. It is an in-

---

[8] Georg Lukács, *Lénine* (Paris, 1965), p. 62.
[9] "The materialist doctrine that men are products of circumstances and upbringing, and that, therefore, changed men are products of other circumstances and changed upbringing, forgets that it is men that change circumstances and that the educator himself needs educating." Karl Marx and Friedrich Engels, *Selected Works* (New York, 1969), p. 28.

strument of dehumanization. This is why, as we affirmed earlier, the pedagogy of the oppressed cannot be developed or practiced by the oppressors. It would be a contradiction in terms if the oppressors not only defended but actually implemented a liberating education.

But if the implementation of a liberating education requires political power and the oppressed have none, how then is it possible to carry out the pedagogy of the oppressed prior to the revolution? This is a question of the greatest importance. . . . One aspect of the reply is to be found in the distinction between *systematic education,* which can only be changed by political power, and *educational projects,* which should be carried out *with* the oppressed in the process of organizing them.

The pedagogy of the oppressed, as a humanist and libertarian pedagogy, has two distinct stages. In the first, the oppressed unveil the world of oppression and through the praxis commit themselves to its transformation. In the second stage, in which the reality of oppression has already been transformed, this pedagogy ceases to belong to the oppressed and becomes a pedagogy of all men in the process of permanent liberation. In both stages, it is always through action in depth that the culture of domination is culturally confronted.[10] In the first stage this confrontation occurs through the change in the way the oppressed perceive the world of oppression; in the second stage, through the expulsion of the myths created and developed in the old order, which like specters haunt the new structure emerging from the revolutionary transformation.

The pedagogy of the first stage must deal with the problem of the oppressed consciousness and the oppressor consciousness, the problem of men who oppress and men who suffer oppression. It must take into account their behavior, their view of the world, and their ethics. A particular problem is the duality of the oppressed: they are contradictory, divided beings, shaped by and existing in a concrete situation of oppression and violence.

Any situation in which "A" objectively exploits "B" or hinders his pursuit of self-affirmation as a responsible person is one of oppression. Such a situation in itself constitutes violence, even when sweetened by false generosity, because it interferes with man's ontological and historical vocation to be more fully human. With the establishment of a relationship of oppression, violence has *already* begun. Never in history has violence been initiated by the oppressed. How could they be the initiators, if they themselves are the result of violence? How could they be the sponsors of something whose objective inauguration called forth their existence as oppressed? There would be no oppressed had there been no prior situation of violence to establish their subjugation

Violence is initiated by those who oppress, who exploit, who fail to recognize others as persons—not by those who are oppressed, exploited, and

35

---

[10] This appears to be the fundamental aspect of Mao's Cultural Revolution.

unrecognized. It is not the unloved who initiate disaffection, but those who cannot love because they love only themselves. It is not the helpless, subject to terror, who initiate terror, but the violent, who with their power create the concrete situation which begets the "rejects of life." It is not the tyrannized who initiate despotism, but the tyrants. It is not the despised who initiate hatred, but those who despise. It is not those whose humanity is denied them who negate man, but those who denied that humanity (thus negating their own as well). Force is used not by those who have become weak under the preponderance of the strong, but by the strong who have emasculated them.

For the oppressors, however, it is always the oppressed (whom they obviously never call "the oppressed" but—depending on whether they are fellow countrymen or not—"those people" or "the blind and envious masses" or "savages" or "natives" or "subversives") who are disaffected, who are "violent," "barbaric," "wicked," or "ferocious" when they react to the violence of the oppressors.

Yet it is—paradoxical though it may seem—precisely in the response of the oppressed to the violence of their oppressors that a gesture of love may be found. Consciously or unconsciously, the act of rebellion by the oppressed (an act which is always, or nearly always, as violent as the initial violence of the oppressors) can initiate love. Whereas the violence of the oppressors prevents the oppressed from being fully human, the response of the latter to this violence is grounded in the desire to pursue the right to be human. As the oppressors dehumanize others and violate their rights, they themselves also become dehumanized. As the oppressed, fighting to be human, take away the oppressors' power to dominate and suppress, they restore to the oppressors the humanity they had lost in the exercise of oppression.

It is only the oppressed who, by freeing themselves, can free their oppressors. The latter, as an oppressive class, can free neither others nor themselves. It is therefore essential that the oppressed wage the struggle to resolve the contradiction in which they are caught; and the contradiction will be resolved by the appearance of the new man: neither oppressor nor oppressed, but man in the process of liberation. If the goal of the oppressed is to become fully human, they will not achieve their goal by merely reversing the terms of the contradiction, by simply changing poles.

This may seem simplistic; it is not. Resolution of the oppressor–oppressed contradiction indeed implies the disappearance of the oppressors as a dominant class. However, the restraints imposed by the former oppressed on their oppressors, so that the latter cannot reassume their former position, do not constitute *oppression*. An act is oppressive only when it prevents men from being more fully human. Accordingly, these necessary restraints do not *in themselves* signify that yesterday's oppressed have become today's oppressors. Acts which prevent the restoration of the oppressive regime cannot be compared with those which create and maintain it, cannot be compared with those by which a few men deny the majority their right to be human.

However, the moment the new regime hardens into a dominating "bu- *40*
reaucracy"[11] the humanist dimension of the struggle is lost and it is no longer
possible to speak of liberation. Hence our insistence that the authentic solution of the oppressor–oppressed contradiction does not lie in a mere reversal
of position, in moving from one pole to the other. Nor does it lie in the replacement of the former oppressors with new ones who continue to subju-
gate the oppressed—all in the name of their liberation.

But even when the contradiction is resolved authentically by a new situation established by the liberated laborers, the former oppressors do not feel
liberated. On the contrary, they genuinely consider themselves to be oppressed. Conditioned by the experience of oppressing others, any situation
other than their former seems to them like oppression. Formerly, they could
eat, dress, wear shoes, be educated, travel, and hear Beethoven; while millions
did not eat, had no clothes or shoes, neither studied nor traveled, much less
listened to Beethoven. Any restriction on this way of life, in the name of the
rights of the community, appears to the former oppressors as a profound violation of their individual rights—although they had no respect for the millions who suffered and died of hunger, pain, sorrow, and despair. For the
oppressor, "human beings" refers only to themselves; other people are "things."
For the oppressors, there exists only one right: their right to live in peace,
over against the right, not always even recognized, but simply conceded, of
the oppressed to survival. And they make this concession only because the
existence of the oppressed is necessary to their own existence.

This behavior, this way of understanding the world and men (which necessarily makes the oppressors resist the installation of a new regime) is explained by their experience as a dominant class. Once a situation of violence
and oppression has been established, it engenders an entire way of life and behavior for those caught up in it—oppressors and oppressed alike. Both are
submerged in this situation, and both bear the marks of oppression. Analysis
of existential situations of oppression reveals that their inception lay in an act
of violence—initiated by those with power. This violence, as a process, is perpetuated from generation to generation of oppressors, who become its heirs
and are shaped in its climate. This climate creates in the oppressor a strongly
possessive consciousness—possessive of the world and of men. Apart from direct, concrete, material possession of the world and of men, the oppressor consciousness could not understand itself—could not even exist. Fromm said of
this consciousness that, without such possession, "it would lose contact with
the world." The oppressor consciousness tends to transform everything surrounding it into an object of its domination. The earth, property, production,

---

[11] This rigidity should not be identified with the restraints that must be imposed on the former
oppressors so they cannot restore the oppressive order. Rather, it refers to the revolution which
becomes stagnant and turns against the people, using the old repressive, bureaucratic State apparatus (which should have been drastically suppressed, as Marx so often emphasized).

the creations of men, men themselves, time—everything is reduced to the status of objects at its disposal.

In their unrestrained eagerness to possess, the oppressors develop the conviction that it is possible for them to transform everything into objects of their purchasing power; hence their strictly materialistic concept of existence. Money is the measure of all things, and profit the primary goal. For the oppressors, what is worthwhile is to have more—always more—even at the cost of the oppressed having less or having nothing. For them, *to be* is *to have* and to be the class of the "haves."

As beneficiaries of a situation of oppression, the oppressors cannot perceive that if *having* is a condition of *being,* it is a necessary condition for all men. This is why their generosity if false. Humanity is a "thing," and they possess it as an exclusive right, as inherited property. To the oppressor consciousness, the humanization of the "others," of the people, appears not as the pursuit of full humanity, but as subversion.

45   The oppressors do not perceive their monopoly on *having more* as a privilege which dehumanizes others and themselves. They cannot see that, in the egoistic pursuit of *having* as a possessing class, they suffocate in their own possessions and no longer *are;* they merely *have.* For them, *having more* is an inalienable right, a right they acquired through their own "effort," with their "courage to take risks." If others do not have more, it is because they are incompetent and lazy, and worst of all is their unjustifiable ingratitude towards the "generous gestures" of the dominant class. Precisely because they are "ungrateful" and "envious," the oppressed are regarded as potential enemies who must be watched.

It could not be otherwise. If the humanization of the oppressed signifies subversion, so also does their freedom; hence the necessity for constant control. And the more the oppressors control the oppressed, the more they change them into apparently inanimate "things." This tendency of the oppressor consciousness to "in-animate" everything and everyone it encounters, in its eagerness to possess, unquestionably corresponds with a tendency to sadism.

> The pleasure in complete domination over another person (or
> other animate creature) is the very essence of the sadistic drive.
> Another way of formulating the same thought is to say that the
> aim of sadism is to transform a man into a thing, something
> animate into something inanimate, since by complete and
> absolute control the living loses one essential quality of life—
> freedom.[12]

Sadistic love is a perverted love—a love of death, not of life. One of the characteristics of the oppressor consciousness and its necrophilic view of the world is thus sadism. As the oppressor consciousness, in order to dominate, tries to

---

[12]Eric Fromm, *The Heart of Man* (New York, 1966), p. 32.

deter the drive to search, the restlessness, and the creative power which characterize life, it kills life. More and more, the oppressors are using science and technology as unquestionable powerful instruments for their purpose: the maintenance of the oppressive order through manipulation and repression.[13] The oppressed, as objects, as "things," have no purposes except those their oppressors prescribe for them.

Given the preceding context, another issue of indubitable importance arises: the fact that certain members of the oppressor class join the oppressed in their struggle for liberation, thus moving from one pole of the contradiction to the other. Theirs is a fundamental role, and has been so throughout the history of this struggle. It happens, however, that as they cease to be exploiters or indifferent spectators or simply the heirs of exploitation and move to the side of the exploited, they almost always bring with them the marks of their origin: their prejudices and their deformations, which include a lack of confidence in the people's ability to think, to want, and to know. Accordingly, these adherents to the people's cause constantly run the risk of falling into a type of generosity as malefic as that of the oppressors. The generosity of the oppressors is nourished by an unjust order, which must be maintained in order to justify that generosity. Our converts, on the other hand, truly desire to transform the unjust order; but because of their background they believe that they must be the executors of the transformation. They talk about the people, but do not trust them; and trusting the people is the indispensable precondition for revolutionary change. A real humanist can be identified more by his trust in the people, which engages him in their struggle, than by a thousand actions in their favor without that trust.

Those who authentically commit themselves to the people must reexamine themselves constantly. This conversion is so radical as not to allow of ambiguous behavior. To affirm this commitment but to consider oneself the proprietor of revolutionary wisdom—which must then be given to (or imposed on) the people—is to retain the old ways. The man who proclaims devotion to the cause of liberation yet is unable to enter into *communion* with the people, whom he continues to regard as totally ignorant, is grievously self-deceived. The convert who approaches the people but feels alarm at each step they take, each doubt they express, and each suggestion they offer, and attempts to impose his "status," remains nostalgic towards his origins.

Conversion to the people requires a profound rebirth. Those who undergo it must take on a new form of existence; they can no longer remain as they were. Only through comradeship with the oppressed can the converts understand their characteristic ways of living and behaving, which in diverse moments reflect the structure of domination. One of these characteristics is the previously mentioned existential duality of the oppressed, who are at the

---

[13] Regarding the "dominant forms of social control," see Herbert Marcuse, *One-Dimensional Man* (Boston, 1964), and *Eros and Civilization* (Boston, 1955).

same time themselves and the oppressor whose image they have internalized. Accordingly, until they concretely "discover" their oppressor and in turn their own consciousness, they nearly always express fatalistic attitudes towards their situation.

> The peasant begins to get courage to overcome his dependence when he realizes that he is dependent. Until then, he goes along with the boss and says "What can I do? I'm only a peasant."[14]

When superficially analyzed, this fatalism is sometimes interpreted as a docility that is a trait of national character. Fatalism in the guise of docility is the fruit of an historical and sociological situation, not an essential characteristic of a people's behavior. It almost always is related to the power of destiny or fate or fortune—inevitable forces—or to a distorted view of God. Under the sway of magic and myth, the oppressed (especially the peasants, who are almost submerged in nature)[15] see their suffering, the fruit of exploitation, as the will of God—as if God were the creator of this "organized disorder."

50   Submerged in reality, the oppressed cannot perceive clearly the "order" which serves the interests of the oppressors whose image they have internalized. Chafing under the restrictions of this order, they often manifest a type of horizontal violence, striking out at their own comrades for the pettiest reasons.

> The colonized man will first manifest this aggressiveness which has been deposited in his bones against his own people. This is the period when the niggers beat each other up, and the police and magistrates do not know which way to turn when faced with the astonishing waves of crime in North Africa. . . . While the settler or the policeman has the right the livelong day to strike the native, to insult him and to make him crawl to them, you will see the native reaching for his knife at the slightest hostile or aggressive glance cast on him by another native; for the last resort of the native is to defend his personality vis-á-vis his brother.[16]

It is possible that in this behavior they are once more manifesting their duality. Because the oppressor exists within their oppressed comrades, when they attack those comrades they are indirectly attacking the oppressor as well.

On the other hand, at a certain point in their existential experience the oppressed feel an irresistible attraction towards the oppressor and his way of life. Sharing this way of life becomes an overpowering aspiration. In their

---

[14]Words of a peasant during an interview with the author.
[15]See Candido Mendes, *Memento dos vivos—A Esquerda católica no Brasil* (Rio, 1966).
[16]Frantz Fanon, *The Wretched of the Earth* (New York, 1968), p. 52.

alienation, the oppressed want at any cost to resemble the oppressor, to imitate him, to follow him. This phenomenon is especially prevalent in the middle-class oppressed, who yearn to be equal to the "eminent" men of the upper class. Albert Memmi, in an exceptional analysis of the "colonized mentality," refers to the contempt he felt towards the colonizer, mixed with "passionate" attraction towards him.

> How could the colonizer look after his workers while peri-odically gunning down a crowd of colonized? How could the colonized deny himself so cruelly yet make such excessive demands? How could he hate the colonizers and yet admire them so passionately? (I too felt this admiration in spite of myself.)[17]

Self-depreciation is another characteristic of the oppressed, which derives from their internalization of the opinion the oppressors hold of them. So often do they hear that they are good for nothing, know nothing and are in-capable of learning anything—that they are sick, lazy, and unproductive—that in the end they become convinced of their own unfitness.

> The peasant feels inferior to the boss because the boss seems to be the only one who knows things and is able to run things.[18]

They call themselves ignorant and say the "professor" is the one who has knowledge and to whom they should listen. The criteria of knowledge im-posed upon them are the conventional ones. "Why don't you," said a peasant participating in a culture circle,[19] "explain the pictures first? That way it'll take less time and won't give us a headache."

Almost never do they realize that they, too, "know things" they have learned in their relations with the world and with other men. Given the cir-cumstances which have produced their duality, it is only natural that they dis-trust themselves.

Not infrequently, peasants in educational projects begin to discuss a gen-erative theme in a lively manner, then stop suddenly and say to the educator: "Excuse us, we ought to keep quiet and let you talk. You are the one who knows, we don't know anything." They often insist that there is no difference between them and the animals; when they do admit a difference, it favors the animals. "They are freer than we are."

It is striking, however, to observe how this self-depreciation changes with the first changes in the situation of oppression. I heard a peasant leader say in an *asentamiento* [20] meeting, "They used to say we were unproductive because

55

---

[17] *The Colonizer and the Colonized* (Boston, 1967), p. x.
[18] Words of a peasant during an interview with the author.
[19] See Chapter 3, p. 113 ff. —Translator's note.
[20] *Asentamiento* refers to a production unit of the Chilean agrarian reform experiment. —Trans-lator's note.

we were lazy and drunkards. All lies. Now that we are respected as men, we're going to show everyone that we were never drunkards or lazy. We were exploited!"

As long as their ambiguity persists, the oppressed are reluctant to resist, and totally lack confidence in themselves. They have a diffuse, magical belief in the invulnerability and power of the oppressor.[21] The magical force of the landowner's power holds particular sway in the rural areas. A sociologist friend of mine tells of a group of armed peasants in a Latin American country who recently took over a latifundium. For tactical reasons, they planned to hold the landowner as a hostage. But not one peasant had the courage to guard him; his very presence was terrifying. It is also possible that the act of opposing the boss provoked guilt feelings. In truth, the boss was "inside" them.

The oppressed must see examples of the vulnerability of the oppressor so that a contrary conviction can begin to grow within them. Until this occurs, they will continue disheartened, fearful, and beaten.[22] As long as the oppressed remain unaware of the causes of their condition, they fatalistically "accept" their exploitation. Further, they are apt to react in a passive and alienated manner when confronted with the necessity to struggle for their freedom and self-affirmation. Little by little, however, they tend to try out forms of rebellious action. In working towards liberation, one must neither lose sight of this passivity nor overlook the moment of awakening.

Within their unauthentic view of the world and of themselves, the oppressed feel like "things" owned by the oppressor. For the latter, *to be* is *to have,* almost always at the expense of those who have nothing. For the oppressed, at a certain point in their existential experience, *to be* is not to resemble the oppressor, but *to be under* him, to depend on him. Accordingly, the oppressed are emotionally dependent.

> The peasant is a dependent. He can't say what he wants. Before
> he discovers his dependence, he suffers. He lets off steam at
> home, where he shouts at his children, beats them, and despairs.
> He complains about his wife and thinks everything is dreadful.
> He doesn't let off steam with the boss because he thinks the
> boss is a superior being. Lots of times, the peasant gives vent to
> his sorrows by drinking. [23]

This total emotional dependence can lead the oppressed to what Fromm calls necrophilic behavior: the destruction of life—their own or that of their oppressed fellows.

60   It is only when the oppressed find the oppressor out and become involved in the organized struggle for their liberation that they begin to believe in

---

[21] "The peasant has an almost instinctive fear of the boss." Interview with a peasant.
[22] See Regis Debray, *Revolution in the Revolution?* (New York, 1967).
[23] Interview with a peasant.

themselves. This discovery cannot be purely intellectual but must involve action; nor can it be limited to mere activism, but must include serious reflection: only then will it be a praxis.

Critical and liberating dialogue, which presupposes action, must be carried on with the oppressed at whatever the stage of their struggle for liberation.[24] The content of that dialogue can and should vary in accordance with historical conditions and the level at which the oppressed perceive reality. But to substitute monologue, slogans, and communiqués for dialogue is to attempt to liberate the oppressed with the instruments of domestication. Attempting to liberate the oppressed without their reflective participation in the act of liberation is to treat them as objects which must be saved from a burning building; it is to lead them into the populist pitfall and transform them into masses which can be manipulated.

At all stages of their liberation, the oppressed must see themselves as men engaged in the ontological and historical vocation of becoming more fully human. Reflection and action become imperative when one does not erroneously attempt to dichotomize the content of humanity from its historical forms.

The insistence that the oppressed engage in reflection on their concrete situation is not a call to armchair revolution. On the contrary, reflection—true reflection—leads to action. On the other hand, when the situation calls for action, that action will constitute an authentic praxis only if its consequences become the object of critical reflection. In this sense, the praxis is the new *raison d'être* of the oppressed; and the revolution, which inaugurates the historical moment of this *raison d'être,* is not viable apart from their concomitant conscious involvement. Otherwise, action is pure activism.

To achieve this praxis, however, it is necessary to trust in the oppressed and in their ability to reason. Whoever lacks this trust will fail to initiate (or will abandon) dialogue, reflection, and communication, and will fall into using slogans, communiqués, monologues, and instructions. Superficial conversions to the cause of liberation carry this danger.

Political action on the side of the oppressed must be pedagogical action in the authentic sense of the word, and, therefore, action *with* the oppressed. Those who work for liberation must not take advantage of the emotional dependence of the oppressed—dependence that is the fruit of the concrete situation of domination which surrounds them and which engendered their unauthentic view of the world. Using their dependence to create still greater dependence is an oppressor tactic.

Libertarian action must recognize this dependence as a weak point and must attempt through reflection and action to transform it into independence. However, not even the best-intentioned leadership can bestow independence as a gift. The liberation of the oppressed is a liberation of men, not

---

[24]Not in the open, of course; that would only provoke the fury of the oppressor and lead to still greater repression.

things. Accordingly, while no one liberates himself by his own efforts alone, neither is he liberated by others. Liberation, a human phenomenon, cannot be achieved by semihumans. Any attempt to treat men as semihumans only dehumanizes them. When men are already dehumanized, due to the oppression they suffer, the process of their liberation must not employ the methods of dehumanization.

The correct method for a revolutionary leadership to employ in the task of liberation is, therefore, *not* "libertarian propaganda." Nor can the leadership merely "implant" in the oppressed a belief in freedom, thus thinking to win their trust. The correct method lies in dialogue. The conviction of the oppressed that they must fight for their liberation is not a gift bestowed by the revolutionary leadership, but the result of their own *conscientização*.

The revolutionary leaders must realize that their own conviction of the necessity for struggle (an indispensable dimension of revolutionary wisdom) was not given to them by anyone else—if it is authentic. This conviction cannot be packaged and sold; it is reached, rather, by means of a totality of reflection and action. Only the leaders' own involvement in reality, within an historical situation, led them to criticize this situation and to wish to change it.

Likewise, the oppressed (who do not commit themselves to the struggle unless they are convinced, and who, if they do not make such a commitment, withhold the indispensable conditions for this struggle) must reach this conviction as Subjects, not as objects. They also must intervene critically in the situation which surrounds them and whose mark they bear; propaganda cannot achieve this. While the conviction of the necessity for struggle (without which the struggle is unfeasible) is indispensable to the revolutionary leadership (indeed, it was this conviction which constituted that leadership), it is also necessary for the oppressed. It is necessary, that is, unless one intends to carry out the transformation *for* the oppressed rather than *with* them. It is my belief that only the latter form of transformation is valid.

70   The object in presenting these considerations is to defend the eminently pedagogical character of the revolution. The revolutionary leaders of every epoch who have affirmed that the oppressed must accept the struggle for their liberation—an obvious point—have also thereby implicitly recognized the pedagogical aspect of this struggle. Many of these leaders, however (perhaps due to natural and understandable biases against pedagogy), have ended up using the "educational" methods employed by the oppressor. They deny pedagogical action in the liberation process, but they use propaganda to convince.

It is essential for the oppressed to realize that when they accept their struggle for humanization they also accept, from that moment, their total responsibility for the struggle. They must realize that they are fighting not merely for freedom from hunger, but for

> ... freedom to create and to construct, to wonder and to venture. Such freedom requires that the individual be active and responsible, not a slave or a well-fed cog in the machine. ...

> It is not enough that men are not slaves; if social conditions
> further the existence of automatons, the result will not be love
> of life, but love of death.[25]

The oppressed, who have been shaped by the death-affirming climate of oppression, must find through their struggle the way to life-affirming humanization, which does not lie *simply* in having more to eat (although it does involve having more to eat and cannot fail to include this aspect). The oppressed have been destroyed precisely because their situation has reduced them to things. In order to regain their humanity they must cease to be things and fight as men. This is a radical requirement. They cannot enter the struggle as objects in order *later* to become men.

The struggle begins with men's recognition that they have been destroyed. Propaganda, management, manipulation—all arms of domination—cannot be the instruments of their rehumanization. The only effective instrument is a humanizing pedagogy in which the revolutionary leadership establishes a permanent relationship of dialogue with the oppressed. In a humanizing pedagogy the method ceases to be an instrument by which the teachers (in this instance, the revolutionary leadership) can manipulate the students (in this instance, the oppressed), because it expresses the consciousness of the students themselves.

> The method is, in fact, the external form of consciousness
> manifest in acts, which takes on the fundamental property of
> consciousness—its intentionality. The essence of consciousness
> is being with the world, and this behavior is permanent and
> unavoidable. Accordingly, consciousness is in essence a "way
> towards" something apart from itself, outside itself, which sur-
> rounds it and which it apprehends by means of its ideational
> capacity. Consciousness is thus by definition a method, in the
> most general sense of the word.[26]

A revolutionary leadership must accordingly practice *co-intentional* education. Teachers and students (leadership and people), co-intent on reality, are both Subjects, not only in the task of unveiling that reality, and thereby coming to know it critically, but in the task of re-creating that knowledge. As they attain this knowledge of reality through common reflection and action, they discover themselves as its permanent re-creators. In this way, the presence of the oppressed in the struggle for their liberation will be what it should be: not pseudo-participation, but committed involvement.

---

[25] Fromm, *op. cit.*, pp. 52–53.

[26] Alvaro Vieira Pinto, from a work in preparation on the philosophy of science. I consider the quoted portion of great importance for the understanding of a problem-posing pedagogy (to be presented in Chapter 2), and wish to thank Professor Vieira Pinto for permission to cite his work prior to publication.

ON PSYCHOLOGICAL OPPRESSION

Sandra Lee Bartky

In *Black Skin, White Masks,* Frantz Fanon offers an anguished and eloquent description of the psychological effects of colonialism on the colonized, a "clinical study" of what he calls the "psychic alienation of the black man." "Those who recognize themselves in it," he says, "will have made a step forward."[1] Fanon's black American readers saw at once that he had captured the corrosive effects not only of classic colonial oppression but of domestic racism too, and that his study fitted well the picture of black America as an internal colony. Without wanting in any way to diminish the oppressive and stifling realities of black experience that Fanon reveals, let me say that I, a white woman, recognize myself in this book too, not only in my "shameful livery of white incomprehension,"[2] but as myself the victim of a "psychic alienation" similar to the one Fanon has described. In this paper I shall try to explore that moment of recognition, to reveal the ways in which the psychological effects of sexist oppression resemble those of racism and colonialism.

To oppress, says Webster, is "to lie heavy on, to weigh down, to exercise harsh dominion over." When we describe a people as oppressed, what we have in mind most often is an oppression that is economic and political in character. But recent liberation movements, the black liberation movement and the women's movement in particular, have brought to light forms of oppression that are not immediately economic or political. It is possible to be oppressed in ways that need involve neither physical deprivation, legal inequality, nor economic exploitation;[3] one can be oppressed psychologically—the "psychic alienation" of which Fanon speaks. To be psychologically oppressed is to be weighed down in your mind; it is to have a harsh dominion exercised over your self-esteem. The psychologically oppressed become their own oppressors; they come to exercise harsh dominion over their own self-esteem. Differently put, psychological oppression can be regarded as the "internalization of intimations of inferiority."[4]

Like economic oppression, psychological oppression is institutionalized and systematic; it serves to make the work of domination easier by breaking the spirit of the dominated and by rendering them incapable of understanding the nature of those agencies responsible for their subjugation. This allows those who benefit from the established order of things to maintain their ascendancy with more appearance of legitimacy and with less recourse to overt acts of violence than they might otherwise require. Now, poverty and powerlessness can destroy a person's self-esteem, and the fact that one occupies an inferior position in society is all too often racked up to one's being an inferior sort of person. Clearly, then, economic and political oppression are themselves psychologically oppressive. But there are unique modes of psychological oppression that can be distinguished from the usual forms of economic and political domination. Fanon offers a series of what are essentially phenomenological descriptions of psychic alienation.[5] In spite of considerable overlapping, the experiences of oppression he describes fall into three categories: stereotyping, cultural domination, and sexual objectification. These, I shall contend, are some of the ways in which the terrible messages of inferiority can be delivered even to those who may enjoy certain material benefits; they are special modes of psychic alienation. In what follows, I shall examine some of the ways in which American women—white women and women of color—are stereotyped, culturally dominated, and sexually objectified. In the course of the discussion, I shall argue that our ordinary concept of oppression needs to be altered and expanded, for it is too restricted to encompass what an analysis of psychological oppression reveals about the nature of oppression in general. Finally, I shall be concerned throughout to show how both fragmentation and mystification are present in each mode of psychological oppression, although in varying degrees: fragmentation, the splitting of the whole person into parts of a person which, in stereotyping, may take the form of a war between a "true" and "false" self—or, in sexual objectification, the form of an often coerced and degrading identification of a person with her body; mystification, the systematic obscuring of both the reality and agencies of psychological oppression so that its intended effect, the depreciated self, is lived out as destiny, guilt, or neurosis.

The stereotypes that sustain sexism are similar in many ways to those that sustain racism. Like white women, black and brown persons of both sexes have been regarded as childlike, happiest when they are occupying their "place"; more intuitive than rational, more spontaneous than deliberate, closer to nature, and less capable of substantial cultural accomplishment. Black men and women of all races have been victims of sexual stereotyping: The black man and the black woman, like the "Latin spitfire," are lustful and hotblooded; they are thought to lack the capacities for instinctual control that distinguish people from animals. What is seen as an excess in persons of color appears as a deficiency in the white woman; comparatively frigid, she has been, nonetheless, defined by her sexuality as well, here her reproductive role or function. In regard to capability and competence, black women have, again, an excess of what in white women is a deficiency. White women have been seen as incapable and incompetent: no matter, for these are traits of the truly feminine woman. Black women, on the other hand, have been seen as overly capable, hence, as unfeminine bitches who threaten, through their very competence, to castrate their men.

Stereotyping is morally reprehensible as well as psychologically oppressive on two counts, at least. First, it can hardly be expected that those who hold a set of stereotyped beliefs about the sort of person I am will understand   *5* my need or even respect my rights. Second, suppose that I, the object of some stereotype, believe in it myself—for why should I not believe what everyone else believes? I may then find it difficult to achieve what existentialists call an authentic choice of self, or what some psychologists have regarded as a state of self-actualization. Moral philosophers have quite correctly placed a high value, sometimes the highest value, on the development of autonomy and moral agency. Clearly, the economic and political domination of women— our concrete powerlessness—is what threatens our autonomy most. But stereotyping, in its own way, threatens our self-determination too. Even when economic and political obstacles on the path to autonomy are removed, a depreciated alter ego still blocks the way. It is hard enough for me to determine what sort of person I am or ought to try to become without being shadowed by an alternate self, a truncated and inferior self that I have, in some sense, been doomed to be all the time. For many, the prefabricated self triumphs over a more authentic self which, with work and encouragement, might sometime have emerged. For the talented few, retreat into the *imago* is raised to the status of art or comedy. Muhammad Ali has made himself what he could scarcely escape being made into—a personification of Primitive Man; while Zsa Zsa Gabor is not so much a woman as the parody of a woman.

Female stereotypes threaten the autonomy of women not only by virtue of their existence but also by virtue of their content.[6] In the conventional portrait, women deny their femininity when they undertake action that is too self-regarding or independent. As we have seen, black women are condemned (often by black men) for supposedly having done this already; white women stand under an injunction not to follow their example. Many women in many places lacked (and many still lack) the elementary right to choose our own mates; but for some women even in our own society today, this is virtually the only major decision we are thought capable of making without putting our womanly nature in danger; what follows ever after is or ought to be a properly feminine submission to the decisions of men. We cannot be autonomous, as men are thought to be autonomous, without in some sense ceasing to be women. When one considers how interwoven are traditional female stereotypes with traditional female roles—and these, in turn, with the ways in which we are socialized—all this is seen in an even more sinister light: White women, at least, are psychologically conditioned not to pursue the kind of autonomous development that is held by the culture to be a constitutive feature of masculinity.

The truncated self I am to be is not something manufactured out there by an anonymous Other which I encounter only in the pages of *Playboy* or the *Ladies' Home Journal;* it is inside of me, a part of myself. I may become infatuated with my feminine persona and waste my powers in the more or less hopeless pursuit of a *Vogue* figure, the look of an *Essence* model, or a home that "expresses my personality." Or I may find the parts of myself fragmented and the fragments at war with one another. Women are only now learning to identify and struggle against the forces that have laid these psychic burdens upon us. More often than not, we live out this struggle, which is really struggle against oppression, in a mystified way: What we are enduring we believe to be entirely intrapsychic in character, the result of immaturity, maladjustment, or even neurosis.

Tyler, the great classical anthropologist, defined culture as all the items in the general life of a people. To claim that women are victims of cultural domination is to claim that all the items in the general life of our people—our language, our institutions, our art and literature, our popular culture—are sexist; that all, to a greater or lesser degree, manifest male supremacy. There is some exaggeration in this claim, but not much. Unlike the black colonial whom Fanon describes with such pathos, women *qua* women are not now in possession of an alternate culture, a "native" culture which, even if regarded by everyone, including ourselves, as decidedly inferior to the dominant culture, we could at least recognize as our own. However degraded or distorted an image of ourselves we see reflected in the patriarchal culture, the culture of our men is still our culture. Certainly in some respects, the condition of women is like the condition of a colonized people. But we are not a colonized people; we have never been more than half a people.[7]

This lack of cultural autonomy has several important consequences for an understanding of the condition of women. A culture has a global character; hence, the limits of my culture are the limits of my world. The subordination of women, then, because it is so pervasive a feature of my culture, will (if uncontested) appear to be natural—and because it is natural, unalterable. Unlike a colonized people, women have no memory of a "time before": a time before the masters came, a time before we were subjugated and ruled. Further, since one function of cultural identity is to allow me to distinguish those who are like me from those who are not, I may feel more kinship with those who share my culture, even though they oppress me, than with the women of another culture, whose whole experience of life may well be closer to my own than to any man's.

Our true situation in regard to male supremacist culture is one of domination and exclusion. But this manifests itself in an extremely deceptive way; mystification once more holds sway. Our relative absence from the "higher" culture is taken as proof that we are unable to participate in it ("Why are there no great women artists?"). Theories of the female nature must then be brought forward to try to account for this.[8] The splitting or fragmenting of women's consciousness which takes place in the cultural sphere is also apparent. While remaining myself, I must at the same time transform myself into that abstract and "universal" subject for whom cultural artifacts are made and whose values and experience they express. This subject is not universal at all, however, but *male*. Thus, I must approve the taming of the shrew, laugh at the mother-in-law or the dumb blonde, and somehow identify with all those heroes of fiction from Faust to the personae of Norman Mailer and Henry Miller, whose *Bildungsgeschichten* involve the sexual exploitation of women. Women of color have, of course, a special problem: The dominant cultural subject is not only male, but *white,* so their cultural alienation is doubled; they are expected to assimilate cultural motifs that are not only masculinist but racist.[9]

Women of all races and ethnicities, like Fanon's "black man," are subject not only to stereotyping and cultural depreciation but to sexual objectification as well. Even though much has been written about sexual objectification in the literature of the women's movement, the notion itself is complex, obscure, and much in need of philosophical clarification. I offer the following preliminary characterization of sexual objectification: A person is sexually objectified when her sexual parts or sexual functions are separated out from the rest of her personality and reduced to the status of mere instruments or else regarded as if they were capable of representing her. On this definition, then, the prostitute would be a victim of sexual objectification, as would the *Playboy* bunny, the female breeder, and the bathing beauty.

To say that the sexual part of a person is regarded as if it could represent her is to imply that it cannot, that the part and the whole are incommensurable. But surely there are times, in the sexual embrace perhaps, when a woman might want to be regarded as nothing but a sexually intoxicating body and when attention paid to some other aspect of her person—say, to her mathematical ability—would be absurdly out of place. If sexual relations involve some sexual objectification, then it becomes necessary to distinguish situations in which sexual objectification is oppressive from the sorts of situations in which it is not.[10] The identification of a person with her sexuality becomes oppressive, one might venture, when such an identification becomes habitually extended into every area of her experience. To be routinely perceived by others in a sexual light on occasions when such a perception is inappropriate is to have one's very being subjected to that compulsive sexualization that has been the traditional lot of both white women and black men and women of color generally. "For the majority of white men," says Fanon, "the Negro is the incarnation of a genital potency beyond all moralities and prohibitions."[11] Later in *Black Skin, White Masks,* he writes that "the Negro is the genital."[12]

One way to be sexually objectified, then, is to be the object of a kind of perception, unwelcome and inappropriate, that takes the part for the whole. An example may make this clearer. A young woman was recently interviewed for a teaching job in philosophy by the academic chairman of a large department. During most of the interview, so she reported, the man stared fixedly at her breasts. In this situation, the woman is a bosom, not a job candidate. Was this department chairman guilty only of a confusion between business and pleasure? Scarcely. He stares at her breasts for his sake, not hers. Her wants and needs not only play no role in the encounter but, because of the direction of his attention, she is discomfited, feels humiliated, and performs badly. Not surprisingly, she fails to get the job. Much of the time, sexual objectification occurs independently of what women want; it is something done to us against our will. It is clear from this example that the objectifying perception that splits a person into parts serves to elevate one interest above another. Now it stands revealed not only as a way of perceiving, but as a way of maintaining dominance as well. It is not clear to me that the sexual and nonsexual spheres of experience can or ought to be kept separate forever (Marcuse, for one, has envisioned the eroticization of all areas of human life); but as things stand now, sexualization is one way of fixing disadvantaged persons in their disadvantage, to their clear detriment and within a narrow and repressive eros.

Consider now a second example of the way in which that fragmenting perception, which is so large an ingredient in the sexual objectification of women, serves to maintain the dominance of men. It is a fine spring day, and with an utter lack of self-consciousness, I am bouncing down the street. Suddenly I hear men's voices. Catcalls and whistles fill the air. These noises are clearly sexual in intent and they are meant for me; they come from across the street. I freeze. As Sartre would say, I have been petrified by the gaze of the Other. My face flushes and my motions become stiff and self-conscious. The body which only a moment before I inhabited with such ease now floods my consciousness. I have been made into an object. While it is true that for these men I am nothing but, let us say, a "nice piece of ass," there is more involved in this encounter than their mere fragmented perception of me. They could, after all, have enjoyed me in silence. Blissfully unaware, breasts bouncing, eyes on the birds in the trees, I could have passed by without having been turned to stone. But I must be *made* to know that I am a "nice piece of ass": I must be made to see myself as they see me. There is an element of compulsion in this encounter, in this being-made-to-be-aware of one's own flesh; like being made to apologize, it is humiliating. It is unclear what role is played by sexual arousal or even sexual connoisseurship in encounters like these. What I describe seems less the spontaneous expression of a healthy eroticism than a ritual of subjugation.

Sexual objectification as I have characterized it involves two persons: the one who objectifies and the one who is objectified. But the observer and the one observed can be the same person. I can, of course, take pleasure in my own body as another might take pleasure in it and it would be naïve not to notice that there are delights of a narcissistic kind that go along with the status "sex object." But the extent to which the identification of women with their bodies feeds an essentially infantile narcissism—an attitude of mind in keeping with our forced infantilization in other areas of life—is, at least for me, an open question. Subject to the evaluating eye of the male connoisseur, women learn to evaluate themselves first and best. Our identities can no more be kept separate from the appearance of our bodies than they can be kept separate from the shadow-selves of the female stereotype. "Much of a young woman's identity is already defined in her kind of attractiveness and in the selectivity of her search for the man (or men) by whom she wishes to be sought."[13] There is something obsessional in the preoccupation of many women with their bodies, although the magnitude of the obsession will vary somewhat with the presence or absence in a woman's life of other sources of self-esteem and with her capacity to gain a living independent of her looks. Surrounded on all sides by images of perfect female beauty—for, in modern advertising, the needs of capitalism and the traditional values of patriarchy are happily married—of course we fall short. The narcissism encouraged by our identification with the body is shattered by these images. Whose nose in not the wrong shape, whose hips are not too wide or too narrow? Anyone who believes that such concerns are too trivial to weigh very heavily with most women has failed to grasp the realities of the feminine condition.

The idea that women ought always to make themselves as pleasing to the eye as possible is very widespread indeed. It was dismaying to come across this passage in a paper written by an eminent Marxist humanist in defense of the contemporary women's movement:

> There is no reason why a woman's liberation activist should
> not try to look pretty and attractive. One of the universal
> human aspirations of all times was to raise reality to the level
> of art, to make the world more beautiful, to be more beautiful
> within given limits. Beauty is a value in itself; it will always be
> respected and will attract—to be sure various forms of beauty
> but not to the exclusion of physical beauty. A woman does not
> become a sex object in herself, or only because of her pretty
> appearance. She becomes a sexual object in relationship, when
> she allows a man to treat her in a certain depersonalizing, de-
> grading way; and vice versa, a woman does not become a sex-
> ual subject by neglecting her appearance.[14]

It is not for the sake of mere men that we women—not just we women, but we women's liberation activists—ought to look "pretty and attractive," but for the sake of something much more exalted: for the sake of beauty. This preoc-cupation with the way we look and the fear that women might stop trying to make themselves pretty and attractive (so as to "raise reality to the level of art") would be a species of objectification anywhere; but it is absurdly out of place in a paper on women's emancipation. It is as if an essay on the black lib-eration movement were to end by admonishing blacks not to forget their nat-ural rhythm, or as if Marx had warned the workers of the world not to neglect their appearance while throwing off their chains.

Markovic's concern with women's appearance merely reflects a larger cultural preoccupation. It is a fact that women in our society are regarded has having a virtual duty "to make the most of what we have." But the imperative not to neglect our appearance suggests that we can neglect it, that it is within our power to make ourselves look better—not just neater and cleaner, but prettier, and more attractive. What is presupposed by this is that we don't look good enough already, that attention to the ordinary standards of hygiene would be insufficient, that there is something wrong with us as we are. Here, the "intimations of inferiority" are clear: Not only must we continue to pro-duce ourselves as beautiful bodies, but the bodies we have to work with are deficient to begin with. Even within an already inferiorized identity (i.e., the identity of one who is principally and most importantly a body), I turn out once more to be inferior, for the body I am to be, never sufficient unto itself, stands forever in need of plucking or painting, of slimming down or fattening up, of firming or flattening.

The foregoing examination of three modes of psychological oppression, so it appears, points up the need for an alteration in our ordinary concept of oppression. Oppression, I believe, is ordinarily conceived in too limited a fashion. This has placed undue restrictions both on our understanding of what oppression itself is and on the categories of persons we might want to classify as oppressed. Consider, for example, the following paradigmatic case of oppression:

> And the Egyptians made the children of Israel to serve with
> rigor; and they made their lives bitter with hard bondage, in
> mortar and in brick, and in all manner of service in the field;
> all their service wherein they made them serve, was with
> rigor.[15]

Here the Egyptians, one group of persons, exercise harsh dominion over the Israelites, another group of persons. It is not suggested that the Israelites, however great their sufferings, have lost their integrity and wholeness *qua* persons. But psychological oppression is dehumanizing and depersonalizing; it attacks the person in her personhood. I mean by this that the nature of psychological oppression is such that the oppressor and oppressed alike come to doubt that the oppressed have the capacity to do the sorts of things that only persons can do, to be what persons, in the fullest sense of the term, can be. The possession of autonomy, for example, is widely thought to distinguish persons from nonpersons; but some female stereotypes, as we have seen, threaten the autonomy of women. Oppressed people might or might not be in a position to exercise their autonomy, but the psychologically oppressed may come to believe that they lack the capacity to be autonomous whatever their position.

Similarly, the creation of culture is a distinctly human function, perhaps the most human function. In its cultural life, a group is able to affirm its values and to grasp its identity in acts of self-reflection. Frequently, oppressed persons, cut off from the cultural apparatus, are denied the exercise of this function entirely. To the extent that we are able to catch sight of ourselves in the dominant culture at all, the images we see are distorted or demeaning. Finally, sexual objectification leads to the identification of those who undergo it with what is both human and not quite human—the body. Thus, psychological oppression is just what Fanon said it was—"psychic alienation"—the estrangement or separating of a person from some of the essential attributes of personhood.

Mystification surrounds these processes of human estrangement. The special modes of psychological oppression can be regarded as some of the many ways in which messages of inferiority are delivered to those who are to occupy

20

an inferior position in society. But it is important to remember that messages of this sort are neither sent nor received in an unambiguous way. We are taught that white women and (among others) black men and women are deficient in those capacities that distinguish persons from nonpersons, but at the same time we are assured that we are persons after all. *Of course* women are persons; *of course* blacks are human beings. Who but the lunatic fringe would deny it? The Antillean Negro, Fanon is fond of repeating, is a *Frenchman*. The official ideology announces with conviction that "all men are created equal"; and in spite of the suspect way in which this otherwise noble assertion is phrased, we women learn that they mean to include us after all.

It is itself psychologically oppressive both to believe and at the same time not to believe that one is inferior—in other words, to believe a contradiction. Lacking an analysis of the larger system of social relations which produced it, one can only make sense of this contradiction in two ways. First, while accepting in some quite formal sense the proposition that "all men are created equal," I can believe, inconsistently, what my oppressors have always believed: that some types of persons are less equal than others. I may then live out my membership in my sex or race in *shame;* I am "only a woman or "just a nigger." Or, somewhat more consistently, I may reject entirely the belief that my disadvantage is generic; but having still to account for it somehow, I may locate the cause squarely within myself, a bad destiny of an entirely private sort—a character flaw, an "inferiority complex," or a neurosis.

Many oppressed persons come to regard themselves as uniquely unable to satisfy normal criteria of psychological health or moral adequacy. To believe that my inferiority is a function of the kind of person I am may make me ashamed of being one of *this* kind. On the other hand, a lack I share with many others just because of an accident of birth would be unfortunate indeed, but at least I would not have to regard myself as having failed uniquely to measure up to standards that people like myself are expected to meet. It should be pointed out, however, that both of these "resolutions"—the ascription of one's inferiority to idiosyncratic or else to generic causes—produces a "poor self-image," a bloodless term of the behavioral sciences that refers to a very wide variety of possible ways to suffer.[16]

To take one's oppression to be an inherent flaw of birth, or of psychology, is to have what Marxists have characterized as "false consciousness." Systematically deceived as we are about the nature and origin of our unhappiness, our struggles are directed inward toward the self, or toward other similar selves in whom we may see our deficiencies mirrored, not outward upon those social forces responsible for our predicament. Like the psychologically disturbed, the psychologically oppressed often lack a viable identity. Frequently we are unable to make sense of our own impulses or feelings, not only because our drama of fragmentation gets played out on an inner psychic stage, but because we are forced to find our way about in a world which presents itself to us in a masked and deceptive fashion. Regarded as persons, yet depersonalized, we are treated by our society the way the parents of some schizophrenics are said by R. D. Laing to treat their children—professing love at the very moment they shrink from their children's touch.

In sum, then, to be psychologically oppressed is to be caught in the double bind of a society which both affirms my human status and at the same time bars me from the exercise of many of those typically human functions that bestow this status. To be denied an autonomous choice of self, forbidden cultural expression, and condemned to the immanence of mere bodily being is to be cut off from the sorts of activities that define what it is to be human. A person whose being has been subjected to these cleavages may be described as "alienated." Alienation in any form causes a rupture within the human person, an estrangement from self, a "splintering of human nature into a number of misbegotten parts."[17] Any adequate theory of the nature and varieties of human alienation, then, must encompass psychological oppression—or, to use Fanon's term once more, "psychic alienation."

Much has been written about alienation, but it is Marx's theory of alienation that speaks most compellingly to the concerns of feminist political theory. Alienation for Marx is primarily the alienation of labor. What distinguishes human beings from animals is "labor"—for Marx, the free, conscious, and creative transformation of nature in accordance with human needs. But under capitalism, workers are alienated in production, estranged from the products of their labor, from their own productive activity, and from their fellow workers.

Human productive activity, according to Marx, is "objectified" in its products. What this means is that we are able to grasp ourselves reflectively primarily in the things we have produced; human needs and powers become concrete "in their products as the amount and type of change which their exercise has brought about."[18] But in capitalist production, the capitalist has a right to appropriate what workers have produced. Thus, the product goes to augment capital, where it becomes part of an alien force exercising power over those who produced it. An "objectification" or extension of the worker's self, the product is split off from this self and turned against it. But workers are alienated not only from the products they produce but from their own laboring activity as well, for labor under capitalism is not, as labor should be, an occasion for human self-realization but mere drudgery which "mortifies the body and ruins the mind."[19] The worker's labor "is therefore not voluntary, but coerced; it is forced labor. It is therefore not the satisfaction of a need; it is merely a means to satisfy needs external to it."[20] When the free and creative productive activity that should define human functioning is reduced to a mere means to sustain life, to "forced labor," workers suffer fragmentation and loss of self. Since labor is the most characteristic human life activity, to be alienated from one's own labor is to be estranged from oneself.

In may ways, psychic alienation and the alienation of labor are profoundly alike. Both involve a splitting off of human functions from the human person, a forbidding of activities thought to be essential to a fully human existence. Both subject the individual to fragmentation and impoverishment. Alienation is not a condition into which someone might stumble by accident; it has come both to the victim of psychological oppression and to the alienated worker from without, as a usurpation by someone else of what is, by rights, *not his to usurp.*[21] Alienation occurs in each case when activities which not only belong to the domain of the self but define, in large measure, the proper functioning of this self, fall under the control of others. To be a victim of alienation is to have a part of one's being stolen by another. Both psychic alienation and the alienation of labor might be regarded as varieties of alienated productivity. From this perspective, cultural domination would be the estrangement or alienation of production in the cultural sphere; while the subjective effects of stereotyping as well as the self-objectification that regularly accompanies sexual objectification could be interpreted as an alienation in the production of one's own person.

All the modes of oppression—psychological, political, and economic—and the kinds of alienation they generate serve to maintain a vast system of privilege—privilege of race, of sex, and of class. Every mode of oppression within the system has its own part to play, but each serves to support and to maintain the others. Thus, for example, the assault on the self-esteem of white women and of black persons of both sexes prepares us for the historic role that a disproportionate number of us are destined to play within the process of production: that of a cheap or reserve labor supply. Class oppression, in turn, encourages those who are somewhat higher in the hierarchies of race or gender to cling to a false sense of superiority—a poor compensation indeed. Because of the interlocking character of the modes of oppression, I think it highly unlikely that any form of oppression will disappear entirely until the system of oppression as a whole is overthrown.

NOTES

1. Frantz Fanon, *Black Skin, White Masks* (New York: Grove Press, 1967), p. 12.
2. Ibid.
3. For an excellent comparison of the concepts of exploitation and oppression, see Judith Farr Tormey, "Exploitation, Oppression and Self-Sacrifice," in *Women and Philosophy,* ed. Carol C. Gould and Marx W. Wartofsky (New York: G. P. Putnam's Sons, 1976), pp. 206–221.
4. Joyce Mitchell Cook, paper delivered at Philosophy and the Black Liberation Struggle Conference, University of Illinois, Chicago Circle, November 19–20, 1970.
5. Fanon's phenomenology of oppression, however, is almost entirely a phenomenology of the oppression of colonized *men.* He seems unaware of the ways in which the oppression of women by their men in the societies he examines is itself similar to the colonization of natives by Europeans. Sometimes, as in *A Dying Colonialism* (New York: Grove Press, 1968), he goes so far as to defend the clinging to oppressive practices, such as the sequestration of women in Moslem countries, as an authentic resistance by indigenous people to Western cultural intrusion. For a penetrating critique of Fanon's attitude toward women, see Barbara Burris, "Fourth World Manifesto," in

Radical Feminism, ed. A. Koedt, E. Levine, and A. Rapone (New York: Quadrangle, 1973), pp. 322–357.

6. I have in mind Abraham Maslow's concept of autonomy, a notion which has the advantage of being neutral as regards the controversy between free will and determinism. For Maslow, the sources of behavior of autonomous or "psychologically free" individuals are more internal than reactive:

> Such people become far more self-sufficient and self-contained. The determinants which govern them are now primarily inner ones. . . . They are the laws of their own inner nature, their potentialities and capacities, their talents, their latent resources, their creative impulses, their needs to know themselves and to become more and more integrated and unified, more and more aware of what they really are, of what they really want, of what their call or vocation or fate is to be. (*Toward a Psychology of Being,* 2d ed. [New York: D. Van Nostrand Co., 1968], p. 35).

It would be absurd to suggest that most men are autonomous in this sense of the term. Nevertheless, insofar as there are individuals who resemble this portrait, I think it likelier that they will be men than women—at least white women. I think it likely that more white men than white women *believe* themselves to be autonomous; this belief, even if false, is widely held, and this in itself has implications that are important to consider. Whatever the facts may be in regard to men's lives, the point to remember is this: women have been thought to have neither the capacity nor the right to aspire to an ideal of autonomy, an ideal to which there accrues, whatever its relation to mental health, an enormous social prestige.

7. Many feminists would object vigorously to my claim that there has been no female culture (see, e.g., Burris, "Fourth World Manifesto"). I am not claiming that women have had no enclaves within the dominant culture, that we have never made valuable contributions to the larger culture, or even that we have never dominated any avenue of cultural expression—one would have to think only of the way in which women have dominated certain forms of folk art (e.g., quilting). What I am claiming is that none of this adds up to a "culture," in the sense in which we speak of Jewish culture, Arapesh culture, or Afro-American culture. Further, the fact that many women are today engaged in the self-conscious attempt to create a female culture testifies, I think, to the situation regarding culture being essentially as I describe it.

8. The best-known modern theory of this type is, of course, Freud's. He maintains that the relative absence of women from the higher culture is the consequence of a lesser ability to sublimate libidinal drives. See "Femininity," in *New Introductory Lectures in Psychoanalysis* (New York: W. W. Norton, 1933).

9. I take it that something like this forms the backdrop to the enjoyment of the average movie. It is daunting to consider the magnitude of the task of neutralization or transformation of hostile cultural messages that must fall constantly to the average female, non-white or even working class white male TV watcher or moviegoer. The pleasure we continue to take in cultural products that may disparage us remains, at least to me, something of a mystery.

10. There might be some objection to regarding ordinary sexual relations as involving sexual objectification, since this use of the term seems not to jibe with its use in more

ordinary contexts. For Hegel, Marx, and Sartre, "objectification" is an important moment in the dialectic of consciousness. My decision to treat ordinary sexual relations or even sexual desire alone as involving some objectification is based on a desire to remain within this tradition. Further, Sartre's phenomenology of sexual desire in *Being and Nothingness* (New York: Philosophical Library, 1966) draws heavily on a concept of objectification in an unusually compelling description of the experienced character of that state:

> The caress by realizing the Other's incarnation reveals to me my own incarnation; that is, I make myself flesh in order to impel the Other to realize for-herself and for-me her own flesh, and my caresses cause my flesh to be born for me in so far as it is for the Other flesh causing her to be born as flesh. I make her enjoy my flesh through her flesh in order to compel her to feel herself flesh. And so possession truly appears as a double reciprocal incarnation. (p. 508)

What I call "objectification," Sartre here calls "incarnation," a refinement not necessary for my purposes. What he call "sadism" is incarnation without reciprocity. Most of my examples of sexual objectification would fall into the latter category.

11. Fanon, *Black Skin, White Masks*, p. 177. Eldridge Cleaver sounds a similar theme in *Soul on Ice* (New York: Dell 1968). The archetypal white man in American society, for Cleaver, is the "Omnipotent Administrator," the archetypal black man the "Super-Masculine Menial."

12. Ibid., p. 180.

13. Erik Erikson, "Inner and Outer Space: Reflections on Womanhood," *Daedalus,* vol. 93, 1961, pp. 582–606.

14. Mihailo Markovic, "Women's Liberation and Human Emancipation," in *Women and Philosophy,* pp. 165–166. In spite of this lapse and some questionable opinions concerning the nature of female sexuality, Markovic's paper is a most compelling defense of the claim that the emancipation of women cannot come about under capitalism.

15. Exod. 1:13–14.

16. The available clinical literature on the psychological effects of social inferiority supports this claim. See William H. Grier and Price M. Cobbs, *Black Rage* (New York: Grosset & Dunlap, 1969); Pauline Bart, "Depression in Middle-Aged Women," in *Women in Sexist Society,* ed. Vivian Gornick and Barbara Moran (New York: New American Library, 1971), pp. 163–186; also Phyllis Chesler, *Women and Madness* (New York: Doubleday, 1972).

17. Bertell Ollman, *Alienation: Marx's Conception of Man in Capitalist Society* (London and New York: Cambridge University Press, 1971), p. 135.

18. Ibid. p. 143.

19. Karl Marx, *The Economic and Philosophical Manuscripts of 1844,* ed. Dirk J. Struik (New York: International Publishers, 1964), p. 111.

20. Ibid.

21. The use of the masculine possessive pronoun is deliberate.

FIVE FACES OF OPPRESSION

Iris Young

*Someone who does not see a pane of glass does not know that he does not see it.
Someone who, being placed differently, does see it, does not know the other does
not see it.*

*When our will finds expression outside ourselves in actions performed by others,
we do not waste our time and our power of attention in examining whether they have
consented to this. This is true for all of us. Our attention, given entirely to the success of
the undertaking, is not claimed by them as long as they are docile. . . .*

*Rape is a terrible caricature of love from which consent is absent. After rape, oppres-
sion is the second horror of human existence. It is a terrible caricature of obedience.*

— SIMONE WEIL

I have proposed an enabling conception of justice. Justice should refer not
only to distribution, but also to the institutional conditions necessary for the
development and exercise of individual capacities and collective communication and cooperation. Under this conception of justice, injustice refers primarily to two forms of disabling constraints, oppression and domination.
While these constraints include distributive patterns, they also involve matters
which cannot easily be assimilated to the logic of distribution: decisionmaking procedures, division of labor, and culture.

Many people in the United States would not choose the term "oppression" to name injustice in our society. For contemporary emancipatory social
movements, on the other hand—socialists, radical feminists, American Indian
activists, Black activists, gay and lesbian activists—oppression is a central category of political discourse. Entering the political discourse in which oppression is a central category involves adopting a general mode of analyzing and
evaluating social structures and practices which is incommensurate with the
language of liberal individualism that dominates political discourse in the
United States.

A major political project for those of us who identify with at least one of
these movements must thus be to persuade people that the discourse of oppression makes sense of much of our social experience. We are ill prepared for
this task, however, because we have no clear account of the meaning of oppression. While we find the term used often in the diverse philosophical literature spawned by radical social movements in the United States, we find little
direct discussion of the meaning of the concept as used by these movements.

In this chapter I offer some explication of the concept of oppression as I
understand its use by new social movements in the United States since the

1960s. My starting point is reflection on the conditions of the groups said by these movements to be oppressed: among others women, Blacks, Chicanos, Puerto Ricans and other Spanish-speaking Americans, American Indians, Jews, lesbians, gay men, Arabs, Asians, old people, working-class people, and the physically and mentally disabled. I aim to systematize the meaning of the concept of oppression as used by these diverse political movements, and to provide normative argument to clarify the wrongs the term names.

5   Obviously the above-named groups are not oppressed to the same extent or in the same ways. In the most general sense, all oppressed people suffer some inhibition of their ability to develop and exercise their capacities and express their needs, thoughts, and feelings. In that abstract sense all oppressed people face a common condition. Beyond that, in any more specific sense, it is not possible to define a single set of criteria that describe the condition of oppression of the above groups. Consequently, attempts by theorists and activists to discover a common description or the essential causes of the oppression of all these groups have frequently led to fruitless disputes about whose oppression is more fundamental or more grave. The contexts in which members of these groups use the term oppression to describe the injustices of their situation suggest that oppression names in fact a family of concepts and conditions, which I divide into five categories: exploitation, marginalization, powerlessness, cultural imperialism, and violence.

In this chapter I explicate each of these forms of oppression. Each may entail or cause distributive injustices, but all involve issues of justice beyond distribution. In accordance with ordinary political usage, I suggest that oppression is a condition of groups. Thus before explicating the meaning of oppression, we must examine the concept of a social group.

OPPRESSION AS A STRUCTURAL CONCEPT

One reason that many people would not use the term oppression to describe injustice in our society is that they do not understand the term in the same way as do new social movements. In its traditional usage, oppression means the exercise of tyranny by a ruling group. Thus many Americans would agree with radicals in applying the term oppression to the situation of Black South Africans under apartheid. Oppression also traditionally carries a strong connotation of conquest and colonial domination. The Hebrews were oppressed in Egypt, and many uses of the term oppression in the West invoke this paradigm.

Dominant political discourse may use the term oppression to describe societies other than our own, usually Communist or purportedly Communist societies. Within this anti-Communist rhetoric both tyrannical and colonialist implications of the term appear. For the anti-Communist, Communism denotes precisely the exercise of brutal tyranny over a whole people by a few rulers, and the will to conquer the world, bringing hitherto independent peoples under that tyranny. In dominant political discourse it is not legitimate to use the term oppression to describe our society, because oppression is the evil perpetrated by the Others.

New left social movements of the 1960s and 1970s, however, shifted the meaning of the concept of oppression. In its new usage, oppression designates the disadvantage and injustice some people suffer not because a tyrannical power coerces them, but because of the everyday practices of a well-intentioned liberal society. In this new left usage, the tyranny of a ruling group over another, as in South Africa, must certainly be called oppressive. But oppression also refers to systemic constraints on groups that are not necessarily the result of the intentions of a tyrant. Oppression in this sense is structural, rather than the result of a few people's choices or policies. Its causes are embedded in unquestioned norms, habits, and symbols, in the assumptions underlying institutional rules and the collective consequences of following those rules. It names, as Marilyn Frye puts it, "an enclosing structure of forces and barriers which tends to the immobilization and reduction of a group or category of people" (Frye, 1983, p. 11). In this extended structural sense oppression refers to the vast and deep injustices some groups suffer as a consequence of often unconscious assumptions and reactions of well-meaning people in ordinary interactions, media and cultural stereotypes, and structural features of bureaucratic hierarchies and market mechanisms—in short, the normal processes of everyday life. We cannot eliminate this structural oppression by getting rid of the rulers or making some new laws, because oppressions are systematically reproduced in major economic, political, and cultural institutions.

The systemic character of oppression implies that an oppressed group *10* need not have a correlate oppressing group. While structural oppression involves relations among groups, these relations do not always fit the paradigm of conscious and intentional oppression of one group by another. Foucault (1977) suggests that to understand the meaning and operation of power in modern society we must look beyond the model of power as "sovereignty," a dyadic relation of ruler and subject, and instead analyze the exercise of power as the effect of often liberal and "humane" practices of education, bureaucratic administration, production and distribution of consumer goods, medicine, and so on. The conscious actions of many individuals daily contribute to maintaining and reproducing oppression, but those people are usually simply doing their jobs or living their lives, and do not understand themselves as agents of oppression.

I do not mean to suggest that within a system of oppression individual persons do not intentionally harm others in oppressed groups. The raped woman, the beaten Black youth, the locked-out worker, the gay man harassed on the street, are victims of intentional actions by identifiable agents. I also do not mean to deny that specific groups are beneficiaries of the oppression of other groups, and thus have an interest in their continued oppression. Indeed, for every oppressed group there is a group that is *privileged* in relation to that group.

The concept of oppression has been current among radicals since the 1960s partly in reaction to Marxist attempts to reduce the injustices of racism and sexism, for example, to the effects of class domination or bourgeois ideology. Racism, sexism, ageism, homophobia, some social movements asserted, are distinct forms of oppression with their own dynamics apart from the dynamics of class, even though they may interact with class oppression. From often heated discussions among socialists, feminists, and antiracism activists in the last ten years a consensus is emerging that many different groups must be said to be oppressed in our society, and that no single form of oppression can be assigned causal or moral primacy (see Gottlieb, 1987). The same discussion has also led to the recognition that group differences cut across individual lives in a multiplicity of ways that can entail privilege and oppression for the same person in different respects. Only a plural explication of the concept of oppression can adequately capture these insights.

Accordingly, I offer below an explication of five faces of oppression as a useful set of categories and distinctions which I believe is comprehensive, in the sense that it covers all the groups said by new left social movements to be oppressed and all the ways they are oppressed. I derive the five faces of oppression from reflection on the condition of these groups. Because different factors, or combinations of factors, constitute the oppression of different groups, making their oppression irreducible, I believe it is not possible to give one essential definition of oppression. The five categories articulated in this chapter, however, are adequate to describe the oppression of any group, as well as its similarities with and differences from the oppression of other groups. But first we must ask what a group is.

THE CONCEPT OF A SOCIAL GROUP

Oppression refers to structural phenomena that immobilize or diminish a group. But what is a group? Our ordinary discourse differentiates people according to social groups such as women and men, age groups, racial and ethnic groups, religious groups, and so on. Social groups of this sort are not simply collections of people, for they are more fundamentally intertwined with the identities of the people described as belonging to them. They are a specific kind of collectivity, with specific consequences for how people understand one another and themselves. Yet neither social theory nor philosophy has a clear and developed concept of the social group (see Turner et al., 1987).

15   A social group is a collective of persons differentiated from at least one other group by cultural forms, practices, or way of life. Members of a group have a specific affinity with one another because of their similar experience or way of life, which prompts them to associate with one another more than with those not identified with the group, or in a different way. Groups are an expression of social relations; a group exists only in relation to at least one other group. Group identification arises, that is, in the encounter and interaction between social collectivities that experience some differences in their

way of life and forms of association, even if they regard themselves as belonging to the same society.

As long as they associated solely among themselves, for example, an American Indian group thought of themselves only as "the people." The encounter with other American Indians created an awareness of difference; the others were named as a group, and the first group came to see themselves as a group. But social groups do not arise only from an encounter between different societies. Social processes also differentiate groups within a single society. The sexual division of labor, for example, has created social groups of women and men in all known societies. Members of each gender have a certain affinity with others in their group because of what they do or experience, and differentiate themselves from the other gender, even when members of each gender consider that they have much in common with members of the other, and consider that they belong to the same society.

Political philosophy typically has no place for a specific concept of the social group. When philosophers and political theorists discuss groups, they tend to conceive them either on the model of aggregates or on the model of associations, both of which are methodologically individualist concepts. To arrive at a specific concept of the social group it is thus useful to contrast social groups with both aggregates and associations.

An aggregate is any classification of persons according to some attribute. Persons can be aggregated according to any number of attributes—eye color, the make of car they drive, the street they live on. Some people interpret the groups that have emotional and social salience in our society as aggregates, as arbitrary classifications of persons according to such attributes as skin color, genitals, or age. George Sher, for example, treats social groups as aggregates, and uses the arbitrariness of aggregate classification as a reason not to give special attention to groups. "There are really as many groups as there are combinations of people and if we are going to ascribe claims to equal treatment to racial, sexual, and other groups with high visibility, it will be more favoritism not to ascribe similar claims to these other groups as well" (Sher, 1987, p. 256).

But "highly visible" social groups such as Blacks or women are different from aggregates, or mere "combinations of people" (see French, 1975; Friedman and May, 1985; May, 1987, chap. 1). A social group is defined not primarily by a set of shared attributes, but by a sense of identity. What defines Black Americans as a social group is not primarily their skin color; some persons whose skin color is fairly light, for example, identify themselves as Black. Though sometimes objective attributes are a necessary condition for classifying oneself or others as belonging to a certain social group, it is identification with a certain social status, the common history that social status produces, and self-identification that define the group as a group.

Social groups are not entities that exist apart from individuals, but neither are they merely arbitrary classifications of individuals according to attributes which are external to or accidental to their identities. Admitting the reality of

20

social groups does not commit one to reifying collectivities, as some might argue. Group meanings partially constitute people's identities in terms of the cultural forms, social situation, and history that group members know as theirs, because these meanings have been either forced upon them or forged by them or both (cf. Fiss, 1976). Groups are real not as substances, but as forms of social relations (cf. May, 1987, pp. 22–23).

Moral theorists and political philosophers tend to elide social groups more often with associations than with aggregates (e.g., French, 1975; May, 1987, chap. 1). By an association I mean a formally organized institution, such as a club, corporation, political party, church, college, or union. Unlike the aggregate model of groups, the association model recognizes that groups are defined by specific practices and forms of association. Nevertheless it shares a problem with the aggregate model. The aggregate model conceives the individual as prior to the collective, because it reduces the social group to a mere set of attributes attached to individuals. The association model also implicitly conceives the individual as ontologically prior to the collective, as making up, or constituting, groups.

A contract model of social relations is appropriate for conceiving associations, but not groups. Individuals constitute associations, they come together as already formed persons and set them up, establishing rules, positions and offices. The relationship of persons to associations is usually voluntary, and even when it is not, the person has nevertheless usually entered the association. The person is prior to the association also in that the person's identity and sense of self are usually regarded as prior to and relatively independent of association membership.

Groups, on the other hand, constitute individuals. A person's particular sense of history, affinity, and separateness, even the person's mode of reasoning, evaluating, and expressing feeling, are constituted partly by her or his group affinities. This does not mean that persons have no individual styles, or are unable to transcend or reject a group identity. Nor does it preclude persons from having many aspects that are independent of these group identities.

The social ontology underlying many contemporary theories of justice is methodologically individualist or atomist. It presumes that the individual is ontologically prior to the social. This individualist social ontology usually goes together with a normative conception of the self as independent. The authentic self is autonomous, unified, free, and self-made, standing apart from history and affiliations, choosing its life plan entirely for itself.

25   One of the main contributions of poststructuralist philosophy has been to expose as illusory this metaphysic of a unified self-making subjectivity, which posits the subject as an autonomous origin or an underlying substance to which attributes of gender, nationality, family role, intellectual disposition, and so on might attach. Conceiving the subject in this fashion implies conceiving consciousness as outside of and prior to language and the context of social interaction, which the subject enters. Several currents of recent philosophy challenge this deeply held Cartesian assumption. Lacanian psychoanaly-

sis, for example, and the social and philosophical theory influenced by it, conceive the self as an achievement of linguistic positioning that is always contextualized in concrete relations with other persons, with their mixed identities (Coward and Ellis, 1977). The self is a product of social processes, not their origin.

From a rather different perspective, Habermas indicates that theory of communicative action also must challenge the "philosophy of consciousness" which locates intentional egos as the ontological origins of social relations. A theory of communicative action conceives individual identity not as an origin but as a product of linguistic and practical interaction (Habermas, 1987, pp. 3–40). As Stephen Epstein describes it, identity is a "socialized sense of individuality, an internal organization of self-perception concerning one's relationship to social categories, that also incorporates views of the self perceived to be held by others. Identity is constituted relationally, through involvement with—and incorporation of—significant others and integration into communities" (Epstein, 1987, p. 29). Group categorization and norms are major constituents of individual identity (see Turner et al., 1987).

A person joins an association, and even if membership in it fundamentally affects one's life, one does not take that membership to define one's very identity, in the way, for example, being Navaho might. Group affinity, on the other hand, has the character of what Martin Heidegger (1962) calls "thrownness": one *finds oneself* as a member of a group, which one experiences as always already having been. For our identities are defined in relation to how others identify us, and they do so in terms of groups which are always already associated with specific attributes, stereotypes, and norms.

From the thrownness of group affinity it does not follow that one cannot leave groups and enter new ones. Many women become lesbian after first identifying as heterosexual. Anyone who lives long enough becomes old. These cases exemplify thrownness precisely because such changes in group affinity are experienced as transformations in one's identity. Nor does it follow from the thrownness of group affinity that one cannot define the meaning of group identity for oneself; those who identify with a group can redefine the meaning and norms of group identity. The present point is only that one first finds a group identity as given, and then takes it up in a certain way. While groups may come into being, they are never founded.

Groups, I have said, exist only in relation to other groups. A group may be identified by outsiders without those so identified having any specific consciousness of themselves as a group. Sometimes a group comes to exist only because one group excludes and labels a category of persons, and those labeled come to understand themselves as group members only slowly, on the basis of their shared oppression. In Vichy France, for example, Jews who had been so assimilated that they had no specifically Jewish identity were marked as Jews by others and given a specific social status by them. These people "discovered" themselves as Jews, and then formed a group identity and affinity with one another (see Sartre, 1948). A person's group identities may be for the most part only a background or horizon to his or her life, becoming salient only in specific interactive contexts.

30   Assuming an aggregate model of groups, some people think that social groups are invidious fictions, essentializing arbitrary attributes. From this point of view problems of prejudice, stereotyping, discrimination, and exclusion exist because some people mistakenly believe that group identification makes a difference to the capacities, temperament, or virtues of group members. This individualist conception of persons and their relation to one another tends to identify oppression with group identification. Oppression, on this view, is something that happens to people when they are classified in groups. Because others identify them as a group, they are excluded and despised. Eliminating oppression thus requires eliminating groups. People should be treated as individuals, not as members of groups, and allowed to form their lives freely without stereotypes or group norms.

This book takes issue with that position. While I agree that individuals should be free to pursue life plans in their own way, it is foolish to deny the reality of groups. Despite the modern myth of a decline of parochial attachments and ascribed identities, in modern society group differentiation remains endemic. As both markets and social administration increase the web of social interdependency on a world scale, and as more people encounter one another as strangers in cities and states, people retain and renew ethnic, locale, age, sex, and occupational group identifications, and form new ones in the processes of encounter (cf. Ross, 1980, p. 19; Rothschild, 1981, p. 130). Even when they belong to oppressed groups, people's group identifications are often important to them, and they often feel a special affinity for others in their group. I believe that group differentiation is both an inevitable and a desirable aspect of modern social processes. Social justice, I shall argue in later chapters, requires not the melting away of differences, but institutions that promote reproduction of and respect for group differences without oppression.

Though some groups have come to be formed out of oppression, and relations of privilege and oppression structure the interactions between many groups, group differentiation is not in itself oppressive. Not all groups are oppressed. In the United States Roman Catholics are a specific social group, with distinct practices and affinities with one another, but they are no longer an oppressed group. Whether a group is oppressed depends on whether it is subject to one or more of the five conditions I shall discuss below.

The view that groups are fictions does carry an important antideterminist or antiessentialist intuition. Oppression has often been perpetrated by a conceptualization of group difference in terms of unalterable essential natures that determine what group members deserve or are capable of, and that exclude groups so entirely from one another that they have no similarities or overlapping attributes. To assert that it is possible to have social group difference without oppression, it is necessary to conceptualize groups in a much more relational and fluid fashion.

Although social processes of affinity and differentiation produce groups, they do not give groups a substantive essence. There is no common nature that members of a group share. As aspects of a process, moreover, groups are fluid; they come into being and may fade away. Homosexual practices have existed in many societies and historical periods, for example. Gay men or lesbians have been identified as specific groups and so identified themselves, however, only in the twentieth century (see Ferguson, 1989, chap. 9; Altman, 1981).

Arising from social relations and processes, finally, group differences usu- *35* ally cut across one another. Especially in a large, complex, and highly differentiated society, social groups are not themselves homogeneous, but mirror in their own differentiations many of the other groups in the wider society. In American society today, for example, Blacks are not a simple, unified group with a common life. Like other racial and ethnic groups, they are differentiated by age, gender, class, sexuality, region, and nationality, any of which in a given context may become a salient group identity.

This view of group differentiation as multiple, cross-cutting, fluid, and shifting implies another critique of the model of the autonomous, unified self. In complex, highly differentiated societies like our own, all persons have multiple group identifications. The culture, perspective, and relations of privilege and oppression of these various groups, moreover, may not cohere. Thus individual persons, as constituted partly by their group affinities and relations, cannot be unified, themselves are heterogeneous and not necessarily coherent.

THE FACES OF OPPRESSION

Exploitation

The central function of Marx's theory of exploitation is to explain how class structure can exist in the absence of legally and normatively sanctioned class distinctions. In precapitalist societies domination is overt and accomplished through directly political means. In both slave society and feudal society the right to appropriate the product of the labor of others partly defines class privilege, and these societies legitimate class distinctions with ideologies of natural superiority and inferiority.

Capitalist society, on the other hand, removes traditional juridically enforced class distinctions and promotes a belief in the legal freedom of persons. Workers freely contract with employers and receive a wage; no formal mechanisms of law or custom force them to work for that employer or any employer. Thus the mystery of capitalism arises: when everyone is formally free, how can there be class domination? Why do class distinctions persist between the wealthy, who own the means of production, and the mass of people, who work for them? The theory of exploitation answers this question.

Profit, the basis of capitalist power and wealth, is a mystery if we assume that in the market goods exchange at their values. The labor theory of value dispels this mystery. Every commodity's value is a function of the labor time necessary for its production. Labor power is the one commodity which in the process of being consumed produces new value. Profit comes from the difference between the value of the labor performed and the value of the capacity to labor which the capitalist purchases. Profit is possible only because the owner of capital appropriates any realized surplus value.

₄₀ In recent years Marxist scholars have engaged in considerable controversy about the viability of the labor theory of value this account of exploitation relies on (see Wolff, 1984, chap. 4). John Roemer (1982), for example, develops a theory of exploitation which claims to preserve the theoretical and practical purposes of Marx's theory, but without assuming a distinction between values and prices and without being restricted to a concept of abstract, homogeneous labor. My purpose here is not to engage in technical economic disputes, but to indicate the place of a concept of exploitation in a conception of oppression.

Marx's theory of exploitation lacks an explicitly normative meaning, even though the judgment that workers are exploited clearly has normative as well as descriptive power in that theory (Buchanan, 1982, chap. 3). C. B. Macpherson (1973, chap. 3) reconstructs this theory of exploitation in a more explicitly normative form. The injustice of capitalist society consists in the fact that some people exercise their capacities under the control, according to the purposes, and for the benefit of other people. Through private ownership of the means of production, and through markets that allocate labor and the ability to buy goods, capitalism systematically transfers the powers of some persons to others, thereby augmenting the power of the latter. In this process of the transfer of powers, according to Macpherson, the capitalist class acquires and maintains an ability to extract benefits from workers. Not only are powers transferred from workers to capitalists, but also the powers of workers diminish by more than the amount of transfer, because workers suffer material deprivation and a loss of control, and hence are deprived of important elements of self-respect. Justice, then, requires eliminating the institutional forms that enable and enforce this process of transference and replacing them with institutional forms that enable all to develop and use their capacities in a way that does not inhibit, but rather can enhance, similar development and use in others.

The central insight expressed in the concept of exploitation, then, is that this oppression occurs through a steady process of the transfer of the results of this labor of one social group to benefit another. The injustice of class division does not consist only in the distributive fact that some people have great wealth while most people have little (cf. Buchanan, 1982, pp. 44–49; Holmstrom 1977). Exploitation enacts a structural relation between social groups. Social rules about what work is, who does what for whom, how work is compensated, and the social process by which the results of work are appropriated operate to enact relations of power and inequality. These relations are produced and reproduced through a systematic process in which the energies of the have-nots are continuously expended to maintain and augment the power, status, and wealth of the haves.

Many writers have cogently argued that the Marxist concept of exploitation is too narrow to encompass all forms of domination and oppression (Giddens, 1981, p. 242; Brittan and Maynard, 1984, p. 93; Murphy, 1985; Bowles and Gintis, 1986, pp. 20–24). In particular, the Marxist concept of class leaves important phenomena of sexual and racial oppression unexplained. Does this mean that sexual and racial oppression are nonexploitative, and that we should reserve wholly distinct categories for these oppressions? Or can the concept of exploitation be broadened to include other ways in which the labor and energy expenditure of one group benefits another, and reproduces a relation of domination between them?

Feminists have had little difficulty showing that women's oppression consists partly in a systematic and unreciprocated transfer of powers from women to men. Women's oppression consists not merely in an inequality of status, power, and wealth resulting from men's excluding them from privileged activities. The freedom, power, status, and self-realization of men is possible precisely because women work for them. Gender exploitation has two aspects, transfer of the fruits of material labor to men and transfer of nurturing and sexual energies to men.

Christine Delphy (1984), for example, describes marriage as a class relation in which women's labor benefits men without comparable remuneration. She makes it clear that the exploitation consists not in the sort of work that women do in the home, for this might include various kinds of tasks, but in the fact that they perform tasks for someone on whom they are dependent. Thus, for example, in most systems of agricultural production in the world, men take to market the goods women have produced, and more often than not men receive the status and often the entire income from this labor.

With the concept of sex-affective production, Ann Ferguson (1979; 1984; 1989, chap. 4) identifies another form of the transference of women's energies to men. Women provide men and children with emotional care and provide men with sexual satisfaction, and as a group receive relatively little of either from men (cf. Brittan and Maynard, pp. 142–48). The gender socialization of women makes us tend to be more attentive to interactive dynamics than men, and makes women good at providing empathy and support for people's feelings and at smoothing over interactive tensions. Both men and women look to women as nurturers of their personal lives, and women frequently complain that when they look to men for emotional support they do not receive it (Easton, 1978). The norms of heterosexuality, moreover, are oriented around male pleasure, and consequently many women receive little satisfaction from their sexual interaction with men (Gottlieb, 1984).

Most feminist theories of gender exploitation have concentrated on the institutional structure of the patriarchal family. Recently, however, feminists have begun to explore relations of gender exploitation enacted in the contemporary workplace and through the state. Carol Brown argues that as men have removed themselves from responsibility for children, many women have become dependent on the state for subsistence as they continue to bear nearly total responsibility for childrearing (Brown, 1981; cf. Boris and Bardaglio,

1983; A. Ferguson, 1984). This creates a new system of the exploitation of women's domestic labor mediated by state institutions, which she calls public patriarchy.

In twentieth-century capitalist economies the workplaces that women have been entering in increasing numbers serve as another important site of gender exploitation. David Alexander (1987) argues that typically feminine jobs involve gender-based tasks requiring sexual labor, nurturing, caring for others' bodies, or smoothing over workplace tensions. In these ways women's energies are expended in jobs that enhance the status of, please, or comfort others, usually men; and these gender-based labors of waitresses, clerical workers, nurses, and other caretakers often go unnoticed and undercompensated.

To summarize, women are exploited in the Marxist sense to the degree that they are wage workers. Some have argued that women's domestic labor also represents a form of capitalist class exploitation insofar as it is labor covered by the wages a family receives. As a group, however, women undergo specific forms of gender exploitation in which their energies and power are expended, often unnoticed and unacknowledged, usually to benefit men by releasing them for more important and creative work, enhancing their status or the environment around them, or providing them with sexual or emotional service.

50   Race is a structure of oppression at least as basic as class or gender. Are there, then, racially specific forms of exploitation? There is no doubt that racialized groups in the United States, especially Blacks and Latinos, are oppressed through capitalist superexploitation resulting from a segmented labor market that tends to reserve skilled, high-paying, unionized jobs for whites. There is wide disagreement about whether such superexploitation benefits whites as a group or only benefits the capitalist class (see Reich, 1981), and I do not intend to enter into that dispute here.

However one answers the question about capitalist superexploitation of racialized groups, is it possible to conceptualize a form of exploitation that is racially specific on analogy with the gender-specific forms just discussed? I suggest that the category of *menial* labor might supply a means for such conceptualization. In its derivation "menial" designates the labor of servants. Wherever there is racism, there is the assumption, more or less enforced, that members of the oppressed racial groups are or ought to be servants of those, or some of those, in the privileged group. In most white racist societies this means that many white people have dark- or yellow-skinned domestic servants, and in the United States today there remains significant racial structuring of private household service. But in the United States today much service labor has gone public: anyone who goes to a good hotel or a good restaurant can have servants. Servants often attend the daily—and nightly—activities of business executives, government officials, and other high-status professionals. In our society there remains strong cultural pressure to fill servant jobs—bellhop, porter, chambermaid, busboy, and so on—with Black and Latino workers. These jobs entail a transfer of energies whereby the servers enhance the status of the served.

Menial labor usually refers not only to service, however, but also to any servile, unskilled, low-paying work lacking in autonomy, in which a person is subject to taking orders from many people. Menial work tends to be auxiliary work, instrumental to the work of others, where those others receive primary recognition for doing the job. Laborers on a construction site for example are at the beck and call of welders, electricians, carpenters, and other skilled workers, who receive recognition for the job done. In the United States explicit racial discrimination once reserved menial work for Blacks, Chicanos, American Indians, and Chinese, and menial work still tends to be linked to Black and Latino workers (Symanski, 1985). I offer this category of menial labor as a form of racially specific exploitation, as a provisional category in need of exploration.

The injustice of exploitation is most frequently understood on a distributive model. For example, though he does not offer an explicit definition of the concept, by "exploitation" Bruce Ackerman seems to mean a seriously unequal distribution of wealth, income, and other resources that is group based and structurally persistent (Ackerman, 1980, chap. 8). John Roemer's definition is narrower and more rigorous: "An agent is exploited when the amount of labor embodied in *any* bundle of goods he could receive, in a feasible distribution of society's net product, is less than the labor he expended" (Roemer, 1982, p. 122). This definition too turns the conceptual focus from institutional relations and processes to distributive outcomes.

Jeffrey Reiman argues that such a distributive understanding of exploitation reduces the injustice of class processes to a function of the inequality of the productive assets classes own. This misses, according to Reiman, the relationship of force between capitalists and workers, the fact that the unequal exchange in question occurs within coercive structures that give workers few options (Reiman, 1987; cf. Buchanan, 1982, pp. 44–49; Holmstrom, 1977). The injustice of exploitation consists in social processes that bring about a transfer of energies from one group to another to produce unequal distributions, and in the way in which social institutions enable a few to accumulate while they constrain many more. The injustices of exploitation cannot be eliminated by redistribution of goods, for as long as institutionalized practices and structural relations remain unaltered, the process of transfer will re-create an unequal distribution of benefits. Bringing about justice where there is exploitation requires reorganization of institutions and practices of decision-making, alteration of the division of labor, and similar measure of institutional, structural, and cultural change.

Marginalization

Increasingly in the United States racial oppression occurs in the form of marginalization rather than exploitation. Marginals are people the system of labor cannot or will not use. Not only in Third World capitalist countries, but also in most Western capitalist societies, there is a growing underclass of people permanently confined to lives of social marginality, most of whom are racially marked—Blacks or Indians in Latin America, and Blacks, East Indians, Eastern Europeans, or North Africans in Europe.

Marginalization is by no means the fate only of racially marked groups, however. In the United States a shamefully large proportion of the population is marginal: old people, and increasingly people who are not very old but get laid off from their jobs and cannot find new work: young people, especially Black or Latino, who cannot find first or second jobs; many single mothers and their children; other people involuntarily unemployed; many mentally and physically disabled people; American Indians, especially those on reservations.

Marginalization is perhaps the most dangerous form of oppression. A whole category of people is expelled from useful participation in social life and thus potentially subjected to severe material deprivation and even extermination. The material deprivation marginalization often causes is certainly unjust, especially in a society where others have plenty. Contemporary advanced capitalist societies have in principle acknowledged the injustice of material deprivation caused by marginalization, and have taken some steps to address it by providing welfare payments and services. The continuance of this welfare state is by no means assured, and in most welfare state societies, especially the United States, welfare redistributions do not eliminate large-scale suffering and deprivation.

Material deprivation, which can be addressed by redistributive social policies, is not, however, the extent of the harm caused by marginalization. Two categories of injustice beyond distribution are associated with marginality in advanced capitalist societies. First, the provision of welfare itself produces new injustice by depriving those dependent on it of rights and freedoms that others have. Second, even when material deprivation is somewhat mitigated by the welfare state, marginalization is unjust because it blocks the opportunity to exercise capacities in socially defined and recognized ways. I shall explicate each of these in turn.

Liberalism has traditionally asserted the right of all rational autonomous agents to equal citizenship. Early bourgeois liberalism explicitly excluded from citizenship all those whose reason was questionable or not fully developed, and all those not independent (Pateman, 1988, chap. 3; cf. Bowles and Gintis, 1986, chap. 2). Thus poor people, women, the mad and the feeble-minded, and children were explicitly excluded from citizenship, and many of these were housed in institutions modeled on the modern prison: poorhouses, insane asylums, schools.

60   Today the exclusion of dependent persons from equal citizenship rights is only barely hidden beneath the surface. Because they depend on bureaucratic institutions for support or services, the old, the poor, and the mentally or physically disabled are subject to patronizing, punitive, demeaning, and arbitrary treatment by the policies and people associated with welfare bureaucracies. Being a dependent in our society implies being legitimately subject to the often arbitrary and invasive authority of social service providers and other public and private administrators, who enforce rules with which the marginal must comply, and otherwise exercise power over the conditions of their lives.

In meeting needs of the marginalized, often with aid of social scientific disciplines, welfare agencies also construct the needs themselves. Medical and social service professionals know what is good for those they serve, and the marginals and dependents themselves do not have the right to claim to know what is good for them (Fraser, 1987a; K. Ferguson, 1984, chap. 4). Dependency in our society thus implies, as it has in all liberal societies, a sufficient warrant to suspend basic rights to privacy, respect, and individual choice.

Although dependency produces conditions of injustice in our society, dependency in itself need not be oppressive. One cannot imagine a society in which some people would not need to be dependent on others at least some of the time: children, sick people, women recovering from childbirth, old people who have become frail, depressed or otherwise emotionally needy persons, have the moral right to depend on others for subsistence and support.

An important contribution of feminist moral theory has been to question the deeply held assumption that moral agency and full citizenship require that a person be autonomous and independent. Feminists have exposed this assumption as inappropriately individualistic and derived from a specifically male experience of social relations, which values competition and solitary achievement (see Gilligan, 1982; Friedman, 1985). Female experience of social relations, arising both from women's typical domestic care responsibilities and from the kinds of paid work that many women do, tends to recognize dependence as a basic human condition (cf. Hartsock, 1983, chap. 10). Whereas on the autonomy model a just society would as much as possible give people the opportunity to be independent, the feminist model envisions justice as according respect and participation in decisionmaking to those who are dependent as well as to those who are independent (Held, 1987). Dependency should not be a reason to be deprived of choice and respect, and much of the oppression many marginals experience would be lessened if a less individualistic model of rights prevailed.

Marginalization does not cease to be oppressive when one has shelter and food. Many old people, for example, have sufficient means to live comfortably but remain oppressed in their marginal status. Even if marginals were provided a comfortable material life within institutions that respected their freedom and dignity, injustices of marginality would remain in the form of uselessness, boredom, and lack of self-respect. Most of our society's productive and recognized activities take place in contexts of organized social cooperation, and social structures and processes that close persons out of participation in such social cooperation are unjust. Thus while marginalization definitely entails serious issues of distributive justice, it also involves the deprivation of cultural, practical, and institutionalized conditions for exercising capacities in a context of recognition and interaction.

The fact of marginalization raises basic structural issues of justice, in particular concerning the appropriateness of a connection between participation in productive activities of social cooperation, on the one hand, and access to the means of consumption, on the other. As marginalization is increasing, with no sign of abatement, some social policy analysts have introduced the idea of a "social wage" as a guaranteed socially provided income not tied to the wage system. Restructuring of productive activity to address a right of participation, however, implies organizing some socially productive activity outside of the wage system (see Offe, 1985, pp. 95–100), through public works or self-employed collectives.

Powerlessness

65 As I have indicated, the Marxist idea of class is important because it helps reveal the structure of exploitation: that some people have their power and wealth because they profit from the labor of others. For this reason I reject the claim some make that a traditional class exploitation model fails to capture the structure of contemporary society. It remains the case that the labor of most people in the society augments the power of relatively few. Despite their differences from nonprofessional workers, most professional workers are still not members of the capitalist class. Professional labor either involves exploitative transfers to capitalists or supplies important conditions for such transfers. Professional workers are in an ambiguous class position, it is true, because they also benefit from the exploitation of nonprofessional workers.

While it is false to claim that a division between capitalist and working classes no longer describes our society, it is also false to say that class relations have remained unaltered since the nineteenth century. An adequate conception of oppression cannot ignore the experience of social division reflected in the colloquial distinction between the "middle class" and the "working class," a division structured by the social division of labor between professionals and nonprofessionals. Professionals are privileged in relation to nonprofessionals, by virtue of their position in the division of labor and the status it carries. Nonprofessionals suffer a form of oppression in addition to exploitation, which I call powerlessness.

In the United States, as in other advanced capitalist countries, most workplaces are not organized democratically, direct participation in public policy decisions is rare, and policy implementation is for the most part hierarchical, imposing rules on bureaucrats and citizens. Thus most people in these societies do not regularly participate in making decisions that affect the conditions of their lives and actions, and in this sense most people lack significant power. At the same time, domination in modern society is enacted through the widely dispersed powers of many agents mediating the decisions of others. To that extent many people have some power in relation to others, even though they lack the power to decide policies or results. The powerless are those who lack authority or power even in this mediated sense, those over whom power is exercised without their exercising it; the powerless are situated so that they must take orders and rarely have the right to give them. Powerlessness also designates a position in the division of labor and the concomitant social position that allow persons little opportunity to develop and exercise skills. The powerless have little or no work autonomy, exercise little creativity or judgment in their work, have no technical expertise or authority, express themselves awkwardly, especially in public or bureaucratic settings, and do not command respect. Powerlessness names the oppressive situations Sennett and Cobb (1972) describe in their famous study of working-class men.

This powerless status is perhaps best described negatively: the powerless lack the authority, status, and sense of self that professionals tend to have. The status privilege of professionals has three aspects, the lack of which produces oppression for nonprofessionals.

First, acquiring and practicing a profession has an expansive, progressive character. Being professional usually requires a college education and the acquisition of a specialized knowledge that entails working with symbols and concepts. Professionals experience progress first in acquiring the expertise, and then in the course of professional advancement and the rise in status. The life of the nonprofessional by comparison is powerless in the sense that it lacks this orientation toward the progressive development of capacities and avenues for recognition.

Second, while many professionals have supervisors and cannot directly influence many decisions or the actions of many people, most nevertheless have considerable day-to-day work autonomy. Professionals usually have some authority over others, moreover—either over workers they supervise, or over auxiliaries, or over clients. Nonprofessionals, on the other hand, lack autonomy, and in both their working and their consumer–client lives often stand under the authority of professionals. *70*

Though based on a division of labor between "mental" and "manual" work, the distinction between "middle class" and "working class" designates a division not ony in working life, but also in nearly all aspects of social life. Professionals and nonprofessionals belong to different cultures in the United States. The two groups tend to live in segregated neighborhoods or even different towns, a process itself mediated by planners, zoning officials, and real estate people. The groups tend to have different tastes in food, decor, clothes, music, and vacations, and often different health and educational needs. Members of each group socialize for the most part with others in the same status group. While there is some intergroup mobility between generations, for the most part the children of professionals become professionals and the children of nonprofessionals do not.

Thus, third, the privileges of the professional extend beyond the workplace to a whole way of life. I call this way of life "respectability." To treat people with respect is to be prepared to listen to what they have to say or to do what they request because they have some authority, expertise, or influence. The norms of respectability in our society are associated specifically with professional culture. Professional dress, speech, tastes, demeanor, all connote respectability. Generally professionals expect and receive respect from others. In restaurants, banks, hotels, real estate offices, and many other such public places, as well as in the media, professionals typically receive more respectful treatment than nonprofessionals. For this reason nonprofessionals seeking a loan or a job, or to buy a house or a car, will often try to look "professional" and "respectable" in those settings.

The privilege of this professional respectability appears starkly in the dynamics of racism and sexism. In daily interchange women and men of color must prove their respectability. At first they are often not treated by strangers with respectful distance or deference. Once people discover that this woman or that Puerto Rican man is a college teacher or a business executive, however, they often behave more respectfully toward her or him. Working-class white men, on the other hand, are often treated with respect until their working-class status is revealed.

I have discussed several injustices associated with powerlessness: inhibition in the development of one's capacities, lack of decisionmaking power in one's working life, and exposure to disrespectful treatment because of the status one occupies. These injustices have distributional consequences, but are more fundamentally matters of the division of labor. The oppression of powerlessness brings into question the division of labor basic to all industrial societies: the social division between those who plan and those who execute.

Cultural Imperialism

75   Exploitation, marginalization, and powerlessness all refer to relations of power and oppression that occur by virtue of the social division of labor—who works for whom, who does not work, and how the content of work defines one institutional position relative to others. These three categories refer to structural and institutional relations that delimit people's material lives, including but not restricted to the resources they have access to and the concrete opportunities they have or do not have to develop and exercise their capacities. These kinds of oppression are a matter of concrete power in relation to others—of who benefits from whom, and who is dispensable.

Recent theorists of movements of group liberation, notably feminist and Black liberation theorists, have also given prominence to a rather different form of oppression, which following Lugones and Spelman (1983) I shall call cultural imperialism. To experience cultural imperialism means to experience how the dominant meanings of a society render the particular perspective of one's own group invisible at the same time as they stereotype one's group and mark it out as the Other.

Cultural imperialism involves the universalization of a dominant group's experience and culture, and its establishment as the norm. Some groups have exclusive or primary access to what Nancy Fraser (1987b) calls the means of interpretation and communication in a society. As a consequence, the dominant cultural products of the society, that is, those most widely disseminated, express the experience, values, goals, and achievements of these groups. Often without noticing they do so, the dominant groups project their own experience as a representative of humanity as such. Cultural products also express the dominant group's perspective on and interpretation of events and elements in the society, including other groups in the society, insofar as they attain cultural status at all.

An encounter with other groups, however, can challenge the dominant group's claim to universality. The dominant group reinforces its position by bringing the other groups under the measure of its dominant norms. Consequently, the difference of women from men, American Indians or Africans from Europeans, Jews from Christians, homosexuals from heterosexuals, workers from professionals, becomes reconstructed largely as deviance and inferiority. Since only the dominant group's cultural expressions receive wide dissemination, their cultural expressions become the normal, or the universal, and thereby the unremarkable. Given the normality of its own cultural expressions and identity, the dominant group constructs the differences which some groups exhibit as lack and negation. These groups become marked as Other.

The culturally dominated undergo a paradoxical oppression, in that they are both marked by stereotypes and at the same time rendered invisible. As remarkable, deviant beings, the culturally imperialized are stamped with an essence. The stereotypes confine them to a nature which is often attached in some way to their bodies, and which thus cannot easily be denied. These stereotypes so permeate the society that they are not noticed as contestable. Just as everyone knows that the earth goes around the sun, so everyone knows that gay people are promiscuous, that Indians are alcoholics, and that women are good with children. White males, on the other hand, insofar as they escape group marking, can be individuals.

Those living under cultural imperialism find themselves defined from the outside, positioned, placed, by a network of dominant meanings they experience as arising from elsewhere, from those with whom they do not identify and who do not identify with them. Consequently, the dominant culture's stereotyped and inferiorized images of the group must be internalized by group members at least to the extent that they are forced to react to behavior of others influenced by those images. This creates for the culturally oppressed the experience that W. E. B. Du Bois called "double consciousness"—"this sense of always looking at one's self through the eyes of others, of measuring one's soul by the tape of a world that looks on in amused contempt and pity" (Du Bois, 1969 [1903], p. 45). Double consciousness arises when the oppressed subject refuses to coincide with these devalued, objectified, stereotyped visions of herself or himself. While the subject desires recognition as human, capable of activity, full of hope and possibility, she receives from the dominant culture only the judgment that she is different, marked, or inferior.

The group defined by the dominant culture as deviant, as a stereotyped Other, *is* culturally different from the dominant group, because the status of Otherness creates specific experiences not shared by the dominant group, and because culturally oppressed groups also are often socially segregated and occupy specific positions in the social division of labor. Members of such groups express their specific group experiences and interpretations of the world to one another, developing and perpetuating their own culture. Double consciousness, then, occurs because one finds one's being defined by two cultures: a dominant and a subordinate culture. Because they can affirm and recognize one another as sharing similar experiences and perspectives on social life, people in culturally imperialized groups can often maintain a sense of positive subjectivity.

Cultural imperialism involves the paradox of experiencing oneself as invisible at the same time that one is marked out as different. The invisibility comes about when dominant groups fail to recognize the perspective embodied in their cultural expressions as a perspective. These dominant cultural expressions often simply have little place for the experience of other groups, at most only mentioning or referring to them in stereotyped or marginalized ways. This, then is the injustice of cultural imperialism: that the oppressed group's own experience and interpretation of social life finds little expression that touches the dominant culture, while that same culture imposes on the oppressed group its experience and interpretation of social life.

Violence

Finally, many groups suffer the oppression of systematic violence. Members of some groups live with the knowledge that they must fear random, unprovoked attacks on their persons or property, which have no motive but to damage, humiliate, or destroy the person. In American society women, Blacks, Asians, Arabs, gay men, and lesbians live under such threats of violence, and in at least some regions Jews, Puerto Ricans, Chicanos, and other Spanish-speaking Americans must fear such violence as well. Physical violence against these groups is shockingly frequent. Rape Crisis Center networks estimate that more than one-third of all American women experience an attempted or successful sexual assault in their lifetimes. Manning Marable (1984, pp. 238–41) catalogues a large number of incidents of racist violence and terror against Blacks in the United States between 1980 and 1982. He cites dozens of incidents of the severe beating, killing, or rape of Blacks by police officers on duty, in which the police involved were acquitted of any wrongdoing. In 1981, moreover, there were at least five hundred documented cases of random white teenage violence against Blacks. Violence against gay men and lesbians is not only common, but has been increasing in the last five years. While the frequency of physical attack on members of these and other racially or sexually marked groups is very disturbing, I also include in this category less severe incidents of harassment, intimidation, or ridicule simply for the purpose of degrading, humiliating, or stigmatizing group members.

Given the frequency of such violence in our society, why are theories of justice usually silent about it? I think the reason is that theorists do not typically take such incidents of violence and harassment as matters of social injustice. No moral theorist would deny that such acts are very wrong. But unless all immoralities are injustices, they might wonder, why should such acts be interpreted as symptoms of social injustice? Acts of violence or petty harassment are committed by particular individuals, often extremists, deviants, or the mentally unsound. How then can they be said to involve the sorts of institutional issues I have said are properly the subject of justice?

What makes violence a face of oppression is less the particular acts themselves, though these are often utterly horrible, than the social context surrounding them, which makes them possible and even acceptable. What makes violence a phenomenon of social injustice, and not merely an individual moral wrong, is its systemic character, its existence as a social practice.

Violence is systemic because it is directed at members of a group simply because they are members of that group. Any woman, for example, has a reason to fear rape. Regardless of what a Black man has done to escape the oppressions of marginality of powerlessness, he lives knowing he is subject to attack or harassment. The oppression of violence consists not only in direct victimization, but in the daily knowledge shared by all members of oppressed groups that they are *liable* to violation, solely on account of their group identity. Just living under such a threat of attack on oneself or family or friends deprives the oppressed of freedom and dignity, and needlessly expends their energy.

Violence is a social practice. It is a social given that everyone knows happens and will happen again. It is always at the horizon of social imagination, even for those who do not perpetrate it. According to the prevailing social logic, some circumstances make such violence more "called for" than others. The idea of rape will occur to many men who pick up a hitch-hiking woman; the idea of hounding or teasing a gay man on their dorm floor will occur to many straight male college students. Often several persons inflict the violence together, especially in all-male groupings. Sometimes violators set out looking for people to beat up, rape, or taunt. This rule-bound, social, and often premeditated character makes violence against groups a social practice.

Group violence approaches legitimacy, moreover, in the sense that it is tolerated. Often third parties find it unsurprising because it happens frequently and lies as a constant possibility at the horizon of the social imagination. Even when they are caught, those who perpetrate acts of group-directed violence or harassment often receive light or no punishment. To that extent society renders their acts acceptable.

An important aspect of random, systematic violence is its irrationality. Xenophobic violence differs from the violence of states or ruling-class repression. Repressive violence has a rational, albeit evil, motive: rulers use it as a coercive tool to maintain their power. Many accounts of racist, sexist, or homophobic violence attempt to explain its motivation as a desire to maintain group privilege or domination. I do not doubt that fear of violence often functions to keep oppressed groups subordinate, but I do not think xenophobic violence is rationally motivated in the way that, for example, violence against strikers is.

90

On the contrary, the violation of rape, beating, killing, and harassment of women, people of color, gays, and other marked groups is motivated by fear or hatred of those groups. Sometimes the motive may be a simple will to power, to victimize those marked as vulnerable by the very social fact that they are subject to violence. If so, this motive is secondary in the sense that it depends on a social practice of group violence. Violence-causing fear or hatred of the other at least partly involves insecurities on the part of the violators: its irrationality suggests that unconscious processes are at work.

Cultural imperialism, moreover, itself intersects with violence. The culturally imperialized may reject the dominant meanings and attempt to assert their own subjectivity, or the fact of their cultural difference may put the lie to the dominant culture's implicit claim to universality. The dissonance generated by such a challenge to the hegemonic cultural meanings can also be a source of irrational violence.

Violence is a form of injustice that a distributive understanding of justice seems ill equipped to capture. This may be why contemporary discussions of justice rarely mention it. I have argued that group-directed violence is institutionalized and systemic. To the degree that institutions and social practices encourage, tolerate, or enable the perpetration of violence against members of specific groups, those institutions and practices are unjust and should be reformed. Such reform may require the redistribution of resources or positions, but in large part can come only through a change in cultural images, stereotypes, and the mundane reproduction of relations of dominance and aversion in the gestures of everyday life.

APPLYING THE CRITERIA

Social theories that construct oppression as a unified phenomenon usually either leave out groups that even the theorists think are oppressed, or leave out important ways in which groups are oppressed. Black liberation theorists and feminist theorists have argued persuasively, for example, that Marxism's reduction of all oppressions to class oppression leaves out much about the specific oppression of Blacks and women. By pluralizing the category of oppression in the way explained in this chapter, social theory can avoid the exclusive and oversimplifying effects of such reductionism.

I have avoided pluralizing the category in the way some others have done, by constructing an account of separate systems of oppression for each oppressed group: racism, sexism, classism, heterosexism, ageism, and so on. There is a double problem with considering each group's oppression a unified and distinct structure or system. On the one hand, this way of conceiving oppression fails to accommodate the similarities and overlaps in the oppressions of different groups. On the other hand, it falsely represents the situation of all group members as the same.

I have arrived at the five faces of oppression—exploitation, marginalization, powerlessness, cultural imperialism, and violence—as the best way to avoid such exclusions and reductions. They function as criteria for determining whether individuals and groups are oppressed, rather than as a full theory of oppression. I believe that these criteria are objective. They provide a means of refuting some people's belief that their group is oppressed when it is not, as well as a means of persuading others that a group is oppressed when they doubt it. Each criterion can be operationalized; each can be applied through the assessment of observable behavior, status relationships, distributions, texts and other cultural artifacts. I have no illusions that such assessments can be value-neutral. But these criteria can nevertheless serve as means of evaluating claims that a group is oppressed, or adjudicating disputes about whether or how a group is oppressed.

The presence of any of these five conditions is sufficient for calling a group oppressed. But different group oppressions exhibit different combinations of these forms, as do different individuals in the groups. Nearly all, if not all, groups said by contemporary social movements to be oppressed suffer cultural imperialism. The other oppressions they experience vary. Working-class people are exploited and powerless, for example, but if employed and white do not experience marginalization and violence. Gay men, on the other hand, are not qua gay exploited or powerless, but they experience severe cultural imperialism and violence. Similarly, Jews and Arabs as groups are victims of cultural imperialism and violence, though many members of these groups also suffer exploitation or powerlessness. Old people are oppressed by marginalization and cultural imperialism, and this is also true of physically and mentally disabled people. As a group women are subject to gender-based exploitation, powerlessness, cultural imperialism, and violence. Racism in the United States condemns many Blacks and Latinos to marginalization, and puts many more at risk, even though many members of these groups escape that condition; members of these groups often suffer all five forms of oppression.

Applying these five criteria to the situation of groups makes it possible to compare oppressions without reducing them to a common essence or claiming that one is more fundamental than another. One can compare the ways in which a particular form of oppression appears in different groups. For example, while the operations of cultural imperialism are often experienced in similar fashion by different groups, there are also important differences. One can compare the combinations of oppressions groups experience, or the intensity of those oppressions. Thus with these criteria one can plausibly claim that one group is more oppressed than another without reducing all oppressions to a single scale.

Why are particular groups oppressed in the way they are? Are there any causal connections among the five forms of oppression? Causal or explanatory questions such as these are beyond the scope of this discussion. While I think general social theory has a place, causal explanation must always be particular and historical. Thus an explanatory account of why a particular group is oppressed in the ways that it is must trace the history and current structure of particular social relations. Such concrete historical and structural explanations will often show causal connections among the different forms of oppression experienced by a group. The cultural imperialism in which white men make stereotypical assumptions about and refuse to recognize the values of Blacks or women, for example, contributes to the marginalization and powerlessness many Blacks and women suffer. But cultural imperialism does not always have these effects.

REFERENCES

Ackerman, Bruce. 1980. *Social Justice and the Liberal State,* New Haven: Yale University Press.

Alexander, David. 1987. "Gendered Job Traits and Women's Occupations." Ph. D. dissertation, Economics, University of Massachusetts.

Boris, Ellen and Peter Bardaglio. 1983. "The Transformation of Patriarchy: The Historic Role of the State." In Irene Diamond, ed., *Families, Politics and Public Policy.* New York: Longman.

Bowles, Samuel and Herbert Gintis. 1986. *Democracy and Capitalism.* New York: Basic.

Brittan, Arthur and Mary Maynard. 1984. *Sexism, Racism and Oppression.* Oxford: Blackwell.

Brown, Carol. 1981. "Mothers, Fathers and Children: From Private to Public Patriarchy." In Lydia Sargent, ed., *Women and Revolution. Boston: South End.*

Buchanan, Allen. 1982. *Marx and Justice.* Totowa, N.J.: Roman and Allanheld.

Coward, Rosalind and John Ellis. 1977. *Language and Materialism.* London: Routledeg and Kegan Paul.

Delphy, Christine. 1984. *Close to Home: A Materialist Analysis of Women's Oppression.* Amherst: University of Massachusetts Press.

Du Bois, W. E. B. 1969 [1903]. *Souls of Black Folk.* New York: New American Library.

Easton, Barbara. 1978. "Feminism and the Contemporary Family." *Socialist Review* 39 (May/June): 11–36.

Epstein, Steven. 1987. "Gay Politics, Ethnic Identity: The Limits of Social Constructionism." *Socialist Review* 17 (May–August) 9–54.

Ferguson, Ann. 1984. "On Conceiving Motherhood and Sexuality: A Feminist Materialist Approach." In Joyce Trebilcot, ed., *Mothering: Essays in Feminist Theory.* Totowa, N.J.: Rowman and Allanheld.

———. 1989. *Blood at the Root.* London: Pandora.

Ferguson, Kathy. 1984. *The Feminist Case against Bureaucracy.* Philadelphia: Temple University Press.

Fiss, Owen. 1976. "Groups and the Equal Protection Clause." *Philosophy and Public Affairs* 5 (Winter): 107–76.

Foucault, Michel. 1977. *Discipline and Punish.* New York: Pantheon.

Fraser, Nancy. 1987a "Women, Welfare, and the Politics of Need Interpretation." *Hypatia: A Journal of Feminist Philosophy* 2 (Winter): 103–22.

———. 1987b. "Social Movements vs. Disciplinary Bureaucracies: The Discourse of Social Needs. "CHS Occasional Paper No. 8. Center for Humanistic Studies, University of Minnesota.

French, Peter., 1975. "Types of Collectivities and Blame." *The Personalist* 56 (Spring): 1960–69.

Friedman, Marilyn. 1985. "Care and Context in Moral Reasoning." In Carol Harding, ed., *Moral Dilemmas: Philosophical and Psychological Issues in the Development of Moral Reasoning.* Chicago: Precedent.

Friedman, Marilyn and Larry May. 1985. "Harming Women as a Group." *Social Theory and Practice* 11 (Summer): 297–34.

Frye, Marilyn. 1983. "Oppression." In *The Politics of Reality*. Trumansburg, N.Y.: Crossing Press.

Giddens, Anthony. 1981. *A Contemporary Critique of Historical Materialism*. Berkeley and Los Angeles: University of California Press.

Gilligan, Carol. 1982. *In a Different Voice*. Cambridge: Harvard University Press.

Gottlieb, Rhonda. 1984. "The Political Economy of Sexuality." *Review of Radical Political Economy* 16 (Spring): 143–65.

Gottlieb, Roger. 1987. *History and Subjectivity*. Philadelphia: Temple University Press.

Habermas, Jürgen. 1987. *The Theory of Communicative Competence*. Vol. 2: *Lifeworld and System*. Boston: Beacon.

Hartsock, Nancy. 1983. *Money, Sex and Power*. New York: Longman.

Heidegger, Martin. 1962. *Being and Time*. New York: Harper and Row.

Held, Virginia. 1987. "A Non-Contractual Society." In Marsha Hanen and Kai Nielsen, eds., *Science, Morality and Feminist Theory*. Calgary: University of Calgary Press.

Holmstrom, Nancy. 1977. "Exploitation." *Canadian Journal of Philosophy* 7 (June): 353–69.

Lugones, Maria C. and Elizabeth V. Spelman. 1983. "Have We Got a Theory for You! Feminist Theory, Cultural Imperialism and the Demand for 'the Woman's Voice.'" *Women's Studies International Forum* 6:573–81.

Macpherson, C. B. 1973. *Democratic Theory: Essays in Retrieval*. Oxford: Oxford University Press.

Marable, Manning. 1984. *Race, Reform and Rebellion: The Second Reconstruction in Black America. 1945–82*. Jackson: University Press of Mississippi.

May, Larry. 1987. *The Morality of Groups: Collective Responsibility, Group-Based Harm, and Corporate Rights*. Notre Dame: Notre Dame University Press.

Murphy, Raymond. 1985. "Exploitation or Exclusion?" *Sociology* 19 (May): 225–43.

Offe, Claus. 1985. *Disorganized Capitalism*. Cambridge: MIT Press.

Pateman, Carole. 1988. *The Sexual Contract*. Stanford: Stanford University Press.

Reich, Michael. 1981. *Racial Inequality*. Princeton: Princeton University Press.

Reiman, Jeffrey. 1987. "Exploitation, Force, and the Moral Assessment of Capitalism: Thoughts on Roemer and Cohen." *Philosophy and Public Affairs* 16 (Winter): 3–41.

Roemer, John. 1982. *A General Theory of Exploitation and Class*. Cambridge: Harvard University Press.

Ross, Jeffrey. 1980. Introduction to Jeffrey Ross and Ann Baker Cottrell, eds., *The Mobilization of Collective Identity*. Lanham, Md.: University Press of America.

Rothschild, Joseph. 1981. *Ethnopolitics*. New York: Columbia University Press.

Sartre, Jean-Paul. 1948. *Anti-Semite and Jew*. New York: Schocken.

Sennett, Richard, and Jonathan Cobb. 1972. *The Hidden Injuries of Class.* New York: Vintage.

Sher, George. 1987. "Groups and the Constitution." In Gertrude Ezorsky, ed., *Moral Rights in the Workplace.* Albany: State University of New York Press.

Symanski, Al. 1985. "The Structure of Race." *Review of Radical Political Economy* 17 (Winter): 106–20.

Turner, John C., Michael A. Hogg, Penelope V. Oakes, Stephen D. Rucher, and Margaret S. Wethrell. 1987. *Rediscovering the Social Group: A Self-Categorization Theory.* Oxford: Blackwell.

Wolff, Robert Paul. 1984. *Understanding Marx.* Princeton: Princeton University Press.

2

Oppression Axis One: Racism

SOMETHING ABOUT THE SUBJECT MAKES IT HARD TO NAME

Gloria Yamato

Racism—simple enough in structure, yet difficult to eliminate. Racism—pervasive in the U.S. culture to the point that it deeply affects all the local town folk and spills over, negatively influencing the fortunes of folk around the world. Racism is pervasive to the point that we take many of its manifestations for granted, believing "that's life." Many believe that racism can be dealt with effectively in one hellifying workshop, or one hour-long heated discussion. Many actually believe this monster, racism, that has had at least a few hundred years to take root, grow, invade our space and develop subtle variations . . . this mind-funk that distorts thought and action, can be merely wished away. I've run into folks who really think that we can beat this devil, kick this habit, be healed of this disease in a snap. In a sincere blink of a well-intentioned eye, presto—poof—racism disappears. "I've dealt with my racism . . . (envision a laying on of hands) . . . Hallelujah! Now I can go to the beach." Well, fine. Go to the beach. In fact, why don't we all go to the beach and continue to work on the sucker over there? Cuz you can't even shave a little piece off this thing called racism in a day, or a weekend, or a workshop.

When I speak of *oppression,* I'm talking about the systematic, institutionalized mistreatment of one group of people by another for whatever reason. The oppressors are purported to have an innate ability to access economic resources, information, respect, etc., while the oppressed are believed to have a corresponding negative innate ability. The flip side of oppression is *internalized oppression*. Members of the target group are emotionally, physically, and spiritually battered to the point that they begin to actually believe that their oppression is deserved, is their lot in life, is natural and right, and that it doesn't even exist. The oppression begins to feel comfortable, familiar enough that when mean ol' Massa lay down de whip, we got's to pick up and whack ourselves and each other. Like a virus, it's hard to beat racism, because by the time you come up with a cure it's mutated to a "new cure-resistant" form. One shot just won't get it. Racism must be attacked from many angles.

The forms of racism that I pick up on these days are (1) aware/blatant racism, (2) aware/covert racism, (3) unaware/unintentional racism, and (4) unaware/self-righteous racism. I can't say that I prefer any one form of racism over the others, because they all look like an itch needing a scratch. I've heard it said (and understandably so) that the aware/blatant form of racism is preferable if one must suffer it. Outright racists will, without apology or confusion, tell us that because of our color we don't appeal to them. If we so choose, we can attempt to get the hell out of their way before we get the sweat knocked out of us. Growing up, aware/covert racism is what I heard many of my elders bemoaning "up north," after having escaped the overt racism "down south." Apartments were suddenly no longer vacant or rents were outrageously high, when black, brown, red, or yellow persons went to inquire about them. Job vacancies were suddenly filled, or we were fired for very vague reasons. It still happens, though the perpetrators really take care to cover their tracks these days. They don't want to get gummed to death or slobbered on by the toothless laws that supposedly protect us from such inequities.

Unaware/unintentional racism drives usually tranquil white liberals wild when they get called on it, and confirms the suspicions of many people of color who feel that white folks are just plain crazy. It has led white people to believe that it's just fine to ask if they can touch my hair (while reaching). They then exclaim over how soft it is, how it does not scratch their hand. It has led whites to assume that bending over backwards and speaking to me in high-pitched (terrified), condescending tones would make up for all the racist wrongs that distort our lives. This type of racism has led whites right to my doorstep, talking 'bout, "We're sorry/we love you and want to make things right," which is fine, and further, "We're gonna give you the opportunity to fix it while we sleep. Just tell us what you need. 'Bye!!"—which *ain't* fine. With the best of intentions, the best of educations, and the greatest generosity of heart, whites, operating on the misinformation fed to them from day one, will behave in ways that are racist, will perpetuate racism by being "nice" the way we're taught to be nice. You can just "nice" somebody to death with naïveté and lack of awareness of privilege. Then there's guilt and the desire to end racism and how the two get all tangled up to the point that people, morbidly fascinated with their guilt, are immobilized. Rather than deal with ending racism, they sit and ponder their guilt and hope nobody notices how awful they are. Meanwhile, racism picks up momentum and keeps on keepin' on.

5   Now, the newest form of racism that I'm hip to is unaware/self-righteous racism. The "good white" racist attempts to shame Blacks into being blacker, scorns Japanese-Americans who don't speak Japanese, and knows more about the Chicano/a community than the folks who make up the community. They assign themselves as the "good whites," as opposed to the "bad whites," and are often so busy telling people of color what the issues in the Black, Asian, Indian, Latino/a communities should be that they don't have time to deal with their errant sisters and brothers in the white community. Which means that people of color are still left to deal with what the "good whites" don't want to . . . racism.

Internalized racism is what really gets in my way as a Black woman. It influences the way I see or don't see myself, limits what I expect of myself or others like me. It results in my acceptance of mistreatment, leads me to believe that being treated with less than absolute respect, at least this once, is to be expected because I am Black, because I am not white. "Because I am (*you fill in the color*)," you think, "life is going to be hard." The fact is life may be hard, but the color of your skin is not the cause of the hardship. The color of your skin may be used as an excuse to mistreat you, but there is no reason or logic involved in the mistreatment. If it seems that your color is the reason, if it seems that your ethnic heritage is the cause of the woe, it's because you've been deliberately beaten down by agents of a greedy system until you swallowed the garbage. That is the internalization of racism.

Racism is the systematic, institutionalized mistreatment of one group of people by another based on racial heritage. Like every other oppression, racism can be internalized. People of color come to believe misinformation about their particular ethnic group and thus believe that their mistreatment is justified. With that basic vocabulary, let's take a look at how the whole thing works together. Meet "the Ism Family," racism, classism, ageism, adultism, elitism, sexism, heterosexism, physicalism, etc. All these isms are systemic, that is, not only are these parasites feeding off our lives, they are also dependent on one another for foundation. Racism is supported and reinforced by classism, which is given a foothold and a boost by adultism, which also feeds sexism, which is validated by heterosexism, and so it goes on. You cannot have the "ism" functioning without first effectively installing its flip-side, the internalized version of the ism. Like twins, as one particular form of the ism grows in potency, there is a corresponding increasing in its internalized form within the population. Before oppression becomes a specific ism like racism, usually all hell breaks loose. War. People fight attempts to enslave them, or to subvert their will, or to take what they consider theirs, whether that is territory or dignity. It's true that the various elements of racism, while repugnant, would not be able to do very much damage, but for one generally overlooked key piece: power/privilege.

While in one sense we all have power, we have to look at the fact that, in our society, people are stratified into various classes and some of these classes have more privilege than others. The owning class has enough power and privilege to not have to give a good whinney what the rest of the folks have on their minds. The power and privilege of the owning class provides the ability to pay off enough of the working class and offer that paid-off group, the middle class, just enough privilege to make it agreeable to do various and sundry oppressive things to other working-class and outright disenfranchised folk, keeping the lid on explosive inequities, at lease for a minute. If you're at the bottom of this heap, and you believe the line that says you're there because that's all you're worth, it is at least some small solace to believe that there are others more worthless than you, because of their gender, race, sexual preference . . . whatever. The specific form of power that runs the show here is the power to intimidate. The power to take away the most lives the quickest, and back it up with legal and "divine" sanction, is the very bottom line. It makes the difference between who's holding the racism end of the stick and who's getting beat with it (or beating others as vulnerable as they are) on the internalized racism end of the stick. What I am saying is, while people of color are welcome to tear up their own neighborhoods and each other, everybody knows that you cannot do that to white folks without hell to pay. People of color can be prejudiced against one another and whites but do not have an ice-cube's chance in hell of passing laws that will get whites sent to relocation camps "for their own protection and the security of the nation." People who have not thought about or refuse to acknowledge this imbalance of power/ privilege often want to talk about the racism of people of color. But then that is one of the ways racism is able to continue to function. You look for someone to blame and you blame the victim, who will nine times out of ten accept the blame out of habit.

So, what can we do? Acknowledge racism for a start, even though and especially when we've struggled to be kind and fair, or struggled to rise above it all. It is hard to acknowledge the fact that racism circumscribes and pervades our lives. Racism must be dealt with on two levels, personal and societal, emotional and institutional. It is possible—and most effective—to do both at the same time. We must reclaim whatever delight we have lost in our own ethnic heritage or heritages. This so-called melting pot has only succeeded in turning us into fast food-gobbling "generics" (as in generic "white folks" who were once Irish, Polish, Russian, English, etc., and "black folks," who were once Ashanti, Bambara, Baule, Yoruba, etc.). Find or create safe places to actually *feel* what we've been forced to repress each time we were a victim of, witness to or perpetrator of racism, so that we do not continue, like puppets, to act out the past in the present and future. Challenge oppression. Take a stand against it. When you are aware of something oppressive going down, stop the show. At least call it. We become so numbed to racism that we don't even think twice about it, unless it is immediately life-threatening.

Whites who want to be allies to people of color: You can educate yourselves via   10 research and observation rather than rigidly, arrogantly relying solely on interrogating people of color. Do not expect that people of color should teach you how to behave non-oppressively. Do not give into the pull to be lazy. Think, hard. Do not blame people of color for your frustration about racism, but do appreciate the fact that people of color will often help you get in touch with that frustration. Assume that your effort to be a good friend is appreciated, but don't expect or accept gratitude from people of color. Work on racism for your sake, not "their" sake. Assume that you are needed and capable of being a good ally. Know that you'll make mistakes and commit yourself to correcting them and continuing on as an ally, no matter what. Don't give up.

People of color, working through internalized racism: Remember always that you and others like you are completely worthy of respect, completely capable of achieving whatever you take a notion to do. Remember that the term "people of color" refers to a variety of ethnic and cultural backgrounds. These various groups have been oppressed in a variety of ways. Educate yourself about the ways different peoples have been oppressed and how they've resisted that oppression. Expect and insist that whites are capable of being good allies against racism. Don't give up. Resist the pull to give out the "people of color seal of approval" to aspiring white allies. A moment of appreciation is fine, but more than that tends to be less than helpful. Celebrate yourself. Celebrate yourself. Celebrate the inevitable end of racism.

overcoming white supremacy: a comment

bell hooks

I

Black people in the United States share with black people in South Africa and with people of color globally both the pain of white-supremacist oppression and exploitation and the pain that comes from resistance and struggle. The first pain wounds us, the second pain helps heal our wounds. It often troubles me that black people in the United States have not risen *en masse* to declare solidarity with our black sisters and brothers in South Africa. Perhaps one day soon—say Martin Luther King's birthday—we will enter the streets at a certain hour, wherever we are, to stand for a moment, naming and affirming the primacy of black liberation.

As I write, I try to remember when the word racism ceased to be the term which best expressed for me exploitation of black people and other people of color in this society and when I began to understand that the most useful term was white supremacy. It was certainly a necessary term when confronted with the liberal attitudes of white women active in feminist movement who were unlike their racist ancestors—white women in the early woman's rights movement who did not wish to be caught dead in fellowship with black women. In fact, these women often requested and longed for the presence of black women. Yet when present, what we saw was that they wished to exercise control over our bodies and thoughts as their racist ancestors had—that this need to exercise power over us expressed how much they had internalized the values and attitudes of white supremacy.

It may have been this contact or contact with fellow white English professors who want very much to have "a" black person in "their" department as long as that person thinks and acts like them, shares their values and beliefs, is in no way different, that first compelled me to use the term white supremacy to identify the ideology that most determines how white people in this society (irrespective of their political leanings to the right or left) perceive and relate to black people and other people of color. It is the very small but highly visible liberal movement away from the perpetuation of overtly racist discrimination, exploitation, and oppression of black people which often masks how all-pervasive white supremacy is in this society, both as ideology and as behavior. When liberal whites fail to understand how they can and/or do embody white-supremacist values and beliefs even though they may not embrace racism as prejudice or domination (especially domination that involves coercive control), they cannot recognize the ways their actions support and affirm the very structure of racist domination and oppression that they profess to wish to see eradicated.

Likewise, "white supremacy" is a much more useful term for understanding the complicity of people of color in upholding and maintaining racial hierarchies that do not involve force (i.e., slavery, apartheid) than the term "internalized racism"—a term most often used to suggest that black people have absorbed negative feelings and attitudes about blackness held by white people. The term "white supremacy" enables us to recognize not only that black people are socialized to embody the values and attitudes of white supremacy, but that we can exercise "white-supremacist control" over other black people. This is important, for unlike the term "uncle tom," which carried with it the recognition of complicity and internalized racism, a new terminology must accurately name the way we as black people directly exercise power over one another when we perpetuate white-supremacist beliefs. Speaking about changing perspectives on black identity, writer Toni Morrison said in a recent interview: "Now people choose their identities. Now people choose to be Black." At this historical moment, when a few black people no longer experience the racial apartheid and brutal racism that still determine the lot of many black people, it is easier for that few to ally themselves politically with the dominant racist white group.

5   Assimilation is the strategy that has provided social legitimation for this shift in allegiance. It is a strategy deeply rooted in the ideology of white supremacy and its advocates urge black people to negate blackness, to imitate racist white people so as to better absorb their values, their way of life. Ironically, many changes in social policy and social attitudes that were once seen as ways to end racial domination have served to reinforce and perpetuate white supremacy. This is especially true of social policy that has encouraged and promoted racial integration. Given the continued force of racism, racial integration translated into assimilation ultimately serves to reinforce and maintain white supremacy. Without an ongoing active movement to end white supremacy, without ongoing black liberation struggle, no social environment can exist in the United States that truly supports integration. When black people enter social contexts that remain unchanged, unaltered, in no way stripped of the framework of white supremacy, we are pressured to assimilate. We are rewarded for assimilation. Black people working or socializing in predominately white settings whose very structures are informed by the principles of white supremacy who dare to affirm blackness, love of black culture and identity, do so at great risk. We must continually challenge, protest, resist while working to leave no gaps in our defense that will allow us to be crushed. This is especially true in work settings where we risk being fired or not receiving deserved promotions. Resisting the pressure to assimilate is a part of our struggle to end white supremacy.

When I talk with audiences around the United States about feminist issues of race and gender, my use of the term "white supremacy" always sparks a reaction, usually of a critical or hostile nature. Individual white people and even some non-whites insist that this is not a white-supremacist society, that racism is not nearly the problem it used to be (it is downright frightening to hear people argue vehemently that the problem of racism has been solved), that there has been change. While it is true that the nature of racist oppression and exploitation has changed as slavery has ended and the apartheid structure of Jim Crow has legally changed, white supremacy continues to shape perspectives on reality and to inform the social status of black people and all people of color. Nowhere is this more evident that in university settings. And often it is the liberal folks in those settings who are unwilling to acknowledge this truth.

Recently in a conversation with a white male lawyer at his home where I was a guest, he informed me that someone had commented to him that children are learning very little history these days in school, that the attempt to be all-inclusive, to talk about Native Americans, blacks, women, etc. has led to a fragmented focus on particular representative individuals with no larger historical framework. I responded to this comment by suggesting that it has been easier for white people to practice this inclusion rather than change the larger framework; that it is easier to change the focus from Christopher Columbus, the important white man who "discovered" America, to Sitting Bull or Harriet Tubman, than it is to cease telling a distorted version of U.S. history which upholds white supremacy. Really teaching history in a new way would require abandoning the old myths informed by white supremacy like the notion that Columbus discovered America. It would mean talking about imperialism, colonization, about the Africans who came here before Columbus (see Ivan Van Sertima's *They Came Before Columbus*). It would mean talking about genocide, about the white colonizers' exploitation and betrayal of Native American Indians; about ways the legal and governmental structures of this society from the Constitution on supported and upheld slavery, apartheid (see Derrick Bell's *And We Are Not Saved*). This history can be taught only when the perspectives of teachers are no longer shaped by white supremacy. Our conversation is one of the many examples that reveal the way black people and white people can socialize in a friendly manner, be racially integrated, while deeply ingrained notions of white supremacy remain intact. Incidents like this make it necessary for concerned folks, for righteous white people, to begin to fully explore the way white supremacy determines how they see the world, even as their actions are not informed by the type of racial prejudice that promotes overt discrimination and separation.

Significantly, assimilation was a term that began to be more commonly used after the revolts against white supremacy in the late 1960s and early 1970s. The intense, passionate rebellion against racism and white supremacy of this period was crucial because it created a context for politicization, for education for critical consciousness, one in which black people could begin to confront the extent of our complicity, our internalization of white supremacy and begin the process of self-recovery and collective renewal.

Describing this effort in his work, *The Search for a Common Ground,* black theologian Howard Thurman commented:

> "Black is Beautiful" became not merely a phrase—it was a
> stance, a total attitude, a metaphysics. In very positive and excit-
> ing terms it began undermining the idea that had developed
> over so many years into a central aspect of white mythology:
> that black is ugly, black is evil, black is demonic. In so doing it
> fundamentally attacked the front line of the defense of the
> myth of white supremacy and superiority.

Clearly, assimilation as a social policy upholding white supremacy was strategically an important counter-defense, one that would serve to deflect the call for radical transformation of black consciousness. Suddenly the terms for success (that is getting a job, acquiring the means to provide materially for oneself and one's family) were redefined. It was not enough for black people to enter institutions of higher education and acquire the necessary skills to effectively compete for jobs previously occupied solely by whites; the demand was that blacks become "honorary whites," that black people assimilate to succeed.

10   The force that gave the social policy of assimilation power to influence and change the direction of black liberation struggle was economic. Economic distress created a climate wherein militancy—overt resistance to white supremacy and racism (which included the presentation of self in a manner that suggests black pride)—was no longer deemed a viable survival strategy. Natural hair styles, African dress, etc. were discarded as signs of militancy that might keep one from getting ahead. A similar regressive, reactionary move was taking place among young white radicals, many of whom had been fiercely engaged in left politics, who suddenly began to seek reincorporation into the liberal and conservative mainstream. Again the force behind their re-entry into the system was economic. On a very basic level, changes in the cost of housing (as in the great apartment one had in 1965 for $100 a month cost $400 by 1975) had a frightening impact on college-educated young people of all ethnicities who thought they were committed to transforming society, but who were unable to face living without choice, without the means to escape, who feared living in poverty. Coupled with economic forces exerting pressure, many radicals despaired of the possibility that this white-supremacist, capitalist patriarchy could really be changed.

Tragically, many radical whites who had been allies in the black liberation struggle began to question whether the struggle to end racism was really that significant, or to suggest that the struggle was over, as they moved into their new liberal positions. Radical white youth who had worked in civil rights struggles, protested the war in Vietnam, and even denounced U.S. imperialism could not reconstruct their ties to prevailing systems of domination without creating a new layer of false consciousness—the assertion that racism was no longer pervasive, that race was no longer an important issue. Similarly, critiques of capitalism, especially those that urged individuals to try and live differently within the framework of capitalism, were also relegated to the back burner as people "discovered" that it was important to have class privilege so that one could better help the exploited.

It is no wonder that black radicals met these betrayals with despair and hopelessness. What had all the contemporary struggle to resist racism really achieved? What did it mean to have this period of radical questioning of white supremacy, of black is beautiful, only to witness a few years later the successful mass production by white corporations of hair care products to straighten black hair? What did it mean to witness the assault on black culture by capitalist forces which stress the production on all fronts of an image, a cultural product that can "cross over"—that is, can speak more directly to the concerns, to the popular imagination of white consumers, while still attracting the dollars of black consumers? And what does it mean in 1987 when television viewers watch a morning talk show on black beauty, where black women suggest that these trends are only related to personal preferences and have no relation to racism; when viewers witness a privileged white male, Phil Donahue, shaking his head and trying to persuade the audience to acknowledge the reality of racism and its impact on black people? Or what does it mean when many black people say that what they like most about the Bill Cosby show is that there is little emphasis on blackness, that they are "just people"? And again to hear reported on national news that little black children prefer playing with white dolls rather than black dolls? All these popular narratives remind us that "we are not yet saved," that white supremacy prevails, that the racist oppression and exploitation which daily assaults the bodies and spirits of black people in South Africa, assaults black people here.

Years ago when I was a high school student experiencing racial desegregation, there was a current of resistance and militancy that was so fierce. It swept over and through our bodies as we—black students—stood, pressed against the red brick walls, watching the national guard with their guns, waiting for those moments when we would enter, when we would break through racism, waiting for the moments of change—of victory. And now even within myself I find that spirit of militancy growing faint; all too often it is assaulted by feelings of despair and powerlessness. I find that I must work to nourish it, to keep it strong. Feelings of despair and powerlessness are intensified by all the images of black self-hate that indicate that those militant 1960s did not have sustained radical impact—that the politicization and transformation of black consciousness did not become an ongoing revolutionary practice in black life. This causes such frustration and despair because it means that we must return to this basic agenda, that we must renew efforts at politicization, that we must go over old ground. Perhaps what is more disheartening is the fear that the seeds, though planted again, will never survive, will never grow strong. Right now it is anger and rage (see Audre Lorde's "The Uses of Anger" in *Sister Outsider*) at the continued racial genocide that rekindles within me that spirit of militancy.

Like so many radical black folks who work in university settings, I often feel very isolated. Often we work in environments predominately peopled by white folks (some of whom are well-meaning and concerned) who are not committed to working to end white supremacy, or who are unsure about what that commitment means. Certainly feminist movement has been one of the places where there has been renewed interest in challenging and resisting racism. There too it has been easier for white women to confront racism as overt exploitation and domination, or as personal prejudice, than to confront the encompassing and profound reality of white supremacy.

15   In talking about race and gender recently, the question most often asked by white women has to do with white women's response to black women or women of color insisting that they are not willing to teach them about their racism—to show the way. They want to know: What should a white person do who is attempting to resist racism? It is problematic to assert that black people and other people of color who are sincerely committed to struggling against white supremacy should be unwilling to help or teach white people. Challenging black folks in the 19th century, Frederick Douglass made the crucial point that "power accedes nothing without demand." For the racially oppressed to demand of white people, of black people, of all people that we eradicate white supremacy, that those who benefit materially by exercising white-supremacist power, either actively or passively, willingly give up that privilege in response to that demand, and then to refuse to show the way is to undermine our own cause. We must show the way. There must exist a paradigm, a practical model for social change that includes an understanding of ways to transform consciousness that are linked to efforts to transform structures.

Fundamentally, it is our collective responsibility as radical black people and people of color, and as white people to construct models for social change. To abdicate that responsibility, to suggest that change is just something an individual can do on his or her own or in isolation with other racist white people is utterly misleading. If as a black person I say to a white person who shows a willingness to commit herself or himself to the struggle to end white supremacy that I refuse to affirm, or help in that endeavor is a gesture that undermines my commitment to that struggle. Many black people have essentially responded in this way because we do not want to do the work for white people, and most importantly we cannot do the work, yet this often seems to be what is asked of us. Rejecting the work does not mean that we cannot and do not show the way by our actions, by the information we share. Those white people who want to continue the dominate/subordinate relationship so endemic to racist exploitation by insisting that we "serve" them—that we do the work of challenging and changing their consciousness—are acting in bad faith. In his work, *Pedagogy in Progress: The Letters to Guinea-Bissau,* Paulo Freire reminds us:

> Authentic help means that all who are involved help each other mutually, growing together in the common effort to understand the reality which they seek to transform.

It is our collective responsibility as people of color and as white people who are committed to ending white supremacy to help one another. It is our collective responsibility to educate for critical consciousness. If I commit myself politically to black liberation struggle, to the struggle to end white supremacy, I am not making a commitment to working only for and with black people, I must engage in struggle with all willing comrades to strengthen our awareness and our resistance. (See *The Autobiography of Malcolm X* and *The Last Year of Malcolm X—The Evolution of a Revolutionary* by George Breitman.) Malcolm X is an important role model for those of us who wish to transform our consciousness for he was engaged in ongoing critical self-reflection, in changing both his words and his deeds. In thinking about black response to white people, about what they can do to end racism, I am reminded of that memorable example when Malcolm X expressed regret about an incident with a white female college student who asked him what she could do and he told her: "nothing." He later saw that there was much that she could have done. For each of us, it is work to educate ourselves to understand the nature of white supremacy with a critical consciousness. Black people are not born into this world with innate understanding of racism and white supremacy. (See John Hodge, ed., *Cultural Bases of Racism and Group Oppression*.)

In recent years, particularly among women active in feminist movement, much effort to confront racism has focussed on individual prejudice. While it is important that individuals work to transform their consciousness, striving to be anti-racist, it is important for us to remember that the struggle to end white supremacy is a struggle to change a system, a structure. Hodge emphasizes in his book "the problem of racism is not prejudice but domination." For our efforts to end white supremacy to be truly effective, individual struggle to change consciousness must be fundamentally linked to collective effort to transform those structures that reinforce and perpetuate white supremacy.

OVERT AND INSTITUTIONAL RACISM

Gertrude Ezorsky

Overt racist action, as conceived here, takes place only if a harm is inflicted or a benefit withheld either because of the perpetrator's racial bias against the victim or because of that perpetrator's obliging the race prejudice of others.[1] (Thus an employer who refuses to hire blacks because of concern for white customers' or white employees' bias is practicing overt racism.) Racially biased persons are disposed to treat blacks in an irrational and negative manner because of their race. The victim of overt racism may be a black group as well as an individual, such as residents of a segregated school district, which because of overt racism is denied equal funding.

How does institutional racism differ from the overt type?

Institutional racism occurs when a firm uses a practice that is race-neutral (intrinsically free of racial bias) but that nevertheless has an adverse impact on blacks as a group. For example, to obtain a position, a worker often needs specific training or skilled work experience. If blacks tend to lack such qualifications, they are excluded disproportionately from employment. Yet job qualification standards are intrinsically free of bias: not only are they used in all-white areas; they would most likely exist in a racially impartial society.

But while competence criteria are inherently bias-free, their negative impact on blacks perpetuates the effects of overt racism. For example, as a result of overtly racist "last-hired, first-fired" policies toward blacks and favoring of whites for on-the-job training, many blacks have been unable to gain work experience, particularly special working skills. Two other widely used hiring practices, selection by personal connections and selection by seniority ranking—also in themselves bias free—tend to bar blacks from desirable positions.

5   The adverse effect on blacks of these neutral practices also contributes to the perpetuation of racist attitudes. Individuals growing up in a society where blacks are visibly predominant in the lowest jobs tend to believe that blacks naturally belong there.

When the adverse impact of bias-free practices occurs in a society where, generally speaking, such impact is in significant part either a result of overt racism, or a contribution to its perpetuation, then that impact is appropriately called *racist impact*. Such impact is characteristic of institutional racism. It is important to remember that those who administer procedures having racist

---

[1]Some points in this book draw on material used in my article "Discrimination," forthcoming in the *Encyclopedia of Ethics* (New York: Garland).

impact may not themselves by racist, that is, they may not personally have racist attitudes.

I have attempted to distinguish the concepts of overt and institutional racism, but in reality they often work together. For example, although qualification requirements are in themselves race-neutral, biased employers or union officials can manipulate them to exclude blacks. Such manipulation was common in the post–1964 Civil Rights Act period, when, as we shall see, employers and some unions fearful of an influx of blacks raised qualification standards in order to keep them out.

OVERT RACISM

Statistics showing that blacks disproportionately occupy low-paying, undesirable jobs conflate the disproportionate effects of both types of racism.

Some methods for detecting overt racism in hiring practices are more effective than others. For example, some sociologists estimate employer racial discrimination by determining whether blacks and whites with equal productive characteristics—for example, education and work experience—receive equal payoffs in employment. Unequal payoffs not explained by unequal productive characteristics define the measure of employment "discrimination."

This method is irrelevant to my analysis, however, because it fails to distinguish the effect of overt employer racism from the powerful racist impact of a significant racially neutral practice—selection by personal connections. The advantage of this widespread recruitment method to whites is very great, for their employed white friends and relatives lead them to remunerative positions. Because of such connections, whites who are no more productive than blacks will tend to receive a better payoff. Recruitment by personal connections, however, does not necessarily reflect overt employer racism. A firm may rely on recruitment by personal contacts because they save job advertising costs or because the employer believes that such referrals are reliable, or because employees are quick to spot opportunities for friends. A better method for assessing overt racism in hiring is the systematic use of "testers," whereby black and white applicants apply for a specific position. The selection can determine whether they are impartially treated by employers. However, no such direct testing has been extensively carried out during the past decade. (But see the Postscript, p. 88.)

Nevertheless, overt racism in employment practices can be assessed indirectly, through extrapolation. If overt racist behavior, as well as racist attitudes—that is, dispositions to such behavior—is widespread in diverse sectors of society generally, it is reasonable to infer that racist attitudes also exist in employment. And abundant evidence shows that overt racism is widespread today.

During the second half of the 1980s, racial violence against blacks increased nationwide. In 1988 a white supremacist movement of violent

10

skin-headed youths, whose weapons included knives, baseball bats, and their own steel-toed boots, sprang up spontaneously in cities throughout the nation. According to academic administrators, there is a "growing pattern of bigotry and animosity towards minority students" at predominantly white schools.[2]

Racist attitudes are also shown by the higher value juries place on a white victim's life. One survey noted in 1986: "In the thirty-two states where the death penalty has been imposed . . . the killer of a white is nearly three times more likely to be sentenced to death than the killer of a black."[3]

A landmark four-year intensive study of racism, *A Common Destiny: Blacks and American Society* (1989), conducted by a panel of distinguished experts, found that despite progress attitudes of racism are still widespread. There is "continuing discriminatory behavior by whites, especially in areas involving close personal contact." Investigation of residential housing markets comparing blacks with whites of similar income shows extensive housing discrimination against blacks. Highly educated blacks also face barriers to living in the same neighborhood with highly educated whites.[4] A University of Chicago investigation showed that because of persistent prejudice suburban blacks are more likely to suffer segregation than other minorities of equal income and social status. There are "strong penalties for being black."[5] The extent of housing discrimination can be gauged from a 1987 estimate by the department of Housing and Urban Development: there are about two million instances of housing discrimination every year.[6]

15   According to a 1981 study black school districts in the black-belt states receive less funding and inferior education by comparison with economically similar white districts, in part as a result of local (white) decision making.[7] Black land-grant colleges and universities receive proportionately lower allotments of federal resources from the Department of Agriculture than do white institutions.[8]

Studies show that 15 to 19 percent of whites would not vote for a qualified black candidate nominated by their own party either for governor or president. According to Linda Williams, senior research associate at the Joint

---

[2]*Newsweek,* January 5, 1987: 24: *Klanwatch Intelligence Report* (Montgomery, Ala: Southern Poverty Law Center, February 1989), p. 1; "Campus Race Incidents Disquiet U. of Michigan," *New York Times,* March 9, 1987; Jon Weiner, "Racial Hatred on Campus," *Nation,* February 27, 1989: 260–64.

[3]Ronald J. Tabak, "The Death of Fairness: The Arbitrary and Capricious Imposition of the Death Penalty in the 1980's," *Review of Law and Social Change* 14 (1986): 826.

[4]*A Common Destiny: Blacks and American Society,* ed. Gerald David Jaynes and Robin M. Williams, Jr., for the Committee on the Status of Black Americans, Commission on Behavioral and Social Sciences and Education, National Research Council (Washington, D.C.: National Academy Press, 1989), pp. 155, 116, 140–46.

[5]"Study Says Prejudice in Suburbs Is Aimed Mostly at Blacks," *New York Times,* November 23, 1988.

[6]"Stepping Up the War on Discrimination," *New York Times,* November 1, 1987.

[7]*A Decade of Frustrations* (Atlanta, Ga.: Southern Regional Council, 1981).

[8]"Latest Charge of Racism Prompts a Debate," *New York Times,* June 30, 1986.

Center for Political Studies, their 1986 national poll showed that "the higher the office, the more whites there were who would admit that they would never vote for a black."[9]

Although the percentage of whites who oppose antimiscegenation laws has risen (from 38 percent in 1963 to 66 percent in 1982), one in three whites still believes that racial intermarriage should be prohibited by law.[10]

It is implausible that racist attitudes, so widespread in contemporary society, should be significantly absent from the world of work where predominantly white employers, supervisors, and union officials decide whether blacks should be rewarded equally with whites. Although enforcement of civil rights laws in the late 1960s and 1970s deterred overt racism in the workplace, such enforcement suffered a dramatic decline after 1980.

INSTITUTIONAL RACISM

The neutral procedures that have had the greatest racist impact within employment are selection by (1) personal connections, (2) qualification standards, and (3) seniority status. As I shall show, although these policies may be administered by racially impartial persons, they are linked to overt racism, past, present, and future. Indeed, in some situations they serve as instruments of overt racism.

Personal Connections

Reliance by employers on friends, relatives, and neighbors—their own or their workers'—has powerful racist impact—first, because of its paramount importance in the world of work, second, because of its links to overt racism.

Numerous studies of workers—blue and white collar, professional and technical—indicate that communicating job information to family, friends, neighbors, and acquaintances by word of mouth is probably the most widely used recruitment method.[11]

Vocational counselors emphasize the importance of making contacts through personal connections.[12] Academic job seekers know the value of having friends in the department of their choice. Referral unions that influence or control hiring for many well-paid jobs in such industries as construction, printing, publishing, and transportation commonly recruit through

20

---

[9]See a Joint Center for Political Studies poll reported in the *New York Times,* February 26, 1989, and Howard Schuman, Charlotte Steh, and Lawrence Bobo, *Racial Attitudes in America* (Cambridge, Mass.: Harvard University Press, 1985), pp. 73–82.

[10]Andrew Hacker, "Black Crime, White Racism," *New York Review of Books,* March 3, 1988: 38, a review of *Racial Attitudes in America.* See pp. 73–76 of that book for a report of the survey.

[11]Joe R. Feagin and Clairece Booher Feagin, *Discrimination, American Style* (Englewood Cliffs, N.J.: Prentice-Hall, 1978), p. 47.

[12]James M. Boros and J. Robert Parkinson, *How to Get a Fast Start in Today's Job Market* (Englewood Cliffs, N.J.: Prentice-Hall, 1980).

personal contacts. Kathleen Parker of the National Center for Career Strategies was reported in 1990 as stating that over 80 percent of executives find their jobs through networking and that about 86 percent of available jobs do not appear in the classified advertisements.[13] The old saying, "It isn't what you know, but who you know" expresses a profound social truth.

Because, for the most part, blacks and whites live as two separate societies, it is not surprising that blacks suffer because of selection by personal contacts. Lacking ties to whites as family, friends, fellow students, neighbors, or club members, blacks tend to be isolated from the networks in which connections to desirable employment—where whites predominate—are forged.

Hence blacks have been outside the channels leading to well-paid jobs controlled by the predominantly white referral unions that recruit by word of mouth. Family or friends had virtually automatic preference for membership cards in such overwhelmingly white labor organizations as the Ironworkers' Union.[14] Such recruitment by referral unions contributed to the virtual exclusion of blacks from employment on public construction projects until affirmative action enforcement in the late 1960s and 1970s brought some improvement in the recruitment of minorities.

25   Blacks also lack personal connections to residents of all-white suburbs where many new jobs have been created. That adverse effect on blacks is exacerbated when suburban employers rely on "walk-in" applicants from these white neighborhoods.

Because whites disproportionately occupy elected government office, especially the more powerful positions, blacks suffer from the widespread use of political patronage to distribute government jobs. For example, according to the *New York Times* New York State Democratic Committee director John A. Marino said that his office funneled three thousand annual job recommendations to the state appointments office, two-thirds of which were minimum-wage seasonal positions. As the article notes, such jobs are "ideal for the children and friends of cooperative politicians."[15] And while small business has generated many of the nation's new jobs during the past decade, blacks live outside the immediate circles from which white owners tend to draw their new workers.

The handicap of exclusion from the white pipeline starts early in life. One study shows that for a young male high-school graduate, the best job route is through relatives. A 1989 comparative ethnographic study by anthropologist Mercer L. Sullivan of three neighborhood groups of young men in New York—ethnic white, hispanic, and black—showed the importance of personal connections for success in the labor market: "The labor market advantages of the . . . [white] youths over their peers in the two minority neigh-

---

[13] *Executive Edge* (Emmaus, Pa., August 1990).
[14] Feagin, p. 50; *Affirmative Action to Open the Doors of Job Opportunity,* Report of the Citizens' Commission on Civil Rights (Washington, D.C., 1984), p. 41; William B. Gould, *Black Workers in White Unions* (Ithaca: Cornell University Press, 1977), p. 341.
[15] "Patronage Takes on Personal Touches as Parties Wane," *New York Times,* January 28, 1989.

borhoods derive not from their greater investment in human capital (e.g., education) but rather from their personal networks. These networks afford them entry into the more desirable sectors of the labor market which recruit not on the basis of education but on the basis of personal connections."[16]

Although the lack of personal connections to the job market is in most cases an institutional barrier to employment for blacks, it arises in large part from segregation created by overtly racist practices. From the period of slavery until the middle of the twentieth century, the segregation of blacks in schools, housing, accommodations, and public and private facilities was imposed by whites throughout the nation, either in ready conformity to explicitly racial laws (as in the South) or to the silent toleration of violence against blacks who dared to cross racial barriers. Today widespread segregation continues as an inherited social structure, excluding blacks from white residential areas and neighborhood schools, where they might develop white connections leading to employment. That structure of "ghettoization" is sustained by pervasive housing discrimination against blacks who wish to move into white areas.

The isolation of blacks from white society is also sustained by widespread racist attitudes that exclude blacks from white clubs and social circles where networks leading to jobs are formed. Even mild unconscious racial prejudice tends to cut blacks off from relations of friendship and intimacy with whites. A University of Chicago study of the nation's ten largest cities showed that blacks and whites rarely interact outside the workplace.[17]

Hiring by personal connections also tends to keep blacks at the bottom of the occupational ladder. Because individuals often hear of openings in their own kind of work, they tend to funnel such information to relatives and acquaintances. Thus both black and white workers informally recruit to *their* types of jobs. Because blacks are disproportionately represented in bottom-level positions, their personal recruitment tends to maintain occupational segregation. Continued perception of blacks in menial, undesirable jobs reinforces the racist conception that blacks belong there.

Thus, although selection by personal connections is intrinsically free of bias, its ties to overt racism—past, present, and future—justify characterization of its adverse impact on blacks as *racist impact*.

Qualification Requirements

Although black–white inequality of educational attainment has been substantially reduced in some respects, such as in the amount of schooling received and the level of reading, nevertheless requirements for a college diploma and

---

[16]Juan Williams, "Racism Revisited," *Utne Reader,* May–June 1987: 56 (reprinted from the *New Republic,* November 10, 1986); Mercer L. Sullivan, *"Getting Paid"* (Ithaca: Cornell University Press, 1989), p. 226. For an analysis of the contribution made by institutions that structure the labor market to the disproportionately higher minority youth crime rate, see Sullivan, chap. 10.
[17]"Study Finds Segregation in Cities Worse Than Scientists Imagined," *New York Times,* August 5, 1989.

for adequate test scores continue to exclude blacks from employment and from postgraduate schools that provide training for desirable positions.[18] Similarly, requirements for certain work experience and vague personality traits have a negative impact in employment.

Overt racism, especially in its contribution to segregating blacks from whites throughout society, makes a significant contribution to the racist impact of qualification requirements on blacks.

Millions of black persons still in the labor force today attended legally segregated public schools in seventeen southern states and the District of Columbia, where a presumption of black inferiority—destructive to their self-confidence—was pervasive, and where, because of gross discrimination in funding, black schools were invariably inferior.[19] And, as indicated earlier, a 1981 study of black-belt states shows that black school districts, by comparison with economically similar white school districts, have continued to receive less funding and inferior education, in part, as a consequence of local (white) government decisions.[20]

35   Many blacks are excluded by requirements for work experience because as students they had been barred from white schools where relevant training was available or had been denied work experience and training by prejudiced supervisors and employers.

In his 1979 *United Steelworkers of America* v. *Weber* case affidavit, Kernell Goudia, a black worker, demonstrated how past overt racism contributed to the racist impact of a "prior experience" requirement set by a Louisiana Kaiser plant for skilled jobs.

> In 1968, upon discharge from the armed services, I applied to
> LSU trade school. I was sent an invitation to come for an inter-

---

[18] *A Common Destiny*, p. 332; *The Reading Report Card* (Washington, D.C.: U.S. Department of Education, Office of Educational Research and Improvement, 1990), p. 15.

[19] See Charles H. Thompson, "Problems in the Achievement of Adequate Educational Opportunity," in *Negro Education in America*, ed. Virgil A. Clift, Archibald W. Anderson and H. Gordon Hullfish (New York: Harper & Row, 1962), p. 176.

[20] Underfunding of black schools is not confined to the black belt. Minority school districts in New York City have also suffered substantially from less than equal funding allocation. A 1987 study of New York City schools showed that such deprivation of educational support—repeatedly perpetrated on the poorest, overwhelmingly black and hispanic districts—extended even to resources designed to fill the urgent needs of disadvantaged students. Since there are to my knowledge no studies that compare funding to economically similar white and minority school districts (outside the black belt), conclusions as to the direct role of overt racism in such funding inequity cannot be drawn. Nevertheless, given pervasive racist attitudes, it is plausible that overt racism contributes to such inequity. But even if less than equal funding is imposed on minority school districts only because they are poor, it is undeniable that a history of overt racism has contributed substantially to the disproportionate impoverishment of blacks. Hence, as poor people, blacks suffer the racist impact of less than equal funding to poor school districts. (For information on underfunding to New York City minority school districts, see Susan Breslin with Eleanor Stier, *Promoting Poverty* [New York: Community Service Society, 1987].)

view, but when I appeared and was seen in person, I was told I would not be interviewed. Louisiana had a system of segregated trade schools, and out of the 27 schools in the state, only two accepted Blacks and their programs were limited to traditionally Black jobs. I had always been interested in getting craft training but due to discrimination I was barred. I understood Kaiser had required prior experience to get into craft positions or training positions, but given the situation in Louisiana this requirement all but excluded Blacks.[21]

Overt housing discrimination affecting all economic classes of blacks works indirectly to reduce the achievement of black youngsters by contributing to the significant racial segregation of neighborhood schools.[22] The psychiatrist Stuart W. Cook informs us that studies show that desegregation in schools, "particularly when begun early and viewed cumulatively, accelerates black achievement gain."[23]

The positive effect of socialization within white families on black children's test scores is indicated in a comparative study of black children adopted by middle-class parents, white and black. The children adopted by white middle-class parents scored significantly higher on the Wechsler Intelligence Scale for Children than did the children adopted by black middle-class parents. The scoring difference is of the magnitude "typically found between the average scores of black and white children."[24]

Noting the history of segregation in the United States, John H. Fischer, past president of Columbia University's Teachers College, stated: "Every Negro child is the victim of the history of his race in this country. On the day he enters Kindergarten, he carries a burden no white child can ever know."[25]

---

[21]Affidavit by Kernell Goudia, sworn on May 6, 1979, and submitted to the Supreme Court for consideration in *United Steelworkers of America* v. *Weber,* 443 U.S. 193 (1979).

[22]For example, in the Yonkers segregation suit the Southern District Court of New York found in 1985 that the city's housing practices, as well as city participation in school affairs, constitute "more than adequate evidence of the city's intentional perpetuation and exacerbation of racial segregation in Yonkers public schools (*United States* v. *Yonkers Board of Education,* 624 F. Supp. 1276 [S.D.N.Y. 1985])." See excerpts from the ruling by Judge Leonard B. Sand in "Judge Finds Yonkers Has Segregation Policy," *New York Times,* November 21, 1985.

[23]Stuart W. Cook, "The 1954 Social Science Statement and School Desegregation: A Reply to Gerard," in *Eliminating Racism,* ed. Phyllis A. Katz and Dalmas A. Taylor (New York and London: Plenum Press, 1988), p. 248.

[24]Elsie G. J. Moore, "Language Behavior in the Test Situation and the Intelligence Test Achievement of Transracially and Traditionally Adopted Black Children," in *The Language of Children Reared in Poverty,* ed. Lynne Feagans and Dale Clark Farran (New York: Academic Press, 1982), p. 152.

[25]John H. Fischer, "Educational Problems of Segregation and Desegregation," in *Education in Depressed Areas,* ed. A. H. Passowe (New York: Teachers College, Columbia University, 1963), p. 291.

40   A 1989 report by the Committee on Policy for Racial Justice, chaired by the historian John Hope Franklin, points out that within the classroom teachers form "negative, inaccurate and inflexible expectations" based on the race as well as on the economic class of their students.[26] Such expectations—injurious to the motivation, self-image, and aspiration of black students—become self-fulfilling prophecies of failure in school and employment.

The racist impact of qualification requirements in employment is the terminus of a cumulative impact that begins in school. Black students are vulnerable to traditional practices such as standardized testing and tracking—that is, ability grouping in schools—which place them disproportionately at the bottom level, sometimes at a very early age, where, deprived of educational resources and instruction in higher-order skills, they have little possibility of moving up.[27]

In the job market the vulnerability of blacks to qualification requirements is exacerbated when employers insist on credentials such as higher-education diplomas that are not related to work performance. Such requirements have had a severe effect on black employment. Irrelevant testing excluded blacks even from such dead-end work as dishwashing. In the post–Civil Rights Act period, the U.S. Equal Employment Opportunity Commission discovered that employers almost uniformly failed to establish that employment requirements reliably measured ability to do the job. The Wonderlic Test, probably the most widely used general intelligence test in industry, had practically no significant value in predicting industrial job performance.[28]

The adverse effect of irrelevant higher education requirements increases when, as in the recessions of the 1970s, college graduates were willing to take traditionally black jobs or, as in 1990, when college graduates—in oversupply—were being hired as clerks, bookkeepers, and so forth.[29]

An important race-neutral qualification standard in the academic marketplace is published research. Taking Harvard University as an example, sociologist Thomas Pettigrew shows how this requirement adversely affects black candidates. In the 1930s, Harvard developed criteria for tenured faculty appointment, which included scholarly publication. The purpose was to ensure a faculty of high quality. Publication requirements, however, worked against the recruitment of black professors because the majority taught heavy course

---

[26] Committee on Policy for Racial Justice, *Visions of a Better Way* (Washington, D.C.: Joint Center for Political Studies Press, 1989), pp. 16–17.

[27] *Visions of a Better Way,* pp. 17–18.

[28] Sources on invalid qualification requirements: "Legal Implications of the Use of Standardized Ability Tests in Employment and Education," *Columbia Law Review* 68 (1968): 691, 701; George Cooper and Richard B. Sobol, "Seniority and Testing under Fair Employment Laws: A General Approach to Objective Criteria of Hiring and Promotion," *Harvard Law Review* 82 (June 1969): 1644.

[29] See Louis Uchitelle, "Surplus of College Graduates Dims Job Outlook for Others," *New York Times,* June 18, 1990.

loads in predominantly black colleges, which limited their time for research and writing.[30] This concentration of blacks in predominantly black colleges has links to a racist past, because black academics were initially excluded by racist attitudes from many white departments. Hence in the 1970s, when some predominantly white universities following affirmative action requirements sought black professors, black college faculty were less able to fill their race-neutral publication requirements.

Although qualification requirements are intrinsically bias-free, they can be manipulated by racist employers and union officials to exclude blacks. Thus while some employers who set irrelevant higher education requirements may simply have undue reverence for diplomas, many are not unhappy that their requirements tend to keep blacks out. According to one legal scholar, raising qualification criteria has been a "common device of employers and construction unions" when, because of civil rights law, hiring and promotion of blacks appeared likely.[31]

Tests plainly not germane to job performance have served the same racist purpose. A classic instance was the attempt by an Ironworkers' local to bar Harold Lewis, a black welder with thirty years' experience, by insisting that he pass a newly introduced and irrelevant knot-tying test.[32]

Vague subjective standards, such as "fitting in," "personality," "vigor," and "self-confidence"—widely used for promotion—easily serve racial prejudice. In *Rowe v. General Motors Co.*, the court stated that promotion procedures that depend on "subjective evaluation" by immediate supervisors are a "ready mechanism" for covert race discrimination. The court expressed skepticism that blacks, dependent on whites for decisive recommendation, can expect impartiality.[33]

Seniority Systems

Seniority status determines promotion, layoff, and job termination for vast numbers of employees: professionals, managers, clericals, skilled, and unskilled workers. A *Harvard Law Review* report states that seniority is one of "the most important bastions of status in our economy": "Enshrined in countless collective bargaining agreements, seniority occupies a unique position in American labor relations."[34]

---

[30] Thomas F. Pettigrew, "Racism and the Mental Health of White Americans: A Social Psychological View," in *Racism in Mental Health,* ed. Charles V. Willie, Bernard M. Kramer, and Bertram S. Brown (Pittsburgh, Pa.: University of Pittsburgh Press, 1973), p. 275.

[31] Albert W. Blumrosen, *Black Employment and the Law* (New Brunswick, N.J.: Rutgers University Press, 1971), p. 32.

[32] Gould, pp. 479–80.

[33] 457 F.2d 348 (5th Cir. 1972); reported by Gould, p. 291.

[34] "Employment Discrimination and the Title VII of the Civil Rights Act of 1964," *Harvard Law Review* 84 (1971): 1156.

Seniority systems have brought significant benefits to American workers. Promotion based on seniority enables harmony, cooperation, and solidarity to replace an ugly scramble for advancement over one's co-workers. Seniority-determined layoff protects workers against arbitrary dismissal due to an employer's whim, malice, or prejudice. Strengthened by such security, many workers have gained in dignity and self-esteem and are less tempted to pander to supervisors or accept humiliating conditions. An older auto worker told me that before the union had negotiated a seniority system his supervisor would invite subordinates over on Sunday to mow his lawn. With the protection of a seniority system, workers can demand to be treated with a measure of respect. Egalitarian philosophers, that is, those committed to equal economic reward, may note that seniority-based benefit systems constitute a significant egalitarian substructure in the hierarchy of employment. Insofar as seniority determines promotion, pay, and job security, protected employees tend to gain equally throughout their working lives.

50   But seniority, in itself race-neutral, has disproportionately benefited white workers. Hired in most cases ahead of blacks, whites have enjoyed higher seniority status.[35] Blacks felt the racist impact of such past hiring discrimination when, as less senior, they were less likely to gain promotion and more likely to lose their jobs in economic recessions. As we shall see, even in industries where blacks entered early, those who achieved high seniority status often suffered the racist impact of departmental seniority arrangements, which locked them into the most miserable jobs.

In the 1970s blacks, hired under affirmative action programs in private and public employment (e.g., as teachers, police, and firefighters), were devastated by seniority-based layoffs—a consequence of three recessions and severe government budget cutbacks.[36] Such layoffs threaten minorities again in the 1990s.

As job losers, blacks tend to move down to unskilled temporary work, or to no work at all. This downward move is facilitated by their lack of significant financial assets, which often makes job retraining unfeasible.[37] Whites have eleven times the wealth of blacks; one-third of all blacks have no major assets whatsoever except for cash on hand.[38] Thus seniority-based layoffs of

---

[35] Philip S. Foner, *Organized Labor and the Black Worker, 1619–1973* (New York: Praeger, 1974), p. 427.

[36] *Last Hired, First Fired: Layoffs and Civil Rights* (Washington, D.C.: U.S. Commission on Civil Rights, 1977), pp. 10–25. The disproportionately high rate of minority job loss due to seniority-based layoff during the 1970s, in both the private and public sector, is documented in this 1977 report: "In some areas where minorities represented only 10–12% of the work force they accounted for 60–70% of those being laid off in 1974" (pp. 24–25). The commission concluded that the "continuing implementation of layoffs by seniority inevitably means the gutting of affirmative action efforts in employment" (p. 61).

[37] *Last Hired, First Fired*, p. 14.

[38] "Whites Own 11 Times the Assets Blacks Have, Census Study Finds," *New York Times,* July 19, 1986.

blacks, including those hired because of affirmative action programs, increases the concentration of blacks at the bottom of the occupational ladder or among the unemployed, thereby reinforcing the racist stereotype of blacks as inferior.

Although long-term black employees have the benefit of high seniority ranking, after the 1964 Civil Rights Act many continued to suffer the racist impact of departmental seniority arrangements. Under such arrangements, a worker who transfers from one department to another loses all seniority credit. Although departmental seniority is a race-neutral practice, it perpetuates the victimizing effect of past overtly racist job assignment. Newly hired blacks in northern and southern plants had traditionally been assigned to segregated departments where they labored in the most undesirable, low-paying jobs, for example, at garbage disposal, the blast furnaces and the coke ovens, and in the foundries. After the 1964 Civil Rights Act, black workers could no longer be legally prevented from transfer to the better, white departments. But under departmental seniority arrangements, transfers were stripped of all seniority, and so they descended to the bottom rung for promotion and layoff. Thus blacks naturally tended to remain in the racially segregated departments, where they had originally been assigned by biased company supervisors.

SUMMARY: THE TIES OF RACE-NEUTRAL PROCEDURES TO OVERT RACISM

Overt racism, past and present, contributes to social and residential segregation, thereby isolating blacks at every income level from white society. Because of such isolation, blacks are vulnerable, by exclusion, to selection by personal connections. The negative impact of qualification standards in employment is sustained by racially biased funding of education and training resources and by the cumulative racist impact of such practices as tracking in schools. Blacks suffer the adverse effects of seniority-based promotion and layoff because of past racist hiring of whites ahead of blacks.

Institutional racism also reinforces future racism by contributing to the disproportionate presence of blacks at the bottom of employment—a presence that helps perpetuate the racist attitude that blacks are inherently inferior. White notions of black people have been formed in a social world where blacks visibly predominate at these bottom levels. Thus they have labored— and continue to labor—as maids and porters, at "hot, heavy, and dirty" jobs in the foundries and paint pits of the auto plants, the boiler rooms of utilities, the dusty basements of tobacco factories, and in the murderous heat of the steel mills' coke ovens.

Today, while some blacks have moved on up, it is still true that the more disagreeable the job, the greater the chance of finding a high proportion of blacks doing it. In 1984, Herman Schwartz, a legal scholar, noted that blacks constitute over 50% of the nation's maids and garbage collectors, but only 4 percent of its managers and 3 percent of its physicians and lawyers.[39]

The racially exclusionary impact of race-neutral policies on employment also contributes to the official black unemployment rate as perpetually double that of whites, thereby reenforcing the racist view of blacks as unwilling to work. Thus these race-neutral policies function as social mechanisms through which the victimizing effects of overt racism, past and present, continue to keep blacks at the bottom levels of employment.

Postscript: In 1991, when this book was in proof, the Urban Institute published the results of an investigation of overt race discrimination in employment. Testers—equally qualified young black and white men, articulate and conventionally dressed—applied through newspaper advertisements for entry-level jobs in Chicago and Washington, D.C. The results showed "widespread and pervasive" race discrimination against young black males. Such discrimination appeared greatest in jobs offering the best wages and future income potential. The investigators concluded that race discrimination contributes to black male unemployment and nonparticipation in the labor force. See Margery Austin Turner, Michael Fix, and Raymond J. Struyk, *Opportunities Denied, Opportunities Diminished: Discrimination in Hiring* (Washington, D.C.: The Urban Institute, 1991) pp. 32–33.

---

[39]Herman Schwartz, "Affirmative Action," in *Minority Report,* ed. Leslie W. Dunbar (New York: Pantheon Books, 1984), p. 61.

OCCUPIED AMERICA

Rodolfo Acuña

Central to the thesis of this monograph is my contention that the conquest of the Southwest created a colonial situation in the traditional sense—with the Mexican land and population being controlled by an imperialistic United States. Further, I contend that this colonization—with variations—is still with us today. Thus, I refer to the colony, initially, in the traditional definition of the term, and later (taking into account the variations) as an internal colony.

From the Chicano perspective, it is obvious that these two types of colonies are a reality. In discussions with non-Chicano friends, however, I have encountered considerable resistance. In fact, even colleagues sympathetic to the Chicano cause vehemently deny that Chicanos are—or have been— colonized. They admit the exploitation and discrimination, but they add that this has been the experience of most "Americans"—especially European and Asian immigrants and Black Americans. While I agree that exploitation and racism have victimized most out-groups in the United States, this does not preclude the reality of the colonial relationship between the Anglo-American privileged and the Chicano.

I feel that the parallels between the Chicanos' experience in the United States and the colonization of other Third World peoples are too similar to dismiss. Attendant to the definition of colonization are the following conditions:

1. The land of one people is invaded by people from another country, who later use military force to gain and maintain control.
2. The original inhabitants become subjects of the conquerors involuntarily.
3. The conquered have an alien culture and government imposed upon them.
4. The conquered become the victims of racism and cultural genocide and are relegated to a submerged status.
5. The conquered are rendered politically and economically powerless.
6. The conquerors feel they have a "mission" in occupying the area in question and believe that they have undeniable privileges by virtue of their conquest.

These points also apply to the relationship between Chicanos and Anglos in Mexico's northwest territory.

5   In the traditional historian's viewpoint, however, there are two differences
that impede universal acceptance of the reality of Anglo-American colonialism in this area.

1. Geographically the land taken from Mexico bordered the United
   States rather than being an area distant from the "mother country."

Too many historians have accepted—subconsciously, if not conveniently—the myth that the area was always intended to be an integral part of
the United States. Instead of conceptualizing the conquered territory as
northern Mexico, they perceive it in terms of the "American" Southwest.
Further, the stereotype of the colonialist pictures him wearing Wellington
boots and carrying a swagger stick, and that stereotype is usually associated
with overseas situations—certainly not in territory contiguous to an "expanding" country.

2. Historians also believe that the Southwest was won in fair and just
   warfare, as opposed to unjust imperialism.

The rationale has been that the land came to the United States as the result of competition, and in winning the game, the country was generous in
paying for its prize. In the case of Texas, they believe Mexico attacked the
"freedom-loving" Anglo-Americans. It is difficult for citizens of the United
States to accept the fact that their nation has been and is imperialistic. Imperialism, to them, is an affliction of other countries.

While I acknowledge the geographical proximity of the area—and the
fact that this is a modification of the strict definition of colonialism—I refute
the conclusion that the Texan and Mexican-American wars were just or that
Mexico provoked them. Further, I illustrate in this monograph that the conditions attendant to colonialism, listed above, accompanied the U.S. take-over
of the Southwest. For these reasons, I maintain that colonialism in the traditional sense did exist in the Southwest, and that the conquerors dominated
and exploited the conquered.

The colonization still exists today, but as I mentioned before, there are
variations. Anglo-Americans still exploit and manipulate Mexicans and still
relegate them to a submerged caste. Mexicans are still denied political and
economic determination and are still the victims of racial stereotypes and
racial slurs promulgated by those who feel they are superior. Thus, I contend
that Mexicans in the United States are still a colonized people, but now the
colonization is *internal*—it is occurring *within* the country rather than being
imposed by an external power. The territories of the Southwest are states
within the United States, and theoretically permanent residents of Mexican
extraction are U.S. citizens. Yet the rights of citizenship are too often circumvented or denied outright.

10   In reality, there is little difference between the Chicano's status in the *traditional colony* of the nineteenth century and in the *internal colony* of the twentieth century. The relationship between Anglos and Chicanos remains the

same—that of master–servant. The principal difference is that Mexicans in the traditional colony were indigenous to the conquered land. Now, while some are descendants of Mexicans living in the area before the conquest, large numbers are technically descendants of immigrants. After 1910, in fact, almost one-eighth of Mexico's population migrated to the United States, largely as a result of the push-and-pull of economic necessity. Southwest agribusinessmen "imported" Mexican workers to fill the need for cheap labor, and this influx signaled the beginning of even greater Anglo manipulation of Mexican settlements or *colonias.*

The original *colonias* expanded in size with the increased immigration and new settlements sprang up. They became nations within a nation, in effect, for psychologically, socially, and culturally they remained Mexican. But the *colonias* had little or no control over their political, economic, or educational destinies. In almost every case, they remained separate and unequal to Anglo-American communities. The elected representatives within the *colonias* were usually Anglo-Americans or Mexicans under their control, and they established a bureaucracy to control the political life of the Mexican settlements—for the benefit of the Anglo privileged.

Further, Anglos controlled the educational system—they administered the schools and taught in the classrooms, and designed the curriculum not to meet the needs of Chicano students but to Americanize them. The police patrolling the *colonia* lived, for the most part, outside the area. Their main purpose was to protect Anglo property. Anglos owned the business and industry in the *colonias,* and capital that could have been used to improve the economic situation within the *colonias* was taken into Anglo-American sectors, in much the same way that capital is drained from underdeveloped countries by foreign economic imperialists. In addition, the *colonias* became employment centers for industrialists, who were assured of a ready supply of cheap labor.

This pattern is one that emerged in most Chicano communities, and one that contradicts the belief in Anglo-American equality. In sum, even though the 1960 census documented that 85 percent of Chicanos are native-born U.S. citizens, most Anglo-Americans still consider them Mexicans and outsiders.

In discussing the traditional and internal colonization of the Chicano, it is not my intention to rekindle hatreds, nor to condemn all Anglo-Americans collectively for the ignominies that the Mexican in the United States has suffered. Rather, my purpose is to bring about an awareness—among both Anglo-Americans and Chicanos—of the forces that control and manipulate seven million people in this country and keep them colonized. If Chicanos can become aware of *why* they are oppressed and *how* the exploitation is perpetuated, they can work more effectively toward ending their colonization.

I realize that the initial stages of such awareness might result in intolerance among some Chicanos. However, I caution the reader that this work does not create a rationale for brown power just because it condemns the injustices of Anglo power. Extended visits in Mexico have taught that Chicano

15

power is no better than any other power. Those who seek power are deprived of their humanity to the point that they themselves become the oppressors. Paulo Friere has written:

> The great humanistic and historical task of the oppressed [is]: to liberate themselves and their oppression as well. The oppressors, who oppress, exploit, and rape by virtue of their power, cannot find in this power the strength to liberate either the oppressed or themselves. Only the power that springs from the weakness of the oppressed will be sufficiently strong to free you.[1]

It is my hope that *Occupied America* can help us perceive the social, political, and economic contradictions of the power that has enabled Anglo-American colonizers to dominate Chicanos—and that has too often made Chicanos accept and, in some instances, support the domination. Awareness will help us take action against the forces that oppress not only Chicanos but the oppressor himself.

---

[1] Paulo Freire, *Pedagogy of the Oppressed* (New York: Herder and Herder, 1972), p. 28.

ENCOUNTERING THE AMERICAN HOLOCAUST

THE POLITICS OF AFFIRMATION AND DENIAL

Ward Churchill

> *The bigger the lie, the greater the likelihood that it will be believed.*
>
> —ADOLF HITLER

During the four centuries spanning the time between 1492, when Christopher Columbus first set foot on the "New World" of a Caribbean beach, and 1892, when the U.S. Census Bureau concluded that there were fewer than a quarter-million indigenous people surviving within the country's claimed boundaries, a hemispheric population estimated to have been as great as 125 million was reduced by something over 90 percent. The people had died in their millions of being hacked apart with axes and swords, burned alive and trampled under horses, hunted as game and fed to dogs, shot, beaten, stabbed, scalped for bounty, hanged on meathooks and thrown over the sides of ships at sea, worked to death as slave laborers, intentionally starved and frozen to death during a multitude of forced marches and internments, and, in an unknown number of instances, deliberately infected with epidemic diseases.[1]

Today, every one of these practices is continued, when deemed expedient by the settler population(s) which have "restocked" the native landbase with themselves, in various locales throughout the Americas. In areas where the indigenous population remains so small or has become so assimilated that it no longer poses a "threat" to the new order which has usurped and subsumed it, it is kept that way through carefully calibrated policies of impoverishment and dispersal, indoctrination and compulsory sterilization. Insofar as native peoples retain lands in these latter regions, it is used as a convenient dumping ground for the toxic industrial waste by-products of the dominant society. The situation is now so acute, and so apparently irreversible, that several major scientific organizations have recommended the terrain be declared "sacrifices" to the interests of national comfort and prosperity. That these places are inhabited by what thus become sacrificial *peoples* is left politely unstated. So, too, are most of the costs borne by the victims which are of benefit to their victimizers.[2]

It was not always that way. Through most of the history of what has happened, the perpetrators, from aristocrats like Jeffrey Amherst to the lowliest private in his army, from the highest elected officials to the humblest of farmers, openly described America's indigenous peoples as vermin, launched literally hundreds of campaigns to effect their extermination, and then reveled in the carnage which resulted. Martial glory was attained by more than a few officers who proudly boasted in later years of having instructed their troops, when attacking essentially defenseless native communities, to "kill and scalp all, little and big [because] nits make lice." The body parts taken by soldiers in such slaughters remain prized possessions, discretely handed down as trophies through the generations of all too many American families.[3] Thus occurred what even dishonest commentators have acknowledged as being "very probably the greatest demographic disaster in history."[4]

Today we discover, while perusing the texts of orthodox scholarship, that much of this never happened, or, to the extent that some things must be at least partially admitted, was "tragic" "unavoidable," and "unintended." The decimated natives were peculiarly responsible for their own demise, having never bothered to develop immunities to the host of pathogens unleashed among them by the ever-increasing numbers of "Old World settlers" swarming to their shores. In North America, where the practice of denial is most accomplished, successive waves of historians and anthropologists harnessed themselves to the common task of advancing the pretense that the aboriginal population of the continent was but a small fraction of its real number. Thus, the deaths of people who never existed need not be explained, nor can there be serious questions as to the original ownership of territory which was uninhabited until the settlers came. The formal term is *territorium rez nullius:* land vacant and therefore open to whomever might wish to claim it.[5]

In the relatively rare instances where even this complex of denial and evasion is insufficient—the 1864 Sand Creek Massacre and its 1890 counterpart at Wounded Knee, for example, are too well known to be simply "disappeared"—orthodoxy frames its discourse in terms of madmen and anomaly. Overall, the nomenclature and emphasis employed is designed to turn the tables entirely. We hear only of "Indian wars," never of "settlers' wars." It is as if the natives, always "warlike" and "aggressive," had invaded and laid waste to London or Castile rather than engaging in desperate and always futile efforts to repel the hordes of "pioneers" and "peaceful settlers" overrunning their homelands—often quite illegally, even in their own terms—from sea to shining sea. It is the kind of historiography one might have expected of nazi academics a century after a German victory in World War II: "When the Poles, led by sullen Jewish chiefs, savagely attacked our innocent troops west of Warsaw in 1939, murdering thousands, we were forced to respond by . . ."[6]

All citizens of the United States (and, to a somewhat lesser extent, Canada) are subjected to indoctrination to this perspective through the elementary and secondary school systems. The outlook they obtain there is substantially reinforced on television, in the "news" media (both print and electronic), in popular literature, and in the well over 2,000 films Hollywood and its Canadian counterparts have produced on such themes during the past seventy years. For those with both means and inclination, higher education builds upon this groundwork, not only through a fleshing out of those nuanced inventories of theory and pseudofact by which "experts" are defined, but psychologically and emotionally as well. Such is the manner in which those interconnecting webs of mythic interpretation and social value known as hegemony are always woven.[7]

Reproduction, evolution, and perfection of any hegemonic structure is inevitable, left to its own devices. Ultimately, what emerges is a sense of triumphalism among the dominant population which is so seamless, pervasive, and pronounced that previously inadmissible facts can begin to be reintegrated with the record, reconciled to and incorporated into the prevailing mythology. Certain aspects of what was done to the first peoples of the Americas, it is now conceded—not just "aberrations" like Sand Creek, but even a few *policies*—may have been "excessive" (as in, "too much of a good thing"). They "went too far" and were therefore "errors" (as in, "We didn't really mean it"). To that extent, but no more, they were "unfortunate," even "dismal" (but never criminally reprehensible).[8]

The falsity of such limited expressions of regret (as in, "Oops!") and accompanying pretenses of sociocultural humility (as in, "We all make mistakes") are, moreover, invariably belied by the assertions that immediately follow such admissions. While there are many variations, they all go in substance to the premise, presented as a foregone conclusion, that, "*however* unfortunate and regrettable the past, it has all worked out for the best" for victim and victimizer alike, given the superlative nature of the civilization we now mutually inhabit. This new—and supposedly vastly superior—mode of existence was created, so the story goes, solely on the basis of obliterating the "squalid, brutish inhumanity" of the old.[9] In this way denial of past realities is used as the crux for imposing an equally firm denial of the present. The voices of our hypothetical postvictory nazi pundits ring through, loud and clear.

DENYING THE AMERICAN HOLOCAUST

The American holocaust was and remains unparalleled, both in terms of its magnitude and the degree to which its goals were met, and in terms of the extent to which its ferocity was sustained over time by not one but several participating groups. The ideological matrix of its denial is also among the most well developed of any genocide—or, more accurately, series of genocides—for which a significant amount of information is readily available (i.e., copious official and unofficial primary records of the processes, explicit statements of intent by perpetrators, published philosophical justifications of the results, and so on).[10] In other words, denial is manifested in more-or-less equal parts at all points on the ideological compass of the dominant society. Am I exaggerating? Being "hyperbolic," "strident," or "shrill" (to borrow the most common terms employed by deniers to dismiss such points without responding to them)?[11]

It would be useful to assess recently stated positions on the matter at each stop along the orthodox political spectrum. Here, we may begin on the right, where we might presume ourselves most likely to encounter reaction and denial. Undisappointed in our expectations, we find then-director of the National Endowment for the Humanities Lynne Cheney, in collaboration with the United States Senate, preparing for the 1992 Columbus quincentenniary by refusing to fund any film production which proposed to use the word "genocide," even in passing, to explain the subsequent liquidation of America's indigenous population. They were joined by then–Secretary of Education William Bennett, who thundered—in a manner worthy of Oswald Spengler—that popularization of such "distortions of history" would signify an undermining of "the Western cultural tradition which has made this great nation what it is today."[12] Such sentiments, which have been ascendant in the United States (and Canada) since 1980, have of course been amply represented in the media. For example:

> Charles Krauthammer, one of *Time* magazine's regular political columnists, used an entire column [on May 27, 1991] to lambaste as "politically correct" opportunists anyone who dared express regret over the killing of millions of innocent people and the destruction of entire ancient cultures in the Americas. What happened in the wake of the European invasion was only what has always characterized human history, Krauthammer claimed, citing the Norman conquest of Britain as an apt (though actually absurd) comparison. "The real question is," he noted, "what eventually grew on this bloodied soil?" For, regardless of the level of destruction and mass murder that was visited upon the indigenous peoples of the Western Hemisphere, it was, in retrospect, entirely justified because in the process it wiped out such alleged barbarisms as the communally based Inca society (which really was only a "beehive," Krauthammer said) and gave the world "a culture of liberty that endowed the individual human being with dignity and sovereignty."[13]

From here, one could anticipate a follow-up column which would explain why, irrespective of the estimated 50 million lives consumed by nazism, its existence should be celebrated rather than condemned. After all, the nazis were responsible for introducing "our civilization" to, among many other things, the wonders of expressways, jet aircraft, missile technologies, synfuels, methamphetamines, the Volkswagen, and the basis for today's genetic engineering. In the process, moreover, nazism managed to permanently eradicate the "insect-like" Jewish culture of Poland and—perhaps most miraculous of all—forced an unprecedented degree of collaboration among Western democracies, the formation of the United Nations, and thus the eventual "New World Order" proclaimed by George Bush (with all the obvious benefits to human dignity, liberty, and sovereignty this has to offer).[14]

Moving leftward, to liberalism, we might expect things to improve at least marginally. What we encounter instead is the denunciation by historian J. H. Elliott in the *New York Review of Books* of what he describes as the "indiscriminate use [of the term] genocide" in depicting the fate of America's indigenous peoples because it carries such "powerful contemporary freight" as to "impede rather than assist genuine understanding" of what happened (but does not bother to explain further). This "wisdom" couples readily to that of noted ethnohistorian James Axtell, who assures us that it is time we "stop flogging ourselves" over "largely imaginary" questions of genocide, a word he habitually situates in quotes wherever American Indians are concerned. Axtell's view, in turn, fits in neatly with that of Arthur Schlesinger, Jr., who, using the pages of *The Atlantic* for the purpose, not only repeats Krauthammer's argument but surpasses it.[15]

> Schlesinger . . . was not content to build his case on the purported shortcomings of the ancient societies of the Americas. No, he gazed into his crystal ball and asserted . . . that without the European conquests and slaughter at least some New World societies today would be sufficiently unpleasant places to live so as to make acceptable the centuries of genocide that were carried out against the native people of the entire Western Hemisphere.[16]

As for left radicals, consider the long-standing postulations of the Revolutionary Communist Party U.S.A., published nearly a decade before the quincentenniary, that the precolumbian population of North America was about half that admitted at the time by even the thoroughly reactionary Smithsonian Institution, that the people were so "primitive" that they were forced to regularly consume their own fecal matter in order to survive, and that only European conquest and colonization had lifted them from their state of perpetual degradation to the level of rudimentary humanity.[17] Nor do socialists deviate appreciably from such naziesque diatribes, a matter evidenced by columnist Christopher Hitchens, writing in a purportedly "dissident weekly, *The Nation,* on October 19, 1992.

> To Hitchens, anyone refusing to join him in celebrating with "great vim and gusto" the annihilation of the native peoples of the Americas was (in his words) self-hating, ridiculous, ignorant, and sinister. People who regard critically the genocide that was carried out in America's past, Hitchens continued, are simply reactionary, since such grossly inhuman atrocities "happen to be the way history is made." And thus "to complain about [them] is as empty as complaint about climactic, geological or tectonic shift." Moreover, he added, such violence is worth glorifying since it more often than not has been for the long-term betterment of mankind—as in the United States today, where the

extermination of [American Indians] has brought about "a nearly boundless epoch of opportunity and innovation."[18]

The same holds true of Euroamerica's supposedly most radical strain, anarchism (or "antiauthoritarianism," as it more often fancies itself these days). Witness self-professed "anarchist's anarchist" Bob Black, author of two books and frequent contributor to such titles as *Anarchy,* addressing native activists as "Taunto" and "Shitting Bull," telling them to "stop whining" about a genocide they "never experienced," and asserting that he has "as much right to this land as any of you, maybe more." Not to be outdone, the more prominent John Zerzan makes the utterly bizarre insinuation that, whatever happened to them, native people have no complaint since they themselves were "guilty" of having "colonized" plantlife in their precolumbian fields.[19]

15   *Sieg heil.* Distinctions in perspective between right, center, left, and extreme left in the United States are quite literally nonexistent on the question of the genocide of indigenous peoples. From all four vantage points, the historical reality is simultaneously denied, justified, and in most cases celebrated. But preposterous as some of the argumentation has become, all of it is outstripped by a substantial component of zionism which contends not only that the American holocaust never happened, but that *no* "true" genocide has ever occurred, other than the Holocaust suffered by the Jews at the hands of the nazis during the first half of the 1940s. In their frenzy to validate the "uniqueness" of their own people's experience, the exclusivism asserted by adherents to this outlook—and they have proven extraordinarily potent in their promotion of it—extends even to the Gypsies, who were subjected to the very same nazi extermination program as they. In kind with the sort of vulgar name-calling practiced by Black, Hitchens, and the RCP, proponents of Jewish exclusivism consistently label anyone referring to a genocide other than their own is an "antisemite."[20]

AFFIRMING THE AMERICAN HOLOCAUST

There have, to be sure, been exceptions to this apparently homogeneous sensibility. Beginning in 1968, the American Indian Movement, for example, following the definition attending Raphaël Lemkin's coinage of the term in 1944, and the legal description of the crime which was adopted by the United Nations in 1948, began to apply the concept of genocide with some precision to American history. AIM was quickly joined in its usage of the term by allied groups within the Black and Chicano liberation movements, the Puerto Rican independence movement, portions of the antiwar movement and at least some elements of the (non-marxist) New Left. By the early 1970s, liberation movements abroad, both in Europe and throughout the Third World, adopted the term with specific reference to the historical devastation of indigenous American societies.[21]

In terms of scholarship, there have also been those who have broken decisively with orthodoxy. Among them have been Carl O. Sauer, Woodrow W. Borah, Sherburn F. Cook, Leslie B. Simpson, Henry F. Dobyns, Noble David Cook, and Russell Thornton, all of whom laboriously excavated the data necessary to reveal the true size of the native population in 1492, both hemispherically and regionally, and entered into the process of honestly describing the means by which it was reduced to almost nothing. Others—notably Richard Drinnon, Francis Jennings, David Stannard, Rupert and Jeanette Henry Costo, Robert F. Heizer, Tzvetan Todorov, Eduardo Galeano, Robert Davis, Mark Zannis, Kirkpatrick Sale, John Grier Varner and Jeanette Johnson Varner, Ann F. Ramenofsky, Lynwood Carranco, Estle Beard, and David Svaldi—have undertaken the effort to document, refine, and amplify these themes in admirable fashion. Because of their work, upon which I rely quite heavily, the veil behind which the American holocaust has been masked for so long has started to slip away.[22]

A LITTLE MATTER OF GENOCIDE

A Little Matter of Genocide, an admittedly sarcastic title provoked by the sort of insistent trivialization described earlier, is intended to contribute to this unmasking. This is not to say that it purports to offer some new body of factual information about the genocide of America's indigenous peoples. Instead, it attempts to present a comprehensive overview of what is already known, bringing several data streams together between two covers for the first time to provide what I hope represents something of the "Big Picture." More important than this synthesizing effort, the book seeks to contextualize the American holocaust through direct comparison to other genocides—most especially the nazi Holocaust—to an extent not previously undertaken on such a scale.[23]

From there, it is possible to advance a definitional typology of genocide which should prove useful in facilitating the analytical apprehension of all holocausts, not only as they've occurred in the past, but as they are unfolding in the present and will likely come about in the future. From there as well, it is possible to offer a concrete illustration, subject to all manner of replication and variation, of how such a misconceptualization of genocide can be applied in the "real world" as an integral component of direct-action strategies designed to stop, or at least blunt, genocidal processes. In other words, a primary underlying objective of *A Little Matter of Genocide* is to assist in the forging of a viable countergenocidal praxis.[24]

Structurally, the body of the book follows a certain progression, leading from definitional considerations through informational array and back again. A pair of overlapping essays, "Assaults on Truth and Memory" and "Lie for Lie," are used to open. This is mainly for purposes of framing the matter of holocaust denial, first by examining its best known element, "revisionist"

20

denial of the nazi Holocaust, and then by comparing the techniques used by proponents of Jewish exclusivism in presenting their doctrine of "uniqueness" to those of the neonazi revisionists. In the second essay, emphasis is placed on the manner in which exclusivism has subverted the very definition of genocide to its own ends, while exploring the hegemonic functions of doing so. In the process of these investigations, every effort is made to restore non-Jewish victims of the Holocaust to their rightful place within it, so that the nazi genocide can be appreciated for what it really was.

With the true scope of what happened in eastern Europe under nazism revealed, and thus available for use as a reference point, we take up the historical realities of the American holocaust. This is approached with three essays—"Deconstructing the Columbus Myth," "Genocide in the Americas," and "Nits Make Lice"—arranged chronologically, according to the historical juncture at which the genocidal process in the geographic area under consideration commenced. Hence, the first essay is devoted to the Caribbean Basin, the second to Iberoamerica, and the third to North America. The last two of the three essays trace the pattern of genocide within their respective regions up to the present moment. The first, however, breaks off in roughly 1540, since by that point the extermination of the indigenous population of the Caribbean was virtually complete.

We turn next, in "Cold War Impacts on Native North America," to the examination of a specifically contemporary phenomenon, the lethal contamination by transient industry of the landbase to which native people are constricted in North America and the consequent declaration of their residual territories as "National Sacrifice Areas." In this interrogation of the linkage between targeted ecocide and collateral genocide, we follow AIM leader Russell Means' 1980 prognosis that declaring Indian reservations to be sacrifice areas equates to sacrificing the indigenous residents themselves. The essay also explores to some extent the question of "spillover" of the by-products of certain industrial processes, intended for containment within reservation boundaries, into the habitat of the nonindigenous population.

By this point, all the essential information has been deployed which seems necessary to allow a fruitful examination of the formal relationship of the United States to the United Nations' legal prohibition against genocide. "The United States and the Genocide Convention" explores why America, alone among the member-states of the United Nations, took forty years to offer even a pretense of ratifying this most fundamental element of international human rights law, and how the exemptions from compliance it sought to provide itself by the instrument of ratification invalidated the Convention's original intent. In effect, the United States—in perfectly Hitlerian fashion—remains to this day outside the law, claiming to transcend mere international legality on its own authority, still refusing to accept the idea that refraining from genocidal activity is not an "abridgment of [its] sovereignty."

The last essay, "Defining the Unthinkable," again follows from everything which has come before. As its title implies, the piece attempts to provide a complete and workable delineation of the term's meaning(s), and to provide illustrations, many of them already discussed in some detail by this juncture, of its various gradients and nuances. Throughout the exposition, we will remain consistent with the definitional criteria worked out by Raphaël Lemkin when he established the concept of genocide—and drafted the International Convention outlawing it—under the presumption that there is no valid basis for conforming it to the preferences or convenience of one or another set of perpetrators (e.g., the U.S. and former Soviet governments) or special-interest groups (e.g., Jewish exclusivists). The result should prove to be something of a precision tool for application to both legal and more purely analytical contexts.

Throughout the book, I have gone out of my way to provide what Noam Chomsky has called "rich footnotes."[25] The reasons for this are several, and devolve not merely upon the usual scholarly fetish with indicating familiarity with "the literature." I *do* believe that when making many of the points I've sought to make, and with the bluntness which typically marks my work, one is well-advised to be thorough in revealing the basis upon which they rest. I also believe it is a matter not just of courtesy, but of ethics, to make proper attribution to those upon whose ideas and research one relies. Most importantly, I want those who read this book to be able to interrogate what I've said, to challenge it and consequently to build on it. The most expedient means to this end is the provision of copious annotation, citing sources both pro and con.

Finally, the obvious should be stated: this is a collection of essays. Hence, unlike most book chapters, each piece was constructed to stand on its own. An inevitable result is that there is a certain amount of repetition from essay to essay—greater here, lesser there—as each strives to establish the context in which its particular point or points will be made. It is, of course, possible to classify this as sheer redundancy, a problem inherent to all such collections (and more than a few booklength treatments as well). In this case, however, I will perhaps be forgiven for suggesting that repetition might be viewed in a more positive light, as what exponents of Freirian pedagogy have termed "recursiveness."[26] In any event, I am of the opinion that, since much of what follows has been said so little, it is worth saying some of it more than once.

QUESTIONS OF MOTIVE

All of this leaves open the question of my motives in undertaking yet another book centering in the genocide of American Indians, or what it is that I hope motivates people to read it. Let me say that, although I readily admit to bearing an abstract allegiance to them, I am not prompted by primarily academic concerns (as in "The Quest for Truth"). Nor, frankly, do I anticipate that *A Little Matter of Genocide* will be favorably received by most academic specialists in its subject area or related disciplines. The positions it advances are far too uncomfortably contrary to theirs for it to find much acceptance in that quarter.

To put it plainly, my goals are unequivocally political. Ironically, it is Deborah Lipstadt, a firm denier of the American holocaust, who, in the process of decrying neonazism's denial of her own people's Holocaust, has most aptly summed up my own reasoning. "The general public tends to accord victims of genocide a certain moral authority. . . . If you devictimize a people you strip them of their moral authority."[27] As an American Indian, as a twenty-year member of the American Indian Movement, and simply as a human being imbued with the conscience and consciousness of such, I believe that American Indians, demonstrably one of the most victimized groups in the history of humanity, are entitled to every ounce of moral authority we can get. My first purpose is, and always has been, to meet my responsibilities of helping deliver that to which my people is due.

At another level, the agenda is rather broader. As Roger Smith, Erik Markusen, and Robert Jay Lifton have pointed out, the denial of *any* genocide contributes to "a false consciousness which can have the most dire reverberations," underpinning a "deadly psychohistorical dynamic in which unopposed genocide begets new genocides."[28] The recent and/or ongoing slaughters in places like Rwanda, Bosnia, and East Timor should be proof enough of that. Assuming that we do not actively embrace such carnage, or believe we can slough it off with banalities about "human nature," we are obligated to find ways and means of stopping it. Here, an insight offered by Frank Chalk and Kurt Jonassohn seems quite germane.

> The major reason for doing comparative research on genocides
> is the hope of preventing them in the future. Such prevention
> will present difficult applied problems, but first it must be based
> on an understanding of the social situations and the social
> structures and the processes that are likely to lead to genocides.
> Only by acquiring such knowledge can we begin to predict
> the likely occurrence of genocides and direct our efforts
> toward prevention.[29]

30   Or, to use Isador Wallimann's and Michael N. Dobkowski's formulation, "Any worthwhile activism with regard to genocide will have to be radically different from other human rights efforts. In order to be of help to the potential victims, it will have to focus solely on prevention . . . [To] prevent such lethal crimes, we would have to be able to predict their occurrence—something that our present state of knowledge does not yet permit. Thus, any efforts at preventing future genocides will have to start with research capable of yielding predictive indicators that would then allow concerted efforts at prevention."[30] With this, I doubt there can be much disagreement, even among those who would deny the nazi Holocaust or claim that it was unique. Since there can be no serious question that *A Little Matter of Genocide* goes very much in the direction indicated, it should be of interest to anyone opposed to the notions of genocide being sometimes a good thing, at least in "certain instances," or that is somehow a "normative human condition."[31] It is, I think,

an absolutely essential book for anyone sharing my own commitment, not just to opposing genocide but to ending it.

NOTES

1. The estimated population range is 112 million to 125 million in 1492; Henry F. Dobyns, "Estimating Aboriginal American Population: An Appraisal of Techniques with a New Hemispheric Estimate," *Current Anthropology,* No. 7, 1966. According to the 1890 federal census, referenced here, the "aboriginal population" in the U.S. portion of North America had been reduced to 248,253; U.S. Bureau of the Census, *Report on Indians Taxed and Indians Not Taxed in the United States (except Alaska) at the Eleventh U.S. Census: 1890* (Washington, D.C.: U.S. Government Printing Office, 1894). The actual nadir was reached around 1900, when the Census Bureau counted only 237,196 surviving Indians; U.S. Bureau of the Census, *Fifteenth Census of the United States, 1930: The Indian Population of the United States and Alaska* (Washington, D.C.: U.S. Government Printing Office, 1937). On causes of death, see generally, David E. Stannard, *American Holocaust: Columbus and the Conquest of the New World* (New York: Oxford University Press, 1992).
2. On impoverishment, see, e.g., U.S. Department of Health, Education and Welfare, *Chart Series Book* (Washington, D.C.: Public Health Service, 1988); on dispersal, see Donald L. Fixico, *Termination and Relocation: Federal Indian Policy, 1945–1960* (Albuquerque: University of New Mexico Press, 1986); on indoctrination, see David Wallace Adams, *Education for Extinction: American Indians and the Boarding School Experience, 1875–1928* (Lawrence: University Press of Kansas, 1995); on sterilization, see Janet Larson, "And Then There Were None: IHS Sterilization Practices," *Christian Century,* No. 94, Jan. 26, 1976; Bill Wagner, "Lo, the Poor and Sterilized Indian," *America* No. 136, Jan. 29, 1977; Brint Dillingham, "Indian Women and IHS Sterilization Practices," *American Indian Journal,* vol. 3, no. 1, Jan. 1977. On national sacrifice areas, see Federal Energy Administration, Office of Strategic Analysis, *Project Independence: A Summary* (Washington, D.C.: U.S. Department of Energy, 1974).
3. In 1991, the American Indian Movement of Colorado removed two Cheyenne scalps from the mantle of a ski lodge in the Rocky Mountains, where the proprietor displayed them for the edification of guests. The man expressed surprise, "never having had any complaints before," that Indians might be upset by such "relics," which he said had been taken by his great-grandfather, a trooper who participated in the 1864 Sand Creek Massacre, and had been "handed down in the family" ever since. Such stories are, unfortunately, not at all uncommon.
4. See, generally, Richard Drinnon, *Facing West: The Metaphysics of Indian Hating and Empire Building* (Minneapolis: University of Minnesota Press, 1980). The order to "kill them all" is attributed to Col. John M. Chivington, commander of the 3rd Colorado Volunteer Cavalry; quoted in Stan Hoig, *The Sand Creek Massacre* (Norman: University of Oklahoma Press, 1961) p. 192. The closing quote is taken from Steven T. Katz, *The Holocaust in Historical Context, Vol. 1: The Holocaust and Mass Death Before the Modern Age* (New York: Oxford University Press, 1992), p. 20.
5. See, e.g., James Axtell, *Beyond 1492: Encounters in Colonial North America* (New York: Oxford University Press, 1992), pp. 261–3. For the best overview of how the "books

were cooked," see Francis Jennings, *The Invasion of America: Indians, Colonialism, and the Cant of Conquest* (Chapel Hill: University of North Carolina Press, 1975), pp. 15–31. Overall, see Robert A. Williams, Jr., *The American Indian in Western Legal Thought: The Discourses of Conquest* (New York: Oxford University Press, 1990).

6. A computer search reveals more than 500 titles including the term "Indian War" or "Wars," but none devoted to "settlers' wars." See, e.g., John Tebbel and Keith Jennison, *The American Indian Wars* (New York: Harper & Row, 1960); T. Harry Williams, *The History of America's Wars from 1745 to 1918* (Baton Rouge: Louisiana State University, 1981); Edwin P. Hoyt, *America's Wars and Military Incursions* (New York: McGraw-Hill, 1987).

7. See, generally, Ralph Friar and Natasha Friar, *"The Only Good Indian . . ." The Hollywood Gospel* (New York: Drama Book Specialists, 1972); Raymond William Stedman, *Shadows of the Indian: Stereotypes in American Culture* (Norman: University of Oklahoma Press, 1982); Ward Churchill, *Fantasies of the Master Race: Literature, Cinema and the Colonization of American Indians* (Monroe, ME: Common Courage Press, 1992). The statement about hegemony is intended in the Gramscian sense; see Walter L. Adamson, *Hegemony and Revolution: A Study of Antonio Gramsci's Political and Cultural Theory* (Berkeley: University of California Press, 1980); Alastair Davidson, *Antonio Gramsci: Towards an Intellectual Biography* (London/Atlantic Highlands, NJ: Merlin Press/Humanities Press, 1977).

8. An unabashed exposition of the sentiments at issue will be found in J. M. Roberts, *The Triumph of the West* (London: British Broadcasting Corporation, 1985). Articulations of the "need" for such intellectual reinforcement of the status quo abound; see, e.g., Arthur M. Schlesinger, Jr., *The Disuniting of America: Reflections on a Multicultural Society* (New York: W. W. Norton, 1992). For useful discussion of the problem and strategies to transcend it, see Edward Said, "The Politics of Knowledge," in Paul Berman, ed., *Debating P.C.: The Controversy Over Political Correctness on College Campuses* (New York: Laurel, 1992). See also, Wilcomb E. Washburn, "Land Claims in the Mainstream of Indian/White Land History," in Imre Sutton, ed., *Irredeemable America: The Indians' Estate and Land Claims* (Albuquerque: University of New Mexico Press, 1985); "Distinguishing History from Moral Philosophy and Public Advocacy," in Calvin Martin, ed., *The American Indian and the Problem of History* (New York: Oxford University Press, 1987). More broadly, see Patricia Nelson Limerick, *The Legacy of Conquest: The Unbroken Past of the American West* (New York: W. W. Norton, 1987); Edward Lazarus, *Black Hills, White Justice: The Sioux Nation versus The United States, 1775 to the Present* (New York: HarperCollins, 1991).

9. For a heavy dose of such characterization, see James E. Clifton, ed., *The Invented Indian: Cultural Fictions and Government Policies* (New Brunswick, NJ: Transaction Books, 1990). Also see *Time, Newsweek,* and other mass-circulation periodicals, 1991–92, inclusive.

10. For a series of apt comparisons of holocausts, see Frank Chalk and Kurt Jonassohn, eds., *The History and Sociology of Genocide: Analyses and Case Studies* (New Haven, CT: Yale University Press, 1990). Excellent analysis of the implications of a parallel example will be found in Roger W. Smith, Eric Markusen, and Robert Jay Lifton, "Professional Ethics and Denial of the Armenian Genocide," *Holocaust and Genocide Studies,* no. 9, 1995.

11. After five solid years of delivering public lectures in this subject area, I can testify that these descriptors—along with the accusation that one is "angry" and/or "emotional"—are used every time, both in Q & A sessions following talks and in such press coverage as may result. Never, in my experience, have those employing such terms attempted to do so in the context of addressing what was actually said. I am thus convinced that the mode of delivery is irrelevant in terms of generating such responses.

12. "Our civilization" is being "brought low by the forces of ignorance, irrationality and intimidation"; quoted in Jack McCurdy, "Bennett Calls Stanford Curriculum Revision Capitulation to Pressure," *Chronicle of Higher Education,* April 27, 1988. The parallels in both logic and rhetoric to those of Spengler, a hero of the nazis, is striking. On Spengler, see Oswald Spengler, *Der Untergang des Abendlandes, Welthistorische und Wirklichkeit* (Münich: C.H. Beck'sche Verlagsbuchhandlung, 1896); published in English translation as *The Decline of the West* (New York: Alfred A. Knopf, 1926).

13. David E. Stannard, "The Politics of Holocaust Scholarship: Uniqueness as Denial," in Alan S. Rosenbaum, ed., *Is the Holocaust Unique? Perspectives on Comparative Genocide* (Boulder, CO: Westview Press, 1996), p. 165.

14. This actually comes fairly close to the arguments presented in contemporary neonazi literature; see, e.g., Christof Friedrich and Eric Thompson, *The Hitler We Loved and Why* (Reedy, WV: White Power Publications, 1978).

15. *New York Review of Books,* June 24, 1993. J.H. Elliott is author of such epic apologia as *The Old World and the New, 1492–1650* (Cambridge, MA: Cambridge University Press, 1970). Axtell, op. cit., p. 263.

16. Stannard, "The Politics of Holocaust Scholarship," op. cit., pp. 165–6; Schlesinger's *Atlantic* piece ran in the September 1992 issue, timed to appear just a month before the Columbian quincentennial.

17. The RCP, "Searching for a Second Harvest," in Ward Churchill, ed., *Marxism and Native Americans* (Boston: South End Press, 1983).

18. Stannard, "The Politics of Holocaust Scholarship," op. cit., p. 166.

19. Although Black's deep-seated racism is an underlying current in much of his published work, it *really* bubbles forth from what he takes to be the privacy of unsolicited personal correspondence, numerous examples of which the author maintains on file. The quotes employed are taken therefrom. Readers are referred to his *Friendly Fire* (Brooklyn, NY: Autonomedia, 1992) and *The Abolition of Work and Other Essays* (Port Townsend, WA: Loompanics, n.d.). See also John Zerzan, *Future Primitive and Other Essays* (Brooklyn, NY: Autonomedia, 1994).

20. With the publication of the first massive volume of his projected three-volume study, *The Holocaust in Historical Context* (op. cit.), Steven T. Katz has probably become the leading exponent of this view; for a more succinct rendering, see his "The Uniqueness of the Holocaust: The Historical Dimension," in Rosenbaum, op. cit. He is followed closely by Yehuda Bauer, the previously reigning "dean" of such distortion; see, e.g., Bauer's *The Holocaust in Historical Perspective* (Seattle: University of Washington Press, 1978). Other heavy-hitters include Elie Wiesel, Lucy Dawidowicz, Leni Yahil, Yisrael Gutman, Robert Marrus, Deborah Lipstadt, and Martin Gilbert. Also, see Lucy Dawidowicz, *The Holocaust and the Historians* (Cambridge: Harvard University Press, 1981), pp. 10–11.

21. On AIM, see Peter Matthiessen, *In the Spirit of Crazy Horse* (New York: Viking, [2nd ed.] 1991). On tie-ins with other liberation movements, see Rex Weyler, *Blood of the Land: The U.S. Government and Corporate War Against the American Indian Movement* (Philadelphia: New Society Publishers, [2nd ed.] 1992).

22. See, e.g., Carl O. Sauer, *Sixteenth Century North America* (Berkeley: University of California Press, 1971); Woodrow W. Borah and Sherburn F. Cook, *The Aboriginal Population of Mexico on the Eve of the Spanish Conquest* (Berkeley: University of California Press, 1963); Sherburn F. Cook, *The Conflict Between the California Indians and White Civilization* (Berkeley: University of California Press, 1976); Sherburn F. Cook and Leslie B. Simpson, *The Population of Central Mexico in the Sixteenth Century* (Berkeley: University of California Press, 1948); Henry F. Dobyns, *Their Numbers Become Thinned: Native American Population Dynamics in Eastern North America* (Knoxville: University of Tennessee Press, 1983); Noble David Cook, *Demographic Collapse: Indian Peru, 1520–1620* (Cambridge: Cambridge University Press, 1981); Russell Thornton, *American Indian Holocaust and Survival: A Population History Since 1492* (Norman: University of Oklahoma Press, 1987); Robert H. Jackson, *Indian Population Decline: The Missions of Northwestern New Spain, 1687–1840* (Albuquerque: University of New Mexico Press, 1995); Drinnon, op. cit.; Jennings, op. cit.; Stannard, *American Holocaust,* op. cit.; Rupert Costo and Jeanette Henry Costo, *The California Missions: A Legacy of Genocide* (San Francisco: Indian Historian Press, 1987); Robert F. Heizer, *They Were Only Diggers: A Collection of Articles from California Newspapers, 1851–1866, on Indian and White Relations* (Ramona, CA: Ballena Press, 1974), revised and republished under the title *The Destruction of California Indians* (Lincoln: University of Nebraska Press, 1993); Tzvetan Todorov, *The Conquest of America: The Question of the Other* (New York: HarperPerennial, 1984); Eduardo Galeano, *The Open Veins of Latin America: Five Centuries of the Pillage of a Continent* (New York: Monthly Review Press, 1973); Robert Davis and Mark Zannis, *The Genocide Machine in Canada: The Pacification of the North* (Montréal: Black Rose Books, 1973); Kirkpatrick Sale, *The Conquest of Paradise: Christopher Columbus and the Columbian Legacy* (New York: Alfred A. Knopf, 1990); John Grier Varner and Jeanette Johnson Varner, *The Dogs of Conquest* (Norman: University of Oklahoma Press, 1983); Ann F. Ramenofsky, *Vectors of Death: The Archaeology of European Contact* (Albuquerque: University of New Mexico Press, 1987); Lynwood Carranco and Estle Beard, *Genocide and Vendetta: The Round Valley Wars of Northern California* (Norman: University of Oklahoma Press, 1981); David Svaldi, *Sand Creek and the Rhetoric of Extermination: A Case Study in Indian–White Relations* (Lanham, MD: University Press of America, 1989). Exposition on the intended meaning of stripping away the veil will be found in J.G. Merquior, *The Veil and the Mask: Essays on Culture and Ideology* (London: Routledge & Keegan Paul, 1979).

23. Stannard in particular, in *American Holocaust,* op. cit., and also in "The Politics of Holocaust Scholarship," op. cit. covers a great deal of ground in this direction. *A Little Matter of Genocide* should be seen as consciously building on his accomplishments. My present effort is also meant to extend the avenues opened up in several of my own earlier books, notably *Struggle for Land: Indigenous Resistance to Genocide, Ecocide and Expropriation in Contemporary North America* (Monroe, ME: Common Courage Press, 1993); *Indians Are US? Culture and Genocide in Native North America* (Monroe, ME:

Common Courage Press, 1994); and *Since Predator Came: Notes from the Struggle for American Indian Liberation* (Littleton, CO: Aigis, 1995).

24. Although it differs sharply with each of them in some respects, the book is meant to be linked to such recent efforts as Chalk and Jonassohn's *The History and Sociology of Genocide* (op. cit.), Leo Kuper's *Genocide: Its Political Use in the Twentieth Century* (New Haven, CT: Yale University Press, 1981), Isidor Wallimann and Michael N. Dobkowski's *Genocide in the Modern Age: Etiology and Case Studies of Mass Death* (Westport, CT: Greenwood Press, 1987), and George Andreopoulos' *Genocide: Conceptual and Historical Dimensions* (Philadelphia: University of Pennsylvania Press, 1994). Philosophical and methodological discussion of praxis will not be undertaken herein. Those interested in such matters should be advised that I subscribe generally to the formulations of Gramsci and the *young* Lukács; for further elaboration, see my "Marxist Theory of Culture: A Cross-Cultural Critique," in Ward Churchill and Elisabeth R. Lloyd, *Culture versus Economism: Essays on Marxism in the Multicultural Arena* (Denver: Fourth World Center for Study of Indigenous Law and Politics, University of Colorado, [2nd ed.] 1989) or Richard Kilminster, *Praxis and Method: A Sociological Dialogue with Lukács, Gramsci and the Early Frankfurt School* (London: Routledge & Keegan Paul, 1979).

25. See the remarks on annotation in Noam Chomsky, *Class Warfare: Interviews with David Barsamian* (Monroe, ME: Common Courage Press, 1996).

26. See, e.g., Paulo Freire, *Education for Critical Consciousness* (New York: Continuum, 1982).

27. Lipstadt, op. cit., pp. 7–8.

28. Smith, Markuson and Lifton, op. cit., p. 16.

29. Chalk and Johansson, op. cit., p. 32.

30. Wallimann and Dobkowski, op. cit., p. 18.

31. If I had a dollar for every time a member of the American professorate had responded in this fashion to my public lectures, at least indirectly and especially with the latter contrivance, I would buy back the hemisphere.

PROPOSED CONVENTION ON PREVENTION AND PUNISHMENT OF THE CRIME OF GENOCIDE (1997)

Ward Churchill

Although it may not involve killing, per se, genocide is a denial of the right of existence of entire human groups, as homicide is the denial of the right to live of individual human beings. Such denial of the right of existence shocks the conscience of mankind, results in great losses to humanity in the form of cultural and other contributions represented by these groups, and its contrary to moral law and the spirit and aim of the United Nations. Many instances of such crimes of genocide have occurred, when racial, religious, political, and other groups have been destroyed, entirely or in part. The punishment of the crime of genocide is therefore a matter of grave international concern.[1]

The United Nations Member States,[2]

    Having considered the declaration made by the General Assembly of the United Nations in its resolution 96(I) dated 11 December 1946 that genocide is a crime under international law, contrary to the spirit and aims of the United Nations and condemned by the civilized world;

    Recognizing that in all periods of history genocide has inflicted great losses on humanity; and

    Being convinced that, in order to liberate mankind from such an odious scourge, international cooperation is required,

    Hereby agree as hereinafter provided:

Article I

The Member States confirm that genocide, whether committed in time of peace or in time of war, is a crime under international law which they undertake to prevent and punish.[3]

Article II

In the present Convention, genocide means the destruction, entirely or in part, of any racial, ethnic, national, religious, cultural, linguistic, political, economic, gender or other human group, however such groups may be defined by the perpetrator.[4] It is understood that, historically, genocide has taken three (3) primary forms, usually, but not always functioning in combination with one another.[5]

(a) *Physical Genocide,* by which is meant killing members of the targeted group(s) either directly, by indirect means, or some combination. Indirect means are understood to include, but are not restricted to, the imposition of slave labor conditions upon the target group(s), denial of fundamental medical attention to group members, and forms of systematic economic deprivation leading to starvation and other deteriorations in the physical well-being of group members.[6]

(b) *Biological Genocide,* by which is meant the prevention of births within target group(s), either directly, indirectly, or both. Direct means are understood to devolve upon the imposition of involuntary sterilization or abortion measures upon group members. Indirect means include the imposition of degrading physical and/or psychological conditions leading to marked declines in birthrate, heightened rates of infant mortality, and the like.[7]

(c) *Cultural Genocide,* by which is meant the destruction of the specific character of the targeted group(s) through destruction or expropriation of its means of economic perpetuation; prohibition or curtailment of its language; suppression of its religious, social or political practices; destruction or denial of use and access to objects of sacred or sociocultural significance; forced dislocation, expulsion or dispersal of its members; forced transfer or removal of its children, or any other means.[8]

It is understood that, insofar as each of these three categories of activity is sufficient in its own right to bring about the complete or partial destruction of human groups, as such, no hierarchy of importance or seriousness can be said to prevail among them. Each will therefore be treated as possessing equal gravity to the other two.[9]

Article III

The following acts shall be punishable:

(a) Genocide;
(b) Conspiracy to commit genocide;
(c) Public incitement to commit or advocacy of genocide;[10]
(d) Attempt to commit genocide;
(e) Complicity in genocide.

Article IV

In keeping with the analogy to murder made in the preamble of this Convention, it is understood that several degrees of culpability pertain to the commission of genocide.[11] These may be taken into consideration for purposes of determining the appropriateness of punishment.

(a) *Genocide in the First Degree,* which consists of instances in which evidence of premeditated intent to commit genocide is present.

15

(b) *Genocide in the Second Degree,* which consists of instance in which evidence of premeditation is absent, but in which it can be reasonably argued that the perpetrator(s) acted with reckless disregard for the probability that genocide would result from their actions.

(c) *Genocide in the Third Degree,* which consists of instances in which genocide derives, however unintentionally, from other violations of international law engaged in by the perpetrator(s).[12]

(d) *Genocide in the Fourth Degree,* which consists of instances in which neither evidence of premeditation nor other criminal behavior is present, but in which the perpetrator(s) acted with depraved indifference to the possibility that genocide would result from their actions and therefore to effect adequate safeguards to prevent it.[13]

Article V

The commission of genocide in any form is not a "right" attending State sovereignty or any other authority. Hence, persons committing genocide or any of the other acts enumerated in Article III shall be punished, whether they are constitutionally responsible rulers, public officials, or private individuals.[14]

Article VI

Insofar as genocide has often been perpetrated as a Crime of State, it may be taken as self-evident that its prosecution lies beyond the competence of the tribunals of individual States. Those charged with genocide in any degree, or with any other act enumerated in Article III of this Convention, shall, therefore, be placed under jurisdiction of an international penal tribunal composed specifically for this purpose. It is this body, not organs of alleged perpetrator states themselves, which shall determine whether sufficient evidence attends given allegations of genocide to warrant their prosecution, and, in instances where this is so, preside over consequent proceedings, pronounce judgments, and affix punishments or other remedies.[15]

Article VII

All Member States hereby agree to undertake such policies and other actions as may be necessary to ensure adherence to and enforcement of the prevention of Article VI of this Convention.[16]

20

Article VIII

It is intended that this instrument shall supercede the United Nations Convention on prevention and Punishment of Genocide (1948).[17]

While it is by no means anticipated that a U.N. member state will suddenly and voluntarily come to the fore in championing these proposed revisions to the Genocide Convention, especially in view of the provision under Article VI stripping all such entities of their present prerogative of engaging in the charade of self-absolution through resort to their own domestic tribunals, the kind of inclusive, flexible, and typologically nuanced definition of the crime advanced here is not without utility. To the extent that it may be adopted and applied in the discourse of scholarly and activist circles, it can have the positive effect of helping expand and reshape public consciousness of what genocide is, how it functions, and the purpose it serves. This is constructive in the sense that to be able to come to grips with any phenomenon, one must first be able to identify it when it is encountered.[18]

With heightened awareness comes heightened expectations for constructive action. Thus it may be that more than one currently recalcitrant state entity will eventually be compelled by a "creeping enlightenment" among its constituents to lobby for such revisions to the convention, even in contradiction to its own perception of sovereign interest.[19] In the alternative, state authority may be circumvented altogether through the sheer outraged force of popular initiative and determination.[20] in either event—and the reality is likely to play out in some symbiotic intertwining of both dynamics—the result will be a giant step toward achieving the mechanisms necessary to lay history's plague of genocidal actions and outlooks to rest, once and for all.

Posterity, which stands to redeem the richest of rewards from any success obtaining in this regard, will inevitably recall those who met their obligations in the matter with the warmest esteem and affection. To those who now move in the opposite direction, seeking for whatever stupid and misguided reasons to diminish and confuse understandings of genocide to the point that it can never be abolished, will accrue the kind of revulsion and contempt among future generations which are reserved now for the likes of the nazis and their apologists. There can be no forgiveness on this score, no room for further toleration of the squirming sophistries of "responsible" scholarship and statist deceit. The stakes are much too high, and the horror has gone on for far too long to bear further iterations of expedient denial.

NOTES

1. With the exception of the first phrase, added for purposes of clarification, this is virtually a recapitulation of the relevant passage contained in U.N. Resolution 96(I).

2. The language here has been changed from "The Contracting Parties" to "The United Nations Member States." My thinking is two-fold. First, insofar as the major elements of international law conform explicitly to the requirements of the U.N. Charter, acceptance of them would seem a concomitant to U.N. membership. Hence, it is arguable that acceptance of instruments such as the Genocide Convention comes with being a member state. Second, insofar as this is true, such instruments constitute customary law, and all states are bound by them, whether or not they have "contracted" to do so.

3. Aside from duplicating the modification of "The Contracting Parties" to "Member States" this is a verbatim recapitulation of the Convention's present language.

4. The itemization of groups used here includes all those put forward since 1946, adhering most closely to that offered by Katz, *Holocaust in Historical Context,* vol. 1, op. cit., p. 131.

5. This imbricated triadic formulation conforms to that put forward by Raphaël Lemkin in his 1947 draft Convention.

6. The delineation of indirect killing techniques conforms to Lemkin's explication in his chapter on genocide in *Axis Rule,* op. cit., as well as the realities of nazi policies bearing on the reduction of Slavic populations in Eastern Europe remarked upon in much of the literature. It also encompasses a range of historical phenomena, such as the effects of the Spanish forced labor system upon the native populations of the Americas, the "death by disease" argument in a number of localities, and so on. At present, this is vaguely addressed under Article II(c) of the 1948 Convention, "inflicting on the group conditions of life calculated to bring about its physical destruction in whole or in part."

7. Although Article II(d) of the 1948 Convention addresses the imposition of "measures intended to prevent births within the group," most literature on genocide fails to mention even sterilization (Katz's massive *Holocaust in Historical Context,* vol. 1, for example, lacks even an index entry on the subject). (Re)incorporation of Lemkin's category in its full dimension should redress this problem, and clarify its overlap with modes of physical genocide (i.e., creating the conditions enumerated in Article II(c) leads not only to deaths, but declining birth rates, etc., a circumstance also bearing on Article II(b), "causing serious bodily or mental harm to members of the group").

8. This again follows from Lemkin's chapter on genocide in *Axis Rule,* as well as his 1947 draft Convention. The provision on expropriation of the means of economic perpetuation plainly overlaps with the same criterion under physical genocide, as well as the provision on creation of conditions causing decline in the rate of childbirth

under biological genocide, and adheres closely to Sartre's linkage of colonialism and genocide; *On Genocide,* op. cit. The provision on forced relocation, expulsion, and dispersal also bears on biological genocide in particular, and, secondarily, on physical genocide; see, e.g., Thayer Scudder et al., *No Place to Go: Effects of Compulsory Relocation on Navajos* (Philadelphia: Institute for Study of Human Issues, 1982).

9. This is consistent with the way the point is made in a fine but little-acknowledged book by Robert Davis and Mark Zannis, *The Genocide Machine in Canada: The Pacification of the North* (Montréal: Black Rose Books, 1973), p. 20: "A culture's destruction is not a trifling matter. . . . If people suddenly lose their 'prime symbol,' the basis of their culture, their lives lose meaning. They become disoriented, with no hope. As social disorganization often follows such a loss, they are unable to ensure their own survival. . . . The cultural mode of group extermination is genocide, a crime. Nor should 'cultural genocide' be used in the game: 'Which is the more horrible, to kill and torture; or, remove the reason and will to live?' Both are horrible."

10. The article is identical to its articulation in the 1948 Convention, except that the requirement that incitement be "direct" has been abandoned, and the word "advocacy" has been added for purposes of clarification. These changes follow the precedent set by the Streicher case at Nuremberg in 1946, and conform to the more general theory advanced by Norman Cohn. . . .

11. Obviously, it makes little sense to analogize genocide to murder—as most analysts have done—unless all the varying degrees by which murder is customarily defined are also incorporated into the definition of genocide. Such gradation of culpability should go far towards resolving the "intentionalist/functionalist controversy.". . . For the original—and to date only—articulation of this concept, see my "Genocide: Toward a Functional Definition," *Alternatives,* vol. XI, no. 3, 1986; reprinted in *Since Predator Came: Notes from the Struggle for American Indian Liberation* (Littleton, CO: Aigis, 1995).

12. The analogous correspondent in U.S. statutory codes would be "felony murder." At issue in connection to genocide, such a charge might devolve upon violations of the laws of war, as suggested by Kuper, among others; e.g., *Genocide,* op. cit., p. 46. Other likely prospects would include violation of the 1960 Declaration on the Granting of Independence to Colonial Countries and Peoples and/or the 1966 International Covenant on Economic, Social and Political Rights, as suggested by Sartre (*On Genocide,* op. cit.), or violation of the 1979 Convention on Elimination of All Forms of Racial Discrimination, as implied *a priori* by William Patterson and other African Americans; William L. Patterson, *The Man Who Cried Genocide: An Autobiography* (New York: International, 1971).

13. The analogous correspondent in U.S. statutory codes would be "negligent homicide."

14. The second sentence herein is the same as it appears in the 1948 Convention. The first sentence has been added in response to concerns raised during U.N. debates on the matter in 1947 that the Convention contain no provision impairing the "sovereign functioning" of any state. Insofar as no state has a right to perpetrate genocide, however, there can be no infringement of legitimate sovereign prerogative entailed in prohibition of it. To argue otherwise is simply to hold that certain entities are entitled to exercise criminal license under international law. While this may be a practical

reality in the world of power politics, it is not a matter deserving of accommodation in the codification of juridical principle.

15. This provision, which may in many ways prove to be the most problematic of all, likely represents the only means by which any semblance of "teeth" can ever be put into the Genocide Convention (or any other element of international criminal law). The basis for a such a tribunal, which has existed since the 1946 United Nations' Affirmation of the Principles of International Law Recognized by the Charter of the Nuremberg Tribunal (U.N.G.A. Res. 95(I), U.N. Doc A/235 at 1144), may also be discerned in the September 13, 1993, order of the World Court that tribunal proceedings be instituted in behalf of Bosnia and Herzegovina against Serbia and Montenegro on charges of violating provisions of the 1948 Convention; reproduced in Francis A. Boyle, *The Bosnian People Charge Genocide: Proceedings of the International Court of Justice Concerning* Bosnia v. Serbia *on the Prevention and Punishment of the Crime of Genocide* (Amherst, MA: Altheia Press, 1996), pp. 341–64. A major sticking point will undoubtedly be the formal 1985 U.S. repudiation of World Court authority over its affairs (although not over the affairs of other countries); "U.S. Terminates Acceptance of ICJ Compulsory Jurisdiction," *U.S. Department of State Bulletins,* Jan. 1986.

16. Again, this is a close paraphrase of existing language.

17. This is not so presumptuous a formulation as it may seem at first glance. Even U.S. rapporteur Ben Whitaker has suggested that some form of supersession of the Convention's current terms and provisions is in order; Ben Whitaker, *Revised and Updated Report on the Question of Prevention and Punishment of the Crime of Genocide* (New York: U.N. Economic and Social Council, Commission on Human Rights [E.CN.4.Sub.2. 1985.6] July 1985).

18. The necessity of such a first step is agreed to by virtually all analysts and commentators; e.g., Chalk and Jonassohn, *History,* op. cit.; Kuper, *The Prevention of Genocide,* op. cit.; Harff, *Genocide and Human Rights,* op. cit.; Fein, "Scenarios of Genocide," op. cit.; Israel W. Charny, "Intervention and Prevention of Genocide," in Israel W. Charny, ed., *Genocide: A Critical Bibliography* (New York/London: Facts on File/Mansell, 1988).

19. This is a prospect suggested by international legal scholar Richard A. Falk, in his *The End of the World Order: Essays on Normative International Relations* (New York: Holmes & Meier, 1983).

20. Such an implication might be drawn from the discussion of the International Peoples' Tribunal formed by Lelio Basso pursuant to the 1976 Algiers Declaration found in Richard A. Falk, *Human Rights and State Sovereignty* (New York: Holmes & Meier, 1981) pp. 200–1.

RACIAL FORMATION

Michael Omi and Howard Winant

In 1982–83, Susie Guillory Phipps unsuccessfully sued the Louisiana Bureau of Vital Records to change her racial classification from black to white. The descendant of an 18th-century white planter and a black slave, Phipps was designated "black" in her birth certificate in accordance with a 1970 state law which declared anyone with at least 1/32nd "Negro blood" to be black.

The Phipps case raised intriguing questions about the concept of race, its meaning in contemporary society, and its use (and abuse) in public policy. Assistant Attorney General Ron David defended the law by pointing out that some type of racial classification was necessary to comply with federal record-keeping requirements and to facilitate programs for the prevention of genetic diseases. Phipps's attorney, Brian Begue, argued that the assignment of racial categories on birth certificates was unconstitutional and that the 1/32nd designation was inaccurate. He called on a retired Tulane University professor who cited research indicating that most Louisiana whites have at least 1/20th "Negro" ancestry.

In the end, Phipps lost. The court upheld the state's right to classify and quantify racial identity.[1]

Phipps's problematic racial identity, and her effort to resolve it through state action, is in many ways a parable of America's unsolved racial dilemma. It illustrates the difficulties of defining race and assigning individuals or groups to racial categories. It shows how the racial legacies of the past—slavery and bigotry—continue to shape the present. It reveals both the deep involvement of the state in the organization and interpretation of race, and the inadequacy of state institutions to carry out these functions. It demonstrates how deeply Americans both as individuals and as a civilization are shaped, and indeed haunted, by race.

Having lived her whole life thinking that she was white, Phipps suddenly discovers that by legal definition she is not. In U.S. society, such an event is indeed catastrophic.[2] But if she is not white, of what race is she? The *state* claims that she is black, based on its rules of classification,[3] and another state agency, the court, upholds this judgment. But despite these classificatory standards which have imposed an either-or logic on racial identity, Phipps will not in fact "change color." Unlike what would have happened during slavery times if one's claim to whiteness was successfully challenged, we can assume that despite the outcome of her legal challenge, Phipps will remain in most of the social relationships she had occupied before the trial. Her socialization, her familial and friendship networks, her cultural orientation, will not change.

She will simply have to wrestle with her newly acquired "hybridized" condition. She will have to confront the "Other" within.

The designation of racial categories and the determination of racial identity is no simple task. For centuries, this question has precipitated intense debates and conflicts, particularly in the U.S.—disputes over natural and legal rights, over the distribution of resources, and indeed, over who shall live and who shall die.

A crucial dimension of the Phipps case is that it illustrates the inadequacy of claims that race is a mere matter of variations in human physiognomy, that it is simply a matter of skin color. But if race cannot be understood in this manner, how *can* it be understood? We cannot fully hope to address this topic—no less than the meaning of race, its role in society, and the forces which shape it—in one chapter, nor indeed in one book. Our goal in this chapter, however, is far from modest: we wish to offer at least the outlines of a theory of race and racism.

WHAT IS RACE?

There is a continuous temptation to think of race as an *essence,* as something fixed, concrete, and objective. And there is also an opposite temptation: to imagine race as a mere *illusion,* a purely ideological construct which some ideal non-racist social order would eliminate. It is necessary to challenge both these positions, to disrupt and reframe the rigid and bipolar manner in which they are posed and debated, and to transcend the presumably irreconcilable relationship between them.

The effort must be made to understand race as an unstable and "decentered" complex of social meanings constantly being transformed by political struggle. With this in mind, let us propose a definition: *race is a concept which signifies and symbolizes social conflicts and interests by referring to different types of human bodies.* Although the concept of race invokes biologically based human characteristics (so-called "phenotypes"), selection of these particular human features for purposes of racial signification is always and necessarily a social and historical process. In contrast to the other major distinction of this type, that of gender, there is no biological basis for distinguishing among human groups along the lines of race.[4] Indeed, the categories employed to differentiate among human groups along racial lines reveal themselves, upon serious examination, to be at best imprecise, and at worst completely arbitrary.

10   If the concept of race is so nebulous, can we not dispense with it? Can we not "do without" race, at least in the "enlightened" present? This question has been posed often, and with greater frequency in recent years.[5] An affirmative answer would of course present obvious practical difficulties: it is rather difficult to jettison widely held beliefs, beliefs which moreover are central to everyone's identity and understanding of the social world. So the attempt to banish the concept as an archaism is at best counterintuitive. But a deeper

difficulty, we believe, is inherent in the very formulation of this schema, in its way of posing race as a *problem,* a misconception left over from the past, and suitable now only for the dustbin of history.

A more effective starting point is the recognition that despite its uncertainties and contradictions, the concept of race continues to play a fundamental role in structuring and representing the social world. The task for theory is to explain this situation. It is to avoid both the utopian framework which sees race as an illusion we can somehow "get beyond," and also the essentialist formulation which sees race as something objective and fixed, a biological datum.[6] Thus we should think of race as an element of social structure rather than as an irregularity within it; we should see race as a dimension of human representation rather than an illusion. These perspectives inform the theoretical approach we call racial formation.

RACIAL FORMATION

We define *racial formation* as the sociohistorical process by which racial categories are created, inhabited, transformed, and destroyed. Our attempt to elaborate a theory of racial formation will proceed in two steps. First, we argue that racial formation is a process of historically situated *projects* in which human bodies and social structures are represented and organized. Next we link racial formation to the evolution of hegemony, the way in which society is organized and ruled. Such an approach, we believe, can facilitate understanding of a whole range of contemporary controversies and dilemmas involving race, including the nature of racism, the relationship of race to other forms of differences, inequalities, and oppression such as sexism and nationalism, and the dilemmas of racial identity today.

From a racial formation perspective, race is a matter of both social structure and cultural representation. Too often, the attempt is made to understand race simply or primarily in terms of only one of these two analytical dimensions.[7] For example, efforts to explain racial inequality as a purely social structural phenomenon are unable to account for the origins, patterning, and transformation of racial difference.

Conversely, many examinations of racial differences—understood as a matter of cultural attributes *à la* ethnicity theory, or as a society-wide signification system, *à la* some poststructuralist accounts—cannot comprehend such structural phenomena as racial stratification in the labor market or patterns of residential segregation.

An alternative approach is to think of racial formation processes as occurring through a linkage between structure and representation. Racial *projects* do the ideological "work" of making these links. *A racial project is simultaneously an interpretation, representation, or explanation of racial dynamics, and an effort to reorganize and redistribute resources along particular racial lines.* Racial projects connect what race *means* in a particular discursive practice and the ways in

15

which both social structures and everyday experiences are racially *organized,* based upon that meaning. Let us consider this proposition, first in terms of large-scale or macro-level social processes, and then in terms of other dimensions of the racial formation process.

Racial Formation as a Macro-Level Social Process

To *interpret the meaning of race is to frame it social structurally.* Consider for example, this statement by Charles Murray on welfare reform:

> My proposal for dealing with the racial issue in social welfare is to repeal every bit of legislation and reverse every court decision that in any way requires, recommends, or awards differential treatment according to race, and thereby put us back onto the track that we left in 1965. We may argue about the appropriate limits of government intervention in trying to enforce the ideal, but at least it should be possible to identify the ideal: Race is not a morally admissible reason for treating one person differently from another. Period.[8]

Here there is a partial but significant analysis of the meaning of race: it is not a morally valid basis upon which to treat people "differently from one another." We may notice someone's race, but we cannot act upon that awareness. We must act in a "color-blind" fashion. This analysis of the meaning of race is immediately linked to a specific conception of the role of race in the social structure: it can play no part in government action, save in "the enforcement of the ideal." No state policy can legitimately require, recommend, or award different status according to race. This example can be classified as a particular type of racial project in the present-day U.S.—a "neoconservative" one.

Conversely, *to recognize the racial dimension in social structure is to interpret the meaning of race.* Consider the following statement by the late Supreme Court Justice Thurgood Marshall on minority "set-aside" programs:

> A profound difference separates governmental actions that themselves are racist, and governmental actions that seek to remedy the effects of prior racism or to prevent neutral government activity from perpetuating the effects of such racism.[9]

Here the focus is on the racial dimensions of *social structure*—in this case of state activity and policy. The argument is that state actions in the past and present have treated people in very different ways according to their race, and thus the government cannot retreat from its policy responsibilities in this area. It cannot suddenly declare itself "color-blind" without in fact perpetuating the same type of differential, racist treatment.[10] Thus, race continues to signify difference and structure inequality. Here, racialized social structure is immediately linked to an interpretation of the meaning of race. This example

too can be classified as a particular type of racial project in the present-day
U.S.—a "liberal" one.

    To be sure, such political labels as "neoconservative" or "liberal" cannot   *20*
fully capture the complexity of racial projects, for these are always multiply
determined, politically contested, and deeply shaped by their historical context. Thus, encapsulated within the neoconservative example cited here are
certain egalitarian commitments which derive from a previous historical context in which they played a very different role, and which are rearticulated in
neoconservative racial discourse precisely to oppose a more open-ended,
more capacious conception of the meaning of equality. Similarly, in the liberal
example, Justice Marshall recognizes that the contemporary state, which was
formerly the architect of segregation and the chief enforcer of racial difference, has a tendency to reproduce those patterns of inequality in a new guise.
Thus he admonishes it (in dissent, significantly) to fulfill its responsibilities to
uphold a robust conception of equality. These particular instances, then,
demonstrate how racial projects are always concretely framed, and thus are always contested and unstable. The social structures they uphold or attack, and
the representations of race they articulate, are never invented out of the air,
but exist in a definite historical context, having descended from previous conflicts. This contestation appears to be permanent in respect to race.

    These two examples of contemporary racial projects are drawn from
mainstream political debate; they may be characterized as center-right and
center-left expressions of contemporary racial politics.[11] We can, however,
expand the discussion of racial formation processes far beyond these familiar
examples. In fact, we can identify racial projects in at least three other analytical dimensions: first, the political spectrum can be broadened to include radical projects, on both the left and right, as well as along other political axes.
Second, analysis of racial projects can take place not only at the macro-level
of racial policy-making, state activity, and collective action, but also at the
micro-level of everyday experience. Third, the concept of racial projects can
be applied across historical time, to identify racial formation dynamics in the
past. We shall now offer examples of each of these types of racial projects.

The Political Spectrum of Racial Formation

We have encountered examples of a neoconservative racial project, in which
the significance of race is denied, leading to a "color-blind" racial politics and
"hands off" policy orientation; and of a "liberal" racial project, in which the
significance of race is affirmed, leading to an egalitarian and "activist" state
policy. But these by no means exhaust the political possibilities. Other racial
projects can be readily identified on the contemporary U.S. scene. For example, "far right" projects, which uphold biologistic and racist views of difference, explicitly argue for white supremacist policies. "New right" projects
overtly claim to hold "color-blind" views, but covertly manipulate racial fears
in order to achieve political gains.[12] On the left, "radical democratic" projects

invoke notions of racial "difference" in combination with egalitarian politics and policy.

Further variations can also be noted. For example, "nationalist" projects, both conservative and radical, stress the incompatibility of racially defined group identity with the legacy of white supremacy, and therefore advocate a social structural solution of separation, either complete or partial.[13] . . . [N]ationalist currents represent a profound legacy of the centuries of racial absolutism that initially defined the meaning of race in the U.S. Nationalist concerns continue to influence racial debate in the form of Afrocentrism and other expressions of identity politics.

Taking the range of politically organized racial projects as a whole, we can "map" the current pattern of racial formation at the level of the public sphere, the "macro-level" in which public debate and mobilization takes place.[14] But important as this is, the terrain on which racial formation occurs is broader yet.

Racial Formation as Everyday Experience

25   At the micro-social level, racial projects also link signification and structure, not so much as efforts to shape policy or define large-scale meaning, but as the applications of "common sense." To see racial projects operating at the level of everyday life, we have only to examine the many ways in which, often unconsciously, we "notice" race.

One of the first things we notice about people when we meet them (along with their sex) is their race. We utilize race to provide clues about *who* a person is. This fact is made painfully obvious when we encounter someone whom we cannot conveniently racially categorize—someone who is, for example, racially "mixed" or of an ethnic/racial group we are not familiar with. Such an encounter becomes a source of discomfort and momentarily a crisis of racial meaning.

Our ability to interpret racial meanings depends on preconceived notions of a racialized social structure. Comments such as, "Funny, you don't look black," betray an underlying image of what black should be. We expect people to act out their apparent racial identities; indeed we become disoriented when they do not. The black banker harassed by police while walking in casual clothes through his own well-off neighborhood, the Latino or white kid rapping in perfect Afro patois, the unending *faux pas* committed by whites who assume that the non-whites they encounter are servants or tradespeople, the belief that non-white colleagues are less qualified persons hired to fulfill affirmative action guidelines, indeed the whole gamut of racial stereotypes—that "white men can't jump," that Asians can't dance, etc., etc.—all testify to the way a racialized social structure shapes racial experience and conditions meaning. Analysis of such stereotypes reveals the always present, already active link between our view of the social structure—its demography, its laws, its customs, its threats—and our conception of what race means.

Conversely, our ongoing interpretation of our experience in racial terms shapes our relations to the institutions and organizations through which we are imbedded in social structure. Thus we expect differences in skin color, or other racially coded characteristics, to explain social differences. Temperament, sexuality, intelligence, athletic ability, aesthetic preferences, and so on are presumed to be fixed and discernible from the palpable mark of race. Such diverse questions as our confidence and trust in others (for example, clerks or salespeople, media figures, neighbors), our sexual preferences and romantic images, our tastes in music, films, dance, or sports, and our very ways of talking, walking, eating, and dreaming become racially coded simply because we live in a society where racial awareness is so pervasive. Thus in ways too comprehensive even to monitor consciously, and despite periodic calls—neoconservative and otherwise—for us to ignore race and adopt "color-blind" racial attitudes, skin color "differences" continue to rationalize distinct treatment of racially identified individuals and groups.

To summarize the argument so far: the theory of racial formation suggests that society is suffused with racial projects, large and small, to which all are subjected. This racial "subjection" is quintessentially ideological. Everybody learns some combination, some version, of the rules of racial classification, and of her own racial identity, often without obvious teaching or conscious inculcation. Thus are we inserted in a comprehensively racialized social structure. Race becomes "common sense"—a way of comprehending, explaining, and acting in the world. A vast web of racial projects mediates between the discursive or representational means in which race is identified and signified on the one hand, and the institutional and organizational forms in which it is routinized and standardized on the other. These projects are the heart of the racial formation process.

Under such circumstances, it is not possible to represent race discursively without simultaneously locating it, explicitly or implicitly, in a social structural (and historical) context. Nor is it possible to organize, maintain, or transform social structures without simultaneously engaging, once more either explicitly or implicitly, in racial signification. Racial formation, therefore, is a kind of synthesis, an outcome, of the interaction of racial projects on a society-wide level. These projects are, of course, vastly different in scope and effect. They include large-scale public action, state activities, and interpretations of racial conditions in artistic, journalistic, or academic fora,[15] as well as the seemingly infinite number of racial judgments and practices we carry out at the level of individual experience.

Since racial formation is always historically situated, our understanding of the significance of race, and of the way race structures society, has changed enormously over time. The processes of racial formation we encounter today, the racial projects large and small which structure U.S. society in so many ways, are merely the present-day outcomes of a complex historical evolution. The contemporary racial order remains transient. By knowing something of how it evolved, we can perhaps better discern where it is heading. We therefore turn next to a historical survey of the racial formation process, and the conflicts and debates it has engendered.

THE EVOLUTION OF MODERN RACIAL AWARENESS

The identification of distinctive human groups, and their association with differences in physical appearance, goes back to prehistory, and can be found in the earliest documents—in the Bible, for example, or in Herodotus. But the emergence of a modern conception of race does not occur until the rise of Europe and the arrival of Europeans in the Americas. Even the hostility and suspicion with which Christian Europe viewed its two significant non-Christian "Others"—the Muslims and the Jews—cannot be viewed as more than a rehearsal for racial formation, since these antagonisms, for all their bloodletting and chauvinism, were always and everywhere religiously interpreted.[16]

It was only when European explorers reached the Western Hemisphere, when the oceanic seal separating the "old" and the "new" worlds was breached, that the distinctions and categorizations fundamental to a racialized social structure, and to a discourse of race, began to appear. The European explorers were the advance guard of merchant capitalism, which sought new openings for trade. What they found exceeded their wildest dreams, for never before and never again in human history has an opportunity for the appropriation of wealth remotely approached that presented by the "discovery."[17]

But the Europeans also "discovered" people, people who looked and acted differently. These "natives" challenged their "discoverers'" pre-existing conceptions of the origins and possibilities of the human species.[18] The representation and interpretation of the meaning of the indigenous peoples' existence became a crucial matter, one which would affect the outcome of the enterprise of conquest. For the "discovery" raised disturbing questions as to whether *all* could be considered part of the same "family of man," and more practically, the extent to which native peoples could be exploited and enslaved. Thus religious debates flared over the attempt to reconcile the various Christian metaphysics with the existence of peoples who were more "different" than any whom Europe had previously known.[19]

35   In practice, of course, the seizure of territories and goods, the introduction of slavery through the *encomienda* and other forms of coerced native labor, and then through the organization of the African slave trade—not to mention the practice of outright extermination—all presupposed a worldview which distinguished Europeans, as children of God, full-fledged human beings, etc., from "Others." Given the dimensions and the ineluctability of the European onslaught, given the conquerors' determination to appropriate both labor and goods, and given the presence of an axiomatic and unquestioned Christianity among them, the ferocious division of society into Europeans and "Others" soon coalesced. This was true despite the famous 16th-century theological and philosophical debates about the identity of indigenous peoples.[20]

Indeed debates about the nature of the "Others" reached their practical limits with a certain dispatch. Plainly they would never touch the essential: nothing, after all, would induce the Europeans to pack up and go home. We cannot examine here the early controversies over the status of American souls. We simply wish to emphasize that the "discovery" signaled a break from the previous proto-racial awareness by which Europe contemplated its "Others" in a relatively disorganized fashion. In other words, the "conquest of America" was not simply an epochal historical event—however unparalleled in its importance. It was also the advent of a consolidated social structure of exploitation, appropriation, domination. Its representation, first in religious terms, but soon enough in scientific and political ones, initiated modern racial awareness.

The conquest, therefore, was the first—and given the dramatic nature of the case, perhaps the greatest—racial formation project. Its significance was by no means limited to the Western Hemisphere, for it began the work of constituting Europe as the metropole, the center, of a group of empires which could take, as Marx would later write, "the globe for a theater."[21] It represented this new imperial structure as a struggle between civilization and barbarism, and implicated in this representation all the great European philosophies, literary traditions, and social theories of the modern age.[22] In short, just as the noise of the "big bang" still resonates through the universe, so the overdetermined construction of world "civilization" as a product of the rise of Europe and the subjugation of the rest of us, still defines the race concept.

FROM RELIGION TO SCIENCE

After the initial depredations of conquest, religious justifications for racial difference gradually gave way to scientific ones. By the time of the Enlightenment, a general awareness of race was pervasive, and most of the great philosophers of Europe, such as Hegel, Kant, Hume, and Locke, had issued virulently racist opinions.

The problem posed by race during the late 18th century was markedly different than it had been in the age of "discovery," expropriation, and slaughter. The social structures in which race operated were no longer primarily those of military conquest and plunder, nor of the establishment of thin beachheads of colonization on the edge of what had once seemed a limitless wilderness. Now the issues were much more complicated: nation-building, establishment of national economies in the world trading system, resistance to the arbitrary authority of monarchs, and the assertion of the "natural rights" of "man," including the right of revolution.[23] In such a situation, racially organized exploitation, in the form of slavery, the expansion of colonies, and the continuing expulsion of native peoples, was both necessary and newly difficult to justify.

The invocation of scientific criteria to demonstrate the "natural" basis of racial hierarchy was both a logical consequence of the rise of this form of   *40* knowledge, and an attempt to provide a more subtle and nuanced account of human complexity in the new, "enlightened" age. Spurred on by the classificatory scheme of living organisms devised by Linnaeus in *Systema Naturae* (1735), many scholars in the 18th and 19th centuries dedicated themselves to the identification and ranking of variations in humankind. Race was conceived as a *biological* concept, a matter of species. Voltaire wrote that "the Negro race is a species of men (sic) as different from ours . . . as the breed of spaniels is from that of greyhounds," and in a formulation echoing down from his century to our own, declared that

> If their understanding is not of a different nature from ours . . . ,
> it is at least greatly inferior. They are not capable of any great
> application or association of ideas, and seem formed neither for
> the advantages nor the abuses of philosophy.[24]

Jefferson, the preeminent exponent of the Enlightenment doctrine of "the rights of man" on North American shores, echoed these sentiments:

> In general their existence appears to participate more of sensa-
> tion than reflection. . . . [I]n memory they are equal to whites,
> in reason much inferior . . . [and] in imagination they are dull,
> tasteless, and anomalous. . . . I advance it therefore . . . that the
> blacks, whether originally a different race, or made distinct by
> time and circumstances, are inferior to the whites. . . . Will not
> a lover of natural history, then, one who views the gradations in
> all the animals with the eye of philosophy, excuse an effort to
> keep those in the department of Man (sic) as distinct as nature
> has formed them.[25]

Such claims of species distinctiveness among humans justified the inequitable allocation of political and social rights, while still upholding the doctrine of "the rights of man." The quest to obtain a precise scientific definition of race sustained debates which continue to rage today. Yet despite efforts ranging from Dr. Samuel Morton's studies of cranial capacity[26] to contemporary attempts to base racial classification on shared gene pools,[27] the concept of race has defied biological definition.

In the 19th century, Count Joseph Arthur de Gobineau drew upon the most respected scientific studies of his day to compose his four-volume *Essay on the Inequality of Races* (1853–1855).[28] He not only greatly influenced the racial thinking of the period, but his themes would be echoed in the racist ideologies of the next one hundred years: beliefs that superior races produced superior cultures and that racial intermixtures resulted in the degradation of the superior racial stock. These ideas found expression, for instance, in the eugenics movement launched by Darwin's cousin, Francis Galton, which had an immense impact on scientific and sociopolitical thought in Europe and the U.S.[29] In the wake of civil war and emancipation, and with immigration from southern and Eastern Europe as well as East Asia running

high, the U.S. was particularly fertile ground for notions such as social darwinism and eugenics.

Attempts to discern the *scientific meaning* of race continue to the present
day. For instance, an essay by Arthur Jensen which argued that hereditary factors shape intelligence not only revived the "nature or nurture" controversy,
but also raised highly volatile questions about racial equality itself.[30] All such
attempts seek to remove the concept of race from the historical context in
which it arose and developed. They employ an *essentialist* approach which
suggests instead that the truth of race is a matter of innate characteristics, of
which skin color and other physical attributes provide only the most obvious,
and in some respects most superficial, indicators.

FROM SCIENCE TO POLITICS

It has taken scholars more than a century to reject biologistic notions of race in
favor of an approach which regards race as a *social* concept. This trend has been
slow and uneven, and even today remains somewhat embattled, but its overall
direction seems clear. At the turn of the century Max Weber discounted biological explanations for racial conflict and instead highlighted the social and
political factors which engendered such conflict.[31] W. E. B. Du Bois argued for
a sociopolitical definition of race by identifying "the color line" as "the problem of the 20th century."[32] Pioneering cultural anthropologist Franz Boas rejected attempts to link racial identifications and cultural traits, labeling as
pseudoscientific any assumption of a continuum of "higher" and "lower" cultural groups.[33] Other early exponents of social, as opposed to biological, views
of race included Robert E. Park, founder of the "Chicago school" of sociology,
and Alain Leroy Locke, philosopher and theorist of the Harlem Renaissance.[34]

Perhaps more important than these and subsequent intellectual efforts,
however, were the political struggles of racially defined groups themselves.
Waged all around the globe under a variety of banners such as anticolonial-
ism and civil rights, these battles to challenge various structural and cultural
racisms have been a major feature of 20th-century politics. The racial horrors
of the 20th century—colonial slaughter and apartheid, the genocide of the
holocaust, and the massive bloodlettings required to end these evils—have
also indelibly marked the theme of race as a political issue *par excellence*.

As a result of prior efforts and struggles, we have now reached the point
of fairly general agreement that race is not a biologically given but rather a
socially constructed way of differentiating human beings. While a tremendous
achievement, the transcendence of biologistic conceptions of race does not
provide any reprieve from the dilemmas of racial injustice and conflict, nor
from controversies over the significance of race in the present. Views of race
as socially constructed simply recognize the fact that these conflicts and controversies are now more properly framed on the terrain of politics. By privileging politics in the analysis which follows we do not mean to suggest that

race has been displaced as a concern of scientific inquiry, or that struggles over cultural representation are no longer important. We do argue, however, that race is now a preeminently political phenomenon. Such an assertion invites examination of the evolving role of racial politics in the U.S. This is the subject to which we now turn.

DICTATORSHIP, DEMOCRACY, HEGEMONY

For more of its existence both as European colony and as an independent nation, the U.S. was a *racial dictatorship*. From 1607 to 1865—258 years—most non-whites were firmly eliminated from the sphere of politics.[35] After the Civil War there was the brief egalitarian experiment of Reconstruction which terminated ignominiously in 1877. In its wake followed almost a century of legally sanctioned segregation and denial of the vote, nearly absolute in the South and much of the Southwest, less effective in the North and far West, but formidable in any case.[36] These barriers fell only in the mid-1960s, a mere quarter-century ago. Nor did the successes of the black movement and its allies mean that all obstacles to their political participation had now been abolished. Patterns of racial inequality have proven, unfortunately, to be quite stubborn and persistent.

It is important, therefore, to recognize that in many respects, racial dictatorship is the norm against which all U.S. politics must be measured. The centuries of racial dictatorship have had three very large consequences: first, they defined "American" identity as white, as the negation of racialized "otherness"—at first largely African and indigenous, later Latin American and Asian as well.[37] This negation took shape in both law and custom, in public institutions and in forms of cultural representation. It became the archetype of hegemonic rule in the U.S. It was the successor to the conquest as the "master" racial project.

Second, racial dictatorship organized (albeit sometimes in an incoherent and contradictory fashion) the "color line" rendering it the fundamental division in U.S. society. The dictatorship elaborated, articulated, and drove racial divisions not only through institutions, but also through psyches, extending up to our own time the racial obsessions of the conquest and slavery periods.

Third, racial dictatorship consolidated the oppositional racial consciousness and organization originally framed by marronage[38] and slave revolts, by indigenous resistance, and by nationalisms of various sorts. Just as the conquest created the "native" where once there had been Pequot, Iroquois, or Tutelo, so too it created the "black" where once there had been Asante or Ovimbundu, Yoruba or Bakongo.

50   The transition from a racial dictatorship to a racial democracy has been a slow, painful, and contentious one; it remains far from complete. A recognition of the abiding presence of racial dictatorship, we contend, is crucial for the development of a theory of racial formation in the U.S. It is also crucial

to the task of relating racial formation to the broader context of political practice, organization, and change.

In this context, a key question arises: in what way is racial formation related to politics as a whole? How, for example, does race articulate with other axes of oppression and difference—most importantly class and gender—along which politics is organized today?

The answer, we believe, lies in the concept of *hegemony*. Antonio Gramsci—the Italian communist who placed this concept at the center of his life's work—understood it as the conditions necessary, in a given society, for the achievement and consolidation of rule. He argued that hegemony was always constituted by a combination of coercion and consent. Although rule can be obtained by force, it cannot be secured and maintained, especially in modern society, without the element of consent. Gramsci conceived of consent as far more than merely the legitimation of authority. In his view, consent extended to the incorporation by the ruling group of many of the key interests of subordinated groups, often to the explicit disadvantage of the rulers themselves.[39] Gramsci's treatment of hegemony went even farther: he argued that in order to consolidate their hegemony, ruling groups must elaborate and maintain a popular system of ideas and practices—through education, the media, religion, folk wisdom, etc.—which he called "common sense." It is through its production and its adherence to this "common sense," this ideology (in the broadest sense of the term), that a society gives its consent to the way in which it is ruled.[40]

These provocative concepts can be extended and applied to an understanding of racial rule. In the Americas, the conquest represented the violent introduction of a new form of rule whose relationship with those it subjugated was almost entirely coercive. In the U.S., the origins of racial division, and of racial signification and identity formation, lie in a system of rule which was extremely dictatorial. The mass murders and expulsions of indigenous people, and the enslavement of Africans, surely evoked and inspired little consent in their founding moments.

Over time, however, the balance of coercion and consent began to change. It is possible to locate the origins of hegemony right within the heart of racial dictatorship, for the effort to possess the oppressor's tools—religion and philosophy in this case—was crucial to emancipation (the effort to possess oneself). As Ralph Ellison reminds us, "The slaves often took the essence of the aristocratic ideal (as they took Christianity) with far more seriousness than their masters."[41] In their language, in their religion with its focus on the Exodus theme and on Jesus's tribulations, in their music with its figuring of suffering, resistance, perseverance, and transcendence, in their interrogation of a political philosophy which sought perpetually to rationalize their bondage in a supposedly "free" society, the slaves incorporated elements of racial rule into their thought and practice, turning them against their original bearers.

Racial rule can be understood as a slow and uneven historical process which has moved from dictatorship to democracy, from domination to hegemony. In this transition, hegemonic forms of racial rule—those based on consent—eventually came to supplant those based on coercion. Of course, before this assertion can be accepted, it must be qualified in important ways. By no means has the U.S. established racial democracy at the end of the century, and by no means is coercion a thing of the past. But the sheer complexity of the racial questions U.S. society confronts today, the welter of competing racial projects and contradictory racial experiences which Americans undergo, suggests that hegemony is a useful and appropriate term with which to characterize contemporary racial rule.

Our key theoretical notion of racial projects helps to extend and broaden the question of rule. Projects are the building blocks not just of racial formation, but of hegemony in general. Hegemony operates by simultaneously structuring and signifying. As in the case of racial opposition, gender- or class-based conflict today links structural inequity and injustice on the one hand, and identifies and represents its subjects on the other. The success of modern-day feminism, for example, has depended on its ability to reinterpret gender as a matter of both injustice and identity/difference.

Today, political opposition necessarily takes shape on the terrain of hegemony. Far from ruling principally through exclusion and coercion (though again, these are hardly absent) hegemony operates by including its subjects, incorporating its opposition. *Pace* both Marxists and liberals, there is no longer any universal or privileged region of political action or discourse.[42] Race, class, and gender all represent potential antagonisms whose significance is no longer given, if it ever was.

Thus race, class, and gender (as well as sexual orientation) constitute "regions" of hegemony, areas in which certain political projects can take shape. They share certain obvious attributes in that they are all "socially constructed," and they all consist of a field of projects whose common feature is their linkage of social structure and signification.

Going beyond this, it is crucial to emphasize that race, class, and gender are not fixed and discrete categories, and that such "regions" are by no means autonomous. They overlap, intersect, and fuse with each other in countless ways. Such mutual determinations have been illustrated by Patricia Hill Collins's survey and theoretical synthesis of the themes and issues of black feminist thought.[43] They are also evident in Evelyn Nakano Glenn's work on the historical and contemporary racialization of domestic and service work.[44] In many respects, race is gendered and gender is racialized. In institutional and everyday life, any clear demarcation of specific forms of oppression and difference is constantly being disrupted.

60   There are no clear boundaries between these "regions" of hegemony, so political conflicts will often invoke some or all these themes simultaneously. Hegemony is tentative, incomplete, and "messy." For example, the 1991 Hill–Thomas hearings, with their intertwined themes of race and gender inequality, and their frequent genuflections before the altar of hard work and upward mobility, managed to synthesize various race, gender, and class projects in a particularly explosive combination.[45]

What distinguishes political opposition today—racial or otherwise—is its insistence on identifying itself and speaking for itself, its determined demand for the transformation of the social structure, its refusal of the "common sense" understandings which the hegemonic order imposes. Nowhere is this refusal of "common sense" more needed, or more imperilled, than in our understanding of racism.

WHAT IS RACISM?

Since the ambiguous triumph of the civil rights movement in the mid-1960s, clarity about what racism means has been eroding. The concept entered the lexicon of "common sense" only in the 1960s. Before that, although the term had surfaced occasionally,[46] the problem of racial injustice and inequality was generally understood in a more limited fashion, as a matter of prejudiced attitudes or bigotry on the one hand,[47] and discriminatory practices on the other.[48] Solutions, it was believed, would therefore involve the overcoming of such attitudes, the achievement of tolerance, the acceptance of "brotherhood," etc., and the passage of laws which prohibited discrimination with respect to access to public accommodations, jobs, education, etc. The early civil rights movement explicitly reflected such views. In its espousal of integration and its quest for a "beloved community" it sought to overcome racial prejudice. In its litigation activities and agitation for civil rights legislation it sought to challenge discriminatory practices.

The later 1960s, however, signaled a sharp break with this vision. The emergence of the slogan "black power" (and soon after, of "brown power," "red power," and "yellow power"), the wave of riots that swept the urban ghettos from 1964 to 1968, and the founding of radical movement organizations of nationalist and Marxist orientation, coincided with the recognition that racial inequality and injustice had much deeper roots. They were not simply the product of prejudice, nor was discrimination only a master of intentionally informed action. Rather, prejudice was an almost unavoidable outcome of patterns of socialization which were "bred in the bone," affecting not only whites but even minorities themselves.[49] Discrimination, far from manifesting itself only (or even principally) through individual actions or conscious policies, was a structural feature of U.S. society, the project of centuries of systematic exclusion, exploitation, and disregard of racially defined minorities.[50] It was this combination of relationships—prejudice, discrimination, and institutional inequality—which defined the concept of racism at the end of the 1960s.

Such a synthesis was better able to confront the political realities of the period. Its emphasis on the structural dimensions of racism allowed it to address the intransigence which racial injustice and inequality continued to exhibit, even after discrimination had supposedly been outlawed[51] and bigoted expression stigmatized. But such an approach also had clear limitations. As Robert Miles has argued, it tended to "inflate" the concept of racism to a point at which it lost precision.[52] If the "institutional" component of racism were so pervasive and deeply rooted, it became difficult to see how the democratization of U.S. society could be achieved, and difficult to explain what progress had been made. The result was a leveling critique which denied any distinction between the Jim Crow era (or even the whole *longue durée* of racial dictatorship since the conquest) and the present. Similarly, if the prejudice component of racism were so deeply inbred, it became difficult to account for the evident hybridity and interpenetration that characterizes civil society in the U.S., as evidenced by the shaping of popular culture, language, and style, for example. The result of the "inflation" of the concept of racism was thus a deep pessimism about any efforts to overcome racial barriers, in the workplace, the community, or any other sphere of lived experience. An overly comprehensive view of racism, then, potentially served as a self-fulfilling prophecy.

65   Yet the alternative view—which surfaced with a vengeance in the 1970s— urging a return to the conception of racism held before the movement's "radical turn," was equally inadequate. This was the neoconservative perspective, which deliberately restricted its attention to injury done to the individual as opposed to the group, and to advocacy of a color-blind racial policy.[53] Such an approach reduced race to ethnicity, and almost entirely neglected the continuing organization of social inequality and oppression along racial lines. Worse yet, it tended to rationalize racial injustice as a supposedly natural outcome of group attributes in competition.[54]

The distinct, and contested, meanings of racism which have been advanced over the past three decades have contributed to an overall crisis of meaning for the concept today. Today, the absence of a clear "common sense" understanding of what racism means has become a significant obstacle to efforts aimed at challenging it. Bob Blauner has noted that in classroom discussions of racism, white and non-white students tend to talk past one another. Whites tend to locate racism in color consciousness and find its absence colorblindness. In so doing, they see the affirmation of difference and racial identity among racially defined minority students as racist. Non-white students, by contrast, see racism as a system of power, and correspondingly ague that blacks, for example, cannot be racist because they lack power. Blauner concludes that there are two "languages" of race, one in which members of racial minorities, especially blacks, see the centrality of race in history and everyday experience, and another in which whites see race as "a peripheral, nonessential reality."[55]

Given this crisis of meaning, and in the absence of any "common sense" understanding, does the concept of racism retain any validity? If so, what view of racism should we adopt? Is a more coherent theoretical approach possible? We believe it is.

We employ racial formation theory to reformulate the concept of racism. Our approach recognizes that racism, like race, has changed over time. It is obvious that the attitudes, practices, and institutions of the epochs of slavery, say, or of Jim Crow, no longer exist today. Employing a similar logic, it is reasonable to question whether concepts of racism which developed in the early days of the post–civil rights era, when the limitations of both moderate reform and militant racial radicalism of various types had not yet been encountered, remain adequate to explain circumstances and conflicts a quarter-century later.

Racial formation theory allows us to differentiate between race and racism. The two concepts should not be used interchangeably. We have argued that race has no fixed meaning, but is constructed and transformed sociohistorically through competing political projects, through the necessary and ineluctable link between the structural and cultural dimensions of race in the U.S. This emphasis on projects allows us to refocus our understanding of racism as well, for racism can now be seen as characterizing some, but not all, racial projects.

A racial project can be defined as *racist* if and only if it *creates or reproduces structures of domination based on essentialist*[56]*categories of race.* Such a definition recognizes the importance of locating racism within a fluid and contested history of racially based social structures and discourses. Thus there can be no timeless and absolute standard for what constitutes racism, for social structures change and discourses are subject to rearticulation. Our definition therefore focuses instead on the "work" essentialism does for domination, and the "need" domination displays to essentialize the subordinated.

Further, it is important to distinguish racial awareness from racial essentialism. To attribute merits, allocate values or resources to, and/or represent individuals or groups on the basis of racial identity, should not be considered racist in and of itself. Such projects may in fact be quite benign.

Consider the following examples: first, the statement, "Many Asian Americans are highly entrepreneurial"; second, the organization of an association of, say, black accountants.

The first racial project, in our view, signifies or represents a racial category ("Asian Americans") and locates that representation within the social structure of the contemporary U.S. (in regard to business, class issues, socialization, etc.). The second racial project is organizational or social structural, and therefore must engage in racial signification. Black accountants, the organizers might maintain, have certain common experiences, can offer each other certain support, etc. Neither of these racial projects is essentialist, and neither can fairly be labeled racist. Of course, racial representations may be biased or misinterpret their subjects, just as racially based organizational efforts may be unfair or unjustifiably exclusive. If such were the case, if for instance in our first example the statement in question were "Asian Americans are naturally entrepreneurial," this would by our criterion be racist. Similarly, if the effort to organize black accountants had as its rationale the raiding of clients from white accountants, it would by our criterion be racist as well.

Similarly, to allocate values or resources—let us say, academic scholar-ships—on the basis of racial categories is not racist. Scholarships are awarded on a preferential basis to Rotarians, children of insurance company employees, and residents of the Pittsburgh metropolitan area. Why then should they not also be offered, in particular cases, to Chicanos or Native Americans?

75　　In order to identify a social project as racist, one must in our view demon-strate a link between essentialist representations of race and social structures of domination. Such a link might be revealed in efforts to protect dominant interests, framed in racial terms, from democratizing racial initiatives.[57] But it might also consist of efforts simply to reverse the roles of racially dominant and racially subordinate.[58] There is nothing inherently white about racism.[59]

Obviously a key problem with essentialism is its denial, or flattening, of differences within a particular racially defined group. Members of subordinate racial groups, when faced with racist practices such as exclusion or discrimi-nation, are frequently forced to band together in order to defend their inter-ests (if not, in some instances, their very lives). Such "strategic essentialism" should not, however, be simply equated with the essentialism practiced by dominant groups, nor should it prevent the interrogation of internal group differences.[60]

Without question, any abstract concept of racism is severely put to the test by the untidy world of reality. To illustrate our discussion, we analyze the following examples, chosen from current racial issues because of their com-plexity and the rancorous debates they have engendered:

■ Is the allocation of employment opportunities through programs restricted to racially defined minorities, so-called "preferential treatment" or affirma-tive action policies, racist? Do such policies practice "racism in reverse"? We think not, with certain qualifications. Although such programs neces-sarily employ racial criteria in assessing eligibility, they do not generally essentialize race, because they seek to overcome specific socially and his-torically constructed inequalities.[61] Criteria of effectiveness and feasibility, therefore, must be considered in evaluating such programs. They must bal-ance egalitarian and context-specific objectives, such as academic potential or job-related qualifications. It should be acknowledged that such programs often do have deleterious consequences for whites who are not personally the source of the discriminatory practices the programs seek to overcome. In this case, compensatory measures should be enacted to vitiate the charge of "reverse discrimination."[62]

■ Is all racism the same, or is there a distinction between white and non-white versions of racism? We have little patience with the argument that racism is solely a white problem, or even a "white disease."[63] The idea that non-whites cannot act in a racist manner, since they do not possess "power," is another variant of this formulation.[64]

80　　For many years now, racism has operated in a more complex fashion than this, sometimes taking such forms as self-hatred or self-aggrandizement at the expense of more vulnerable members of racially subordinate groups.[65] Whites can at times be the victims of racism—by other whites or non-whites—as is the case with anti-Jewish and anti-Arab prejudice. Furthermore, unless one is prepared to argue that there has been no transformation of the U.S. racial order over the years, and that racism consequently has remained unchanged—an essentialist position *par excellence*—it is difficult to contend that racially defined minorities have attained no power or influence, especially in recent years.

Having said this, we still do not consider that all racism is the same. This is because of the crucial importance we place in situating various "racisms" within the dominant hegemonic discourse about race. We have little doubt that the rantings of a Louis Farrakhan or Leonard Jeffries—to pick two currently demonized black ideologues—meet the criteria we have set out for judging a discourse to be racist. But if we compare Jeffries, for example, with a white racist such as Tom Metzger of the White Aryan Resistance, we find the latter's racial project to be far more menacing than the former's. Metzger's views are far more easily associated with an essentializing (and once very powerful) legacy: that of white supremacy and racial dictatorship in the U.S., and fascism in the world at large. Jeffries's project has far fewer examples with which to associate: no more than some ancient African empires and the (usually far less bigoted) phase of the black power movement.[66] Thus black supremacy may be an instance of racism, just as its advocacy may be offensive, but it can hardly constitute the threat that white supremacy has represented in the U.S., nor can it be so easily absorbed and rearticulated in the dominant hegemonic discourse on race as white supremacy can. All racisms, all racist political projects, are not the same.

■ Is the redrawing—or gerrymandering—of adjacent electoral districts to incorporate large numbers of racially defined minority voters in one, and largely white voters in the other, racist? Do such policies amount to "segregation" of the electorate? Certainly this alternative is preferable to the pre–Voting Rights Act practice of simply denying racial minorities the franchise. But does it achieve the Act's purpose of fostering electoral equality across and within racial lines? In our view such practices, in which the post–1990 redistricting process engaged rather widely—are vulnerable to charges of essentialism. They often operate through "racial lumping," tend to freeze rather than overcome racial inequalities, and frequently subvert or defuse political processes through which racially defined groups could otherwise negotiate their differences and interests. They worsen rather than ameliorate the denial of effective representation to those whom they could not effectively redistrict—since no redrawing of electoral boundaries is perfect, those who get stuck on the "wrong side" of the line are particularly disempowered. Thus we think such policies merit the designation of "tokenism"—a relatively mild form of racism—which they have received.[67]

Parallel to the debates on the concept of race, recent academic and political controversies about the nature of racism have centered on whether it is primarily an ideological or structural phenomenon. Proponents of the former position argue that racism is first and foremost a matter of beliefs and attitudes, doctrines and discourse, which only then give rise to unequal and unjust practices and structures.[68] Advocates of the latter view see racism as primarily a matter of economic stratification, residential segregation, and other institutionalized forms of inequality which then give rise to ideologies of privilege.[69]

From the standpoint of racial formation, these debates are fundamentally misguided. They frame the problem of racism in a rigid "either-or" manner. We believe it is crucial to disrupt the fixity of these positions by simultaneously arguing that ideological beliefs have structural consequences, and that social structures give rise to beliefs. Racial ideology and social structure, therefore, mutually shape the nature of racism in a complex, dialectical, and overdetermined manner.

85 Even those racist projects which at first glance appear chiefly ideological turn out upon closer examination to have significant institutional and social structural dimensions. For example, what we have called "far right" projects appear at first glance to be centrally ideological. They are rooted in biologistic doctrine, after all. The same seems to hold for certain conservative black nationalist projects which have deep commitments to biologism.[70] But the unending stream of racist assaults initiated by the far right, the apparently increasing presence of skinheads in high schools, the proliferation of neo-Nazi computer bulletin boards, and the appearance of racist talk shows on cable access channels, all suggest that the organizational manifestations of the far right racial projects exist and will endure.[71] Perhaps less threatening but still quite worrisome is the diffusion of doctrines of black superiority through some (though by no means all) university-based African American Studies departments and student organizations, surely a serious institutional or structural development.

By contrast, even those racisms which at first glance appear to be chiefly structural upon closer examination reveal a deeply ideological component. For example, since the racial right abandoned its explicit advocacy of segregation, it has not seemed to uphold—in the main—an ideologically racist project, but more primarily a structurally racist one. Yet this very transformation required tremendous efforts of ideological production. It demanded the rearticulation of civil rights doctrines of equality in suitably conservative form, and indeed the defense of continuing large-scale racial inequality as an outcome preferable to (what its advocates have seen as) the threat to democracy that affirmative action, busing, and large-scale "race-specific" social spending would entail.[72] Even more tellingly, this project took shape through a deeply manipulative coding of subtextual appeals to white racism, notably in a series of political campaigns for high office which have occurred over recent decades. The retreat of social policy from any practical commitment to racial justice, and the relentless reproduction and divulgation of this theme at the level of everyday life—where whites are now "fed up" with all the "special treatment" received by non-whites, etc.—constitutes the hegemonic racial project at this time. It therefore exhibits an unabashed structural racism all the more brazen because on the ideological or signification level, it adheres to a principle of "treating everyone alike."

In summary, the racism of today is no longer a virtual monolith, as was the racism of yore. Today, racial hegemony is "messy." The complexity of the present situation is the product of a vast historical legacy of structural inequality and invidious racial representation, which has been confronted during the post–World War II period with an opposition more serious and effective than any it had faced before. The result is a deeply ambiguous and contradictory spectrum of racial projects, unremittingly conflictual racial politics, and confused and ambivalent racial identities of all sorts.

NOTES

1. *San Francisco Chronicle,* 14 September 1982, 19 May 1983. Ironically, the 1970 Louisiana law was enacted to supersede an old Jim Crow statute which relied on the idea of "common report" in determining an infant's race. Following Phipps' unsuccessful attempt to change her classification and have the law declared unconstitutional, a legislative effort arose which culminated in the repeal of the law. See *San Francisco Chronicle,* 23 June 1983.
2. Compare the Phipps case to Andrew Hacker's well-known "parable" in which a white person is informed by a mysterious official that "the organization he represents has made a mistake" and that ". . . [a]ccording to their records . . . , you were to have been born black: to another set of parents, far from where you were raised." How much compensation, Hacker's official asks, would "you" require to undo the damage of this unfortunate error? See Hacker, *Two Nations: Black and White, Separate, Hostile, Unequal* (New York: Charles Scribner's Sons, 1992), pp. 31–32.
3. On the evolution of Louisiana's racial classification system, see Virginia Dominguez, *White By Definition: Social Classification in Creole Louisiana* (New Brunswick: Rutgers University Press, 1986).
4. This is not to suggest that gender is a biological category while race is not. Gender, like race, is a social construct. However, the biological division of humans into sexes—two at least, and possibly intermediate ones as well—is not in dispute. This provides a basis for argument over gender divisions—how "natural," etc.—which does not exist with regard to race. To ground an argument for the "natural" existence of race, one must resort to philosophical anthropology.
5. "The truth is that there are no races, there is nothing in the world that can do all we ask race to do for us. . . . The evil that is done is done by the concept, and by easy—yet impossible—assumptions as to its application." (Kwame Anthony Appiah, *In My Father's House: Africa in the Philosophy of Culture* [New York: Oxford University Press, 1992].) Appiah's eloquent and learned book fails, in our view, to dispense with the race concept, despite its anguished attempt to do so; this indeed is the source of its

author's anguish. We agree with him as to the non-objective character of race, but fail to see how this recognition justifies its abandonment. This argument is developed below.

6. We understand essentialism as *belief in real, true human, essences, existing outside or impervious to social and historical context*. We draw this definition, with some small modifications, from Diana Fuss, *Essentially Speaking: Feminism, Nature, & Difference* (New York: Routledge, 1989), p. xi.

7. Michael Omi and Howard Winant, "On the Theoretical Status of the Concept of Race," in Warren Crichlow and Cameron McCarthy, eds., *Race, Identity, and Representation in Education* (New York: Routledge, 1993).

8. Charles Murray, *Losing Ground: American Social Policy, 1950–1980* (New York: Basic Books, 1984), p. 223.

9. Justice Thurgood Marshall, dissenting in *City of Richmond v. J. A. Croson Co.*, 488 U.S. 469 (1989).

10. See, for example, Derrick Bell, "Remembrances of Racism Past: Getting Past the Civil Rights Decline," in Herbert Hill and James E. Jones, Jr., eds., *Race in America: The Struggle for Equality* (Madison: The University of Wisconsin Press, 1993), pp. 75–76; Gertrude Ezorsky, *Racism and Justice: The Case for Affirmative Action* (Ithaca: Cornell University Press, 1991), pp. 109–111; David Kairys, *With Liberty and Justice for Some: A Critique of the Conservative Supreme Court* (New York: The New Press, 1993), pp. 138–41.

11. Howard Winant has developed a tentative "map" of the system of racial hegemony in the U.S. circa 1990, which focuses on the spectrum of racial projects running from the political right to the political left. See Winant, "Where Culture Meets Structure: Race in the 1990s," in idem, *Racial Conditions: Politics, Theory, Comparisons* (Minneapolis: University of Minnesota Press, 1994).

12. A familiar example is use of racial "code words." Recall George Bush's manipulations of racial fear in the 1988 "Willie Horton" ads, or Jesse Helms's use of the coded term "quota" in his 1990 campaign against Harvey Gantt.

13. From this perspective, far right racial projects can also be interpreted as "nationalist." See Ronald Walters, "White Racial Nationalism in the United States," *Without Prejudice*, vol. 1, no. 1 (Fall 1987).

14. To be sure, any effort to divide racial formation patterns according to social structural location—"macro" vs. "micro," for example—is necessarily an analytic device. In the concrete, there is no such dividing line. See Winant, "Where Culture Meets Structure."

15. We are not unaware, for example, that publishing this work is in itself a racial project.

16. Antisemitism only began to be racialized in the 18th century, as George L. Mosse clearly shows in his important *Toward the Final Solution: A History of European Racism* (New York: Howard Fertig, 1978).

17. As Marx put it:

> The discovery of gold and silver in America, the extirpation, enslavement, and entombment in mines of the aboriginal population, the beginning of the conquest and looting of the East Indies, the turning of Africa into a warren for the commercial hunting of blackskins, signalized the rosy dawn of the era of capital-

ist production. These idyllic proceedings are the chief momenta of primitive accumulation. (Karl Marx, *Capital*, vol. I (New York: International Publishers, 1967) p. 751.)

David E. Stannard argues that the wholesale slaughter perpetrated upon the native peoples of the Western hemisphere is unequalled in history, even in our own bloody century. See his *American Holocaust: Columbus and the Conquest of the New World* (New York: Oxford University Press, 1992).

18. Winthrop Jordan provides a detailed account of the sources of European attitudes about color and race in *White Over Black: American Attitudes Toward the Negro, 1550–1812* (New York: Norton, 1977 [1968], pp. 3–43.

19. In a famous instance, a 1550 debate in Valladolid pitted the philosopher and translator of Aristotle, Ginés de Sepúlveda, against the Dominican Bishop of the Mexican state of Chiapas, Bartolomé de Las Casas. Discussing the native peoples, Sepúlveda argued that:

> In wisdom, skill, virtue and humanity, these people are as inferior to the Spaniards as children are to adults and women to men; there is as great a difference between them as there is between savagery and forbearance, between violence and moderation, almost—I am inclined to say, as between monkeys and men (Sepúlveda, *Democrates Alter,* quoted in Tsvetan Todorov, *The Conquest of America: The Question of the Other* (New York: Harper and Row, 1984), p. 153).

In contrast, Las Casas defended the humanity and equality of the native peoples, both in terms of their way of life—which he idealized as one of innocence, gentleness, and generosity—and in terms of their readiness for conversion to Catholicism, which for him as for Sepúlveda was the true and universal religion (Las Casas, "Letter to the Council of the Indies," quoted ibid, p. 163). William E. Connolly interrogates the linkages proposed by Todorov between early Spanish colonialism and contemporary conceptions of identity and difference in *Identity/Difference: Democratic Negotiations of Political Paradox* (Ithaca: Cornell University Press, 1991), pp. 40–48.

20. In Virginia, for example, it took about two decades after the establishment of European colonies to extirpate the indigenous people of the greater vicinity; fifty years after the establishment of the first colonies, the elaboration of slave codes establishing race as *prima facie* evidence for enslaved status was well under way. See Jordan, *White Over Black*.

21. Marx, *Capital,* p. 751.

22. Edward W. Said, *Culture and Imperialism* (New York: Alfred A. Knopf, 1993).

23. David Brion Davis, *The Problem of Slavery in The Age of Revolution* (Ithaca: Cornell University Press, 1975).

24. Quoted in Thomas F. Gossett, *Race: The History of an Idea in America* (New York: Schocken Books, 1965), p. 45.

25. Thomas Jefferson, *Notes on Virginia* [1787], in Merrill D. Peterson, *Writings of Thomas Jefferson* (New York: The Library of America, 1984), pp. 264–66, 270. Thanks to Kimberly Benston for drawing our attention to this passage.

26. Proslavery physician Samuel George Morton (1799–1851) compiled a collection of 800 crania from all parts of the world which formed the sample for his studies of

race. Assuming that the larger the size of the cranium translated into greater intelligence, Morton established a relationship between race and skull capacity. Gossett reports that "In 1849, one of his studies included the following results: the English skulls in his collection proved to be the largest, with an average cranial capacity of 96 cubic inches. The Americans and Germans were rather poor seconds, both with cranial capacities of 90 cubic inches. At the bottom of the list were the Negroes with 83 cubic inches, the Chinese with 82, and the Indians with 79." Gossett, *Race,* p. 74. More recently, Steven Jay Gould has reexamined Morton's data, and shown that his research data were deeply, though unconsciously, manipulated to agree with his "a priori conviction about racial ranking" (Gould, *The Mismeasure of Man* (New York: W. W. Norton, 1981), pp. 50–69).

27. Definitions of race founded upon a common pool of genes have not held up when confronted by scientific research which suggests that the differences *within* a given human population are every bit as great as those *between* populations. See L. L. Cavalli-Sforza, "The Genetics of Human Population," *Scientific American* (September 1974), pp. 81–89.

28. A fascinating summary critique of Gobineau is provided in Tsvetan Todorov, *On Human Diversity: Nationalism, Racism, and Exoticism in French Thought,* trans. Catherine Porter (Cambridge, MA: Harvard University Press, 1993), esp. pp. 129–40.

29. Two recent histories of eugenics are Allen Chase, *The Legacy of Malthus* (New York: Knopf, 1977); Daniel J. Kevles, *In the Name of Eugenics: Genetics and the Uses of Human Heredity* (New York: Knopf, 1985).

30. Arthur Jensen, "How Much Can We Boost IQ and Scholastic Achievement?" *Harvard Educational Review 39* (1969), pp. 1–123.

31. See Weber, *Economy and Society,* vol. I (Berkeley: University of California Press, 1978), pp. 385–87; Ernst Moritz Manasse, "Max Weber on Race," *Social Research,* vol. 14 (1947), pp. 191–221.

32. Du Bois, *The Souls of Black Folk* (New York: Penguin, 1989 [1903]), p. 13. Du Bois himself wrestled heavily with the conflict between a fully sociohistorical conception of race, and the more essentialized and deterministic vision he encountered as a student in Berlin. In "The Conservation of Races" (1897) we can see his first mature effort to resolve this conflict in a vision which combined racial solidarity and a commitment to social equality. See Du Bois, "The Conservation of Races," in Dan S. Green and Edwin D. Driver, eds., *W. E. B. Du Bois On Sociology and the Black Community* (Chicago: University of Chicago Press, 1978), pp. 238–49; Manning Marable, *W. E. B. Du Bois: Black Radical Democrat* (Boston: Twayne, 1986), pp. 35–38. For a contrary, and we believe incorrect reading, see Appiah, *In My Father's House,* pp. 28–46.

33. A good collection of Boas's work is George W. Stocking, ed., *The Shaping of American Anthropology, 1883–1911: A Franz Boas Reader* (Chicago: University of Chicago Press, 1974).

34. Robert E. Park's *Race and Culture* (Glencoe, IL: Free Press, 1950) can still provide insight; see also Stanford H. Lyman, *Militarism, Imperialism, and Racial Accommodation: An Analysis and Interpretation of the Early Writings of Robert E. Park* (Fayetteville: University of Arkansas Press, 1992); Locke's views are concisely expressed in Alain Leroy Locke, *Race Contacts and Interracial Relations,* ed. Jeffrey C. Stewart (Washington, DC: Howard University Press, 1992), originally a series of lectures given at Howard University.

35. Japanese, for example, could not become naturalized citizens until passage of the 1952 McCarran-Walter Act. It took over 160 years, since the passage of the Law of 1790, to allow all "races" to be eligible for naturalization.
36. Especially when we recall that until around 1960, the majority of blacks, the largest racially defined minority group, lived in the South.
37. Toni Morrison, *Playing in the Dark: Whiteness and the Literary Imagination* (Cambridge, MA: Harvard University Press, 1992); Richard Drinnon, *Facing West: The Metaphysics of Indian-Hating and Empire-Building* (Minneapolis: University of Minnesota Press, 1980); Michael Paul Rogin, *Fathers and Children: Andrew Jackson and the Subjugation of the American Indian* (New York: Knopf, 1975).
38. This term refers to the practice, widespread throughout the Americas, whereby runaway slaves formed communities in remote areas, such as swamps, mountains, or forests, often in alliance with dispossessed indigenous peoples.
39. Antonio Gramsci, *Selections from the Prison Notebooks,* edited and translated by Quintin Hoare and Geoffrey Nowell Smith (New York: International Publishers, 1971), p. 182.
40. Anne Showstack Sassoon, *Gramsci's Politics,* 2nd ed. (London: Hutchinson, 1987); Sue Golding, *Gramsci's Democratic Theory: Contributions to Post-Liberal Democracy* (Toronto: University of Toronto Press, 1992).
41. Ralph Ellison, *Shadow and Act* (New York: New American Library, 1966), p. xiv.
42. Chantal Mouffe makes a related argument in "Radical Democracy: Modern or Postmodern?" in Andrew Ross, ed., *Universal Abandon: The Politics of Postmodernism* (Minneapolis: University of Minnesota Press, 1988).
43. Patricia Hill Collins, *Black Feminist Thought: Knowledge, Consciousness, and the Politics of Empowerment* (New York and London: Routledge, 1991).
44. Evelyn Nakano Glenn, "From Servitude to Service Work: Historical Continuities in the Racial Division of Paid Reproductive Labor," *Signs: Journal of Women in Culture & Society,* vol. 18, no. 1 (Autumn 1992).
45. Toni Morrison, ed., *Race-ing Justice, En-gendering Power: Essays on Anita Hill, Clarence Thomas, and the Construction of Social Reality* (New York: Pantheon, 1992).
46. For example, in Magnus Hirschfeld's prescient book, *Racism* (London: Victor Gollancz, 1938).
47. This was the framework, employed in the crucial study of Myrdal and his associates; see Gunnar Myrdal, *An American Dilemma: The Negro Problem and Modern Democracy,* 20th Anniversary Edition (New York: Harper and Row, 1962 [1944]). See also the articles by Thomas F. Pettigrew and George Fredrickson in Pettigrew et al., *Prejudice: Selections from The Harvard Encyclopedia of American Ethnic Groups* (Cambridge, MA: The Belknap Press of Harvard University, 1982).
48. On discrimination, see Frederickson in ibid. In an early essay which explicitly sought to modify the framework of the Myrdal study, Robert K. Merton recognized that prejudice and discrimination need not coincide, and indeed could combine in a variety of ways. See Merton, "Discrimination and the American Creed," in R. M. McIver, ed., *Discrimination and National Welfare* (New York: Harper and Row, 1949).
49. Gordon W. Allport, *The Nature of Prejudice* (Cambridge, MA: Addison-Wesley, 1954) remains a classic work in the field; see also Philomena Essed, *Understanding Everyday Racism: An Interdisciplinary Theory* (Newbury Park, CA: Sage, 1991). A good overview

of black attitudes toward black identities is provided in William E. Cross, Jr., *Shades of Black: Diversity in African-American Identity* (Philadelphia: Temple University Press, 1991).

50. Stokely Carmichael and Charles V. Hamilton first popularized the notion of "institutional" forms of discrimination in *Black Power: The Politics of Liberation in America* (New York: Vintage, 1967), although the basic concept certainly predated that work. Indeed, President Lyndon Johnson made a similar argument in his 1965 speech at Howard University:

> But freedom is not enough. You do not wipe away the scars of centuries by saying: Now you are free to go where you want, do as you desire, and choose the leaders you please.
>
> You do not take a person who, for years, has been hobbled by chains and liberate him (sic), bring him up to the starting line of a race and then say, "You are free to compete with all the others," and still justly believe that you have been completely fair.
>
> Thus it is not enough just to open the gates of opportunity. All our citizens must have the opportunity to walk through those gates.
>
> This is the next and more profound stage of the battle for civil rights. We seek not just freedom but opportunity—not just legal equity but human ability—not just equality as a right but equality as a fact and as a result. (Lyndon B. Johnson, "To Fulfill These Rights," reprinted in Lee Rainwater and William L. Yancey, *The Moynihan Report and the Politics of Controversy* [Cambridge, MA: MIT Press, 1967, p. 125].)

This speech, delivered at Howard University on June 4, 1965, was written in part by Daniel Patrick Moynihan. A more systematic treatment of the institutional racism approach is David T. Wellman, *Portraits of White Racism* (New York: Cambridge University Press, 1977).

51. From the vantage point of the 1990s, it is possible to question whether discrimination was ever effectively outlawed. The federal retreat from the agenda of integration began almost immediately after the passage of civil rights legislation, and has culminated today in a series of Supreme Court decisions making violation of these laws almost impossible to prove. See Ezorsky, *Racism and Justice;* Kairys, *With Liberty and Justice for Some.* As we write, the Supreme Court has further restricted antidiscrimination laws in the case of *St. Mary's Honor Center v. Hicks.* See Linda Greenhouse, "Justices Increase Workers' Burden in Job-Bias Cases," *The New York Times,* 26 June 1993, p. 1.

52. Robert Miles, *Racism* (New York and London: Routledge, 1989), esp. chap. 2.

53. The *locus classicus* of this position is Nathan Glazer, *Affirmative Discrimination: Ethnic Inequality and Public Policy,* 2nd ed. (New York: Basic Books, 1978); for more recent formulations, see Murray, *Losing Ground;* Arthur M. Schlesinger, *The Disuniting of America: Reflections on a Multicultural Society* (New York: W. W. Norton, 1992).

54. Thomas Sowell, for example, has argued that one's "human capital" is to a large extent culturally determined. Therefore the state cannot create a false equality which runs counter to the magnitude and persistence of cultural differences. Such attempts at social engineering are likely to produce negative and unintended results: "If social

processes are transmitting real differences—in productivity, reliability, cleanliness, sobriety, peacefulness [!]—then attempts to impose politically a very different set of beliefs will necessarily backfire. . . ." (Thomas Sowell, *The Economics and Politics of Race: An International Perspective* (New York: Quill, 1983) p. 252).

55. Bob Blauner "Racism, Race, and Ethnicity: Some Reflections on the Language of Race" (unpublished manuscript, 1991).

56. Essentialism, it will be recalled, is understood as belief in real, true human essences, existing outside or impervious to social and historical context.

57. An example would be the "singling out" of members of racially defined minority groups for harsh treatment by authorities, as when police harass and beat randomly chosen ghetto youth, a practice they do not pursue with white suburban youth.

58. For example, the biologistic theories found in Michael Anderson Bradley, *The Iceman Inheritance: Prehistoric Sources of Western Man's Racism, Sexism, and Aggression* (Toronto: Dorset, 1978), and in Frances Cress Welsing, *The Isis (Yssis) Papers* (Chicago: Third World Press, 1991).

59. "These remarks should not be interpreted as simply an effort to move the gaze of African-American studies to a different site. I do not want to alter one hierarchy in order to institute another. It is true that I do not want to encourage those totalizing approaches to African-American scholarship which have no drive other than the exchange of dominations—dominant Eurocentric scholarship replaced by dominant Afrocentric scholarship. More interesting is what makes intellectual domination possible; how knowledge is transformed from invasion and conquest to revelation and choice; what ignites and informs the literary imagination, and what forces help establish the parameters of criticism." (Toni Morrison, *Playing in the Dark,* p. 8; emphasis original.)

60. Lisa Lowe states: "The concept of 'strategic essentialism' suggests that it is possible to utilize specific signifiers of ethnic identity, such as Asian American, for the purpose of contesting and disrupting the discourses that exclude Asian Americans, while simultaneously revealing the internal contradictions and slippages of Asian Americans so as to insure that such essentialisms will not be reproduced and proliferated by the very apparatuses we seek to disempower." Lisa Lowe, "Heterogeneity, Hybridity, Multiplicity: Marking Asian American Differences," *Diaspora,* Vol. 1, no. 1 (Spring 1991) p. 39.

61. This view supports Supreme Court decisions taken in the late 1960s and early 1970s, for example in *Griggs v. Duke Power,* 401 U.S. 424 (1971). We agree with Kairys that only ". . . [F]or that brief period in our history, it could accurately be said that governmental discrimination was prohibited by law" (Kairys, *With Liberty and Justice For Some,* p. 144).

62. This analysis draws on Ezorsky, *Racism and Justice.*

63. See for example, Judy H. Katz, *White Awareness: Handbook for Anti-Racism Training* (Norman: University of Oklahoma Press, 1978).

64. The formula "racism equals prejudice plus power" is frequently invoked by our students to argue that only whites can be racist. We have been able to uncover little written analysis to support this view (apart from Katz, ibid., p. 10), but consider that it is itself an example of the essentializing approach we have identified as central to racism. In the modern world, "power" cannot be reified as a thing which some possess and

others don't, but instead constitutes a relational field. The minority student who boldly asserts in class that minorities cannot be racist is surely not entirely powerless. In all but the most absolutist of regimes, resistance to rule itself implies power.

65. To pick but one example among many: writing before the successes of the civil rights movement, E. Franklin Frazier bitterly castigated the collaboration of black elites with white supremacy. See Frazier, *Black Bourgeoisie: The Rise of a New Middle Class in the United States* (New York: The Free Press, 1957).

66. Interestingly, what they share most centrally seems to be their anti-Semitism.

67. Having made a similar argument, Lani Guinier, Clinton's nominee to head the Justice Department's Civil Rights Division was savagely attacked and her nomination ultimately blocked. See Guinier, "The Triumph of Tokenism: The Voting Rights Act and the Theory of Black Electoral Success," *Michigan Law Review* (March 1991).

68. See Miles, *Racism,* p. 77. Much of the current debate over the advisability and legality of banning racist hate speech seems to us to adopt the dubious position that racism is primarily an ideological phenomenon. See Mari J. Matsuda et al., *Words That Wound: Critical Race Theory, Assaultive Speech, and the First Amendment* (Boulder, CO: Westview Press, 1993).

69. Or ideologies which mask privilege by falsely claiming that inequality and injustice have been eliminated. See Wellman, *Portraits of White Racism.*

70. Racial teachings of the Nation of Islam, for example, maintain that whites are the product of a failed experiment by a mad scientist.

71. Elinor Langer, "The American Neo-Nazi Movement Today," *The Nation,* July 16/23, 1990.

72. Such arguments can be found in Nathan Glazer, *Affirmative Discrimination,* Charles Murray, *Losing Ground,* and Arthur M. Schlesinger, Jr., *The Disuniting of America,* among others.

3

Oppression Axis Two: Sexism

■ ■ ■

TOWARDS A DEFINITION OF PATRIARCHY

Heidi Hartmann

We can usefully define patriarchy as a set of social relations between men, which have a material base, and which, though hierarchical, establish or create interdependence and solidarity among men that enable them to dominate women. Though patriarchy is hierarchical and men of different classes, races, or ethnic groups have different places in the patriarchy, they also are united in their shared relationship of dominance over their women; they are dependent on each other to maintain that domination. Hierarchies "work" at least in part because they create vested interests in the status quo. Those at the higher levels can "buy off" those at the lower levels by offering them power over those still lower. In the hierarchy of patriarchy, all men, whatever their rank in the patriarchy, are bought off by being able to control at least some women. There is some evidence to suggest that when patriarchy was first institutionalized in state societies, the ascending rulers literally made men the heads of their families (enforcing their control over their wives and children) in exchange for the men's ceding some of their tribal resources to the new rulers.[1] Men are dependent on one another (despite their hierarchical ordering) to maintain their control over women.

The material base upon which patriarchy rests lies most fundamentally in men's control over women's labor power. Men maintain this control by excluding women from access to some essential productive resources (in capitalist societies, for example, jobs that pay living wages) and by restricting women's sexuality.[2] Monogamous heterosexual marriage is one relatively

143

recent and efficient form that seems to allow men to control both these areas. Controlling women's access to resources and their sexuality, in turn, allows men to control women's labor power, both for the purpose of serving men in many personal and sexual ways and for the purpose of rearing children. The services women render men, and which exonerate men from having to perform many unpleasant tasks (like cleaning toilets) occur outside as well as inside the family setting. Examples outside the family include the harassment of women workers and students by male bosses and professors as well as the common use of secretaries to run personal errands, make coffee, and provide "sexy" surroundings. Rearing children, whether or not the children's labor power is of immediate benefit to their fathers, is nevertheless a crucial task in perpetuating patriarchy as a system. Just as class society must be reproduced by schools, work places, consumption norms, etc., so must patriarchal social relations. In our society children are generally reared by women at home, women socially defined and recognized as inferior to men, while men appear in the domestic picture only rarely. Children raised in this way generally learn their places in the gender hierarchy well. Central to this process, however, are the areas outside the home where patriarchal behaviors are taught and the inferior position of women enforced and reinforced: churches, schools, sports, clubs, unions, armies, factories, offices, health centers, the media, etc.

The material base of patriarchy, then, does not rest solely on childrearing in the family, but on all the social structures that enable men to control women's labor. The aspects of social structures that perpetuate patriarchy are theoretically identifiable, hence separable from their other aspects. Gayle Rubin has increased our ability to identify the patriarchal element of these social structures enormously by identifying "sex/gender systems":

> a "sex/gender system" is the set of arrangements by which a society
> transforms biological sexuality into products of human activity, and
> in which these transformed sexual needs are satisfied.[3]

We are born female and male, biological sexes, but we are created woman and man, socially recognized genders. *How* we are so created is that second aspect of the *mode* of production of which Engels spoke, "the production of human beings themselves, the propagation of the species."

How people propagate the species is socially determined. If, biologically, people are sexually polymorphous, and society were organized in such a way that all forms of sexual expression were equally permissible, reproduction would result only from some sexual encounters, the heterosexual ones. The strict division of labor by sex, a social invention common to all known societies, creates two very separate genders and a need for men and women to get together for economic reasons. It thus helps to direct their sexual needs toward heterosexual fulfillment, and helps to ensure biological reproduction. In more imaginative societies, biological reproduction might be ensured by other techniques, but the division of labor by sex appears to be the universal solution to date. Although it is theoretically possible that a sexual division of labor not imply inequality between the sexes, in most known societies, the socially acceptable division of labor by sex is one which accords lower status to women's work. The sexual division of labor is also the underpinning of sexual subcultures in which men and women experience life differently; it is the material base of male power which is exercised (in our society) not just in doing housework and in securing superior employment, but psychologically as well.

How people meet their sexual needs, how they reproduce, how they inculcate social norms in new generations, how they learn gender, how it feels to be a man or a woman—all occur in the realm Rubin labels the sex/gender system. Rubin emphasizes the influence of kinship (which tells you with whom you can satisfy sexual needs) and the development of gender specific personalities via childrearing and the "oedipal machine." In addition, however, we can use the concept of the sex/gender system to examine all other social institutions for the roles they play in defining and reinforcing gender hierarchies. Rubin notes that theoretically a sex/gender system could be female dominant, male dominant, or egalitarian, but declines to label various known sex/gender systems or to periodize history accordingly. We choose to label our present sex/gender system patriarchy, because it appropriately captures the notion of hierarchy and male dominance which we see as central to the present system.

Economic production (what marxists are used to referring to as *the* mode of production) and the production of people in the sex/gender sphere both determine "the social organization under which the people of a particular historical epoch and a particular country live," according to Engels. The whole of society, then, can be understood by looking at both these types of production and reproduction, people and things.[4] There is no such thing as "pure capitalism," nor does "pure patriarchy" exist, for they must of necessity coexist. What exists is patriarchal capitalism, or patriarchal feudalism, or egalitarian hunting/gathering societies, or matriarchal horticultural societies, or patriarchal horticultural societies, and so on. There appears to be no necessary connection between *changes* in the one aspect of production and changes in the other. A society could undergo transition from capitalism to socialism, for example, and remain patriarchal. Common sense, history, and our experience tell us, however, that these two aspects of production are so closely intertwined, that change in one ordinarily creates movement, tension, or contradiction in the other.

Racial hierarchies can also be understood in this context. Further elaboration may be possible along the lines of defining color/race systems, arenas of social life that take biological color and turn it into a social category, race. Racial hierarchies, like gender hierarchies, are aspects of our social organization, of how people are produced and reproduced. They are not fundamentally ideological; they constitute that second aspect of our mode of production, the production and reproduction of people. It might be most accurate then to refer to our societies not as, for example, simply capitalist, but as patriarchal capitalist white supremacist.

Capitalist development creates the places for a hierarchy of workers, but traditional marxist categories cannot tell us who will fill which places. Gender and racial hierarchies determine who fills the empty places. *Patriarchy is not simply hierarchical organization,* but hierarchy in which *particular* people fill *particular* places. It is in studying patriarchy that we learn why it is women who are dominated and how. While we believe that most known societies have been patriarchal, we do not view patriarchy as a universal, unchanging phenomenon. Rather patriarchy, the set of interrelations among men that allow men to dominate women, has changed in form and intensity over time. It is crucial that the hierarchy among men, and their differential access to patriarchal benefits, be examined. Surely, class, race, nationality, and even marital status and sexual orientation, as well as the obvious age, come into play here. And women of different class, race, national, marital status, or sexual orientation groups are subjected to different degrees of patriarchal power. Women may themselves exercise class, race, or national power, or even patriarchal power (through their family connections) over men lower in the patriarchal hierarchy than their own male kin.

To recapitulate, we define patriarchy as a set of social relations which has a material base and in which there are hierarchical relations between men and solidarity among them which enable them in turn to dominate women. The material base of patriarchy is men's control over women's labor power. That control is maintained by excluding women from access to necessary economically productive resources and by restricting women's sexuality. Men exercise their control in receiving personal service work from women, in not having to do housework or rear children, in having access to women's bodies for sex, and in feeling powerful and being powerful. The crucial elements of patriarchy as we *currently* experience them are: heterosexual marriage (and consequent homophobia), female childrearing and housework, women's economic dependence on men (enforced by arrangements in the labor market), the state, and numerous institutions based on social relations among men—clubs, sports, unions, professions, universities, churches, corporations, and armies. All of these elements need to be examined if we are to understand patriarchal capitalism.

10   Both hierarchy and interdependence among men and the subordination of women are *integral* to the functioning of our society; that is, these relationships are *systemic.* We leave aside the question of the creation of these relations and ask, can we recognize patriarchal relations in capitalist societies? Within capitalist societies we must discover those same bonds between men which both bourgeois and marxist social scientists claim no longer exist or are, at the most, unimportant leftovers. Can we understand how these relations among men are perpetuated in capitalist societies? Can we identify ways in which patriarchy has shaped the course of capitalist development?

NOTES

1. See Viana Muller, "The Formation of the State and the Oppression of Women: Some Theoretical Considerations and a Case Study in England and Wales," *Review of Radical Political Economics,* vol. 9, no. 3 (Fall 1977), pp. 7–21.

2. The particular ways in which men control women's access to important economic resources and restrict their sexuality vary enormously, both from society to society, from subgroup to subgroup, and across time. The examples we use to illustrate patriarchy in this section, however, are drawn primarily from the experience of whites in western capitalist countries. The diversity is shown in *Toward an Anthropology of Women,* ed. Rayna Rapp Reiter (New York: Monthly Review Press, 1975), *Woman, Culture and Society,* ed. Michelle Rosaldo and Louise Lamphere (Stanford, California: Stanford University Press, 1974), and *Females, Males, Families: A Biosocial Approach,* by Liba Leibowitz (North Scituate, Massachusetts: Duxbury Press, 1978). The control of women's sexuality is tightly linked to the place of children. An understanding of the demand (by men and capitalists) for children is crucial to understanding changes in women's subordination.

   Where children are needed for their present or future labor power, women's sexuality will tend to be directed toward reproduction and childrearing. When children are seen as superfluous, women's sexuality for other than reproductive purposes is encouraged, but men will attempt to direct it towards satisfying male needs. The Cosmo girl is a good example of a woman "liberated" from childrearing only to find herself turning all her energies toward attracting and satisfying men. Capitalists can also use female sexuality to their own ends, as the success of Cosmo in advertising consumer products shows.

3. Gayle Rubin, "The Traffic in Women," in *Anthropology of Women,* ed. Reiter, p. 159.

4. Himmelweit and Mohun point out that both aspects of production (people and things) are logically necessary to describe a mode of production because by definition a mode of production must be capable of reproducing itself. Either aspect alone is not self-sufficient. To put it simply the production of things requires people, and the production of people requires things. Marx, though recognizing capitalism's need for people did not concern himself with how they were produced or what the connections between the two aspects of production were. See Himmelweit and Mohun, "Domestic Labour and Capital."

DIFFERENCE AND DOMINANCE: ON SEX DISCRIMINATION

Catharine A. MacKinnon

What is a gender question a question of? What is an inequality question a question of? These two questions underlie applications of the equality principle to issues of gender, but they are seldom explicitly asked. I think it speaks to the way gender has structured thought and perception that mainstream legal and moral theory tacitly gives the same answer to them both: these are questions of sameness and difference. The mainstream doctrine of the law of sex discrimination that results is, in my view, largely responsible for the fact that sex equality law has been so utterly ineffective at getting women what we need and are socially prevented from having on the basis of a condition of birth: a chance at productive lives of reasonable physical security, self-expression, individuation, and minimal respect and dignity. Here I expose the sameness/difference theory of sex equality, briefly show how it dominates sex discrimination law and policy and underlies its discontents, and propose an alternative that might do something.

According to the approach to sex equality that has dominated politics, law, and social perception, equality is an equivalence, not a distinction, and sex is a distinction. The legal mandate of equal treatment—which is both a systemic norm and a specific legal doctrine—becomes a matter of treating likes alike and unlikes unlike; and the sexes are defined as such by their mutual unlikeness. Put another way, gender is socially constructed as difference epistemologically; sex discrimination law bounds gender equality by difference doctrinally. A built-in tension exists between this concept of equality, which presupposes sameness, and this concept of sex, which presupposes difference. Sex equality thus becomes a contradiction in terms, something of an oxymoron, which may suggest why we are having such a difficult time getting it.

Upon further scrutiny, two alternate paths to equality for women emerge within this dominant approach, paths that roughly follow the lines of this tension. The leading one is: be the same as men. This path is termed gender neutrality doctrinally and the single standard philosophically. It is testimony to how substance gets itself up as form in law that this rule is considered formal equality. Because this approach mirrors the ideology of the social world, it is considered abstract, meaning transparent of substance; also for this reason it is considered not only to be *the* standard, but *a* standard at all. It is so far the leading rule that the words "equal to" are code for, equivalent to, the words "the same as"—referent for both unspecified.

To women who want equality yet find that you are different, the doctrine provides an alternate route: be different from men. This equal recognition of difference is termed the special benefit rule or special protection rule legally, the double standard philosophically. It is in rather bad odor. Like pregnancy, which always calls it up, it is something of a doctrinal embarrassment. Considered an exception to true equality and not really a rule of law at all, this is the one place where the law of sex discrimination admits it is recognizing something substantive. Together with the Bona Fide Occupational Qualification (BFOQ), the unique physical characteristic exception under ERA policy, compensatory legislation, and sex-conscious relief in particular litigation, affirmative action is thought to live here.[1]

The philosophy underlying the difference approach is that sex *is* a difference, a division, a distinction, beneath which lies a stratum of human commonality, sameness. The moral thrust of the sameness branch of the doctrine is to make normative rules conform to this empirical reality by granting women access to what men have access to: to the extent that women are no different from men, we deserve what they have. The differences branch, which is generally seen as patronizing but necessary to avoid absurdity, exists to value or compensate women for what we are or have become distinctively as women (by which is meant, unlike men) under existing conditions.

My concern is not with which of these paths to sex equality is preferable in the long run or more appropriate to any particular issue, although most discourse on sex discrimination revolves about these questions as if that were all there is. My point is logically prior: to treat issues of sex equality as issues of sameness and difference *is to take a particular approach*. I call this the difference approach because it is obsessed with the sex difference. The main theme in the fugue is "we're the same, we're the same, we're the same." The counterpoint theme (in a higher register) is "but we're different, but we're different, but we're different." Its underlying story is: on the first day, difference was; on the second day, a division was created upon it; on the third day, irrational instances of dominance arose. Division may be rational or irrational. Dominance either seems or is justified. Difference *is*.

There is a politics to this. Concealed is the substantive way in which man has become the measure of all things. Under the sameness standard, women are measured according to our correspondence with man, our equality judged by our proximity to his measure. Under the difference standard, we are measured according to our lack of correspondence with him, our womanhood judged by our distance from his measure. Gender neutrality is thus simply the male standard, and the special protection rule is simply the female standard, but do not be deceived: masculinity, or maleness, is the referent for both. Think about it like those anatomy models in medical school. A male body is the human body; all those extra things women have are studied in ob/gyn. It truly is a situation in which more is less. Approaching sex discrimination in this way—as if sex questions are difference questions and equality questions are sameness questions—provides two ways for the law to hold women to a male standard and call that sex equality.

Having been very hard on the difference answer to sex equality questions, I should say that it takes up a very important problem: how to get women access to everything we have been excluded from, while also valuing everything that women are or have been allowed to become or have developed as a consequence of our struggle either not to be excluded from most of life's pursuits or to be taken seriously under the terms that have been permitted to be our terms. It negotiates what we have managed in relation to men. Legally articulated as the need to conform normative standards to existing reality, the strongest doctrinal expression of its sameness idea would prohibit taking gender into account in any way.

    Its guiding impulse is: we're as good as you. Anything you can do, we can do. Just get out of the way. I have to confess a sincere affection for this approach. It has gotten women some access to employment[2] and education,[3] the public pursuits, including academic,[4] professional,[5] and blue-collar work;[6] the military;[7] and more than nominal access to athletics.[8] It has moved to change the dead ends that were all we were seen as good for and has altered what passed for women's lack of physical training, which was really serious training in passivity and enforced weakness. It makes you want to cry sometimes to know that it has had to be a mission for many women just to be permitted to do the work of this society, to have the dignity of doing jobs a lot of other people don't even want to do.

10   The issue of including women in the military draft[9] has presented the sameness answer to the sex equality question in all its simple dignity and complex equivocality. As a citizen, I should have to risk being killed just like you. The consequences of my resistance to this risk should count like yours. The undercurrent is: what's the matter, don't you want me to learn to kill . . . just like you? Sometimes I see this as a dialogue between women in the afterlife. The feminist says to the soldier, "we fought for your equality." The soldier says to the feminist, "oh, no, *we* fought for *your* equality."

    Feminists have this nasty habit of counting bodies and refusing not to notice their gender. As applied, the sameness standard has mostly gotten men the benefit of those few things women have historically had—for all the good they did us. Almost every sex discrimination case that has been won at the Supreme Court level has been brought by a man.[10] Under the rule of gender neutrality, the law of custody and divorce has been transformed, giving men an equal chance at custody of children and at alimony.[11] Men often look like better "parents" under gender-neutral rules like level of income and presence of nuclear family, because men make more money and (as they say) initiate the building of family units.[12] In effect, they get preferred because society advantages them before they get into court, and law is prohibited from taking that preference into account because that would mean taking gender into account. The group realities that make women more in need of alimony are not permitted to matter, because only individual factors, gender-neutrally considered, may matter. So the fact that women will live their lives, as individuals, as members of the group women, with women's chances in a sex-discriminatory society, may not count, or else it is sex discrimination. The equality principle in this guise mobilizes the idea that the way to get things for women is to get them for men. Men have gotten them. Have women? We still have not got equal pay,[13] or equal work,[14] far less equal pay for equal work,[15] and we are close to losing separate enclaves like women's schools through this approach.[16]

Here is why. In reality, which this approach is not long on because it is liberal idealism talking to itself, virtually every quality that distinguishes men from women is already affirmatively compensated in this society. Men's physiology defines most sports,[17] their needs define auto and health insurance coverage, their socially designed biographies define workplace expectations and successful career patterns, their perspectives and concerns define quality in scholarship, their experiences and obsessions define merit, their objectification of life defines art, their military service defines citizenship, their presence defines family, their inability to get along with each other—their wars and rulerships—defines history, their image defines god, and their genitals define sex. For each of their differences from women, what amounts to an affirmative action plan is in effect, otherwise known as the structure and values of American society. But whenever women are, by this standard, "different" from men and insist on not having it held against us, whenever a difference is used to keep us second class and we refuse to smile about it, equality law has a paradigm trauma and it's crisis time for the doctrine.

What this doctrine has apparently meant by sex inequality is not what happens to us. The law of sex discrimination that has resulted seems to be looking only for those ways women are kept down that have *not* wrapped themselves up as a difference—whether original, imposed, or imagined. Start with original: what to do about the fact that women actually have an ability men still lack, gestating children in utero. Pregnancy therefore is a difference. Difference doctrine says it is sex discrimination to give women what we need, because only women need it. It is not sex discrimination not to give women what we need because then only women will not get what we need.[18] Move into imposed: what to do about the fact that most women are segregated into low-paying jobs where there are no men. Suspecting that the structure of the marketplace will be entirely subverted if comparable worth is put into effect, difference doctrine says that because there is no man to set a standard from which women's treatment is a deviation, there is no sex discrimination here, only sex difference. Never mind that there is no man to compare with because no man would do that job if he had a choice, and of course he has because he is a man, so he won't.[19]

Now move into the so-called subtle reaches of the imposed category, the de facto area. Most jobs in fact require that the person, gender neutral, who is qualified for them will be someone who is not the primary caretaker of a preschool child.[20] Pointing out that this raises a concern of sex in a society in which women are expected to care for the children is taken as day one of taking gender into account in the structuring of jobs. To do that would violate the rule against not noticing situated differences based on gender, so it never emerges that day one of taking gender into account was the day the job was structured with the expectation that its occupant would have no child care responsibilities. Imaginary sex differences—such as between male and female applicants to administer estates or between males aging and dying and females aging and dying[21]—I will concede, the doctrine can handle.

15   I will also concede that there are many differences between women and men. I mean, can you imagine elevating one half of a population and denigrating the other half and producing a population in which everyone is the same? What the sameness standard fails to notice is that men's differences from women are equal to women's differences from men. There is an *equality* there. Yet the sexes are not socially equal. The difference approach misses the fact that hierarchy of power produces real as well as fantasied differences, differences that are also inequalities. What is missing in the difference approach is what Aristotle missed in his empiricist notion that equality means treating likes alike and unlikes unlike, and nobody has questioned it since. Why should you have to be the same as a man to get what a man gets simply because he is one? Why does maleness provide an original entitlement, not questioned on the basis of *its* gender, so that it is women—women who want to make a case of unequal treatment in a world men have made in their image (this is really the part Aristotle missed)—who have to show in effect that they are men in every relevant respect, unfortunately mistaken for women on the basis of an accident of birth?

The women that gender neutrality benefits, and there are some, show the suppositions of this approach in highest relief. They are mostly women who have been able to construct a biography that somewhat approximates the male norm, at least on paper. They are the qualified, the least of sex discrimination's victims. When they are denied a man's chance, it looks the most like sex bias. The more unequal society gets, the fewer such women are permitted to exist. Therefore, the more unequal society gets, the *less* likely the difference doctrine is to be able to do anything about it, because unequal power creates both the appearance and the reality of sex differences along the same lines as it creates its sex inequalities.

The special benefits side of the difference approach has not compensated for the differential of being second class. The special benefits rule is the only place in mainstream equality doctrine where you get to identify as a woman and not have that mean giving up all claim to equal treatment—but it comes close. Under its double standard, women who stand to inherit something when their husbands die have gotten the exclusion of a small percentage of the inheritance tax, to the tune of Justice Douglas waxing eloquent about the difficulties of all women's economic situation.[22] If we're going to be stigmatized as different, it would be nice if the compensation would fit the disparity. Women have also gotten three more years than men get before we have to be advanced or kicked out of the military hierarchy, as compensation for being precluded from combat, the usual way to advance.[23] Women have also gotten excluded from contact jobs in male-only prisons because we might get raped, the Court taking the viewpoint of the reasonable rapist on women's employment opportunities.[24] We also get protected out of jobs because of our fertility. The reason is that the job has health hazards, and somebody who might be a real person some day and therefore could sue—that is, a fetus—might be hurt if women, who apparently are not real persons and therefore can't sue either for the hazard to our health or for the lost employment opportunity, are given jobs that subject our bodies to possible harm.[25] Excluding women is always an option if equality feels in tension with the pursuit itself. They never seem to think of excluding men. Take combat.[26] Somehow it takes the glory out of the foxhole, the buddiness out of the trenches, to imagine us out there. You get the feeling they might rather end the draft, they might even rather not fight wars at all than have to do it with us.

The double standard of these rules doesn't give women the dignity of the single standard; it also does not (as the differences standard does) suppress the gender of its referent, which is, of course, the female gender. I must also confess some affection for this standard. The work of Carol Gilligan on gender differences in moral reasoning[27] gives it a lot of dignity, more than it has ever had, more, frankly, than I thought it ever could have. But she achieves for moral reasoning what the special protection rule achieves in law: the affirmative rather than the negative valuation of that which has accurately distinguished women from men, by making it seem as though those attributes, with their consequences, really are somehow ours, rather than what male supremacy has attributed to us for its own use. For women to affirm difference, when difference means dominance, as it does with gender, means to affirm the qualities and characteristics of powerlessness.

Women have done good things, and it is a good thing to affirm them. I think quilts are art. I think women have a history. I think we create culture. I also know that we have not only been excluded from making what has been considered art; our artifacts have been excluded from setting the standards by which art is art. Women have a history all right, but it is a history both of what was and of what was not allowed to be. So I am critical of affirming what we have been, which necessarily is what we have been permitted, as if it is women's, ours, possessive. As if equality, in spite of everything, already ineluctably exists.

I am getting hard on this and am about to get harder on it. I do not think that the way women reason morally is morality "in a different voice."[28] I think it is morality in a higher register, in the feminine voice. Women value care because men have valued us according to the care we give them, and we could probably use some. Women think in relational terms because our existence is defined in relation to men. Further, when you are powerless, you don't just speak differently. A lot, you don't speak. Your speech is not just differently articulated, it is silenced. Eliminated, gone. You aren't just deprived

20

of a language with which to articulate your distinctiveness, although you are; you are deprived of a life out of which articulation might come. Not being heard is not just a function of lack of recognition, not just that no one knows how to listen to you, although it is that; it is also silence of the deep kind, the silence of being prevented from having anything to say. Sometimes it is permanent. All I am saying is that the damage of sexism is real, and reifying that into differences is an insult to our possibilities.

So long as these issues are framed this way, demands for equality will always appear to be asking to have it both ways: the same when we are the same, different when we are different. But this is the way men have it: equal and different too. They have it the same as women when they are the same and want it, and different from women when they are different and want to be, which usually they do. Equal and different too would only be parity.[29] But under male supremacy, while being told we get it both ways, both the specialness of the pedestal and an even chance at the race, the ability to be a woman and a person, too, few women get much benefit of either.

There is an alternative approach, one that threads its way through existing law and expresses, I think, the reason equality law exists in the first place. It provides a second answer, a dissident answer in law and philosophy, to both the equality question and the gender question. In this approach, an equality question is a question of the distribution of power. Gender is also a question of power, specifically of male supremacy and female subordination. The question of equality, from the standpoint of what it is going to take to get it, is at root a question of hierarchy, which—as power succeeds in constructing social perception and social reality—derivatively becomes a categorical distinction, a difference. Here, on the first day that matters, dominance was achieved, probably by force. By the second day, division along the same lines had to be relatively firmly in place. On the third day, if not sooner, differences were demarcated, together with social systems to exaggerate them in perception and in fact, *because* the systematically differential delivery of benefits and deprivations required making no mistake about who was who. Comparatively speaking, man has been resting ever since. Gender might not even code as difference, might not mean distinction epistemologically, were it not for its consequences for social power.

I call this the dominance approach, and it is the ground I have been standing on in criticizing mainstream law. The goal of this dissident approach is not to make legal categories trace and trap the way things are. It is not to make rules that fit reality. It is critical of reality. Its task is not to formulate abstract standards that will produce determinate outcomes in particular cases. Its project is more substantive, more jurisprudential than formulaic, which is why it is difficult for the mainstream discourse to dignify it as an approach to doctrine or to imagine it as a rule of law at all. It proposes to expose that which women have had little choice but to be confined to, in order to change it.

The dominance approach centers on the most sex-differential abuses of women as a gender, abuses that sex equality law in its difference garb could not confront. It is based on a reality about which little of a systematic nature was known before 1970, a reality that calls for a new conception of the problem of sex inequality. This new information includes not only the extent and intractability of sex segregation into poverty, which has been known before, but the range of issues termed violence against women, which has not been. It combines women's material desperation, through being relegated to categories of jobs that pay nil, with the massive amount of rape and attempted rape—44 percent of all women—about which virtually nothing is done;[30] the sexual assault of children—38 percent of girls and 10 percent of boys— which is apparently endemic to the patriarchal family;[31] the battery of women that is systematic in one quarter to one third of our homes;[32] prostitution, women's fundamental economic condition, what we do when all else fails, and for many women in this country, all else fails often;[33] and pornography, an industry that traffics in female flesh, making sex inequality into sex to the tune of eight billion dollars a year in profits largely to organized crime.[34]

These experiences have been silenced out of the difference definition of sex equality largely because they happen almost exclusively to women. Understand: for this reason, they are considered *not* to raise sex equality issues. Because this treatment is done almost uniquely to women, it is implicitly treated as a difference, the sex difference, when in fact it is the socially situated subjection of women. The whole point of women's social relegation to inferiority as a gender is that for the most part these things aren't done to men. Men are not paid half of what women are paid for doing the same work on the basis of their equal difference. Everything they touch does not turn valueless because they touched it. When they are hit, a person has been assaulted. When they are sexually violated, it is not simply tolerated or found entertaining or defended as the necessary structure of the family, the price of civilization, or a constitutional right.

Does this differential describe the sex difference? Maybe so. It does describe the systematic relegation of an entire group of people to a condition of inferiority and attribute it to their nature. If this differential were biological, maybe biological intervention would have to be considered. If it were evolutionary, perhaps men would have to evolve differently. Because I think it is political, I think its politics construct the deep structure of society. Men who do not rape women have nothing wrong with their hormones. Men who are made sick by pornography and do not eroticize their revulsion are not underevolved. This social status in which we can be used and abused and trivialized and humiliated and bought and sold and passed around and patted on the head and put in place and told to smile so that we look as though we're enjoying it all is not what some of us have in mind as sex equality.

This second approach—which is not abstract, which is at odds with socially imposed reality and therefore does not look like a standard according to the standard for standards—became the implicit model for racial justice applied by the courts during the sixties. It has since eroded with the erosion of judicial commitment to racial equality. It was based on the realization that the condition of Blacks in particular was not fundamentally a matter of rational or irrational differentiation on the basis of race but was fundamentally a matter of white supremacy, under which racial differences became invidious as a consequence.[35] To consider gender in this way, observe again that men are as different from women as women are from men, but socially the sexes are not equally powerful. To be on the top of a hierarchy is certainly different from being on the bottom, but that is an obfuscatingly neutralized way of putting it, as a hierarchy is a great deal more than that. If gender were merely a question of difference, sex inequality would be a problem of mere sexism, of mistaken differentiation, of inaccurate categorization of individuals. This is what the difference approach thinks it is and is therefore sensitive to. But if gender is an inequality first, constructed as a socially relevant differentiation in order to keep that inequality in place, then sex inequality questions are questions of systematic dominance, of male supremacy, which is not at all abstract and is anything but a mistake.

If differentiation into classifications, in itself, is discrimination, as it is in difference doctrine, the use of law to change group-based social inequalities becomes problematic, even contradictory. This is because the group whose situation is to be changed must necessarily be legally identified and delineated, yet to do so is considered in fundamental tension with the guarantee against legally sanctioned inequality. If differentiation is discrimination, affirmative action, and any legal change in social inequality, is discrimination— but the existing social differentiations which constitute the inequality are not? This is only to say that, in the view that equates differentiation with discrimination, changing an unequal status quo is discrimination, but allowing it to exist is not.

Looking at the difference approach and the dominance approach from each other's point of view clarifies some otherwise confusing tensions in sex equality debates. From the point of view of the dominance approach, it becomes clear that the difference approach adopts the point of view of male supremacy on the status of the sexes. Simply by treating the status quo as "the standard," it invisibly and uncritically accepts the arrangements under male supremacy. In this sense, the difference approach is masculinist, although it can be expressed in a female voice. The dominance approach, in that it sees the inequalities of the social world from the standpoint of the subordination of women to men, is feminist.

30   If you look through the lens of the difference approach at the world as the dominance approach imagines it—that is, if you try to see real inequality through a lens that has difficulty seeing an inequality as an inequality if it also appears as a difference—you see demands for change in the distribution of power as demands for special protection. This is because the only tools that the difference paradigm offers to comprehend disparity equate the recognition of a gender line with an admission of lack of entitlement to equality

under law. Since equality questions are primarily confronted in this approach as matters of empirical fit[36]—that is, as matters of accurately shaping legal rules (implicitly modeled on the standard men set) to the way the world is (also implicitly modeled on the standard men set)—any existing differences must be negated to merit equal treatment. For ethnicity as well as for gender, it is basic to mainstream discrimination doctrine to preclude any true diversity among equals or true equality within diversity.

To the difference approach, it further follows that any attempt to change the way the world actually is looks like a moral question requiring a separate judgment of how things ought to be. This approach imagines asking the following disinterested question that can be answered neutrally as to groups: against the weight of empirical difference, should we treat some as the equals of others, even when they may not be entitled to it because they are not up to standard? Because this construction of the problem is part of what the dominance approach unmasks, it does not arise with the dominance approach, which therefore does not see its own foundations as moral. If sex inequalities are approached as matters of imposed status, which are in need of change if a legal mandate of equality means anything at all, the question whether women should be treated unequally means simply whether women should be treated as less. When it is exposed as a naked power question, there is no separable question of what ought to be. The only real question is what is and is not a gender question. Once no amount of difference justifies treating women as subhuman, eliminating that is what equality law is for. In this shift of paradigms, equality propositions become no longer propositions of good and evil, but of power and powerlessness, no more disinterested in their origins or neutral in their arrival at conclusions than are the problems they address.

There came a time in Black people's movement for equality in this country when slavery stopped being a question of how it could be justified and became a question of how it could be ended. Racial disparities surely existed, or racism would have been harmless, but at that point—a point not yet reached for issues of sex—no amount of group difference mattered anymore. This is the same point at which a group's characteristics, including empirical attributes, become constitutive of the fully human, rather than being defined as exceptions to or as distinct from the fully human. To one-sidedly measure one group's differences against a standard set by the other incarnates partial standards. The moment when one's particular qualities become part of the standard by which humanity is measured is a millenial moment.

To summarize the argument: seeing sex equality questions as matters of reasonable or unreasonable classification is part of the way male dominance is expressed in law. If you follow my shift in perspective from gender as difference to gender as dominance, gender changes from a distinction that is presumptively valid to a detriment that is presumptively suspect. The difference approach tries to map reality; the dominance approach tries to challenge and change it. In the dominance approach, sex discrimination stops being a question of morality and starts being a question of politics.

You can tell if sameness is your standard for equality if my critique of hierarchy looks like a request for special protection in disguise. It's not. It envisions a change that would make possible a simple equal chance for the first time. To define the reality of sex as difference and the warrant of equality as sameness is wrong on both counts. Sex, in nature, is not a bipolarity; it is a continuum. In society it is made into a bipolarity. Once this is done, to require that one be the same as those who set the standard—those which one is already socially defined as different from—simply means that sex equality is conceptually designed never to be achieved. Those who most need equal treatment will be the least similar, socially, to those whose situation sets the standard as against which one's entitlement to be equally treated is measured. Doctrinally speaking, the deepest problems of sex inequality will not find women "similarly situated"[37] to men. Far less will practices of sex inequality require that acts be intentionally discriminatory.[38] All that is required is that the status quo be maintained. As a strategy for maintaining social power first structure reality unequally, then require that entitlement to alter it be grounded on a lack of distinction in situation; first structure perception so that different equals inferior, then require that discrimination be activated by evil minds who *know* they are treating equals as less.

35   I say, give women equal power in social life. Let what we say matter, then we will discourse on questions of morality. Take your foot off our necks, then we will hear in what tongue women speak. So long as sex equality is limited by sex difference, whether you like it or don't like it, whether you value it or seek to negate it, whether you stake it out as a grounds for feminism or occupy it as the terrain of misogyny, women will be born, degraded, and die. We would settle for that equal protection of the laws under which one would be born, live, and die, in a country where protection is not a dirty word and equality is not a special privilege.

NOTES

1. The Bona Fide Occupational Qualification (BFOQ) exception to Title VII of the Civil Rights Act of 1964, 42 U.S.C. § 2000 e-(2)(e), permits sex to be a job qualification when it is a valid one. The leading interpretation of the proposed federal Equal Rights Amendment would, pursuing a similar analytic structure, permit a "unique physical characteristic" exception to its otherwise absolute embargo on taking sex into account. Barbara Brown, Thomas I. Emerson, Gail Falk, and Ann E. Freedman, "The Equal Rights Amendment: A Constitutional Basis for Equal Rights for Women," 80 *Yale Law Journal* 893 (1971).
2. Title VII of the Civil Rights Act of 1964, 42 U.S.C. § 2000 e; Phillips v. Martin-Marietta, 400 U.S. 542 (1971). Frontiero v. Richardson, 411 U.S. 484 (1974) is the high-water mark of this approach. *See also* City of Los Angeles v. Manhart, 435 U.S. 702 (1978); Newport News Shipbuilding and Dry Dock Co. v. EEOC, 462 U.S. 669 (1983).

3. Title IX of the Education Amendments of 1972, 20 U.S.C. § 1681; Cannon v. University of Chicago, 441 U.S. 677 (1981); Mississippi University for Women v. Hogan, 458 U.S. 718 (1982); *see also* De La Cruz v. Tormey, 582 F.2d 45 (9th Cir. 1978).

4. My impression is that women appear to lose most academic sex discrimination cases that go to trial, although I know of no systematic or statistical study on the subject. One case that won eventually, elevating the standard of proof in the process, is Sweeney v. Board of Trustees of Keene State College, 439 U.S. 29 (1979). The ruling for the plaintiff was affirmed on remand, 604 F.2d 106 (1st Cir. 1979).

5. Hishon v. King & Spalding, 467 U.S. 69 (1984).

6. *See, e.g.,* Vanguard Justice v. Hughes, 471 F. Supp. 670 (D. Md. 1979); Meyer v. Missouri State Highway Commission, 567 F.2d 804, 891 (8th Cir. 1977); Payne v. Travenol Laboratories Inc., 416 F. Supp. 248 (N.D. Mass. 1976). *See also* Dothard v. Rawlinson, 433 U.S. 321 (1977) (height and weight requirements invalidated for prison guard contact positions because of disparate impact on sex).

7. Frontiero v. Richardson, 411 U.S. 484 (1974); Schlesinger v. Ballard, 419 U.S. 498 (1975).

8. This situation is relatively complex. *See* Gomes v. R.I. Interscholastic League, 469 F. Supp. 659 (D. R.I. 1979); Brenden v. Independent School District, 477 F.2d 1292 (8th Cir. 1973); O'Connor v. Board of Education of School District No. 23, 645 F.2d 578 (7th Cir. 1981); Cape v. Tennessee Secondary School Athletic Association, 424 F. Supp. 732 (E.D. Tenn. 1976), *rev'd,* 563 F.2d 793 (6th Cir. 1977); Yellow Springs Exempted Village School District Board of Education v. Ohio High School Athletic Association, 443 F. Supp. 753 (S.D. Ohio 1978); Aiken v. Lieuallen, 593 P.2d 1243 (Or. App. 1979).

9. Rostker v. Goldberg, 453 U.S. 57 (1981). *See also* Lori S. Kornblum, "Women Warriors in a Men's World: The Combat Exclusion," 2 *Law and Inequality: A Journal of Theory and Practice* 353 (1984).

10. David Cole, "Strategies of Difference: Litigating for Women's Rights in a Man's World," 2 *Law & Inequality: A Journal of Theory and Practice* 34 n.4 (1984) (collecting cases).

11. Devine v. Devine, 398 So. 2d 686 (Ala. Sup. Ct. 1981); Danielson v. Board of Higher Education, 358 F. Supp. 22 (S.D.N.Y. 1972); Weinberger v. Wiesenfeld, 420 U.S. 636 (1975); Stanley v. Illinois, 405 U.S. 645 (1971); Caban v. Mohammed, 441 U.S. 380 (1979); Orr v. Orr, 440 U.S. 268 (1979).

12. Lenore Weitzman, "The Economics of Divorce: Social and Economic Consequences of Property, Alimony and Child Support Awards," 28 *U.C.L.A. Law Review* 1118, 1251 (1982), documents a decline in women's standard of living of 73 percent and in increase in men's of 42 percent within a year after divorce.

13. Equal Pay Act, 29 U.S.C. § 206(d)(1) (1976) guarantees pay equality, as does case law, *but cf.* data on pay gaps, "Introduction," note 2.

14. Examples include Christenson v. State of Iowa, 563 F.2d 353 (8th Cir. 1977); Gerlach v. Michigan Bell Tel. Co., 501 F. Supp. 1300 (E.D. Mich. 1980); Odomes v. Nucare, Inc., 653 F.2d 246 (6th Cir. 1981) (female nurse's aide denied Title VII remedy because her job duties were not substantially similar to those of better-paid male orderly);

Power v. Barry County, Michigan, 539 F. Supp. 721 (W.D. Mich. 1982); Spaulding v. University of Washington, 740 F.2d 686 (9th Cir. 1984).

15. County of Washington v. Gunther, 452 U.S. 161 (1981) permits a comparable worth–type challenge where pay inequality can be proven to be a correlate of intentional job segregation. *See also* Lemons v. City and County of Denver, 17 FEP Cases 910 (D. Colo. 1978), *aff'd*, 620 F.2d 228 (10th Cir. 1977), *cert. denied*, 449 U.S. 888 (1980); AFSCME v. State of Washington, 770 F.2d 1401 (9th Cir. 1985). *See generally* Carol Jean Pint, "Value, Work and Women," 1 *Law & Inequality: A Journal of Theory and Practice* 159 (1983).

16. Combine the result in Bob Jones University v. United States, 461 U.S. 547 (1983), with Mississippi University for Women v. Hogan, 458 U.S. 718 (1982), and the tax-exempt status of women-only schools is clearly threatened.

17. A particularly pungent example comes from a case in which the plaintiff sought to compete in boxing matches with men, since there were no matches sponsored by the defendant among women. A major reason that preventing the woman from competing was found not to violate her equality rights was that the "safety rules and precautions [were] developed, designed, and tested in the context of all-male competition." Lafler v. Athletic Board of Control, 536 F. Supp. 104, 107 (W.D. Mich. 1982). As the court put it: "In this case, the real differences between the male and female anatomy are relevant in considering whether men and women may be treated differently with regard to their participating in boxing. The plaintiff *admits* that she wears a protective covering for her breasts while boxing. Such a protective covering . . . would violate Rule Six, Article 9 of the Amateur Boxing Federation rules currently in effect. The same rule *requires* contestants to wear a protective cup, a rule obviously designed for the unique anatomical characteristics of men." Id. at 106 (emphasis added). The rule is based on the male anatomy, therefore not a justification for the discrimination but an example of it. This is not considered in the opinion, nor does the judge discuss whether women might benefit from genital protection, and men from chest guards, as in some other sports.

18. This is a reference to the issues raised by several recent cases which consider whether states' attempts to compensate pregnancy leaves and to secure jobs on return constitute sex discrimination. California Federal Savings and Loan Assn. v. Guerra, 758 F.2d 390 (9th Cir. 1985), *cert. granted* 54 U.S.L.W. 3460 (U.S. Jan. 13, 1986); *see also* Miller-Wohl v. Commissioner of Labor, 515 F. Supp. 1264 (D. Montana 1981), *vacated and dismissed*, 685 F.2d 1088 (9th Cir. 1982). The position argued in "Difference and Dominance" here suggests that if these benefits are prohibited under Title VII, Title VII is unconstitutional under the equal protection clause.

This argument was not made directly in either case. The American Civil Liberties Union argued that the provisions requiring pregnancy to be compensated in employment, without comparable coverage for men, violated Title VII's prohibition on pregnancy-based classifications and on sex. Montana had made it illegal for an employer to "terminate a woman's employment because of her pregnancy" or to "refuse to grant to the employee a reasonable leave of absence for such pregnancy." Montana Maternity Leave Act § 49-2-310(1) and (2). According to the ACLU, this provision "grants pregnant workers certain employment rights not enjoyed by other workers . . .

Legislation designed to benefit women has . . . perpetuated destructive stereotypes about their proper roles and operated to deny them rights and benefits enjoyed by men. The [Montana provision] deters employers from hiring women who are or may become pregnant, causes resentment and hostility in the workplace, and penalizes men." Brief of American Civil Liberties Union, et al. *amicus curiae,* Montana Supreme Court No. 84-172, at 7. The National Organization for Women argued that the California provision, which requires employers to give pregnant workers unpaid disability leave with job security for up to four months, would violate Title VII should Title VII be interpreted to permit it. Brief of National Organization for Women, et al., United States Court of Appeals for the Ninth Circuit, 685 F.2d 1088 (9th Cir. 1982).

When Congress passed the Pregnancy Discrimination Act, amending Title VII, 42 U.S. C. § 2000 e(k), it defined "because of sex" or "on the basis of sex" to include "because of or on the basis of pregnancy, childbirth, or related medical conditions; and women affected by pregnancy, childbirth, or related medical conditions shall be treated the same for all employment-related purposes." In so doing, Congress arguably decided that one did not have to be the same as a man to be treated without discrimination, since it guaranteed freedom from discriminatory treatment on the basis of a condition that is not the same for men as it is for women. It even used the word "women" in the statute.

Further, Congress made this decision expressly to overrule the Supreme Court decision in General Electric v. Gilbert, 429 U.S. 125 (1976), which had held that failure to cover pregnancy as a disability was not sex discrimination because the line between pregnant and nonpregnant was not the line between women and men. In rejecting this logic, as the Court found it did expressly in Newport News Shipbuilding and Dry Dock Co. v. EEOC, 462 U.S. 669, 678 (1983), Congress rejected the implicit measuring of women's entitlement to equality by a male standard. Nor need all women be the same, that is, pregnant or potentially so, to have pregnancy-based discrimination be sex-based discrimination.

Upholding the California pregnancy leave and job security law, the Ninth Circuit opinion did not require sameness for equality to be delivered: "The PDA does not require states to ignore pregnancy. It requires that women be treated equally . . . [E]quality under the PDA must be measured in employment opportunity, not necessarily in amounts of money expended—or in amounts of days of disability leave expended. Equality . . . compares coverage to actual need, not coverage to hypothetical identical needs." California Federal v. Guerra, 758 F.2d 390 (9th Cir. 1985) (Ferguson, J.). "We are not the first court to announce the goal of Title VII is equality of employment opportunity, not necessarily sameness of treatment." Id. at 396 n.7.

19. Most women work at jobs mostly women do, and most of those jobs are paid less than jobs that mostly men do. *See, e.g.,* Pint, note 15 above, at 162–63 nn.19, 20 (collecting studies). To the point that men may not meet the male standard themselves, one court found that a union did not fairly represent its women in the following terms: "As to the yard and driver jobs, defendants suggest not only enormous intellectual requirements, but that the physical demands of those jobs are so great as to be beyond the capacity of any female. Again, it is noted that plaintiffs' capacity to perform those jobs was never tested, despite innumerable requests therefor. It is also

noted that defendants have never suggested *which* of the innumerable qualifications they list for these jobs (for the first time) the plaintiffs might fail to meet. The court, however, will accept without listing here the extraordinary catalogue of feats which defendants argue must be performed in the yard, and as a driver. That well may be. However, one learns from this record that one cannot be too weak, too sick, too old and infirm, or too ignorant to perform these jobs, *so long as one is a man.* The plaintiffs appear to the layperson's eye to be far more physically fit than many of the drivers who moved into the yard, over the years, according to the testimony of defense witnesses.... In short, they were all at least as fit as the men with serious physical deficits and disabilities who held yard jobs." Jones v. Cassens Transport, 617 F. Supp. 869, 892 (1985) (emphasis in original).

20. Phillips v. Martin-Marietta, 400 U.S. 542 (1971).
21. Reed v. Reed, 404 U.S. 71 (1971) held that a statute barring women from administering estates is sex discrimination. If few women were taught to read and write, as used to be the case, the gender difference would not be imaginary in this case, yet the social situation would be even more sex discriminatory than it is now. Compare City of Los Angeles v. Manhart, 434 U.S. 815 (1978), which held that requiring women to make larger contributions to their retirement plan was sex discrimination, in spite of the allegedly proven sex difference that women on the average outlive men.
22. Kahn v. Shevin, 416 U.S. 351, 353 (1974).
23. Schlesinger v. Ballard, 419 U.S. 498 (1975).
24. Dothard v. Rawlinson, 433 U.S. 321 (1977); *see also* Michael M. v. Sonoma County Superior Court, 450 U.S. 464 (1981).
25. Doerr v. B.F. Goodrich, 484 F. Supp. 320 (N.D. Ohio 1979). Wendy Webster Williams, "Firing the Woman to Protect the Fetus: The Reconciliation of Fetal Protection with Employment Opportunity Goals Under Title VII," 69 *Georgetown Law Journal* 641 (1981). *See also* Hayes v. Shelby Memorial Hospital, 546 F. Supp. 259 (N.D. Ala. 1982); Wright v. Olin Corp., 697 F.2d 1172 (4th Cir. 1982).
26. Congress requires the Air Force (10 U.S.C. § 8549 [1983]) and the Navy (10 U.S.C. § 6015 [1983]) to exclude women from combat, with some exceptions. Owens v. Brown, 455 F. Supp. 291 (D.D.C. 1978), had previously invalidated the prior Navy combat exclusion because it prohibited women from filling jobs they could perform and inhibited Navy's discretion to assign women on combat ships. The Army excludes women from combat based upon its own policies under congressional authorization to determine assignment (10 U.S.C. § 3012 [e] [1983]).
27. Carol Gilligan, *In a Different Voice* (1982).
28. Ibid.
29. I argued this in Appendix A of my *Sexual Harassment of Working Women: A Case of Sex Discrimination* (1979). That book ends with "Women want to be equal and different, too." I could have added "Men are." As a standard, this would have reduced women's aspirations for equality to some corresponding version of men's actualities. But as an observation, it would have been true.
30. Diana Russell and Nancy Howell, "The Prevalence of Rape in the United States Revisited," 8 *Signs: Journal of Women in Culture and Society* 689 (1983) (44 percent of women in 930 households were victims of rape or attempted rape at some time in their lives).

31. Diana Russell, "The Incidence and Prevalence of Intrafamilial and Extrafamilial Sexual Abuse of Female Children," 7 *Child Abuse & Neglect: The International Journal* 133 (1983).

32. R. Emerson Dobash and Russell Dobash, *Violence against Wives: A Case against the Patriarchy* (1979); Bruno v. Codd, 90 Misc. 2d 1047, 396 N.Y.S. 2d 974 (Sup. Ct. 1977), *rev'd,* 64 A.D. 2d 582, 407 N.Y.S. 2d 165 (1st Dep't 1978), *aff'd* 47 N.Y. 2d 582, 393 N.E. 2d 976, 419 N.Y.S. 2d 901 (1979).

33. Kathleen Barry, *Female Sexual Slavery* (1979); Moira K. Griffin, "Wives, Hookers and the Law: The Case for Decriminalizing Prostitution," 10 *Student Lawyer* 18 (1982); Report of Jean Fernand-Laurent, Special Rapporteur on the Suppression of the Traffic in Persons and the Exploitation of the Prostitution of Others (A United Nations report), in *International Feminism: Networking against Female Sexual Slavery* 130 (Kathleen Barry, Charlotte Bunch, and Shirley Castley eds.) (Report of the Global Feminist Workshop to Organize against Traffic in Women, Rotterdam, Netherlands, Apr. 6–15, 1983 [1984]).

34. Galloway and Thornton, "Crackdown on Pornography—A No-Win Battle," *U.S. News and World Report,* June 4, 1984, at 84. *See also* "The Place of Pornography," *Harper's,* November 1984, at 31 (citing $7 billion per year).

35. Loving v. Virginia, 388 U.S. 1 (1967), first used the term "white supremacy" in invalidating an antimiscegenation law as a violation of equal protection. The law equally forbade whites and Blacks to intermarry. Although going nowhere near as far, courts in the athletics area have sometimes seen that "same" does not necessarily mean "equal" nor does "equal" require "same." In a context of sex inequality like that which has prevailed in athletic opportunity, allowing boys to compete on girls' teams may diminish overall sex equality. "Each position occupied by a male reduces the female participation and increases the overall disparity of athletic opportunity which generally exists." Petrie v. Illinois High School Association, 394 N.E. 2d 855, 865 (Ill. 1979). "We conclude that to furnish exactly the same athletic opportunities to boys as to girls would be most difficult and would be detrimental to the compelling governmental interest of equalizing general athletic opportunities between the sexes." Id.

36. The scholars Tussman and tenBroek first used the term "fit" to characterize the necessary relation between a valid equality rule and the world to which it refers. J. Tussman and J. tenBroek, "The Equal Protection of the Laws," 37 *California Law Review* 341 (1949).

37. Royster Guano Co. v. Virginia, 253 U.S. 412, 415 (1920): "[A classification] must be reasonable, not arbitrary, and must rest upon some ground of difference having a fair and substantial relation to the object of the legislation, so that all persons similarly circumstanced shall be treated alike." Reed v. Reed, 404 U.S. 71, 76 (1971): "Regardless of their sex, persons within any one of the enumerated classes . . . are similarly situated. . . . By providing dissimilar treatment for men and women who are thus similarly situated, the challenged section violates the Equal Protection Clause."

38. Washington v. Davis, 426 U.S. 229 (1976) and Personnel Administrator of Massachusetts v. Feeney, 442 U.S. 256 (1979), require that intentional discrimination be shown for discrimination to be shown.

SEXUAL TERRORISM: THE SOCIAL CONTROL OF WOMEN

Carole J. Sheffield

At a time when the media, the political right, and many of my students, male and female, have proclaimed the end of the women's movement, we must ask some hard, direct questions about the status of women in American society. In an era when women are indeed exercising hard-won options in areas such as employment, childbearing, and politics, they often seem to be limited in simpler choices—whether to go to the movies alone, where to walk or jog, whether to answer the door or telephone. Can we measure the success of a social movement for equality if we do not include an assessment of the quality of life of the affected groups? No aspect of well-being is more fundamental than freedom from personal harm motivated by hatred or fear of one's ascribed characteristics, that is, freedom from ideologically justified violence against one's person. Without such freedom it is impossible to implement other choices. To the extent that women's personal freedom is still restricted and denied, we can continue to speak of oppression.

All systems of oppression employ violence or the threat of violence as an institutionalized mechanism for ensuring compliance. "Inferior" peoples—whether they be blacks in South Africa, peasants in South America, or females in the United States—are kept in place by fear, which is generated by periodic displays of force. Subordination, as described by Dworkin (1985), is a social/political dynamic consisting of hierarchy, objectification, submission, and violence. This [reading] is largely concerned with the last element—violence—as a crucial element in the ongoing process of female subordination.

Sexual terrorism is the system by which males frighten, and by frightening, dominate and control females. It is manifested through actual and implied violence. All females are potential victims—at any age, any time, or any place, and through a variety of means: rape, battery, incest, sexual abuse of children, sexual harassment, prostitution, and sexual slavery. The subordination of women in all other spheres of the society rests on the power of men to intimidate and to punish women sexually.

In this [reading] we will analyze the ways in which male dominance is established and maintained through sexual terrorism, primarily as manifested in our society today. That is, we shall consider terrorism as a crucial strategy in sustaining the power relationships of *patriarchy*, whereby maleness is glorified and femaleness denigrated. As the institutionalized mechanism for the social control of women, sexual terrorism operates at several levels: through (1) the normative dichotomy of good woman/bad woman; (2) the production of fear through expressions of the popular culture—rituals of degradation, music, literature, films, television, advertising, pornography; and (3) providing legitimation and social support for those who act out their contempt for women (e.g., rapists, men who beat "nagging" wives, and so forth).

Thus, while sexual terrorism is the objective condition of female exis- 5 tence—that is, living in fear of bodily harm—it also provides a theoretical framework for examining how patriarchal social orders are created and maintained. The three levels at which sexual terrorism operates—normative, cultural, and social—can be integrated into a broader conceptual model of terrorism in general, in which five basic components have been identified: ideology, propaganda, indiscriminate violence, "voluntary compliance," and perceptions of victim and oppressor characteristics.

IDEOLOGY

Terrorism must be "explicitly rationalized and justified by some philosophy, theory, or ideology—however crude" (Johnson, 1978: 273), and indeed no bomb thrower or world power is without a claim to a "higher principle" or "greater good." In the case of sexual terrorism, the ideological underpinnings of patriarchal power relationships serve as ample justification for violence against women. If maleness is superior to femaleness, then females must be described in terms of some basic flaw, some trait that makes their subordination both necessary and legitimate. Many feminist thinkers (e.g., Tavris and Wade, 1984) have identified this presumed "basic flaw" as female sexuality itself— tempting and seductive, and therefore disruptive; capable of reproducing life itself, and therefore powerful. Out of their own fear, men have sought to bring this threatening force under control by both physical and psychological means.

Although there is still much debate over the original basis for male dominance and the role of sheer physical force in that equation, by the time of full-fledged archaic states the ideological components were well in place. The story of Adam and Eve, along with its counterparts throughout the world, can stand as the basic cautionary tale of the dire consequences of unfettered female sexuality.

Moreover, if maleness becomes the standard of normality, femaleness (whether manifest by females or males) is necessarily abnormal. The definition of female behavior as somehow non-normative, a neat example of the social construction of deviance (Schur, 1984), sets in motion the process of stigmatization, which in turn becomes the rationalization for both gender stratification (patriarchy) and sexual terrorism.

The concept of female "deviance" reflects—indeed, some structuralists would claim that it is the original instance of—a basic division of the world into dichotomous types: female/male, nature/culture, emotion/reason, body/brains, and so forth. Not only is masculinity defined in opposition to femininity, but males are seen as self-reliant, courageous, competent, and rational. In contrast, females must therefore be dependent, sensual, emotional, and evil. If man is the maker of history, the one who does things, woman is "the mediating force between man and nature, a remainder of his childhood, a reminder of the body, and a reminder of sexuality, passion, and human connectedness . . . the repository of emotional life and of all the nonrational elements of human experience" (Lowe and Hubbard, 1983: 12). To the extent that men must not harbor such traits and must distance themselves from femininity, contempt and fear of femaleness are logical concomitants of this dualistic conception of gender.

10   Yet another dichotomy lies *within* the construct of femininity itself: between the "good" woman and the "bad" woman. Somehow, some women are going to have to become "good" enough to serve as marriage partners. Apparently, this is achieved by accepting their limitations, controlling their basically evil nature, and placing themselves under the protection of a man. The "good" woman becomes the wife; or more likely, the wife is compelled to have these attributes as one outcome of the complex historical process whereby women are transformed into private property (Firestone, 1972).

The pressure to achieve "goodness" is a powerful mechanism of social control; one must work constantly to earn the label of "lady," an accolade that can only be bestowed by men (Fox, 1977). Although some women may achieve instant respectability through wealth or lineage, most must strive to acquire and maintain that status. Further, becoming a good woman in order to secure protection from male violence is a rather dubious bargain; the home is hardly a haven from sexual assaults, nor does marriage shield a woman from nonfamily attacks.

The good woman/bad woman dichotomy has particularly troublesome consequences for black women in our society. In general, racism and sexual violence, particularly rape, are part of the same oppressive structure. Historically, U.S. rape laws were enacted to maintain the property rights of white men and to control black men and women. Although it was a capital offense for a black man to rape a white woman, the rape of a black woman (by either a black or a white man) was not considered a crime. According to the racist ideology, the black woman was inherently inferior and could therefore never achieve goodness. Thus, "to assault her and exploit her sexually . . . carried with it none of the normal sanctions against such behavior" (Lerner, 1973: 163).

Hooks (1981: 108) carries the argument one step further, to suggest that black women have had great difficulty forming alliances with men from either group in order to gain protection from the other. Neither the abolition of slavery nor the 120 years of American history since the Civil War have had much effect on the way in which black women are regarded, especially by white men. Their "blackness" continues to define their sexuality. Given the continued pervasiveness of racism in our society, it is reasonable to assume that women of color experience additional humiliation when they encounter the predominantly male judicial system.

In sum, all aspects of male supremacist ideology provide a justification for sexual terrorism as a means of keeping women in their place and thus reinforcing the gender stratification system of patriarchy across time and place. But the effectiveness of ideologies depends on how broadly and thoroughly they are disseminated and on how they are given concreteness.

PROPAGANDA

The second component of terrorism is propaganda—the methodical dissemination of information promoting this ideology. By definition, the information is biased, even false, designed to present one point of view and to discredit all contrary opinion (LaBelle, 1980). "Terrorism must not be defined only in terms of violence, but also in terms of propaganda. . . . Violence of terrorism is a coercive means for attempting to influence the thinking and actions of people. Propaganda is a persuasive means for doing the same thing" (Watson, 1976: 15).

Other [writings] suggest the degree to which patriarchal ideology has shaped what passes for "knowledge" in such diverse realms as anthropology, sociology, psychology, economics, political science, medicine, and the law. These are all areas in which the new feminist scholarship has questioned and corrected many misconceptions (although the public remains largely unaware of this reshaping and restructuring of knowledge).

The avenues of propaganda central to the theme of this [reading] are those of the modern mass media: television, radio, films, music, and advertising. It is not difficult to find telling examples in which the theme of violence toward women dominates. Battered women appear nightly on television (and even the programs presumably devoted to "educating the public" have a high titillation factor). Moviemakers such as Brian DePalma outdo one another in finding ever more gory ways to mutilate female bodies (a recent one being with a power saw). Lyrics for rock music have become offensive enough to elicit an agreement from record companies to provide warning labels. Pictures of women in bondage appear on album covers, in the pages of *Vogue* magazine, and in the windows of Bloomingdale's department store.

But the propaganda of sexual terrorism is most fully embodied in the books and films and paraphernalia exclusively devoted to the sexual degradation of women—pornography. The word itself is derived from the Greek *porne,* referring to the lowest class of sexual slave. Here the line between good and bad women may be erased, as all female bodies and all parts of the body exist for the pleasure of men. To its most severe critics, then, pornography teaches men not only what they can do with/to whores but also what can be done with/to one's wife, lover, or daughter (Barry, 1979; Russell, 1982). This view has received support from recent research on the link between exposure to pornography and subsequent tolerance of violence against women (Donnerstein 1980; Malamuth, 1981).

There is no question that most pornography today articulates a male fantasy world in which women are typically depicted as depraved and insatiable, and therefore appropriate objects for rape, bondage, mutilation, and even murder. But there is a very heated controversy among feminists about the effects of pornography, the distinction between eroticism and pornography, the threat to civil liberties of antiobscenity campaigns, and the dangers of alliances with antifeminists.[1]

20   Pornography, however is more than a sexual—or even legal—issue; it is also about power. Its economic power is immense; it's a multi-billion-dollar industry, involving a network of producers, distributors, retailers, and consumers. Even more important, pornography is about the power of naming, or naming women as body parts and their sexuality as depraved, thus literally "doing the dirty work" in the spread of the ideology of patriarchy.

The ultimate power of pornography is terrorization. Pornography embodies acts of sexual terrorism (rape, battery, incestuous assault, bondage, torture), symbols of sexual terrorism (gun, knife, fist, whip, etc.), and the legend of sexual terrorism (the male as dangerous; Dworkin, 1979). The extreme manifestations of physical violence found in much of contemporary pornography are considered by many people, feminist and antifeminist alike, to pose a threat to the safety of women and girls insofar as these images normalize sexual abuse and raise the level of tolerance for such behavior.

INDISCRIMINATE AND AMORAL VIOLENCE

According to classic theories of political terrorism, an ideology and its spread through propaganda are both necessary *and* sufficient causes of overt violence directed at people who possess a particular ascribed characteristic that legitimates their victimization. As described by Wilkinson (1974: 17), all terrorism involves "indiscriminateness, unpredictability, arbitrariness, ruthless destructiveness and amorality." Sexual terrorism, then, is violence perpetrated on girls and women *simply because they are female,* as when the threat of sexual assault keeps many girls and women in a state of fear, regardless of their actual risks (Warr, 1985).

The element of amorality can be seen in the fact that only rarely do those who commit acts of sexual violence perceive themselves as having done "wrong"—even child molesters and incestuous fathers. Rather, like the rapists studied by Scully and Marolla (1985), they construct a vocabulary of motives and rationales from the surrounding culture that they feel will be acceptable to others. That this vocabulary is often shared by police officers, lawyers, and judges can be seen in the low rate of prosecution of crimes of sexual violence in our society (Polk, 1985). Indeed, the rationalizations may also be shared by an entire community. In the case of the New Bedford, Massachusetts, gang rape, for example, the largely Portuguese community interpreted the prosecution of rapists as an incident of ethic discrimination rather than a response to sexual violence.

Although from the viewpoint of women sexual terrorism could be defined inclusively, public perception will often be based on those acts that fall within the criminal law (keeping in mind that each state defines its own standards of appropriate sexual behavior, and that the federal law may hold to yet another standard). Despite such diversity, there is at least one unifying strand: The laws have been promulgated by male-dominated legislatures and interpreted by a male-dominated judiciary (MacKinnon, 1983; Bart and Schepple, 1980). Changing these laws to take into account women's own definitions of their experience is perhaps the most difficult yet most crucial task for feminist activists in the coming decades.

At the moment, however, the generally recognized acts of sexual violence *25* that have been prohibited by law include the following: rape, wife assault, sexual abuse of children, sexual harassment, and sexual slavery. And each has been defined from a male point of view.

RAPE   The definition of rape, for example, was originally drawn to exclude the possibility of marital sexual assaults on the assumption that a wife's sexual services were part and parcel of the marriage contract (Russell, 1982). That is, the laws were designed precisely to protect a husband's sexual property.

In addition, the description of the forbidden act was based on the traditional model of sexual intercourse (i.e., vaginal-penile penetration), thus obscuring the whole context of violence in which the act takes place. This exclusive focus on the sexual component, then, requires some evidence that the victim was not "willing," in other words, that she resisted. For no other crime is a victim required to prove nonconsent; rape, however, is still viewed largely in terms of women's sexuality rather than men's coercion (Stanko, 1985). Women must prove that they resisted, or consent is presumed. Yet at the same time they are warned of potential bodily harm that their resistance might encourage—a veritable "catch-22": If you fight back you'll get hurt, but if you don't we'll think you welcomed the attack. Yet recent research strongly suggests that women who physically resist are more likely than nonresisters to *avoid* being raped, without necessarily increasing the rapist's level of violence (Bart and O'Brien, 1984).

Redefining rape to include forms of sexual violation other than intercourse would be a first step in directing attention to the inherent violence and degradation of the phenomenon but would not necessarily advance a deeper understanding of the victimization of women. The value of Brownmiller's (1975: 5) claim that rape is a "more or less conscious process of intimidation by which *all* men keep *all* women in a state of fear" is that it draws attention to the power dimension of the act. But power relationships are themselves a function of complex historical/economic processes.

Other social scientists have argued that not all men are potential rapists and not all cultures provide a vocabulary of motives; rather, we should look to the links among socioeconomic inequality, general levels of violence in a society, and variations in gender stratification systems (e.g., Leacock, 1981;

Sanday, 1981; Schwendinger and Schwendinger, 1983). The general finding from these reviews of the anthropological and sociological literature is that rape is part of the entire sociocultural complex in which men lose control over their own destinies and in which violence toward women is a response to powerlessness in other spheres of activity.

30   Yet when looking at contemporary America, Brownmiller's thesis receives qualified support from rape researchers Holmstrom and Burgess (1983: 36), who conclude that while it would have been more accurate to say that "rape is one way in many (but not all) societies that men *as a class* oppress and control women *as a class*," it is a fact that "macho" values are institutionalized in the United States today and that "male-dominated patterns of aggressive behavior and male-dominated institutions oppress and control women" (1983: 36).

WIFE-ASSAULT   Here again in dealing with behavior that takes place within the privacy of the marriage, the law—and public opinion—often reflect the traditional assumptions of appropriate gender roles and power relationships. Yet much has changed over the past two decades as certain types of family violence have been redefined as "social problems," with the result that both public opinion and the law are changing.

As analyzed by Breines and Gordon (1983), these changes in the perception and definition of family violence are the result of a number of societal trends, including the feeling that intrafamily violence is a symptom of a deeper "crisis" in the American family: the notion of child-centered parenthood, which makes the violence toward children less acceptable than in the past; the feminist emphasis on the family as source of oppression and on the translation of the personal into the public; and the growing acceptance of a "confessional mode" in which people are encouraged to "tell all." It would be a mistake, however, to lump all family violence together, as there are very different historical developments in both the incidence and the recognition of each type as a social problem. Note, however, that as these acts receive public attention they are also being privatized through the use of terms such as "family" or "domestic" violence (i.e., that these are really personal problems of unhappy individuals, and most likely due to a failure on the part of the wife/mother whose task it is precisely to maintain harmony in the home). This language also obscures the primary victims (Bush, 1985). Russell (1982) makes a similar point by suggesting that the term "wife-rape" is preferable to either "marital rape" or "spousal rape" specifically because wife-rape is not gender neutral.

The recognition of wife-assault as a social problem, for example, is primarily a product of the women's movement (Tierney, 1982) and has been the object of an outpouring of feminist research and analysis over the past 15 years (reviewed in Breines and Gordon, 1983; Pagelow, 1985). The theme has also been taken up by the mass media, although not without an element of voyeurism and typically in a way that emphasizes the psychological problems of the abuser or of the marital pair. So while the personal has become public, it has not yet been transformed into the political. A feminist analysis of gender-power relationships in the wider society is still missing. Instead, violence against women has typically been treated by clinicians, law enforcement personnel, and the judiciary as a consequence of victim characteristics that either arouse or anger the batterers (i.e., the "victim provocation" thesis). It follows from this view that the solution lies in training women to watch themselves—to become, as it were, the monitors of their own actions. This is victimization internalized. Also, the simplistic solution to wife-abuse—that women should leave batterers—suggests that women are to blame if they do not leave. Blame, then, comes back on the victim for "accepting" this behavior. Only rarely, and only in the feminist literature, are the roots of such violence located in culture and social structure—the gender stratification system, the socioeconomic system, or the structure of the family (for this type of analysis see Schechter, 1982; Schwendinger and Schwendinger, 1983).

Yet as women begin to speak out and as others realize the extent of the phenomenon, pressures are generated on lawmakers and judges, who, despite their patriarchal interests, are slowly changing the legal definitions of appropriate marital behavior. Only a few states define wife-abuse as a felony per se, and in most other states the general assault statutes apply to violence directed against a wife. But lawmakers are loath to tackle the subject of wife-rape, particularly if the couple is living together, and in a few states a husband cannot be charged even if the couple is legally separated (Russell, 1982).

Although it is difficult to estimate the incidence or prevalence of wife-rape—in part because the wife may not interpret the situation in those terms—it is interesting to note that when researcher Irene Frieze (1983) sought a matched sample to compare with a group of 137 women who had reported being physical assaulted by their husbands, she discovered that close to 30% of the presumably violence-free comparison group had also experienced marital attacks. The findings from this study of wives indicate that wife-rape is strongly associated with other acts of personal violence; that wives do *not* precipitate such incidents by refusing sex or being unfaithful; and that husbands who rape appear to like violent sex and lots of it, and feel they have the right to demand it.

SEXUAL ABUSE OF CHILDREN   This category includes a number of different types of behavior, from incest to indecent exposure. Again, the statutes vary from state to state with regard to what acts are included, how they are defined, and how the offense will be treated (as felony, misdemeanor, or a form of assault). In general, the phrases most often used to describe the sexual abuse of children are the following: (by definition) statutory rape, incest, molestation, carnal knowledge, indecent liberties, and impairing the morals of a minor. It is assumed that a child cannot give informed consent, even though it is possible that some adolescents are willing partners. In the case of incest, Butler (1978) argues that the term "incestuous assault" is more useful because it implies nonconsensual, essentially coercive behavior. Increasingly the use of children as models in pornography is specifically included in the statutes, although this behavior also falls well within several of the existing definitions.

It is impossible to know the true extent of sexual abuse of children; estimates vary from 1% to 10% for man/girl incest to 25% of all females being victims of some form of "sexual molestation" by the time they reach 18 years of age (data reviewed in Breines and Gordon, 1983: 521–522). The sexual abuse of children, unlike child abuse in general, is overwhelmingly committed by men against girls, a fact that the clinical literature succeeded in ignoring until the recent wave of feminist scholarship. By denying the male-dominant nature of incest, for example, the clinical establishment could continue to consider it a problem of individual psychopathology—on the part of the victim who may have acted "seductively," or on the part of the mother who "failed" to protect her daughter or who "collaborated" with her partner in "allowing" the assault—and not on the part of the assailant, who was only following his sexual nature.

Despite the existence of statutory prohibitions (and certain types of incest have always been criminalized), the sexual abuse of children is notoriously difficult to prosecute. The victims, if they recognize themselves as such, are relatively powerless; adults employ denial mechanisms; the perpetrator has the power to punish: and few outsiders can pierce the veil of privacy that protects the modern family. As in the case of wife-assault, the women's movement has given many women the courage to speak out about their own childhood experiences, making it quite clear that they were not willing participants, that it was not pleasurable (a common male fantasy), and that they still bear deep psychological scars. Feminism has also spurred an analysis based on cultural and societal variables, to which gendered power relationships are central. Childhood victimization is a powerful socialization to that fear so essential to the entire system of sexual terrorism.

SEXUAL HARASSMENT Although coined only recently, "sexual harassment" (Farley, 1978) is a phenomenon with which women were well acquainted before it was named. Sexual harassment refers to a wide range of coercive and intimidating behaviors that reinforce the basic fears of women by implying the ultimate use of force.

40   Although sexual assaults, in the work place or anywhere else, were already covered by the criminal law, other less physical but nonetheless threatening behaviors are now also forbidden. The common legal definition includes any deliberate, repeated, or unwelcome verbal comments, gestures, or physical contracts of a sexual nature. A specific definition covering academic sexual harassment is that of the National Advisory Council on Women's Educational Programs: "The use of authority to emphasize the sexuality or sexual identity of a student in a manner which prevents or impairs that student's full enjoyment of educational benefits, climate, or opportunities" (Till, 1980: 7).

Under 1980 federal guidelines, sexual harassment has been subsumed under the rubric of discrimination as an unfair impediment to an individual's ability to get a job done or to advance on one's own merits. Many organizations now have written rules spelling out the proscribed conduct and providing channels for handling complaints, which may provide women with some protection or redress. However, the fact that sexual harassment is analogous to rape in that it is less an expression of sexuality than of power and represents a process of intimidation must not be overlooked. Only in the feminist literature and scholarship do we find the link to the larger system of gender stratification.

There is, therefore, some question about the effectiveness of antiharassment laws given the "combined effects of occupational segregation, employment discrimination, and economic dependency [that] force women to remain in workplace situations that are decidedly threatening and coercive" (Schneider, 1985: 26). As Schneider also points out, because workplace harassment occurs almost by definition among people who know one another, the victim has the same problem as the victim of "acquaintance rape" in interpreting the event as totally unprovoked and in being believed by others.

With respect to antiharassment regulations drawn up by universities, Crocker (1983) notes that they cover a wide spectrum of actions, acknowledge the potentially damaging consequences for victims, provide ample warning to possible violators, and also raise community consciousness—all generally constructive outcomes. Yet Crocker also suggests that using the words "inappropriate" or "unwelcome" implies that there are appropriate or welcome leers and pinches that will not be considered harassment. Similarly, the use of words such as "coercion" and "force" implies that unforced sexual favors are acceptable. But is it really possible, given the power of professors over students, that even uncoerced sexual favors are truly willingly bestowed? Then, too, the ranking of offenses—the general assumption that threat of punishment ("fuck or flunk") is a more serious offense than promise of reward ("A for a lay")—makes little difference to the student, who may not even need to have the alternatives articulated in order to protect herself (Crocker, 1983).

In other words, in both the work place and academe, sexual harassment regulations may alert women to their rights, may restrain some men, and may raise the general level of consciousness of all members of the community, but as long as the gender stratification system remains intact, sexual threats will continue to characterize the lives of women outside the family as well as within.

SEXUAL SLAVERY Sexual terrorism may well reach its ultimate form in the practice of what Barry (1979) calls "female sexual slavery"—the international traffic in women and forced street prostitution. Although prostitution is illegal in most jurisdictions, our legal conception is actually very limited and misleading. Prostitution was defined as illegal in order to protect man (primarily from disease) and is viewed as a crime that women commit willingly. Barry argues that "female sexual slavery is present in all situations where women or girls cannot change the immediate conditions of their existence; where regardless of how they got into those conditions, they cannot get out; and where they are subject to sexual violence and exploitation" (1979: 33).

Another form of sexual slavery, practiced by individual pimps who employ intimidation or overt violence to force women and girls to sell their bodies for his profit, is more well known. The situation of runaway girls has recently been exploited by the mass media, along with general concern over the potential sexual abuse of "missing children"—both boys and girls (although we suspect that cases of male prostitutes receive disproportionate attention).

Procurers employ a variety of subtle as well as openly coercive techniques to attach their women to them, including both emotional and drug dependencies. Among urban blacks, where so many other forms of achievement are systematically blocked, Bell Hooks (1981: 108) notes that "the male who overtly reveals his hatred and contempt of women is admired," so that the pimp becomes a hero.

The newest pimp may be the broker who arranges marriages between American men and Asian women. These brokers, who sell women for a lifetime rather than for an hour or an evening or who arrange for increasingly popular sex tours of Southeast Asia, combine racism—that is, the stereotypical view of submissive and exotic Asian women—with the traditional view of women as chattel.

Barry (1979) also extends the definition of sexual slavery to include situations where fathers and husbands use force to keep wives and daughters submissive and powerless. As we have noted for other types of family violence, it is often difficult to prove that victims were not volunteers, and the authorities are far more prone to see complicity rather than coercion. Few have asked the crucial question posed by Barry (1979: 70): "Are these women able to change the conditions of their existence?" If not, their complicity cannot be assumed.

VOLUNTARY COMPLIANCE

50 An institutionalized system of terror requires mechanisms other than sustained violence to achieve its goals. Sexual terrorism is maintained by a system of sex-role socialization that encourages men to be terrorists in the name of masculinity and women to be victims in the name of femininity. Therefore, the fourth element in the model of terrorism, "voluntary compliance," is almost an automatic assumption in cases of sexual terrorism. Not only do women "ask for" this type of treatment, but deep down they really "want it"—a belief bolstered by the pseudo-scientific authority of psychoanalysis. To the extent that the essence of femininity is defined as an innate masochism, coerciveness is rationalized away. This image is perhaps the quintessential aspect of the ideology, the basic theme of so much propaganda, a key to the vocabulary of motives, and an effective means of interjecting fear.

As long as each women clutches her self-doubts to herself, the line between compliance and coercion can be blurred. In one recent study of the responses of victims of sexual violence, Stanko (1985) found three common reactions among women, whether they were raped, battered, harassed, or incestuously assaulted: self-blame, shame, and guilt (responsibility). Such feelings complete the circle of the self-fulfilling prophecy as women internalize the identity of "bad women," the one who must deserve her fate (see also Burgess, 1985). This is also one way to resolve the cognitive dissonance of maintaining the image of a good woman while recognizing that awful things have been done to you: Either you're not all that good or what's happened to you isn't all that bad.

A third possibility is to realize that you are good and that you don't deserve to be attacked—neither perception being nurtured in the patriarchy. And here is precisely where the feminist reconstruction of reality can begin to erode the forces of fear. As Bart and O'Brien (1984) found, the women who resisted rapists also defied the traditional vocabulary of motives, and whether their resistance was successful or not, were less likely than other victims to feel depressed or to blame themselves. It is not quite clear what led to the original decision to resist, but there is no question that the experience of having resisted brought a psychic liberation. If rape is the purest expression of male dominance, than resisting (not just avoiding) rape is a powerful statement of self-worth.

PERCEPTIONS OF VICTIMS AND TERRORISTS

Among the major goals of any system of terror are the erosion of public support for victims and acquisition of respectability for one's own cause. The effectiveness of all the other elements of terrorism can be judged by an examination of societal responses. With regard to sexual terrorism, the evidence is that such acts are the least reported of crimes and that when reported are least likely to be brought to trial or to result in conviction.

In addition, the exclusive focus of the law and the media is on the sexual nature of the crime; and because the victim and terrorist are usually known to one another, sexual assaults are treated as "acquaintance crimes" (i.e., the result of some personal problem between the individuals involved).

Yet sexual violence is pervasive (Stanko, 1985; Finklehor, 1984; Straus et al., 1980) and cuts across lines of age, religion, ethnicity, and social class. Although some research suggests no relationship to social class (e.g., Adler, 1985), other scholars disagree (e.g., the studies reviewed by Schwendinger and Schwendinger, 1983). These mixed findings reflect, in part, a political agenda. That is, if you see sexual violence as a response to socioeconomic conditions—at the macro and micro levels—you have a vested interest in finding that lower status subgroups are most likely to engage in sexual terrorism. If, conversely, you believe that sexually aggressive behavior is a generalized male trait or that all men in a society benefit from the patriarchal system, you will look for support in the finding of no social class effect.

It is always comforting to believe that crimes and other antisocial behaviors are restricted to people unlike those who make and enforce the laws—poor, uneducated, or nonwhite people. And it is easy to deny disconfirming evidence. Thus it seems likely that sexual terrorism is more widely distributed across the social class structure than is commonly assumed. But it is also possible that the proximate causes of sexual violence are disproportionately experienced by the less affluent.

In any event, whoever commits the crime stands very little chance of having a complaint filed or of being prosecuted. For example, in 1984, over 84,000 rapes were reported to the police (FBI, 1985), a 7% increase over 1983 and 50% increase since 1975. It is doubtful that, in such a short time span, this increase reflects only a greater willingness to report a rape or more effective law enforcement. The FBI calculates that, correcting for under-reporting, a rape occurs every two minutes. Yet rape has the lowest conviction rate of all violent crime.

As with rape, the true prevalence of wife-assault is unknown because the crime is so seldom reported. Although wife-assault is not yet an FBI crime category, federal analysts recognize that it is widespread and estimate that it is three times as common as rape. Russell's (1982) random sample of 644 women revealed that 21% had been subjected to physical violence by a husband. In their national study of American homes, Straus et al. (1980) found husbands violent in 27% of marriages analyzed. They suggest, however, that the true rate is much higher.

Similarly, the incidence of the sexual abuse of children is unknown. Finklehor (1984) estimates that 75% to 90% of the incidents are never reported. In spite of this, studies clearly suggest that child sexual abuse is of great magnitude. Reviewing the evidence from five surveys on incest between 1940 and the present, Herman (1981) found that one-fifth to one-third of all the respondents reported that they had had some kind of childhood sexual encounter with an adult male; between 4% and 12% reported a sexual encounter with a relative, and 1 female in 100 reported having had a sexual experience with her father or step-father. In spite of the acknowledged prevalence of wife-assault and child sexual abuse, arrest and prosecution is arduous and discouraging and convictions are rare.

60   An identical pattern emerges when examining the data on sexual harassment. While accurate data are impossible to obtain, studies suggest that sexual harassment is pervasive. Farley (1978) found that within the federal government, accounts of sexual harassment are extensive, and that surveys of working women in the private sector suggest a "dangerously high rate of incidence of this abuse." The U.S. Merit System's Protection Board surveyed 23,000 federal employees in 1981 and found that within the two years prior to the survey 42% of the respondents experienced sexual harassment (Stanko, 1985). Moreover, younger, single women reported a higher incidence of harassment.

According to Dziech and Weiner's (1984) study of academic sexual harassment, 20% to 30% of female students are victims of sexual harassment during their college years. While victims of sexual harassment are increasingly breaking the silence and some are even successful in bringing cases to court, adjudication and conviction in these cases are rare.

CONCLUSIONS

As the task of confronting men's power to intimidate and violate females is manifold, the agenda for feminist research and activism must be diverse and bold. Therefore, in an effort to deepen and broaden our understanding of sexual terrorism, I would like to offer suggestions for further research.

First, we must expand our understanding of the definitions and scope of sexual violence. Since 1971 when the first speak-out on rape was held, both feminist scholars and courageous survivors of sexual terrorism have broken silence on the darkest aspects of patriarchy. In the past 15 years we have pierced the curtain of ignorance of what W. W. Visser't Hofft (1982) calls "the twilight between knowing and not knowing." The breaking of the tradition of silence surrounding rape, wife-assault, wife-rape, sexual harassment, sexual slavery, incestuous assault, and pornography is truly revolutionary. Because women have been constructed within a male-dominated society, women's experiences of sexual violence have been viewed through a patriarchal lens, resulting in an illusion of at best insignificance, and at worst complicity. What was lost—or rather, what was denied—was a woman-defined understanding of sexual terrorism. As feminist theory comes largely from the experience of women, the breaking of silence has informed and transformed the study of violence against women. While the gap between women's experiences of male violence and men's definition of sexual violence still must be bridged, the recognition that violence must be defined, in large measure, by those who experience it provides a meaningful foundation for future research.

We still need, however, to know more about the actual extent of violence against women. Hence a national random incidence survey is imperative. Such a study should not be limited to the conventional criminal categories, but should include the opportunity for women and girls to provide subjective understanding and definitions.

Second, we need to bring together the various forms of violence against females in order to see the patterns. In furthering our understanding of the commonalities of forms of sexual violence, we can then examine areas of women's oppression that have been previously neglected in the literature on violence. For example, the link between medicine and sexual violence has yet to be fully explored. Corea's (1985) analysis of medicine as a form of social control, and the work of Stark et al. (1979) on the treatment of battered women in a hospital emergency room, represent an important introduction to this uncharted terrain. Additionally, the diagnosis and treatment of women in psychiatric care should be analyzed from the perspective of societal attitudes toward sexual violence and the role of violence in keeping women subordinate in institutions of care.

65   We need to know more about multiple personality syndrome and its connection to sexual violence. Similarly, an investigation of female self-abusers and studies of suicide and attempted suicide relative to sexual violence are necessary. Research into these areas would not only enlarge the scope of our understanding of sexual violence but would provide insight into the coping/survival strategies of victims and the ways sexual violence is processed by agencies of the culture.

Third, the role of violence in structuring and maintaining male–female relationships remains inadequately considered. This needs to be addressed at the macro level, where force and the threat of violence are functional to male supremacy and provide the foundation for other forms of domination and control. At the micro level we need to study the psychosexual processes that underscore the heterosexual social system. From this perspective, Hamner and Saunders (1984) suggest that we look at the concepts of authority and obedience in personal relationships. Also, we should continue exploring the interconnections between the socially constructed dependencies of women and the further powerlessness engendered by physical intimidation and violence.

Moreover, the study of women should illuminate the study of men. This is generally, and notably, not the case in the study of sexual violence. For example, the majority of offenders are known to the victims, yet the significance of this has yet to be explored. To date, most of the studies involving offenders (Groth, 1979; Scully and Marolla, 1985) have been done with *convicted* sex offenders. Given that victims are least likely to report when the offender is known to them, and acquaintance rapes rarely result in conviction, studies on convicted offenders are limited to their ability to inform us about the complexities inherent in the phenomenon of men committing violence against women and girls whom they profess to love.

Fourth, there is a need for much more research into the legal system and its response to offenders and victims. While there has been both evidentiary and statutory reform in the legal codes, the greater problem in the litigation of sexual violence seems to be discriminatory enforcement. The chasm between legislative reform and women's experiences of the legal process as "the second assailant" (Stanko, 1985) remains wide.

Finally, I believe that the continuing study of the relationships between sexual terrorism and popular culture is crucial. The expressions of popular culture—literature, films, television, music, advertising, and so on—are vehicles for the transmission of patriarchal myths and attitudes.

70   Furthermore, the level of violence against females is not only at an all-time high, but indications are that it is increasing. To say that it is pervasive is not enough; acts of sexual violence are more severe and brutal than ever before. There is an apparent increase in gang rapes, serial rapes, and murders (which often involve dismemberment of women's bodies). This alarming

phenomenon should be analyzed in relation to the propaganda of sexual terrorism and the production of fear.

Strategies to free women must be based on a thorough understanding of the roots and range of the system of sexual terrorism. The task of feminist scholarship is to forward the search for truth and, in so doing, develop a body of knowledge and a new curriculum about women, and to inform public policy. As Kathleen Barry (1979: 11) put it, "knowing the worst frees us to hope and strive for the best."

NOTES

1. This debate on "sex war," as explained by Ferguson et al. (1981) hinges on two radically different visions of feminist sexual morality. One group, the "radical feminists," perceives not only pornography but all forms of sexuality based on dominance and power inequality as supportive of the patriarchal sex/gender system. The other group—"libertarian feminists"—argues that feminism must stand for liberation from the narrow confines of male-defined traditional sexuality, that women must be allowed to find sexual pleasure in a variety of hitherto forbidden ways, provided only that the relationships are consensual.

   Libertarians claim that the antipornography activists would turn the clock back to a repressive morality in which female sexuality would be once more stifled. The radicals perceive libertarians as reinforcers of brutality in the larger society and among women. The debate among feminists, however, may make it possible to find some third path to defining a female sexuality that is both liberating and noncoercive.

   In addition, many feminists doubt the effectiveness of using the law to control pornography when both are defined by male perspectives. Nonetheless, other feminists have written and promoted local ordinances that would define pornography as a threat to women's rights to move freely in the community and to enjoy equal protection of the laws (Blakely, 1985).

   The antifeminists have, of course, an entirely different agenda in their crusade against "obscenity," one that has more to do with a fear of rampant sexuality (echoing the basic patriarchal position) than with the issue of gender power (Diamond, 1980). There is, then, a way in which the suppression of pornography, along with the suppression of contraception and access to abortion, could herald a new wave of puritanism that would once more deny to women the ability to define and control their own sexuality.

REFERENCES

Adler, C. (1985) "An exploration of self-reported sexually aggressive behavior." *Crime and Delinquency* 31, 2: 306–331.

Barry, K. (1979) *Female Sexual Slavery.* Englewood Cliffs, NJ: Prentice-Hall.

Bart, P. B. and P. H. O'Brien (1984) "Stopping rape: Effective avoidance strategies." *Signs* 10, 1: 82–101.

Bart, P. B. and K. L. Scheppele (1980) "There ought to be a law: Women's definitions and legal definitions of sexual assault." Presented at the American Sociological Association meeting.

Blakely, M. K. (1985) "Is one woman's sexuality another woman's pornography?" *Ms.* (April).

Breines, W. and L. Gordon (1983) "The new scholarship on family violence." *Signs* 8, 3: 490–531.

Brownmiller, S. (1975) *Against Our Will: Men, Women and Rape.* New York: Simon & Schuster.

Burgess, A. W. (1985) *Rape and Sexual Assault.* New York and London: Garland Publishing.

Bush, D. M. (1985) "Doublethink and newspeak in the real 1984: Rationalizations for violence against women." *Humanity and Society,* 9(3): 308–327.

Corea, G. (1985) *The Hidden Malpractice: How American Medicine Mistreats Women.* New York: Harper & Row.

Crocker, P. L. (1983) "An analysis of university definitions of sexual harassment." *Signs* 8, 4: 696–707.

Diamond, I. (1980) "Pornography and repression: A reconsideration of who and what," in Laura Lederer (ed.) *Take Back the Night: Women on Pornography.* New York: William Morrow.

Donnerstein, E. (1980) "Aggressive erotica and violence against women." *Journal of Personality and Social Psychology* 39, 2: 269–277.

Dworkin, A. (1979) *Pornography: Men Possessing Women.* New York: Perigree Books.

Dworkin, A. (1985) "A word people don't understand." *Ms.* (April).

Dziech, B. W. and L. Weiner (1984) *The Lecherous Professor.* Boston: Beacon.

Farley, I. (1978) *Sexual Shakedown: The Sexual Harassment of Women on the Job.* New York: McGraw-Hill.

Ferguson, A. I. Phillipson, I. Diamond, L. Quinby, C. S. Vance, and A. B. Snitow (1984) "The feminist sexuality debates." *Signs* 10, 1: 102–153.

Finkelhor, D. (1984) *Child Sexual Abuse: New Theory and Research.* New York: Free Press.

Firestone, S. (1972) *The Dialectic of Sex.* New York: Bantam.

Fox, G. L. (1977) "Nice girl: Social control of women through a value construct." *Signs* 2, 4: 805–817.

Frieze, I. H. (1983) "Investigating the causes and consequences of marital rape." *Signs* 8, 3: 532–553.

Groth, N. (1979) *Men Who Rape: The Psychology of the Offender.* New York: Plenum.

Hamner, J. and S. Saunders (1984) *Well-Founded Fear: A Community Study of Violence to Women.* London: Hutchinson.

Herman, J. I. with L. Hirschman (1981) *Father-Daughter Incest.* Cambridge, MA: Harvard University Press.

Holmstrom, L. and A. W. Burgess (1983) "Rape and everyday life." *Society* (July/August): 33–40.

Hooks, B. (1981) *Ain't I a Woman: Black Women and Feminism.* Boston: South End Press.

Johnson, C. (1978) "Perspectives on terrorism," in Walter Laqueur (ed.) *The Terrorism Reader*. Philadelphia: Temple University Press.

LaBelle, B. (1980) "The propaganda of misogyny," in Laura Lederer (ed.) *Take Back the Night: Women on Pornography*. New York: William Morrow.

Leacock, E. B. [ed.] (1981) *Myths of Male Dominance: Collected Articles on Women Cross-Culturally*. New York: Monthly Review Press.

Lerner, G. [ed.] (1973) *Black Women in White America: A Documentary History*. New York: Vintage Books.

Lowe, M. and R. Hubbard (1983) *Women's Nature: Rationalizations of Integrity*. New York: Pergamon.

MacKinnon, C. A. (1983) "Feminism, Marxism, method and the state: Toward feminist jurisprudence." *Signs* 8, 4: 635–658.

Malamuth, N. M. (1981) "Rape proclivity among males." *Journal of Social Issues* 37: 138–157.

Pagelow, M. D. with L. W. Pagelow (1985) *Family Violence*. New York: Praeger.

Polk, K. (1985) "Rape reform and criminal justice processing." *Crime and Delinquency* 31, 2: 191–205.

Russell, D. F. H. (1982) *Rape in Marriage*. New York: Macmillan.

Sanday, P. R. (1981) "The socioculture context of rape." *Journal of Social Issues* 37, 1.

Schehier, S. (1982) *Woman and Male Violence: The Visions and Struggles of the Battered Women Movement*. Boston: South End Press.

Schneider, B. E. (1984) "Put up and shut up: Workplace sexual assaults." Presented at the American Sociological Association meeting.

Schur, F. M. (1984) *Labeling Women Deviant: Gender, Stigma, and Social Control*. New York: Random House.

Schwendinger, R. J. R. and H. Schwendinger (1983) *Rape and Inequality*. Newbury Park, CA: Sage.

Scully, D. and J. Marolla (1985) "Riding the bull at Gilley's: Convicted rapists describe the rewards of rape." *Social Problems* 32, 3: 251–263.

Stanko, F. A. (1985) *Intimate Intrusions: Women's Experience of Male Violence*. London: Routledge & Kegan Paul.

Stark, F., A. Flitcraft, and W. Fraziew (1979) "Medicine and patriarchal violence: The social construction of a 'private' event." *International Journal of Health Services* 9, 3: 461–492.

Straus, M., R. Giles, and S. Steinmetz (1980) *Behind Closed Doors*. Garden City, NY: Anchor/Doubleday.

Tavris, C. and C. Wade (1984) *The Longest War: Sex Differences in Perspectives*. New York: Harcourt Brace Jovanovich.

Tierney, K. J. (1982) "The battered women's movement and the creation of the wife beating problem." *Social Problems* 26, 2: 207–220.

Till, F. J. (1980) *Sexual Harassment: A Report on the Sexual Harassment of Students*. Washington, DC: National Advisory Council on Women's Educational Programs.

U.S. Department of Justice, Federal Bureau of Investigation (1985) *Uniform Crime Report.* Washington, DC: U.S. Government Printing Office.

Visser't Hofft, W. W. (1982) *The Terrible Secret: The Suppression of the Truth About Hitler's Final Solution.* New York: Penguin.

Warr, M. (1985) "Fear of rape among urban women." *Social Problems* 32, 3: 238–250.

Watson, F. M. (1976) *Political Terrorism: The Threat and the Response.* Washington, DC: R. B. Luce.

Wilkinson, P. (1974) *Political Terrorism.* New York: John Wiley.

■ ■ ■ ■

OPPRESSION

Marilyn Frye

It is a fundamental claim of feminism that women are oppressed. The word "oppression" is a strong word. It repels and attracts. It is dangerous and dangerously fashionable and endangered. It is much misused, and sometimes not innocently.

The statement that women are oppressed is frequently met with the claim that men are oppressed too. We hear that oppressing is oppressive to those who oppress as well as to those they oppress. Some men cite as evidence of their oppression their much-advertised inability to cry. It is tough, we are told, to be masculine. When the stresses and frustrations of being a man are cited as evidence that oppressors are oppressed by their oppressing, the word "oppression" is being stretched to meaninglessness; it is treated as though its scope includes any and all human experience of limitation or suffering, no matter the cause, degree or consequence. Once such usage has been put over on us, then if ever we deny that any person or group is oppressed, we seem to imply that we think they never suffer and have no feelings. We are accused of insensitivity; even of bigotry. For women, such accusation is particularly intimidating, since sensitivity is one of the few virtues that has been assigned to us. If we are found insensitive, we may fear we have no redeeming traits at all and perhaps are not real women. Thus are we silenced before we begin: the name of our situation drained of meaning and our guilt mechanisms tripped.

But this is nonsense. Human beings can be miserable without being oppressed, and it is perfectly consistent to deny that a person or group is oppressed without denying that they have feelings or that they suffer.

We need to think clearly about oppression, and there is much that mitigates against this. I do not want to undertake to prove that women are oppressed (or that men are not), but I want to make clear what is being said when we say it. We need this word, this concept, and we need it to be sharp and sure.

I

The root of the word "oppression" is the element "press." *The press of the crowd; pressed into military service; to press a pair of pants; printing press; press the button.* Presses are used to mold things or flatten them or reduce them in bulk, sometimes to reduce them by squeezing out the gasses or liquids in them. Something pressed is something caught between or among forces and barriers which are so related to each other that jointly they restrain, restrict or prevent the thing's motion or mobility. Mold. Immobilize. Reduce.

183

The mundane experience of the oppressed provides another clue. One of the most characteristic and ubiquitous features of the world as experienced by oppressed people is the double bind—situations in which options are reduced to a very few and all of them expose one to penalty, censure or deprivation. For example, it is often a requirement upon oppressed people that we smile and be cheerful. If we comply, we signal our docility and our acquiescence in our situation. We need not, then, be taken note of. We acquiesce in being made invisible, in our occupying no space. We participate in our own erasure. On the other hand, anything but the sunniest countenance exposes us to being perceived as mean, bitter, angry or dangerous. This means, at the least, that we may be found "difficult" or unpleasant to work with, which is enough to cost one's livelihood; at worst, being seen as mean, bitter, angry or dangerous has been known to result in rape, arrest, beating and murder. One can only choose to risk one's preferred form and rate of annihilation.

Another example: It is common in the United States that women, especially younger women, are in a bind where neither sexual activity nor sexual inactivity is all right. If she is heterosexually active, a woman is open to censure and punishment for being loose, unprincipled or a whore. The "punishment" comes in the form of criticism, snide and embarrassing remarks, being treated as an easy lay by men, scorn from her more restrained female friends. She may have to lie and hide her behavior from her parents. She must juggle the risks of unwanted pregnancy and dangerous contraceptives. On the other hand, if she refrains from heterosexual activity, she is fairly constantly harassed by men who try to persuade her into it and pressure her to "relax" and "let her hair down"; she is threatened with labels like "frigid," "uptight," "man-hater," "bitch" and "cocktease." The same parents who would be disapproving of her sexual activity may be worried by her inactivity because it suggests she is not or will not be popular, or is not sexually normal. She may be charged with lesbianism. If a woman is raped, then if she has been heterosexually active she is subject to the presumption that she liked it (since her activity is presumed to show that she likes sex), and if she has not been heterosexually active, she is subject to the presumption that she liked it (since she is supposedly "repressed and frustrated"). Both heterosexual activity and heterosexual nonactivity are likely to be taken as proof that you wanted to be raped, and hence, of course, weren't *really* raped at all. You can't win. You are caught in a bind, caught between systematically related pressures.

Women are caught like this, too, by networks of forces and barriers that expose one to penalty, loss or contempt whether one works outside the home or not, is on welfare or not, bears children or not, raises children or not, marries or not, stays married or not, is heterosexual, lesbian, both or neither. Economic necessity; confinement to racial and/or sexual job ghettos; sexual harassment; sex discrimination; pressures of competing expectations and judgments about *women, wives* and *mothers* (in the society at large, in racial and ethnic subcultures and in one's own mind); dependence (full or partial) on husbands, parents or the state; commitment to political ideas; loyalties to racial or ethnic or other "minority" groups; the demands of self-respect and responsibilities to others. Each of these factors exists in complex tension with every other, penalizing or prohibiting all of the apparently available options. And nipping at one's heels, always, is the endless pack of little things. If one dresses one way, one is subject to the assumption that one is advertising one's sexual availability; if one dresses another way, one appears to "not care about oneself" or to be "unfeminine." If one uses "strong language," one invites categorization as a whore or slut; if one does not, one invites categorization as a "lady"—one too delicately constituted to cope with robust speech or the realities to which it presumably refers.

The experience of oppressed people is that the living of one's life is confined and shaped by forces and barriers which are not accidental or occasional and hence avoidable, but are systematically related to each other in such a way as to catch one between and among them and restrict or penalize motion in any direction. It is the experience of being caged in: all avenues, in every direction, are blocked or booby trapped.

Cages. Consider a birdcage. If you look very closely at just one wire in the cage, you cannot see the other wires. If your conception of what is before you is determined by this myopic focus, you could look at that one wire, up and down the length of it, and be unable to see why a bird would not just fly around the wire any time it wanted to go somewhere. Furthermore, even if, one day at a time, you myopically inspected each wire, you still could not see why a bird would have trouble going past the wires to get anywhere. There is no physical property of any one wire, *nothing* that the closest scrutiny could discover, that will reveal how a bird could be inhibited or harmed by it except in the most accidental way. It is only when you step back, stop looking at the wires one by one, microscopically, and take a macroscopic view of the whole cage, that you can see why the bird does not go anywhere; and then you will see it in a moment. It will require no great subtlety of mental powers. It is perfectly *obvious* that the bird is surrounded by a network of systematically related barriers, no one of which would be the least hindrance to its flight, but which, by their relations to each other, are as confining as the solid walls of a dungeon.

It is now possible to grasp one of the reasons why oppression can be hard to see and recognize: one can study the elements of an oppressive structure with great care and some good will without seeing the structure as a whole, and hence without seeing or being able to understand that one is looking at a cage and that there are people there who are caged, whose motion and mobility are restricted, whose lives are shaped and reduced.

The arresting of vision at a microscopic level yields such common confusion as that about the male door-opening ritual. This ritual, which is remarkably widespread across classes and races, puzzles many people, some of whom do and some of whom do not find it offensive. Look at the scene of the two people approaching a door. The male steps slightly ahead and opens the door. The male holds the door open while the female glides through. Then the male goes through. The door closes after them. "Now how," one innocently asks, "can those crazy womenslibbers say that is oppressive? The guy *removed* a barrier to the lady's smooth and unruffled progress." But each repetition of this ritual has a place in a pattern, in fact in several patterns. One has to shift the level of one's perception in order to see the whole picture.

The door-opening pretends to be a helpful service, but the helpfulness is false. This can be seen by noting that it will be done whether or not it makes any practical sense. Infirm men and men burdened with packages will open doors for able-bodied women who are free of physical burdens. Men will impose themselves awkwardly and jostle everyone in order to get to the door first. The act is not determined by convenience or grace. Furthermore, these very numerous acts of unneeded or even noisome "help" occur in counterpoint to a pattern of men not being helpful in many practical ways in which women might welcome help. What *women* experience is a world in which gallant princes charming commonly make a fuss about being helpful and providing small services when help and services are of little or no use, but in which there are rarely ingenious and adroit princes at hand when substantial assistance is really wanted either in mundane affairs or in situations of threat, assault or terror. There is no help with the (his) laundry; no help typing a report at 4:00 a.m.; no help in mediating disputes among relatives or children. There is nothing but advice that women should stay indoors after dark, be chaperoned by a man, or when it comes down to it, "lie back and enjoy it."

The gallant gestures have no practical meaning. Their meaning is symbolic. The door-opening and similar services provided are services which really are needed by people who are for one reason or another incapacitated—unwell, burdened with parcels, etc. So the message is that women are incapable. The detachment of the acts from the concrete realities of what women need and do not need is a vehicle for the message that women's actual needs and interests are unimportant or irrelevant. Finally, these gestures imitate the behavior of servants toward masters and thus mock women, who are in most respects the servants and caretakers of men. The message of the false helpfulness of male gallantry is female dependence, the invisibility or insignificance of women, and contempt for women.

15   One cannot see the meanings of these rituals if one's focus is riveted upon the individual event in all its particularity, including the particularity of the individual man's present conscious intentions and motives and the individual woman's conscious perception of the event in the moment. It seems sometimes that people take a deliberately myopic view and fill their eyes with things seen microscopically in order not to see macroscopically. At any rate, whether it is deliberate or not, people can and do fail to see the oppression of women because they fail to see macroscopically and hence fail to see the various elements of the situation as systematically related in larger schemes.

As the cageness of the birdcage is a macroscopic phenomenon, the oppressiveness of the situation in which women live our various and different lives is a macroscopic phenomenon. Neither can be *seen* from a microscopic perspective. But when you look macroscopically you can see it—a network of forces and barriers which are systematically related and which conspire to the immobilization, reduction and molding of women and the lives we live.

II

The image of the cage helps convey one aspect of the systematic nature of oppression. Another is the selection of occupants of the cages, and analysis of this aspect also helps account for the invisibility of the oppression of women.

It is as a woman (or as a Chicana/o or as a Black or Asian or lesbian) that one is entrapped.

"Why can't I go to the park; you let Jimmy go!"
"Because it's not safe for girls."

"I want to be a secretary, not a seamstress; I don't want to learn
    to make dresses."
"There's no work for negroes in that line; learn a skill where
    you can earn your living."[1]

When you question why you are being blocked, why this barrier is in your path, the answer has not to do with individual talent or merit, handicap or failure; it has to do with your membership in some category understood as a "natural" or "physical" category. The "inhabitant" of the "cage" is not an individual but a group, all those of a certain category. If an individual is oppressed, it is in virtue of being a member of a group or category of people that is systematically reduced, molded, immobilized. Thus, to recognize a person as oppressed, one has to see that individual *as* belonging to a group of a certain sort.

There are many things which can encourage or inhibit perception of someone's membership in the sort of group or category in question here. In particular, it seems reasonable to suppose that if one of the devices of restriction and definition of the group is that of physical confinement or segregation, the confinement and separation would encourage recognition of the group as a group. This in turn would encourage the macroscopic focus which enables one to recognize oppression and encourages the individuals' identification and solidarity with other individuals of the group or category. But physical confinement and segregation of the group as a group is not common to all oppressive structures, and when an oppressed group is geographically and demographically dispersed the perception of it as a group is inhibited. There may be little or nothing in the situations of the individuals encouraging the macroscopic focus which would reveal the unity of the structure bearing down on all members of that group.[2]

A great many people, female and male and of every race and class, simply do not believe that *woman* is a category of oppressed people, and I think that this is in part because they have been fooled by the dispersal and assimilation of women throughout and into the systems of class and race which organize

20

---

[1] This example is derived from *Daddy Was a Number Runner,* by Louise Meriwether (Englewood Cliffs, N.J.: Prentice-Hall, 1979), p. 144.
[2] Coerced assimilation is in fact one of the *policies* available to an oppressing group in its effort to reduce and/or annihilate another group. This tactic is used by the U.S. government, for instance, on the American Indians.

men. Our simply being dispersed makes it difficult for women to have knowledge of each other and hence difficult to recognize the shape of our common
cage. The dispersal and assimilation of women throughout economic classes
and races also divides us against each other practically and economically and
thus attaches *interest* to the inability to see: for some, jealousy of their benefits,
and for some, resentment of the others' advantages.

To get past this, it helps to notice that in fact women of all races and
classes *are* together in a ghetto of sorts. There is a women's place, a sector,
which is inhabited by women of all classes and races, and it is not defined by
geographical boundaries but by function. The function is the service of men
and men's interests as men define them, which includes the bearing and rearing of children. The details of the service and the working conditions vary by
race and class, for men of different races and classes have different interests,
perceive their interests differently, and express their needs and demands in different rhetorics, dialects and languages. But there are also some constants.

Whether in lower, middle or upper-class home or work situations,
women's service work always includes personal service (the works of maids,
butlers, cooks, personal secretaries),[3] sexual service (including provision for
his genital sexual needs and bearing his children, but also including "being
nice," "being attractive for him," etc.), and ego service (encouragement, support, praise, attention). Women's service work also is characterized everywhere by the fatal combination of responsibility and powerlessness: we are
held responsible and we hold ourselves responsible for good outcomes for
men and children in almost every respect though we have in almost no case
power adequate to that project. The details of the subjective experience of
this servitude are local. They vary with economic class and race and ethnic
tradition as well as the personalities of the men in question. So also are the
details of the forces which coerce our tolerance of this servitude particular to
the different situations in which different women live and work.

All this is not to say that women do not have, assert and manage sometimes to satisfy our own interests, nor to deny that in some cases and in some
respects women's independent interests do overlap with men's. But at every
race/class level and even across race/class lines men do not serve women as
women serve men. "Women's sphere" may be understood as the "service sector," taking the latter expression much more widely and deeply than is usual
in discussions of the economy.

III

It seems to be the human condition that in one degree or another we all suffer
frustration and limitation, all encounter unwelcome barriers, and all are damaged

---

[3]At higher class levels women may not *do* all these kinds of work, but are generally still responsible for hiring and supervising those who do it. These services are still, in these cases, women's
responsibility.

and hurt in various ways. Since we are a social species, almost all of our behavior and activities are structured by more than individual inclination and the conditions of the planet and its atmosphere. No human is free of social structures, nor (perhaps) would happiness consist in such freedom. Structure consists of boundaries, limits and barriers; in a structured whole, some motions and changes are possible, and others are not. If one is looking for an excuse to dilute the word "oppression," one can use the fact of social structure as an excuse and say that everyone is oppressed. But if one would rather get clear about what oppression is and is not, one needs to sort out the sufferings, harms and limitations and figure out which are elements of oppression and which are not.

From what I have already said here, it is clear that if one wants to determine whether a particular suffering, harm or limitation is part of someone's being oppressed, one has to look at it *in context* in order to tell whether it is an element in an oppressive structure: one has to see if it is part of an enclosing structure of forces and barriers which tends to the immobilization and reduction of a group or category of people. One has to look at how the barrier or force fits with others and to whose benefit or detriment it works. As soon as one looks at examples, it becomes obvious that not everything which frustrates or limits a person is oppressive, and not every harm or damage is due to or contributes to oppression.

If a rich white playboy who lives off income from his investments in South African diamond mines should break a leg in a skiing accident at Aspen and wait in pain in a blizzard for hours before he is rescued, we may assume that in that period he suffers. But the suffering comes to an end; his leg is repaired by the best surgeon money can buy and he is soon recuperating in a lavish suite, sipping Chivas Regal. Nothing in this picture suggests a structure of barriers and forces. He is a member of several oppressor groups and does not suddenly become oppressed because he is injured and in pain. Even if the accident was caused by someone's malicious negligence, and hence someone can be blamed for it and morally faulted, that person still has not been an agent of oppression.

Consider also the restriction of having to drive one's vehicle on a certain side of the road. There is no doubt that this restriction is almost unbearably frustrating at times, when one's lane is not moving and the other lane is clear. There are surely times, even, when abiding by this regulation would have harmful consequences. But the restriction is obviously wholesome for most of us most of the time. The restraint is imposed for our benefit, and does benefit us; its operation tends to encourage our *continued* motion, not to immobilize us. The limits imposed by traffic regulations are limits most of us would cheerfully impose on ourselves given that we knew others would follow them too. They are part of a structure which shapes our behavior, not to our reduction and immobilization, but rather to the protection of our continued ability to move and act as we will.

Another example: The boundaries of a racial ghetto in an American city serve to some extent to keep white people from going in, as well as to keep ghetto dwellers from going out. A particular white citizen may be frustrated

25

or feel deprived because s/he cannot stroll around there and enjoy the "exotic" aura of a "foreign" culture, or shop for bargains in the ghetto swap shops. In fact, the existence of the ghetto, of racial segregation, does deprive the white person of knowledge and harm her/his character by nurturing unwarranted feelings of superiority. But this does not make the white person in this situation a member of an oppressed race or a person oppressed because of her/his race. One must look at the barrier. It limits the activities and the access of those on both sides of it (though to different degrees). But it is a product of the intention, planning and action of whites for the benefit of whites, to secure and maintain privileges that are available to whites generally, as members of the dominant and privileged group. Though the existence of the barrier has some bad consequences for whites, the barrier does not exist in systematic relationship with other barriers and forces forming a structure oppressive to whites; quite the contrary. It is part of a structure which oppresses the ghetto dwellers and thereby (and by white intention) protects and furthers white interests as dominant white culture understands them. This barrier is not oppressive to whites, even though it is a barrier to whites.

Barriers have different meanings to those on opposite sides of them, even though they are barriers to both. The physical walls of a prison no more dissolve to let an outsider in than to let an insider out, but for the insider they are confining and limiting while to the outsider they may mean protection from what s/he takes to be threats posed by insiders—freedom from harm or anxiety. A set of social and economic barriers and forces separating two groups may be felt, even painfully, by members of both groups and yet may mean confinement to one and liberty and enlargement of opportunity to the other.

30   The service sector of the wives/mommas/assistants/girls is almost exclusively a woman-only sector; its boundaries not only enclose women but to a very great extent keep men out. Some men sometimes encounter this barrier and experience it as a restriction on their movements, their activities, their control or their choices of "lifestyle." Thinking they might like the simple nurturant life (which they may imagine to be quite free of stress, alienation and hard work), and feeling deprived since it seems closed to them, they thereupon announce the discovery that they are oppressed, too, by "sex roles." But that barrier is erected and maintained by men, for the benefit of men. It consists of cultural and economic forces and pressures in a culture and economy controlled by men in which, at every economic level and in all racial and ethnic subcultures, economy, tradition—and even ideologies of liberation—work to keep at least local culture and economy in male control.[4]

The boundary that sets apart women's sphere is maintained and promoted by men generally for the benefit of men generally, and men generally do benefit from its existence, even the man who bumps into it and complains of the incon-

---

[4]Of course this is complicated by race and class. Machismo and "Black manhood" politics seem to help keep Latin or Black men in control of more cash than Latin or Black women control; but these politics seem to me also to ultimately keep the larger economy in *white* male control.

venience. That barrier is protecting his classification and status as a male, as superior, as having a right to sexual access to a female or females. It protects a kind of citizenship which is superior to that of females of his class and race, his access to a wider range of better paying and higher status work, and his right to prefer unemployment to the degradation of doing lower status or "women's" work.

If a person's life or activity is affected by some force or barrier that person encounters, one may not conclude that the person is oppressed simply because the person encounters that barrier or force; nor simply because the encounter is unpleasant, frustrating or painful to that person at that time; nor simply because the existence of the barrier or force, or the processes which maintain or apply it, serve to deprive that person of something of value. One must look at the barrier or force and answer certain questions about it. Who constructs and maintains it? Whose interests are served by its existence? Is it part of a structure which tends to confine, reduce and immobilize some group? Is the individual a member of the confined group? Various forces, barriers and limitations a person may encounter or live with may be part of an oppressive structure or not, and if they are, that person may be on either the oppressed or the oppressor side of it. One cannot tell which by how loudly or how little the person complains.

IV

Many of the restrictions and limitations we live with are more or less internalized and self-monitored, and are part of our adaptations to the requirements and expectations imposed by the needs and tastes and tyrannies of others. I have in mind such things as women's cramped postures and attenuated strides and men's restraint of emotional self-expression (except for anger). Who gets what out of the practice of those disciplines, and who imposes what penalties for improper relaxations of them? What are the rewards of this self-discipline?

Can men cry? Yes, in the company of women. If a man cannot cry, it is in the company of men that they cannot cry. It is men, not women, who require this restraint; and men not only require it, they reward it. The man who maintains a steely or tough or laid-back demeanor (all are forms which suggest invulnerability) marks himself as a member of the male community and is esteemed by other men. Consequently, the maintenance of that demeanor contributes to the man's self-esteem. It is felt as good, and he can feel good about himself. The way this restriction fits into the structures of men's lives is as one of the socially required behaviors which, if carried off, contribute to their acceptance and respect by significant others and to their own self-esteem. It is to their benefit to practice this discipline.

Consider, by comparison, the discipline of women's cramped physical postures and attenuated stride. This discipline can be relaxed in the company of women; it generally is at its most strenuous in the company of men.[5] Like men's emotional restraint, women's physical restraint is required by men. But unlike the case of men's emotional restraint, women's physical restraint is not rewarded. What do we get for it? Respect and esteem and acceptance? No. They mock us and parody our mincing steps. We look silly, incompetent, weak and generally contemptible. Our exercise of this discipline tends to low esteem and low self-esteem. It does not benefit us. It fits in a network of behaviors through which we constantly announce to others our membership in a lower caste and our unwillingness and/or inability to defend our bodily or moral integrity. It is degrading and part of a pattern of degradation.

Acceptable behavior for both groups, men and women, involves a required restraint that seems in itself silly and perhaps damaging. But the social effect is drastically different. The woman's restraint is part of a structure oppressive to women; the man's restraint is part of a structure oppressive to women.

V

One is marked for application of oppressive pressures by one's membership in some group or category. Much of one's suffering and frustration befalls one partly or largely because one is a member of that category. In the case at hand, it is the category, *woman*. Being a woman is a major factor in my not having a better job than I do; being a woman selects me as a likely victim of sexual assault or harassment; it is my being a woman that reduces the power of my anger to a proof of my insanity. If a woman has little or no economic or political power, or achieves little of what she wants to achieve, a major causal factor in this is that she is a woman. For any woman of any race or economic class, being a woman is significantly attached to whatever disadvantages and deprivations she suffers, be they great or small.

None of this is the case with respect to a person's being a man. Simply being a man is not what stands between him and a better job; whatever assaults and harassments he is subject to, being male is not what selects him for victimization; being male is not a factor which would make his anger impotent—quite the opposite. If a man has little or no material or political power, or achieves little of what he wants to achieve, his being male is not part of the explanation. Being male is something he has going *for* him, even if race or class or age or disability is going against him.

Women are oppressed, *as women*. Members of certain racial and/or economic groups and classes, both the males and the females, are oppressed *as* members of those races and/or classes. But men are not oppressed *as men*.

40 . . . and isn't it strange that any of us should have been confused and mystified about such a simple thing?

---

[5]Cf., *Let's Take Back Our Space: "Female" and "Male" Body Language as a Result of Patriarchal Structures,* by Marianne Wex (Frauenliteratureverlag Hermine Fees, West Germany, 1979), especially p. 173. This remarkable book presents literally thousands of candid photographs of women and men, in public, seated, standing and lying down. It vividly demonstrates the very systematic differences in women's and men's postures and gestures.

INEQUALITY AND DIFFERENCE

THE SOCIAL CONSTRUCTION OF GENDER RELATIONS

Michael S. Kimmel

Society is a masked ball, where everyone hides his real character, and reveals it by hiding.
—RALPH WALDO EMERSON, "Worship" (1860)

My self . . . is a dramatic ensemble.

—PAUL KLEE

In one of its most thoughtful definitions, sociology was defined by C. Wright Mills as the intersection of biography and history. In his view, the goal of a sociological perspective would be to locate an individual in both time and space, to provide the social and historical contexts in which a person constructs his or her identity. In that sense, sociology's bedrock assumption, upon which its analyses of structures and institutions rests, is that individuals shape their lives within both historical and social contexts. We do not do so simply because we are biologically programmed to act in certain ways, nor because we have inevitable human tasks to solve as we age. Rather, we respond to the world we encounter—shaping, modifying, and creating our identities through those encounters with other people and within social institutions.

Sociological perspectives on gender assume the variability of gendered identities that anthropological research has explored, the biological "imperatives" toward gender identity and differentiation (though sociology locates the source of these imperatives less in our bodies and more in our environments), and the psychological imperatives toward both autonomy and connection that modern society requires of individuals in the modern world. To a sociologist, both our biographies (identities) and history (evolving social structures) are gendered.

Like other social sciences, sociology begins with a critique of biological determinism. Instead of observing our experiences as the expressions of inborn, interplanetary differences, the social sciences examine the variations among men and among women, as well as the differences between them. The social sciences thus begin with the explicitly social origin of our patterns of development.

Our lives depend on social interaction. Literally, it seems. In the thirteenth century, Frederick II, emperor of the Holy Roman Empire, decided to perform an experiment to see if he could discover the "natural language of man."

What language would we speak if no one taught us language? He selected some newborn babies, and decreed that no one speak to them. The babies were suckled and nursed and bathed as usual, but speech and songs and lullabies were strictly prohibited. All the babies died. And you've probably heard those stories of "feral children"—babies who were abandoned and raised by animals became suspicious of people and could not be socialized to live in society after age six or so. In all the stories, the children died young, as did virtually all the "isolates," those little children who are locked away in closets and basements by sadistic or insane parents.[1] What do such stories tell us? True or apocryphal, they suggest that biology alone—that is, our anatomical composition—does not determine our development as we might have thought. We need to interact, to be socialized, to be part of society. It is that interaction, not our bodies, that makes us who we are.

5   Often, the first time we hear that gender is socially constructed, we take it to mean that we are, as individuals, not responsible for what we do. "Society made me like this," we might say. "It's not my fault." (This is often the flip side of the other response one often hears: "In America an individual can do anything he or she wants to do," or "It's a free country and everyone is entitled to his or her own opinion.") Both of these rhetorical strategies—what I call reflexive passivity and impulsive hyperindividualism—are devices that we use to deflect individual accountability and responsibility. They are both, therefore, misreadings of the sociological mandate. When we say that gender identity is socially constructed, what we do mean is that our identities are a fluid assemblage of the meanings and behaviors that we construct from the values, images, and prescriptions we find in the world around us. Our gendered identities are both voluntary—we choose to become who we are—and coerced—we are pressured, forced, sanctioned, and often physically beaten into submission to some rules. We neither make up the rules as we go along, nor do we glide perfectly and effortlessly into preassigned roles.

For some of us, becoming adult men and women in our society is a smooth and almost effortless drifting into behaviors and attitudes that feel as familiar to us as our skin. And for others of us, becoming masculine or feminine is an interminable torture, a nightmare in which we must brutally suppress some parts of ourselves to please others—or simply, to survive. For most of us, though, the experience falls somewhere in between: There are parts we love and wouldn't part with, and other parts where we feel we've been forced to exaggerate one side at the expense of others. It's the task of the sociological perspective to specify the ways in which our own experiences, our interactions with others, and the institutions combine to shape our sense of who we are. Biology provides the raw materials, while society and history provide the context, the instruction manual, that we follow to construct our identities.

Definitions of masculinity and femininity vary, first, from culture to culture, and, second, in any one culture over historical time. Thus, social constructionists rely on the work of anthropologists and historians to identify the commonalities and the differences in the meanings of masculinity and femininity from one culture to another, and to describe how those differences change over time.

Third, gender definitions also vary over the course of a person's life. The issues confronting women when they are younger—their marketability in both the workplace and the marriage market, for example—will often be very different from the issues they face at menopause or retirement. And the issues confronting a young man about proving himself and achieving what he calls success, and the social institutions in which he will attempt to enact those experiences will change throughout his life. For example, men often report a "softening," the development of greater interest in care-giving and nurturing when they become grandfathers than when they became fathers—often to the puzzlement and distress of their sons. But in their sixties and seventies, when their children are having children, these men may not feel the same pressures to perform, to leave a mark, to prove themselves. Their battles are over, and they can relax and enjoy the fruits of their efforts. Thus, we rely on developmental psychologists to specify the normative "tasks" that any individual must successfully accomplish as he or she matures and develops, and we also need scholars in the humanities to explore the symbolic record that such men and women leave us as evidence of their experiences.

Finally, definitions of masculinity and femininity will vary within any one culture at any one time—by race, class, ethnicity, age, sexuality, education, region of the country. You'll recall that it seemed obvious that an older gay black man in Chicago would have a different idea of what it meant to be a man than a heterosexual white teenager in rural Iowa.

Social constructionism thus builds on the other social and behavioral sciences, adding specific dimensions to the exploration of gender. What sociology contributes are the elements that the social psychology of sex roles cannot explain adequately: difference, power, and the institutional dimensions of gender. To explain difference, social constructionism offers an analysis of the plurality of gender definitions; to explain power, it emphasizes the ways in which some definitions become normative through the struggles of different groups for power, including the power to define. Finally, to explain the institutional dimension, social constructionism moves beyond socialization of gendered individuals who occupy gender-neutral sites, to the study of the interplay between gendered individuals and gendered institutions.

10

BEYOND SEX ROLE THEORY

Social psychologists located the process of acquisition of gender identity in the developmental patterns of individuals in their families and in early childhood interaction. Specifically, sex role theorists explored the ways in which individuals come to be gendered, and the ways in which they negotiate their ways toward some sense of internal consistency and coherence, despite contradictory role definitions. Still, however, the emphasis is on the gendering of individuals, and occasionally on the inconsistent cultural blueprints with which those individuals must contend. Sociological understandings of gender begin, historically, with a critique of sex role theory, with sociologists arguing that such theory is inadequate to fully understand the complexities of gender as a social institution. Sociologists have identified several significant problems with sex role theory—problems that require its modification.

First, the use of the idea of role has the curious effect of actually minimizing the importance of gender. Role theory uses drama as a metaphor—we learn our roles through socialization and then perform them for others. But to speak of a gender role makes it sound almost too theatrical, and thus too easily changeable. Gender, as Helena Lopata and Barrie Thorne write: "is not a role in the same sense that being a teacher, sister, or friend is a role. Gender, like race or age, is deeper, less changeable, and infuses the more specific roles one plays; thus, a female teacher differs from a male teacher in important sociological respects (e.g., she is likely to receive less pay, status and credibility)." *To make gender a role like any other role is to diminish its power in structuring our lives.*[2]

Second, sex role theory posits singular normative definitions of masculinity and femininity. If the meanings of masculinity and femininity vary across cultures, over historical time, among men within any one culture, and over the life course, we cannot speak of masculinity or femininity as though each was a constant, singular, universal essence. Personally, when I read what social psychologists wrote about the "male sex role" I always wondered whom they were writing about. "Who, me?" I thought. Is there really only *one* male sex role and only one female sex role?

One of the key themes about gender identity is the ways in which other differences—race, class, ethnicity, sexuality, age, region—all inform, shape, and modify our definitions of gender. To speak of one male or one female sex role is to compress the enormous variety of our culture's ideals into one, and to risk ignoring the other factors that shape our identities. In fact, in those early studies of sex roles, social psychologists did just that, suggesting that, for example black men or women, or gay men or lesbians evidenced either "too much" or "too little" adherence to their appropriate sex role. In that way, homosexuals or people of color were seen as expressing sex role problems; since their sex roles differed from the normative, it was they who had the problem. (The most sophisticated sex role theorists understand that such normative definitions are internally contradictory, but they still mistake the normative for the "normal.")

15   By positing this false universalism, sex role theory assumes what needs to be explained—how the normative definition is established and reproduced—and explains away all the differences among men and among women. Sex role theory cannot fully accommodate these differences among men or among women. A more satisfying investigation must take into account these different definitions of masculinity and femininity constructed and expressed by different groups of men and women. Thus, we speak of *masculinities* and *femininities*. What's more, sociologists see the differences among masculinities or feminini-

ties as expressing exactly the opposite relationship than do sex role theorists. Sex role theorists, if they can accommodate differences at all, see these differences as aberrations, as the failure to conform with the normal sex role. Sociologists, on the other hand, believe that the differences among definitions of masculinity or femininity are themselves the outcome of the ways in which those groups interact with their environments. Thus, sociologists contend that one cannot understand the differences in masculinity or femininity based on race or ethnicity without first looking at the ways in which institutional and interpersonal racial inequality structures the ways in which members of those groups actively construct their identities. Sex role theorists might say, for example, that black men, lesbians, or older Latinas experience discrimination because their definitions of masculinity and femininity are "different" from the norm. To a sociologist, that's only half right. A sociologist would add that these groups develop different definitions of masculinity and femininity in active engagement with a social environment in which they are discriminated against. Thus, their differences are more the product of discrimination than its cause.

This leads to a third arena in which sociologists challenge sex role theory. Gender is not only plural, it also relational. Sex role theory posits two separate spheres, as if sex role differentiation were more a matter of sorting a herd of cattle into two appropriate pens for branding. Boys get herded into the masculine corral, girls the feminine. But such a static model also suggests that the two corrals have virtually nothing to do with one another. "The result of using the role framework is an abstract view of the *differences* between the sexes and their situations, not a concrete one of the *relations* between them."[3] But what surveys indicate is that men construct their ideas of what it means to be men *in constant reference* to definitions of femininity. What it means to be a man is to be unlike a woman; indeed, social psychologists have emphasized that while different groups of men may disagree about other traits and their significance in gender definitions, the "antifemininity" component of masculinity is perhaps the single dominant and universal characteristic.

Fourth, because gender is plural and relational, it is also situational. What it means to be a man or a woman varies in different contexts. Those different institutional contexts demand and produce different forms of masculinity and femininity. "Boys may be boys," cleverly comments feminist legal theorist Deborah Rhode, "but they express that identity differently in fraternity parties than in job interviews with a female manager."[4] Gender is thus not a property of individuals, some "thing" one has, but a specific set of behaviors that are produced in specific social situations. And thus gender changes as the situation changes.

Sex role theory cannot adequately account for either the differences among women and men, or their different definitions of masculinity and femininity in different situations, without implicitly assuming some theory of deviance. Nor can it express the relational character of those definitions. In addition, sex role theory cannot fully account for the power relationships between women and men, and among different groups of women and different groups of men. Thus, the fifth and perhaps most significant problem in sex role theory is that it *depoliticizes* gender, making gender a set of individual attributes and not an aspect of social structure. "The notion of 'role' focuses attention more on individuals than on social structure, and implies that 'the female role' and 'the male role' are complementary (i.e., separate or different but equal)," write sociologists Judith Stacey and Barrie Thorne. "The terms are depoliticizing: they strip experience from its historical and political context and neglect questions of power and conflict."[5]

But how can one speak of gender without speaking of power? A pluralistic and relational theory of gender cannot pretend that all masculinities and femininities are created equal. All American women and all American men must also contend with a singular vision of both masculinity and femininity, specific definitions that are held up as models against which we all measure ourselves. These are what sociologist R. W. Connell calls the "hegemonic" definition of masculinity and the "emphasized" version of femininity. These are normative constructions, the ones against which others are measured and, almost invariably, found wanting. (Connell's trenchant critique of sex role theory, therefore, hinges on his contention that sex role psychologists do not challenge but in fact reproduce the hegemonic version as the "normal" one.) The hegemonic definition is a "particular variety of masculinity to which others—among them young and effeminate as well as homosexual men—are subordinated."[6] We thus come to know what it means to be a man or a woman in American culture by setting our definitions in opposition to a set of "others"—racial minorities, sexual minorities, and so on. One of the most fruitful areas of research in sociology today is trying to specify exactly how these hegemonic versions are established, and how different groups negotiate their ways through problematized definitions.

20   Sex role theory proved inadequate to explore the variations in gender definitions, which requires adequately theorizing of the variations *within* the category men or women. Such theorizing makes it possible to see the relationships between and among men, or between and among women as structured relationships as well. Tension about gender was earlier theorized by sex role theory as a tension between an individual and the expectations that were established by the sex role—that is, between the individual and an abstract set of expectations.

This leads to the sixth and final problem with sex role theory: its inadequacy in comprehending the dynamics of change. In sex role theory, movements for social change, like feminism or gay liberation, become movements to expand role definitions, and to change role expectations. Their goal is to expand role options for individual women and men, whose lives are constrained by stereotypes. But social and political movements are not only about expanding the opportunities for individuals to break free of the constraints of inhibiting sex roles, to allow their "true" selves to emerge: They are about the redistribution of power in society. They demand the reallocation of resources, and end to forms of inequality that are embedded in social institutions as well as sex role stereotypes. Only a perspective that begins with an analysis of

power can adequately understand those social movements. A social constructionist approach seeks to be more concrete, specifying tension and conflict
not between individuals and expectations, but between and among groups of
people within social institutions. Thus social constructionism is inevitably
about power.

What's wrong with sex role theory can, finally, be understood by analogy.
Why is it, do you suppose, no reputable scholars today use the terms *race roles*
or *class roles* to describe the observable aggregate differences between members of different races or different classes? Are such "race roles" specific behavioral and attitudinal characteristics that are socialized into all members of
different races? Hardly. Not only would such a term flatten all the distinctions
and differences among members of the same race, but it would also ignore the
ways in which the behaviors of different races—to the extent that they might
be seen as different in the first place—are the products of racial inequality and
oppression, and not the external expression of some inner essence.

The positions of women and blacks have much in common, as sociologist Helen Hacker pointed out in her groundbreaking article "Women as a
Minority Group," which was written nearly half a century ago. Hacker argued that systematic structural inequality produces a "culture of self-hatred"
among the target group. And yet we do not speak of "race roles." Such an
idea would be absurd, because (1) the differences within each race are far
greater than the differences between races; (2) what it means to be white or
black is always constructed in relationship to the other; (3) those definitions
make no sense outside the context of the racially based power that white
people, as a group, maintain over people of color, as a group. Movements for
racial equality are about more than expanding role options for people of color.

Ultimately, to use role theory to explain race or gender is a form of blaming
the victim. If our gendered behaviors "stem from fundamental personality differences, socialized early in life," suggests psychologist David Tresemer, then responsibility must lie at our own feet. This is what R. Stephen Warner and his
colleagues call the "Sambo theory of oppression"—"the victims internalize the
maladaptive set of values of the oppressive system. Thus behavior that appears
incompetent, deferential, and self-degrading is assumed to reflect the crippled
capabilities of the personality."[7] In this world view, social change must be left to
the future, when a more egalitarian form of childhood socialization can produce children better able to function according to hegemonic standards. Social
change comes about when the oppressed learn better the ways of their oppressors. If they refuse, and no progress is made, well, whose fault is that?

A NOTE ABOUT POWER

One of the central themes of this book is that gender is about difference and
also about inequality, about power. At the level of gender relations, gender is
about the power that men as a group have over women as a group, and it is

25

also about the power that some men have over other men (or that some women have over other women). It is impossible to explain gender without adequately understanding power—not because power is the consequence of gender difference, but because power is what produces those gender differences in the first place.

To say that gender is a power relation—the power of men over women and the power of some men or women over other men or women—is among the more controversial arguments of the social constructionist perspective. In fact, the question of power is among the most controversial elements in all explanations of gender. Yet it is central; all theories of gender must explain both difference and domination. While other theories explain male domination as the result of sex differences, social constructionism explains differences as the result of domination.

Yet a discussion about power invariably makes men, in particular, uncomfortable or defensive. How many times have we heard a man say, when confronted with women's anger at gender-based inequality and discrimination, "Hey, don't blame me! I never raped anyone!" (This is analogous to white people's defensive response denying that one's family ever owned or continues to own slaves, when confronted with the contemporary reality of racial oppression.) When challenged by the idea that the gender order means that men have power over women, men often respond with astonishment. "What do you mean, men have all the power? What are you talking about? I have no power at all. I'm completely powerless. My wife bosses me around, my children boss me around, my boss bosses me around. I have no power at all!" Most men, it seems, do not feel powerful.

Here, in a sense, is where feminism has failed to resonate for many men. Much of feminist theory of gender-based power derived from a symmetry between the structure of gender relations and women's individual experiences. Women, as a group, were not *in* power. That much was evident to anyone who cared to observe a corporate board, a university board of trustees, or a legislative body at any level anywhere in the world. Nor, individually, did women *feel* powerful. In fact, they felt constrained by gender inequality into stereotypic activities that prevented them from feeling comfortable, safe, and competent. So women were neither in power nor did they feel powerful.

That symmetry breaks down when we try to apply it to men. For although men may be *in* power everywhere one cares to look, individual men are not "in power," and they do not *feel* powerful. Men often feel themselves to be equally constrained by a system of stereotypic conventions that leave them unable to live the lives to which they believe they are entitled. Men as a group are in power (when compared with women), but do not feel powerful. The feeling of powerlessness is one reason why so many men believe that they are the victims of reverse discrimination and oppose affirmative action. Or why some men's movement leaders comb through the world's cultures for myths and rituals to enable men to claim the power they want but do not feel they have. Or even why many yuppies took to wearing "power ties" while they munched their "power lunches" during the 1980s and early 1990s—as if power were a fashion accessory for those who felt powerless.

Pop psychologist Warren Farrell called male power a "myth," since men *30* and women have complementary roles, and equally defamatory stereotypes of "sex object" and "success object." Farrell often uses the analogy of the chauffeur to illustrate his case. The chauffeur is in the driver's seat. He knows where he's going. He's wearing the uniform. You'd think, therefore, that he is in power. But from his perspective, someone else is giving the orders; he's not powerful at all. This analogy does have some limited value: Individual men are not powerful, at least none but a small handful of individual men. But what if we ask one question of our chauffeur, and try to shift the frame just a little. What if we ask him: What is the gender of the person who is giving the orders? (The lion's share of riders in chauffeur-driven limousines are, after all, upper-class white men.) When we shift from the analysis of the individual's experience to a different context, the relations between and among men emerge also as relations of power—power based on class, race, ethnicity, sexuality, age, and the like. "It is particular groups of men, not men in general, who are oppressed within patriarchal sexual relations, and whose situations are related in different ways to the overall logic of the subordination of women to men."[8]

Like gender, power is not the property of individuals—a possession that one has or does not have—but a property of group life, of social life. Power *is*. It can neither be willed away or ignored. Here is how the philosopher Hannah Arendt put it:

> Power corresponds to the human ability not just to act but to act in concert. Power is never the property of an individual; it belongs to a group and remains in existence only so long as the group keeps together. When we say of somebody that he is "in power" we actually refer to his being empowered by a certain number of people to act in their name. The moment the group, from which the power originated to begin with . . . disappears, "his power" also vanishes.[9]

To a sociologist, power is neither attitude nor possession; it's not really a "thing" at all. It cannot be "given up" like an ideology that's been outgrown. Power creates as well as destroys. It is deeply woven into the fabric of our lives—it is the warp of our interactions and the weft of our institutions. And it is so deeply woven into our lives that it is most invisible to those who are most empowered.

GENDER AS AN INSTITUTION

My argument that power is the property of a group, not an individual, is related to my argument that gender is as much a property of institutions as it is part of our individual identities. One of the more significant sociological points of departure from sex role theory concerns the institutional level of analysis. As we've seen, sex role theory holds that gender is a property of individuals—that gendered people acquire their gender identity and move outward, into society, to populate gender-neutral institutions. To a sociologist, however, those institutions are themselves gendered. Institutions create gendered normative standards, express a gendered institutional logic, and are major factors in the reproduction of gender inequality. The gendered identity of individuals shapes those gendered institutions, and the gendered institutions express and reproduce the inequalities that compose gender identity.

To illustrate this, let us undertake a short thought experiment. To start with, let's assume that (1) men are more violent than women (whether biologically derived or socialized, this is easily measurable by rates of violent crime); that (2) men occupy virtually all the positions of political power in the world (again, easily measurable by looking at all political institutions); and that (3) there is a significant risk of violence and war at any moment.

Now, imagine that when you awaken tomorrow morning, all of those power positions in all those political institutions—every president and prime minister, every mayor and governor, every state, federal, or local official, every member of every House of Representatives and every Parliament around the world—was held by a woman. Do you think the world would be any safer from the risk of violence and war? Do you think you'd sleep better that night?

35   Biological determinists and psychologists of sex roles would probably have to answer yes. Whether from fundamental biological differences in levels of testosterone, brain chemistries, or evolutionary imperatives, a biological perspective would probably conclude that since females are less violent and aggressive than men, the world would be safer. (It is ironic, then, that the same people who believe these biological differences are also often the least likely to support female candidates for political office.) And those who observe that different socialization produces women who are more likely to avoid hierarchy and competition and search instead for peaceful solutions by another gendered value system would also breathe a collective sigh of relief.

"But," I hear some of you saying, "what about the women who have already *been* heads of state. What about Golda Meir, Indira Gandhi, and Margaret Thatcher? They're not exactly poster girls for a pacific ethic of care, are they?"

Indeed, not. And part of the reason that they were so "unladylike" in political office is that the office itself demands a certain type of behavior, independent of the gender of the person who holds it. Often it seems that no matter who occupies those positions, he—or she—can do little to transform them.

This observation is the beginning of a sociological perspective—the recognition that the institutions themselves express a logic, a dynamic, that reproduces gender relations between women and men and the gender order of hierarchy and power. Men *and* women have to express certain traits to occupy a political office, and his or her failure to do so will make the officeholder seem ineffective and incompetent. (These criteria apply to men also, as anyone who witnessed the gendered criticisms launched against Jimmy Carter for being frightened by a scurrying rabbit or for his failure to invade Iran during the hostage crisis in 1979–80 can testify.)

To argue that institutions are gendered is *only* the other half of the story. It's as simplistic to argue that the individuals who occupy those positions are genderless as it is to argue that the positions they occupy are gender-neutral. Gendered individuals occupy places within gendered institutions. And thus it is quite likely that if all the positions were filled with the gender that has been raised to seek peaceful negotiations instead of the gender that is accustomed to drawing lines in the sand, the gendered mandates of those institutions would be affected, modified, and moderately transformed. In short, if all those positions were filled with women, we might well sleep more peacefully at night—at least a little bit more peacefully.

Another example will illustrate this in a different way. Barbara McClin- *40* tock, the Nobel Prize–winning research cytogeneticist, . . . came upon her remarkable discovery of the behavior of molecules by a very different route than that used by her male colleagues. While earlier models had always assumed a hierarchically ordered relationship, McClintock, using what she called "feminine methods," and relying on her "feeling for the organism," discovered that instead of each cell being ruled by a "master molecule," cells were driven by a complex interaction among molecules. In this case, the gender of the person collided with the gendered logic of scientific inquiry to generate a revolutionary, and Nobel Prize–winning, insight.[10]

To say, then, that gender is socially constructed requires that we locate individual identity within a historically and socially specific and equally gendered place and time, and that we situate the individual within the complex matrix of our lives, our bodies, and our social and cultural environments. A sociological perspective examines the ways in which gendered individuals interact with other gendered individuals in gendered institutions. As such, sociology examines the interplay of those two forces—identities and structures—through the prisms of socially created difference and domination.

Gender revolves around these themes—identity, interaction, institution—in the production of gender difference and the reproduction of gender inequality. These themes are quite complex and the relationships between and among them are also complex. These are the processes and experiences that form core elements of our personalities, our interactions with others, and the institutions that shape our lives. These experiences are shaped by our societies, and we return the favor, helping to reshape our societies. We are gendered people living in gendered societies.

A social constructionist perspective however goes one step further than even this. Not only do gendered individuals negotiate their identities within gendered institutions, but also those institutions produce the very differences we assume are the properties of individuals. Thus, "the extent to which women and men do different tasks, play widely disparate concrete social roles, strongly influences the extent to which the two sexes develop and/or are expected to manifest widely disparate personal behaviors and characteristics."

Different structured experiences produce the gender differences which we often attribute to people.[11]

Let me illustrate this phenomenon, first with a mundane example and then with a more analytically complex one. At the most mundane level, think about public restrooms. In a clever essay on the "arrangement between the sexes," the late sociologist Erving Goffman playfully suggested the ways in which these public institutions produce the very gender differences they are supposed to reflect. Though men and women are "somewhat similar in the question of waste products and their elimination," Goffman observes, in public, men and women use sex-segregated rest rooms, clearly marked "gentlemen" and "ladies." These rooms have very different spatial arrangements, such as urinals for men and more elaborate "vanity tables" and other grooming facilities for women. We think of these as justifiably "separate but equal."

45   But in the privacy of our own homes, we use the same bathrooms, and feel no need for separate space. What is more, virtually no private homes have urinals for men, and few have separate and private vanity tables for women. (And of course, in some cultures, these functions are performed publicly, with no privacy at all.) Had these needs been biologically based, Goffman asks, why are they so different in public and in private? The answer, of course, is that they are not biologically based at all:

> The *functioning* of sex differentiated organs is involved, but there
> is nothing in this functioning that biologically recommends
> segregation; *that* arrangement is a totally cultural matter. . . .
> Toilet segregation is presented as a natural consequence of the
> difference between the sex-classes when in fact it is a means of
> honoring, if not producing, this difference.[12]

In other words, by using separate facilities, we "become" the gentlemen and ladies who are supposed to use those separate facilities. The physical separation of men and women creates the justification for separating them—not the other way around.

At the less mundane, but certainly no less important level, take the example of the workplace. In her now-classic work, *Men and Women of the Corporation,* Rosabeth Moss Kanter demonstrated that the differences in men's and women's behaviors in organizations had far less to do with their characteristics as individuals, than it had to do with the structure of the organization. Organizational positions "carry characteristic images of the kinds of people that should occupy them," she argued, and those who do occupy them, whether women or men, exhibited those necessary behaviors. Though the criteria for evaluation of job performance, promotion, and effectiveness seem to be gender neutral, they are, in fact, deeply gendered. "While organizations were being defined as sex-neutral machines," she writes, "masculine principles were dominating their authority structures." Once again, masculinity, the norm, was invisible.[13]

In a series of insightful essays, sociologist Joan Acker has expanded on Kanter's early insights, and specified the interplay of structure and gender. It is through our experiences in the workplace, Acker maintains, that the differences between women and men are reproduced and by which the inequality between women and men is legitimated. Institutions are like factories, and what they produce is gender difference. The overall effect of this is the reproduction of the gender order as a whole. Thus, an institutional level cannot be left out of any explanation of gender, because institutions are fundamentally involved in both gender difference and gender domination. "Gender is not an addition to ongoing processes, conceived as gender neutral," she argues. "Rather, it is an integral part of those processes."[14]

Institutions accomplish the creation of gender difference and the reproduction of the gender order, Acker argues, through several "gendered processes." These gendered processes mean that "advantage and disadvantage, exploitation and control, action and emotion, meaning and identity, are patterned through and in terms of a distinction between male and female, masculine and feminine." She observes five of these processes:

1. The production of gender divisions—the ways in which "ordinary organizational practices produce the gender patterning of jobs, wages, and hierarchies, power and subordination." In the very organization of work, gender divisions are produced and reinforced, and hierarchies maintained—often despite the intentions of well-meaning managers and supervisors.

2. The construction of symbols and images "that explain, express, reinforce, or sometimes oppose those divisions." Gender images, such as advertisements, reproduce the gendering of positions so that the image of successful manager or business executive is almost always an image of a well-dressed, powerful man.

3. The interactions between individuals—women and men, women and women, men and men, in all the forms and patterns that express dominance and submission. For example, conversations between supervisors and subordinates typically involve power dynamics, such as interruptions, sentence completion, and setting the topic for conversation, which, given the gendered positions within the organization will reproduce observable conversational gender differences.

4. The internal mental work of individuals "as they consciously construct their understandings of the organization's gendered structure of work and opportunity and the demands for gender-appropriate behaviors and attitudes." This might include patterns of dress, speech, and general presentation of self.

5. The ongoing logic of organizations themselves—how the seemingly gender-neutral theories of organizational dynamics, bureaucracy, and

50

organizational criteria for evaluation and advancement are actually very gendered criteria masquerading as "objective" and gender-neutral.[15]

As we've seen, sex role theory assumed that gendered individuals enter gender-neutral sites, thus maintaining the invisibility of gender-as-hierarchy, and specifically the invisible masculine organizational logic. On the other hand, many organizational theories assume that genderless "people" occupy those gender-neutral sites. The problem is that such genderless people are assumed to be able to devote themselves single-mindedly to their jobs, have no children or family responsibilities, and may even have familial supports for such single-minded workplace devotion. Thus, the genderless job-holder turns out to be gendered as a man. Once again, the invisibility of masculinity as the unexamined norm turns out to reproduce the power differences between women and men.

55   One or two more examples should suffice. Many doctors complete college by age twenty-one or twenty-two, medical school by age twenty-five to twenty-seven, and then endure three more years of internship and residency, during which time they are occasionally on call for long stretches of time, sometimes, even two or three days straight. They thus complete their residencies by their late twenties or early thirties. Such a program is designed for a male doctor—one who is not pressured by the ticking of a biological clock, for whom the birth of children will not disrupt these time demands, and who may even have someone at home taking care of the children while he sleeps at the hospital. No wonder women in medical school—who number nearly one-half of all medical students today—began to complain that they were not able to balance pregnancy and motherhood with their medical training. (The real wonder is that the male medical school students had not noticed this problem earlier!)

Similarly, lawyers just out of law school and who take jobs with large corporate law firms are expected to bill up to fifty to sixty hours per week—a process that probably requires working eighty to ninety hours per week. Assuming at least six hours of sleep per night, a one-hour round-trip commute, and one half-day of rest, these young lawyers are going to have a total of about seventeen hours per week to eat, cook, clean their houses, talk with and/or make love with their spouse (or date if they're single), and spend time with their children. Without that half-day off on the weekend, they have about one hour per day for everything else. Failure to submit to this regime places a lawyer on a "mommy track" or a "daddy track," which means that everyone will think well of you for being such an involved parent, but that you are certain never to be promoted to partner, to join all the rest of lawyers who made such sacrifices for their careers.

Or take university life. In a typical academic career, a scholar completes a Ph.D. about six to seven years after the B.A., or roughly by one's early thirties. Then he or she begins a career as an assistant professor and has six more years to earn tenure and promotion. This is usually the most intense academic work period of a scholar's life—he or she works night and day to publish enough scholarly research and prepare and teach his or her courses. The early thirties are also the most likely childbearing years for professional women. The academic tenure clock is thus timed to a man's rhythms—and not just any man, but one who has a wife or other family supports to relieve him of family obligations as he works to establish his credentials. Remember the adage "publish or perish"? Often, to academics struggling to make tenure, it feels as though publishing requires that family life perish.

In other occupations, the process of "gendering" through gendered institutions is similar. Not only are the demands of becoming a fire-fighter, police-man, or skilled worker most difficult and demanding during one's earliest years of apprenticeship and entry-level work, but also these occupations actually see themselves as actively developing a gendered individual. Thus among those men who work in dangerous professions—fire-fighting, police, military—the exclusion of women was often an essential component of reassuring these men that they had successfully mastered their masculine role. Similarly, unions served as a "masculinizing" force for workers who otherwise would have been left helpless and dependent in their inability to negotiate fair labor contracts. Unions provided "muscle"—strength in numbers. If individual union members were "weak" as men, the union, as the old song goes, "makes us strong." Since the institutions actually engage in gendering individuals, the femininity of any woman who entered those occupations was suspect.

Observing the institutional dimension also offers the possibility to observe adjustment and readjustment within institutions as they are challenged. Sometimes, their boundaries prove more permeable than originally expected. For example, what happens when the boundaries between work and home become permeable, when women leave the home and enter the gendered workplace? Judith Gerson and Kathy Peiss suggest that boundaries "*within* the workplace (occupation segregation) and interactional microlevel boundaries assume increased significance in defining the subordinate position of women." Thus occupational segregation can reproduce gender difference *and* gender inequality by assigning women to secondary statuses within organizations. For those women who enter nontraditional positions, though, microlevel boundary maintenance would come into play—"the persistence of informal group behavior among men (after-work socializing, the uses of male humor, modes of corporate attire)—act to define insiders and outsiders, thus maintaining gender-based distinctions."[16]

Embedded in organizational structures that are gendered, subject to gendered organizational processes, and evaluated by gendered criteria, then, the differences between women and men appear to be the differences solely between gendered individuals. When gender boundaries seem permeable, other dynamics and processes can reproduce the gender order. When women do not meet these criteria (or, perhaps more accurately, when the criteria do not meet women's specific needs), we see a gender segregated workforce and wage, hiring, and promotional disparities as the "natural" outcomes of already-present differences between women and men. It is in this way that those differences are generated and the inequalities between women and men are legitimated and reproduced.

(One should, of course, note that it is through these same processes that the "differences" between working-class and professional men, between whites and people of color, and between heterosexuals and homosexuals are also produced, and the inequalities based on class or race or sexuality are legitimated and reproduced. Making gender visible in these organizational processes ought not to blind us to the complex interactions with other patterns of difference and principles of inequality. Just as a male pattern becomes the unexamined norm, so too does a white, heterosexual and middle-class pattern become the unexamined norm against which others' experiences and performances are evaluated.)

The idea of organizational gender neutrality, then, is the vehicle by which the gender order is reproduced. "The theory and practice of gender neutrality," writes Acker, "covers up, obscures, the underlying gender structures, allowing practices that perpetuate it to continue even as efforts to reduce gender inequality are also under way."[17] Organizations reflect and produce gender differences; gendered institutions also reproduce the gender order by which men are privileged over women and some men—white, middle class, heterosexual—are privileged over other men.

"DOING GENDER"

There remains one more element in the sociological explanation of gender. According to sex role theory, we acquire our gender identity through socialization, and afterward, we are socialized to behave in masculine or feminine ways. It is thus the task of society to make sure that the men act in the masculine manner, and that the women act in the feminine manner. Our identity is fixed, permanent, and, now, inherent in our personalities. We can no more cease being men or women than we can cease being human.

In an important contribution to the social constructionist perspective, sociologists Candace West and Don Zimmerman argued that gender was less a component of identity—fixed, static—that we take with us into our interactions, but rather the product *of* those interactions. They argued that "a person's gender is not simply an aspect of what one is, but, more fundamentally, it is something that one *does,* and does recurrently, in interaction with others." We are constantly "doing" gender, performing the activities and exhibiting the traits that are prescribed for us.[18]

65   If our sex role identity were inherent, West and Zimmerman might ask, in what does it inhere? What are the criteria by which we sort people into those sex roles to begin with? Typically, our answer returns us to biology, and more specifically, to the primary sex characteristics that we believe determines which gender one will become. Biological sex—externally manifested

genitalia—becomes socialized gender role. Those with male genitalia are classified in one way; those with female genitalia are classified in another way. These two sexes become different genders, which are assumed to have different personalities and require different institutional and social arrangements to accommodate their natural—and now, socially acquired—differences.

Most of the time, we carry around these types of commonsense understandings. We see primary sex characteristics (those present at birth) as far more decisive than secondary sex characteristics (those that develop at puberty) for the assignment of gender role identity. But how do we know? When we see someone on the street, it is his or her *secondary* sex characteristics that we observe—breast development, facial hair, musculature. Even more than that, it is through the behavioral presentation of self—how he or she dresses, moves, talks—that signals for us whether that someone is a man or a woman. It would be a strange world, indeed, if we had constantly to ask to see people's genitals to make sure they were who they appeared to be!

One method that sociologists developed to interrogate this assumption has been to imagine that primary and secondary sex characteristics did not match. In many cases, "intersexed" infants, or hermaphrodites—whose primary sex characteristics cannot be easily discerned visually—have their genitals surgically reconstructed, depending upon the size of the penis, and not on the presence or absence of Y chromosomes. To these surgeons "chromosomes are less relevant in determining gender than penis size." Therefore to be labeled "male" does not necessarily depend upon having one Y and one X chromosome, nor upon the production of sperm, "but by the aesthetic condition of having an appropriately sized penis." The surgeons assume that no "male" would want to live as a man with such minute genitalia, and so they

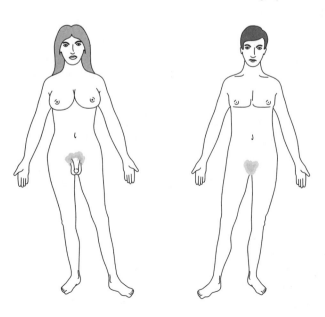

"correct" what will undoubtedly be perceived as a problem. (These surgically constructed females go on to live their lives as women.) It would appear then that size really does matter—at least to the doctors![19]

In a brilliantly disconcerting study, *Gender: An Ethnomethololological Approach,* Suzanne Kessler and Wendy McKenna proposed two images in which primary and secondary sex characteristics did not match.

Which one is the "man" and which is the "woman"? How can you tell? If you base your decision on primary sex characteristics—the genitals—you would have to conclude that many of the people with whom you interact in daily life might be hiding their true selves. But, if you base your decision on what you see "above the waist," which is more visible in daily life, you would have to conclude that many people may actually be a different sex from that which they appear to be.

70   Looking at those images, one might be tempted to dismiss this as the stuff of fantasy. After all, in real life, people's genitals match their secondary sex characteristics, and we are always able to tell the difference, right? Well, maybe not always. Recall the consternation in the popular film *The Crying Game,* when it was revealed, to both the audience and the film's protagonist simultaneously, that Dil, the woman he was in love with, was actually a man. And remember everyone's reaction when Dustin Hoffman revealed that Emily Kimberly was in fact Edward Kimberly in *Tootsie;* or the Broadway play *M. Butterfly,* which was about a man who lived with a "woman" for more than thirty years *without ever realizing that he was actually a man.* And think of the commotion and confusion about Marilyn Manson in recent years. And what about the consternation and disgust expressed by men who pay cross-dressing prostitutes for oral sex and then find out that "she" is actually "he." Such confusion is often the basis for comedy. Knowing whether someone is male or female is far more important to the observer than it often is to the observed, as fans of the television program *Saturday Night Live* will recall with the ambiguous character "Pat." People who interacted with Pat were constantly trying to trick him/her into revealing what he/she "really" was, while Pat nonchalantly answered their questions and eluded every rhetorical trap.

Of course, these are all media creations and in real life, "passing" is far more difficult and far less common. But one reason we enjoy such a parade of such ambiguous characters is because gender certainty is so important to us. Without it, we feel as if we have lost our social bearings in the world, and are threatened with a kind of "gender vertigo," in which the dualistic conceptions that we believe are the foundations of our social reality turn out to be more fluid than we believed or hoped.[20] It's as though our notions of gender are anchored in quicksand. One sociologist reported how she became disturbed by the sexual ambiguity of a computer salesperson:

The person who answered my questions was truly a sales
person. I could not categorize him/her as a woman or a man.

What did I look for? (1) Facial hair: She/he was smooth
skinned, but some men have little or no facial hair. (This
varies by race; Native Americans and blacks often have none.)
(2) Breasts: She/he was wearing a loose shirt that hung from
his/her shoulders. And, as many women who suffered through
a 1950s adolescence know to their shame, women are often
flat-chested. (3) Shoulders: His/hers were small and round for
a man, broad for a woman. (4) Hands: Long and slender fingers,
knuckles a bit large for a woman, small for a man. (5) Voice:
Middle range, unexpressive for a woman, not at all the exaggerated tones some gay males affect. (6) His/her treatment of me:
Gave off no signs that would let me know if I were the same or
different sex as this person. There were not even any signs that
he/she knew his/her sex would be difficult to categorize and
I wondered about this even as I did my best to hide these questions so I would not embarrass him/her while we talked to
computer paper. I left still not knowing the sex of my sales
person, and was disturbed by the unanswered question (child
of my culture that I am).[21]

Transvestites and cross-dressers reveal the artifice of gender. Gender is a
performance, a form of drag, by which, through the successful manipulation
of props, signs, symbols, behaviors, and emotions, we attempt to convince
others of our successful acquisition of masculinity or femininity. Or by which
we play with the conventions of successful gender acquisition, as in the antics
of pro basketball player Dennis Rodman.

By contrast, transgendered people who have had genital reconstructive
surgery often reinstate anatomy as the chief signifier of gender identity, as if a
man could not be a "real" woman as long as he possessed a penis, or a woman
could not be a "real" man as long as she did not possess one. Often transgendered people, or transsexuals, enact an exaggerated set of gendered traits of
their newly reconstructed biological sex. Male-to-female transsexuals often
become hyperfeminine, prissy, and passive; female-to-male transsexuals may
become assertively and aggressively masculine.

Cross-dressers know better, or rather, know different: As "social constructionists," they know that successfully being a man or a woman simply means
convincing others that you are what you appear to be. Just ask RuPaul, who
seems to float almost effortlessly between the two. (I say "seems" advisedly, since
it probably takes "him" as long to accomplish the male presentation of self as it
does to accomplish the female.) Or ask Alison Laing, a husband and a father,
who spends about 80 percent of his time dressed in women's clothes and 20
percent dressed as a man. "We don't have to live in gender boxes," he says.[22]

Most of us find the walls of those boxes enormously comforting. We learn
gender performance early in childhood, and it remains with us virtually all
our lives. When our gender identities are threatened, we will often retreat to

exaggerated displays of hypermasculinity or exaggerated femininity. And when our sense of others' gender identity is disrupted or dislodged, we can become anxious, even violent. "We're so invested in being men or women that if you fall outside that easy definition of what a man or woman is, a lot of people see you as some kind of monster," commented Susan Stryker, who is a male-to-female transsexual. Many transsexuals are murdered or attacked every year.[23]

The fascinating case of "Agnes" reported by Harold Garfinkel also demonstrates these themes. Agnes was first encountered in the late 1950s by a psychiatrist, Robert Stoller and by Garfinkel, a sociologist. Though Agnes appeared in every way to be a very feminine woman, she also had a penis, which she regarded as a biological mistake. Agnes "knew" she was a woman, and acted (and demanded to be treated) as a woman. "I have always been a girl," she proclaimed to her interviewers, and regarded her early childhood socialization as a relentless trauma of being forced to participate in activities for boys, like sports. Since genitals were not "the essential signs of her femininity," Agnes instead referred to her prominent breasts and her lifelong sense that she was, in fact, female. "Her self-described feminine feelings, behavior, choices of companions, and the like were never portrayed as matters of decision or choice but were treated as *given* as a natural fact," writes Garfinkel (Reavealingly, Garfinkel refers to Agnes, as I have, with a feminine pronoun, although biologically Agnes possessed male genitalia.)[24]

Understanding how we do gender, then, requires that we make visible the performative elements of identity, and also the audience for those performances. It also opens up unimaginable possibilities for social change; as Suzanne Kessler points out in her study of "intersexed people" (hermaphrodites):

> If authenticity for gender rests not in a discoverable nature but in someone else's proclamation, then the power to proclaim something else is available. If physicians recognized that implicit in their management of gender is the notion that finally, and always, people construct gender as well as the social systems that are grounded in gender-based concepts, the possibilities for real social transformations would be unlimited.[25]

Kessler's gender utopianism does raise an important issue in the sociological perspective. In saying that we "do" gender we are saying that gender is more than something that is done to us. We create and re-create our own gendered identities within the contexts of our interactions with others and within the institutions we inhabit.

A SOCIOLOGY OF RAPE

Some evolutionary biologists explain rape as an evolutionary reproductive strategy for "losers" who are unable to pass on their genetic inheritance by old-fashioned seduction. (It is therefore evolutionary biologists, not mainstream feminists who insist that rape and sex are the same thing!) And anthropologists undermine such biological arguments, suggesting instead that rape varies dramatically from one culture to another, and what causes the differences between rape-prone and rape-free societies is the status of women. Where women are valued and honored, rape rates are exceptionally low. Where women are degraded and devalued, rape rates are high.

Psychologists enable us to differentiate between rapists and nonrapists by understanding the psychodynamic processes that lead an individual man to such aberrant behavior. Whether because of childhood trauma, unresolved anger at his mother, a sense of inadequate gender identity, rapists are characterized by their deviance from the norm. "Rape is always a symptom of some psychological dysfunction, either temporary and transient, or chronic and repetitive." In the popular view, rapists are "sick individuals."[26]

As we have seen, the sociological perspective builds upon these other perspectives. But it offers a radical departure from them, as well. Rape is particularly illustrative because it is something that is performed almost exclusively by one gender—men—although it can be and is done to both men and women. Thus, it is particularly useful for teasing out the dynamics of both difference (since only men do it) and dominance (since its primary function is the domination of either women or men). Instead of seeing a collection of sick individuals, sociologists look at how ordinary, how "normal," rapists can be—and then at the culture that legitimates their behaviors. It also assesses the process and dynamics that force all women to confront the possibility of sexual victimization—a process that reproduced both gender division and gender inequality.

Sociological studies of rapists have found that many are married or have steady, regular partners. Studies of gang rape reveal an even more "typical" guy who sees himself simply as going along with his friends. Rapists see their actions in terms that express power differentials between women and men. They see what they do to women as their "right," a sense of entitlement to women's bodies. And they often see their behavior in light of their relationship with other men. For example, the members of Spur Posse, a group of teenage boys in Southern California accused of numerous acts of date and acquaintance rape, kept score of their "conquests" using athletes' uniform numbers—which only the other boys could understand. And during wartime, the rape of vanquished women becomes a form of communication between the victor and the loser, and women's bodies are the "spoils of war."

While rape is an act of aggression by an individual man, or a group of men, it is also a social problem women, as a group, face. Women may deal with rape as individuals—by changing their outfits, their patterns of walking and talking, their willingness to go to certain places at certain times—but rape affects all women. Rape is a form of "sexual terrorism," writes legal theorist Carol Sheffield, a "system of constant reminders to women that we are vulnerable and targets solely by virtue of our gender. The knowledge that such things can and do happen serves to keep all women in the psychological condition of being aware that they are potential victims."[27]

To the sociologist, then, rape thus expresses both a structure of relations *and* an individual event. At the individual level, it is the action of a man (or group of men) against a woman. It is sustained by a cultural apparatus that interprets it as legitimate and justified. It keeps women in a position of vulnerability as potential targets. In this way, rape produces both gender difference (women as vulnerable and dependent upon men for protection, women afraid to dare to enter male spaces such as the street for fear of victimization) and gender inequality.

TOWARD AN EXPLANATION OF THE SOCIAL CONSTRUCTION OF GENDER RELATIONS

So, how shall we think about gender from a sociological perspective? The elements of a definition seem clear enough. We shall explore three related levels—(1) identity, (2) interaction, and (3) institution—and the interactions among them, in order to explain the related phenomena: gender difference and gender inequality.

85   First, we understand that gender is not a "thing" that one possesses, but a set of activities that one *does*. When we "do" gender, we do it in front of other people; it is validated and legitimated by the evaluations of others. Gender is less a property of the individual than it is a product of our interactions with others. West and Zimmerman call gender a "managed property," which is "contrived with respect to the fact that others will judge and respond to us in particular ways." Women and men are distinct social groups, constituted in "concrete, historically changing—and generally unequal—social relationships." What the great British historian E. P. Thompson once wrote about class applies equally to gender. Gender "is a relationship, not a thing"—and like all relationships we are active in their construction. We do not simply inherit a male or female sex role, but we actively—interactively—constantly define and redefine what it means to be men or women in our daily encounters with one another. Gender is something one *does,* not something one *has*.[28]

Second, we understand that we do gender in every interaction, in every situation, in every institution in which we find ourselves. Gender is a situated accomplishment, as much an aspect of interaction as it is of identity. As Messerschmidt puts it, "gender is a situated accomplishment in which we produce forms of behavior seen by others in the same immediate situation as masculine or feminine." Gender is what we bring to these interactions and what is produced in them as well.[29]

Nor do we do gender in a genderless vacuum, but, rather, in a gendered world, in gendered institutions. Our social world is a built on systemic, structural inequality based on gender; social life reproduces both gender differences and gender inequality. We need to think of masculinity and femininity "not as a single object with its own history, but as being constantly constructed within the history of an evolving social structure." As Katherine Pyke defines it, gender is:

> an emergent property of situated interaction rather than a role or attribute. Deeply held and typically nonconscious beliefs about men's and women's essential nature shape how gender is accomplished in everyday interactions. Because those beliefs are molded by existing macrostructural power relations, the culturally appropriate ways of producing gender favor men's interests over those of women. In this manner, gendered power relations are reproduced.[30]

In short, sociology is uniquely equipped to understand both what is really different between women and men, and what is not really different but only seems to be, as well as the ways in which gender difference is the product of, and not the cause of, gender inequality. We are gendered people living gendered lives in a gendered society—but we do actually live on the same planet. (In fact it may be that only on this planet would such differences make a difference.)

NOTES

1. M. Pines, "Civilizing of Genes," *Psychology Today* (September 1981).
2. Helen Z. Lopata and Barrie Thorne, "On The Term 'Sex Roles,'" *Signs* 3 (1978): 719.
3. Tim Carrigan, Bob Connell, and John Lee, "Toward a New Sociology of Masculinity," *Theory and Society* 14 (1985). See also R. W. Connell, *Gender and Power* (Stanford: Stanford University Press, 1987); R. W. Connell, *Masculinities* (Berkeley: University of California Press, 1995); Judith Stacey and Barrie Thorne, "The Missing Feminist Revolution in Sociology," *Social Problems* 32(4) (1985) for elaboration and summaries of the sociological critique of sex role theory.
4. Deborah Rhode, *Speaking of Sex* (Cambridge: Harvard University Press, 1997), p. 42.
5. Stacey and Thorne, "Missing Feminist Revolution," p. 307.
6. Carrigan, Connell, and Lee, "Toward a New Sociology," p. 587; see also Connell, *Gender and Power.*
7. Helen Hacker, "Women as a Minority Group," *Social Forces* 30 (1951); David Tresemer, "Assumptions Made about Gender Roles," in *Another Voice: Feminist Perspectives on Social Life and Social Science,* M. Millman and R. M. Kanter, eds. (New York: Anchor Books, 1975), p. 323; R. Stephen Warner, David Wellman, and Leonore Weitzman, "The Hero, the Sambo and the Operator: Three Characterizations of the Oppressed," *Urban Life and Culture* 2 (1973).
8. Carrigan, Connell, and Lee, "Toward a New Sociology," p. 587.
9. Hannah Arendt, *On Revolution* (New York: Viking 1976).
10. Evelyn Fox Keller, *A Feeling for the Organism* (New York: W. H. Freeman, 1985).
11. Janet Saltzman Chafetz, "Toward a Macro-Level Theory of Social Stratification," *Current Perspectives in Social Theory* 1 (1980).

12. Erving Goffman, "The Arrangement between the Sexes," *Theory and Society* 4 (1977): 316.
13. Rosabeth Moss Kanter, *Men and Women of the Corporation* (New York: Basic Books, 1977). See also Rosabeth Moss Kanter, "Women and the Structure of Organizations: Explorations in Theory and Behavior," in *Another Voice,* Millman and Kanter, eds.
14. Joan Acker, "Hierarchies, Jobs, Bodies: A Theory of Gendered Organizations," *Gender & Society* 4(2): 146 (1990); see also Joan Acker, "Sex Bias in Job Evaluation: A Comparable Worth Issue," in *Ingredients for Women's Employment Policy,* C. Bose and G. Spitze, eds. (Albany: SUNY Press, 1987); "Class, Gender and the Relations of Distribution," *Signs* 13 (1988); *Doing Comparable Worth: Gender, Class and Pay Equity* (Philadelphia: Temple University Press, 1989); and Joan Acker and Donald R. Van Houten, "Differential Recruitment and Control: The Sex Structuring of Organizations," *Administrative Science Quarterly* 19(2) (1974).
15. Acker, "Hierarchies, Jobs, Bodies," pp. 146–47.
16. Judith Gerson and Kathy Peiss, "Boundaries, Negotiation, Consciousness: Reconceptualizing Gender Relations," *Social Problems* 32(4): 320 (1985).
17. Acker, "Hierarchies, Jobs, Bodies," p. 258.
18. Candace West and Don Zimmerman, "Doing Gender," *Gender & Society* 1(2): 140 (1987)
19. Suzanne J. Kessler, "The Medical Construction of Gender: Case Management of Intersexed Infants," *Signs* 16(1): 12, 13 (1990).
20. The phrase comes from R. W. Connell; I take it from the title of Barbara Risman, *Gender Vertigo* (New Haven: Yale University Press, 1998).
21. Cited in West and Zimmerman, "Doing Gender," pp. 133–34.
22. Carey Goldberg, "Shunning 'He' and 'She,' They Fight for Respect." *The New York Times,* 8 Sept 1996, p. A24.
23. Cited in Goldberg, "Shunning 'He' and 'She,'" p. A24.
24. Harold Garfinkel, *Studies in Ethnomethodology* (Englewood Cliffs, N.J.: Prentice-Hall, 1967), pp. 128, 132.
25. Kessler, "The Medical Construction of Gender," p. 25.
26. Nicholas Groth, Ann Bergess, and Suzanne Sgroi, *Sexual Assault of Children and Adolescents* (San Francisco: Jossey-Bass, 1978).
27. Carol Sheffield, *Feminist Jurisprudence* (New York: Routlege, 1997), p. 203.
28. West and Zimmerman, "Doing Gender," p. 140; Barrie Thorne, "Children and Gender: Constructions of Difference," in *Theoretical Pespectives on Sexual Difference,* D. Rhode, ed. (New Haven: Yale University Press, 1990), p. 110; E. P. Thompson, *The Making of the English Working Class* (New York: Pantheon, 1963), p. 11
29. James Messerschmidt, *Masculinities and Crime* (Lanham, Md.: Rowman and Littlefield, 1993), p. 121
30. Carrigan, Connell, and Lee, "Toward a New Sociology," p. 589; Karen D. Pyke, "Class-Based Masculinities: The Interdependence of Gender, Class and Interpersonal Power," *Gender & Society* 10(5): 530 (1996).

Oppression Axis Three: Heterosexism/ Homophobia

4

■ ■ ■ ■

NOT FOR LESBIANS ONLY

Charlotte Bunch

The following is an expanded and revised version of a speech given at the Socialist-Feminist Conference, Antioch College, Yellow Springs, Ohio, July 5, 1975. Many of the ideas expressed here about lesbian-feminist politics were first developed several years ago in The Furies. Nevertheless, I am continually discovering that most feminists, including many lesbians, have little idea what lesbian-feminist politics is. This speech takes those basic political ideas and develops them further, particularly as they relate to socialist-feminism.

I am listed in your program as Charlotte Bunch-Weeks—a rather ominous slip-of-the-tongue (or slip in historical timing), which reflects a subject so far avoided at this conference that I, for one, want to talk about.

Five years ago, when I *was* Charlotte Bunch-Weeks, and straight, and married to a man, I was also a socialist-feminist. When I left the man and the marriage, I also left the newly developing socialist-feminist movement—because, for one reason, my politics then, as now, were inextricably joined with the way I lived my personal, my daily life. With men, with male politics, I was a socialist; with women, engaged in the articulation of women's politics, I became a lesbian-feminist—and, in the gay–straight split, a lesbian-feminist separatist. It's that gay–straight split that no one here seems to want to remember—and I bring it up now, not because I want to relive a past painful to all concerned, but because it is an essential part of our political history which, if ignored, will eventually force lesbians to withdraw again from other

217

political women. There were important political reasons for that split, reasons explicitly related to the survival of lesbians, and those reasons and the problems causing them are still with us. It is important—especially for political groups who wish to give credence and priority to lesbian issues—to remember why separation happened, why it is not a historical relic but still vital to the ongoing debate over lesbianism and feminism.

In my own personal experience, I and the other women of The Furies collective left the women's movement because it had been made clear to us that there was no space to develop a lesbian-feminist politics and life style without constant and nonproductive conflict with heterosexual fear, antagonism, and insensitivity. This was essentially the same experience shared by many other lesbian-feminists at about the same time around the country. What the women's movement could not accept then—and still finds it difficult to accept—is that lesbianism is political: this is the essence of lesbian-feminist politics. Sounds simple. Yet most feminists still view lesbianism as a personal decision or, at best, as a civil rights concern or a cultural phenomenon. Lesbianism is more than a question of civil rights and culture, although the daily discrimination against lesbians is real and its alleviation through civil-libertarian reforms is important. Similarly, although lesbianism is a primary force in the emergence of dynamic women's culture, it is much more. Lesbian-feminist politics is a political critique of the institution and ideology of heterosexuality as a cornerstone of male supremacy. It is an extension of the analysis of sexual politics to an analysis of sexuality itself as an institution. It is a commitment to women as a political group, which is the basis of a political/economic strategy leading to power for women, not just an "alternative community."

There are many lesbians still who feel that there is no place in socialist-feminist organizations in particular, or the women's movement in general, for them to develop that politics or live that life. Because of this, I am still, in part, a separatist; but I don't want to be a total separatist again: few who have experienced that kind of isolation believe it is the ultimate goal of liberation. Since unity and coalition seem necessary, the question for me is unity on what terms? with whom? and around what politics? For instance, to unify the lesbian-feminist politics developed within the past four years with socialist-feminism requires more than token reference to queers. It requires an acknowledgement of lesbian-feminist analysis as central to understanding and ending woman's oppression.

5 The heart of lesbian-feminist politics, let me repeat, is a recognition that heterosexuality as an institution and an ideology is a cornerstone of male supremacy. Therefore, women interested in destroying male supremacy, patriarchy and capitalism must, equally with lesbians, fight heterosexual domination—or we will never end female oppression. This is what I call "the heterosexual question"—it is *not* the lesbian question.

Although lesbians have been the quickest to see the challenge to heterosexuality as a necessity for feminist's survival, straight feminists are not precluded from examining and fighting against heterosexuality. The problem is that few have done so. This perpetuates lesbian fears that remaining tied to men prevents women from seeing the function of heterosexuality and acting to end it. It is not lesbianism (women's ties to women) but heterosexuality (women's ties to men), and thus men themselves, which divides women politically and personally. This is the "divisiveness" of the lesbian issue to the women's movement. We won't get beyond it by demanding that lesbians retreat, politics in hand, back into the closet. We will only get beyond it by struggling over the institutional and ideological analysis of lesbian-feminism. We need to discover what lesbian consciousness means for any woman, just as we struggle to understand what class or race consciousness means for women of any race or class. And we must develop strategies that will destroy the political institutions that oppress us.

It is particularly important for those at this conference to understand that heterosexuality—as an ideology and as an institution—upholds all those aspects of female oppression that have been discussed here. For example, heterosexuality is basic to our oppression in the workplace. When we look at how women are defined and exploited as secondary, marginal workers, we recognize that this definition assumes that all women are tied to men. I mention the workplace because it upset me yesterday at the economics panel that no one made that connection; and further, no one recognized that a high percentage of women workers are lesbian and therefore their relationship to and attitudes toward work are fundamentally different from those assumed by straight workers. It is obvious that heterosexuality upholds the home, housework, the family as both a personal and economic unit. It is apparently not so obvious that the whole framework of heterosexuality defines our lives, that it is fundamental to the negative self-image and self-hatred of women in this society. Lesbian-feminism is based on a rejection of male definitions of our lives and is therefore crucial to the development of a positive woman-identified identity, of redefining who we are supposed to be in every situation, including the workplace.

What is that definition? Basically, heterosexuality means men first. That's what it's all about. It assumes that every woman is heterosexual; that every woman is defined by and is the property of men. Her body, her services, her children belong to men. If you don't accept that definition, you're a queer—no matter who you sleep with; if you do not accept that definition in this society, you're queer. The original imperialist assumption of the right of men to the bodies and services of women has been translated into a whole variety of forms of domination throughout this society. And as long as people accept that initial assumption—and question everything *but* that assumption—it is impossible to challenge the other forms of domination.

What makes heterosexuality work is heterosexual privilege—and if you don't have a sense of what that privilege is, I suggest that you go home and announce to everybody that you know—a roommate, your family, the people you work with, everywhere you go—that you're a queer. Try being a queer for a week. Do not walk out on the street with men; walk only with women, especially at night. For a whole week, experience life as if you were a lesbian, and I think you will know what heterosexual privilege is very quickly. And, hopefully, you will also learn that heterosexual privilege is the method by which women are given a stake in male supremacy—and that it is therefore the method by which women are given a stake in their own oppression. Simply stated, a woman who stays in line—by staying straight or by refusing to resist straight privileges—receives some of the benefits of male privilege indirectly and is thus given a stake in continuing those privileges and maintaining their source—male supremacy.

10   Heterosexual women must realize—no matter what their personal connection to men—that the benefits they receive from men will always be in diluted form and will ultimately result in their own self-destruction. When a woman's individual survival is tied to men, she is at some intrinsic place separate from other women and from the survival needs of those other women. The question arises not because of rhetorical necessity—whether a woman is personally loyal to other women—but because we must examine what stake each of us has in the continuation of male supremacy. For example, if you are receiving heterosexual benefits through a man (or through his social, cultural, or political systems), are you clear about what those benefits are doing for you, both personally and in terms of other women? I have know women who are very strong in fighting against female job discrimination, but when the battle closes in on their man's job, they desert that position. In universities, specifically, when a husband's job is threatened by feminist hiring demands, I have seen feminists abandon their political positions in order to keep the privileges they receive from their man's job.

This analysis of the function of heterosexuality in women's oppression is available to any woman, lesbian or straight. Lesbian-feminism is not a political analysis "for lesbians only." It is a political perspective and fight against one of the major institutions of our oppression—a fight which heterosexual women can engage in. The problem is that few do. Since lesbians are materially oppressed by heterosexuality daily, it is not surprising that we have seen and understood its impact first—not because we are more moral, but because our reality is different, and it is a *materially* different reality. We are trying to convey this fact of our oppression to you because, whether you feel it directly or not, it also oppresses you, and because if we are going to change society and survive, we must all attack heterosexual domination.

CLASS AND LESBIANISM

There is another important aspect of lesbian-feminism which should be of interest to a socialist-feminist conference: the connection between lesbianism and class. One of the ways lesbianism has affected the movement is in changing women's individual lives. Those of us who are out of the closet have, in particular, learned that we must create our own world—we haven't any choice in the matter, because there is no institution in this society that is created for us. Once we are out, there is no place that wholeheartedly accepts us. Coming out is important, partly because it puts us in a materially different reality in terms of what we have to do. And it is the impact of reality that moves anyone to understand and change. I don't believe that idealism is the primary force that moves people; necessity moves people. And lesbians who are out are moved by necessity—not by choice—to create our own world. Frequently (and mistakenly), that task has been characterized as cultural. While the culture gives us strength, the impetus is economic: the expression of necessity is always material. For middle-class women this is especially true—lesbianism means discovering that we have to support ourselves for the rest of our lives, something that lower- and working-class women have always known. This discovery makes us begin to understand what lower- and working-class women have been trying to tell us all along: "What do you know about survival?"

I heard a lot about class analysis when I was in the Left, and some of it was helpful. But it wasn't until I came out as a lesbian and had to face my own survival on that basis—as an outlaw, as a woman alone—that I learned about class in my own life. Then I learned what the Left had never taught me—what my middle-class assumptions were and the way in which my background crippled me as a woman. I began to understand how my own middle-class background was holding me back personally and the ways in which middle-class assumptions were holding back the growth of our movement. Class affects the way we operate every day—as has been obvious in much of what has happened at this conference. And theories of class should help us understand that. The only way to understand the function of class in society, as far as I'm concerned, is to understand how it functions right here, on the spot, day to day, in our lives.

Another way in which class consciousness has occurred in the lesbian community—and I want to acknowledge it because it is frequently one of the things kept locked in the bedroom closet—is the cross-class intimacy that occurs among lesbians. This intimacy usually leads to an on-the-spot analysis of class oppression and conflict based on the experience of being hit over the head with it. Understand that I am not advising every middle-class woman to go out and get herself a lower-class lesbian to teach her about class-in-the-raw; but also understand that I am saying that there's no faster way to learn how class functions in our world.

Cross-class contact occurs all the time in the lesbian community, frequently without any self-conscious politics attached to it. For example, in lesbian bars, a political process that is often misinterpreted as a purely social process is going on in women's lives. Because there are no men in that environment, the conflicts around class and race—those issues basic to women's survival—become crystal clear, if you understand them not in rhetorical or theoretical terms but in the ways that women's lives are interacting with each other's. This is one reason why a lot of class analysis, particularly the practical kind, has come out of the lesbian-feminist movement—analysis based on our experience of class contact and conflict, our recognition of it, and our integration of its meanings in the way we live our lives. This material experience

15

of class realities produces real commitment to struggle and to the class question, not out of idealism but as integral to our survival. Idealism can be abandoned at any time. Survival cannot.

I want to be clear about what it is that I am *not* saying. I am not saying that all lesbians are feminists; all lesbians are not politically conscious. I am saying that the particular material reality of lesbian life makes political consciousness more likely; we can build on the fact that it is not in the interests of lesbians to maintain and defend the system as it is.

I am also *not* saying that the only way to have this political analysis is to be a lesbian. But I am saying that so far most of the people with lesbian-feminist politics who have challenged heterosexuality are lesbians. But ours is not the only way, and we've got to make it not the only way. We, as lesbians, are a minority. We cannot survive alone. We will not survive alone, but if we do not survive the entire women's movement will be defeated and female oppression will be re-enacted in other forms. As we all understand survival more clearly, we see that the politics and analysis of women's oppression coming out of the lesbian's life experience have got to be integrated into the politics of socialist-feminism and the rest of the women's movement.

It is not okay to be queer under patriarchy—and the last thing we should be aiming to do is to make it okay. Nothing in capitalist-patriarchal America works to our benefit and I do not want to see us working in any way to integrate ourselves into that order. I'm not saying that we should neglect work on reforms—we must have our jobs, our housing, and so on. But in so doing we must not lose sight of our ultimate goal. Our very strength as lesbians lies in the fact that we are outside of patriarchy; our existence challenges its life. To work for "acceptance" is to work for our own disintegration and an end to the clarity and energy we bring to the women's movement.

It is not okay, and I do not want it ever to be okay, to be queer in patriarchy. The entire system of capitalism and patriarchy must be changed. And essential to that change is an end to heterosexual domination. Lesbians cannot work in movements that do not recognize that heterosexuality is central to all women's oppression: that would be to work for our own self-destruction. But we can coalesce with groups which share the lesbian-feminist analysis and are committed to the changes essential to our survival. This is the basis upon which we can begin to build greater unity and a stronger, more powerful feminist movement.

HOMOPHOBIA

Timothy Beneke

Straight men especially have a strange paranoia about feelings, and they fear what they perceive in themselves and in gay men as weakness: femininity, softness, crying too easily. And you know, that's their limitation that's coming out. What they twitch from in us is what we have to nourish and make even stronger.

PAUL MONETTE, in Mark Thompson's *Gay Soul*

Homophobia is entirely about extinguishing the feminine and extinguishing the child. Because what are the two enemies of the masculine myth—the woman and the child!

ANDREW HARVEY, in Mark Thompson's *Gay Soul*

GAY HATING

The record of straight men's behavior toward gays and lesbians has been, and largely remains, abominable. It ought to be easy to see that straights have systematically abused and oppressed gay people and continue to do so, but this perception eludes most straight men. Such a perception is intellectually obvious; the obstacles to its achievement lie outside the realm of mere intellection.

We have no single word for the hatred of gays—this fact alone reflects our unwillingness to acknowledge the problem. "Homophobia" psychologizes the problem; "heterosexism" addresses structural issues of oppression and the privileging of heterosexuals; but neither addresses the intensity of the hatred. Growing up in the deep South in the 1950s, the most powerful hatred I encountered was directed not at blacks but at gays. Though racism was rampant, it was partially balanced by a sense among some that racism was wrong; there were real black people around whose humanity was visible, and simple human decency could at times prevail. But gays were not visible and were thus available as repositories of the most horrendous projections.

I don't know at what age it started but by sixth grade this hatred was going full blaze:

"When you wake up in the morning do you have hair between your teeth?"

"No."

"You're a professional."

If you said yes, you were told you were an amateur. And epithets spewed out of boys' mouths: "Q-ball! Queerball! Queer!" And a little later, "Cocksucker!" or "That sucks!" It was rampant around boys my age until I was eighteen and left for college, where other perspectives began to prevail.

The insecurity of straight men about our heterosexuality/masculinity is, to judge from our behavior, enormous and even hysterical. As Jeffrey Weeks points out, heterosexuality is embroiled in a deep contradiction.[1] Heterosexuality is at once presented as the most natural thing in the world, and yet so many straight men behave as if it were perpetually fragile, and in danger of being undercut by any association with gays. How can something so supposedly "natural" be threatened by something so supposedly "unnatural"? Part of the answer lies in the fact that heterosexuality is equated with masculinity, which I have argued is, for many men, under perpetual psychic threat. The uncoupling of heterosexuality and masculinity would itself be a force against homophobia—if heterosexual desire and activity did not prove masculinity, homosexual desire and activity would not disprove it.

It is useful to be struck by—and not easy to be struck by—another contradiction: the existence of as many gay men as possible is, from the perspective of the mentality of sexual scarcity that afflicts so many straight men, in their objective, rational self-interest; and yet so few straight men welcome the existence of gays. We are so accustomed to the hostility of straights to gays that we rarely notice that straight men—especially adolescent and postadolescent straight men—compete, sometimes desperately, for the attention of women and benefit from the existence of men who offer no competition. This suggests the degree to which the hatred of gays is motivated by psychological needs. One can argue that racism and sexism are in the very narrowly conceived self-interest of those who propagate them, but it is harder to see this about homophobia.

10   Presumably, the fear of being raped by other men is an objective danger implicit in the very existence of gays, as Terry Kupers suggests.[2] Arguably, we should distinguish homophobia in straight men that focuses on the fear of being raped by strong macho gays, from homophobia that is threatened by gay effeminacy.[3] Straight men realize how hostile their own lust for women can be and fear being on the receiving end of that lust from men. Still, the sources of homophobia must be sought not in the objective self-interests of straights but in the realm of the psychological and irrational.

It is important to distinguish homophobia as an anxiety in straight men about their possible, or actual, homoerotic feelings and fantasies, from homophobia as the enacted oppression of gays by straights. The ability of straights to acknowledge and explore homophobia in the first sense is a step toward ending it in the second. Experiencing one's homophobia in the first sense is to be encouraged; enacting it in the second is to be condemned and its institutionalization, where possible, politically and legally remedied.[4] This distinction is important; if straight men are to become the allies of gay men they may have to confront their discomfort with their (real or, more likely, imagined) homoerotic sides. I take it that most straight men possess homophobic anxieties, whether consciously admitted or not; to simply label such feelings as "homophobia" and therefore "bad" closes off the possibilities of psychological and political exploration needed for straight men to engage in antihomophobic actions and to achieve self-knowledge. The more friendly straight men are with their homophobic anxieties, the more friendly they are likely to be toward gay men. Far too much pro-gay writing conflates homophobic oppression with homophobic anxiety in straight men, and uselessly condemns the latter.

I take it as true that, generally, men who oppress gays are likely to be men who oppress women, and likely to be more compulsively masculine; that homophobia and sexism have in common difficulty empathizing with and treating as fully human, people who have sex with men—gays and (most) women. And that homophobia essentially is grounded in the hatred of any appearance of what is regarded as "feminine" in men. Straight men in part fear the feminine in men because they fear possible arousal, or the attempt at arousal, by effeminate gay men.

Homophobia and sexism are thus best understood in relation to each other. Homophobic anxiety sometimes eats away at straight men. It is in part the fear that something arduously and painfully achieved, masculinity, will be forever lost if one gives in to certain impulses. It is in part inexorably tied to shame—the fear of being seen as gay by other men. Many straight men so strongly conjoin sexual object choice and achieved masculinity that they have great difficulty separating them.

PSYCHOANALYTIC SOURCES OF HOMOPHOBIA

Predominantly mother-raised boys begin life more or less identified with their mothers and, at a certain point, must make a shift in identification to a remote father, and to grandiose stereotypes of masculinity. This shift is never quite successful; hence masculinity remains problematic throughout life.

Following the important work of gay psychoanalyst Richard Isay, I believe that we come into the world with biologically based impulses to be sexually attracted to either the same or the opposite sex, or in varying degrees, both, and that social context and the social generally can powerfully, sometimes transiently, influence object choice. (I will not argue this point here.)[5] But the process of psychosexual development allow for complex motives for attraction or pseudoattraction, or lustless sexual fantasy, grounded in, among other things, processes of gender identification. There is a tendency to assume that sexual object choice as enacted in behavior, private sexual fantasy, felt gender identity, displayed gender identity, mode of sexual satisfaction, and biological sex will be in natural "alignment." That is, a biological male will act straight, have straight fantasies, feel internally like a "man" and act like one, and prefer conventional intercourse. But all of these characteristics can manifest in different forms and combinations. And sexual desire and fantasy can mean many things. Fantasies of engaging in sexual acts may not express sexual desire.

15

I want to distinguish among the following. First, there is lust toward one's own sex that is driven toward orgasm, something I take to be biologically impelled and a powerful source of fantasy. Such lust may be attached to any number of emotions. Second, there is an affectional consciousness toward members of one's own sex in which identification and attraction are difficult to separate. Third, there are fantasies of sexual activity with members of one's own sex that are not charged with lust and do not lead to orgasm. One's ability to relate to such distinctions will be constrained by one's experience. Lust centers around genital arousal and the desire to discharge in orgasm. An affectional consciousness is not driven by lust. And fantasies of erotic acts uncharged by lust are driven by psychological motivation usually related to processes of identification.

With these distinctions in mind, I want to explore three developmental moments that may motivate heterosexual men (men biologically impelled toward heterosexuality) toward forms of erotic or eroticized consciousness of men in ways that are likely to threaten manhood. All of them center around the concept of identification; one relates to the original identification with mother; a second relates to the process of shifting identification to father; and a third relates to the process of identifying with mother's models of masculinity.

These are meant only to be conceptually distinct; in life they may work together in a number of ways.

The first point has been expressed well by Michael Kimmel: "If the pre-oedipal boy identifies with mother, he *sees the world through his mother's eyes*. . . . He sees the father as his mother sees his father, with a combination of awe, wonder, terror, *and desire.* He simultaneously sees the father as he, the boy, would like to see him—as the object not of desire but of emulation."[6]

20   This presumes what I take to be true—that there exists a pre-oedipal stage of "safe" identification with the mother, where she is recognized as of different gender. This is arguably the strongest source of homophobia; it is not lust for the father so much as a mediated *erotic perception* of the father. The boy represses this erotic perception as he identifies with the father. The threat of regressing and identifying with his mother is a threat of loss of masculinity and loss of heterosexuality, or at least the awakening of an eroticized perception of his father. The two become psychically inseparable. Disidentifying with women and the "feminine" and disidentifying with gay men—twin sources of both sexism and homophobia—become necessary defenses.

Men become terrified of being seen as gay or feminine—a *fag, queer, wimp, sissy,* and so on. The animating emotion is shame. In shame we imagine we are being seen in a diminished way; we shrink and want to disappear or crawl into a hole and die; we curse our visibility. It is the eyes of others upon them that homophobic men fear, both of men perceiving them as less than masculine and gay men viewing them with lust.

The more tenuous the identification with father, the greater the fear of regression and identification with mother, and the stronger the need to resist.

Obviously the more comfortable men are with their "feminine side" and their residual identification with mother, the less they need sexism and homophobic oppression.

The second distinction and developmental moment is a little more elusive. When the boy transfers identification to the father (and to grandiose stereotypes of masculinity) he also transfers attraction; as he seeks to incorporate the father, to become him, he also idealizes him and masculinity itself. This idealized identification carries with it a form of attraction. In admiring and wanting to possess the muscles and skill and swagger of men, one experiences a kind of attraction. Again this is to be distinguished from lust.

The third distinction and developmental moment recapitulates the first. As the boy grows up, the mother presents a vision of men for him to identify with. In so doing she encourages the boy to identify with her image of a good man, and her image of a good man is, assuming she is heterosexual, necessarily an eroticized one. One identifies with masculinity in part through mother's eyes. In sharing her vision of the man she wants him to be, a boy shares her attraction. In striving to identify with such men, boys perpetuate a certain erotic perception of them.

HOMOEROTIC FANTASY IN STRAIGHT MEN

We are very familiar with the idea that sex can be symbolized in various fantasies and acts not themselves explicitly sexual. It is also possible and arguably common for nonsexual feelings to be symbolized sexually. As Willard Gaylin points out we commonly use sexual language to express nonsexual feelings. When a man says "Fuck you!" to another man, or "I got screwed by my boss!" he is using the sexual to express the nonsexual.

It is possible to have lustless erotic fantasies, just as we lustlessly speak of "getting screwed" or say "Fuck you." Isay lucidly argues that among straight men homoerotic fantasies often express unconscious desires to be like women— from my perspective, to regress and identify with mother. Anal and oral fantasies toward men, fantasies with clear sexual content, can be experienced without lust attached to them or the desire to enact them, because they express desires to identify with women and not desires for sex with men. As Isay points out, "The unconscious at times expresses identification with the mother as fantasies of performing fellatio or being the receptive partner in anal sex."[7]

In Isay's experience, this is more common among straight men who "perceive their fathers as powerful, authoritarian, and frightening, and their mothers as submissive, dominated and demeaned by their husbands."[8] The fear of the father translates into a desire not to compete for mother's attention, not to be a man.

If homoerotic fantasy in straight men is typically motivated by a desire to identify with the mother, it is not surprising that homophobia and sexism are

25

so deeply conjoined. Overcoming sexism means men empathizing with women—something men will be afraid to do if it means seeing men through women's eyes.

I want to briefly address two often conjoined assumptions regarding homophobia. The first is the assumption that if two straight men love or care deeply about each other, or enjoy hugging or being held by each other, they must be sublimating genital lust for each other, or be "latently homosexual." The second is the assumption that if men experience homophobic anxiety, or enact homophobic oppression, they must be repressing or struggling with homoerotic lust.

30   Both assumptions strike me as not only intellectual mystifications, but potentially injurious to straight men. If heterosexuality and homosexuality are both primarily genetically based, there is no reason to believe that straight men who care about each other possess homoerotic lust for each other. It may be understandably gratifying for gay or antihomophobic straight men and women to imagine the existence of such lust, but it is without clear foundation. Profeminist straight men sometimes, in reality or in imagination, try out a gay experience, seeking to find homoerotic lust within themselves simply because they believe it is supposed to be there. To establish an antihomophobic culture, straight men must be able to care for each other without needing to inspect themselves for evidence of lust.

If this analysis is correct, homophobic anxiety is driven not by a lust for men, but by a terrifying *fear* of lust for men—a fear that behind one's affection for men is sexual desire. Behind this is a fear of losing masculinity—and behind this, ultimately, a fear of losing identity itself.

Finally, I want to observe some ways that homophobia constrains and harms straight men. Given the enormous suffering—largely unacknowledged by straights—that homophobia causes gays and lesbians, it may seem indulgent to go on about the ways it harms straight men. But in fact it does, and straight men largely don't know it. Or rather, have to be prodded to acknowledge it. If straights are to stop oppressing gays, it will help if they see it as in their self-interest.

The pains that straight men take not to appear gay or effeminate are substantial, unacknowledged, and self-destructive. Sociologist Michael Kimmel asks his students to list all the things that count as evidence that a man is gay. They mention, among other things, effeminate gaits or gestures, flamboyant or colorful dress, expressing affection toward other men, expressing psychological sensitivity about anything, expressing "vulnerable" emotions like sadness or grief, expressing strong aesthetic reactions, and engaging in traditionally feminine activities like cooking or sewing. By implication, all of these also serve as tacit injunctions that burden men and tell them what *not* to do. The acknowledgment of such a burden by straight men is an important antihomophobic step that needs to be taken.

Straight men choke themselves off from so many realms of expression in striving to prove manhood. It is hard for a straight man to live a full emotional life while straining to appear straight. Ridding the world of homophobic oppression will help free straights as well as gays.

NOTES

1. Jeffrey Weeks, *Sexuality and Its Discontents: Meanings, Myths and Modern Sexuality* (London: Routledge and Kegan Paul, 1985.)
2. Terry Kupers, *Revisioning Masculinity* (New York: Guilford Press, 1993), chap. 3.
3. Here I draw upon Young-Bruehl's typology of homophobias in *The Anatomy of Prejudices.* According to her, "Researchers using questionnaires and interviews have developed a profile of the homophobic person. He or she is authoritarian, status conscious, intolerant of ambiguity, and both cognitively and sexually rigid. . . .Those who are least homophobic support equality between the sexes" (152). The research suggests that the homophobe is a sexist and the nonhomophobe is an antisexist.
4. We could start by instituting strong antidiscrimination laws and legalizing gay marriage.
5. Daryl Bem recently offered a fascinating theory of the sources of sexual orientation, meant to apply to everyone, that he summarizes in the phrase "exotic becomes erotic." Bem argues that biology, in the form of genes and prenatal hormones, drives childhood temperament, which leads boys and girls to prefer to play with those of similar temperament. Most choose to play with those of the same gender, but some boys and girls prefer to play with those of the opposite gender. As a result of this, the same gender is experienced as alien and strange. We know that around those who are alien and strange, we experience autonomic arousal. When genital sexuality kicks in at adolescence, this autonomic arousal becomes sexualized, according to Bem—the exotic becomes erotic. Bem's argument is subtle and elaborate and worthy of much attention. It may be that some such mediation of biological temperament is at work in the development of sexual orientation, rather than a direct, inherited impulsion toward a given sexual object. See "Exotic Becomes Erotic: A Developmental Theory of Sexual Orientation," *Psychological Review* 103, no. 2 (1996):320–335.
6. Michael Kimmel, "Masculinity as Homophobia: Fear, Shame, and Silence in the Construction of Gender Identity," in *Theorizing Masculinities,* ed. Harry Brod and Michael Kaufman (Thousand Oaks, California: Sage Publications, 1994), 130.
7. Richard A. Isay, *Being Homosexual* (New York: Avon Books, 1990), 77. Also, see Isay's fine book, *Becoming Gay* (New York: Pantheon Books, 1996), which contains a poignant account of his own evolution and coming out.
8. Isay, *Becoming Gay,* 77.

GENDER TREACHERY: HOMOPHOBIA, MASCULINITY, AND THREATENED IDENTITIES[1]

Patrick D. Hopkins

One of my first critical insights into the pervasive structure of sex and gender categories occurred to me during my senior year of high school. The seating arrangement in my American Government class was typical—the "brains" up front and at the edge, the "jocks" at the back and in the center. Every day before and after class, the male jocks bandied insults back and forth. Typically, this "good-natured" fun included name-calling. Name-calling, like most pop-cultural phenomena, circulates in fads, with various names waxing and waning in popularity. During the time I was taking this class, the most popular insult/name was used over and over again, *ad nauseam*. What was the insult?

It was simply, "girl."

Suggestively, "girl" was the insult of choice among the male jocks. If a male student was annoying, they called him "girl." If he made a mistake during some athletic event, he was called "girl." Sometimes "girl" was used to challenge boys to do their masculine best ("don't let us down, girl"). Eventually, after its explicitly derogatory use, "girl" came to be used among the male jocks as merely a term of greeting ("hey, girl").

But the blatantly sexist use of the word "girl" as an insult was not the only thing that struck me as interesting in this case. There was something different about this school, which in retrospect leads to my insight. My high school was a conservative Christian institution; no profanity (of a defined type) was allowed. Using "bad" words was considered sinful, was against the rules, and was formally punished. There was, therefore, a regulated lack of access to the more commonly used insults available in secular schools. "Faggot," "queer," "homo," or "cocksucker" were not available for use unless one was willing to risk being overheard by school staff, and thus risk being punished. However, it is important to note that, for the most part, these words were not restricted merely because of any sense of hurtfulness to a particular group or because they expressed prejudice. They were restricted merely because they were "dirty" words, "filthy" words, gutter-language words, like "shit" or "asshole." "Girl" was not a dirty word, and so presented no risk. It was used flagrantly in the presence of staff members, and even used by staff members themselves.[2]

5   In a curious twist, the very restriction of discursive access to these more common profanities (in the name of morality and decency) reveals a deeper structure of all these significations. "Girl," as an allowable, non-profane substitute for "faggot," "homo," and "cocksucker," mirrors and thus reveals a com-

mon essence of these insults. It signifies "not–male," and as related to the male speaker, "not-me."

"Girl," like these other terms, signifies a failure of masculinity, a failure of living up to a gendered standard of behavior, and a gendered standard of identity. Whether it was the case that a "failure of masculinity" actually occurred (as in fumbling the football) or whether it was only the "good-natured" intimation that it would occur (challenging future masculine functioning), the use of such terms demonstrates that to levy a successful insult, it was enough for these young men to claim that their target was insufficiently male; he was inadequately masculine, inadequately gendered.[3]

This story can, of course, be subjected to countless analyses, countless interpretations. For my purposes here, however, I want to present this story as an illustration of how important gender is to the concept of one's self. For these young males, being a man was not merely another contingent feature of their personhood. They did not conceive of themselves as people who were also male. They were, or wanted to be, *Men*. "Person" could only be a less descriptive, more generic way of talking about humans in the abstract. But there are no abstract humans; there are no "persons," rigorously speaking. There are only men and women. Or so we believe.

In what follows, I use this insight into gendered identity to make a preliminary exploration of the relationships between masculinity and homophobia. I find that one way to read homophobia and heterosexism in men is in terms of homosexuality's threat to masculinity, which in light of the connection between gender and personal identity translates into a threat to what constitutes a man's sense of self. To form a genuine challenge to homophobia, therefore, will not result from or result in merely increased social tolerance, but will be situated in a fundamental challenge to traditional concepts of masculinity itself.

WHAT IT MEANS TO BE (A) GENDERED ME

Categories of gender, in different ways, produce a multiplicity of other categories in a society. They affect—if not determine—labor, reproduction-associated responsibilities, childrearing roles, distributions of political power, economic status, sexual practices, uses of language, application of certain cognitive skills, possession of personality traits, spirituality and religious beliefs, and more. In fact, all members of a given society have their material and psychological statuses heavily determined by their identification as a particular gender. However, not only individuals' physical, economic, and sexual situations are determined by gender categories, but also their own sense of personal identity—their personhood. I use "personhood" here as a metaphor for describing individuals' beliefs about how they fit into a society, how they fit into a world, who and what they think they *are*[4] Personhood is critically linked (or perhaps worse, uncritically linked) to the influence of the gender categories under which an individual develops.

10   Individuals' sense of personhood, their sense-of-self, is largely a result of their construction as members of particular social groups within society-at-large: religions, ethnicities, regional affinities, cultural heritages, classes, races, political parties, family lineages, etc. Some of the most pervasive, powerful, and hidden of these identity-constructing "groups" are the genders; pervasive because no individual escapes being gendered, powerful because so much else depends on gender, and hidden because gender is uncritically presented as a natural, biological given, about which much can be discovered but little can (or should) be altered. In most cultures, though not all, sex/gender identity, and thus much of personal identity, is regulated by a binary system—man and woman.[5] Men and women are constructed from the socially raw material of newborn human bodies—a process that masquerades as natural rather than constructive.[6] To a very large extent, what it means to be a member of society, and thus what it means to be a person, *is* what it means to be a girl or a boy, a man or a woman. There is no such thing as a sexually or gender undifferentiated person.[7]

Identity is fundamentally relational. What it means to have a particular identity depends on what it means not to have some other identity, and by the kinds of relationships one has to other possible and actual identities. To have personhood, sense-of-self, regulated by a binary sex/gender system means that the one identity must be different from the other identity; a situation requiring that there be identifiable, performative, behavioral, and psychological characteristics that allow for clear differentiation. Binary identities demand criteria for differentiation.

For a "man" to qualify as a man, he must possess a certain (or worse, uncertain) number of demonstrable characteristics that make it clear that he is not a woman, and a woman must possess characteristics demonstrating she is not a man. These characteristics are, of course, culturally relative, and even intraculturally dynamic, but in late twentieth-century U.S. culture the cluster of behaviors and qualities that situate men in relation to women include the by now well-known litany: (hetero)sexual prowess, sexual conquest of women, heading a nuclear family, siring children, physical and material competition with other men, independence, behavioral autonomy, rationality, strict emotional control, aggressiveness, obsession with success and status, a certain way of walking, a certain way of talking, having buddies rather than intimate friends, etc.[8]

Because personal identity (and all its concomitant social, political, religious, psychological, biological, and economic relations) is so heavily gendered, any threat to sex/gender categories is derivatively (though primarily non-consciously) interpreted as a threat to personal identity—a threat to what it means to *be* and especially what it means to *be me.* A threat to manhood (masculinity) is a threat to personhood (personal identity). Not surprisingly then, a threat to established gender categories, like most other serious threats, is often met with grave resistance, for challenging the regulatory operations of a gender system means to destabilize fundamental social, political, and personal categories (a profoundly anxiety-producing state), and society is always prejudiced toward the protection of established categories. Inertia is a force in culture as well as in physics.

There are many different threats to gendered identity, but I think they can all be generally grouped together under the rubric of "gender treachery."[9] A gender traitor can be thought of as anyone who violates the "rules" of gender identity/gender performance, i.e., someone who rejects or appears to reject the criteria by which the genders are differentiated.[10] At its most obvious, gender treachery occurs as homosexuality, bisexuality, cross-dressing, and feminist activism. Any of these traitorous activities may result in a serious reaction from those individuals and groups whose concept of personal and political identity is most deeply and thoroughly sexed by traditional binary categories.[11] However, homosexuality is particularly effective in producing the extreme (though not uncommon) reaction of homophobia—a response that is often manifested in acts of physical, economic, and verbal assault against perceived gender traitors, queers.[12] Homosexuals, intentionally or not, directly challenge assumptions concerning the relational aspects of the binary categories of sex/gender, and as such threaten individual identities. Since the homophobic reaction can be lethal and so theoretically suggestive, it deserves serious attention.

HOMOPHOBIA/HETEROSEXISM

Theorists debate the value of using the term "homophobia." For some, the "phobia" suffix codes anti-gay and anti-lesbian activity as appertaining to psychiatric discourse—the realm of irrationality, uncontrollable fear, a realm where moral responsibility or political critique seems inapplicable due to the clinical nature of the phobia.[13] We do not punish people for being claustrophobic; we do not accuse agoraphobics or ignorance or intolerance; why should we treat homophobics any differently?

Other terms have been used to describe the aggregation of prejudices against gays and lesbians, including homoerotophobia, homosexism, homonegativism, anti-homosexualism, anti-homosexuality, and homohatred.[14] "Heterosexism" has become the terminology of choice for some theorists, emphasizing similarities to racism and sexism. "Heterosexism" characterizes a political situation in which heterosexuality is presented and perceived as natural, moral, practical, and superior to any non-heterosexual option. As such, heterosexuals are *justly* accorded the privileges granted them—political power, sexual freedom, religious sanction, moral status, cultural validation, psychiatric and juridical non-interference, occupational and tax privilege, freedom to have or adopt children and raise families, civil rights protection, recourse against unfair hiring practices, public representatives in media and entertainment industries, etc.

For many of us, however, "heterosexism," though accurate and useful, does not possess the rhetorical and emotional impact that "homophobia"

15

does. "Heterosexism" is appropriate for describing why all television couples are straight, why marriage and joint tax returns are reserved for heterosexuals, why openly lesbian or gay candidates face inordinate difficulty in being elected to office, or why only heterosexuals can adopt children or be foster parents. But "heterosexism," though perhaps still technically accurate, does not seem strong enough to describe the scene of ten Texas teenage boys beating a gay man with nail-studded boards and stabbing him to death.[15] The blood pooling up on the ground beneath the dying body is evidence for something more than the protection of heterosexual privilege. It is evidence for a radical kind of evil.

It is neither my goal nor my desire here to set out specific definitions of homophobia. Though I will use the term primarily with reference to physical violence and strong verbal, economic, and juridical abuse against gays, I do not claim to establish a clear boundary between homophobia and heterosexism. No stable boundary could be set, nor would it be particularly useful to try to do so—they are not discrete. "Homophobia" and "heterosexism" are political words, political tools; they are ours to use as specific situations present specific needs.

However, for my purposes here, heterosexism—loosely characterized as valorizing and privileging heterosexuality (morally, economically, religiously, politically)—can be seen as the necessary precursor to homophobia. Heterosexism is the backdrop of the binary division into heterosexual and homosexual (parasitic on the man/woman binary), with, as usual, the first term of the binary good and second term bad. Heterosexism constructs the field of concepts and behaviors so that some heterosexists' hierarchical view of this binary will be reactionary, for a variety of reasons, thus becoming homophobic (read: violent/abusive/coercive). In the same way that a person doesn't have to be a member of a white supremacist organization to be racist, a person doesn't have to be homophobic to be heterosexist. This is not to say that heterosexism is not as bad as homophobia, but rather that though heterosexism presents less of an obvious, direct, personal physical threat to gays, it nonetheless situates the political arena such that homophobia can and is bound to exist. Heterosexism is culpable for the production of homophobics. Heterosexists are politically culpable for the production of homophobics.

20   But even when we choose to use the term "homophobia" for cases of brutality, fanatic claims, petitions for fascistic laws, or arbitrarily firing gay employees, this does not mean that we must always characterize homophobia as an irrational, psychiatric/clinical response. Such a characterization would be grossly inadequate. "Homophobia" has evolved as primarily a political term, not as a psychiatric one, and does not parallel claustrophobia or agoraphobia, for the political field is not the same.

Religious and political rhetorics of moral turpitude and moral danger do not attach to closed-in spaces or wide-open spaces in the way they attach to same-sex eroticism. In other words, the fear and abhorrence of homosexuals is often taught as a moral and practical virtue and political oppression is massed against gays and lesbians. As a result, oppositional strategies to homophobia must be located in political discourse, not just psychiatric or pop-psychiatric discourse. Homophobia is supported and subsidized by cultural and governmental institutions in ways that demand the need for a variety of analyses. Though homophobia may often seem irrational or semi-psychotic in appearance, it must not be dismissed as simply an obsessive individual psychological aberration. Homophobia is a product of institutional heterosexism and gendered identity.

How do people explain homophobia? And especially, though not exclusively, how do people in queer communities explain homophobia? Being the victims of it, what do they see in it? Why is it that some men react so strongly and so virulently to the mere presence of gay men?

The Repression Hypothesis

One of the most common explanations of homophobia among gay men is that of repressed homosexuality. Men who constantly make anti-gay slurs, tell anti-gay jokes, use anti-gay language, obsess about the dire political and moral impact of homosexuality on the family and country, or even who are known to attack gays physically are often thought to be repressing their own sexual attraction toward men. As a result of their terror in coming to grips with their own sexuality, they overcompensate, metastasizing into toxic, hypermasculine, ultra-butch homophobes who seem to spend far more time worrying about homosexuality than openly gay men do.

This kind of repressed-homosexual explanation was aptly demonstrated by one of my straight undergraduate ethics professors. While teaching a section on sexual ethics, my professor and the entire class read a series in the college newspaper by our Young Republican student editor about how "the homosexuals" were taking over the country and converting all the children. Finally, after yet another repetition of the "but they can't have babies and they're unnatural" columns, my exasperated professor wrote a response to the paper, and after a lengthy list of counterarguments, ended by saying simply, "Methinks thou doth protest too much."

His intimation was clear. He believed that the Young Republican's arguments were more for his benefit than for his readers'. As the typical response goes among gays who hear men constantly ranting about the perils of homosexuality and the virtues of heterosexuality—"He's not trying to convince us. He's trying to convince himself."

I think for many men this theory of repression is accurate. It is not unusual for openly gay men to talk about their days in the closet and report that they were assertively heterosexist/homophobic—and that yes, they were desperately trying to convince themselves that they were really heterosexual. Sadly enough, many of these repressed homosexuals manage to maintain their repression at great cost to themselves and often at great cost to others. Some marry and live a lie, unfulfilled emotionally and sexually, deceiving their wives and children, sometimes having furtive, sexual affairs with other men. They manage psychologically to compartmentalize their erotic orientation and same-sex sexual experiences so radically that they live two separate, torturous lives. Some repressives become anti-gay activists and spend their lives trying to force gays and lesbians back into the closet, working against gay civil rights and protections.[16] Horrifyingly, some others undergo an even worse schism in their personalities, resulting in a bizarre, malignant, and persistent internalized war between homophobia and homophilia. This war can culminate in what John Money calls the exorcist syndrome, in which the repressive picks up, seduces, or even rapes a gay man, and then beats him or kills him in order to exorcise the repressive's "homosexual guilt."[17]

But while the repressive hypothesis is certainly accurate for some men, it is not accurate for all. I have no doubt that there are indubitably heterosexual men who hate and assault gays. To some extent, the explanation of repressed homosexuality may be wish fulfillment on the part of some gays. Forced by necessity of survival to be secretive and cryptic themselves, many gay men find it eminently reasonable to suspect any man of potential homosexual desire, and in fact, want such to be the case. It is reasonable, if optimistic, to hope that there are really more of you than there seem to be. And in light of the fact that many openly gay men report that they used to be homophobic themselves, the repression theory seems to be both empirically sound as well as emotionally attractive. There is also a certain sense of self-empowerment resulting from the repression hypothesis—out gays may see themselves as morally, cognitively, and emotionally superior to the men who continue to repress their sexuality. But homophobia is not so simple. What about those homophobes who clearly are not repressing their own homosexuality? What explanation fits them?

The Irrationality/Ignorance Hypothesis

Another explanation, one in perfect keeping with the roots of the word, is that homophobia is an irrational fear, based on ignorance and resulting from social training. [18] This explanation is also popular among liberal heterosexuals as well as liberal lesbians and gays. The stereotype of this kind of cultural/developmental homophobia is that of a little boy who grows up in a poorly educated, very conservative family, often in a rural area, who hears his parents and other relatives talk about the fags on TV or the homo child molester they caught in the next county and how he ought to be "strung up and shot." As the little boy grows, he models his parents' behavior, identifying with their emotions and desiring to emulate them. Although the boy has no idea of what a "fag" or "homo" is, he nevertheless learns the appropriate cues for application of those terms to situations and individuals, and the emotions associated with that application. He begins to use them himself, often as a general-use insult (like young children calling each other "nigger" even when they do not know what it means). He learns that certain kinds of behaviors elicit being called a fag and that he can achieve a degree of peer approval when he uses those terms. So he stands on the playground at recess and calls the boy who takes piano lessons a homo; his friends laugh. He asks the girls who are jumping rope with another boy why they are playing with a faggot; his friends laugh. Simultaneously, of course, the boy is learning all the other dictums of traditional heteromasculinity—girls are weak, boys are strong, girls play stupid games, boys play real games, girls that want to play football are weird, boys that do not want to play football are faggots. Eventually the boy learns the more complete definition of "faggot," "homo," "queer." Homos aren't just sissies who act like girls; they aren't just weak. They like to "do things" with other boys. Sick things. Perverted things.

A little knowledge is a very dangerous thing and the boy becomes a full-fledged homophobe who thinks boys who play the piano and do not like football want to touch him "down there." He learns that grown-up homos like to grab young boys and "do bad things to them." He learns that just as one can become a tougher, stronger, more masculine man by killing a deer and by "slaughtering" the guys on the opposing football team, one can become more masculine, or prove one's masculinity, by verbally abusing or beating up queers.

Though this scenario may seem hyperbolic, it certainly does occur. I have seen it happen myself. The lesson that gets learned is that of the recurring conflict of essence and performance.

Essence: You (the little boy) have a natural, core, normal, good, essential identity; you are a *boy*, a *young man,* male, not-a-girl. This is just what you are. You are born this way. Little girls will like you. You have buddies. You're lucky. You are our *son*. It's natural and obvious that you will grow up and get married and be a *daddy*.

Performance: But even though you just *are* a little *boy,* even though it's perfectly natural, you must make sure you do not act (how? why?) like a girl. You must always make sure that you exhibit the right behavior for a boy (but isn't it natural?). Don't ever act like not-a-boy! Don't betray that which you are naturally, comfortable, normally. Don't not-be what you are. Perform like a man.

The stage is set. The child knows that he is a he and that being a he is a good, normal, natural thing. Being a he requires no effort. You just are a boy. But at the same time, there is lingering on the horizon the possibility, amorphous and not always spoken, that you might do something which violates what you are. It might be quiet—"Now put those down, son. Boys don't play with dolls." It might be loud—"What the hell are you doing playing with dolls like some sissy??!!" The little boy internalizes the expectations of masculinity.

This kind of explanation of homophobia, though useful and accurate for many purposes, tends to characterize homophobia as learned but completely irrational, unfounded, arbitrary, ignorant, counterproductive, and dysfunctional. However, such a simple analysis excludes much of the experience of the homophobe. It is not actually the case that the poor mindless homophobe

simply veers through life distorting reality and obsessing over nothing, froth-
ing at the mouth and seeing faggots behind every corner and homosexual
conspiracies in every liberal platform, ruining his own life as well as others. In
fact, homophobia is not dysfunctional in the way that agoraphobia is. Homophobia has functional characteristics.[19]

35   For example, in the story given above, the boy does not simply "catch"
the obsessive, dysfunctional view of the world that his parents have. He learns
that certain kinds of behaviors elicit rewarding emotions not only from his
parents directly, but also from within himself when away from his parents.
When the little boy plays with toy soldiers and pretends to slaughter communists or Indians, his parents smile, encourage him, and even play with him
sometimes. If he plays house with his little sister, he is always the daddy and
she is always the mommy and he pretends to get home from work and she
pretends to have supper fixed for him—a game in which roles are correctly
modeled and are thus emotionally rewarding—"I'm just like my daddy."

However, the emotional (and sometimes corporal) punishments function
in the same way. If the boy is caught playing with dolls, or pretending to be
the mommy, he may be told that he is doing something wrong, or be punished, or may simply detect a sense of worry, disapproval, or distaste from his
parents. Homophobic tendencies will be carried along with all the other traits
of conservative masculinity. He will be "just like his daddy" when he calls
some effeminate boy a sissy—an emotionally rewarding experience. He will
receive approval from his peers when he pushes the class homo around—he
will be tough and formidable in their eyes. And perhaps most importantly, he
will be clearly and unambiguously performing the masculine role he perceives (correctly in context) to be so valued—an advantage in power, safety,
admiration, and self-esteem. It is also in no small sense that homophobia can
be functional in keeping other heterosexuals in line. The potential to accuse
another boy of being a faggot, to threaten ostracism or physical assault, is a
significant power.[20]

Thus, it is not the case that homophobia is somehow obviously dysfunctional on an individual or group level.[21] Homophobic activity carries with it
certain rewards and a certain power to influence. In the case of the repressed
homosexual, it externalizes the intra-psychic conflict and reaffirms a man's
appearance of heterosexuality and thus his sense of stability, safety, and self. In
the case of childhood modeling, homophobic activity wins approval from
peers and authority figures, protects one from becoming the target of other
homophobes, and reaffirms one's place in a larger context of gender appropriate behavior—protecting one's personal identity.

The Political Response Hypothesis

The recognition that there are rational, functional aspects of homophobia (in
a heteropatriarchal context) leads to a third explanation of homophobia that
reverses the second. This theory says that queers are a genuine political threat

to heterosexuals and really do intend to eliminate heterosexual privilege. Homophobia, therefore, is a rational political response.[22] Radical feminist lesbians and certain radical gay men directly challenge the hetero-male-dominated structure of society, rejecting patriarchal rule, conventional morality, and patriarchal modes of power distribution. All of the primary institutional sites of power that have maintained patriarchal domination—the state, the church, the family, the medical profession, the corporation—are being challenged from without by queers who do not want merely to be accepted, or tolerated, or left alone, but who want to dismantle heteropatriarchal society and build something different in its place. In response to liberal heterosexuals who promote the irrationalist theory of homophobia, supporters of this theory might say that many of the so-called "ignorant" and "false" stereotypes of queers are in fact correct, but they are not bad stereotypes; they are good and should be praised, should be revered, should replace heterosexual values. Yes, lesbians do hate men. Yes, fags do want to destroy the nuclear family. Yes, dykes do want to convert children. Yes, homos are promiscuous.

The impetus for this theory of homophobia comes from lesbians and gays who view their sexuality as primarily a political identity, having chosen to reject heterosexuality and become lesbian or gay as a political act of resistance. They have chosen this identification because they want to fight, destroy, or separate from hetero-male-dominated society. According to this theory, homophobia is a perfectly rational, reasonable reaction to the presence of queers, because queers pose a genuine threat to the status of heterosexual privilege. It is only logical that heterosexuals would fight back because if they do not fight back, their privilege, their power, and their dominance will be stripped away all the sooner.

There are people who seem, at least partially, to confirm this theory. It has been interesting to see that over the past ten years or so, it has become common for neo-conservative activist organizations to use the word "family" in their names. Among many gay, lesbian, and feminists activists, any organization with "Family" as part of its name is automatically suspected to be anti-gay, anti-lesbian, anti-feminist.[23] The frequency of the word "family" as an identification tag is seen as signifying a belief in the moral superiority of the traditional, heterosexual, nuclear family. This suggests that some "pro-family" activists trace and justify their anti-homosexual activism to the belief that lesbians and gays are threatening to destroy The Family and thus to destroy heterosexual morality.

It is also true that over the past twenty years or so, lesbian and gay thought has become radicalized in a variety of ways. Lesbians and gays have moved away from merely the hope of demedicalization and decriminalization to the hope of building cultures, ethics, practices, and politics of their own, hopes that include the destruction of heterosexist, or even heterosexual society. There are some radical, separatist lesbians and separatist gays who view most human behavior in terms of rational, political aims, and for them homophobia is a predictable political response to their own oppositional politics. Nineteen ninety-two Republican presidential candidate Pat Buchanan was not simply being hyperbolic when he gravely predicted that the 1990's would be the decade of the radical homosexual. One of his campaign ads, featuring a film clip of near-nude, dancing, gay leathermen, formed the background for the attack on the grant policies of the National Endowment for the Arts. Such ads demonstrate that his homophobia is partially directed against queer-specific political and sexual challenges to his conservative Christian morality.

However, the political response hypothesis, like the others, accounts only for some homophobes, and I think, relatively few. This hypothesis suffers from too great a dose of modernist political rationalism. Like many traditional models of political activity, it overrationalizes the subjects involved. It assumes that members of the oppressor class interpret the world in political terms similar to that of members of an oppositional movement. Thus, the characterization of a homophobe is that of a rational individual with immoral goals, who recognizes that the particular oppositional group of gays and lesbians is a genuine political threat to his or her power and privilege, and as such must take an active stand against that insurgent group. One of the best tactics for resisting the insurgents is terror—on individual levels with violence, on institutional levels with oppressive laws, and on sociocultural levels with boogeyfag propaganda.[24]

While this model has merit and may be partially accurate in accounting for some homophobia, it endows homophobes (and homosexuals) with a hyperrationality that does not seem to be in evidence. Most homophobes, even those who openly admit their involvement in physical and verbal attacks on gays and lesbians, do not consider their activity to be political. Most of them, in fact, do not perceive any obvious threat from the people they attack. Gary Comstock claims that perpetrators of anti-queer violence typically list the "recreational, adventuresome aspect of pursuing, preying upon, and scaring lesbians and gay men" as the first and foremost reason for their behavior. Only secondarily and less often do they list things like the "wrongness of homosexuality" as a reason for their activity. But even this "wrongness" is not listed as an explanation or political justification for their behavior as much as a background assumption that functions as cultural permission.[25]

A recent television news program interviewed a perpetrator of antigay violence and, like Comstock's interviewee, he had little or no explanation for why he was doing what he was doing except that it was fun. When asked how he could have fun hurting people, he said that he had never really thought of queers as real people. I think this suggests that interpreting all, or even most, homophobic violence as conscious political activity ignores that much of the "reasoning" behind homophobia, when there is any active reasoning at all, relies on a very abstract and loosely integrated background of heterosexist assumptions. Many homophobes view gays and lesbians as politically, morally, and economically insignificant. For those who have never had any personal interaction (positive or negative) with openly gay or lesbian folk, lesbian/gay people may be such an abstract other that they do not enter into one's political and moral consideration any more than people who kick dogs for fun consider the political and moral significance of dogs, except perhaps in terms of legal consequences.

PERFORMING GENDER
AND GENDER TREACHERY

All three explanations of homophobia have one thing in common. They re-   *45* side on a field of unequal, binary, sexual and gender differentiation. Behind all homophobia, regardless of its development, expression, or motivation, is the background of heterosexism. Behind all heterosexism is the background of gendered identities.

The gender category of men constructs its members around at least two conflicting characterizations of the essence of manhood. First, your masculinity (being-a-man) is natural and healthy and innate. But second, you must stay masculine—do not ever let your masculinity falter. So, although being a man is seen as a natural and automatic state of affairs for a certain anatomical makeup, masculinity is so valued, so valorized, so prized, and its loss such a terrible thing, that one must always guard against losing it. Paradoxically, then, the "naturalness" of being a man, of being masculine, is constantly guarding against the danger of losing itself. Unaware, the "naturalness," the "rightness," of masculinity exposes its own uncertainties in its incessant self-monitoring— a self-monitoring often accomplished by monitoring others. In fact, although the stable performance of masculinity is presented as an *outcome* of being a man, what arises in looking at heterosexism/homophobia is that being a man, or continuing to be a man, is the *outcome* of performing masculinity. But of course, not just anybody can make the performance. Anatomy is seen as prior even as the performance is required to validate the anatomy. Thus the performance produces the man, but the performance is also limited to and compulsory for a "man."[26]

The insults of the male high school jocks are telling. Even though one is recognized as a man (or boy) prior to evidenced masculinity, evidence must be forthcoming in order to merit that continued "unproblematic" status. Whether performative evidence is provided with ease or with difficulty, it is nonetheless a compulsory performance, as compulsory as the initial anatomically based gender assignment. But because (proof of) masculinity has to be maintained not merely by anatomical differentiation but by performance, the possibility of failure in the performance is always there. It is enough to insult, to challenge, to question personal identity, by implying that one is not being masculine enough.

The logic of masculinity is demanding—protect and maintain what you are intrinsically, or you could lose it, mutate, become something else. The insults of my student peers suggest that the "something else" is being a girl— a serious enough demotion in a patriarchal culture. But of course, this is metaphor. One does not actually become a girl: the power of prior anatomy is too spellbinding, even when the performance fails. The "something else" is a male without masculinity, a monster, a body without its essential spirit, a mutation with no specifiable identity.[27]

So one mutation, which is so offensive it becomes the template of all mutations, occurs when a man finds that his erotic orientation is toward other men.[28] If he acts on that erotic orientation, he violates a tenet of masculinity, he fails at masculinity, and most importantly, appears to reject standards by which real men are defined as selves, as subjects. In a binary gender system, however, to be unmasculine means to be feminine; that is the only other possibility. But even as a cultural transformation into the feminine is attempted, it appears to be seriously problematic; it is not without resistance that the unmasculine male is shunted off to the realm of the feminine, for though femininity is devalued as the repository of the unmasculine, its presence as a discernible nonmasculine essense/performance is required to maintain the boundary of masculinity, and "feminine essences" do not easily coincide with "male" bodies.

50   The male body, which is supposed to house masculine essence from the first time it is identified as male, is out of place in the realm of unmasculine. That body is a manifestation of confusion, a reminder of rejection, an arrogant affront to all that is good and true about men, real men, normal men, natural men. How could this "man" give up his natural power, his natural strength, his real self? Why is he rejecting what he should be, what I am?

If the male is neither masculine nor feminine enough, what is he? He becomes a homosexual, a member of that relatively new species of creature, originally delineated by psychiatry, which does not simply engage in unmasculine behavior, but which has an essential, unmasculine essence; no positive essence of his own, mind you, but rather a negative essence, an absence of legitimate essence, and thus the absence of legitimate personhood.[29] But what is the response to a creature with the husk of a man but with the extremely present absence of masculinity? That depends entirely on the situatedness of the responder in the distribution of gender identities and personal identities.

The repressive sees and fears becoming *that,* and must distance himself from *that* by any means necessary, often overcompensating, revealing his repression through his obsession, sometimes through active malignancy—assaulting or killing or merely registering disgust at that which he hates embodied in that which he desires.[30]

The ignorant will dismiss *those* as not really human, creatures so unidentified that they do not merit the response given to genuine identities (whether positive or negative—even enemies have genuine, if hated, identities). *It* can be killed, can be beaten, can be played with, can be dismissed.

The heterosupremacist reactionary will raise the warning—*They* are dangerous! *They* are getting out of hand! *They* are here! *They* are threatening your homes, your churches, your families, your children! And in some sense that threat may be real; *they* really do reject many of the beliefs upon which the heterosupremacists' political and personal identities are maintained.

Fortunately, the logic of masculinity, like any other logic, is neither universal nor irresistibly stable. Not every individual classified as a male in this culture will be adequately represented in my sketchy characterization of masculine personhood. My characterization is not to be interpreted so much as an empirically accurate description of all men in society as it is a description of the mythology of masculinity that informs all constructions of men, the masculine "self" in Western culture, and that which could threaten them. I do not claim that all heterosexual males are homophobic (although I do think that the vast majority of heterosexual males are heterosexist). While I describe three homophobic reactions to the identity threat represented by gay men (repression, abusive ignorant bigotry, political reactionism), these in no way exhaust the variety of male reactions.

Some men, though they hate and are sickened by gays, lack the bravado to do anything more about their hate than make private slurs. Others, particularly liberals, are tolerantly heterosexist; they have no "real" problem with gays provided they are discreet and replicate the model of conventional heterosexual morality and family. And then there is the rare, genuinely subversive heterosexual man, a kind of gender traitor himself, whose identity is not co-extensive with his assignment as a man. Although comfortable with himself, he wouldn't mind being gay, or mind being a woman—those are not the categories by which he defines, or wants do define, his personhood.

Do not, however, take this as a disclaimer to the effect that homophobia is the exception, the out-of-nowhere, the unusual case. Heterosexism may be the father of homophobia, modeling in public what is done more blatantly in hiding, but hidden does not mean rare. Do not think that homophobes, even violent ones, are few and far between—occasional atavistics "suffering" from paleolithic conceptions of sex roles. Even though many instances of anti-gay/anti-lesbian crime go unreported due to fear of outing, lack of proof, fear of retaliation, or police hostility, evidence is accumulating that such crime is widespread and that violent attack is higher among gays and lesbians than for the population at large. In a recent Philadelphia study, 24 percent of gay men and 10 percent of lesbians *responding* said that they had been physically attacked—a victimization rate twice as high for lesbians and four times as high for gay men than for women and men in the urban population at large.[31] Economic threat and verbal assault are, of course, even more common.

The gender demographics of physical homophobic attack suggest something about the correlation between masculinity and homophobia. Consider the findings in a recent study on violence against lesbians and gays by Gary Comstock: (1) 94 percent of all attackers were male; (2) 99 percent of the perpetrators who attacked gay men were male, while 83 percent of those who attacked lesbians were male; (3) while 15 percent of attacks on lesbians were made by women, only 1 percent of attacks on gay men were made by women.[32]

Homophobic violence seems to be predominantly a male activity. What is the relationship between homophobia and masculinity? Is the man who attacks gay men affirming or reaffirming, consciously or subconsciously, his own masculinity/heterosexuality and thus has own sense of self? How is masculinity implicated in homophobia?

60   I have suggested in this essay that one reading of homophobia is that queers pose a threat to (compulsory) masculinity and as such, pose a threat to men whose personhood is coextensive with their identity as men. Certainly, homophobia could not exist without the background assumptions of (heterosexist) masculine identity. There could be no fear or hatred of gays and lesbians if there were no concept of a proper gender identity and a proper sexual orientation. Masculinity assumes, essentializes, naturalizes, and privileges heterosexuality. A violation of heterosexuality can be see as treachery against masculinity, which can register as an affront or threat to a man's core sense of self, a threat to his (male) identity. In this sense, homophobia requires masculinity (and femininity); it is necessarily parasitic on traditional categories of sex/gender identity. Homophobia is the malignant "correction" to a destabilizing deviation, Without gendered standards of identity, there could be nothing from which to deviate, and thus nothing to "correct."

If this reading is accurate, homophobia is not just a social prejudice (on the xenophobic/minoritarian model) that can be eliminated by education or tolerance training.[33] It will not be eliminated just by persuading people to be "more accepting." While these approaches may be helpful, they do not get at the basis of homophobia—binary gender systems and heterosexism. The only way to ensure that heterosexism and its virulent manifestation homophobia are genuinely eliminated is to eliminate the binary itself—challenge the assumption that one must be sexed or gendered to be a person. Eliminate the binary and it would be impossible to have heterosexism or homophobia, because hetero and homo would have no meaning. This does not mean humans would have to be "fused" into some androgynous entity ("androgyny" has no meaning without the binary). It means simply that identities would no longer be distributed according to anatomically based "sexes."

While this hope may seem utopian and may have theoretical problems of its own, it nonetheless suggests an approach to studies of masculinity that may be incommensurable with other approaches. When using the model of masculinity (and femininity) as a social construct that has no intrinsic interpretation, there seems to be little use in trying to reconstruct masculinity into more "positive" forms, at least as long as masculinity is somehow viewed as an intrinsically appropriate feature of certain bodies. To make masculinity "positive" could easily devolve into retracing the boundaries of appropriate behavior without challenging the compulsory nature of that behavior. Delving into mythology and folklore (along the lines of some sort of the men's movement models) to "rediscover" some archetypal masculine image upon which to base new male identities is not so much wrong or sexist as it is arbitrary. Discovering what it means, or should mean, to be a "real man" is an exercise in uselessness. A "real man" is nothing. A "real man" could be anything. This is not to say that searching through mythohistory for useful metaphors for living today is not useful. I believe that it is.[34] But such a search will never get anyone closer to being a "real man" or even to being just a "man." There is no such thing. Nor should there be.

For some of us who have been embattled our entire lives because our desires/performances/identities were "immorally" or "illegally" or "illegitimately" cross-coded with our anatomies, we fear the flight into "rediscovering" masculinity will be a repetition of what has gone before. Gendered epistemologies will only reproduce gendered identities. I personally do not want to be a "real man," or even an "unreal man." I want to be unmanned altogether. I want to evaluate courses of behavior and desire open to me on their pragmatic consequences, not on their appropriateness to my "sex." I want to delve into the wisdom of mythology, but without the prior restrictions of anatomy.

I want to betray gender.

NOTES

1. I want to thank Larry May for his encouragement and editing suggestions throughout the writing of this paper. I also want to make it clear that although I think some of this essay is applicable to hatred and violence directed against lesbians (sometimes called lesbophobia), for the purposes of a volume specifically on masculinity I have deliberately (though not exclusively) focused on males and hatred and violence directed against gay males. Even with this focus, however, I am indebted to work on homophobia by lesbian researchers and theorists. In a future, more comprehensive project I will explore the oppression and marginalization of a wider variety of gender traitors.

2. Although the scope of this essay prevents a lengthy discussion, it should be pointed out that many male teachers and coaches call their students and team members "girls": to be playful, to be insulting, or to shame them into playing more roughly.

3. It should also be pointed out that gay men often use the word "girl" to refer to each other. In these cases however, signifying a lack of masculinity is not registering insult. Often, it is expressing a sentiment of community—a community formed by the shared rejection of compulsory heterosexuality and compulsory forms of masculinity.

4. I deliberately sidestep the philosophical debate over the existence of a "self" in this discussion. While I am quite skeptical of the existence of any stable, core self, I do not think the argument in this paper turns on the answer to that problem. "Self" could simply be interpreted as a metaphor for a social situatedness. In any case, I do not mean to suggest that subverting gender is a way to purify an essential human "self."

5. For work on Native American societies that do not operate with a simple gender binary, see Walter L. Williams, *The Spirit and the Flesh: Sexual Diversity in American Indian Culture* (Boston: Beacon Press, 1986), and Will Roscoe (ed.), *Living the Spirit: A Gay American Indian Anthology* (New York: St. Martin's Press, 1988).

6. For works on the social construction of gender and sexuality see: Judith Butler, *Gender Trouble: Feminism and the Subversion of Identity* (New York: Routledge, 1990); Michel Foucault, *Herculine Barbin: Being the Recently Discovered Memoirs of a Nineteenth Century*

French Hermaphrodite (New York: Pantheon, 1980); Michel Foucault, *The History of Sexuality: Volume 1, An Introduction* (New York: Vintage Books, 1980); Monique Wittig, *The Straight Mind and Other Essays* Boston: Beacon Press, 1992).

7. In the United States and many other countries, if a baby is born with anatomical genital features that do not easily lend themselves to a classification within the gender/sex system in place, they are surgically and hormonally altered to fit into the categories of male and female, girl or boy.

8. I am grateful to Bob Strikwerda for pointing out that none of these characteristics taken by itself is absolutely necessary to be perceived as masculine in contemporary U. S. culture (except perhaps heterosexuality). In fact, a man who possessed every characteristic would be seen as a parody.

9. I borrow the insightful term "gender treachery" from Margaret Atwood. In her brilliant dystopian novel, *The Handmaid's Tale* (Boston: Houghton Mifflin, 1986), set in a post-fundamentalist Christian takeover America, criminals are executed and hanged on a public wall with the name of their crime around their necks for citizens to see. Homosexuals bear the placard "gender traitor."

10. It doesn't matter if this rejection is "deliberate" or not it the sense of direct refusal. Any deviant behavior can be seen as treacherous unless perhaps the individual admits "guilt" and seeks a "cure" or "forgiveness."

11. Someone might ask: But why those people most *thoroughly* sexed rather than those most insecure in their sexuality? My point here is a broad one about the categories of gender. Even those people who are insecure in their sexuality will be laboring under the compulsory ideal of traditional binary gender identities.

12. "Queers"—the name itself bespeaks curiosity, treachery, radical unidentifiability, the uncategorized, perverse entities, infectious otherness.

13. See Gregory M. Herek, "On Heterosexual Masculinity: Some Psychical Consequences of the Social Construction of Gender and Sexuality," *American Behavioral Scientist,* vol. 29, no. 5, May/June 1986, 563–77.

14. For all these terms except "homohatred," see Gregory M. Herek, "Stigma, Prejudice, and Violence Against Lesbians and Gay Men," pp. 60–80, in J. C. Gonsiorek and J. D. Weinrich (eds.), *Homosexuality: Research Implications for Public Policy* (London: Sage Publications, Inc., 1991). For "homohatred," see Marshall Kirk and Hunter Madsen, *After the Ball: How America Will Conquer Its Fear & Hatred of Gays in the 90's* (New York: Penguin Books, 1989).

15. See Jacob Smith Yang's article in *Gay Community News,* August 18–24, vol. 19, no. 6, 1991, p. 1. The brutal July 4 murder of Paul Broussard sparked an uproar in Houston's queer community over anti-gay violence and police indifference. To "quell the recent uproar," Houston police undertook an undercover operation in which officers posed as gay men in a well-known gay district. Although police were skeptical of gays' claims of the frequency of violence, within one hour of posing as gay men, undercover officers were sprayed with mace and attacked by punks wielding baseball bats.

16. See Kirk and Madsen, p. 127. They mention the case of Rose Mary Denman, a United Methodist minister who was a vocal opponent of the ordinations of gays and lesbians until she eventually acknowledged her own lesbianism. Upon announcing this, however, she was defrocked. Kirk and Madsen quote a *New York Times* article that states:

"In retrospect, she attributed her previous vehement stand against ordaining homosexuals to the effects of denying her unacknowledged lesbian feelings."

17. See John Money, *Gay, Straight and In-Between: The Sexology of Erotic Orientation* (Oxford: Oxford University Press, 1988), pp. 109–110.

18. See Suzanne Pharr, *Homophobia: A Weapon of Sexism* (Little Rock, AR: Chardon Press, 1988), and also Kirk and Madsen, *After the Ball*. The stereotypical story is one I have elaborated on from Kirk and Madsen's book, chap. 2.

19. See Herek, "On Heterosexual Masculinity . . .", especially pp. 572–73.

20. One can think of the typical scene where one boy challenges another boy to do something dangerous or cruel by claiming that if he does not do so, he is afraid—a sissy. Similarly, boys who are friends/peers of homophobes may be expected to engage in cruel physical or verbal behavior in order to appear strong, reliable, and most importantly of all, not faggots themselves. They know what happens to faggots.

21. See Herek, *On Heterosexual Masculinity,* p. 573.

22. See Celia Kitzinger, *The Social Construction of Lesbianism* (London: Sage Publications, Inc., 1987).

23. For example, in my own area of the country we have Rev. Don Wildmon's American Family Association, headquartered in Tupelo, Mississippi—an ultraconservative media watchdog group dedicated to the elimination of any media image not in keeping with right-wing Christian morality. Also, in Memphis, Tennessee, there is FLARE (Family Life America for Responsible Education Under God, Inc.), a group lobbying for Christian prayer in public schools, the elimination of sex-education programs, and the installation of a "Family Life Curriculum" in public schools that would stress sexual abstinence and teach that the only form of morally acceptable sexual activity is married, heterosexual sex.

24. I borrow the term "boogeyfag" from David G. Powell's excellent unpublished manuscript, *Deviations of a Queen: Episodic Gay Theory.* Powell deconstructs California Congressman Robert Dornan's claim that "The biggest mass murderers in history are gay."

25. Gary David Comstock, *Violence Against Lesbians and Gay Men* (New York: Columbia University Press, 1991), p. 172.

26. For this analysis of masculinity and performance, I owe much to insights garnered from Judith Butler's article "Imitation and Gender Insubordination," in Diana Fuss, *Inside/Out: Lesbian Theories, Gay Theories* (New York: Routledge, 1991).

27. I use the term "monster" here in a way similar to that of Donna Haraway in her essay "A Cyborg Manifesto: Science, Technology, and Socialist-Feminism in the Late Twentieth Century," reprinted in her book *Simians, Cyborgs, and Women: The Reinvention of Nature* (New York: Routledge, 1991). Haraway says: "Monsters have always defined the limits of community in Western imaginations. The Centaurs and Amazons of ancient Greece established the limits of the centred polis of the Greek male human by their disruption of marriage and boundary pollutions of the warrior with animality and woman" (p. 180). I loosely use "monster" in referring to homosexuality in the sense that the homosexual disrupts gender boundaries and must therefore be categorized into its own species so as to prevent destabilizing those boundaries.

28. Aquinas, for example, viewed the "vice of sodomy" as the second worst "unnatural vice," worse even than rape—a view echoed in contemporary legal decisions such as

Bowers v. Hardwick (106 S. Ct. 2841, 1986), which upheld the criminal status of homosexuality. See Arthur N. Gilbert. "Conceptions of Homosexuality and Sodomy in Western History," in Salvatore J. Licata and Robert P. Peterson (eds.), *The Gay Past: A Collection of Historical Essays* (New York: Harrington Park Press, 1985) pp. 57–68.

29. On the creation of homosexuality as a category, see Foucault, *The History of Sexuality.*

30. In this sense: The repressive hates the species "homosexual," but nonetheless desires the body "man." It is only an historically contingent construction that desiring a certain kind of body "makes" you a certain kind of person, "makes" you have a certain kind of "lifestyle." Unfortunately, it is also true that being a certain "kind" of person can carry with it serious dangers, as is the case for homosexuals.

31. See Comstock, p. 55.

32. See Comstock, p. 59.

33. This is not to say that gays and lesbians are not often treated as a minority; good arguments have been made that they are. See Richard D. Mohr, "Gay Studies as Moral Vision," *Educational Theory,* vol. 39, no. 2, 1989.

34. In fact, I very much enjoy studies in applied mythology, particularly the work of Joseph Campbell. However, I am extremely skeptical about any application of mythology that characterizes itself as returning us to some primal experience of masculinity that contemporary culture has somehow marred or diminished. There is always the specter of essentialism in such moves.

THE FAILURE TO TRANSFORM: HOMOPHOBIA IN THE BLACK COMMUNITY

Cheryl Clarke

That there is homophobia among black people in America is largely reflective of the homophobic culture in which we live. The following passage from the proposed "Family Protection Act" (1981, S. 1378, H.R. 3955), a venomous bill before the U.S. Congress, vividly demonstrates the depth of the ruling class' fear and hatred of homosexuals, homosexuality, and the homosexual potential in everyone (themselves included).

> No federal funds may be made available under any provision of
> federal law to any public or private individual, group, founda-
> tion, commission, corporation, association, or other entity for
> the purpose of advocating, promoting, or suggesting homosex-
> uality, male or female, as a lifestyle (p. 9, line 13, section 108)

Yet, we cannot rationalize the disease of homophobia among black people as the white man's fault, for to do so is to absolve ourselves of our responsibility to transform ourselves. When I took my black lesbian feminist self to the First National Plenary Conference on Self-Determination (December 4, 5, 6, 1981) in New York City, thinking surely that this proclaimed "historic meeting of the Black Liberation Movement" must include black lesbian feminists, I was struck by a passage from the printed flyer left on every seat:

> Revolutionary nationalists and genuine communists cannot
> uphold homosexuality in the leadership of the Black Liberation
> Movement nor uphold it as a correct practice. Homosexuality
> is a genocidal practice. . . . Homosexuality does not produce
> children. . . . Homosexuality does not birth new warriors for
> liberation. . . . homosexuality cannot be upheld as correct or
> revolutionary practice. . . . The practice of homosexuality is an
> accelerating threat to our survival as a people and as a nation.

Compare these two statements—the first from the ultra(white)-right and the second from self-proclaimed black "revolutionaries and genuine communists." Both reflect a decidedly similar pathology: homophobia. If I were a "revolutionary nationalist" or even a "genuine communist," I would be concerned if my political vision in any way supported the designs of my oppressors, the custodians of white male privilege. But it is these black macho intellectuals and politicos, these heirs of Malcolm X, who have never expanded Malcolm's revolutionary ideals beyond the day of his death, who consciously

249

or unwittingly have absorbed the homophobia of their patriarchal slavemasters. It is they who attempt to propagate homophobia throughout the entire black community. And it is they whom I will address in this writing.

Since 1965, the era which marked a resurgence of radical black consciousness in the United States, many black people of the post–World War II generation began an all-consuming process of rejecting the values of WASP America and embracing our African and Afro-American traditions and culture. In complete contrast to the conservative black bourgeoisie and to bourgeois reformist civil right proponents, the advocates of Black Power demanded progressive remedies to the accumulated ills of Black folk in America, viewed racism as international in scope, rescued Afro-American culture from anonymity, and elevated the black man to the pedestal of authority in the black liberation movement. In order to participate in this movement one had to be black (of course), be male-oriented, and embrace a spectrum of black nationalist, separatist, Pan Africanist sentiments, beliefs, and goals. Rejection of white people was essential as well as rejection of so-called white values, which included anything from reading Kenneth Clark's *Civilization* to eating a t.v. dinner.

5   While the cult of Black Power spurned the assimilationist goals of the politically conservative black bourgeoisie, its devotees, nevertheless, held firmly to the value of heterosexual and male superiority. As Michele Wallace states in her controversial essay, "Black Macho" (1979):

> . . . the contemporary black man no longer exists for his people
> or even for himself. . . . He has become a martyr. And he has
> arrived in this place, not because of the dependency inflicted
> upon him in slavery, but because his black perspective, like the
> white perspective, supported the notion that manhood is more
> valuable than anything else. (p. 79)

It is ironic that the Black Power movement could transform the consciousness of an entire generation of black people regarding black self-determination and, at the same time, fail so miserably in understanding the sexual politics of the movement and of black people across the board.

Speaking of the "sexual-racial antagonisms" dividing the Student Nonviolent Coordinating Committee during the 1960s, Manning Marable assesses the dilemma of the black movement of that era:

> . . . The prevailing popular culture of racism, the sexist stereo-
> types held by black men and women, and the psychological
> patterns of dependency which exploitation creates over several
> generations could not be uprooted easily. In the end the Move-
> ment may have failed to create a new interracial society in the
> South because its advocates had first failed to transform them-
> selves. (1980, p. 125)

Like all Americans, black Americans live in a sexually repressive culture. And we have made all manner of compromise regarding our sexuality in order to live here. We have expended much energy trying to debunk the racist mythology which says our sexuality is depraved. Unfortunately, many of us have overcompensated and assimilated the Puritan value that sex is for procreation, occurs only between men and women, and is only valid within the confines of heterosexual marriage. And, of course, like everyone else in America who is ambivalent in these respects, black folk have to live with the contradictions of this limited sexual system by repressing or closeting any sexual/ erotic urges, feelings, or desires.

Dennis Altman, in his pivotal work, *Homosexuality: Oppression and Liberation* (1971), says the following of Western culture:

> The repression of polymorphous perversity in Western
> societies has two major components: the removal of the erotic
> from all areas of life other than the explicitly sexual and the de-
> nial of out inherent bisexuality. (p. 79)

That Western culture is limiting, few can deny. A tremendous amount of pressure is brought to bear on men, women, and children to be heterosexual to the exclusion of every other erotic impulse. I do not begrudge heterosexuals the right to express themselves, but rabid sexual preference is a stone drag on anybody's list. That the black community is homophobic and rabidly heterosexual is a reflection of the black movement's failure to "transform" its proponents with regard to the boundless potential of human sexuality. And this failure has prevented critical collaboration with politically motivated black lesbians and gay men. Time and again homophobia sabotages coalitions, divides would-be comrades, and retards the mental restructuring, essential to evolution, which black people need so desperately.

The concept of the black family has been exploited since the publication of the infamous Moynihan report, *The Negro Family: A Case for National Action* (1965). Because the insular, privatized nuclear family is upheld as the model of Western family stability, all other forms—for example, the extended family, the female-headed family, the lesbian family—are devalued. Many black people, especially middle-class black people, have accepted the male-dominated nuclear family model, though we have had to modify it because black women usually work outside the home. Though "revolutionary nationalists and genuine communists" have not accepted the nuclear family model per se, they have accepted African and Eastern patriarchal forms of the family, including polygamy (offering the specious rationalization that there are more black women than black men). Homosexuality is viewed as a threat to the continued existence of the heterosexual family, because homosexual unions do not, in and of themselves, produce offspring—as if one's only function within a family, within a relationship, or in sex were to produce offspring. Black family lifestyles and homosexual lifestyles are not antithetical. Most black lesbians and gay men grew up in families and are still critically involved with their families. Many black lesbians and gay men are raising children. Why must the black family be so strictly viewed as the result of a heterosexual dyad?

10   And finally, why is the black male so-called left so vehement in its propagation of these destructive beliefs, and why have its proponents given such relentless expression to the homophobic potential in the mass of black people? Because the participation of open black lesbians and gay men in the black so-called liberation movement is a threat to the continued hegemony of dogmatic, doctrinaire black men who have failed to reject the Western institution of heterosexuality and the Christian fundamentalist notion of sex as "sin," no matter what doctrine or guru they subscribe to. Homophobic black intellectuals and politicos are so charged with messianic fervor that they seem like a perversion of the W.E.B. DuBois concept of the "Talented Tenth," the hypothesis that "the Negro race . . . is going to be saved by its exceptional men." Indeed, this homophobic cult of black men seems to view itself as the "exceptional men" who will save the black liberation movement from homosexual "contamination." Furthermore, the black intellectual/political man, by dint of his knowledge, training, and male privilege—and in spite of racism—has access to numerous bourgeois resources (such as television, radio, the stage, the podium, publications, and schools) whereby he can advance his reactionary ideologies and make his opinions known to the public at large.

Let us examine the rhetoric and ravings of a few notable black heterosexuals.

Chairman Baraka, Imamu Baraka, LeRoi Jones—whatever patriarchal designation he assumes—is a rabid homophobe. Whenever he makes his homophobic statements, his sexist invective is not far behind. From his early works on, this chameleon, the patriarch of the "new black poetry" of the 1960s, has viewed homosexuality as a symbol of a decadent establishment, as defectiveness, as weakness, as a strictly white male flaw.

In his first book of poems, *Preface to a Twenty Volume Suicide Note* (1961), in which he reveals himself as a versatile though imitative poet, Jones is homophobic and woman-hating. In a wildly imagistic poem, "To a Publisher . . . cut out," he free-associates:

> . . . Charlie Brown spent most his time whacking his doodle, or
> having weird relations with that dopey hound of his (though
> that's a definite improvement over . . . that filthy little lesbian
> he's hung up with). (p. 19)

In the same poem, Jones debunks the myth of the black woman's superior sexual prowess: "I have slept with almost every mediocre colored woman/On 23rd St. . . . " (p. 19).

In his notorious essay "American Sexual Reference: Black Male" (*Home*, 1965) Jones lays the ultimate disparagement on the American white man and white woman:

> Most American men are trained to be fags. . . . That red flush,
> those silk blue faggot eyes. So white women become men-
> things, a weird combination sucking male juices to build a
> navel orange, which is themselves. (p. 216)

But Jones is at his heterosexist best in the essay "Black Woman" (*Raise Race Rays Raze,* 1971), which should have been titled, "One Black Macho Man's Narcissistic Fantasy." He commands the black woman, with arrogant conde-scension, to "complement" her man, to "inspire" her man. He is laughable in his smugness, his heterosexist presumptions—to say nothing of his obvious contempt for women. It seems that his homophobic and misogynist attitudes have not abated since he embraced Marxism. Leroi-Imamu-Chairman-Jones-Baraka is an irreversible homophobe. Methinks he protests too much.

In another classic example of sixties-style black woman-hatred, playwright   15
Ed Bullins attempts a portrayal of a lesbian relationship in *Clara's Ole Man* (1965). The action is set in the North Philadelphia flat of Clara and Big Girl, Clara's "Ole Man" who is stereotypically "butch." Clara and Big Girl are not disparaged by their "ghetto" community, symbolized by two older, alcoholic black women who stay upstairs and by three juvenile delinquents, Stoogie, Bama, and Hoss, who take refuge from a police chase in the couple's apartment, a familiar haunt. It is only Jack, an outsider and ex-Marine in pursuit of upward mobility through college prep courses, who is too narcissistic to understand the bond between the two women. Jack, whose intention is to date Clara, "retches" when he realizes Clara and Big Girl are lovers. *Clara's Ole Man* is a substanceless rendering of the poor black community, a caricature of lesbianism, and a per-petuation of the stereotype of the pathological black community. But Ed Bullins gained a great deal of currency among black and white "avant garde" intellec-tuals for his ability to replicate and create caricatures of black life.

In that same year (1965), a pivotal year in the political development of black people, Calvin Hernton discusses the interrelationship of sex and racism in his popular book, *Sex and Racism in America.* Hernton does not address the issue of homosexuality in any of his four essays, "The White Woman," "The Negro Male," "The White Male," and "The Negro Woman." In several ho-mophobic asides Hernton is alternately dismayed by, presumptuous about, and intrigued by his observations of homosexual behavior:

> The extent to which some white women are attracted to
> Negro lesbians is immensely revealing—even the Negro lesbian
> is a "man." It is not and uncommon sight (in Greenwich
> Village, for instance) to see these "men" exploiting this image
> of themselves to the zenith. (p. 113)

> . . . One man who seemed *effeminate* put coins into the
> jukebox, *swished* along side me. (p. 114)

> He had the appearance of a business man or a politician—
> except for his eyes, which seem to hold some dark secret,
> something in them that made me wonder . . . maybe this man
> was a homosexual. (p. 89) [Ital. mine.]

We can see from the few passages cited above that homophobia in the black community has not only a decidedly bourgeois character but also a markedly male imprint. Which is not to say, however, that homophobia is limited to the psyche of the black intellectual male, but only that it is he who institutionalizes the illness within our political/intellectual community. And rest assured, we can find his homophobic counterpart in black women, who are, for the most part, afraid of risking the displeasure of their homophobic brothers were they to address, seriously and in a principled way, homosexuality. Black bourgeois female intellectuals practice homophobia by omission more often than rabid homophobia.

Michele Wallace's *Black Macho and the Myth of the Superwoman* is a most obvious example. This brave and scathing analysis of the sexual politics of the black political community after 1965 fails to treat the issues of gay liberation, black lesbianism, or homophobia vis à vis the black liberation or the women's liberation movement. In "Black Macho," the opening essay, Wallace addresses the homophobia of Eldridge Cleaver and Amiri Baraka, but she neither calls it "homophobia" nor criticizes these attitudes as a failing of the black liberation movement. For the sake of her own argument re the black macho neurosis, Wallace exploits the popular conception of male homosexuality as passivity, the willingness to be fucked (preferably by a white man, according to Cleaver). It is then seen as antithetical to the concept of black macho, the object of which is to do the fucking. Wallace does not debunk this stereotype of male homosexuality. In her less effective essay, "The Myth of the Superwoman," Wallace omits any mention of black lesbians. In 1979, when asked at a public lecture at Rutgers University in New Jersey why the book had not addressed the issues of homosexuality and homophobia, the author responded that she was not an "expert" on either issue. But Wallace, by her own admission, was also not an "expert" on the issues she *did* address in her book.

The black lesbian is not only absent from the pages of black political analysis, her image as a character in literature and her role as a writer are blotted out from or trivialized in literary criticism written by black women. Mary Helen Washington's otherwise useful anthologies are a prime example of this omission of black lesbianism and black lesbian writers. In both *Black Eyed Susans* (1975) and *Midnight Birds* (1980), the editor examines the varied roles black women have played in the black community and how these roles are more authentically depicted in the fiction of black women than in the fiction of black men.

20   In her introduction to *Midnight Birds,* Washington speaks of the major themes of the material presented in this anthology: "women's reconciliation with one another," antagonisms with men, "areas of commonality among black and white women." Now, one would think with all the mention of these women–identified themes that there would be a lesbian story or two in the anthology. But, again, we are disappointed. There is no mention of lesbianism in the introduction, there are no open lesbian contributors to the anthology, and there is no lesbian story in the collection. And yet, we know there is certainly plenty of available work by black lesbian writers. For exam-

ple, Audre Lorde's lesbian fiction piece, "Tar Beach," which appeared in *Conditions: Five, The Black Woman's Issue* in 1979—prior to the publication of *Midnight Birds*—would have powerfully enhanced the collection. Washington knows that black lesbian writers exist. In a footnote to the previously mentioned introduction (p. xxv), Washington credits Barbara Smith's essay, "Toward a Black Feminist Criticism" (*Conditions:Two,* 1977), as one of two pieces of writing which has challenged and shaped her thinking. Smith is a lesbian and she writes about lesbianism. The other piece Washington refers to, Adrienne Rich's "Disloyal to Civilization: Feminism, Racism, Gynephobia" (*On Lies, Secrets, and Silence,* 1979) is written by a lesbian as well.

One of the most recent books to appear in the name of feminism is bell hooks' *Ain't I a Woman: Black Women and Feminism.* hooks seems to purposely ignore the existence and central contributions of black lesbians to the feminist movement. Aside from a gross lack of depth in her analysis of the current women's movement in America, the most resounding shortcoming of this work of modern feminism is its omission of any discussion of lesbian feminism, the radicalizing impact of which distinguishes this era of feminism from the previous eras. hooks does not even mention the word *lesbian* in her book. This is unbearable. Ain't lesbians women too? Homophobia in the black movement and in the woman's movement is not treated, yet lesbians historically have been silenced and repressed in both. In her statement, "Attacking heterosexuality does little to strengthen the self-concept of the masses of women who desire to be with men" (p. 191), hooks delivers a backhanded slap at lesbian feminists, a considerable number of whom are black. hooks would have done well to attack the institution of heterosexuality, as it is a prime tool of black woman's oppression in America. Like the previously discussed writers, hooks fears alienating the black community cum the black bourgeois intellectual/political establishment. And there is the fear of transformation, the fear that the word will generate the deed. Like her black male counterpart, the black woman intellectual is afraid to relinquish heterosexual privilege. So little else is guaranteed black people.

I must confess that, in spite of the undeniably homophobic pronouncements of black intellectuals, I sometimes become impatient with the accusations of homophobia hurled at the black community by many gay men and lesbians, as if the whole black community were more homophobic than the heterosexist culture we live in. The entire black community gets blamed for the reactionary postures of a few petit-bourgeois intellectuals and politicos. Since no one has bothered to study the black community's attitudes on homosexuals, homosexuality, or homosexual lifestyles, it is not accurate to attribute homophobia to the mass of black people.

Prior to the growth of the contemporary black middle class, which has some access to the white world, the black community—due to segregation North and South—was even more diverse, encompassing a world of black folk of every persuasion, profession, status, and lifestyle. There have always been upwardly mobile blacks, but until the late 1950s and early sixties there had never been so many opportunities to reap the tenuous fruits of affluence outside the traditional black community. The cordoning off of all types of black people into a single community because of race may be one influence on black attitudes toward difference.

The poor and working-class black community, historically more radical and realistic than the reformist and conservative black middle class and the atavistic, "blacker-than-thou" (bourgeois) nationalists, has often tolerated an individual's lifestyle prerogatives, even when that lifestyle was disparaged by the prevailing culture. Though lesbians and gay men were exotic subjects of curiosity, they were accepted as part of the community (neighborhood)—or at least, there were no manifestos calling for their exclusion from the community.

25   I can recall being about twelve years old when I first saw a black lesbian couple. I was walking down the street with my friend Kathy. I saw two young women walking together in the opposite direction. One wore a doo-rag, a Banlon buttondown, and high-top sneakers. The other woman wore pink brush rollers, spit curls plastered with geech, an Oxford-tailored shirt, a mohair sweater, fitted skirt with a kick pleat, black stockings, and the famous I. Miller flat, sling-back shoe, the most prestigious pair of kicks any Dee Cee black girl could own. I asked Kathy, "Who are they?" "Bulldaggers," she answered. "What's that?" I asked again. "You know, they go with each other," Kathy responded. "Why?" I continued. "Protection," Kathy said casually. "Protection?" I repeated. "Yeah, at least they won't get pregnant," Kathy explained.

It is my belief that poor black communities have often accepted those who would be outcast by the ruling culture—many times to spite the white man, but mainly because the conditions of our lives have made us empathic. And, as it stands now, the black political community seems bereft of that humanity which has always been a tradition among Afro-American freedom fighters, the most illustrious of whom have come from the grass roots.

As a group and as individuals, black lesbians and gay men—sometimes obvious sometimes not—have been as diverse as the communities we've lived in. Like most other people, we have been workers, church-goers, parents, hustlers, and upwardly mobile. Since gay black men and lesbians have always been viable contributors to our communities, it is exceedingly painful for us to face public denunciation from black folk—the very group who should be championing our liberation. Because of the level of homophobia in the culture in general, many black gay men and lesbians remain in the closet, passing as heterosexuals. Thus, when public denunciation of our lifestyles are made by other black people, we remain silent in the face of their hostility and ignorance. The toll taken on us because we repress our rage and hurt makes us distrustful of all people whom we cannot identify as lesbian or gay. Also, for those of us who are isolated from gay or lesbian community, the toll is greater self-hate, self-blame, and belief in the illness theory of homosexuality.

In the face of this, open and proud gay black men and lesbians must take an assertive stand against the blatant homophobia expressed by members of the black intellectual and political community who consider themselves custodians of the revolution. For if we will not tolerate the homophobia of the culture in general, we cannot tolerate it from black people, no matter what their positions in the black liberation movement. Homophobia is a measure of how far removed we are from the psychological transformation we so desperately need to engender. The expression of homophobic sentiments, the threatening political postures assumed by black radicals and progressives of the nationalist/communist ilk, and the seeming lack of any willingness to understand the politics of gay and lesbian liberation collude with the dominant white male culture to repress not only gay men and lesbians, but also to repress a natural part of all human beings, namely the bisexual potential in us all. Homophobia divides black people as political allies, it cuts off political growth, stifles revolution, and perpetuates patriarchal domination.

The arguments I have presented are not definitive. I hope that others may take some of the issues raised in this essay into consideration for further study. The sexual politics of the black liberation movement have yet to be addressed by its advocates. We will continue to fail to transform ourselves until we reconcile the unequal distribution of power in our political community accorded on the basis of gender and sexual choice. Visions of black liberation which exclude lesbians and gay men bore and repel me, for as a black lesbian I am obligated and dedicated to destroying heterosexual supremacy by "suggesting, promoting, and advocating" the rights of gay men and lesbians wherever we are. And we are everywhere. As political black people, we bear the twin responsibilities of transforming the social, political, and economic systems of oppression as they affect all our people—not just the heterosexuals—and of transforming the corresponding psychological structure that feeds into these oppressive systems. The more homophobic we are as a people the further removed we are from any kind of revolution. Not only must black lesbians and gay men be committed to destroying homophobia, but *all* black people must be committed to working out and rooting out homophobia in the black community. We begin to eliminate homophobia by engaging in dialogue with the advocates of gay and lesbian liberation, educating ourselves about gay and lesbian politics, confronting and correcting homophobic attitudes, and understanding how these attitudes prevent the liberation of the total being.

REFERENCES

Baldwin, James. *Another Country.* New York: Dial Press, 1968.

Baraka, Imamu Amiri. *Raise Race Rays Raze: Essays Since 1965.* New York: Random House, 1971.

Bullins, Ed. *Five Plays by Ed Bullins.* New York: Bobbs-Merrill Co. Inc., 1968.

Hernton, Calvin. *Sex and Racism in America.* New York: Grove Press, 1965.

Jones, LeRoi. *Preface to a Twenty Volume Suicide Note.* New York: Totem/Corinth, 1961.

Jones, LeRoi. *The Dead Lecturer.* New York: Grove Press, 1964.

Jones, LeRoi. "American Sexual Preference: Black Male." *Home.* New York: William Morrow and Co, Inc., 1966.

Staples, Robert. "Mystique of Black Sexuality." In Staples (ed.) *The Black Family: Essays and Studies.* Belmont, California: Wadsworth Publishing Co., Inc. 1977.

Wallace, Michele. *Black Macho and the Myth of the Superwoman.* New York, Dial Press, 1979.

Washington, Mary Helen, "In Pursuit of Our Own History," in M. H. Washington (ed.) *Midnight Birds.* New York: Anchor Books, 1980.

HOMOPHOBIA: A WEAPON OF SEXISM

Suzanne Pharr

Homophobia—the irrational fear and hatred of those who love and sexually desire those of the same sex. Though I intimately knew its meaning, the word homophobia was unknown to me until the late 1970s, and when I first heard it, I was struck by how difficult it is to say, what an ugly word it is, equally as ugly as its meaning. Like racism and anti-Semitism, it is a word that calls up images of loss of freedom, verbal and physical violence, death.

In my life I have experienced the effects of homophobia through rejection by friends, threats of loss of employment, and threats upon my life; and I have witnessed far worse things happening to other lesbian and gay people: loss of children, beatings, rape, death. Its power is great enough to keep ten to twenty percent of the population living lives of fear (if their sexual identity is hidden) or lives of danger (if their sexual identity is visible) or both. And its power is great enough to keep the remaining eighty to ninety percent of the population trapped in their own fears.

Long before I had a word to describe the behavior, I was engaged in a search to discover the source of its power, the power to damage and destroy lives. The most common explanations were that to love the same sex was either abnormal (sick) or immoral (sinful).

My exploration of the sickness theory led me to understand that homosexuality is simply a matter of sexual identity, which, along with heterosexual identity, is formed in ways that no one conclusively understands. The American Psychological Association has said that it is no more abnormal to be homosexual than to be lefthanded. It is simply that a certain percentage of the population *is.* It is not healthier to be heterosexual or righthanded. What is unhealthy—and sometimes a source of stress and sickness so great it can lead to suicide—is homophobia, that societal disease that places such negative messages, condemnation, and violence on gay men and lesbians that we have to struggle throughout our lives for self-esteem.

The sin theory is a particularly curious one because it is expressed so often and with such hateful emotion both from the pulpit and from laypeople who rely heavily upon the Bible for evidence. However, there is significant evidence that the approximately eight references to homosexuality in the Bible are frequently read incorrectly, according to Dr. Virginia Ramey Mollenkott in an essay in *Christianity and Crisis:*

> Much of the discrimination against homosexual persons is
> justified by a common misreading of the Bible. Many English
> translations of the Bible contain the word homosexual in

extremely negative contexts. But the fact is that the word *homosexual* does not occur anywhere in the Bible. No extant text, no manuscript, neither Hebrew nor Greek, Syriac, nor Aramaic, contains the word. The terms *homosexual* and *heterosexual* were not developed in any language until the 1890's when for the first time the awareness developed that there are people with a lifelong, constitutional orientation toward their own sex. Therefore the use of the word *homosexuality* by certain English Bible translators is an example of the extreme bias that endangers the human and civil rights of homosexual persons. (*pp. 383–4, Nov. 9, 1987*)

Dr. Mollenkott goes on to add that two words in I Corinthians 6:9 and one word in Timothy 1:10 have been used as evidence to damn homosexuals but that well into the 20th century the first of these was understood by everyone to mean masturbation, and the second was known to refer to male prostitutes who were available for hire by either women or men. There are six other Biblical references that are thought by some to refer to homosexuals but each of these is disputed by contemporary scholars. For instance, the sin in the Sodom and Gomorrah passage (Genesis 19:1–10) is less about homosexuality than it is about inhospitality and gang rape. The law of hospitality was universally accepted and Lot was struggling to uphold it against what we assume are heterosexual townsmen threatening gang rape to the two male angels in Lot's home. While people dwell on this passage as a condemnation of homosexuality, they bypass what I believe is the central issue or, if you will, *sin:* Lot's offering his two virgin daughters up to the men to be used as they desired for gang rape. Here is a perfectly clear example of devaluing and dehumanizing and violently brutalizing women.

The eight Biblical references (and not a single one by Jesus) to alleged homosexuality are very small indeed when compared to the several hundred references (and many by Jesus) to money and the necessity for justly distributing wealth. Yet few people go on a rampage about the issue of a just economic system, using the Bible as a base.

Finally, I came to understand that homosexuality, heterosexuality, bisexuality are *morally neutral.* A particular sexual identity is not an indication of either good or evil. What is important is not the gender of the two people in relationship with each other but the content of that relationship. Does that relationship contain violence, control of one person by the other? Is the relationship a growthful place for the people involved? It is clear that we must hold all relationships, whether opposite sex or same sex, to these standards.

The first workshops that I conducted were an effort to address these two issues, and I assumed that if consciousness could be raised about the invalidity of these two issues then people would stop feeling homophobic and understand homophobia as a civil rights issue and work against it. The workshops took a high moral road, invoking participants' compassion, understanding, and outrage at injustice.

The eight-hour workshops raised consciousness and increased partici- *10* pants' commitment to work against homophobia as one more oppression in a growing list of recognized oppressions, but I still felt something was missing. I felt there was still too much unaccounted for power in homophobia even after we looked at the sick and sinful theories, at how it feels to be a lesbian in a homophobic world, at why lesbians choose invisibility, at how lesbian existence threatens male dominance. All of the pieces seemed available but we couldn't sew them together into a quilt.

As I conducted more workshops over the years I noticed several important themes that led to the final piecing together:

1. Women began to recognize that economics was a central issue connecting various oppressions;
2. Battered women began talking about how they had been called lesbians by their batterers;
3. Both heterosexual and lesbian women said they valued the workshops because in them they were given the rare opportunity to talk about their own sexuality and also about sexism in general.

Around the same time (1985–86), the National Coalition Against Domestic Violence (NCADV) entered into a traumatic relationship with the U.S. Department of Justice (DOJ), requesting a large two-year grant to provide domestic violence training and information nationally. At the time the grant was to be announced, NCADV was attacked by conservative groups such as the Heritage Foundation as a "pro-lesbian, pro-feminist, anti-family" organization. In response to these attacks, the DOJ decided not to award a grant; instead they formulated a "cooperative agreement" that allowed them to monitor and approve all work, and they assured conservative organizations that the work would not be pro-lesbian and anti-family. The major issue between NCADV and the DOJ became whether NCADV would let an outside agency define and control its work, and finally, during never-ending concern from the DOJ about "radical" and "lesbian" issues, the agreement was terminated by NCADV at the end of the first year. Throughout that year, there were endless statements and innuendoes from the DOJ and some members of NCADV's membership about NCADV's lesbian leadership and its alleged concern for only lesbian issues. Many women were damaged by the cross fire, NCADV's work was stopped for a year, and the organization was split from within. It was lesbian baiting at its worst.

As one of NCADV's lesbian leadership during that onslaught of homophobic attacks, I was still giving homophobia workshops around the country, now able to give even more personal witness to the virulence of the hatred and fear of lesbians and gay men within both institutions and individuals. It was a time of pain and often anger for those of us committed to creating a world free of violence, and it was a time of deep distress for those of us under personal attack. However, my mother, like many mothers, had always said, "All things work for the good," and sure enough, it was out of the accumulation of these experiences that the pieces began coming together to make a quilt of our understanding.

On the day that I stopped reacting to attacks and gave my time instead to visioning, this simple germinal question came forth for the workshops: "What will the world be like without homophobia in it—for everyone, female and male, whatever sexual identity?" Simple though the question is, it was at first shocking because those of us who work in the anti-violence movement spend most of our time working with the damaging, negative results of violence and have little time to vision. It is sometimes difficult to create a vision of a world we have never experienced, but without such a vision, we cannot know clearly what we are working toward in our social change work. From this question, answer led to answer until a whole appeared of our collective making, from one workshop to another.

15   Here are some of the answers women have given:

- Kids won't be called tomboys or sissies; they'll just be who they are, able to do what they wish.
- People will be able to love anyone, no matter what sex; the issue will simply be whether or not she/he is a good human being, compatible, and loving.
- Affection will be opened up between women and men, women and women, men and men, and it won't be centered on sex; people won't fear being called names if they show affection to someone who isn't a mate or potential mate.
- If affection is opened up, then isolation will be broken down for all of us, especially for those who generally experience little physical affection, such as unmarried old people.
- Women will be able to work whatever jobs we want without being labeled masculine.
- There will be less violence if men do not feel they have to prove and assert their manhood. Their desire to dominate and control will not spill over from the personal to the level of national and international politics and the use of bigger and better weapons to control other countries.
- People will wear whatever clothes they wish, with the priority being comfort rather than the display of femininity or masculinity.
- There will be no gender roles.

It is at this point in the workshops—having imagined a world without homophobia—that the participants see the analysis begin to fall into place. Someone notes that all the things we have been talking about relate to sexual gender roles. It's rather like the beginning of a course in Sexism 101. The next question is: Imagine the world with no sex roles—sexual identity, which may be in flux, but no sexual gender roles." Further: imagine a world in which opportunity is not determined by gender or race. Just the imagining makes women alive with excitement because it is a vision of freedom, often just glimpsed but always known deep down as truth. Pure joy.

We talk about what it would be like to be born in a world in which there were no expectations or treatment based on gender but instead only the expectation that each child, no matter what race or sex, would be given as many options and possibilities as society could muster. Then we discuss what girls and boys would be like at puberty and beyond if sex role expectations didn't come crashing down on them with girls' achievement levels beginning to decline thereafter; what it would be for women to have the training and options for economic equity with men; what would happen to issues of power and control, and therefore violence, if there were real equality. To have no prescribed sex roles would open the possibility of equality. It is a discussion women find difficult to leave. Freedom calls.

Patriarchy—an enforced belief in male dominance and control—is the ideology and sexism the system that holds it in place. The catechism goes like this: Who do gender roles serve? Men and the women who seek power from them. Who suffers from gender roles? Women most completely and men in part. How are gender roles maintained? By the weapons of sexism: economics, violence, homophobia.

Why then don't we ardently pursue ways to eliminate gender roles and therefore sexism? It is my profound belief that all people have a spark in them that yearns for freedom, and the history of the world's atrocities—from the Nazi concentration camps to white dominance in South Africa to the battering of women—is the story of attempts to snuff out that spark. When that spark doesn't move forward to full flame, it is because the weapons designed to control and destroy have wrought such intense damage over time that the spark has been all but extinguished.

Sexism, that system by which women are kept subordinate to men, is kept   20
in place by three powerful weapons designed to cause or threaten women with pain and loss. As stated before, the three are economics, violence, and homophobia. The stories of women battered by men, victims of sexism at its worst, show these three forces converging again and again. When battered women tell why they stayed with a batterer or why they returned to a batterer, over and over they say it was because they could not support themselves and their children financially, they had no skills for jobs, they could not get housing, transportation, medical care for their children. And how were they kept controlled? Through violence and threats of violence, both physical and verbal, so that they feared for their lives and the lives of their children and doubted their own abilities and self-worth. And why were they beaten? Because they were not good enough, were not "real women," were dykes, or because they stood up to him as no "real woman" would. And the male batterer, with societal backing, felt justified, often righteous, in his behavior—for his part in keeping women in their place.

Economics must be looked at first because many feminists consider it to be the root cause of sexism. Certainly the United Nations study released at the final conference of the International Decade on Women, held in Nairobi,

Kenya, in 1985, supports that belief: of the world's population, women do 75% of the work, receive 10% of the pay and own 1% of the property. In the United States it is also supported by the opposition of the government to the idea of comparable worth and pay equity, as expressed by Ronald Reagan who referred to pay equity as "a joke." Obviously, it is considered a dangerous idea. Men profit not only from women's unpaid work in the home but from our underpaid work within horizontal female segregation such as clerical workers or upwardly mobile tokenism in the workplace where a few affirmative action promotions are expected to take care of all women's economic equality needs. Moreover, they profit from women's bodies through pornography, prostitution, and international female sexual slavery. And white men profit from both the labor of women and of men of color. Forced economic dependency puts women under male control and severely limits women's options for self-determination and self-sufficiency.

This truth is borne out by the fact that according to the National Commission on Working Women, on average, women of all races working year round earn only 64 cents to every one dollar a man makes. Also, the U.S. Census Bureau reports that only 9 percent of working women make over $25,000 a year. There is fierce opposition to women gaining employment in the nontraditional job market, that is, those jobs that traditionally employ less than 25 percent women. After a woman has gained one of these higher paying jobs, she is often faced with sexual harassment, lesbian baiting, and violence. It is clear that in the workplace there is an all-out effort to keep women in traditional roles so that the only jobs we are "qualified" for are the low-paid ones.

Actually, we have to look at economics not only as the root cause of sexism but also as the underlying, driving force that keeps all the oppressions in place. In the United States, our economic system is shaped like a pyramid, with a few people at the top, primarily white males, being supported by large numbers of unpaid or low-paid workers at the bottom. When we look at this pyramid, we begin to understand the major connection between sexism and racism because those groups at the bottom of the pyramid are women and people of color. We then begin to understand why there is such a fervent effort to keep those oppressive systems (racism and sexism and all the ways they are manifested) in place to maintain the unpaid and low-paid labor.

Susan DeMarco and Jim Hightower, writing for *Mother Jones,* report that *Forbes* magazine indicated that "the 400 riches families in America last year had an average net worth of $550 million each. These and less than a million other families—roughly one percent of our population—are at the prosperous tip of our society. . . . In 1976, the wealthiest 1 percent of America's families owned 19.2 percent of the nation's total wealth. (This sum of wealth counts all of America's cash, real estate, stocks, bonds, factories, art, personal property, and anything else of financial value.) By 1983, those at this 1 percent tip of our economy owned 34.3 percent of our wealth. . . . *Today, the top 1 percent of Americans possesses more net wealth than the bottom 90 percent.*" (My italics.) (*May, 1988, pp. 32–33*)

In order for this top-heavy system of economic inequity to maintain it-   *25*
self, the 90 percent on the bottom must keep supplying cheap labor. A very
complex, intricate system of institutionalized oppressions is necessary to maintain the status quo so that the vast majority will not demand its fair share of
wealth and resources and bring the system down. Every institution—schools,
banks, churches, government, courts, media, etc.—as well as individuals must
be enlisted in the campaign to maintain such a system of gross inequity.

What would happen if women gained the earning opportunities and
power that men have? What would happen if these opportunities were distributed equitably, no matter what sex one was, no matter what race one was
born into, and no matter where one lived? What if educational and training
opportunities were equal? Would women spend most of our youth preparing
for marriage? Would marriage be based on economic survival for women?
What would happen to issues of power and control? Would women stay with
our batterers? If a woman had economic independence in a society where
women had equal opportunities, would she still be thought of as owned by
her father or husband?

Economics is the great controller in both sexism and racism. If a person
can't acquire food, shelter, and clothing and provide them for children, then
that person can be forced to do many things in order to survive. The major
tactic, worldwide, is to provide unrecompensed or inadequately recompensed
labor for the benefit of those who control wealth. Hence, we see women performing unpaid labor in the home or filling low-paid jobs, and we see people
of color in the lowest-paid jobs available.

The method is complex: limit educational and training opportunities for
women and for people of color and then withhold adequate paying jobs with
the excuse that people of color and women are incapable of filling them.
Blame the economic victim and keep the victim's self-esteem low through
invisibility and distortion within the media and education. Allow a few people
of color and women to succeed among the profit-makers so that blaming
those who don't "make it" can be intensified. Encourage those few who succeed in gaining power now to turn it against those who remain behind rather
than to use their resources to make change for all. Maintain the myth of
scarcity—that there are not enough jobs, resources, etc., to go around—among
the middleclass so that they will not unite with laborers, immigrants, and the
unemployed. The method keeps in place a system of control and profit by a
few and a constant source of cheap labor to maintain it.

If anyone steps out of line, take her/his job away. Let homelessness and
hunger do their work. The economic weapon works. And we end up saying,
"I would do this or that—be openly who I am, speak out against injustice,
work for civil rights, join a labor union, go to a political march, etc.—if I
didn't have this job. I can't afford to lose it." We stay in an abusive situation
because we see no other way to survive.

In the battered women's movement abusive relationships are said to be   *30*
about power and control and the way out of them is through looking at the

ways power and control work in our lives, developing support, improving self-esteem, and achieving control over our decisions and lives. We have yet to apply these methods successfully to our economic lives. Though requiring massive change, the way there also lies open for equality and wholeness. But the effort will require at least as much individual courage and risk and group support as it does for a battered woman to leave her batterer, and that requirement is very large indeed. Yet battered women find the courage to leave their batterers every day. They walk right into the unknown. To break away from economic domination and control will require a movement made up of individuals who possess this courage and ability to take risks.

Violence is the second means of keeping women in line, in a narrowly defined place and role. First, there is the physical violence of battering, rape, and incest. Often when battered women come to shelters and talk about their lives, they tell stories of being not only physically beaten but also raped and their children subjected to incest. Work in the women's anti-violence movement during almost two decades has provided significant evidence that each of these acts, including rape and incest, is an attempt to seek power over and control of another person. In each case, the victim is viewed as an object and is used to meet the abuser's needs. The violence is used to wreak punishment and to demand compliance or obedience.

Violence against women is directly related to the condition of women in a society that refuses us equal pay, equal access to resources, and equal status with males. From this condition comes men's confirmation of their sense of ownership of women, power over women, and assumed right to control women for their own means. Men physically and emotionally abuse women because they *can,* because they live in a world that gives them permission. Male violence is fed by their sense of their *right* to dominate and control, and their sense of superiority over a group of people who, because of gender, they consider inferior to them.

It is not just the violence but the threat of violence that controls our lives. Because the burden of responsibility has been placed so often on the potential victim, as women we have curtailed our freedom in order to protect ourselves from violence. Because of the threat of rapists, we stay on alert, being careful not to walk in isolated places, being careful where we park our cars, adding incredible security measures to our homes—massive locks, lights, alarms, if we can afford them—and we avoid places where we will appear vulnerable or unprotected while the abuser walks with freedom. Fear, often now so commonplace that it is unacknowledged, shapes our lives, reducing our freedom.

As Bernice Reagon of the musical group Sweet Honey in the Rock said at the 1982 National Coalition Against Domestic Violence conference, women seem to carry a genetic memory that women were once burned as witches when we stepped out of line. To this day, mothers pass on to their daughters word of the dangers they face and teach them the ways they must limit their lives in order to survive.

Part of the way sexism stays in place is the societal promise of survival,   *35*
false and unfulfilled as it is, that women will not suffer violence if we attach
ourselves to a man to protect us. A woman without a man is told she is vulnerable to external violence and, worse, that there is something wrong with
her. When the male abuser calls a woman a lesbian, he is not so much labeling
her as a woman who loves women as he is warning her that by resisting him,
she is choosing to be outside society's protection from male institutions and
therefore from wide-ranging, unspecified, ever-present violence. When she
seeks assistance from woman friends or a battered women's shelter, he recognizes the power in woman bonding and fears loss of her servitude and loyalty:
the potential loss of his control. The concern is not affectional/sexual identity: the concern is disloyalty and the threat is violence.

The threat of violence against women who step out of line or who are
disloyal is made all the more powerful by the fact that women do not have to
do anything—they may be paragons of virtue and subservience—to receive
violence against our lives: the violence still comes. It comes because of the
woman-hating that exists throughout society. Chance plays a larger part than
virtue in keeping women safe. Hence, with violence always a threat to us,
women can never feel completely secure and confident. Our sense of safety is
always fragile and tenuous.

Many women say that verbal violence causes more harm than physical
violence because it damages self-esteem so deeply. Women have not wanted
to hear battered women say that the verbal abuse was as hurtful as the physical abuse: to acknowledge that truth would be tantamount to acknowledging
that *virtually every woman is a battered woman.* It is difficult to keep strong
against accusations of being a bitch, stupid, inferior, etc., etc. It is especially
difficult when these individual assaults are backed up by a society that shows
women in textbooks, advertising, TV programs, movies, etc., as debased, silly,
inferior, and sexually objectified, and a society that gives tacit approval to
pornography. When we internalize these messages, we call the result "low
self-esteem," a therapeutic individualized term. It seems to me we should use
the more political expression: when we internalize these messages, we experience *internalized sexism,* and we experience it in common with all women
living in a sexist world. The violence against us is supported by a society in
which woman-hating is deeply imbedded.

In "Eyes on the Prize," a 1987 Public Television documentary about the
Civil Rights Movement, an older white woman says about her youth in the
South that it was difficult to be anything different from what was around her
when there was no vision for another way to be. Our society presents images
of women that say it is appropriate to commit violence against us. Violence is
committed against women because we are seen as inferior in status and in
worth. It has been the work of the women's movement to present a vision of
another way to be.

Every time a woman gains the strength to resist and leave her abuser, we
are given a model of the importance of stepping out of line, of moving toward freedom. And we all gain strength when she says to violence, "Never

again!" Thousands of women in the last fifteen years have resisted their abusers to come to this country's 1100 battered women's shelters. There they have sat down with other women to share their stories, to discover that their stories again and again are the same, to develop an analysis that shows that violence is a statement about power and control, and to understand how sexism creates the climate for male violence. Those brave women are now a part of a movement that gives hope for another way to live in equality and peace.

40   Homophobia works effectively as a weapon of sexism because it is joined with a powerful arm, heterosexism. Heterosexism creates the climate for homophobia with its assumption that the world is and must be heterosexual and its display of power and privilege as the norm. Heterosexism is the systemic display of homophobia in the institutions of society. Heterosexism and homophobia work together to enforce compulsory heterosexuality and that bastion of patriarchal power, the nuclear family. The central focus of the rightwing attack against women's liberation is that women's equality, women's self-determination, women's control of our own bodies and lives will damage what they see as the crucial societal institution, the nuclear family. The attack has been led by fundamentalist ministers across the country. The two areas they have focused on most consistently are abortion and homosexuality, and their passion has led them to bomb women's clinics and to recommend deprogramming for homosexuals and establishing camps to quarantine people with AIDS. To resist marriage and/or heterosexuality is to risk severe punishment and loss.

It is not be chance that when children approach puberty and increased sexual awareness they begin to taunt each other by calling these names: "queer," "faggot," "pervert." It is at puberty that the full force of society's pressure to conform to heterosexuality and prepare for marriage is brought to bear. Children know what we have taught them, and we have given clear messages that those who deviate from standard expectations are to be made to get back in line. The best controlling tactic at puberty is to be treated as an outsider, to be ostracized at a time when it feels most vital to be accepted. Those who are different must be made to suffer loss. It is also at puberty that misogyny begins to be more apparent, and girls are pressured to conform to societal norms that do not permit them to realize their full potential. It is at this time that their academic achievements begin to decrease as they are coerced into compulsory heterosexuality and trained for dependency upon a man, that is, for economic survival.

There was a time when the two most condemning accusations against a woman meant to ostracize and disempower her were "whore" and "lesbian." The sexual revolution and changing attitudes about heterosexual behavior may have led to some lessening of the power of the word *whore,* though it still has strength as a threat to sexual property and prostitutes are stigmatized and abused. However, the word *lesbian* is still fully charged and carries with it the full threat of loss of power and privilege, the threat of being cut asunder, abandoned, and left outside society's protection.

To be a lesbian is to be *perceived* as someone who has stepped out of line, who has moved out of sexual/economic dependence on a male, who is woman-identified. A lesbian is perceived as someone who can live without a man, and who is therefore (however illogically) against men. A lesbian is perceived as being outside the acceptable, routinized order of things. She is seen as someone who has no societal institutions to protect her and who is not privileged to the protection of individual males. Many heterosexual women see her as someone who stands in contradiction to the sacrifices they have made to conform to compulsory heterosexuality. A lesbian is perceived as a threat to the nuclear family, to male dominance and control, to the very heart of sexism.

Gay men are perceived also as a threat to male dominance and control, and the homophobia expressed against them has the same roots in sexism as does homophobia against lesbians. Visible gay men are the objects of extreme hatred and fear by heterosexual men because their breaking ranks with male heterosexual solidarity is seen as a damaging rent in the very fabric of sexism. They are seen as betrayers, as traitors who must be punished and eliminated. In the beating and killing of gay men we see clear evidence of this hatred. When we see the fierce homophobia expressed toward gay men, we can begin to understand the ways sexism also affects males through imposing rigid, de-humanizing gender roles on them. The two circumstances in which it is le-gitimate for men to be openly physically affectionate with one another are in competitive sports and in the crisis of war. For many men, these two experi-ences are the highlights of their lives, and they think of them again and again with nostalgia. War and sports offer a cover of all-male safety and dominance to keep away the notion of affectionate openness being identified with ho-mosexuality. When gay men break ranks with male roles through bonding and affection outside the arenas of war and sports, they are perceived as not being "real men," that is, as being identified with women, the weaker sex that must be dominated and that over the centuries has been the object of male hatred and abuse. Misogyny gets transferred to gay men with a vengeance and is increased by the fear that their sexual identity and behavior will bring down the entire system of male dominance and compulsory heterosexuality.

If lesbians are established as threats to the status quo, as outcasts who must be punished, homophobia can wield its power over all women through les-bian baiting. Lesbian baiting is an attempt to control women by labeling us as lesbians because our behavior is not acceptable, that is, when we are being in-dependent, going our own way, living whole lives, fighting for our rights, de-manding equal pay, saying no to violence, being self-assertive, bonding with and loving the company of women, assuming the right to our bodies, insist-ing upon our own authority, making changes that include us in society's deci-sion-making; lesbian baiting occurs when women are called lesbians because we resist male dominance and control. And it has little or nothing to do with one's sexual identity.

To be named as lesbian threatens all women, not just lesbians, with great loss. And any woman who steps out of role risks being called a lesbian. To

45

understand how this is a threat to all women, one must understand that any woman can be called a lesbian and there is no real way she can defend herself: there is no way to credential one's sexuality. ("The Children's Hour," a Lillian Hellman play, makes this point when a student asserts two teachers are lesbians and they have no way to disprove it.) She may be married or divorced, have children, dress in the most feminine manner, have sex with men, be celibate—but there are lesbians who do all those things. *Lesbians look like all women and all women look like lesbians.* There is no guaranteed method of identification, and as we all know, sexual identity can be kept hidden. (The same is true for men. There is no way to prove their sexual identity, though many go to extremes to prove heterosexuality.) Also, women are not necessarily born lesbian. Some seem to be, but others become lesbians later in life after having lived heterosexual lives. Lesbian baiting of heterosexual women would not work if there were a definitive way to identify lesbians (or heterosexuals).

We have yet to understand clearly how sexual identity develops. And this is disturbing to some people, especially those who are determined to discover how lesbian and gay identity is formed so that they will know where to start in eliminating it. (Isn't it odd that there is so little concern about discovering the causes of heterosexuality?) There are many theories: genetic makeup, hormones, socialization, environment, etc. But there is no conclusive evidence that indicates that heterosexuality comes from one process and homosexuality from another.

We do know, however, that sexual identity can be in flux, and we know that sexual identity means more than just the gender of people one is attracted to and has sex with. To be a lesbian has as many ramifications as for a woman to be heterosexual. It is more than sex, more than just the bedroom issue many would like to make it: it is a woman-centered life with all the social interconnections that entails. Some lesbians are in long-term relationships, some in short-term ones, some date, some are celibate, some are married to men, some remain as separate as possible from men, some have children by men, some by alternative insemination, some seem "feminine" by societal standards, some "masculine," some are doctors, lawyers and ministers, some laborers, housewives and writers: what all share in common is a sexual/affectional identity that focuses on women in its attractions and social relationships.

If lesbians are simply women with a particular sexual identity who look and act like all women, then the major difference in living out a lesbian sexual identity as opposed to a heterosexual identity is that as lesbians we live in a homophobic world that threatens and imposes damaging loss on us for being *who we are,* for choosing to live whole lives. Homophobic people often assert that homosexuals have the choice of not being homosexual; that is, we don't have to act out our sexual identity. In that case, I want to hear heterosexuals talk about their willingness not to act out their sexual identity, including not just sexual activity but heterosexual social interconnections and heterosexual privilege. It is a question of wholeness. It is very difficult for one to be denied the life of a sexual being, whether expressed in sex or in physical affection, and to feel complete, whole. For our loving relationships with humans feed the life of the spirit and enable us to overcome our basic isolation and to be interconnected with humankind.

If, then, any woman can be named a lesbian and be threatened with ter- 50 rible losses, what is it she fears? Are these fears real? Being vulnerable to a homophobic world can lead to these losses:

- *Employment.* The loss of job leads us right back to the economic connection to sexism. This fear of job loss exists for almost every lesbian except perhaps those who are self-employed or in a business that does not require societal approval. Consider how many businesses or organizations you know that will hire and protect people who are openly gay or lesbian.

- *Family.* Their approval, acceptance, love.

- *Children.* Many lesbians and gay men have children, but very, very few gain custody in court challenges, even if the other parent is a known abusers. Other children may be kept away from us as though gays and lesbians are abusers. There are written and unwritten laws prohibiting lesbians and gays from being foster parents or from adopting children. There is an irrational fear that children in contact with lesbians and gays will become homosexual through influence or that they will be sexually abused. Despite our knowing that 95 percent of those who sexually abuse children are heterosexual men, there are no policies keeping heterosexual men from teaching or working with children, yet in almost every school system in America, visible gay men and lesbians are not hired through either written or unwritten law.

- *Heterosexual privilege and protection.* No institutions, other than those created by lesbians and gays—such as the Metropolitan Community Church, some counseling centers, political organizations such as the National Gay and Lesbian Task Force, the National Coalition of Black Lesbians and Gays, and Lambda Legal Defense and Education Fund, etc.—affirm homosexuality and offer protection. Affirmation and protection cannot be gained from the criminal justice system, mainline churches, educational institutions, the government.

- *Safety.* There is nowhere to turn for safety from physical and verbal attacks because the norm presently in this country is that it is acceptable to be overtly homophobic. Gay men are beaten on the streets; lesbians are kidnapped and "deprogrammed." The National Gay and Lesbian Task Force, in an extended study, has documented violence against lesbians and gay men and noted the inadequate response of the criminal justice system. One of the major differences between homophobia/heterosexism and racism and sexism is that because of the Civil Rights Movement and the women's movement racism and sexism are expressed more covertly (though with great harm); because there has not been a major, visible lesbian and gay movement, it is permissible to be overtly homophobic in any institution or public forum. Churches spew forth homophobia in the same way they did racism prior to the Civil Rights Movement. Few laws are in place to protect lesbians and gay men, and the criminal justice system is wracked with homophobia.

■ *Mental health.* An overtly homophobic world in which there is full permission to treat lesbians and gay men with cruelty makes it difficult for lesbians and gay men to maintain a strong sense of well-being and self-esteem. Many lesbians and gay men are beaten, raped, killed, subjected to aversion therapy, or put in mental institutions. The impact of such hatred and negativity can lead one to depression and, in some cases, to suicide. The toll on the gay and lesbian community is devastating.

■ *Community.* There is rejection by those who live in homophobic fear, those who are afraid of association with lesbians and gay men. For many in the gay and lesbian community, there is a loss of public acceptance, a loss of allies, a loss of place and belonging.

■ *Credibility.* This fear is large for many people: the fear that they will no longer be respected, listened to, honored, believed. They fear they will be social outcasts.

The list goes on and on. But any one of these essential components of a full life is large enough to make one deeply fear its loss. A black woman once said to me in a workshop, "When I fought for Civil Rights, I always had my family and community to fall back on even when they didn't fully understand or accept what I was doing. I don't know if I could have borne losing them. And you people don't have either with you. It takes my breath away."

What does a woman have to do to get called a lesbian? Almost anything, sometimes nothing at all, but certainly anything that threatens the status quo, anything that steps out of role, anything that asserts the rights of women, anything that doesn't indicate submission and subordination. Assertiveness, standing up for oneself, asking for more pay, better working conditions, training for and accepting a non-traditional (you mean a man's?) job, enjoying the company of women, being financially independent, being in control of one's life, depending first and foremost on oneself, thinking that one can do whatever needs to be done, but above all, working for the rights and equality of women.

In the backlash to the gains of the women's liberation movement, there has been an increased effort to keep definitions man-centered. Therefore, to work on behalf of women must mean to work against men. To love women must mean that one hates men. A very effective attack has been made against the word *feminist* to make it a derogatory word. In current backlash usage, *feminist* equals *man-hater* which equals *lesbian.* This formula is created in the hope that women will be frightened away from their work on behalf of women. Consequently, we now have women who believe in the rights of women and work for those rights while from fear deny that they are feminists, or refuse to use the word because it is so "abrasive."

So what does one do in an effort to keep from being called a lesbian? She steps back into line, into the role that is demanded of her, tries to behave in such a way that doesn't threaten the status of men, and if she works for women's rights, she begins modifying that work. When women's organizations begin doing significant social change work, they inevitably are lesbian-baited; that is, funders or institutions or community members tell us that they can't work with us because of our "man-hating attitudes" or the presence of lesbians. We are called too strident, told we are making enemies, not doing good.

The battered women's movement has seen this kind of attack: the pressure has been to provide services only, without analysis of the causes of violence against women and strategies for ending it. To provide only services without political analysis or direct action is to be in an approved "helping" role; to analyze the causes of violence against women is to begin the work toward changing an entire system of power and control. It is when we do the latter that we are threatened with the label of man-hater or lesbian. For my politics, if a women's social change organization has not been labeled lesbian or communist, it is probably not doing any significant work; it is only "making nice."

Women in many of these organizations, out of fear of all the losses we are threatened with, begin to modify our work to make it more acceptable and less threatening to the male-dominated society which we originally set out to change. The work can no longer be radical (going to the root cause of the problem) but instead must be reforming, working only on the symptoms and not the cause. Real change for women becomes thwarted and stopped. The word *lesbian* is instilled with the power to halt our work and control our lives. And we give it its power with our fear.

In my view, homophobia has been one of the major causes of the failure of the women's liberation movement to make deep and lasting change. (The other major block has been racism.) We were fierce when we set out but when threatened with the loss of heterosexual privilege, we began putting on brakes. Our best-known nationally distributed women's magazine was reluctant to print articles about lesbians, began putting a man on the cover several times a year, and writing articles about women who succeeded in a man's world. We worried about our image, our being all right, our being "real women" despite our work. Instead of talking about the elimination of sexual gender roles, we stepped back and talked about "sex role stereotyping" as the issue. Change around the edges for middleclass white women began to be talked about as successes. We accepted tokenism and integration, forgetting that equality for all women, for all people—and not just equality of white middleclass women with white men—was the goal that we could never put behind us.

But despite backlash and retreats, change is growing from within. The women's liberation movement is beginning to gain strength again because there are women who are talking about liberation for all women. We are examining sexism, racism, homophobia, classism, anti-Semitism, ageism, ableism, and imperialism, and we see everything as connected. This change in point of view represents the third wave of the women's liberation movement, a new direction that does not get mass media coverage and recognition. It has been initiated by women of color and lesbians who were marginalized or rendered invisible by the white heterosexual leaders of earlier efforts. The first wave was the 19th and early 20th century campaign for the vote; the second, beginning in the 1960s, focused on the Equal Rights Amendment and abortion rights. Consisting of predominantly white middleclass women, both failed in recognizing issues of equality and empowerment for all women. The third wave of the movement, multi-racial and multi-issued, seeks the transformation of the world for us all. We know that we won't get there until everyone gets there; that we must move forward in a great strong line, hand in hand, not just a few at a time.

We know that the arguments about homophobia originating from mental health and Biblical/religious attitudes can be settled when we look at the sexism that permeates religious and psychiatric history. The women of the third wave of the women's liberation movement know that *without the existence of sexism, there would be no homophobia.*

60   Finally, we know that as long as the word lesbian can strike fear in any woman's heart, then work on behalf of women can be stopped; the only successful work against sexism must include work against homophobia.

Summing Up: Axes
of Oppression

BLAMING THE VICTIM

William Ryan

Twenty years ago, Zero Mostel used to do a sketch in which he impersonated a Dixiecrat Senator conducting an investigation of the origins of World War II. At the climax of the sketch, the senator boomed out, in an excruciating mixture of triumph and suspicion, "What was Pearl Harbor *doing* in the Pacific?" This is an extreme example of Blaming the Victim.

Twenty years ago, we could laugh at Zero Mostel's caricature. In recent years, however, the same process has been going on every day in the arena of social problems, public health, anti-poverty programs, and social welfare. A philosopher might analyze this process and prove that, technically, it is comic. But it is hardly ever funny.

Consider some victims. One is the miseducated child in the slum school. He is blamed for his own miseducation. He is said to contain within himself the causes of his inability to read and write well. The shorthand phrase is "cultural deprivation," which, to those in the know, conveys what they allege to be inside information: That the poor child carries a scanty pack of intellectual baggage as he enters school. He doesn't know about books and magazines and newspapers, they say. (No books in the home: the mother fails to subscribe to *Reader's Digest*.) They say that if he talks at all—an unlikely event since slum parents don't talk to their children—he certainly doesn't talk correctly. (Lower-class dialect spoken here, or even—God forbid—Southern Negro. *Ici on parle nigra.*) If you can manage to get him to sit in a chair, they say, he squirms and looks out the window. (Impulsive-ridden, these kids, motoric rather than verbal.) In a word he is "disadvantaged" and "socially deprived," they say, and this, of course, accounts for his failure (*his* failure, they say) to learn much in school.

Note the similarity to the logic of Zero Mostel's Dixiecrat Senator. What is the culturally deprived child *doing* in the school? What is wrong with the victim? In pursing this logic, no one remembers to ask questions about the collapsing buildings and torn textbooks; the frightened, insensitive teachers; the six additional desks in the room; the blustering, frightened principals; the relentless segregation; the callous administrator; the irrelevant curriculum; the bigoted or cowardly members of the school board; the insulting history book; the stingy taxpayers; the fairy-tale readers; or the self-serving faculty of the local teachers' college. We are encouraged to confine our attention to the child and to dwell on all his alleged defects. Cultural deprivation becomes an omnibus explanation for the educational disaster area known as the inner-city school. This is Blaming the Victim.

5   Pointing to the supposedly deviant Negro family as the "fundamental weakness of the Negro community" is another way to blame the victim. Like "cultural deprivation," "Negro family" has become a shorthand phrase with stereotyped connotations of matriarchy, fatherlessness, and pervasive illegitimacy. Growing up in the "crumbling" Negro family is supposed to account for most of the racial evils in America. Insiders have the word, of course, and know that this phrase is supposed to evoke images of growing up with a long-absent or never-present father (replaced from time to time perhaps by a series of transient lovers) and with bossy women ruling the roost, so that the children are irreparably damaged. This refers particularly to the poor, bewildered male children, whose psyches are fatally wounded and who are never, alas, to learn the trick of becoming upright, downright, forthright all-American boys. Is it any wonder the Negroes cannot achieve equality? From such families! And, again, by focusing our attention on the Negro family as the apparent *cause* of racial inequality, our eye is diverted. Racism, discrimination, segregation, and the powerlessness of the ghetto are subtly, but thoroughly, downgraded in importance.

The generic process of Blaming the Victim is applied to almost every American problem. The miserable health care of the poor is explained away on the grounds that the victim has poor motivation and lacks health information. The problems of slum housing are traced to the characteristics of tenants who are labeled as "Southern rural migrants" not yet "acculturated" to life in the big city. The "multiproblem" poor, it is claimed, suffer the psychological effects of impoverishment, the "culture of poverty," and the deviant value system of the lower classes; consequently, though unwittingly, they cause their troubles. From such a viewpoint, the obvious fact that poverty is primarily an absence of money is easily overlooked or set aside.

The growing number of families receiving welfare are fallaciously linked together with the increased number of illegitimate children as twin results of promiscuity and sexual abandon among members of the lower orders. Every important social problem—crime, mental illness, civil disorder, unemployment—has been analyzed within the framework of the victim-blaming ideology. . . .

I have been listening to the victim-blamers and pondering their thought processes for a number of years. That process is often very subtle. Victim-blaming is cloaked in kindness and concern, and bears all the trappings and statistical furbelows of scientism; it is obscured by a perfumed haze of human-itarianism. In observing the process of Blaming the Victim, one tends to be confused and disoriented because those who practice this art display a deep concern for the victims that is quite genuine. In this way, the new ideology is very different from the open prejudice and reactionary tactics of the old days. Its adherents include sympathetic social scientists with social consciences in good working order, and liberal politicians with a genuine commitment to reform. They are very careful to dissociate themselves from vulgar Calvinism or crude racism; they indignantly condemn any notions of innate wickedness or genetic defect. "The Negro is *not born* inferior," they shout apoplectically. "Force of circumstance," they explain in reasonable tones, "has *made* him in-ferior." And they dismiss with self-righteous contempt any claims that the poor man in America is plainly unworthy or shiftless or enamored of idle-ness. No, they say, he is "caught in the cycle of poverty." He is trained to be poor by his culture and his family life, endowed by his environment (perhaps by his ignorant mother's outdated style of toilet training) with those unfortu-nately unpleasant characteristics that make him ineligible for a passport into the affluent society.

Blaming the Victim is, of course, quite different from old-fashioned con-servative ideologies. The latter simply dismissed victims as inferior, genetically defective, or morally unfit: the emphasis is on the intrinsic, even hereditary, defect. The former shifts its emphasis to the environmental causation. The old-fashioned conservative could hold firmly to the belief that the oppressed and the victimized were born that way—"that way" being defective or inade-quate in character or ability. The new ideology attributes defect and inade-quacy to the malignant nature of poverty, injustice, slum life, and racial difficulties. The stigma that marks the victim and accounts for his victimiza-tion is an acquired stigma, a stigma of social, rather than genetic, origin. But the stigma, the defect, the fatal difference—though derived in the past from environmental forces—is still located *within* the victim, inside his skin. With such an elegant formulation, the humanitarian can have it both ways. He can, all at the same time, concentrate his charitable interest on the defects of the victim, condemn the vague social and environmental stresses that produced the defect (some time ago), and ignore the continuing effect of victimizing social forces (right now). It is a brilliant ideology for justifying a perverse form of social action designed to change, not society, as one might expect, but rather society's victim.

As a result, there is a terrifying sameness in the programs that arise from this kind of analysis. In education, we have programs of "compensatory edu-cation" to build up the skills and attitudes of the ghetto child, rather than 10 structural changes in the schools. In race relations, we have social engineers who think up ways of "strengthening" the Negro family, rather than methods of eradicating racism. In health care we develop new programs to provide health information (to correct the supposed ignorance of the poor) and to reach out and discover cases of untreated illness and disability (to compensate for their supposed unwillingness to seek treatment). Meanwhile, the gross inequities of our medical care delivery systems are left completely unchanged. As we might expect, the logical outcome of analyzing social problems in terms of the deficiencies of the victim is the development of programs aimed at correcting those deficiencies. The formula for action becomes extraordinarily simple: change the victim.

All of this happens so smoothly that it seems downright rational. First, identify a social problem. Second, study those affected by the problem and discover in what ways they are different from the rest of us as a consequence of deprivation and injustice. Third, define the differences as the cause of the social problem itself. Finally, of course, assign a government bureaucrat to invent a humanitarian action program to correct the differences.

Now no one in his right mind would quarrel with the assertion that social problems are present in abundance and are readily identifiable. God knows it is true that when hundreds of thousands of poor children drop out of school—or even graduate from school—they are barely literate. After spending some ten thousand hours in the company of professional educators, these children appear to have learned very little. The fact of failure in their education is undisputed. And the racial situation in America is usually acknowledged to be a number one item on the nation's agenda. Despite years of marches, commissions, judicial decisions, and endless legislative remedies, we are confronted with unchanging or even widening racial differences in achievement. In addition, despite our assertions that Americans get the best health care in the world, the poor stubbornly remain unhealthy. They lose more work because of illness, have more carious teeth, lose more babies as a result of both miscarriage and infant death, and die considerably younger than the well-to-do.

The problems are there, and there in great quantities. They make us uneasy. Added together, these disturbing signs reflect inequality and a puzzlingly high level of unalleviated distress in America totally inconsistent with our proclaimed ideals and our enormous wealth. This thread—this rope—of inconsistency stands out so visibly in the fabric of American life, that it is jarring to the eye. And this must be explained, to the satisfaction of our conscience as well as our patriotism. Blaming the Victim is an ideal, almost painless, evasion.

The second step in applying this explanation is to look sympathetically at those who "have" the problem in question, to separate them out and define them in some way as a special group, a group that is *different* from the population in general. This is a crucial and essential step in the process, for that difference is in itself hampering and maladaptive. The Different Ones are seen as less competent, less skilled, less knowing—in short, less human. The ancient Greeks deduced from a single characteristic, a difference in language, that the barbarians—that is, the "babblers" who spoke a strange tongue—were wild, uncivilized, dangerous, rapacious, uneducated, lawless, and, indeed, scarcely more than animals. Automatically labeling strangers as savages, weird and inhuman creatures (thus explaining difference by exaggerating difference) not infrequently justifies mistreatment, enslavement, or even extermination of the Different Ones.

Blaming the Victim depends on a very similar process of identification (carried out, to be sure, in the most kindly, philanthropic, and intellectual manner) whereby the victim of social problems is identified as strange, different—in other words, as a barbarian, a savage. Discovering savages, then, is an essential component of, and prerequisite to, Blaming the Victim, and the art of Savage Discovery is a core skill that must be acquired by all aspiring Victim Blamers. They must learn how to demonstrate that the poor, the black, the ill, the jobless, the slum tenants, are different and strange. The must learn to conduct or interpret the research that shows how "these people" think in different forms, act in different patterns, cling to different values, seek different goals, and learn different truths. Which is to say that they are strangers, barbarians, savages. This is how the distressed and disinherited are redefined in order to make it possible for us to look at society's problems and to attribute their causation to the individuals affected. . . .

Blaming the victim can take its place in a long series of American ideologies that have rationalized cruelty and injustice.

Slavery, for example, was justified—even praised—on the basis of a complex ideology that showed quite conclusively how useful slavery was to society and how uplifting it was for the slaves.[1] Eminent physicians could be relied upon to provide the biological justification for slavery since after all, they said, the slaves were a separate species—as, for example, cattle are a separate species. No one in his right mind would dream of freeing the cows and fighting to abolish the ownership of cattle. In the view of the average American of 1825, it was important to preserve slavery, not simply because it was in accord with his own group interests (he was not fully aware of that), but because reason and logic showed clearly to the reasonable and intelligent man that slavery was good. In order to persuade a good and moral man to *do* evil, then, it is not necessary first to persuade him to *become* evil. It is only necessary to teach him that he is doing good. No one, in the words of a legendary newspaperman, thinks of himself as a son of a bitch.

In late-nineteenth-century America their flowered another ideology of injustice that seemed rational and just to the decent, progressive person. But Richard Hofstadter's analysis of the phenomenon of Social Darwinism[2] shows clearly its functional role in the preservation of the *status quo*. One can scarcely imagine a better fit than the one between this ideology and the purposes and actions of the robber barons, who descended like piranha fish on the America of this era and picked its bones clean. Their extraordinarily unethical operations netted them not only hundreds of millions of dollars but also, perversely, the adoration of the nation. Behavior that would be, in any more rational land (including today's America), more than enough to have landed them all in jail, was praised as the very model of a captain of modern industry. And the philosophy that justified their thievery was such that John D. Rockefeller could actually stand up and preach it in church. Listen as he speaks in, of all places, Sunday school: "The growth of a large business is merely a survival of the fittest. . . . The American Beauty rose can be produced in the splendor and fragrance which bring cheer to its beholder only by sacrificing the early buds which grow up around it. This is not an evil tendency in business. It is merely the working-out of a law of nature and a law of God."[3]

This was the core of the gospel, adapted analogically from Darwin's writings on evolution. Herbert Spencer and, later, William Graham Sumner and other beginners in the social sciences considered Darwin's work to be directly applicable to social processes: ultimately as a guarantee that life was progressing toward perfection but, in the short run, as a justification for an absolutely uncontrolled laissez-faire economic system. The central concepts of "survival of the fittest," "natural selection," and "gradualism" were exalted in Rockefeller's preaching to the status of laws of God and Nature. Not only did this ideology justify the criminal rapacity of those who rose to the top of the industrial heap, defining them automatically as naturally superior (this was bad enough), but as the same time it also required that those at the bottom of the heap be labeled as patently *unfit*—a label based solely on their position in society. According to the law of natural selection, they should be, in Spencer's judgment, eliminated. "The whole effort of nature is to get rid of such, to clear the world of them and make room for better."

20 For a generation, Social Darwinism was the orthodox doctrine in the social sciences, such as they were at that time. Opponents of this ideology were shut out of respectable intellectual life. The philosophy that enabled John D. Rockefeller to justify himself self-righteously in front of a class of Sunday school children was not the product of an academic quack or a marginal crackpot philosopher. It came directly from the lectures and books of leading intellectual figures of the time, occupants of professorial chairs at Harvard and Yale. Such is the power of an ideology that so neatly fits the needs of the dominant interests of society.

If one is to think about ideologies in America in 1970, one must be prepared to consider the possibility that a body of ideas that might seem almost self-evident is, in fact, highly distorted and highly selective; one must allow that the inclusion of a specific formulation in every freshman sociology text does not guarantee that the particular formulation represents abstract Truth rather than group interest. It is important not to delude ourselves into thinking that ideological monstrosities were constructed by monsters. They were not; they are not. They are developed through a process that shows every sign of being valid scholarship, complete with tables of numbers, copious foot-notes, and scientific terminology. Ideologies are quite often academically and socially respectable and in many instances hold positions of exclusive validity, so that disagreement is considered unrespectable or radical and risks being la-beled as irresponsible, unenlightened, or trashy.

Blaming the Victim holds such a position. It is central in the mainstream of contemporary American social thought, and its ideas pervade our most crucial assumptions so thoroughly that they are hardly noticed. Moreover, the fruits of this ideology appear to be fraught with altruism and humanitarian-ism, so it is hard to believe that it has principally functioned to block social change.

A major pharmaceutical manufacturer, as an act of humanitarian concern, has distributed copies of a large poster warning "LEAD PAINT CAN KILL!" The poster, featuring a photograph of the face of a charming little girl, goes on to explain that if children *eat* lead paint, it can poison them, they can develop se-rious symptoms, suffer permanent brain damage, even die. The health depart-ment of a major American city has put out a coloring book that provides the same information. While the poster urges parents to prevent their children from eating paint, the coloring book is more vivid. It labels as neglectful and thoughtless the mother who does not keep her infant under constant surveil-lance to keep it from eating paint chips.

Now, no one would argue against the idea that it is important to spread knowledge about the danger of eating paint in order that parents might act to forestall their children from doing so. But to campaign against lead paint *only* in these terms is destructive and misleading and, in a sense, an effective way to support and agree with slum landlords—who define the problem of lead poi-soning in precisely these terms.

This is an example of applying an exceptionalistic solution to a universal- 25 istic problem. It is not accurate to say that lead poisoning results from the ac-tions of individual neglectful mothers. Rather, lead poisoning is a social phenomenon supported by a number of social mechanisms, one of the most tragic by-products of the systematic toleration of slum housing. In New Haven, which has the highest reported rate of lead poisoning in the country, several small children have died and many others have incurred irreparable brain damage as a result of eating peeling paint. In several cases, when the landlord failed to make repairs, poisonings have occurred time and again through a succession of tenancies. And the major reason for the landlord's neglect of this problem was that the city agency responsible for enforcing the housing code did nothing to make him correct this dangerous condition.

The cause of the poisoning is the lead in the paint on the walls of the apartment in which the children live. The presence of the lead is illegal. To use lead paint in a residence is illegal; to permit lead paint to be exposed in a residence is illegal. It is not only illegal, it is potentially criminal since the housing code does provide for criminal penalties. The general problem of lead poisoning, then, is more accurately analyzed as the result of a systematic program of lawbreaking by one interest group in the community, with the toleration and encouragement of the public authority charged with enforcing that law. To ignore these continued and repeated law violations, to ignore the fact that the supposed law enforcer actually cooperates in lawbreaking, and then to load a burden of guilt on the mother of a dead or dangerously-ill child is an egregious distortion of reality. And to do so under the guise of public-spirited and humanitarian service to the community is intolerable.

But this how Blaming the Victim works. The righteous humanitarian concern displayed by the drug company, with its poster, and the health department, with its coloring book, is a genuine concern, and this is a typical feature of Blaming the Victim. Also typical is the swerving away from the central target that requires systematic change and, instead, focusing in on the individual affected. The ultimate effect is always to distract attention from the basic causes and to leave the primary social injustice untouched. And, most telling, the proposed remedy for the problem is, of course, to work on the victim himself. Prescriptions for cure, as written by the Savage Discovery set, are invariably conceived to revamp and revise the victim, never to change the surrounding circumstances. They want to change his attitudes, alter his values, fill up his cultural deficits, energize his apathetic soul, cure his character defects, train him and polish him and woo him from his savage ways.

Isn't all of this more subtle and sophisticated than such old-fashioned ideologies as Social Darwinism? Doesn't the change from brutal ideas about survival of the fit (and the expiration of the unfit) to kindly concern about characterological defects (brought about by stigmas of social origin) seem like a substantial step forward? Hardly. It is only a substitution of terms. The old reactionary exceptionalistic formulations are replaced by new progressive, humanitarian exceptionalistic formulations. In education, the outmoded and unacceptable concept of racial or class differences in basic inherited intellectual ability simply gives way to the new notion of cultural deprivation: there is very little functional difference between these two ideas. In taking a look at the phenomenon of poverty, the old concept of unfitness or idleness or laziness is replaced by the newfangled theory of the culture of poverty. In race relations, plain Negro inferiority—which was good enough for old-fashioned conservatives—is pushed aside by fancy conceits about the crumbling Negro family. With regard to illegitimacy, we are not so crass as to concern ourselves with immorality and vice, as in the old days; we settle benignly on the explanation of the "lower-class pattern of sexual behavior," which no one condemns as evil, but which is, in fact, simply a variation of the old explanatory idea. Mental illness is no longer defined as the result of hereditary taint or congenital character flaw; now we have new causal hypotheses regarding the ego-damaging emotional experiences that are supposed to be the inevitable consequence of the deplorable child-rearing practices of the poor.

In each case, of course, we are persuaded to ignore the obvious: the continued blatant discrimination against the Negro, the gross deprivation of contraceptive and adoption services to the poor, the heavy stresses endemic in the life of the poor. And almost all our make-believe liberal programs aimed at correcting our urban problems are off target; they are designed either to change the poor man or to cool him out.

We come finally to the question, Why? It is much easier to understand the *30* process of Blaming the Victim as a way of thinking than it is to understand the motivation for it. Why do Victim Blamers, who are usually good people, blame the victim? The development and application of this ideology, and of all the mythologies associated with Savage Discovery, are readily exposed by careful analysis as hostile acts—one is almost tempted to say acts of war—directed against the disadvantaged, the distressed, the disinherited. It is class warfare in reverse. Yet those who are most fascinated and enchanted by this ideology tend to be progressive, humanitarian, and in the best sense of the word, charitable persons. They would usually define themselves as moderates or liberals. Why do they pursue this dreadful war against the poor and the oppressed?

Put briefly, the answer can be formulated best in psychological terms—or, at least, I, as a psychologist, am more comfortable with such a formulation. The highly-charged psychological problem confronting this hypothetical progressive, charitable person I am talking about is that of reconciling his own self-interest with the promptings of this humanitarian impulses. This psychological process of reconciliation is not worked out in a logical, rational, conscious way; it is a process that takes place far below the level of sharp consciousness, and the solution—Blaming the Victim—is arrived at subconsciously as a compromise that apparently satisfies both his self-interest and his charitable concerns. Let me elaborate.

First, the question of self-interest or, more accurately, class interest. The typical Victim Blamer is a middle class person who is doing reasonably well in a material way; he has a good job, a good income, a good house, a good car. Basically, he likes the social system pretty much the way it is, at least in broad outline. He likes the two-party political system, though he may be highly skilled in finding a thousand minor flaws in its functioning. He heartily approves of the profit motive as the propelling engine of the economic system despite his awareness that there are abuses of that system, negative side effects, and substantial residual inequalities.

On the other hand, he is acutely aware of poverty, racial discrimination, exploitation, and deprivation, and, moreover, he wants to do something concrete to ameliorate the condition of the poor, the black, and the disadvantaged. This is not an extraneous concern; it is central to his value system to insist on the worth of the individual, the equality of men, and the importance of justice.

What is to be done, then? What intellectual position can he take, and what line of action can he follow that will satisfy both of these important motivations? He quickly and self-consciously rejects two obvious alternatives, which he defines as "extremes." He cannot side with an openly reactionary, repressive position that accepts continued oppression and exploitation as the price of a privileged position for his own class. This is incompatible with his own morality and his basic political principals. He finds the extreme conservative position repugnant.

35   He is, if anything, more allergic to radicals, however, than he is to reactionaries. He rejects the "extreme" solution of radical social change, and this makes sense since such radical social change threatens his own well-being. A more equitable distribution of income might mean that he would have less— a smaller or older house, with fewer yews or no rhododendrons in the yard, a less enjoyable job, or, at the least, a somewhat smaller salary. If black children and poor children were, in fact, reasonably educated and began to get high S.A.T. scores, they would be competing with *his* children for the scarce places in the entering classes of Harvard, Columbia, Bennington, and Antioch.

So our potential Victim Blamers are in a dilemma. In the words of an old Yiddish proverb, they are trying to dance at two weddings. The are old friends of both brides and fond of both kinds of dancing, and they want to accept both invitations. They cannot bring themselves to attack the system that has been so good to them, but they want so badly to be helpful to the victims of racism and economic injustice.

Their solution is a brilliant compromise. They turn their attention to the victim in his post–victimized state. They want to bind up wounds, inject penicillin, administer morphine, and evacuate the wounded for rehabilitation. They explain what's wrong with the victim in terms of social experiences *in the past,* experiences that have left wounds, defects, paralysis, and disability. And they take the cure of these wounds and the reduction of these disabilities as the first order of business. They want to make the victims less vulnerable, send them back into battle with better weapons, thicker armor, a higher level of morale.

In order to do so effectively, of course, they must analyze the victims carefully, dispassionately, objectively, scientifically, empathetically, mathematically, and hardheadedly, to see what make them so vulnerable in the first place.

What weapons, now, might they have lacked when they went into battle? Job skills? Education?

40   What armor was lacking that might have warded off their wounds? Better values? Habits of thrift and foresight?

And what might have ravaged their morale? Apathy? Ignorance? Deviant low class cultural patterns?

This is the solution of the dilemma, the solution of Blaming the Victim. And those who buy this solution with a sigh of relief are inevitably blinding themselves to the basic causes of the problems being addressed. They are, most crucially, rejecting the possibility of blaming, not the victims, but themselves. They are all unconsciously passing judgments on themselves and bringing in a unanimous verdict of Not Guilty.

If one comes to believe that the culture of poverty produces persons *fated* to be poor, who can find any fault with our corporation-dominated economy? And if the Negro family produces young men *incapable* of achieving equality, let's deal with that first before we go on to the task of changing the pervasive racism that informs and shapes and distorts our every social institution. And if unsatisfactory resolution of one's Oedipus complex accounts for all emotional distress and mental disorder, then by all means let us attend to that and postpone worrying about the pounding day-to-day stresses of life on the bottom rungs that drive so many to drink, dope, and madness.

That is the ideology of Blaming the Victim, the cunning Art of Savage Discovery. The tragic, frightening truth is that it is a mythology that is winning over the best people of our time, the very people who must resist this ideological temptation if we are to achieve non-violent change in America.

NOTES

1. For a good review of this general ideology, see I. A. Newby, *Jim Crow's Defense* (Baton Rouge: Louisiana State Univerity Press, 1965).
2. Richard Hofstadter, *Social Darwinism in American Thought* (revised ed., Boston: Beacon Press, 1955).
3. William J. Ghent, *Our Benevolent Feudalism* (New York: The Macmillan Co., 1902), p. 29.

IF EVERYBODY'S RESPONSIBLE, THEN NOBODY IS

Peg O'Connor

In this [reading], I continue the discussion that I began [earlier] about the responsibility for extreme acts of racism such as the recent burnings of African-American churches in the South. I do not deny that it is appropriate to assign responsibility to those who actually set the fires. These acts cause a great deal of harm and suffering while at the same time reinforcing a background of racism. Individual harmful and oppressive acts are made possible and intelligible by existing practices, and they reinforce these practices. It is a mistake to assign responsibility only to those who actually set the fires. Doing so, I argue, keeps the focus and moral outrage on particular actions rather than on the conditions that make such acts possible and intelligible. Those of use who hold racist attitudes and beliefs and participate in racist practices are, in some way, responsible for creating a combustible environment. That combustibility makes the burnings possible and intelligible. We must, therefore, conceive of responsibility for practices, and not just actions.

After I read an early version of my paper "Conspiracies and Connect the Dots" at a conference on race sponsored by the Radical Philosophy Association, one person challenged the view I articulated. This [reading] is a sustained response to his challenge. First I lay out my interlocutor's objections and reveal the account of moral responsibility I take to underlie his criticisms. I call this underlying account the linked chain, and I describe this account, pointing to where it works well, and where it does not. To further explicate this linked chain account, I turn to Larry May's work, *Sharing Responsibility*. May's account, while an improvement on the original linked chain account, is not adequate to the task of addressing responsibility for racist practices.

In formulating an alternative both to the original linked chain and to May's account, I stretch the chain to include attitudes and unintentional actions. I also expand upon May's notions of collective and shared responsibility.

THE CRITICISMS

The main criticisms leveled at my claims in "Conspiracies" revolve around the coherence of my claim, given a traditional account of responsibility. For the sake of simplicity and clarity, I have boiled down my critic's argument into three main points:

1. My view rests on a paradox: if all of us are responsible, then none of us is.

2. My view that all white people share responsibility stretches the concept of responsibility to meaninglessness. How could I use the same concept to evaluate the actions of the arsonists and the actions (and inactions) of other white people? I call this the dilution view. Responsibility, when spread so thin because it is spread over so many people, loses its potency and effectiveness. Responsibility works best when it can be heaped on particular individuals in light of their actions and inactions.

3. My position engenders a form of helplessness. Suppose that my view that all white people bear some responsibility is right; then what are we individual white people supposed to do? We cannot change the system by ourselves, therefore there is nothing we can do.

These three criticisms are fundamentally connected: Responsibility attaches to individuals, and by extension, to groups. But, in order to spread responsibility as far as I want, it must be spread thinly. Spread thus, it loses its effectiveness because the motivational force of responsibility for individuals requires a certain dosage. $_5$

LINKED CHAIN PARADIGM

The three young white men who first burgled an African-American church and torched it, and who then went to another African-American church and set it ablaze while yelling racial epithets, are responsible for these actions. Such cases are paradigms for how responsibility works. The intentions played a causal role in the actions undertaken. These actions were freely chosen on the basis of one's attitudes and intentions. The consequences of these acts were harmful. There was a direct causal chain between the intentions of the individuals, their actions, and the consequences of them. Most importantly, all three elements—intention, action, and consequence—are linked together. I call this model the "linked chain account."

It is true that in much of traditional moral theory, responsibility attaches to the intentional acts of individuals and, by extension, to the consequences of these acts. The dominant moral theories (Kantianism, Utilitarianism, rights-based), though they differ in very important ways with respect to content, all share a similar form. Margaret Urban Walker calls this shared form the theoretical-juridical model.[1] According to Walker, "The regnant type of moral theory in contemporary ethics is a codifiable (and usually compact) set of moral formulas (or procedures for selecting formulas) that can be applied by any agent to a situation to yield a justified and determinate action-guiding judgment. The

---

[1] Margaret Urban Walker, *Moral Understandings: A Feminist Study in Ethics* (New York: Routledge, 1998); hereafter cited in the text.

formulas or procedures (if there is more than one) are typically seen as rules or principles at a high level of generality. Application of these formulas is typically seen as something like deduction or instantiation. The formulas and their applications yield the same for all agents indifferently" (52).

The picture is that morality is an individually acting guiding system within or for a person (61). Given the application of an abstract rule, whether it is in the form of Kant's Categorical Imperative where motivation or intention is key, or the utilitarian's maximization principle where consequences are the focus, it makes sense that the linked chain is the regnant model of moral responsibility.

The three elements taken together will determine the kind or degree of responsibility that an individual or group has for actions. All three elements in one action present the strongest case. If, for example, there is some question about the voluntariness of the action, or the intentions are not clear, or the consequences of the action are not all that bad, then we often say that these mitigate and lessen the degree of responsibility. What is important is that intentions and consequences are linked by the action. In the absence of action, there is little cause to assign responsibility. Intentions without action are impotent, and it is actions that have consequences.

10   A particular conception of agency underlies this linked chain account. Full agency involves the ability and opportunity to make choices freely. A person who has reached a certain degree of maturation, demonstrates appropriate rational behavior, and finds herself evaluating and choosing acts, is exercising full moral agency. Agency requires intentional acts freely chosen; agency is manifest in intentional actions. Unintentional acts, mere reactions, and coerced acts do not demonstrate full agency.

This linked chain paradigm provides a formula for the moral evaluation of events. In the case mentioned above, those of us who did not light the fires can discern the intentions of the arsonists. The racial epithets they yelled as they set the fires are evidence of their intentions and attitudes. The actions that resulted from these intentions are the fires. Some of the consequences, such as the destroyed buildings, can clearly be seen, while other consequences are not so easily noticed, such as the church members' feelings of fear and anger. This paradigm encourages us to look for the links between intentions, actions, and consequences. When we can see these links, we can make judgments of responsibility.

This linked chain account of responsibility is also equipped to address groups' responsibilities for the actions of their members. A group, according to Iris Young, is "a collection of persons that recognize themselves and one another as in a unified relation with one another. . . . Members of the group, that is, are united by *action* that they undertake together. In acknowledging himself or herself as a member of the group, an individual acknowledges himself or herself as oriented toward the same goals as the others; each individual thereby assumes the common project as a project for his or her individual action."[2] The project of a group is collective; each member recognizes that it is best undertaken by a group. As examples of such collective projects best undertaken by a group, Young includes storming the Bastille, organizing a women's conference, and achieving women's suffrage.

Obviously, groups can be organized around projects that are not morally defensible in the ways that organizing for women's suffrage or a women's conference are. The Ku Klux Klan is a group whose members have a shared project of asserting the supremacy of white Christian people and the inferiority of all other races. In those few cases where the arsonists were found to be members of hate groups, many people would say that all the members of that groups are responsible, even those individuals who did not participate in those particular arsons. Though they did not actually light a fire, these other individuals created and cultivated an environment in which such racist acts were sanctioned, and perhaps rewarded. By holding all members of hate groups responsible, we are saying that they have been creating an atmosphere which they ought not to have through their actions and attitudes, and this resulted in some of its members undertaking overtly racist actions such as the church burnings. This notion of group responsibility is being utilized within the legal system to redress wrongs and injuries perpetrated by individual members of certain groups.

The Southern Poverty Law Center has adopted a strategy of suing hate groups such as the United Klans of America and the White Aryan Resistance (WAR) in civil court. In 1987, the law center won a seven-million-dollar judgment against the Klan and all the Klansmen who had played a role in the lynching of Michael Donald in Mobile, Alabama. The suit was filed on behalf of Donald's mother, Beulah Mae Donald. As a result of the court's decision, the United Klans of American had to turn over its headquarters to Beulah Mae Donald.

In October 1990, a jury awarded twelve and half million dollars to the family of Mulugeta Seraw, an Ethiopian who had been killed by members of a Portland, Oregon, skinhead group. The suit was filed against WAR and its leaders, Tom and John Metzger. Prior to the killing of Seraw, the members of that skinhead group had been at a training organized by the top recruiter for WAR. Morris Dees of the Southern Poverty Law Center argued that the Metzgers had a preexisting relationship with the perpetrators and that the Metzgers did occupy a position of authority over the Portland skinheads.

Assigning responsibility to a group such the Ku Klux Klan and WAR keeps us within the linked chain paradigm, except that the actions of groups instead of the actions of an individual are the relevant ones in question. The intentions of individual members are formed and organized against a backdrop of the

15

---

[2] Iris Marion Young, *Intersecting Voices: Dilemmas of Gender, Political Philosophy, and Policy* (Princeton: Princeton University Press, 1997), 23; hereafter cited in the text.

intentions of the larger group. The civil suits filed on behalf of the victims or families of victims appeal to what Larry May calls collective responsibility.[3] In the cases of the church arsonists and the Ku Klux Klan mentioned above, the linked chain account works very well. But there are instances when it does not work so well, yet we still hold on to it. Each link in the chain has weaknesses.

The importance of evaluating intentions shows up most clearly in Kant's moral philosophy. According to Kant in *Grounding for the Metaphysics of Morals,* the moral goodness of an action comes solely from the intention from which the action springs.[4] Furthermore, the content of the intention matters. The only action that is morally good is the action that is done for the sake of the moral law; mere conformity with the moral law is not sufficient (3). Furthermore, he says, "The moral worth depends, therefore, not on the realization of the object of the action, but merely on the principle of volition according to which, without regard to any objects of the faculty of desire, that action has been done" (13). Inclinations do not matter, nor do the consequences of the actions. What is necessary is that the principle of volition be from duty. It is also necessary that the intention be clearly identifiable.

However, in many cases, the intentions or attitudes of the agent are clear neither to the agent himself nor to others around him evaluating the act. Intentions are complicated phenomena, and so, too, must be the search for the intention or the set of intentions that caused the agent to choose one course of action over another. We often attribute internationality in an after-the-fact manner. The intention reveals itself to the agent and others after the act is done. On the basis of a particular act, we say that must have been the intention. In other cases, though, an act can be made to accord with a variety of intentions, and choosing one as the cause may be a matter of caprice or convenience.

In order to evaluate the moral permissibility and praiseworthiness of an action, the intention must be recognizable to both the agent and others

---

[3]Larry May, *Sharing Responsibility* (Chicago: University of Chicago Press, 1992); hereafter cited in the text. In his chapter "Groups and Personal Value Transformation," May notes that there are two main ways that a group changes the values of its members. First, the organizational structure or decision-making process (or lack thereof) brings about a conformity in values of the group. Second, conformity is bred by the feelings of camaraderie, solidarity, and alienation from or aversion to what adversely affects the group as a whole (75).

Values reside in individuals and not in a group. May is careful to assert that groups are not some superentities that are reifications of individuals. Talking about groups influencing the values and behaviors of individuals is a way of speaking in shorthand. Rather, "its is individuals within groups, operating through the formal and informal relationships or structures of the group, who influence the values of their fellow members" (75). While I agree that organizational structure and social identification are two means to bring about individuals' conformity to group values, I am neither convinced that values are solely the possession of individuals nor that groups do not influence the values of its members.

[4]Immanuel Kant, *Grounding for the Metaphysics of Morals,* trans. James Ellington (Indianapolis: Hackett, 1993).

around him. Wittgenstein might say that this would have to mean that the agent sees the causal connection from the inside and the observers from the outside (*PI* §631). But here it is appropriate to ask exactly what is being seen or ascertained by the agent and others. We can ask both about the transparency of an intention and its location. Consider the following set of passages:

> "I am not ashamed of what I did then, but of the intention which I had."—And didn't the intention lie also in what I did? What justifies the shame? The whole history of the incident.
>
> "For a moment I meant to . . ." That is, I had a particular feeling, an inner experience; and I remember it.—And now remember *quite precisely!* Then the 'inner experience' of intending seems to vanish again. Instead one remembers thoughts, feelings, movements, and also connexions with earlier situations.
>
> It is as if one had altered the adjustment of a microscope. One did not see before what is now in focus.
>
> "Well, that only shews that you have adjusted your microscope wrong. You were supposed to look at a particular section of the culture, and you are seeing a different one."
>
> There is something right about that. But suppose that (with a particular adjustment of the lenses) I did remember a *single* sensation; how have I the right to say that is what I call the "intention"? It might be that (for example) a particular tickle accompanied every one of my intentions.
>
> What is the natural expression of an intention?—Look at a cat when it stalks a bird; or a beast when it wants to escape. (*PI* §§644–47)

. . . [A]n intention cannot be understood as a mental process that causes or accompanies an action. Searching for some discrete sensation or mental process that one identifies as *the* intention causing the action is misguided. Wittgenstein might remind us that we couldn't really be sure what we were looking for, or when we had found it. It would be as futile as seeking the core of an onion by peeling away its layers. When we "look for intention" we need to take into account "the whole history of the incident," and this involves looking at context, which entails looking at the practices that shape our behaviors and attitudes.

With regard to actions, the linked chain can handle cases of inaction of a particular sort. In the linked chain account, inaction is a species of action. Inaction involves choosing not to act in a particular situation. But this is not the only brand of inaction. [20]

Perhaps the biggest weakness of the intention/attitude and action link is the assumption that all acts suitable for evaluation are caused by an intention. Many acts lack an intention, but nevertheless should be the object of moral analysis. Evaluating consequences is a very tricky undertaking, one that has been the subject of great concern since the development of Utilitarianism and Consequentialism. It is not always possible to draw a clear line between an act and its consequences. Nor is it possible to draw a ring around all those things that are consequences of a particular act. When is something a consequence of *this* act and not of *that* act?

But even though the linked chain cannot address all moral situations, it still has a hold on us. When it works, it works extremely well. But sometimes in the interests of assigning responsibility, we make the case fit the paradigm by bracketing some considerations in favor of others, or redefining the situation, or making some features *the* defining ones.

COLLECTIVE AND SHARED RESPONSIBILITY

Larry May, in *Sharing Responsibility,* stretches the linked chain so that he can address the issue of responsibility for racist attitudes. I turn now to an examination of how he stretches this chain, which will be useful for me as I stretch it even further.

COLLECTIVE RESPONSIBILITY

Larry May argues that the responsibility that the Ku Klux Klan has for the actions of its members is collective responsibility. May defines collective responsibility as "nondistributed responsibility of a group structured in such a way that action can occur that would not occur if the members were acting outside the group" (106). With collective responsibility, the group as a whole is responsible. This does not entail that all, if any, are individually responsible for the harm (38). When a group is collectively responsible for a harm, the group as a whole must have done something, or failed to do something, that contributed to the harm. One example that May offers is the collective responsibility that the United States bears for the downing of an Iranian passenger plane by the U.S. military (106). A corporation also bears responsibility for the actions of its employees because the corporate decisions shape the attitudes and behaviors of its employees. And the absence of a company policy on sexual abuse, for instance, might be taken as a tacit condoning of it by employees (75–76).

Shared Responsibility

25   May offers one other kind of responsibility that will be useful in making my argument about the responsibility that white people qua whites have for acts of racism. Shared responsibility, according to May, is "the aggregated responsibility of individuals, all of whom contribute to a result and for that reason are personally responsible, albeit to different degrees, for a given harmful result" (106). When responsibility is shared, responsibility attaches to each individual

member of a collective. Shared responsibility does not even depend upon the existence of a cohesive group because it concerns aggregated personal responsibility (38). For example, those people who are at a beach but do not attempt to rescue a drowning child share responsibility for the harm of the child. Similarly, those people who hear a person shouting for help but do not call the police share responsibility for the harm done to that person. The residents of a New York apartment building who failed to do anything (including calling the police) while a woman was being murdered outside their building chose not to do anything. They have shared responsibility for their inaction (8).

Part of May's project is expanding the scope of moral responsibility to include attitudes. He asserts that "those who have racist attitudes, as opposed to those who do not, create a climate of attitudes in which harm is more likely to occur . . . members of a community who share racist attitudes also share in the responsibility for racially motivated harms produced by some of the members because of this climate for racist attitudes" (46). In expanding responsibility, May also advocates an expanded notion of agency that includes "those attitudes and dispositions that make overt behavior, even the behavior of others, more likely to occur" (51). On May's account, people who continue to hold racist views, even when they recognize the harm these attitudes can bring about, are exercising their agency. They are demonstrating a kind of moral recklessness because they are posing a threat to others, while refusing to do anything to lessen this risk (49). Such people contribute to the production of racial violence indirectly by helping to create an environment in which overt behaviors are more likely to occur.

With these notions of collective and shared responsibility, May has broadened the scope of responsibility. But his account remains in the linked chain paradigm and has too restricted a scope to enable me to justify the claim I make about whites' responsibility for racism.

May restricts his account by his emphasis on individual choice and his conception of the role and nature of attitudes: "[I]n arguing for the view that the attitudes and beliefs we choose, and not just our overt behaviors, are relevant to judgments of responsibility, I remain committed to the view that people should only be judged morally responsible for those things that are under our control; but control here does not necessarily mean that one could make the world a different place" (44). On May's view, one is in control when she can freely and voluntarily choose her attitudes and behaviors.

This emphasis on individuals' control—what they choose to believe and how they choose to act—is overly narrow. May, in his discussions of collective responsibility, is primarily concerned with groups. The groups he discusses and uses in examples—a college community, a corporation, the mob, health-care institutions, and the United States—have fairly clear criteria for membership. With the possible exception of the United States, they are all groups to which people voluntarily choose to belong. But there is another way people can be connected to each other. This alternative form of association will enable me to combine elements of both collective and shared responsibility which in turn will address the broader social practices in which actions and attitudes have their lives.

30   Underlying May's position is the assumption that it is possible for a person not to have racist attitudes. However, given my analysis throughout this work, this position just isn't tenable. Against a long history of racist and oppressive practices, it is not possible for any person not to have racist attitudes. These attitudes are part of the worldviews we inherit.

May understands attitudes to be not just cognitive states but affective states in which a person is, under normal circumstances, moved to behave (46). The person who acts out of racist attitudes causes direct harm for which he ought to be held morally responsible. Other people who share these attitudes but do not act, according to May, cause indirect harm because they bring about conditions in which others will cause harm.

This distinction between direct and indirect harm makes me uneasy. It would appear that harm attaches primarily to actions, so what we are really evaluating are the harmful consequences of actions. This brings us right back again to the linked chain account. In May's view, the harmfulness of an attitude is a function of its being instrumental to action. The harm is indirect, and perhaps only potential. If the attitude does not bring about an action causing direct harm, then should we conclude that the attitude was not harmful? I want to avoid this conclusion and address the ways attitudes are harmful in and of themselves, and not just because they lead to harmful actions. Attitudes in the absence of actions can be quite harmful.

The racist climate is maintained in a variety of ways, and so the account of moral responsibility we need is one that is broader than the linked chain paradigm and incorporates elements of both collective and shared responsibility. My account expands the ways in which people ought to be responsible. Like shared responsibility, there must be an aggregate quality because it is individuals who act and who have attitudes. I also recognize that responsibility must also be collective because individuals' actions and attitudes are made possible by and do reflect broader social practices and structures.

The alternative account that I offer includes unintentional actions, unintentional inactions, and the harmfulness of attitudes, even in the absence of action. This account decenters the direct causal chain of intention→action→consequences. More specifically, under this new paradigm, unintentional actions can have harmful consequences for which people ought to bear responsibility. Also, intentions and attitudes in the absence of actions can have harmful consequences.

UNINTENTIONAL ACTIONS AND HABITS

35   Some actions and habits are so familiar that they do not need to be accompanied by any intention in order to be undertaken. Such actions help maintain and reinforce the racist system in which we live. That I speak more nervously

about racism when there are students of color in my classes, that I grimace when a group of African-American girls seems to be talking so loudly, and that I get defensive when my privilege is named by others, are all actions that are unintentional. . . . [T]hese bodily expressions are beliefs and attitudes that are open to the public. Attitudes have public expression and meaning. I will return to this point below.

By "unintentional" I mean not intending harm, and in some cases, actually intending something good. Those who argued for a gradual ending of slavery on the basis of the belief that Black people were like children and unable to care and provide for themselves did not intend to harm Black people. To the contrary, they saw themselves as doing something good because they were trying to end slavery. Their approach, however, was harmful to Blacks because it did not abolish slavery immediately, thus prolonging the abuse and suffering of many. Further, the notion that Black people are like children dependent on white people for their well-being has been used not only as a justification of slavery, but also as a justification for their continued exclusion from certain jobs and careers. As I have argued, beliefs such as this can begin to function normatively, becoming ones around which others will cluster. In this role, they recede from view and doubt.

Another example of unintentional actions that are harmful even though the intentions may have been good is the food stamp program. Food stamps often require that the bearer purchase a certain foodstuff, sometimes even specifying the brand. Such programs remove any choice because it is assumed that either the people who need this kind of assistance are not able to make a choice or that the choices they would make are bad ones.[5] Losing the opportunity to make choices affects one's ability to make choices. Perhaps this isn't the greatest harm that one can suffer (especially when weighted against the "benefit" of having food), but it is a harm nevertheless. The loss of opportunity and ability to make choices results in more people becoming dependent on others (federal, state, and local agencies) at a time when programs are being cut and needs are growing. These unintentional actions are often difficult to name because the intentions that accompany them are often, in some sense, good. These cases show how actions have their meaning in their use and role in our communal life rather than in the intentions of individual actors.

UNINTENTIONAL INACTIONS

The linked chain paradigm is primarily concerned with intentional actions. Inaction can similarly be intentional. One can choose not to stop an arsonist because she does not care if a church is torched or she does not want to get

---

[5] See Nancy Fraser, "Women, Welfare, and the Politics of Need Interpretation," in *Unruly Practices: Power, Discourse, and Gender in Contemporary Social Theory* (Minneapolis: University of Minnesota Press, 1989).

involved. Inaction such as this is often partly evaluated on the intentions that accompany it. The possibility of being harmed if she intervenes is a reason for not acting to prevent the fires. Talking about inaction in this way still preserves the relationship between intention and action. Many inactions, however, are not accompanied by such explicit intentions. Inactions such as these are important to evaluate because they are part of the oppressive foreground and background.

One kind of inaction involves actions that would never occur to a person. Something not occurring to me may be a consequence of my privilege; I am not forced to pay attention to certain things. For example, a native speaker of English may never have to think about taking classes and achievement/ aptitude tests in a different language. California's Proposition 227 (which was passed in June 1988) requires that after one year in an English immersion class, all students be put into English-only classes. California also requires that all children, regardless of their first language, time lived in the United States, and time spent learning English, take math and reading achievement tests in English.[6]

40   It might not occur to a native speaker of English that such a test might not reliably measure what a child knows. The test scores of nonnative speakers could be significantly lower than their native English-speaking counterparts. Politicians and educational administrators put a huge emphasis on these tests. The results are use to place or track students through their elementary and secondary school careers. They are also used in diagnosing all sorts of social "problems" and prescribing remedies for these problems. Such remedies often involve more traditional subject matters, teaching methods, and forms of discipline.

HARMFULNESS OF ATTITUDES IN THE ABSENCE OF ACTIONS

My critic might say that attitudes, without actions, are like the ornamental knobs that spin on a machine but don't engage with any part of it. In some sense, they just don't *do* anything. One can have whatever she wants in her heart, so long as she doesn't act on it.

Underlying this position is the assumption that there is a clear connection between having an attitude, forming an intention on the basis of that attitude,

---

[6] The San Francisco school district refused to administer these tests to non-English speakers in academic year 1997–98. The State Board of Education and the Department of Education petitioned the court to force San Francisco to administer these tests. Superior Court Judge David Garcia denied the petition in a terse, four-sentence ruling. Unfortunately, Garcia's ruling applied only to the San Francisco district. A bill in the state assembly that would have exempted immigrant students with less than thirty months of English instruction from having to take such tests was vetoed by Governor Pete Wilson in August 1998.

and the action that springs from it. "Acting on an intention" or "acting out of an attitude" means acting in a way that attempts to achieve the desired outcome. This is certainly one way that actions are connected to intentions and attitudes. But there are other ways that actions can attach to attitudes.

Consider a white person who tends to doubt that a Black person is having difficulty securing a homeowner's loan because that person is Black, no matter what sort of evidence is produced. This white person may seek out and then parade a variety of explanations for the refusal—the person may have bad credit history or too much debt, or the house is in a "bad" neighborhood. For the white person, the refusal does not have anything to do with the race of the person, but only with that person's financial history. Or the refusal may have nothing to do with the person but rather with the neighborhood. The neighborhood is the problem, not race. It just wouldn't make good business sense to give homeowners' loans for houses in certain neighborhoods. Banks have obligations to their customers.

To the person who replies that financial history is closely connected to race (including the opportunity to get good-paying jobs, obtain credit cards to build that all-important history, and have a pension plan) and that neighborhoods are often segregated along race lines, and that most banks are not located in such neighborhoods (pawn shops and check-cashing businesses have started to play the role of banks), this doubting white may express exasperation and exclaim that Black people are making everything be about race when clearly (at least to him) most things are not. Blacks are playing the race card too much and blaming too much on race. The initial disbelief can turn into frustration. Uttering this sentiment is harmful, I believe. A child hears these comments often enough, especially from an authority figures such as a parent, admired adult, or even a radio personality, and the child will take them as true. It is only after a child has reached a certain point of maturation that she may begin to question the veracity of such claims.

Many people might be tempted to say that a person who just says something like this isn't really doing anything. The person saying such things isn't the one keeping people from getting loans. But how sharply is the line drawn between saying and doing? Using my imaginary critic, I want to show how this distinction breaks down. My critic might assert that uttering a statement like the one above is an action. Talking is an action and not an attitude. What, then, about a person's facial expressions? A frown or a grimace certainly conveys attitudes such as sadness or disapproval. Here, my critic might say that frowning or grimacing is an action; she is doing something with her face. But if my critic defines actions this broadly, what is left for attitudes? The only thing an attitude could be is what is manifested in the privacy of my own mind. Attitudes could include all and only mental processes. Everything falls to the action side of the divide. Attitudes could never be reflected alone in the real world but only in the privacy of one's mind. Once they move outside the privacy of one's mind, they cease to be attitudes and become actions. Attitudes are phantasms or chimeras.

Presuming a sharp distinction between attitudes and actions while asserting that only actions have consequences for which we ought to bear responsibility means that one does not have responsibility for attitudes. But when the action/attitude distinction breaks down, and when we do not limit ourselves to the linked chain paradigm, attitudes clearly become things for which we ought to bear responsibility.

A racist climate is harmful in itself; its very existence is harmful. A racist climate is a toxic one for people and the environment. Paulo Freire in *Pedagogy of the Oppressed* says that oppression dehumanizes both the oppressed and the oppressors, albeit in radically different ways.[7] To be an oppressor and exercise power and authority over others requires that some part of you becomes warped. Not being able to see the humanity of others requires that your own humanity be compromised.

A racist climate destroys the social environment by creating hierarchies and divisions. It sets parameters (if you are an oppressor) and high, razor wire fences (if you are oppressed) around the social relations into which you can enter. Finally, a racist climate helps to destroy the physical world. From the lack of adequate sewage treatment to the location of toxic waste sites in predominantly Black geographical areas in the United States to the use of biological warfare and land mines to widespread poverty and disease, a racist climate is destroying the world in ways that we have not yet come to realize. The harmful effects of a racist climate are long lasting and never localized.[8]

---

[7] Paulo Freire, *Pedagogy of the Oppressed* (New York: Continuum, 1970), 28.

[8] For several good articles about racism and the physical environment, see Laura Westra and Peter Wenz, eds., *Faces of Environmental Racism: Confronting Issues of Global Justice* (Lanham, Md.: Rowman and Littlefield, 1995).

Part II
Theorizing Privilege

INTRODUCTION

Part II focuses on the "flip side" or companion concept of oppression, *privilege*. Why is privilege the relevant companion to oppression? What does it mean to say that if you flip over an instance of oppression, you'll find an instance of privilege on the other side?

Not everyone will agree that privilege is the relevant term. Some will argue that *domination* is the companion concept of oppression; they assert that if you are not a member of a particular oppressed group, then you are automatically a dominator. (You encountered this notion is some of the readings in Part I.) The concept of domination presupposes that a group or an individual exercises power over another group in very obvious and *overt* ways. (Think, for example, of the relationship between a master and a slave; the master has power *over* the slave, and may exercise that power in both subtle and brutal ways.)

But domination isn't a concept that is flexible or broad enough to be paired with the concept of oppression that emerged in Part I; it cannot account for all the kinds of situations we want to be able to describe. For instance, it does not give us a way to explain situations in which people who are not the targets of oppression, and are also not actively dominating over others, nevertheless *benefit* from the oppressive conditions in place. The readings in Part I showed that oppression has many different faces; it is created in all kinds of social practices, structures, and institutions. In many instances of oppression, we may not be able to point to any person or group of persons who are actively engaged in dominating the oppressed group the way that slaveholders dominate their slaves.

We need a companion concept that has as many different faces as does oppression. The concept of privilege will fill the bill; its multiple aspects allow us to describe and understand the roles that different "unoppressed" groups play in the maintenance of oppressive systems.

The readings in this section examine white privilege, male privilege, and heterosexual privilege. Privilege, like oppression, is a consequence of one's membership in a particular group. One feature that is common to these different forms is that privilege is often invisible to those who have it. Privilege obscures itself, making it very difficult to identify and name when you have it. Most often privilege, like oppression, is "explained" in terms of natural or given traits. People with privilege tend to appeal to those traits in an attempt to justify having the privilege in the first place. But as these readings reveal, privilege is not something natural or "God-given"; like oppression, it is created, and granted to certain groups of people.

People with privilege can learn to be "disloyal" to it, and such disloyalty can be an effective means of challenging systems of oppression. This is an idea that was first introduced in Part I; we will return to it in earnest in Part IV, when we turn to the topic of resistance.

6

Privilege: General Theories

■ ■ ■

PRIVILEGE: EXPANDING ON MARILYN FRYE'S "OPPRESSION"

Alison Bailey

Marilyn Frye's "Oppression" (1983) is essential reading in most courses with political and feminist content. One of the merits of her essay is the way in which examples such as men opening doors for women, metaphors that equate oppression with a double-binds, and birdcage-like social structures get tied to the meaning of oppression. Anyone who teaches this essay knows how difficult it is to get students initially to understand how Frye uses the term "oppression" to refer to systems. Each time I teach this essay I try to move the conversation one step further to make connections between oppression and privilege so that, in Frye's words, these terms do not get "stretched to mean-inglessness" (1983, 1). Yet when I suggest that the oppression of people of color is systematically held in place by white privilege, or that women's sub-ordination makes male privilege possible, or that homophobia holds hetero-sexual privilege in place, students who otherwise embrace Frye's analysis become reluctant to extend it to cover their own unearned advantages. To my surprise, conversations about what it means to have privilege are met with re-sponses parallel to those Frye mentions at the beginning of her essay. "Blacks and other minorities are privileged too; they get athletic scholarships and af-firmative action benefits," my students say. Or, "women are privileged too; they don't have to register for the selective service and men pay for their din-ner on dates." Or, "gays and lesbians are privileged; current city ordinances for domestic partnership give them special rights." If students really do under-stand oppression as the product of systematically related barriers and forces not of one's own making, then why do they abandon Frye's analysis when I raise issues of privilege to explain how the oppression of one group can be used to generate privilege for another? It would appear that they have not understood the structural features of oppression well enough to grasp how their use of "privilege" to describe mere advantages such as having someone pay for your dinner, puts the term "privilege" in danger of being stretched to meaninglessness. I've come to conclude that any understanding of oppression is incomplete without recognition of the role privilege plays in maintaining systems of domination.

This essay continues the conversation Frye began in a way that makes connections between oppression and privilege. It is my hope that by providing a parallel account of privilege in general—and white, heterosexual, male privilege in particular—I can extend Fry's analysis to clarify the political dimensions of privilege.

1. FRYE'S STRUCTURAL ANALYSIS OF OPPRESSION

In her careful analysis of oppression, Marilyn Frye argues that one of the reasons people fail to see oppression is that they focus on particular events, attitudes, and actions that strike them as harmful, but they do not place these incidents in the context of historical, social, and political *systems*. According to Frye, members of oppressed groups commonly experience "double-binds," that is, they are faced daily with situations in which their options are reduced to a very few, all of which expose them to penalty, censure, or deprivation[1] (1983, 2). These binds are created and shaped by forces and barriers which are neither accidental nor avoidable, but are systematically related to each other in ways that confine individuals to the extent that movement in any direction is penalized. To make visible the systemic character of the barriers shaping the double-bind Frye uses the metaphor of a birdcage.

> [Oppression is] the experience of being caged in. . . . Consider a birdcage. If you look very closely at just one wire, you cannot see the other wires. If your conception of what is before you is determined by this myopic focus, you could look at that one wire, up and down the length of it, and be unable to see why a bird would not just fly around the wire. . . . it is only when you step back, stop looking at the wires one by one, microscopically, and take a macroscopic view of the whole cage, that you can see why the bird does not go anywhere; and then you will see it in a moment. (1983, 5–6)

Ignoring the systemic and interlocking nature of what I call complex systems of domination (e.g., racism, ableism, sexism, anti-Semitism, or homophobia) has misleading consequences. When the effects of sexism, for example, are not understood macroscopically as the products of systemic injustices, they are understood microscopically as the exclusive problems of particular women who have made bad choices, have poor attitudes, are too sensitive, or who are overreacting to a random incident. Failure to examine sexism, homophobia, racism, and anti-Semitism as harms produced by systematically related forces and barriers blurs the distinction between harm and oppression.

For oppression to be useful as a concept, Frye argues, the differences between harm and oppression need to be sharpened. All persons who are oppressed are in some way harmed, but not all persons who are harmed are oppressed. Men who cannot cry in public or whites who are ineligible for minority loan programs may feel harmed by these restrictions, but they are not oppressed. The gender roles which make public tearfulness inappropriate for men are unfair and may indeed be harmful to men's emotional well-being, but there is no network of forces or barriers which says both crying and not crying are unacceptable and that to do either is to expose oneself to "penalty, censure or deprivation" (1983, 2). Similarly, whites who are ineligible for loan programs designated for racial or ethnic minority applicants are only oppressed if there are no other reasonable means of securing a loan open to them. If whites are eligible for a variety of existing loan options, having one avenue closed to them may feel unfair, but it does not mean they are oppressed in Frye's sense of the word. Whites who find options for financing their education severely limited may be oppressed by their class, but not by their race. There is nothing in these cases to suggest racial barriers or forces that leave loan-seeking whites optionless.

Since oppression is a structural phenomenon that devalues the work, experiences, and voices of members of marginalized social groups, it might be said that oppression is experienced by persons *because* they are members of particular social groups. In the language of Frye's cage metaphor: "The 'inhabitant' of the 'cage' is not an individual but a group. . . . Thus, to recognize a person as oppressed, one has to see that individual *as* belonging to a group of a certain sort" (1983, 8). Before turning to my analysis of the concept of privilege, I wish to make two important comments regarding Frye's observations about group membership and its role in systems of oppression. First, because individuals are rarely members of one community, oppression is not a unified phenomenon. Group differences in race/ethnicity, sexual orientation, gender, or class cut across individual lives to the point that privilege and oppression are often experienced simultaneously. The felt experience of oppression of a working-class white woman, for example, will be different than the felt oppression experienced by a middle-class African American male. Because of the complexity of these intersections, Iris Young argues that to be oppressed persons must experience at least one or a combination of as many as five conditions: economic exploitation, social/cultural marginalization, political powerlessness, cultural imperialism, and violence (1990, 48–63). The double-bind may be *a* characteristic of an individual's experiences of oppression, but it is not *the* defining feature. Both Frye and Young, I think, would argue that the strength of the bind depends upon which of these oppressive conditions are present in a person's life, how many conditions are present, how long they are present, and whether the individual is privileged in ways that might weaken or mediate the binds.

Next, to say that women are oppressed as members of the group women, or that lesbians are oppressed as lesbians, or that African Americans, Cherokees, or Chicano/as are oppressed as members of particular racial-ethnic group suggests that sexism, heterosexism, and racism require identifiable sexes, sexual orientations, and racial-ethnic groups. Yet to understand how oppression is experienced by these marginalized groups, it is not necessary for social groups to have fixed boundaries. In fact understanding the systemic nature of oppression requires just the opposite: it requires that one understand how the *lack* of a rigid definition of social groups is part of complex systems of domination. One of the features of privilege is the ability of dominant groups to construct, define, and control the construction of categories. In the United States, for example, the invention of the category "white" illustrates how systems of oppression are held in place by purposely unstable racial categories. The word "white" began appearing in legal documents around 1680 as a direct result of legislation enforcing the hereditary bond servitude of Negroes, antimiscegenation laws, and new anti-Negro attitudes. In time, the idea of a homogeneous "white" race was adopted as a political means of generating cohesion among European explorers, traders, migrants, and settlers of eighteenth-century North America. The borders constructed between races have never been static. Racial borders are well guarded but intentionally porous: the political nature racial classification requires that these borders be redrawn as patterns of immigration challenge them and new candidates for whiteness arise. Racial designations, then, historically shift to preserve power and privilege of those who have the authority to define who counts as white.

2. THE VIEW FROM OUTSIDE THE BIRDCAGE: PRIVILEGE AND EARNED ADVANTAGES

When I argue that members of dominant groups—men, whites, heterosexuals, or the wealthy—have privilege by virtue of their being members of particular social groups, I do not mean "privilege," as Joel Feinberg defines it, in its philosophical broad juridical sense as synonymous with *mere* liberties or the absence of duty.[2] In this sense to say that person P is privileged or at liberty to do action A means that P has no duty to refrain from doing A. To say that I am privileged or at liberty to take a job in Seattle means that I have no obligations to refrain from taking a job in Seattle. Although privilege, in the sense I will be using the word, does imply a greater freedom of movement and choice, there is nothing about belonging to a group such as whites or men that would imply that one does or does not have duty to refrain from choosing to move to Seattle.

Neither am I using privilege in the sense of a legal benefit that is not a right. Privilege in this sense offers valuable benefits granted to persons or organizations by institutions (e.g., the state of Illinois, the federal government, or the Catholic Church) at the discretion of those institutions. Having a driver's license, being a naturalized citizen, or holding public office are common examples of privilege in this sense. Because my driving or voting privilege may be revoked at any time, say, for speeding or treason, the privileges to drive or to vote count as *mere* privileges; the state does not have a duty to grant these to me. I have neither a prior right to get a license nor a right to retain it once I pass the examination. While legal structures have historically played a role in holding heterosexual privilege, male privilege, or white privilege in place, privilege in this sense is not captured by legal language.

My interest is in a narrower sense of privilege as unearned assets conferred systematically. My aim is to fashion a distinction between privilege and advantages that parallels Frye's distinction between oppression and harm. Just as all oppression counts as harm, but not all harms count as oppression, I want to suggest that all privilege is advantageous, but that not all advantages count as privilege. Like the difference between harms and oppression, the difference between advantages and privilege has to do with the systematically conferred nature of these unearned assets. If we want to determine whether a particular harm qualifies as oppression, Frye argues that we have to look at that harm in context (macroscopically) to see what role, if any, it plays in an maintaining a structure that is oppressive. Likewise, if we want to determine whether a particular advantage qualifies as a privilege, we need to look at that advantage macroscopically in order to observe whether it plays a role in keeping complex systems of domination in place. We need to know if the advantage enables members of privileged groups to avoid the structured system of forces and barriers which serve to immobilize members of marginalized groups.

I am interested in providing an account of privilege and advantages that further clarifies Peggy McIntosh's distinction between "earned strength" and "unearned power conferred systematically." As McIntosh argues: 10

> Power from unearned privilege can look like strength when
> it is, in fact, permission to escape or to dominate. But not all
> privileges . . . are inevitably damaging. Some, like the expec-
> tation that neighbors will be decent to you, or that your race
> will not count against you in court, should be the norm in
> a just society and should be considered as the entitlement of
> everyone. Others, like the privilege not to listen to less power-
> ful people, distort the humanity of the holders as well as the
> ignored groups. Still others, like finding one's staple foods
> everywhere may be a function of a numerical majority. Others
> have to do with not having to labor under pervasive negative
> stereotyping and mythology. (1991, 78)

McIntosh's explanation suggests that strength is something necessarily earned and that power is something unearned. She explains that the power of unearned privilege can appear as strength, when in reality it is just permission to escape or to dominate. And later, she says that privilege may confer power, but not moral strength.

McIntosh's distinction between strength and power puzzles me. Her point can be stated more simply by distinguishing between two kinds of assets: (unearned) privilege and earned advantages. The general distinction I will make between privilege and earned advantages begins with an etymology of privilege and rests on four related claims: (1) benefits granted by privilege are always unearned and conferred *systematically* to members of dominant social groups; (2) privilege granted to members of dominant groups simply because they are members of these groups is almost never justifiable; (3) most privilege is invisible to, or not recognized as such by, those who have it; and (4) privilege has an unconditional "wild card" quality that extends benefits to cover a wide variety of circumstances and conditions.

To understand how the benefits granted by privilege are always unearned and conferred systematically to members of dominant social groups, privilege must first be understood as a class of advantages. The words "advantage" and "advance" have a common Latin root—*abante* meaning "in front of" or "before." To possess any kind of advantage is to have a skill, talent, asset, or condition acquired—either by accident of birth or by intentional cultivation—that allows a person or a group to rise to a higher rank, to bring themselves forward, to lift themselves up, or otherwise to make progress. Privilege, in the sense that I will be using the word, is by definition advantageous, but not all advantages count as privilege. Advantages that are not privilege I will call *earned advantages.* Earned advantages are strengths which refer to any earned condition, skill, asset, or talent that benefits its possessor and which under restricted conditions helps to advance that person. Earned advantages include things such as being awarded extra frequent flyer miles, learning a second language, working hard so that you afford to live in a neighborhood with a good school system, or dutifully attending athletic practice in order to be eligible for a volleyball scholarship.

The difference between earned advantages and privilege is not hard and fast; but I want to hang onto the distinction in a way that recognizes how privilege and earned advantages do not operate independently from one another, and at the same time highlight the connections between them. So the distinction between privilege and advantages becomes less clear when it is challenged by cases where, for example, class oppression diminishes the currency of white or male privilege. Consider the role privilege plays in one's ability to get good work, to afford to fly, to buy a house, or to rent an apartment. To earn frequent flyer miles, for instance, assumes that one can afford to fly. Regardless of race, the homeless have few, if any, chances to take advantage of opportunities to earn frequent flyer miles. Working long hours so you can afford to buy a house in a good neighborhood also assumes that you are able to get a high-paying job, that real estate agents will show you houses in the "good parts of town," and that the owners of those houses will sell to you. Regardless of economic class, practices like redlining commonly keep families of color that can afford to live in middle- or upper-class suburbs from purchasing real estate and moving into those areas. In addition, malicious stereotypes of African Americans or Puerto Ricans as lazy, dirty, or untrustworthy, or stereotypes of gays and lesbians as pedophiles, promiscuous, or diseased also discourage landowners from renting to these individuals even if they are good tenants.

The distinction between privilege and advantage is also blurred by instances where, for example, class, race, or heterosexual oppression are temporarily transcended or overlooked. I have in mind here the gay community leader or the working-class philanthropist who, by virtue of outstanding community service, earns a good reputation in the community and is granted the status and authority commonly associated with heterosexual or class privilege. Or the African American who has elevated her economic status to the point where she is granted privileges commonly associated with well-to-do whites. In these cases members of dominant groups are often willing to make exceptions for certain individuals because of their economic success, community visibility, or civic reputation. There are also instances where closeted gays or light-skinned Latinas and African Americans are granted privileges because they can pass as straight or white.

Perhaps the point here is not that earned advantages and privilege are   15
necessarily distinct, but rather that some advantages are more easily earned if they are accompanied by gender, heterosexual, race, or class privilege. Privilege and earned advantages are connected in the sense that privilege places one in a better position to earn more advantages. The link between earned advantages and unearned privilege generates a situation in which privileged groups can earn assets (e.g., control of resources, skills, a quality education, the attention of the mayor, a good reputation, a prestigious well-paying job, political power, or a safe place to live) more easily and more frequently than those who don't have white, male, heterosexual, or economic privilege. Failure to recognize the differences between earned and unearned assets allows privileged groups to interpret *all* privilege on the same footing as earned advantages. Ann Richards' insightful remark, "George Bush was born on third base, and to this day he believes he hit a triple," is telling illustration of the failure to make this distinction.[3]

The cases of the black entrepreneur, the working-class activist, or the gay community leader weaken the tie between privilege and birth. Privilege also helps to move a person forward, but unlike the advantages described above, privilege is *granted* and birth is the easiest way of being granted privilege. In this sense, for a person to have privilege is to be granted benefits automatically by virtue of their perceived or actual class, sex, race or sexual status that others not of that status have had to earn. Suffrage, for example, was initially granted to white property-owing males; white women and emancipated Negroes, Native Americans, and immigrants had to struggle to earn this privilege. Marriage is also a highly regulated privilege which is granted exclusively to heterosexual couples. Gay, lesbian, and bisexual couples are currently struggling to secure this privilege in ways similar to Mildred Jeter Loving and her husband, Richard, who struggled to have their interracial marriage recognized by the Commonwealth of Virginia in the early 1960s. Being granted the privilege to marry because you are heterosexual, or the privilege to vote because you own land, are male, or are white, then, is unearned in the same way that having a friend or relative who will work on your car for nothing, or having good-natured and caring neighbors is unearned; they both seem to be largely a matter of luck. In spite of their significant differences the words privilege and advantage are used interchangeably. For this reason I want to be clear about how my use of privilege—as unearned advantages or assets conferred systematically—differs from standard philosophical and conversational usage.

Like McIntosh, I recognize and am disturbed by the misleading ordinary language connotations of privilege as something positive. The privilege that gives some people the freedom to be thoughtless at best, and murderous at worst, should not be thought of as desirable (1988, 77). The etymology of the word "privilege" helps to clarify my use of privilege as unearned advantages conferred systematically. "Privilege" itself is derived from the Latin *privilegium,* a law or bill in favor of or against an individual, from *priv-us,* meaning private, individual, or peculiar, and from *lex,* or law. So, privilege literally means private or individual law.[4] As one legal definition holds: "Privileges are special rights belonging to the individual or class, and not to the mass."[5] The etymological roots of privilege as private law or special rights reveals the worrisome nature of privilege. Historically, to have a privilege meant to have a right or immunity granting a peculiar benefit, advantage, or favor, such as a right or an immunity attached to a particular position or office. The exemption of ambassadors and members of Congress from arrest while going to, returning from, or attending to their public duties is an example of this. Here, having privilege means that holders of particular offices such as queen, police officer, senator, judge, parliamentarian, or bishop are either exempt from the usual operations of public law or accountable to a less formal set of private laws (sometimes of their own making) or both. In this sense to have a privilege means that a particular individual, like the president of the United States, or a specific group, say members of the Senate, are exempt from particular burdens or liabilities of public law (e.g., having to pay their parking tickets); their activities are governed by an individual or private set of immunity-granting rules. If the contemporary connotations of privilege strike us as too positive, then surely the denotations reveal the disturbing origins of this term.

Second, since exemptions and benefits of offices are sometimes understood as arbitrary favoritism, privilege in this sense has pejorative connotations; but it could be argued that some exemptions, and thus some privilege, is justified. For example, it is reasonable to grant ambulance drivers immunity from speeding laws, since emergency care requires getting to the hospital as quickly as possible. In this sense paramedics may be said to have special rights in the sense that they are granted temporary immunity from speeding laws while they are on duty. The extension of privilege to particular practices such as ambulance driving, which enable emergency care to continue efficiently, are generally regarded as justifiable. However, by most standards of fairness it is not justifiable to grant immunities to persons simply because they are perceived to be white, heterosexual, or male. Laws granting immunities to individuals because they are perceived to be members of dominant groups, if they can be justified at all, certainly ought not to be justified on the grounds that these private laws are needed for members of dominant racial or economic groups to move through the world safely at the expense of others.

Dominant group privilege is a particular class of unearned benefits and immunities enjoyed by individuals who, by moral luck, belong to groups with race, heterosexual, gender, or class privilege. I refer to groups such as men, whites, and heterosexuals as dominant not because of their numbers, but by virtue of that fact that historically their lives and experiences define the standard for what is deemed valuable or "normal." Dominant group privileges can, as I have argued, also be extended to individuals outside of these groups. Dominant group privilege is established partly through legislation and public policy but also through informal and subtle expressions of speech, bodily reactions and gestures, malicious stereotypes, aesthetic judgments, and media images. In this way privilege is systematically created and culturally reinforced.

My third point is that one of the functions of privilege is to structure the 　*20* world so that mechanisms of privilege are invisible—in the sense that they are unexamined—to those who benefit from them. What Frye's birdcage metaphor does for oppression, Peggy McIntosh's invisible knapsack and Jona Olsson's computer metaphor do for privilege.[6] The systemic and unexamined nature of what it means to have dominant group privilege is made clearer by McIntosh's metaphor of the "invisible knapsack." White privilege, she argues,

> [is] an invisible package of unearned assets that I can count on cashing in each day, but about which I was "meant" to remain oblivious. White privilege is like an invisible weightless knapsack of special provisions, assurances, tools, maps, guides, code books, passports, visas, clothes, compass, emergency gear, and blank checks. (1988, 71)

It is worth highlighting some of the common examples of privilege in this sense. Briefly white privilege includes:

- I can if I wish arrange to be in the company of people of my race most of the time.
- I can be sure that my children will be given curricular material that testifies to the existence of their race.
- I am never asked to speak for all the people of my racial group.
- I can dress any way I want and not have my appearance explained by the perceived tastes of my race.
- Whether I use checks, credit cards, or cash I can be fairly sure that my skin color will not count against the appearance of my financial reliability.
- In most instances I can be assured of having the public trust. (1991, 78)

Heterosexual privileges include:

- Being able to publicly show affection for one's partner without fear of public harm or hostility.
- Being assured that most people will approve of one's relationship.
- Not having to self-censor gender pronouns when talking about one's partner.

The structural nature of privilege is made visible by Jona Olsson, who compares privilege to having a very user-friendly word processing program. When I open up a new document in this program, the font, margins, page length, type point size, spacing, and footnote style are set in a commonly accepted format for me. I do not have to do anything: this preset style is the default mode. I expect this service when I open up a new document, so much so that I take the professional shape and appearance of my document for granted. The structured invisibility of the word processing program insures that the flawless professional presentation of my documents will be attributed to my own talents and individual merits, rather than to my software. Privilege offers a default mode not unlike the default position on my word processing program. White, male, and heterosexual privilege are default positions. Either I can choose to be aware of these default positions or I can ignore them and decide to experiment with new fonts, margins, or document styles. If I become unhappy or frustrated with these new modes, I can always go back to the default positions.

Like the default mode on a word processing program, the bars on the birdcage are especially difficult to see from outside of the cage. The structured invisibility of privilege insures that a person's individual accomplishments will be recognized more on the basis of individual merit than on the basis of group membership.[7] Redirecting attention away from the unearned nature of privilege and toward individual merit allows persons born on third base to believe sincerely that they hit a triple. In fact, the maintenance of heterosexual, white, or male privilege as positions of structural advantage lie largely in the silence surrounding the mechanisms of privilege. For persons situated inside the borders of privilege, the privilege associated with being white, male, wealthy, or heterosexual is difficult to name, yet for those situated outside of these borders, the benefits of privilege are seen all too clearly.[8] White, heterosexual, or male survival do not depend upon an awareness of default positions and invisible knapsacks, so whites are not encouraged to recognize or acknowledge the effects of racialization on white lives, men have difficulty seeing the effects of sexism or women's lives, and heterosexuals rarely understand the impact of homophobia on gay, bisexual, and lesbian communities. Reflecting on the racial heterogeneity within her own family, for example, Cherríe Moraga uncomfortably acknowledges that her güera (light-skinned) appearance is something she can use to her advantage in a wide variety of difficult situations.

> Then [my friend] Tavo says to me, "you see at any time [you] decide to use your light skinned privilege [you] can."

I say, "uh huh. Uh huh." He says, "You can decide that you are suddenly no Chicana."

That I can't say, but once my light skin and good English saved my lover from arrest. And I'd use it again. I'd use it to the hilt over and over to save our skins.

"You get to choose." Now I want to shove those words right back into his face. You call this a choice! To constantly push against a wall of resistance from your own people or to fall nameless into the mainstream of this country, running with our common blood?[9]

The invisibility of the default position here means that whites are rarely aware of the times light skin and/or clear English benefits us. Since whites rarely examine their privilege, we rarely perceive the barriers and hassles faced by those who appear to others as "nonwhite."

The final claim I want to make is that privilege facilitates one's movement through the world in a way that earned advantages do not. The systemic nature of privilege gives it a wild card quality, which means that privilege has a broader currency than earned advantages. Most earned advantages will advance a person under limited conditions. For example, frequent flyer miles are only an advantage if I need to travel, living in a neighborhood with a good school system is only an asset if I have children, and being bilingual is only beneficial to me if I live in or travel to communities where speaking two languages facilitates my daily activities. Unlike earned advantages, playing the privilege card (e.g., using the passports, checks, and codebooks in my knapsack) grants extra advantages to holders in a broader variety of circumstances. This is to say that being heterosexual, male, or white will almost always count in one's favor. To have white, heterosexual, or male privilege means that the immunities and benefits you have because of your race, sexual orientation, or sex extend beyond the boundaries of your comfort zones, neighborhood, circles of friends, or what María Lugones calls "worlds" in which you are at ease.[10] Although privileged persons feel ill at ease outside of their own worlds, they rarely lose privilege outside of their comfort zones. The meaning of privilege as "special rights" or "private laws" should now be clear: immunity granting passports, checks, and tickets in the knapsack are wild cards in the sense that they are accepted almost everywhere. Regardless of where I am, being a member of a dominant group will almost always count in my favor.

Andrew Hacker (1992) has designed a particularly effective exercise to illustrate the extent to which whites unconsciously understand the wild card character of white privilege. He asks his white students to imagine that they will be visited by an official they have never met. The official informs them that his organization has made a terrible mistake and that according to official records you were to have been born black. Since this mistake must be rectified immediately, at midnight you will become black and can expect to live out the rest of your life—say fifty years—as a black person in America. Since this is the agency's error, the official explains that you can demand compensation. Hacker then asks his white students: How much financial recompense would you request? The figures white students give in my class—usually between $250,000. to $50 million—demonstrates the extent to which white privilege is valued.

3. POSITIVE AND NEGATIVE DIMENSIONS OF WHITE PRIVILEGE

The wild card quality of privilege points to the possibility that dominant group privilege is more complex than simple immunities from the systemic barriers of which Frye speaks. Members of dominant groups not only receive benefits from the default options and knapsack tools they use to maneuver themselves around barriers, they also receive *additional* benefits. Barriers are put in place with the intention of creating privilege, but it is here that we encounter the limits of Frye's barrier metaphor. The collective package of privileges given to members of dominant groups takes two distinct forms: *negative privilege,* which can be understood simply as the absence of barriers, and *positive privilege,* which can be understood as the presence of additional perks that cannot be described in terms of immunities alone.

25   The distinction between positive and negative privilege is not merely two ways of expressing the same phenomenon. I first became aware of this distinction during a conversation I had with a young white male student in my "Introduction to Women's Studies" class. Once he became aware of the unearned aspects of his male privilege, this student was eager to use it in politically useful ways. He suggested that one way to do this would be to accompany women on a Take Back the Night March, a historically women-only demonstration against sexual violence. Since men can go out at night with little risk of sexual assault, he reasoned, he might use this unearned privilege to, in his words, "protect the women as they marched." What this student had in mind, no doubt, was to exercise his role as protector to defend the marching women against members of his gender with predatory leanings. In other words, he wanted to use his privileged protector status in a way that supported feminist projects.

But, it might be objected, what is wrong with wanting to use male privilege to help women and girls demonstrate for their right to safe access to the streets at night? Shouldn't our male allies use privilege to open up opportunities for women and to advance feminist causes? Certainly, in some cases persons with privilege should actively seek ways of using privilege supportively, but this is not one of them. The purpose of Take Back the Night Marches is to give women and girls the opportunity to reclaim the night in ways that do not rely on male protection. On a practical level, when male protectors step in, the symbolism of the march is undermined; with male protection the marchers no longer experience the autonomy and empowerment which come with walking around at night and feeling safe.

On a theoretical level, the problem is that the gendered roles of both "protector" and "predator" are the products of the ideology of hetero-patriarchal dominance. The student fails to understand how the protector role that heterosexual male privilege grants him is the product of the systemic nature of heterosexism; that is, the benefits of the protector role depend on and cannot be secured independently of the heterosexual paradigm which cast women in male-serving subordinate roles. As Sarah Hoagland argues, "there can be no protectors unless there is a danger. A man cannot identify himself in the role of protector unless there is something which needs protection" (1988, 30). In his eagerness to help the cause he does not notice the systemic links between his heterosexual male privilege as a protector and women's oppression. He does not notice how his offer of protective services reinscribes the function of the hetero-patriarchal protector/predator gender role as assigned to men.[11] In attempting to supportive he falls into his scripted role as a protector.

Protector status is a wild card which can be played in a wide variety of circumstances beyond the example of the march. By virtue of a hetero-patriarchal system that cast men in the role of protector, men are granted additional credibility and power. It is expected that males will be protectors; being a protector is understood as a natural innate male trait. Men who deviate from this role are often thought of as cowardly or as sissies. The unquestioned presupposition here is that men's so-called "natural protector" status gives them additional benefits beyond protectorship. It suggests that men, by virtue of their "natural" role, are automatically the rightful heads of households, the proper leaders, the best organizers, administrators, and educators. Thus, the Take Back the Night March example reveals the tightly intertwined nature of positive and negative privilege. First, this student was aware that male privilege meant that, *as a man* he saw no barriers to his being able to move about at night (a negative privilege). Second, the student was also aware on some level that male privilege conferred upon him the status of protector (a positive privilege) that is not characterized by the absence of barrier alone.

The unearned privilege accorded to whites can also be explained in terms of both negative and positive privilege. Whiteness—the expression of white privilege—means more than just being granted immunity from demeaning stereotypes and the removal of barriers to housing or high-paying jobs. Since privilege and oppression intersect all identities, having light skin and whitely mannerisms does not automatically grant one immunity from misfortune or failure, but even for those whites who are poor or unemployed, being white does have some value. If whiteness is associated with "being an American," hardworking, or a trustworthy neighbor, then to be white in America is to have a culturally valued identity. The positive dimension of white privilege captures what, for lack of a better phrase, might be called a reputational interest in being regarded as white. In fact, this reputational interest was used as grounds for Plessy's case in *Plessy vs. Ferguson*. When Homer A. Plessy, a light-skinned man of European and African descent, boarded a railway car reserved for whites, he was arrested for violating a Louisiana Jim Crow statute mandating separate cars for white and "colored" passengers. Plessy's gripe was not that he has an additional barrier placed in his path. He charged that the refusal to seat him on the white passenger car deprived him of "the reputation [of being white] which has an actual pecuniary value."[12] Because Plessy appeared to be white, not allowing him to ride on that car reserved for whites deprived him of the white privilege to which he felt entitled. The entitlements Plessy gained from being regarded as white are not expressed negatively in terms of being denied freedom of access to the best seats on the train, but being denied this status (or positive privilege) associated with being treated as a person worthy of respect. To treat persons with respect and dignity is to listen to what they have to say, to respond to their requests, or to give their needs and concerns priority. The unquestioned presupposition that whites are in most cases hardworking, honest, good trustworthy citizens may suggest that white people will be better candidates for jobs, scholarships, and public office.[13] By virtue of a system that understands white and male superiority to be the natural state of affairs, Plessy is granted the credibility and respect appropriate to white men.

30   If the structural features of oppression generate privilege, then a complete understanding of oppression requires that we also be attentive to the ways in which complex systems of domination rely on the oppression of one group to generate privilege for another. A complete understanding of the systematic features of oppression requires not only that we understand the differences between oppression and harm, but also that we understand both the differences between privilege and earned advantages and the connections between oppression and privilege. Silence about privilege is itself a function of privilege and it has a chilling effect on political discourse. Conversations that focus exclusively on oppression reinforce the structured invisibility of privilege. White women who focus solely on their oppression as women, for example, generate incomplete accounts of oppression when they fail to explore the role white privilege plays in the subordination of their sisters of color. Attention to the construction of privilege, then, is a necessary component for a full account of oppression as well as a way to make visible the role of privilege in maintaining hierarchies.

This paper has benefited greatly from conversations I've had on privilege and oppression. In particular I would like to thank Charlotte Brown, Susan Feldman, Marilyn Frye, Kay Leigh Hagan, Lisa Heldke, Sarah Hoagland, Amber Katherine, Jona Olsson, Mark Siderits, and Nancy Tuana for their comments on earlier drafts of this project. This essay is dedicated to the loving memory of Linda Weiner Morris.

NOTES

1. Maria Lugones has challenged Frye's account and Marxist accounts of oppression that leave oppressed groups in the discouraging position of the double-bind. In response to these theories she suggests a more liberatory "contradictory desiderata" for oppression theory which rests on embracing a pluralist notion of the self. See "Structure and Anti-Structure: Agency under Oppression," *The Journal of Philosophy*, 88:10 (October 1990), p. 500.

2. See Joel Feinberg, *Social Philosophy,* Englewood Cliffs, N.J.: Prentice Hall, 1963, pp. 58–59, and *Black's Law Dictionary,* 6th ed., St. Paul, Minn: West Publishing, 1990, pp. 1197–98. My remarks follow Feinberg's examples here.

3. I am grateful to Jona Olsson for demonstrating the appropriateness of Richards's remark in this context.

4. My definition here follows the *Oxford English Dictionary.* Privilege: [from old French and middle English] *privilegium* a bill in favor of or against an individual; fr. L. *priv-us,* private, peculiar + *lex, legem* law.

5. Given this definition it is ironic that current struggles for equality on the part of historically disenfranchised groups are described as "special rights" by conservatives. See, *Loans v. State, 50 Tenn.* (3 Heisk.) cited in *Words and Phrases,* permanent edition, 1658 to Date, vol. 33A, St. Paul, Minn.: West Publishing, 1995, p. 494.

6. The word processing metaphor comes from Jona Olsson's unpublished work on white antiracism. "White Privilege" Workshop. August 10, 1994. 19th Annual Womyn's Music Festival. Hart, Michigan.

7. The term "structural invisibility" comes from Ruth Frankenburg, *White Women, Race Matters: The Social Construction of Whiteness,* Minneapolis, Minn.: University of Minneapolis Press, 1993. In another context Frye refers to this phenomenon as "structured ignorance." See Marilyn Frye, "Critique," *Philosophy and Sex,* eds. Robert Baker and Frederick Elliston, New York, N.Y.: Prometheus Books, 1984, p. 447. I'm grateful to Mark Siderits for having called my attention to Frye's phrase.

8. For instance, contrast bell hooks's account of whiteness with that of Judith Levine or Minnie Bruce Pratt. See hooks, "Representations of Whiteness in the Black Imagination," in *Black Looks: Race and Representation,* Boston: South End Press, 1992, pp. 165–79. Judith Levine, "White Like Me," *Ms. Magazine* (March/April 1994), pp. 22–24. Minnie Bruce Pratt, "Identity: Skin, Blood, Heart," *Yours in Struggle: Three Feminist Perspectives on Anti-Semitism and Racism,* ed. Elly Bulkin, Minnie Bruce Pratt, and Barbara Smith, Ithaca, N.Y.: Firebrand Books, 1984, pp. 11–63.

9. Cherrie Moraga, *Loving in the War Years, Lo Que Nunca Paso por Sus Labios.* Boston: South End Press, 1983, p. 97.

10. I'm using "world" in the sense that Maria Lugones uses it in her essay "Playfulness, World Traveling and Loving Perception." For those unfamiliar with Lugones's notion of world traveling, "worlds" are not utopias; they may be an actual society as it is constructed by either dominant or nondominant groups. Worlds need not be constructions of whole societies, they may be just small parts of that society (e.g., a barrio in Chicago, Chinatown in New York, a lesbian bar, a women's studies class, an elegant country club, or a migrant farmworkers community). The notion of "worlds" is useful in that it helps us to understand why we are constructed differently in worlds in which we are not at ease. Lugones's own example is of being constructed as "serious" in Anglo/white worlds where she is ill at ease and as "playful" in Latina worlds where she is at ease. The shift from being one person in one world, to being another person in a different world is what she calls travel. See Maria Lugones, "Playfulness, World-Traveling, and Loving Perception," *Hypatia,*2:2 (Summer 1987), pp. 3–18. Lugones's observations are supported by sociologist Joe Feagin's research on the "black tax" or the added hassles African Americans face in getting through the day. See Feagin, "The

Continuing Significance of Race: Antiblack Discrimination in Public Places," *American Sociological Review,* 56 (February 1991), pp. 101–22.

11. Some ways of using male and heterosexual privilege may reinscribe privilege, but it is not obvious that all will. The fact that the male student could not use the privilege his protector status afforded him in this instance does not mean that male or heterosexual privilege can never be used in traitorous ways. It does not mean that men should never use their privileges to protect women and it would be foolish for women not to ask for protection in some instances.

12. See Derek Bell, "Property Rights in Whiteness—Their Legacy, Their Economic Costs," in *Critical Race Theory: The Cutting Edge,* ed. Richard Delgado, Philadelphia, Penn.: Temple University Press, 1995, pp. 75–83; Cheryl Harris, "Whiteness as Property," *Harvard Law Review,* vol. 106, no. 8 (June 1993), p. 1746; and Andrew Hacker, *Two Nations: Black and White, Separate, Hostile and Unequal,* New York, N.Y.: Scribner's, 1992, exp. pp. 31–49.

13. The political significance of whiteness as I have described it in the Plessy case is highly gendered. For example, had a Mrs. Plessy taken a seat on the train that day, the reaction would have been very different because reputation and respect have different values for women. As Frye explains: "Being rational, righteous, and [law abiding] . . . do for some of us some of the time buy a ticket to a higher level of material well-being than we might otherwise be permitted. . . . But the reason, right, and rules are not of our own making; white men may welcome our whiteliness as an endorsement of their own values and as an expression of our loyalty to them (that is, as proof of their power over us), and because it makes us good helpmates to them, but if our whiteliness commands any respect, it is only in the sense that a woman who is chaste and obedient is called . . . 'respectable.'" See Frye "White Woman Feminist," *Willful Virgin: Essays in Feminism,* Freedom, Calif.: Crossing Press, 1992, p. 161.

REFERENCES

Frye, Marilyn. *The Politics of Reality.* Freedom, Calif.: Crossing Press, 1983, 1–16.

———. "White Woman Feminist." *In Willful Virgin: Essays in Feminism.* Freedom, Calif.: Crossing Press, 1992, 147–69.

Hacker, Andrew. *Two Nations: Black and White, Separate, Hostile and Unequal.* New York: Scribner's, 1992.

Hoagland, Sarah, *Lesbian Ethics: Toward New Value.* Palo Alto, Calif.: Institute of Lesbian Studies, 1988.

McIntosh, Peggy. "White Privilege and Male Privilege: A Personal Account of Coming to See Correspondences Through Work in Women's Studies." In *Race, Class and Gender: An Anthology,* eds. Margaret L. Andersen and Patricia Hill Collins. N.Y.: Wadsworth, 1991.

Moraga, Cherrie. *Loving in the War Years, Lo Que Nunca Paso por Sus Labios.* Boston: South End Press, 1983.

Young, Iris Marion. *Justice and the Politics of Difference,* Princeton, N.J.: Princeton University Press, 1990.

Privilege Axis One: White Privilege

7

■ ■ ■ ■

WHITE PRIVILEGE AND MALE PRIVILEGE

A PERSONAL ACCOUNT OF COMING TO SEE CORRESPONDENCES THROUGH WORK IN WOMEN'S STUDIES

Peggy McIntosh

Through work to bring materials and perspectives from Women's Studies into the rest of the curriculum, I have often noticed men's unwillingness to grant that they are overprivileged in the curriculum, even though they may grant that women are disadvantaged. Denials that amount to taboo surround the subject of advantages that men gain from women's disadvantages. These denials protect male privilege from being fully recognized, acknowledged, lessened, or ended.

Thinking through unacknowledged male privilege as a phenomenon with a life of it's own, I realized that since hierarchies in our society are interlocking, there was most likely a phenomenon of white privilege that was similarly denied and protected, but alive and real in its effects. As a white person, I realized I had been taught about racism as something that puts others at a disadvantage, but had been taught not to see one of its corollary aspects, white privilege, which puts me at an advantage.

I think whites are carefully taught not to recognize white privilege, as males are taught not to recognize male privilege. So I have begun in an untutored way to ask what it is like to have white privilege. This paper is a partial record of my personal observations and not a scholarly analysis. It is based on my daily experiences within my particular circumstances.

I have come to see white privilege as an invisible package of unearned assets that I can count on cashing in each day, but about which I was "meant" to remain oblivious. White privilege is like an invisible weightless knapsack of special provisions, assurances, tools, maps, guides, codebooks, passports, visas, clothes, compass, emergency gear, and blank checks.

5   Since I have had trouble facing white privilege, and describing its results in my life, I saw parallels here with men's reluctance to acknowledge male privilege. Only rarely will a man go beyond acknowledging that women are disadvantaged to acknowledging that men have unearned advantage, or that unearned privilege has not been good for men's development as human beings, or for society's development, or that privilege systems might ever be challenged and *changed*.

I will review here several types or layers of denial that I see at work protecting, and preventing awareness about, entrenched male privilege. Then I will draw parallels, from my own experience, with the denials that veil the facts of white privilege. Finally, I will list forty-six ordinary and daily ways in which I experience having white privilege, by contrast with my African American colleagues in the same building. This list is not intended to be generalizable. Others can make their own lists from within their own life experiences.

Writing this paper has been difficult, despite warm receptions for the talks on which *it* is based.[1] For describing white privilege makes one newly accountable. As we in Women's Studies work to reveal male privilege and ask men to give up some of their power, so one who writes about having white privilege must ask, "Having described it, what will I do to lessen or end it?"

The denial of men's overprivileged state takes many forms in discussions of curriculum change work. Some claim that men must be central in the curriculum because they have done most of what is important or distinctive in life or in civilization. Some recognize sexism in the curriculum but deny that it makes male students seem unduly important in life. Others agree that certain *individual* thinkers are male oriented but deny that there is any *systemic* tendency in disciplinary frameworks or epistemology to overempower men as a group. Those men who do grant that male privilege takes institutionalized and embedded forms are still likely to deny that male hegemony has opened doors for them personally. Virtually all men deny that male overreward alone can explain men's centrality in all the inner sanctums of our most powerful institutions. Moreover, those few who will acknowledge that male privilege systems have overempowered them usually end up doubting that we could dismantle these privilege systems. They may say they will work to improve women's status, in the society or in the university, but they can't or won't support the idea of lessening men's. In curricular terms, this is the point at which they say that they regret they cannot use any of the interesting new scholarship on women because the syllabus is full. When the talk turns to giving men less cultural room, even the most thoughtful and fair-minded of the men I know will tend to reflect, or fall back on, conservative assumptions about the inevitability of present gender relations and distributions of power, calling on precedent or sociobiology and psychobiology to demonstrate that male domination is natural and follows inevitably from evolutionary pressures. Others resort to arguments from "experience" or religion or social responsibility or wishing and dreaming.

After I realized, through faculty development work in Women's Studies, the extent to which men work from a base of unacknowledged privilege, I understood that much of the oppressiveness was unconscious. Then I remembered the frequent charges from women of color that white women whom they encounter are oppressive. I began to understand why we are justly seen as oppressive, even when we don't see ourselves that way. At the very least, obliviousness of one's privileged state can make a person or group irritating to be with. I began to count the ways in which I enjoy unearned skin privilege and have been conditioned into oblivion about its existence, unable to see that it put me "ahead" in any way, or put my people ahead, overrewarding us and yet also paradoxically damaging us, or that it could or should be changed.

My schooling gave me no training in seeing myself as an oppressor, as an unfairly advantaged person, or as a participant in a damaged culture. I was taught to see myself as an individual whose moral state depended on her individual moral will. At school, we were not taught about slavery in any depth; we were not taught to see slaveholders as damaged people. Slaves were seen as the only group at risk of being dehumanized. My schooling followed the pattern which Elizabeth Minnich has pointed out: whites are taught to think of their lives as morally neutral, normative, and average, and also ideal, so that when we work to benefit others, this is seen as work that will allow "them" to be more like "us." I think many of us know how obnoxious this attitude can be in men. 10

After frustration with men who would not recognize male privilege, I decided to try to work on myself at least by identifying some of the daily effects of white privilege in my life. It is crude work, at this stage, but I will give here a list of special circumstances and conditions I experience that I did not earn but that I have been made to feel are mine by birth, by citizenship, and by virtue of being a conscientious law-abiding "normal" person of goodwill. I have chosen those conditions that I think in my case *attach somewhat more to skin-color privilege* than to class, religion, ethnic status, or geographic location, though these other privileging factors are intricately intertwined. As far as I can see, my Afro-American co-workers, friends, and acquaintances with whom I come into daily or frequent contact in this particular time, place, and line of work cannot count on most of these conditions.

1. I can, if I wish, arrange to be in the company of people of my race most of the time.

2. I can avoid spending time with people whom I was trained to mistrust and who have learned to mistrust my kind or me.

3. If I should need to move, I can be pretty sure of renting or purchasing housing in an area which I can afford and in which I would want to live.

4. I can be reasonably sure that my neighbors in such a location will be neutral or pleasant to me.

5. I can go shopping alone most of the time, fairly well assured that I will not be followed or harassed by store detectives.

6. I can turn on the television or open to the front page of the paper and see people of my race widely and positively represented.

7. When I am told about our national heritage or about "civilization," I am shown that people of my color made it what it is.

8. I can be sure that my children will be given curricular materials that testify to the existence of their race.

9. If I want to, I can be pretty sure of finding a publisher for this piece on white privilege.

10. I can be fairly sure of having my voice heard in a group in which I am the only member of my race.

11. I can be casual about whether or not to listen to another woman's voice in a group in which she is the only member of her race.

12. I can go into a book shop and count on finding the writing of my race represented, into a supermarket and find the staple foods that fit with my cultural traditions, into a hairdresser's shop and find someone who can deal with my hair.

13. Whether I use checks, credit cards, or cash, I can count on my skin not to work against the appearance that I am financially reliable.

14. I could arrange to protect our young children most of the time from people who might not like them.

15. I did not have to educate our children to be aware of systemic racism for their own daily protection.

16. I can be pretty sure that my children's teachers and employers will tolerate them if they fit school and workplace norms; my chief worries about them do not concern others' attitudes toward their race.

17. I can talk with my mouth full and not have people put this down to my color.

18. I can swear, or dress in secondhand clothes, or not answer letters, without having people attribute these choices to the bad morals, the poverty, or the illiteracy of my race.

19. I can speak in public to a powerful male group without putting my race on trial.

20. I can do well in a challenging situation with being called a credit to my race.

21. I am never asked to speak for all the people of my racial group.

22. I can remain oblivious to the language and customs of persons of color who constitute the world's majority without feeling in my culture any penalty for such oblivion.

23. I can criticize our government and talk about how much I fear its policies and behavior without being seen as a cultural outsider.

24. I can be reasonably sure that if I ask to talk to "the person in charge," I will be facing a person of my race.

25. If a traffic cop pulls me over or if the IRS audits my tax return, I can be sure I haven't been singled out because of my race.

26. I can easily buy posters, postcards, picture books, greeting cards, dolls, toys, and children's magazines featuring people of my race.

27. I can go home from most meetings of organizations I belong to feeling somewhat tied in, rather than isolated, out of place, outnumbered, unheard, held at a distance, or feared.

28. I can be pretty sure that an argument with a colleague of another race is more likely to jeopardize her chances for advancement than to jeopardize mine.

29. I can be fairly sure that if I argue for the promotion of a person of another race, or a program centering on race, this is not likely to cost me heavily within my present setting, even if my colleagues disagree with me.

30. If I declare there is a racial issue at hand, or there isn't a racial issue at hand, my race will lend me more credibility for either position than a person of color will have.

31. I can choose to ignore developments in minority writing and minority activist programs, or disparage them, or learn from them, but in any case, I can find ways to be more or less protected from negative consequences of any of these choices.

32. My culture gives me little fear about ignoring the perspectives and powers of people of other races.

33. I am not made acutely aware that my shape, bearing, or body odor will be taken as a reflection on my race.

34. I can worry about racism without being seen as self-interested or self-seeking.

35. I can take a job with an affirmative action employer without having my co-workers on the job suspect that I got it because of my race.

36. If my day, week, or year is going badly, I need not ask of each negative episode or situation whether it has racial overtones.

37. I can be pretty sure of finding people who would be willing to talk with me and advise me about my next steps, professionally.

38. I can think over many options, social, political, imaginative, or professional, without asking whether a person of my race would be accepted or allowed to do what I want to do.

39. I can be late to a meeting without having the lateness reflect on my race.

40. I can choose public accommodation without fearing that people of my race cannot get in or will be mistreated in the places I have chosen.

41. I can be sure that if I need legal or medical help, my race will not work against me.

42. I can arrange my activities so that I will never have to experience feelings of rejection owing to my race.

43. If I have low credibility as a leader, I can be sure that race is not the problem.

44. I can easily find academic courses and institutions that give attention only to people of my race.

45. I can expect figurative language and imagery in all of the arts to testify to experiences of my race.

46. I can choose blemish cover or bandages in "flesh" color and have them more or less match my skin.

I repeatedly forgot each of the realizations on this list until I wrote it down. For me, white privilege has turned out to be an elusive and fugitive subject. The pressure to avoid it is great, for in facing it I must give up the myth of meritocracy. If these things are true, this is not such a free country; one's life is not what one makes it; many doors open for certain people through no virtues of their own. These perceptions mean also that my moral condition is not what I had been led to believe. The appearance of being a good citizen rather than a troublemaker comes in large part from having all sorts of doors open automatically because of my color.

A further paralysis of nerve comes from literary silence protecting privilege. My clearest memories of finding such analysis are in Lillian Smith's unparalleled *Killers of the Dream* and Margaret Andersen's review of Karen and Mamie Fields' *Lemon Swamp*. Smith, for example, wrote about walking toward black children on the street and knowing they would step into the gutter; Andersen contrasted the pleasure that she, as a white child, took on summer driving trips to the south with Karen Fields' memories of driving in a closed car stocked with all necessities lest, in stopping, her black family should suffer "insult, or worse." Adrienne Rich also recognizes and writes about daily experiences of privilege, but in my observation, white women's writing in this area is far more often on systemic racism than on our daily lives as light-skinned women.[2]

In unpacking this invisible knapsack of white privilege, I have listed conditions of daily experience that I once took for granted, as neutral, normal, and universally available to everybody, just as I once thought of a male-focused curriculum as the neutral or accurate account that can speak for all. Nor did I think of any of these perquisites as bad for the holder. I now think that we need a more finely differentiated taxonomy of privilege, for some of these varieties are only what one would want for everyone in a just society, and others give license to be ignorant, oblivious, arrogant, and destructive. Before proposing some more finely tuned categorization, I will make some observations about the general effects of these conditions on my life and expectations.

In this potpourri of examples, some privileges make me feel at home in the world. Others allow me to escape penalties or dangers that others suffer. Through some, I escape fear, anxiety, insult, injury, or a sense of not being welcome, not being real. Some keep me from having to hide, to be in disguise, to feel sick or crazy, to negotiate each transaction from the position of being an outsider or, within my group, a person who is suspected of having too close links with a dominant culture. Most keep me from having to be angry.

I see a pattern running through the matrix of privilege, a pattern of assumptions that were passed on to me as a white person. There was one main piece of cultural turf; it was my own turf, and I was among those who could control the turf. I could measure up to the cultural standards and take advantage of the many options I saw around me to make what the culture would call a success of my life. My *skin color was an asset for any move I was educated to want to make. I* could think of myself as "belonging" in major ways and of making social systems work for me. I could freely disparage, fear, neglect, or be oblivious to anything outside of the dominant cultural forms. Being of the main culture, I could also criticize it fairly freely. My life was reflected back to me frequently enough so that I felt, with regard to my race, if not to my sex, like one of the real people. 15

Whether through the curriculum or in the newspaper, the television, the economic system, or the general look of people in the streets, I received daily signals and indications that my people counted and that others *either didn't exist or must be trying, not very successfully, to be like people of my race. I* was given cultural permission not to hear voices of people of other races or a tepid cultural tolerance for hearing or acting on such voices. I was also raised not to suffer seriously from anything that darker-skinned people might say about my group, "protected," though perhaps I should more accurately say *prohibited,* through the habits of my economic class and social group, from living in racially mixed groups or being reflective about interactions between people of differing races.

In proportion as my racial group was being made confident, comfortable, and oblivious, other groups were likely being made unconfident, uncomfortable, and alienated. Whiteness protected me from many kinds of hostility, distress, and violence, which I was being subtly trained to visit in turn upon people of color.

For this reason, the word "privilege" now seems to me misleading. Its connotations are too positive to fit the conditions and behaviors which "privilege systems" produce. We usually think of privilege as being a favored state, whether earned, or conferred by birth or luck. School graduates are reminded they are privileged and urged to use their (enviable) assets well. The word "privilege" carries the connotation of being something everyone must want.

Yet some of the conditions I have described here work to systematically overempower certain groups. Such privilege simply *confers dominance,* gives permission to control, because of one's race or sex. The kind of privilege that gives license to some people to be, at best, thoughtless and, at worst, murderous should not continue to be referred to as a desirable attribute. Such "privilege" may be widely desired without being in any way beneficial to the whole society.

Moreover, though "privilege" may confer power, it does not confer moral strength. Those who do not depend on conferred dominance have traits and qualities that may never develop in those who do. Just as Women's Studies courses indicate that women survive their political circumstances to lead lives that hold the human race together, so "underprivileged" people of color who are the world's majority have survived their oppression and lived survivors' lives from which the white global minority can and must learn. In some groups, those dominated have actually become strong through *not* having all of these unearned advantages, and this gives them a great deal to teach the others. Members of so-called privileged groups can seem foolish, ridiculous, infantile, or dangerous by contrast.

20   I want, then, to distinguish between earned strength and unearned power conferred systemically. Power from unearned privilege can look like strength when it is, in fact, permission to escape or to dominate. But not all of the privileges on my list are inevitably damaging. Some, like the expectation that neighbors will be decent to you, or that your race will not count against you in court, should be the norm in a just society and should be considered as the entitlement of everyone. Others, like the privilege not to listen to less powerful people, distort the humanity of the holders as well as the ignored groups. Still others, like finding one's staple food everywhere, may be a function of being a member of a numerical majority in the population. Others have to do with not pervasive-negative stereotyping and mythology.

We might at last start by distinguishing between positive advantages that we can work to spread, to the point where they are not advantages at all but simply part of the normal civic and social fabric, and negative types of advantage that unless rejected will always reinforce our present hierarchies. For example, the positive "privilege" of belonging, the feeling that one belongs within the human circle, as Native Americans say, fosters development and should not be seen as a privilege for a few. It is, let us say, an entitlement that none of us should have to earn; ideally it is an *unearned entitlement.* At present, since only a few have it, it is an *unearned advantage* for them. The negative "privilege" that gave me cultural permission not to take darker-skinned Others seriously can be seen as arbitrarily conferred dominance and should not be desirable for anyone. This paper results from a process of coming to see that some of the power that I originally saw as attendant on being a human being in the United States consisted in *unearned advantage* and *confirmed dominance,* as well as other kinds of special circumstances not universally taken for granted.

In writing this paper I have also realized that white identity and status (as well as class identity and status) give me considerable power to choose whether to broach this subject and its trouble. I can pretty well decide whether to disappear and avoid and not listen and escape the dislike I may engender in other people through this essay, or interrupt, answer, interpret, preach, correct, criticize, and control to some extent what goes on in reaction to it. Being white, I am given considerable power to escape many kinds of danger or penalty as well as to choose which risks I want to take.

There is an analogy here, once again, with Women's Studies. Our male colleagues do not have a great deal to lose if they oppose it either. They simply have the power to decide whether to commit themselves to more equitable distributions of power. They will probably feel few penalties whatever choice they make; they do not seem, in any obvious short-term sense, the ones at risk, though they and we are all at risk because of behaviors that have been.

Through Women's Studies work I have met very few men who are truly distressed about systemic, unearned male and confirmed dominance. And so one question for me and others like me is whether we will be like them, or whether we will get truly distressed, even outraged, about unearned race advantage and conferred dominance and if so, what we will do to lessen them. In any case, we need to do more work in identifying how they actually affect our daily lives. We need more down-to-earth writing by people about these taboo subjects. We need more understanding of the ways in which white "privilege" damages white people, for these are not the same ways in which it damages the victimized. Skewed white psyches are an inseparable part of the picture, though I do not want to confuse the kinds of damage done to the holders of special assets and to those who suffer the deficits. Many, perhaps most, of our white students in the United States think that racism doesn't affect them because they are not people of color; they do not see "whiteness" as a racial identity. Many men likewise think that Women's Studies does not bear on their own existence because they are not female; they do not see themselves as having gendered identities. Insisting on the universal "effects" of "privilege" systems, then, becomes one of our chief tasks, and being more explicit about the particular effects in particular contexts is another. Men need to join us in this work.

In addition, since race and sex are not the only advantaging systems at work, we need to similarly examine the daily experience of having age advantage, or ethnic advantage, or physical ability, or advantage related to nationality, religion, or sexual orientation. Professor Marnie Evans suggested to me that in many ways the list I made also applies directly to heterosexual privilege. This is a still more taboo subject than race privilege: the daily ways in which heterosexual privilege makes some persons comfortable or powerful, providing supports, assets, approvals, and rewards to those who live or expect to live in heterosexual pairs. Unpacking that content is still more difficult, owing to the deeper imbeddedness of heterosexual advantage and dominance and stricter taboos surrounding these.

But to start such an analysis I would put this observation from my own experience: The fact that I live under the same roof with a man triggers all kinds of societal assumptions about my worth, politics, life, and values and triggers a host of unearned advantages and powers. After recasting many elements from the original list I would add further observations like these:

1. My children do not have to answer questions about why I live with my partner (my husband).

2. I have no difficulty finding neighborhoods where people approve of our household.

3. Our children are given texts and classes that implicitly support our kind of family unit and do not turn them against my choice of domestic partnership.

4. I can travel alone or with my husband without experiencing embarrassment or hostility in those who deal with us.

5. Most people I meet will see my marital arrangements as an asset to my life or as a favorable comment on my likability, my competence, or my mental health.

6. I can talk about the social events of a weekend without fearing most listeners' reactions.

7. I will feel welcomed and "normal" in the usual walks of public life, institutional and social.

8. In many contexts, I am seen as "all right" in daily work on women because I do not live chiefly with women.

Difficulties and dangers surrounding the task of finding parallels are many. Since racism, sexism, and heterosexism are not the same, the advantages associated with them should not be seen as the same. In addition, it is hard to isolate aspects of unearned advantage that derive chiefly from social class, economic class, race, religion, sex, or ethnic identity. The oppressions are both distinct and interlocking, as the Combahee River Collective statement of 1977 continues to remind us eloquently.[3]

One factor seems clear about all of the interlocking oppressions. They take both active forms that we can see and embedded forms that members of the dominant group are taught not to see. In my class and place, I did not see myself as racist because I was taught to recognize racism only in individual acts of meanness by members of my group, never in invisible systems conferring racial dominance on my group from birth. Likewise, we are taught to think that sexism or heterosexism is carried on only through intentional, individual acts of discrimination, meanness, or cruelty, rather than in invisible systems conferring unsought dominance on certain groups. Disapproving of the systems won't be enough to change them. I was taught to think that racism could end if white individuals changed their attitudes; many men think sexism can be ended by individual changes in daily behavior toward women. But a man's sex provides

advantage for him whether or not he approves of the way in which dominance has been conferred on his group. A "white" skin in the United States
opens many doors for whites whether or not we approve of the way the dominance has been conferred on us. Individual acts can palliate, but cannot end,
these problems. To redesign social systems, we need first to acknowledge their
colossal unseen dimensions. The silences and denials surrounding privilege are
the key political tool here. They keep the thinking about equality or equity
incomplete, protecting unearned advantage and conferred dominance by making these taboo subjects. Most talk by whites about equal opportunity seems
to me now to be about equal opportunity to try to get into a position of dominance while denying that *systems* of dominance exist.

Obliviousness about white advantage, like obliviousness about male advantage, is kept strongly inculturated in the United States so as to maintain
the myth of meritocracy, the myth that democratic choice is equally available
to all. Keeping most people unaware that freedom of confident action is there
for just a small number of people props up those in power and serves to keep
power in the hands of the same groups that have most of it already. Though
systemic change takes many decades, there are pressing questions for me and I
imagine for some others like me if we raise our daily consciousness on the
perquisites of being light-skinned. What will we do with such knowledge? As
we know from watching men, it is an open question whether we will choose
to use unearned advantage to weaken invisible privilege systems and whether
we will use any of our arbitrarily awarded power to try to reconstruct power
systems on a broader base.

NOTES

1. This paper was presented at the Virginia Women's Studies Association conference in
   Richmond in April 1986, and the American Educational Research Association conference in Boston in October 1986, and discussed with two groups of participants in
   the Dodge seminars for Secondary School Teachers in New York and Boston in the
   spring of 1987.
2. Andersen, Margaret, "Race and the Social Science Curriculum: A Teaching and
   Learning Discussion," *Radical Teacher* (November 1984), pp. 17–20. Smith, Lillian,
   Killers of the Dream.
3. "A Black Feminist Statement," The Combahee River Collective, pp. 13–22 in
   G. Hull, P. Scott, B. Smith, eds., *All the Women Are White, All the Blacks Are Men, But
   Some of Us Are Brave: Black Women's Studies* (Old Westbury, N.Y.: The Feminist Press,
   1982).

THE PATHOLOGY OF RACISM: A CONVERSATION WITH THIRD WORLD WIMMIN

Doris Davenport

A few years ago in New Haven, I tried to relate to feminism through a local women's center (located in a Yale basement). I was politely informed that I should "organize" with Black wimmin. In other words, get out. I wanted to start several projects that would include more third world wimmin, but I was told to talk to black wimmin about that. In short, white only. Then, the socialist study group I was interested in was suddenly closed just at the time I wanted to join. And once, in a wimmin's group when a discussion of men came up, it was revealed that half the white wimmin there feared black men, which included me (from the way they glared at me). In other words: *nigger, go home.*

Last year in Los Angeles, after volunteering to work for a local white feminist magazine, repeatedly offering my services and having my ideas and poems rejected, I was finally called to be one of the few token black wimmin at a reception for Ntozake Shange. And the beat, like the song says, goes on. From coast to coast, the feminist movement is racist, but that news is old and stale by now. It is increasingly apparent that the problem is white wimmin.

We, third world wimmin, always discuss this fact. (Frankly, I'm a little tired of it). However, we usually discuss the varied, yet similar manifestations of racism, without going into *why* white wimmin are racist.

In this article, which I conceive of as a conversation with third world wimmin, I want to explore the whys. I don't see the point of further cataloguing my personal grievances against white racist feminists. You know. Whatever you have experienced, I have too. Extrapolate a little. I think that one of our limitations in dealing with this issue is that we stay on the surface. We challenge symptoms of the disease while neglecting the causes. I intend to examine the causes.

5   If I were a white feminist and somebody called me a racist, I'd probably feel insulted (especially if I knew it was at least partially true). It's like saying someone has a slimey and incurable disease. Naturally I would be reactionary and rake out my health department/liberal credentials, to prove I was clean. But the fact is, the word "racism" is too simplistic, too general, and too easy. You can use the word and not say that much, unless the term is explained or clarified. Once that happens, racism looks more like a psychological problem (or pathological aberration) than an issue of skin color.

By way of brief clarification, we experience white feminists and their organizations as elitist, crudely insensitive, and condescending. Most of the feminist groups in this country are examples of this elitism. (This anthology came to be as a result of that.) It is also apparent that white feminists still perceive us as the "Other," based on a menial or sexual image: as more sensual, but less cerebral; more interesting, perhaps, but less intellectual, and more oppressed, but less political than they are. (If you need specific examples of this, think about your own experiences with them.)

When we attend a meeting or gathering of theirs, we are seen in only one of two limited or oppressive ways: as being white-washed and therefore sharing all their values, priorities, and goals, etc; or, if we (even accidentally) mention something particular to the experience of black wimmin, we are seen as threatening, hostile, and subversive to their interests. So when I say racist, these are some of the things I mean. I know this, and so do many white feminists. Because of their one-dimensional and bigoted ideas, we are not respected as feminists or wimmin. Their perverse perceptions of black wimmin mean that they continue to see us as "inferior" to them, and therefore, treat us accordingly. Instead of alleviating the problems of black wimmin, they add to them.

Although black and white feminists can sometimes work together for a common goal with warmth and support, and even love and respect each other occasionally, underneath there is still another message. That is that white feminists, like white boys and black boys, are threatened by us. Moreover, white feminists have a serious problem with truth and "accountability" about how/why they perceive black wimmin as they do.

For example, in a long, and long-winded article, "Disloyal to Civilization, Feminism, Racism, and Gynephobia"[1] Adrienne Rich attempted to address an issue similar to this one. Instead she did what she accused other feminists of doing, she "intellectualized the issue." She evaded it, after apologetically (or proudly, it's hard to tell) saying that "the most unconditional, tender . . . intelligent love I received was given me by a black woman." (Translated, she had a black mammy as a child.) Then, she hid behind a quasi-historical approach that defused the subject. After about fifteen pages, she got close, but apparently also got scared, and backed off. It seems she found it hard, after all, to tell the truth and be "accountable."

On the other hand, and as a brief but necessary digression, black wimmin *10* don't always tell the whole truth about and to white wimmin. We know, for example, that we have at least three distinct areas of aversion to white wimmin which affect how we perceive and deal with them: aesthetic, cultural, and social/political. Aesthetically (& physically) we frequently find white wimmin repulsive. That is, their skin colors are unaesthetic (ugly, to some people). Their hair, stringy and straight, is unattractive. Their bodies: rather like misshapen

---

[1]Adrienne Rich, *On Lies, Secrets, and Silence* (New York: Norton, 1979), p. 9.

lumps of whitish clay or dough, that somebody forgot to mold in certain areas. Furthermore, they have a strange body odor.

Culturally, we see them as limited and bigoted. They can't dance. Their music is essentially undanceable too, and un-pleasant. Plus, they are totally saturated in western or white american culture with little knowledge or respect for the cultures of third world people. (That is, unless they intend to exploit it.) The bland food of white folks is legendary. What they call partying is too low keyed to even be a wake. (A wake is when you sit up all night around the casket of a dead person.) And it goes on and on.

Socially, white people seem rather juvenile and tasteless. Politically they are, especially the feminists, naive and myopic. Then too, it has always been hard for us (black folk) to believe that whites will transcend color to make political alliances with us for any reason. (The women's movement illustrates this point.)

We have these aversions for one thing, because we saw through the "myth" of the white womon. The myth was that white wimmin were the most envied, most desired (and beautiful), most powerful (controlling white boys) wimmin in existence. The truth is that black people saw white wimmin as some of the least enviable, ugliest, most despised and least respected people, period. From our "close encounters" (i.e., slavery, "domestic" workers, etc.) with them, white people increasingly did seem like beasts or subnormal people. In short, I grew up with a certain kind of knowledge that all black folk, especially wimmin, had access to.

This knowledge led to a mixture of contempt and repulsion. I honestly think that most black feminists have some of these feelings. Yet, we constantly keep them hidden (at least from white wimmin), try to transcend them, and work towards a common goal. A few of us even see beyond the so-called privilege of being white, and perceive white wimmin as very oppressed, and ironically, invisible. This perception has sometimes been enough for us to relate to white feminists as sisters.

15   If *some* of us can do this, it would seem that some white feminists could too. Instead, they cling to their myth of being privileged, powerful, and less oppressed (or equally oppressed, whichever it is fashionable or convenient to be at the time) than black wimmin. Why? Because that is all they have. That is, they have defined, or re-defined themselves and they don't intend to let anything or anybody interfere. Somewhere deep down (denied and almost killed) in the psyche of racist white feminists there is some perception of their real position: powerless, spineless, and invisible. Rather than examine it, they run from it. Rather than seek solidarity with wimmin of color, they pull rank within themselves. Rather than attempt to understand our cultural and spiritual differences, they insist on their own limited and narrow views. In other words, they act out as both "white supremacists" and as a reactionary oppressed group.

As white supremacists, they still try to maintain the belief that white is right, and "godly" (sic). No matter how desperately they try to overcome it, sooner or later it comes out. They really have a hard time admitting that white skin does not insure a monopoly on the best in life, period.

Such a "superiority complex" is obviously a result of compensation. I mean, if whites really knew themselves to be superior, racism could not exist. They couldn't be threatened, concerned, or bothered. I am saying that the "white supremacist" syndrome, especially in white feminists, is the result of a real inferiority complex, or lack of self-identity. Just as a macho male uses wimmin to define himself or to be sure he exists, white feminists use wimmin of color to prove their (dubious) existence in the world.

Anyone familiar with the literature and psychology of an oppressed or *colonized* group knows that as they initially attempt to redefine themselves, they react. Their immediate mental, spiritual, and physical environment is chaotic and confused. The fact is white wimmin are oppressed; they have been "colonized" by white boys, just as third world people have. Even when white wimmin "belonged" to white boys they had no reality. They belonged as objects, and were treated as such. (As someone else has noted, the original model for colonization was the treatment of white wimmin.) Nobody has yet sufficiently researched or documented the collective psychology of oppressed white wimmin. So consider this as a thesis: they know. And so do I. The reality of their situation is the real pits. Lately, having worked free of the nominal and/or personal control of white boys, white wimmin are desperately reactionary. As a result, they identify with and encourage certain short-sighted goals and beliefs. Their infatuation with the word "power" in the abstract is an example of this: power to them mainly means external established power or control. They have minimal, if any, knowledge of personal power. But most importantly, as a reactionary oppressed group, they exhibit a strange kind of political bonding or elitism, where white wimmin are the only safe or valid people to be with; all others are threatening. Clearly, this state of mind is a political dead end, and the reasons for it stem from their great confusion.

So this is my contribution to the conversation. The cause of racism in white feminists is their bizarre oppression (and suppression). This, I contend, is what lies beneath the surface. This pathological condition is what *they* have to admit and deal with, and what we should start to consider and act on. Too often we discuss their economic freedom while ignoring other aspects of life. We sometimes dwell at length on their color, forgetting that they are still wimmin in a misogynist culture. They have been seriously mutated as a result.

In other words, their elitism and narrowminded rigidity are defense *20* mechanisms and that, in part, is why they create "alternatives" for themselves and put up psychological signs saying **white women only.** Part of the reason is fear, as a result of centuries of living with dogs and having no identities. Now, they are threatened by anyone different from them in race, politics, mannerisms, or clothing. It's partly a means of self-protection but that does not excuse it. Feminism either addresses itself to all wimmin, or it becomes even more so just another elitist, prurient white organization, defeating its own purposes.

As a partial solution to some of the above, and to begin to end some of the colossal ignorance that white feminists have about us, we (black and white feminists) could engage in "c.r." conversations about and with each other. If done with a sense of honesty, and a sense of *humor,* we might accomplish something. If overcoming our differences were made a priority, instead of the back burner issue that is usually is, we might resolve some of our problems.

On the other hand, my experiences with white feminists prevent me from seeing dialogue as anything but a naive beginning. I honestly see our trying to "break into" the white feminist movement as almost equivalent to the old, outdated philosophy of integration and assimilation. It is time we stopped this approach. We know we have no desire to be white. On the other hand, we know we have some valid concerns and goals that white feminists overlook. By now, in fact, a few of their organizations are as rigid and stagnant as any other "established" institution, with racism included in the by-laws.

So, sisters, we might as well give up on them, except in rare and individual cases where the person or group is deliberately and obviously more evolved mentally and spiritually. That is, un-racist. We should stop wasting our time and energy, until these wimmin evolve. Meanwhile, we can re-channel our energies toward ourselves.

We can start to develop a feminist movement based on the realities and priorities of third world wimmin. Racism would have to be a priority. Misogyny is another major problem of third world wimmin. Not only that, many of our communities are more homophobic (or "lesbophobic") than white ones. Also, a lot of our sisters are straight, and have no intention of changing. We cannot afford to ignore them and their need, nor the needs of many third world wimmin who are both feminists and nationalists; that is, concerned with our sex, and also our race. Finally, a lot of third world wimmin are ignorant about each other. We have yet to make our own realities known to ourselves, or anyone else. So we really do have a lot more to concentrate on beside the pathology of white wimmin. What we need to do is deal with us, first, then maybe we can develop a wimmin's movement that is more international in scope and universal in application.

25   It is time we stopped letting the rest of this oppressive society dictate our behavior, devour our energies, and control us, body, and soul. It is time we dealt with our own energies, and our own revolutionary potential, like the constructive and powerful forces that they are. When we *do* act on our power and potential, there will be a *real* feminist movement in this country, one that will finally include all wimmin.

WHITE WOMEN, RACE MATTERS

THE SOCIAL CONSTRUCTION OF WHITENESS

Ruth Frankenberg

INTRODUCTION: POINTS OF ORIGIN, POINTS OF DEPARTURE

My argument in this book is that race shapes white women's lives. In the same way that both men's and women's lives are shaped by their gender, and that both heterosexual and lesbian women's experiences in the world are marked by their sexuality, white people *and* people of color live racially structured lives. In other words, any system of differentiation shapes those on whom it bestows privilege as well as those it oppresses. White people are "raced," just as men are "gendered." And in a social context where white people have too often viewed themselves as nonracial or racially neutral, it is crucial to look at the "racialness" of white experience. Through life history interviews, the book examines white women's places in the racial structure of the United States at the end of the twentieth century and views white women's lives as sites both for the reproduction of racism and for challenges to it.

If race shapes white women's lives, the cumulative name that I have given to that shape is "whiteness." Whiteness, I will argue in the pages that follow, has a set of linked dimensions. First, whiteness is a location of structural advantage, of race privilege. Second, it is a "standpoint," a place from which white people look at ourselves, at others, and at society.[1] Third, "whiteness" refers to a set of cultural practices that are usually unmarked and unnamed. This book seeks to begin exploring, mapping, and examining the terrain of whiteness.

There are two analytic dimensions to the book. In beginning to research the significance of race in white women's lives, I expected to learn about, and document, the daily experience of racial structuring and the ways race privilege might be crosscut by other axes of difference and inequality: class, culture, ethnicity, gender, and sexuality. From there, I hoped to comprehend how that daily experience shapes white women's perceptions of the significance of race in the social structure as a whole. As my work proceeded however, a second dimension of analysis became equally significant, for it became clear that, as much as white women are located in—and speak from—physical environments shaped by race, we are also located in, and perceive our environments by means of, a set of discourses on race, culture, and society whose history spans this century and, beyond it, the broader sweep of Western expansion and colonialism.[2]

The material and discursive dimensions of whiteness are always, in practice, interconnected. Discursive repertoires may reinforce, contradict, conceal, explain, or "explain away" that materiality or the history of a given situation. Their interconnection, rather than material life alone, is in fact what generates "experience"; and, given this, the "experience" of living as a white woman in the United States is continually being transformed. Analytically, chapters of the book at times foreground that which is clearly concrete, tangible, and material about white women's experience of race—childhood, interracial relationships, political activism. At other times my focus is on issues of discourse—the meaning and apparent emptiness of "white" as a cultural identity; the political contexts, strengths, and limitations of different ways of "thinking through race"; the persistence of a discourse against interracial relationships.

Points of Origin

5   This book emerged out of the 1980s, the decade in which white feminist women like myself could no longer fail to notice the critique of white feminist racism by feminist/radical women of color (a critique that had, in fact, marked the entire "second wave" of feminism).[3] More specifically, the research project had as its inception my own passage through that decade, and my own despair over the confused mess that white feminist women's response to charges of racism had collectively become by 1983–84. At worst—and it appeared from where I was standing that "worst" was much of the time—it seemed as though we white feminists had a limited repertoire of responses when we were charged with racism: confusion over accusations of racism; guilt over racism; anger over repeated criticism; dismissal; stasis. Feminist/radical women of color would also, it seemed, go through phases: anger over racism; efforts to communicate with white women about racism, despite it; frustration; and the temptation (acted upon temporarily or permanently) to withdraw from multiracial work.

Sites of productive multiracial feminist dialogue and activity existed, but they were few and far between.[4] Too often, I witnessed situations in which, as predominantly white feminist workplaces, classrooms, or organizations tried to move to more multiracial formats or agendas, the desire to work together rapidly deteriorated into painful, ugly processes in which racial tension and conflict actually seemed to get worse rather than better as the months went by. There were, it appeared, multiple ways in which racism of the wider culture was simply being replayed in feminist locations.

Increasingly, this generated for a me a sense of contradiction, a need to know more. As a white feminist, I knew that I had not previously known I was "being racist" and that I had never set out to "be racist." I also knew that these desires and intentions had had little effect on outcomes. I, as a coauthor, in however modest a way, of feminist agendas and discourse, was at best failing to challenge racism, and, at worst, aiding and abetting it. How had feminism, a movement that, to my knowledge, intended to support and benefit all women, turned out not to be doing so?

In the early 1980s, I found myself straddling two sides of a "race line." On the one hand, I spent time sitting with white feminist university friends (roughly my age, roughly my class), at times in discussion groups and at other times more informally, as we struggled to make sense of the "racism question." The issue was anything but trivial to us. For one thing, it was startling in its implication that we were about to lose our newly found grip on the reins of liberation. (My friends and I were mostly socialist feminists. I, for one, liked the idea that, as women—apparently racially undefined—we had a distinctively radical purview of society, premised in part upon our status as structurally oppressed in relation to men—again apparently racially undefined. We were, however, analytically honest enough to realize that analyses such as that proposed by the Combahee River Collective, pointing to the structural subordination of women of color, and the potentially radical standpoint arising out of that position, changed all that!)[5] Because we were basically well-meaning individuals, the idea of being part of the problem of racism (something I had associated with extremists or institutions but not with myself) was genuinely shocking to us. And the issue was also terrifying, in the sense that we constantly felt that at any second we might err again with respect to racism, that we didn't know the rules and therefore didn't know how to prevent what was happening. There was, perhaps, a way racism was disembodied in our discussions, sometimes an issue of standpoint, sometimes one of etiquette, and definitely an issue that provoked the intense frustration that came of not being able to "get it," or to "get it right."

Meanwhile, I was also spending a great deal of time with a friendship/support network of working-class women of color and white women, some of whom I had also first met through the university. These women were mainly parents (I was not), as well as older, poorer, and positioned very differently than I in the relations of racism in the United States. As I sat with them and traveled their daily pathways—thanks to an unexpectedly profound connection to one woman in particular—an inventory of meanings of racism, of racist behaviors began, de facto, to accumulate in my consciousness. In part, the inventory felt necessary to my ability to cope in those gatherings without offending anyone, but in part my friend made it her business to educate me. I learned by proximity what it means to navigate through a largely hostile terrain, to deal with institutions that do not operate by one's own logic nor in ones interests, and to need those institutions to function in one's favor if one is to survive, let alone to achieve. I realized for almost the first time in my life the gulf of experience and meaning between individuals differentially positioned in relation to systems of domination, and the profundity of cultural difference. (I say *almost* the first time because the culture shock of moving to the United States from Britain at the age of twenty-one had opened my eyes to the latter.)

10   Uniting the divergent experiences of being both a part of that network and a graduate student was, and remains, beyond my capability. In any case, doing so, and especially conveying the experiences of women of color, in general or particular, is not my goal in any direct way.[6] More relevant here is the multifaceted impact of both affiliations, and their disjunction, on my own understanding of racism and on the genesis of this project. When my white sisters and I struggled to comprehend a situation we did not understand and had not meant to create, critical questions for me were: How did this happen? How did we get into this mess? What do "they" mean when they tell us white feminism is racist? Translated into research, the same questions looked something like this:

> (How) does racism shape white women's lives?
>
> What are the social processes through which white women are created as social actors primed to reproduce racism within the feminist movement?
>
> (How) can white women's lives become sites of resistance to the reproduction of racism?

Socialist feminism had also given me an analytical commitment to three axioms: first, that in "societies structured in dominance"[7] we, as feminists, must always remember that we act from within the social relations and subject positions we seek to change; second, that experience constructs identity; and, third, that there is a direct relationship between "experience" and "worldview" or "standpoint" such that any system of domination can be seen most clearly from the subject positions of those oppressed by it. As the project developed, applying those axioms to positions of privilege or domination, or to subjects simultaneously privileged and oppressed, required me to complicate the second and third of these axioms. The first remained not only intact but even more challenging than it had appeared at the outset.

From the network predominantly made up of women of color, of which I was in some way part, I carried into the research three realizations: first, that there is frequently a gulf of experience of racism between white people and people of color; second, that white women might have a range of awareness in relation to racism, with greater awareness based on, among other things, their long-term connectedness to communities of color (I did not, I should perhaps clarify, include myself in the latter category at the time); third, that there *is* a cultural/racial specificity to white people, at times more obvious to people who are not white than to white individuals.

What's in a Name?

When I began to work on this book, I described it as one that would examine the relationship between white women and racism. In the years between then and now, I have added another conceptualization of it, one that perhaps overlaps, without displacing, my earlier description. For I now also describe this book as a study of the social construction of whiteness.

Calling the project a study of white women and racism marked out the set of concerns that motivated me to begin it, namely, emphasizing that racism was and is something that shapes white women's lives. Rather than something that people of color have to live and deal with in a way that bears no relationship or relevance to the lives of white people. For when white people—and I was especially concerned about white feminists, since the project had its origins in the feminist movement—look at racism, we tend to view it as an issue that people of color face and have to struggle with, but not as an issue that generally involves or implicates us. Viewing racism in this way has serious consequences for how white women look at racism, and for how antiracist work might be framed. With this view, white women can see antiracist work as an act of compassion for an "other," an optional, extra project but not one intimately and organically linked to our own lives. Racism can, in short, be conceived as something external to us rather than as a system that shapes our daily experiences and sense of self.

The "and" in "white women and racism" implies, but does not really de- 15
fine, a link between the two terms. The need to speak of whiteness further specifies what is at stake in speaking of racism in relation to white people. To speak of the "social construction of whiteness" asserts that there are locations, discourses, and material relations to which the term "whiteness" applies. I argue in this book that whiteness refers to a set of locations that are historically, socially, politically, and culturally produced and, moreover, are intrinsically linked to unfolding relations of domination. Naming "whiteness" displaces it from the unmarked, unnamed status that is itself an effect of its dominance. Among the effects on white people both of race privilege and of the dominance of whiteness are their seeming normativity, their structured invisibility. This normativity is, however, unevenly effective. I will explore and seek to explain the invisibility and modes of visibility of racism, race difference, and whiteness. To look at the social construction of whiteness, then, is to look head-on at a site of dominance. (And it may be more difficult for white people to say "Whiteness has nothing to do with me—I'm not white" than to say "Race has nothing to do with me—I'm not racist.") To speak of whiteness is, I think, to assign everyone a place in the relations of racism. It is to emphasize that dealing with racism is not merely an option for white people—that, rather, racism shapes white people's lives and identities in a way that is inseparable from other facets of daily life.

To name whiteness also broadens the focus of my study, first because it makes room for the linkage of white subjects to histories not encompassed by, but connected to, that of racism: histories of colonialism and imperialism, and, secondarily, histories of assimilationism in the United States. Second, it allows me to view certain practices and subject positions as racialized (that is, structured by relations of race, usually alongside other structuring principles) rather than necessarily racist—although whiteness is for the most part racialized in the context of racism. Third, by examining and naming the terrain of whiteness, it may, I think, be possible to generate or work toward antiracist forms of whiteness, or at least toward antiracist strategies for reworking the terrain of whiteness.

Several distinct but, I believe, compatible theoretical and methodological orientations have been distilled into my approach. First, I share in a feminist commitment to drawing on women's daily lives as a resource for analyzing society. Second, I also share what is, in a sense, the converse of that commitment (and also an approach adopted by feminists): the belief that women's daily life experiences can only be adequately understood by "mapping" them onto broader social processes. Third, then, in order to better comprehend the social processes involved in the construction of whiteness, I have drawn on both theoretical and substantive analyses of race, racism, and colonialism in the United States and beyond.

Feminism: Personal, Political, Theoretical

My decision, in 1984, to being to explore whiteness through white women's life histories drew on a strong current of feminist thought that has used accounts of women's experience as ground for the construction and critique of theory and strategy. Since the consciousness-raising groups of the late 1960s, feminists have transformed accounts of personal experience into politicized and theorized terrain.[8] Through this process, the private, the daily, and the apparently trivial in women's activities came to be understood as shared rather than individual experiences, and as socially and politically constructed. The personal, in short, became political.

In addition to anchoring theories of gender and of society in general, women's accounts of personal experience have served as leverage points from which to criticize canons, whether of social theory or of political movements' agenda for change. During the "second wave" of feminism, from the late 1960s to the present, this kind of critique has challenged at least two canons that are especially relevant here. First, white feminists and feminist/radical women of color have criticized the lack of attention to gender domination—and effective male-centeredness—of left and antiracist movements. Second, feminist/radical women of color have challenged feminisms dominated by white-centered accounts of female experience. As women activists of a range of racial identities criticized theory based on male standpoints, it became clear that such standpoints obscured or ignore female subordination. And again, as women of color challenged a white feminist accounts of "women's place" in society, the partiality of those accounts became visible.

20   Theorizing "from experience" rested on several key epistemological claims that, over time, became staples of feminist "common sense." The first of these was a critique of "objectivity" or "distance" as the best stances from which to generate knowledge. For, feminists argued, there is a link between where one stands in society and what one perceives. In addition, this epistemological stance made another, stronger claim: that the oppressed can see with the greatest clarity not only their own position but also that of the oppressor/privileged, and indeed the shape of social systems as a whole.[9]

To theorize "from experience" is thus to propose that there is no firm separation to be drawn between woman as member of society and woman as thinker, theorist, or activist. And therefore, as became clear in the context of a critique of white feminist racism, there are multiple problems in attempting (by default) to use white women's lives as a resource for analyzing gender domination in its entirety. Through the 1980s and into the present, work predominantly by women of color has been transforming feminist analysis, drawing attention to the white-centeredness, and more generally the false universalizing claims, of much feminist discourse.[10] Ethnocentrism based on the racial specificity of white women's lives, it was pointed out, limits feminist analysis and strategy in relation to issues such as the family[11] and reproductive rights.[12] In the realm of theory, women of color were the first to advocate advance frameworks for understanding the intersection in women's lives of gender, sexuality, race, and class[13] as well as visions and concepts of multiracial coalition work.[14]

The issue here was not only that white women's daily experiences *differed* from those of our sisters of color. If that had been the case, simply adding more accounts by women from a variety of racial locations would have resolved the problem. Instead, it became clear that white feminist women accounting for our experience were missing its "racialness" and that we were not seeing what was going on around us: in other words, we lacked an awareness of how our positions in society were constructed in relation to those of women—and men—of color.

One of my concerns, as I looked at white women's lives through a specifically racial lens, was, as a result, trying to comprehend those lacunae in perception. I needed to understand not only how race is lived, but also how it is seen—or more often, in my immediate political and social networks, *not* seen. In 1983 (before beginning the interviews for this book) I argued that the extent to which white women were "missing" or "not getting" the significance of race in either our or anyone else's experience had everything to do with a standpoint: because we were race privileged, I argued, we were not in a structural position to see the effects of racism on our lives, nor the significance of race in the shaping of the U.S. society.[15]

But by themselves, the material, daily relations of race cannot adequately explain whether, when, and in what terms white women perceive race as structuring either their own or anyone else's experience. The "dailiness" of racial separation and the inescapability of whiteness as a position of relative privilege cannot explain the *content* of white women's descriptions of others and of themselves—the ways, for example, masculinity and femininity are divided in racial and cultural terms. Similarly, they cannot explain why some white women learn or contest explicitly racist attitudes from childhood onward, while for others racial inequality is, in the words of the one of the women I interviewed, "a reality enjoyed, but not acknowledged, a privilege lived, but unknown."

Through the second half of the 1980s, several ongoing areas of feminist work were critical as I interviewed white women and analyzed their narratives. *25*

First, feminist scholars, mainly women of color, engaged in the painstaking work of refracting gender through the lenses of race and culture: examining, for example, how constructions of womanhood have always been racially and culturally marked and, in a racist society, even racially exclusive.[16] This work of rigorous specification exposes the universalism of the second wave of feminism as largely false—and calls, I suggest, for the reciprocal specification of *white* womanhood.[17] Second, feminists of all racial groups (but, as noted earlier, in a process initiated by women of color) made richer and more complex our theorizations of subjectivity and of society in general. Thus, for example, theorists described the "simultaneity" of the impact of race, class, and gender in shaping the lives of women of color[18] (and, I would add, white women too) and emphasized that subjectivity is "[displaced] across a multiplicity of discourses"[19] rather than produced out of the single axis of gender domination or the twin poles of capitalism and patriarchy. Third, more complex views of the subject produced correspondingly complex epistemologies, understood as emerging out of multifaceted political locations.[20]

While feminist women of color have worked to specify their histories and the contemporary shape of their lives in gendered and racial terms, however, a corresponding particularism has too often been lacking on the part of white feminism women. Thus, as white feminists participate alongside women of color in developing new theoretical articulations of "difference" and the "multiplicity" of women's experiences, there is, I fear, a danger that while increasingly theorists of color speak from concrete conceptualizations of what that multiplicity means to them, for white women visions of "difference" and "multiplicity" may remain abstract.

There are critical exceptions here. In a productive approach to questions about white women and racism, some white feminists began in the late 1970s and 1980s to examine through autobiography the ways race privilege and racism have shaped their own lives.[21] Thus, as these women and others like them continue to articulate feminist practice, they do so with a more multifaceted understanding of the social forces that made them who they are.

My study, and the exploration of white women's life histories upon which this book is based, share these women's commitment to careful and detailed analysis of how racism enters and shapes white women's lives, and to making more visible how our lives are embedded in a range of histories, political struggles, and social forces. My assumption here is one I have held since I first came to politics in the 1970s: that knowledge about a situation is a critical tool in dismantling it.

Theorizing Race

In analyzing the life narratives of white women, I attempt as thoroughly as possible to situate them in relation both to the material relations of racism at specific times and places in the United States, and to the circulation and shifting salience of a range of discourses on race. In the narratives that serve as the primary resource for this book, it is clear that, indeed, race privilege translated directly into forms of social organization that shaped daily life (for example, the de jure and, later, de facto residential, social, and educational segregation that characterized most of these women's childhoods), and that these in turn shaped the women's perception of race.

In order to think about white women and race, then, it is critical to re-   *30* flect on the meaning and history, in the United States, of the category of "race" itself, and similarly that of the idea of "racism." I have found most useful those analyses that view race as a socially construed rather than inherently meaningful category, one linked to relations of power and processes of struggle, and one whose meaning changes over time.[22] Race, like gender, is "real" in the sense that it has real, though changing, effects in the world and real, tangible, complex impact on individuals' sense of self , experiences, and life chances. In asserting that race and racial difference are socially constructed, I do not minimize their social and political reality, but rather insist that their reality is, precisely, social and political rather than inherent or static.

Historical research underscores the instability of racial categorizing. Michael Omi and Howard Winant point out, for example, that:

> [In the U.S. census] Japanese Americans have moved from categories such as "non-white," "Oriental" or simply "Other," to recent inclusion as a specific ethnic group under the broader category of "Asian and Pacific Islanders." The variation both reflects and in turn shapes racial understanding and dynamics.[23]

Again, Jewish Americans, Italian Americans, and Latinos have at different times and from varying political standpoints, been viewed as both "white" and "nonwhite." And as the history of "interracial" marriage and sexual relationships demonstrates, "white" is as much as anything else an economic and political category maintained over time by a changing set of exclusionary practices, both legislative and customary.[24]

The women I interviewed replicated another dimension of racial discourse worth noting at this preliminary stage. Racist discourse, I suggest, frequently accords a hypervisibility to African Americans and a relative *invisibility* to Asian Americans and Native Americans; Latinos are also relatively less visible than African Americans in discursive terms. Needless to say, neither mode of expression of racism is more desirable, or more unpleasant in its effects, than the other. Two white women explicitly singled out African Americans as "racial others," in contrast to Latinos and Asians, viewed as "culturally" but not "racially" different from white people. Elsewhere, the women described Asian Americans and Latinos as somehow less different from whites in racial terms. They also at times had more to say about Black-white relations, and more elaborate constructions of African Americans, than any about other communities of color. This pattern was in part an effect of the regions in which individual women had grown up: those raised on the West Coast of the United States, for example, explored questions about race and identity in relation to Chicanas and Chicanos as often as to African American men and women.

In this book, I define race difference in a way that is avowedly historically specific, politically engaged, and provisional. I thus view groups who are currently targets of racism—Native Americans, Latinos, African Americans, and Asian/Pacific Americans, as well as other nonwhite immigrants—as being racially different from white people, and from each other. (The study is also premised on the notion that white people, as much as people of color, are racialized.) Part of my concern is, of course, to explore how white women described race and cultural difference, and how their descriptions reflect different moments in the history of race.

Racial naming is also in part an effect of communities' own collective struggles to claim or rearticulate identity. The shifts in census classification of Japanese Americans, for example, resulted in large part from the demands of Asian/Pacific Americans themselves. And in fact, this book bears the marks of a more recent community-initiated "renaming" process, for in the years 1984 to 1986, when the interviews for this book took place, the name "African American" was not yet current, so it was not used by the women I interviewed to describe men and women of African descent living in the United States.

35   U.S. history is marked by an unevenly evolving history of discourses on race difference. Central to completing analyses of race have been assertions of, and challenges to, a range of claims about differences between people, including psychological or genetic differences, cultural differences, and differences in access to power. One can, in fact, identify a chronological movement in the history of ideas about race in the United States, if only to qualify and complicate that chronology immediately afterward. In a synthesis that has been crucial to this book, Omi and Winant divide that chronology into three stages.[25] For the greater part of U.S. history, as they point out, arguments for the biological inferiority of people of color represented the dominant discourse (or in their terms, paradigm) for thinking about race.[26] Within this discourse, race was constructed as a biological category, and the assertion of white biological superiority was used to justify economic and political inequities ranging from settler colonialization to slavery.

Beginning in the 1920s, a new clustering of concepts gained currency: race difference came to be named in cultural and social terms instead of, or simultaneously with, biological ones. Here, Omi and Winant argue, the notion of "ethnicity" displaced "race" as a descriptor of difference.[27] Within this new paradigm, belonging to an ethnic group came to be understood more behaviorally than biologically (although, since a cultural group continued to be understood in terms of descent rather than practice, one could add that biology continued to underwrite conceptions of identity). Alongside the ethnicity paradigm came an "assimilationist" analysis of what would and should happen to people of color in the United States: like white immigrants, it was argued, people of color would gradually assimilate into the "mainstream" of U.S. society. Ultimately, ethnicity theorists believed, a meritocracy would be achieved. Vital to this perspective was the belief that racial inequality was incompatible with American society, which, within this view, was understood to be fundamentally adequate as a democracy.

The posing of demands for racial equality in terms of the ideal of democracy in the United States also provided the rhetorical and moral force of the early civil rights movement. However, radical antiracist and cultural nationalist movements of the late 1960s and early 1970s—Black Power, La Raza, and the American Indian Movement—brought about a resurgence, reevaluation, and transformation of notions of the *differentness* of peoples of color from the white dominant culture, along with an analysis and critique of racial inequality as a fundamentally structuring feature of U.S. society. Omi and Winant characterize this third phase as one of class- and nation-based paradigms for understanding race and racism.[28] Here, in fact, we come full circle to the second wave of feminism. For, as Omi and Winant (among others) point out, these class- and nation-based movements were themselves the inspiration and in some ways provided the moment of origin for second-wave feminism or "women's liberation." Not only did they provide models for the women's movement,[29] but many women activists either moved from antiracist movements into the feminist movement or participated simultaneously in both.[30] The obvious question here is why, given these origins, by the mid-1970s the most clearly audible feminist discourses were those that failed to address racism. The answer to that question is lengthy and beyond the scope of this book, although related to it.

One way to describe these three moments, paradigms, or discourses is in terms of shifts from "difference" to "similarity," and then "back" to difference radically redefined. The first shift, then, is from a first moment that I will call "essentialist racism," with its emphasis on race difference understood in hierarchical terms of essential, biological inequality to a discourse of essential "sameness" popularly referred to as "color blindness"—which I have chosen to name as a double move toward "color evasiveness" and "power evasiveness."[31] This second movement asserts that we are all the same under the skin; that, culturally, we are converging; that, materially, we have the same chances in U.S. society; and that—the sting in the tail—any failure to achieve is therefore that fault of the people of color themselves. The third moment insists once again on difference, but in a form very different from that of the first moment. Where the terms of essentialist racism were set by the white dominant culture, in the third moment they are articulated by people of color. Where difference within the terms of essentialist racism alleges the inferiority of people of color, in the third moment difference signals autonomy of culture, values, aesthetic standards, and so on. And, of course, inequality in this third moment refers no to ascribed characteristics, but to the social structure. I will refer to this discursive repertoire as one of "race cognizance."

Having begun this discussion with a chronological description of the emergence of three distinct modes of thinking through race, I should stress that the transitions from one to the next cannot be viewed as paradigm shifts in any total sense, for elements of all three can be found in today's literature on race and racism in the Untied States and in the rhetoric of activists both for and against racism.[32] Moreover, while it may be fair to say that at a certain point in U.S. history a color- and power-evasive public language of race displaced essentialist racism as the dominant discourse on race, color- and power-evasive discourse remains dominant today; it has not been displaced in its turn by race cognizance. Although continually challenged by the third mode of thinking through race, the color- and power-evasive paradigm has incorporated elements of race cognizance into itself, rather than being in any significant way displaced by it. . . .

40   The claim that evasion of color and power is dominant is, perhaps, at first sight counterintuitive at a time when conservative cultural critics are arguing that the United States is being overrun by the new orthodoxy of "multiculturalism"—ostensibly a product of race cognizance. But the situation is much more complicated than conservative critics would claim. First, efforts to move popular discourse toward multiculturalism have thus far been limited in scope and, while having some impact in education and mass media, are not yet a part of most people's daily thought or practice. Second, despite the conservatives' claims, it has in practice proven to be extremely difficult to establish multiculturalist or pluralist approaches to curricula or media in the context of continued structural and institutional white leadership. Proposals for the development of pluralist or multiculturalist curricula are often "watered down" in their pathways through institutional bureaucracies. The versions of multiculturalism that emerge as educational or representational practice are for the most part rearrangements of the selective engagement that evasion of color represents, and are little less power-evasive than the policies and practices that arise out of classical "color-blindness." One can, in fact, argue that struggles between power evasion and race cognizance are being fought on the terrain of multiculturalism.

. . . [E]lements of all three modes of thinking through race were present in the narratives of the women I interviewed. In analyzing the ways in which they circulated in the narratives, I have found it helpful to characterize as "discursive repertoires" the clusterings of discursive elements upon which the women drew. "Repertoire" captures, for me, something of the way in which strategies for thinking through race were learned, drawn upon, and enacted, repetitively but not automatically or by vote, chosen but by no means freely so.[33] . . .

NOTES

1. Following Nancy Hartsock, "The Feminist Standpoint: Developing the Ground for a Specifically Feminist Historical Materialism," in *Discovering Reality,* ed. Sandra Harding and Merrill B. Hintikka (Dordrecht: D. Riedel, 1983), 283–310, the word "standpoint" has two linked meanings. The first is the perspective that arises out of a class's or gender's received and unanalyzed engagement with its material environment, perceived through the worldview of the dominant group. The second is the self-

conscious perspective on self and society that arises out of a class (or gender) grouping's critical apprehension of itself and its location in relation to the system it inhabits. With respect to gender, Hartsock styles the former "women's standpoint" and the latter "feminist standpoint." No such distinction is currently available for my purposes. In referring to whiteness as a standpoint, I intend, loosely, an analogy with Hartsock's "women's standpoint." The most appropriate analogy for Hartsock's "feminist standpoint" would be "white antiracist standpoint." At points in this book, I and some interviewees articulate elements of a white antiracist standpoint. Finally, it should be emphasized that the analogy is by no means perfect, since both "feminist" and "proletarian" standpoints refer to the self-conscious engagements of oppressed groups with their own positioning, whereas, of course, "a white antiracist standpoint" refers to self-conscious and self-critical engagement with a *dominant* position in the racial order.

2. "Discourses" may be understood in this book as historically constituted bodies of ideas providing conceptual framework for individuals, made material in the design and creation of institutions and shaping daily practices, interpersonal interactions, and social relations. "Western" is capitalized here to draw attention to its status as a discursive rather than a geographical construct. In the geographical sense, "west" is of course a relative term (tied to "east," "north," and "south," as well as to a particular point in space from which a given calculation emanates). But "west," *in* the West, tends to be understood to refer to the capitalist European countries, North America, Australia, New Zealand, and, on occasion, Japan(!). Discursively, too, "West" and "Western" are regional terms, constructed out of opposition to non-Western Others or "Orientals." Westernness implies a particular, dominative relationship to power, colonial expansion, a belonging to center rather than margin in a global capitalist system, and a privileged relationship to institutions—be they academic or oriented to mass communication—for the production of knowledge. Not all people in the (pseudogeographical) West/west are, within the terms of a discourse on West–non-West, Westerners. This is because the cultural content of Westernness draws on Christian, rationalist, north and west European customs and patterns of thought and because, discursively, Westerness is racially exclusive and tends to mean only Caucasian. Thus, for example, Ward Churchill, in describing the stages of European colonization of Native Americans, remarks that, "In the beginning, troops arrive to butcher the indigenous population. Later, the 'savages' are seen as worthy of being 'educated' and 'civilized' to white, *Western* standards, dealing a devastating blow to the cultures possessed by the survivors of the slaughter." Ward Churchill, *Fantasies of the Master Race: Literature, Cinema, and the Colonization of American Indians,* ed. Annette Jaimes (Monroe, Maine: Common Courage Press, 1992), 264 (emphasis mine).

3. I use "second wave" to refer to feminism from the late 1960s to the present. "Third wave" has at times been used to characterize, optimistically, the emergence of distinctively multiracial feminisms through the 1980s.

4. Examples of the published record of Black–white feminist dialogue in particular are Tia Cross, Frieda Klein, Barbara Smith, and Beverley Smith, "Face-to-Face, Day-to-Day: Racism CR (Consciousness Rating)," *Heresies* 3:3, 66–67; Elly Bulkin, Minnie Bruce Pratt, and Barbara Smith, *Yours in Struggle: Three Feminist Perspectives on Anti-Semitism and Racism* (Brooklyn, N.Y.: Long Haul Press 1984; Ithaca, N.Y.: Firebrand,

1988); Gloria I. Joseph and Jill Lewis, *Common Differences: Conflicts in Black and White Feminist Perspectives* (Garden City, N.Y.: Anchor, 1981). See also Chandra Talpade Mohanty, Ann Russo, and Lourdes Torres, eds., *Third World Women and the Politics of Feminism* (Bloomington: Indiana University Press, 1991), ix, for reference to the conference Common Differences: Third World Women and Feminist Perspectives, University of Illinois, Urbana-Champaign, April 1983.

5. Combahee River Collective, "A Black Feminist Statement," in *Capitalist Patriarchy and the Case for Socialist Feminism,* ed. Zillah R. Eisenstein (New York: Monthly Review Press, 1979), 362–72. The statement argues for the need to analyze U.S. society in terms of four interlocking axes of oppression based on race, class, gender, and sexuality. It also articulates an identity politics that linked the positioning of Black women who are targets of all four systems of domination with a unique purview and political agency.

6. In fact, bell hooks and Chela Sandoval, two women I met at the same time at the University of California, Santa Cruz, have written precisely about the political and strategic implications for women of color of their positioning within webs of power and systems of domination. Both of these women have been critical to my thinking about racism, and Sandoval's work has been crucial to my thinking about power and political strategy. bell hooks, *Ain't I a Woman? Black Women and Feminism* (Boston: South End Press, 1981); *Feminist Theory: From Margin to Center* (Boston: South End Press, 1984); *Talking Back: Thinking Feminist, Thinking Black* (Boston: South End Press, 1989). Chela Sandoval, "The Struggle Within: Women Respond to Racism—Report on the National Women's Studies Conference, Storrs Connecticut" (Oakland, California: Occasional Paper, Center for Third World Organizing, 1982) (revised version of this paper is published in *Making Face, Making Soul, Haciendo Caras: Creative and Critical Perspectives by Women of Color,* ed. Gloria Anzaldúa, [San Francisco: Aunt Lute, 1990], 55–71; "U.S. Third World Feminism: The Theory and Method of Oppositional Consciousness in the Postmodern World," *Genders* 10 (Spring 1991): 1–24.

7. I owe this term to Stuart Hall, "Race, Articulation, and Societies Structured in Dominance," in *UNESCO: Sociological Theories, Race, and Colonialism* (Paris: UNESCO Press, 1980), 305–45.

8. For accounts of the uses and effectiveness of consciousness raising in the second wave of feminism, see Anna Coote and Beatrix Campbell, *Sweet Freedom: The Struggle for Women's Liberation* (London: Picador, 1982): Alice Echols, *Daring to Be Bad: Radical Feminism in America, 1967–75* (Minneapolis: University of Minnesota Press, 1989); Katie King, "The Situation of Lesbianism as Magical Sign: Contests for Meaning in the U.S. Women's Movement, 1968–72," *Communications* 9 (1986) 65–91.

9. From a white feminist perspective, the clearest articulation of this position is Hartsock, "The Feminist Standpoint." Articulations of a similar epistemological stance by U.S. women of color include Combahee River Collective. "A Black Feminist Statement"; Aida Hurtado, "Relating to Privilege: Seduction and Rejection in the Subordination of White Women and Women of Color," *Signs* 14, no. 4 (1989): 833–55; and Patricia Hill Collins, "The Social Construction of Black Feminist Thought," *Signs* 14, no. 4 (1989): 745–73.

10. A key text here is Cherríe Moraga and Gloria Anzaldúa, eds. *This Bridge Called My Back: Writings by Radical Women of Color* (Watertown, Mass.: Persephone, 1981; New York: Kitchen Table Women of Color Press, 1983).

11. Among others, see Hazel Carby, "White Women Listen! Black Feminism and the Boundaries of Sisterhood," Center for Contemporary Cultural Studies, *The Empire Strikes Back: Race and Racism in '70s Britain* (London: Hutchinson, 1981), 212–35; Kum Kum Bhavnani and Margaret Coulson, "Transforming Socialist Feminism: The Challenge of Racism," *Feminist Review* 23 (Summer 1986): 81–92.

12. See, for example, Angela Y. Davis, *Women, Race, and Class* (New York: Random House, 1981) 202–21.

13. The founding text here is, I believe, the Combahee River Collective's "A Black Feminist Statement." I will discuss more recent contributions later.

14. For example, Bernice Johnson Reagon, "Coalition Politics: Turning the Century," in *Home Girls: A Black Feminist Anthology,* ed. Barbara Smith (New York: Kitchen Table Women of Color Press, 1983), 356–69; Cherríe Moraga and Gloria Anzaldúa's concept of "El Mundo Zurdo/The Left Handed World," *This Bridge Called My Back,* 195–96.

15. Ruth Frankenberg, "Different Perspectives: Interweaving Theory and Practice in Women's Work," qualifying essay, Board of Studies in the History of Consciousness, University of California, Santa Cruz, 1983.

16. Among such developments, Chicana scholars have examined how the figure of La Malinche constructs Chicana femininity (for example, Norma Alarcon, "Chicana's Feminist Literature: A Revision Through Malintzin/or Malintzin: Putting Flesh Back on the Object," Moraga and Anzaldúa, *This Bridge Called My Back,* 182–90. Similarly, Hortense Spillers builds on the work of African American historians to show how, given the material conditions of Black women's lives, they were "excluded" from racially dominant notions of femininity. "Mama's Baby, Papa's Maybe: An American Grammar Book," *Diacritics,* Summer 1987: 65–81. Rayna Green, in "The Pocahontas Perplex: The Image of Indian Women in American Culture," in *Unequal Sisters,* ed. Ellen Carol DuBois and Vicki L. Ruiz (New York: Routledge, 1990), 15–21, analyzes the ideological constructions of the figure of Native American women within a colonial matrix.

17. Such work has been undertaken by, for example, Gloria I. Joseph and Jill Lewis, *Common Differences,* who examine the differences in perspective, experience, and sense of self between white and Black women; Vron Ware, *Beyond the Pale: White Women, Racism, and History* (London: Verso, 1992), who articulates in particular the place of white womanhood in the discursive economies of racism and imperialism; and Teresa L. Amott and Julie A. Matthaei, *Race, Gender, and Work: A Multicultural History of Women in the United States* (Boston: South End Press, 1991), who by juxtaposing and contrasting the histories of U.S. women across racial and ethnic lines enable greater attention to the specification of gender by race and class.

18. Patricia Zavella, "The Problematic Relationship of Feminism and Chicana Studies," *Women's Studies* 17 (1988): 123–34.

19. Norma Alarcon, "The Theoretical Subjects of *This Bridge Called My Back* and Anglo-American Feminism," in *Haciendo Caras,* ed. Anzaldúa, 356–69.

20. Chandra Talpade Mohanty, "Feminist Encounters: Locating the Politics of Experience," *Copyright* 1, no. 1 (1984); Donna J. Haraway, "Situated Knowledges: The Science Question and the Privilege of Partial Perspective," in Donna J. Haraway, *Simians, Cyborgs, and Women: The Reinvention of Nature* (New York: Routledge, 1991), 183–202.

21. Foremost in this regard were Elly Bulkin ("Hard Ground: Jewish Identity, Racism and Anti-Semitism") and Minnie Bruce Pratt ("Identity: Skin, Blood, Heart") in Bulkin,

Pratt, and Smith, *Yours in Struggle,* 89–228 and 9–64; Mab Segrest, *My Mama's Dead Squirrel: Lesbian Essays on Southern Culture* (Ithaca, N.Y.: Firebrand, 1985); Adrienne Rich, "Disloyal to Civilization: Feminism, Racism, Gynephobia," in Adrienne Rich, *On Lies, Secrets and Silence: Selected Prose, 1966–1978* (New York: Norton, 1979), 275–310; and Adrienne Rich, "Notes Toward a Politics of Location," in Adrienne Rich *Blood, Bread and Poetry: Selected Prose, 1979–1985* (New York: Norton, 1986), 210–31.

22. Among the works I have found extremely helpful in this regard, see Stuart Hall, "Race, Articulation"; Centre for Contemporary Cultural Studies, *The Empire Strikes Back;* Michael Omi and Howard Winant, *Racial Formation in the United States: From the 1960s to the 1980s* (New York: Routledge and Kegan Paul, 1986); Cornel West, "Race and Social Theory: Towards a Genealogical Materialist Analysis," in *The Year Left, 2, Towards a Rainbow Socialism—Essays on Race, Ethnicity, Class, and Gender,* ed. Mike Davis et al. (London: Verso, 1987), 74–90; Paul Gilroy, *There Ain't No Black in the Union Jack* (London: Hutchinson, 1987); David Theo Goldberg, ed. *Anatomy of Racism* (Minneapolis: University of Minnesota Press, 1990).

23. Omi and Winant, *Racial Formation,* 3.

24. See, for example, Virginia R. Dominguez, *White by Definition: Social Classification in Creole Louisiana* (New Brunswick, N.J.: Rutgers University Press, 1986); Peggy Pascoe, "Race, Gender, and Intercultural Relations: The Case of Interracial Marriage," *Frontiers* 12, no. 1 (Summer 1991).

25. I am very much indebted to the work of Michael Omi and Howard Winant (in *Racial Formation*) for their periodization of U.S. race discourse. However, my analysis diverges from theirs in a range of ways, including the names I have given to specific periods or tendencies, my emphasis on the continued salience of "essentialist racism," and my focus on daily life rather than on intellectual movements, political processes, and social movements.

26. Omi and Winant, *Racial Formation,* 14–15.

27. Ibid., 14–24.

28. Ibid., 25–51.

29. Ibid., 4.

30. Toni Cade, *The Black Woman: An Anthology* (New York: Mentor, 1970); Sara Evans, *Personal Politics: The Origins of the Women's Liberation Movement in the Civil Rights Movement and the New Left* (New York: Vintage, 1980); Paula Giddings, *When and Where I Enter: The Impact of Black Women on Race and Sex in America* (New York: Bantam, 1984); Alma Garcia, "The Development of Chicana Feminist Discourse, 1970–1980," in *Unequal Sisters,* ed. DuBois and Ruiz, 418–31.

31. The term "color-blindness" is in some ways convenient because it is commonly used. I find it troubling, however, partly because it places a value judgment on physical disability, and partly because it offers a quasi-physiological description of what is in fact a complex of social and political processes. Moreover, as I argue in later chapters of this book, differences of racial identity and their connections to positions of dominance and subordination are, for the most part, evaded within this discursive repertoire rather than literally not seen.

32. See, for example, Cornel West, "Race and Social Theory."

33. I am indebted to Chetan Bhatt for suggesting to me the term "repertoire."

8

Privilege Axis Two: Male Privilege

HOW MEN HAVE (A) SEX

AN ADDRESS TO COLLEGE STUDENTS

John Stoltenberg

In the human species, how many sexes are there?

Answer A: There are two sexes.
Answer B: There are three sexes.
Answer C: There are four sexes.
Answer D: There are seven sexes.
Answer E: There are as many sexes as there are people.

I'd like to take you, in an imaginary way, to look at a different world, some-where else in the universe, a place inhabited by a life form that very much re-sembles us. But these creatures grow up with a peculiar knowledge. They know that they have been born in an infinite variety. They know, for instance, that in their genetic material they are born with hundreds of different chromosome formations at the point in each cell that we would say determines their "sex." These creatures don't just come in XX or XY; they also come in XXY and XYY and XXX plus a long list of "mosaic" variations in which some cells in a creature's body have one combination and other cells have another. Some of these creatures are born with chromosomes that aren't even quite X or Y be-cause a little bit of one chromosome goes and gets joined to another. There are hundreds of different combinations, and though all are not fertile, quite a number them are. The creatures in this world enjoy their individuality; they delight in the fact that they are not divisible into distinct categories. So when another newborn arrives with an esoterically rare chromosomal formation, there is a little celebration: "Aha," they say, "another sign that we are each unique."

These creatures also live with the knowledge that they are born with a vast range of genital formations. Between their legs are tissue structures that vary along a continuum, from clitorises with a vulva through all possible combinations and gradations to penises with a scrotal sac. These creatures live with an understanding that their genitals all developed prenatally from exactly the same little nub of embryonic tissue called a genital tubercle, which grew and developed under the influence of varying amounts of the hormone androgen. These creatures honor and respect everyone's natural-born genitalia—including what we would describe as a microphallus or a clitoris several inches long. What these creatures find amazing and precious is that because everyone's genitals stem from the same embryonic tissue, the nerves inside all their genitals got wired very much alike, so these nerves of touch just go crazy upon contact in a way that resonates completely between them. "My gosh," they think, "you must feel something in your genital tubercle that intensely resembles what I'm feeling in my genital tubercle." Well, they don't exactly *think* that in so many words; they're actually quite heavy into their feeling at that point; but they do feel very connected—throughout all their wondrous variety.

I could go on. I could tell you about the variety of hormones that course through their bodies in countless different patterns and proportions, both before birth and throughout their lives—the hormones that we call "sex hormones" but that they call "individuality inducers." I could tell you how these creatures think about reproduction: For part of their lives, some of them are quite capable of gestation, delivery, and lactation; and for part of their lives, some of them are quite capable of insemination; and for part or all of their lives, some of them are not capable of any of those things—so these creatures conclude that it would be silly to lock anyone into a lifelong category based on a capability variable that may or may not be utilized and that in any case changes over each lifetime in a fairly uncertain and idiosyncratic way. These creatures are not oblivious to reproduction; but nor do they spend their lives constructing a self-definition around their variable reproductive capacities. They don't have to because what is truly unique about these creatures is that they are capable of having a sense of personal identity without struggling to fit into a group identity based on how they were born. These creatures are quite happy, actually. They don't worry about sorting *other* creatures into categories, so they don't have to worry about whether they are measuring up to some category they themselves are supposed to belong to.

These creatures, of course, have sex. Rolling and rollicking and robust sex, and sweaty and slippery and sticky sex, and trembling and quaking and tumultuous sex, and tender and tingling and transcendent sex. They have sex fingers to fingers. They have sex belly to belly. They have sex genital tubercle to genital tubercle. They *have* sex. They do not have *a* sex. In their erotic lives, they are not required to act out their status in a category system—because there *is* no category system. There are no sexes to belong to, so sex between creatures is free to be between genuine individuals—not representatives of a category. They have sex. They do not have a sex. Imagine life like that.

Perhaps you have guessed the point of this science fiction: Anatomically, each creature in the imaginary world I have been describing could be an identical twin of every human being on earth. These creatures, in fact, *are us*—in every way except socially and politically. The way they are born is the way we are born. And we are not born belonging to one or the other of two sexes. We are born into a physiological continuum on which there is no discrete and definite point that you can call "male" and no discrete and definite point that you can call "female." If you look at all the variables in nature that are said to determine human "sex," you can't possibly find one that will unequivocally split the species into two. Each of the so-called criteria of sexedness is itself a continuum—including chromosomal variables, genital and gonadal variations, reproductive capacities, endocrinological proportions, and any other criterion you could think of. Any or all of these different variables may line up in any number of ways, and all of the variables may vary independently of one another.[1]

What does all this mean? It means, first of all a logical dilemma: Either human "male" and human "female" actually exist in nature as fixed and discrete entities and you can credibly base an entire social and political system on those absolute natural categories, or else the variety of human sexedness if infinite. As Andrea Dworkin wrote in 1974:

> The discovery is, of course, that "man" and "woman" are fictions, caricatures, cultural constructs. As models they are reductive, totalitarian, inappropriate to human becoming. As roles they are static, demeaning to the female, dead-ended for male and female both.[2]

The conclusion is inescapable:

> *We are, clearly, a multisexed species which has its sexuality spread along a vast continuum where the elements called male and female are not discrete.*[3]

"*We are . . . a multisexed species.*" I first read those words a little over ten years ago—and that liberating recognition saved my life.

All the time I was growing up, I knew that there was something really problematical in my relationship to manhood. Inside, deep inside, I never believed I was fully male—I never believed I was growing up enough of a man. I believed that someplace out there, in other men, there was something that was genuine authentic all-American manhood—the real stuff—but I didn't have it: not enough of it to convince *me* anyway, even if I managed to be fairly convincing to those around me. I felt like an impostor, like a fake. I agonized a lot about not feeling male enough, and I had no idea then how much I was not alone.

Then I read those words—those words that suggested to me for the first time that the notion of manhood is a cultural delusion, a baseless belief, a false front, a house of cards. It's not true. The category I was trying so desperately to belong to, to be a member of in good standing—it doesn't exist. Poof. Now you see it, now you don't. Now you're terrified you're not really part of it; now you're free, you don't have to worry anymore. However removed you feel inside from "authentic manhood," it doesn't matter. What matters is the center inside yourself—and how you live, and how you treat people, and what you can contribute as you pass through life on this earth, and how honestly you love, and how carefully you make choices. Those are the things that really matter. Not whether you're a real man. There's no such thing.

The idea of the male sex is like the idea of an Aryan race. The Nazis believed in the idea of an Aryan race—they believed that the Aryan race really exists, physically, in nature—and they put a great deal of effort into making it real. The Nazis believed that from the blond hair and blue eyes occurring naturally in the human species, they could construe the existence of a separate *race*—a distinct category of human beings that was unambiguously rooted in the natural order of things. But traits do not a race make; traits only make traits. For the idea to be real that these physical traits comprised a race, the race had to be socially constructed. The Nazis inferiorized and exterminated those they defined as "non-Aryan." With that, the notion of an Aryan race began to seem to come true. That's how there could be a political entity known as an Aryan race, and that's how there could be for some people a personal, subjective sense that they belonged to it. This happened through hate and force, through violence and victimization, through treating millions of people as things, then exterminating them. The belief system shared by people who believed they were all Aryan could not exist apart from that force and violence. The force and violence created a racial class system, *and* it created those people's membership in the race considered "superior." The force and violence served their class interest in large part because it created and maintained the class itself. But the idea of an Aryan race could never become metaphysically true, despite all the violence unleashed to create it, because there simply *is* no Aryan race. There is only the idea of it—and the consequences of trying to make it seem real. The male sex is very like that.

10   Penises and ejaculate and prostate glands occur in nature, but the notion that these anatomical traits comprise a sex—a discrete class, separate and distinct, metaphysically divisible form some other sex, *the* "other sex"—is simply that: a notion, an idea. The penises exist; the male sex does not. The male sex is socially constructed. It is a political entity that flourishes only through acts of force and sexual terrorism. Apart from the global inferiorization and subordination of those who are defined as "nonmale," the ideas of personal membership in the male sex class would have no recognizable meaning. It would make no sense. No one could be a member of it and no one would think they *should* be a member of it. There would be no male sex to belong to. That doesn't mean there wouldn't still be penises and ejaculate and prostate glands

and such. It simply means that the center of our selfhood would not be required to reside inside an utterly fictitious category—a category that only seems real to the extent that those outside it are put down.

We live in a world divided absolutely into two sexes, even though nothing about human nature warrants that division. We are sorted into one category or another at birth based solely on a visual inspection of our groins, and the only question that's asked is whether there's enough elongate tissue around your urethra so you can pee standing up. The presence or absence of a long-enough penis is the primary criterion for separating who's to grow up male from who's to grow up female. And among all the ironies in that utterly whimsical and arbitrary selection process is the fact that *anyone* can pee both sitting down and standing up.

Male sexual identity is the conviction or belief, held by most people born with penises, that they are male and not female, that they belong to the male sex. In a society predicated on the notion that there are two "opposite" and "complementary" sexes, this idea not only makes sense, it *becomes* sense; the very idea of a male sexual identity produces sensation, produces the meaning of sensation, becomes the meaning of how one's body feels. The sense and the sensing of a male sexual identity is at once mental and physical, at once public and personal. Most people born with a penis between their legs grow up aspiring to feel and act unambiguously male, longing to belong to the sex that is male and daring not to belong to the sex that is not, and feeling the urgency for a visceral and constant verification of their male sexual identity—for a fleshy connection to manhood—as the driving force of their life. The drive does not originate in the anatomy. The sensations derive from the idea. The idea gives the feelings social meaning; the idea determines which sensations shall be sought.

People born with penises must strive to make the idea of male sexual identity personally real by doing certain deeds, actions that are valued and chosen because they produce the desired feeling of belonging to a sex that is male and not female. Male sexual identity is experienced only in sensation and action, in feeling and doing, in eroticism and ethics. The feeling of belonging to a male sex encompasses both sensations that are explicitly "sexual" and those that are not ordinarily regarded as such. And there is a tacit social value system according to which certain acts are chosen because they make an individual's sexedness feel real and certain other acts are eschewed because they numb it. That value system is the ethics of male sexual identity—and it may well be the social origin of all injustice.

Each person experiences the idea of sexual identity as more or less real, more or less certain, more or less true, depending on two very personal phenomena: one's feelings and one's acts. For many people, for instance, the act of fucking makes their sexual identity feel more real than it does at other times, and they can predict from experience that this feeling of greater certainty will last for at least a while after each time they fuck. Fucking is not the only such act, and not only so-called sex acts can result in feelings of certainty about sexual identity; but the act of fucking happens to be a very good example of the correlation between *doing* a specific act in a specific way and *sensing* the specificity of the sexual identity to which one aspires. A person can decide to do certain acts and not others just because some acts will have the payoff of a feeling of greater certainty about sexual identity and others will give the feedback of a feeling of less. The transient reality of one's sexual identity, a person can know, is always a function of what one does and how one's acts make one feel. The feeling and the act must conjoin for the idea of the sexual identity to come true. We all keep longing for surety of our sexedness that we can feel; we all keep striving through our actions to make the idea real.

15   In human nature, eroticism is not differentiated between "male" and "female" in any clear-cut way. There is too much to a continuum, too great a resemblance. From all that we know, the penis and the clitoris are identically "wired" to receive and retransmit sensations from throughout the body, and the congestion of blood within the lower torso during sexual excitation makes all bodies sensate in a remarkably similar manner. Simply put, we all share all the nerve and blood-vessel layouts that are associated with sexual arousal. Who can say, for instance, that the penis would not experience sensations the way that a clitoris does if this were not a world in which the penis is supposed to be hell-bent on penetration? By the time most men make it through puberty, they believe that erotic sensation is supposed to *begin* in their penis; that if engorgement has not begun there then nothing else in their body will heat up either. There is a massive interior dissociation from sensations that do not explicitly remind a man that his penis is still there. And not only there as sensate, but *functional and operational.*

So much of most men's sexuality is tied up with gender-actualizing—with feeling like a real man—that they can scarcely recall an erotic sensation that had no gender-specific cultural meaning. As most men age, they learn to cancel out and deny erotic sensations that are not specifically linked to what they think a real man is supposed to feel. An erotic sensation unintentionally experienced in a receptive, communing mode—instead of in an aggressive and controlling and violative mode, for instance—can shut down sensory systems in an instant. An erotic sensation unintentionally linked to the "wrong" sex of another person can similarly mean sudden numbness. Acculturated male sexuality has a built-in fail-safe: Either its political context reifies manhood or the experience cannot be felt as sensual. Either the act creates his sexedness or it does not compute as a sex act. So he tenses up, pumps up, steels himself against the dread that he be found not male enough. And his dread is not stupid; for he sees what happens to people when they are treated as nonmales.

My point is that sexuality does not *have* a gender; it *creates* a gender. It creates for those who adapt to it in narrow and specified ways the confirmation for the individual of belonging to the idea of one sex or the other. So-called male sexuality is a learned connection between specific physical sensations and the idea of a male sexual identity. To achieve this male sexual identity requires that an individual *identify with* the class of males—that is, accept as one's own the values and interests of the class. A fully realized male sexual identity also requires *nonidentification with* that which is perceived to be

nonmale, or female. A male must not identify with females; he must not associate with females in feeling, interests, or action. His identity as a member of
the sex class men absolutely depends on the extent to which he repudiates
the values and interests of the sex class "women."

I think somewhere inside us all, we have always known something about the
relativity of gender. Somewhere inside us all, we know that our bodies harbor
deep resemblances, that we are wired inside to respond in a profound harmony to the resonance of eroticism inside the body of someone near us. Phys-
iologically, we are far more alike than different. The tissue structures that have
become labial and clitoral or scrotal and penile have not forgotten their common ancestry. Their sensations are of the same source. The nerve networks
and interlock of capillaries throughout our pelvises electrify and engorge as if
plugged in together and pumping as one. That's what we feel when we feel
one another's feelings. That's what can happen during sex that is mutual,
equal, reciprocal, profoundly communing.

So why is it that some of us with penises think it's sexy to pressure someone into having sex against their will? Some of us actually get harder the
harder the person resists. Some of us with penises actually believe that some
of us without penises want to be raped. And why is it that some of us with
penises think it's sexy to treat other people as objects, as things to be bought
and sold, impersonal bodies to be possessed and consumed for our sexual
pleasure? Why is it that some of us with penises are aroused by sex tinged
with rape, and sex commoditized by pornography? Why do so many of us
with penises want such antisexual sex?

There's a reason, of course. We have to make a lie seem real. It's a very big   *20*
lie. We each have to do our part. Otherwise the lie will look like the lie that it
is. Imagine the enormity of what we each must do to keep the lie alive in each
of us. Imagine the awesome challenge we face to make the lie a social fact. It's
a lifetime mission for each of us born with a penis: to have sex in such a way
that the male sex will seem real—and so that we'll feel like a real part of it.

We all grow up knowing exactly what kind of sex that is. It's the kind of sex
you can have when you pressure or bully someone else into it. So it's a kind of
sex that makes your will more important than theirs. That kind of sex helps the
lie a lot. That kind of sex makes you feel like someone important and it turns
the other person into someone unimportant. That kind of sex makes you feel
real, not like a fake. It's a kind of sex men have in order to feel like a real man.

There's also the kind of sex you can have when you force someone and
hurt someone and cause someone suffering and humiliation. Violence and
hostility in sex help the lie a lot too. Real men are aggressive in sex. Real
men get cruel in sex. Real men use their penises like weapons in sex. Real men
leave bruises. Real men think it's a turn-on to threaten harm. A brutish push
can make an erection feel really hard. That kind of sex helps the lie a lot. That
kind of sex makes you feel like someone who is powerful and it turns the
other person into someone powerless. That kind of sex makes you feel dangerous and in control—like you're fighting a war with an enemy and if you're

mean enough you'll win but if you let up you'll lose your manhood. It's a kind of sex men have *in order to have* a manhood.

There's also the kind of sex you can have when you pay your money into a profit system that grows rich displaying and exploiting the bodies and body parts of people without penises for the sexual entertainment of people with. Pay your money and watch. Pay your money and imagine. Pay your money and get real turned on. Pay your money and jerk off. That kind of sex helps the lie a lot. It helps support an industry committed to making people with penises believe that people without are sluts who just want to be ravished and reviled—an industry dedicated to maintaining a sex-class system in which men believe themselves sex machines and men believe women are mindless fuck tubes. That kind of sex helps the lie a lot. It's like buying Krugerrands as a vote of confidence for white supremacy in South Africa.

And there's one more thing: That kind of sex makes the lie indelible— burns it onto your retinas right adjacent to your brain—makes you remember it and makes your body respond to it and so it makes you believe that the lie is in fact true: You really are a real man. That slavish and submissive creature there spreading her legs is really not. You and that creature have nothing in common. That creature is an alien inanimate thing, but your penis is com- pletely real and alive. Now you can come. Thank god almighty—you have a sex at last.

25   Now, I believe there are many who are sick at heart over what I have been describing. There are many who were born with penises who want to stop collaborating in the sex-class system that needs us to need these kinds of sex. I believe some of you want to stop living out the big lie, and you want to know how. Some of you long to touch truthfully. Some of you want sexual relation- ships in your life that are about intimacy and joy, ecstasy and equality—not antagonism and alienation. So what I have to say next I have to say to you.

When you use sex to have a sex, the sex you have is likely to make you feel crummy about yourself. But when you have sex in which you are not struggling with your partner in order to act out "real manhood," the sex you have is more likely to bring you close.

This means several specific things:

1. *Consent is absolutely essential.* If both you and your partner have not freely given your informed consent to the sex you are about to have, you can be quite certain that the sex you go ahead and have will make you strangers to each other. How do you know if there's con- sent? You ask. You ask again if you're sensing any doubt. Consent to do one thing isn't consent to do another. So you keep communicat- ing, in clear words. And you don't take anything for granted.

2. *Mutuality is absolutely essential.* Sex is not something you do *to* some- one. Sex is not a one-way transitive verb, with a subject, you, and an object, the body you're with. Sex that is mutual is not about doing and being done to; it's about being-with and feeling-with. You have

to really be there to experience what is happening between and within the two of you—between every part of you and within both your whole bodies. It's a matter of paying attention—as if you are paying attention to someone who matters.

3. *Respect is absolutely essential.* In the sex that you have, treat your partner like a real person who, like you, has real feelings—feelings that matter as much as your own. You may or may not love—but you must always respect. You must respect the integrity of your partner's body. It is not yours for the taking. It belongs to someone real. And you do not get ownership of your partner's body just because you are having sex—or just because you have had sex.

For those who are closer to the beginning of your sex lives than to the middle or the end, many things are still changing for you about how you have sex, with whom, why or why not, what you like or dislike, what kind of sex you want to have more of. In the next few years, you are going to discover and decide a lot. I say "discover" because no one can tell you what you're going to find out about yourself in relation to sex—and I say "decide" because virtually without knowing it you are going to be laying down habits and patterns that will probably stay with you for the rest of your life. You're at a point in your sexual history that you will never be at again. You don't know what you don't know yet. And yet you are making choices whose consequences for your particular sexuality will be sealed years from now.

I speak to you as someone who is closer to the middle of my sexual history. As I look back, I see that I made many choices that I didn't know I was making. And as I look at men who are near my age, I see that what has happened to many of them is that their sex lives are stuck in deep ruts that began as tiny fissures when they were young. So I want to conclude by identifying what I believe are three of the most important decisions about your sexuality that you can make when you are at the beginning of your sexual history. However difficult these choices may seem to you now, I promise you they will only get more difficult as you grow older. I realize that what I'm about to give is some quite unsolicited nuts-and-bolts advice. But perhaps it will spare you, later on in your lives, some of the obsessions and emptiness that have claimed that sexual histories of many men just a generation before you. Perhaps it will not help, I don't know; but I hope very much that it will.

First, you can start choosing now not to let your sexuality be manipulated by the   30
pornography industry. I've heard many unhappy men talk about how they are so hooked on pornography and obsessed with it that they are virtually incapable of a human erotic contact. And I have heard even more men talk about how, when they do have sex with someone, the pornography gets in the way, like a mental obstacle, like a barrier preventing a full experience of what's really happening between them and their partner. The sexuality that the pornography industry needs you to have is not about communicating and caring; it's about "pornographizing" people—objectifying and conquering them, not being with them as a person. You do not have to buy into it.

Second, you can start choosing now not to let drugs and alcohol numb you through your sex life. Too many men, as they age, become incapable of having sex with a clear head. But you need your head clear—to make clear choices, to send clear messages, to read clearly what's coming in on a clear channel between you and your partner. Sex is no time for your awareness to sign off. And another thing: Beware of relying on drugs or alcohol to give you "permission" to have sex, or to trick your body into feeling something that it's not, or so you won't have to take responsibility for what you're feeling or for the sex that you're about to have. If you can't take sober responsibility for your part in a sexual encounter, you probably shouldn't be having it—and you certainly shouldn't be zonked out of your mind *in order* to have it.

Third, you can start choosing now not to fixate on fucking—especially if you'd really rather have sex in other, noncoital ways. Sometimes men have coital sex—penetration and thrusting then ejaculating inside someone—not because they particularly feel like it but because they feel they *should* feel like it: It's expected that if you're the man, you fuck. And if you don't fuck, you're not a man. The corollary of this cultural imperative is that if two people don't have intercourse, they have not had real sex. That's baloney, of course, but the message comes down hard, especially inside men's heads: Fucking is *the* sex act, the act in which you act out what sex is supposed to be—and what sex you're supposed to be.

Like others born with a penis, I was born into a sex-class system that requires my collaboration every day, even in how I have sex. Nobody told me, when I was younger, that I could have noncoital sex and that it would be fine. Actually, much better than fine. Nobody told me about an incredible range of other erotic possibilities for mutual lovemaking—including rubbing body to body, then coming body to body; including multiple, nonejaculatory orgasms; including the feeling you get when even the tiniest place where you and your partner touch becomes like a window through which great tidal storms of passion ebb and flow, back and forth. Nobody told me about the sex you can have when you stop working at having a sex. My body told me, finally. And I began to trust what my body was telling me more than the lie I was supposed to make real.

I invite you too to resist the lie. I invite you too to become an erotic traitor to male supremacy.

NOTES

1. My source for the foregoing information about so-called sex determinants in the human species is a series of interviews I conducted with the sexologist Dr. John Money in Baltimore, Maryland, in 1979 for an article I wrote called "The Multisex Theorem," which was published in a shortened version as "Future Genders" in *Omni* magazine, May 1980, pp. 67–73 ff.
2. Dworkin, Andrea. *Woman Hating* (New York: Dutton, 1974), p. 174.
3. Dworkin, *Woman Hating,* p. 183 (Italics in original).

COMING APART

Alice Walker

These three paragraphs by Alice Walker tell why she wrote Coming Apart:

"Many Black men see pornography as progressive because the white woman, formerly taboo, is, via pornography, made available to them. Not simply available, but in a position of vulnerability to all men. These availability and vulnerability diminishes the importance and power of color among men and permits a bonding with white men as men, which Black men, striving to be equal, not content with being different, apparently desire.

"Many Black women also consider pornography progressive and are simply interested in equal time. But in a racist society, where Black women are on the bottom, there is no such thing as equal time or equal quality of exposure. It is not unheard of to encounter 'erotica' or pornography in which a Black woman and a white woman are both working in 'a house of ill-repute,' but the Black woman also doubles as the white woman's maid.[1] The Black man who finds himself 'enjoying' pornography of this sort faces a split in himself that allows a solidarity of gender but promotes a rejection of race. 'Beulah, peel me a grape' has done untold harm to us all.

"I have, as we all have, shared a part of my life—since the day I was born—with men whose concept of woman is a degraded one. I have also experienced, like the woman in this piece, Forty-second Street; I felt demeaned by the selling of bodies, threatened by the violence, and furious that my daughter must grow up in society in which the debasement of women is actually enjoyed."

A middle-aged husband comes home after a long day at the office. His wife greets him at the door with the news that dinner is ready. He is grateful. First, however, he must use the bathroom. In the bathroom, sitting of the commode, he opens up the *Jiveboy* magazine he has brought home in his briefcase. There are a couple of Jivemate poses that particularly arouse him. He studies the young women—blonde, perhaps (the national craze), with elastic waists and inviting eyes—and strokes his penis. At the same time, his bowels stir with the desire to defecate. He is in the bathroom a luxurious ten minutes. He emerges spent, relaxed—hungry for dinner.

His wife, using the bathroom later, comes upon the slightly damp magazine. She picks it up with mixed emotions. She is a brownskin woman with black hair and eyes. She looks at the white blondes and brunettes. Will he be thinking of them, she wonders, when he is making love to me? Will he be

"Why do you need these?" she asks.

"They mean nothing," he says.

---

[1]Ed. Note: This is the situation in the movie version of *The Story of O.*

5   "But they hurt me somehow," she says.

"You are being (a) silly, (b) a prude, and (c) ridiculous," he says. "You know I love you."

She cannot say to him: But they are not me, those women. She cannot say she is jealous of pictures on a page. That she feels invisible. Rejected. Overlooked. She says instead, to herself: He is right. I will grow up. Adjust. Swim with the tide.

He thinks he understands her, what she has been trying to say. It is *Jiveboy,* he thinks, the white women.

Next day he brings home *Jivers,* a Black magazine, filled with bronze and honey-colored women. He is in the bathroom another luxurious ten minutes.

10   She stands, holding the magazine: on the cover are the legs and shoes of a well-dressed Black man, carrying a briefcase and a rolled *Wall Street Journal* in one hand. At his feet—she turns the magazine cover around and around to figure out how exactly the pose is accomplished—there is a woman, a brown-skin woman like herself, twisted and contorted in such a way that her head is not even visible. Only her glistening body—her back and derriere—so that she looks like a human turd at the man's feet.

He is on a business trip to New York. He has brought his wife along. He is eagerly sharing Forty-second Street with her. "Look!" he says, "how *free* everything is! A far cry from Bolton!" (The small town they are from.) He is elated to see the blonde, spaced-out hookers, with their Black pimps, trooping down the street. Elated at the shortness of the Black hooker's dresses, their long hair, inevitably false and blonde. She walks somehow behind him, so that he will encounter these wonders first. He does not notice until he turns a corner that she has stopped in front of a window that has caught her eye. While she is standing alone, looking, two separate pimps ask her what stable she is in or if in fact she is in one. Or simply "You workin'?"

He struts back and takes her elbow. Looks hard for the compliment implied in these questions, then shares it with his wife: *"You* know you're foxy?"

She is immovable. Her face suffering and wondering. "But look," she says, pointing. Four large plastic dolls—one a skinny Farrah Fawcett (or so the doll looks to her) posed for anal inspection; one, an oriental, with her eyes, strangely, closed, but her mouth, a pouting red suction cup, open; an enormous eskimo woman—with fur around her neck and ankles, and vagina; and a Black woman dressed entirely in a leopard skin, complete with tail. The dolls are life-size, and the efficiency of their rubber genitals is explained in detail on a card visible through the plate glass.

For her this is the stuff of nightmares because all the dolls are smiling. She will see them for the rest of her life. For him the sight is also shocking, but arouses a prurient curiosity. He will return, another time, alone. Meanwhile, he must prevent her from seeing such things, he resolves, whisking her briskly off the street.

Later, in their hotel room, she watches TV as two Black women sing their   *15*
latest hits: the first woman, dressed in a gold dress (because her song is now
"solid gold!"), is nonetheless wearing a chain around her ankle—the wife
imagines she sees a chain—because the woman is singing: "Free me from my
freedom, chain me to a tree!"

"What do you think that?" she asks her husband.

"She's a fool," says he.

But when the second woman sings: "Ready, aim, fire, my name is desire,"
with guns and rockets going off all around her, he thinks the line "Shoot me
with your love!" explains everything.

She is despondent.

She looks in a mirror at her plump brown and blackskin body, crinkly   *20*
hair and black eyes and decides, foolishly, that she is not beautiful. And that
she is not hip, either. Among her other problems is the fact that she does not
like the word "nigger" used by anyone at all, and is afraid of marijuana. These
restraints, she feels, make her old, too much like her own mother, who loves
sex (she has lately learned) but is highly religious and, for example, thinks
cardplaying wicked and alcohol deadly. Her husband would not consider her
mother sexy, she thinks. Since she herself is aging, this thought frightens her.
But, surprisingly, while watching herself become her mother in the mirror,
she discovers that *she* considers her mother—who carefully braids her average
length, average grade, graying hair every night before going to bed; the braids
her father still manages to fray during the night—*very* sexy.

At once she feels restored.

Resolves to fight.

"You're the only Black woman in the world that worries about any of
this stuff," he tells her, unaware of her resolve, and moody at her months of
silent studiousness.

She says, "Here, Colored Person, read this essay by Audre Lorde."

He hedges. She insists.   *25*

He comes to a line about Lorde "moving into sunlight against the body
of woman I love," and bridles. "Wait a minute," he says. "What kind of a name
is 'Audre' for a man? They must have meant 'André.' "

"It *is* the name of a woman," she says. "Read the rest of that page."

"No dyke can tell me anything," he says, flinging down the pages.

She has been calmly waiting for this. She brings in *Jiveboy* and *Jivers*. In
both, there are women eating women they don't even know. She takes up the
essay and reads:

This brings me to the last consideration of the erotic. To share
the power of each other's feelings is different from using
another's feelings as we would use a Kleenex. And when we
look the other way from our experience, erotic or otherwise,

we use rather than share the feelings of those others who participate in the experience with us. And use without consent of the used is abuse.

30   He looks at her with resentment, because she is reading this passage over again, silently, absorbedly, to herself, holding the pictures of the phony lesbians (a favorite, though unexamined, turn on) absentmindedly on her lap. He realizes he can never have her again sexually, the way he has had her since their second year of marriage, as though her body belonged to someone else. He sees, down the road, the dissolution of the marriage, a constant search for more perfect bodies, or dumber wives. He feels oppressed by her incipient struggle, and feels somehow as if her struggle to change the pleasure he has enjoyed is a violation of his rights.

Now she is busy pasting Audre Lorde's words on the cabinet over the kitchen sink.

When they make love she tries to look him in the eye, but he refuses to return her gaze.

For the first time he acknowledges the awareness that the pleasure of coming without her is bitter and lonely. He thinks of eating stolen candy alone, behind the barn. And yet, he thinks greedily, it is better than nothing, which he considers her struggle's benefit to him.

The next day she is reading another essay when he comes home from work. It is called "A Quite Subversion," and is by Luisah Teish. "Another dyke?" he asks.

35   "Another one of your sisters," she replies, and begins to read aloud, even before he's had dinner:

> During the Black Power Movement, much cultural education was focused on the Black physique. One of the accomplishments of that period was the popularization of African hairstyles and the Natural. Along with (the Natural) came a new self-image and way of relating. It suggested that Black people should relate to each other in respectful and supportive ways. Then the movie industry put out *Superfly,* and the Lord Jesus Look and the Konked head, and an accompanying attitude ran rampant in the Black community. . . . Films like *Shaft* and *Lady Sings the Blues* portray Black "heroes" as cocaine-snorting, fast-life fools. In these movies a Black woman is always caught in a web of violence. . . .
>
> A popular Berkeley, California, theater featured a pornographic movie entitled *Slaves of Love.* Its advertisement portrayed two Black women, naked, in chains, and a white man standing over them with a whip! How such *racist* pornographic material escapes the eye of Black activists presents a problem. . . .

Typically, he doesn't even hear the statement about the women. "What does the bitch know about the Black Power Movement?" he fumes. He is angry at

his wife for knowing him so long and so well. She knows, for instance, that because of the Black Power Movement (and really because of the Civil Rights
Movement before it) and not because he was at all active in it—he holds the
bourgeois job he has. She remembers when his own hair was afro-ed. Now it is
loosely curled. It occurs to him that, because she knows him as he was, he cannot make love to her as she is. Cannot, in fact, *love* her as she is. There is a way
in which, in some firmly repressed corner of his mind, he considers his wife to
be *still* Black, whereas he feels himself to have moved to some other plane.

(This insight, a glimmer of which occurs to him, frightens him so much
that he will resist it for several years. Should he accept it at once, however unsettling, it would help him understand the illogic of his acceptance of pornography used against Black women: that he has detached himself from his own
blackness in attempting to identify Black women only by their sex.)

The wife has never considered herself a feminist—though she is, of
course, a "womanist." A "womanist" is a feminist, only more common.[2] So
she is surprised when her husband attacks her as a "women's liber," a "white
women's lackey," a "pawn" in the hands of Gloria Steinem, an incipient bra-
burner! What possible connection could there be, he wants to know, between
her and white women—those overprivileged hags, now (he's recently read in
Newsweek) marching and preaching their puritanical horseshit up and down
Times Square!

(He remembers only the freedom he felt there, not her long pause before
the window of the plastic doll shop.) And if she is going to make a lot of new
connections with dykes and whites, where will that leave him, the Black man,
the most brutalized and oppressed human being on the face of the earth? (*Is
it because he can now ogle white women in freedom and she has no similar outlet of
expression that he thinks of her as still Black and himself as something else?* This
thought underlines what he is actually saying, and his wife is unaware of it.)
Didn't she know it is over these very same white bodies he has been lynched
in the past, and is lynched still, by the police and the U.S. prison system,
dozens of times a year *even now!?*

The wife has cunningly saved Tracey A. Gardner's essay for just this moment. Because Tracey A. Gardner has thought about it *all,* not just presently,
but historically, and she is clear about all the abuse being done to herself as a

---

[2] "Womanist" encompasses "feminist" as it is defined in Webster's, but also means *instinctively* pro-
woman. It is not in the dictionary at all. Nonetheless, it has a strong root in Black women's culture.
It comes (to me) from the word "womanish," a word our mothers used to describe, and attempt to
inhibit, strong, outrageous or outspoken behavior when we were children: "You're acting *womanish!*" A labeling that failed, for the most part, to keep us from acting "womanish" whenever we
could, that is to say, like our mothers themselves, and like other women we admired.

An advantage of using "womanist" is that, because it is from my own culture, I needn't
preface it with the word "Black" (an awkward necessity and a problem I have with the word
"feminist"), since Blackness is implicit in the term; just as for white women there is apparently
no felt need to preface "feminist" with the word "white," since the word "feminist" is accepted
as coming out of white women's culture.

Black person and as a woman, and she is bold and she is cold—she is furious. The wife, given more to depression and self-abnegation than to fury, basks in the fire of Gardner's high-spirited anger.

40   She begins to read:[3]

> Because from my point of view, racism is everywhere, includ-ing the Women's Movement, and the only time I really need to say something special about it is when I *don't* see it—and the first time that happens, I'll tell you about it.

The husband, surprised, thinks this very funny, not to say pertinent. He slaps his knee and sits up. He is dying to make some sort of positive dyke comment, but nothing comes to mind

> American slavery relied on the denial of the humanity of Black folks, on the undermining of our sense of nationhood and fam-ily, on the stripping away of the Black man's role as protector and provider, and on the structuring of Black men and women into the American system of *white* male domination.

"In other words," she says, "white men think they have to be on top. Other men have been known to savor life from other positions."

> The end of the Civil War brought the end of a certain "form" of slavery for Black folks. It also brought the end of any "job security" and the loss of the protection of their white enslaver. Blacks were now free game, and the terrorization and humilia-tion of Black people, especially Black men, began. Now the Black man could have his family and prove his worth, but he had no way to support or protect them, or himself.

As she reads, he feels ashamed and senses his wife's wounded embarrass-ment, for him and for herself. For their history together. But doggedly, she continues to read:

> After the Civil War, "Popular justice" (which meant there usu-ally was no trial and no proof needed) began its reign in the form of the castration, burning at the stake, beheading, and lynching of Black men. As many as 5,000 white people turned out to witness these events, as though going to a celebration. *(She pauses, sighs: beheading?)* Over 2,000 Black men were lynched in the ten-year period from 1889–1899. There were also a number of Black women who were lynched. *(She reads this sentence quickly and forgets it.)* Over 50 percent of the lynched Black males were charged with rape or attempted rape.

---

[3] The excerpts that follow are taken from an earlier, longer version of Tracey A. Gardner's essay, "Racism in Pornography and the Women's Movement."

He cannot imagine a woman being lynched. He has never even considered the possibility. Perhaps this is why the image of a Black woman chained and bruised excites rather than horrifies him? It is the fact that the lynching of her body has never stopped that forces the wife, for the time being, to blot out the historical record. She is not prepared to connect her own husband with the continuation of that past.

She reads:

If a Black man had sex with a consenting white woman, it was rape. *(Why am I always reading about, thinking about, worrying about, my man having sex with white women? she thinks, despairingly, underneath the reading.)* If he insulted a white woman by looking at her, it was attempted rape.

"Yes," he says softly, as if in support of her dogged reading, "I've read Ida B.—what's her last name?" [4]

"By their lynching, the white man was showing that he hated the Black man carnally, biologically; he hated his color, his features, his genitals. Thus he attacked the Black man's body, and like a lover gone mad, maimed his flesh, violated him in the most intimate, pornographic fashion. . . ."

I believe that his obscene, inhuman treatment of Black men by white men . . . has a direct correlation to white men's increasingly obscene and inhuman treatment of women, particularly white women, in pornography and real life. White women, working toward their own strength and identity, their own sexuality and independence, have in a sense become "uppity niggers." As the Black man threatens the white man's masculinity and power, so now do women.

"That girl's onto something," says the husband, but thinks, for the first time in his life, that when he is not thinking of fucking white women—fantasizing over *Jiveboy* or clucking at them on the street—he is very often thinking of ways to degrade them. Then he thinks that, given his history as a Black man in America, it is not surprising that he has himself confused fucking them *with* degrading them. But what does that say about how he sees himself? This thought smothers his inward applause for Gardner, and instead he casts a bewildered, disconcerted look at his wife. He knows that to make love to his wife as she really is, as who she really is—indeed, to make love to any other human being as they really are—will require a soul-rendering look into himself, and the thought of this virtually straightens his hair.

---

[4] Ida B. Wells, also known as Ida Wells Barnett, Black radical investigative reporter and publisher of the Memphis-based *Free Speech*. She wrote *On Lynchings: A Red Record, Mob Rule in New Orleans: Southern Horrors* (New York: Arno Press, 1969; first published 1892), a brilliant analysis of lynching in America. Wells led the anti-lynching movement in this country.

His wife continues:

> Some Black men, full of the white man's perspective and val-
> ues, see the white woman or Blond Goddess as part of the
> American winning image. Sometimes when he is with the
> Black woman, he is ashamed of how she has been treated, and
> how he has been powerless, and that they have always had to
> work together and protect each other. (*Yes, she thinks, we were
> always all we had, until now.*)
>
> (*He thinks: We are all we have still, only now we can live without
> permitting ourselves to know this.*)
>
> Frantz Fanon said about white women, "By loving me she
> proves that I am worthy of white love. I am loved like a white
> man. I am a white man. I marry the culture, white beauty,
> white whiteness. When my restless hands caress those white
> breasts, they grasp white civilization and dignity and make
> them mine." (*She cannot believe he meant to write "white dignity."*)

She pauses, looks at her husband: "'So how does a Black woman feel
when her Black man leaves *Playboy* on the coffee table?'"

For the first time he understands fully a line his wife read the day before:
"This pornography industry's exploitation of the Black woman's body is *qualitatively* different from that of the white woman," because she is holding the
cover of *Jivers* out to him and asking: "What does this woman look like?"

50   What he has refused to see—because to see it would reveal yet another
area in which he is unable to protect or defend Black women—is that where
white women are depicted in pornography as "objects," Black women are depicted as animals. Where white women are at least depicted as human bodies
if not beings, Black women are depicted as shit.

He begins to feel sick. For he realizes that he has bought some if not all
of the advertisements about women, Black and white. And further, inevitably,
he has bought the advertisements about himself. In pornography the Black
man is portrayed as being capable of fucking anything . . . even a piece of shit.
He is defined solely by the size, readiness and unselectivity of his cock.

Still, he does not know how to make love without the fantasies fed to
him by movies and magazines. Those movies and magazines (whose character's pursuits are irrelevant or antithetical to his concerns) that have insinuated
themselves between him and his wife, so that the totality of her body, her entire corporeal reality is alien to him. Even to clutch her in lust is to automatically shut his eyes. Shut his eyes, and . . . he chuckles bitterly . . . dream of
England. For years he has been fucking himself.

At first, reading Lorde together, they reject celibacy. Then they discover
they need time apart to clear their heads. To search out damage. To heal. In

any case, she is unable to fake response—he is unwilling for her to do so. She goes away for a while. Left alone, he soon falls hungrily on the magazines he had thrown out. Strokes himself raw over the beautiful women, spread like so much melon (he begins to see how stereotypes transmute) before him. But he cannot refuse what he knows—or what he knows his wife knows, walking along a beach in some Black country where all the women are bleached and straightened and the men never look at themselves; and are ugly, in any case, in their imitation of white men.

Long before she returns he is reading her books and thinking of her— and of her struggles alone and his fear of sharing them—and when she returns, it is 60% *her* body that he moves against in the sun, her own Black skin affirmed in the brightness of his eyes.

9

Privilege Axis Three: Heterosexual Privilege

■░■░■

STRAIGHT TALK: MALE HETEROSEXUAL PRIVILEGE

Bruce Ryder[*]

Heterosexual men's relation to the movement for lesbian and gay liberation, like our relation to feminism, produces epistemological and political dilemmas. As members of an oppressor class, how can we contribute in good faith to the struggle to end heterosexist and sexist oppression? The dilemmas are real and troubling; in particular, if white heterosexual men's ("W.H.M.'s") ways of knowing and seeing the world have traditionally masqueraded as objective truth, how can we speak and act without reinscribing the epistemic and political dominance of our particular brand of masculinity? As a person committed to political struggles to overcome oppression in all its forms, I admittedly have a stake in believing that we progressive, white, straight men are not a collection of oxymorons.[1] My own view is that W.H.M.s *must* speak, that we have a responsibility to speak out against sexism and heterosexism. This involves, for example, relying upon and contributing to bodies of knowledge developed by feminist and gay theorists that have exposed the structures of domination by which heterosexual men are privileged, and the ways in which our privilege is sustained and rationalized in legal and other discourses. In doing so, we must speak and write with great care, acknowledging our privilege and using it and the authority that comes with it in a manner which is attentive to the limitations of our particular knowledge and experiences. We W.H.M.s have been speaking for others for too long—we have defined gender, sexual, racial, and other differences in unspeakable ways. In many contexts, it is time that we shut up and listened to the majority. But we not only have to learn to talk less about (before we have listened to) others, we also have to learn to talk more about ourselves and about the structures of domination that sustain our privilege. After all, masculinity is a problem. Heterosexuality is a problem. Male heterosexuality is double trouble.

My purpose below is to explore the dilemmas of our participation in anti-sexist and anti-heterosexist movements that result from our position of dual dominance captured in the notion of male heterosexual privilege. I will begin by outlining my understanding of the meanings of heterosexuality and heterosexual privilege, and of how they are sustained and rationalized in legal discourse. I will conclude with some thoughts which I hope will be useful to other heterosexual men in thinking through our position regarding the struggles to end sexist and heterosexist oppression.

HETEROSEXUALITY, HETEROSEXUAL PRIVILEGE AND THE LAW

Heterosexuality as the Institutionalization of Dual Hierarchy

Many feminist theorists have identified heterosexuality as a political institution which disempowers women.[2] In Catharine MacKinnon's words,

> [s]exuality . . . is a form of power. Gender, as socially constructed, embodies it, not the reverse. Women and men are divided by gender, made into the sexes as we know them, by the social requirements of its dominant form, heterosexuality, which institutionalizes male sexual dominance and female submission.[3]

The gender hierarchy institutionalized in heterosexuality is supported and rationalized by sexism, a system of beliefs and practices premised on the assumption that natural and fundamental differences exist between men and women; for example, that men are naturally sexually dominant and women naturally sexually submissive.

Heterosexuality is also supported by heterosexism, the system of beliefs and practices which suppresses, denies, and penalizes homosexuality on the grounds that only sexual attraction to members of the opposite sex is natural and normal. The range of social, economic, and criminal mechanisms that create pressure to conform to the requirements of heterosexual desire have led feminists, following Adrienne Rich's influential essay,[4] to describe the institution of heterosexuality as "compulsory." Gay male theorists have demonstrated the necessity of exploring the ways in which heterosexism structures relationships of power among men, and creates pressure on all men to conform to the dominant form of male heterosexuality predicated, amongst other things, on the continuing objectification and subordination of women and gay men.[5] "[T]he proof of 'manhood' must be continuous. . . ."[6]

> The limits of "acceptable" masculinity are in part defined by
> comments like "What are you, a fag?" As boys and men we
> have heard such expressions and the words "queer," "faggot,"
> and "sissy" all our lives. These words encourage certain types
> of male behaviour and serve to define, regulate, and limit our
> lives, whether we consider ourselves straight or gay.[7]

On my understanding, informed by feminist and gay theorists, heterosexuality is founded on two fundamental oppositions constructed as hierarchies:
male/female and heterosexual/homosexual. Gender and sexual hierarchies
are explained as natural, not political, by sexism and heterosexism respectively.
These two ideologies combine to produce a ". . . model of gender intelligibil-
ity that assumes that for bodies to cohere and make sense there must be a stable sex expressed through a stable gender . . . that is oppositionally and
hierarchically defined through the compulsory practice of heterosexuality."[8]

5   In contrast to the naturalizing discourses of sexism and heterosexism,
gender and sexuality are understood in my analysis as historically and culturally specific socially constructed identities, subject to a constant dialectic of
challenge and redefinition. A stable sense of gender and sexuality in the binary system of heterosexuality can be maintained only by an ongoing process
of denial and exclusion. That means that the identity, for example, of male
heterosexuals needs to be constantly reaffirmed through the denial in themselves of homosexual desire and of traits gendered feminine. Thus the hatred
and fear directed by male heterosexuals at women and gays (misogyny and
homophobia respectively) can be understood as a product of male heterosexuals' fear of the unsettling presence of "the enemies within"—the "feminine"
and the homosexual in themselves.[9] In men, then, misogyny and homophobia are the most aggressive and violent manifestations of the psychic damage
caused by sexism and heterosexism.[10]

Some feminist theorists would not agree with the characterization of
heterosexuality as the institutionalization of dual hierarchy. For example, an
important and influential body of radical feminist thought sees gender and
sexual hierarchy as one and the same. As Catharine MacKinnon puts it,

> [i]f heterosexuality is the dominant gendered form of sexuality
> in a society where gender oppresses women through sex, sexu-
> ality and heterosexuality are essentially the same thing. This
> does not erase homosexuality, it merely means that sexuality in
> that form may be no less gendered.[11]

Radical feminist theorists committed to analyzing sexual hierarchy as a consequence of gender oppression have argued that lesbians are punished for resisting heterosexuality, and that gay men are punished for not participating fully
in its daily maintenance of women's subordination. In other words, the social
penalties imposed on lesbians and gay men can be understood as a response
to the gender treachery inherent in failing to adhere to the requirements of
heterosexual desire.

Such explanations are valuable, not least because they locate links between sexual and gender oppression, and reveal the necessity of joining anti-sexist and anti-heterosexist struggle. Gender is obviously a large and integral part of the story of heterosexist oppression; my point is simply that it cannot be the whole story. The attempt to describe the effects of heterosexuality solely in terms of a gendered dynamic of dominance and submission fails to provide a complete account of the social consequences of sexual identity that place gay and heterosexual men, and lesbians and heterosexual women, in very different positions. I would maintain that if one attempts to fit sexuality (or race, or class) into a gender analysis, one finds the box won't pack without strains and omissions.[12] For example, it is possible, although certainly not easy, to explain on a gender analysis alone why it is that single, celibate men are not stigmatized in the same way, or at least half as much, as gay men. The fact that celibate men are called bachelors, monks or priests, rather than faggots or queers, suggests that heterosexist oppression has effects which cannot be explained solely by reference to their functional relationship to the maintenance of gender hierarchy. At the same time, sexist and heterosexist oppression cannot be adequately theorized in isolation from each other because they are clearly linked by a requirement that the sexed bodies of men and women adhere to strict gender roles. I believe that gender and sexuality must be treated as interlocking vectors of oppression, each with its own interrelated yet distinct set of mechanisms and effects.[13]

Heterosexual Privilege

"Heterosexual privilege" refers to the range of perks and incentives with which heterosexually identified persons[14] are rewarded for conforming to the dominant sexuality. What heterosexism gives straight men and women, what it takes away from lesbians and gays, is heterosexual privilege. Heterosexual privilege, in other words, describes the effects of heterosexism on the position of heterosexually identified persons. It follows that straight people must recognize their privilege as a precondition to joining the struggle to end heterosexist oppression.

It is easy for us male heterosexuals to take our privilege for granted, for it is as much part of our worlds as the air we breathe. But one has only to imagine for a moment how gays and lesbians experience a heterosexist world to get a sense of its all-pervasive and painful contours. A few of the privileges we have that readily come to my mind are the fact that my partner and I qualify as "spouses" and therefore can benefit from our employers' health, dental, and pension plans as well as a range of statutory benefits, rights, and powers.[15] As she and I pursue our educations, we are entitled to deduct each other's tuition fees from our incomes. We need not fear that public displays of affection or otherwise revealing our sexuality in North American society will provoke violence, harassment, or criminal charges. Nor do our wedding rings provoke cold stares, hostile actions, or violence; rather, they make us "normal" and "acceptable," more worthy of admiration and respect from our heterosexually identified families, friends, and colleagues. As Charlotte Bunch has said:

> [w]hat makes heterosexuality work is heterosexual privilege—
> and if you don't have a sense of what privilege is, I suggest
> that you go home and announce to everybody that you
> know—a roommate, your family, the people you work with—
> everywhere that you go—that you're a queer. Try being a
> queer for a week.[16]

While heterosexual privilege is a pervasive feature of heterosexist society, it has different effects on people's lives depending upon factors such as their gender, race, and class. In thinking about the effects of heterosexual privilege, I find it useful to bear in mind the dual hierarchies of gender and sexuality embodied in heterosexuality. While it is true that heterosexism, or heterosexual privilege, does benefit both straight men and women at the expense of gay men and lesbians, this is only part of the story. For heterosexuality not only embodies a hierarchy between those inside and those outside privileged heterosexual relationships, it is also characterized by gender hierarchy within those relationships.

10   Thus, straight women are both oppressed by virtue of their gender, and enjoy some privileges by virtue of their heterosexuality relative to lesbians. Heterosexual women, especially if they are married, do enjoy a degree of social status and economic benefits not conferred upon women choosing to live their lives free of primary emotional and sexual attachments to men. However, for straight women, social acceptance may often come at the expense of elements of financial, emotional, and physical security in their intimate relationships. Many of the "privileges" enjoyed by straight women may be quite illusory, if, for example, the economic benefits remain in the control and at the disposal of their male partners. Studies of women's economic status following divorce would give anyone pause before asserting anything other than contingent economic advantages in heterosexual relationships for women.[17] Indeed, for straight women, "[m]ost heterosexual privilege is diminished when compared to the degree of exploitation and oppression a woman is likely to encounter in most heterosexual relationships."[18] Thus, in contrast to popular images of heterosexual love, it is important to emphasize that the overall result of heterosexual relationships on women's lives is not likely to be the conferral of privileges.

Thus, the notion of women's heterosexual privilege does not refer to the overall effect of heterosexual relationships on women's lives; rather, it draws attention to the kinds of privileges straight women have by virtue of their heterosexual identification that lesbians are denied. Used contextually, the expression describes the position of heterosexual women in certain aspects of their lives relative to women living free of primary emotional attachments to men. Straight women benefit from the social recognition and acceptance of their primary relationships, and are granted a degree of legitimacy denied to lesbians by heterosexist culture. Thus, for example, they are likely to have less difficulty finding acceptance in workplaces dominated by heterosexually identified men (i.e., most workplaces) than lesbians do, and straight women's voices are less devalued than those of lesbians in a sexist and heterosexist society. Of course, for straight women a different form of oppression than that confronted by lesbians is still oppression, not privilege.

While heterosexual women's relationship to heterosexuality contains elements of privilege and exploitation, the same is not true for heterosexual men. The gender and sexual hierarchies embodied in heterosexuality work together to give us power; our position of dual dominance within heterosexuality is captured by the unproblematic notion of male heterosexual privilege. However, while all heterosexual men benefit in some way from sexism and heterosexism, we do not all benefit equally. Male heterosexual privilege has different effects on men of, for example, different races and classes. Recent studies have begun the task of deconstructing the categories "men" and "masculinity" to reveal the multiplicity of masculinities they obscure, and the power relations that exist among and between groups of men.[19] In our society, the dominant or "hegemonic" form of masculinity to which our masculinities are subordinated is white, middle-class, and heterosexual.[20] This means that the heterosexual privilege of, say, straight black men takes a very different shape in their lives than it does for straight white men. For one, black men have to contend with the fact that the "prevailing Western concept of sexuality already contains racism"[21]; in racist ideology, black men's bodies are made to bear a disproportionate responsibility for the brutality of male sexuality in a sexist society. In James Baldwin's words, "[t]he white man's unadmitted—and apparently, to him, unspeakable—private fears and longing are projected onto the Negro."[22] For another, many of the economic advantages that accrue to heterosexuals relative to gays and lesbians may be overshadowed by the economic effects of racism on black men's lives. As Kenneth Clatterbaugh puts it,

> [j]ust as the dominant masculinity is shaped by privilege and
> anti-black racism, black masculinity is shaped by poverty and
> oppression. The white patriarchal gender ideals that are held
> out to black men in a racist society create double binds. . . .
> The message to black men from patriarchy is to "be a man";
> the message from capitalism is "no chance."[23]

While all heterosexual men benefit, albeit unequally, from sexism and heterosexism, the situation of gay men is contradictory in relation to the dual hierarchy constructed by heterosexuality. As Gary Kinsman puts it,

> [w]hile gay men share with straight men the privilege of being
> in a dominant position in relation to women, we are at the
> same time in a subordinate position in the institution of het-
> erosexuality. As a result, gay men's lives and experiences are not
> the same as those of heterosexual men. For instance, while we
> share with straight men the economic benefits of being men

in a patriarchal society, we do not participate as regularly in
the everyday interpersonal subordination of women in the
realms of sexuality and violence.[24]

Gay men, as men, are accorded male privilege by sexism, yet they are oppressed
by heterosexism. Even though they live outside of the social status and legitimacy accorded by heterosexual relationships, they benefit from the gendered
division of labour in capitalist patriarchy and the dominance of men in political institutions. The contradictory position of gay men in relationship to the
dual hierarchy embodied in heterosexuality is well illustrated by considering
the nature of their exposure to public acts of violence. Unlike women, most
gay men need not consider the constant and unavoidable threat of sexual violence in structuring their lives. At the same time, gay men, or men who risk
being identified as gay, must consider the danger posed by the growing incidence of homophobic violence fostered by a heterosexist society.

Lesbians bear the assaults of both sexist and heterosexist oppression. Thus,
for example, the combination of misogyny and homophobia renders lesbians
particularly susceptible to male violence. The distinct position of lesbians—
doubly subordinated by the construction of dual hierarchy embodied in heterosexuality—means that their position has to be theorized in a manner that
takes into account their differences from both straight women and gay men, for
the latter two groups have a contradictory relationship to the dual construction
of male and heterosexual dominance institutionalized in heterosexuality.

The Legal Construction of Heterosexual Privilege

The law contributes to the construction of heterosexual privilege by conferring a vast range of rights, powers, privileges, benefits, and obligations exclusively on "spouses," a legal category open only to married persons or
cohabiting heterosexuals.[25] The common law definition of marriage as the
union of a man and a woman[26] ensures that access to marriage, and therefore
to the current legislative definition of spouse in Canada, is restricted to heterosexuals, or to persons conforming to or feigning the outward requirements
of heterosexual cohabitation.

15   The law maintains a resounding silence regarding lesbian and gay exis-
tences. "Homosexuals" have been mentioned but once in Canadian legislation—in the 1952 amendments to the *Immigration Act* which prohibited the
entry of "prostitutes, homosexuals or persons living on the avails of prostitution or homosexualism" into the country.[27] Gay sexuality has been penalized
under the *Criminal Code* in varying degrees since the late nineteenth century
under provisions criminalizing "buggery" (now "anal intercourse"[28]), "gross
indecency" (now repealed), "indecent acts,"[29] and keeping or being an "in-
mate" in a "bawdy-house."[30] Gay men are represented in the criminal reports
alternately as powerful victimizers, deserving weak victims, or as the perpetrators of unmentionable indecent acts. Apart from these few stigmatizing

representations, lesbians and gay men do not appear as subjects in Canadian legislation.

The legal denial of lesbian and gay personhood has a number of effects. At an ideological level, it naturalizes heterosexuality and renders all other sexualities suspect. At a psychic level, gays and lesbians cannot count on state support or on official recognition of their interests at times of crisis in their intimate relationships. At a material level, gays and lesbians are deprived of financial benefits conferred on heterosexuals. Gays and lesbians, in aggregate, are paying a higher proportion of tax on their income than heterosexuals, and yet they receive nothing in return in terms of family pensions, survivor's or dependent's benefits.[31] In other words, lesbians and gays are forced to subsidize heterosexual privilege. In terms of physical security, heterosexism, legal and otherwise, by devaluing lesbian and gay lives, provokes and legitimates acts of violence against gay men and lesbians, and makes it more likely that these crimes will go unreported, or, if reported, taken less seriously by the police and the public at large.

The irrational and pervasive fear that heterosexually identified legislators seem to have about enacting into law even the mildest positive image or signal regarding lesbian and gay lives was evident in the debates regarding the 1969 reforms of the *Criminal Code* partially decriminalizing gay sexuality,[32] and in the 1986 and 1987 debates regarding the addition of sexual orientation to the human rights legislation of Ontario and Manitoba respectively.[33] Another recent example of heterosexism in the legislative process was provided by the debate in the U.S. Congress surrounding the passage of the *Hate Crimes Statistics Act* in 1990.[34] The purpose of the Act is to authorize the collection of data on hate crimes against, amongst other groups, lesbians and gay men. The bill was delayed for years in part as a result of fears on the part of heterosexually identified members of Congress that it would amount to a "subtle affirmation of homosexuality."[35] It would, presumably, because it entails, for some, the novel proposition that the dead and injured gay men and lesbians are worth counting.[36]

The Rationalization of Heterosexual Privilege in Legal and Heterosexist Discourse

Heterosexuality is rationalized by heterosexism in a manner analogous to the way that gender inequality is rationalized in sexist discourse, namely by reference to biology, nature, or some other source of apparent transcendent truth, like the Bible or the Oxford English Dictionary. Perhaps the most common argument used to rationalize the oppression of lesbians and gays is the fact that their sexuality is not procreative. As Jonathan Ward argues, "the nature of heterosexuality is 'nature' itself,"[37] and that nature is characterized, made sense of, by its purpose: procreation. "The procreative function has conventionally decided between 'natural' and 'unnatural' sexual practice, and today lends its authority to heterosexual supremacy."[38] As women's capacity for pregnancy is to sexism, the lack of a connection between procreation and sexuality is to heterosexism. From a male heterosexual perspective, both are biological differences that have been used to rationalize and justify oppression.[39]

The dominant approach to same-sex sexual activity in western capitalist countries used to be a "sin model" rooted in theological tradition. It was replaced by a "sickness model," dominant until the early 1970's, which views heterosexuality as the measure of a healthy, mature sexuality. Lesbians and gays have accordingly failed to attain a heterosexual idea of sexual development; they are "sick" or "deviant." Neither the "sin" nor the "sickness" model are currently dominant in academic or professional circles,[40] yet the tendency for heterosexuals to believe that nature, biology, or the family has somehow failed the homosexual remains. The explanation for why heterosexual persons tend to find comfort in such explanations for homosexuality lies, I suspect, in our failure to interrogate, or our fear of interrogating, the "naturalness" of our own sexuality. This tendency finds absurd expression in studies like the one reported last year finding a correlation between being left-handed and being gay. Such biologistic explanations serve to rationalize heterosexuality and insulate it from critical examination. It allows heterosexuals to avoid the difficult work of examining our sexuality at an individual and collective level. In so avoiding the social construction of sexuality, heterosexuals can also avoid confronting the fact of socially constructed privilege and the possibility of change.

20   One consequence of the attempt to naturalize heterosexuality is the emergence of a compassion/condonation dichotomy in heterosexist discourse. A rough caricature of this line of thought goes as follows: since nature has failed gays and lesbians, they deserve compassion from us normal heterosexuals who have not been handicapped by such a trick of fate. Therefore, we witness growing support for human rights protection on the basis of sexual orientation, or at least for the idea that a woman or man should not be deprived of her or his home, job, children, right to services, solely because of her or his sexual orientation. One can adhere to this basic principal of fairness without acknowledging heterosexual privilege—the frame of human rights legislation allows one to continue to believe, if it suits one's view of the world, that heterosexuals need and deserve this protection as much as lesbians and gay men do.

At the same time, heterosexually identified people do have some awareness that sexuality is, at least in part, within individual or social control. Rather than deploying this awareness to examine critically the social construction of heterosexual privilege, it is used to portray gay men and lesbians as a threat to the natural order of heterosexuality.[41] Hence, the common heterosexist refrain "I feel sorry for them, but I cannot condone their lifestyle." In heterosexist discourse, heterosexuality is, paradoxically, both a "natural" institution and an extremely vulnerable institution, likely to collapse like a house of cards if any legal recognition is granted to other sexualities.

The compassion/condonation dichotomy in heterosexist thinking was abundantly evident in the statements of legislators in debates in Manitoba and Ontario when sexual orientation was added as a prohibited ground of discrimination to those provinces' human rights legislation.[42] Indeed, the intensity of the concerns expressed in Manitoba that extending human rights protection to lesbians and gays would "condone their lifestyle" and undermine the "naturalness" of heterosexuality led to the addition of a clause to the act making clear that "nothing in this Act shall be interpreted as condoning or condemning any beliefs, values or lifestyles" associated, inter alia, with sexual orientation.[43] The compassion/condonation framework of heterosexist discourse also explains the paradoxical existence of legal guarantees against discrimination on the basis of sexual orientation sitting side-by-side in the statue books with a plethora of laws that confer benefits solely on heterosexual spouses. Prohibitions on the denial of access to housing, employment, and services on the grounds of a person's sexual orientation represents the limited compassionate side of the heterosexist coin; the refusal to extend to gays and lesbians benefits currently available only to heterosexuals represents the flipside of "no condonation." Judges have dismissed arguments that laws or policies granting benefits exclusively to heterosexuals are discriminatory on the grounds that only heterosexuals can form families and that those families are favoured by the legal system because they are the "natural" site of procreation and child-rearing.[44] This is true even for same-sex couples who are parenting.[45] The presumed superiority of heterosexual family units provides the explicit or implicit framework through which judges in custody cases have assessed a gay or lesbian parent's claim to access or custody of the children of a prior heterosexual relationship. The case law involving lesbian parents indicates that they are at serious risk of losing custody of their children if they actively affirm the value of lesbian lives or politics.[46] In these and other ways, legal discourse is characterized by a willingness to condone heterosexuality and a concomitant refusal to condone homosexuality.

THE DILEMMAS POSED BY HETEROSEXUAL MEN'S PARTICIPATION IN ANTI-SEXIST AND ANTI-HETEROSEXIST MOVEMENT

Deconstructing White Male Heterosexual Discourse

In thinking through our position relative to anti-sexist and anti–heterosexist struggle, it is important to bear in mind the embodiment in heterosexuality of the dual hierarchies of gender and sexuality, and the ways these relations are depicted as natural, not political, in sexist and heterosexist discourses, as outlined above. It is also important to understand the epistemological dominance of the white, male, heterosexual point of view. Because our ways of knowing and seeing the world have been dominant in western societies, *both* talking and silence are problematic. Talking about gender and sexuality risks reinscribing our epistemological dominance, yet, as straight men, to not confront male heterosexual privilege is collaboration in sexist and heterosexist oppression. Whether we want our sexuality to be invested with such meaning or not, we cannot avoid embodying and benefitting from heterosexual privilege if our primary sexual relationships are with women. Similarly, whether or not we want it, as males in sexist society, we benefit from all the advantages that maleness brings. As Sheila McIntyre has said, "[t]there is no outside of gender."[47]

The dilemmas of our position regarding anti-sexist and anti-heterosexist struggles, then, flow from the fact that until sexism and heterosexism have been eradicated, we heterosexual men are unavoidably part of the problem. However, it is also worth emphasizing that, if we are not part of the solution, then we are a bigger part of the problem. I raise the dilemmas in our relation to anti-sexist and anti-heterosexist struggle not as an excuse for inaction, but to open up a dialogue with those involved in that struggle about the ways in which we can and should participate.

25   Feminist theorists have long criticized the transcendental pretences of "objective" male reasoning. In Catharine MacKinnon's words, the male point of view, or the "male epistemological stance,"[48] is "the standard for point-of-viewlessness, its particularity the meaning of universality."[49] The power of male, objectivist epistemology is evident in many discourses, not least in the law.[50] Thus, a principle aim of Canadian feminist legal scholarship has been to demonstrate that ". . . so-called objectivity is only one mode of subjectivity, and that is male privilege that transforms masculist subjectivity into (universalist) objectivity."[51]

Moreover, men do not have a monopoly on the totalizing and imperialistic features of masculinist disourse; these features are present in any discourse that subsumes relations of, for example, class, race and sexuality. Just as feminists have critiqued the erasure of women's point of view by the male epistemological stance, and the erasure of lesbianism in heterosexist discourse,[52] so too have feminist theorists criticized the tendency in the writing of white, bourgeois feminists to be inattentive to racial and class differences between women.[53] Feminists have also been criticized for obscuring differences between men based on race, class, and sexuality in their accounts of gender oppression.[54] Feminists have criticized gay theorists for failing adequately to theorize gender hierarchy, which results, for example, in the erasure of the distinct position of lesbians within the generic categories "gay" or "homosexual."[55] Black gays and lesbians have criticized white gay liberationists for failing to bring race into their analyses.[56] Gay black men and black feminists have criticized black communities for failing to address sexism and heterosexism.[57] Gay men and men of colour have not felt comfortable joining men's anti-sexist groups that have theorized from the position of white heterosexual men and have thus failed to take account of the differences between men produced by heterosexism and racism.[58]

These are just some examples of the continuing struggles in progressive movements to develop theories and practices that are responsive to all structures of oppression. The "simultaneity of oppression"[59] experienced by members of all but the most privileged groups in society means that no progressive movement can afford to prioritize the struggle to end one form of oppression over another by positing an "essential" or "generic" woman, lesbian, gay man, black heterosexual man, etc. It is oppressed peoples' relationship to structures of domination that is relevant to how they theorize about changing them, so naturally it is peoples' differing relationships to these structures that has inscribed debates in progressive communities in these terms. In Joan W. Scott's words, "power is constructed on and so must be challenged from the ground of difference."[60]

The challenge to essentialist discourses in progressive movements mirrors the challenge to essentialism developed by feminists in response to the totalizing and exclusionary frame of male epistemology.[61] The challenge will continue within movements defined by difference that themselves purport to speak across differences which have formed the basis of oppression within interlocking structures of domination. The goal is the development of a language and a practice that accounts for all the effects of oppressive practices and discourses, and that prioritizes none of them in the struggle for change. In other words, the notion that progressive discourses are fracturing and turning in on themselves is the point of view only of those who thought earlier essentialist discourses responded to their struggles adequately in the first place. The dynamic reformulation of progressive discourses and movements to take account of all structures of oppression is necessary to an inclusive, and therefore an effective, politics. This process is as necessary, as dynamic, as essential, and as finite as the enumeration of grounds of historical disadvantage in anti-discrimination laws must also be all of these things.

What does this say about the position of straight men? First of all, that we are a diverse category, and our situations for the purposes of theorizing are very different depending upon factors such as our race, ability, and our class. Those of us who are white, heterosexual, christian, middle-class, and able bodied men are especially used to thinking in a manner that could be called epistemological imperialism.[62] This is not to say that colonizing discourse has been solely our preogative; but we are the ones who are least likely to be aware of the exclusionary tendencies within its universality masking its (our) singularity. Most people are aware of discontinuities between W.H.M. discourse and their own lived experiences and aspirations, simply because most people are not W.H.M.s. When it comes to the project of decolonizing discourse— learning not to speak for the experiences and aspirations of others—we W.H.M.s have by far the most work to do, yet we have thus far done the least. Also, we will be the group most likely to resist the challenge to objectivist male epistemology because it is a language that has suited us just fine, thank you. For example, Bruce Feldthusen has perceptively described male legal academics' failure to take seriously or grant legitimacy to feminist theory as an exercise of their "right not to know."[63] W.H.M.s feel about as much need to theorize about the dominant male epistemology as fish do about water.

Standing Aside, Listening and Problematizing Heterosexuality

30 W.H.M.s have traditionally spoken in a universalist discourse that obscures our particularity by assuming it. We have also had the power, in the supposedly neutral and objective languages of science, medicine, psychoanalysis, the law, etc., to describe and produce the particularities of others. For example, we have been trying for many years to define "the causes and consequences" of gay sexuality, and to figure out how lesbians have sex without us; we have come up with lurid definitions of the difference of women, people of colour, people of different abilities, and so on. In both our universalist and particularist discourses, we, our bodies, remain peculiarly unspoken.[64] The result is, in Victor Seidler's words, "a blindness around the particular experience of heterosexual men"[65]; we become "strangely invisible"[66] to ourselves. As Jonathan Rutherford puts it, ". . . heterosexual men have inherited a language which can define the lives and sexualities of others, but fails us when we have to deal with our own heterosexuality and masculine identities."[67]

To overcome the negative effects of W.H.M. epistemology, in my view W.H.M. legal academics need to concentrate on three related goals in the context of debates concerning sexuality: standing aside, listening to gays and lesbians, and problematizing male heterosexuality.

First, we can help to create spaces in which gay men and lesbians can define their own differences, free of the imperialistic tendencies of W.H.M. discourse. This means standing aside in both an epistemological and institutional sense.[68] As legal scholars, we should support and encourage the interests and careers of gay and lesbian scholars whose perspectives are vastly underrepresented on law faculties, mirroring the silence and absence of positive images of gay men or of lesbians in Canadian law. And, in my view, our contribution should not be along the lines of prescribing or advocating particular solutions to existing forms of legal discrimination—it should be left to lesbians and gay men to work out for themselves the place of law and law reform in their political movements.

Which brings me to my second point, which is that we should listen carefully to debates within lesbian and gay communities, to the changes those communities are seeking in political and legal institutions, and then support in whatever ways we can challenges to heterosexist oppression. And we should catch up on the enormous body of exciting and challenging scholarship produced by feminist, including lesbian-feminist, and gay theorists; we should read their work carefully, seriously, and critically. We have a great deal to learn about how our conception of white, heterosexual masculinity has been defined in opposition to others: for example, in opposition to women gendered inferior, in opposition to gay men sexualized "deviant," and in opposition to black masculinity represented as "uncivilized" in racist discourse. Listening to the voices of the heterogeneous majority is a good place to start to understand the dominance and colonizing tendencies inherent in W.H.M. practices and discourses.[69] And we should incorporate the insights of feminist and gay theorists into our teaching and scholarship. In doing so, we must take special care to attribute ideas to their source, because anti-sexist and anti-heterosexist ideas are far less threatening when they come from a heterosexual man. We get listened to. All we have to do is wash the dishes to get credit for making the dinner.

Thirdly, we have to learn to speak and problematize our own gender and sexuality which have been obscured in universals or projected onto others.[70] We can, we must, talk, but in doing so we must make space for other voices, and not speak with authority about the meaning of lesbian and gay experiences. We can begin by acknowledging our privilege and working to change it, and by taking the radical step of publicly affirming the value of lesbian and gay lives. And we need to examine ourselves, not for the purpose of finding the "hairy beast" or the "wild man" within,[71] but to discover the ways in which our lives have been shaped by sexism, heterosexism, and other structures of oppression, and to find strength and meaning in working towards a better world.

It is also crucial, in my view, that we contribute to the problematizing of heterosexuality; that is, to exposing it as an oppressive political institution. This could entail exploring it origins, its history, the nature of its ongoing privilege, and its rationalization in legal and other heterosexist discourses. Male heterosexual scholars, by leaving the exploration of heterosexuality to feminists and gay theorists,[72] and by focusing on "the woman problem" or "the homosexual problem,"[73] may unwittingly ratify the normality of heterosexuality. As Jonathan Katz has argued:

> [b]y not studying the heterosexual idea in history, analysts of
> sex, gay and straight, have continued to privilege the "normal"
> and "natural" at the expense of the "abnormal" and "unnatural."
> Such privileging of the norm accedes to its domination, pro-
> tecting it from questions. By making the normal the object of
> a thoroughgoing historical study we simultaneously pursue a
> pure truth and a sex-radical and subversive goal: we upset basic
> preconceptions. We discover that the heterosexual, the normal,
> and the natural have a history of changing definitions. Studying
> the history of the term challenges its power.[74]

What's In It for Us?

While I believe that we have a responsibility to make efforts to change ourselves and to challenge the construction of heterosexuality as dual hierarchy, we must do so with careful attention to our motivations. Is it possible that in

35

our desire to be relevant to feminist and anti-heterosexist struggle we are really seeking approval and admiration? In Stephen Heath's words, ". . . do I write from desire-fear, to say simply in the last analysis 'love me'?"[75] In learning the language and rhetoric of feminist and gay theory, are we motivated by competitive impulses to "one-up" those theorists?[76] Are we competing with or distancing ourselves from other heterosexual men who are potential allies by setting up hierarchies of awareness and "political correctness"? Are we trying to set ourselves up as the latest chivalrous white knights in shining armour? Is our interest sincere, or it is ". . . a form of critical cross-dressing, a fashion risk of the 1980s [and 1990s] that is both radical chic and power play?"[77] These are not questions to which there are easy answers—rather they are ones with which we should continuously challenge ourselves.

Cleansing our own "penis guilt," or otherwise focusing on our own wounded or defensive feelings as we come to grips with the effects of sexism and heterosexism, is not a motivation that will foster progressive change.[78] For example, consider Tim Carrigan, Bob Connell and John Lee's observation regarding one of the 1970's men's pro-feminist books,[79]

> [o]ne gets the impression that being subject to constant criticism by feminists is the emotional center of this book, and that the response is to bend over backwards, and backwards again. A relationship with feminism is indeed crucial to any counter-sexist politics among heterosexual men; but a series of back somersaults is not a strong position from which to confront the patriarchal power structure.[80]

Heterosexual men can best contribute to the struggle against sexism and heterosexism from a position of strength and security in ourselves. Alice Jardine's words of advice to pro-feminist men are apt here:

> [i]f you will forgive me my directness, we do not want you to *mimic* us, to become the same as us; we don't want your pathos or your guilt; and we don't even want your admiration (even if it's nice to get it once in a while). What we want, I would even say what we need, is your *work*. We need you to get down to serious work. And like all serious work, that involves struggle and pain.[81]

Part of the work we need to do as heterosexual men is very personal. For example, why do we consider ourselves to be heterosexual? We should seriously question the extent to which we have not felt prepared to love *any* person, man or woman, based on the quality of our interpersonal interactions. To what extent have we been prepared to renounce heterosexual privilege? For those of us in committed relationships with women, this question raises particularly troubling tensions and contradictions. We may feel, as I do, that our relationships with our partners are worth celebrating in-so-far as they are based on mutual love and respect. In this sense, I feel that my relationship with my partner is worth celebrating not because it is heterosexual, but despite its heterosexuality. The problem is, of course, that it is not possible to celebrate and honour our love for each other without further entrenching heterosexuality and heterosexual privilege. Renouncing all heterosexual privilege would involve not cohabiting in a sexual relationship, and thus avoiding being seen as "spouses" in the eyes of society and the law. Choosing to get married, as I have, allows my partner and I to share our commitment with our community of friends and family, but in doing so we enter an institution that excludes gays and lesbians and that brings with it a host of new privileges. The choices I have made are a source of personal joy and pride; they are also politically problematic. The unavoidable conflict between my commitment to overcoming heterosexism and my commitment to being true to my experience of love and joy with a member of the opposite sex is personally a very troubling one.

This conflict will exist for heterosexual men so long as we live in a heterosexist society that compromises sexual choice. Heterosexual men need to confront honestly, without retreating into defensive heterosexual posturing, the fact that it is simply not possible to have full confidence in heterosexual "choices" in a society organized around compulsory heterosexuality.[82] I believe that the most constructive responsive we can make as heterosexual men is to join gays and lesbians in challenging a heterosexist society that impoverishes the meaning of the "choice" by which we heterosexuals have constructed our intimate lives.

An awareness of the myriad forces privileging heterosexuality should prompt heterosexual men to work toward a society where the meaning of choice in sexuality is not so impoverished, where it is possible to celebrate a loving relationship with a member of the opposite sex without simultaneously celebrating a form of institutionalized discrimination, and where our daily interactions with others are not restricted by heterosexism. Heterosexism is a mechanism, as Eve Kosofsky Sedgwick has observed, ". . . for regulating the behaviour of the many by the specific oppression of the few."[83] And as Gary Kinsman has said:

> [h]eterosexual men interested in seriously transforming the
> fabric of their lives have to stop seeing gay liberation as simply
> a separate issue for some men that has nothing to say to them.
> They should begin to ask what the experience of gay men can
> bring into view for them. As we break the silence and move
> beyond liberal tolerance toward gays and lesbians, we can begin
> to see how 'queer baiting' and the social taboo against pleasure,
> sex, and love between men serves to keep all men in line,
> defining what proper masculinity is for us.[84]

We have to come to grips with the ways in which sexism and heterosexism cause pain in and diminish our lives without equating those effects with the oppression of women and gay men. We also have to acknowledge that straight men as a group will lose power. And that giving up power is easier to do for those of us who already have a lot of it. Tenured male professors like myself, for example, can confront male heterosexual privilege from the relatively secure position provided by our already having reaped many of its benefits. Whatever else can be said about it, there is certainly no heroism in speaking out from such a position. It is, nonetheless, irresponsible, in my view, to fail to use the privileged positions we have to work towards the democratic dispersal of power.

Being Straight About Being Straight

40   Heterosexual men taking gay- or lesbian-positive positions must continually deal with the question of whether or not to reveal their heterosexuality. The dilemma arises because there is a widespread assumption in both gay and straight communities that any man who says anything supportive about issues of concern to lesbian or gay communities must be gay himself—an understandable response for the very simple reason that so few heterosexuals make such minimal gestures. I do not think there is an easy answer to the dilemma of whether to disclose one's heterosexuality. The answer is certainly not never or always; rather, I think heterosexual men must make their decisions in a manner sensitive to the particular context, and to the political value of letting people think you are gay, or being straight about being straight, or keeping them guessing.[85] My own rather tentative conclusions are as follows: I am coming to understand that as a general rule it is important to situate myself in debates when I speak or write so as not to mislead people into believing that I am speaking with the authority of experience about gay concerns.[86] Being up front about one's heterosexuality is desirable to avoid the potential for distorting or appropriating gay experience. Moreover, self-identified gay-positive heterosexuals can send out the important message that heterosexism should be as much of an issue for straight people as racism should be for white people. At the same time, in social and professional contexts in which I am not speaking to an audience, I normally choose to not reveal that I have a female partner in order to avoid claiming (as much as that is possible for someone who has already made a decision to marry) heterosexual privilege. Thus, I refer to my "partner" rather than my "spouse" or "wife." It strikes me as important for heterosexual men to overcome fears of being mistakenly identified as gay, for otherwise we are likely to consciously or unconsciously reproduce behavior typical of the dominant masculinity. For example, there have been times when, baited by homophobes, I have decided that proudly claiming a gay identity seems preferable to pleading my heterosexuality.

CONCLUSION

The feminist, lesbian and gay movements have given the white male heterosexual stance a cause. What we used to take for granted has to be justified—or changed. As Arthur Brittan elaborates:

[n]ow that feminism and the gay movement directly challenge "hierarchic heterosexuality" in the political and cultural arenas, it is clear that its defences are being strengthened and reinforced by more sophisticated discourses and practices. Indeed, the "discovery" of heterosexualism has given the "male epistemological stance" a cause.

The incorrigible propositions of gender now have a useful name, a name which is invoked whenever the family or marriage is threatened by other sexualities and practices. Heterosexualism is now being constructed and articulated in a very self-conscious and deliberate fashion.[87]

"Hierarchic heterosexuals" are seeking to put homosexuality back in the closet and reaffirm a naturalist heterosexist discourse. Thus, the conservative philosopher Roger Scruton has argued in a recent work that women's role is properly the domestication and constraint of the natural vagrancy of male sexuality within the socially constructed institution of heterosexuality.[88] In 1988, the British Parliament passed an amendment to the *Local Government Act* making it illegal for a local authority to "intentionally promote homosexuality" or "to promote the teaching . . . of the acceptability of homosexuality as a pretended family relationship."[89] The hard edge of the reactionary spectrum is represented by the increasing incidence of physical attacks by the defenders of heterosexual dominance on men and women perceived to be gay or lesbian.

In such a social context, it is all the more critical that progressive heterosexuals speak out against attempts to intimidate or silence gays and lesbians. We straight men are in a uniquely powerful position either to abet the reaction or to work alongside gays and lesbians to give voice and legitimacy to oppositional sexualities. It is crucial that heterosexual men counter the reaction by revealing, exploring, and critiquing their privilege, thereby providing a role model for other men, demonstrating that this can be done and one's penis will *not* fall off, one's sense of self will not wither away without heterosexuality as dual hierarchy. Indeed, to deny that there is a problem with the manner in which male heterosexuality is constructed in this society, in the face of rather compelling evidence to the contrary, is the path that can lead to self-deception and self-hatred. The truly challenging work, the truly exciting work, is to remake ourselves and the world in creative struggle within and against structures of oppression.

When we do attempt to work seriously for change, when we do attempt to examine and change our privilege, we need both the criticisms and the support of lesbians and gays. We need criticisms because, like everyone else, we will make mistakes. Indeed, one of the points of this paper has been to argue that the gaps and omissions in male heterosexuals' understanding of gender and sexuality are likely to be greater because we have, many of us, spent our lives in blissful ignorance, believing our gender and sexuality were, well, natural.

If male heterosexuality is socially constructed then it can re-form itself. With this knowledge, and a commitment to equality, I believe that we heterosexual men can play a positive role in the struggle to dismantle the gender and sexual hierarchies embodied in the social institution of heterosexuality. And one day, when these goals are accomplished, we will, happily, cease to exist as straight men. It will be the end of the gendered world as we know it, and I'll feel fine.

NOTES

* Associate Professor, Osgoode Hall Law School, York University. This paper is based on comments presented at the "Heterosexual Privilege" panel of the conference on lesbian and gay legal issues, Justice For All, held at Queen's University on 20 October 1990.

1. I have attempted to use the pronoun "we" carefully throughout this paper, that is, taking care to make clear for whom and to whom I presume to speak (usually heterosexual men or privileged sub-categories of heterosexual men). Occasionally I use a more wishful-thinking "we," which, perhaps presumptively, is meant to include all those who share my desire for progressive coalition-building across differences.

2. See, for example, Sheila Jeffreys, *Anticlimax: A Feminist Perspective on the Sexual Revolution* (London: Women's Press, 1990); Celia Kitsinger, *The Social Construction of Lesbianism* (London: Sage Publications, 1987); Catharine A. MacKinnon, *Toward a Feminist Theory of the State* (Cambridge, Mass.: Harvard University Press, 1990): Adrienne Rich, "Compulsory Heterosexuality and Lesbian Existence" in *Blood, Bread and Poetry. Selected Prose 1979–1985* (New York: Norton, 1986) 23 at 23.

3. Catharine MacKinnon, ibid. at 113.

4. Adrienne Rich, supra, note 2.

5. See, for example, Gary Kinsman, "Men Loving Men: The Challenge of Gay Liberation" in Michael Kaufman, ed., *Beyond Patriarchy: Essays By Men on Pleasure, Power, and Change* (Toronto: Oxford University Press, 1987) 103; Ned Lyttelton, "Men's Liberation, Men Against Sexism and Major Dividing Lines" (1983–1984) 12(4) *Resources for Feminist Research* 33; Tim Carrigan et al., "Hard and Heavy: Toward a New Sociology of Masculinity," in Kaufman, supra. 139; John Neirenberg, "Misogyny: Gay and Straight" in Franklin Abbott, ed., *New Men, New Minds* (Freedom, Cal.: Crossing Press, 1987) 130; Gay Left Collective, ed., *Homosexuality: Power and Politics* (London: Allison & Busby, 1980); Gregory K. Lehne, "Homophobia Among Men" in Deborah S. David & Robert Brannon, eds., *The Forty-Nine Percent Majority: The Male Sex Role* (Reading, Mass.: Addison-Wesley, 1976) 66.

6. Gregory Lehne, ibid at 79.

7. Gary Kinsman, supra, note 5 at 103.

8. Judith Butler, *Gender Trouble: Feminism and the Subversion of Identity* (New York: Routledge, 1990) at 151, note 6.

9. Lynne Segal, *Slow Motion: Changing Masculinities, Changing Men* (New Brunswick, N.J.: Rutgers University Press, 1990) at 158; Jonathan Dollimore, "Homophobia and Sexual Difference" (1986) 8 *Oxford Literary Rev.* 5 (noting at 5 that ". . . homosexuality is so strangely integral to the self-same heterosexual cultures which obsessively denounce it . . .").

10. Several lesbian, gay, and anti-heterosexist theorists have emphasized that the term "heterosexism" should be used rather than "homophobia" to place emphasis where it

belongs, namely on the social and political system of oppression rather than on an individual pathology. As Celia Kitzinger puts it, ". . . classifying homophobes as sick is far less threatening than any attempt to look at the issue in political terms." Supra, note 2 at 61. See also Arthur Brittan, *Masculinity and Power* (New York: Basil Blackwell, 1989) at 173–74; Gary Kinsman, *The Regulation of Desire: Sexuality in Canada* (Montreal: Black Rose Books, 1987) at 29; Joseph Neisen. "Heterosexism or Homophobia: The Power of the Language We Use" (1990) 10 Out/Look 36.

Rather than jettisoning the concept of homophobia altogether, I prefer to understand it in light of its political and social origins, that is, as an irrational fear and hatred manifest in many heterosexual individuals that is one of the consequences of heterosexism. I find persuasive Diana Fuss' emphasis on

> . . . the importance of the psychoanalytic insight which holds that homosexuality is not opposed to heterosexuality but lies within it—as its very precondition since all identity is based on exclusion. Dismissals of homophobia in favour of heterosexism overlook the fact that homosexual desire plays a role in *all* psychical identity formations. . . . Investigating the precise relation between homophobia and heterosexism strikes me as one of the most productive lines of research gay and lesbian studies might pursue in the future.

Diana Fuss, *Essentially Speaking: Feminism, Nature and Difference* (New York: Routledge, 1989) at 110 (emphasis in original).

11. *Feminism Unmodified: Discourses on Life and Law* (Cambridge, Mass.: Harvard University Press, 1987) at 60. See also Catharine A. MacKinnon, "Legal Perspectives on Sexual Difference" in Deborah Rhode, ed., *Theoretical Perspectives on Sexual Difference* (New Haven: Yale University Press, 1990) 213 at 225.

> The issue is the social meaning of the sexuality of women and men, the gender of women and men, not their sexuality or gender "itself"—if such a distinction can be made.

12. See Adrienne Rich, supra, note 2 at xiv: ". . . the woman trying to fit racism and class into a strictly radical-feminist analysis finds that the box won't pack." While I have borrowed Rich's metaphor, I am not sure she would agree with the proposition in the text.
13. Important work by gay and gay-positive theorists, relying heavily on the pioneering work of Michel Foucault on the social construction of sexuality, is informed by an understanding of sexuality as a discursive realm with distinct mechanisms and effects. Michel Foucault, *The History of Sexuality, Volume 1: An Introduction* (New York: Vintage Books, 1980). See, for example, Gary Kinsman, supra, note 5; Gary Kinsman, supra, note 10; Gay Left Collective, supra, note 5; Jon Ward, "The Nature of Heterosexuality," in Gillian E. Hanscombe & Martin Humphries, eds., *Heterosexuality* (London: GMP Publishers, 1987) 145; Jonathan Ned Katz, "The Invention of Heterosexuality" (1990) 90(1) Socialist Rev. 7; Lorna Weir & Leo Casey, "Subverting Power in Sexuality" (1984) 14(3–4) *Socialist Rev.* 139; Jeffrey Weeks, *Sex, Politics and Society: The Regulation of Sexuality Since 1800,* 2nd ed. (New York: Longman, 1989); Gayle Rubin, "Thinking Sex: Notes for a Radical Theory of the Politics of Sexuality" in Carole S. Vance, ed., *Pleasure and Danger: Exploring Female Sexuality* (Boston: Routledge & Kegan Paul, 1984) 267 at 300–09.

Unfortunately, Rubin suggests in the latter article that feminism is a theory which is limited to the analysis of gender oppression; her static conception of feminism is at odds with recent feminist work that has demonstrated the importance, indeed the necessity, of not theorizing gender in isolation form other interlocking vectors of oppression. For example, Elizabeth Spelman cautions us about the dangers of "add-on" feminist theories that do not dislocate the priority of gender when dealing with interlocking and interdependent systems of oppression. (I am grateful to Annie Bunting for this formulation.) See Elizabeth V. Spelman, *Inessential Woman: Problems of Exclusion in Feminist Thought* (Boston: Beacon Press, 1988) at 125.

Similar criticisms have been made of gay male theorists, who on some occasions have erased gender (for example, Foucault, supra) or failed to theorize adequately gender oppression or the distinct position of lesbians "outside the generic pretences of 'gay' or 'homosexual.'" Diana Fuss, supra, note 10 at 111; see also Sheila Jeffreys, supra, note 2 at 167; Adrienne Rich, supra, note 2 at 52–53.

14. I use the expression "heterosexually identified persons" (rather than simply "heterosexuals") to refer to people claiming a heterosexual public identity. My purpose in adopting this language is to underline the fact that, given the enormous costs that accompany a public disclosure of gay or lesbian identity, one should not assume that a heterosexual public identity expresses a lived sexual reality rather than a decision to not publicly disclose an oppositional sexuality.

15. For an overview, see Bruce Ryder, "Equality Rights and Sexual Orientation: Confronting Heterosexual Family Privilege" (1990) 9(1) Can. J. Fam. Law 39 at 46–63.

16. "Not for Lesbians Only." Quoted in Kinsman, supra, note 5 at 105.

17. For example, Lenore J. Weitzman, *The Divorce Revolution: The Unexpected Social and Economic Consequences for Women and Children in America* (New York: The Free Press, 1985).

18. bell hooks, *Feminist Theory: From Margin to Center* (Boston: South End Press, 1984) at 154.

19. Arthur Brittan, supra, note 10: Harry Brod, ed., *The Making of Masculinities: The New Men's Studies* (Boston: Allen & Unwin, 1987); Harry Brod, ed., *A Mensch Among Men: Explorations in Jewish Masculinity* (Freedom, CA: Crossing Press, 1988); Rowena Chapman & Jonathan Rutherford, eds., *Male Order: Unwrapping Masculinity* (London: Lawrence & Wishart, 1988); Kenneth C. Clatterbaugh, *Contemporary Perspectives on Masculinity: Men, Women, and Politics in Modern Society* (Boulder, Col.: Westview, 1990); Robert W. Connell, *Gender and Power: Society, the Person and Sexual Politics* (Cambridge: Polity Press, 1997); Jeff Hearn, *The Gender of Oppression: Men, Masculinity, and the Critique of Marxism* (Brighton: Wheatsheaf, 1987); Jeff Hearn & David Morgan, eds., *Men, Masculinities and Social Theory* (London: Unwin Hyman, 1990); Michael Kaufman, supra, note 5; Lynne Segal, supra, note 9; Michael Kimmel, ed., *Changing Men: New Directions in Research on Men and Masculinity* (London: Sage, 1987); Michael Kimmel & Michael Messner, eds., *Men's Lives* (New York: Macmillan, 1989); Robert Stables, *Black Masculinity: The Black Male's Role in American Society* (San Francisco, Black Scholar, 1982).

20. On the notion of "hegemonic masculinity," see Tim Carrigan, supra, note 5; Robert Connell, ibid.

21. Kobena Mercer & Isaac Julien, "Race, Sexual Politics and Black Masculinity," in Chapman & Rutherford, supra note 19, 97 at 106.

22. James Baldwin, "The Fire Next Time" in *The Price of the Ticket* (London: Michael Joseph, 1985) at 375.
23. Kenneth Clatterbaugh, supra, note 19 at 142–43. For further analyses of black masculinity, see Kobena Mercer & Issac Julien, supra, note 21; Lynne Segal, supra, note 9 at 168–204; Clyde W. Franklin II, "Surviving the Institutional Decimation of Black Males: Causes, Consequences and Intervention" in Harry Brod, ed., supra, note 19 at 155–69; Jewelle T. Gibbs, *Young, Black and Male in America: An Endangered Species* (Dover, Del Auburn House, 1988); Manning Marable, *How Capitalism Underdeveloped Black America* (Boston: South End, 1983); Note, *Invisible Man: Black and Male Under Title VII,* (1991) 104 Harv. L. Rev. 749.
24. Gary Kinsman, supra, note 5 at 104–05.
25. The Ontario government may soon be the first Canadian jurisdiction to end the heterosexual-exclusivity of the legislative definition of spouse. In a December 1990 announcement, Government Services Minister Frances Lankin announced that the government would make family employment benefits available to the same sex partners of its employees, and that the government was undertaking a review of "all pertinent laws and policies pertaining to spousal benefits" in light of the principal that ". . . all of Ontario's laws and programs must treat people fairly, regardless of the nature of their personal relationships or of their family unit." See Paul Todd, "Ontario Gives Job Benefits to Civil Servants' Gay Partners" *Toronto Star* (21 December 1990) A1; Paula Todd, "NDP Faces Battle Over Gay Rights" *Toronto Star* (1 January 1991) A1.
26. For example, *North v. Matheson,* (1976) 20 R.F.L. 112 (Man. Co. Ct.) *Singer v. Hara,* 11 Wash. App. 247, 522 P.2d 1187 (1974), *Baker v. Nelson,* 291 Minn. 310, 191 N.W.2d 185 (1971), appeal dismissed, 409 U.S. 810; Jones v. Hallahan, 501 S.W.2d 588 (Ky. 1973); *Corbett v. Corbett,* [1970] 2 All E.R. 33. Denmark is presently the only country in which same sex couples are accorded formal legal status at the national level. See "The Complete List of Countries Where Lesbians and Gay Men Legally Can Get Married" (1990) 9 Out/Look 81, and Linda Nielsen, "Family Rights and the 'Registered Partnership' in Denmark" (1990) 4 Int'l J. Law & Family 297.
27. This provision was repealed by the *Immigration Act, 1976,* S.C. 1976–77, c. 52 See Philip Girard, "From Subversion to Liberation: Homosexuals and the Immigration Act, 1952–1977" (1987) 2 Can. J. Law & Society 1.
28. *Criminal Code.* R.S.C. 1985, c. C-46, s. 159.
29. Section 173.
30. Sections 197(1) and 210.
31. Bruce Ryder, supra, note 15 at 48–52.
32. For an analysis, see Gary Kinsman, supra, note 10 at 164–72.
33. See Bruce Ryder, supra, note 15 at 65–73. Becki Ross, "Sexual Dis/Orientation or Playing House: To Be or Not To Be Coded Human" in Sharon D. Stone, ed., *Lesbians in Canada* (Toronto: Between the Lines, 1990) 133; David Rayside, "Gay Rights and Family Values: The Passage of Bill 7 in Ontario" (1988) 26 Studies in Pol. Econ 109.
34. Pub. L. No. 101-275 (1990).
35. Editors of the Harvard Law Review, *Sexual Orientation and the Law* (Cambridge, Mass.: Harvard University Press, 1990) at 167, note 36 (quoting Rep. Dannemeyer).

36. Senators found it necessary to amend the final version of the Act to add a clause stating that "nothing in the Act shall be construed . . . to promote or encourage homosexuality." 136 Cong. Rec. (8 February 1990) (Debate on S1169-01).

37. Jon Ward, supra, note 13 at 145.

38. Ibid. at 162.

39. Bruce Ryder, supra, note 15 at 87–89.

40. In her thorough study of social scientific discourses, Celia Kitzinger has argued that the conceptualization of same-sex activity as a medical pathology has been displaced since the early 1970's by a psychological ". . . model of lesbianism (and male homosexuality) as a normal, natural and healthy sexual preference or lifestyle, and the issue of pathology has shifted to the diagnosis and cure of the new disease of 'homophobia' (fear of homosexuals)." Supra, note 2 at 33.

41. Arthur Brittan's explanation for the hostility many heterosexuals display towards gays and lesbians is similar:

> "hierarchic heterosexuals" understand at some subliminal level that all gender ascriptions and typification are tentative and fragile, and that, therefore, the only way to hold on to what they have is to use force and other coercive means. The universal acknowledgement that gender is a social construction would lead to the breakdown of the existing gender order. Moreover, such an acknowledgement would entail admitting that their own heterosexuality is suspect and flawed. To suspect that you are like those you hate and despise is tantamount to hating and despising yourself. "Hierarchic heterosexuals" find it threatening to come to terms with these suspicions. In a sense, "hierarchic heterosexualism" is built upon the idea of the unity of the male self, the "seamless" self. It sees itself, as rational, transcendental and completely sure of its place in the world. Such a self cannot tolerate contradiction and ambiguity. To have doubts about one's sexuality and moral authority is to lose control of one's intentionality.

Supra, note 10 at 172.

42. For a more detailed discussion, see Bruce Ryder, supra, note 15 at 65–73.

43. S.M. 1987–88, c. 45, s. 9(5). Not surprisingly, the wording of the amendments did not satisfy opponents of the bill, who insisted that government policy should both condone heterosexuality and condemn homosexuality.

44. For example, *Andrews v. Ontario (Ministry of Health),* (1988) 64 O.R. (2d) 258 (H.C.C.) [hereinafter *Andrews*]; *A.-G. of Canada v. Mossop,* (1990) 32 C.C.E.L. 276 (Fed. C.A.), leave to appeal to S.C.C. granted. For critical examinations of the issues raised by the same-sex spousal benefits litigation, see Mary Eaton & Cynthia Peterson, Comment on *Andrew v. Ontario,* (1987–1988) 2(2) C.J.W.L. 421; Didi Herman, "Are We Family? Lesbian Rights and Women's Liberation" (1990) 28(4) Osgoode Hall L.J. 789.

45. For example, *Andrews,* ibid.

46. Katherine Arnup, "'Mothers Just Like Others': Lesbians, Divorce, and Child Custody in Canada" (1989) 3(1) C.J.W.L. 8; Wendy Gross, "Judging the Best Interests of the Child: Custody and the Homosexual Parent" (1986) 1(2) C.J.W.L. 505; Margaret Leopold & Wendy King, "Compulsory Heterosexuality, Lesbians, and the Law: The Case for Constitutional Protection" (1985) 1(1) C.J.W.L. 163 at 170–76; Bruce Ryder, supra, note 15 at 57–59.

47. Sheila McIntyre, "Promothea Unbound: A Feminist Perspective on Law in the University" (1989) 38 U.N.B.L.J. 157 at 173.

48. Catharine MacKinnon, supra, note 2 at 121.

49. Ibid. at 116–17.

50. "Objectivist epistemology is the law of law." Catharine MacKinnon, ibid. at 163.

51. Kathleen Lahey, ". . . Until Women Themselves Have Told All That They Have to Tell . . ." (1985) 23(3) Osgoode Hall L. J. 519 at 533 See also Christine Boyle, "Teaching Law As If Women Really Mattered, or, What About the Washrooms?" (1986) 2(1) C.J.W.L. 96; Bruce Feldthusen, "The Gender Wars: 'Where the Boys Are'" (1990) 4(1) C.J.W.L. 66; Sheila McIntyre, "Gender Bias Within the Law School 'The Memo' and Its Impact" (1987–1988) 2 C.J.W.L. 362; Sheila McIntyre, supra, note 47; Mary O'Brien & Sheila McIntyre, "Patriarchal Hegemony and Legal Education" (1986) 2(1) C.J.W.L. 69; Mary Jane Mossman, "Feminism and Legal Method: The Difference It Makes" (1987) 3 Wisc. Women's L.J. 147; Mary Jane Mossman, "'Otherness' and the Law School: A Comment on Teaching Gender Equality" (1985) 1(1) C.J.W.L. 213; Toni Pickard, "Is Real Life Finally Happening?" (1986) 2(1) C.J.W.L. 150; Ann Robinson, "Thémis retrouve l'usage de la vue" (1989) 3(1) C.J.W.L. 211.

52. For example, Adrienne Rich, supra, note 2; Monique Wittig, "The Straight Mind" (1980) 1 Feminist Issues 103.

53. For example, Patricia Hill Collins, *Black Feminist Thought, Knowledge, Consciousness and Politics of Empowerment* (Boston: Unwin Hyman, 1990); Angela P. Harris, "Race and Essentialism in Feminist Legal Theory" (1990) 42(3) Stanford L. Rev. 581; bell hooks, supra, note 18; bell hooks, *Ain't I a Woman: Black Women and Feminism* (Boston: South End Press, 1981); Marlee Kline, "Race, Racism, and Feminist Legal Theory" (1989) 12 Harvard Women's L.J. 115; Elizabeth Spelman, supra, note 13.

54. For example, bell hooks, "Men: Comrades in Struggle" in supra, note 18, c 5; Diana Fuss, supra, note 10; Gayle Rubin, supra, note 13.

55. For example, Adrienne Rich, supra, note 2 at 52–53; Sheila Jeffreys, supra, note 2 at 145–226. Diana Fuss, supra, note 10 at 110–11

56. For example, Kobena Mercer & Isaac Julien, supra, note 21; Jackie Goldsby, "What It Means to Be Colored Me" (1990) 9 Out/Look 8.

57. Kobena Mercer & Isaac Julien, ibid; bell hooks, "Homophobia in Black Communities," in *Talking Back: Thinking Feminist, Thinking Black* (Toronto: Between the Lines, 1988) 120; Patricia Hill Collins, supra, note 53 at 192–96; Audre Lorde, "Age, Race, Class, and Sex: Women Redefining Difference," in *Sister Outsider: Essays and Speeches* (Trumansburg, NY: Crossing Press, 1984) 114.

58. For example, Kenneth Clatterbaugh, supra, note 19 at 127–50; Gary Kinsman, supra, note 5 at 103–04; Michael Kimmel, "After Fifteen Years: The Impact of the Sociology of Masculinity on the Masculinity of Sociology" in Hearn & Morgan, supra, note 19 at 93.

59. See, for example, Patricia Monture, "Ka-Nin-Geh-Gah-E-Sa-Nonh-Yah-Gah" (1986) 2(1) C.J.W.L. 159 at 167; Esmeralda Thornhill, "Focus on Black Women" (1985) 1(1) C.J.W.L. 153; Hazel V. Carby, "White Women Listen: Black Feminism and the Boundaries of Sisterhood" in University of Birmingham Centre for Contemporary Cultural Studies, ed.; *The Empire Strikes Back: Race and Racism in 70s Britain* (London, Hutchinson, 1982) 213; Audre Lorde, supra, note 57; Adrienne Rich, supra, note 2 at xii.

60. Joan W. Scott, "Deconstructing Equality-Versus-Difference: Or the Uses of Poststructuralist Theory for Feminism" in Marianne Hirsch & Evelyn Fox Keller, ed., *Conflicts in Feminism* (New York: Routledge, 1990) 134 at 146.

61. In Gayatri Spivak's words: "We are deeply interested in the tropological deconstruction of masculist universalism. But when questions of the inscription of feminine subject-effects arise we do not want to be caught within the institutional performance of the imperialist lie . . . the critique must be persistent." Gayatri Chakravorty Spivak, "Imperialism and Sexual Difference" (1986) 8 Oxford Literary Rev. 225 at 238.

62. Cf. Richard Delgado, "The Imperial Scholar: Reflections on a Review of Civil Rights Literature" (1984) 132 U. l'a L. Rev. 561.

63. Bruce Feldthusen, supra, note 51 at 79:

> Of all the barriers to mutual respect and tolerance, to meaningful equality within the law schools, the exercise of the male right not to know is the most immediately pressing. It renders any further civil progress impossible. It goes beyond a trivialization of women's experience to the point of denying the existence of women's experience.

See also Jonathan Rutherford, "Who's That Man?" in Rowena Chapman & Jonathan Rutherford, eds., supra, note 19, 21 at 25: "Exposed to a growing questioning men have used their silence as the best form of retaining the status quo."

64. In Rowena Chapman and Jonathan Rutherford's words,

> . . . this [i.e., W.H.] masculinity remains the great unsaid. The contestation is over the bodies of black and gay people and women. Masculinity remains somehow removed, like a crumbling castle around which the battle against the Other rages—the cause but not the site of struggle.

"The Forward March of Men Halted" in Rowena Chapman & Jonathan Rutherford, supra, note 19, 9 at 11.

65. Victor J. Seidler, *Rediscovering Masculinity: Reason, Language and Sexuality* (New York: Routledge, 1989) at 3.

66. Ibid at 4.

67. Supra, note 63 at 22.

68. Richard Delgado, supra, note 62 at 577; Lee Maracle, "Moving Over" (1989) 14 Trivia 9.

69. See Bruce Feldthusen, supra, note 51 at 92:

> Men, especially white middle class men, must take responsibility to discover social reality as it is experienced by others. This process has two stages. First, men must abandon their right not to know. Then, they must come to grips with knowing.

70. See Paul Smith, "Men in Feminism: Men and Feminist Theory" in Alice Jardine & Paul Smith, eds., *Men in Feminism* (New York: Methuen, 1987) 33 at 37, noting that men have been absolved from "the responsibility of speaking their own bodies"; Alice Jardine, "Men in Feminism: Odor di Uomo Or Compagnons de Route?" in Alice Jardine & Paul Smith, ibid., 54 at 60, suggests that pro-feminist men consider the words of Hélène Cixous:

... a sentence which, to my knowledge, has not been taken seriously by our allies at all: "Men still have everything to say about their own sexuality." *You still have everything to say about your sexuality,* that's a challenge ..."

(Emphasis in original.)

71. I am referring to the "Wild Man" movement, associated with the American poet Robert Bly, whose blend of mysticism and Jungian psychology has produced the idea that men can descend into their spirits and make contact with the wildman archetype (not to be confused with the "savage man" who represents the limitations of familiar macho masculinity). Robert Bly, *Iron John: A Book About Men* (Reading: Addison-Wesley, 1990). For a discussion, see Kenneth Clatterbaugh, supra, note 19 at 85. It seems to me that the effort to create "new men," "wild" or otherwise, is doomed to recreate misogyny and familiar patriarchal roles if it is not informed by a fundamental commitment to overcoming sexism and heterosexism. As one journalist described his impressions of a wildman gathering: "Whatever this wildman was, I thought he still seemed to be an abstraction. We'd been far more convincing as savages." Trip Gabriel, "Call of the Wildmen," *New York Times Magazine* (14 October, 1990), 36 at 47.

72. See, for example, the works cited, supra, in notes 2, 10, 13, and 19. Heterosexual men have recently made contributions to the analysis of the effects of sexism and heterosexism on heterosexual men. See, for example, Howard Buchbinder et al., *Who's On Top?: The Politics of Heterosexuality* (Toronto: Garamond Press, 1987); Jeff Hearn, supra, note 19; Jonathan Rutherford, supra, note 63; Victor Seidler, supra, note 65; Victor J. Seidler, *Recreating Sexual Politics: Men, Feminism and Politics* (London: Routledge, 1991).

In Canada, a few heterosexual male legal academics have started to address sexism, but generally heterosexism remains beyond our theoretical grasp—that is, it is left to inform our analyses in an unexamined manner.

73. As Jonathan Rutherford has remarked, the predominant attitude of heterosexual men is that "sexual politics is all about women and gay men and not ourselves." Supra, note 63 at 43.

74. Jonathan Katz, supra, note 13 at 8. For an interesting volume of essays engaged in the task of problematizing heterosexuality, see Hanscombe & Humphries, supra, note 13, and especially Alan Wakeman's amusing flip of conventional wisdom, "What Exactly Is Heterosexuality ... and What Causes It?" at 17.

75. Stephen Heath, "Male Feminism" in Alice Jardine & Jonathan Smith, eds., supra, note 70, 1 at 6. See also Joyce E. Canaan & Christine Griffin, "The New Men's Studies: Part of the Problem or Part of the Solution?" in Jeff Hearn & David Morgan, supra, note 19, 206 at 213:

> having been cast as rebellious daughters by male academics, feminists are now being set up as mother figures, expected to provide nurturance and approval for the boys' ideas, even, or perhaps especially, when these ideas threaten our very existence.

And see, Jonathan Rutherford, supra, note 63 at 59: "Because heterosexual men repress our own homoerotic desires we fetishize gay men."

I worry that the measure of this paper can be reduced to the style of an ad in a personals column: "W.H.M. seeks validation of role as ally alongside persons engaged in anti-sexist and anti-heterosexist struggle. Positive responses only to Box # ..."

76. As Elaine Showalter notes, ". . . there is more than a hint in some recent critical writing that it's time for men to step in and show the girls how to do it, a swaggering tone that reminds me of a recent quip in the *Yale Alumni Magazine* about a member of the class of 1955, Renée Richards. "When better women are made, Yale men will make them." "Critical Cross-Dressing: Male Feminists and the Woman of the Year" in Alice Jardine & Paul Smith, eds., supra, note 70, 116 at 119.

77. Elaine Showalter, ibid at 120.

78. Cf. Michael Kaufman, "The Construction of Masculinity and the Triad of Men's Violence" in Michael Kaufman, ed., supra, note 5, 1 at 25:

> An awareness of oppressive behavior is important, but too often it only leads to guilt about being a man. Guilt is a profoundly conservative emotion and as such is not particularly useful for bringing about change. From a position of insecurity and guilt, people do not change or inspire others to change.

79. Jon Snodgrass, ed., *For Men Against Sexism: A Book of Readings* Albion, CA: Times Change Press, 1977).

80. Tim Carrigan, supra, note 5 at 163.

81. Alice Jardine, supra, note 70 at 60.

82. As Adrienne Rich has stated, ". . . the absence of choice remains the great unacknowledged reality, and in the absence of choice, women will remain dependent upon the chance or luck of particular relationships and will have no collective power to determine the meaning and place of sexuality in their lives." Supra, note 2 at 67. See also Catharine MacKinnon, supra, note 11 at 61: "Those who think that one chooses heterosexuality under conditions that make it compulsory should either explain why it is not compulsory or explain why choice can be meaningful here."

83. Eve Kosofsky Sedgwick, *Between Men: English Literature and Male Homosocial Desire* (New York: Columbia University Press, 1985) at 88.

84. Gary Kinsman, supra, note 5 at 105.

85. Another option is to deny the relevance of the categories altogether. However, I believe this is a disingenuous position for men to take if their primary sexual relationships are with women. Not only does it deny the reality of heterosexual privilege, which cannot be washed away by good intentions, it is simply not possible to know, in a sexist and heterosexist society, that your love of and desire for an opposite sex partner is somehow independent of the social construction of gender and sexuality. I cannot speak for celibate or bisexual men, who must confront a different set of dilemmas.

86. An earlier article I wrote is a good example of a failure to do so. Bruce Ryder, supra, note 15.

87. Arthur Brittan, supra, note 10 at 170–71.

88. Roger Scruton, *Sexual Desire* (London: Weidenfeld & Nicolson, 1986).

89. *Local Government Act 1988* (U.K.), c. 9, s. 28. For an analysis, see Madeleine Colvin, *Section 28: A Practical Guide to the Law and Its Implications* (London: National Council for Civil Liberties, 1989); Jeffery Weeks, supra, note 13 at 293–96.

STRAIGHT OUT OF THE CLOSET: MEN, FEMINISM, AND MALE HETEROSEXUAL PRIVILEGE

Devon Carbado

The essays in this collection reveal how Black men prioritize and negotiate gender sexuality in their antiracist politics. The collection does not, however, constitute a Black male feminist text. For one thing, not all the essays reflect feminist ideological commitments. For another, not all the essays reflect feminist ideological commitments. For another, not all the contributors would identify as feminists or profeminists. A Black male feminist collection remains to be published.

However, several of the contributors to this volume, most notably Michael Awkward and Luke Harris, have begun the project of theorizing about the possibilities for a contemporary (Black) male feminist criticism. This epilogue is my contribution to this effort. Here, I urge antiracist men to embrace and assert a feminist political identity. Male assertions of feminist identity are, of course, controversial. Such assertions raise serious concerns about: (1) territory (whether feminism is women's political terrain); (2) "safe spaces" (whether feminism is a place for women to escape male epistemological dominance); and (3) authenticity (whether feminism is constructed on, and intended to be a voice for, women's experience). Significantly, in arguing that men should identify as feminists, I am not suggesting that men should endeavor to speak in a "different" (read: women's) voice; male feminism should not attempt to replicate female feminism. The last thing we want or need is more men—under the guise and ostensible legitimacy of feminism—presuming to define the nature of women's experiences. Women "do not want you [men] to mimic us, to become the same as us; we don't want your pathos or your guilt; and we don't even want your admiration (even if it's nice to get it once in a while). What we do want, I would say what we need, is your work. And like all serious work, that involves struggle and pain."[1]

Part of the work of male feminism, the "struggle and the pain," should involve men coming to terms with and challenging male and heterosexual privilege. This, then, is the focus of this epilogue—exposing and contesting the male experiential side of hetero-patriarchy.

I want to begin by addressing the men and feminism controversy. As Kimberlé Crenshaw observes in her foreword, feminist discourse about men and feminism is, by and large, a discourse about white men and white feminism. There are very few voices of color. My contribution will attempt to explicitly racialize the debate, identify some of the concerns Black feminists might have about Black men's relationship to Black feminist theory, and provide an indication of how Black male feminists might respond to these concerns.

MALE FEMINIST OR OXYMORON?

5   It might indeed be the case that "men's relationship to feminism is an impossible one,"[2] that men cannot be feminists. This "impossibility thesis" is quite arresting. There is, however, an explanation:

> Women are the subjects of feminism, its initiators, its makers, its force; the move and the join from being a woman to being a feminist is a grasp of that subjecthood. Men are the objects of the analysis, agents of the structure to be transformed, representatives in, carriers of the patriarchal mode; and my desire to be a subject there too in feminism—to be a feminist—is then only also the last feint in the long history of their colonization.

Assuming that this male-object/female-subject dichotomy is accurate (I tend to think that women and men are subjects and objects of feminism, though not in the same way), the analysis avoids the fundamental normative question: Conceding that women were the "initiators" of feminism, "its makers, its force," do we want it to remain so? Proponents of the "impossibility thesis" seem to suggest that quite apart from what we might want, it must be so; the impossibility of men's relationship to feminism stems from the fact that "I am not where they [women] are and I cannot be." Because "there is no equality, no symmetry . . . there can be no reversing: it is for women now to reclaim and redefine sexuality [and feminism], for us [men] to learn from them."[3] Importantly, this argument is not suggesting political abdication—"that I can do nothing in my life, that I cannot respond to and change for feminism."[4] Rather, the argument is that "Male feminism is not just different from feminism (how ludicrous it would be to say "female feminism"), it is a contradiction in terms."[5] Fundamental to this argument, then, is the idea that because women are the "natives" of feminism men necessarily are the "colonists."[6] There is no male exit from patriarchy.

    I am not persuaded that "men's relationship to feminism is an impossible one." It is certainly true that men and women have different social realities. Yet, the very fact that men are not "where women are" might be a starting point for male feminism. Men's realization of gender "difference" and gender hierarchy, can provide us with the opportunity to theorize about gender from the gender-privileged position(s) we occupy as men. Indeed, men's contestation of gender should be grounded in men's and women's positional "difference"—the extent to which it is socially constructed and contingent, the extent to which it corresponds to power and marginalization, the extent to which men, and not just women, live the difference. Male feminism need not attempt to "speak" in a "different voice." Instead, male feminist criticism should be *explicitly* informed by men's experiential "differences." These "differences" could be the basis for consciousness raising among and between men. I am not speaking here about consciousness raising "for the purpose of finding the 'hairy beast' or the 'wild man' within."[7] Rather, consciousness raising should be a way for men to examine the multiple ways in which they are privileged and then to challenge the social practices in their lives that reproduce, entrench, and at the same time normalize patriarchy. It is not clear to me that male feminism would merely "reproduce what has come before."[8] On the contrary, a male feminist project could engender men, forcing us "to articulate the 'me' in 'men.'"[9] Part of the problem with discourses produced by men is that they are presented as ungendered discourses, purportedly neutral discourses, abstracted from any experiential reality. Employing feminism, "the male critic may find that his voice no longer exists as an abstraction, but that it in fact inhabits a body: its own sexual textual body."[10]

The personal is political—one of feminism's first principles. The personal, epistemological grounding of feminism *could be* the basis for male feminist criticism. This criticism could be centered on the male subject as a problematic identity. It is easier for men to acknowledge the realities of gender subordination in women's lives than it is for us to acknowledge the realities of gender privilege in our own. Generally speaking, men don't perceive themselves to be en-gendered.[11] "Gender," for men, is a term that relates to women and women's experiences; it is synonymous with "female." Thus, men have not paid much attention to the ways in which the social constructions of gender shape and define men's experiences as "men." Indeed, men accept their identities are pre-political givens. The gender question, when it is addressed, is rarely about the nature and consequences of male privilege but rather about the nature and consequences of female disadvantages.

A male feminist project could challenge men's tendency to conceptualize gender outside of their own experiences as men. As Hélène Cixous has observed, "men still have everything to say about their own sexuality."[12] It remains the "dark continent."[13] A male engagement *in* feminism (assuming men can be feminist) or *with* feminism (assuming they cannot), rather than portending the reinscription of [male] epistemological dominance,[14] could portend the "decoding" of the male subject and the production of a male epistemological self-criticism. This self-criticism could include an examination of the specific ways that men reproduce patriarchy interpersonally, and institutionally and the material consequences of that reproduction for women. As Michael Awkward observers, "to identify the writing self as biologically[15] male is to emphasize the desire not to be ideologically male; it is to explore the process of rejecting the phallocentric perspectives by which men traditionally have justified the subjugation of women."[16]

Significantly, patriarchy is not just "out there," external to our relationships and experiences; it is manifested and constituted by the ways in which we structure those relationships and experiences. Part of a male feminist project, then, should be to persuade men to *see themselves* as body-coded (as distinct from naturally created) men, and to identify how the social, patriarchal codes of manhood are re-enacted and naturalized in their everyday interactions with other men and with women.

10   But even if men's relationship to feminism is *not* impossible, which is what I am suggesting, feminism is not unproblematically available to men. Because men are the beneficiaries of patriarchy, it might be entirely appropriate to refer to a male feminist as "a[n] . . . oxymoronic entity."[17] There is, after all, the tendency on the part of men to control. To dominate. To silence. To appropriate and redefine. The "male feminist" must thus be mindful of the fact that his participation in feminism does not go "without saying."[18]

The "political terrain/safe space" concept raises additional concerns if we *explicitly* racialize the discussion so that the question becomes: What is Black men's relationship to Black feminism? This Black-centered framing of the discussion is especially important given the (mis)treatment of Black feminists and feminism in antiracist discourse. It is not hyperbolic to say that Black feminists occupy an outsider status within traditional Black antiracist discourse. This outsider status results from the construction of Black feminists either as racially disloyal—*women* who conspire with *white* feminists to "emasculate" *Black* men,[19] or as racially naïve—women who ignore or fail to appreciate the extent to which American law and social policy is designed to destroy the Black family via the destruction of Black men. As a result of these constructions, Black female assertions of feminist identity are to some degree race negating.

At least two questions emerge from Black feminists' subordinate status in Black antiracist discourse: (1) Do Black male feminists occupy this subordinate status as well; and (2) how have Black (female) feminists responded to Black male assertions of feminist political identity. Both questions are difficult to answer, because there is not yet a self-consciously defined Black male feminist community. However, in a recent essay,[20] Black feminist Joy James suggests that concerns about political terrain, safe space, and authenticity do not disappear when the men and feminist debate is rearticulated as the Black men and Black feminism debate.

With respect to authenticity, James asserts that she "prefer[s] the terms *feminism* or *feminist* for female and *profeminism* or *profeminist* for male advocates of gender equality."[21] She is "reluctant" to "concede" men "the use of the label 'feminism' given that it now requires the qualifiers *male* and *female* to distinguish advocates for an ideology associated with females."[22] James recognizes that "perhaps my uneasiness with male feminists is tied to my desire to biologize this ideology."[23] Women can be feminist because they are women; men can't be feminist because they are men. Sex is both qualifying and disqualifying here. But James points out that her concerns about men and feminism transcend biology; she is worried about male epistemological dominance as well. The fact that "Gender Studies" is replacing "Women's Studies," and more men are engaging feminism is not, for James, "necessarily a sign of counter-progressive politics."[24] Yet, she is not at all persuaded that these changes are (in the literal and more campy sense of the term) "all good." She writes:

Although I welcome the departure of exclusionary disciplines and Manichean depictions of the oppressed and their oppressor(s), I am still left with the uncomfortable perception that if the validity of an area of knowledge, for instance, women's studies or ethnic studies, garners legitimacy only to the extent that privileged intellectuals, for example, men or whites, shape the discourse, then the exegetical and institutional strengths that allegedly safeguard against subversion or mutation are not as powerfully entrenched as [some] would like us to believe.[25]

For James, the question is not whether we should be worried about (Black) men in (Black) feminism but rather what we should be worried about.[26]

As an example of what we might be worried about, James refers to Michele Wallace's critique of Henry Louis Gates, Jr., regarding the extent to which he is shaping and defining the African American literary canon, including Black feminist literary theory. Wallace employs Gates's intellectual career as an example of male control of discourse. According to Wallace, Gates is "single-handedly reshaping, codifying and consolidating the entire field of Afro-American studies, including black feminist studies." Wallace argues that the results of Gates's intellectual monopoly "are inevitably patriarchal. Having established himself as the father of Afro-American Literary Studies, with the help of the *New York times Book Review,* he now proposes to become the phallic mother of the newly depolicitized, mainstreamed, and commodified black feminist literary criticism."[27] Wallace's argument, with which James agrees, is that Black men still have "greater access and authority as intellectuals and thinkers" than Black women.[28] Black men's greater access and authority can result in the displacement of Black female feminists. This displacement of women by men entrenches the notion that men are the leaders of political movements, the force behind political ideologies, the intellectual movers and shakers, and the agents of social change. James' analysis suggests that while she finds "it is difficult to argue against naturalizing coalitions between feminists and black male profeminists," [29] she would doubtless agree with the idea that (Black) men's participation in (Black) feminism does not go without saying.

Not all feminists are as worried as James is about male participation in feminism. Some, for example, "see no reason why a man should not proclaim himself a feminist."[30] To illustrate why men's relationship to feminism is neither impossible nor inexorably problematic, these feminists distinguish between feminism and women. They maintain that while men can be feminists, "they cannot be women. The parallel here is the struggle against racism: whites can—indeed ought to be—antiracist, but they cannot be black."[31] For these feminists, the "important thing for men is not to spend their time worrying about definition and essences ('am I really a feminist?') but to take up recognizable anti-patriarchal positions."[32] To state the point a little differently, the question about men and feminism need not be a question about political terrain or gender essentialism ("whether men should [or can] be in feminism")[33] but rather about political vision ("whether [men] should be against patriarchy").[34]

bell hooks, an influential Black feminist, insists that feminism is (or should be) about revolutionary politics.[35] Women and men have a stake in transforming gender relations; feminism provides an ideological vehicle for women and men to do so. hooks suggests that there are two problems with the notion that feminism is for "women only." First, it provides men with a political out, creating the impression that feminism is "women's work." According to hooks, "Even as [feminists] were attacking sex role divisions of labor, the institutionalized sexism that assigns unpaid, devalued, and 'dirty' work to women, they were assigning to women yet another sex role task: making a feminist revolution."[36] hook argues that this sexual division of political labor is problematic; she reasons that men whose personal politics reflect feminist ideological commitments are "comrades" in a feminist movement— "they have a place" in feminism.[37] "Since men are the primary agents of maintaining and supporting sexism, [sexism] can only be successfully eradicated if men are compelled to assume responsibility for transforming their consciousness and the consciousness of society as a whole."[38]

hooks identifies a second problem with the notion of a "women's only" feminist movement: the idea is often buttressed by the conceptualization of "all men" as "the enemy."[39] This conceptualization ignores the fact that men are differently situated with respect to patriarchy because of race, gender, class, sexuality, and political commitment. "Assertions like 'all men are the enemy,' 'all men hate women' lump all groups of men in one category, thereby suggesting that they share equally in all forms of male privilege."[40] These assertions, moreover, are based largely on white, upper- and middle-class women's relationships with white, upper- and middle-class men. According to hooks, "Despite sexism, black women have continually contributed equally to the antiracist struggle, and frequently, before the contemporary black liberation effort, black men recognized this contribution." [41] hook's argument regarding Black male acknowledgement of Black female contributions to Black antiracist efforts is certainly contestable, but her broader point is that feminist theories on the possibilities for male feminist engagements often are white and middle class centered.

I am persuaded that the men and feminism debate should be about political vision *and* action. Nevertheless, I do believe that concerns about political terrain are important. For feminism might very well be "a room of one's own"—a place for "women to claim for themselves, a space from which to speak, a space within which to develop their voices as thinkers and writers, to cultivate that warm intellectual glow of the poets that circumstances and ideology [has] stifled for so long."[42] A strong case can be made, then, that feminism should indeed be for women only. Thus, the male feminist criticism that I have in mind would respect the need for "women only" social, political, and intellectual organization. Male feminism, as I imagine it, would reject the idea that men have "the right" to participate in female feminists' political groups.

But what, more fundamentally, does the male feminist criticism I am proposing entail? What is my male feminist methodology? And how might this methodology facilitate the dismantling of male heterosexual privilege? Let me now turn directly to these questions.

BECOMING FEMINISTS TO UNBECOME MEN

A fundamental goal of male feminism should be to facilitate the process of   *20* men unbecoming men, the process of men unlearning the patriarchal ways in which they have learned to become men. Ever since Simone de Beauvoir articulated the idea that women are not born women, but rather become women, feminists have been grappling with ways to strip the category "women" of its patriarchal ideological trappings, to find the pre- (or post-) socially constructed, pre- (or post-) patriarchal woman, the woman who has not been, as Tania Modleski puts it, "saturate[d]" . . . with [her] sex.[43] Significantly, de Beauvoir is not suggesting that, outside of patriarchy, there is some true female essence—the "real woman." (It might not even be meaningful to refer to the woman who has not been saturated with her sex as a "woman.") Her point is rather that people who are body-coded female cannot experience their personhood outside of the social construction of gender, and the social construction of gender for women is agency-denying and subordinating.

Of course, gender for men is also socially constructed. One must learn to be a "man" in this society, precisely because "manhood" is a socially produced category.[44] Manhood is a performance. A script. It is accomplished and re-enacted in everyday relationships. Yet, men have been much less inclined to theorize about the sex/gender category we inhabit, reproduce, and legitimize, much less inclined to theorize about the constructability and contingency of the social meanings associated with being "men," and much less inclined to search for, or even imagine, the pre (or post-) patriarchal man, the man who is not saturated with his sex. We (men) sometimes theorize about gender inequality, but rarely about gender privilege, as though our privileges as men were not politically up for grabs, as though they were social givens—inevitably "just there."

I think it is important for men to challenge the social construction of gender employing our privileged experiences as men as a starting point. These contestations should not displace or replace victim-centered or bottom-up accounts of sexism. That is to say, men's articulation of the ways in which they are the beneficiaries of patriarchy should not be a substitute for women's articulations of the ways in which they are the victims of patriarchy. Both narratives need to be told. The telling of both narratives gives content to patriarchy and helps to make clear that patriarchy is bi-directional: Patriarchy gives to men what it takes away from women; the disempowerment of women is achieved through the empowerment of men.[45] Patriarchy effectuates and maintains this relational difference. The social construction of women as the second sex requires the social construction of men[46] as the first.

Heterosexism, too, effectuates and maintains a relational difference that is based on power. There is no disadvantage without a corresponding advantage, no marginalized group without the empowered, no subordinate identity without a dominant identity. Power and privilege are relational, so, too, are our identities. What "heterosexism takes away from lesbians and gays . . . it gives to straight men and women."[47] The normalization of heterosexuality is only achieved through the "abnormalization" of homosexuality.

Yet, rarely do heterosexuals, especially heterosexual men, theorize about their identities as heterosexual, about their sexual identity privilege. Indeed, even pro–gay rights heterosexuals conceive of sexual identity as something that *other* people have, something that disadvantages *other* people, rather than something that heterosexuals have which advantages them.

25   Nor should male heterosexual articulations of gender and sexual identity privilege function to legitimize otherwise "untrustworthy" and "self-interested" accounts of discrimination by straight women and lesbians and gays. There is a tendency on the part of dominant groups (e.g., males and heterosexuals) to discount the experiences of subordinate groups (e.g., straight women and lesbians and gays) unless those experiences are authenticated or legitimized by a member of the dominant group. It is one thing for me, a Black man, to say I was discriminated against in a particular social setting; it is quite another for my white colleague to say I was discriminated against in that same social setting. My telling of the story is suspect because I am Black. My white colleague's telling of the story is less suspect because he is white. Male heterosexuals who participate in discourses on gender and sexuality should avoid creating the (mis)impression that, because they are outsiders to the subordinating effects of patriarchy and heterosexism, their critiques of patriarchy and/or heterosexism are more valid than the critiques offered by lesbians, straight women, and gay men.

A MALE FEMINIST METHOD: IDENTIFYING EVERYDAY PRIVILEGE

> It's up to him [man] to say where his masculinity and femininity are at. —Hélène Cixous[48]

Thus far I've suggested that, though the issue is far from uncontroversial, men can be feminists. I've suggested, too, that a male feminist project should not attempt to replicate "female feminism" in the sense of trying to articulate the nature of women's experiences. Rather, male feminism should be male centered, striving to give content to the very specific ways men benefit from patriarchy. For example, a white heterosexual male's engagement in feminism might begin by acknowledging that He (the white heterosexual male) is the norm. "Mankind." The baseline. "He" is our reference. We are all defined with Him in mind. We are the same as or different from Him.[49]

A clear and now fairly uncontroversial illustration of the male norm in operation is revealed in the debates about women's equality. Essentially, two competing paths exist to pursue women's equality in the United States: demonstrate that women are the "same" or "different" from men. "The main theme in the fugue is 'we're the same, we're the same, we're the same.' The counterpoint theme (in a higher register) is 'but we're different, but we're different, but we're different.'"[50] As Catharine MacKinnon observes, both of these conceptions of gender have "man" as their reference. "Under the sameness standard, women are measured according to our correspondence with man. . . . Under the difference standard, we are measured according to our lack of correspondence with him.[51]

Unfortunately, men are often unaware of, or reluctant to acknowledge, this baseline privilege. Indeed, we "are taught not to recognize [it]."[52] We are even taught to deny it. Self-interestedly, men accept present-day social arrangements and ideologies about gender as necessary, pre-political, and inevitable.

And there are "taboos against . . . male self-analysis."[53] Consequently, men, generally speaking, fail to consider or choose to ignore the extent to which they are "unfairly advantaged,"[54] even if they agree that women are unfairly disadvantaged. Stated differently,

> "[r]arely will a man go beyond acknowledging that women are disadvantaged to acknowledging that men have unearned advantage, or that unearned privilege has not been good for men's development."[55]

Men must begin to understand that male privilege is "an invisible package of unearned assets that men can count on cashing in each day."[56] A male feminist project should include a commitment to expose and contest these privileges. Men might begin, for example, by carefully examining their personal lives for examples of the ways in which they do not experience certain everyday disadvantages precisely because they are men. Here is an example of what I have in mind.

1. I can walk in public, alone, without fear of being sexually violated.
2. Prospective employers will never ask me if I plan on having children.
3. I can be confident that my career path will never be tainted by accusations that I "slept my way to the top" (though it might be "tainted" by the fact that I am a beneficiary of affirmative action).
4. I don't have to worry about whether I am being paid less than my female colleagues (though I might be worried about whether I'm being paid less than my white male colleagues).
5. When I get dressed in the morning, I don't worry about whether my clothing "invites" sexual harassment.

6. I can be moody, irritable, or brusque without it being attributed to my sex, or to biological changes in my life, to being "on the rag"—"PMS" (though it might be attributable to my "preoccupation" with race).

7. My career opportunities are not dependent on the extent to which I am perceived to be the same as a woman (though they may be dependent upon the extent to which I am perceived to be "a good black"—i.e., racially assimilable).

8. I don't have to choose between having a family or having a career.

9. I don't have to worry about being called selfish for having a career instead of having a family.

10. It will almost always be the case that my supervisor will be a man (though rarely will my supervisor be Black).

11. I can express outrage without being perceived as irrational, emotional, or too sensitive (except if I am expressing outrage about race).

12. I can fight for my country without controversy.

13. No one will qualify my intellectual or technical ability with the phrase "for a man" (though they may qualify my ability with the phrase "for a Black man").

14. I can be outspoken without being called a "bitch" (though I might be referred to as uppity).

15. I don't have to concern myself with finding the line between assertive and aggressive.

16. I don't have to think about whether my race comes before my gender, about whether I am Black first and a man second.

17. The politics of dress—to wear or not to wear make-up, high heels, or trousers, to straighten or not to straighten, to braid or not to braid my hair—affects me less than it does women.

18. More is known about "male" diseases and how medicine affects male bodies.

19. I was not "supposed" to change my name upon getting married.

20. I am rewarded for vigorously and aggressively pursuing my career.

21. I don't have to worry about female strangers or close acquaintances committing gender violence against me (though I do have to worry about racial violence).

22. I am not less manly because I play sports.

23. My reputation does not diminish with each person I have sex with.

24. There is no societal pressure for me to marry before the age of thirty.

25. I can dominate a conversation without being perceived as domineering.
26. I am praised for spending time with my children, cooking, cleaning, or doing other household chores.
27. I will rarely have to worry whether compliments from my boss contain a sexual subtext (though they may very well contain a racial subtext).

This list does not reflect the male privileges of all men. It is both under and over inclusive. Class, race, and sexual orientation impact male identities, shaping the various dimensions of male privilege. For example, the list does not include as a privilege the fact that men are automatically perceived as authority figures. While this may be a true of white men, it has not been my experience as a Black man. Moreover, my list clearly reveals the fact that I am middle class. My relationship to patriarchy is thus not the same as for a working class Black male. In constructing a list of male privilege, then, one has to be careful not to universalize "man," present him as a "cohesive identity"[57] in ways that deny, obscure, or threaten the recognition of male multiplicity.

But even taking male multiplicity into account, the preceding list of male advantages still leaves an awful lot out. Specifically, the foregoing items do not directly address male patriarchal agency—the extent to which men make choices that entrench male advantages and contribute to women's disadvantages. The privileges I've identified are the products of the cumulative choices men make everyday in their personal and professional lives. Thus, men must do more than identify male privileges; they must come to realize how they *actively* re-enact them interpersonally (in the workplace, in the street, and in relationships) and institutionally as well. Men must come to recognize their own complicity in the normalization of male hegemony.

UNPACKING HETEROSEXUAL PRIVILEGE (AND ITS RELATIONSHIP TO RACE PRIVILEGE)

I am a Negro Faggot, if I believe what movies, TV, and rap music say about me. Because of my sexuality, I cannot be Black. A strong, proud, Afrocentric Black man is resolutely heterosexual, not even bi-sexual. Hence I remain a Negro. My sexual difference is . . . a testament to weakness, passivity, the absence of real guts—balls. Hence I remain a sissy, punk, faggot. I cannot be a Black Gay Man because, by the tenets of Black Macho, a Black Gay Man is a triple negation.
—Marlon T. Riggs[58]

Straight men—even "progressive" straight men—might be reluctant to challenge heterosexual privilege to the extent that such challenges call into question their (hetero)sexual orientation. As Lee Edelman observes in a related context, there "is a deeply rooted concern on the part of . . . heterosexual males about the possible meanings of [men subverting gender roles]."[59] According to Edelman, heterosexual men consider certain gender role inversions potentially dangerous because they portend not only a "[male] feminization that would destabilize or question gender"[60] but also a "feminization that would challenge one's (hetero)sexuality."[61]

Edelman's observations suggest that straight men want to preserve the presumption of heterosexual identity; they want to preserve this presumption not so much because of what heterosexuality signifies in a positive sense but rather because of what it signifies in the negative—*not* being homosexual. And straight Black men might be especially concerned about preserving the presumption of heterosexuality—though I am not at all confident that I'm right about this, and I am certainly not suggesting that straight Black men are more homophobic than straight men of other races. But it is the case that heterosexual privilege is one of the few privileges that straight Black men *know* they have—not being a "sissy, punk, faggot." This is not to say, of course, that Black male heterosexuality has the normative standing of white male heterosexuality. It does not; straight Black men continue to be perceived as heterosexually deviant (potential rapist of white women)[62] and heterosexually irresponsible (jobless fathers of children out of wedlock). Still, black heterosexuality is closer to white male heterosexual normalcy and normativity than is Black gay sexuality. And many straight (or closeted) Black men will want to avoid even the suspicion of homosexuality, because that carries with it the "Black Gay [Male] . . . triple negation" to which Marlon Riggs refers. Challenging heterosexual privilege creates (homo)sexual identity suspicion.

35   Most of us, I think, recognize that our identities, via their social constructions, signify. That is to say, our socially constructed identities have social meanings to others, and even ourselves. Some of these meanings are more entrenched in the American psyche than others. Race, gender, and sexuality-based assumptions about personhood are especially difficult to dismantle. For example, when I walk into a department store, my identity signifies not only that I am Black and male but also that I am a potential criminal. My individual identity is lost in the social construction of Black manhood. I can try to adopt race-negating strategies to challenge this dignity-destroying social meaning. I can dress "respectable" when I go shopping. There is, after all, something to the politics of dress, particularly in social contexts in which race matters—that is to say, every American social context; I can *appear* less "Black" in a social meaning sense if I am professionally or semi-formally dressed.

Purchasing an item—something expensive—immediately upon entering the store is another strategy I can employ to disabuse people of my "Blackness." This strategy will reveal to the department store's security personnel what might not otherwise be apparent because of my race and gender: that

I am a shopper. If I am not in the mood to dress-up and I don't want to spend any money, there is a third strategy I can employ: solicit the assistance of a white sales associate. This, too, must be done early in the shopping experience. A white sales person would not be suspected of facilitating or contributing to Black shoplifting and can be trusted to keep an eye on me (a Black man).

White people don't have to worry about employing these strategies. Nor should they have to—no one should have to. However, white people should recognize and grapple with the fact that they don't have to employ or think about employing these strategies. This is a necessary first step for white people to come to terms with White privilege. Barbara Flagg and Peggy McIntosh—two white women—make similar arguments. Their self-referential interrogation of whiteness is the analytical analogue to the self-referential interrogation of heterosexuality I am proposing.

According to Barbara Flagg, "[t]here is a profound cognitive dimension to the material and social privilege that attaches to whiteness in this society, in that a white person has an everyday option not to think of herself in racial terms at all."[63] This, reasons Flagg, is indeed what defines whiteness: "to be white is not to think about it.[64] Flagg refers to the propensity of whites not to think in racial terms as "transparency phenomenon."[65]

Importantly, Flagg does not suggest that white people are unmindful of the racial identities of other whites or the racial "difference" of nonwhites; "Race is undeniably a powerful determinant of social status and so is always noticed, in a way that eye color, for example, may not be."[66] Rather, her point is that because whiteness operates as the racial norm, whites are able "to relegate our own racial specificity to the realm of the subconscious."[67] As a result, racial distinctiveness is Black, is Asian, is Latina/o, is Native America, but it is not white.[68] To address transparency, Flagg suggests the "[r]econceptualization of white race consciousness . . . [to create] a positive white racial identity, one neither founded on the implicit acceptance of white racial domination nor productive of distributive effects that systematically advantage white."[69]

Peggy McIntosh's work provides a specific indication of some of the "distributive effects" of white racial privilege. Thinking about how male privilege is normalized in everyday life but denied and protected by men, McIntosh "realized that since hierarchies in our society are interlocking, there was most likely a phenomenon of white privilege that was similarly denied and protected."[70] To illustrate the extent to which white privilege structures and is implicated in everyday social encounters, McIntosh exposes the "unearned" advantages that accrue to her on a daily basis because she is white.[71] The following are a few examples:

1. I can, if I wish, arrange to be in the company of people of my race most of the time.

   . . .

40

6. I can turn on the television or open to the front page of the paper and see people of my race widely represented.

. . .

15. I did not have to educate our children to be aware of systemic racism for their own daily physical protection.

. . .

17. I can talk with my mouth full and not have people put this down to my color.

. . .

25. If a traffic cop pulls me over or if the IRS audits my tax return, I can be sure I haven't been singled out because of my race.[72]

McIntosh is careful to point out that the term "privilege" is something of a misnomer: "We usually think of privilege as being a favored state, whether earned, or conferred by birth or luck. . . . The word 'privilege' carries the connotation of something I want. Yet some of the conditions I described here work to systematically overempower certain groups." Accordingly, McIntosh distinguishes between "positive advantages that we can work to spread . . . and negative types of advantage that unless rejected will always reinforce our present hierarchies."[73]

Flagg's and McIntosh's interrogation of whiteness can inform an interrogation of heterosexuality. Like whiteness, heterosexuality operates as an identity norm; it functions as the "what is" or "what is supposed to be" of sexuality. This is illustrated, for example, by the Nature versus Nurture debate. The question about the cause of sexuality is almost always formulated in terms of whether *homosexuality* is or is not biologically determined rather than whether *sexual orientation* (which includes heterosexuality) is or is not biologically determined. Scientists are searching for a gay, not a heterosexual or sexual orientation, gene. Like non-whiteness, then, homosexuality signifies "difference"—more specifically, sexual identity distinctiveness. It is homosexuality, not heterosexuality, that must be "specified, pointed out."[74]

Perhaps heterosexuals should develop a practice of "pointing out" their heterosexuality to destabilize the notion of homosexual difference. Perhaps heterosexuals should be encouraged to "come out" as heterosexuals. One argument to support this practice would be that the more heterosexuals explicitly invoke their heterosexuality the less it operates as an unstated norm. This argument has some force. Yet, I am uncomfortable with the idea of heterosexuals "coming out." My uneasiness is unrelated to concerns about whether individual acts of heterosexual signification undermine political efforts to establish a privacy norm around (*homo*)sexuality. The argument here would go something like the following: to the extent that heterosexuals are "closeted" (i.e., private) about their (*hetero*)sexuality, they help to send a message that (*homo*)sexuality is a private matter and should be irrelevant to social and political decision making.

I am not persuaded by this sexual identity privacy argument. It is functionally analogous to race neutrality arguments: Not invoking race, ignoring race, keeping race "private," helps to delegitimize the invidious employment of race as a relevant social category. It seems to me that keeping race private—removing it from public discourses—is not a sensible way to address the realities of racism. Race matters; therefore, we ought to talk about it—and publicly. Nor am I persuaded that avoiding public discussions about (homo- and hetero-) sexuality is a sensible way to address homophobia. Sexuality matters; therefore, we ought to discuss *it*—and publicly.

My concerns about heterosexuals "coming out" relate to the social meaning of that act. Individual acts of heterosexual signification contribute to the growing tendency on the part of people who are not gay or lesbian to employ the term "coming out" to reveal some usually uncontroversial or safe aspect of their personhood. Nowadays, people are "coming out" as chocolate addicts, as yuppies, as soap opera viewers, and even as trekies. Sometimes the "outing" is more political—"I 'out' myself as a conservative," I heard someone say recently. This appropriation and redeployment of the term is problematic to the extent that it obscures the economical, psychological, and physical harms that potentially attend the gay and lesbian coming out (or outing) process.[75] Although context would clearly matter, there is usually little, if any, vulnerability to "coming out" as a conservative, as a yuppie, as trekies, etc. Nor is there usually any vulnerability to "coming out" as a heterosexual. The assertion of heterosexuality, without more, merely re-authenticates heterosexual normalcy.[76]

Yet, more and more heterosexuals are "coming out," and often with good intentions. This "coming out" is performed explicitly and implicitly—affirmatively and by negation. Consider, for example, the way Houston Baker comes out in a panel discussion about gender, sexuality, and Black images: "I am not gay, but I have many gay friends."[77] When asked about his decision to reveal his sexual identity in the negative (Baker did not say, "'I am a heterosexual,' but 'I am not gay'"[78]), Baker responds that in thinking about our identities, "You decide what you are not, rather than leaping out of the womb saying, "I am this."[79]

The questions about whether Baker should have "come out" as a heterosexual in the affirmative or the negative obscures the fact that it is the "coming out" itself that is potentially problematic. As Bruce Ryder points out, "heterosexual men taking gay or lesbian positions must continually deal with the question of whether or not to reveal their heterosexuality."[80] On the one hand, self-identifying as a heterosexual is a way to position oneself within a discourse so as not to create the (mis)impression of gay authenticity.[81] Moreover, revealing one's heterosexuality can help to convey the idea that "heterosexism should be as much an issue for straight people as racism should be for white people."[82] On the other hand, "coming out" as a heterosexual can be a heteronormative move to avoid gay and lesbian stigmatization. It can function not simply as a denial of same sex desire but to preempt the attribution of

45

certain stereotypes to one's sexual identity. The assertion of heterosexuality, stated differently, is (functionally, if not intentionally) both an affirmative and a negative assertion about sexual preferences ("I sleep with persons of the opposite, *not* the same sex") and an affirmative and a negative assertion about the normalcy of one's sexual relationships ("therefore I am normal, *not* abnormal"). In this sense, I do not completely agree with Keith Boykin, director of the Black Gay and Lesbian Leadership Forum,[83] who maintains that because heterosexual orientation "has become so ingrained in our social customs, so destigmatized of our fears about sex, . . . we sometimes fail to make any connection between heterosexuality and sex."[84]

Boykin is only half right here. The socially constructed normalcy of heterosexuality is not due to the desexualization of heterosexuality in mainstream political and popular culture, but rather is due to the sexualization of heterosexuality as normative—"destigmatized," to employ Boykin's term. And it is not simply that homosexuality is sexed that motivates or stimulates homophobic fears about gay and lesbian relationships, but rather that homosexuality is sexed deviant—stigmatized, as it were. The disparate social meanings that attach to gay and lesbian identities on the one hand, and straight identities on the other, make explicit or implicit individual acts of heterosexual signification cause for concern.

Recently, I participated in a workshop where one of the presenters "came out" as a heterosexual in the context of giving his talk. This sexual identity disclosure engendered a certain amount of whispering in the back row. Up until that moment, I think many people had assumed that the presenter was gay.[85] After all, he was sitting on a panel discussing sexual orientation and had participated in the Gay and Lesbian Section of the American Association of Law Schools (AALS). There were three other heterosexuals on the panel, but everyone knew they were not gay because everyone *knew* them; they have all been in teaching for a while, two are very senior, and everyone knew of their spouses or partners. Everyone also knew that there was a lesbian on the panel. She, too, has been in teaching for some time and had been "out" for many years. Apparently, few of the workshop participants knew very much about the presenter who "came out." Because "there is a widespread assumption in both gay and straight communities that any man who says something supportive about issues of concern to lesbian or gay communities must be gay himself," [86] there was, at the very least, a question mark about his sexuality. Whatever his intentions were for "coming out," whatever his motivations, his assertion of heterosexuality removed the question mark.

50 And it is the politics behind the removal of the question mark—the politics of sexual identity signification—that we always have to be concerned with here. Is it an act of resistance or does it reflect an acquiescence to existing sexual identity social meanings? Consider, for example, the television situation comedy *Spin City*, in which Michael Boatman plays the role of Carter Heywood, an openly gay Black male character. Boatman is clearly very comfortable with the role and is "believably gay"—perhaps, for some, "too believably gay." Thus, in a recent article in *Essence* about Boatman we learn rather

quickly that Boatman is not in fact gay—he just plays one on television.[87] We learn, too, that it was not Heywood's sexuality that attracted Boatman to the role (he hadn't set out to play a gay man), but rather Heywood's career. The relevant text reads: "It was Heywood's job description (a civil rights attorney who joins the mayor's office) rather than his sexuality that attracted the 32-year-old actor to the groundbreaking sitcom. . . . 'we've been exposed to the stereotype of swishy gay men,' explains the *happily married* acting veteran."[88] The question mark about Boatman's (homo)sexuality is removed.

I became sensitized to the politics of heterosexuals "coming out" in the context of reading about James Baldwin. Try to find a piece written about Baldwin and count the number of lines before the author comes out as heterosexual. Usually, it's not more than a couple of paragraphs, so the game ends fast. The "coming out" seems inevitable nevertheless. The following introduction from a recently published essay about Baldwin is one indication of what I'm talking about: "The last time I saw James Baldwin was late autumn of 1985, when my wife and I attended a sumptuous book party."[89] In this case, the game ends immediately. Independent of any question of intentionality on the author's part, his wife functions as an identity signifier to subtextually "out" his heterosexuality. We *see* "wife" we *think* heterosexual. My point here is not to suggest that the essay's overall tone is heterosexually defensive; I simply find it suspicious when heterosexuals speak of their spouses so quickly (in this case the very first sentence of the essay) when a subject (a topic or a personality—here, James Baldwin) directly or indirectly implicates homosexuality.

After reading that introduction, I thought about a book review I had read a year or so ago where the reviewer, after describing how generous Baldwin had been to him as young man in Paris, casually drops the line, "I met a young American woman on a train and we made love." No mention of the woman again. No mention of any other women either. These weren't recollections of his Paris days, but were recollections of his relationship with Baldwin. But that single sentence served its intended purpose. There is no point wondering what he was "doing" with Baldwin in Paris. The game is over. The possibility of a gay subtextual reading of the text vis-à vis the author's relationship with Baldwin and/or the author's sexual identity is rendered untenable by the rhetorical deployment of the "young American woman." Her presence in the text operates not only to signify and authenticate the author's heterosexual subject position but also to signify and functionally (if not intentionally) stigmatize Baldwin's gay subject position. The author engages in what I refer to as "the politics of the 3Ds"—disassociation, disidentification and differentiation. The author is "different" from Baldwin (the author sleeps with women), and this difference, based as it is on sexual identity, compels the author to disassociate himself from and disidentify with what it is that makes Baldwin "different" (Baldwin sleeps with men).

I do not believe that heterosexual significations always reflect the politics of the 3Ds. It is possible for heterosexuals to "point out" their heterosexual privilege without re-authenticating heterosexuality. Consider the way Peggy McIntosh signifies on her heterosexuality to challenge heterosexual privilege:

1. My children do not have to answer questions about why I live with my partner (my husband).

2. I have no difficulty finding neighborhoods where people approve of our household.

3. Our children are given texts and classes that implicitly support our kind of family unit and do not turn them against my choice of domestic partnership.

4. I can travel alone with my husband without expecting embarrassment or hostility in those who deal with us.

5. Most people I meet will see my marital arrangements as an asset to my life or as a favorable comment on my likeability, my competence, or my mental health.

6. I can talk about the social event of a weekend without fearing most listeners' reactions.

7. I will feel welcomed and "normal" in the usual walks of public life, institutional and social.

8. In many contexts, I am seen as "all right" in the daily work on women because I do not live chiefly with women.[90]

Although the above items clearly reveal McIntosh's sexual identity, they do not normalize heterosexuality. Thus, I want to expand upon her list. I think it is a useful methodology for exposing and deconstructing sexual identity hierarchy. As with my list on gender privilege, I do not suggest that this list is complete or that it will apply to all heterosexuals. As Bruce Ryder observes:

> Male heterosexual privilege has different effects on men of, for example, different races and classes. . . . In our society, the dominant or "hegemonic" form of masculinity to which other masculinities are subordinated is white, middle-class, and heterosexual. This means that the heterosexual privilege of, say, straight black men takes a very different shape in their lives than it does for straight white men.[91]

My hope in presenting this list, then, is not to represent "every heterosexual man," but to intervene in the normalization of heterosexual privilege in everyday life, and to challenge the pervasive tendency of heterosexuals to see homophobia as something that puts others at a disadvantage and not something that actually advantages them.[92]

Heterosexual Privileges: A List

1. Whether on T.V. or at the movies, heterosexuality is always affirmed as healthy and/or normal.

2. Without making a special effort to, heterosexuals are surrounded by other heterosexuals everyday.

3. A husband and wife can comfortably express affection in any, and even predominantly gay, social settings.

4. The children of a heterosexual couple will not have to explain why their parents have different genders—why they have a mummy and a daddy.

5. Heterosexuals are not blamed for creating and spreading the AIDS virus.

6. Heterosexuals don't have to worry about people trying to "cure" their sexual orientation.

7. Black heterosexual males did not have to worry about whether they would be accepted at the Million Man March.

8. Rarely, if ever, will a doctor upon learning that her patient is heterosexual inquire as to whether the patient has ever taken an AIDS test and if so, how recently.

9. Medical service will never be denied to heterosexuals because they are heterosexuals.

10. Friends of heterosexuals generally don't refer to heterosexuals as their "straight friends."

11. A heterosexual couple can enter a restaurant on their anniversary and be fairly confident that staff and fellow diners will warmly congratulate them if an announcement is made.

12. Heterosexuals don't have to worry about whether a fictional film villain who is heterosexual will reflect negatively on their heterosexuality.

13. Heterosexuals are entitled to legal recognition of their marriage throughout the U.S. and the world.

14. Within the Black community, Black male heterosexuality does not engender comments like "what a waste," or "there goes another good Black man," or "if they're not in jail, they're faggots."

15. Heterosexuals can take a job with most companies without worrying about whether their spouse will be included in the benefits package.

16. Child molestation by heterosexuals does not confirm the deviance of heterosexuality.

17. Black rap artists do not make songs suggesting that heterosexuals should be shot or beaten-up because they are heterosexuals.

18. Black male heterosexuality does not undermine a Black heterosexual male's ability to be a role model for Black boys.

19. Heterosexuals can join the military without hiding their sexual identity.

20. Children will be taught in school (explicitly or implicitly) about the naturalness of heterosexuality.

21. Conversations on Black liberation will always include concerns about heterosexual men.

22. Heterosexuals can adopt children without being perceived as selfish and without anyone questioning their motives.

23. Heterosexuals are not denied custody or visitation rights of their children because they are heterosexuals.

24. Heterosexual men are welcomed as leaders of Boy Scout troops.

25. Heterosexuals can go home, visit their parents and family as who they are, and take their spouses, partners, or dates with them to family functions.

26. Heterosexuals can talk matter-of-factly about their relationship with their partners without people commenting that they are "flaunting" their sexuality.

27. A Black heterosexual couple would be welcomed as members of any Black church.

28. Heterosexual couples don't have to worry about whether kissing each other in public or holding hands in public will render them vulnerable to violence.

29. Heterosexuals don't have to struggle with "coming out" or worry about being "outed."

30. The parents of heterosexuals don't love them "in spite of" their sexual orientation, and they don't blame themselves for their children's heterosexuality.

31. Heterosexuality is affirmed in every religious tradition.

32. Heterosexuals can introduce their spouses to colleagues and not worry about whether the decision will have a detrimental impact on their careers.

33. A Black heterosexual male doesn't have to choose between being Black and being heterosexual.

34. Heterosexuals can prominently display their spouses' photographs at work without causing office gossip or hostility.

35. (White) Heterosexuals don't have to worry about "positively" representing heterosexuality.

36. Few will take pity on a heterosexual upon hearing that she is straight, or will feel the need to say, "that's O.K."

37. (Male) Heterosexuality is not considered to be symptomatic of the "pathology" of the Black family.

38. Heterosexuality is never mistaken as a lifestyle but is merely one more component of one's personal identity.

39. Heterosexuals don't have to worry over the impact their sexuality will have personally on their children's lives, particularly as it relates to their social life.

40. Heterosexuals don't have to worry about being "bashed" after leaving a social event with other heterosexuals.

41. Everyday is "Heterosexual Pride Day."

CONCLUSION: RESISTING PRIVILEGES

In some ways, the "identity privilege" lists in this essay represent the very early stages in a complicated process of dismantling male heterosexual privilege. The lists reveal that our identity privileges are legitimized through the personal choices we make everyday. All of us make choices that facilitate discriminatory practices. Many of us get married and/or go to weddings, notwithstanding that gay marriages are unrecognized. Others of us have racially monolithic social encounters, live in white only (or predominantly white) neighborhoods, and send our kids to white only (or predominantly white) schools; still others of us have "straight only" associations. These choices are not just personal, they are political as well. And the cumulative effect of these micro-political choices is the entrenchment of the very social practices—racism, sexism, classism, and homophobia—we profess to abhor.[93]

My purpose in constructing the "identity privilege" lists is to suggest that identity privilege should be self-referentially contested. We have to remake ourselves if we are to remake our institutions. We cannot hope to institutionalize our political commitments unless we localize our politics. Joining a de facto white only country club and challenging the politics of racial segregation won't do. The former helps to facilitate the latter.

The value of conceptualizing privilege micro-politically is that it forces all of us to think about the extent to which, on a very personal level, we are "unjustly enriched" because of certain aspects of our identities. If we observe and come to terms with the "unjustly enriched" aspects of our personal lives, we are more likely to take notice of the ways in which unjust enrichment operates systemically.

Of course, there are material costs incidental to the repudiation of personal privileges. People have little incentive to see themselves as unjustly enriched, for that carries with it the possibility of disgorgement. And what would it mean to resist privilege anyway? With respect to gay marriages, for example, does resistance to heterosexual privilege require heterosexuals to refrain from getting married and/or attending weddings? This essay does not explore these hard issues. I leave to others the task of theorizing about the various forms that critical resistance to identity privileges might take.

NOTES

1. Alice Jardine, "Men in Feminism: Odor di Uomo or Compagnons de Route?" in Alice Jardine and Paul Smith, eds., *Men in Feminism* (New York: Methuen, 1987).
2. Stephen Heath, "Male Feminism," in *Men in Feminism*, supra note 1, at 1.
3. Ibid. at 14.

4. Ibid. at 28.

5. Ibid.

6. Joseph A. Boone and Michael Cadden, eds., *Engendering Men: The Question of Male Feminist Criticism* (New York: Routledge, 1990): 3.

7. Bruce Ryder, "Straight Talk: Male Heterosexual Privilege," 16 *Queens L.J.* (1991): 289, 300.

8. Alice Jardine, supra note 1, at 60.

9. *Engendering Men,* supra note 6, at 2.

10. Ibid. at 12.

11. Alice Jardine, supra note 1, at 60 (observing that "It is much easier [for a man] to speak about women than to speak [about himself] as a body-coded male").

12. Ibid.

13. Rosalind Coward, *Female Desire* (London: Paladin, 1984): 227.

14. Bruce Ryder, supra note 7, at 296.

15. I would add "socially constructed" here.

16. Michael Awkward, "A Black Man's Place in Black Feminist Criticism," 362, this book.

17. Ibid. at 365.

18 Ibid. at 364.

19. Perhaps the most classic articulation of this perspective is Robert Staple's controversial 1979 essay, "The Myth of Black Macho: A Response to Angry Black Feminists," in *The Black Scholar: Journal of Black Studies and Research No. 6* (March/April 1979).

20. Joy James, "Antiracist (Pro)Feminisms and Coalition Politics: 'No Justice, No Peace,'" in Tom Digby, ed., *Men Doing Feminism* (New York: Routledge, 1998).

21. Ibid. at 240.

22. Ibid.

23. Ibid.

24. Ibid. at 241.

25. Ibid.

26. Ibid.

27. Ibid. at 282.

28. Ibid.

29. Ibid. at 240.

30. Toril Moi, "Men Against Patriarchy," in Linda Kauffman, ed., *Gender Theory: Dialogues on Feminist Criticism* (New York: Blackwell, 1989): 181.

31. Ibid. at 183.

32. Ibid. at 184.

33. Ibid.

34. Ibid.

35. bell hooks, *Feminist Theory: From Margin to Center* (Boston: South End Press, 1989): 67.

36. Ibid.

37. Ibid. at 80.

38. Ibid. at 81.

39. Ibid. at 68.

40. Ibid.

41. Ibid. at 69.

42. David Porter, *Between Men and Feminism* (New York: Routledge, 1992): introduction (commenting on Virginia Woolf's appeal to women to find a "safe" place from which to write).

43. Tania Modleski, "Feminism Without Women: Culture and Criticism," in *A Postfeminist Age* (New York: Routledge, 1991): 17.

44. See Henry Louis Gates, Jr., *Loose Canons: Notes on the Culture Wars* (New York: Oxford University Press, 1992): 101.

45. Of course, not all men are empowered by patriarchy in the same way. Race, class, and sexual orientation shape the nature of men's relationships to patriarchal privilege. Perhaps is it more accurate to say, then, that patriarchy gives to (some) men (more than others) what it takes away from (some) women (more than others); the disempowerment of (some) women (more than others) is achieved through the empowerment of (some) men (more than others).

46. Here, too, my comments about race, class, and sexual orientation pertain. See ibid.

47. Bruce Ryder, supra note 7, at 290.

48. Hélène Cixous, "The Laugh of Medusa," *Signs* (Summer 1976).

49. "The norms and the dynamics of the natural world—the ways its biological, evolutionary, and even chemical and physical properties are explained—embody unstated male reference points." Martha Minow, "Feminist Reason: Getting It and Losing It," 38 *J. Legal. Educ.* (1988): 47, 48. Of course, I am engaging in a crude form of essentialism to the extent that I am suggesting that heterosexual white men—unmodified (or as such)—operate as the norm. Quite obviously, there are other aspects of identity—class, ethnicity, religious affiliation—that complicate the notion of white heterosexual male privilege.

50. Catharine A. MacKinnon, "On Difference and Dominance," in Leslie Bender and Dan Braveman, eds., *Power Privilege and Law: A Civil Rights Reader* (Minn: West Publishing Co., 1995): 24.

51. Ibid. at 23.

52. Peggy McIntosh, "White Privilege and Male Privilege: A Personal Account of Coming to See Correspondences through Work in Women's Studies," in Leslie Bender and Dan Braveman, eds., *Power Privilege and Law: A Civil Rights Reader* (Minn: West Publishing Co. 1995): 23.

53. Elaine Showalter, "Introduction: The Rise of Gender," in *Speaking of Gender* (New York: Routledge, 1989): 6.

54. Peggy McIntosh, supra note 52, at 24.

55. Ibid. at 22, 23.

56. Ibid. at 23.

57. Robert Vorlicky, "(In)visible Alliances: Conflicting Chronicles of Feminism," in *Engendering Men,* supra note 6, 275–276.

58. Marlon T. Riggs, "Black Macho Revisited: Reflections of a Snap Queen," in Essex Hemphill, ed., *Brother to Brother: Collected Writings by Black Gay Men* (Los Angeles: Alyson Books, 1991): 253.

59. Lee Edelman, "Redeeming the Phallus: Wallace Stevens, Frank Lentricchia, and the Politics of (Hetero)Sexuality," in *Engendering Men,* supra note 6, at 50.

60. Ibid.

61. Ibid.

62. For a thoughtful discussion of Black male and female sexuality, see generally Charles R. Lawrence, III, "The Message of the Verdict: A Three-Act Morality Play Starring Clarence Thomas, Willie Smith, and Mike Tyson," 212, this book.

63. Barbara Flagg, "Was Blind, But Now I See: White Race Consciousness and the Requirement of Discriminatory Intent," 91 *Mich. L. Rev.* 953 (1994): 969.

64. Ibid.

65. Ibid. at 957.

66. Ibid. at 970–971.

67. Ibid. at 971.

68. Ibid.

69. Ibid. at 957.

70. Peggy McIntosh, supra note 52, at 23.

71. Ibid. at 25–26. For a discussion of the legal legitimation of white privilege, see Cheryl Harris, "Whiteness as Property," 106 *Harv. L. Rev.* 1707 (1993); Ian F. Haney López, *White By Law: The Legal Construction of Race* (New York: NYU Press, 1996); Stephanie M. Wildman et al., *Privilege Revealed: How Invisible Preference Undermines America* (New York: NYU Press, 1996).

72. Peggy McIntosh, supra note 52, at 23.

73. Ibid.

74. Martha Minow, supra note 49, at 48 (observing that feminist analyses have often presumed that a white middle class, heterosexual, Christian, and able-bodied person is the norm behind women's experience. Anything else must be specified, "pointed out").

75. See, e.g., Ann Yuri Ueda, "Mother Tongue," in Mona Oikawa et al., eds., *Resist!: Essays Against a Homophobic Culture* (Toronto: Women's Press, 1994): 23 (noting that her family has not spoken to her since she came out).

76. In some sense, heterosexuals are out all the time—kissing comfortably in public, sharing wedding pictures at work, announcing anniversaries, etc. These are not the practices I am referring to when I suggest that, perhaps, heterosexuals should develop a practice of "coming out." For none of the foregoing heterosexual significations challenge the socially constructed normalcy of heterosexuality. Further along in the essay, I provide an indication of how heterosexuals *might* be able to assert their heterosexuality without further entrenching heterosexual normalcy.

77. See Houston A. Baker, Jr., "'You Cain't Trus' It'": Experts Witnessing in the Case of Rap, in Gina Dent, ed., *Black Popular Culture* (Seattle: Bay Press, 1992): 132.

78. Ibid. at 139.

79. Ibid.

80. Bruce Ryder, supra note 7, at 303.

81. Ibid.

82. Ibid.

83. See Keith Boykin, *One More River to Cross: Black and Gay in America* (New York: Anchor Books, 1997).

84. Ibid. at 42.

85. A colleague relayed a similar experience to me. He was sitting on a panel discussing his school's anti–sexual orientation discrimination policy. At the end of his presenta-

tion, he was asked by his colleague from another department whether his wife knew that he was gay.

86. Bruce Ryder, supra note 7, at 303.
87. "Michael Boatman Acting Out," *Essence,* September 1997, at 78 (emphasis added).
88. Ibid.
89. "Evidences of Jimmy Baldwin," in *Leon Forrest, The Furious Voice for Freedom: Essays on Life* (Wakefield: Asphodel Press, 1994): 267.
90. Peggy McIntosh, supra note 52, at 32.
91. Bruce Ryder, supra note 7, at 292.
92. Peggy McIntosh, supra note 52, at 23 (commenting that "As a white person, I realized I had been taught about racism as something that puts others at a disadvantage, but had been taught not to see [as] one of its corollary aspects white privilege, which puts me at an advantage").
93. Karen D. Pyke, "Class-Based Masculinities: The Interdependence of Gender, Class, & Interpersonal Power," 10 *Gender & Society* 527 (October, 1996) observing that "Conventional theoretical perspectives on power . . . view microlevel power practices as simply derivative of macrostructural inequalities and overlook how power in day-to-day interactions shapes broader structures."

Part III Complicating Theories of Oppression and Privilege

INTRODUCTION

The readings in Parts I and II have given you a working set of ideas about oppression and privilege. Those readings have tended to characterize oppression and privilege as standing in opposition to each other, and as affecting entirely different groups of people. According to that understanding, either you're a member of an oppressed group, or you're a member of a privileged group—never both at the same time, and never neither one. Furthermore, the readings have tended to isolate the various axes of oppression, leaving one with the impression that any given individual will be affected by only one axis at any given time. (Either you're Black or you're gay.)

But of course these categories are not hermetically sealed from each other; no doubt many of you have already been reflecting on your own situation and thinking, "Well, I seem to be a member of both oppressed groups and privileged groups. Does that make me privileged or oppressed? How do the models we're reading account for people who stand on both sides of this divide?" Or perhaps you've wondered, "How can theories of racism that only talk about Blacks and whites address my experience as a Latino?" Or "How can theories that separate racism from sexism account for my life as an Asian woman?" Clearly, we need to complicate our theories of oppression and privilege, if they are going to be useful to us to describe people's actual lived experience.

The readings in Part III explore the myriad ways that these axes of oppression and privilege overlap and influence each other. These readings complicate the more "neat and tidy" theories of Parts I and II, and in the process they help make the concepts of oppression and privilege more descriptively accurate and useful for explaining more kinds of situations and experiences.

We complicate the theories of oppression and privilege in three different but related ways. The readings in Chapter 10 complicate our concepts by rejecting the either/or dichotomies that characterize much of our thinking about racism, sexism, and heterosexism. Think, for instance, of the tendency to talk about racism only in terms of Blacks and whites; the tendency to understand sexual identity as consisting of only the categories of heterosexuality and homosexuality; and, perhaps most fundamentally, the overpowering presumption that every human being is either a male or a female, never neither and never anything "in between." Some theorists in this section ask if an either/or way of characterizing race, sexuality, or gender is descriptively accurate. One invites us to consider the possibility that, instead of two mutually exclusive sexes, it would be more accurate to consider sex a continuum, on which "male" and "female" stand as endpoints, between which lie a number of other sexes. Other theorists point out the ways in which dichotomous thinking produces models of oppression that leave out entire groups of people; for instance, white/Black models of race and racism may be entirely inadequate for addressing the forms of racism experienced by Native Americans or Latinos/as.

Chapter 11 explores a second way to complicate the theories of privilege and oppression; namely, challenging the tendency of those theories to compartmentalize an individual's race, sex, and sexuality, and to treat each one separately. We sometimes think and talk as if we can understand a person's racial identity independently of her or his sexual identity, and independently of her or his sex/gender identity. This picture makes it seem as if a person's lived reality is a sum total of discrete parts not in interaction with one another. This kind of thinking leads to questions like "Do you think you were targeted for that harassment because you were Black, or because you were a woman?" Theorists in this section attempt to bring all of the axes of oppression together, and to use all of them simultaneously to interpret their own and others' experience. In the process, they reveal some of the limitations and shortcomings of the theories of oppression and privilege with which we're working.

A third sort of complicating is represented by the readings in Chapter 12. These readings explore and theorize about situations in which individuals are members of groups that are targets of oppression and groups that are systematically privileged, simultaneously. This is the reality of many—perhaps even most—people's lives, and theorists must be able to address this reality in ways that provide insight into it. The theories in this section work to create a more interactive and integrative model of oppression and privilege, exploring the ways that these opposing forces coexist in the experiences of a given individual, and the struggles that result for people who face the reality of their privilege and oppression.

Part III leaves us with many more loose ends and conundrums that we were left with in Parts I and II. It also leaves us with more nuanced, flexible, and workable understandings of our two central concepts, oppression and privilege. Recognizing that such "complications" are the norm, and not the exception, will enable you to continue to develop stronger and more useful theories of oppression and privilege that will account for the conditions of your own lives.

Equipped with these more complex concepts, we turn in Part IV to the project of theorizing resistance to oppression and privilege.

10

Challenging Dichotomous Thinking

■■■■

RACE, BIRACIALITY, AND MIXED RACE—IN THEORY

Lewis R. Gordon

> *"You, who are a doctor," said I to my [American] interlocutor, "you do not believe, however, that the blood of blacks has some specific qualities?"*
>
> *He shrugged his shoulders: "There are three blood types," he responded to me, "which one finds nearly equally in blacks and whites."*
>
> *"Well?"*
>
> *"It is not safe for black blood to circulate in our veins."*
>
> JEAN-PAUL SARTRE, "Return from the United States"

An African American couple found themselves taking their child, a few months of age, to a physician for an ear infection. Since their regular physician was out, an attending physician took their care. Opening the baby girl's files, he was caught by some vital information. The charts revealed a diagnosis of "H level" alpha thalassemia, a genetic disease that is known to afflict 2 percent of northeast Asian populations. He looked at the couple.

The father of the child, noticing the reticence and awkwardness of the physician, instantly spotted a behavior that he experienced on many occasions. "It's from me," he said. "She's got the disease from me."

"Now, how could she get the disease from you?" the physician asked with some irritation.

5   "My grandmother is Chinese," the father explained.

The physician's face suddenly shifted to an air of both surprise and relief. Then he made another remark. "Whew!" he said. "I was about to say, 'But— you're *black.*'"

The couple was not amused.

Realizing his error, the physician continued, "I mean, I shouldn't have been surprised. After all, I know Hispanics who are also Asians, so why not African Americans?"

Yes. Why not?

The expression "mixed race" has achieved some popularity in contemporary discussions of racial significations in the United States, Canada, and the United Kingdom.[1] It is significant that these three countries are marked by the dominance of an Anglo-cultural standpoint. In other countries, particularly with Spanish, Portuguese, and French influences, the question of racial mixture has enjoyed some specificity and simultaneous plurality. For the Anglos, however, the general matrix has been in terms of "whites" and "all others," the consequence of which has been the rigid binary of whites and nonwhites. It can easily be shown, however, that the specific designations in Latin and Latin American countries are, for the most part, a dodge and that, ultimately, the primary distinctions focus on being either white or at least not being black.

We find in the contemporary Anglophone context, however, a movement that is not entirely based on the question of racial mixture per se. The current articulation of racial mixture focuses primarily upon the concerns of *biracial* people. Biracial mixture pertains to a specific group within the general matrix of racial mixing, for a biracial identity can only work once, as it were. If the biracial person has children with, say, a person of supposedly a pure race, the "mixture," if you will, will be between a biracial "race" and a pure one. But it is unclear what race the child will then designate (a mixture of biraciality and *X*, perhaps, which means being a new biracial formation?).

To understand both mixed race and its biracial specification and some of the critical race theoretical problems raised by both, we need first to understand both race and racism in contemporary race discourse.

Much of contemporary race discourse is muddled, confusing, and premised on an ongoing project of evading the core issues of race and racism. Texts that racialize everyone with equal-opportunity racism tend to achieve some popularity because of the carrot they offer the contemporary sentiment on race matters. There is desire to speak about race, that is, but not about racism. Consequently, as race is spoken of in ways that offer multiple sites of oppression (consider the current vogue of the term *racisms*), we find persistent racializing of every site of oppression. Thus, even where race isn't the proper marker nor concern, the terms *race* and *racism* are evoked as legitimating expression for acts of condemnation. One reason for this tendency is the historic role race and racism have played in the construction of oppression in Anglo societies. For example, given the historical significance of slavery and the civil rights struggle in the United States, the operating metaphor for oppression has been and continues to be race and racism. Thus, race discourse is projected onto any location of group oppression, the consequence of which is that race and racism are spoken of in contexts ranging from Irish–Anglo conflicts to black–Korean conflicts.

Yet, if we were to deconstruct the order of racial signifiers in these contexts, we will notice the persistence of the metaphor "the blacks of. . . ." If one has to be "the black" in or of a particular context in order to designate a racial and a racist formation, then the rug that slips away beneath one's feet becomes apparent with the Fanonian historical "lived-experience" (*l'expérience vécue*) of the black: Although there are people who function as "the blacks" of particular contexts, there is a group of people who function as the blacks everywhere.[2] They are called, in now-archaic language—*Negroes.* Negroes are the blacks of everywhere, the black blacks, the blackest blacks.

15   Blackness functions as the prime racial signifier. It is the element that enters a room and frightens Reason out. The popular effort to articulate racial specificity through rubrics such as "racial formation," as emerged in the 1980s in work like that of Michael Omi and Howard Winant, fails, then, to address the lived reality of what race and racism are about.[3] Their theory, which they call racial formation, is premised on the view that race must now be analyzed beyond its historical associations with ethnicity, class, or nation.[4] The biological paradigm of racial formation is limited and limiting, they argue, because it supposedly presumes a static meaning to a historically shifting concept. "*Race is,*" they claim, "*a concept which signifies and symbolizes social conflicts and interests by referring to different types of human bodies. . . .* We define *racial formation* as the sociohistorical process by which racial categories are created, inhabited, transformed, and destroyed" (p. 55, emphasis in original). They define racism thus: A racial project can be defined as *racist* if and only if it *creates or reproduces structures of domination based on essential categories of race"* (p. 71). Fanon's sociogenic turn supports this interpretation. But the historical specificity of blackness as a point *from which* the greatest distance must be forged entails its status as metaphor. The formal structure of racism could be articulated thus:

$$\underline{} \quad <\!\!\text{---}\!\! \quad \underline{}$$

The underlined blanks are asymmetric points. The arrow points to a direction at which to aim. That direction goes away from the direction to avoid. Color contingently occupies these relations. Distance is relationally understood here, as are race and racism. This distance transcends logic ironically through a logic of its own. For instance, the call for black existence as unjustified existence need not appeal to essentialist racial categories.[5] Couldn't a structure of domination based on an *absence of essential categories* emerge—especially where an essential category is "humanness"?

Note further that the concept of racial formation is based on a distinction between social constructivity (which is an ontological claim about reference) and racial meaning (which pertains to the concept of race and is a claim about sense). Omi and Winant are antipathetic, on social constructivity grounds, to biological interpretations of race, even though a social construction can have biological connotations or senses. It is like a physicist who claims that what is meant by "table" is its collection of atoms. It may be correct that physical particles comprise a table, but that in no way determines a table's meanings. Thus, although meaning may be a function of societal conditions—how, for example, language is manifested—it doesn't follow that what is "meant" is social. Think of the distinction between a belief and a belief about or on the basis of that belief. Both race and racism, for instance, emerge when the physical or the biological is invoked. Groups are therefore racialized at the point at which the values attributed to them are treated as material attributes of who or "what" they are. There are formations that will not collapse into the "racial" category without a special set of signifiers, which the racial formation theory was designed to reject.[6]

In his famous *Oration on the Dignity of Man,* Pico Della Mirandola constructed a schema that is instructive for the understanding of race and racism.[7] According to Pico, the human being stood between the gods above and animals below. Although racism is generally spoken about in terms of hatred of other races, one should note the difference between hatred of other races and racism. One can hate another race on the basis of the conviction that that other race is one's racial superior. With such hatred there is no construction of the other race as less than human. In fact, with such a construction, there is a danger of one's own race being less so. To be more precise on our use of the term *racism,* then, we shall use racism to refer to (1) the conviction that there is a race that is superior to other races and (2) the institutional practice of treating that race as superior to others. Pico's schema becomes instructive, in that the implications of a superior race and an inferior race fall into the schema, in terms of which each group is pushed in relation to the gods and animals. The teleological implication of a superior race is its closer place to the gods, and the implication of an inferior race is its closer place to animals.[8]

The consequence of such a schema is that the conditions of being human are transformed into conditions of being gods or at least godlike. An instructive example of such conditions is Hitler's logic in *Mein Kampf.*[9] There, Hitler argues that the proof of a superior group's superiority is its ability to exercise its will over inferior groups. Thus, a superior group "is" superior by virtue of its place under that status quo. An implication of this superiority is its freedom from constraints. The superior group is literally boundless. It thus serves as the criterion for its own justification, whereas the inferior groups can only be "justified" in terms of the superior group. In effect, then, the category of superiority demands the impossible of the inferiors. They are to prove the validity of their existence, which, in effect, means to demonstrate, beyond using themselves as justification, that their existence is justified. Recall that Fanon identified this phenomenon in *Les damnés de la terre* when he writes:

> Because it is a systematic negation of the other, a resolute
> decision to refuse the other all the attributes of humanity,
> colonialism compels the dominated people constantly to ask
> the question: In reality, who am I? (p. 300).

Although Fanon is talking about colonialism, his points have a corollary in racism. For racism compels the designated inferior race to ask constantly not only in reality who am I, but also, "In reality, *what* am I?"

20 Without the transition of an interrogated "what," a what that signals a call for one's place in the scheme of human identification, neither racism nor race is born. On the same page, Fanon adds a distinction between domination and colonialism. To be dominated is not identical with being colonized, for it is still possible for one's humanity to be acknowledged (as, for example, in the case of being under the authority of a legitimate government). It is when one's humanity is wiped out of the scheme of human affairs, to the point of functioning as a natural phenomenon among other natural phenomena—in other words, among the land, plants, and animals—that the racist schema evinces itself. Both race and racism, then, are functions below the sphere of normativity. The consequence is that the dominant "race" is, as it were, *raceless.*

Race-neutrality is loaded with coded racial designations. If the standpoint of "man" is the dominant group, then that group stands as the leitmotif of all human significations. If white stands at the top of the value scheme of a society, we will find that many supposedly racially neutral terms also carry a white subtext. Arguably, in most of the world, except northeast Asia and India, the terms *man, woman, person, child,* and a host of other supposedly racially neutral terms, usually mean white man, white woman, white person, and white child.[10] Thus, to be equal to white means to be raceless. Race, then, is a feature of all other groups, and racism becomes a uniquely white possibility and perspective on these groups.

We can now explore the question of how both mixed race and biraciality can be understood in this context. In the United States, the significant factor of differentiation is premised on whites in an epicenter of swirling colors. In effect, then, to be "mixed" is a function of colored realities, not white ones, on the level of "race." Although whites may speak of being "mixed" with various European ethnicities and religions, racial mixture and white identity are antipathetic to each other. Whiteness, in other words, usually signifies purity. The "child," if you will, of white-nonwhite liaisons exists as an onto-biological point of difference from at least one parent. One finds, in such circumstances, a rigid order of hierarchies according to social subordination. Thus, in all matrices it is the white parent who loses onto-racial connection to his or her offspring. But in other matrices—for example, Northeast Asians ("mongoloids") with blacks—it is the Asian parent who loses the connection.[11] In terms of membership, then, the black parent finds a permanent racial connection with the child. (Of course, there are children who reject the racial designation and, in effect, reject, although not intentionally, their parents. But our concern here is the social reality of the hierarchies.)

One finds, then, that offsprings who are biracial mixtures with blacks are pretty much excluded from most racial categories except for black. Although it can be shown that among Native Americans the story differs—for Native

American and African American offsprings are often both (Native American and black)—there is still the social reality of the different quality of life available for a child who is a result of Native American unions with whites or Asians versus blacks. I recall speaking at a state university in Tennessee. A member of the audience introduced himself as a redneck with a Confederate flag on his truck. He also identified himself as part Cherokee by virtue of his grandmother, and he added that that has posed no problem at efforts to recruit him at Ku Klux Klan and right-wing militia rallies. I asked him to consider what his affiliations may have been if his grandmother were black or Asian. I also asked him to think about the significance of his Confederate flag as a sign of willingness to join right-wing and racist organizations. And finally, I asked him why he was so proud of being taken by such people as someone who is ideologically in their camp. Before he could respond, a woman in the audience, who announced herself as part Cherokee as well, voiced her objection. "Indians aren't white," she said. "There are whites with some Indian in them. But to be Indian, that's another story. Go to the reservations. You'll see."

Later that year, I found myself having lunch with a prominent couple from Toronto, Canada, one of whom regarded herself as being a biracial mixture of European and Chinese parentage. Her husband was white. As we discussed matters of race and theory, I eventually asked her and her husband to consider this: Most racially mixed marriages in North America occur between white men and Asian women. I recall a Chinese male associate in San Francisco lamenting that, in order to marry an Asian woman in California, he would have to find a way to become white. If the possibility of having children is still a central concern in most marriages, and if people consider the possibility of desirable children in their choice of matrimonial partners, why don't white men seem to worry about having children with Asian women? Why is the least mixture between blacks and every other group, and the highest mixture between whites and every other group except blacks?[12] And finally, why is there such a qualitatively different life in racial terms for Asians who are mixed with blacks versus Asians mixed with whites? Do we find Asians (and Latin Americans) rushing to wed blacks to uplift their gene pool, as seems to be the case with their marrying whites? Blackness, in the end, functions as a constant, underlying mark of racialization as does no other racial designation. Its persistence suggests that the fluidity of racial identities points upward in continuing spirals of potential whiteness.

But blackness also points to a history of mixed racialization that, although always acknowledged among blacks, is rarely understood or seen among other groups. I have argued elsewhere, for instance, that to add the claim of "mixture" to blacks in both American continents would be redundant, because blacks are their primary "mixed" populations to begin with. Mixture among blacks, in particular, functions as an organizing aesthetic, as well as a tragic history. On the aesthetic level, it signifies the divide between beauty and ugliness. On the social level, the divide is between being just and unjust, virtuous and vicious; "fair skin" is no accidental, alternative term for "light skin." And on the historical level, the divide signifies concerns that often are denied. Consider the striking similarity of the subtext of the following two observations—the first by El-Haji Malik El-Shabazz and the second by Frantz Fanon:

> Out in the world later, in Boston and New York, I was among the millions of Negroes who were insane enough to feel that it was some kind of status symbol to be light-complexioned—that one was actually fortunate to be born thus. But, still later, I learned to hate every drop of that white rapist's blood that is in me.[13]

> And Mayotte Capécia has [a good] reason [for being elated at having a white grandmother]: It is an honor to be the daughter of a white woman. That shows that she was not "made in the bushes." (This expression is reserved for all illegitimate children of the upper class in Martinique. They are known to be extremely numerous: Aubery, for example, is reputed to have fathered fifty.) (*Peau noire*, p. 37, n. 5)

In these two passages, we find both an aesthetic and moral tale that is indicative of the dynamics that emerge on questions of racial mixture. On the one hand, there is the prevailing significance of what Fanon calls "denegrification" (*dénégrification*), the phenomenon in which blackness is treated as a Manichæan quantity to be either eliminated from one's body or at least reduced. But on the other hand, there are the facts of historical social reality. In the El-Shabazz/Malcom X passage, there is historical reality of rape that signals the wisdom of the contemporary black expression, "All of us have a little bit of white in us." In Fanon's discussion, however, there is the more nuanced reality of the dynamics of power and gender difference. For Fanon's point is not only that social status enables one to "have one's way" with groups of lower social status, but that even among the upper classes, gender genealogies are of different significance.[14] A white female parent or grandparent shifts the meaning of the source of whiteness. It is not that one's genesis cannot have a history of violence (for the source of violence could also be from the black father and forefathers), but that if violence were present against a white forebear, consequences would have been different. The victimological narrative on both rape and lynching are so focused on white females for the former and black males for the latter in the Americas that an invisible history of predatory white males reaping the advantages of legally rejected black female bodies became the organizing principles behind any social consciousness of interracial realities. We find, then, a history of a touch of whiteness being a mark of blackness in the Americas.[15] As one U.S. woman of African descent puts it:

> While some have recently overthrown this term [Black American] in favor of African American, I have not. I find it too simplistic. I am not an African with American citizenship. Please

do not misunderstand. I embrace my African roots. However,
the term African American excludes the Native American,
White Protestant, and Jewish components of my distant ances-
try. And, I identify most strongly with a culture rooted in the
American South. Since I have not come up with a better term,
I still call myself Black.[16]

This woman makes no denial of being "mixed." Yet she defines herself as
black, and she uses the term *black* in the way most U.S. blacks actually use the
term. (In countries like Brazil, however, blackness refers to a mythical, "pure"
blackness because of the existence of the various populations of recognized
mixtures that differentiate themselves from blacks. To this point we shall
return.) In the North American context, then, awareness of being mixed has
taken on a kind of banality in black communities. What is often overlooked,
however, is the extent to which mixture-in-itself also has functioned as a site
of value. The general view is that people of color's preferential treatment for
lightness of skin and eyes and straightness of hair are signs of their preference
for or desire to become white. Consider Fanon's rather pithy observation:

For several years, some laboratories have been trying to
discover a serum for "denegrification"; these laboratories,
with all the seriousness in the world, have rinsed their test
tubes, checked their scales, and begun research that might make
it possible for the miserable Negroes to whiten themselves and
thus to throw off the burden of that corporeal malediction
(*Peau noire,* pp. 89–90).

These remarks on the technology of denegrification signal the matrices
of value in a world that is conditioned by two fundamental convictions: (1) it
is best to be white, and (2) it is worst to be black. The logic leads to obvious
conclusions of rational action. Failing to become white, one can at least
increase the distance between oneself and blackness. Thus, there are skin
creams for lighter skin, hair devices and chemicals for straight, "pretty," more
"manageable" hair, blue- and hazel-eyed contact lenses, and surgical techniques for the transformation of lips, hips, thighs, and any dimension of the
body that is interpreted as a signifier of blackness.[17] Yet in spite of the seemingly obvious aim of becoming white, I suggest that another step in the analysis is needed to understand how such phenomena are, in phenomenological
terms, *lived.* The way such phenomena are lived alludes less to becoming
white than to gaining certain aesthetic and political-economic resources that
pertain to being white. Many blacks, in short, simply want to be beautiful and
successful. But because no black can be white, it follows that there must be
some *other,* achievable point of being beautiful and successful that is aimed at
in such activity, and I have argued that that achievable point is ironically one
that is already embodied by the people trying to achieve it. One has, in other
words, a phenomenon of black people aiming to not pass for being white, but

instead to pass for being *mixed,* which is ironic because most people of color in North and South America as well as Europe and Australia, are, in fact, already mixed. That being mixed needs to be apparent—that is, it is important to *look* like one's mixture, to be, in a word, "authentically" mixed—provides a demand for the technology of mixed-race constructions.[18] Within the white social sphere, the technological innovation is ironically similar: The objective, whether in Bo Derek's wearing corn-rows or the current wave of hairstyle and tanning techniques to don the *look* of mixed race, is not to be taken for being mixed in the sense of parentage or heredity, but in the sense of *playing* mixture—literally, wearing it.

Appearing mixed offers something for both poles of the racial matrix. A touch of mixedness, which announces blackness, functions like black leather or lingerie in a bedroom—wearing it elicits associations and desires that are necessary but purged and relegated elsewhere in a bad-faith social order.[19] If blacks are socially acceptable sites of sexual and biological release, then one needs to wear one's blackness to be set "free."[20] The mixture emerges, then, as whiteness in colored clothing. In popular culture, examples abound: Whites in "darky" or blackface make-up, superheroes and heroines who don dark garbs, sexy vampire ghouls in dark clothing, or even the recent popular film, *The Mask* (1994), in which the personality released by the protagonist's wearing the possessed mask during the night abounds with peculiarly African American and Afro-Caribbean cultural formations, music such as jazz, rhumba, salsa, and the language of hipsters like Cab Calloway and the youthful Detroit Red (Malcolm X). The libidinous release achieved through rock 'n' roll has its genesis, after all, in white participation in black musical productions.[21]

30   In black communities, power and superiority have long been invested in children whose mixture was, let us say, phenomenologically apparent. To wear one's mixedness offered instant satisfaction. Even if one were not affluent or successful, simply appearing mixed signaled that one ought to have been so. One's existence takes on that added, almost-human element that shifts one's condition from the banal to the unjust and eventually to the tragic—as in the case of the "tragic mulatto."

Recall our discussion of Pico's schema. Individuals who are a mixture of white and black find themselves in more than a construction of mixture in and of itself. They find themselves facing a mixture of clearly unequal terms. For even if their whiteness is toppled from the stage of whiteness, it will stand, nevertheless, on the level of a human existence. But the prevailing ideology offers no hope in the other direction, where blackness is located on a lower point of the evolutionary scale. The conclusion is devastating: One is more of a human being to the extent to which one is less black.

The consequence of such an ideology is a set of existential and political considerations that provide tensions in the current movements of mixed-race identifications, to which we shall now turn.

Race talk is dirty business, primarily because race discourse exists in a racist context, a context that is occasioned by such a desire to deny what it is that its mode of operation is to play on ambiguities of the human condition in order to avoid getting to the heart of the matter. Consequently, diversions constitute a vast body of the literature. One is on the road to sobriety, however, when one begins to interrogate the keepers of the gate, for at least then one can discern the purpose of the practice.

Race discourse today can be divided into groups who find the very concept of race repugnant and groups who find race itself to be less of an issue and racism to be a primary concern.[22] Between these two groups of theorists, however, I would add a group I shall call *everyday people*. For the most part, everyday people do not think about races. They instead think about groups of people who are identified as races by people who theorize about what human beings are and what they do. Thus, for the typical antiblack racist, it is not races that bother him. It is *the blacks. The blacks* are an idealization that is seen in the body of certain people throughout the day. *The blacks* signal the extreme category of the nonwhites. As a character announced in a wonderful German cinematic allegory on racism and immigration: "As if it weren't bad enough that we had the Italians and the Turks. Now we have the Africans!"[23] Similarly, children learn about groups to hate, although they have no clue about what races are. I make these remarks because it is important to understand the extent to which race is a designation that usually emerges in contexts of explanation, whereas racism is simply the lived, ongoing practice that stimulates such explanation. The antirace people therefore miss the point. Even if they show that race is a social construction, even if they show that races are no more than cultural or social formations, even if they show that races are pseudoscientific fictions, they still need to address the ways in which phenomena understood as racial phenomena are lived. Not all black people know what races are, but they know what hatred of black people is. They read it in the symbols of value and the objective sites of power and lack thereof in which they are immersed in their waking moments, and even in their dreams. Even if every scientific claim about the existence of races is true, the antiracism people can retort, and rightly I would say, that such claims will have no impact on the task of fighting racism.[24] The fight against racism is an existential/moral phenomenon. Proof is found in the nineteenth century, when people who actually believed in the scientific validity of the concept of race simultaneously fought against slavery, genocide, and exploitation, and the myriad of ways in which *racism* is made manifest. Against Anthony Appiah's position then, where it is claimed that racism needs to be rejected because of the scientific invalidity (which for him constitutes the ontological illegitimacy) of the concept of race, the obvious conclusion here is that the scientific invalidity is not the relevant point.[25]

The antirace gatekeepers have had an unfortunate relationship with the evolution of one dimension of mixed-race movements and contemporary biracial politics. As we've seen, the whole point is not to be the darkest/most inferior.

So, given the existential dimensions of what we have discussed thus far, what, may we say, are the goals and possibilities available for a critical theory of mixed race?

35

Some claims that can be asserted in favor of a critical race theory premised on mixed race identity are:

1. Accuracy and consistency of racial ideology demand a mixed-race standpoint, for if whites and blacks are "pure," then mixtures signify other forms of race. (This argument supports the reasoning behind constructing separate racial categories for mixed-race people.)

2. The question of accuracy raises questions of affiliation: Filial recognition plays an important role in our self-identities. The need to recognize fully one's ancestry calls for recognition of mixture. Saying that one's ancestry is all-black because of the "one drop rule," for instance, fails to identity relatives whose lineage is multiracial beyond their African ancestry.

3. On the biracial end, there is the fact of converging embodiments to consider: A biracial offspring "is" biologically and often culturally both of her or his parents.

4. If race *means* black or white, the mixture becomes an enigma. It signifies "racelessess." (This argument goes both ways. In favor of a separate category for mixed-race people, it is advanced as a way of eliminating their exclusion from racial matrices by making such a provision. Against a category of mixed-race people, it is advanced to claim that even a racial designation will be an inaccurate articulation of their reality. And there are those who argue that it provides a critique of racial categories to being with and perhaps point to a [raceless] future.)[26]

5. On the practical end, biraciality and mixed-race designations can serve an antiracist strategy: recognition of racial mixture dilutes identities premised on conceptions of "purity" and can therefore be an important stage on the road to a raceless or more racially free future.

6. And finally, but not exhaustively, there is the existential claim: Mixed and biracial people have unique experiences that can be shared and cultivated through a recognized group identification. (This existential turn is also, of course, support for the political implications designated by the first claim.)

Now, recall my point about the two dominant principles of racist ideology: (1) be white, but above all, (2) don't be black. We can call the first *the principle of white supremacy;* and we can call the second *the principle of black inferiority.* Given these two principles, the following responses can be made to our six aforementioned claims.

First, we have already shown that to be racialized means not to be "white." And in fact, when white is spoken of as a race, many whites experience discomfort for good reason; it violates their place in the social order. Thus when all is said and done, the question of mixed-race people being an "other" race is only significant in regard to principle (2), which signifies the importance of not being black. Now, although this principle doesn't apply to biracial and mixed people along Euro–Asian or Euro–Native American lines—and given the racial hierarchies, it is rare, very rare indeed, that we find principle (2) being articulated in relation to any group other than blacks—it becomes clear that the "other" race argument is really about not being black.[27] Since the practice is geared toward adhering to principle (2), the political consequence will be an institutionalization of a certain place in the racial hierarchy. There will, in short, be an institutionally recognized group of nonblacks. One can readily see why certain groups of blacks are very suspicious of such a move, for its consequence is, after all, a quantitative reduction, by a legal stroke, of the population of designated black people. A whole group of black people will, that is, legally disappear.

Perhaps the best critical response to this move stems from our articulation of racism as a desire for black people to disappear. The first claim about accuracy requiring a mixed-race standpoint has the consequence of facilitating such a process, at least in terms of legal measures that can be taken. Such a consequence clearly violates W.E.B. DuBois' famous admonition against problematizing people instead of responding to the social problems that people experience.[28] There is nothing in the first claim that can reject the conclusion that the world will be better off if it had a lot less black folks, especially since the number of white people in the world will in no way diminish from such a move.

The second claim about affiliation seems to me to be correct but also in need of other considerations, for the question of filial recognition pertains primarily to *white* affiliation. The history of ancestral denial and rejecting descendants hasn't been a problem of colored folks. It is a white problem. There are whites who deny black ancestry and whites who reject black descendants; the issues pertains to the principle of white supremacy. But the principle of black inferiority also emerges through the lack of appreciation of black filial recognition. In black communities, for instance, talk of ancestry nearly always pertains to nonblack ancestry. It was only during brief moments of African ancestral pride, periods under attack today as "nationalist" and "Afrocentric," that a search for specificity of African lineage emerged. There are, however, surprising sites of such recognition. On a research visit to Cuba, for instance, my U.S. colleagues and I were astonished by a tour guide's response to a question raised by a member of our delegation: "Are there any Cuban Indians still around?" The guide, without missing a beat, responded, "Native Caribbeans were killed off within a century of Columbus's landing. All Cubans are of African and European ancestry." Because Cubans, at least the Cubans who remain on the island, are for the most part a "colored" people, the point of colored recognition is here affirmed. But even in Cuba, there are clearly black-designated people. There, as in most of the Caribbean, Central American, and South America, such people hardly stand as racially superior. The project of the ancestral claim, then, is to affirm *mixture* itself, which is to establish the force of the principle of black inferiority.

40

The third claim is clearly true. Biracial offsprings are from both parents biologically and often culturally. But again, once one introduces a racial designation other than white, the principle of black inferiority becomes the dominant factor. The biracial person can embody white superiority if the current group of people who are designated white people disappear. But in that case, whoever is next on the racial hierarchical scale will become white people. This turn, then, affirms the principle of black inferiority only because of the *current* limitations of embodying the principle of superior whiteness. In countries such as Brazil and Mexico, this is exactly what occurs. I recall a colleague of mine being shocked, for instance, while staying with a family in Guatemala. The family, whom he saw as not only colored but "mixed," categorically hated black people. What were they? Their answer was simple: white.

Moreover, the biracial offspring who attempts to affirm both identities faces a social reality of both identities existing on unequal terms. In short, to affirm whiteness on the level of blackness has the consequence of equalizing whiteness, which, in effect, is to "blacken" it. There is thus the catch-22 of being able to affirm their white side *as white* without encountering two perversions of reality: Either the white side is treated as superior or it is treated as a form of nonwhite whiteness; as, in a word, colored. These considerations bring us to the fourth claim, which addresses the supposed racelessness of mixed groups.

The fourth claim is subject to all the criticisms of race-neutrality. Since whites function as normative standpoints of humanity, they normally live as raceless. Angela Y. Davis, in a public lecture, phrased the situation thus: If colored means not to be white, then white means to be colorless.[29] Thus, to declare, as Michael Jackson did in his song "Black or White," "I don't want to spend my life being a color," means, in effect, to spend one's life surreptitiously being white. The problem with using this route as a means to a raceless future, then, is that it affirms a future premised on both principles by ultimately advocating the elimination of black people .

In an essay entitled, "White Normativity and the Racial Rhetoric of Equal Protection," Robert Westley unmasks some insidious dimensions of racelessness in the present age.[30] When the search for a legal remedy to racism took the form of *equal* protection, many whites suddenly gained the consciousness of being *racialized*. In the previous world, there were only human beings and coloreds—at the bottom of which were *the blacks*. Today, the law says that blacks are equal to every other group, which for these groups means that the law considers them equal to blacks. A strange equality: blacks move up while everyone else moves "down." For many whites, the metaphor of being treated "like the blacks" became a source of deeply rooted anxiety. In effect, social policy demanded that they take, as Adam and Eve apparently did, a "fall." Needless to say, many whites couldn't take it, and a full-scale attack on affirmative action and an array of antirace and so-called reverse-discrimination constructions emerged. The goal of this attack is supposedly a raceless future, but because racism can persist without race, such a future holds the key to a special nightmare of exploitation and invisibility without reference. It problematizes race, ultimately to preserve racism.

The fifth claim, which sees an antiracist strategy in which racelessness is *45* the carrot at the end of the rod, is problematic for the same reasons as the fourth one: It portends a world without blacks.

The sixth claim, that biracial and mixed-race people have a unique existential situation, strikes me as correct. Mixed-race and biracial people do have unique experiences that are functions of their existential situation. For the biracial child, the anonymous white man may be, in his specific instantiation, Daddy. And all the literature and cultural knowledge of victimized femininity—white, pure, rapable—may be Mommy. Similarly, the complex social forces that say that one is more one's black parent than one's white parent (or one's Asian or Native American parent) raises a complex question of who one is by virtue of one's choice and that choice's relation to one's social situation. Since black Americans and Native Americans are already mixed peoples (what is a "pure" New World black and Native American today?), the question relates mostly to people of color elsewhere: African Americans, for example, experience a profound anxiety when they travel to "black" countries; they seem, in those places, to be the least or lesser blacks; they carry with them, that is, the United States as a history of white domination and, for the most part, the masculine history of white "insemination."

On the existential level, biracial people at least have the unique experience of living the racial realities of more than one group in the course of their innermost private lives. That reality alone substantiates something unique, since among all other groups, "others" function anonymously. "God knows what they do in their homes!" is not a rhetorical appeal in biracial people's lived realities.

The question of the political significance of the sixth claim is undermined, however, by our critique of the other claims, especially the first. After all, having a unique situation does not mean that the principle of white superiority and the principle of black inferiority should be affirmed. For the biracial child stands below whiteness and, by virtue of biraciality, in affirmation of black inferiority. The impact of building policy on the uniqueness of biracial people, then, is that it fails to account for political realities that are already in place against people who are clear and present violators of the principle against blackness—in a word, *blacks.*

In spite of contemporary resistance to "binary" analyses, a critical discussion of mixed-race categories calls for an understanding of how binary logic functions in discourses on race and racism. Without binaries, no racism will exist. We have seen the politics of mixed-racialization come to the fore, for instance, on matters of legal recognition of multiple categories. There, principle (2), which affirms the importance of not being black, is the most significant principle. That is because there are social benefits in not being designated black. It is a waste of time to discuss the social losses of being designated white, since the distribution of resources on a global scale falls disproportionately in favor of whites. Affirming principle (2), therefore, affirms the whole racist hierarchy that we may be attempting to avoid. It solidifies the significance of the expression, "Well, at least you're not black."

50   The struggle against racism from a mixed-race critical position cannot work, then, through simply a rejection of principle (1). To reject the importance of being white in no way addresses the social revulsion with being black. A mixed-race racial position is compatible with the rejection of principle (1), but it is not compatible with the rejection of principle (2). That is because there is no way to reject the thesis that there is something wrong with being black beyond the willingness to "be" black—not in terms of convenient fads of playing blackness, but by paying the social costs of antiblackness on a global scale. Against the raceless credo, then, racism cannot be rejected without a dialectic in which humanity experiences a blackened world. But therein lies the suicidal irony of a *critical* mixed-race theory.

NOTES

1. See, for example, Naomi Zack's *Race and Mixed Race* (Philadelphia: Temple University Press, 1993) and her edited volume *American Mixed Race* (Lanham, MD: Rowman and Littlefield, 1995), as well as the February 13, 1995, issue of *Newsweek* for some discussion of this phenomenon. One also can argue that the popularity of the term *hybridity* in postmodern and postcolonial cultural studies is indicative of this phenomenon, where, in an effort to evade the peculiarly biological dimensions of race, *cultural* mixture becomes the focus in a tale of political ambiguity. That cultures are not homogenous in not new to cultural anthropologists. Its contemporary popularity is premised on a false academic history of hegemonic purity. For discussion, see Paul Gilroy's *The Black Atlantic: Modernity and Double Consciousness* (Cambridge, MA: Harvard University Press, 1993). Although Gilroy's position is a sound critique of cultural reductionism and cultural purity (homogeneity may have been a value of cultures, but not a reality of their evolution), some of his readers' interests stem not from the social logic of his argument but from a fascination with a form of privileged hybridity or mixture. One need only consult the contemporary mystique of mixture, particularly of the female biracial variety in British popular films over the past two decades. For discussion, see Joy Ann James, *Resisting State Violence in U.S. Culture* (Minneapolis: University of Minnesota Press, 1996), and Lisa Anderson, *Mammies No More!* (Lanham, MD): Rowman & Littlefield, 1997). Finally, on the matter of political ambiguity, I think context and relevance are the best appeals. Sometimes circumstances are without ambiguity. Only those with tenuous access to power can afford ambiguity in their political relations.
2. See Fanon, *Peau noire, masques blancs,* chap. 5. For discussion, see *Bad Faith and Antiblack Racism,* part III.
3. Michael Omi and Howard Winant, *Racial Formations in the United States: From the 1960s to the 1990s,* 2nd ed. (New York and London: Routledge, 1994).
4. We argue that sex and gender are two categories that also apply.

5. I discuss this dimension of antiblack racism in parts III and IV of *Bad Faith and Antiblack Racism*. See also, "Introduction: Black Existential Philosophy" in *Existence in Black*.

6. For discussion, see treatments of the spirit of seriousness in chap. 6 and the discussion of "meaning" and racism in Parts II and III of *Bad Faith and Antiblack Racism,* as well as the critique, in *Fanon and the Crisis of European Man,* chap. 3, of the current misuse of the term *social construction*. See also Fanon's discussion of blacks as an *"objet phobogène"* (phobogenic object) and the point at which *"commence le cycle du biologique"* (the cycle of the biological begins) in *Peau noire,* pp. 123, 131. For critical discussion of Omi and Winant's notion of racial formation, see also David Theo Goldberg's *Racist Culture: Philosophy and the Politics of Meaning* (Oxford: Blackwell, 1993), especially p. 88.

7. See Count Giovanni Pico Della Mirandola, *Oration on the Dignity of Man,* trans. Elizabeth L. Forbes, in *The Renaissance Philosophy of Man,* ed. Ernst Cassirer, Paul Oskar Kristeller, and John Herman Randall, Jr. (Chicago: University of Chicago Press, 1939).

8. For some readers, Lovejoy's discussion of the Great Chain of Being may come to mind. For discussion of that ontological schema, see Daniel Wideman, "The 'African Origin' of AIDS: De-constructing Western Biomedical Discourse," in *Black Texts and Textuality: Constructing and De-Constructing Blackness,* ed. with an intro. By Lewis R. Gordon and Renée T. White (Lanham, MD: Rowman & Littlefield, 2004). See also Robert Westley, "White Normativity and the Rhetoric of Equal Protection" in *Existence in Black.*

9. For discussion of this "logic," see C.W. Cassinelli, *Total Revolution: A Comparative Study of Germany under Hitler, the Soviet Union under Stalin, and China under Mao* (Santa Barbara and Oxford: Clio Books, 1976), part II.

10. One can argue that they mean these categories in those other societies as well, but the argument requires a demonstration of the relation between historical reality and phenomenology of "race seeing." For such a phenomenology, see *Bad Faith and Antiblack Racism,* chaps. 13–14.

11. For some discussion of Afro-Asian dynamics, see Ernest Allen Jr., "When Japan Was 'Champion of the Darker Races': Satokata Takahashi and the Flowering of Black Messianic Nationalism." *The Black Scholar* 24, no. 1 (Winter 1994): 23–46, and Joy Ann James, *Resisting State Violence in U.S. Culture* (Minneapolis: University of Minnesota Press, 1996), chap. 15. For specifically Northeast Asian encounters with racial mixture in the United States, see Stephen Satris, "'What Are They?'" in *American Mixed Race: The Culture of Microdiversity,* ed. Naomi Zack (Lanham, MD: Rowman & Littlefield, 1995), pp. 53–60. Satris argues that children of European (caucasian) and Northeast Asian (mongoloid) descent tend to be regarded as Asian only when mongoloid morphology is visually apparent. Children who don't appear as such are regarded and treated by the white and Asian communities as white.

12. According to the U.S. Census, as of 1993, only 2% of interracial marriages were between blacks and "other" races, 20% between blacks and whites, but the number of interracial marriages between whites and non-black "others" was 77%. See also Connie Leslie, Regina Elam, Allison Samuels, and Danzy Senna, "The Loving Generation: Biracial Children Seek Their Own Place," *Newsweek* (February 13, 1995), p. 72, where these figures also are cited.

13. From *The Autobiography of Malcolm X as Told to Alex Haley* (New York: Ballantine Books, 1965), p. 2.

14. The impact of class on interracial relationships hasn't received significant study. And in fact, most of the constructions of interracial liaisons are premised on either a white male boss with a colored female subordinate, or affluent men of color with affluent white women. But note: relationships are most likely to occur where people are compelled to live. Because the black poor and the white poor have few options over where they can live, and because the urban poor tend to be located in black areas of cities, it follows that interracial relationships should have a greater probability of emerging in poor or working-class communities: In fact, there are no black American communities that have not had a white population, however small.

15. For discussion, see Fanon's essay "Antillais et africains" in his *Pour la révolution africaine: écrits politiques* (Paris: François Maspero, 1979), pp. 22–31. The essay appears as "West Indians and Africans" in the English edition, *Toward the African Revolution: Political Essays,* trans. Haakon Chevalier (New York: Grove Press, 1967), pp. 17–27. . . .

16. Victoria Holloway, "President's Message," *The Drum: The SNMA–Yale Chapter Newsletter* (October 1991): 1.

17. The question of transforming the body takes special forms with the Northeast Asians. There is, for instance, the phenomenon of surgically "fixing" the eyes. But note, the normative point is white eyes. The probability of Asians transforming their bodies to look more "black" is very small. For discussion of Northeast Asian Americans' identity formations, see Brian Locke, "The Impact of the Black–White Binary on Asian American Identity," *Radical Philosophy Review,* 1, no. 2 (1998). Locke argues that an apocalyptic subtext of the U.S. black–white binary structures Asian Americans as foreign.

18. In this regard, the appeal to mixed race as a model for resisting appeals to racial and cultural "authenticity" appears misguided, for the problem of authenticity—as "being *authentically* mixed" demonstrates—is quite resilient.

19. For more discussion of playing blackness, see bell hooks, *Black Looks: Race and Representation* (Boston: South End Press, 1992), chap. 1.

20. See, for example, bell hook's criticism of Camille Paglia: "'Black' Pagan or White Colonizer?" chap. 7 of hooks's *Outlaw Culture* (New York and London: Routledge, 1994).

21. One also finds the phenomenon of mixture in philosophy itself, where there is antipathy on the part of the dominant, Anglo-Analytical philosophy toward any of the pluralistic, "mixed" conceptions of philosophy ranging from pragmatism and European continental philosophy, on the one hand, to Africana philosophies and Eastern philosophies on the other. Departments that offer both are "mixed." Interestingly enough, certain "mixtures" exist in the form of Anglo-Analytical approaches to Africana philosophy, the most noted proponent of which is Kwame Anthony Appiah and the analytical race theorists who follow his path.

22. Theorists who focus on the concept of race are Michael Omi and Howard Winant, K. Anthony Appiah, Jorge Klor de Alva, and Naomi Zack. Theorists who focus on racism are Lucius Outlaw, Paget Henry, David Theo Goldberg, Cornel West, and myself, among others. This distinction doesn't mean, however, that the two groups do not touch on dimensions of each other's position. The former group argues that the

elimination of the discourse of race is a necessary step toward the elimination of racism. The latter takes two stands on that issue. First, some argue for the existential complexity of race. Second, some argue that racism can exist without race. In either event, both groups end up addressing race and racism, but the first group, unlike the second, wants to eliminate both categories.

23. *Schwartzfahren* (1992). In contemporary Eastern Europe (and Europe generally), the digression seems to take a definite form: first, xenophobic (anti-immigration) and, eventually, racist (antiblack). The argument is that immigration policies pollute the state by leading to an influx of blacks. For discussion, see Paul Hockenos, *Free to Hate: The Rise of the Right in Post-Communist Eastern Europe* (New York and London: Routledge, 1993). We also may note that in California the pattern is strikingly similar: Proposition 187 is anti-immigrants legislation that has been followed by a so-called Civil Rights Initiative, which is an anti–Affirmative Action legislation that is primarily antiblack.

24. A classic instance of a thinker and activist against racism who nevertheless believes in race is Franz Boas. Boas believed not only in the existence of races but also that blacks were to some extent less intellectually capable than whites, yet he fought vehemently against the status of second-class citizenship of blacks. For discussion, see Vernon Williams, Jr., *Rethinking Race: Franz Boas and His Contemporaries* (Lexington: University of Kentucky Press, 1996). See also Amy Guttman's "Responding to Racial Injustice" in Anthony Appiah and Amy Guttman, *Color Conscious: The Political Morality of Race,* with an intro. by David B. Wilkins (Princeton: Princeton University Press, 1996), p. 64.

25. For discussion, see K. Anthony Appiah's "Racisms" in *Anatomy of Racism,* ed. David Theo Goldberg (Minneapolis: University of Minnesota Press 1990), pp. 3–17; Appiah's *In My Father's House: Africa in the Philosophy of Culture* (New York and Oxford: Oxford University Press), pp. 13–15; and "Race, Culture, and Identity: Misunderstood Connections," in *Color Conscious. . . .*

26. All of these possibilities are discussed in Naomi Zack's *Mixed Race* and *American Mixed Race.*

27. On the nonracial level, a correlative is in religious-cultural affiliation, where the goal of the assimilating Jew is not to be Jewish. The closest similarity to the racial question emerges when the assimilating Jew of "mixed" Gentile-Jewish parentage experiences this question through having a Jewish mother. . . .

28. W.E.B. Du Bois, *The Souls of Black Folks,* with introductions by Nathan Hare and Alvin F. Poussaint, revised and updated bibliography (New York and Scarborough, Ontario: New American Library, 1982 [originally published, 1903]), chap. 1.

29. Angela Y. Davis, Keynote Address, *10th Annual Empowering Women of Color Conference: Reaping Fruit, Throwing Seed* (22 April 1995), University of California at Berkeley.

30. Robert Wesley, "White Normativity and the Rhetoric of Equal Protecting" in *Existence in Black.*

A COUNTRYLESS WOMAN

THE EARLY FEMINISTA

Ana Castillo

> *I would have spoken these words as a feminist who "happened" to be a white United States citizen, conscious of my government's proven capacity for violence and arrogance of power, but as self-separated from the government, quoting without second thought Virginia Woolf's statement in* The Three Guineas *that "as a woman I have no country. As a woman I want no country. As a woman my country is the whole world." This is not what I come [here] to say in 1984. I come here with notes but without absolute conclusions. This is not a sign of loss of faith or hope. These notes are the marks of a struggle to keep moving, a struggle for accountability.*
> —ADRIENNE RICH, "Notes toward a Politics of Location," *Blood, Bread, and Poetry*

I cannot say I am a citizen of the world as Virginia Woolf, speaking as an Anglo woman born to economic means, declared herself; nor can I make the same claim to U.S. citizenship as Adrienne Rich does despite her universal feeling for humanity. As a mestiza born to the lower strata, I am treated at best, as a second class citizen, at worst, as a non-entity. I am commonly perceived as a foreigner everywhere I go, including in the United States and in Mexico. This international perception is based on my color and features. I am neither black nor white. I am not light skinned and cannot be mistaken for "white"; because my hair is so straight I cannot be mistaken for "black." And by U.S. standards and according to some North American Native Americans, I cannot make official claims to being india.

Socioeconomic status, genetic makeup and ongoing debates on mestisaje aside, if in search of refuge from the United States I took up residence on any other continent, the core of my being would long for a return to the lands of my ancestors. My ethereal spirit and my collective memory with other indigenas and mestizo/as yearn to *claim* these territories as homeland. In the following pages, I would like to review our socioeconomic status, our early activism and feminismo, and to begin the overall discussion that moves toward a Xicanista vision.

In the 1980s, leftists and liberals recognized the atrocities of U.S. intervention in Central America, as similar sympathizers did with Viet Nam in the 1960s. Their sympathy is reminiscent of North American leftists and liberals who in the 1930s struggled against fascism during the Spanish Civil War. In each instance, there is the implication that these liberal individuals are not in any way responsible for the persecution, and that it is all their government's fault. These same humanists have vaguely and apologetically acknowledged the injustice done to the descendants of their country's former slaves and to the Native Americans who have been all but obliterated through genocide and dispossession.

Yet, mestizo/as, those who are Mexican citizens as well as those who are U.S. born, are viewed less sympathetically. We are advised to assimilate into white dominant society or opt for invisibility—an invisibility that we are blamed for because of our own lack of ability to take advantage of the supposedly endless opportunities available through acculturation.

Racism has been generally polarized into a black-white issue. U.S. mestizo/as of Mexican background, therefore, are viewed by many white people, by many African Americans and yes, by some Native Americans as having the potential to "pass" for white, in theory, at will. This general view is based on the assumptions, lack of information and misinformation that accompanies policies, media control, and distorted historical documentation disseminated to the general populace by the white male dominated power system that has traditionally governed this country. The United States cannot deny its early history of importing Africans as slaves, which explains the presence of African Americans throughout the Americas. However, censorship continues regarding the extent of genocide of Native Americans. As for mestizo/as, we were identified as a mongrel race, a mixture of the dispensable Amerindian race and the lowly Spaniard. Little is known by the general public regarding how these attitudes caused ongoing persecution of Mexic Amerindians and mestizo/as in what was once Mexico and later became United States territory. For example, while it is well known that in the South there were lynchings and hangings of African Americans, it isn't common knowledge that Mexicans were also lynched and hung in Texas and throughout the Southwest.

Most people in the United States have little awareness of this government's ongoing dominant-subordinate relationship with Mexico since, of course, this is not taught in schools as part of United States history. The general public assumes that all Mexicans are immigrants and therefore, *obligated* to assimilate just as European immigrants did and do.

Most members of dominant society have very little understanding of the numerous ways a country, especially one supposedly based on the free enterprise system and democracy, systematically and quite effectively disenfranchises much of its population. While some white members of society have an understanding of this from an economic and historical standpoint, they do not or will not recognize that there are, to this day, economic inequities based on racism. Many more do not understand or refuse to accept that today all women suffer, in one way or another, as a result of the prevalent misogyny legislated and expounded in this society.

For the last twenty years the leaders of the U.S. government have tried to convince its population that the Civil Rights Movement succeeded in creating a true democracy and that increasing poverty and unemployment are primarily a question of world economics. If indications of the growing frustration on the part of women and people of color who cannot overcome job and educational inequities based on race, gender, and limited economic resources were not evident enough to the federal government, the national riots after the Rodney King verdict serve as the final argument.

While I have more in common with a Mexican man than with a white woman, I have much more in common with an Algerian woman than I do with a Mexican man. This opinion, I'm sure, chagrins women who sincerely believe our female physiology unequivocally binds all women throughout the world, despite the compounded social prejudices that daily affect us all in different ways. Although women everywhere experience life differently from men everywhere, white women are members of a race that has proclaimed itself globally superior for hundreds of years. We live in a polarized world of contrived dualisms, dichotomies and paradoxes: light vs. dark and good vs. evil. We as Mexic Amerindians/mestizas are the dark. We are the evil . . . or at least, the questionable.

10   Ours is a world imbued with nationalism, real for some, yet tenuous as paper for others. A world in which from the day of our births, we are either granted citizenship or relegated to the netherstate of serving as mass production drones. Non-white women—Mexicans/Chicanas, Filipinas, Malaysians, and others—who comprise eighty percent of the global factory work force, are the greatest dispensable resource that multinational interests own. The women are in effect, represented by no country.

Feminists of color in the United States (and around the world) are currently arduously re-examining the very particular ways our non-Western cultures use us and how they view us. We have been considered opinionless and the invariable targets of every kind of abusive manipulation and experimentation. As a mestiza, a resident of a declining world power, a countryless woman, I have the same hope as Rich who, on behalf of her country aims to be accountable, flexible, and learn new ways to gather together earnest peoples of the world without the defenses of nationalism.

I was born, raised, and spent most of my life in one of the largest cities in the United States. Despite its distance from Mexico, Chicago has a population of approximately a quarter of a million people of Mexican background. It is also the third most frequent U.S. destination of Mexican migrants after El Paso and Los Angeles. The greatest influx of Mexicans occurred during the first half of this century when the city required cheap labor for its factories, slaughterhouses, and steel mill industry.

In an effort to minimize their social and spiritual alienation, the Mexican communities there developed and maintained solid ties to Mexican culture and traditions. This was reinforced by the tough political patronage system in Chicago, which was dependent upon ethnically and racially divisive strategies to maintain its power. Thus I grew up perceiving myself to be Mexican despite the fact that I born in the United States and did not visit Mexico until the age of ten.

Assimilation into dominant culture, while not impossible, was not encouraged nor desired by most ethnic groups in Chicago—Mexicans were no exception. We ate, slept, talked, and dreamed Mexican. Our parishes were Mexican. Small Mexican-owned businesses flourished. We were able to replicate Mexico to such a degree that the spiritual and psychological needs of a people so despised and undesired by white dominant culture were met in our own large communities.

Those who came up north to escape destitution in Mexico were, in general, dark-skinned mestizos. In the face of severe racism, it's no wonder we maintained such strong bonds to each other. But even those who were not as outwardly indentifiably Mexican were usually so inherently Mexican by tradition that they could not fully assimilate. Not a few refused to "settle in" on this side of the border with the pretense that they would eventually return to their home towns in Mexico.

As I was growing up, Mexicans were the second largest minority in Chicago. There was also a fair size Puerto Rican community and a fair amount of Cubans and other Latin Americans. But in those years, before the blatant military disruption of Latin American countries such as Chile and El Salvador, a person with "mestiza" characteristics was considered Mexican. When one had occasion to venture away from her insulated community to say, downtown, impressive and intimidating with its tremendous skyscrapers and evidently successful (white) people bustling about, she felt as if she were leaving her village to go into town on official matters. Once there she went about her business with a certain sense of invisibility, and even hoped for it, feeling so out of place and disoriented in the presence of U.S. Anglo, profit-based interests, which we had nothing to do with except as mass-production workers. On such occasions, if she were to by chance to run across another mestiza (or mestizo), there was a mutual unspoken recognition and, perhaps, a reflexive avoidance of eye contact. An instantaneous mental communication might sound something like this:

> I know you. You are Mexican (like me). You are brown-skinned (like me). You are poor (like me). You probably live in the same neighborhood as I do. You don't have anything, own anything. (Neither do I.) You're no one (here). At this moment I don't want to be reminded of this, in the midst of such luxury, such wealth, this disorienting language; it makes me ashamed of the food I eat, the flat I live in, the only clothes I can afford to wear, the alcoholism and defeat I live with. You remind me of all of it.
>
> You remind me that I am not beautiful—because I am short, round bellied and black-eyed. You remind me that I will never ride in that limousine that just passed us because we are going to board the same bus back to the neighborhood where

15

we both live. You remind me of why the foreman doesn't move me out of that tedious job I do day after day, or why I got feverish and too tongue-tied to go to the main office to ask for that Saturday off when my child made her First Holy Communion.

When I see you, I see myself. You are the mirror of this despicable, lowly sub-human that I am in this place far from our homeland which scarcely offered us much more since the vast majority there live in destitution. None of the rich there look like us either. At least here we feed our children; they have shoes. We manage to survive. But don't look at me. Go on your way. Let me go on pretending my invisibility, so that I can observe close up all the possibilities—and dream the gullible dreams of a human being.[1]

At seventeen, I joined the Latino/Chicano movement. I went downtown and rallied around City Hall along with hundreds of other youth screaming, "¡Viva La Raza!" and "Chicano Power!" until we were hoarse. Our fears of being recognized as lowly Mexicans were replaced with socioeconomic theories that led to political radicalism. Yet our efforts to bring unity and courage to the majority of our people were short lived; they did not embrace us. Among the factors contributing to this were the ability of some to assimilate more easily on the basis of lighter skin color and the consumer-fever that overrides people's social needs. The temptations of the rewards of assimilation and the internalization of racism by the colonized peoples of the United States was and is devastating. Society has yet to acknowledge the trauma it engenders.

The Hispanic population in the U.S. totaled 22,354,509, according to the 1990 U.S. Department of Commerce report. 13,495,938 of that total were of Mexican origin. (We can estimate therefore that when we are discussing the woman of Mexican origin we are referring to a population of about seven million women in the United States.) According to the 1989 report immigration constituted half of the recent Hispanic population growth. I am personally glad to see the U.S. Department of Commerce gives this reason to explain the disproportionate growth of Hispanics as compared to non-Hispanics, as opposed to the 1987 Department of Labor Report, which states that there are so many Hispanics because Hispanic women tend to be more fertile than non-Hispanic women. These figures, of course, do not include the undocumented Latino population. The U.S. Immigration and Naturalization Service estimated 1.2 million apprehensions at the border in 1986.

Hispanic as the ethnic label for all people who reside in the U.S. with some distant connection with the culture brought by the Spaniards during the conquest of the Americas is a gross misnomer. The word promotes an official negation of people called "Hispanic" by inferring that their ethnicity or race is exclusively European rather than partly Native American (as are most

Chicano/as), or African American (as are those descendants of the African slave trade along the Caribbean coasts).

The term Hispanic is a misnomer because one-fifth of South America—Brazil—does not speak Spanish. A large population of Guatemala speaks indigenous dialects as a first language and maintains its own indigenous culture. Chicano/as and Puerto Ricans may have little or no fluency in Spanish having been brought up in an English-dominant society, having attended its monolingual schools, and having been discouraged, in general, from pursuing the language of their ancestors. In fact, despite the provisions made by the Treaty of Guadalupe Hidalgo of 1848 to allow Spanish speakers in the Southwest to retain their native tongue, Spanish was prohibited in schools and workplaces. The debate rages on among educators and government alike.

If Hispanic refers to all natives and descendants of Latin America, it is including no less than twenty countries—whose shared patterns of colonization may allow them to be called Pan-American, but whose histories and cultural attitudes are nevertheless diverse in very particular ways.   20

How can people from the Caribbean states, whose economies depended on slave trade be generically called Hispanic? Is it because they are from states that are presently Spanish speaking or were once colonized by the Spaniards, although they may presently be under another country's dominion? In the Caribbean, Hispanic includes Puerto Ricans, Cubans, and Dominicans. While Cuba's official language has remained Spanish since Spanish rule, many of its people are of African ancestry. Citizens of the Dominican Republic are considered Hispanic because they speak Spanish, but the residents of the other side of their island, Haiti, speak French (and more commonly, as I understand, patois). Are there enough major racial differences between these two nationalities on the same island to justifiably classify one as Hispanic but not the other? The Philippines were once colonized by Spain and now have English as a dominant language, but they are not classified as Hispanic. They are placed in another catch-all group, Asian.

Hispanic gives us all one ultimate paternal cultural progenitor: Spain. The diverse cultures already on the American shores when the Europeans arrived, as well as those introduced because of the African slave trade, are completely obliterated by the term. Hispanic is nothing more than a concession made by the U.S. legislature when they saw they couldn't get rid of us. If we won't go away, why not at least Europeanize us, make us presentable guests at the dinner table, take away our feathers and rattles and civilize us once and for all.

This erroneous but nationally accepted label invented by a white supremacist bureaucracy essentially is a resignation to allow, after more than two hundred years of denial, some cultural representation of the conquistadors who originally colonized the Southwest. Until now, in other words, only Anglo-Saxons were legitimate informants of American culture.

To further worsen the supposition that we can be Hispanic—simply long forgotten descendants of Europeans just as white people are—is the horrific history of brutal and inhuman subjugation that not only Amerindians experienced under Spanish and other European rules in Mexico and throughout Latin America and the Carribbean, but all those of mixed blood. Indeed, shortly after the Conquest of Mexico, Spanish rule set up a complex caste system in which to be of mixed-blood virtually excluded you from full rights as citizens and protection by the law. Jews and Moors in that Catholic society also experienced racist attitudes.[2] Just as with today's African-Americans, among mestizo/as and Amerindians, the result of such intense, legislated racism throughout centuries is demoralization. As one historian puts it regarding the Mexic Amerindian people, "Trauma and neuroses linger still, and may not be entirely overcome. For Spaniards, in Mexico, did not commit genocide; they committed culturcide."[3]

25   Among Latino/as in the United States today there is a universe of differences. There is a universe of difference, for example, between the experience of the Cuban man who arrived in the United States as a child with his parents after fleeing Castro's revolution and the Puerto Rican woman who is a third generation single mother on the Lower East side. There is a universe of difference between the young Mexican American aspiring to be an actor in Hollywood in the nineties and the community organizer working for rent control for the last ten years in San Francisco, although both may be sons of farmworkers. There is a universe of difference between Carolina Herrera, South American fashion designer and socialite, and a Guatemalan refugee who has hardly learned to speak Spanish but must already adapt to English in order to work as a domestic in the United States. Picture her: She is not statuesque or blonde (like Ms. Herrera). She is short, squat, with a moon face, and black, oily hair. She does not use six pieces of silverware at the dinner table, but one, if any, and a tortilla. There is a universe of differences among all of these individuals, yet Anglo society says they all belong to the same ethnic group: Hispanic.

A study by the University of Chicago shows that deep divisions based on race exist between black Hispanics and white Hispanics in the United States. The black/white dichotomy of the United States causes black Hispanics to relate more to Africa Americans than to non-black Hispanics. It is also revealed that "black Hispanics are far more segregated from U.S. whites than are white Hispanics."[4] *Color,* rather than saying simply ethnicity, in addition to class and gender, as well as *conscientización,* all determine one's identity and predict one's fate in the United States.

Except for the historical period characterized by "Manifest Destiny" fate is not part of United States Anglo Saxon ideology. But the United States does have a fate.

Sir John Glubb in his book *A Short History of the Arab Peoples* suggests reviewing world history to see how frequently great empires reach and fall from their pinnacle of power, all within two hundred to three hundred years. According to Glubb, for example, the Greek Empire (330 B.C. to about 100 B.C.) lasted two hundred and thirty years; the Spaniards endured for (1556 to 1800) two hundred and forty four years; and the British Empire lasted two hundred and thirty years (1700 to 1930). It is sobering to note that no great power simply lost its position as number one slipping into second or third place, nor has any former great power ever resumed its original, unchallenged position. They all have ceased to exist as a world power. After the fall of the Roman Empire, Italy has been little more than the home of the Pope for the past fifteen centuries. Moreover, regarding his figures Glubb tells us, "It is not desired to insist on rigid numbers, for many outside factors influence the fates of great nations. Nevertheless, the resemblance between the lives of so many and such varied empires is extremely striking, and is obviously entirely unconnected with the development of those mechanical devices of which we are so proud."[5] "Mechanical devices" means military might.

Signs of the decline of the United States as the leading world power are most apparent in the phenomenal growth of the public debt in the 1980s: during the Reagan-Bush years, the public debt of the United States went from 907.7 billion dollars in 1980 to over 3 trillion dollars in 1990 (as reported by the United States Department of the Treasury).

The United States, being a relatively young, therefore resilient country, can and eventually will allow for the representation of people of color in the institutions that influence and mandate people's lives—government, private industry, and universities, for example. It will gradually relent with its blatant refusal to fulfill its professed democratic ideals and include the descendants of its slave trade, the Native Americans, mestizo/as, and Asians (who also come from a wide variety of countries and social and economic backgrounds and who, due to various political circumstances, are immigrating to the United States at an exorbitant rate). It will do so because the world economy will not permit anything short of it. Nevertheless, most assuredly among those who will get further pushed down as the disparity between the few wealthy and the impoverished grows, will be our gente.

The largest movement in the history of the United States ever to force the government to reckon with its native Latino population was the Chicano/Latino Movement of the late 1960s and 1970s. Because of its force there is today a visible sector of Latinos who are college degreed, who have mortgages on decent houses, and who are articulate in English. (In Spanish, when a person has facility in a language to get by, we say we can "defend" ourselves; we now have a substantial number of Latinos who are defending themselves against Anglophile culture.) The generation that came of age in the 1980s was given the general message that acculturation can be rewarding. Yes, the status quo will always reward those who succumb to it, who serve it, and who do not threaten its well being.

In 1980 when the Republicans and the Reagan administration came to office, their tremendous repression quashed the achievements of the Chicano/Latino Movement, which has been based on collectivism and the retention of our Mexican/Amerindian culture. Community projects and grassroots programs dependent on government funding—rehabilitation and training, child care, early education and alternative schooling, youth counseling, cultural projects that supported the arts and community artists, rehab-housing for low income families, and women's shelters—shut down.

In their place the old "American Dream"—a WASP male philosophy on which this country was founded at the expense of third world labor—was reinstated. As in U.S. society before the Civil Rights Movement, material accumulation equaled self-worth.

The new generation of Chicanos and Latinos who came of age in the 1980s had a radically different attitude than the collective mentality of the 1970s activists, believing that after two hundred years of racist and ethnic exploitation, the age of the "Hispanic" had finally come. Their abuelos, tios, parents (some who had been in the Chicano/Latino Movement) had paid the dues for the American Dream. Now they could finally claim their own place in society. They acculturated.

35 Encouraged by media hype announcing our arrival in the 1980s as the "Decade of the Hispanic," for the first time in U.S. history, ad campaigns took the Latino/a consumer into consideration. Magazines, billboards and even television commercials (Coors comes to mind) showed young, brown, beautiful Latina models in flashy wear reaping some of the comforts and pleasures of a democracy based on free enterprise. Also, there was the unprecedented tokenism of Latino/as in visible and high level government posts and private industry that further convinced many among the new generation that each individual indeed had the ability to fulfill his or her own great master plan for material success. The new generation was not alone. The previous generation became more conservative along with immigrating Latinos who also believed in the Republican administration and the trickle down theory of Reaganomics.

It is difficult to generalize why so many Latino/as moved toward conservative, if not overtly right wing, views. Personal disillusionment with leftist ideology may explain in part the change in attitude and goals for some. But for many, I believe it is basically a matter of desiring material acquisitions. It is difficult to maintain a collective ideology in a society where possessions and power-status equal self-worth.

Unfortunately, the continuous drop of the U.S. dollar in the world trade market caused the economy to worsen each year. In the 1980s, jobs were lost, companies closed down and moved out of the country, banks foreclosed on mortgages, and scholarships and grants once available to needy college students in the 1970s were taken away. These were only a few of the losses experienced not only by Latino/as but by much of the population.

Simultaneously, the cost of living went up. The much coveted trendy lifestyle of the white yuppie moved further away from the grasp of young and upwardly mobile Reagan-Bush generation. The nineties ushered a new generation cognizant of the white hegemonic atmosphere entrenched in colleges and universities and with a vigor reminiscent of the student movements of two decades earlier, have begun protests on campuses throughout the country. The acceleration of gang violence in cities, drug wars, cancer on the rise and AIDS continue to be the backdrop, while the new decade's highlights so far for living in these difficult times were the Persian Gulf War Espectáculo and the Rodney King riots that resounded throughout the world—sending out a message that his is indeed a troubled country.

El Movimiento Chicano/Latino saw its rise and fall within a time span of less than two decades on these territories where our people have resided for thousands of years. El Movimiento (or La Causa) was rooted to a degree in Marxist oriented theory (despite the strong ties activists felt to their Catholic upbringings) because it offered some response to our oppression under capitalism. Socialist and communist theories which were based on late nineteenth century ideas on the imminent mass industrialization of society, did not foresee the high technology world of the late twentieth century—one hundred years later—or fully consider the implications of race, gender, and sexual-preference differences on that world. Wealth accumulation no longer simply stays within the genteel class but our aristocracy now includes athletes, rock stars, and Hollywood celebrities.

The early feminista, as the Chicana feminist referred to herself then, had been actively fighting against her socioeconomic subjugation as a Chicana and as a woman since 1968, the same year the Chicano Movement was announced. I am aware that there have been Chicana activists throughout U.S. history, but I am using as a date of departure an era in which women consciously referred to themselves as *feministas*. 40

An analysis of the social status of la Chicana was already underway by early feministas, who maintained that racism, sexism, and sexist racism were the mechanisms that socially and economically oppressed them. But, for reasons explained here, they were virtually censored. The early history of la feminista was documented in a paper entitled, "La Feminista," by Anna Nieto Gómez and published in *Encuentro Feminil: The First Chicana Feminist Journal,* which may now be considered, both article and journal, archival material.[6]

The early feminista who actively participated in the woman's movement had to educate white feminist groups on their political, cultural, and philosophical differences. Issues that specifically concerned the feminista of that period were directly related to her status as a non-Anglo, culturally different, often Spanish-speaking woman of lower income. Early white feminism compared sexism (as experienced by white middle-class women) to the racism that African Americans are subjected to. But African American feminists, such as those of the Rio Combahee Collective,[7] pointed out that this was not only an inaccurate comparison but revealed an inherent racist attitude on the part of white feminists who did not understand what it was to be a woman *and* black in America.

By the same token, brown women were forced into a position in which we had to point out similar differences as well as continuously struggle against a prevalent condescension on the part of white middle-class women toward women of color, poor women, and women whose first language is Spanish and whose culture is not mainstream American. *This Bridge Called My Back,* first published in 1981, as well as other texts by feminists of color that followed serve as excellent testimonies regarding these issues and the experiences of feminists of color in the 1970s.

At the same time, according to Nieto Gómez, feministas were labeled as *vendidas* (sell-outs) by activists within *La Causa.* Such criticism came not solely from men but also from women, whom Nieto Gómez calls Loyalists. These Chicanas believed that racism not sexism was the greater battle. Moreover, the Loyalists distrusted any movement led by any sector of white society. The early white women's movement saw its battle based on sex and gender, and did not take into account the race and class differences of women of color. The Loyalists had some reason to feel reluctant and cynical toward an ideology and organizing effort that at best was condescending toward them. Loyalists told the feministas that they should be fighting such hard-hitting community problems as police brutality, Viet Nam, and La Huelga, the United Farm workers labor strike. But white female intellectuals were largely unaware of these issues. While the Chicana resided in a first world nation, indeed the most powerful nation at that time, she was part of a historically colonized people.

45   I am referring to the approximate period between 1968 through the 1970s. However, more than twenty years later, the Chicana—that is a brown woman of Mexican descent, residing in the United States with political consciousness—is still participating in the struggle for recognition and respect from white dominant society. Residing throughout her life in a society that systematically intentionally or out of ignorance marginalizes her existence, often stereotypes her when she does "appear," suddenly represented (for example by mass-media or government sources), and perhaps more importantly, relegates her economic status to among the lowest paid according to the U.S. Census Bureau, the Chicana continues to be a countryless woman. She is— I am, we are—not considered to be, except marginally and stereotypically, United States citizens.

Nevertheless, according to las feministas, feminism was "a very dynamic aspect of the Chicana's heritage and not at all foreign to her nature."[8] Contrary to ethnographic data that portrays Chicanas as submissive followers who are solely designated to preserve the culture, the feminista did not see herself or other women of her culture as such. While the feminist dialogue remained among the activists in el Movimiento, one sees in *Encuentro Feminil* that there indeed existed a solid initiative toward Chicana feminist thought, that is, recognition of sexism as a primary issue, as early on as the late 1960s. Clarifying the differences between the needs of the Anglo feminist and the feminista was part of the early feminista's tasks.

And if the focus of the Chicano male-dominated movement with regard to women had to do with family issues, the feminista zeroed in on the very core of what those issues meant. For instance, the feministas believed that women would make use of birth control and abortion clinics if in fact they felt safe going for these services; that is, if they were community controlled. Birth control and abortion are pertinent issues for all women, but they were particularly significant to the Chicana who had always been at the mercy of Anglo controlled institutions and policies.

Non-consenting sterilizations of women—poor white, Spanish speaking, welfare recipients, poor women of color—women in prison among them— during the 1970s were being conducted and sponsored by the U.S. government. One third of the female population of Puerto Rico was sterilized during that period.[9] The case of ten Chicanas (*Madrigal v. Quilligan*) against the Los Angeles County Hospital who were sterilized without their consent led to activism demanding release of the Health, Education and Welfare (HEW) guidelines for sterilizations. During that period, HEW was financing up to 100,000 sterilizations a year.[10]

The feminista also wanted a bicultural and bilingual child care that would validate their children's culture and perhaps ward off an inferiority complex before they had a chance to start public school; traditionally, monolingual and anglocentric schools had alienated children, causing them great psychological damage.[11]

The early feminista understood the erroneous conceptions of the White Woman's Movement that equated sexism to racism because she was experiencing its compounding effects in her daily life. The feministas were fighting against being a "minority" in the labor market. According to Nieto Gómez, more Anglo women had jobs than did women of color. We must keep in mind that most women of color in this country have always needed employment to maintain even a level of subsistence for their families.

According to the 1991 U.S. Dept. of Commerce Census Bureau Report, income figures for 1989 show that "Hispanic" women are still among the lowest paid workers in the United States, earning less than African American women:

WEEKLY INCOME

Hispanic women	$269.00
Black women	301.00
White women	334.00
Hispanic men	315.00
Black men	348.00
All Other Women	361.00

The mestiza still ranks in the labor force among the least valued in this country. In Susan Faludi's best-selling *Backlash,* which focuses on the media's backlash against the white feminist movement, the only noteworthy observation of women of color refers to our economic status in the 1980s. Faludi states that overall income did not increase for the African American woman and for the Hispanic woman, it actually got worse.

CLASHING OF CULTURES   We need not look very far back or for very long to see that we have been marginalized in every sense of the word by U.S. society. But an understanding of the U.S. economic system and its relationship to Mexico is essential in order that we understand our inescapable role as a productive/reproductive entity within U.S./Mexican society for the past two hundred years.

The transnational labor force into which most of us are born was created out of Mexico's neocolonialist relationship to the United States.[12] Throughout the history of the United States, Mexicans have served as a labor reserve controlled by U.S. policy. Mexico encourages the emigration of this labor force to alleviate its own depressed economy, and the United States all too willingly consumes this labor without giving it the benefits enjoyed by U.S. residents.

Contrary to the ideological claim of the United States that insists that all immigrants (which by legislature and action meant European) pay their dues before being able to participate fully in its melting pot economy, the underpaid Mexican worker is crucial to the survival of the profit-based system of the United States. The maquiladoras illustrate this point.[13]

55   Since the late sixties, U.S. production has undergone a transfer of manufacturing to less industrialized nation, such as Mexico.[14] The U.S.-Mexican border has been an appealing site for such assembly operations. Unskilled women pressed with dire economic necessity serve as a reserve for these industries. A continuing influx of labor from the interior of Mexico provides competition and keeps wages at a base minimum. Daily wage for a maquiladora *rose* to a mere $3.50 per day in 1988.[15] An unofficial border source told me that that figure had risen to $3.75 per day in 1992. The outrageously low wages for working in dangerous and unregulated conditions are among the strongest arguments against the free-trade agreements between United States, Mexico, and Canada.

The cultural and religious beliefs that maintain that most Latinas on either side of the border are (and should be) dependent on their men for economic survival are not only unrealistic, evidence shows they do not reflect reality. On this side of the border, according to the 1987 Department of Labor Report, one million "Hispanic" households were headed by women. Their average income was $337.00 per week. Fifty-two percent of these households headed by women survive below poverty level.

Any woman without the major support of the father of her children and who has no other resources, must, in order to survive, commodify her labor. Even most Chicano/Latino men do not earn enough to support their families; their wives must go outside the home to earn an income (or bring it home in the form of piece work). Furthermore, statistics show that many mothers do not live with the father of their children and do not receive any kind of financial assistance from him.

Most Chicanas/Latinas are not conscienticized. The majority of the populace, on either side of the border, in fact, is not actively devoted to real social change. That sense of inferiority, as when two people were confronted with their mexicanidad on the streets of downtown Chicago, permeates most Chicanas' self-perceptions. Lack of concientización is what makes the maquiladora an ideal worker for the semi-legal, exploitative operations of multi-national factory production.

At an early age we learn that our race is undesirable. Because of possible rejection, some of us may go to any length to deny our background. But one cannot cruelly judge such women who have resorted to negation of their own heritage; constant rejection has accosted us since childhood. Certain women indeed had contact early on in their lives with México and acquired enough identification with its diverse culture and traditions to battle against the attempts of white, middle class society to usurp all its citizens into an abstract culture obsessed with material gain.

But many women born in the United States or brought here during childhood have little connection with the country of our ancestors. The umbilical cord was severed before we could develop the intellectual and emotional link to México, to the astonishing accomplishments of its indigenous past, to its own philosophical and spiritual nature so much at odds with that of the WASP. Instead we flounder between invisibility and a tacit hope that we may be accepted here and awarded the benefits of acculturation. 60

Looking different, that is, not being white nor black but something in between in a society that has historically acknowledged only a black/white racial schism is cause for great anxiety. Our internalized racism causes us to boast of our light coloring, if indeed we have it, or imagine it. We hope for light-skinned children and brag no end of those infants who happen to be born güeros, white looking, we are downright ecstatic if they have light colored eyes and hair. We sometimes tragically reject those children who are dark.

On the subject of color and internal conflicts there are also those who, despite identification with Latino heritage are light-skinned because of their dominating European genes or because one parent is white. For some this may be an added reason for internalizing racism, particularly when young (since it is difficult to explain the world to yourself when you are growing up). But for others, while their güero coloring may cause them to experience less racial tension in broad society, it may cause tension for a variety of reasons in their home, chosen communities, and when politically active against racism.

Let us consider for a moment a woman who does not necessarily desire marriage or bearing children, and works instead to attain a higher standard of living for herself. She must still interact with and quite often be subordinate to white people, and occasionally African Americans. I do not want to elaborate on the dynamics of her relationships with African Americans since it is understood here that institutionalized racism has not allowed either race to have real domination over the other. My own experience has been one of cultural difference rather than a racial one since there are also "black hispanos." But I will note that she will in all likelihood still feel "foreign" with African Americans who have an acknowledged history in the United States. Because of slavery, white people *know* why African Americans are here. They also *know* why Native Americans are here, yet they *assume* mestizos have all migrated here for economic gain as their own people did.

To compound our anxiety over our foreign-like identity in the United States is the fact that Mexican Americans are also not generally accepted in México. We are derogatorily considered *pochos,* American Mexicans who are either among the traitors or trash of Mexico because we, or previous generations, made the United States home. Unlike the experiences that many African Americans have had in "returning" and being welcomed in Africa,[16] many U.S.-born mestizo/as have found themselves more unwelcome by mexicanos than white gringos.

65   Aside from skin color, language can add to the trauma of the Chicana's schizophrenic-like existence. She was educated in English and learned it is the only acceptable language in society, but Spanish was the language of her childhood, family, and community. She may not be able to rid herself of an accent; society has denigrated her first language. By the same token, women may also become anxious and self-conscious in later years if they have no or little facility in Spanish. They may feel that they had been forced to forfeit an important part of their personal identity and still never found acceptability by white society.

Race, ethnicity, and language are important factors for women who aspire to decent standard of living in our anglocentric, xenophobic society. Gender compounds their social dilemma and determines the very nature of their lifestyle regardless of the ability to overcome all other obstacles set against them.

Feminism at its simplest has not ever been solely a political struggle for women's rights, i.e., equal pay for equal work. The early feminista's initial attempts at placing women-related issues at the forefront were once viewed with suspicion by Marxist-oriented activists as The Woman Question was seen to be separate from or less significant than race and class issues by most activists, and along with gay issues, even thought to be an indication of betrayal to La Causa. Along those lines, in the 1990s, while issues of sexuality have come to the forefront, most recently with the national debate of permitting gays in the military, there remains a strong heterosexist bias among Chicano/Hispanic/Latino based organizations and our varying communities.

With the tenacious insistence at integrating a feminist perspective to their political concientización as Chicanas, feminist activistas, and intellectuals are in the process of developing what I call Xicanisma. On a pragmatic level, the basic premise of Xicanisma is to reconsider behavior long seen as inherent in the Mexic Amerindian woman's character, such as, patience, perseverance, industriousness, loyalty to one's clan, and commitment to our children. Contrary to how those incognizant of what feminism is, we do not reject these virtues. We may not always welcome the taxing responsibility that comes with our roles as Chicanas. We've witnessed what strain and limitations they often placed on our mothers and other relatives. But these traits often seen as negative and oppressive to our growth as women, as well as having been translated to being equal to being a drone for white society and its industrial interests, may be considered strengths. Simultaneously, as we redefine (not categorically reject) our roles within our families, communities at large, and white dominant society, our Xicanisma helps us to be self-confident and assertive regarding the pursuing of our needs and desires.

As brown-skinned females, often bilingual but not from a Spanish speaking country (not a Mexican citizen yet generally considered to not really be American), frequently discouraged in numerous ways from pursuing formal education, usually with limited economic means, therefore made to compete in a racist and sexist lower skilled work force, we continue to be purposely rendered invisible by society except as a stereotype and in other denigrating ways. The U.S. Women's Movement, which in fact began long before the Civil Rights Movement and the ensuing Chicano Movement, is now incorporating a more expansive vision that includes the unique perceptions and experiences of all peoples heretofore excluded from the democratic promise of the United States. Until we are all represented, respected, and protected by society and the laws that govern it, the status of the Chicana will be that of a countryless woman.

NOTES

1. As a young poet in 1974, I wrote something similar to this in "Our Tongue Was Nahuatl," in *New Worlds of Literature,* ed. J. Beaty and J. P. Hunter (New York: W. W. Norton, 1989).
2. T. R. Fehrenback, *Fire and Blood: A History of Mexico* (New York: Bonanza Books, 1973), 234.
3. Fehrenback, *Fire and Blood,* 238 and 162.
4. Hispanic Link Weekly Report, Nov. 6, 1989.
5. Please refer to John Glubb, *A Short History of the Arab Peoples* (New York: Dorset Press, 1969).
6. *Encuentro Femenil: The First Chicana Feminist Journal* 1 (1974): no. 2. (CA: Hijas de Cuauhtemoc). I can't recall how, but it seems fortuitously for me, this document came into my hands in Chicago around this time.
7. Please read their essay in *This Bridge Called My Back: Writings by Radical Women of Color,* ed. Cherrie Moraga and Gloria Anzaldúa (Watertown, Mass.: Persephone Press, 1981).
8. Anna Nieto Gómez, "La Feminista," *Encuentro Feminil: The First Chicana Feminist Journal* 1 (1974): no. 2, 38.
9. See Angela Davis, *Women, Culture and Politics* (New York: Random House, 1989).
10. Thomas Shapiro, *Population Control Politics: Women, Sterilization and Reproductive Choice* (Philadelphia: Temple University Press, 1985), 91–93.
11. I am reminded of two stories I have heard from U.S.-born Spanish-speaking women who went to public schools in the United States. One was sent with her sister, upon starting school, to the class for the hearing impaired. Another, attending a school with a majority Chicano population was sent to "girls' math" class. For further reading on the education of Chicanos please refer to Fernando Penalosa's *Chicano Linguistics.*

12. Marlene Dixon, "Chicanas and Mexicanas in a Transnational Working Class," in *The Future of Women* (San Francisco: Synthesis Publications, 1980).
13. Susan Tiano, "Maquiladoras, Women's Work, and Unemployment in Northern Mexico," *Aztlan* 15, no. 2 (1984): 341–78.
15. Figure quoted as of Dec. 1988 by International Trade and Finance Assn., Laredo State Univ., Tx. I will also note that maquiladoras suffer exposure to deadly chemicals due to lack of health regulations. Please refer to "The Maquiladoras and Toxics: The Hidden Costs of Production South of the Border" by Leslie Kochan, published in a report by the AFL-CIO, 815 Sixteen St., N.W., Washington, D.C., 20006.
16. Michael Jackson being crowned king in Africa comes to mind.

THE OTHER COLORS OF WHITENESS: A TRAVELOGUE

Lisa Tessman and Bat-Ami Bar On

We—Ami, an expatriate immigrant from Israel to the United States, and Lisa, born and raised in the United States—are on an extended visit to Israel where we are immersed in a racial/ethnic system different from that of the United States. The two countries' configurations of ethnicity/race as well as our relationships to each country, as original home, adopted home, or supposed "homeland," shape these reflections of the significance of whiteness. We are both Jewish—in the quite different ways that a Sabra (native-born Israeli Jew) and an American can be Jewish—and in the United States we are both white. But as it turns out, it is also in our whiteness that we are so very different from each other.

Ami: On this visit to Israel I am quickly reminded in subtle and unsubtle ways that, contrary to the United States, here color is not the most important marker of racial or ethnic distinctions and, hence, not the most useful marker for ethnically or racially based discrimination. Being white here, while signaling Jewish-European ancestry (generally referred to as *Ashkenazi* ancestry), counts socially only if one is from the right European countries and during the right time—for example, at present a new immigrant from Russia.[1]

What marks one more than color here are things that signal not distance from blackness but rather a national kind of distance from the local, from the cultures of Southwest Asia (the Middle East), North Africa, and the cultures of the Balkans. In short, what matters is the distance from Arab and strongly Arab-influenced cultures, including even cultures where some form of Arab rule, specifically that of Turkey, continued into the nineteenth and twentieth centuries. Not that this distance did not have in the past an East European flavor and now has a West European/North American flavor, insofar as it is the proximity to them rather than to Southeast Asia, the rest of Africa, or South America that is considered better. This flavoring, especially its more current versions, has not yet fully colored ethnic/racial distinctions.[2]

Lisa: I think that as Jewish Israeli and American Jew you and I see through eyes trained by systems with different constructions of us/them. The us/them division that I learned growing up is white/black. Since I was raised quite assimilated, it is a stretch for me to think of the central division as Jew/Gentile, and even then, Gentile tends to mean Christian rather than Muslim. But from here in Israel, as I reflect on the patterns of racial formation in the United States[3]—the patterns familiar to me—they appear strange. This is something I realize upon shifting imaginatively into the local, unfamiliar framework:

us/them is primarily national and is thus Jewish/Arab. The visuals of this binary do not work for me: I cannot, unless they are marked by traditional dress or sometimes language (an unreliable marker since some Jews speak Arabic and many Palestinians speak Hebrew), distinguish Jews from Arabs, and "black" still cues "difference" to me though they are Jewish and hence "us" rather than "them."

I have frequent encounters with this startling shift into the local binary. In one such incident we are at the Central Bus Station in Tel Aviv, where a few Israeli Defense Force (IDF) soldiers mill around waiting to board buses. Unaccustomed to the sight, my eyes are always drawn to their assault rifles, carried so naturally they appear to be part of their clothing. Their uniformed presence is supposed to make me feel protected against the enemy, and if I look down at the photograph on the front page of the newspaper I am carrying, I see exactly that: IDF soldiers aiming their weapons at Palestinians in Hebron. "We" are firing rubber bullets and "they" are throwing stones; two of "us" and fifteen of "them" were wounded yesterday. In the bus station the uniforms and rifles tell me that I am to think of these young women and men as "us," but as I look at one, an Ethiopian Jew whom I would have called "black" in the States, I recall a phrase a white student of mine used as she described first encountering blacks. She had been puzzled, at about age six, when witnessing her parents' friendliness to a black acquaintance, and wondered to herself, "But aren't we at war with them?" She had apparently gathered an awareness that whites in the United States are indeed in a warlike destruction of black lives.

5   I shift back: "we" (namely whites, which includes at least those Jews who are Ashkenazi and assimilated enough) are not at war with "them" (blacks, which must include this Ethiopian Jew, as skin color tells me within a U.S. racial framework), but rather "we" (Jews of any skin color and any ethnicity or background, and here in Israel, the majority of Jews are shades of lightish brown) are united against an Arab other who, like the Jews, would officially be white within the U.S. framework.[4]

Nevertheless, while supposedly united in this nationalist project here in Israel, the Jewish "we" is also hierarchically divided in some ways that mirror U.S. racism and in other ways that diverge from it. For instance, Ethiopian Jews seem to both count and not count as black and to experience a racism both similar to and different from what blacks in the U.S. experience. A (*Sabra, Mizrachi,* lesbian) friend tells us that Ethiopians are treated "like niggers" but when I ask, to clarify, whether they are thought of as black (as opposed to white), another friend (of similar social position) insists that they are not black—they are *"shoko"* (chocolate). The conversation continues: we are told that yes, there is terrible racism against the Ethiopians, just like there is racism against the new Russian immigrants, and just like there is racism against homosexuals. The term *racism* is used without any intended correspondence to what might be called a "race."[5] Given this stretched usage of the word *racism,* which now seems to mean discrimination against any sort of group, it is still unclear what being white signifies in Israel. What is clear is that to focus on whiteness as of primary significance in determining where one stands with respect to racism here would be to (mis)apply a framework imported from elsewhere.

Ami: Following the same conversation you have already described, I feel the perhaps perverse need to reexamine what race/ethnicity may mean here now and begin to wonder about my last claim regarding the local situation. Namely, am I right to believe that the Jewish Israeli orientation toward Europe and North America just flavors but does not fully color the local ethnic/racial distinctions? There is obviously antiblack racism here and now that targets most harshly non-Jewish African guest workers who have been deployed as replacement for the cheap labor force from Palestine (the West Bank and Gaza Strip). They are treated badly, particularly when here illegally, and are called *kushim,* literally meaning people from Kush, a biblical name for Africa. In local parlance, especially when used by children, *kushim* is meant to insult.[6] Still, the local form of antiblack racism is not the same as antiblack racism in the United States, which seems so totalizing because it colors one wholly black under the "one drop rule."[7] In light of U.S. understandings, the local form of antiblack racism is not too intelligible because what is perceived as one's biological Jewishness seems to affect one's color, acting perhaps as a "reverse one drop rule" that "lightens" one's color (as is clear from the case of the *"shoko"* Ethiopian Jews). This is perceived biological Jewishness, and cultural Jewishness like that of the convert, may, however, act quite differently. Instead of functioning as a kind of a "reverse one drop rule," Jewishness may displace color as the primary and most significant marker of racial/ethnic distinctions recentering what still counts much more here, the nation, and therefore the Jewish/Arab binary.

There is something else, though, that needs to be taken into consideration, which is the possibility that while the Jewish/Arab binary is still primary here, Israel, like other countries in the global socioeconomic center and its immediate borders, is also experiencing the development of additional forms of racism.[8] Such a change may be facilitated by socioeconomic shifts including, locally, the introduction of guest workers who, though not Jewish and also not Arab, require different ways to be marked as unlike in a society where marking the other as other is an ingrained habit. This may explain, at least in part, why the term *racism* is used here so vaguely and seems to encompass any form of discrimination or bad attitude based on group membership. Thus, for example, secular Israeli Jews are accused of racism against the very Jewish orthodox, the *haredim,* who are both *Ashkenazi* and *Mizrachi* (meaning Eastern or Oriental and used interchangeably with *Spharadi,* a term that in the past was reserved to refer to Ladino-speaking Jews who traced their ancestry back to Spain and their legacy to the Spanish expulsion of Jews in 1492). In part, though, the extended domain of the term *racism* may be simply the result of the fact that from the beginning it was used without much precision. The term was borrowed in the late 1960s from U.S. discourses by local activists organizing themselves in protest of discrimination against *Mizrachi* Jews along U.S. models and even naming themselves the Black Panthers. Prior to that, the discrimination against *Mizrachi* Jews was discussed with reference to ethnicity but not to the idea of race, as was the discrimination against Arabs. The spread of support for antidiscrimination demands seems to have brought with it a popularization and very elastic use of the term *racism.*

But why am I talking about racism, even the local kind, when what I wanted to do when I started to describe whiteness as not very significant in the Israeli fabric of social meanings was to begin to explain my confusion about whiteness as a category, even after so many years in the United States? This confusion began when I had to fill out the first U.S. form that asked me what my race was. It was a confusion that I could not resolve with the answer given to me when I requested help: that since I was by nationality Israeli, hence, from the Middle East, I was Caucasian or white.

10　　Having a formula to rely on when asked by a form about my race is not the same as knowing that I have a race, an idea that my education implied was at best bizarre, as well as terribly dangerous, as should have been rather clear from World War II and the Nazi Judeocide. Moreover, were I to have a race, the one I was supposed to have by virtue of *my* history was not included on the form; I was Jewish and not white or Caucasian.

Lisa: I have been apprehensive about light-skinned, generally *Ashkenazi* Jews in the United States who claim to not quite be white, including immigrants such as you who report that although they know they are considered white in the United States, such classification feels imposed and foreign and not a right fit. In the context of discussions of U.S. racism, such claims have seemed both irrelevant and evasive of responsibility for white racism.[9] When I first heard you claim that it still felt strange to you to be labeled "white," I could not really believe that your reluctance to accept the designation could have its source in something other than evasion. I could not imagine this other source because I could not fully conceive of the black/white binary as decentered and therefore could not see how the importance of being white—and the responsibility for acknowledging oneself as white—could be diminished. Now, from here in the Middle East, I can finally understand how "whiteness" can be of less than primary importance; while not completely absent, whiteness conceived as a racial marker is far from central. From within the shifted perspective that I have even as a visitor here, my reflections on myself as someone who has learned to think of myself as white reveal a strangeness.

Here in Israel, it seems that nobody actually learns to *be* white—to experience themselves as white—in any very meaningful sense. Coming from here to the United States, a Jewish Israeli would "become" white in one magical moment of encountering the Immigration and Naturalization Service but would have missed out on all the training that makes it seem natural to be white, all the training in which a self-concept as white becomes inseparable from one's experience of the rest of the world. The moment is magical in that it signifies a becoming-white that takes place all at once; it is an official granting of whiteness where before there was none. It is a promise, too, that one will be treated as white every day in the new country—a promise made, though, to someone who has not yet come to know firsthand its importance. But the whiteness that is granted magically like this is not the same whiteness that has become internal to those of us who grew up with it.

I want to get at the difference between these two kinds of whiteness because my sense is that one cannot reduce being white to having white privilege. To do so is to fail to notice the difference between learning to experience oneself as white, with whiteness as fundamental to one's self (as in my case), and missing out on that learning, yet appearing externally indistinguishable from someone who has done the learning (as in your case). It is true that (light-skinned, generally *Ashkenazi*) Jews, whether immigrant or raised in an unassimilated way in the United States, are largely taken to be white, both in official contexts and everyday "commonsense" ways (on the street, on the job market, in social situations),[10] and they are accorded what can be called white privilege, especially when the right class factors figure in. Nonetheless, there is something distinct and additional about experiencing oneself as white. It seems that certain things, such as being an immigrant from a country without a racial state (or with a different one), or being raised as clearly an ethnic outsider within the United States (such as Jews can be if they are not assimilated, especially in those parts of the United States where "white," "Christian," and "American" function inseparably), can create a void in which one *is* not fully white though one is treated as white.

What, then, does one learn when one learns to *be* white in the United States? What did I learn (being assimilated enough) that makes me fully white, that you never got to learn, and that makes you less than fully fitted into whiteness (i.e., not "properly" socialized)? To be fully white is to have the habits of whiteness, habits that most whites in the United States probably begin practicing in childhood and that seem to involve learning how to distinguish oneself from specific others, especially blacks, and to distinguish as one distinguishes the superior from the inferior, the norm from the aberration, the trustworthy from the scary, the valuable from the dispensable. Perhaps these early-learned habits are among the things that an adult immigrant can never really attain, even after substantial assimilation. I have often noticed that you do not catch my references to the details of a U.S. childhood—such things as nursery rhymes and taunts and children's books and games, or standing in grade-school classrooms where one is expected to recite "I pledge of allegiance to the flag of the United States of America . . ."—and even if I tell you about them they will not be a part of you as they are a part of me, for they will not make you smile or cringe with memories; you may read *Goodnight Moon* aloud now to a friend's child, but it will reverberate with nothing from your past; you may be called upon to salute the American flag—and refuse— but it brings forth no memories, as it does for me, of refusing to do so as a child. And so it dawned on me that along with missing out on early effective training in such things, you were not trained at a young age in how to experience yourself as white. Whatever you learned about being white as an adult has no childhood or adolescent reference point. Without this, there must be no undercurrent feeling of loss in struggling to rid oneself of the sense of superiority that comes with a white identity.

15   My sense of whiteness always has a childhood or adolescent reference point. My sense of myself as white is inseparable from my sense of being from Newton, Massachusetts, a town that blacks could only enter as outsiders. It was certainly as outsiders that the METCO kids—black students bussed in from Boston—came to the Newton public schools; we (white, middle- and upper-class youth, self-confident in our belonging in the town and the schools) never called them black, referring to them only as "the METCO kids." And though we were liberal and therefore thought of ourselves as very, very different from those racist white people who had thrown stones at the buses, and though we were quite cognizant of and sometimes active against the racist practice of tracking "the METCO kids" into the lowest-level classes, the messages of who we were as whites had sunk in. Despite the euphemistic terms we used to mask it, we knew ourselves as white in relation to our opposite, black. My image of "us" (here many whites get excluded from my "we" because "they" were not the right class; nevertheless, my deepest sense of being white is indeed this elite one, undoubtedly a different sense of whiteness than those with different class backgrounds have) was that we were smart, sometimes so smart that others would resent it and tease us; we did not get pregnant and drop out; we did drugs, but the fun, recreational kind, not the kind that one must be desperate to go near; we had professional parents at home; we were profound thinkers and read the best literature; we were not loud and did not take up the whole hallway at school by walking in a tight throng; the best of us did not even watch television. While there were many divisions among groups of kids when I was growing up, based on class, ethnicity, and just plain popularity, they were not *all* unbridgeable. However, one was absolutely unbridgeable: I knew of not one single friendship between any of us white students and any of "the METCO kids."

Once when I was in college, a midwestern liberal arts college where friendships between blacks and whites were at least possible, I met a black student who introduced himself as being from Roxbury, one of the parts of Boston from which "the METCO kids" were bussed to the suburbs including Newton. Suddenly the weight of having a childhood reference point for race bore down on me. There I was in college, raised consciousness and all, in the middle of the passionate if misguided process of trying to jump out of my white skin to avoid being one of the bad guys in the racist schema of things. I knew that if I said at that moment where I was from, my whiteness in the face of his blackness would be overwhelming, inescapable, and somehow terribly wrong. It was not that *any* whiteness and *any* blackness could have had this effect. It was that the whiteness that I was, that I had learned early on, was meant to be superior to the blackness that he was. It seemed that there could be, for me, no undoing of that sense of superiority—felt now by me as racist and shameful—as long as I was thrown back by what presented themselves as simple facts: I was from Newton; he was from Roxbury.

What would it be like to be suddenly designated white and yet have none of this early weighted socialization in what it means to be white?

Ami: To me the designation "white" has yet to seem fitting in just the right way, because it feels so shallow, especially in comparison to my designation as an Jewish Israeli. I am not certain how to describe the difference of feeling one as "shallow" and the other as "deep" except by pointing out that when "hailed" as white, I am still surprised and have to tell myself that yes it is me who is "hailed." I experience a similar surprise only when I am not "hailed" as Jewish Israeli, which now happens sometimes during the first days back in Israel, when my Hebrew is still American English accented. But resisting the designation of "white," which I did for a while after arriving in the United States, eventually put me in an ethicopolitically peculiar place. I understood the antiracist struggle in the United States, and especially the feminist one (being so identity based), as requiring that I identify publicly as white to be seen as a credible ally. Nonetheless, as my experience of the failure of "hailing" suggests, this identification is quite formulaic: I identify publicly as a being that falls under a social category, but I do not have much of a sense of myself as a being that falls under that category, perhaps because this sense is a function of the play of complex micro and macro social forces, many of which, as you point out, shape one's feel of self during early socialization.

What has been less formulaic for me is learning that I am a being who is most usually accorded a measure of white privilege in the United States and who is there granted certain courtesies, deferences, opportunities, and safeties. Because I have grown us as a Jewish Israeli, I have also been socialized into a variety of privileges that are part of the Israeli scene, with its ethnic hierarchies.[11] Thus, for example, I was quite used to being treated in a friendly enough fashion by salespersons, unlike Jews in North Africa, and to not being suspected by the police when taking a walk through the neighborhood no matter how late at night, which no Palestinian in Israel can take for granted when not in Jewish Israeli company.

While these examples may seem quite innocuous, they are about suspicion, and suspicion of Palestinians as harboring danger to Jews undergirds elaborate surveillance routines in the Israeli situation, many of which are performed by every Jewish Israeli citizen automatically. Like all other Jewish Israelis, I have been mobilized by the state since I was very young and taught to "recognize Arabs" (we did not "recognize" Palestinians because we denied their national identity), to use almost imperceptible kinds of difference to succeed in performing these acts of "recognition," and always be alert to the possibility of their "passing." Though burdened with vigilance, as long as I embodied the gestures, posture, modes of talking and modes of dress of the *Sabra,* I was free from suspicion by others. This freedom, requiring as it does the fashioning of the body in distinction from other bodies, is a Jewish Israeli privilege that makes some white privileges familiar.

20

Being accorded white privilege, especially when social privilege is familiar, may tempt immigrants who do not come from countries in which whiteness is a particularly significant marker of identity to begin to develop a sense of ourselves as white and hence refashion ourselves into people with white identities. This temptation is hard to resist because some level of assimilation, or of hybridization, is simply necessary for survival in one's new country. Our transformations into white-identified people may, however, come about much less consciously, since being designated white may slowly interpolate us into whiteness. White privilege is accorded as part of a practice, and practice subjectifies through habituation. So, while being white is different from merely being designated white, one may become used to whiteness precisely because one is designated and treated as if one is white.

I do not think, though, that because one can be and is interpolated into whiteness through practices that accord one white privilege, one becomes the same kind of white as one who has been socialized to be white from early on. What one will continue to lack are the multiple ways in which early socialization gives one's racialized self a sense of depth. While in the context of U.S. antiracist struggle it does not seem to be such a bad thing to lack depth in one's sense of whiteness, for an immigrant, the lack is a reminder of her or his foreignness, of something about her or him that is forever inassimilable. One can choose to celebrate this, and yet one must recognize that there is always something psychologically costly to *being* "other."

NOTES

1. A recent radio poll has shown that the new immigrants from Russia are resented by more than 50 percent of the established Jewish Israeli population. Among the things believed by respondents is that they compete with Jewish Israelis for work, they cheapen labor, and their professional degrees are a sham. Thirty-four percent of the respondents even found the new Russian immigrants frightening. See the July 10, 1997, summary of findings in the *Jerusalem Post,* p. 4.

2. See Ella Shohat, "Spharadim in Israel: Zionism from the Standpoint of Its Jewish Victims," *Social Text* 7, nos. 1–2 (Fall 1988): 1–36.

3. I borrow this terminology from Michael Omi and Howard Winant, *Racial Formation in the Untied States: From the 1960s to the 1990s* (New York: Routledge, 1994).

4. According to the definitions used by the U.S. federal government, one is "WHITE (Not of Hispanic Origin)" if one is "a person having origins in any of the original peoples of Europe, North Africa, or the Middle East."

5. For instance, the National Union of Students, in their antiracism campaign, focuses on eliminating the use of what it refers to as "racist" slogans such as "Dirty Ethiopian," "Manic Ashkenazi," "Slippery Moroccan," and "Russian Whore" and, after being criticized by Arab students for a glaring omission, claims to have also intended targeting the slogan, "A Good Arab Is a Dead Arab." See "City Lights," supplement to the *Jerusalem Post* 5, no. 179 (July 11,1997): 2.

6. There gave been several newspaper reports about this. See, for example, a series of articles about the new Tel Aviveans in *Ha'ir,* June and July 1997.

7. See Ian F. Haney Lopez, *White by Law: The Legal Construction of Race* (New York: New York University Press, 1996). At the same time, though, the "one drop rule" is under attack by the "mixed-race" movement. While its politics needs examining (see Lisa Tessman, "The Racial Politics of Mixed Race," *Journal of Social Philosophy* 30, no. 2 [Fall 1999]), the fact of its organization and its growing success together with the organization and success of other ethnic/racial groups in the United States, may indicate a change of the racial/ethnic formation of the United States.

8. Zigmunt Bauman calls attention to changes of this kind in Europe in his discussion of anti-Semitism in *Life in Fragments: Essays in Postmodern Morality* (Oxford: Blackwell, 1995, 206–22. See also Etienne Balibar's "Is There a Neo-Racism?" in *Race, Nation, Class: Ambiguous Identities,* ed. Etienne Balibar and Immanuel Wallerstein (Paris: Editions La Découverte, 1988; London: Verso, 1991), 17–28.

9. See, for instance, Gloria Anzaldúa's complaints about those whom she calls "white Jewishwomen" (which she distinguishes from "Jewish women-of-color"), who, in a class she taught about women of color, "did not want to identify as white." She writes, "Some declared they felt they 'belonged' more to the women-of-color group than they did to the white group. Because they felt isolated and excluded, they felt that their oppressions were the same or similar to those of women-of-color." "Haciendo Caras, una Entrada," in *Making Faces, Making Soul/Haciendo Caras: Creative and Critical Perspectives by Women of Color,* ed. Gloria Anzaldúa (San Francisco: Aunt Lute, 1990), xx. Anzaldúa saw this as a failure to be accountable for white racism. A very nuanced consideration of whether and how Jews are white in the United States (an account that in fact quelled some of my apprehension) can be found in Melanie Kaye/Kantrowitz, "Jews, Class, Color, and the Cost of Whiteness," in *The Issue is Power* (San Francisco: Aunt Lute, 1992), and "Jews in the U.S.: The Rising Costs of Whiteness," in *Names We Call Home: Autobiography on Racial Identity,* ed. Becky Thompson and Sangeeta Tyagi (New York: Routledge, 1996).

10. Some dark-skinned Jews may be in an especially interesting position of being officially classified as white yet not counting as white in "commonsense" ways.

11. In her "White Privilege: Unpacking the Invisible Knapsack," *Peace and Freedom* (July/August 1989): 10–12, Peggy McIntosh list twenty-six items that exemplify white privilege in the United States. The list can work with appropriate adjustments when thinking through Jewish Israeli privilege relative to Palestinian Israeli, *Ashkenazi* privilege relative to *Mizrachi,* as well as about aspects of class privilege.

NOTES ON THE CONFLATION OF SEX, GENDER, AND SEXUAL ORIENTATION

A QUEERCRIT AND LATCRIT PERSPECTIVE

Francisco Valdes

Because sex, gender, and sexual orientation are central concepts in our society's sex/gender system, their histories and meanings are significant and complex. However, the conflation of this trio, and its effects, have gone largely unnoticed both in law and society. The conflation comprises three constructs: sex, gender, and sexual orientation. The first leg of this triangle is the conflation of sex and gender; the second, that of gender and sexual orientation. The third is the conflation of sex and sexual orientation.

The first leg, conflating sex and gender, holds that every person's sex is also that person's gender. This leg, or its disruption, produces "sissies" and "tomboys." The second leg, conflating sex-derived gender and sexual orientation, is less familiar, at least initially. This leg is the generally recognizable linkage between "queers" and "sissies" on the one hand, and "dykes" and "tomboys" on the other, suggesting that some correlation between sex-determined gender and sexual orientation *is* at work.

The conflation's third leg may be the least familiar, but is discernible and demonstrable nonetheless. The conflation of sex and sexual orientation is shown by the way in which sexual orientation is directly surmised by the sameness or difference of sex(es) within a coupling: a sameness of sex within a coupling results directly in conclusions of homosexual orientation for each participant whereas a difference of sexes within a coupling produces conclusions of heterosexual orientation.

In this conflationary scheme, "sex" refers to external genitalia, usually as observed at birth, while "gender" signifies the composite of personal appearance and social behaviors, characteristics and roles imputed to all persons at birth on the basis of sex. These attributes are organized into an active/male and passive/female paradigm that extends both to social *and* sexual identities. In other words, the conflationary manifestation or performance of sex-determined gender, in the form of "active/male" or "passive/female" personality, is expected and demanded in both social ("public") settings as well as in sexual ("private") relations. In this scheme, "sexual orientation" effectively represents the sexual dimension or performance of gender: sexual orientation denotes the sense and enactment of erotic desire or personality, which is cast as either "active" or "passive" under the sexed and gendered dictates of the active/passive paradigm. Moreover, in the active/passive hierarchy of this scheme, masculinity structurally is valorized over femininity and cross-sex couplings structurally are valorized over same-sex couplings. The conflation's sex/gender ideology therefore is heteropatriarchy—the intertwining of andro-sexism and heterosexism to validate malecentric and heterocentric biases.

As these socio-legal definitions indicate, the conflation of the three constructs begins with and pivots on "sex," and on its assignment at birth. And because gender is deduced from and fixed by sex, this conflationary scheme constructs the social and sexual dimensions of "gender" as both deductive and intransitive. It bears emphasis that these basic definitions, and their anchoring to active/passive ideology, are entrenched in Euro-American history, and they continue to prevail in the United States as a matter of clinical practice, cultural custom and legal doctrine.[1]

The courts have faced these conflations in several modern cases. In one, *Strailey v. Happy Times Nursery Sch., Inc.,*[2] the Ninth Circuit confronted all three legs at once. In that case, Strailey alleged that he "was fired by Defendants in September 1975 because he [was] a homosexual and failed to present a proper male image," and that this action violated Title VII. He further alleged that his employer "refused[d] to employ anyone it [knew to be] homosexual, including persons it believed[d] [did] not present a proper male or (or female) image, despite their abilities to teach and to deal with children effectively."[3] As such, the claim asserted that the school maintained a "policy and practice of denying equal employment opportunities to homosexual applicants and employees because of their sex and sexual orientation."[4] This framing linguistically used "sex" when meaning "gender" because conceptually this claim sought to describe effeminacy—the social display of "female" gender by a person of a "male" sex. Strailey's effeminacy/"sissy" and homosexuality/"queer" claims thus invoked the conflation's first and second legs, respectively.

Further, Strailey asserted that "[d]iscrimination based on sexual orientation is based upon the gender of the plaintiffs as well as that of their sexual partners, just as discrimination based on hetero-racial relationships is based upon the race of each party to such relationships."[5] Conversely, this framing linguistically used "gender" when meaning "sex" because conceptually this claim sought to analogize homo-sexual couplings to hetero-racial ones. Without directly implicating gender, this claim characterized discrimination against same-sex couples as based on "sex" in the same way that discrimination against cross-race couples is based on "race."

In support of this claim, Strailey relied on cases decided during the 1960s that had invalidated anti-miscegenation statutes. Defenders of those statutes had argued then that because the prohibition against cross-race relations applied "equally" to both races, the laws did not "discriminate" on the basis of race. The courts resolutely rejected that reasoning, discerning that the anti-miscegenation statutes were intended and employed as a means of preserving racial hierarchies that subordinated minority races. Thus, judicial rejection of this sophistry in the miscegenation setting was based on a recognition that the abstract equality on the face of the statutes masked and perpetuated race-based inequalities in practice.

In effect, Strailey's third claim advanced and presaged an analogy between sex and race: since Strailey's framing and assertion of this claim, this "miscegenation analogy" has received scholarly attention and development. Here, as in the subsequent scholarship, this analogy was employed to train the court(s) on the direct, unmediated inter-connection between sex and sexual orientation in order to obtain judicial recognition of sexual orientation discrimination as a sub-set of sex-based discrimination. This claim, and the analogy as later developed, thus introduce Leg Three of the conflation into the sex/gender record of legal culture.

10 In this vein, Strailey's brief went on to analogize this claim to EEOC decisions dealing with discrimination based on an employee's "associations" with persons of another race. Specifically, it referred to a 1971 decision in which the EEOC considered the claim of a white employee who had been discharged, in the former employee's words, "because of her friends."[6] The EEOC in that case had concluded that the discharge was based unlawfully on the employee's "interracial dating," an association that was "clearly protected by Title VII."[7]

Unfortunately, the *Strailey* court's response to this analogizing disregarded the reasoning of precedent, and was as strained and superficial as the rest of its opinion. The court asserted that Strailey's analogy had not claimed that his employer would "terminate anyone with a male (or female) friend."[8] Rather, the court maintained, Strailey had claimed that his employer "discriminate[d] against employees who have a certain type of relationship—i.e., homosexual relationship—with certain friends."[9] This distinction—presumable between "friends" on the one hand and "certain relationships . . . with certain friends" on the other—seems slippery, and is incongruent with the statute's anti-discrimination principals because it serves to license rather than to limit bigotry.

Still, even as reformulated by the court, Strailey's associational claim seems precisely analogous to cross-race intimacy. Anti-miscegenation statutes, as well as the discharge of employees who had "friends" of other races, discriminated against persons who had a certain type of relationship—i.e., a hetero-racial relationship—with certain friends. In each instance, the discrimination sought to regulate intimate interactions with sexual or affectional partners. In each instance the discrimination was calculated to subordinate minority groups. Finally, in each instance the discrimination succeeded in doing just that (and nothing else).

The conflation today remains as firmly entrenched in sexual minority communities as it is in mainstream American society and its legal culture. This entrenchment is exemplified by the continuing sway of identifications like "butch" or "femme" or "queen" that project various conflationary configurations of sex, gender, and sexual orientation. And though the butch-femme debate is often most directly associated with lesbian identity, its sex/gender issues extend to gay male identity as well because both female and male same-sex couples necessarily confront male/husband and female/wife roles and issues defined by traditionalist active/passive standards.

For instance, both female and male same-sex couples frequently encounter queries from friends, relatives, or acquaintances in the sexual majority asking, "Who plays the 'wife's' role?" This query, in effect, seeks to determine who is the "butch" and who is the "femme"; in other words, who conforms and who does not—who is socially *and* sexually gender typical and who is socially *and* sexually gender atypical. Of course, this query effectively signals underlying confusion (or incredulity) over the possibility that sex-determined gender and sexual orientation are not necessarily correlated or conflated either socially/publicly or sexually/privately.

Perhaps the most familiar example of the butch-femme issue in specifically gay male subculture might be the still-ubiquitous "drag" shows that glorify cross-dressing and other social gender-bending affectations as a means of representing sexual orientation to the audience. Much as we saw in the 1982 film, *Victor, Victoria,* these shows feature lip-sync impersonations of hyper-glamorous female performers, replete with wigs, makeup, gowns, and gestures. Major cities often have at least one establishment specializing in the presentation of this type of activity, and many other bars or lounges across the country include such fare in their regular entertainment schedules. Literally and normatively, these shows place gender squarely at center stage in the cultural life of communities apparently defined by sexual orientation, and thereby project active/passive traditions represented and reproduced jointly by the first and second legs of the conflation.

The ongoing butch-femme debate in lesbian communities, which contests the pros and cons of acting out sex-based gender roles socially and/or sexually within an all-female coupling, likewise attests to the conflation's hardiness. For example, JoAnn Loulan's groundbreaking surveys of lesbians throughout the country illustrate the phenomenon well: her most recent data, from 1989–1990, show 44 percent of the 589 lesbians interviewed electing to adopt a socially and/or sexually gendered role within the relationship, with 19 percent identifying themselves as butch (the male role) and 25 percent as femme (the female role). The conflation thus persists among sizable segments of lesbian communities, coexisting with the growing recognition that butch-femme categorizing often serves to perpetuate androsexist as well as hetero-sexist images. In short, under the first and second legs of the conflation, internalized active/passive traditions regarding sex and gender continue to drive, at least in part, the personal(ized) constructions of sexual orientation among many lesbians living today.

In both male and female same-sex settings, the butch/femme/queen discourse manifests an awareness of and an acquiescence to official active/passive sex/gender themes and traditions, even when "bending" them. Among both the men and the women, sex is viewed as gender's determinant. Among

15

both sexes, gender is understood to comprise social/public and sexual/private personality. Among both gay men and lesbians, social gender atypicality is associated with sexual gender atypicality. Thus, Leg One and Leg Two of the conflation remain jointly in place among both male and female segments of sexual minority communities.

In like vein, sexual minorities of color continue to live the conflation in much the same way that Eric Garber depicted in his study of early-to-mid-1900s Harlem. Indeed, the costumed events that Garber described now have evolved into the highly stylized recent innovation known as "voguing." Popularized by Madonna's 1990 pop music hit single, *Vogue,* this activity involves "striking a pose" which, more often than not, amounts to glamorized and exaggerated social gender posturing; the voguing balls of today, as with their earlier equivalents, are characterized by flamboyant social gender regalia and props.

The popularity of voguing and balls among African-American and Latino sexual minorities in New York City was depicted in movingly graphic detail in the 1990 film *Paris Is Burning.* The film documents the "houses" that play central roles in the production of balls; each is headed by a "mother" who directs his/her house's participation in the events. Participants compete in categories such as "Butch Queen," "Pretty Girl," and "Miss Cheesecake." One set of categories, "Realness," focuses on the ability of the competitors to emulate the subjects of the category; for instance, "Looking Like a Girl Going to School" or "Executive Man." In an especially revealing comment on these categories of competition, one participant explains that the object of the latter category is to "look like a real man, a straight man." Indeed, under the conflation's configuration and depiction of active/passive human identities and personalities, "real" men (and women) are "straight" men (and women).

20   Not surprisingly, then, social/public gender affectations provide much of the film's thematic centerpiece, attesting to the continuing vitality of the conflation's first and second legs even among youngsters unequipped to (re)cognize them: throughout the film, we repeatedly encounter young males in interviews and escapades who self-identify as gay, and who uniformly conceive and articulate that sexual identity by adopting in both outlandish and discreet ways the social/public attributes associated with femininity. This film, in fact, portrays individuals for whom sex-determined gender and sexual orientation are indistinguishable, and who live their lives *today* on that basis; these are persons who today define themselves as sexually and therefore socially cross-gendered, or vice versa, and who thereby apply to their beings and lives the active/passive dictates corresponding both to the first and to the second leg of the conflation.

Finally, there is Jacob's story. As an African American growing up in the southeast just as the integration of public schools was getting underway, Jacob was a star student who excelled both in academics and in extracurricular activities.[10] Fearful that his "effeminate mannerisms" (coupled with his apparent lack of interest in girls) and general timidity toward sports might label him as gay, Jacob used his studies and activities to insulate himself from suspicion: he deflected any questioning of his closeted (homo)sexuality by raising his "bookworm" persona as a shield. Additionally, he steered clear of any association with the "hard-core faggots" in his high school, characterizing the group as "very effeminate acting." As Jacob's story indicates, for him as well as for his peers among both the "faggots" and nonfaggots, social effeminacy (in the form of mannerisms, activities, or talents) stood for, and therefore was interpreted as, same-sex desire. Social effeminacy, in other words, signaled and was tantamount to sexual effeminacy, and vice versa.

To avoid identification with the latter attribute of his personality, Jacob strategically deployed and disguised the former attributes of his personality. In doing so, Jacob displayed an intuitive understanding of the way(s) in which active/passive sex/gender traditions under the conflation's first and second legs operate(d) in tandem to shape his peers' and his family's (mis)perceptions of him, both socially and sexually. He intuited that society officially and culturally regards gender as deductive and intransitive; in turn, Jacob understood that his personal survival and prosperity depended on deflecting suspicion over his sexual/private personality which, by his own account, he consciously set out to do by disguising his apparently atypical or cross-gendered social/public personality.

Confirming this intuition, Jacob's calculated disguises succeeded. Though he engaged in same-sex liaisons throughout his high school years, Jacob was able to "pass for straight" in the eyes of both friends and family. In this way, Jacob enabled himself to avoid (some of) the stigma and prejudice heaped on persons who somehow—socially, sexually, or both—are deemed cross-gendered; persons who are devalued or denigrated because they personify the violation or disruption of one or more of the conflation's legs.

Both voguing and Jacob display yet again the way(s) in which contemporary sexual minorities—including those living in communities of color—comply with traditionalist sex/gender conceptions, even as they bend or break official or cultural sex/gender rules accompanying those conceptions. In both instances, sex was understood to fix gender. In both instances, gender was understood to encompass both social/public sexual/private components. In both instances, gender transitivity that was social was associated with the sexual version. And, in both instances, society's problematization of gender atypicality socially and/or sexually was intuitively, if not intellectually, understood. Thus, while indulging, both socially and sexually, in various forbidden cross-gender attributes or activities, the individuals in these instances clearly were aware of—and accepted and accommodated—the official premises and the cultural power of the first and second legs of the conflation.

Although the history of the conflation in modern Euro-American culture presented above is necessarily oversimplified, it points to the inescapable conclusions that the conflation of sex, gender, and sexual orientation envelops our intellectual and attitudinal environment and shapes our personal and collective sensibilities. The conflation's embodiment and enforcement of active/passive sex/gender themes and traditions are so pervasive, so ingrained, 25 so institutionalized, so internalized, that even our children unknowingly collect epithets like "queer," "sissy," "dyke," and "tomboy" in single, automatic breaths. These epithets, in turn, display how heteropatriarchy is imprinted in the collective psyche of each generation.

In short, this nation's sex/gender system is designed, built, and maintained precisely along the conflation's traditionalist active/passive fault lines, both socially and sexually. These official and cultural fault lines do not operate randomly: in practice, they operate to secure the social/public and sexual/private intransitivity of deductive gender, and thereby to secure the hierarchical imperatives that underlie and drive the Euro-American sex/gender system and its heteropatriarchal ideology. Unthinking schoolyard comments only reflect and confirm the conflationary system's continuing grip on the nation's senses, while underscoring traditionalist fear and loathing of social or sexual challenges to conflationary arrangements that (might) disrupt the sex/gender status quo.

In Latina/o culture or settings, both within and beyond the United States, this conflationary dynamic and its sex/gender ideology are also present, and perhaps even more virulently so due to the prevalence of a strong "machismo" norm. Terms like "marimacha" and "maricon"—meaning dyke and queer, respectively—reflect and reify the conflation's sway over Latina/o sex/gender norms and sexual orientation identities: the former connotes a mannish female, the latter an effeminate man. Both are devalued because they enact nonconforming combinations of sex, gender, and sexuality. Thus, as in Euro-American contexts, all three legs of the conflation operate, and in combination construct social and sexual identifications: sex establishes gender expectations, and gender a/typically is construed and mis/treated as homo/heterosexual orientation. As in Euro-American culture, social or sexual disruption of any leg is censured. Moreover, as these terms imply, Latina/o sex/gender hierarchies are not only heterocentric, they also are androcentric. Thus, as in the Euro-American sex/gender system, Latina/o ideas and values instill and demand conformity to the conflation's active/passive heteropatriarchal bent.

Accordingly, resistance to this conflation and its ideology must be recognized as central to the anti-subordination strategy of Queer legal theory. But this strategy also must guard against our prior internalization of conflationary beliefs or associations. In particular, concerns over gay male androsexism, and the dangers that it poses for Queer theorizing, should serve constructively to heighten our individual and collective vigilance against the potential for a wholesale or creeping influence of androsexism within Queer critiques. Because it counters the tradition of male supremacy that has run through Western history, this heightened vigilance may not come easily, but it is also not impossible. Indeed, by definition, the term "Queer" reflects and invokes this type of heightened awareness for sex/gender egalitarianism and against sex/gender imperialism. The key, then, is to live up to the standards of the term, and the challenge is to join in the fulfillment of the ideals underlying this commitment.

However, to do so we also must take into account other issues raised by Queer legal theory. American culture employs "queer" to denigrate persons suspected of being gay, but in recent years "Queer," has come to signify principally a rebellious resistance to heterosexist customs and precepts. As a result, "Queer," like "queer," tends to indicate minority "sexual orientation." But it need (and should) not be so: "Queer" is a description of consciousness regarding sexuality and its relationship to one's self and to one's culture.[11] Thus, even though most persons who self-identify as Queer today probably are gay, lesbian, bisexual, or trans/bi-gendered, one *can* be gay or lesbian or bisexual or trans/bi-gendered without being Queer; Queer consciousness is neither innate nor uniform among sexual minorities. Likewise, Queer subjectivity may be articulated from a sexual majority position.

Queer legal theory likewise must and can avoid the similar danger of carelessly (or intentionally) reiterating the racist biases that, like androsexism, pervade our social and legal environments. The vigilance of Queer legal theory against racism is again especially important due to our cultural backdrop: the larger Queer social movement already has experienced problems with racial (dis)harmony because it has not (fully) excised racist overtones and undertones from its ranks. This failure excludes people of color from Queer venues, replicating and compounding the race divisions of the sexual majority. This failure thus demonstrates how deeply we are mired in acculturation, and how crucial it is for queer legal theory to intercede during these formative times on behalf of Queers of color. Queer as legal theory, using queer cultural politics and studies as its point of departure, has the opportunity and obligation to discontinue, interrupt, and condemn the replication of racism both in sexual minority cultural venues and legal projects.

This opportunity is also an obligation because the exclusion or marginalization of people of color within Queer settings is antithetical to the inclusiveness and expansiveness that is definitive and constitutive of Queerness. As in the case of androsexism, Queer undertakings proactively must show and apply a heightened sensitivity to, and an uncompromising opposition against, the omission of race, ethnicity, and class from Queer critiques. Queer as legal theory cannot tolerate or ignore any show of wholesale or creeping racism, ethnocentrism, or classism. The inclusiveness and egalitarianism of Queerness demand that Queer legal theory not ignore the lives and presence of Queers of color, or varying ethnic backgrounds, or of (dis)advantaged backgrounds: to do so would be to lend support to the oppression that subordinates groups based on race, ethnicity, or class more generally. As legal theory, the Queer enterprise must take a proactive stance toward race, ethnicity, and class, toward their particularized intersections with (homo/bi)sexuality, and toward their broader intertwining with sex/gender issues.

At the threshold—where we stand today—this concern therefore necessitates nothing less than a sustained effort to make the historic and unfinished fight against racism, ethnocentrism, and classism integral to Queer critiques of the law. This effort in turn requires an affirmative interrogation of why and

30

how Queerness plays differently in different racial, ethnic, or class contexts, as much as it requires an interrogation of where and when racism, ethnocentrism, and classism—perhaps even of the unconscious type—confine Queer theorizing in arbitrary or unproductive ways. From the outset, Queer legal critiques therefore must take the time and make the effort expressly to discuss and expose the role of race, ethnicity, and class in the (mis)fortunes visited by the law on Queer (and other) lives. In this way "Queer" as legal theory can avoid importing the assumed and imposed whiteness of "queer" as cultural epithet and also align itself with the greater anti-subordination civil rights movement for equality in color and class relations.

Finally, these notes make plain that the conflation's androcentric and heterocentric prejudice is replicated and disseminated not only through Anglo, but also through Hispanic, norms. For Latinas/os in the United States, and especially for those who identify as lesbian, gay, bisexual or trans/bi-gendered, this social combination is a "double whammy." In other words, Latina/o members of sexual minorities in the United States are socially and legally marginalized through the conflationary precepts and practices of the two systems that constitute our beings and structure our environments.

These notes thus make plain that this conflation concerns more than Queer legal theory; the conflation's impact specifically on Latina/o sexual minority communities implicates LatCrit theory as well. The conflation's heteropatriarchal biases are directly relevant to the anti-subordination mission of LatCrit theory because the LatCrit enterprise is explicitly and self-consciously dedicated to the cause of social justice for *all* Latinas/os; LatCrit theory insistently embraces and celebrates the multiple diversities of "Latinas/os," rejecting both single-axis analyses that essentialize Latinas/os as well as internal and external ideologies of subordination.[12] Because the conflation's promotion of adrosexism and heterosexism subordinates many Latinas/os, these notes suggest that LatCrit theory and Queer legal theory share a common interest in the transformation of today's sex/gender system, a transformation that unites the QueerCrit and LatCrit goals of a just post-subordination society. These notes, in sum, invite LatCrit interrogation of this conflation, an interrogation that properly is deemed integral to the LatCrit anti-subordination agenda.

NOTES

1. Francisco Valdes, "Queers, Sissies, Dykes and Tomboys: Deconstructing the Conflation of "Sex," "Gender," and "Sexual Orientation" in Euro-American Law and Society," 83 *Calif. L. Rev.* 1, 36–55 (1995).
2. 608 F.2d 327 (9th Cir. 1979).
3. Complaint at 3, Strailey v. Happy Times Nursery Sch., Inc. (N.D. Cal.) (Civil Action No. 76-1088).
4. Ibid.
5. Complaint at 3–4.
6. EEOC Decision No. 71-1902, 3 Fair Empl. Pac. Cas. (BNA) 1244, 1244–45 (1971).

7. Ibid.
8. Strailey, 608 F.2d at 331.
9. Ibid.
10. James T. Sears, *Growing Up Gay in the South: Race, Gender, and Journeys of the Spirit* 117–29 (1991).
11. See generally Lauren Berlant & Elizabeth Freeman, *Queer Nationality,* in Queer Planet: Queer Politics and Social Theory (Michael Warner ed., 1993) at 193.
12. See generally Symposium, *LatCrit Theory: Naming and Launching a New Discourse of Critical Legal Scholarship,* 2 Harv. Latino L. Rev. 1 (1997); Symposium, *LatCrit Theory: Latinas/os and the Law,* 85 Calif. L. Rev. (forthcoming 1998).

THE FIVE SEXES: WHY MALE AND FEMALE ARE NOT ENOUGH

Anne Fausto-Sterling

In 1843 Levi Suydam, a twenty-three-year-old resident of Salisbury, Connecticut, asked the town board of selectmen to validate his right to vote as a Whig in a hotly contested local election. The request raised a flurry of objections from the opposition party, for reasons that must be rare in the annals of American democracy: it was said that Suydam was more female than male and thus (some eighty years before suffrage was extended to women) could not be allowed to cast a ballot. To settle the dispute a physician, one William James Barry, was brought in to examine Suydam. And, presumably upon encountering a phallus, the good doctor declared the prospective voter male. With Suydam safely in their column the Whigs won the election by a majority of one.

Barry's diagnosis, however, turned out to be somewhat premature. Within a few days he discovered that, phallus notwithstanding, Suydam menstruated regularly and had a vaginal opening. Both his/her physique and his/her mental predispositions were more complex than was first suspected. S/he had narrow shoulders and broad hips and felt occasional sexual yearnings for women. Suydam's "feminine propensities, such as a fondness for gay colors, for pieces of calico, comparing and placing them together, and an aversion for bodily labor, and an inability to perform the same, were remarked by many," Barry later wrote. It is not clear whether Suydam lost or retained the vote, or whether the election results were reversed.

Western culture is deeply committed to the idea that there are only two sexes. Even language refuses other possibilities: thus to write about Levi Suydam I have had to invent conventions—*s/he and his/her*—to denote someone who is clearly neither male nor female or who is perhaps both sexes at once. Legally, too, every adult is either man or woman, and the difference, or course, is not trivial. For Suydam it meant the franchise; today it means being available for, or exempt from, draft registration, as well as being subject, in various ways, to a number of laws governing marriage, the family and human intimacy. In many parts of the United States, for instance, two people legally registered as men cannot have sexual relations without violating anti-sodomy statutes.

But if the state and the legal system have an interest in maintaining a two-party sexual system, they are in defiance of nature. For biologically speaking, there are many gradations running from female to male; and depending on how one calls the shots, one can argue that along that spectrum lie at least five sexes—and perhaps even more.

For some time medical investigators have recognized the concept of the 5
intersexual body. But the standard medical literature uses the term *intersex* as a
catch-all for three major subgroups with some mixture of male and female
characteristics: the so-called true hermaphrodites, whom I call herms, who
possess one testis and one ovary (the sperm- and egg-producing vessels, or
gonads); the male pseudohermaphrodites (the "merms"), who have testes and
some aspects of the female genitalia but no ovaries; and the female pseudohermaphrodites (the "ferms"), who have ovaries and some aspects of the male
genitalia but lack testes. Each of those categories is in itself complex; the percentage of male and female characteristics, for instance, can vary enormously
among members of the same subgroup. Moreover, the inner lives of the
people in each subgroup—their special needs and their problems, attractions
and repulsions—have gone unexplored by science. But on the basis of what is
known about them I suggest that the three intersexes, herm, merm and ferm,
deserve to be considered additional sexes each in its own right. Indeed, I
would argue further that sex is a vast, infinitely malleable continuum that defies the constraints of even five categories.

Not surprisingly, it is extremely difficult to estimate the frequency of intersexuality, much less the frequency of each of the three additional sexes: it is
not the sort of information one volunteers on a job application. The psychologist John Money of Johns Hopkins University, a specialist in the study of
congenital sexual-organ defects, suggests intersexuals may constitute as many
as 4 percent of births. As I point out to my students at Brown University, in a
student body of about 6,000 that fraction, if correct, implies there may be as
many as 240 intersexuals on campus—surely enough to form a minority caucus of some kind.

In reality though, few such students would make it as far as Brown in
sexually diverse form. Recent advances in physiology and surgical technology
now enable physicians to catch most intersexuals at the moment of birth. Almost at once such infants are entered into a program of hormonal and surgical management so that they can slip quietly into society as "normal"
heterosexual males or females. I emphasize that the motive is in no way con-
spiratorial. The aims of the policy are genuinely humanitarian, reflecting the
wish that people be able to "fit in" both physically and psychologically. In the
medical community, however, the assumptions behind that wish—that there
be only two sexes, that heterosexuality alone is normal, that there is one true
model of psychological health—have gone virtually unexamined.

The word *hermaphrodite* comes from the Greek names Hermes, variously
known as the messenger of the gods, the patron of music, the controller of
dreams or the protector of livestock, and Aphrodite, the goddess of sexual
love and beauty. According to Greek mythology, those two gods parented
Hermaphroditus, who at age fifteen became half male and half female when
his body fused with the body of a nymph he fell in love with. In some true
hermaphrodites the testis and the ovary grow separately but bilaterally; in
others they grow together within the same organ, forming an ovo-testis. Not

infrequently, at least one of the gonads functions quite well, producing either sperm cells or eggs, as well as functional levels of the sex hormones—androgens or estrogens. Although in theory it might be possible for a true hermaphrodite to become both father and mother to a child, in practice the appropriate ducts and tubes are not configured so that egg and sperm can meet.

In contrast with the true hermaphrodites, the pseudohermaphrodites possess two gonads of the same kind along with the usual male (XY) or female (XX) chromosomal makeup. But their external genitalia and secondary sex characteristics do not match their chromosomes. Thus merms have testes and XY chromosomes, yet they also have a vagina and a clitoris, and at puberty they often develop breasts. They do not menstruate, however. Ferms have ovaries, two X chromosomes and sometimes a uterus, but they also have at least partly masculine external genitalia. Without medical intervention they can develop beards, deep voices and adult-size penises. . . .

10   Intersexuality itself is old news. Hermaphrodites for instance, are often featured in stories about human origins. Early biblical scholars believed Adam began life as a hermaphrodite and later divided into two people—a male and a female—after falling from grace. According to Plato there once were three sexes—male, female, and hermaphrodite—the third sex was lost with time.

Both the Talmud and the Tosefta, the Jewish books of law, list extensive regulations for people of mixed sex. The Tosefta expressly forbids hermaphrodites to inherit their fathers' estates (like daughters), to seclude themselves with women (like sons) or to shave (like men). When hermaphrodites menstruate they must be isolated from men (like women); they are disqualified from serving as witnesses or as priests (like women), but the laws of pederasty apply to them.

In Europe a pattern emerged by the end of the Middle Ages that, in a sense, has lasted to the present day: hermaphrodites were compelled to choose an established gender role and stick with it. The penalty for transgression was often death. Thus, in the 1600s a Scottish hermaphrodite living as a woman was buried alive after impregnating his/her master's daughter.

For questions of inheritance, legitimacy, paternity, success to title and eligibility for certain professions to be determined, modern Anglo-Saxon legal systems require that newborns be registered as either male or female. In the U.S. today sex determination is governed by state laws. Illinois permits adults to change the sex recorded on their birth certificates should a physician attest to having performed the appropriate surgery. The New York Academy of Medicine, on the other hand, has taken an opposite view. In spite of surgical alterations of the external genitalia, the academy argued in 1966, the chromosomal sex remains the same. By that measure, a person's wish to conceal his or her original sex cannot outweigh the public interest in protection against fraud.

During this century the medical community has completed what the legal world began—the complete erasure of any form of embodied sex that does not conform to a male–female, heterosexual pattern. Ironically, a more sophisticated knowledge of the complexity of sexual systems has led to the repression of such intricacy.

In 1937 the urologist Hugh H. Young of Johns Hopkins University pub- 15
lished a volume titled *Genital Abnormalities, Hermaphroditism and Related Adrenal Diseases.* The book is remarkable for its erudition, scientific insight and open-mindedness. In it Young drew together a wealth of carefully documented case histories to demonstrate and study the medical treatment of such "accidents of birth." Young did not pass judgment on the people he studied, nor did he attempt to coerce into treatment those intersexuals who rejected that option. And he showed unusual even-handedness in referring to those people who had had sexual experiences as both men and women as "practicing hermaphrodites."

One of Young's more interesting cases was hermaphrodite named Emma who had grown up as a female. Emma had both a penis-size clitoris and a vagina, which made it possible for him/her to have "normal" heterosexual sex with both men and women. As a teenager Emma had had sex with a number of girls to whom s/he was deeply attracted: but at the age of nineteen s/he had married a man. Unfortunately, he had given Emma little sexual pleasure (although *he* had had no complaints), and so throughout that marriage and subsequent ones Emma had kept girlfriends on the side. With some frequency s/he had pleasurable sex with them. Young describes his subject as appearing "to be quite content and even happy." In conversation Emma occasionally told him of his/her wish to be a man, a circumstance Young said would be relatively easy to bring about. But Emma's reply strikes a heroic blow for self-interest:

> Would you have to remove that vagina? I don't know about
> that because that's my meal ticket. If you did that, I would have
> to quit my husband and go to work, so I think I'll keep it and
> stay as I am. My husband supports me well, and even though
> I don't have any sexual pleasure with him, I do have lots with
> my girlfriends.

Yet even as Young was illuminating intersexuality with the light of scientific reason, he was beginning its suppression. For his book is also an extended treatise on the most modern surgical and hormonal methods of changing intersexuals into either males or females. Young may have differed from his successors in being less judgmental and controlling of the patients and their families, but he nonetheless supplied the foundation on which current intervention practices were built.

By 1969, when the English physicians Christopher J. Dewhurst and Ronald R. Gordon wrote *The Intersexual Disorders,* medical and surgical approaches to intersexuality had neared a state of rigid uniformity. It is hardly surprising that such a hardening of opinion took place in the era of the feminine mystique—of the post–Second World War flight to the suburbs and the strict division of family roles according to sex. That the medical consensus was not quite universal (or perhaps that it seemed poised to break apart again) can be gleaned from the near-hysterical tone of Dewhurst and Gordon's book, which contrasts markedly with the calm reason of Young's founding work. Consider their opening description of an intersexual newborn:

> One can only attempt to imagine the anguish of the parents. That a newborn should have a deformity . . . [affecting] so fundamental an issue as the very sex of the child . . . is a tragic event which immediately conjures up visions of a hopeless psychological misfit doomed to live always as a sexual freak in loneliness and frustration.

Dewhurst and Gordon warned that such a miserable fate would, indeed, be a baby's lot should the case be improperly managed; "but fortunately," they wrote, "with correct management the outlook is infinitely better than the poor parents—emotionally stunned by the event—or indeed anyone without special knowledge could ever imagine."

20   Scientific dogma has held fast to the assumption that without medical care hermaphrodites are doomed to a life of misery. Yet there are few empirical studies to back up that assumption, and some of the same research gathered to build a case for medical treatment contradicts it. Francies Benton, another of Young's practicing hermaphrodites, "had not worried over his condition, did not wish to be changed, and was enjoying life." The same could be said of Emma, the opportunistic hausfrau. Even Dewhurst and Gordon, adamant about the psychological importance of treating intersexuals at the infant stage, acknowledged great success in "changing the sex" of older patients. They reported on twenty cases of children reclassified into a different sex after the supposedly critical age of eighteen months. They asserted that all the reclassifications were "successful," and they wondered then whether reregistration could be "recommended more readily than [had] been suggested so far."

The treatment of intersexuality in this century provides a clear example of what the French historian Michel Foucault has called biopower. The knowledge developed in biochemistry, embryology, endocrinology, psychology and surgery has enabled physicians to control the very sex of the human body. The multiple contradictions in that kind of power call for some scrutiny. One the one hand, the medical "management" of intersexuality certainly developed as part of an attempt to free people from perceived psychological pain (though whether the pain was the patient's, the parents' or the physician's is unclear). And if one accepts the assumption that in a sex-divided culture people can realize their greatest potential for happiness and productivity only if they are sure they belong to one of only two acknowledged sexes, modern medicine has been extremely successful.

On the other hand, the same medical accomplishments can be read not as progress but as a mode of discipline. Hermaphrodites have unruly bodies. They do not fall naturally into a binary classification; only a surgical shoehorn can put them there. But why should we care if a "woman," defined as one who has breasts, a vagina, a uterus, and ovaries and who menstruates, also has a clitoris large enough to penetrate the vagina of another woman? Why should we care if there are people whose biological equipment enables them to have sex "naturally" with both men and women? The answers seem to lie in a cultural need to maintain clear distinctions between the sexes. Society mandates the control of intersexual bodies because they blur and bridge the great divide. Inasmuch as hermaphrodites literally embody both sexes, they challenge traditional beliefs about sexual difference, they possess the irritating ability to live sometimes as one sex and sometimes the other, and they raise the specter of homosexuality.

But what if things were altogether different? Imagine a world in which the same knowledge that has enabled medicine to intervene in the management of intersexual patients has been placed at the service of multiple sexualities. Imagine that the sexes have multiplied beyond currently imaginable limits. It would have to be a world of shared powers. Patient and physician, parent and child, male and female, heterosexual and homosexual—all those oppositions and others would have to be dissolved as sources of division. A new ethic of medical treatment would arise, one that would permit ambiguity in a culture that had overcome sexual division. The central mission of medical treatment would be to preserve life. Thus hermaphrodites would be concerned primarily not about whether they can conform to society but about whether they might develop potentially life-threatening conditions—hernias, gonadal tumors, salt imbalance caused by adrenal malfunction—that sometimes accompany hermaphroditic development. In my ideal world medical intervention for intersexuals would take place only rarely before the age of reason; subsequent treatment would be a cooperative venture between physician, patient and other advisers trained in issues of gender multiplicity.

I do not pretend that the transition to my utopia would be smooth. Sex, even the supposedly "normal," heterosexual kind, continues to cause untold anxieties in Western society. And certainly a culture that has yet to come to grips—religiously and, in some states, legally—with the ancient and relatively uncomplicated reality of homosexual love will not readily embrace intersexuality. No doubt the most troublesome arena by far would be the rearing of children. Parents, at least since the Victorian era, have fretted, sometimes to the point of outright denial, over the fact that their children are sexual beings.

All that and more amply explains why intersexual children are generally squeezed into one of the two prevailing sexual categories. But what would be the psychological consequences of taking the alternative road—raising children as unabashed intersexuals? On the surface that tack seems fraught with peril. What, for example, would happen to the intersexual child amid the unrelenting cruelty of the school yard? When the time came to shower in gym class, what horrors and humiliations would await the intersexual as his/her anatomy was displayed in all its nontraditional glory? In whose gym class would s/he register to begin with? What bathroom would s/he use? And how on earth would Mom and Dad help shepherd him/her through the mine field of puberty? 25

In the past thirty years those questions have been ignored, as the scientific community has, with remarkable unanimity, avoided contemplating the alternative route of unimpeded intersexuality. But modern investigators tend to overlook a substantial body of case histories, most of them compiled between 1930 and 1960, before surgical intervention became rampant. Almost without exception, those reports describe children who grew up knowing they were intersexual (though they did not advertise it) and adjusted to their unusual status. Some of the studies are richly detailed—described at the level of gym-class showering (which most intersexuals avoided without incident); in any event, there is not a psychotic or a suicide in the lot.

Still, the nuances of socialization among intersexuals cry out for more sophisticated analysis. Clearly, before my vision of sexual multiplicity can be realized, the first openly intersexual children and their parents will have to be brave pioneers who will bear the brunt of society's of growing pains. But in the long view—though it could take generations to achieve—the prize might be a society in which sexuality is something to be celebrated for its subtleties and not something to be feared or ridiculed.

11

Recognizing Multiple Axes of Oppression

■▪■▪■

GENDER & RACE: THE AMPERSAND PROBLEM IN FEMINIST THOUGHT

Elizabeth V. Spelman

> *You don't really want Black folks, you are just looking for yourself with a little color to it.*
>
> —BERNICE JOHNSON REAGON

In earlier chapters we have examined how attempts to focus on gender in isolation from other aspects of identity such as race and class can work to obscure the effect race, class, and gender have on each other.[1] In particular, we've looked at how gender can be treated in a way that obscures the race and class identity of privileged women—for example, of contemporary white middle-class women or the free women of ancient Greece—and simultaneously makes it hard to conceive of women who are not of that particular class and race as "women." Precisely insofar as a discussion of gender and gender relations is really, even if obscurely, about a particular group of women and their relation to a particular group of men, it is unlikely to be applicable to any other group of women. At the same time, the particular race and class identity of those referred to simply as "women" becomes explicit when we see the inapplicability of statements about "women" to women who are not of that race or class.

. . . [S]ome of these points are illustrated tellingly in an article in the *New York Times* about how "women and Blacks" have fared in the U.S. military.[2] The author of the article does not discuss women who are Black or Blacks who are women. Indeed, it is clear that the "women" referred to are white, the "Blacks" referred to are male, even though, in a chart comparing the numbers and the placement of "women" and "Blacks," a small note appears telling the reader that Black women are included in the category "Blacks."[3] There are several things to note about the sexual and racial ontology of the article. The racial identity of those identified as "women" does not become explicit until reference is made to Black women, at which point it also becomes clear that the category "women" excludes Black women. In the contrast between "women" and "Blacks" the usual contrast between "men" and "women" is dropped, even though the distinction is in effect between a group of men and a group of women. But the men in question are not called men. They are called "Blacks."

It is not easy to think about gender, race, and class in ways that don't obscure or underplay their effects on one another. The crucial question is how the links between them are conceived. So, for example, we see that de Beauvoir tends to talk about comparisons between sex and race, or between sex and class, or between sex and culture; she describes what she takes to be comparisons between sexism and racism, between sexism and classism, between sexism and anti-Semitism. In the work of Chodorow and others influenced by her, we observe a readiness to look for links between sexism and other forms of oppression depicted as distinct from sexism. In both examples, we find an additive analysis of the various elements of identity and various forms of oppression: there's sex *and* race *and* class; there's sexism *and* racism *and* classism. In both examples, attempts to bring in elements of identity other than gender, to bring in kinds of oppression other than sexism, still have the effect of obscuring the racial and class identity of those described as "women," still make it hard to see how women not of a particular race and class can be included in the description.

In this chapter we shall examine in more detail how additive analyses of identity and of oppression can work against an understanding of the relations between gender and other elements of identity, between sexism and other forms of oppression. In particular we will see how some very interesting and important attempts to link sexism and racism themselves reflect and perpetuate racism. Ironically, the categories and methods we may find most natural and straightforward to use as we explore the connections between sex and race, sexism and racism, confuse those connections rather than clarify them.

5   As has often been pointed out, what have been called the first and second waves of the women's movement in the United States followed closely on the heels of women's involvement in the nineteenth-century abolitionist movement and the twentieth-century civil rights movement. In both centuries, challenges to North American racism served as an impetus to, and model for, the feminist attack on sexist institutions, practices, and ideology. But this is not to say that all antiracists were antisexists, or that all antisexists were antiracists. Indeed, many abolitionists of the nineteenth century and civil rights workers of the twentieth century did not take sexism seriously, and we continue to learn about the sad, bitter, and confusing history of women who in fighting hard for feminist ends did not take racism seriously.[4]

Recent feminist history has not totally ignored white racism, though white feminists have paid much less attention to it than have Black feminists.

Much of feminist theory has reflected and contributed to what Adrienne Rich has called "white solipsism": the tendency "to think, imagine, and speak as if whiteness described the world."[5] While solipsism is "not the consciously held belief that one race is inherently superior to all others, but a tunnel-vision which simply does not see nonwhite experience or existence as precious or significant, unless in spasmodic, impotent guilt-reflexes, which have little or no long-term, continuing momentum or political usefulness."[6]

In this chapter I shall focus on what I take to be instances and sustaining sources of this tendency in recent theoretical works by, or of interest to, feminists. In particular, I examine certain ways of comparing sexism and racism in the United States, as well as habits of thought about the source of women's oppression and the possibility of our liberation. I hope that exposing some of the symptoms of white solipsism—especially in places where we might least expect to find them—will help to eliminate tunnel vision and to widen the descriptive and explanatory scope of feminist theory. Perhaps we might hasten the day when it will no longer be necessary for anyone to have to say, as Audre Lorde has, "How difficult and time-consuming it is to have to reinvent the pencil every time you want to send a message."[7]

I shall not explicitly be examining class and classism, though at a number of points I suggest ways in which considerations of class and classism affect the topic at hand. Many of the questions I raise about comparisons between sexism and racism could also be raised about comparison between sexism and classism or racism and classism.

I

It is perhaps inevitable that comparisons of sexism and racism include, and often culminate in, questions about which form of oppression is more "fundamental."[8] Whether or not one believes that this way of thinking will bear any strategic or theoretic fruit, such comparisons have come to inform analyses of the nature of sexism and the nature of racism. To begin, I will examine some recent claims that sexism is more fundamental than racism, a highly ambiguous argument. In many instances the evidence offered in support turns out to refute the claim; and this way of comparing sexism and racism often presupposes the nonexistence of Black women, insofar as neither the description of sexism nor that of racism seems to apply to them. This is a bitter irony indeed, since Black women are the victims of both sexism and racism.

We need to ask first what "more fundamental" means in a comparison of racism and sexism. It has meant or might mean several different though related things:[9]

> It is harder to eradicate sexism than it is to eradicate racism.
>
> There might be sexism without racism but not racism without sexism: any social and political changes that eradicate sexism will eradicate

racism, but social and political changes that eradicate racism will not eradicate sexism.

Sexism is the first form of oppression learned by children.

Sexism predates racism.

Sexism is the cause of racism.

Sexism is used to justify racism.

Sexism is the model for racism.

We can trace these arguments in the work of two important feminist theorists: Kate Millet in *Sexual Politics* and Shulamith Firestone in *The Dialectic of Sex*. It is worth remembering that these authors did not ignore race and racism. But their treatments of the subjects enable us to see that as long as race is taken to be independent of sex, racism as independent of sexism, we are bound to give seriously misleading descriptions of gender and gender relations .

In *Sexual Politics*, Kate Millet seems to hold that sexism is more fundamental than racism in three senses: it is "sturdier" than racism and so presumably is harder to eradicate; it has a more "pervasive ideology" than racism, and so those who are not racists may nevertheless embrace sexist beliefs; and it provides our culture's "most fundamental concept of power."[10] But as Margaret Simons has pointed out, Millet ignores the fact that Black women and other women of color do not usually describe their own lives as ones in which they experience sexism as more fundamental than racism.[11] There is indeed something very peculiar about the evidence Millett offers in behalf of her view that sexism is the more endemic oppression.

On the one hand, she states that everywhere men have power over women. On the other hand, she notes with interest that some observers have described as an effect of racism that Black men do not have such power over Black women, and that only when racism is eradicated will Black men assume their proper position of superiority. She goes on to argue that "the military, industry, technology, universities, science, political office, and finance—in short, every avenue of power within society, including the coercive force of the police, is entirely in male hands."[12] But surely that is white male supremacy. Since when did Black males have such constitutionally based power, in what Millet calls "our culture"? She thus correctly describes as sexist the hope that Black men could assume their "proper authority" over Black women, but her claim about the pervasiveness of sexism is belied by her reference to the lack of authority of Black males.

There is no doubt that Millet is right to view as sexist the hope that racial equity will be established when Black males have authority over Black females, but it is also correct to describe as racist the hope—not uncommonly found in feminist arguments—that sexual equity will be established when women can be presidents or heads of business. That is no guarantee that they will not be running racist countries and corporations. As Elizabeth F. Hood said: "Many white women define liberation as the access to those thrones traditionally occupied by white men—positions in the kingdoms which support racism."[13] Of course, one might insist that any truly antisexist vision also is an antiracist vision, for it requires the elimination of all forms of oppression against all women, white or Black. But, similarly, it can be said that any truly antiracist vision would have to be antisexist, for it requires the elimination of all forms of oppression against all Blacks and other people of color, women or men.

In arguing for the position in *The Dialectic of Sex* that racism is "extended sexism," Shulamith Firestone provides another variation on the view that sexism is more fundamental:

> Racism is sexism extended. . . . Let us look at race relations is America, a macrocosm of the hierarchical relations within the nuclear family: the white man is the father, the white woman wife-and-mother, her status dependent on his; the blacks, like children, are his property, their physical differentiation branding them the subservient class, in the same way that children form so easily distinguishable a servile class vis-à-vis adults. The power hierarchy creates the psychology of racism, just as, in the nuclear family, it creates the psychology of sexism.[14]

It is clear that Firestone sees sexism as the model for racism; as the cause of racism, so that racism cannot disappear unless sexism does; and as the historical precursor racism. Moreover, with this model she sees the goal of the Black man (male child) to be to usurp the power of the white man (father), which means that the restoration of the authority of the Black man will involve his domination of women.[15] Hence sexism according to Firestone is more fundamental than racism, in the sense that the eradication of racism is portrayed as compatible with the continuation of sexism.

Here, as in the case of Millett, the evidence Firestone offers actually undermines her claim. First of all, she points out, and her analogy to the family requires, that the Black man is not really "the *real* man."[16] However much the Black man tries to act like the white man, and however much his treatment of Black women resembles the white man's treatment of white women and Black women, he isn't really The Man. Now if this is so, it seems odd to claim that sexism is more fundamental than racism, since according to Firestone's own account the Black man's identity as a man is obscured or erased by his identity as Black. Thus according to her own account, the racial identity of being an inferior assigned him by racists is more fundamental than the sexual identity of being a superior assigned him by sexists.

Firestone also claims that "the All-American Family is predicated on the existence of the black ghetto whorehouse. The rape of the black community in America makes possible the existence of the family structure of the larger white community."[17] But to say in these ways that racism makes sexism possible is to say that in the absence of racism, sexism could not exist—surely just the opposite of the claim that sexism is more fundamental than racism, the claim Firestone wishes to establish.

15

II

If Millett's and Firestone's accounts tend to ignore facts about the status of Black men, other similar accounts ignore the existence of Black women. In the process of comparing racism and sexism, Richard Wasserstrom describes the ways in which women and Blacks have been stereotypically conceived of as less fully developed than white men: In the United States, "men and women are taught to see men as independent, capable, and powerful; men and women are taught to see women as dependent, limited in abilities, and passive."[18] But who is taught to see Black men as "independent, capable, and powerful," and by whom are they taught? Are Black men taught that? Black women? White men? White women? Similarly, who is taught to see Black women as "dependent, limited in abilities, and passive"? If this stereotype is so prevalent, why then have Black women had to defend themselves against the images of matriarch and whore?

Wasserstrom continues:

> As is true for race, it is also a significant social fact that to be a female is to be an entity or creature viewed as different from the standard, fully developed person who is male as well as white. But to be female, as opposed to being black, is not to be conceived of as simply a creature of less worth. That is one important thing that differentiates sexism from racism: the ideology of sex, as opposed to the ideology of race, is a good deal more complex and confusing. Women are both put on a pedestal and deemed not fully developed persons.[19]

He leaves the room for the Black woman. For a Black woman cannot be "female, as opposed to being Black"; she is female *and* Black. Since Wasserstrom's argument proceeds from the assumption that one is either female or Black, it cannot be an argument that applies to Black women. Moreover, we cannot generate a composite image of the Black women from Wasserstrom's argument, since the description of women as being on a pedestal, or being dependent, never generally applied to Black women in the United States and was never meant to apply to them.

Wasserstrom's argument about the priority of sexism over racism has an odd result, which stems from the erasure of Black women in his analysis. He wishes to claim that in this society sex is a more fundamental fact about people than race. Yet his description of women does not apply to the Black woman, which implies that being Black is a more fundamental fact about her than being a woman and hence that her sex is not a more fundamental fact about her than her race. I am not saying that Wasserstrom actually believes this is true, but that paradoxically the terms of his theory force him into that position. If the terms of one's theory require that a person is either female or Black, clearly there is no room to describe someone who is both.

A similar erasure of the Black woman, through failure to note how sexist stereotypes are influenced by racist ones, is found in Laurence Thomas's comparison of sexism and racism.[20] Like Wasserstrom, Thomas believes that sexism is more deeply ingrained in our culture. Racist attitudes, he says, are easier to give up than sexist ones for two reasons: First, "sexism, unlike racism, readily lends itself to a morally unobjectionable description" and second, "the positive self-concept of men has been more centrally tied to their being sexists that has been the positive self-concept of whites to their being racist."[21]

Thomas argues that it is not morally objectionable that "a natural outcome of a sexist conception of women" is the role of men as benefactors of women—part of men's role vis-à-vis women is to "protect women and to provide them with the comforts of life."[22] But at best, Thomas's claim about the man's role as benefactor of woman only applies to men and women of the same race (and probably of the same class). It is of course difficult to explain how claims about roles are established, but the history of race relations in the United States surely makes ludicrous the idea that the role of white men is to be the benefactors of Black women—to "protect" them and to "provide them with the comforts of life." This neither describes what white men have done, nor what they have been told they ought to have done, with respect to Black women.

Thomas's description of sexism in relations between women and men leaves out the reality of racism in relations between Blacks and whites. If he wishes to insist that his analysis was only meant to apply to same-race sexual relations, then he cannot continue to speak unqualifiedly about relations between men and women. My point is not that Black men cannot in any way be sexist to white or to Black women, for indeed they can, just as white women can be racist to Black men or to Black women. My point, rather, is that a theory of sexism that describes men's and women's roles can itself reflect the racist society in which it develops, insofar as it is based on erasure of the realties of white racism.

Thomas also holds that sexism is more central to the positive self-concept of men than racism has been to the positive self-concept of whites. He claims that, although being benefactors of women is essential to men's self-esteem as "real" men, for whites it is not necessary to own slaves or to hate blacks in order to be "really" white.[23] Once again, we have to see what happens to Thomas's claim when we put "Black" or "white" in front of "men" or "women" in his formula: "For white men, being benefactors of Black women is essential to their self-esteem as 'real' men." That is false. Indeed, in a racist society, white men's self-esteem requires the opposite position and attitude toward Black women.

Reflection on this leads to doubts about the second part of Thomas's claim—that whites don't have to be racists in order to be "really" white. Does he mean to say that in our society a white man feels no threat to his self-esteem if a Black man gets the job for which they both are candidates? That a white man feels no threat to his self-esteem if a Black man marries the white woman the white man was hoping to marry? That a white man feels no threat to his self-esteem if he lives in a neighborhood with Blacks? Certainly not all white men's self-esteem is so threatened. But this is a racist society, and generally, the self-esteem of white people is deeply influenced by their difference from and supposed superiority to Black people.[24] Those of us who are white may not think of ourselves as racists, because we do not own slaves or hate Blacks, but that does not mean that much of what props up our sense of self is not based on the racism that unfairly distributes benefits and burdens to whites and Blacks.

25   For example, think for a moment about a case of self-esteem that seems on the surface most unlikely to be supported by racism: the self-esteem that might be thought to attend sincere and serious philosophical reflections on the problems of racism. How could this be said to based on racism, especially if the philosopher is trying to eliminate racism? As the editors of the *Philosophical Forum* in an issue on philosophy and the Black experience pointed out, "Black people have to a disproportionate extent supplied the labor which has made possible the cultivation of philosophical inquiry."[25] A disproportionate amount of the labor that makes it possible for some people to have philosophy as a profession has been done by Blacks and others under conditions that can only be described as racist. If the connection between philosophy and racism is not very visible, that invisibility itself is a product of racism. Any feminist would recognize a similar point about sexism: it is only in footnotes and prefaces that we see a visible connection between a man's satisfaction in having finished an article or book and a woman's having made that completion possible.[26]

At several points early in his essay, Thomas says that he is going to consider the "way in which sexism and racism each conceives of its object: women and Blacks, respectively."[27] But there are many difficulties in talking about sexism and racism in this way, some of which we have noted, and others to which we now turn.

III

First of all, sexism and racism do not have different "objects" in the case of Black women. It is highly misleading to say, without further explanation, that Black women experience "sexism and racism." For to say merely that suggests that Black women experience one form of oppression, as Blacks (the same thing Black men experience) and that they experience another form of oppression, as women (the same thing white women experience). While it is true that images and institutions that are described as sexist affect both Black and white women, they are affected in different ways, depending upon the extent to which they are affected by other forms of oppression. Thus, as noted earlier, it will not do to say that women are oppressed by the image of the "feminine" woman as fair, delicate, and in need of support and protection by men. As Linda Brent succinctly puts it, "That which commands admiration in the white woman only hastens the degradation of the female slave."[28] More specifically, as Angela Davis reminds us, "the alleged benefits of the ideology of femininity did not accrue" to the Black female slave—she was expected to toil in the fields for just as long and hard as the male was.[29]

Reflection on the experience of Black women also shows that it is not as if one form of oppression is merely piled upon another. As Barbara Smith has remarked, the effect of multiple oppression "is not merely arithmetic."[30] This additive method informs Gerda Lerner's analysis of the oppression of Black women under slavery: "Their work and duties were the same as that of men, while childbearing and rearing fell upon them as an added burden."[31] But as Angela Davis has pointed out, the mother/housewife role (even the words seem inappropriate) doesn't have the same meaning for women who experience racism as it does for those who are not so oppressed:

> In the infinite anguish of ministering to the needs of the men
> and children around her (who were not necessarily members
> of her immediate family), she was performing the only labor of
> the slave community which could not be directly and immedi-
> ately claimed by the oppressor.[32]

The meaning and the oppressive nature of the "housewife" role has to be understood in relation to the roles against which it is contrasted. The work of mate/mother/nurturer has a different meaning depending on whether it is contrasted to work that has high social value and ensures economic independence or to labor that is forced, degrading, and unpaid. All of these factors are left out in a simple additive analysis. How one form of oppression is experienced is influenced by and influences how another form is experienced. An additive analysis treats the oppression of a Black woman in society that is racist as well as sexist as if it were a further burden when, in fact, it is a different burden. As the work of Davis, among others, shows, to ignore the difference is to deny the particular reality of the Black woman's experience.

If sexism and racism must be seen as interlocking, and not as piled upon each other, serious problems arise for the claim that one of them is more fundamental than the other. As we saw, one meaning of the claim that sexism is more fundamental than racism is that sexism causes racism: racism would not exist if sexism did not, while sexism could and would continue to exist even in the absence of racism. In this connection, racism is sometimes seen as something that is both derivative from sexism and in the service of it: racism keeps women from uniting in allegiance against sexism. This view has been articulated by Mary Daly in *Beyond God the Father*. According to Daly, sexism is the "root and paradigm" of other forms of oppression such as racism. Racism is a "deformity *within* patriarchy. . . . It is most unlikely that racism will be eradicated as long as sexism prevails."[33]

Daly's theory relies on an additive analysis, and we can see again why such an analysis fails to describe adequately Black women's experience. Daly's

30

analysis makes it look simply as if both Black women and white women experience sexism, while Black women also experience racism. Black women, Daly says, must come to see what they have in common with white women—shared sexist oppression—and see that they are all "pawns in the racial struggle, which is basically not the struggle that will set them free as free women."[34] But insofar as she is oppressed by racism in a sexist context and sexism in a racist context, the Black woman's struggle cannot be compartmentalized into two struggles—one as a Black and one as a woman. Indeed, it is difficult to imagine why a Black woman would think of her struggles this way except in the face of demands by white women or by Black men that she do so. This way of speaking about her struggle is required by a theory that insists not only that sexism and racism are distinct but that one might be eradicated before the other. Daly rightly points out that the Black woman's struggle can easily be, and has usually been, subordinate to the Black man's struggle in antiracist organizations. But she does not point out that Black woman's struggle can easily be, and usually has been, subordinated to the white woman's struggle in antisexist organizations.

Daly's line of thought also promotes the idea that, were it not for racism, there would be no important differences between Black and white women. Since, according to her view, sexism is the fundamental form of oppression and racism works in its service, the only significant differences between Black and white women are differences that men (Daly doesn't say whether she means white men or Black men or both) have created and that are the source of antagonism between women. What is really crucial about us is our sex; racial distinctions are one of the many products of sexism, of patriarchy's attempt to keep women from uniting. According to Daly, then, it is through our shared sexual identity that we are oppressed together; it is through our shared sexual identity that we that we shall be liberated together.

This view not only ignores the role women play in racism and classism, but it seems to deny the positive aspects of racial identities. It ignores the fact that being Black is a source of pride, as well as an occasion for being oppressed. It suggests that once racism is eliminated, Black women no longer need be concerned about or interested in their Blackness—as if the only reason for paying attention to one's Blackness is that it is the source of pain and sorrow and agony. The assumption that there is nothing positive about having a Black history and identity is racism pure and simple. Recall the lines of Nikki Giovanni:

> and I really hope no white person ever has cause
> to write about me
>   because they never understand Black love is
> Black wealth and they'll
>   probably talk about my hard childhood
> and never understand that
>   all the while I was quite happy.[35]

Or recall the chagrin of the central character in Paule Marshall's story "Reena," when she discovered that her white boyfriend could only see her Blackness in terms of her suffering and not as something compatible with taking joy and pleasure in life.[36] I think it is helpful too in this connection to remember the opening lines of Pat Parker's "For the white person who wants to know how to be my friend":

> The first thing you do is to forget that i'm Black.
> Second, you must never forget that i'm Black.[37]

Perhaps it does not occur to feminists who are white that celebrating being white has anything to do with our celebrating being women. But that may be so because celebrating being white is already taken care of by the predominantly white culture in which we live in North America. Certainly feminist theory and activity on the whole have recognized that it is possible, if difficult, to celebrate being a woman without at the same time conceiving of woman in terms of the sexist imagery and lore of the centuries. (That celebrating womanhood is a tricky business we know from the insidiousness of the "two-sphere" ideology of the nineteenth century and of the image of the "total woman"—in Daly's wonderful phrase, the "totaled woman"—of the twentieth century: as if by celebrating what men tell us we are, the burden magically disappears because we embrace it.) But just as it is possible and desirable to identify oneself as a woman and yet think of and describe oneself in ways that are not sexist, so it is possible and desirable to identify oneself as a Black woman and yet think of oneself in ways that are not racist.

In sum, according to an additive analysis of sexism and racism, all women are oppressed by sexism; some women are further oppressed by racism. Such an analysis distorts Black women's experiences of oppression by failing to note important differences between the contexts in which Black women and white women experience sexism. The additive analysis also suggests that a woman's racial identity can be "subtracted" from her combined sexual and racial identity: "We are all women." But this does not leave room for the fact that different women may look to different forms of liberation just because they are white or Black women, rich or poor women, Catholic or Jewish women.

IV

... [F]eminist leaders such as Elizabeth Cady Stanton used racist arguments in pleas to better the condition of "women." Though such blatant racism is not likely to appear in contemporary feminism, that doesn't mean that visions of a nonsexist world will also be visions of a nonracist world. In the rest of the chapter I will explore how some ways of conceiving women's oppression and liberation contribute to the white solipsism of feminist theory.

As I have argued in detail elsewhere, feminist theorists as politically diverse as Simone de Beauvoir, Betty Friedan, and Shulamith Firestone have described the conditions of women's liberation in terms that suggest that identification of woman with her body has been the source of our oppression, and hence that the source of our liberation lies in sundering that connection.[38] For example, de Beauvoir introduces *The Second Sex* with the comment that woman has been regarded as "womb"; and she later observes that woman is thought of as planted firmly in the world of "immanence," that is, the physical world of nature, her life defined by the dictates of her "biologic fate."[39] In contrast, men live in the world of "transcendence," actively using their minds to create "values, mores, religions."[40] Theirs is the world of culture as opposed to the world of nature. Among Friedan's central messages is that women should be allowed and encouraged to be "culturally" as well as "biologically" creative, because the former activities, in contrast to childbearing and rearing, are "mental" and are of "highest value to society"—"mastering the secrets of atoms, or the stars, composing symphonies, pioneering a new concept in government or society."[41]

This view comes out especially clearly in Firestone's work. According to her, the biological difference between men and women is at the root of women's oppression. It is woman's body—in particular, our body's capacity to bear children—that makes, or makes possible, the oppression of women by men. Hence we must disassociate ourselves from our bodies—most radically—by making it possible, or even necessary, to conceive and bear children outside the womb, and by otherwise generally disassociating our lives from the thankless tasks associated with the body.[42]

40   In predicating women's liberation on a disassociation from our bodies, Firestone oddly enough joins the chorus of male voices that has told us over the centuries about the disappointments entailed in being embodied creatures. What might be called "somatophobia" (fear of and disdain for the body) is part of a centuries-long tradition in Western culture. As de Beauvoir so thoroughly described in *The Second Sex,* the responsibility for being embodied creatures has been assigned to women: we have been associated, indeed virtually identified, with the body; men (or some men) have been associated and associated and virtually identified with the mind. Women have been portrayed as possessing bodies in a way men have not. It is as if women essentially, men only accidentally, have bodies. It seems to me that Firestone's (as well as Friedan's and de Beauvoir's) prescription for women's liberation does not challenge the negative attitude toward the body; it only hopes to end the association between the body, so negatively characterized, and women.

I think the somatophobia we see in the work of Firestone and others is a force that contributes to white solipsism in feminist thought, in at least three related ways. First, insofar as feminists ignore, or indeed accept, negative views of the body in prescriptions for women's liberation, we will also ignore an important element in racist thinking. For the superiority of men to women (or, as we have seen, of some men to some women) is not the only hierarchical relationship that has been linked to the superiority of the mind to the body. Certain kinds, or "races," of people have been held to be more body-like than others, and this has meant that they are perceived as more animal-like and less god-like. For example, in *The White Man's Burden,* Winthrop Jordan describes ways in which white Englishman portrayed black Africans as beastly, dirty, highly sexual beings.[43] Lillian Smith tells us in *Killers of the Dream* how closely run together were her lessons about the evil of the body and the evil of Blacks.[44]

We need to examine and understand somatophobia and look for it in our own thinking, for the idea that the work of the body and for the body has no part in real human dignity has been part of racist as well as sexist ideology. That is, oppressive stereotypes of "inferior races" and of women (notice that even in order to make the point in this way, we leave up in the air the question of how we shall refer to those who belong to both categories) have typically involved images of their lives as determined by basic bodily functions (sex, reproduction, appetite, secretions, and excretions) and as given over to attending to the bodily functions of others (feeding, washing, cleaning, doing the "dirty work"). Superior groups, we have been told from Plato on down, have better things to do with their lives. It certainly does not follow from the presence of somatophobia in a person's writings that she or he is a racist or a sexist. But disdain for the body historically has been symptomatic of sexist and racist (as well as classist) attitudes.

Human groups know that the work of the body and for the body is necessary for human existence, and they make provisions for that necessity. Thus even when a group views its liberation in terms of being free of association with, or responsibility for, bodily tasks, its own liberation is likely to be predicated on the oppression of other groups—those assigned to do the body's work. For example, if feminists decide that women are not going to be relegated to doing such work, who do we think is going to do it? Have we attended to the role that racism and classism historically have played in settling that question? We may recall why Plato and Aristotle thought philosophers and citizens needed leisure from this kind of work and who they thought ought to do it.

Finally, if one thinks—as de Beauvoir, Friedan, and Firestone do—that the liberation of women requires abstracting the notion of woman from the notion of a woman's body, then one might logically think that the liberation of Blacks requires abstracting the notion of a Black person from the notion of a Black body. Since the body, or at least certain of its aspects, may be thought to be the culprit, the solution may seem to be: Keep the person and leave the occasion for oppression behind. Keep the woman, somehow, but leave behind her woman's body; keep the Black person but leave the Blackness behind. Once one attempts to stop thinking about oneself in terms of having a body, then one will not only stop thinking in terms of characteristics such as womb and breast, but also will stop thinking in terms of skin and hair. We would expect to find that any feminist theory based in part on a disembodied view of human identity would regard blackness (or any other physical characteristic that may serve as a centering post for one's identity) as of temporary and negative importance.

45   Once the concept of woman is divorced from the concept of woman's body, conceptual room is made for the idea of a women who is no particular historical woman—she has no color, no accent, no particular characteristics that require having a body. She is somehow all and only woman; that is her identifying feature. And so it will seem inappropriate or beside the point to think of women in terms of any physical characteristics, especially if their oppression has been rationalized by reference to those characteristics.

None of this is to say that the historical and cultural identity of being Black or white is the same thing as, or is reducible to, the physical feature of having black or white skin. Historical and cultural identity is not constituted by having a body with particular identifying features, but it cannot be comprehended without such features and the significance attached to them.

V

Adrienne Rich was perhaps the first well-known contemporary white feminist to have noted "white solipsism" in feminist theorizing and activity. I think it is no coincidence that she also noticed and attended to the strong strain of somatophobia in feminist theory. *Of Woman Born* updates the connection between somatophobia and misogyny/gynephobia that Simone de Beauvoir described at length in *The Second Sex*.[45] But unlike de Beauvoir or Firestone, Rich refuses to throw out the baby with the bathwater: she sees that the historical negative connection between woman and body (in particular, between woman and womb) can be broken in more than one way. Both de Beauvoir and Firestone wanted to break it by insisting that women need be no more connected—in thought or deed—with the body than men have been. In their view of embodiment as a liability, de Beauvoir and Firestone are in virtual agreement with the patriarchal cultural history they otherwise question. Rich, however, insists that the negative connection between woman and body be broken along other lines. She asks us to think about whether what she calls "flesh-loathing" is the only attitude it is possible to have toward our bodies. Just as she explicitly distinguishes between motherhood as experience and motherhood as institution, so she implicitly asks us to distinguish between embodiment as experience and embodiment as institution. Flesh-loathing is part of the well-entrenched beliefs, habits, and practices epitomized in the treatment of pregnancy as a disease. But we need not experience our flesh, our body, as loathsome.

I think it is not a psychological or historical accident that having examined the way women view their bodies, Rich also focused on the failure of white women to see Black women's experiences as different from their own. For looking at embodiment is one way (though not the only one) of coming to recognize and understand the particularity of experience. Without bodies we could not have personal histories. Nor could we be identified as woman or man, Black or white. This is not to say that reference to publicly observable bodily characteristics settles the question of whether someone is woman or man, Black or white; nor is it to say that being a woman or man, Black or white, just means having certain bodily characteristics (this is one reason some Blacks want to capitalize the term; "Black" refers to a cultural identity, not simply a skin color). But different meanings are attached to having certain characteristics, in different places and at different times and by different people, and those differences affect enormously the kinds of lives we lead or experiences we have. Women's oppression has been linked to the meanings assigned to having a woman's body by male oppressors. Blacks' oppression has been linked to the meanings assigned to having a black body by white oppressors. (Note how insidiously this way of speaking once again leaves unmentioned the situation for Black women.) We cannot hope to understand the meaning of a person's experiences, including her experiences of oppression, without first thinking of her as embodied, and second thinking about the particular meanings assigned to that embodiment. If, because of somatophobia, we think and write as if we are not embodied, or as if we would be better off if we were not embodied, we are likely to ignore the ways in which different forms of embodiment are correlated with different kinds of experience.

Rich—unlike de Beauvoir—asks us to reflect on the culturally assigned differences between having a Black or white body, as well as on the differences between having the body of a woman or of a man. Other feminists have reflected on the meaning of embodiment and recognized the connection between flesh-loathing and woman-hatred, but they have only considered it far enough to try to divorce the concept of woman from the concept of flesh. In effect, they have insisted that having different bodies does not or need not mean men and women are any different as humans; and having said that, they imply that having different colored bodies does not mean that Black women and white women are any different. Such statements are fine if interpreted to mean that the differences between woman and man, Black and white, should not be used against Black women and white women and Black men. But not paying attention to embodiment and to the cultural meanings assigned to different forms of it is to encourage sexblindness and colorblindness. These blindnesses are vicious when they are used to support the idea that all experience is male experience or that all experience is white experience. Rich does not run away from the fact that women have bodies, nor does she wish that women's bodies were not so different from men's. That healthy regard for the ground of our differences from men is logically connected to—though of course does not ensure—a healthy regard for the ground of the differences between Black women and white women.

> "Colorblindness" . . . implies that I would look at a Black
> woman and see her as white, thus engaging her in white
> solipsism to the utter erasure of her particular reality.[46]

Colorblindness denies the particularity of the Black woman and rules out the possibility both that her history has been different and that her future might be different in any significant way from the white woman's.

VI

50   I have been discussing the ways in which some aspects of feminist theory exhibit what Adrienne Rich has called "white solipsism." In particular, I have been examining ways in which some prominent claims about the relation between sexism and racism ignore the realities of racism. I have also suggested that there are ways of thinking about women's oppression and about women's liberation that reflect and encourage white solipsism, but that thinking differently about women and about sexism might lead to thinking differently about Blackness and about racism.

First, we have to continue to reexamine the traditions which reinforce sexism and racism. Though feminist theory has recognized the connection between somatophobia and misogyny/gynephobia, it has tended to challenge the misogyny without challenging the somatophobia, and without fully appreciating the connection between somatophobia and racism.

Second, we have to keep a cautious eye on discussions of racism versus sexism. They keep us from seeing ways in which what sexism means and how it works is modulated by racism, and ways in which what racism means is modulated by sexism. Most important, discussions of sexism versus racism tend to proceed as if Black women—to take one example—do not exist. None of this is to say that sexism and racism are thoroughly and in every context indistinguishable. Certain political and social changes may point to the conclusion that some aspects of racism will disappear sooner than some aspects of sexism (see, for example, the statistics Diane Lewis cites in "A Response to Inequality: Black Women, Racism, and Sexism").[47] Other changes may point to the conclusion that some aspects of sexism will disappear sooner than aspects of racism (e.g., skepticism about the possible effects of passage of the ERA on the lives of Black women in the ghetto). And there undoubtedly is disagreement about when certain changes should be seen as making any dent in sexism or racism at all. But as long as Black women and other women of color are at the bottom of the economic heap (which clearly we cannot fully understand in the absence of a class analysis), and as long as our descriptions of sexism and racism themselves reveal racist and sexist perspectives, it seems both empirically and conceptually premature to make grand claims about whether sexism or racism is "more fundamental." For many reasons, then, it seems wise to proceed very cautiously in this inquiry.

Third, it is crucial to sustain a lively regard for the variety of women's experiences. On the one hand, what unifies women and justifies us in talking about the oppression of women is the overwhelming evidence of the worldwide and historical subordination of women to men. On the other, while it may be possible for us to speak about women in a general way, it also is inevitable that any statement we make about women in some particular place at some particular time is bound to suffer from ethnocentrism if we try to claim for it more generality than it has. So, for example, to say that the image of woman as frail and dependent is oppressive is certainly true. But it is oppressive to white women in the United States in quite a different way than it is oppressive to Black women, for the sexism Black women experience is in the context of their experience of racism. In Toni Morrison's *The Bluest Eye,* the causes and consequences of Pecola's longing to have blue eyes are surely quite different from the causes and consequences of a white girl with brown eyes having a similar desire.[48] More to the point, the consequences of *not* having blue eyes are quite different for the two. Similarly, the family may be the locus of oppression for white middle-class women, but to claim that it is the locus of oppression for all women is to ignore the fact that for Blacks in America the family has been a source of resistance against white oppression.[49]

In short, the claim that all women are oppressed is fully compatible with, and needs to be explicated in terms of, the many varieties of oppression that different populations of women have been subject to. After all, why should oppressors settle for uniform kinds of oppression, when to oppress their victims in many different ways—consciously or unconsciously—makes it more likely that the oppressed groups will not perceive it to be in their interest to work together?

Finally, it is crucial not to see Blackness only as the occasion for oppression—any more than one sees being a woman only as the occasion for oppression. No one ought to expect the forms of our liberation to be any less various than the forms of our oppression. We need to be at least as generous in imagining what women's liberation will be like as our oppressors have been in devising what women's oppression has been. 55

NOTES

1. This chapter is a slightly revised edition of my "Theories of Race and Gender: The Erasure of Black Women," in *Quest: a feminist quarterly 5,* no. 4 (1982): 36–62.
2. Halloran, "Women, Blacks, Spouses Transforming the Military."
3. See also Gloria T. Hull, Patricia Bell Scott, and Barbara Smith, eds. *All the Women Are White, All the Blacks Are Men, But Some of Us Are Brave: Black Women's Studies* (Old Westbury, N.Y.: Feminist Press, 1982).
4. See Eleanor Flexner, *Century of Struggle* (New York: Atheneum, 1972), especially chapter 13, on the inhospitality of white women's organizations to Black women, as well as Aileen S. Kraditor's *The Ideas of the Woman Suffrage Movement, 1890–1920* (Garden City, N.Y.: Doubleday, 1971). See also DuBois, *Feminism and Suffrage;* Sara Evans, *Personal Politics* (New York: Vintage, 1979), on sexism in the civil rights movement; Dorothy Sterling, *Black Foremothers* (Old Westbury, N.Y.: Feminist Press, 1979), 147, on Alice Paul's refusal to grant Mary Church Terrell's request that Paul endorse enforcement of the Nineteenth Amendment for all women; Davis, *Women, Race, and Class;* Bettina Aptheker, *Women's Legacy: Essays on Race, Sex, and Class in American History* (Amherst: University of Massachusetts Press, 1982); Paula Giddings, *When and Where I Enter: The Impact of Black Women on Race and Sex in America* (New York: Morrow, 1984).
5. Adrienne Rich, "Disloyal to Civilization: Feminism, Racism, Gynephobia," in her *On Lies, Secrets, and Silence* (New York: Norton, 1979), 299 and passim. In the philosophical

literature, solipsism is the view according to which it is only one's self that is know-able, or it is only one's self that constitutes the world. Strictly speaking, of course, Rich's use of the phrase "white solipsism" is at odds with the idea of there being only the self, insofar as it implies that there are other white people; but she is drawing from the idea of there being only one perspective on the world—not that of one person, but of one "race." (For further comment on the concept of race, see references in note 23 below.)

6. Ibid., 306.

7. Audre Lorde, "Man Child: A Black Lesbian Feminist's Response," *Conditions* 4 (1979): 35. My comments about racism apply to the racism directed against Black people in the United States. I do not claim that all my arguments apply to the racism experi-enced by other people of color.

8. See Margaret A. Simons, "Racism and Feminism: A Schism in the Sisterhood," *Femi-nist Studies 5,* no. 2 (1979): 384–401.

9. A somewhat similar list appears in Alison M. Jaggar and Paula Rothenberg's introduc-tion to part 2 of *Feminist Frameworks,* 2nd ed. (New York: McGraw-Hill, 1984), 86.

10. Kate Millet, *Sexual Politics,* (New York: Ballantine, 1969), 33–34.

11. Simons, "Racism and Feminism."

12. Millett, *Sexual Politics,* 33–34.

13. Elizabeth F. Hood, "Black Women, White Women: Separate Paths to Liberation," *Black Scholar,* April 1978, 47.

14. Shulamith Firestone, *The Dialectic of Sex* (New York: Bantam, 1970), 108.

15. Ibid., 117–18.

16. Ibid., 115. Emphasis on the original.

17. Ibid., 116.

18. Richard A. Wasserstrom, "Racism and Sexism," in *Philosophy and Women,* ed. Sharon Bishop and Marjorie Weinzweig (Belmont, Cal.: Wadsworth, 1979), 8. Reprinted from "Racism, Sexism, and Preferential Treatment: An Approach to the Topics," *UCLA Law Review* (February 1977); 581–615.

19. Ibid.

20. Laurence Thomas, "Sexism and Racism: Some Conceptual Differences," *Ethics* 90 (1980): 239–50.

21. I shall here leave aside the question of whether Thomas succeeds in offering a de-scription of sexism that is not of something morally objectionable (see B.C. Postow's reply to Thomas, "Thomas on Sexism," *Ethics* 90 [1980]: 251–56). I shall also leave aside the question of to whom such a description is or is not morally objectionable, as well as the question of how its moral objectionableness is to be measured.

22. Thomas, "Sexism and Racism," 239 and passim.

23. Thomas says that "one very important reason" for this lack of analogy is that racial identity, unlike sexual identity, is "more or less settled by biological considerations" (ibid, 248). If Thomas means by this that there are such things as "races," and that the question of what race one belongs to is settled by biology, one must point out in reply that it is far from clear that this is so. See Ashley Montagu, "The Concept of Race: Part 1," *American Anthropologist* 64, no. 5 (1962), reprinted in *Anthropology: Contempo-rary Perspectives,* ed. David E. Hunter and Phillip Whitten (Boston: Little, Brown, 1975),

83–95; and Frank B. Livingstone, "On the Nonexistence of Human Races," *The Concept of Race,* ed. Ashley Montagu (New York: Collier, 1964), reprinted in Hunter and Whitten. The existence of racism does not require that there are races; it requires the belief that there are races.

24. This is the kind of superiority that de Beauvoir described.
25. *Philosophical Forum,* 9, no. 2–3 (1977–78): 113.
26. See Carol Christ and Judith Plaskow Goldenberg, "For the Advancement of My Career: A Form Critical Study in the Art of Acknowledgement," *Bulletin of the Council for Religious Studies* (June 1972), for a marvelous study of the literary form of the "acknowledgement to the wife." See also the gruesomely delightful "Collecting Scholar's Wives," by Marilyn Hoder-Salmon, in *Feminist Studies* 4, no. 3 (n.d.): 107–14.
27. Thomas, "Sexism and Racism," 242–43.
28. Linda Brent, "The Trials of Girlhood," in *Root of Bitterness,* ed. Nancy F. Cott (New York: Dutton, 1972), 201.
29. Angela Y. Davis, "Reflections on the Black Woman's Role in the Community of Slaves," *Black Scholar* 3 (1971): 7.
30. Barbara Smith, "Notes For Yet Another Paper on Black Feminism, or Will the Real Enemy Please Stand Up," *Conditions* 5 (1979): 123–32. See also "The Combahee River Collective Statement," *Capitalist Patriarchy and the Case for Socialist Feminism,* ed. Zillah Eisenstein (New York: Monthly Review Press, 1979), 362–72.
31. Gerda Lerner, ed., *Black Woman in White America* (New York: Vintage, 1973), 15.
32. Davis, "Reflections on the Black Woman's Role," 7. Davis revises this slightly in *Women, Race, and Class.*
33. Mary Daly, *Beyond God the Father* (Boston: Beacon Press, 1975), 56–57.
34. Ibid.
35. Nikki Giovanni, "Nikki Rosa," in *The Black Woman,* ed. Toni Cade (New York: New American Library, 1980), 16.
36. Paule Marshall, "Reena," in *The Black Woman,* 28.
37. Pat Parker, *Womanslaughter* (Oakland: Diana Press, 1978), 13.
38. Spelman, "Woman as Body."
39. De Beauvoir, *The Second Sex,* xii, 57.
40. Ibid., 119.
41. Friedan, *The Feminine Mystique,* 247–77.
42. Firestone, *The Dialectic of Sex,* chap. 10.
43. Winthrop P. Jordan, *The White Man's Burden* (New York: Oxford University Press, 1974), chap. 1.
44. Smith *Killers of the Dream,* 83–98.
45. Adrienne Rich, *Of Woman Born* (New York: Norton, 1976).
46. Rich, "Disloyal to Civilization," 300.
47. Diane Lewis, "A Response to Inequality: Black Women, Racism, and Sexism," *Signs* 3, no. 2 (1977): 339–61.
48. Toni Morrison, *The Bluest Eye* (New York: Pocketbooks, 1972).
49. See, for example, Carol Stack, *All Our Kin* (New York: Harper and Row, 1974).

INEQUALITY IN AMERICA

THE FAILURE OF THE AMERICAN SYSTEM FOR PEOPLE OF COLOR

Edna Bonacich

INTRODUCTION

Right before Christmas 1987 a Chicana was fired from food services on our campus, where she had been working as an assistant cook. She is a single mother with three children.[1] Her own mother suffers from epilepsy. She was making $150 a week and when she was fired she was faced with the prospect of not being able to pay next month's rent, let alone celebrating Christmas.

According to university rules, food services have to be self-supporting, but cannot be run profitably on a campus of our size. For years the university lost money on it—around $50,000 a year. So they decided to bail out and subcontract to a private firm, the Marriott Corporation.

The decision to subcontract happens to have coincided with a union election victory among service workers in the University of California system, the first such victory in the system. When the union would actually be able to negotiate a pay raise was immaterial. Indeed the union was exceedingly weak and did not represent the self-organization of the workers. Instead, it operated as a Washington-based bureaucracy that saw the thousands of UC workers as a plum in its own organizational growth. Still, the university administration was quick to preclude any pay raises among the food services staff.

Marriott is managing to turn a losing operation into a profitable one. This miracle is achieved by paying the workers well below the university wage scale. Most of their employees, at least on our campus, are women of color.

---

[1] The style of this paper is more informal than most academic papers. This is purposeful. I am eager to get away from the dry abstraction of academic discourse. As I see it, the style of western academic writing is very much a part of the "white man's civilization," with its dualistic idealism, or division between thought and life. I am seeking a more integrated world view and want my method of communication to match the content. I realize that the imperatives of careerism often force us to speak and write in ways that are not authentic to us, and I am resisting this form of coercion. I hope that my audience will not close their ears to what I say just because my manner of presentation does not meet their preconceptions. Instead, I hope you will listen to its substance and check it against your own experience, against what you know in your hearts to be true.

There are not a lot of other people who are "willing" to work for minimum wage and no benefits. Marriott is, of course, non-union.

The case against the woman who was fired consisted of tardiness and ab- 5 sences on the job. Perhaps the accusations had some validity. When a person is earning close to minimum wage there is not a lot of incentive to be a perfectly disciplined, eagerly loyal employee. Besides, her family circumstances made it difficult always to be punctual. There was no give in the situation that could allow for the exigencies of this employee's life. The management of food services claimed that they had given her every break, but they were operating on a tight budget and could not afford to hold on to an inefficient worker. The results might be unfortunate for this individual, but they were not a charity. They had a business to run. They had to balance their books.

And so the woman was left without a job right before Christmas. A group of us took her case to the campus administrator in charge of sub-contracting. He heard it and rejected it, siding with management that they could not afford to keep a nonpunctual worker. After learning of his decision, I went back alone one more time to make a humanitarian plea. I tried to draw a parallel to homelessness. Did he sanction it? Did he believe that, if persons could not pay their rent, they should be thrown out on the streets? Was not his action similar in this case? But I was wasting my time. "You can't coddle employees," he said. "We're in business to make money." He would not consider taking her back and giving her another chance. She was "poison" in his eyes, I assume because she had dared to challenge her firing and had managed to get a group around her to support her case. A politically aroused employee was indeed poison to this man.

Marriott claims it is not making a profit off food services on our campus, yet they take out six percent of the gross in "management fees," and the woman who manages the cafeteria for them makes a good salary. Money is certainly being made in this enterprise; it just is not going to the workers.

I am telling this little story in such detail because it illustrates some of the dynamics of capitalism and its racist manifestations. And it shows that even such seemingly benign institutions as the university are accomplices in the perpetuation of racial oppression in their daily operations. By handing over food services to Marriott, the University has allowed a kind of sweatshop to develop in its midst, a sweatshop that depends on the exploitation of women of color.

The university could have decided to subsidize food services. If they feel this is an important service to provide to the campus, they should be willing to pay for it. Other non-academic services, such as health and counseling centers, are supported by the campus and their employees are paid the university salary rates. But since food service workers are generally paid low wages, the competitive rates permit the university to save money. They can and do justify the special treatment of these workers by citing market conditions. If food service workers everywhere are paid poorly, why should campus food service employees be an exception?

10   So the poorly paid labor of a group of women of color is used to "subsidize" the mighty University of California. Wealth, as usual, is taken from the poor and transferred to the wealthy and privileged. The pathways of this transfer may be complicated and indirect, but the transfer occurs nonetheless. The university, Marriott, students, and faculty all have a little more money in their pockets because these women live so close to the margin.

Jesse Jackson captured this reality eloquently when he said to a group of poor people: "You are not the bottom. You are the foundation." What a profound inversion of the way this society normally looks at itself! And yet, how true are his words. As in the example I have just presented, the whole magnificent edifice of wealth and privilege in this society has been built on the suffering of poor people, large numbers of whom are people of color. . . .

INEQUALITY IN AMERICA

The United States is an immensely unequal society in terms of the distribution of material wealth, and consequently, in the distribution of all the benefits and privileges that accrue to wealth—including political power and influence. This inequality is vast irrespective of race. However, people of color tend to cluster at the bottom so that inequality in this society also becomes racial inequality. I believe that racial inequality is inextricably tied to overall inequality, and to an ideology that endorses vast inequality as justified and desirable. The special problems of racial inequality require direct attention in the process of attacking inequality in general, but I do not believe that the problem of racial inequality can be eliminated within a context of the tremendous disparities that our society currently tolerates. And even if some kind of racial parity, at the level of averages, could be achieved, the amount of suffering at the bottom would remain undiminished, hence unconscionable.

How unequal is the distribution of rewards in the United States? Typically this question is addressed in terms of occupation and income distribution rather than the distribution and control of property. By the income criterion, the United States is one of the more unequal of the Western industrial societies, and it is far more unequal than the countries of the eastern European socialist bloc. The Soviet Union, for instance, has striven to decrease the discrepancy in earnings between the highest paid professionals and managers and the lowest paid workers, and as a consequence, has a much flatter income distribution than the United States (Szymanski 1979, pp. 63–9).

To take an extreme example from within the United States, in 1987 the minimum wage was $3.35 an hour, and 6.7 million American workers were paid at that level. That comes to $6,968 a year. In contrast, the highest paid executive, Lee Iacocca, received more than $20 million in 1986, or $9,615 per hour. In other words, the highest paid executive received more in an hour than a vast number of workers received in a year (Sheinkman 1987).

The excessive differences in income are given strong ideological justifica-   15
tion—they serve, supposedly, as source of incentive. Who will work hard if
there is no pot of gold at the end, a pot that can be bigger than anyone else's?
The striving for achievement leads to excellence, and we all are the beneficiaries of the continual improvements and advances that result.

Or are we? I believe a strong case can be made for the opposite. First of
all, the presumed benefits of inequality do not trickle down far enough. The
great advances of medical science, for example, are of little use to those people
who cannot afford even the most basic health care. Second, instead of providing incentive, our steep inequalities may engender hopelessness and despair
for those who have no chance of winning the big prize. When you have no
realistic chance of winning the competition, and when there are no prizes for
those who take anything less than fourth place, why should you run all out?
Third, one can question how much inequality is necessary to raise incentives.
Surely fairly modest inducements can serve as motivators. Does the person
who makes $100,000 a year in any sense work that much harder than the per-
son who makes the annual $7,000 wage? Altogether, it would seem that the
justifications for inequality are more rationalizations to preserve privilege
than they are a well-reasoned basis of social organization. The obvious wholesale waste of human capability (let alone life in and for itself) that piles up at
the bottom of our system of inequality is testimony to the failure.

Even more fundamental than income inequality is inequality in the ownership of property. Here not only are the extremes much more severe, but the
justification of incentives for achievement grow exceedingly thin. First, large
amounts of property are simply inherited and the owner never did a stitch of
work in his or her life to merit any of it. Second, and more important, wealth
in property expands at the expense of workers. Its growth depends not on the
achievements of the owner so much as on his or her ability to exploit other
human beings. The owner of rental property, for example, gets richer simply
because other people who have to work for a living cannot afford to buy their
own housing and must sink a substantial portions of their hard-earned wages
into providing shelter. The ownership of property provides interest, rent or
profit simply from the fact of ownership. The owner need only put out the
capital itself to have the profits keep rolling in for the rest of his or her life.

The concentration of property in the United States is rarely studied—I
assume because its exposure is politically embarrassing and even dangerous to
those in power (who overlap substantially with, or are closely allied to those
who own property). Only two such studies have been undertaken in the last
25 years, one in 1963 and one in 1983. The 1983 study was commissioned by
the Democratic staff of the Congressional Joint Economic Committee (U.S.
Congress 1986). It seems it may have been a political hot potato since shortly
after its appearance, a brief 19-line article appeared in the *Los Angeles Times*
stating that the committee withdrew some of its conclusions because of "an
error in the figures" (*Los Angeles Times* 1986).

The 1983 study found that the top 0.5 percent of families in the United States owned over 35 percent of the net wealth of this nation. If equity in personal residences is excluded from consideration, the same 0.5 percent of households owned more than 45 percent of the privately held wealth. In other words, if this county consisted of 200 people, one individual would own almost half of the property held among all 200. The other 199 would have to divide up the remainder.

20   The remainder was not equally divided either. The top 10 percent of the country's households owned 72 percent of its wealth, leaving only 28 percent for the remaining 90 percent of families. If home equity is excluded, the bottom 90 percent only owned 17 percent of the wealth.

The super-rich top half of one percent consisted of 420,000 families. These families owned most of the business enterprises in the nation. They owned 58 percent of unincorporated businesses and 46.5 percent of all personally owned corporate stock. They also owned 77 percent of the value of trusts and 62 percent of state and local bonds. They owned an average of $8.9 million apiece, ranging from $2.5 million up to hundreds of times that amount.

Forbes publishes an annual list of the 400 richest Americans (*Los Angeles Times* 1986). In 1986, 25 individuals owned over a billion dollars in assets. The richest owned $4.5 billion. That is a 10-digit figure. The four-hundredth person on the list owned $180 million. So the concentration of wealth at the very top is even more extreme than the Congressional study reveals. In 1986, for the first time, a Black man made the *Forbes* list—he owned $185 million in assets. The super rich property owners of this country are generally an all-white club.

By 1987, the number of billionaires in the country (as counted by *Forbes*) had grown from 26 in 1986 to 49 (*Forbes* 1987). The average worth of the top 400 had grown to $220 million apiece, a jump of 41 percent in one year. The top individual now owned $8.5 billion. Together, these 400 individuals commanded a net worth of $220 billion, comparable to the entire U.S. military budget in 1986, and more than the U.S. budget deficit, or total U.S. investment abroad.

RACIAL INEQUALITY

The gross inequalities that characterize American society are multiplied when race and ethnicity are entered into the equation. Racial minorities, especially Blacks, Latinos, and Native Americans, tend to be seriously overrepresented at the bottom of the scale in terms of any measure of material well-being.

25   In the distribution of occupations Whites are substantially overrepresented in the professional and managerial stratum. They are almost twice as likely as Blacks (1.71 times) and Latinos (1.97 times) to hold these kinds of jobs. On the other hand, Blacks and Latinos are much more concentrated in

the lower paid service sector, and the unskilled and semiskilled of operators, fabricators and laborers. Whereas only 27 percent of White employees fall into these combined categories, 47 percent of Blacks and 43 percent of Latinos are so categorized. Finally, even though the numbers are relatively small, Blacks are more than three times and Latinos more than twice as likely as Whites to work as private household servants. This most demeaning of occupations remains mainly a minority preserve (U.S. Department of Labor 1987).

Occupational disadvantage translates into wage and salary disadvantage. The median weekly earning of White families in 1986 was $566, compared to $412 for Latino families and $391 for Black families. In other words, Black and Latino families made about 70 percent of what White families made. Female-headed households of all groups made substantially less money. Both Black and Latino female-headed families made less than half of what the average White family (including married couples) made (U.S. Department of Labor 1987).

Weekly earnings only reflect the take-home pay of employed people. In addition, people of color bear the brunt of unemployment in this society. In 1986, 14.8 percent of Black males, 14.2 percent of Black females, 10.5 percent of Latino males, and 10.8 percent of Latino females were unemployed officially. This compares to 6 percent of White males and 6.1 percent of White females (U.S. Department of Labor 1987).

The absence of good jobs or any jobs at all, and the absence of decent pay for those jobs that are held translates into poverty. Although the poverty line is a somewhat arbitrary figure, it nevertheless provides some commonly accepted standard for decent living in our society.

As of 1984, over one-third of Black households lived in poverty. If we include those people who live very close to the poverty line, the near poor, then 41 percent, or two out of five Blacks, are poor or near poor. For Latinos the figures are only slightly less grim, with over 28 percent living in poverty and 36 percent, or well over one-third, living in or near poverty. This compares to an official poverty rate of 11 percent for Whites.

Female-headed households, as is commonly known, are more likely to *30*
live in or near poverty. Over half of Black and Latino female-headed families are forced to live under the poverty line, and over 60 percent of each group live in or near poverty. The figures for White female-headed families are also high with over one-third living in or near poverty. But the levels for people of color are almost twice as bad (U.S. Bureau of the Census 1986).

The degree of racial inequality in property ownership is stark—more stark than the income and employment figures. . . . The average White family has a net worth of about $39,000, more than ten times the average net worth of about $3,000 for Black families. Latino families are only slightly better off, with an average net worth of about $5,000. The differences are even more marked among female-headed households. The average Black and Latino female-headed households have a net worth of only $671 and $478 respectively, less than 2 percent of the net worth of the average White household.

...The richest man in this country owned $8.5 billion in wealth in 1987 and there are a handful of others close behind him. Meanwhile, the average—not the poorest but the average—Black and Latino female-headed household only commands a few hundred dollars. How can one even begin to talk about equality of opportunity under such circumstances? What power and control must inevitably accompany the vast holdings of the billionaires, and what scrambling for sheer survival must accompany the dearth of resources at the bottom end? ...

CAPITALISM AND RACISM

I want to consider the ways in which the American political-economic system is bound to racism. It is my contention that the racism of this society is linked to capitalism and that, so long as we retain a capitalist system, we will not be able to eliminate racial oppression. This is not to say that racism will automatically disappear if we change the system. If we were to transform to a socialist society, the elimination of racism would have to be given direct attention as a high priority. I am not suggesting that its elimination would be easily achieved within socialism, but it is impossible under capitalism.[2]

Stripped of all its fancy rationalizations and complexities, the capitalist system depends upon the exploitation of the poor by the rich. Property owners need an impoverished class of people so that others will be forced to work for them. We can see this in food services on my campus. And we can see it on a world-wide scale, where, for example, poor Latin American countries sent to American investors and lenders (between 1982 and 1987) $145 billion more than they took in. And they still owe a principal of $410 billion in foreign debt, and all the billions of dollars of interest payments that will accrue to that (*Los Angeles Times* 1987).

35   Capitalism depends on inequality. The truth is, the idea of equality cannot even be whispered around here. It is too subversive, too completely undermining of the "American way." Liberals, conservatives, Democrats, and Republicans are all committed to the idea of inequality and so, no matter how much they yell at each other in Congressional hearings, behind the scenes they shake hands and agree that things are basically fine and as they should be.

Perhaps not everyone agrees with my formulation, but I do not think anyone can disagree that there is a commitment to economic inequality in

---

[2]There is a major debate around the question of race versus class. See, for example, Alphonso Pinkney (1984) and Michael Omi and Howard Winant. The question is raised: Which is more important, race or class? Some argue that race cannot be "reduced" to class and that it has independent vitality. A similar argument is made by some feminists regarding gender. I do not contend that race can be reduced to class, but I do not think that race and class are independent systems that somehow intersect with one another. This imagery is too static.

this system and that no attempt is made to hide it. It is part of the official ideology. However the same cannot be said for racial inequality today. At least at the official level it is stated that race should not be the basis of any social or economic distinction. Thus it should, in theory, be possible to eliminate racial inequality within the system, even if we do not touch overall inequality.

Even though an open commitment to racial inequality has been made illegitimate in recent years as a consequence of the Civil Rights and related social movements, I believe that it remains embedded in this system. Before getting into the present dynamics of the system, however, let me point out how deeply racism is embedded in the historical evolution of capitalism. First of all, one can make the case that, without racism, without the racial domination implicit in the early European "voyages of discovery," Europe would never have accumulated the initial wealth for its own capitalist "take off." In other words, capitalism itself is predicated on racism (Williams 1966).

But setting aside this somewhat controversial point, European capitalist development quickly acquired an expansionist mode and took over the world, spreading a suffocating blanket of White domination over almost all the other peoples of the globe. The motive was primarily economic, primarily the pursuit of markets, raw materials, cheap labor, and investment opportunities. The business sector of Europe, linked to the state, wanted to increase its profits. They sought to enhance their wealth (see Cheng and Bonacich 1984).

The belief in the inferiority of peoples of color, the belief that Europeans were bringing a gift of civilization, salvation, and economic development, helped justify the conquest. They were not, they could think to themselves, hurting anyone. They were really benefactors, bringing light to the savages.

The world order that they created was tiered. On the one hand, they exploited the labor of their own peoples, creating from Europe's farmers and craftsmen an ownerless White working class. On the other hand, of the conquered nationalities they created a super-exploited work-force, producing the raw materials for the rising European industries, and doing the dirtiest and lowest paid support jobs in the world economy. Because they had been conquered and colonized, the peoples of color could be subjected to especially coercive labor systems, such as slavery, indentured servitude, forced migrant labor and the like.

Both groups of workers were exploited in the sense that surplus was taken from their labor by capitalist owners. But White "free labor" was in a relatively advantaged position, being employed in the technically more advanced and higher paid sectors. To a certain extent, White labor benefited from the super-exploitation of colonized workers. The capital that was drained from the colonies could be invested in industrial development in Europe or the centers of European settlement (such as the United States, Canada, Australia, New Zealand, and South Africa). The White cotton mill workers in Manchester and New England depended on the super-exploitation of cotton workers in India and the slave South, producing the cheap raw material on which their industrial employment was built.

Although the basic structure of the world economy centered on European capital and the exploitation of colonized workers in their own homelands, the expansion of European capitalism led to movement of peoples all over the globe to suit the economic needs of the capitalist class. Internal colonies, the products of various forms of forced and semiforced migrations, replicated the world system within particular territories.

The basic stratification of world capitalism, with workers of color at the foundation, remains in effect today. Women of color, in particular, are the most exploited of workers around the globe (see Fuentes and Ehrenreich 1983; Fernandez-Kelly 1983). Although race may not be overtly invoked in the exploitation of Third World peoples, the fact is that they are peoples of color who suffer external domination and must labor for "White" capitalists. In the case of South Africa, specifically racial oppression is openly enforced. And the U.S. government's extremely weak response to this reality suggests the degree of their commitment to ending racism. But even if the racist government of South Africa collapses, as it inevitably will, U.S. capital still exploits people of color from Asia to Africa to Latin America, supporting regimes that enforce their ability to suck these nations dry.

Still, we can ask: Is it not possible that within the United States, a redistribution could occur that would eliminate the racial character of inequality? Could we not, with the banning of racial discrimination and even positive policies like affirmative action, restructure our society such that color is no longer correlated with wealth and poverty? This is what is meant by racial equality within capitalism. The total amount of human misery would remain unaltered, but its complexion would change.

Assimilationism

45 It seems to me that, even if people of color are fully distributed along the capitalist hierarchy, resembling the distribution of White people, that does not necessarily spell the end of racism. The very idea of such absorption is assimilationist. It claims that people of color must abandon their own cultures and communities and become utilitarian individualists like the White men. They must compete on the white man's terms for the White man's values.

The notion that the American system can be "color blind," a common conservative position, is, of course, predicated on the idea that one is color blind within a system of rules, and those rules are the White man's. Even though he claims they are without cultural content, this is nonsense. They are his rules, deriving from his cultural heritage, and he can claim that they are universal and culturally neutral only because he has the power to make such a claim stick. There is an implicit arrogance that the White man's way is the most advanced, and that everyone else ought to learn how to get along in it as quickly as possible. All other cultures and value systems are impugned as backward, primitive or dictatorial. Only Western capitalism is seen as the pinnacle of human social organization, the height of perfection (see Bonacich 1987 and Bonacich 1989).

The absurdity of such a position need scarcely be mentioned. The White man's civilization has not only caused great suffering to oppressed nationalities around the globe, but also to many of its own peoples. It has not only murdered and pillaged other human beings but has also engaged in wanton destruction of our precious planet, so that we can now seriously question how long human life will be sustainable at all.

Let me give an example of the way in which the White man's seemingly universal rules have been imposed. In 1887 the U.S. government passed the Allotment Act, authored by Senator Henry Dawes. This law terminated communal land ownership among American Indians by allotting private parcels of land to individuals. Dawes articulated the philosophy behind this policy:

> The head chief [of the Cherokee] told us that there was not a family in that whole nation that had not a home of its own. There was not a pauper in that nation, and the nation did not owe a dollar. . . . Yet the defect in the system was apparent. They have got as far as they can go, because they own their land in common. . . . There is no enterprise to make your home any better than that of your neighbor's. There is no self-ishness, which is at the bottom of civilization. Until this people consent to give up their lands and divide them among their citizens so that each can own the land he cultivates, they will not make much progress (Wexler 1982).

Needless to say, the plans to coerce American Indians into participation in the White man's system of private property did not work out according to official plan. Instead, White people came in and bought up Indian land and left the Indians destitute. People who had not been paupers were now pauperized. It is a remarkably familiar story. The workings of an apparently neutral marketplace have a way of leaving swaths of destruction in their wake.

The Role of the Middle Class

The growth of a Black, Latino and Native American middle class in the last few decades also does not negate the proposition that racial inequality persists in America. In order to understand this, we need to consider the role that the middle class, or professional-managerial stratum, plays in capitalist society, irrespective of race. In my view, middle class people (including myself) are essentially the sergeants of the system. We professionals and managers are paid by the wealthy and powerful, by the corporations and the state, to keep things in order. Our role is one of maintaining the system of inequality. Our role is essentially that of controlling the poor. We are a semi-elite. We are given higher salaries, social status, better jobs, and better life chances as payment for our service to the system. If we were not useful to the power elite, they would not reward us. Our rewards prove that we serve their interests. Look at who pays us. That will give you a sense of whom we are serving (see Ehrenreich and Ehrenreich 1979).

We middle class people would like to believe that our positions of privilege benefit the less advantaged. We would like to believe that our upward mobility helps others, that the benefits we receive somehow "trickle down." But this is sheer self-delusion. It is capitalist ideology, which claims that the people at the top of the social system are really the great benefactors of the people at the bottom. The poor should be grateful to the beneficent rich elites for all their generosity. The poor depend on the wealthy; without the rich elites, where would the poor be? But of course, this picture stands reality on its head. Dependency really work the other way. It is the rich that depend on the poor for their well-being. And benefit, wealth and privilege flow up, not down.

The same basic truths apply to the Black and Latino middle class with some added features. People of color are, too often, treated as tokens. Their presence in higher level positions is used to "prove" that the American system is open to anyone with talent and ambition. But the truth is, people of color are allowed to hold more privileged positions if and only if they conform to the "party line." They are not allowed real authority. They have to play the White man's game by the White man's rules or they lose their good jobs. They have to give up who they are, and disown their community and its pressing needs for change, in order to "make it" in this system. . . .

The rising Black and Latino middle class is, more often than not, used to control the poor and racially oppressed communities, to crush oppression and prevent needed social change. The same is the case, as I have said, with the White middle class. However, there was an implicit promise that the election of Black and Latino political officials, and the growth of a professional and business stratum, would trickle down to the benefit of their communities. This has worked as well as trickle down theory in general. Regardless of the intentions of the Black and Latino middle class, the institutional structures and practices of capitalism have prohibited the implementation of any of the needed reforms. Black mayors, for example, coming in with plans of social progress, find themselves trapped in the logic of the private profit system and cannot implement their programs (see Lembcke 1989).

This state of affairs is manifest on my campus. There has been little progress in terms of affirmative action among the staff. However, if you look more closely, you discover that almost all of the Black and Chicano staff work under White administrators. Furthermore, those people with professional positions are highly concentrated in minority-oriented programs, like Student Affirmative Action, Immediate Outreach, Black and Chicano Student Programs and the like. Even here they are under the direction of White supervisors who ultimately determine the nature and limits of these programs.

55 What happens, more often than not, is that professional staff who are people of color become shock-absorbers in the system. They take responsibility for programs without having the authority to shape them. If recruitment or retention of students from racially oppressed communities does not produce results, it is the Black, Chicano and Native American professional staff who are held accountable, even though they could not shape a program that had any chance of succeeding. The staff people of color must accept the indi-

vidualistic, meritocratic ethic of the institution and cannot push for programs that would enhance community development or community participation in the shaping of the university. They simply have to implement the bankrupt idea of plucking out the "best and brightest" and urging them to forsake their families and communities in the quest to "make it" in America.

Still, even if the ruling class can make use of people of color in middle class positions, I believe there are real limits to their willingness to allow enough redistribution to occur so that the averages across groups would become the same. The powerful and wealthy White capitalist class may be able to tolerate and even endorse "open competition" in the working and middle classes. However, they show no sign whatsoever of being willing to relinquish their own stranglehold on the world economy. They can play the game of supporting a recarving up of the tiny part of the pie left over after they have taken their share. Indeed, it is probably good business to encourage various groups to scramble for the crumbs. They will be so busy attacking each other that they will not think to join together to challenge the entire edifice.

The White establishment manipulates racial ideology. Even when it uses the language of colorblindness and equal opportunity, the words need to be stripped of their underlying manipulation. Right now it pays that establishment to act as though they are appalled by the use of race as a criterion for social allocation. But not too long ago, certainly within my memory, they were happy to use it openly. Have they suffered a real change of heart? Is a system that was openly built on racial oppression and that still uses it on a world scale, suddenly free from this cancer?

The truth is, a system driven by private profit, by the search for individual gain, can never solve its social problems. The conservatives promise that market forces will wipe out the negative effects of a history of racial discrimination. But this is a mirage. Wealth accrues to the already wealthy. Power and wealth enhance privilege. Nothing in the market system will change the fact that women of color are exploited in food services on my campus. The market system will not iron out this oppression. On the contrary, its operation sustains it. Only political opposition, only a demand for social justice, will turn this situation around. . . .

REFERENCES

Bonacich, Edna. 1989. "Racism in the Deep Structure of U.S. Higher Education: When Affirmative Action Is Not Enough." In *Affirmative Action and Positive Policies in the Education of Ethnic Minorities,* ed. Sally Tomlinson and Abraham Yogev. Greenwich, CT: JAI Press.

———. 1987. "The Limited Social Philosophy of Affirmative Action." *Insurgent Sociologist* 14:99–116.

Cheng, Lucie and Edna Bonacich. 1984. *Labor Immigration Under Capitalism: Asian Workers in the United States Before World War II.* Berkeley: University of California Press.

Ehrenreich, Barbara and John, 1979. "The Professional-Managerial Class." Pp. 5–45 in *Between Labor and Capital,* ed. Pat Walker. Boston: South End Press.

Fernandez-Kelly, Maria Patricia. 1983. *For We Are Sold, I and My People: Women and Industry in Mexico's Frontier.* Albany: State University of New York.

Forbes. 1987. "The 400 Richest People in America." 140 (October): 106–110.

Fuentes, Annette and Barbara Ehrenreich. 1983. *Women in the Global Factory.* Boston: South End Press.

Lembcke, Jerry. 1989. *Race, Class, and Urban Change.* Greenwich, CT: JAI Press.

Los Angeles Times. "Hemisphere in Crisis." December 29, 1987.

———. "'Super Rich' Control Misstated by Study." August 22, 1986.

———. "Walton Still Tops Forbes List of 400 Richest Americans." October 14, 1986.

Omi, Michael and Harold Winant. 1986. *Racial Formation in the United States: From the 1960s to the 1980s.* New York: Routledge and Kegan Paul.

Pinkney, Alphonso. 1984. *The Myth of Black Progress.* Cambridge: Cambridge University Press.

Sacks, Karen Brodkin and Dorothy Remy. 1984. *My Troubles Are Going to Have Trouble with Me: Everyday Trials and Triumphs of Women Workers.* New Brunswick, New Jersey: Rutgers University Press.

Sheinkman, Jack. 1987. "Stop Exploiting Lowest-Paid Workers." *Los Angeles Times* September 9.

Szymanski, Albert. 1979. *Is the Red Flag Flying? The Political Economy of the Soviet Union.* London: Zed Press.

U.S. Bureau of Census. 1986. Current Population Reports, Series P-60, No. 152. *Characteristics of the Population Below the Poverty Level: 1984.* Washington, D.C.: U.S. Government Printing Office.

U.S. Congress Joint Economic Committee. 1986. *The Concentration of Wealth in the United States: Trends in the Distribution of Wealth Among American Families.* Washington, D.C.: U.S. Government Printing Office.

U.S. Department of Labor, Bureau of Labor Statistics. 1987. *Employment and Earnings* 34:212. Washington, D.C.: U.S. Government Printing Office.

Wexler, Rex. 1982. *Blood of the Land: The Government and Corporate War Against the American Indian Movement.* New York: Vintage.

Williams, Eric. 1966. *Capitalism and Slavery.* New York: Capricorn.

BLACK MACHO REVISITED

REFLECTIONS OF A SNAP! QUEEN

Marlon T. Riggs

Negro faggotry is in fashion.
  SNAP!
  Turn on your television and camp queens greet you in living color.
  SNAP!
  Turn to cable and watch America's most bankable modern minstrel ex- 5
pound on getting "fucked in the ass" or his fear of faggots.
  SNAP!
  Turn off the TV, turn on the radio: Rotund rapper Heavy D, the self-
styled "overweight lover MC," expounds on how *his* rap will make you "happy
like a faggot in jail." Perhaps to preempt questions about how he would
know—you might wonder what kind of "lover" he truly is—Heavy D reas-
sures us that he's just "extremely intellectual, not bisexual."
  Jelly-roll SNAP!
  Negro faggotry is in vogue. Madonna commodified it into a commercial
hit. Mapplethorpe photographed it, and art galleries drew fire and record
crowds in displaying it. Black macho movie characters dis'—or should we say
dish?—their antagonists with unkind references to it. Indeed, references to,
and representations of, Negro faggotry seem a rite of passage among contemporary black male rappers and filmmakers.
  Snap-swish-and-dish divas have truly arrived, giving Beauty Shop drama 10
at center stage, performing the read-and-snap two-step as they sashay across
the movie screen, entertaining us in the castles of our home—like court
jesters, like eunuchs—with their double entendres and dead-end lusts, and,
above all, their relentless hilarity in the face of relentless despair. Negro faggotry is the rage! Black gay men are not. For in the cinematic and television
images of and from black America, as well as the lyrics and dialogue that now
abound and *seem* to address my life as a black gay man, I am struck repeatedly
by the determined, unreasoning, often irrational desire to discredit my claim
to blackness and hence to black manhood.
  Consequently, the terrain black gay men navigate in the quest for self and
social identity is, to say the least, hostile. What disturbs, no, enrages me is not
so much the obstacles set before me by whites, which history conditions me
to expect, but the traps and pitfalls planted by my so-called brothers, who, because of the same history, should know better.

I am a Negro faggot, if I believe what movies, TV, and rap music say of me. My life is game for play. Because of my sexuality, I cannot be black. A strong, proud, "Afrocentric" black man is resolutely heterosexual, not *even* bisexual. Hence, I remain a Negro. My sexual difference is considered of no value; indeed, it's a testament to weakness, passivity, the absence of real guts—balls. Hence, I remain a sissy, punk, faggot. I cannot be a black gay man because, by the tenets of black macho, black gay man is a triple negation. I am consigned, by these tenets, to remain a Negro faggot. And, as such, I am game for play, to be used, joked about, put down, beaten, slapped, and bashed, not just by illiterate homophobic thugs in the night but by black American culture's best and brightest.

In a community where the dozens, signifying, dis'ing, and *dishing* are revered as art form, I ask myself: What does this obsession with Negro faggotry signify? What is its significance?

What lies at the heart, I believe, of black America's pervasive cultural homophobia is the desperate need for a convenient Other within the community, yet not truly of the community; an Other to which blame for the chronic identity crises afflicting the black male psyche can be readily displaced; an indispensable Other that functions as the lowest common denominator of the abject, the base line of transgression beyond which a Black Man is no longer a man, no longer black; an essential Other against which black men and boys maturing, struggling with self-doubt, anxiety, feelings of political, economic, social, and sexual inadequacy—even impotence—can always measure themselves and by comparison seem strong, adept, empowered, superior.

15 Indeed, the representation of Negro faggotry disturbingly parallels and reinforces America's most entrenched racist constructions around African American identity. White icons of the past signifying "Blackness" share with contemporary icons of Negro faggotry a manifest dread of the deviant Other. Behind the Sambo and the SNAP! Queen lies a social psyche in torment, a fragile psyche threatened by deviation from its egocentric-ethnocentric construct of self and society. Such a psyche systematically defines the Other's "deviance" by the essential characteristics that make the Other distinct, then invests those differences with intrinsic defect. Hence, blacks are inferior because they are not white. Black gays are unnatural because they are not straight. Majority representations of both affirm the view that blackness and gayness constitute a fundamental rupture in the order of things, that our very existence is an affront to nature and humanity.

For black gay men, this burden of (mis)representation is compounded. We are saddled by historic caricatures of the black male, now fused with newer notions of the Negro faggot. The resultant dehumanization is multilayered and profound.

What strikes me as most insidious and paradoxical is the degree to which popular African American depictions of us as black gay men so keenly resonate with American majority depictions of us as black people. Within the black gay community, for example, the SNAP! contains a multiplicity of coded meaning: as in—SNAP!—"Got your point." Or—SNAP!—"Don't even try it." Or—SNAP!—"You fierce!" Or—SNAP!—"Get out my face." Or—SNAP!—"Girlfriend, pleeease." The snap can be as emotionally and politically charged as a clenched fist, can punctuate debate and dialogue like an exclamation point, a comma, an ellipse, or altogether negate the need for words among those who are adept at decoding its nuanced meanings.

But the particular appropriation of the snap by Hollywood's Black Pack deflates the gesture into rank caricature. Instead of a symbol of communal expression and, at times, cultural defiance, the snap becomes part of a simplistically reductive Negro faggot identity; it functions as a mere signpost of effeminate, cute, comic homosexuality. Thus robbed of its full political and cultural dimension, the snap, in this appropriation, descends to stereotype.

Is this any different from the motives and consequences associated with the legendary white dramatist T. D. Rice, who more than 150 years ago appropriated the tattered clothes and dance style of an old crippled black man, then went on stage and imitated him, thus shaping in the popular American mind an indelible image of blacks as simplistic and poor, yet given, without exception, to "natural" rhythm and happy feet?

A family tree displaying dominant types in the cultural iconography of Black men would show, I believe, an unmistakable line of descent from Sambo to the SNAP! Queen and, in parallel lineage from the brute Negro to the AIDS-infected Black Homo-Con-Rapist. 20

What the members of this pantheon share in common is an extreme displacement and distortion of sexuality. In Sambo and the SNAP! Queen, sexuality is repressed, arrested. Laughter, levity, and a certain childlike disposition cement their mutual status as comic eunuchs. Their alter egos, the Brute Black and the Homo Con, are but psychosocial projections of an otherwise tamed sexuality run amuck—bestial, promiscuous, pathological.

Contemporary proponents of black macho thus converge with white supremacist D.W. Griffith in their cultural practice, deploying similar devices toward similarly dehumanizing ends. In its constructions of "unnatural" sexual aggression, Griffith's infamous chase scene in *Birth of a Nation,* in which a lusting "Brute Negro" (a white actor in black face) chases a white Southern virgin to her death, displays a striking aesthetic kinship to the homophobic jail rape—or, should I say, attempted rape?—in Reginald and Warrington Hudlin's *House Party.*

The resonances go deeper. Pseudoscientific discourse fused with popular icons of race in the late-nineteenth-century America to project a social fantasy of black men, not simply as sexual demons but, significantly, as intrinsically corrupt. Diseased, promiscuous, destructive—of self and others—our fundamental nature, it was widely assumed, would lead us to extinction.

Against this historical backdrop consider the highly popular comedy routines of Eddie Murphy, which unite Negro Faggotry, "Herpes Simplex 10"—

and AIDS—into an indivisible modern icon of sexual terrorism. Rap artists and music videos resonate with this perception, fomenting a social psychology that blames the *victim* for his degradation and death.

25   The sum total of prime-time fag pantomimes, camp queens as culture critics, and the proliferating bit-part swish-and-dish divas who, like the ubiquitous black maids and butlers in fifties Hollywood films, move along the edges of the frame, seldom at the center, manifests the persistent psychosocial impulse toward control, displacement, and marginalization of the black gay Other. This impulse, in many respects, is no different from the phobic, distorted projections that motivated blackface minstrelsy.

This is the irony: there are more black filmmakers and rap artists than ever, yet their works display a persistently narrow, even monolithic, construction of the black male identity.

"You have to understand something," explained Professor Griff of the controversial and highly popular rap group Public Enemy, in an interview. "In knowing and understanding black history, African history, there's not a word in any African language which describes homosexual, y'understand what I'm saying? You would like to make them part of the community, but that's something brand-new to black people."

And so black macho appropriates African history, or, rather, a deeply reductive, mythologized view of African history, to rationalize homophobia. Pseudoacademic claims of "Afrocentricity" have now become a popular invocation when black macho is pressed to defend its essentialist vision of the race. An inheritance from Black Cultural Nationalism of the late sixties, and Negritude before that, today's Afrocentrism, as popularly theorized, premises an historical narrative that runs thus: before the white man came, African men were strong, noble, protectors, providers, and warriors for their families and tribes. In precolonial Africa, men were truly men, and women were women. Nobody was lesbian. Nobody was feminist. Nobody was gay.

This distortion of history, though severe, has its seductions. Given the increasingly besieged state of black men in America, and the nation's historic subversion of an affirming black identity, it is no wonder that a community would turn to pre-Diasporan history for metaphors of empowerment. But the embrace of the African warrior ideal—strong, protective, impassive, patriarchal—has cost us. It has sent us down a perilous road of cultural and spiritual redemption and distorted or altogether deleted from the historical record the multiplicity of identities around color, gender, sexuality, and class that informs the African and the African American experience.

30   It is to me supremely revealing that in black macho's popular appropriation of Malcolm X (in movies, music, rap videos), it is consistently Malcolm before Mecca—militant, macho, "by any means necessary" Malcolm—who is quoted and idolized, not Malcolm after Mecca, when he became more critical of himself and of exclusivist Nation of Islam tenets and embraced a broader, multicultural perspective on nationalist identity.

By the tenets of black macho, true masculinity admits little or no space for self-interrogation or multiple subjectivities around race. Black macho prescribes an inflexible ideal: strong black men—"Afrocentric" black men—don't flinch, don't weaken, don't take the blame or shit, take charge, step-to when challenged, and defend themselves without pause for self-doubt. Black macho counterpoises this warrior model of masculinity with the emasculated Other: the Other as a punk, sissy, Negro faggot, a status with which any man, not just those who are in fact gay, can be and are branded should one deviate from rigidly prescribed codes of hypermasculine conduct.

"When I say Gamma, you say Fag. Gamma. Fag. Gamma. Fag." In the conflict between the frat boys and the "fellas" in Spike Lee's *School Daze,* verbal fag bashing becomes the weapon of choice in the fellas' contest for male domination. In this regard, Lee's movie not only resonates with a poisonous dynamic in contemporary black male relations but, worse, it glorifies black male homophobia.

Spike Lee and others like him count on the complicit silence of those who know better, who know the truth of their own lives as well as the diverse truths that inform the total black experience.

Notice is served. Our silence has ended. SNAP!

REPORT FROM THE BAHAMAS

June Jordan

I am staying in a hotel that calls itself the Sheraton British Colonial. One of the photographs advertising the place displays a middle-aged Black man in a waiter's tuxedo, smiling. What intrigues me most about the picture is just this: while the Black man bears a tray full of "colorful" drinks above the his left shoulder, both of his feet, shoes and trouserlegs, up to ten inches above his ankles, stand in the also "colorful" Caribbean salt water. He is so delighted to serve you he will wade into the water to bring you Banana Daquiris while you float! More precisely, he will wade into the water, fully clothed, oblivious to the ruin of his shoes, his trousers, his health and he will do it with a smile.

I am in the Bahamas. On the phone in my room, a spinning complement of plastic pages offers handy index clues such as CAR RENTALS and CASINOS. A message from the Ministry of Tourism appears among these travellers tips. Opening with a paragraph of "WELCOME," the message proceeds to "A PAGE OF HISTORY," which reads as follows:

> New World History begins on the same day that modern
> Bahamian history begins—October 12, 1492. That's when
> Columbus stepped ashore—British influence came first
> with the Eleutherian Adventurers of 1647—After the Revo-
> lutions, American Loyalists fled from the newly independent
> states and settled in the Bahamas. Confederate blockade-
> runners used the island as a haven during the War between
> the States, and after the War, a number of Southerners moved
> to the Bahamas. . . .

There it is again. Something proclaims itself a legitimate history and all it does is track white Mr. Columbus to the British Eleutherians through the Confederate Southerners as they barge into the New World surf, land on New World turf, and nobody saying one word about the Bahamian people, the Black peoples, to whom the only thing new in their island world was this weird succession of crude intruders and its colonial consequences.

This is my consciousness of race as I unpack my bathing suit in the Sheraton British Colonial. Neither this hotel nor the British nor the long ago Italians nor the white Delta airline pilots belong here, of course. And every time I look at the photograph of that fool standing in the water with his shoes on I'm about to have a West Indian fit, even though I know he's no fool; he's a middle-aged Black man who needs a job and this is his job—pretending himself a servile ancillary to the pleasures of the rich. (Compared to his options in life, I am a rich woman. Compared to most of the Black Americans arriving for this Easter weekend on three nights four days' deal of bargain rates, the middleaged waiter is a poor Black man.)

We will jostle with the other (white) visitors and join them in the tee shirt shops or, laughing together, learn ruthless rules of negotiations as we, Black Americans as well as white, argue down the price of handwoven goods at the nearby straw market while the merchants, frequently toothless Black women seated on the concrete in their only presentable dress, humble themselves to our careless games:

"Yes? You like it? Eight dollar."   5

"Five."

"I give it to you. Seven."

And so it continues, the weird succession of crude intruders that, now, includes me and my brothers and my sisters from the North.

This is my consciousness of class as I try to decide how much money I can spend on Bahamian gifts for my family back in Brooklyn. No matter that these other Black women incessantly weave words and flowers into the straw hats and bags piled beside them on the burning dusty street. No matter that these other Black women must work their sense of beauty into these things that we will take away as cheaply as we dare, or they will do without food.

We are not white after all. The budget is limited. And we are harmlessly   10
killing time between the poolside rum punch and "The Native Show on the Patio" that will play tonight outside the hotel restaurant.

This is my consciousness of race and class and gender identity as I notice the fixed relations between these other Black women and myself. They sell and I buy or I don't. They risk not eating. I risk going broke on my first vacation afternoon.

We are not particularly women anymore; we are parties to a transaction designed to set us against each other.

"Olive" is the name of the Black woman who cleans my hotel room. On my way to the beach I am wondering what "Olive" would say if I told her why I chose The Sheraton British Colonial; if I told her I wanted to swim. I wanted to sleep. I did not want to be harassed by the middleaged waiter, or his nephew. I did not want to be raped by anybody (white or Black) at all and I calculated that my safety as a Black woman alone would best be assured by a multinational hotel corporation. In my experience, the big guys take customer complaints more seriously than the little ones. I would suppose that's one reason why they're big; they don't like to lose money anymore than I like to be bothered when I'm trying to read a goddamned book underneath a palm tree I paid $264 to get next to. A Black woman seeking refuge in a multinational corporation may seem like a contradiction to some, but there you are. In this case, it's a coincidence of entirely different self-interests: Sheraton/cash = June Jordan's short run safety.

Anyway, I'm pretty sure "Olive" would look at me as though I came from someplace as far away as Brooklyn. Then she'd probably allow herself one indignant query before righteously removing her vacuum from the room; "and why in the first place you come down you without your husband?"

15   I cannot imagine how I would begin to answer her.

My "rights" and my "freedom" and my "desire" and a slew of other New World values; what would they sound like to this Black woman described on the card atop my hotel bureau as "Olive the Maid"? "Olive" is older than I am and I may smoke a cigarette while she changes the sheets on my bed. Whose rights? Whose freedom? Whose desire?

And why should she give a shit about mine unless I do something, for real, about hers?

It happens that the book that I finished reading under a palm tree earlier today was the novel, *The Bread Givers,* by Anzia Yezierska. Definitely autobiographical, Yezierska lays out the difficulties of being both female and "a person" inside a traditional Jewish family at the start of the 20th century. That any Jewish woman became anything more than the abused servant of her father or her husband is really an improbable piece of news. Yet Yezierska managed such an unlikely outcome for her own life. In *The Bread Givers,* the heroine also manages an important, although partial, escape from traditional, Jewish female destiny. And in the unpardonable, despotic father, the Talmudic scholar of that Jewish family, did I not see my own and hate him twice, again? When the heroine, the young Jewish child, wanders the streets with a filthy pail she borrows to sell herring in order to raise the ghetto rent and when she cries, "Nothing was before me but the hunger in our house, and no bread for the next meal if I didn't sell the herring. No longer like a fire engine, but like a houseful of hungry mouths my heart cried, 'herring—herring! Two cents apiece!'" who would doubt the ease, the sisterhood of conversation possible between that white girl and the Black women selling straw bags on the streets of a paradise because they do not want to die. And it was not obvious that the wife of that Talmudic scholar and "Olive," who cleans my room here at the hotel, have more in common than I can claim with either one of them?

This is my consciousness of race and class and gender identity as I collect wet towels, sunglasses, wristwatch, and head towards a shower.

20   I am thinking about the boy who loaned this novel to me. He's white and he's Jewish and he's pursuing an independent study project with me, at the State University where I teach whether or not I feel like it, where I teach without stint because, like the waiter, I am no fool. It's my job and either I work or I do without everything you need money to buy. The boy loaned me the novel because he thought I'd be interested to know how a Jewish-American writer used English so that the syntax, and therefore the cultural habits of mind expressed by the Yiddish language, could survive translation. He did this because he wanted to create another connection between us on the basis of language, between his knowledge/his love of Yiddish and my knowledge/my love of Black English.

He has been right about the forceful survival of the Yiddish. And I had become excited by this further evidence of the written voice of spoken language protected from the monodrone of "standard" English, and so we had grown closer on this account. But then our talk shifted to student affairs more generally, and I had learned that this student does not care one way or the other about currently jeopardized Federal Student Loan Programs because, as he explained it to me, they do not affect him. He does not need financial help outside his family. My own son, however, is Black. And I am the only family help available to him and that means, if Reagan succeeds in eliminating federal programs to aid minority students, we will have to forget about furthering his studies, or he and I or both of us will have to hit the numbers pretty big. For these reasons of difference, the student and I had moved away from each other, even while we continued to talk.

My consciousness turned to race, again, and class.

Sitting in the same chair as the boy, several weeks ago, a graduate student came to discuss her grade. I praised the excellence of final paper, indeed it had seemed to me an extraordinary pulling together of recent left brain/right brain research with the themes of transcendental poetry.

She told me that, for her part, she'd completed her reading of my political essays. "You are so lucky!" she exclaimed.

"What do you mean by that?" 25

"You have a cause. You have a purpose to your life."

I looked carefully at this white woman; what was she really saying to me?

"What do you mean?" I repeated.

"Poverty. Police violence. Discrimination in general."

(Jesus Christ, I thought: Is that her idea of lucky?) 30

"And how about you?" I asked.

"Me?"

"Yeah, you. Don't you have a cause?"

"Me? I'm just a middle aged woman: a housewife and a mother. I'm nobody."

For a while, I made no response. 35

First of all, speaking of race and class and gender in one breath, what she said meant that those lucky preoccupations of mine, from police violence to nuclear wipe-out, were not shared. They were mine and not hers. But here she sat, friendly as an old stuffed animal, beaming good will or more "luck" in my direction.

In the second place what this white woman said to me meant that she did not believe she was "a person" precisely because she had fulfilled the traditional female functions revered by the father of that Jewish immigrant, Anzia Yezierska. And the woman in front of me was not a Jew. That was not the connection. The link was strictly female. Nevertheless, how should that woman and I, another female connect, beyond this bizarre exchange?

If she believed me lucky to have regular hurdles of discrimination then why shouldn't I insist that she's lucky to be a middle class white Wasp female who lives in such well-sanctioned and normative comfort that she even has the luxury to deny the power of the privileges that paralyze her life.

If she deserts me and "my cause" where we differ, if, for example, she abandons me to "my" problems of race, then why should I support her in "her" problems of housewife oblivion?

40 Recollection of this peculiar moment brings me to the shower in the bathroom cleaned by "Olive." She reminds me of the usual Women's Studies curriculum because it has nothing to do with her or her job: you won't find "Olive" listed anywhere on the reading list. You will likewise seldom hear of Anzia Yezierska. But yes, you will find, from Florence Nightingale to Adrienne Rich, a white procession of independently well-to-do women writers. (Gertrude Stein/Virginia Woolf/Hilda Doolittle are standard names among the "essential" women writers.)

In other words, most of the women of the world—Black and First World and white who work because we must—most of the women of the world persist far from the heart of the usual Women's Studies syllabus.

Similarly, the typical Black History course will slide by the majority experience it pretends to represent. For example, Mary McLeod Bethune will scarcely receive as much attention as Nat Turner, even though Black women who bravely and efficiently provided for the education of Black people hugely outnumber those few Black men who led successful or doomed rebellions against slavery. In fact, Mary McLeod Bethune may not receive even honorable mention because Black History too often apes those ridiculous white history courses which produce such dangerous gibberish as The Sheraton British Colonial "history" of the Bahamas. Both Black and white history courses exclude from their central consideration those people who neither killed nor conquered anyone as the means to new identity, those people who took care of every one of the people who wanted to become "a person," those people who still take care of the life at issue: the ones who wash and who feed and who teach and who diligently decorate straw hats and bags with all of their historically unrequired gentle love: the women.

Oh the old rugged cross
on a hill far away
Well I cherish the old rugged cross

It's Good Friday in the Bahamas. Seventy-eight degrees in the shade. Except for Sheraton territory, everything's closed.

It so happens that for truly secular reasons I've been fasting for three days. My hunger has now reached nearly violent proportions. In the hotel sandwich shop, the Black woman handling the counter complains about the tourists; why isn't the shop closed and why don't the tourists stop eating for once in their lives. I'm famished and order chicken salad and cottage cheese and lettuce and tomato and a hard boiled egg and a hot cross bun and apple juice.

She eyes me with disgust.

45 To be sure the timing of my stomach offends her serious religious practices. Neither one of us apologizes to the other. She seasons the chicken salad

to the peppery max while I listen to the loud radio gospel she plays to console herself. It's a country Black version of "The Old Rugged Cross."

As I heave much chicken into my mouth, tears start. It's not the pepper. I am, after all, a West Indian daughter. It's the Good Friday music that dominates the humid atmosphere.

Well I cherish the old rugged cross

And I am back, faster than a 747, in Brooklyn, in the home of my parents where we are wondering, as we do every year, if the sky will darken until Christ has been buried in the tomb. The sky should darken if God is in His heavens. And then, around 3 p.m., at the conclusion of our mournful church service at the neighborhood St. Phillips, and even while we dumbly stare at the black cloth covering the gold altar and the slender unlit candles, the sun should return through the high gothic windows and vindicate our waiting faith that the Lord will rise again, on Easter.

How I used to bow my head at the very name of Jesus: ecstatic to abase myself in deference to His majesty.

My mouth is full of salad. I can't seem to eat quickly enough. I can't think how I should lessen the offense of my appetite. The other Black woman on the premises, the one who disapprovingly prepared this very tasty break from my fast, makes no remark. She is no fool. This is a job that she needs. I suppose she notices that at least I included a hot cross bun among my edibles. That's something in my favor. I decide that's enough.

I am suddenly eager to walk off the food. Up a fairly steep hill I walk without hurrying. Through the pastel desolation of the little town, the road brings me to a confectionary pink and white plantation house. At the gates, an unnecessarily large statue of Christopher Columbus faces me down, or tries to. His hand is fisted to one hip. I look back at him, laugh without deference, and turn left.

It's time to pack it up. Catch my plane. I scan the hotel room for things not to forget. There's that white report card on the bureau. 50

"Dear Guests:" it says, under the name "Olive." "I am your maid for the day. Please rate me: Excellent. Good. Average. Poor. Thank you."

I tuck this momento from the Sheraton British Colonial into my notebook. How would "Olive" rate *me*? What would it mean for us to seem "good" to each other? What would that rating require?

But I am hastening to leave. Neither turtle soup nor kidney pie nor any conch shell delight shall delay my departure. I have rested, here, in the Bahamas, and I'm ready to return to my usual job, usual work. But the skin on my body has changed and so has my mind. On the Delta flight home I realize I am burning up, indeed.

So far as I can see, the usual race and class concepts of connection, or gender assumptions of unity, do not apply very well. I doubt that they ever did. Otherwise why would Black folks forever bemoan our lack of solidarity when the deal turns real. And if unity on the basis of sexual oppression is something natural, then why do we women, the majority people on the planet, still have a problem?

55   The plane's ready for takeoff. I fasten my seatbelt and let the tumult inside my head run free. Yes: race and class and gender remain as real as the weather. But what they must mean about the contact between two individuals is less obvious and, like the weather, not predictable.

And when these factors of race and class and gender absolutely collapse is whenever you try to use them as automatic concepts of connection. They may serve well as indicators of commonly felt conflict, but as elements of connection they seem about as reliable as precipitation probability for the day after the night before the day.

It occurs to me that much organizational grief could be avoided if people understood that partnership in misery does not necessarily provide for partnership for change. *When we get the monsters off our backs all of us may want to run in very different directions.*

And not only that: even though both "Olive" and "I" live inside a conflict neither one of us created, and even though both of us therefore hurt inside that conflict, I may be one of the monsters she needs to eliminate from her universe and, in a sense, she may be one of the monsters in mine.

I am reaching for the words to describe the difference between a common identity that has been imposed and the individual identity any one of us will choose, once she gains that chance.

60   That difference is the one that keeps us stupid in the face of new, specific information about somebody else with whom we are supposed to have a connection because a third party, hostile to both of us, has worked it so that the two of us, like it or not, share a common enemy. *What happens beyond the idea of that enemy and beyond the consequences of that enemy?*

I am saying that the ultimate connection cannot be the enemy. The ultimate connection must be the need that we find between us. It is not only who you are, in other words, but what we can do for each other that will determine the connection.

I am flying back to my job. I have been teaching contemporary women's poetry this semester. One quandary I have set myself to explore with my students is the one of taking responsibility without power. We had been wrestling ideas to the floor for several sessions when a young Black woman, a South African, asked me for help after class.

Sokutu told me she was "in a trance" and she'd been unable to eat for two weeks.

"What's going on?" I asked her, even as my eyes startled at her trembling and emaciated appearance.

65   "My husband. He drinks all the time. He beats me up. I go to the hospital. I can't eat. I don't know what/anything."

In my office, she described her situation. I did not dare let her sense my fear and horror. She was dragging about, hour by hour, in dread. Her husband, a young Black South African, was drinking himself into more and more deadly violence with her.

Sokutu told me how she could keep nothing down. She already weighed 90 pounds at the outside, as she spoke to me. She'd already been hospitalized as a result of her husband's battering rage.

I knew both of them because I had organized a campus group to aid the liberation struggles of Southern Africa.

Nausea rose in my throat. What about this presumable connection: this husband and this wife fled from that homeland of hatred against them, and now what? He was destroying himself. If not stopped, he would certainly murder his wife.

She needed a doctor right away. It was a medical emergency. She needed   70
protection. It was a security crisis. She needed refuge for battered wives and personal therapy and legal counsel. She needed a friend.

I got on the phone and called every number in the campus directory that I could imagine might prove helpful. Nothing worked. There were no institutional resources designed to meet her enormous, multifaceted, and ordinary woman's need.

I called various students. I asked the Chairperson of the English Department for advice. I asked everyone for help.

Finally, another one of my students, Cathy, a young Irish woman active in campus IRA activities, responded. She asked for further details. I gave them to her.

"Her husband," Cathy told me, "is an alcoholic. You have to understand about alcoholics. It's not the same as anything else. And it's a disease you can't treat any old way."

I listened, fearfully. Did this mean there was nothing we could do?   75

"That's not what I'm saying" she said. "But you do have to keep the alcoholic part of the thing central in everyone's mind, otherwise the husband will kill her. Or he'll kill himself."

She spoke calmly, I felt there was nothing to do but assume she knew what she was talking about.

"Will you come with me?" I asked her, after a silence. "Will you come with me and help us figure out what to do next?"

Cathy said she would but she felt shy: Sokutu comes from South Africa. What would she think about Cathy.

"I don't know," I said, "But let's go."   80

We left to find a dormitory room for the young battered wife.

It is late, now, and dark outside.

On Cathy's VW that I followed behind with my own car, was the sticker that reads BOBBY SANDS FREE AT LAST. My eyes blurred as I read and reread the words. This was another connection: Bobby Sands and Martin Luther King, Jr. and who would believe it? I would not have believed it; I grew up terrorized by Irish kids who introduced me to the word "nigga."

And here I was following an Irish woman to the room of a Black South African. We were going to that room to try and save a life together.

85   When we reached the little room, we found ourselves awkward and large. Sokutu attempted to treat us with the utmost courtesy, as though we were honored guests. She seemed surprised by Cathy, but mostly Sokutu was flushed with relief and joy because we were there, with her.

I did not know how we should ever terminate her heartfelt courtesy and address, directly, the reason for our visit: her starvation and her extreme physical danger.

Finally, Cathy sat on the floor and reached out her hands to Sokutu.

"I'm here," she said quietly. "Because June has told me what has happened to you. And I know what it is. Your husband is an alcoholic. He has a disease. I know what it is. My father was an alcoholic. He killed himself. He almost killed my mother. I want to be your friend."

"Oh," was the only small sound that escaped from Sokutu's mouth. And then she embraced the other student. And then everything changed and I watched all of this happen so I know that this happened: this connection.

90   And after we called the police and exchanged phone numbers and plans were made for the night and for the next morning, the young South African woman walked down the dormitory hallway, saying goodbye and saying thank you to us.

I walked behind them, the young Irish woman and the young South African, and I saw them walking as sisters walk, hugging each other, whispering and sure of each other and I felt how it was not who they were but what they both know and what they were both preparing to do about what they know that was going to make them both free at last.

And I look out the windows of the plane and I see clouds that would not kill me and I know that someday soon other clouds may erupt to kill us all.

And I tell the stewardess No thanks to the cocktails she offers me. But I look about the cabin at the hundred strangers drinking as they fly and I think even here and even now I must make the connection real between me and these strangers everywhere before those other clouds unify this ragged bunch of us, too late.

12

Being Both Privileged and Oppressed

■▪■▪■

TOWARD A NEW VISION: RACE, CLASS, AND GENDER AS CATEGORIES OF ANALYSIS AND CONNECTION

Patricia Hill Collins

The true focus of revolutionary change is never merely the oppressive situations which
we seek to escape, but that piece of the oppressor which is planted deep within us.
—AUDRE LORDE, *Sister Outsider,* 123

Audre Lorde's statement raises a troublesome issue for scholars and activists working for social change. While many of us have little difficulty assessing our own victimization within some major system of oppression, whether it be by race, social class, religion, sexual orientation, ethnicity, age or gender, we typically fail to see how our thoughts and actions uphold someone else's subordination. Thus, white feminists routinely point with confidence to their oppression as women but resist seeing how much their white skin privileges them. African-Americans who possess eloquent analyses of racism often persist in viewing poor White women as symbols of white power. The radical left fares little better. "If only people of color and women could see their true class interests," they argue, "class solidarity would eliminate racism and sexism." In essence, each group identifies a type of oppression with which it feels most comfortable as being fundamental and classifies all other types as being of lesser importance.

Oppression is full of such contradictions. Errors in political judgment that we make concerning how we teach our courses, what we tell our children, and which organizations are worthy of our time, talents and financial support flow smoothly from errors in theoretical analysis about the nature of oppression and activism. Once we realize that there are few pure victims or oppressors, and that each one of us derives varying amounts of penalty and privilege from the multiple systems of oppression that frame our lives, then we will be in a position to see the need for new ways of thought and action.

To get at the "piece of the oppressor which is planted deep within each of us," we need at least two things. First, we need new visions of what oppression is, new categories of analysis that are inclusive of race, class, and gender as distinctive yet interlocking structures of oppression. Adhering to a stance of comparing and ranking oppressions—the proverbial, "I'm more oppressed than you"—locks us all into a dangerous dance of competing for attention, resources, and theoretical supremacy. Instead, I suggest that we examine our different experiences within the more fundamental relationship of domination and subordination. To focus on the particular arrangements that race or class or gender take in our time and place without seeing these structures as sometimes parallel and sometimes interlocking dimensions of the more fundamental relationship of domination and subordination may temporarily ease our consciences. But while such thinking may lead to short term social reforms, it is simply inadequate for the task of bringing about long term social transformation.

While race, class and gender as categories of analysis are essential in helping us understand the structural bases of domination and subordination, new ways of thinking that are not accompanied by new ways of acting offer incomplete prospects for change. To get at that "piece of the oppressor which is planted deep within each of us," we also need to change our daily behavior. Currently, we are all enmeshed in a complex web of problematic relationships that grant our mirror images full human subjectivity while stereotyping and objectifying those most different than ourselves. We often assume that the people we work with, teach, send our children to school with, and sit next to . . . will act and feel in prescribed ways because they belong to given race, social class or gender categories. These judgments by category must be replaced with fully human relationships that transcend the legitimate differences created by race, class and gender as categories of analysis. We require new categories of connection, new visions of what our relationships with one another can be. . . .

5   [This discussion] addresses this need for new patterns of thought and action. I focus on two basic questions. First, how can we reconceptualize race, class and gender as categories of analysis? Second, how can we transcend the barriers created by our experiences with race, class and gender oppression in order to build the types of coalitions essential for social exchange? To address these question I contend that we must acquire both new theories of how race, class and gender have shaped the experiences not just of women of color, but of all groups. Moreover, we must see the connections between these categories of analysis and the personal issues in our everyday lives, particularly our scholarship, our teaching and our relationships with our colleagues and students. As

Audre Lorde points out, change starts with self, and relationships that we have with those around us must always be the primary site for social change.

HOW CAN WE RECONCEPTUALIZE RACE, CLASS AND GENDER AS CATEGORIES OF *ANALYSIS*?

To me, we must shift our discourse away from additive analyses of oppression (Spelman 1982; Collins 1989). Such approaches are typically based on two premises. First, they depend on either/or, dichotomous thinking. Persons, things and ideas are conceptualized in terms of their opposites. For example, Black/White, man/woman, thought/feeling, and fact/opinion are defined in oppositional terms. Thought and feeling are not seen as two different and interconnected ways of approaching truth that can coexist in scholarship and teaching. Instead, feeling is defined as antithetical to reason, as its opposite. In spite of the fact that we all have "both/and" identities (I am both a college professor and a mother—I don't stop being a mother when I drop my child off at school, or forget everything I learned while scrubbing the toilet), we persist in trying to classify each other in either/or categories. I live each day as an African-American woman—a race/gender specific experience. And I am not alone. Everyone in this room has a race/gender/class specific identity. Either/or, dichotomous thinking is especially troublesome when applied to theories of oppression because every individual must be classified as being either oppressed or not oppressed. The both/and position of simultaneously being oppressed and oppressor becomes conceptually impossible.

A second premise of additive analyses of oppression is that these dichotomous differences must be ranked. One side of the dichotomy is typically labeled dominant and the other subordinate. Thus, Whites rule Blacks, men are deemed superior to women, and reason is seen as being preferable to emotion. Applying this premise to discussions of oppression leads to the assumption that oppression can be quantified, and that some groups are oppressed more than others. I am frequently asked, "Which has been most oppressive to you, your status as a Black person or your status as a woman?" What I am really being asked to do is divide myself into little boxes and rank my various statuses. If I experience oppression as a both/and phenomenon, why should I analyze it any differently?

Additive analyses of oppression rest squarely on the twin pillars of either/or thinking and the necessity to qualify and rank all relationships in order to know where one stands. Such approaches typically see African-American woman as being more oppressed than everyone else because the majority of Black women experience the negative effects of race, class and gender oppression simultaneously. In essence, if you add together separate oppressions, you are left with a grand oppression greater than the sum of its parts.

I am not denying that specific groups experience oppression more harshly than others—lynching is certainly objectively worse than being held up as a sex object. But we must be careful not to confuse this issue of the saliency of one type of oppression in people's lives with a theoretical stance positing the interlocking nature of oppression. Race, class and gender may all structure a situation but may not be equally visible and/or important in people's self-definitions. In certain contexts, such as the antebellum American South and contemporary South America, racial oppression is more visibly salient, while in other contexts, such as Haiti, El Salvador and Nicaragua, social class oppression may be more apparent. For middle class White women, gender may assume experiential primacy unavailable to poor Hispanic women struggling with the ongoing issues of low paid jobs and the frustrations of the welfare bureaucracy. This recognition that one category may have salience over another for a given time and place does not minimize the theoretical importance of assuming that race, class and gender as categories of analysis structure all relationships.

10   In order to move toward new visions of what oppression is, I think that we need to ask new questions. How are relationships of domination and subordination structured and maintained in the American political economy? How do race, class and gender function as parallel and interlocking systems that shape this basic relationship of domination and subordination? Questions such as these promise to move us away from futile theoretical struggles concerned with ranking oppressions and towards analyses that assume race, class and gender are all present in any given setting, even if one appears more visible and salient than the others. Our task becomes redefined as one of reconceptualizing oppression by uncovering the connections among race, class and gender as categories of analysis.

1. Institutional Dimension of Oppression

Sandra Harding's contention that gender oppression is structured along three main dimensions—the institutional, the symbolic, and the individual—offers a useful model for more comprehensive analysis encompassing race, class and gender oppression (Harding 1989). Systemic relationships of domination and subordination structured through social institutions such as schools, businesses, hospitals, the work place, and government agencies represent the institutional dimension of oppression. Racism, sexism and elitism all have concrete institutional locations. Even though the workings of the institutional dimension of oppression are often obscured with ideologies claiming equality of opportunity, in actuality, race, class and gender place Asian-American women, Native American men, White men, African-American women, and other groups in distinct institutional niches with varying degrees of penalty and privilege.

Even though I realize that many in the [first Bush] administration would not share this assumption, let us assume that the institutions of American society discriminate whether by design or by accident. While many of us are familiar with how race, gender and class operate separately to structure inequality, I want to focus on how these three systems interlock in structuring the institutional dimension of oppression. To get at the interlocking nature of race, class and gender, I want you to think about the antebellum plantation as a guiding metaphor for a variety of American social institutions. Even though slavery is typically analyzed as a racist institution, and occasionally as a class institution, I suggest that slavery was a race, class, gender specific institution. Removing any one piece from our analysis diminishes our understanding of the true nature of relations of domination and subordination under slavery.

Slavery was a profoundly patriarchal institution. It rested on the dual tenets of White male authority and White male property, a joining of the political and economic within the institution of the family. Heterosexism was assumed and all Whites were expected to marry. Control over affluent White women's sexuality remained key to slavery's survival because property was to be passed on to the legitimate heirs of the slave owner. Ensuring affluent White women's virginity and chastity was deeply intertwined with maintenance of property relations.

Under slavery, we see varying levels of institutional protection given to affluent White women, working class and poor White women, and enslaved African women. Poor White women enjoyed few of the protections held out to their upper class sisters. Moreover, the devalued status of Black women was key in keeping all White women in their assigned places. Controlling Black women's fertility was also key to the continuation of slavery, for children born to slave mothers themselves were slaves.

African-American women shared the devalued status of chattel with their husbands, fathers and sons. Racism stripped Blacks as a group of legal rights, education and control over their own persons. African-Americans could be whipped, branded, sold, or killed, not because they were poor, or because they were women, but because they were Black. Racism ensured that Blacks would continue to serve Whites and suffer economic exploitation at the hands of all Whites. *15*

So we have a very interesting chain of command on the plantation—the affluent White master as the reigning patriarch, his White wife helpmate to serve him, help him manage his property and bring up his heirs, his faithful servants whose production and reproduction were tied to requirements of the capitalist political economy, and largely propertyless, working class White men and women watching from afar. In essence, the foundations for the contemporary roles of elite White women, poor Black women, working class White men, and a series of other groups can be seen in stark relief in this fundamental American social institution. While Blacks experienced the most harsh treatment under slavery, and thus made slavery clearly visible as a racist institution, race, class, and gender interlocked in structuring slavery's systemic organization of domination and subordination.

Even today, the plantation remains a compelling metaphor for institutional oppression. Certainly the actual conditions of oppression are not as severe now as they were then. To argue, as some do, that things have not changed all that much denigrates the achievements of those who struggled for social change before us. But the basic relationships among Black men, Black women, elite White women, elite White men, working class White men and working class White women as groups remain essentially intact.

A brief analysis of key American social institutions most controlled by elite White men should convince us of the interlocking nature of race, class and gender in structuring the institutional dimension of oppression. For example, if you are from an American college or university, is your campus a modern plantation? Who controls your university's political economy? Are elite White men over represented among the upper administrators and trustees controlling your university's finances and policies? Are elite White men being joined by growing numbers of elite White women helpmates? What kinds of people are in your classrooms grooming the next generation who will occupy these and other decision-making positions? Who are the support staff that produce the mass mailings, order the supplies, fix the leaky pipes? Do African-Americans, Hispanics or other people of color form the majority of the invisible workers who feed you, wash your dishes, and clean up your offices and libraries after everyone else has gone home?

If your college is anything like mine, you know the answers to these questions. You may be affiliated with an institution that has Hispanic women as vice-presidents for finance, or substantial numbers of Black men among the faculty. If so, you are fortunate. Much more typical are colleges where a modified version of the plantation as a metaphor for the institutional dimension of oppression survives.

2. The Symbolic Dimension of Oppression

20 Widespread, societally-sanctioned ideologies used to justify relations of domination and subordination comprise the symbolic dimension of oppression. Central to this process is the use of stereotypical or controlling images of diverse race, class and gender groups. In order to assess the power of this dimension of oppression, I want you to make a list, either on paper or in your head, of "masculine" and "feminine" characteristics. If your list is anything like that compiled by most people, it reflects some variation of the following:

Masculine	Feminine
aggressive	passive
leader	follower
rational	emotional
strong	weak
intellectual	physical

Not only does this reflect either/or dichotomous thinking and the need to rank both sides of the dichotomy, but ask yourself exactly which men and women you had in mind when compiling these characteristics. This list applies almost exclusively to middle class White men and women. The allegedly "masculine" qualities that you probably listed are only acceptable when exhibited by elite White men, or when used by Black and Hispanic men against each other or against women of color. Aggressive Black and Hispanic men are seen as dangerous, not powerful, and are often penalized when they exhibit any of the allegedly "masculine" characteristics. Working class and poor white men fare slightly better and are also denied the allegedly "masculine" symbols of leadership, intellectual competence, and human rationality. Women of color and working class and poor White women are also not represented on this list, for they have never had the luxury of being "ladies." What appear to be universal categories representing all men and women instead are unmasked as being applicable to only a small group.

It is important to see how the symbolic images applied to different race, class and gender groups interact in maintaining systems of domination and subordination. If I were to ask you to repeat the same assignment, only this time, by making separate lists for Black men, Black women, Hispanic women, and Hispanic men, I suspect that your gender symbolism would be quite different. In comparing all of the lists, you might begin to see the interdependence of symbols applied to all groups. For example, the elevated images of White womanhood need devalued images of Black womanhood in order to maintain credibility.

While the above exercise reveals the interlocking nature of race, class and gender in structuring the symbolic dimension of oppression, part of its importance lies in demonstrating how race, class and gender pervade a wide range of what appears to be universal language. Attending to diversity in our scholarship, in our teaching, and in our daily lives provides a new angle of vision on interpretations of reality thought to be natural, normal and "true." Moreover, viewing images of masculinity and femininity as universal gender symbolism, rather than as symbolic images that are race, class and gender specific, renders the experience of people of color and of non-privileged White women and men invisible. One way to dehumanize an individual or a group is to deny the reality of their experiences. So when we refuse to deal with race or class because they do not appear to be directly relevant to gender, we are actually becoming part of someone else's problem.

Assuming that everyone is affected differently by the same interlocking set of symbolic images allows us to move forward toward new analyses. Women of color and White women have different relationships to White male authority and this difference explains the distinct gender symbolism applied to both groups. Black women encounter controlling images such as the mammy, the matriarch, the mule and the whore, that encourage others to reject us as fully human people. Ironically, the negative nature of these images simultaneously encourages us to reject them. In contrast, White women are offered seductive images, those that promise to reward them for supporting the status quo. And yet seductive images can be equally controlling. Consider, for example, the views of Nancy White, a 73-year old Black woman, concerning images of rejection and seduction:

> My mother used to say that the black woman is the white man's mule and the white woman is his dog. Now, she said that to say this: we do the heavy work and get beat whether we do it well or not. But the white woman is closer to the master and he pats them on the head and lets them sleep in the house, but he ain't gon' treat neither one like he was dealing with a person. (Gwaltney, 148)

25   Both sets of images stimulate particular political stances. By broadening the analysis beyond the confines of race, we can see the varying levels of rejection and seduction available to each of us due to our race, class and gender identity. Each of us lives with an allotted portion of institutional privilege and penalty, and with varying levels of rejection and seduction inherent in the symbolic images applied to us. This is the context in which we make our choices. Taken together, the institutional and symbolic dimensions of oppression create a structural backdrop against which all of us live our lives.

3. The Individual Dimension of Oppression

Whether we benefit or not, we all live within institutions that reproduce race, class and gender oppression. Even if we never have any contact with members of other race, class and gender groups, we all encounter images of these groups and are exposed to the symbolic meanings attached to those images. On this dimension of oppression, our individual biographies vary tremendously. As a result of our institutional symbolic statuses, all of our choices became political acts.

Each of us must come to terms with the multiple ways in which race, class and gender as categories of analysis frame our individual biographies. I have lived my entire life as an African-American woman from a working class family and this basic fact has had a profound impact on my personal biography. Imagine how different your life might have been if you were born Black, or White, or poor, or a different race/class/gender group than the one with which you are most familiar. The institutional treatment you have received and the symbolic meanings attached to your very existence might differ dramatically from what you now consider to be natural, normal and part of everyday life. You might be the same, but your personal biography might have been quite different.

I believe that each of us carries around the cumulative effect of our lives within multiple structures of oppression. If you want to see how much you have been affected by this whole thing, I ask you one simple question—who are your close friends? Who are the people with whom you share your hopes, dreams, vulnerabilities, fears, and victories? Do they look like you? If they are all the same, circumstance may be the cause. For the first seven years of my life I saw only low income Black people. My friends from those years reflected the composition of my community. But now that I am an adult, can the defense of circumstance explain the patterns of people that I trust as my friends and colleagues? When given other alternatives, if my friends and colleagues reflect the homogeneity of one race, class and gender group, then these categories of analysis have indeed become barriers to connection.

I am not suggesting that people are doomed to follow the paths laid out to them by race, class and gender as categories of analysis. While these three structures certainly frame my opportunity structure, I as an individual always have the choice of accepting things as they are, or trying to change them. As Nikki Giovanni points out, "we've got to live in the real world. If we don't like the world we're living in, change it. And if we can't change it, we change ourselves. We can do something" (Tate 1983, 68). While a piece of the oppressor may be planted deep within each of us, we each have the choice of accepting that piece or challenging it as part of the "true focus of revolutionary change."

HOW CAN WE TRANSCEND THE BARRIERS CREATED BY OUR EXPERIENCES WITH RACE, CLASS AND GENDER OPPRESSION IN ORDER TO BUILD THE TYPES OF COALITIONS ESSENTIAL FOR SOCIAL CHANGE?

Reconceptualizing oppression and seeing the barriers created by race, class and gender as interlocking categories of analysis is a vital first step. But we must transcend these barriers by moving toward race, class and gender as categories of connection, by building relationships and coalitions that will bring about social change. What are some the issues involved in doing this?

1. Differences in Power and Privilege

First, we must recognize that our differing experiences with oppression create problems in the relationships among us. Each of us lives within a system that vests us with varying levels of power and privilege. These differences in power, whether structured along axes of race, class, gender, age or sexual orientation, frame our relationships. African-American writer June Jordan describes her discomfort on a Caribbean vacation with Olive, the Black woman who cleaned her room:

> ... even though both "Olive" and "I" live inside a conflict neither one of us created, and even though both of us therefore hurt inside that conflict, I may be one of the monsters she needs to eliminate from her universe and, in a sense, she may be one of the monsters in mine. (1985, 47)

Differences in power constrain our ability to connect with one another even when we think we are engaged in dialogue across differences. Let me give you an example. One year, the students in my course "Sociology of the Black Community" got into a heated discussion about the reasons for the upsurge of racial incidents on college campuses. Black students complained vehemently about the apathy and resistance they felt most White students expressed about examining their own racism. Mark, a White male student, found their comments particularly unsettling. After claiming that all the Black people he had ever known had expressed no such beliefs to him, he questioned how representative the viewpoints of his fellow students actually were. When pushed further, Mark revealed that he had participated in conversations over the years with the Black domestic worker employed by his family. Since she had never expressed such strong beliefs about White racism, Mark was genuinely shocked by class discussions. Ask yourselves whether that domestic worker was in a position to speak freely. Would it have been wise for her to do so in a situation where the power between the two parties was so unequal?

In extreme cases, members of privileged groups can erase the very presence of the less privileged. When I first moved to Cincinnati, my family and I went on a picnic at a local park. Picnicking next to us was a family of White Appalachians. When I went to push my daughter on the swings, several of the children came over. They had missing, yellowed and broken teeth, they wore old clothing and their poverty was evident. I was shocked. Growing up in a large eastern city, I had never seen such awful poverty among Whites. The segregated neighborhoods where I grew up made White poverty all but invisible. More importantly, the privileges attached to my newly acquired social class position allowed me to ignore and minimize the poverty among Whites that I did encounter. My reactions to those children made me realize how confining such phrases as "well, at least they're not Black," had become for me. In learning to grant human subjectivity to the Black victims of poverty, I had simultaneously learned to demean White victims of poverty. By applying categories of race to the objective conditions confronting me, I was qualifying and ranking oppressions and missing the very real suffering which, in fact, is the real issue.

One common pattern of relationships across differences in power is one that I label "voyeurism." From the perspective of the privileged, the lives of people of color, of the poor, and of women are interesting for their entertainment value. The privileged become voyeurs, passive onlookers who do not relate to the less powerful, but who are interested in seeing how the "different" live. Over the years, I have heard numerous African-American students complain about professors who never call on them except when a so-called Black issue is being discussed. The students' interest in discussing race or qualifications for doing so appear unimportant to the professor's efforts to use Black students' experiences as stories to make the material come alive for the White student audience. Asking Black students to perform on cue and provide a Black experience for their white classmates can be seen as voyeurism at its worst.

35   Members of subordinate groups do not willingly participate in such exchanges but often do so because members of dominant groups control the

institutional and symbolic apparatuses of oppression. Racial/ethnic groups, women, and the poor have never had the luxury of being voyeurs of the lives of the privileged. Our ability to survive in hostile settings has hinged on our ability to learn intricate details about the behavior and world view of the powerful and adjust our behavior accordingly. I need only point to the difference in perception of those men and women in abusive relationships. Where men can view their girlfriends and wives as sex objects, helpmates and a collection of stereotyped categories of voyeurism—women must be attuned to every nuance of their partners' behavior. Are women "naturally" better in relating to people with more power than themselves, or have circumstances mandated that men and women develop different skills? . . .

Coming from a tradition where most relationships across difference are squarely rooted in relations of domination and subordination, we have much less experience relating to people as different but equal. The classroom is potentially one powerful and safe space where dialogues among individuals of unequal power relationships can occur. The relationship between Mark, the student in my class, and the domestic worker is typical of a whole series of relationships that people have when they relate across differences in power and privilege. The relationship among Mark and his classmates represents the power of the classroom to minimize those differences so that people of different levels of power can use race, class and gender as categories of analysis in order to generate meaningful dialogues. In this case, the classroom equalized racial difference so that the Black students who normally felt silenced spoke out. White students like Mark, generally unaware of how they had been privileged by their whiteness, lost that privilege in the classroom and thus became open to genuine dialogue. . . .

2. Coalitions Around Common Causes

A second issue in building relationships and coalitions essential for social change concerns knowing the real reasons for coalition. Just what brings people together? One powerful catalyst fostering group solidarity is the presence of a common enemy. African-American, Hispanic, Asian-American, and women's studies all share the common intellectual heritage of challenging what passes for certified knowledge in the academy. But politically expedient relationships and coalitions like these are fragile because, as June Jordan points out:

> It occurs to me that much organizational grief could be
> avoided if people understood that partnership in misery does
> not necessarily provide for partnership for change: When we
> get the monsters off our backs all of us may want to run in
> very different directions. (1985, 47)

Sharing a common cause assists individuals and groups in maintaining relationships that transcend their differences. Building effective coalitions involves struggling to hear one another and developing empathy for each other's points of view. The coalitions that I have been involved in that lasted and that worked have been those where commitment to a specific issue mandated collaboration as the best strategy for addressing the issue at hand.

Several years ago, masters degree in hand, I chose to teach in an inner city, parochial school in danger of closing. The money was awful, the conditions were poor, but the need was great. In my job, I had to work with a range of individuals who, on the surface, had very little in common. We had White nuns, Black middle class graduate students, Blacks from the "community," some of whom had been incarcerated and/or were affiliated with a range of federal anti-poverty programs. Parents formed another part of this community, Harvard faculty another, and a few well-meaning White liberals from Colorado were sprinkled in for good measure.

40   As you might imagine, tension was high. Initially, our differences seemed insurmountable. But as time passed, we found a common bond that we each brought to the school. In spite of profound differences in our personal biographies, differences that in other settings would have hampered our ability to relate to one another, we found that we were all deeply committed to the education of Black children. By learning to value each other's commitment and by recognizing that we each had different skills that were essential to actualizing that commitment, we built an effective coalition around a common cause. Our school was successful, and the children we taught benefited from the diversity we offered them.

. . . None of us alone has a comprehensive vision of how race, class and gender operate as categories of analysis or how they might be used as categories of connection. Our personal biographies offer us partial views. Few of us can manage to study race, class and gender simultaneously. Instead, we each know more about some dimensions of this larger story and less about others. . . . Just as the members of the school had special skills to offer to the task of building the school, we have areas of specialization and expertise, whether scholarly, theoretical, pedagogical or within areas of race, class or gender. We do not all have to do the same thing in the same way. Instead, we must support each other's efforts, realizing that they are all part of the larger enterprise of bringing about social change.

3. Building Empathy

A third issue involved in building the types of relationships and coalitions essential for social change concerns the issue of individual accountability. Race, class and gender oppression form the structural backdrop against which we frame our relationship—these are the forces that encourage us to substitute voyeurism . . . for fully human relationships. But while we may not have created this situation, we are each responsible for making individual, personal choices concerning which elements of race, class and gender oppression we will accept and which we will work to change.

One essential component of this accountability involves developing empathy for the experiences of individuals and groups different than ourselves.

Empathy begins with taking an interest in the facts of other people's lives, both as individuals and as groups. If you care about me, you should want to know not only the details of my personal biography but a sense of how race, class and gender as categories of analysis created the institutional and symbolic backdrop for my personal biography. How can you hope to assess my character without knowing the details of the circumstances I face?

Moreover, by taking a theoretical stance that we have all been affected by race, class and gender as categories of analysis that have structured our treatment, we open up possibilities for using those same constructs as categories of connection in building empathy. For example, I have a good White woman friend with whom I share common interests and beliefs. But we know that our racial differences have provided us with different experiences. So we talk about them. We do not assume that because I am Black, race has only affected me and not her or that because I am a Black woman, race neutralizes the effect of gender in my life while accenting it in hers. We take those same categories of analysis that have created cleavages in our lives, in this case, categories of race and gender, and use them as categories of connection in building empathy for each other's experiences.

Finding common causes and building empathy is difficult, no matter which side of privilege we inhabit. Building empathy from the dominant side of privilege is difficult, simply because individuals from privileged backgrounds are not encouraged to do so. For example, in order for those of you who are White to develop empathy for the experiences of people of color, you must grapple with how your white skin has privileged you. This is difficult to do, because it not only entails the intellectual process of seeing how whiteness is elevated in institutions and symbols, but it also involves the often painful process of seeing how your whiteness has shaped your personal biography. Intellectual stances against the institutional and symbolic dimensions of racism are generally easier to maintain than sustained self-reflection about how racism has shaped all of our individual biographies. Were and are your fathers, uncles, and grandfathers really more capable than mine, or can their accomplishments be explained in part by the racism members of my family experienced? Did your mothers stand silently by and watch all of this happen? More importantly, how have they passed on the benefits of their whiteness to you?

These are difficult questions, and I have tremendous respect for my colleagues and students who are trying to answer them. Since there is no compelling reason to examine the source and meaning of one's own privilege, I know that those who do so have freely chosen this stance. They are making conscious efforts to root out the piece of the oppressor planted within them. To me, they are entitled to the support of people of color in their efforts. Men who declare themselves feminists, members of the middle class who ally themselves with anti-poverty struggles, heterosexuals who support gays and lesbians, are all trying to grow, and their efforts place them far ahead of the majority who never think of engaging in such important struggles.

Building empathy from the subordinate side of privilege is also difficult, but for different reasons. Members of the subordinate groups are understandably reluctant to abandon a basic mistrust of members of powerful groups because this basic mistrust has traditionally been central to their survival. As a Black woman, it would be foolish for me to assume that White women, or Black men, or White men, or any other group with a history of exploiting African-American women have my best interests at heart. These groups enjoy varying amounts of privilege over me and therefore I must carefully watch them and be prepared for a relation of domination and subordination.

Like the privileged, members of subordinate groups must also work toward replacing judgments by category with new ways of thinking and acting. Refusing to do so stifles prospects for effective coalition and social change. Let me use another example from my own experiences. When I was an undergraduate, I had little time or patience for the theorizing of the privileged. My initial years at a private, elite institution were difficult, not because the coursework was challenging (it was, but that wasn't what distracted me) or because I had to work while my classmates lived on family allowances (I was used to work). The adjustment was difficult because I was surrounded by so many people who took their privilege for granted. Most of them felt entitled to their wealth. That astounded me.

I remember one incident of watching a White woman down the hall in my dormitory trying to pick out which sweater to wear. The sweaters were piled up on her bed in all the colors of the rainbow, sweater after sweater. She asked my advice in a way that let me know choosing a sweater was one of the most important decisions she had to make on a daily basis. Standing knee-deep in her sweaters, I realized how different our lives were. She did not have to worry about maintaining a solid academic average so that she could receive financial aid. Because she was in the majority, she was not treated as a representative of her race. She did not have to consider how her classroom comments or basic existence on campus contributed to the treatment her group would receive. Her allowance protected her from having to work, so she was free to spend her time studying, partying, or in her case, worrying about which sweater to wear. The degree of inequality in our lives and her unquestioned sense of entitlement concerning that inequality offended me. For a while, I categorized all affluent White women as being superficial, arrogant, overly concerned with material possessions, and part of my problem. But had I continued to classify people this way, I would have missed out on making some very good friends whose discomfort with their inherited or acquired social class privileges pushes them to examine their position.

50   Since I opened with the words of Audre Lorde, it seems appropriate to close with another of her ideas. . . .

> Each of us is called upon to take a stand. So in these days
> ahead, as we examine ourselves and each other, our works, our
> fears, our differences, our sisterhood and survivals, I urge you to

tackle what is most difficult for us all, self-scrutiny of our complacencies, the idea that since each of us believes she is on the side of right, she need not examine her position. (1985)

I urge you to examine your position.

REFERENCES

Butler, Johnnella. 1989. "Difficult Dialogues." *The Women's Review of Books* 6, no. 5.

Collins, Patricia Hill. 1989. "The Social Construction of Black Feminist Thought." *Signs.* Summer 1989.

Harding, Sandra. 1986. *The Science Question in Feminism.* Ithaca, New York: Cornell University Press.

Gwalatney, John Langston. 1980. *Drylongso: A Self-Portrait of Black America.* New York: Vintage.

Jordan, June. 1985. *On Call: Political Essays.* Boston: South End Press.

Lorde, Audre. 1984. *Sister Outsider.* Trumansburg, New York: The Crossing Press.

———. 1985 "Sisterhood and Survival." Keynote address, conference on the Black Woman Writer and the Diaspora, Michigan State University.

Spelman, Elizabeth. 1982. "Theories of Race and Gender: The Erasure of Black Women." *Quest* 5: 36–32.

Tate, Claudia, ed. 1983. *Black Women Writers at Work.* New York: Continuum.

GAY SEXISM

Timothy Beneke

Relatively little has been written by gay men about gay sexism; gays have their hands full resisting a gay-hating culture and coping with the tragedy of AIDS. In this chapter, I want to write from a distance as a straight man about gay sexism.[1] In doing so I do not mean to imply that most or all gay men are sexist . . . I believe straight men have much of value to learn from gays and much to benefit from their liberation. I equally believe that straight men could learn a lot from the capacity of some gay men to empathize with women.

The first and most obvious thing to say about gay sexism is that gay men who are sexist are likely to be sexist because they are men and partake of the privileges that men partake of in this society. Whatever sexism exists in gay men derives from this more than anything else. But I want to ask two questions. Is there anything distinctive about the ways that gay men are sexist? And if there is, is there anything common to the personal and familial and social structures of gay experience that predispose gay men to these particular forms of sexism?

What seems to be distinctive about the sexism that can be found in gay men? My answer derives substantially, though not exclusively, from discussions with feminist women. I will focus on three things: (1) A certain willful, and tacitly hostile, ignoring of women; (2) a certain appropriation and mocking of, and competitiveness toward, the "feminine" and women's heteroerotic attractiveness; (3) a certain denigration of the "feminine" by gay men, as it is found in gay men. It is hard to separate this denigration from internalized homophobia.

As to the first type of gay sexism. A feminist friend was at a conference attended by many gay men. It was her observation that the gay men present, who were politically active, seemed to have no interest at all in the struggles of women that were being articulated. When she confronted them on this, they seemed to have no idea what she was talking about.

5   Another woman described a situation at her workplace where several gay men would totally ignore her in the halls and elevators, failing to adhere to even minimal standards of cordiality and civility.[2] It is only gay men who have treated her this particular way in any workplace. Other women coworkers had similar experiences.

Recently, a gay man I know, who has a Ph.D. in sociology and moves in progressive circles, did not know what PMS was; for someone in his social milieu not to know this can only be a willful achievement.

The second point refers in part to certain forms of drag, which some women experience as a put-down of women. Some gay men appear to appropriate and mock straight women's attractiveness, an act sometimes coupled with a seeming lack of interest in the lives of real women. My point is that drag *can* be sexist and is at times experienced as sexist by women (and men). The debate over when, how, and why drag is sexist is a complicated one that I will only briefly engage here. Men wearing women's clothes may encompass many things: gay men in drag; straight men transvestites seeking sexual pleasure (and perhaps paradoxically proving manhood);[3] joyous gender anarchy performed in any number of spirits; the transsexual longing of a biological male to be and be seen as, a woman; straight men resisting the oppressions of gender; and no doubt many other things as well. A variegated political content attends gay men in drag or gay men expressing a "feminine" persona. Drag can simultaneously subvert the gender order and support sexism. At its best, it may express hostility toward the gender system, may demonstrate the performed nature of all gender. It may reflect a certain awareness on the part of gay men of the rather arbitrary "performativity of gender" (grounded in years of gay men passing as straight), and may express affection for women. And yet, drag sometimes expresses and gratifies hostility toward women, both by those who perform it and by those who enjoy it.

A third type of gay sexism occurs when gay men refer to other gay men as feminine—as "she," "her," "queen," or by a woman's name—often with an element of derision present. Effeminate gay men are often denigrated. It is not clear whether (or when) this should be seen as internalized homophobia or sexism, but it speaks of an implicit hostility toward women. Homophobia and sexism are not always easily differentiated.

What might be structurally common to the experiences of gay men that might lead to the sexism described above? I will suggest four things. The first two are rather simple.

First, gay men are not attracted to women and (mostly) do not form primary economic and affectional bonds with them as mates. As such they lack one motivation straight men possess to relate to and understand women. This of course excludes them from certain forms of sexism straight men engage in—they do not (as far as I know) rape or sexually harass or batter women. But lacking such a motivation to relate to women makes it easier for gay men who do not like women to ignore them.

Gay men's lack of attraction and primary bonding to women is also a reason why gay men may be *less* sexist than straight men. They are less embroiled in the war between the sexes; they do not compete for control and resources in relationships with women as straight men do. And gay men are attracted to men and often critical of traditional forms of masculinity, which gives them a basis for identifying with and forming friendships with straight women.

Second, many women—straight women in particular—are homophobic and denigrating of gay men. This gives gay men good reason to feel angry toward some straight women; it does not legitimate the prejudgment of any particular woman, but it is an inevitable source of distrust.

The final two points require considerable elaboration. The first is psycho-analytic; the second, "socioanalytic"—it looks at the possible effects of social structures on the psyches of gay men.

Third, the psychoanalytic point is an extension of the wonderfully lucid and sensible work of gay psychoanalyst Richard Isay.... Isay believes, as I do, that for gay men sexual object choice is for the most part genetically deter-mined.[4] Environment may influence how sexuality is expressed, but for the most part not object choice. He defines homosexuality in terms of the con-tent of the sexual fantasies that impel a person toward sex with either men or women. If a man has predominant same-sex sexual fantasies, for Isay, he is homosexual.

15   Isay, working with some forty gay men in analysis or analytic therapy, has arrived at several clinical findings.[5] There is no evidence that the parenting of gay boys is more aberrant than the parenting of straights. Gay boys, some-where between the ages of three and six, develop a sexual attraction toward their fathers; often, they adopt "feminine" mannerisms in identification with their mothers in an attempt to gain their father's attraction. Some, during adolescence, give up these "feminine" mannerisms.[6] While straight boys iden-tify with their fathers and cultural stereotypes of masculinity in part as a way of seeking their mothers' attraction, gay boys lack this motivation and are likely to reject mainstream masculinity. They tend to be more sensitive and gentle, to cry more easily, to be more aesthetically oriented, and to reject ag-gressive masculine pursuits. Their fathers, consciously or unconsciously, sense that their gay sons are "different" and tend to withdraw from them, and may direct greater attention to other siblings. This withdrawal typically results in a lifelong wound for gay men, the denial or repression of which can be an in-hibiting force in the expression of sexuality.[7]

The scene that Isay describes offers one potential source of gay sexism. If gay men are attracted to their fathers at a young age, they are of necessity in competition with their mothers and with women. As Isay puts it:

> Gay men may also be envious of and competitive with women,
> a feeling that they are often not aware of which originates in the
> rivalry with the mother for the father's attention. The descrip-
> tion some gay men give of their mothers as being overbearing
> or binding, or as keeping them from their fathers, at times stems
> from anger at and envy of her closeness to the father.[8]

I said that drag often appears to appropriate and mock the heteroerotic attractiveness of women, and is experienced by some women as hostile and sexist. It appears to simultaneously denigrate and compete with women's at-tractiveness. One can find structural sources of such feelings in the childhood scenario Isay delineates, in which boys feel rivalry toward and envious of their mothers with whom they compete for father's attention.

Fourth, the socioanalytic point, which echoes the psychoanalytic one, relates to gay men's experience of their desired object's failure to be attracted to them. As a straight man, I try to imagine what it would be like to be gay. I can imagine life in one or another closet, the attraction to those with the same genitalia, the pain of being victimized by heterosexist oppression, the impersonation of false straight selves, the agony of coming out, alien and threatening (to me) oral and anal sexual practices, and the freedom to be affectionate toward other men.[9]

But I want to contemplate a particular social reality: for gay men 90+ percent of the people they are in principle attracted to—men—are by self-definition at least, attracted to women; and (something like) 90+ percent of the people who *are* in principle attracted to gay men are women, to whom gay men are not attracted.[10] (As a shorthand, I will refer to this as the Sexual Attraction Ratio, or SAR.) I take it that some such reality holds true in American society today, while acknowledging the reality of bisexuality and the imperfection of these categories, which are, here at least, roughly serviceable. I want to argue that the SAR must have a considerable, ponderable—if incommensurable—effect on the social construction of gay sexuality, gender, and gay sexism, and that it will echo and exacerbate the envy and competitiveness gay men may feel toward women as a result of the childhood scenario Isay describes. I will argue that the SAR will be of far greater importance in a homophobic world in which gays are driven into the closet than a world with no closet. Thus, homophobic oppression, both through its expression in women and its mediation through the SAR, can be seen as a cause of gay sexism.

Please note: I am not arguing that gay men prefer straight men to other gays. To the contrary, as I will explore later, I believe gays establish a psychic sexual economy, facilitated by the opening of the closet, by which they are much more able to recognize, and shape their attraction to, other gays.

An imperfect analogy may be useful for straight men. What would it be like if the SAR were reversed: if 90+ percent of those one was attracted to, women, were lesbians and 90+ percent of those one was not attracted to, men, were gay? How would this affect one's experience of gender and desire? What emotions and satisfactions might it animate? What defenses might it lead to? Take it a step farther and suppose one's attraction to women was totally closeted by a culture that ostracized one's sexuality, and the only public attraction to and from women one witnessed emanated from other women.[11]

Would this different SAR alone have important psychic implications for straight men? It is impossible for me to imagine that it would not; and it is difficult to specify what they would be—my imagination begins to break down, in part because I have to imagine a different "I." It is important to imagine not simply how some constant "I" (the same "I" as "me" now) would feel if the world were this way, but who I would be, how I might be differently constructed. I would probably be angry at lesbian women in such a world, and I might be motivated to identify with women. If I wanted women

20

to be attracted to me and the only attraction I saw was exchanged between women, I would have a motivation to act like women—and a resentment of women's attractiveness. I would receive a lot of rejection from lesbian women and a lot of unwanted attraction from gay men. I might find it gratifying to put down lesbian women by mocking them. It has been argued that gay and straight men have more in common sexually than either of them realize, that gender is a prime organizer of sexuality. I do not dispute this, but there is another side.

Consider the erotic flux of social life, something that for the most part occurs in the background, something almost always present but only occasionally represented. We regularly give and receive desire in all kinds of subtle ways. Gay men, particularly in a closeted world, give unrequited desire to men and receive unwanted desire from women as a (perhaps hidden) part of daily social experience. This will vary according to each man's place in society, his relation to the closet, his point in history and culture, and so on. And some gay men have painful crushes on straight men and receive unwanted crushes from straight women.

Consider further that part of the nature of sexual desire is to desire to be desired by the object of desire, the desire to be recognized and mirrored as a sexual being in the desiring response of the desired. If I am a gay man attracted to men attracted to women, does this motivate me to want to possess women's heteroerotic attractiveness?

25   Consider the experience of receiving unwanted desire from the object of desire of one's desired—gay men receiving desire from women. While some may find this flattering, some respond negatively, especially given that the source of unwanted desire—women—attract 90+ percent of those one is attracted to. Women's heteroerotic attractiveness has a dual meaning for gay men: it is simultaneously directed toward them and is unwanted, and it attracts many of those one is attracted to, who are not attracted to them.

I take it that the SAR will necessarily have psychic consequences for gay men, or at least I cannot imagine that it would have no consequences, especially in a homophobic world. The first evident consequence will be to replicate the early childhood scenario described earlier. Isay describes a scene in which gay boys are attracted to a father who is attracted to their mother and who withdraws from them. Gay men are in varying degrees likely to carry internal images of this conflict that can be touched off by the SAR, though I think the SAR in itself must be a powerful motivator of psychic gratifications.

And the feelings such a scene might animate? Presumably a general resentment and envy of attractive women. And specifically, it would be psychically gratifying to appropriate the heteroerotic attractiveness of women in an exaggerated mocking way, because:

1.   To do so is to mock and satirize and satisfy resentment against sexy straight women for so often being the desired object of the object of one's desire. One simultaneously possesses women's attractiveness, while ridiculing it.

2. To do so is to satisfy a perhaps weaker desire to satisfy a perhaps weaker resentment toward women for the distress caused by their unwanted attraction to one.

3. To do so is to satisfy one's frustrated desire to arouse such men, that is, to satisfy one's desire to be the object of desire of the desired.

4. To do so is to satisfy the desire for revenge against straight men who arouse and frustrate one, by arousing and frustrating them in turn. And as straight homophobic men recognize that they are attracted to gay men impersonating women, homophobic panic may ensue. This is a way gay men can vengefully inflict homophobic pain and self-hate on homophobic straight men.

All of these satisfactions, and others, may be at work at once.

By the satisfactions of drag I refer to the satisfactions both of drag queens themselves and those gay men who enjoy them. Relatively few gay men practice drag, but it is celebrated in parts of gay culture. It is noteworthy that some famous feminine icons for gays—Mae West, Greta Garbo, Marlene Dietrich—typically possessed considerable sexual power over straight men while holding them in contempt.

I am also talking about a more general gratification in assuming womanliness, "feminine" personas, something Isay describes in young gay boys. Sexual desire and gender invite each other. Gender identity is invited by the response to one's desire, just as desire invites, creates, animates gender. Someone's desire is said to make one *feel like a woman* or (less often) *a man*. If gay men are attracted to men who give off sexual vibrations meant to make women feel like women, such vibrations may make gay men feel like women. Clark Gable's unabashed, dimpled gaze made women feel like women and made them want to look and seem like whatever they regarded as feminine. His attractiveness was directed to and, in a sense, generated womanliness. If one is attracted to straight men—or if in a closeted world there are few visible gay men—can such a desire also be generated? Playwright Harvey Fierstein has commented that he loved Clark Gable as Rhett Butler—"I mean if I was in love with Clark Gable, then I must be Vivien Leigh."[12] For a long time, sexual desire was supposed to inhere in men, and women were supposed to respond passively to this desire. In the past thirty years, we have seen a flowering of women's expressed desire. If men have been the containers of desire they have also been, to a degree, the definers of gender.

Presumably, to invoke a stereotype, part of the pleasure of being a gay hairdresser is to enhance, and identify with, the power of women's sexiness for men; likewise, the pleasure involved in being a gay fashion designer who designs women's clothes. I take it as objectively true that a disproportionate number of male hairdressers and fashion designers are gay.

There is a fairly simple reason why the SAR is likely to motivate sexism in gay men. The SAR is a force that drives gay men—partly in search of sexual partners—to live in certain urban "gay ghettos" apart from women. The less experience gay men have of women, the easier it will be to dismiss them.[13] (Of course homophobic oppression also drives gay men into gay enclaves.)

The SAR would be substantially less important if there were no closet. Consider the closeted world first. Outside highly sequestered subcultures, the only public display of sexual heat men can exhibit is toward women, and the only public sexual heat men can respond to is that exhibited by women. In such a world, gay men have women as their only models of sexual attraction *to* men, and women as their only models of objects of sexual attraction *for* men. Both as sexual subjects and objects, their only models are women.

Such a world will encourage gay men to adopt feminine gender displays for the simple reason that the public models of attraction directed at men all come from women, and the public models of desire coming from men all are directed toward women. Hence gay men will be motivated to identify with women's desire for men. I want to be desired by men; I only see men desiring women; I want to be womanly. I desire men; I see only women desiring men; I identify with women. I am simultaneously motivated to identify with women's sexual power over men and motivated to envy and resent women for possessing it. Such an SAR, combined with an omnipresent closet, will produce more sexism than a world with no closet.

Take the other pole, a world with no closet and no oppression of gays by straights. In such a world, there would be many public models of attraction of men to men, and men from men, for gay men to identify with. A psychic economy would come into play whereby attraction to straight men would be limited and less compelling. Where public sexual heat is freely displayed between men, attraction to straight men will be less important and the feelings of resentment, envy, and jealousy toward straight women's sexiness will be limited. One would expect less of a need for gay men to gratify angry dealings toward women, to adopt "effeminate" gestures or to do drag in a world with no closet. Of course, drag can also celebrate a certain joyous anarchic spirit toward gender, and the loss of the closet should be accompanied by the loss of gender as well.

35   A world without a closet is one in which gay men will be less sexist and less resentful of women. Of course, if straight women are no longer homophobic, that too provides a motive for gay men to feel less resentful of women, so it will be difficult to disentangle these effects. And if straight men no longer enact homophobic oppression, fathers will inflict fewer wounds on their gay sons and gay boys will feel less desperately competitive toward their mothers. A world without a closet is one in which more gay men will more easily show empathy toward women.

NOTES

1. In this essay, I do something some may object to. I, a straight man, speculate—somewhat uneasily—about some possible social causes of gay sexism and displays of gen-

der. I want to suggest, among other things, that the oppression of gays increases gay sexism in structural ways. But first I want to be clear: I regard all sexuality and gender as worth explaining or at least understanding and all sexism and heterosexism as urgently in need of explaining.

It may be that what intuitively strikes me as likely sources of gay sexism are simply wrong; that, as a straight man, an outsider, I am blind to gay experience and I project feelings and conflicts that do not exist in gays. Even if that is the case, I still think it is worth exploring my intuitions. First, my intuitions are ones that a straight person contemplating gay sexism is likely to have. If they are wrong, they need to be demystified and disposed of as part of a conversation between gays and straights. Second, it is useful to understand the sources of plausibility in the intuitions that derive from straight contemplation of gay experience. In that sense, what follows may be seen, or may turn out to be, an example of homophobia, or at least a form of straight blindness to gay experience. I hope my openness to this possibility is not disingenuous.

So I present the arguments in this chapter not simply as arguments per se, but as arguments-constructed-through-a-straight-man's-eyes. I have tried to present a little of the process and phenomenology that lead me to find them compelling.

2. The question can be legitimately raised to what extent some women gain self-esteem from the attentions and attractions of men and thus might be particularly angered by the lack of cordiality of gay men in the workplace, or elsewhere. This damage to self-esteem may result in hostility from women and may feed some women's homophobic attitudes toward gay men. However, in the examples here adduced I do not see that at work.

3. Psychoanalyst Robert Stoller argues from clinical experience that the arousal that transvestite men feel wearing women's clothes is a way of proving manhood—if they can remain real heterosexual men, attracted to women while dressed as women, they must truly be men. For a discussion of this, see Marjorie Garber, "Spare Parts: The Surgical Construction of Gender," in *Theorizing Feminism,* ed. Anne C. Herrmann and Abigail J. Stewart (Boulder: Westview Press, 1994).

4. It is likely that homosexuality is more genetically coded in gay men than lesbians, given the strong existence of political lesbianism—lesbianism motivated by an alliance with women and a rejection of patriarchy. In this section I rely heavily on the work of Isay, *Being Homosexual.*

5. I am of course aware of the intellectual vulnerability attendant upon any reliance on psychoanalytic "clinical findings." Supposed "clinical findings" have taught us much that is wrong and oppressive: that women who report childhood sexual abuse are expressing their own sexual fantasies; that gay men are gay because of overidentification with their mothers. So, why rely on Isay's findings? Ultimately, I can only say that they make good sense to me. If one starts from the assumption that gay men are gay for genetic reasons (and straight men likewise), the rest falls into place.

6. Richard Isay has recently, through what he describes (in conversation) as a "different kind of listening" to his patients, come to believe that most gay men are constitutionally more effeminate and thus drawn to identify with their mothers. Genetic affinities may exist between some gay men and their mothers that predispose them toward "femininity" and further identification with their mothers. This is an intriguing

observation that awaits further research. If this is the case, then this genetic affinity, more than competition for the father's attraction, is more likely to be driving gay men's feminine identification. I think one must remain particularly open to new research and theorizing on this matter.

7. The reader may wonder how the much discussed issue of "hypermasculine" gays fits into this discussion. It is not clear to me that such gay men are in any way unique regarding sexism. Anthropologist Gayle Rubin in a study of the gay leather culture observed (in conversation) that gay men involved in the leather scene struck her as no more or less sexist than other men.

8. Isay, *Being Homosexual*, 42.

9. Paul Monette's remarkable, relentlessly searching and honest book, *Becoming a Man: Half a Life Story* (New York: Harcourt Brace Jovanovich, 1992), more than anything else I have read, gives me a sense of what it is like growing up in at least one closet.

10. I am using the 90+ figure to stand in for a general social science finding that somewhat over 90 percent of the population, by self-report, is heterosexual. No one can be confident that people being surveyed on their sex lives are telling the truth, and there are always problems of definition, but at least by self-report the 90+ percent figure is the best we have. The most recent, and arguably most rigorous, study comes out of the University of Chicago. See Robert T. Michael, John H. Gagnon, Edward O. Laumann, and Gina Kolata, *Sex in America* (New York: Little, Brown and Company, 1994).

11. The disanalogies in this imagined world are strong here, too. Those one is most attracted to, women, presumably in such a world would continue to have less power, whereas the straight men that gays are attracted to retain power.

12. Quoted in Michael Bronski, *Culture Clash* (Boston: South End Press, 1984), 96.

13. I am indebted to sociologist Joshua Gamson for this observation.

AGE, RACE, CLASS, AND SEX: WOMEN REDEFINING DIFFERENCE[1]

Audre Lorde

Much of western european history conditions us to see human differences in simplistic opposition to each other: dominant/subordinate, good/bad, up/down, superior/inferior. In a society where the good is defined in terms of profit rather than in terms of human need, there must always be some group of people who, through systematized oppression, can be made to feel surplus, to occupy the place of the dehumanized inferior. Within this society, that group is made up of Black and Third World people, working-class people, older people, and women.

As a forty-nine-year-old Black lesbian feminist socialist mother of two, including one boy, and a member of an interracial couple, I usually find myself a part of some group defined as other, deviant, inferior, or just plain wrong. Traditionally, in american society, it is the members of oppressed, objectified groups who are expected to stretch out and bridge the gap between the actualities of our lives and the consciousness of our oppressor. For in order to survive, those of us for whom oppression is as american as apple pie have always had to be watchers, to become familiar with the language and manners of the oppressor, even sometimes adopting them for some illusion of protection. Whenever the need for some pretense of communication arises, those who profit from our oppression call upon us to share our knowledge with them. In other words, it is the responsibility of the oppressed to teach the oppressors their mistakes. I am responsible for educating teachers who dismiss my children's culture in school. Black and Third World people are expected to educate white people as to our humanity. Women are expected to educate men. Lesbians and gay men are expected to educate the heterosexual world. The oppressors maintain their position and evade responsibility for their own actions. There is a constant drain of energy which might be better used in redefining ourselves and devising realistic scenarios for altering the present and constructing the future.

Institutionalized rejection of difference is an absolute necessity in a profit economy which needs outsiders as surplus people. As members of such an economy, we have *all* been programmed to respond to the human differences between us with fear and loathing and to handle that difference in one of

---

[1] Paper delivered at the Copeland Colloquium, Amherst College, April 1980.

three ways: ignore it, and if that is not possible, copy it if we think it is dominant, or destroy it if we think it is subordinate. But we have no patterns for relating across our human differences as equals. As a result, those differences have been misnamed and misused in the service of separation and confusion.

Certainly there are very real differences between us of race, age, and sex. But it is not those differences between us that are separating us. It is rather our refusal to recognize those differences, and to examine the distortions which result from our misnaming them and their effects upon human behavior and expectation.

5   *Racism, the belief in the inherent superiority of one race over all others and thereby the right to dominance. Sexism, the belief in the inherent superiority of one sex over the other and thereby the right to dominance. Ageism. Heterosexism. Elitism. Classism.*

It is a lifetime pursuit for each one of us to extract these distortions from our living at the same time as we recognize, reclaim, and define those differences upon which they are imposed. For we have all been raised in a society where those distortions were endemic within our living. Too often, we pour the energy needed for recognizing and exploring difference into pretending those differences are insurmountable barriers, or that they do not exist at all. This results in a voluntary isolation, or false and treacherous connections. Either way, we do not develop tools for using human difference as a springboard for creative change within our lives. We speak not of human difference, but of human deviance.

Somewhere, on the edge of consciousness, there is what I call a *mythical norm,* which each one of us within our hearts knows "that is not me." In america, this norm is usually defined as white, thin, male, young, heterosexual, christian, and financially secure. It is with this mythical norm that the trappings of power reside within this society. Those of us who stand outside that power often identify one way in which we are different, and we assume that to be the primary cause of all oppression, forgetting other distortions around difference, some of which we ourselves may be practicing. By and large within the women's movement today, white women focus upon their oppression as women and ignore differences of race, sexual preference, class, and age. There is a pretense to a homogeneity of experience covered by the word *sisterhood* that does not in fact exist.

Unacknowledged class differences rob women of each others' energy and creative insight. Recently a women's magazine collective made the decision for one issue to print only prose, saying poetry was a less "rigorous" or "serious" art form. Yet even the form our creativity takes is often a class issue. Of all the art forms, poetry is the most economical. It is the one which is the most secret, which requires the least physical labor, the least material, and the one which can be done between shifts, in the hospital pantry, on the subway, and on scraps of surplus paper. Over the last few years, writing a novel on tight finances, I came to appreciate the enormous differences in the material demands between poetry and prose. As we reclaim our literature, poetry has been the major voice of poor, working class, and Colored women. A room of one's own may be a necessity for writing prose, but so are reams of paper, a typewriter, and plenty of time. The actual requirements to produce the visual arts also help determine, along class lines, whose art is whose. In this day of inflated prices for material, who are our sculptors, our painters, our photographers? When we speak of a broadly based women's culture, we need to be aware of the effect of class and economic differences on the supplies available for producing art.

As we move toward creating a society within which we can each flourish, ageism is another distortion of relationship which interferes without vision. By ignoring the past, we are encouraged to repeat its mistakes. The "generation gap" is an important social tool for any repressive society. If the younger members of a community view the older members as contemptible or suspect or excess, they will never be able to join hands and examine the living memories of the community, nor ask the all important question, "Why?" This gives rise to a historical amnesia that keeps us working to invent the wheel every time we have to go to the store for bread.

We find ourselves having to repeat and relearn the same old lessons over and over that our mothers did because we do not pass on what we have learned, or because we are unable to listen. For instance, how many times has this all been said before? For another, who would have believed that once again our daughters are allowing their bodies to be hampered and purgatoried by girdles and high heels and hobble skirts?   10

Ignoring the differences of race between women and the implications of those differences presents the most serious threat to the mobilization of women's joint power.

As white women ignore their built-in privilege of whiteness and define *woman* in terms of their own experience alone, then women of Color become "other," the outsider whose experience and tradition is too "alien" to comprehend. An example of this is the signal absence of the experience of women of Color as a resource for women's studies courses. The literature of women of Color is seldom included in women's literature courses and almost never in other literature courses, nor in women's studies as a whole. All too often, the excuse given is that the literatures of women of Color can only be taught by Colored women, or that they are too difficult to understand, or that classes cannot "get into" them because they come out of experiences that are "too different." I have heard this argument presented by white women of otherwise quite clear intelligence, women who seem to have no trouble at all teaching and reviewing work that comes out of the vastly different experiences of Shakespeare, Molière, Dostoyefsky, and Aristophanes. Surely there must be some other explanation.

This is a very complex question, but I believe one of the reasons white women have such difficulty reading Black women's work is because of their reluctance to see Black women as women and different from themselves. To examine Black women's literature effectively requires that we be seen as whole people in our actual complexities—as individuals, as women, as human—

rather than as one of those problematic but familiar stereotypes provided in this society in place of genuine images of Black women. And I believe this holds true for the literatures of other women of Color who are not Black.

The literatures of all women of Color recreate the textures of our lives, and many white women are heavily invested in ignoring the real differences. For as long as any difference between us means one of us must be inferior, then the recognition of any difference must be fraught with guilt. To allow women of Color to step out of stereotypes is too guilt provoking, for it threatens the complacency of those women who view oppression only in terms of sex.

15   Refusing to recognize difference makes it impossible to see the different problems and pitfalls facing us as women.

Thus, in a patriarchal power system where whiteskin privilege is a major prop, the entrapments used to neutralize Black women and white women are not the same. For example, it is easy for Black women to be used by the power structure against Black men, not because they are men, but because they are Black. Therefore, for Black women, it is necessary at all times to separate the needs of the oppressor from our own legitimate conflicts within our communities. This same problem does not exist for white women. Black women and men have shared racist oppression and still share it, although in different ways. Out of that shared oppression we have developed joint defenses and joint vulnerabilities to each other that are not duplicated in the white community, with the exception of the relationship between Jewish women and Jewish men.

On the other hand, white women face the pitfall of being seduced into joining the oppressor under the pretense of sharing power. This possibility does not exist in the same way for women of Color. The tokenism that is sometimes extended to us is not an invitation to join power; our racial "otherness" is a visible reality that makes that quite clear. For white women there is a wider range of pretended choices and rewards for identifying with patriarchal power and its tools.

Today, with the defeat of ERA, the tightening economy, and increased conservatism, it is easier once again for white women to believe the dangerous fantasy that if you are good enough, pretty enough, sweet enough, quiet enough, teach the children to behave, hate the right people, and marry the right men, then you will be allowed to co-exist with patriarchy in relative peace, at least until a man needs your job or the neighborhood rapist happens along. And true, unless one lives and loves in the trenches it is difficult to remember that the war against dehumanization is ceaseless.

But Black women and our children know the fabric of our lives is stitched with violence and with hatred, that there is no rest. We do not deal with it only on the picket lines, or in dark midnight alleys, or in the places where we dare to verbalize our resistance. For us, increasingly, violence weaves through the daily tissues of our living—in the supermarket, in the classroom, in the elevator, in the clinic and the schoolyard, from the plumber, the baker, the saleswoman, the bus driver, the bank teller, the waitress who does not serve us.

Some problems we share as women, some we do not. You fear your children will grow up to join the patriarchy and testify against you, we fear our children will be dragged from a car and shot down in the street, and you will turn your backs upon the reasons they are dying. *20*

The threat of difference has been no less blinding to people of color. Those of us who are Black must see that the reality of our lives and our struggle does not make us immune to the errors of ignoring and misnaming difference. Within Black communities where racism is a living reality, differences among us often seem dangerous and suspect. The need for unity is often misnamed as a need for homogeneity, and a Black feminist vision mistaken for betrayal of our common interests as a people. Because of the continuous battle against racial erasure that Black women and Black men share, some Black women still refuse to recognize that we are also oppressed as women, and that sexual hostility against Black women is practiced not only by the white racist society, but implemented within our Black communities as well. It is a disease striking the heart of Black nationhood, and silence will not make it disappear. Exacerbated by racism and the pressures of powerlessness, violence against Black women and children often becomes a standard within our communities, one by which manliness can measured. But these woman-hating acts are rarely discussed as crimes against Black women.

As a group, women of Color are the lowest paid wage earners in america. We are the primary targets of abortion and sterilization abuse, here and abroad. In certain parts of Africa, small girls are still being sewed shut between their legs to keep them docile and for men's pleasure. This is known as female circumcision, and it is not a cultural affair as the late Jomo Kenyatta insisted, it is a crime against Black women.

Black women's literature is full of the pain of frequent assault, not only by a racist patriarchy, but also by Black men. Yet the necessity for and history of shared battle have made us, Black women, particularly vulnerable to the false accusation that antisexist is anti-Black. Meanwhile, womanhating as a recourse of the powerless is sapping strength from Black communities, and our very lives. Rape is on the increase, reported and unreported, and rape is not aggressive sexuality, it is sexualized aggression. As Kalamu ya Salaam, a Black male writer points out, "As long as male domination exists, rape will exist. Only women revolting and men made conscious of their responsibility to fight sexism can collectively stop rape."[2]

Differences between ourselves as Black women are also being misnamed and used to separate us from one another. As a Black lesbian feminist comfortable with the many different ingredients of my identity, and a woman

---

[2] From "Rape: A Radical Analysis, An African-American Perspective" by Kalamu ya Salaam in *Black Books Bulletin,* vol. 6, no. 4 (1980).

committed to racial and sexual freedom from oppression, I find I am constantly being encouraged to pluck out some one aspect of myself and present this as the meaningful whole, eclipsing or denying the other parts of self. But this is a destructive and fragmenting way to live. My fullest concentration of energy is available to me only when I integrate all the parts of who I am, openly, allowing power from particular sources of my living to flow back and forth freely through all my different selves, without the restrictions of externally imposed definition. Only then can I bring myself and my energies as a whole to the service of those struggles which I embrace as part of my living.

25   A fear of lesbians, or of being accused of being a lesbian, has led many Black women into testifying against themselves. It has led some of us into destructive alliances, and others into despair and isolation. In the white women's communities, heterosexism is sometimes a result of identifying with the white patriarchy, a rejection of that interdependence between women-identified women which allows the self to be, rather than to be used in the service of men. Sometimes it reflects a die-hard belief in the protective coloration of heterosexual relationships, sometimes a self-hate which all women have to fight against, taught us from birth.

Although elements of these attitudes exist for all women, there are particular resonances of heterosexism and homophobia among Black women. Despite the fact that woman-bonding has a long and honorable history in the African and African-american communities, and despite the knowledge and accomplishments of many strong and creative women-identified Black women in the political, social, and cultural fields, heterosexual Black women often tend to ignore or discount the existence and work of Black lesbians. Part of this attitude has come from an understandable terror of Black male attack within the close confines of Black society, where the punishment for any female self-assertion is still to be accused of being a lesbian and therefore unworthy of the attention or support of the scarce Black male. But part of this need to misname and ignore Black lesbians comes from a very real fear that openly women-identified Black women who are no longer dependent upon men for their self-definition may well reorder our whole concept of social relationships.

Black women who once insisted that lesbianism was a white woman's problem now insist that Black lesbians are a threat to Black nationhood, are consorting with the enemy, are basically un-Black. These accusations, coming from the very women to whom we look for deep and real understanding, have served to keep many Black lesbians in hiding, caught between the racism of white women and the homophobia of their sisters. Often, their work has been ignored, trivialized, or misnamed, as with the work of Angelina Grimke, Alice Dunbar-Nelson, Lorraine Hansberry. Yet women-bonded women have always been some part of the power of Black communities, from our unmarried aunts to the amazons of Dahomey.

And it is certainly not Black lesbians who are assaulting women and raping children and grandmothers on the streets of our communities.

Across this country, as in Boston during the spring of 1979 following the unsolved murders of twelve Black women, Black lesbians are spearheading movements against violence against Black women.

What are the particular details within each of our lives that can be scrutinized and altered to help bring about change? How do we redefine difference for all women? It is not our differences which separate women, but our reluctance to recognize those differences and to deal effectively with the distortions which have resulted from the ignoring and misnaming of those differences.

As a tool of social control, women have been encouraged to recognize only one area of human difference as legitimate, those differences which exist between women and men. And we have learned to deal across those differences with the urgency of all oppressed subordinates. All of us have had to learn to live or work or coexist with men, from our fathers on. We have recognized and negotiated these differences, even when this recognition only continued the old dominant/subordinate mode of human relationship, where the oppressed must recognize the masters' difference in order to survive.

But our future survival is predicated upon our ability to relate within equality. As women, we must root out internalized patterns of oppression within ourselves if we are to move beyond the most superficial aspects of social change. Now we must recognize differences among women who are our equals, neither inferior nor superior, and devise ways to use each others' difference to enrich our visions and our joint struggles.

The future of our earth may depend upon the ability of all women to identify and develop new definitions of power and new patterns of relating across difference. The old definitions have not served us, nor the earth that supports us. The old patterns, no matter how cleverly rearranged to imitate progress, still condemn us to cosmetically altered repetitions of the same old exchanges, the same old guilt, hatred, recrimination, lamentation, and suspicion.

For we have, built into all of us, old blueprints of expectation and response, old structures of oppression, and these must be altered at the same time as we alter the living conditions which are a result of those structures. For the master's tools will never dismantle the master's house.

As Paulo Freire shows so well in *The Pedagogy of the Oppressed*,[3] the true focus of revolutionary change is never merely the oppressive situations which we seek to escape, but that piece of the oppressor which is planted deep within each of us, and which knows only the oppressors' tactics, the oppressors' relationships.

Change means growth, and growth can be painful. But we sharpen self-definition by exposing the self in work and struggle together with those

---

[3] Seabury Press, New York, 1970.

whom we define as different from ourselves, although sharing the same goals. For Black and white, old and young, lesbian and heterosexual women alike, this can mean new paths to our survival.

> *We have chosen each other*
> *and the edge of each other's battles*
> *the war is the same*
> *if we lose*
> *someday women's blood will congeal*
> *upon a dead planet*
> *if we win*
> *there is no telling*
> *we seek beyond history*
> *for a new and more possible meeting.*[4]

---

[4] From "Outlines," unpublished poem.

Part IV   Theorizing Resistance

INTRODUCTION

Parts I through III have examined the nature of oppression and privilege, and have begun to reveal the complicated ways they function together. The results of that examination can be quite daunting and may leave you, the reader, feeling as if you should do something to resist or challenge oppression, but stymied, confused, or even hopeless about what *to* do. Racism, sexism, and heterosexism are enormous, multifaceted systems of oppression; the actions of any one individual, no matter how noble her intentions, cannot make these systems "go away"—not even in the life of an individual. Such a realization cannot fail to be disheartening.

But if the analysis of systems of oppression tells us anything, it tells us that there exist many ways to resist—because oppression is not just one thing. And for all its power and comprehensiveness, this multifaceted system is also full of holes, gaps, missing threads, inconsistencies, and other lacunae—the ideal locations from which to work to resist and undermine it. Part IV examines the theories underlying six strategies for resisting—strategies that respond to different dimensions of the system. Some strategies are more appropriate for individuals, whereas others have a more collective focus. Some strategies may also be in tension with one another—a fact that is unsurprising when we remember the many faces of oppression.

The first strategy, discussed in Chapter 13, is *education*. Theorists in this section address both schooling in the formal sense and other, more informal instances of education. Given the fact that schooling in the United States is mandatory, schools are an obvious place in which to begin to challenge oppressive structures and practices. One theorist in this section examines the ways that schools can reinforce oppression, and also their promise for undermining oppression. Schools might look quite different indeed if they were conceived as institutions in the business of challenging racism, sexism, and heterosexism. Other theorists consider the informal education that occurs when people get together and begin to put a name to their experiences, or to understand their experiences in a new framework. This sort of education can be quite empowering and can help people to make new sense of their lives and roles in the world.

Chapter 14 explores the second strategy: *treason, traitorousness,* and *disloyalty*—to systems of oppression and to the parts of our lives that have given us privilege. Our analysis of oppression and privilege has made clear that these systems are constituted in ways that give many of us a stake in Things Remaining the Way They Are. The strategy of disloyalty invites people with privilege to reject or disrupt the privileges they are given by the systems. It also invites oppressed people to disrupt or stymie expectations of them to which the system of oppression gives rise. Theorists explore the way in which both humor and anger can be used as tools in this undertaking.

The third strategy for resistance, explored in Chapter 15, is *separatism* and *identity politics*. This strategy is often closely connected with disloyalty and traitorousness. Once a person has decided to become disloyal to a system, she or he might embrace an identity that has been scorned within the dominant system. One who embraces this identity might also choose to separate from the dominant system in a variety of ways or to varying degrees. Separatism is not a simple "bowing out" of oppressive systems but, rather, an active strategy that creates communities intentionally organized around principles or identities.

Chapter 16 considers *revolution*. Paulo Freire warns oppressed people to beware of revolts, which [can] merely reverse the positions of oppressor and oppressed. A reversal of positions is not a revolution to end oppression, precisely because it preserves the oppressive system. A revolution to end oppression must involve a fundamental restructuring so that domination and subordination are not the fundamental relations of social, economic, political, and moral life.

The fifth strategy (Chapter 17) is *coalition building*. Relations of oppression and privilege work in such a way as to leave our interests at odds with one another. What happens when former foes unite in response to a shared need or a common enemy? Coalitions, especially those formed among groups that are very different from one another or that have a history of hostility, offer radical potential because they disrupt the "divide and conquer" approach that pits one form of oppression against another. However, coalitions, because of their very nature, are difficult to form and even more difficult to maintain. Although a common foe might be an immediate reason for forming a coalition, it is not enough to sustain an effective one.

The sixth strategy, explored in Chapter 18, is *neither/nor* thinking. This strategy is particularly responsive to the issues raised in Chapter 10, "Challenging Dichotomous Thinking." Those readings challenged the dichotomies of male/female, white/black, heterosexual/homosexual that are taken for granted and function normatively. The neither/nor strategy advocates undermining these powerful dichotomies by adopting, acknowledging, and fostering the growth of identities and practices that don't fit either side of the dichotomy. Such an approach opens up new spaces and identities for people and communities, and disrupts the hierarchical thinking inherent in the dichotomies.

Oppression and privilege can't be overcome overnight. Nor can they be transformed by the work of individuals acting entirely in isolation from one another. Recognizing the systematic, structural nature of oppression, however, can enable us to develop theories and practices of resistance that address these realities, and work effectively to undermine them. We leave you with the invitation to refine these strategies for yourself, and to develop and disseminate new strategies for resisting oppression and privilege.

13

Resistance Strategy One: Education

■·■·■

ANTIRACISM, MULTICULTURALISM, AND INTERRACIAL COMMUNITY

THREE EDUCATIONAL VALUES FOR A MULTICULTURAL SOCIETY

Lawrence Blum

In the past year and a half or so multicultural education has garnered an extraordinary amount of media attention, most of it negative. My own involvement in this area predates the recent hoopla and has its source in my own children's working their way through the public schools of Cambridge, Massachusetts. I have been struck by how extraordinarily different their educational and social experience has been, and will continue to be, than was my own, attending almost all-white schools in the 1950s. Charges of so-called political correctness cannot mask the extraordinary demographic and social changes our society is undergoing that ground the need for a philosophy of education suited to an increasingly multiracial, multicultural society.

I approach that task from my own background in moral philosophy and the philosophy of value. I want to ask what values I would want my own and other children to be taught in schools, as well as in their families, to prepare them for life in the multicultural United States. I assume here that moral and value education must be a part of precollege education, and in doing so I ally myself with educators across a wide political spectrum.

My work in this area does not by and large focus on education at the college level, though I assume that *some* of what I have to say will have implications for colleges and their curricula. I also think it instructive for adults concerned with our current and future state of racial and ethnic relations to focus on younger children, where we sometimes get a glimpse of possibilities otherwise difficult to envision.

I want to argue that there are a *plurality* of values that one would want taught in schools and families. None of these can be reduced to the others, nor can any take the place of the others. Without claiming comprehensiveness for my list I want to suggest that there are at least four values, or families of values, essential to a program of value education for a multiracial society. I will describe all four values briefly and will then talk about each in more detail. (I recognize that the labels on these are somewhat arbitrary.)

I realize that multicultural education has its critics and detractors. I will not attempt today to defend or justify the four values but only to articulate them, so that it will be clearer what it is that needs defense and justification.

The first value is *antiracism* or *opposition to racism:*

Racism is the denial of the fundamental moral equality of all human beings. It involves the expression of attitudes of superior worth or merit justifying or underpinning the domination or unjust advantage of some groups over others. Antiracism as a value involves striving to be without racist attitudes oneself as well as being prepared to work against both racist attitudes in others and racial injustice in society more generally.

The second value is *multiculturalism:*

Multiculturalism involves an understanding, appreciation and valuing of one's own culture, and an informed respect and curiosity about the ethnic culture of others. It involves a valuing of other cultures, not in the sense of approving of all aspects of those cultures, but of attempting to see how a given culture can express value to its own members.

The third value is a sense of *community,* and in particular an *interracial community:*

This involves a sense, not necessarily explicit or articulated, that one possesses human bonds with persons of other races and ethnicities. The bonds may, and ideally should, be so broad as to encompass all of humanity; but they may also be limited to the bonds formed in friendships, schools, workplaces, and the like.

The fourth value is *treating persons as individuals:*

This involves recognizing the individuality of each person—specifically, that while an individual person is a member of an ethnic or racial group, and while that aspect may be an important part of who she is, she is more than that ethnic or racial identity. It is the lived appreciation of this individuality, not simply paying lip service to it, that constitutes the value I will call treating persons as individuals. (I will not have the opportunity to discuss this value further on this occasion.)

10 Again, I claim that these four are distinct though related values, and that all of them are essential to multicultural value education. Failure to appreciate their distinctness poses the danger that one of them will be neglected in a value education program. At the same time there are natural convergences and complementarities among the four values taken in any combination; there are ways of teaching each value that support the promotion of each one of the other values. On the other hand, I will claim, there can also be tensions, both practical and theoretical, between various of the values; that is, some ways of teaching one of the values may work against the conveying of one of the others. Since the values can be either convergent or in tension, it will be crucial to search for ways of teaching them that minimize the tension and support the convergences.

I have designated *antiracism* as the first value for this value education. In contrast to the three others, this one is stated negatively—in opposition to something rather than as a positive goal to be striven for. Why do I not refer to this value positively as "racial equality" or "racial justice"? One reason is that the oppositional definition brings out that a central aspect of the value of antiracism involves countering an evil and not just promoting a good. An important component of what children need to be taught is how to notice, to confront, to oppose, and to work toward the elimination of manifestations of racism. Particular moral abilities and traits of character involving certain forms of empowerment are required for activities of *opposition* that are not required merely for the promotion of a good goal. Of course, antiracism does presuppose the positive value of racial justice; hence, the positive element is implicitly contained in the value of antiracism.

To understand the value of antiracism we must first understand *racism*. The term racism, while a highly charged and condemnatory one, has no generally agreed upon meaning. On the other hand all can agree that using a racial slur, telling a Chicano student that one does not like Chicanos and wishes they were not in one's school, or carving "KKK" on the door of the African-American student, are racist acts. At the same time the conservative writer Dinesh D'Souza has given voice to a suspicion, shared I am sure by others, that the term "racism" is in danger of losing its meaning and moral force through a too broad usage.

I agree that there has sometimes been a tendency to inflate the meaning of the word racism so it becomes virtually a catchall term for any behavior concerning race or race relations that its user strongly condemns. This development ill serves those like myself who wish racism to be taken more seriously than it presently is. Like the boy who cried "wolf," the inflation of the concept of racism to encompass phenomena with questionable connection to its core meaning desensitizes people to the danger, horror, and wrongfulness of true racism.

Here is my definition of racism, which I present without further defense: Racism refers both to an institutional or social structure of racial domination or injustice—as when we speak of a racist institution—and also to individual actions, beliefs, and attitudes whether consciously held or not, which express, support or justify the superiority of one racial group to another. Thus, on both the individual levels, racism involves denying or violating the equal dignity and worth of all human beings independent of race, and on both levels, racism is bound up with dominance and hierarchy.

Note that on my definition several practices or attitudes sometimes 15 thought of as automatically racist are not (necessarily) racist, though they may involve racism in particular instances. One is *racial ignorance* or *insensitivity,* an example being a black high school student, who had what he thought were good white friends; but when Martin Luther King's birthday came around the white students did not understand why the black student cared about the celebration of King's birthday. This seems to be an example of racial ignorance or insensitivity, but not of racism. A second is *making racial distinctions.* We are all familiar with the view that merely to make a distinction between people on the basis of race is itself racist. A related example is when simply mentioning or noticing someone's race is seen as racist. A false model of nonracism as "color blindness" leads us to confuse making racial distinctions with racism itself. But unless making the racial distinction is grounded in an attribution of inferiority or lesser worth to one of the groups involved, racism (on my definition) is not present.

A third example is *racial exclusiveness* on the part of people of color, as when African-American or Hispanic students sit together in the school cafeteria. This too is not normally a racist practice, for it is not normally premised on an attitude of superiority toward nonblacks (or non-Hispanics), but may be simply a sense of comfort with those like oneself. A final example is *racial discomfort,* that is, a discomfort with people of other races; this too is not necessarily racist, though, of course, it can be.

Some of these practices or attitudes may be objectionable or regrettable without being racist. After all, ignorance and insensitivity are bad things. And racial exclusiveness can be detrimental to a sense of interracial community. But conflating them with racism makes it difficult to deal *either* with racism or with whatever *other* disvalue these practices may involve.

The point I am making here—and one I mean to emphasize in my work on multiculturalism—is that there are a *plurality* of values needed in a multicultural society, and, conversely, a plurality of things that can go wrong in multicultural and multiracial interaction.

There are three components of (the value of) *antiracism* as I see it.

One is the belief in the equal worth of all persons regardless of race, not 20 just as an intellectual matter, but rooted more deeply in one's attitudes and emotions; this is to have what one might call a *nonracist* moral consciousness. But it is not enough to learn to be nonracist as an individual; students must also be taught to *understand* the particularity of racism as a psychological and historical phenomenon. This is partly because one aspect of antiracism is learning to perceive racism and to recognize when it is occurring. Just being nonracist cannot guarantee this. For one may sincerely subscribe to the right principles of racial justice and yet not see particular instances of racism right under one's nose, in either institutional or individual forms; for example, not recognizing unintended patterns of exclusion of people of color, or not recognizing a racial stereotype.

There are three components to this second feature of antiracism (understanding racism). The first is the *psychological* dynamic of racism, such as scapegoating and stereotyping, rigidity and fear of difference, rationalization of privilege and power, projecting of unwanted wishes onto others, and other psychological processes contributing to racist attitudes. The second is the *historical* dynamic of racism in its particular forms: slavery, colonialism, segregation, Nazism, the mistreatment of native Americans, and the like. Involved also must be learning about movements *against* racism, such as abolitionism, civil rights movements, and the black power movement; and learning about institutional racism as well. The third component is the role of *individuals* in sustaining or resisting racist institutions, patterns, and systems—how individuals can change racist structures; how they may contribute to or help to perpetuate racist patterns even if they themselves are not actually racist.

Studying the historical dynamics of racism necessarily involves teaching the victimization of some groups by others. While some conservative critics of multicultural education ridicule and derogate focusing on a group's history as victims of racism, it would nevertheless be intellectually irresponsible not to do so. One can hardly understand the historical experience of African-Americans without slavery, of Jews without the Holocaust, of Asian-Americans without the historic barriers to citizenship and to family life and without the World War II internment camps.

Nevertheless, from the point of view of historical accuracy as well as that of value education, it is vital not to *confine* the presentation of a group to its status as victim. One needs to see subordinate groups as agents in their own history—not just as suffering victimization but as responding to it, sometimes by active resistance both cultural and political, sometimes by passive resistance, sometimes by accommodation. The study of social history is invaluable here in providing the framework for seeing that victims made their own history in the face of their victimization, and for giving concrete embodiment to the philosophical truth that human beings retain the capacity for agency even when oppressed and dominated by others.

The third component of antiracist education (in addition to nonracism and understanding racism) is *opposition to racism;* for nonracism implies only that one does all one can to avoid racism in *one's own* actions and attitudes. This is insufficient, for students need also to develop a sense of responsibility concerning manifestations of racism in other persons and in the society more generally. For example, since students will almost inevitably witness racist acts, to confine their own responsibility simply to ensuring that they individually do not participate in such actions themselves is to give students a mixed message about how seriously they are being asked to take racism.

A teacher in my children's school elicited from her class occasions on which they had witnessed racist remarks. Two examples were of store clerks, one of whom said, "You Puerto Ricans are always stealing things; get out of my store," and the other, "Don't be a dirty Jew—give him the money." As this teacher did, truly antiracist education should help pupils think through what they themselves might do in such situations, how to assess the gains and risks of various courses of action. Discussions of this sort might help secure two goals. The first is that by encouraging students to bring up incidents of racism and by discussing them seriously, the teacher conveys to the class that racism is serious business, and is everyone's responsibility. The second is that such conversations help to develop students' own skills, abilities, and sense of competence in the complex tasks of active engagement with a society and world far from embodying ideals of racial justice.

Let me now examine antiracist education in the context of "citizenship" education, currently being touted across a broad political spectrum as an important component of secondary school education. A very useful text here is the *California History/Social Science Framework,* officially adopted by the state of California as a guideline for the writing and the adoption of textbooks for secondary schools.[1] (Some textbooks have now been adopted that conform to this framework.) This is an intellectually and pedagogically impressive document, written by a variety of educators and scholars, including Diane Ravitch, an influential educational historian and theorist, and currently an Assistant U.S. Education Secretary.

The *History/Social Science Framework* sees the development of the commitments and skills of active citizenship—a citizenship whose purpose is to sustain and protect democratic institutions—as a central task of secondary school education. The *Framework* also takes up racial issues much more fully than, say, the education that I received in the 1950s. Yet there is very little recognition in the *Framework* that the responsibilities of citizenship in a democratic society should include antiracist commitments. To give just one illustration, the *Framework* speaks of learning to respect the rights of the minority, even a minority of one. But how about learning when to *be* such a minority of one, oneself? When should one be the person to speak out, to call attention to an injustice that others prefer not to think about?

James Baldwin in his book *The Fire Next Time,* powerfully describes an incident from the early sixties in his own life that exemplifies such a failure of citizenship in the area of race.[2]

A civilization is not destroyed by wicked people; it is not necessary that people be wicked but only that they be spineless.

> I and two Negro acquaintances, all of us well past thirty, and
> looking it, were in the bar in Chicago's O'Hare airport several
> months ago, and the bartender refused to serve us, because, he
> said, we looked too young. It took a vast amount of patience
> not to strangle him and great insistence and some luck to get
> the manager, who defended the bartender, on the ground that
> he was "new" and had not yet, presumably, learned how to dis-
> tinguish a Negro "boy" of twenty and a Negro "boy" of thirty-
> seven. Well, we were served finally, of course, but by this time
> no amount of Scotch would have helped us. The bar was very
> crowded and our altercation had been very noisy, yet not one
> customer in the bar had done anything to help us. 77 f.

One goal of citizenship education should surely be for people to come to believe that they ought to intervene in some way in such situations, and to come
away from their education with some guidelines about how to do so. On this,
antiracist, feature of citizen education the *California History / Social Science
Framework* is almost entirely silent.

The *Framework*'s failure here has two interconnected aspects. First, its conception of the forms of activity appropriate to a citizenry committed to upholding justice (as a feature of a democratic society) is too limited. It largely
omits citizens' responsibility to *counter injustices* in their society. The second
failure is the inadequate attention to racism as a *primary instance* of the sort of
injustice that a future democratic citizenry needs to be educated to understand and to counteract.

30   The second educational value, *multiculturalism,* encompasses the following
three subvalues: (1) affirming one's own cultural identity; learning about and
valuing one's own cultural heritage; (2) respecting and desiring to understand
and learn about (and from) cultures other than one's own; (3) valuing and taking delight in cultural diversity itself; that is, regarding the existence of distinct
cultural groups within one's own society as a positive good to be treasured
and nurtured. The kind of respect involved in the second condition (respecting others) is meant to be an informed (and not uncritical) respect grounded
in an understanding of another culture. It involves an attempt to see the culture from the point of view of its members and in particular to see how members of that culture value the expression of their own culture. It involves an
active interest in and ability in some way to enter into and to enjoy the cultural expressions of other groups.

Such an understanding of another culture in no way requires an affirmation of every feature of that culture as positively good, as some critics of multiculturalism fear (or at least charge). It does not preclude criticism, on the
basis either of norms of that culture itself which particular practices in that
culture might violate, or of standards external to that culture. Of course when
it is legitimate to use a standard external to a culture (e.g. a particular standard

of equality between men and women drawn from the Western liberal tradition) is a complex issue. And multiculturalism always warns both against using a legitimate criticism of some feature of a culture as moral leverage to condemn the culture as a whole—declaring it not worthy of serious curricular attention, or disqualifying it as a source of moral insight to those outside that culture, for example—as well as alerting us to the difficult-to-avoid failure to scrutinize the basis of that criticism for its own cultural bias. Nevertheless, multiculturalism need not and should not identify itself with the view that members of one culture never have the moral standing to make an informed criticism of the practices of another culture.

The outward directedness of the second feature of multiculturalism (respecting other cultures) is an important complement to the inward focus of the first feature (learning about and valuing one's own culture). This dual orientation meets the criticism sometimes made of multiculturalism that it creates divisions between students. For the second feature prescribes a reaching out beyond one's own group and thus explicitly counters the balkanizing effect of the first dimension of multiculturalism alone. Nevertheless, that first feature—learning about and valuing one's own culture—is an integral part of multiculturalism, not merely something to be tolerated, treated as a response to political pressure, or justified simply on the grounds of boosting self-esteem. An individual's cultural identity is a deeply significant element of herself, and understanding of her own culture should be a vital part of the task of education. An understanding of one's own culture as contributing to the society of which one is a part is a significant part of that first element of multiculturalism.

The third component of multiculturalism is the valuing of diversity itself. Not only do we want our young people to respect specific other cultures but also to value a school, a city, a society in which diverse cultural groups exist. While this diversity may certainly present problems for young people, one wants them to see the diversity primarily as something to value, prefer, and cherish.

Three dimensions of culture seem to be deserving of curricular and other forms of educational attention in schools. The first is the *ancestor culture* of the ethnic group, nation, or civilization of origin. For Chinese-Americans this would involve understanding Chinese culture, including ancient Chinese cultures, philosophies, religions, and the like. For Irish-Americans it would be Irish history and culture. For Mexican-Americans it would include attention to some of the diverse cultures of Mexico—the Aztec, the Mayan, as well as the Spanish, and then the hybrid Spanish/indigenous culture which forms modern Mexican culture.

While all ethnic cultures have an ancestor culture, not all current groups bear the same relationship to that ancestor culture. For example, African-Americans' connection to their ancestor culture is importantly different from that of immigrant groups like Italians, Eastern European Jews, and Irish. Although scholars disagree about the actual extent of influence of various African cultures on current African-American cultural forms, it was a general

35

feature of American slavery systematically to attempt to deprive African slaves of their African culture. By contrast voluntary immigrant groups brought with them an intact culture, which they renegotiated in the new conditions of the United States. In fact the label "African-American" can be seen as an attempt to forge a stronger analogy between the experience of black Americans and that of other immigrant groups than do other expressions such as "black" or even "Afro-American." The former conceptualization emphasizes that American blacks are not simply a product of America but do indeed possess an ancestor culture, no matter how brutally that culture was attacked. Note, however, that there is an important difference between this use of "African-American" and that applied, for example, to second-generation Ethiopian-Americans. The latter is a truer parallel to white ethnic "hyphenate Americans."

Other differences among groups, such as the current ethnic group's distance in time from its original emigration, variations and pressures to assimilate once in the United States, and the effects of racism affect the significance of the ancestor culture for a current ethnic group. Nevertheless ancestor culture plays some role for every group.

A second dimension of culture to be encompassed by multicultural education is the *historical experience* of the ethnic group within the United States. Generally it will attend to the historical experiences, ways of life, triumphs and setbacks, art and literature, contributions and achievements, of ethnic groups in the United States. The latter point is uncontroversial; all proponents of multicultural education agree in the need to correct the omission in traditional curricula and text books of many ethnic groups' experiences and contributions to our national life. But distinguishing this dimension from the ancestor culture and giving attention to both of them is crucial. For the culture of the Chinese-American is *not* the same as the culture of traditional or modern China; it is a culture with its own integrity: neither the purer form of ancestor culture nor that of middle-America. It can be called "intercultural," influenced by more than one culture (as indeed the ancestor culture itself may have been), yet forming a culture in its own right.

A third dimension of culture is the *current ethnic culture* of the group in question. This is the dimension most directly embodied in the student member of that culture. This current ethnic culture—family ethnic rituals, foods, customs regarding family roles and interactions, values, musical and other cultural preferences, philosophies of life, and the like—bears complex relationships to the ancestor culture as well as to the group's historical ethnic experience in the United States. It changes over time and is affected in myriad ways by the other society. As with ancestor culture and historical ethnic experience, the student's current ethnic culture must be given respect. What such respect consists in is a complex matter, as the following examples indicate.

In one case respect can involve allowing Arab girls to wear traditional headgear in school if they so desire. In another it can mean seeing a child's remark in class as containing an insight stemming from her cultural perspective that might otherwise be missed or seem off the mark. Another form of respect for culture involves, for example, recognizing that a Vietnamese child's failure to look a teacher in the eye is not a sign of evasiveness or lack of interest but a way of expressing a deference to teachers and authority, culturally regarded as appropriate. Thus, respect for ethnic cultures sometimes involves a direct valorizing of a part of that culture; at other times neither valorizing nor disvaluing, but allowing for its expression because it is important to the student. In another context, it can involve reshaping one's own sense of what is educationally essential, to take into account another culture's difference. Finally, it can sometimes involve seeing a cultural manifestation as a genuine obstacle to learning but respecting the cultural setting in which it is embedded and the student's own attachment to that cultural feature, and finding ways to work with or around that obstacle to accomplish an educational goal.

In summary, ancestor culture, ethnic historical experience in the United States, and current ethnic culture are three dimensions of ethic culture requiring attention in a multicultural education. They are all dimensions that children need to be taught and taught to respect—both in their own and others' cultures.

The context of multicultural education presupposes a larger society consisting of various cultures. Thus, teaching an attitude of appreciation toward a particular one of these cultures in the three dimensions just mentioned will have both a particular and a general aspect. We will want students to appreciate cultures in their own right, but also in their relationship to the larger society. This simple point can help us to avoid two familiar, and contrasting, pitfalls of multicultural education, that can be illustrated with the example of Martin Luther King, Jr.

One pitfall would be exemplified by a teacher who portrayed King as an important leader of the black community, but who failed to emphasize that he should be seen as a great *American* leader more generally—as a true hero for all Americans, indeed, for all humanity, and not *only* for or of African-Americans. The teacher fails to show the non-African-American students that they too have a connection with King simply as Americans.

Yet an exactly opposite pitfall is to teach appreciation of the contribution of members of particular cultures *only* insofar as those contributions can be seen in universal terms or in terms of benefiting the entire society. This pitfall would be exemplified by seeing Dr. King only in terms of his contribution to humanity or to American society more generally, but *not* acknowledging him as a product and leader specifically of the African-American community. Multicultural education needs to enable non-African-American students, whether white or not, to be able to appreciate a leader of the African-American community in that role itself, and not *only* by showing that the leader in question made a contribution to everyone in the society. Thus, multicultural education needs to emphasize both the general or full society dimension of each culture's contributions and heroes and also the particular or culture-specific dimension.

Many people associate multiculturalism with the idea of moral *relativism* or cultural relativism and specifically with the view that because no one from one culture is in a position to judge another culture, no one is in a position to say which culture should be given priority in the allocation of respect, curricular inclusion, and the like. Therefore, according to this way of thinking, every culture has a claim to equal inclusion and respect, because no one is in a position to say which ones are *more* worthy of respect. While the philosophic relativism on which this version of multiculturalism rests needs to be taken seriously—it has a long and distinguished philosophic history—there is an alternative, quite different and nonrelativistic, philosophic foundation for multiculturalism as well. This view—which might be called *pluralistic*—agrees that cultures manifest different values but affirms that the values of a given culture can be, or can come to be, appreciated (as well as assessed) by someone from a different culture. Thus, while cultures are different, they are at least partly accessible to one another.

45   According to this pluralist, nonrelativist line of thought, multicultural education should involve exposing students to, and helping them to appreciate the range of, values embodied in different cultures. Both whites and Cambodian immigrant students can come to appreciate Toni Morrison's novels of black life in America. African-American students can come to understand and appreciate Confucian philosophy. This pluralist view should not minimize the work often necessary to see beyond the parochial assumptions and perspectives of one's own culture in order to appreciate the values of another culture. Indeed, one of the undoubted contributions of the multicultural movement has been to reveal those obstacles as well as the dominant culture's resistance to acknowledging them. Nevertheless, the fact that such an effort can be even partially successful provides a goal of multicultural education that is barely conceivable within the pure relativist position.

I want now to explore the complex relationship between the two values that I have discussed so far—antiracism and multiculturalism. First, to establish the differences: Both multiculturalism and antiracism are concerned with groups and group identities; but the groups are constituted differently from an antiracist than from a multicultural standpoint. From an antiracist standpoint a group is constituted by its place in the hierarchy of racial dominance (roughly, by whether it is a dominant group or a subordinate group). Thus, in the United States whites, as a racial group, are dominant, while African-Americans, Native-Americans, and Latinos or Hispanics are subordinate. But from a multicultural perspective African-Americans, Latinos, and Native-Americans are not single cultural groups. Mexicans are culturally very different from Puerto Ricans though both are Latino. Black Americans whose roots in this country go back to slavery are culturally distinct from much more recent immigrants, for example, from Haiti, whose native language is Haitian Creole, as well as from English-speaking blacks from other Caribbean countries. Haitians have a heritage as citizens of the first black republic in the New World and the only one set up as a result of a successful slave revolt. This gives Haitians a very different sense of the significance of their race and racial history than that of United States slave descendants. Elaine Pinderhughes, an African-American professor of social work and the author of *Understanding Race, Ethnicity, and Power,* quotes a Haitian-American whose racial and ethnic identity illustrates this: "As a child I never understood why my father insisted on identifying himself as Haitian whenever the issue of race came up. Later I understood that he wanted us to dissociate ourselves from black Americans."[3]

In fact, it is partly because racist attitudes are generally *not* sensitive to these cultural and ethnic distinctions that an antiracist perspective divides groups up in a somewhat different way from a multicultural perspective. This point is made powerfully and tragically by the case of a Chinese-American, Vincent Chin, who was killed by a white autoworker resentful towards the Japanese because competition from the Japanese auto industry contributed to unemployment of American auto workers. The point suggested by a documentary film concerning this incident (*The Killing of Vincent Chin*) is not so much that the white killer mistook a Chinese-American for a Japanese-American, as that he had no clear sense that there was a difference between these two Asian-American groups. So racism's existence gives subordinate groups that are culturally distinct, common cause to identify and unite on a common racial basis in opposition to, for example, anti-Asian racism.

This difference between the antiracist and the multicultural perspectives applies to the categorization of dominant groups as well as to that of subordinate or vulnerable ones, in that the antiracist perspective ignores cultural differences within the dominant groups. Jewish-, Polish-, and Irish-Americans exemplify this. Irish-Americans, once viciously discriminated against by Anglo-Protestants in this country and viewed in derogatory terms similar to African-Americans, are no long a victimized group; rather, Irish-Americans are now part of, are seen by nonwhite minorities as part of, and generally see themselves as part of the majority white group—a group which in fact perpetuates disadvantage and injustice to nonwhite groups.

Yet, despite the common racial designation as "white," Irish-Americans are a culturally distinct group from Jewish-Americans and Polish-Americans; they have a distinct ancestor culture and historic ethnic experience, distinctive music, rituals, language, backgrounds, foods and the like. These deserve to be valued and appreciated by members of other ethnic groups, including nonwhite ethnic groups, as part of a multicultural program. Yet from a purely antiracist perspective Irish-Americans have no distinct group identity; they are just "white." White students often object to being lumped together, as discussions of racism may do. The multicultural perspective is meant to speak to one legitimate source of this discomfort or protest. (Another is socioeconomic class, a large factor in this context, but unfortunately one beyond my scope here.) Whites aren't *just* whites; they too have ethnicities that are important sources of identity and that differentiate them from other whites. Nevertheless, the classification yielded by the lens of race—of Irish-Americans or

Polish-Americans as "white" is not a *false* one: it is simply *partial*. Antiracism and multiculturalism constitute two distinct and complementary lenses, yielding different categorizations of a common social reality. Both lenses highlight a truth about that reality. *Antiracism:* the truth that groups are arranged in a hierarchy of dominance and subordination, security and vulnerability, advantage and disadvantage; *multiculturalism:* the truth that groups have distinct cultures.

50   The metaphor of antiracism and multiculturalism as complementary lenses on a complex reality should not mislead us as to the reality of race and ethnicity. The identities of both racial and ethnic cultural groups are not simply givens but are historical and social constructs. What people at a given time think of as distinct racial or ethnic groups is a product of social categorization both situationally determined and subject to change. Thus, southern and eastern European immigrant groups in this country in the early part of the twentieth century are now regarded unequivocally as white, but at that time were often seen as distinct races; they were thought by many to have racially based psychological characteristics, such as industry, irresponsibility, intelligence, and the like. To the extent that the notions of "white" and "black" were used, members of these immigrant groups did not always think of themselves as either one. Another example: in England the term "black" is currently used to refer to east Asians as well as to Afro-Caribbeans; in the United States only the latter are regarded as "black."

A third difference is that multiculturalism and antiracism involve distinct approaches to the study of a particular cultural group that has been a target of racism. While antiracism highlights victimization and resistance, multiculturalism highlights cultural life, cultural expression, achievements, and the like.

In particular the two perspectives yield distinct (though complementary) approaches to the study of the *contributions* of different groups. Multiculturalism's thrust is to highlight (especially hitherto neglected or undervalued) contributions. Yet merely highlighting contributions of different cultural groups does not, by itself, address the deficiencies in traditional education that the multicultural education movement (broadly construed) hopes to address. For one effect of racism has been to prevent subordinate groups from fully developing their capacities for such accomplishments and contributions. Indeed, what it means for a society to be characterized by systemic and institutional racism is precisely for it to place obstacles, on the basis of race, in the way of equal opportunity to develop precisely those capacities that allow a cultural group to make contributions both to their own people and to the wider society. Hence, the multicultural perspective is needed to highlight (often neglected or underappreciated) contributions of a group, while the antiracist perspective focuses on the racist obstacles in the path of that group's development toward (among other things) making such contributions.

A fourth difference between the antiracist and the multicultural perspectives lies in the basic values in which each is grounded and which guide the forms of education under each rubric. Antiracism is grounded in the idea of the equal dignity of all persons and of the consequent wrongness of any group dominating or suppressing any other. Equal dignity is a value rooted in a *sameness* among persons; a humanity *shared* by all persons. By contrast, multiculturalism is a value rooted in *differences* among persons; multiculturalism calls for a respect for cultures, not in spite of their differences from oneself, but precisely *for* those differences. Both of these values—of shared humanity, and of cultural difference—are essential; neither one encompasses the other. The strength of antiracism—in its grounding in individual dignity and shared humanity—is also the source of its limitation. While antiracism says that it is wrong for one group to dominate or persecute another because of race, it does not by itself involve a positive appreciation of ethnic groups as embodying distinct *cultures* which deserve to be valued. Common dignity can be affirmed without a positive valuing of the individual's culture in its concrete particularity. Multiculturalism involves the converse value limitation, for while highlighting respect and appreciation for cultural difference, it does *not* focus on our common humanity or shared dignity. These two values are not inconsistent with one another; children can and need to learn both what they share with others as well as an appreciation of their differences.

A striking example of the difference between multiculturalism and antiracism regarding this valuational foundation can be found in a comprehensive study of non-Jewish rescuers of Jews during the Holocaust, a book called *The Altruistic Personality,* by Samuel and Pearl Oliner.[4]

Most of the rescuers of Jews studied by the Oliners—people of various nationalities and occupations—expressed in some way an appreciation of the equal dignity of all persons and the irrelevance of race, nationality, and religion to that dignity. It was this acute appreciation of dignity, this strong antiracist consciousness, that provided an important part of their willingness to put themselves at great personal risk to rescue Jews during the Nazi occupation. However, only rarely did any rescuers show an appreciation of Jewishness as a cultural form having value in its own right. The rescuees were seen as having dignity *independent of,* and even *despite* their Jewishness. The Jewishness was not seen as a source of value, a value that was at risk in Hitler's attempt to exterminate Jewishness as well as Jews. The rescuers either lacked a general sense of multicultural value or failed to appreciated that value in the case of Jews. Similar points can be made about Turkish rescuers of Armenians during the Armenian genocide of 1915–16, according to research by Richard Hovanissian.

A final significant difference between the antiracist and the multicultural perspectives is that while antiracism directly challenges racial domination and racial injustice, multiculturalism, by contrast, poses no strong or pointed challenge to inequalities of power and opportunity between groups. Multiculturalism tends to promote the attitude of respect for other cultures, primarily within the existing structure and inequality between groups. While some multicultural education theorists, such as Christine Sleeter and Carl Grant, have argued that a fully realized program of multicultural education does challenge inequalities of power,[5] I think this point is better put by saying that a multicultural program needs to have a strong and central antiracist component, as well as a multicultural one in the sense I have outlined here.

I hope I have succeeded in showing both that antiracism and multiculturalism provide distinct perspectives and guiding values; that these perspectives are complementary; and that both are essential to a value education for a multiracial, multiethnic society.

The third value for an educational program that I want to discuss is the *sense of community*—specifically a sense of community that embraces racial and cultural differences. While the idea of a multiracial integrated community has historically been linked with the struggle against racism, I think there is reason for focusing on it as a value distinct from antiracism. The sense of community that I mean involves a sense of bond with other persons, a sense of shared identification with the community in question (be it a class, a school or workplace), a sense of loyalty to and involvement with this community. I will make the further assumption that the experience of interracial community in such institutions is an important contributor to being able fully to experience members of other races and cultures as fellow citizens and fellow human beings throughout one's life.

It is true that the achievement of or the experience of interracial community is likely to contribute to a firm commitment to nonracist and antiracist values. Nevertheless, there is an important difference between the two families of values. A sense of community is defeated not only by racist attitudes, in which members of one group feel themselves superior to members of another group, but simply by experiencing members of other races and cultural groups as *other,* as distant from oneself, as people with whom one does not feel comfortable, and has little in common. As I suggested earlier, racial discomfort, racial sensitivity, and racial ignorance should be distinguished from racism itself; yet all of the former run contrary to a sense of interracial community. What defeats a sense of community is to see members of a group primarily as a *they,* as a kind of undifferentiated group counterposed to a *we,* defined by the group one identifies with oneself. One becomes blind to the individuality of members of the *they* group. One experiences this group as deeply different from oneself, even if one cannot always account for or explain that sense of difference. This anticommunal consciousness can exist in the absence of actual racist attitudes toward the other group, although the former is a natural stepping stone toward the latter. I think many students in schools, of all races and cultures, never do achieve the experience of interracial community, never learn to feel comfortable with members of other racial and ethnic groups, even though these students do not really have racist attitudes in the strict sense. Rather, the sense of group difference simply overwhelms any experiencing of commonality and sharing that is necessary for developing a sense of community.

60   Moreover, and unfortunately, despite the ways that antiracism and interracial community can be mutually supportive, there can also be tensions

between certain aspects of antiracist education and the achievement of interracial community. On the most general level, antiracist education puts racial identity in the forefront of concern; one talks about groups—whites, blacks, Hispanic, etc. Yet, an overfocus on racial identity can give children a message that the most important thing about persons is their racial identity, and that people who differ from oneself racially necessarily differ in all kinds of other fundamental ways. It is perhaps ironic that an antiracist perspective that affirms the shared humanity and equal dignity of all persons independent of race can sometimes contribute to this *we/they* consciousness. Nevertheless, this "racialization" of consciousness, to use Michael Omi and Howard Winant's term,[6] can contribute to a sense of distance and estrangement, or at least to a lack of comfort with members of other races. It can thereby harm the achievement of interracial community. This is not of course an argument against antiracist education, for, even if the two values were irrevocably in tension—and I will argue that they aren't—it might be interracial community that should be sacrificed to the more urgent task of antiracist education.

This tension presents a situation in which the tasks of value education might appear different to members of subordinate groups than of dominant groups, especially to parents in those different groups. African-American and other parents of color face the difficult task of teaching their children to be wary of and prepared for the racism that they will probably experience at some point, while yet not becoming so paranoid as to lump all whites together and to be entirely distrustful of them. I bring this point up partly because I think many white people fail to recognize, or don't take seriously enough, the pervasive and often subtle racism experienced by people of color, and incorrectly regard this self-protective attitude on their part as hypersensitivity. Because of their greater stake in countering racism, the ideal of interracial community might seem like a luxury to a subordinate group parent; nevertheless, I think it is a value that needs to have some place in their children's education as well.

Fortunately, we need not choose between the values of interracial community and antiracism; rather, we should search for ways of teaching antiracist values that minimize the potential for harming or preventing interracial community. I will briefly mention two general guidelines in this regard. One is constantly to emphasize the internal variety within a group being studied; not to say "whites" and "blacks" all the time as if these were monolithic groups. For example, in discussing slavery, make clear that not all blacks were slaves during the period of slavery, that there were many free blacks. Similarly, most whites did *not* own slaves, and a few whites even actively aligned themselves with the cause of abolition, aiding free blacks who organized the underground railroads and the like. Exhibiting such internal variety within "white," "black," and other groups helps to prevent the formation of rigid or undifferentiated images of racial groups that lend themselves readily to a *we/they* consciousness that undermines community.

A second guideline is to try to give students the experience (in imagination at least) of being both discriminated against, excluded, or demeaned, and also being the discriminator, the excluder, the advantaged one. One first grade teacher I know discusses discrimination and racism by asking all the children in her class if they feel that they have been discriminated against in any way. Children feel discriminated against, excluded, or vulnerable to exclusion for all sorts of reasons—because they are short, or because they once didn't have a certain toy that other children had, or didn't know the characters of some television program being discussed. In one discussion in this teacher's class, a heavyish boy said that other kids made fun of him because of his size. In discussing this all the children were helped to see and to be sensitized in a personal, meaningful way to the damage done by all sorts of discrimination; and this is a lesson that this teacher extended to other forms of discrimination as well, including more socially significant ones, such as racism and sexism.

Encouraging students to attempt as much as possible to experience the vantage points of advantaged and disadvantaged, included and excluded, and the like, provides an important buffer to a "we/they" consciousness in the racial domain. This buffering is accomplished not so much by encouraging, as the first guideline does, the appreciation of internal diversity in a given group, as by bridging the gulf between the experience of the dominant and that of the subordinate. This is achieved by showing children that there is at least *some* dimension of life on which they occupy the dominant, and on others the subordinate, position (even if these dimensions are not of equal significance).

65   There is a similar process of potential convergence as well as potential tension between *community* and *multiculturalism*. These are distinct values. The positive bond and sense of connection involved in interracial community is not guaranteed by multiculturalism, which emphasizes *respect, interest,* and *understanding;* while such attitudes may help to inform and enrich a sense of community, they are quite compatible with its absence, and with a sense of distance from those of the respected, interesting "other culture." Some forms of multicultural education can even further divide students from one another while teaching respect, by *overemphasizing* cultural differences and mutual inaccessibility of different cultures to one another. Analogously to antiracism, this kind of faulty teaching of multiculturalism can lead to a similarly rigidified *we/they* consciousness.

The converse is true as well. Interracial community can not provide all the values involved in multiculturalism. For, while interracial community does encompass people who are culturally, racially, different from one another, it does not by itself promote a definite, positive appreciation of cultural differences and of distinct cultural values. And a single-minded attempt to foster interracial community can lead easily to an avoidance of fully acknowledging these racial/cultural differences, for fear that such acknowledgment will foster a we/they attitude inimical to community.

Thus, interracial community and multiculturalism are distinct values that are both essential to a value education program, but that can be in tension with one another. Nevertheless, there are ways of teaching multiculturalism that minimize these tensions. Some broad guidelines are the following: (1) Invite children's participation in cultures studied, so as to make "other" cultures as accessible as possible to nonmembers. For example, have children in the class interview one another, posing questions about each others' cultures that the questioners feel will help them to comprehend the culture in question. Establish an "intercultural dialogue" among students. This approach will use a recognition of genuine cultural differences to bring children together rather than keep them apart. (2) Recognize cultures' internal variety (even contradictory strands within a given culture), their change over time, and (where appropriate) their interaction with other cultures—rather than presenting cultures as frozen in time, monolithic, and totally self-contained. (3) Recognize cultural universals and commonalities. It is not contrary to the spirit of multiculturalism—to the acknowledgment of authentic cultural differences—to see that distinct cultures may share certain broad features. For example, every culture responds to certain universal features of human life, such as birth, death, the rearing of children, a search for meaning in life. Both (2) and (3) prevent an inaccurate and community-impairing "theyness" in the presentation of other cultures.

Finally, our conception of interracial community must itself allow for the recognition of difference. A powerful, but misleading, tradition in our thinking about community is that people only feel a sense of community when they think of themselves as "the same" as the other members of the community. On this view, recognition of difference is threatening to community. But, as Robert Bellah and his colleagues argue in *Habits of the Heart,* the kind of community needed in the United States is *pluralistic* community, one which involves a sense of bond and connection stemming from shared activity, condition, task, location, and the like—and grounded ultimately in an experience of shared humanity—yet recognizing and valuing cultural differences (and other kinds of differences as well).[7]

I have discussed three crucial educational values for a multiracial, multicultural society: opposition to racism, multiculturalism, and interracial community. I have argued that these are distinct values, and that all three are essential to a responsible program of value education in a multicultural society. I have argued also that there can be tensions between different values. But the values can also be mutually supportive, and I have suggested some guidelines for maximizing the support and minimizing the tensions.

NOTES

1. *History—Social Science Framework for California Public Schools, Kindergarten Through Grade Twelve* (Sacramento: California State Department of Education, 1988).
2. James Baldwin, *The Fire Next Time* (New York: Dell, 1962).
3. Elaine Pinderhughes, *Understanding Race, Ethnicity, and Power: The Key to Efficacy in Clinical Practice* (New York: Free Press, 1989).

4. Samuel and Pearl Oliner, *The Altruistic Personality: Rescuers of Jews in Nazi Europe* (New York: Free Press, 1988).
5. See among other writings, Carl Grant and Christine Sleeter, "An analysis of Multicultural Education in the United States," *Harvard Educational Review* (Nov. 1987).
6. Michael Omi and Howard Winant, *Racial Formation in the United States: From the 1960's to the 1980's* (New York: Routledge, 1986).
7. Robert Belah et al., *Habits of the Heart: Individualism and Commitment in American Life* (Berkeley: University of California Press, 1985).

WHY WE READ:
CANON TO THE RIGHT OF ME . . .

Katha Pollitt

For the past couple of years we've all been witness to a furious debate about the literary canon. What books should be assigned to students? What books should critics discuss? What books should the rest of us read, and who are "we" anyway? Like everyone else, I've given these questions some thought, and when an invitation came my way, I leaped to produce my own manifesto. But to my surprise, when I sat down to write—in order to discover, as E. M. Forster once said, what I really think—I found that I agreed with all sides in the debate at once.

Take the conservatives. Now this rather dour collection of scholars and diatribists—Allan Bloom, Hilton Kramer, John Silber and so on—are not a particularly appealing group of people. They are arrogant, they are rude, they are gloomy, they do not suffer fools gladly, and everywhere they look, fools are what they see. All good reasons not to elect them to public office, as Massachusetts voters decided when they rejected Silber's 1990 gubernatorial bid. But what is so terrible, really, about what they are saying? I, too, believe that some books are more profound, more complex, more essential to an understanding of our culture than others; I too, am appalled to think of students graduating from college not having read Homer, Plato, Virgil, Milton, Tolstoy—all writers, dead white Western men though they be, whose works have meant a great deal to me. As a teacher of literature and of writing, I too have seen at first hand how ill-educated many students are, and how little they are aware of this important fact about themselves. Last year I taught a graduate seminar in the writing of poetry. None of my students had read more than a smattering of poems by anyone, male or female, published more than ten years ago. Robert Lowell was as far outside their frame of reference as Alexander Pope. When I gently suggested to one student that it might benefit her to read some poetry if she planned to spend her life writing it, she told me that yes, she knew she should read more but when she encountered a really good poem, it only made her depressed. That contemporary writing has a history which it profits us to know in some depth, that we ourselves were not born yesterday, seems too obvious even to argue.

But ah, say the liberals, the canon exalted by the conservatives is itself an artifact of history. Sure, some books are more rewarding than others, but why can't we change our minds about which books those are? The canon itself was not always as we know it today: Until the 1920s, *Moby-Dick* was shelved with the boys' adventure stories. If T. S. Eliot could single-handedly dethrone the

Romantic poets in favor of the neglected Metaphysicals and place John Webster alongside Shakespeare, why can't we dip into a sea of stories and fish out Edith Wharton or Virginia Woolf? And this position, too, makes a great deal of sense to me. After all, alongside the many reasons for a book to end up on the required-reading shelf are some rather suspect reasons for its exclusion; because it was written by a woman and therefore presumed to be too slight; because it was written by a black person and therefore presumed to be too unsophisticated or to reflect too special a case. By all means, say the liberals, let's have great books and a shared culture. But let's make sure that all the different kinds of greatness are represented and that the culture we share reflects the true range of human experience.

If we leave the broadening of the canon up to the conservatives, this will never happen, because to them change only means defeat. Look at the recent fuss over the latest edition of the Great Books series published by Encyclopedia Britannica, headed by that old snake-oil salesman Mortimer Adler. Four women have now been added to the series: Virginia Woolf, Willa Cather, Jane Austen, and George Eliot. That's nice, I suppose, but really! Jane Austen has been a certified Great Writer for a hundred years! Lionel Trilling said so! There's something truly absurd about the conservatives earnestly sitting in judgment on the illustrious dead, as though up in Writer's Heaven Jane and George and Willa and Virginia were breathlessly waiting to hear if they'd finally made it into the club, while Henry Fielding, newly dropped from the list, howls in outer darkness and the Brontës, presumably, stamp their feet in frustration and hope for better luck in twenty years, when *Jane Eyre* and *Wuthering Heights* will suddenly turn out to have qualities of greatness never before detected in their pages. It's like Poet's Corner at Manhattan's Cathedral of St. John the Divine, where mortal men—and a woman or two—of letters actually vote on which immortals to honor with a plaque, a process no doubt complete with electoral campaigns, compromise candidates and all the rest of the underside of literary life. "No, sorry, I just can't vote for Whitman. I'm a Washington Irving man myself."

5   Well, a liberal is not a very exciting thing to be, and so we have the radicals, who attack the concepts of "greatness," "shared," "culture," and "lists." (I'm overlooking here the ultraradicals, who attack the "privileging" of "texts," as they insist on calling books, and think one might as well spend one's college years deconstructing "Leave It to Beaver.") Who is to say, ask the radicals, what is a great book? What's so terrific about complexity, ambiguity, historical centrality and high seriousness? If *The Color Purple,* say, gets students thinking about their own experience, maybe they ought to read it and forget about ————, and here you can fill in the name of whatever classic work you yourself found dry and tedious and never got around to finishing. For the radicals the notion of a shared culture is a lie, because it means presenting as universally meaningful and politically neutral books that reflect the interests and experience and values of privileged white men at the expense of those of others—women, blacks, Latinos, Asians, the working class, whomever. Why

not scrap the one-list-for-everyone idea and let people connect with books that are written by people like themselves about people like themselves? It will be a more accurate reflection of a multifaceted and conflict-ridden society, and will do wonders for everyone's self-esteem, except, of course, living white men—but they have too much self-esteem already.

Now, I have to say that I dislike the radicals' vision intensely. How foolish to argue that Chekhov has nothing to say to a black woman—or, for that matter, to me—merely because he is Russian, long dead, a man. The notion that one reads to increase one's self-esteem sounds to me like more snake oil. Literature is not an aerobics class or session at the therapist's. But then I think of myself as a child, leafing through anthologies of poetry for the names of women. I never would have admitted that I needed a role model, even if that awful term had existed back in the prehistory of which I speak, but why was I so excited to find a female name, even when, as was often the case, it was attached to a poem of no interest to me whatsoever? Anna Laetitia Barbauld, author of "Life! I know not what thou art / But know that thou and I must part!"; Lady Anne Lindsey, writer of plaintive ballads in incomprehensible Scots dialect, and the other minor female poets included by chivalrous Sir Arthur Quiller-Couch in the old *Oxford Book of English Verse:* I have to admit it, just by their presence in that august volume they did something for me. And although it had not much to do with reading or writing, it was an important thing they did.

Now, what are we to make of this spluttering debate, in which charges of imperialism are met by equally passionate accusations of vandalism, in which each side hates the others, and yet each one seems to have its share of reason? Perhaps what we have here is one of those debates in which the opposing sides, unbeknownst to themselves, share a myopia that will turn out to be the most telling feature of the whole discussion: a debate, for instance, like that of our Founding Fathers over the nature of the franchise. Think of all the energy and passion spent pondering the question of property qualifications or direct versus legislative elections, while all along, unmentioned and unimagined, was the fact—to us so central—that women, not to mention slaves, were never considered for any kind of vote.

Something is being overlooked: the state of reading, and books, and literature in our country at this time. Why, ask yourself, is everyone so hot under the collar about what to put on the required-reading shelf? It is because while we have been arguing so fiercely about which books make the best medicine, the patient has been slipping deeper and deeper into a coma.

Let us imagine a country in which reading is a popular voluntary activity. There, parents read books for their own edification and pleasure, and are seen by their children at this silent and mysterious pastime. These parents also read to their children, give them books for presents, talk to them about books and underwrite, with their taxes, a public library system that is open all day, every day. In school—where an attractive library is invariably to be found—the children study certain books together but also have an active reading life of their own. Years later it may even be hard for them to remember if they read *Jane Eyre* at home and Judy Blume in class, or the other way around. In college young people continue to be assigned certain books, but far more important are the books they discover for themselves, browsing in the library, in bookstores, on the shelves of friends, one book leading to another, back and forth in history and across languages and cultures. After graduation they continue to read, and in the fullness of time produce a new generation of readers. Oh, happy land! I wish we all lived there.

10   In that other country of real readers—voluntary, active, self-determined readers—a debate like the current one over the canon would not be taking place. Or if it did, it would be as a kind of parlor game: What books would *you* take to a desert island? Everyone would know that the top-ten list was merely a tiny fraction of the books one would read in a lifetime. It would not seem racist or sexist or hopelessly hidebound to put Hawthorne on the syllabus and not Toni Morrison. It would be more like putting oatmeal and not noodles on the breakfast menu—a choice part arbitrary, part a nod to the national past, part, dare one say it, a kind of reverse affirmative action: School might frankly be the place where one read the books that are a little offputting, that have gone a little cold, that you might pass over because they do not address, in reader-friendly contemporary fashion, the issues most immediately at stake in modern life, but that, with a little study, turn out to have a great deal to say. Being on the list wouldn't mean so much. It might even add to a writer's cachet *not* to be on the list, to be in one way or another too heady, too daring, too exciting to be ground up into institutional fodder for teenagers. Generations of high school students have been spoiled for George Eliot by being forced to read *Silas Marner* at a tender age. One can imagine a whole new readership for her if grown-ups were left to approach *Middlemarch* and *Daniel Deronda* with open minds, at their leisure.

Of course, they rarely do. In America today the assumption underlying the canon debate is that the books on the list are the only books that are going to be read, and if the list is dropped no books are going to be read. Becoming a textbook is a book's only chance; all sides take that for granted. And so all agree not to mention certain things that they themselves, as highly educated people and, one assumes, devoted readers, know perfectly well. For example, that if you read only twenty-five, or fifty, or a hundred books, you can't understand them, however well chosen they are. And if you don't have an independent reading life—and very few students do—you won't *like* reading the books on the list and will forget them the minute you finish them. And that books have, or should have, lives beyond the syllabus—thus, the totally misguided attempt to put current literature in the classroom. How strange to think that people need professional help to read John Updike or Alice Walker, writers people actually do read for fun. But all sides agree: If it isn't taught, it doesn't count.

Let's look at the canon question from another angle. Instead of asking what books we want others to read, let's ask why we read books ourselves. I think the canon debaters are being a little disingenuous here, are suppressing, in the interest of their own agendas, their personal experience of reading. Sure, we read to understand our American culture and history, and we also read to recover neglected masterpieces, and to learn more about the accomplishments of our subgroup and thereby, as I've admitted myself, increase our self-esteem. But what about reading for the aesthetic pleasures of language, form, image? What about reading to learn something new, to have a vicarious adventure, to follow the workings of an interesting, if possibly skewed, narrow and ill-tempered mind? What about reading for the story? For an expanded sense of sheer human variety? There are a thousand reasons why a book might have a claim on our time and attention other than its canonization. I once infuriated an acquaintance by asserting that Trollope, although in many ways a lesser writer than Dickens, possessed some wonderful qualities Dickens lacked: a more realistic view of women, a more skeptical view of good intentions, a subtler sense of humor, a drier vision of life which I myself found congenial. You'd think I'd advocated throwing Dickens out and replacing him with a toaster. Because Dickens is a certified Great Writer, and Trollope is not.

Am I saying anything different from what Randall Jarrell said in his great 1953 essay, "The Age of Criticism"? Not really, so I'll quote him. Speaking of the literary gatherings of the era, Jarrell wrote:

> If, at such parties, you wanted to talk about *Ulysses* or *The Castle* or *The Brothers Karamazov* or *The Great Gatsby* or Graham Greene's last novel—Important books—you were at the right place. (Though you weren't so well off you wanted to talk about *Remembrance of Things Past*. Important, but too long.) But if you wanted to talk about Turgenev's novelettes, or *The House of the Dead*, or *Lavengro*, or *Life on the Mississippi*, or *The Old Wives' Tale*, or *The Golovlyov Family*, or Cunningham-Grahame's stories, or Saint-Simon's memoirs, or *Lost Illusions*, or *The Beggar's Opera*, or *Eugen Onegin*, or *Little Dorrit*, or the *Burnt Njal Saga*, or *Persuasion*, or *The Inspector-General*, or *Oblomov*, or *Peer Gynt*, or *Far from the Madding Crowd*, or *Out of Africa*, or the *Parallel Lives*, or *A Dreary Story*, or *Debits and Credits*, or *Arabia Deserta*, or *Elective Affinities*, or *Schweik*, or— any of a thousand good or interesting but Unimportant books, you couldn't expect a very ready knowledge or sympathy from most of the readers there. They had looked at the big sights, the current sights, hard, with guides and glasses; and those walks in the country, over unfrequented or thrice-familiar territory, all alone—those walks from which most of the joy and good of reading come—were walks that they hadn't gone on very often.

I suspect that most canon debaters have taken those solitary rambles, if only out of boredom—how many times, after all, can you reread the *Aeneid*, or *Mrs. Dalloway*, or *Cotton Comes to Harlem* (to pick one book from each column)? But those walks don't count, because of an another assumption all sides hold in common, which is that the purpose of reading is none of the many varied and delicious satisfactions I've mentioned; it's medicinal. The chief end of reading is to produce a desirable kind of society. A respectful, high-minded citizen of a unified society for the conservatives, an up-to-date and flexible sort for the liberals, a subgroup-identified, robustly confident one for the radicals. How pragmatic, how moralistic, how American! The culture debaters turn out to share a secret suspicion of culture itself, as well as the anti-pornographer's belief that there is a simple, one-to-one correlation between books and behavior. Read the conservatives' list and produce a nation of sexists and racists—or a nation of philosopher kings. Read the liberals' list and produce a nation of spineless relativists—or a nation of open-minded world citizens. Read the radicals' list and produce a nation of psychobabblers and ancestor-worshippers—or a nation of stalwart proud-to-be-me pluralists.

15   But is there any list of a few dozen books that can have such a magical effect, for good or for ill? Of course not. It's like arguing that a perfectly nutritional breakfast cereal is enough food for the whole day. And so the canon debate is really an argument about what books to cram down the resistant throats of a resentful captive populace of students; and the trick is never to mention the fact that, in such circumstances, one book is as good, or as bad, as another. Because, as the debaters know from their own experience as readers, books are not pills that produce health when ingested in measured doses. Books do not shape character in any simple way—if, indeed, they do so at all—or the most literate would be the most virtuous instead of just the ordinary run of humanity with larger vocabularies. Books cannot mold a common national purpose when, in fact, people are honestly divided about what kind of country they want—and are divided, moreover, for very good and practical reasons, as they always have been.

For these burly and strenuous purposes, books are all but useless. The way books affect us is an altogether more subtle, delicate, wayward and individual, not to say private, affair. And that reading is being made to bear such an inappropriate and simplistic burden speaks to the poverty of both culture and of frank political discussion in our time.

On his deathbed, Dr. Johnson—once canonical, now more admired than read—is supposed to have said to a friend who was energetically rearranging his bedclothes, "Thank you, this will do all that a pillow can do." One might say that the canon debaters are all asking of their chosen books that it do a great deal more than any handful of books can do.

FACE-TO-FACE, DAY-TO-DAY—RACISM CR

Tia Cross, Freada Klein, Barbara Smith, and Beverly Smith

On April 4, 1979, four women met to discuss consciousness-raising guidelines for women's groups working on the issue of racism. All of us— Tia Cross, Freada Klein, Barbara Smith, and Beverly Smith—had had experiences as white and Black women thinking and talking about racism with white women's groups, or participating in ongoing racism groups ourselves. We taped our discussion, and the ideas and guidelines that follow are based upon it.

We feel that using consciousness-raising to explore our racism is particularly useful and appropriate. It is a feminist form based upon the ways women have always talked and listened to each other. The CR format encourages personal sharing, risk-taking, and involvement, which are essential for getting at how each of us is racist in a daily way; and it encourages the "personal" change that makes political transformation and action possible. The women's movement has begun to address racism in a way that no previous movement has, because we have a growing understanding that our racism often manifests itself in how we interact with other women. Doing CR acknowledges that how we feel can inhibit or lead to action, and that how we actually treat people does make a difference.

Theoretical and analytical comprehension of the political and historical cause of racism is essential, but this understanding on an intellectual level doesn't always help to make face-to-face meetings with women of color real, productive, or meaningful. We need both a political understanding of racism and a personal-political understanding of how it affects our daily lives. Many women start doing CR about racism because they are already confronting it in other areas of their lives and need a place to explore what is happening. CR about racism is not merely talk, talk, talk, and no action, but the essential talking that will make action possible. Doing CR is based upon the fact that as a person you simply cannot do political action without personal interaction.

We also want to stress, however, that these guidelines are not instant solutions. You cannot spend fifteen minutes on each topic and assume that you're done. Racism is much too complex and brutal a system for that. The absence of language to explore our own racism contributes to the difficulty and is in itself part of the problem. Only one term, "racism," exists to describe the range of behavior from subtle, nonverbal daily experiences to murders by the Ku Klux Klan. "Racism" covers individual acts and institutional patterns. But this stumbling block of language presents another theme to explore, not a reason to give up. CR is just one step in the whole process of changing the legacy of oppression (based upon difference) that white-male rule has imposed on us.

5   Actions can grow out of the CR group directly. For example, the group can find out about and publicize the resources which exist in their area, such as other CR groups, study groups, Third World women's groups, and coalitions of Third World and white women. The group can compile reading lists about Black women, racism, and white women's antiracist activity. It can spread the word about the CR process through writing articles, and by giving workshops and talks. It can also compile its own CR guidelines. The legacy of racism in this country is long. It will take a great deal of time and ongoing commitment to bring about change, to alter the insidious and deep-rooted patriarchal attitudes we learn from the time we are children. It is important to show other women what is possible.

The following guidelines are divided into three sections: (1) Early Memories/Childhood Experiences, (2) Adolescence/Early Adulthood, and (3) Becoming a Feminist/Racism in the Women's Movement. The group should plan to spend a substantial amount of time sharing personal histories and feelings in order to build trust, especially at the beginning. It is good to pose questions constantly that make women backtrack and remember their own pasts. General questions which can be applied to any topic and which should be raised along the way are: "How do you experience yourself as a white person?" "What were your fears and what was your anger?" "What did you do with your fears and anger?"

We have included some guidelines that deal with anti-Semitism, but the primary focus of the guidelines is white racism against Black people. It is important for groups to discuss the ways in which anti-Semitism in America is similar to and different from racism aimed against Black people. It is also important to connect racism aimed at Afro-Americans with the racism and oppression aimed at all people of color and with the discrimination aimed at white nationality groups who are not Anglo-Saxon Protestants. Insights about how class identity connects with racism should also provide an ongoing topic for discussion.

EARLY MEMORIES/CHILDHOOD EXPERIENCES

1. When were you first aware that there was such a thing as race and racial differences? How old were you? Recall an incident if you can. How did you feel?
2. What kind of contact did you have with people of different races? Were they adults, children, playmates?
3. How did you experience your own ethnic identity?
4. How did you first experience racism? From whom did you learn it? What did it mean to you? How did it function in your perception of yourself? How did it make you feel? How did it affect you in relation to other people?

5. When did you first notice yourself treating people of color in a different way?
6. When were you first aware that there was such a thing as anti-Semitism? How old were you? Recall an incident. How did you feel?
7. What did you learn at home about Black people and other people of color?
8. What did you learn about Jewish people?
9. How was what you learned about Black people and what you learned about Jewish people connected?
10. What terms did your parents use to refer to Black people and other people of color? If these terms were negative, how did hearing these terms make you feel—curious, uncomfortable, angry?
11. In the group say out loud and make a collective list of *all* the terms you were ever taught or heard about people of color. Also do the same activity with all the terms used for other ethnic and religious groups.

ADOLESCENCE/EARLY ADULTHOOD

1. What kinds of messages did you get about race as you entered adolescence? Did your group of friends change?
2. Discuss the connections between coming of age sexually and racial separation. (When the four of us discussed being a teenager, one woman pinpointed the sexual-racial dichotomy by saying, "It's about who you can't date!")
3. If you went to integrated schools, what messages did you get about Black people in general and about Black males specifically?
4. In what ways was race used by you or your friends as a subject of so-called teenage rebellion?
5. How did different groups of students get along in your school? Were you aware of divisions by race and class? How did it feel?
6. How were different groups of students treated by teachers and the school administration?
7. When you were growing up, what kind of information did you get about Black people through the media? How much of it was specifically about Black men?
8. If you had interactions with Black people through work during the 50s and 60s, through political groups, or socially, what proportion of these interactions were with Black men? With Black women?
9. What were your experiences as white women with Black men? What were the racial-sexual dynamics of these relationships? In what ways did these experiences help you to explore your own racism? In what ways did they fuel your own racism? How did they affect your developing feminism?

BECOMING A FEMINIST/RACISM IN THE WOMEN'S MOVEMENT

10

1. When did you being to make the connection between your own experiences and the experiences of other women?
2. As you became a feminist, to what degree did you feel connected to women of all different backgrounds and lifestyles?
3. How do you see yourself as different than a white woman? How do you see yourself as the same?
4. Think about your relationships with Black and white women who are co-workers, neighbors, and acquaintances. What are the differences resulting from race in these relationships? Have you ever had a really close woman friend who was Black? Can you imagine having such a friendship? Why or why not? Have you ever had a sexual relationship with a Black woman? Can you imagine having such a relationship? Why or why not?
5. How does your class background affect your racism and making connections with women different from yourself? What are the barriers you have to overcome to connect?
6. Everyone in the group fills in the blanks in the following statements. This exercise could be done out loud or by each person writing her response down first before hearing the group. "Black women always _____." "When I am with Black people I always feel or usually feel _____." "I wouldn't want Black people to _____." "When I'm with Black people I'm afraid that _____." "I'm afraid I will _____." "I'm afraid they will _____."
7. Discuss different values you think white and Black women have about family, sexuality, childrearing, clothes, food, money, upward or downward mobility, and other issues.
8. How does racism affect your daily life as a white woman? The group could discuss Lillian Smith's statement (from *The Winner Names the Age*), "Back door treatment is humiliation to all who participate in it. Both leave stains on the soul."
9. Each week the group has the "homework assignment" of noticing racist situations—things each member sees, hears, or reads. Begin each session by sharing the things you have noticed.
10. Discuss what happens when you confront another white woman about her racism. What are your fears? How does it feel to do this?
11. In what way does being a lesbian connect to the whole issue of racism between white and Black women? What kinds of racism have you noticed in all-women's social situations, at bars and at cultural events? In what ways can shared lesbian oppression be used to build connections between white women and women of color?

12. Discuss the ways in which white women lower their standards for being feminist for Black and other Third World women. Do you find yourself "hiding" your feminism is a situation where there are Third World women? Are you afraid to confront Black women's antifeminism?

13. Discuss issues that the women's movement has worked on which might be considered racist because they did not address the experiences of women of color. Discuss feminist issues that cut across racial and class lines, touching the lives of all women. Which of these issues have you worked on or considered a priority?

ANTI-SEXIST CONSCIOUSNESS-RAISING GROUPS FOR MEN

Paul Carlo Hornacek

RATIONALE

Anti-sexist men's consciousness-raising groups are beginning to appear in various parts of our country as a complement to and in support of the women's liberation (feminist) movement. These groups are not to be confused or mistakenly identified with the recent and more popular men's liberation movement. Proponents of men's liberation espouse the view that sexism is a societally pervasive institution which oppresses both women and men by prescribing stereotypical sex-role behaviors which are dehumanizing and which cause great emotional suffering. They encourage C-R sessions as a vehicle by which men can get in touch with their emotions, free themselves of sex-role assignments, learn to be more open with and caring for other men, and struggle together to fight the external (re) imposition upon themselves of the socially oppressive male role. In this manner they learn a way of relating in more rewarding ways to women and to other men.

In direct contrast to this, men who are participating in what some have called anti-sexist (or pro-feminist) men's C-R groups maintain that sexism is an institutionalized way of life in which women, gay people, and children are systematically oppressed and disempowered by heterosexual men. They agree that sexism and the external imposition of stereotypical sex-role behavior which accompanies it is dehumanizing to all people, but feel that while heterosexual men are alienated and limited by sexism, they are not oppressed by it. By definition, those who gain substantial material, psychic and other benefits by the subordination of another group are recognized as the oppressors, not as the oppressed. This distinction is not merely a semantic disagreement; it is a major difference in the purpose of the group. Anti-sexist men's C-R is designed to support women's liberation by changing men's male supremacist consciousness. Men's liberation C-R, on the other hand, supports male domination by reinforcing men's sexist consciousness. Surrendering male privilege requires a recognition of the compensatory gains for economic class differences that males are afforded by sexism. Men in our culture (and especially heterosexual men) are by birthright the benefactors of the oppressive societal institution of sexism—which was created and is maintained in their interest.

Members of anti-sexist men's C-R groups see the need for men to meet together to discuss the ways in which sexism pervades their daily lives, and how their conscious and unconscious sexist behaviors limit and alienate themselves and oppress women, gay people, and children. They recognize the inherent contradiction in men getting together and forming supportive groups in our society which is already dominated by powerful privileged male groups. The justification for men getting together in this way comes from the purpose and methods of the group which are designed to insure a commitment to the struggle against male privilege. Unity in the struggle against male supremacist consciousness is different from traditional male bonding because it is aware of the contradiction and specifically and intentionally designed to oppose male solidarity. Anti-sexist men's C-R is one of the first positive steps men can take on their own, following the example and the leadership articulated by feminists, toward a unified female and male struggle to smash sexism. In being freed from their own sex roles men can free others who are oppressed by them. Only by recognizing and struggling with this contradiction can the urge to perpetuate rather than to eradicate sexism and male privilege be overcome.

To help insure that the C-R experience does not become just one more instrument by which patriarchy further strengthens itself, anti-sexist men's C-R groups need to build the following three conditions into their structure: (1) a period of criticism and self-criticism wherein at the end of each session, group members reflect upon their own and others' sexism as was demonstrated during that meeting (this is the period when any sexist male bonding within the group is challenged), (2) a commitment to bring forth sexual change by personal and political activity against sexism, and (3) an acceptance of the principles and tenets of the feminist movement. (This means a recognition that sexism is an inequality between women and men in which all men benefit from the subordination of women.)

PRACTICE

Anti-sexist consciousness-raising is an activity which permits participants to see   *5* clearly the ways in which their individual situation reflects the total social process around them. It allows people to examine and come to understand how the institutions of patriarchy foster and perpetuate the devastatingly dehumanizing effects of sexism. My experience in several anti-sexist men's C-R groups over the past five years has led me to subscribe to a structured rather than an unstructured format for C-R group conduct for men. The structure which I have found most useful is borrowed in large part from the feminist movement and its female creators to who I am indebted for many of the ideas this paper expresses. Outlined below is a method of forming and participating in C-R groups which allow men to emerge feeling good about the fact that they are struggling with other men to give up the male-oppressor role. This format is designed to prevent competition, male dominance, the abuse of authority, and the misuse of aggression. It provides an atmosphere of trust and support wherein men can learn non-traditional ways of relating to women, to children, and to other men. Where women's groups have stressed the importance of flexibility and lack of formal structure in order to counterbalance the effects that male supremacist power structures have had upon their lives, it is important that men's C-R groups adhere to a pre-determined format which assures that anti-sexist principles and self-critical vigilance are ever-present in the process. A C-R group is qualitatively different from a rap, encounter, or therapy group because of the structure which it follows.

Men have reported a variety of different reasons for deciding to seek a C-R group, all of which have an underlying link to the feminist movement. Most are experiencing emotional pain as a result of their male sex-role and are dissatisfied with it. Some have had confrontations with radical feminists in public or private encounters and have been repeatedly criticized for being sexists. Some come as a result of their commitment to social change and their recognition that sexism and patriarchy are elements of an intolerable social system that needs to be altered. Male classmates, co-workers, relatives, friends and neighbors are all potentially good candidates for an anti-sexist men's C-R group. All men in our society have been socialized into the masculine role, all have been taught to objectify and dominate women, all have been continually exposed to a public media which teaches violence, misogyny, and the misuse of power and aggression toward women, children and other men.

The ideal size of a C-R group seems to be about six to eight people. Larger groups do not afford the degree of intimacy necessary to develop honest self-disclosure and progress toward change. Smaller groups tend to become too informal and allow little room for absence or attrition, and groups which are too small contradict the basic assumption of consciousness-raising, which is to learn by hearing the experiences of several people.

Meetings should be conducted on a regular basis, preferably once a week, in order to facilitate continuity of thought and content. Each meeting should last for a specific pre-designated length of time, usually two and a half to three hours. This time is to be divided according to the size of the group. Most people decide to have ten or fifteen minutes for each speaker to address the topic of the session, leaving fifteen or twenty minutes for discussion and analysis, and fifteen minutes at the end of the meeting for a criticism and self-criticism period. Most groups also like to have five minutes at the beginning of the meeting for each member to say how he feels that evening and whether there are any pressing issues in his life which might interfere with his participation in the C-R session. It is important to begin and end a C-R group on time and to require full attendance at every meeting. A true commitment to fighting sexism is reflected in the fact that the C-R group meeting holds a priority in members' schedules.

Groups use members' homes as meeting places, and rotate on a weekly basis so that everyone has an opportunity to learn a little about the environment in which the other members live. Rotation of the meeting also creates an opportunity for group members to share the responsibility of hosting the sessions (perhaps providing a beverage and a snack).

While many women's C-R groups have formed and met successfully *10* without a leader or facilitator, on the premise that all women are oppressed by sexism and therefore they themselves are best able to find their way to a liberating theory, men cannot follow the same practice. Since men are socialized into the sexual-oppressor role, it is important that when they meet to struggle against that role they have an experienced, feminist-conscious person to guide them for the first few sessions. This facilitator can be a man who has experienced anti-sexist C-R groups and who appreciates the three organizational principles of men's C-R outlined above, or a feminist who is willing to meet with a men's group for a few times to help them to get started.

During the first meeting participants introduce themselves and usually give a brief autobiographical sketch to help others to begin to know them on a personal level. After this, the real work of discovering feelings and inexpressiveness begins. To enable the sharing of emotional reactions and personal information, it is essential that group members agree to a pact of strict confidentiality. Only by this agreement can an atmosphere of trust develop. Trust is necessary for the honest sharing of personal information and for the persistent struggle against the enemy within ourselves. Members may choose to share information with outside people about the group process and structure or general topic, but not about the group content.

For successive meetings, the format is a very simple one. Topics are selected according to group preference a week in advance. During the session itself the topic is addressed by each person until it is exhausted. All topics must relate to the socialization of males and females within our society which leads to the perpetuation of sexist behaviors. The person who chooses to speak first discusses the subject by speaking in the first person, i.e., only making "I" statements based on his own experience. He expresses how the topic in question has affected his life, attempting to be honest about revealing personal information and trying to stay as close to the topic as possible. Intellectualization, a defensive maneuver by which men avoid feelings and emotional statements, is to be avoided.

The role of the members who are not speaking is very important. They are to give their full attention to the speaker and attempt to understand what is being expressed. Listeners should silently note experiences and feelings with which they too are familiar. No one is to interrupt the speaker. Questions of clarification can be raised when the speaker indicates that he is finished. Speakers are not to be confronted or challenged. If a member hears sexist language or a report of sexist behavior, he is to make a mental or written note and bring it up during the criticism/self-criticism period described below.

When one person has finished speaking, another begins until all the members have addressed the topic. When the round has been accomplished, a discussion and analysis period begins. Members try to find a pattern to their experiences and draw conclusions from what has been discussed. During this period it is important to try to understand how their abstract, aggressive, un-emotional masculine role has affected their lives and the lives of women and children to whom they relate. The consciousness-raising process is one in which shared personal experiences come to be seen as a consistent product of societally imposed sex-role stereotyping, rather than natural or idiosyncratic personal behaviors. Finding a pattern to shared personal experiences is easier and more meaningful when men try to relate what they reported to what they have read in feminist writings. Consequently it is important for an anti-sexist men's C-R group to simultaneously involve itself in the study of feminist theory.

15   The final portion of the meeting should be devoted to criticism and self-criticism, a process in which members attempt to point out the sexism in their own and others' statements. This is not a time for hostile remarks or advice giving. Criticisms are to be accepted and digested, and not responded to defensively.

After several months of meeting in this fashion, most groups begin to search for a larger purpose. Their activity may take the form of political action against sexism, formal study of feminist literature, the seeding of new C-R groups, reaching out to women's or gay groups in an attempt to meet and work together, or other specific forms of anti-sexist practice. Usually one or more of these activities begin to occur in addition to an on-going C-R group experience. Time restrictions are such that for some people, the anti-sexist political activity replaces the C-R group meeting altogether. The friendships and close ties that develop as a result of participation in an anti-sexist men's C-R group often are both profound and long-lasting. The personal insights that are gained are invaluable. The politicized views of sex-role stereotyping are enlightening, and the various actions in support of women's liberation which are the result can hasten the revolution which feminists have initiated.

TEN ESSENTIAL MEN'S C-R TOPICS

Childhood training for sex-roles

Marriage, monogamy, jealousy

Work and housework

Fathers and sons

Rape

Homosexuality, heterosexuality, bisexuality

The nuclear family as a bastion of sexism

Maleness and masculinity

Sensuality and sexuality

Intimacy with women; intimacy with men

REFERENCES

Dreifus, Claudia. *Women's Fate: Raps from a Feminist Consciousness-Raising Group.* New York: Bantam Books, Inc., 1973.

Koedt, Anne; Levine, Ellen; Rapone, Anita, eds. *Radical Feminism.* New York: Quadrangle—The New York Times Book Co., 1973.

Pleck, Joseph H., and Sawyer, Jack. *Men and Masculinity.* New Jersey: Prentice-Hall, Inc., 1974.

Rush, Anne Kent. *Getting Clear—Body Work for Women.* New York: Random House, 1973.

Stoltenberg, John, "Toward Gender Justice," *Social Policy* (May/June, 1975): pp. 35–39.

DANGERS WITH MEN'S CONSCIOUSNESS-RAISING GROUPS

Leonard Schein

The formation of men's consciousness raising groups must be seen as a positive step in the struggle against sexism. At this time it is extremely important for men to start working with other men in new ways that destroy traditional "male bonding." Men working with other men is a necessary and good direction for three main reasons.

First, men have a long history, when working with women, of cooptation, of treating women in a sexist manner, of channeling a movement's energy into male directions, and of making male issues the priorities. A few examples demonstrate this cooption process. The New Left political movement has always argued in loud and large terms about how we must fight the oppression of people throughout the world. But this same New Left was very late to recognize women's oppression. Then it developed an empty rhetoric about supporting women's liberation, but whenever priorities were set, women's issues always took last place. The New Left is only interested in the welfare of certain oppressed people. Those people are the ones who fit the traditional Marxian analysis: (male) worker, (male) third-world people, and (male) people of color in North America. The struggle of women to gain human status has never been taken seriously by people in the New Left. We have a situation in which energies are devoted to freeing oppressed males.

Not only did the New Left not work for the political benefit of women, its "Macho Marx" male consciousness perpetuated and reinforced the worst of patriarchal role division. Male chauvinism was the New Left's "little red book": the movement was completely authoritarian and male dominated. Men did the important work while women were stuck doing the domestic and office shit-work. The male radical "leaders" became like rock stars with their following of "groupies" to sexually nurture them after a hard day fighting imperialism.

The Gay Liberation Front is another example of a political struggle where men have co-opted the Movement away from women. In the beginning, the Gay Liberation Front was a movement of both male and female homosexuals, but after a while it was clear to lesbians that they could no longer work politically with gay males. The gay men channeled their energies and priorities into male directions and took political stances that were degrading to women (supporting pornography, sadism/masochism, and refusing to deal with butch/femme role division). Gay males were sexist toward the women and ran the movement in an authoritarian manner. The male consciousness of the gay males, in the same manner as in the New Left, prevented lesbians from being taken seriously in their own right as full human beings.

The straight world has its examples also. In the 1972 Democratic National Convention, when the crunch came, George McGovern sold women's issues down the river. Another example is that of the American Civil Liberties Union and the President's Commission on Obscenity and Pornography which, under the guise of supporting freedom of speech and press, have been the foremost champions of the legalization of pornography and prostitution. Pornography and prostitution oppress women, establish anti-female models of sexuality, and further male domination and misogyny. Male politicians and political parties have always sold "their" women supporters short because of "political reality."

The second important reason for men to work together is our need to directly confront male violence and misogyny. We can no longer take the easy way out, by relating to women and being nurtured by them and draining them emotionally, but must face directly the violence and hatred toward women which is inside ourselves. We must confront our misogyny as fundamental to our consciousness, in order to fully understand the fears that we force women to live with every day.

The third reason is that we have similar experiences, consciousness, perceptions, and world views to share with each other. We have all been socialized in masculine roles. Together we can best explore the depth of our male consciousness—two heads are better than one. We also need each other to learn new ways of relating to people as full human beings: emotionally and caringly, without competition, aggression and power-tripping, in open, vulnerable, equal and supportive relationships. We know our experience best, and we can no longer pretend to help others with "their" oppression (especially women) because *we* are the ones who need the help; *we* are the ones who are the enemy; *we* are the ones who oppress and objectify women; and *we* are the incomplete, crippled human beings.

I believe there should be three fundamental principles as a foundation for men's consciousness-raising groups. Before any man joins a group, he should agree to these essential propositions. First, the full acceptance of radical feminism in theory and practice. By this I mean that we must agree that patriarchy is the *prime* contradiction from which all other models of oppression come—capitalism, imperialism, slavery, racism, etc. The role division that our society forces upon males and females through socialization must be actively struggled against (theory put into practice). In addition, we must see male consciousness and its concrete expressions as the main opponents of full humanism in the world, and we must realize the privilege we enjoy as a class/caste over women. We must also recognize that although both males and females suffer under patriarchal rule, our suffering is not the same, and in fact is qualitatively less than that of women. The emptiness, self-loss, powerlessness, and violations that women endure are far more insidious than our masculine role suffering. Even as incomplete, unalive human beings, we enjoy privilege and power: the world, God, and culture are all made in our own image.

The second principle is the acceptance of emotionality as a valid and necessary part of the new man we are trying to create. We must appreciate the limitations of logical-intellectual-rational discussion, and concentrate our energy on discovering and exploring our emotional potential.

10   The third principle is that we as men can never speak for women. Antisexist men cannot co-opt or take control of the Feminist Movement. We must realize our debt to feminism and that, for most of us, our main motivation for dealing with sexism comes from women who have forced us to, and that feminism has already provided the theory, structure, and models for us. Presently, women in the feminist movement are so far beyond men in terms of full human consciousness that we cannot bring them down to our level but must instead attempt to raise ourselves to theirs.

My experience in men's consciousness-raising groups has taught me to be aware of four dangers. The first danger is that the men's group may be used to collude against women. Since more often than not we in a men's group have common women friends, it is important that we not team up in our groups against these women. Most of us join our first consciousness-raising group because women with whom we are involved will no longer accept our sexism. In order to have fulfilling relationships and become whole, we have to deal seriously with our maleness. In entering these groups, we are coming from a place of feeling very hurt, afraid, and confused, and so we look for allies to support us emotionally. There is a tendency for us to betray women to gain sympathy and reassurance and to rebuild our deflated egos. There is also a tendency to put our own position in the best light (especially in the beginning of the group, before trust is really established) without realizing the consequences of these untruths to our female partners. There is also a tendency to play ego games with women friends: "See, I'm not as bad as John . . . See, Bill agrees with me . . . Ralph tells me that Carole does this sexually with him. . . ."

The experience of the "Brother" collective in Berkeley, California, illustrates a further aspect of colluding against women. John, a bisexual, was married to Scottie for eight years and they had two children. Their relationship was monogamous until the men's group, when John "fell in love" with Bill, a gay member of the group. The following is Bill's revealing perception of Scottie's feelings:

> After that (John and Bill becoming lovers) Scottie became
> lovers with another man. I feel that to some extent Scottie felt
> pressured to agree to what John wanted to do this past year—
> open up their marriage to other lovers, and specifically male
> lovers for himself. . . . Yet Scottie has felt through this year less
> loved by John than ever before. She saw that John's love for me
> and other men was more emotional, more feeling—there

seemed to be more loving strokes for these men than for herself. Scottie was hurt and oppressed by this inequity. . . . But because she has felt less loved and because she is not bisexual, I
have found myself editing my gayness for her so it would be
less threatening. John has also done some editing of his gayness
though less than I. I feel deceitful both to myself and to Scottie
and feel this is an oppressive element for each of us in the relationship. John, Scottie, and their two children are planning to
leave this area. It has been projected by John and by myself that
I would join them after the summer. I have talked to Scottie
about this a number of times. She is being put in a very difficult position. If she says she doesn't want me to join them,
she risks that John will be unhappy and resentful. If she gives
her approval, she continues for herself an uncomfortable experiment from which she'd like some distance. I feel that as a man
and as her partner's lover, I am unavoidably oppressive to her in
this situation. I continue to be lovers with John because that is
what I want and he wants and what Scottie has *agreed to* (emphasis mine).

Joel, another gay member of the group, seemed to recognize the obvious
oppression of Scottie in the John-Bill-Scottie triangle. Yet he and the other
members of the men's group *did nothing* to censor and stop the sexism of John
and Bill. The group gave tacit approval for the continuation of men fucking
over women by tolerating their relationship and being uncritical. If "Brother"
were really serious about fighting sexism, it would not have been a party to
such destructive sexist consciousness and behavior. Women, being typically less
powerful and more vulnerable in any relationship with a man, lose (both economically and emotionally) when men bond together in their own interest.
John wins everything; he holds his relationship with Bill over Scottie's head
(forcing her to take another "sexual" lover). John is even oppressive to gay males
(especially Bill) by not taking them seriously in an equal emotional relationship while "he gets his rocks off in a new way." It is clear that John is continuing to force Scottie into compromises and situations she does not freely choose
in order for her and the two children to survive. Men's groups should attempt
to prevent the recurrence of this unfortunate "Brother" experience.

The second danger we have to watch for in these groups is the misdirec-
tion of anger toward the women who have forced us to confront our sexism.
Our past experience with anger has been to turn it into violence. Now, as
men we are at a loss to find a new, sane method of dealing with our hostility.
In opening up to our emotionality as never before, we do not quite know
what to do with our anger, especially since women are no longer available to
maintain our fragile egos. Groups have to be careful to direct anger towards
its real source, the patriarchal society and masculinist socialization which
forces every man (including "sensitive, gentle us") to have a male supremacist

consciousness. Our anger is inside us. We must take responsibility for it and struggle to change. This anger cannot be smoothed over or directed towards women. It is a fundamental core of our psyche, and we have to face it squarely to become fully human.

15   The third danger is that we may not continue to struggle with our individual sexism. After the group meets for some period of time, we begin to develop a method of nurturing each other and having closer ties emotionally. As we become more sensitive and are more aware of our vulnerability, there is a tendency to backslide away from fighting our sexism because we do not want to hurt those we care a lot about. It is important to learn nurturing and caring, but these cannot be uncritical and unconditional. Unconditional caring is a trap for ourselves and the men we care about. The absence of criticism is not only dishonest, it allows us to give up the struggle against sexism when it becomes particularly painful. We develop a more hidden, sophisticated system of sexism to hide our male privileges behind false illusions.

The fourth danger is that our consciousness-raising may exist exclusively inside the group. The analysis and new consciousness that we learn in our groups must lead to political practice in order to destroy patriarchal authority, sexism, and role division. We must change the way we relate with our friends—both males and females—and we must criticize our friends' sexism. We must be willing to drop our sexist friends if the contradiction is too great. This challenge must take place at our jobs and in our social life. We must also publicly bring to the attention, especially of males, that sexism is prevalent in our society. Facing the men in the streets who are violating women (whistling, derogatory remarks, sexual objectification) is a difficult but necessary task. We cannot let the threat of male violence scare us away from our responsibility to combat sexism in other men. We need collective support because as sensitive individuals it is hard to deal with male violence alone. We must also rechannel our priorities in terms of political action into those issues which are seen by macho male consciousness as "just women's issues:" childcare, contraception, abortion, rape laws, the Equal Rights Amendment, etc. These are not women's issues or side issues, but issues that go to the very core of role division in patriarchal society. If we are really serious about our priorities, we must deal with political issues that challenge patriarchal rule.

For the best understanding of consciousness-raising groups, see Kathie Sarachild's "Program for Feminist Consciousness-Raising" in *Notes from the Second Year: Women's Liberation* and "Consciousness-Raising: A Radical Weapon" in *Feminist Revolution*.

14

Resistance Strategy Two: Disloyality/Disobedience/ Traitorousness

TREASON TO WHITENESS IS LOYALTY TO HUMANITY

Noel Ignatiev

An interview with Noel Ignatiev of Race Traitor *Magazine*

What is a race traitor anyway?

A traitor to the white race is someone who is nominally classified as white, but who defies the rules of whiteness so flagrantly as to jeopardize his or her ability to draw upon the privileges of the white skin.

"Race" has meant various things in history. We use the term to mean a group that includes all social classes, in a situation where the most degraded member of a dominant group is exalted over any member of a subordinate group. That formation was first successfully established in the 17th century. By then there already existed a trade across the Atlantic in laborers. Traders from both Europe and Africa sold their countrymen and were not held back because they were of the same color as those they sold. Slavery was a matter of economics. At the time it was the most efficient way of guaranteeing a labor force—provided it could be enforced.

As Theodore Allen points out in *Invention of the White Race,* the white race meant not only that no European-Americans were slaves, but also that all European-Americans, even laborers, were by definition enforcers of slavery. In the Chesapeake Bay Colony (Virginia and Maryland), people from Africa and people from Europe worked together in the tobacco fields. They mated with each other, ran away and rebelled together, at first. At the end of the 1600s, people of African descent, even those who were free, lost certain rights they had

605

had before and that even the poorest and most downtrodden person of European descent continued to enjoy. In return for these privileges, European-Americans of all classes came to be part of the apparatus that maintained Afro-Americans in chattel slavery (and themselves in unfreedom). That was the birth of "race," as we use the term.

What do you mean when you say that race is a social construction?

We mean that it is the result of social distinctions. Many black people have European ancestors, and plenty of so-called whites have African or American Indian ancestors. No biologist has ever been able to provide a satisfactory definition of race—that is, a definition that includes all the members of a given "race" and excludes all others. Attempts to do so lead to absurdities: mothers and children of different races, or the phenomenon that a white woman can give birth to a black child, but a black woman can never give birth to a white child. The only possible conclusion is that people are members of different races because they are assigned to them. Of course, differences exist between individuals, and the natives of West Africa in general had darker skin and so forth than the natives of the British Isles, but groups are formed by social distinctions, not nature.

Can you provide an example of a people suddenly becoming "white"?

5   The Irish are as clear an example as any. In Ireland, under the Protestant Ascendancy, Catholic Irish were the victims of discrimination identical to what we in America call racial, and were even referred to as a "race." Karl Marx, writing from England, reported that the average English worker looked down on the Irish the way poor whites in the American South looked upon Afro-Americans. Yet over here the Irish became "whites," by gaining the right to vote while free Negroes were losing it, by supporting the Democratic Party (the party of the slaveholders), and by preventing free Afro-Americans from competing with them for jobs. The overcoming of anti-Irish prejudice meant that the Irish were admitted to the privileges of whiteness.

What do you mean by the "new abolitionism"?

We believe that so long as the white race exists, all movements against what is called "racism" will fail. Therefore, our aim is to abolish the white race.

How does your position on race and whiteness differ from the standard political stance of anti-racism?

Racism is a pretty vague term. It has come to mean little more than a tendency to dislike people for the color of their skin. Most anti-racists, even while they oppose discrimination, believe that racial status is fixed and eternal. We hold that without social distinctions, "race" is a fiction. The only race is the human race.

Even if a person declares him/herself a "race traitor," to the vast majority of people in this society, he/she is still white and therefore allowed all the privileges of the "white club." Is it possible to abolish the white race, ironically, only as white people?

The white race does not like to relinquish a single member, so that even those who step out of it in one situation find it virtually impossible not to rejoin it later, if only because of the assumptions of others—unless, like John Brown, they have the good fortune to be hanged before that happens. So-called whites have special responsibilities to abolition that only they can fulfill. Only they can dissolve the white race from within, by rejecting the poisoned bait of white-skin privileges. If that is what you mean by abolishing the white race "as whites," then we have no quarrel.

What is the relationship between capitalism and racism?

Capital itself is color-blind, and the capitalist system, as such, recognizes nothing but atomized individuals acting independently in the market. There are places in the world where it exists without race. In this country race is central to the system of social control: It leads some workers to settle for being "white" when they could, with some effort, be free.

Is there such a thing as a "white culture"?

No. There is Italian culture, and Polish, Irish, Yiddish, German, and Appalachian culture. There is youth culture and drug culture and queer culture; but there is no "white" culture—unless you mean Wonder Bread and television game shows. Whiteness is nothing but an expression of race privilege. It has been said that the typical "white" American male spends his childhood as an Indian, his adolescence as an Afro-American, and only becomes white when he reaches the age of legal responsibility.

In an autobiographical essay, Joel Gilbert says that most of this whiteness has washed away and that he has "plenty of black inside." How is it possible for a white person to have "plenty of black" inside? How is it possible for whites to wash away their whiteness? Should a black person accept a white person's claim to have "a lot of black inside"?

Politically, whiteness is the willingness to seek a comfortable place within the system of race privilege. Blackness means total, implacable, and relentless opposition to that system. To the extent so-called whites oppose the race line, repudiate their own race privileges, and jeopardize their own standing in the white race, they can be said to have washed away their whiteness and taken in some blackness. Probably a black person should not accept a white person's claim to have done that, but should watch how that person acts.

A common theme in Race Traitor *is that of whites "crossing over" into black culture, or what you have called "black assimilation." A lot of the examples you cite of people "refusing to be white" involve white people—especially youth—imitating black cultural forms. The line between "crossing over" into black culture and ripping off black culture is a mighty fine one; where do you draw it? Is there a necessary connection between "crossover" and the abandonment of whiteness? What makes white "crossover" in the '90s different from white youths and big businesses "crossing over" and ripping off black music in the '40s and '50s?*

In culture, the line between rip-off and respect is the willingness to pay the dues, if necessary to forgo the social advantages of being white, in order to achieve genuineness of expression. There is no necessary connection between cultural assimilation and rejection of whiteness: The crowds at professional basketball games prove that; and on the other hand, immigrants to this country may speak no English and have no interest in American culture and still refuse to take part in the oppression of black people. But for many, the rejection of whiteness seems to entail some engagement with Afro-American culture, because that is the first cultural expression of resistance they encounter, and it speaks powerfully to them. You are right to point out that whites have been ripping off Afro-American culture for years. Fundamentally, the crossover of the '90s may not be different from that of the past, although it may make a difference that the process of social dissolution is now more advanced. By itself, crossover represents a potential for race treason, not the actuality.

How does wanting to abolish racial classifications avoid doing away with cultural differences, which is what most liberal attempts to "confront racism" do?

For us, black and white are political categories, separate from, although not unrelated to, culture. One of the effects of white supremacy is that it represses the cultures of Afro-Americans and other peoples of color. If that repression were removed, who knows how they would flourish. Moreover, American culture is, as Albert Murray has pointed out, incontestably mulatto. Without race prejudice, Americans might discover that culturally they are all Afro-American, as well as Native American, and so forth.

Abolition also brings up issues of identity. People of color, in struggling against oppression, often turn toward their precolonial cultures and earlier examples of resistance to find an identity that can inspire them today. What can a so-called white person turn to after abandoning whiteness? Does s/he seek inspiration in prewhite cultures such as Judaism, Celtic or Germanic tribes, in ethnic identities such as Irish, Italian-American, etc.? In committing treason against the white race, must we seek these "intermediate" identities, abandon all identities in favor of a universal humanism, or something else?

I don't know. So far as I am concerned, there is nothing wrong with people seeking out the Celtic or Germanic tribes, or ethnicity, or anything else that can provide them with a vital alternative to whiteness, although I have my doubts about how real these are or can be made to be for modern Americans, and the last time somebody built a mass movement around Germanic tribal myths it led to big trouble. We might do better to promote models of amalgamation. The Seminole Indians, as I understand it, were composed of the remnants of several native groups who had earlier been dispersed, plus a number of runaway slaves, plus some deserters from the army. They came together and fought three wars against the U.S. government. They were never really defeated. The Seminole tribe might be a model that could inspire people. Time will tell.

In being a race traitor, to whom do you announce your treason—fellow so-called whites? Is it ever appropriate to tell a person of color that you have abandoned your whiteness?

I would never say that, although I might say I was working on it.   *15*

What kinds of relations with people of color are implied when one becomes a race traitor? How does a race traitor act politically with people of color?

Relations must be based on solidarity. People of color have a wealth of experience with white supremacy from which others can learn, but the fight against white supremacy is not something to engage in as a favor to anyone. All people who wish to be free have an equal stake—yes, an equal stake—in overturning the system of white supremacy. I'm reminded of the old IWW [Industrial Workers of the World, the "Wobblies"] slogan, "An injury to one is an injury to all." Decades of distortion have reduced the message of those words to the idea that you should oppose injustice against others today because if you don't it will come your way tomorrow. We believe in the original intent of the slogan. The Bible offers the same instruction: "Remember them that are in bonds as bound with them."

Race Traitor does an excellent job of providing examples of individuals rejecting their whiteness and joining the human race, but there is little there of collective resistance. Where is the collective political strategy in a politics of abolition? How do we, collectively, abolish the white race?

For the white race to be effective, it must be unanimous, or nearly so. The reason is that if the cops and the courts and so forth couldn't be sure that every person who looked white was loyal to the system, then what would be the point of extending race privileges to whites? And if they stopped extending race privileges, what would happen to the white race? Our strategy seeks to bring together a determined minority, willing to defy white rules so flagrantly they make it impossible to pretend that all those who look white are loyal to the system of racial oppression.

We wish we could cite more example of collective resistance. The whites who joined the rebellions in Los Angeles and elsewhere were a good example. The Attica prison rebellion was another. The initiative by Love and Rage to launch a campaign culminating in a day of action against immigration controls and anti-immigrant violence was a good project, but unfortunately it never got off the ground. Collectively struggle is crucial, but at some point every white person has to choose, like Huck Finn, between being white and striking out for freedom.

In some articles you literally break the world down into a matter of black and white. Have you ever been accused of ignoring the struggles and perspectives of nonblack people of color and how do you respond to this charge?

Yes, I have been. I think that the line between black and white determines race in this country, and all groups get defined in relation to that line. Don't forget, I am using black and white as political, not cultural, categories. I do not mean to neglect the real and independent histories of people of color who are not of African descent. But in some cases the talk about "people of color" obscures the essence of racial oppression. Chinese are people of color and in the past they suffered fierce oppression in this country, and still suffer the effects of prejudice, but would anyone argue that Chinese in America today constitute an oppressed race? They have been defined as an ethnic group, indeed the "model minority," as shown by the high rate of social mobility among them, the high proportion of marriages with European-Americans, and the presence among them of a substantial number of capitalists who function outside of a segregated market—all in contrast to the situation of Afro-Americans. Of course they might become an oppressed race again. Or they might choose to identify as black in the struggle against white power, as many of the so-called coloureds of South Africa have done.

It seems from your journal and from thinking about your ideas that abolishing the white race would bring about widespread, radical changes in other aspects of social life. Is race treason necessarily revolutionary in that it threatens not only white supremacy but class rule as well?

20 It would be good if people could forget that they are white and pursue their interests as workers, or women, or whatever else moves them. The problem is that American society does not allow anyone to forget, but injects race into every political controversy. For those in power, the privileges granted whites are a small price to pay for the stability of an unjust social system. While not all forms of injustice can be collapsed into whiteness, undermining white race solidarity opens the door to fundamental social change in other areas. For so-called whites, treason to the white race is the most subversive act I can imagine.

INDIAN HUMOR

Vine Deloria, Jr.

One of the best ways to understand a people is to know what makes them laugh. Laughter encompasses the limits of the soul. In humor life is redefined and accepted. Irony and satire provide much keener insights into a group's collective psyche and values than do years of research.

It has always been a great disappointment to Indian people that the humorous side of Indian life has not been mentioned by professed experts on Indian Affairs. Rather the image of the granite-faced grunting redskin has been perpetuated by American mythology.

People have little sympathy with stolid groups. Dick Gregory did much more than is believed when he introduced humor to the Civil Rights struggle. He enabled non-blacks to enter into the thought world of the black community and experience the hurt it suffered. When all people shared the humorous but ironic situation of the black, the urgency and morality of Civil Rights was communicated.

The Indian people are sometimes the opposite of the popular stereotype. I sometimes wonder how anything is accomplished by Indians because of the apparent overemphasis on humor within the Indian world. Indians have found a humorous side of nearly every problem and the experiences of life have generally been so well defined through jokes and stories that they have become a thing in themselves.

For centuries before the white invasion, teasing was a method of control   5
of social situations by Indian people. Rather than embarrass members of the tribe publicly, people used to tease individuals they considered out of step with the consensus of tribal opinion. In this way egos were preserved and disputes within the tribe of a personal nature were held to a minimum.

Gradually people learned to anticipate teasing and began teasing themselves as a means of showing humility and at the same time advocating a course of action the deeply believed in. Men would depreciate their feats to show they were not trying to run roughshod over tribal desires. This method of behavior served to highlight their true virtues and gain them a place of influence in tribal policy-making circles.

Humor has come to occupy such a prominent place in national Indian affairs that any kind of movement is impossible without it. Tribes are being brought together by sharing humor of the past. Columbus jokes gain great sympathy among all tribes, yet there are no tribes extant who had anything to do with Columbus. But the fact of white invasion from which all tribes have suffered has created a common bond in relation to Columbus jokes that gives a solid feeling of unity and purpose to the tribes.

The more desperate the problem, the more humor is directed to describe it. Satirical remarks often circumscribe problems so that possible solutions are drawn from the circumstances that would not make sense if presented in other than a humorous form.

Often people are awakened and brought to a militant edge through funny remarks. I often counseled people to run for the Bureau of Indian Affairs in case of an earthquake because nothing could shake the BIA. And I would watch as younger Indians set their jaws, determined that they, if nobody else, would shake it. We also had a saying that in case of fire call the BIA and they would handle it because they put a wet blanket on everything. This also got a warm reception from people.

10   Columbus and Custer jokes are the best for penetration into the heart of the matter, however. Rumor has it that Columbus began his journey with four ships. But one went over the edge so he arrived in the new world with only three. Another version states that Columbus didn't know where he was going, didn't know where he had been, and did it all on someone else's money. And the white man has been following Columbus ever since.

It is said that when Columbus landed, one Indian turned to another and said, "Well, there goes the neighborhood." Another version has two Indians watching Columbus land and one saying, "Maybe if we leave them alone they'll go away." A favorite cartoon in Indian country a few years back showed a flying saucer landing while an Indian watched. The caption was, "Oh, no, not again."

The most popular and enduring subject of Indian humor is, of course, General Custer. There are probably more jokes about Custer and the Indians than there were participants in the battle. All tribes, even those thousands of miles from Montana, feel a sense of accomplishment when thinking of Custer. Custer binds together implacable foes because he represented the Ugly American of the last century and he got what was coming to him.

Some years ago we put out a bumper sticker which read, "Custer Died for Your Sins." It was originally meant as a dig at the National Council of Churches. But as it spread around the nation it took on additional meaning until everyone claimed to understand it and each interpretation was different.

Originally, the Custer bumper sticker referred to the Sioux Treaty of 1868 signed at Fort Laramie in which the United States pledged to give free and undisturbed use of the lands claimed by Red Cloud in return for peace. Under the covenants of the Old Testament, breaking a covenant called for a blood sacrifice for the United States breaking the Sioux treaty. That, at least, was the original meaning of the slogan.

15   Custer jokes, however, can barely be categorized, let alone sloganized. Indians say that Custer was well-dressed for the occasion. When the Sioux found his body after the battle, he had on an Arrow shirt.

Many stories are derived from the details of the battle itself. Custer is said to have boasted that he could ride through the entire Sioux nation with his Seventh Cavalry and he was half right. He got half-way through.

One story concerns the period immediately after Custer's contingent had been wiped out and the Sioux and Cheyennes were zeroing in on Major Reno and his troops several miles south of the Custer battlefield.

The Indians had Reno's troopers surrounded on a bluff. Water was scarce, ammunition was nearly exhausted, and it looked like the next attack would mean certain extinction.

One of the white soldiers quickly analyzed the situation and shed his clothes. He covered himself with mud, painted his face like an Indian, and began to creep toward the Indian lines.

A Cheyenne heard some rustling in the grass and was just about to shoot.   20

"Hey, chief," the soldier whispered, "don't shoot, I'm coming over to join you. I'm going to be on your side."

The warrior looked puzzled and asked the soldier why he wanted to change sides.

"Well," he replied, "better red than dead."

Custer's Last Words occupy a revered place in Indian humor. One source states that as he was falling mortally wounded he cried, "Take no prisoners!" Other versions, most of them off color, concentrate on where those * * * * Indians are coming from. My favorite last saying pictures Custer on top of a hill looking at a multitude of warriors charging up the slope at him. He turns resignedly to his aide and says, "Well, it's better than going back to North Dakota."

Since the battle it has been a favorite technique to boost the numbers on   25 the Indian side and reduce the numbers on the white side so that Custer stands out as a man fighting against insurmountable odds. One question no pseudo-historian has attempted to answer, when changing the odds to make the little boy in blue more heroic, is how what they say were twenty thousand Indians could be fed when gathered into one camp. What a tremendous pony herd that must have been that gathered there, what a fantastic herd of buffalo must have been nearby to feed that amount of Indians, what an incredible source of drinking water must have been available for fifty thousand animals and some twenty thousand Indians!

Just figuring water-needs to keep that many people and animals alive for a number a days must have been incredible. If you estimated correctly, you will see that the Little Big Horn was the last great *naval* engagement of the Indian Wars.

The Sioux tease other tribes a great deal for not being at Little Big Horn. The Crows, traditional enemies of the Sioux, explain their role as Custer's scouts as one of bringing Custer where the Sioux could get at him! Arapahos and Cheyennes, allies of the Sioux in that battle, refer to the time they "bailed the Sioux out" when they got in trouble with the cavalry.

Even today variations of the Custer legend are bywords in Indian country. When an Indian gets too old and becomes inactive, people say he is "too old to muss the Custer anymore."

The early reservation days were times when humorous incidents abounded as Indians tried to adapt to the strange new white ways and occasionally found themselves in great dilemmas.

30   At Fort Sisseton, in Dakota territory, Indians were encouraged to enlist as scouts for the Army after the Minnesota Wars. Among the requirements for enlistment were a working knowledge of English and having attained twenty-one years of age. But these requirements were rarely met. Scouts were scarce and the goal was to keep a company of scouts at full strength, not to follow regulations from Washington to the letter.

In a very short time the Army had a company of scouts who were very efficient but didn't know enough English to understand a complete sentence. Washington, finding out about the situation, as bureaucracies occasionally do, sent an inspector to check on the situation. While he was en route, orders to disband the scouts arrived, and so his task became one of closing the unit and making the mustering-out payments.

The scouts had lined up outside the command officer's quarters and were interviewed one by one. They were given their choice of taking money, horses, or a combination of the two as their final severance pay from the Army. Those who could not speak English were severely reprimanded and tended to get poorer horses in payment because of their obvious disregard of the regulations.

One young scout, who was obviously in violation of both requirements, was very worried about his interview. He quizzed the scouts who came from the room about the interview. To a man they repeated the same story: "You will be asked three questions, how old you are, how long have you been with the scouts, and whether you want money or horses for your mustering-out pay."

The young scout memorized the appropriate answers and prepared himself for his turn with the inspector. When his turn came he entered the room, scared to death but determined to do his best. He stood at attention before the man from Washington, eager to give his answers and get out of there.

35   The inspector, tired after a number of interviews, wearily looked up and inquired:

"How long have you been in the scouts?"

"Twenty years," the Indian replied with a grin.

The inspector stopped short and looked at the young man. Here was a man who looked only eighteen or twenty, yet he had served some twenty years in the scouts. He must have been one of the earliest recruits. It just didn't seem possible. Yet, the inspector thought, you can't tell an Indian's age from they way he looks, they sure can fool you sometimes. Or was he losing his mind after interviewing so many people in so short a time? Perhaps it was the Dakota heat. At any rate, he continued the interview.

"How old are you?" he continued.

40   "Three years."

A look of shock rippled across the inspector's face. Could this be some mysterious Indian way of keeping time? Or was he now delirious.

"Am I crazy or are you?" he angrily asked the scout.

"Both" was the reply and the scout relaxed, smiled, and leaned over the desk, reaching out to receive his money.

The horrified inspector cleared the window in one leap. He was seen in Washington, D.C., the following morning, having run full speed during the night. It was the last time Indian scouts were required to know English and applications for interpreter were being taken the following morning.

The problems of the missionaries in the early days provided stories which   45
have become classics in Indian country. They are retold over and over again wherever Indians gather.

One story concerns a very obnoxious missionary who delighted in scaring the people with tales of hell, eternal fires, and everlasting damnation. This man was very unpopular and people went out of their way to avoid him. But he persisted to contrast heaven and hell as a carrot-and-stick technique of conversion.

One Sunday after a particularly fearful description of hell he asked an old chief, the main holdout of the tribe against Christianity, where he wanted to go. The old chief asked the missionary where he was going. And the missionary replied that, of course, he as a missionary of the gospel was going to heaven.

"Then I'll go to hell," the old chief said, intent on having peace in the world to come if not in this world.

On the Standing Rock reservation in South Dakota my grandfather served as the Episcopal missionary for years after his conversion to Christianity. He spent a great deal of his time trying to convert old Chief Gall, one of the strategists of Custer's demise, and a very famous and influential member of the tribe.

My grandfather gave Gall every argument in the book and some outside   50
the book but the old man was adamant in keeping his old Indian ways. Neither the joys of heaven nor the perils of hell would sway the old man. But finally, because he was fond of my grandfather, he decided to become an Episcopalian.

He was baptized and by Christmas of that year was ready to take his first communion. He fasted all day and attended the Christmas Eve services that evening.

The weather was bitterly cold and the little church was heated by an old wood stove placed in the center of the church. Gall, as the most respected member of the community, was given the seat of honor next to the stove where he could keep warm.

In deference to the old man, my grandfather offered him communion first. Gall took the chalice and drained the entire supply of wine before returning to his seat. The wine had been intended for the entire congregation and so the old man had a substantial amount of spiritual refreshment.

Upon returning to his seat by the stove, it was not long before the wine took its toll on the old man who by now had had nothing to eat for nearly a day.

55   "Grandson," he called to my grandfather, "now I see why you wanted me to become a Christian. I feel fine, so nice and warm and happy. Why didn't you tell me you Christians do this every Sunday. If you would have told me about this, I would have joined your church years ago."

Needless to say, the service was concluded as rapidly as possible and attendance skyrocketed the following Sunday.

Another missionary was traveling from Gallup to Albuquerque in the early days. Along the way he offered a ride to an Indian who was walking to town. Feeling he had a captive audience, he began cautiously to promote his message, using a soft-sell approach.

"Do you realize," he said, "that you are going to a place where sinners abound?"

The Indian nodded his head in assent.

60   "And the wicked dwell in the depths of their iniquities?"

Again a nod.

"And sinful women who have lived a bad life go?"

A smile and then another nod.

"And no one who lives a good life goes there?"

65   A possible conversion, thought the missionary, and so he pulled out his punch line: "And do you know what we call that place?"

The Indian turned, looked the missionary in the eye, and said, "Albuquerque."

Times may have changed but difficulties in communications seem to remain the same. At Santee, Nebraska, the people tell of a full blood who had a great deal of trouble understanding English. He used the foreign tongue as little as possible and managed to get along. But he knew only a few phrases of broken English, which he used when bargaining for his necessities of life.

One day he approached a white farmer and began bargaining for a fine rooster that the farmer owned. The old timer had brought two large bags filled with new potatoes and he motioned to the farmer that he wanted to trade them for the rooster.

Pointing from one to the other, he anxiously inquired, "potato rooster, potato rooster?" Soon the white farmer got the message and decided that it would be a good trade.

70   "Sure, chief," he replied, "I'll trade you."

So the Indian picked up the rooster, looked at it with satisfaction, tucked the rooster under his arm, and then started to walk away.

As he was leaving, the white farmer began to think about the exchange. Obviously the rooster would be of little value without some hens for it. The potatoes were more than adequate to pay for a number of chickens, so he called after the Indian:

"Chief, do you want a pullet?"

The Indian turned around, tucked the rooster tighter under his arm, and said, "No, I can carry it."

75   In the Southwest, Indians like to talk about a similar play on words. One favorite story concerns a time when the Apaches and the settlers were fight-

ing for control of Arizona territory. The chief of one Apache band was the last one needed to sign the peace treaty. Scout after scout had urged him to sign so the territory could have peace. But to no avail.

One day the chief took sick and, because he realized his days were numbered, he called his three sons together and made them pledge not to make peace unless all three signed the treaty. Soon after that the old man died and his three sons, Deerfoot, Running Bear, and Falling Rocks, all left to seek their fortunes with portions of the original band.

Scouts quickly found Deerfoot and Running Bear and convinced them they should sign the treaty. But they were unable to find Falling Rocks. Years went by and everyone in the territory sought the missing band so the treaty could be concluded. Falling Rocks was not to be found.

Eventually everyone gave up except the state highway department. They continued looking for him. And that is why as you drive through the mountain passes of Arizona you will see large signs that read, "Look out for Falling Rocks."

The years have not changed the basic conviction of the Indian people that they are still dealing with the United States as equals. At a hearing on Civil Rights in South Dakota a few years ago a white man asked a Sioux if they still considered themselves an independent nation. "Oh, yes," was the reply, "we could still declare war on you. We might lose but you'd know you'd been in a terrible fight. Remember the last time in Montana?"

During the 1964 elections Indians were talking in Arizona about the relative positions of the two candidates, Johnson and Goldwater. A white man told them to forget about domestic policies and concentrate on foreign policies of the two men. One Indian looked at him coldly and said that from the Indian point of view it was all foreign policy.

The year 1964 also saw the emergence of the Indian vote on a national scale. Rumors reached us that on the Navajo reservation there was more enthusiasm than understanding of the political processes. Large signs announced, "All the Way with LJB."

The current joke is that a survey was taken and only 15 percent of the Indians thought the United States should get out of Vietnam. Eighty-five percent thought they should get out of America!

One of the most popular topics of Indian humor is the Bureau of Indian Affairs. When asked what was the biggest joke in Indian country, a man once said, "the BIA." During the years of termination, no matter how many tribes were being terminated the BIA kept adding employees. Since the thrust of termination was to cut government expenditures, the continual hiring of additional people led Indians to believe that such was not the real purpose. The rumor began that the BIA was phasing out Indians and would henceforth provide services only for its own employees.

A favorite story about the BIA concerns the time when Interior tried to merge the Standing Rock and Cheyenne River Sioux agencies in an economy move. A Sioux from Cheyenne River told an investigating committee the following story.

85   One day an Indian went to the Public Health Service because he had a bad headache. The PHS doctor decided to operate on him and he cut the Indian's head open and took out the brain to examine it.

Just then a man came in the door and shouted, "Joe, your house is on fire."

Joe, lying on the operating table, urged the doctor to sew his head so that he could go and fight the fire. The doctor did as requested and Joe headed for the door.

"Wait, Joe," the doctor yelled, "you forgot your brain."

"I don't need any brain, Joe answered as he went out the door. "After I get the fire put out, I'm going to work for the BIA."

90   An additional story about the BIA concerns the Indian who wanted a new brain. He walked into the PHS clinic and asked for an operation whereby he could exchange his brain for a better one.

The doctor took him into a room that contained many shelves upon which were rows of jars containing brains. Each jar had a price tag on it. A doctor's brain sold for ten dollars an ounce, a professor's brain sold for fifteen dollars an ounce. Similar brains from professional people ranged higher and higher until, at the very end of the back of the rows, there was a jar marked one thousand dollars an ounce.

The Indian asked why that type of brain was so expensive and wanted to know what kind of brain it was. The doctor said the jar contained brains of the BIA, and added, "You know it takes so many of them to make an ounce."

In 1967 we had a conference on manpower at Kansas City. One panel on employment had well-known BIA representative moderating it. He made an excellent presentation and then asked for questions. For a long time the assembled delegates just sat and looked at him. So again he asked for questions, mentioned a few things he thought were important, and waited for a response from the audience. Nothing.

Finally he said, "I really didn't want a discussion. I just wanted to show that the BIA can come to a conference and stand here without saying anything."

95   "You proved that during your speech," one of the Indians retorted.

Perhaps the most disastrous policy, outside of termination, ever undertaken by the Bureau of Indian Affairs was a program called Relocation. It began as a policy of the Eisenhower administration as a means of getting Indians off the reservation and into the slums where they could fade away.

Considerable pressure was put on reservation Indians to move into the cities. Reservation people were continually harassed by bureau officials until they agreed to enter the program. Sometimes the BIA relocation officer was so eager to get the Indians moved off the reservation that he would take the entire family into the city himself.

But the Indians came back to the reservation as soon as they saw what the city had to offer. Many is the story by BIA people of how the Indians got back to the reservations before the BIA officials who had taken them to the city returned.

When the space program began, there was great talk about sending men to the moon. Discussion often centered about the difficulty of returning men from the moon to earth, as re-entry procedures were considered to be very tricky. One Indian suggested they send an Indian to the moon on relocation. "He'll figure out some way to get back."

Chippewas always tease the Sioux about the old days when they ran the   *100* Sioux out of Minnesota. It was, they claim, the first successful relocation program. In turn, the tribes that were pushed aside by the Sioux when they invaded the plains are ribbed about the relocation program which the Sioux conducted.

One solution to the "Indian problem" advocated in the Eisenhower years was closing the rolls of Indians eligible to receive federal services. Instead of federal services, each Indian would receive a per capita share of the total budget. As each Indian died off the total budget would be reduced. When all of the eligible Indians died off, that would be the end of federal–Indian relationships.

This plan was the favorite of Commissioner Glenn Emmons, who was heading the bureau at that time. But try as he might, he couldn't sell the program to anyone.

An agency superintendent from the Rosebud Sioux reservation in South Dakota had to go to Washington on business and so he decided to drive. As long as he was going he decided to take an old full blood with him and let the old man see the nation's capital.

The old man was very excited to be going to Washington and he made up his mind to see the Commissioner when he arrived there. So the superintendent began to suggest that the old man might have some solution to the Indian problem that he could share with the Commissioner. The old Indian discussed several ideas but admitted that they would probably be rejected.

Finally the superintendent outlined Emmon's plan to distribute the fed-   *105* eral budget being spent on Indians among those then eligible for services. The old man pondered the idea for some time. Then he said, "That's the craziest idea I ever heard of. If I said something like that to the Commissioner, he would have me thrown out of his office."

Later the superintendent said he had always wished that the old man had suggested the plan to Emmons. "I always wanted," he told me, "to see the look on Emmon's face when an uneducated full blood suggested his own plan to him. I'd bet my last dollar that things would have changed at the BIA."

Frequently, without intending any humor, Indians can create a situation so funny that it is nearly impossible to believe. At the Manpower Conference in Kansas City in 1967 a series of events set up a hilarious incident. At least, looking back at it, Indians still chuckle over the results of the conference.

In 1966, after Philleo Nash had been Commissioner and had been fired for protecting the tribes, Udall gathered all of his top people and began to plan for a massive new program for "his" Indians. The administration also planned a comprehensive survey of Indian problems, perhaps realizing that Interior would once again draw a blank.

All of 1966 a secret Presidential Task Force surveyed Indian Affairs. By late December of that year they had compiled their report which, among other things, advocated a transfer of the Bureau of Indian Affairs to Health,

Education and Welfare. Rumors began to fly in Indian country about the impending transfer and so the administration sent John Gardner, then Secretary of HEW, to Kansas City to present the idea to the assembled tribes.

110   In spite of all we could do to get HEW to advance the idea to a series of small conferences made up of influential tribal leaders, HEW insisted on presenting the idea to the entire group of assembled tribes—cold. So Gardner embarked for Kansas City with the usual entourage of high officialdom to present the message.

The tribal chairmen were greatly concerned about the possible loss of treaty rights which might occur during the transfer. When Gardner finished his presentation he opened the floor for questions and the concerned chairmen began.

The first man to know if all treaty rights would be protected. The secretary of HEW assured him that treaty rights would be protected by law. The second man said that he had had such assurances before and now he wanted Gardner to give his personal assurance so he could go back and talk to his people. Gardner gave him the personal assurances he wanted.

The next chairman wanted Gardner's assurance that nothing would be changed in the method of operations. The third wanted Gardner's assurance that no part of the existing structure would be changed, but that only the name plates would be different. The man following again wanted assurance that nothing would be changed, absolutely nothing. Wearily Gardner explained that *nothing* would be changed, everything would remain the same.

Eight straight chairmen questioned Gardner, asking for assurances that the basic structure would remain absolutely as it had been under Interior. Not a jot or a tittle, according to Gardner, would be changed at all. There was no possible way that anything could be changed. Everything was to remain just as it was.

115   The ninth questioner brought down the house. "Why," he inquired, "if there are to be no changes at all, do you want to transfer the bureau to HEW? It would be the same as it is now," he concluded.

It suddenly occurred to everyone that the chairmen had successfully trapped Gardner in a neat box from which there was no escape. Suffice to say, there was no transfer.

Not only the bureau, but other agencies, became the subject of Indian humor. When the War on Poverty was announced, Indians were justly skeptical about the extravagant promises of the bureaucrats. The private organizations in the Indian field, organized as the Council on Indian Affairs, sponsored a Capital Conference on Poverty in Washington in May of 1966 to ensure that Indian poverty would be highlighted just prior to the passage of the poverty program in Congress.

Tribes from all over the nation attended the conference to present papers on the poverty existing on their reservations. Two Indians from the plains area were asked about their feelings on the proposed program.

"Well," one said, "if they bring that War on Poverty to our reservation, they'll know they've been in a fight."

At the same conference, Alex Chasing Hawk, a nationally famous Indian   *120*
leader from Cheyenne River and a classic storyteller, related the following tale
about poverty.

It seemed that a white man was introduced to an old chief in New York
City. Taking a liking to the old man, the white man invited him to dinner.
The old chief hadn't eaten a good steak in a long time and eagerly accepted.
He finished one steak in no time and still looked hungry. So the white man
offered to buy him another steak.

As they were waiting for the steak, the white man said, "Chief, I sure wish
I had your appetite."

"I don't doubt it, white man," the chief said. "You took my land, you took
my mountains and streams, you took my salmon and my buffalo. You took
everything I had except my appetite and now you want that. Aren't you ever
going to be satisfied?"

At one conference on urban renewal, an Indian startled the audience
when he endorsed the program. All day he had advocated using the poverty
program to solve Indian problems on the reservation. Then, when the discussion got around to urban renewal, he abruptly supported the program.

He was asked why he wanted the program. It was, he was assured, per-   *125*
fectly natural for blacks and Mexican people to support urban renewal because so many of their people live in the cities. But it didn't make sense to the
conference participants what good an urban program would do for reservation Indians.

"I know," the Indian replied, "that a great many blacks and Mexicans want
the program because so many of their people live in the cities and these cities
must be rebuilt to give them a better life. But the program would also mean a
better life for my people. You see, after the cities are rebuilt and everyone is
settled there, we are going to fence them off and run our buffalo all over the
country again."

People are always puzzled when they learn that Indians are not involved
in the Civil Rights struggle. Many expect Indians to be marching up and
down like other people, feeling that all problems of poor groups are basically
the same.

But Indian people, having treaty rights of long standing, rightly feel protection of existing rights is much more important to them. Yet intra-group jokes
have been increasing since the beginning of the Civil Rights movement and
few Indians do not wryly comment on movements among the other groups.

An Indian and a black man were in a bar one day talking about the problems of their respective groups. The black man reviewed all of the progress his
people had made over the past decade and tried to get the Indian inspired to
start a similar movement of activism among the tribes.

Finally the black man concluded, "Well, I guess you can't do much, there   *130*
are so few of you."

"Yes," said the Indian, "and there won't be many of you if they decide to
play cowboys and blacks."

Another time, an Indian and a black man were talking about their respective races and how they had been treated by the white man. Each was trying to console the other about the problem and each felt the other group had been treated worse.

The Indian reminded the black man how his people had been slaves, how they had not had a chance to have a good family life, and how they were so persecuted in the South.

The black man admitted all of the sufferings of his people, but he was far more eloquent in reciting the wrongs against the Indians. He reviewed the broken treaties, the great land thefts, the smallpox infected blankets given to the tribes by the English, and the current movement to relocate all the Indians in the cities, far from their homelands.

135 Listening to the vivid description, the Indian got completely carried away in remorse. As each wrong was recited he nodded sorrowfully and was soon convinced that there was practically no hope at all for his people. Finally he could stand it no more.

"And do you know," he told the black man, "there was a time in the history of this country when they used to shoot us *just to get feathers!*"

During the riots, an Indian and a black man were talking about the terrible things going on. The black man said that the Indians could have prevented all this grief if they had only stopped the white men at the Allegheny Mountains in the early days. Then there would have been no expansion of white influence and perhaps even slavery would not have been started. Why, the black man wanted to know, hadn't the Indians stopped the white man when it was possible for them to do so.

"I know, I know," the Indian answered, "but every time we tried to attack their forts, they had "Soul Brother" painted on them, so we never got the job done."

Because there is little communication between minority communities, inter-group jokes always have the great danger of being misunderstood. In 1966, beside the Custer cards, we put out a card which read "We Shall Overrun," which, at least to us, harked to the scenes in Western movies where a small group of Indians mysteriously grows as it is outlined along the rim of a canyon until appears as if several thousand warriors have sprung from the initial group of a dozen.

140 When we showed the card to various blacks in the Civil Rights movement they didn't know how to take it and several times there was a tense situation until the card was explained.

Such is not the case when tribes tease each other. Then everything is up for grabs. Sioux announce that safe-conduct passes are available to Chippewas at the registration desk. Chippewas retort that if the Sioux don't behave they will have to relocate them again. Southwestern tribes innocently proclaim that their chili is very mild when in reality they are using asbestos pottery to serve it in. And the northern tribes seem always to take large helpings, which they somehow manage to get down amid tears and burnt mouths.

In the old days, after the buffalo were gone, the Sioux were reduced to eating dogs to keep alive. They had no meat of any kind and rabbits on the reservation were rare. Other tribes keep up the ribbing by announcing that the chef has prepared a special treat for the Sioux present at the annual banquet through the special cooperation of the local dog pound.

In 1964, Billy Mills, a Sioux from Pine Ridge, South Dakota, won the ten thousand meter run at the Olympics in Tokyo. Justly proud of Billy, the Sioux went all out to inform other tribes of his achievement. One day we were bragging about Billy's feat to the Coeur d'Alenes of Idaho, who politely nodded their heads in agreement.

Finally the wife of the chairman, Leona Garry, announced that Mills' running ability did not really surprise the Coeur d'Alenes. "After all," she said, "up here in Idaho, Sioux have to run far, fast, and often if they mean to stay alive." That ended the discussion of Sioux athletic ability for the evening.

Clyde Warrior, during this time, was perhaps the single greatest wit in Indian country. One day he announced that the bureau was preparing a special training program for the other tribes. When quizzed about how it differed from other programs in existence, he noted that it had a restriction of only a half-hour lunch period. "Otherwise," Clyde said, "they would have to be retrained after lunch."

Providing information to inquisitive whites has also proved humorous on occasion. At a night club in Washington, D.C., a group of Indians from North Dakota were gathered, taking the edge off their trip before heading home. One man, a very shy and handsome Chippewa, caught the eye of one of the entertainers. She began to talk with him about Indian life.

Did Indians still live in tents, she inquired. He admitted shyly that he sometimes lived in a tent in the summertime because it was cooler than a house. Question after question came and was answered by the same polite responses. The girl took quite a fancy to the Chippewa and he got more and more embarrassed at the attention.

Finally she wanted to know if Indians still raided wagon trains. He said no, they had stopped doing that a long time ago. She was heartbroken at hearing the news. "I sure would like to be raided by you," she said, and brought down the house.

Louie Sitting Crow, an old timer from Crow Creek, South Dakota, used to go into town and watch the tourists who traveled along Highway 16 in South Dakota to get to the Black Hills. One day at a filling station a car from New York pulled up and began filling its tank for the long drive.

A girl came over to talk to Louie. She asked him a great many questions about the Sioux and Louie answered as best he could. Yes, the Sioux were fierce warriors. Yes, the Sioux had once owned all of the state. Yes, they still wished for the old days.

Finally the girl asked if the Indians still scalped people. Louie, weary of the questions, replied, "Lady, remember, when you cross that river and head west, you will be in the land of the fiercest Indians on earth and you will be very lucky to get to the Black Hills alive. And you ask me if they still scalp. Let me tell you, its worse than that. Now they take the whole head."

As Louie recalled, the car turned around and headed east after the tank was full of gas.

Southwestern Indians can get off a good one when they are inspired. A couple of years ago I was riding a bus from Santa Fe to Albuquerque late at night. The bus was late leaving Santa Fe and it seemed like it was taking forever to get on its way.

Two old men were from one of the pueblos between the two cities were aboard and obviously feeling contented after their night in town. They filled the time we were waiting for the bus to depart by telling stories and as the bus got under way they began to make comments on its snail's pace.

155   The bus driver was in no humor to withstand a running commentary on the speed of the bus that night so he turned around and said, "If you don't like the speed we're making, why don't you get out and walk?"

"Oh, we couldn't do that," one of the men said. "They don't expect us home until the bus gets in."

An Indian in Montana was arrested for driving while intoxicated and he was thrown in jail for the night. The following morning he was hauled before a judge for his hearing. Not knowing English very well, the Indian worried about the hearing, but he was determined to do the best he could.

The judge, accustomed to articulate, English-speaking people appearing before him, waited for the man to make his plea. The Indian stood silently waiting for the judge to say something. As the two looked at each other the silence began to become unbearable and the judge completely forgot what the man was being tried for.

Finally he said, "Well, speak up, Indian, why are you here?"

160   The Indian, who had been planning to plead not guilty, was also completely off balance. He gulped, looked at the judge and said, "Your honor, I was arrested for driving a drunken car."

One-line retorts are common in Indian country. Popovi Da, the great Pueblo artist, was quizzed one day on why the Indians were the first ones on this continent. "We had reservations," was his reply. Another time, when questioned by an anthropologist on what the Indians called America before the white man came, an Indian said simply, *"Ours."* A young Indian was asked one day at a conference what a peace treaty was. He replied, "That's when the white man wants a piece of your land."

The best example of Indian humor and militancy I have ever heard was by Clyde Warrior one day. He was talking with a group of people about the National Indian Youth Council, of which he was then president, and its program for revitalization of Indian life. Several in the crowd were skeptical about the idea of rebuilding Indian communities along traditional Indian lines.

"Do you realize," he said, "that when the United States was founded, it was only 5 percent urban and 95 percent rural and now it is 70 percent urban and 30 percent rural?"

His listeners nodded solemnly but didn't seem to understand what he was driving at.

"Don't you realize what this means?" he rapidly continued. "It means we are pushing them into the cities. Soon we will have the country back again." 165

Whether Indian jokes will eventually come to have more significance than that, I cannot speculate. Humor, all Indians will agree, is the cement by which the coming Indian movement is held together. When a people can laugh at themselves and laugh at others and hold all aspects of life together without letting anybody drive them to extremes, then it seems to me that people can survive.

15

Resistance Strategy Three: Separatism and Identity Politics

■ ■ ■ ■

BLACK POWER: A SCIENTIFIC CONCEPT WHOSE TIME HAS COME

James Boggs

Black Power. Black Power. This is what is being written about and talked about in all strata of the population of the United States of America. Not since the spector of Communism first began to haunt Europe over one hundred years ago has an idea put forward by so few people frightened so many in so short a time. Liberals and radicals, Negro civil rights leaders and politicians, reporters and editorial writers—it is amazing to what degree all of them are fascinated and appalled by Black Power.

The fact that these words were first shouted out by the little-known Willie Ricks and then by Stokely Carmichael to a crowd of blacks during a march to Jackson, Mississippi, in the spring of 1966 has heightened the tension surrounding the phrase. For earlier in the year the Student Non-Violent Coordinating Committee (SNCC), which Carmichael heads and of which Ricks is an organizer, had issued a public statement on American foreign policy condemning the war in Vietnam as a racist war and connecting the black movement in this country with the anti-imperialist movement in Asia. In that same period, SNCC had begun to analyze the role white liberals and radicals could play in the movement, aptly characterizing it as one of supporting rather than decision-making. Coming after these statements, the cry of Black Power was seen by most people as deepening the gulf between the pro-integrationists and the nationalists. Whether or not Carmichael had intended this cannot really be determined since the phrase had scarcely left his lips before the press and every so-called spokesman for the movement were making their own interpretations to fit their own prejudices or programs.

When Malcolm X was assassinated in February 1965, every radical in the country and every group in the movement began to seize on some slogan Malcolm had raised or some speech he had made or some facet of his personality in order to identify themselves with him or to establish support for some plank in their own program. The same process of attempted identification is now taking place with Black Power. The difference, however, is that Black Power is not just a personality or a speech or a slogan, as most radicals, liberals, and Negro leaders would like to regard it. The immediate and instinctive reaction of the average white American and the white extremist or fascist is far sounder than that of the liberal, radical, and civil rights leader. For these average whites reacted to the call for Black Power simply and honestly by reaffirming "white power." Their concern is not civil rights (which are, after all, only the common rights which should be guaranteed to everyone by the state and its laws). They are concerned with power, and they recognize instinctively that once the issue of power is raised it means one set of people who are powerless replacing another set of people who have the power. Just as Marx's concept of workers' power did not mean workers becoming a part of or integrating themselves into capitalist power, so Black Power does not mean black people becoming a part of or integrating themselves into white power. Power is not something that a state or those in power bestow upon or guarantee those who have been without power because of morality or a change of heart. It is something that you must make or take from those in power.

It is significant that practically nobody in the United States has tried to seek out the extensive theoretical work that has been done on the concept of Black Power. Actually, most of those writing for and against Black Power don't want to investigate further. They would rather keep the concept vague than grapple with the systematic analysis of American capitalism out of which the concept of Black Power has developed. In *The American Revolution: Pages from a Negro Worker's Notebook,* I stated my belief that if Marx were living today he would have no problem facing the contradictions which have developed since his original analysis because his method of analysis was itself historical. I said further that I considered it the responsibility of any serious Marxist to advance Marx's theory to meet today's historical situation, in which the underdeveloped—i.e., the super-exploited—nations of the world, which are in fact a world under-class, confront the highly developed capitalist countries in which the working classes for the most part have been incorporated or integrated into pillars of support for the capitalist system. Yet such an analysis has not been seriously attempted by either European or American Marxists. European Marxists have not seriously grappled with: (1) the fact that Marx specifically chose England (at the time the most advanced country industrially in the world) as the basis of his analysis of the class struggle in terms of the process of production; and (2) the fact that at the same time that the European workers were beginning to struggle as a class against the capitalist enemy at home, this same class enemy was expanding its colonial exploitation of Africa, Asia, and Latin America and thereby acquiring the means with which to make concessions to and integrate the working class into the system at home. Therefore, the working classes in the advanced countries were to a significant degree achieving their class progress at home at the expense of the under-class of the world. It was Lenin who dealt with this question most seriously when the European workers supported their capitalist governments in the first imperialist world war, and it was Lenin who, finding it necessary to deal seriously with the anti-colonialist revolutionary struggle after the Russian Revolution, recognized the nationalist and anti-colonialist character of the black struggle in the United States. Yet today, nearly a half century after the Russian Revolution and after two generations of European workers have shown themselves just as opposed to independence for the peoples of Africa and Asia as their capitalist oppressors, European Marxists are still using the slogan "workers of the world, unite" and evading the scientific question of which workers they are calling on.

5   Who is to unite? And with whom? The under-class of Africa, Asia, and Latin America which makes up the colonized, ex-colonized, and semi-colonized nations? Or the workers of highly developed Europe and America whose improved conditions and higher standard of living have been made possible by colonial exploitation of the world under-class? Isn't it obvious that the working classes of Europe and America are like the petty bourgeoisie of Marx's time and that they collaborate with the power structure and support the system because their high standard of living depends upon the continuation of this power structure and this system?

The United States has been no exception to this process of advanced nations advancing through exploitation of an under-class excluded from the nation. The only difference has been that its under-class was inside the country, not outside. Black men were brought into this country by a people dedicated to the concept that all blacks were inferior, subhuman savages and natives to be used as tools in the same way that machines are used today. The phrase "all men" defined in the Constitution as "created equal" did not include black men. By definition, blacks were not men but some kind of colored beings. It took 335 years, from 1619 to 1954, before an effort was made to extend the definition of manhood to blacks. Yet American radicals have sought to propagate the concept of "black and white, unite and fight" as if black and white had common issues and grievances, systematically evading the fact that every immigrant who walked off the gangplank into this country did so on the backs of the indigenous blacks and had the opportunity to advance precisely because the indigenous blacks were being systematically deprived of the opportunity to advance by both capitalist and workers.

The United States has a history of racism longer than that of any other nation on earth. Fascism, or the naked oppression of a minority race not only by the state but by the ordinary citizens of the master majority race, is the normal, natural way of life in this country. The confusion and bewilderment of old radicals in the face of the Black Power concept is therefore quite natural. United States and European radicals accept white power as so natural that they do not even see its color. They find it perfectly natural to exhort blacks to integrate into white society and the white structure but cannot conceive of its being the other way around. Integration has been an umbrella under which American radicals have been able to preach class collaboration without appearing to do so. Under the guise of combating the racism of whites, they have actually been trying to bring about collaboration between the oppressed race and the oppressing race, thus sabotaging the revolutionary struggle against oppression which, by virtue of the historical development of the United States, requires a mobilization of the oppressed blacks for struggle against the oppressing whites.

There is no historical basis for the promise, constantly made to blacks by American radicals, that the white workers will join with them against the capitalist enemy. After the Civil War the white workers went homesteading the West while the Southern planters were being given a free hand by Northern capitalists to re-enslave the blacks systematically. White workers supported this re-enslavement just as the German working class supported Hitler in his systematic slaughter of the Jews. The gulf between blacks and white workers in the United States is just as great as that between the Jews and the German workers under Hitler. The difference is that Hitler lasted only a few years while systematic oppression and unceasing threat of death at the hands of ordinary whites have been the lot of blacks in the United States for nearly 400 years. The present so-called white backlash is just white people acting like white people and just as naturally blaming their white hate and white anger not on themselves but on the blacks wanting too much too soon.

Despite their slavish allegiance to the concept of "black and white, unite and fight," most radicals and liberals are well aware that they do not constitute a serious social force in the United States. Few, it any of them, would dare go into a white working-class neighborhood and advocate that slogan. They would be about as safe doing it there as they would be in South Africa. That they go so easily into the black community with the slogan but steer clear of white communities is just another example of how naturally they think white. For whether they admit it to themselves or not, if anyone wanted to build a quick mass organization in a white working-class neighborhood today, his best bet would be to go in as a Ku Klux Klan or White Citizens' Council organizer to mobilize white workers to unite and fight against blacks. Out of self-mobilization white workers have already come up with the slogan: "Fight for what is white and right!"

Revolutionaries must face the fact that the black revolt is now under way and is not waiting for that "someday" when the white workers will have changed their minds about blacks. Like it or not, they must face the fact that the historical and dialectical development of the United States in particular has made the blacks the chief social force for the revolt against American capitalism and that the course of this black revolt itself will decide which side the white workers will be on. The more powerful the black revolt, the more blacks move toward black power, the greater the chances of the white workers'

10

accepting revolutionary change. On the other hand, the more the black revolt is weakened, diluted, and deluded by class collaboration (e.g., "black and white, unite and fight" and "integration"), the more chance there is of the white workers remaining counter-revolutionary.

Black Power in the United States raises the question that Stalin could not tolerate from Mao: Would the revolution in China come from the urban workers or from the peasantry? Mao pursued his theory, based upon the specific conditions in China, and was proven right by the revolution itself. In the United States today, the question is whether the blacks (over 75 percent of whom are now concentrated in the heart of the nation's largest cities) will lead the revolution or whether they must wait for the white workers. In the twentieth century the United States has advanced rapidly from a semi-urban, semi-rural society into an overwhelmingly urban society. The farms which at the beginning of the century still employed nearly half the working population have now become so mechanized that the great majority of those who formerly worked on the land have had to move into the cities. Their land is now the city streets. Meanwhile, industry itself has been automated, with the result that black labor, which over the centuries has been systematically deprived of the opportunity to become skilled, had become economically and socially unnecessary. Unemployed or underemployed, the now expendable blacks are a constant threat to the system. Not only must they be fed in order to cool off the chances of their rebelling, but they occupy the choicest and most socially critical land in the heart of the nation's cities from which the racist white population has fled in order to remain lily white. Moreover, since blacks have become a majority in the inner-city population, they are now in line to assume the political leadership of the cities in accordance with the historical tradition whereby the largest ethnic minorities have successively run the cities. The city is now the black man's land, and the city is also the place where the nation's most critical problems are concentrated.

Confronted with this dilemma, the power structure, from its highest echelons to the middle classes, is seeking to incorporate or integrate a few elite Negroes into the system and thereby behead the black movement of its leadership. At the same time the power structure has devised ingenious methods for mass "Negro removal." Under the pretext of "urban renewal," it condemns and breaks up entire black communities, bulldozes homes, and scatters the black residents to other black communities which in turn are judged to need "urban renewal." Meanwhile, under the auspices of white draft boards black youths are sent as cannon fodder to die in the counter-revolutionary wars which the United States is carrying on all over the world as it replaces the old European colonial powers. Today the sun never sets on an American Empire which maintains bases in at least fifty-five different worldwide locations. The war in Vietnam is a war of sections of the world under-class fighting one another, for it is the poor, uneducated, unemployed who are drafted and the privileged (mainly white) who are deferred. This United States counter-revolution all over the world has the support not only of the general population but of organized labor. A peace demonstration in any white working-class or middle-class neighborhood brings out a hostile mob which is sure to come even when the peace demonstrators are all allegedly guarded by police.

Those progressives who are honestly confused by the concept of Black Power are in this state of confusion because they have not scientifically evaluated the present stage of historical development in relation to the stage of historical development when Marx projected the concept of workers' power vs. capitalist power. Yesterday the concept of workers' power expressed the revolutionary social force of the working class organized inside the process of capitalist production. Today the concept of Black Power expresses the new revolutionary social force of the black population concentrated in the black belt of the South and in the urban ghettos of the North—a revolutionary social force which must struggle not only against the capitalist but against the workers and middle classes who benefit by and support the system which has oppressed and exploited blacks. To expect the Black Power struggle to embrace white workers inside the black struggle is in fact to expect the revolution to welcome the enemy into its camp. To speak of the common responsibility of all Americans, white and black, to fight for black liberation is to sponsor class collaboration.

The uniqueness of Black Power stems from the specific historical development of the United States. It has nothing to do with any special moral virtue in being black, as some black nationalists seem to think. Nor does it have to do with the special cultural virtues of the African heritage. Identification with the African past is useful insofar as it enable black Americans to develop a sense of identity independent of the Western civilization which has robbed them of their humanity by robbing them of any history. But no past culture ever created a revolution. Every revolution creates a new culture out of the process of revolutionary struggle against the old values and culture which an oppressing society has sought to impose upon the oppressed.

The chief virtue in being black at this juncture in history stems from the fact that the vast majority of the people in the world who have been deprived of the right of self-government and self-determination are people of color. Today these people of color are not only the wretched of the earth but people in revolutionary ferment, having arrived at the decisive recognition that their underdevelopment is not the result of ethnic backwardness but of their systematic confinement to backwardness by the colonial powers. The struggle against this systematic deprivation is what has transformed them into a social force or an under-class. 15

The clarion call "black people of the world, unite and fight" is only serious if it is also a call to black people to organize. The call for Black Power in the United States at this juncture in the development of the movement has gone beyond the struggle for civil rights to a call for black people to replace white people in power. Black people must organize the fight for power. They have nothing to lose but their condition as the wretched of the earth.

The call for Black Power is creating—had to create—splits within the movement. These splits are of two main kinds. The first is between the Black Power advocates and the civil rights advocates. The civil rights advocates, sponsored, supported, and dependent upon the white power structure, are committed to integrate blacks into the white structure without any serious changes in that structure. In essence, they are simply asking to be given the same rights which whites have had and blacks have been denied. By equality they mean just that and no more: being equal to white Americans.

This is based on the assumption that the American way of life (and American democracy) is itself a human way of life, and ideal worth striving for. Specifically and concretely and to a large extent consciously, the civil rights advocates evade the fact the American way of life is a way of life that has been achieved through systematic exploitation of others (chiefly the black people inside this country and the Latin Americans), and is now being maintained and defended by counter-revolutionary force against blacks everywhere, particularly in Asia and Africa.

Inside the Black Power movement there is another growing split between the idealists or romanticists and the realists. The romanticists continue to talk and hope to arouse the masses of black people through self-agitation, deluding themselves and creating the illusion that one set of people can replace another set of people in power without building an organization to take active steps toward power, while at the same time agitating and mobilizing the masses. Masses and mass support come only when masses of people not only glimpse the desirability and possibility of serious improvement in their condition, but can *see* the force and power able to bring this about.

20   The realists in the movement for Black Power base themselves first and foremost on a scientific evaluation of the American system and of revolution, knowing that Black Power cannot come from the masses doing what they do when they feel like doing it, but must come from the painstaking, systematic building of an organization to lead the masses to power. The differentiation now taking place inside the Black Power movement between idealists and realists is comparable to the classic differentiation which took place inside the Russian revolutionary movement between the Mensheviks, who were opposed to building disciplined organization, and Bolsheviks, who insisted upon it.

The organization for Black Power must concentrate on the issue of political power and refuse to redefine and explain away Black Power as "black everything except black political power." The development of technology in the United States has made it impossible for blacks to achieve economic power by the old means of capitalist development. The ability of capitalists today to produce in abundance not only makes competition with them on an economic capitalist basis absurd but has already brought the United States technologically to the threshold of a society where each can have according to his needs. Thus black political power, coming at this juncture in the economically advanced United States, is the key not only to black liberation but to the introduction of a new society to emancipate economically the masses of the people in general. For black political power will have to decide on the kind of economy and the aims and direction of the economy for the people.

. . . [T]he type of organization which would be in tune with the struggle for Black Power . . . must be clearly distinguished not only from the traditional civil rights organizations which have been organized and financed by whites to integrate blacks into the system, and thereby save it, but also from the *ad hoc* organizations which have sprung up in the course of the struggle, arousing the masses emotionally around a particular issue and relying primarily on the enthusiasm and good will of their members and supporters for their continuing activity. By contrast, an organization for Black Power must be a cadre-type organization whose members have a clear understanding, allegiance, and dedication to the organization's perspectives and objectives and who have no illusions about the necessities of a struggle for power.

A cadre organization cannot be made up of just enthusiastic and aroused people. Its essential core must be cold, sober individuals who are ready to accept discipline and who recognize the absolute necessity of a strong leadership which can organize and project a strategy of action to mobilize the conscious and-not-so-conscious masses around their issues and grievances for a life-and-death struggle against those in power. Such a cadre must be able to continue the revolutionary struggle despite the inevitable setbacks because they believe that only through the revolution will their own future be assured.

At the same time that it recognizes the inevitability of setbacks, such an organization must build itself consciously upon a perspective of victory. This is particularly necessary in the United States, where the idea of the defeat of the black man has been so systematically instilled into the black people themselves that a tendency toward self-destruction or martyrdom will lurk unconsciously within the organization unless it is systematically rooted out of every member, leader, and supporter. The movement for Black Power cannot afford to lose other Malcolms, other Emmett Tills, other Medgar Everses, and it must build the kind of organization which has the strength and discipline to assure that there will be no more of these.

Nor can such an organization build itself on the counter-revolution's mistakes or abuses of the masses as the civil rights movement has done. Rather it must seriously plot every step of its course—when to act, when to retreat, when to seize upon an issue or a mistake by the ruling power and when not to.

Within such a cadre there must be units able to match every type of unit that the counter-revolution has at its disposal, able not only to pit themselves against these but to defend them. Colonialism, whether in Asia, Africa, Latin America, or inside the United States, was established by the gun and is maintained by the gun. But it has also been able to hold itself together because it had skilled, disciplined colonizers and administrators well versed in the art of ruling and able to make the decisions inseparable from rule.

There will be many fundamental questions and problems facing such an organization as it moves toward power. How will it create new national and international ties with other people within the country and without? What will it do about industry when its take-over is imminent and those in power resist? What will it do about the armed forces and how will it win them over? In what cities or localities should a base first be built? What will it do when confronted by those in power as they respond to the threat of replacement? What segments of the old apparatus can be useful and which should be destroyed? And most important, how can it expose its alleged friends as the real enemies they are? These are all questions of strategy and tactics which every serious organization for power has to work out but which no serious organization for power would write too much about.

. . . [T]he tragedy is that so few see the urgency of facing up to this reality. But as I also said, that is what makes a revolution: two sides—the revolution and the counter-revolution—and the people on both sides.

LESBIANISM: AN ACT OF RESISTANCE

Cheryl Clarke

For a woman to be a lesbian in a male-supremacist, capitalist, misogynist, racist, homophobic, imperialist culture, such as that of North America, is an act of resistance. (A resistance that should be championed throughout the world by all the forces struggling for liberation from the same slave master.) No matter how a woman lives out her lesbianism—in the closet, in the state legislature, in the bedroom—she has rebelled against becoming a slave master's concubine, viz. the male-dependent female, the female heterosexual. This rebellion is dangerous business in patriarchy. Men at all levels of privilege, of all classes and colors have the potential to act out legalistically, moralistically, and violently when they cannot colonize women, when they cannot circumscribe our sexual, productive, reproductive, creative prerogatives and energies. And the lesbian—that woman who, as Judy Grahn says, "has taken a woman lover"[1]—has succeeded in resisting the slave master's imperialism in that one sphere of her life. The lesbian has decolonized her body. She has rejected a life of servitude implicit in Western, heterosexual relationships and has accepted the potential of mutuality in a lesbian relationship—*roles* notwithstanding.

Historically, this culture has come to identify lesbians as women, who over time, engage in a range and variety of sexual-emotional relationships with women. I, for one, identify a woman as a lesbian who says she is. Lesbianism is a recognition, an awakening, a reawakening of our passion for each (woman) other (woman) and for same (woman). This passion will ultimately reverse the heterosexual imperialism of male culture. Women, through the ages, have fought and died rather than deny that passion. In her essay, "The Meaning of Our Love for Women Is What We Have Constantly to Expand" Adrienne Rich states:

> . . . Before any kind of feminist movement existed, or could exist, lesbians existed: women who loved women, who refused to comply with behavior demanded of women, who refused to define themselves in relation to men. Those women, our fore-sisters, millions whose names we do not know, were tortured and burned as witches, slandered in religious and later in "scientific" tracts, portrayed in art and literature as bizarre, amoral, destructive, decadent women. For long time, the lesbian has been a personification of feminine evil.
>
> . . . Lesbians have been forced to live between two cultures, both male-dominated, each of which has denied and endangered our existence. . . . Heterosexual, patriarchal culture

has driven lesbians into secrecy and guilt, often to self-hatred and suicide.[2]

The evolving synthesis of lesbianism and feminism—two women-centered and powered ideologies—is breaking that silence and secrecy. The following analysis is offered as one small cut against that stone of silence and secrecy. It is not intended to be original or all-inclusive. I dedicate this work to all the women hidden from history whose suffering and triumph have made it possible for me to call my name out loud.[3]

The woman who embraces lesbianism as an ideological, political, and philosophical means of liberation of all women from heterosexual tyranny must also identify with the world-wide struggle of all women to end male-supremacist tyranny at all levels. As far as I am concerned, any woman who calls herself a feminist must commit herself to the liberation of *all* women from *coerced* heterosexuality as it manifests itself in the family, the state, and on Madison Avenue. The lesbian-feminist struggles for the liberation of all people from patriarchal domination through heterosexism and for the transformation of all socio-political structures, systems, and relationships that have been degraded and corrupted under centuries of male domination.

5 However, there is no one kind of lesbian, no one kind of lesbian behavior, and no one kind of lesbian relationship. Also there is no one kind of response to the pressures that lesbians labor under to survive as lesbians. Not all women who are involved in sexual-emotional relationships with women call themselves lesbians or identify with any particular lesbian community. Many women are only lesbians to a particular community and *pass* as heterosexuals as they traffic among enemies. (This is analogous to being black and passing for white with only one's immediate family knowing one's true origins.) Yet, those who hide in the closet of heterosexual presumption are sooner or later discovered. The "nigger in the woodpile" story retells itself. Many women are politically active as lesbians, but may fear holding hands with their lovers as they traverse heterosexual turf. (This response to heterosexual predominance can be likened to the reaction of the black student who integrates a predominately white dormitory and who fears leaving the door of her room open when she plays gospel music.) There is the woman who engages in sexual-emotional relationships with women and labels herself *bisexual*. (This is comparable to the Afro-American whose skin-color indicates her mixed ancestry yet who calls herself "mulatto" rather than black.) Bisexual is a safer label than lesbian, for it posits the possibility of a relationship with a man, regardless of how infrequent or non-existent the female bisexual's relationships with men might be. And then there is the lesbian who is a lesbian anywhere and everywhere and who is in direct and constant confrontation with heterosexual presumption, privilege, and oppression. (Her struggle can be compared to that of the Civil Rights activist of the 1960's who was out there on the streets for freedom, while so many of us viewed the action on the television.)

Wherever we, as lesbians, fall along this very generalized political continuum, we must know that the institution of heterosexuality is a die-hard custom through which male-supremacist institutions insure their own perpetuity and control over us. Women are kept, maintained, and contained through terror, violence, and spray of semen. It is profitable for our colonizers to confine our bodies and alienate us from our own life processes as it was profitable for the European to enslave the African and destroy all memory of a prior freedom and self-determination—Alex Haley notwithstanding. And just as the foundation of Western capitalism depended upon the North Atlantic slave trade, the system of patriarchal domination is buttressed by the subjugation of women through heterosexuality, So, patriarchs must extol the boy–girl dyad as "natural" to keep us straight and compliant in the same way the European had to extol Caucasian superiority to justify the African slave trade. Against the historic backdrop, *the woman who chooses to be a lesbian lives dangerously.*

As a member of the largest and second most oppressed group of people of color, as a woman whose slave and ex-slave foresisters suffered some of the most brutal racist, male-supremacist imperialism in Western history, the black lesbian has had to survive also the psychic mutilation of heterosexual superiority. The black lesbian is coerced into the experience of institutional racism—like every other nigger in America—and must suffer as well the homophobic sexism of the black political community, some of whom seem to have forgotten so soon the pain of rejection, denial, and repression sanctioned by racist America. While most political black lesbians do not give a damn if white America is negrophobic, it becomes deeply problematic when the contemporary black political community (another male-dominated and male-identified institution) rejects us because of our commitment to women and women's liberation. Many black male members of that community seem still not to understand the historic connection between the oppression of African peoples in North America and the universal oppression of women. As the women's rights activist and abolitionist, Elizabeth Cady Stanton, pointed out during the 1850's, racism and sexism have been produced by the same animal, viz. "the white Saxon man."

Gender oppression (i.e., the male exploitation and control of women's productive and reproductive energies on the specious basis of a biological difference) originated from the first division of labor, viz. that between women and men, and resulted in the accumulation of private property, patriarchal usurpation of "mother right" or matrilineage, and the duplicitous, male-supremacist institution of heterosexual monogamy (for women only). Sexual politics, therefore, mirror the exploitative, class-bound relationship between the white slave master and the African slave—and the impact of both relationships (between black and white and woman and man) has been residual beyond emancipation and suffrage. The ruling class white man had a centuries-old model for his day-to-day treatment of the African slave. Before he learned to justify the African's continued enslavement and the ex-slave's continued disfranchisement with arguments of the African's divinely ordained mental and moral inferiority to himself (a smokescreen for his capitalist greed) the white man learned, within the structure of heterosexual monogamy and under the system of patriarchy, to relate to black people—slave or free—as a man *relates* to a woman, viz. as property, as a sexual commodity, as a servant, as a source of free or cheap labor, and as an innately inferior being.

Although counter-revolutionary, Western heterosexuality, which advances male-supremacy, continues to be upheld by many black people, especially black men, as the most desired state of affairs between men and women. This observation is borne out on the pages of our most scholarly black publications to our most commercial black publications, which view the issue of black male and female relationships through the lens of heterosexual bias. But this is to be expected, as historically heterosexuality was one of our only means of power over our condition as slaves and one of two means we had at our disposal to appease the white man.

10   Now, as ex-slaves, black men have more latitude to oppress black women, because the brothers no longer have to compete directly with the white man for control of black women's bodies. Now, the black man can assume the "master" role, and he can attempt to tyrannize black women. The black man may view the lesbian—who cannot be manipulated or seduced sexually by him—in much the same way the white slave master once viewed the black male slave, viz. as some perverse caricature of manhood threatening his position of dominance over the female body. This view, of course, is a "neurotic illusion" imposed on black men by the dictates of male supremacy, which the black man can never fulfill because he lacks the capital means and racial privilege.

> Historically, the myth in the Black world is that there are only two free people in the United States, the white man and the black woman. The myth was established by the Black man in the long period of his frustration when he longed to be free to have the material and social advantages of his oppressor, the white man. On examination of the myth this so-called freedom was based on the sexual prerogatives taken by the white man on the Black female. It was fantasied by the Black man that she enjoyed it.[4]

While lesbian-feminism does threaten the black man's predatory control of black women, its goal as a political ideology and philosophy is not to take the black man's or any man's position on top.

Black lesbians who do work within "by-for-about-black-people" groups or organizations either pass as "straight" or relegate our lesbianism to the so-called "private" sphere. The more male-dominated or black nationalist bourgeois the organization or group, the more resistant to change, and thus, the more homophobic and anti-feminist. In these sectors, we learn to keep a low profile.

In 1979, at the annual conference of a regional chapter of the National Black Social Workers, the national director of that body was given a standing ovation for the following remarks:

> Homosexuals are even accorded minority status now. . . . And
> white women, too. And some of you black women who call
> yourselves feminists will be sitting up in meetings with the
> same white women who will be stealing your men on the sly.

This type of indictment of women's revolution and implicitly of lesbian liberation is voiced throughout the bourgeois black (male) movement. But this is the insidious nature of male supremacy. While the black man may consider racism his primary oppression, he is hard-put to recognize that sexism is inextricably bound up with the racism the black woman must suffer, nor can he see that no women (or men for that matter) will be liberated from the original "master–slave" relationship, viz., that between men and women, until we are all liberated from the false premise of heterosexual superiority. This corrupted, predatory relationship between men and women is the founda-tion of the master–slave relationship between white and black people in the United States.

The tactic many black men use to intimidate black women from embrac-   15
ing feminism is to reduce the conflicts between white women and black women to a "tug-o'-war" for the black penis. And since the black lesbian, as stated previously, is not interested in his penis, she undermines the black man's only source of power over her, viz. his heterosexuality. Black lesbians and all black women involved in the struggle for liberation must resist this manipulation and seduction.

The black dyke, like every dyke in America, is everywhere—in the home, in the street, on the welfare, unemployment and social security rolls, raising children, working in factories, in the armed forces, on television, in the public school system, in all the professions, going to college or graduate school, in middle-management, et al. The black dyke, like every other non-white and working class and poor woman in America, has not suffered the luxury, privilege or oppression of being dependent on men, even though our male counterparts have been present, have shared our lives, work and struggle, and in addition have undermined our "human dignity" along the way like most men in patriarchy, the imperialist family of man. But we could never depend on them "to take care of us" on their resources alone—and, of course, it is another "neurotic illusion" imposed on our fathers, brothers, lovers, husbands that they are supposed to "take care of us" because we are women. Translate: "to take care of us" equals "to control us." Our brothers', fathers', lovers', husbands' only power is their manhood. And unless manhood is somehow embellished by white skin and generations of private wealth, it has little currency in racist, capitalist patriarchy. The black man, for example, is accorded native elite or colonial guard or vigilante status over black women in imperialist patriarchy. He is an overseer for the slave master. Because of his maleness he is given access to certain privileges, e.g. employment, education, a car, life insurance, a house, some nice vines. He is usually a rabid heterosexual. He is, since emancipation, allowed to raise a "legitimate" family, allowed to have his piece of turf, viz. his wife and children. That is far as his dictatorship extends for, if his wife decides that she wants to leave that home for whatever reason, he does not have the power or resources to seduce her otherwise if she is determined to throw off the benign or malicious yoke of dependency. The ruling class white man on the other hand, has always had the power to count women among his pool of low-wage labor, his means of production. Most recently, he has "allowed" women the right to sue for divorce, to apply for AFDC, and to be neocolonized.

Traditionally, poor black men and women who banded together and stayed together and raised children together did not have the luxury to cultivate dependence among the members of their families. So, the black dyke, like most black women, has been conditioned to be self-sufficient, i.e. not dependent on men. For me personally, the conditioning to be self-sufficient and the predominance of female role models in my life are the roots of my lesbianism. Before I became a lesbian, I often wondered why I was expected to give up, avoid, and trivialize the recognition and encouragement I felt from women in order to pursue the tenuous business of heterosexuality. And I am not unique.

As political lesbians, i.e. lesbians who are resisting the prevailing culture's attempts to keep us invisible and powerless, we must become more visible (particularly black and other lesbians of color) to our sisters hidden in their various closets, locked in prisons of self-hate and ambiguity, afraid to take the ancient act of woman-bonding beyond the sexual, the private, the personal. I am not trying to reify lesbianism or feminism. I am trying to point out that lesbian-feminism has the potential of reversing and transforming a major component in the system of women's oppression, viz. predatory heterosexuality. If radical lesbian-feminism purports an anti-racist, anti-classist, anti-woman-hating vision of bonding as mutual, reciprocal, as infinitely negotiable, as freedom from antiquated gender prescriptions and proscription, *then all people struggling to transform the character of relationships in this culture have something to learn from lesbians.*

The woman who takes a woman lover lives dangerously in patriarchy. And woe betide her even more if she chooses as her lover a woman who is not of her race. The silence among lesbian-feminists regarding the issue of lesbian relationships between black and white women in America is caused by none other than the centuries-old taboo and laws in the United States against relationships between people of color and those of the Caucasian race. Speaking heterosexually, the laws and taboos were a reflection of the patriarchal slave master's attempts to control his property via controlling his lineage through the institution of monogamy (for women only) and justified the taboos and laws with the argument that purity of the Caucasian race must be preserved (as well as its supremacy). However, we know that his racist and racialist laws and taboos did not apply to him in terms of the black slave woman just as his classist laws and taboos regarding the relationship between the ruling class and the indentured servants did not apply to him in terms of the white woman servant he chose to rape. The offspring of any unions between the white ruling class slave master and the black slave woman or white woman indentured servant could not legally inherit their white or ruling class sire's property or name, just their mothers' condition of servitude.

The taboo against black and white people relating at any other level than master–slave, superior–inferior has been propounded in America to keep black women and men and white women and men, who share a common oppression at the hands of the ruling class white man, from organizing against that common oppression. We, as black lesbians, must vehemently resist being bound by the white man's racist, sexist laws, which have endangered potential intimacy of any kind between whites and blacks. [20]

It cannot be presumed that black lesbians involved in love, work, and social relationships with white lesbians do so out of self-hate and denial of our racial-cultural heritage, identities, and oppression. Why should a woman's commitment to the struggle be questioned or accepted on the basis of her lover's or comrade's skin color? White lesbians engaged likewise with black lesbians or any lesbians of color cannot be assumed to be acting out of some perverse, guilt ridden racialist desire.

I personally am tired of going to events, conferences, workshops, planning sessions that involve a coming together of black and other lesbians of color for political for even social reasons and listening to black lesbians relegate feminism to white women, castigate black women who propose forming coalitions with predominantly white feminist groups, minimize the white woman's oppression and exaggerate her power, and then finally judge that a black lesbian's commitment to the liberation of black women is dubious because she does not sleep with a black woman. All of us have to accept or reject allies on the basis of politics not on the specious basis of skin color. *Have not black people suffered betrayal from our own people?*

Yes, black women's experiences of misogyny are different from white women's. However, they all add up to how the patriarchal slave master decided to oppress us. We both fought each other for his favor, approval, and protection. Such is the effect of imperialist, heterosexist patriarchy. Shulamith Firestone, in the essay, "Racism: the Sexism of the Family of Man," purports this analysis of the relationship between white and black women:

> How do the women of this racial Triangle feel about each
> other? Divide and conquer: Both women have grown hostile
> to each other, white women feeling contempt for the "sluts"
> with no morals, black women feeling envy for the pampered
> "powder puffs." The black woman is jealous of the white
> woman's legitimacy, privilege, and comfort, but she also feels
> deep contempt. . . . Similarly the white woman's contempt for
> the black woman is mixed with envy: for the black woman's

greater sexual license, for her gutsiness, for her freedom from the marriage bind. For after all, the black woman is not under the thumb of a man, but is pretty much her own boss to come and go, to leave the house, to work (much as it is degrading work) or to be "shiftless." What the white woman doesn't know is that the black woman, not under the thumb of *one* man, can now be squashed by all. There is no alternative for either of them than the choice between being public or private property, but because each still believes that the other is getting away with something both can be fooled into mis-channeling their frustration onto each other rather than onto the real enemy, "The Man."[5]

Though her statement of the choices black and white women have under patriarchy in America has merit, Firestone analyzes only a specific relationship i.e. between the ruling class white woman and slave or ex-slave black woman.

25 Because of her whiteness, the white woman of all classes has been accorded, as the black man has because of his maleness, certain privileges in racist patriarchy, e.g. indentured servitude as opposed to enslavement, exclusive right to public assistance until the 1960's, "legitimate" offspring and (if married into the middle/upper class) the luxury to live on her husband's income, etc.

The black woman, having neither maleness nor whiteness, has always had her heterosexuality, which white men and black men have manipulated by force and at will. Further, she, like all poor people, has had her labor, which the white capitalist man has also taken and exploited at will. These capabilities have allowed black women minimal access to the crumbs thrown at black men and white women. So, when the black woman and the white woman become lovers, we bring that history and all those questions to the relationship as well as other people's problems with the relationships. The taboo against intimacy between white and black people has been internalized by us, and simultaneously defied by us. If we, as lesbian-feminists, defy the taboo, then we begin to transform the history of relationships between black women and white women.

In her essay, "Disloyal to Civilization: Feminism, Racism, Gynephobia," Rich calls for feminists to attend to the complexities of the relationship between black and white women in the United States. Rich queries:

> What caricatures of bloodless fragility and broiling sensuality still imprint our psyches, and where did we receive these imprintings? What happened between the several thousand northern white women and southern black women who together taught in the schools founded under Reconstruction by the Freedmen's Bureau, side by side braving the Ku Klux Klan harassment, terrorism, and the hostility of white communities?[6]

So, all of us would do well to stop fighting each other for our space at the bottom, because there ain't no more room. We have spent so much time hating ourselves. Time to love ourselves. And that, for all lesbians, as lovers, as comrades, as freedom fighters, is the final resistance.

NOTES

1. Judy Grahn, "The Common Woman," *The Work of a Common Woman* (Oakland: Diana Press, 1978), p. 67.
2. Adrienne Rich, *On Lies, Secrets, and Silence: Selected Prose 1966–1978.* (New York: W. W. Norton, 1979), p. 225.
3. I would like to give particular acknowledgment to the Combahee River Collective's "A Black Feminist Statement." Because this document espouses "struggling against racial, sexual, heterosexual, and class oppression," it has become a manifesto of radical feminist thought, action and practice.
4. Pat Robinson and Group, "Poor Black Women's Study Papers by Poor Black Women of Mount Vernon, New York," in T. Cade, ed., *The Black Woman: An Anthology* (New York: New American Library, 1970), p. 194.
5. Shulamith Firestone, *The Dialectic of Sex: The Case for Feminist Revolution.* (New York: Bantam Books, 1972), p. 113.
6. Rich, op. cit., p. 298. One such example is the Port Royal Experiment (1862), the precursor of the Freedmen's Bureau. Port Royal was a program of relief for "freed men and women" in the South Carolina Sea Islands, organized under the auspices of the Boston Education Commission and the Freedmen's Relief Assoc. in New York and the Port Royal Relief Assoc. in Philadelphia, and sanctioned by the Union Army and the Federal Government. See *The Journal of Charlotte Forten* on the "Port Royal Experiment" (Boston: Beacon Press, 1969). Through her Northern bourgeois myopia, Forten recounts her experiences as a black teacher among the black freed men and women and her Northern white women peers.

A BLACK FEMINIST STATEMENT

Combahee River Collective

The Combahee River Collective is a Black feminist group in Boston whose name comes from the guerrilla action conceptualized and led by Harriet Tubman on June 2, 1863, in the Port Royal region of South Carolina. This action freed more than 750 slaves and is the only military campaign in American history planned and led by a woman.

We are a collective of Black feminists who have been meeting together since 1974.[1] During that time we have been involved in the process of defining and clarifying our politics, while at the same time doing political work within our own group and in coalition with other progressive organizations and movements. The most general statement of our politics at the present time would be that we are actively committed to struggling against racial, sexual, heterosexual, and class oppression and see as our particular task the development of integrated analysis and practice based upon the fact the major systems of oppression are interlocking. The synthesis of these oppressions creates the conditions of our lives. As Black women we see Black feminism as the logical political movement to combat the manifold and simultaneous oppressions that all women of color face.

We will discuss four major topics in the paper that follows: (1) the genesis of contemporary black feminism; (2) what we believe, i.e., the specific province of our politics; (3) the problems in organizing Black feminists, including a brief herstory of our collective; and (4) Black feminist issues and practice.

1. THE GENESIS OF CONTEMPORARY BLACK FEMINISM

Before looking at the recent development of Black feminism we would like to affirm that we find our origins in the historical reality of Afro-American women's continuous life-and-death struggle for survival and liberation. Black women's extremely negative relationship to the American political system (a system of white male rule) has always been determined by our membership in two oppressed racial and sexual castes. As Angela Davis points out in "Reflections on the Black Woman's Role in the Community of Slaves," Black women have always embodied, if only in their physical manifestation, an adversary stance to white male rule and have actively resisted its inroads upon them and their communities in both dramatic and subtle ways. There have always been Black women activists—some known, like Sojourner Truth, Harriet Tubman, Frances E. W. Harper, Ida B. Wells Barnett, and Mary Church Terrell, and thousands upon thousands unknown—who had a shared awareness of how their sexual identity combined with their racial identity to make their whole life situation and the focus of their political struggles unique. Contemporary Black feminism is the outgrowth of countless generations of personal sacrifice, militancy, and work by our mothers and sisters.

A black feminist presence has evolved most obviously in connection with the second wave of the American women's movement beginning in the late 1960s. Black, other Third World, and working women have been involved in the feminist movement from its start, but both outside reactionary forces and racism and elitism within the movement itself have served to obscure our participation. In 1973 Black feminists, primarily located in New York, felt the necessity of forming a separate Black feminist group. This became the National Black Feminist Organization (NBFO).

Black feminist politics also have an obvious connection to movements for   5
Black liberation, particularly those of the 1960s and 1970s. Many of us were active in those movements (civil rights, Black nationalism, the Black Panthers), and all of our lives were greatly affected and changed by their ideology, their goals, and the tactics used to achieve their goals. It was our experience and disillusionment within these liberation movements, as well as experience on the periphery of the white male left, that led to the need to develop a politics that was antiracist, unlike those of white women, and antisexist, unlike those of Black and white men.

There is also undeniably a personal genesis for Black feminism, that is, the political realization that comes from the seemingly personal experiences of individual Black women's lives. Black feminists and many more Black women who do not define themselves as feminists have all experienced sexual oppression as a constant factor in our day-to-day existence. As children we realized that we were different from boys and that we were treated differently. For example, we were told in the same breath to be quiet both for the sake of being "ladylike" and to make us less objectionable in the eyes of white people. As we grew older we became aware of the threat of physical and sexual abuse of men. However, we had no way of conceptualizing what was so apparent to us, what we *knew* was really happening.

Black feminists often talk about their feelings of craziness before becoming conscious of the concepts of sexual politics, patriarchal rule, and most importantly, feminism, the political analysis and practice that we women use to struggle against our oppression. The fact that racial politics and indeed racism are pervasive factors in our lives did not allow us, and still does not allow most Black women, to look more deeply into our own experiences and, from that sharing and growing consciousness, to build a politics that will change our lives and inevitably end our oppression. Our development must also be tied to the contemporary economic and political position of Black people. The post World War II generation of Black youth was the first to be able to minimally partake of certain educational and employment options, previously closed completely to Black people. Although our economic position is still at the very bottom of the American capitalistic economy, a handful of us have been able to gain certain tools as a result of tokenism in education and employment which potentially enable us to more effectively fight our oppression.

A combined antiracist and antisexist position drew us together initially, and as we developed politically we addressed ourselves to hetero-sexism and economic oppression under capitalism.

2. WHAT WE BELIEVE

Above all else, our politics initially sprang from the shared belief that Black women are inherently valuable, that our liberation is a necessity not as an adjunct to somebody else's but because of our need as human persons for autonomy. This may seem so obvious as to sound simplistic, but it is apparent that no other ostensibly progressive movement has ever considered our specific oppression as a priority or worked seriously for the ending of that oppression. Merely naming the pejorative stereotypes attributed to Black women (e.g., mammy, matriarch, Sapphire, whore, bulldagger), let alone cataloguing the cruel, often murderous, treatment we receive, indicates how little value has been placed upon our lives during four centuries of bondage in the Western hemisphere. We realize that the only people who care enough about us to work consistently for our liberation is us. Our politics evolve from a healthy love for ourselves, our sisters and our community which allows us to continue our struggle and work.

10   This focusing upon our own oppression is embodied in the concept of identity politics. We believe that the most profound and potentially the most radical politics come directly out of our own identity, as opposed to working to end somebody else's oppression. In the case of black women this is a particularly repugnant, dangerous, threatening, and therefore revolutionary concept because it is obvious from looking at all the political movements that have preceded us that anyone is more worthy of liberation than ourselves. We reject pedestals, queen-hood, and walking ten paces behind. To be recognized as human, levelly human, is enough.

We believe that sexual politics under patriarchy is as pervasive in Black women's lives as are the politics of class and race. We also often find it difficult to separate race from class from sex oppression because in our lives they are most often experienced simultaneously. We know that there is such a thing as racial-sexual oppression which is neither solely racial nor solely sexual, e.g., the history of rape of Black women by white men as a weapon of political repression.

Although we are feminists and lesbians, we feel solidarity with progressive Black men and do not advocate the fractionalization that white women who are separatists demand. Our situation as Black people necessitates that we have solidarity around the fact of race, which white women of course do not need to have with white men, unless it is their negative solidarity as racial oppressors. We struggle together with Black men against racism, while we also struggle with Black men about sexism.

We realize that the liberation of all oppressed peoples necessitates the destruction of the political-economic systems of capitalism and imperialism as well as patriarchy. We are socialists because we believe the work must be organized for the collective benefit of those who do the work and create the products, and not for the profit of the bosses. Material resources must be equally distributed among those who create these resources. We are not convinced, however, that a socialist revolution that is not also a feminist and antiracist revolution will guarantee our liberation. We have arrived at the necessity for developing an understanding of class relationships that takes into account the specific class position of Black women who are generally marginal in the labor force, while at this particular time some of us are temporarily viewed as doubly desirable tokens at white-collar and professional levels. We need to articulate the real class situation of persons who are not merely raceless, sexless workers, but for whom racial and sexual oppression are significant determinants in their working/economic lives. Although we are in essential agreement with Marx's theory as it applied to the very specific economic relationships he analyzed, we know that his analysis must be extended further in order for us to understand our specific economic situation as Black women.

A political contribution which we feel we have already made is the expansion of the feminist principle that the personal is political. In our consciousness-raising sessions, for example, we have in many ways gone beyond white women's revelations because we are dealing with the implications of race and class as well as sex. Even our Black women's style of talking/testifying in Black language about what we have experienced has a resonance that is both cultural and political. We have spent a great deal of energy delving into the cultural and experiential nature of our oppression out of necessity because none of these matters has ever been looked at before. No one before has ever examined the multilayered texture of Black women's lives. An example of this kind of revelation/conceptualization occurred at a meeting as we discussed the ways in which our early intellectual interests had been attacked by our peers, particularly Black males. We discovered that all of us, because we were "smart" had also been considered "ugly", *i.e.,* "smart-ugly." "Smart-ugly" crystallized the way in which most of us had been forced to develop our intellects at great cost to our "social" lives. The sanctions in the Black and white communities against Black women thinkers is comparatively much higher than for white women, particularly ones from the educated middle and upper classes.

As we have already stated, we reject the stance of lesbian separatism because it is not a viable political analysis or strategy for us. It leaves out far too much and far too many people, particularly Black men, women, and children.   *15*

We have a great deal of criticism and loathing for what men have been social-ized to be in this society: what they support, how they act, and how they op-press. But we do not have the misguided notion that it is their maleness, per se—i.e., their biological maleness—that makes them what they are. As Black women we find any type of biological determination a particularly dangerous and reactionary basis upon which to build a politic. We must also question whether lesbian separatism is an adequate and progressive political analysis and strategy, even for those who practice it, since it so completely denies any but the sexual sources of women's oppression negating the facts of class and race.

3. PROBLEMS IN ORGANIZING BLACK FEMINISTS

During our years together as a Black feminist collective we have experienced success and defeat, joy and pain, victory and failure. We have found that it is very difficult to organize around Black feminist issues, difficult even to an-nounce in certain contexts that we *are* Black feminists. We have tried to think about the reasons for our difficulties, particularly since the white women's movement continues to be strong and to grow in many directions. In this section we will discuss some of the general reasons for the organizing prob-lems we face and also talk specifically about the stages in organizing our own collective.

The major source of difficulty in our political work is that we are not just trying to fight oppression on one front or even two, but instead to address a whole range of oppressions. We do not have racial, sexual, heterosexual, or class privilege to rely upon, nor do we have even the minimal access to resources and power that groups who possess any one of these types of privi-lege have.

The psychological toll of being a Black woman and the difficulties this presents in reaching political consciousness and doing political work can never be underestimated. There is a very low value placed upon Black women's psy-ches in this society, which is both racist and sexist. As an early group member once said, "We are all damaged people merely by virtue of being Black women." We are dispossessed psychologically and on every other level, and we feel the necessity to struggle to change the condition of all Black women. In "A Black Feminist's Search for Sisterhood," Michele Wallace arrives at this conclusion:

> We exist as women who are Black who are feminists, each
> stranded for the moment, working independently because there
> is not yet an environment in this society remotely congenial to
> our struggle—because, being on the bottom, we would have to
> do what no one else has done: we would have to fight the
> world.[2]

Wallace is pessimistic but realistic in her assessment of Black feminists' position, particularly in her allusion to the nearly classic isolation most of us face. We might use our position at the bottom, however, to make a clear leap into revolutionary action. If Black woman were free, it would mean that everyone else would have to be free since our freedom would necessitate the destruction of all the systems of oppression.

Feminism is, nevertheless, very threatening to the majority of Black people because it calls into question some of the most basic assumptions about our existence, i.e., that sex should be a determinant of power relationships. Here is the way male and female voices were defined in a Black nationalist pamphlet from the early 1970's.

> We understand that it is and has been traditional that the man is the head of the house. He is the leader of the house/nation because his knowledge of the world is broader, his awareness is greater, his understanding is fuller and his application of this information is wiser. . . . After all, it is only reasonable that the man be the head of the house because he is able to defend and protect the development of his home. . . . Women cannot do the same things as men—they are made by nature to function differently. Equality of men and women is something that cannot happen even in the abstract world. Men are not equal to other men, i.e. ability, experience or even understanding. The value of men and women can be seen as in the value of gold and silver—they are not equal but both have great value. We must realize that men and women are a complement to each other because there is no house/family without a man and his wife. Both are essential to the development of any life.[3]

The material conditions of most Black women would hardly lead them to upset both economic and sexual arrangements that seem to represent some stability in their lives. Many Black women have a good understanding of both sexism and racism, but because of the everyday constrictions of their lives cannot risk struggling against them both.

The reaction of Black men to feminism has been notoriously negative. They are, of course, even more threatened than Black women by the possibility that Black feminists might organize around our own needs. They realize that they might not only lose valuable and hardworking allies in their struggles but that they might also be forced to change their habitually sexist ways of interacting with and oppressing Black women. Accusations that Black feminism divides the Black struggle are powerful deterrents to the growth of an autonomous Black women's movement.

Still, hundreds of women have been active at different times during the three-year existence of our group. And every Black woman who came, came out of a strongly-felt need for some level of possibility that did not previously exist in her life.

When we first started meeting early in 1974 after the NBFO first eastern regional conference, we did not have a strategy for organizing, or even a focus. We just wanted to see what we had. After a period of months of not meeting, we began to meet again late in the year and started doing an intense variety of consciousness-raising. The overwhelming feeling that we had is that after years and years we had finally found each other. Although we were not doing political work as a group, individuals continued their involvement in Lesbian politics, sterilization abuse and abortion rights work, Third World Women's International Women's Day activities, and support for the trials of Dr. Kenneth Edelin, Joan Little, and Inéz García. During our first summer, when membership had dropped off considerably, those of us remaining devoted serious discussion to the possibility of opening a refuge for battered women in a Black community. (There was no refuge in Boston at that time.) We also decided around that time to become an independent collective since we had serious disagreements with NBFO's bourgeois-feminist stance and their lack of a clear political focus.

25   We also were contacted at that time by socialist feminists, with whom we had worked on abortion rights activities, who wanted to encourage us to attend the National Socialist Feminist Conference in Yellow Springs. One of our members did attend and despite the narrowness of the ideology that was promoted at that particular conference, we became more aware of the need for us to understand our own economic situation and to make our own economic analysis.

In the fall, when some members returned, we experienced several months of comparative inactivity and internal disagreement which were first conceptualized as a Lesbian–straight split but which were also the result of class and political differences. During the summer those of us who were still meeting had determined the need to do political work and to move beyond consciousness-raising and serving exclusively as an emotional support group. At the beginning of 1976, when some of the women who had not wanted to do political work and who also voiced disagreements stopped attending of their own accord, we again looked for a focus. We decided at that time, with the addition of new members, to become a study group. We had always shared our reading with each other, and some of us had written papers on Black feminism for group discussion a few months before this decision was made. We began functioning as a study group and also began discussing the possibility of starting a Black feminist publication. We had a retreat in the late spring which provided a time for both political discussion and working out interpersonal issues. Currently we are planning to gather together a collection of Black feminist writing. We feel that it is absolutely essential to demonstrate the reality of our politics to other Black women and believe that we can do this through writing and distributing our work. The fact that individual Black feminists are living in isolation all over the country, that our own numbers are small, and that we have some skills in writing, printing, and publishing makes us want to carry out these kinds of projects as a means of organizing Black feminists as we continue to do political work in coalition with other groups.

4. BLACK FEMINIST ISSUES AND PROJECTS

During our time together we have identified and worked on many issues of particular relevance to Black women. The inclusiveness of our politics makes us concerned with any situation that impinges upon the lives of women, Third World and working people. We are of course particularly committed to working on those struggles in which race, sex, and class are simultaneous factors in oppression. We might, for example, become involved in workplace organizing at a factory that employs Third World women or picket a hospital that is cutting back on already inadequate health care to a Third World community, or set up a rape crisis center in a Black neighborhood. Organizing around welfare and daycare concerns might also be a focus. The work to be done and the countless issues that this work represents merely reflect the pervasiveness of our oppression.

Issues and projects that collective members have actually worked on are sterilization abuse, abortion rights, battered women, rape, and health care. We have also done many workshops and educationals on Black feminism on college campuses, at women's conferences, and most recently for high school women.

One issue that is of major concern to us and that we have begun to publicly address is racism in the white women's movement. As Black feminists we are made constantly and painfully aware of how little effort white women have made to understand and combat their racism, which requires among other things that they have a more than superficial comprehension of race, color, and black history and culture. Eliminating racism in the white women's movement is by definition work for white women to do, but we will continue to speak to and demand accountability on this issue.

In the practice of our politics we do not believe that the end always justifies the means. Many reactionary and destructive acts have been done in the name of achieving "correct" political goals. As feminists we do not want to mess over people in the name of politics. We believe in collective process and a nonhierarchical distribution of power within our own group and in our vision of a revolutionary society. We are committed to a continual examination of our politics as they develop through criticism and self-criticism as an essential aspect of our practice. In her introduction to *Sisterhood Is Powerful* Robin Morgan writes:

> I haven't the faintest notion what possible revolutionary role
> white heterosexual men could fulfill, since they are the very
> embodiment of reactionary-vested-interest-power.

30

As Black feminists and Lesbians we know that we have a very definite revolutionary task to perform and we are ready for the lifetime of work and struggle before us.

NOTES

1. This statement is dated April 1977.
2. Michele Wallace, "A Black Feminist's Search for Sisterhood," *The Village Voice,* 28 July 1975, pp. 6–7.
3. Mumininas of Committee for Unified Newark, Mwanamke Mwananchi (The Nationalist Woman), Newark, N.J., © 1971, pp. 4–5.

WILLFUL VIRGIN OR DO YOU HAVE TO BE A LESBIAN TO BE A FEMINIST?[1]

Marilyn Frye

The connection between lesbianism and feminism has made many women nervous. Many believe that if they associate themselves with feminism they will be associated with lesbianism, and for some that is a frightening, even a disgusting, thought. There is a fear of being suspected of approving lesbians or lesbianism, fear of being identified with lesbians, fear of being suspected of being a lesbian, fear of being lesbian. And there is anger at lesbians for being present, active and assertive as feminists, and for insisting on a connection between lesbianism and feminism.

I will directly provoke and address these fears and this anger here. They are homophobic, more specifically, *gyn*ophobic and lesbian-hating, and they make me impatient. I am going to speak plainly, out of impatience and also out of my own peculiar and slightly perverse optimism.

Every term in my feminism classes, a time comes when heterosexual women students articulate a question: Do I have to be a lesbian to be a feminist? I don't know how much other teachers of Women's Studies hear this question. My classroom is a situation which brings the connection between feminism and lesbianism to one's attention. I am a lesbian, I am "out" to my Women's Studies students, and I expose them to a great deal of strong and empowering feminist thinking by feminists of many cultures and locales who are lesbians. In the classroom, this question signals our arrival at a point where newcomers to feminism are beginning to grasp that sexual acts, sexual desire, and sexual dread and taboo are profoundly political and that feminist politics is as much about the disposition of bodies, the manipulation of desire and arousal, the bonds of intimacy and loyalty as it is about gender stereotypes, economic opportunity, and legal rights. In my classes, this question is a moment of students' coming to terms with the fact that the political is indeed personal, very personal. But what goes one in my class is clearly not the only thing that gives rise to this question. For many students it has already arisen outside this class; they have elsewhere encountered people who apparently believe that if you are a feminist you must be a lesbian. Some students have just been waiting for the chance to pose this question. I usually ask women in my Women's Studies classes if they have ever been called lesbians or dykes or been accused of being lesbian, and always many, often a majority, say they have. One woman was a called a lesbian when she rejected the attentions of a man in a bar; another was called "butch" when she opened and held a door for a male friend; another was asked if she was a lesbian when she challenged a man's sexist description of another woman. A woman told her date that she did not want to have sex with him and he called her a dyke. A young woman told her mother that she was going to Washington D.C. for the big pro-choice march; her mother, disapproving and fearing for her daughter's safety, said, "Oh, so now you're going to go off and become a lesbian." A woman who divorced her husband and lives on her own is gossiped about in a way that spreads the suggestion that she is a lesbian. A woman says she is frequently assumed to be a lesbian because of her athletic build and refusal to wear skirts. A women who does not experience sexual arousal or orgasm with her husband is quizzed about her lesbian tendencies by her doctor and her therapist. A woman reports that her friends refer to her Women's Studies as her "lesbian class"; several other women say some of their friends do that too.

The message of these exchanges is clearly that a women who is a feminist or does anything or betrays any attitude or desire which expresses her autonomy or deviance from conventional femininity is a lesbian. Hearing this message in these contexts, women are likely to "consider the source"—the message has come from people who are anti-feminist, misogynistic, or at least unreflective defenders of male privilege or the gender status quo. One might think they are inventing this equation just to intimidate women who are "out of line." But it is more complicated that that. These are not the only people who suggest to newly feminist women that they can't be feminists without being lesbians. Paradoxically, heterosexual feminists suggest the same thing to them in many ways. Consider what may go on, what often does go on, in the context of Women's Studies in universities and colleges.

5   In a Women's Studies program somewhere in the U.S. students register with the Women's Studies advisory committee the complaint that their courses are not challenging and radical enough, and a key faculty member surmises that the students who are dissatisfied are lesbian. The dissatisfied students, few of whom are lesbian, pick up on this response, and those who are not lesbian learn that they are out of step because they want their radicalness and rebellion nurtured and they are not lesbian.

Another example: Some students who have been exposed to the thinking and lives of feminist lesbians bring ideas from there into a Women's Studies course and those ideas are denigrated by that teacher, who identifies them as ideas only a lesbian separatist would consider. Some of those students are not lesbian and yet they have considered those ideas and found them interesting, even compelling, and have found themselves empowered just by thinking about those ideas. They are being told these ideas belong to lesbians, and heterosexual women don't believe those things or even take them seriously.

In many Women's Studies contexts, students are exposed to heterosexual feminist teachers (and sometimes closeted lesbian teachers who are passing as heterosexuals) who model conformity to man-made norms of femininity in appearance, bearing and voice, who argue against any action or politics that would alienate men or non-feminist women, who do not model, approve, or encourage any radical insubordination, any blasphemy against men and their gods, any uncareful enactment of anger. In academic settings it is common that women see these things modeled, hear the violences of men against women unqualifiedly named and condemned, and hear witty mockery of men's arrogances, only by feminists who are lesbian—usually students, more rarely, teachers.

In colleges and universities in the U.S., there is now, after 20 years of work, a great deal of feminist knowledge and analysis available to students and there are many students eagerly acquiring a rich understanding of women's subordination in U.S. cultures. Students who are exposed to the well-known data on wife-battering, street rape and acquaintance rape, pornography, child sexual assault, incest and other violences against women, and to any deep and acute feminist analysis of the patriarchal structures of marriage, reproduction and mothering—students who are exposed to feminist analyses of patriarchal religions and of the mythology propagated by popular culture in contemporary societies—students who understand something about women's paid and unpaid work in various modern economies and the practices and institutions which determine the accumulation and distribution of wealth—students who have some idea of the scope and intent of historical conspiracies against women such as the Inquisition, the erasure of women from history, the post–World War II propaganda campaign in the U.S. to convert women workers into housewife-consumers—such students catch on that what we are dealing with here is profound, that it goes to the root of this society and what is called "civilization" and is etched into the deepest sources of our own thoughts and passions. They get it that any adequate response to this is going to require radical analysis, radical strategies and radical imagination, and the rebellion will be dangerous and costly. Feminists in the academy have helped students to appreciate the character and magnitude of the problems; students then look to these feminists for resources for responding to the problems— intellectual, spiritual, artistic, emotional, political resources. But when they express this need they often are told, either implicitly or explicitly, that only lesbians offer these. They are being told that a strong and angry feminism that will settle for nothing but going to the root of the matter belongs to lesbians. Heterosexual women associated with Women's Studies to a great extent leave the whole task of "being radical" to lesbians, leave the burden, the hopefulness and the excitement of pushing the limits to lesbians. They leave rage and ecstasy to lesbians.

In a variety of contexts, newly feminist women find their assertions and demands met with this implicit or explicit connecting of sexuality and politics. It is a sort of implicit theory of women's sexuality according to which a women who largely adheres to patriarchal feminine norms in act and attitude and who does not radically challenge or rebel against patriarchal institutions is heterosexual, and a woman who does not comply with feminine norms or who seriously challenges or rebels against patriarchal institutions is a lesbian. The difference between the explicit accusations of lesbianism on the part of non- or anti-feminists and the implicit association of feminist radicalness with lesbianism that occurs in many academic contexts is only a difference in the degree and kind of non-compliance it takes to earn the attributed status of lesbian. Feminists are, by definition, to some degree non-compliant with the patriarchal norms of femininity and rebellious against patriarchal institutions; so by this theory, feminists are to some degree lesbian. It would follow logic that those who are *very* feminist, *uncompromisingly* feminist, *extremely* feminist, *radically* feminist, must BE lesbians, flat out.

10   For the newly feminist woman who is not lesbian, this connecting of feminism (or any sign of female autonomy or rebellion) with lesbianism is very likely to have the effect of making her back off from any radicalness, censor in herself any extremeness of anti-patriarchal thought or action. She has lived all her life in a social climate that makes her believe she herself is not and could never be lesbian. If she is a member of a racialized group, she may also have some sense that to be a lesbian would be disloyal to her home community, or she may have the impression that lesbianism simply does occur among her people. In such contexts, the equation of feminism and lesbianism is a very effective way to place a very narrow and constraining limit on feminism.

But even though the linking of feminism and lesbianism actually does work—in conjunction with women's homophobia and lesbian-hating—to restrain feminism, and even though our contemporary concept of lesbianism is rooted in theories of sexuality which were invented in a period of fearful and extreme reaction against 19th century feminism, I want to suggest that this notion of a connection between feminism and lesbianism is *not* merely an *ad hoc* fiction invented by patriarchal loyalists to vilify feminism and intimidate feminists. An intrinsic connection between feminism and lesbianism in a contemporary Euro-American setting is just a historically specific manifestation of an ancient and intrinsic connection between patriarchal/fraternal social order and female heterosexuality.

I believe that all feminist theory and practice eventually conveys one to this proposition: that a central constitutive dynamic and key mechanism of the global phenomenon of male domination, oppression, and exploitation of females, is near-universal female heterosexuality. All of the institutions and practices which constitute and materialize this domination (and simultaneously organize males' lives in relation to each other) either presuppose almost-universal female heterosexuality or manufacture, regulate and enforce female heterosexuality, or both.

In saying this, I am using a term, "heterosexuality," which has a particular meaning in contemporary Euro-American cultures and does not translate in any simple way into other cultural contexts. In some cultures the physical intimacy between women which we here think of as central to the concept *les-*

bian are not tabooed as they are here—they may not be socially recognized at all, even negatively.[2] But in almost all cultures for at least the last couple of thousands years, to the best of my knowledge, virtually every woman is strenuously required by tradition, law, more and taboo to be in some form of availability, servitude or marriage to a man or men in which she can unconditionally or almost unconditionally sexually accessible to that man or men and in the context of which she carries and bears his or their children. In cultures most shaped by male domination, wives' (females slaves', or servants) compulsory sexual accessibility and service is of a piece with their economic and domestic service and subordination to the man or men to whom they are attached and in some cases to those men's whole fraternity, family, or clan.[3] Even though, in many cultures a distinction between two female sexualities, "hetero-" and "lesbian," is not operative, my use of the term "heterosexual" is suitable because I am referring to life-situations and dispositions of female bodies which are defined and determined in terms of female sexual accessibility to males and not in terms of the whole female's *own* desire, affectional ties or erotic intimacies, whatever their objects. The point is that virtually all women in patriarchal cultures are rigorously required to be sexual with and for men. When I speak of "the patriarchal institution of female heterosexuality" and suggest that in some sense "it" exists widely across cultures and time, I speak of a nearly global pattern using a term which strictly designates just one of its local manifestations.[4]

For females to be subordinated and subjugated to males on a global scale, and for males to organize themselves and each other as they do, billions of female individuals, virtually all who see life on this planet, must be reduced to a more-or-less willing toleration of subordination and servitude to men. The primary sites of this reduction are the sites of heterosexual relation and encounter—courtship and marriage-arrangement, romance, sexual liaisons, fucking, marriage, prostitution, the normative family, incest and child sexual assault. It is on this terrain of heterosexual connection that girls and women are habituated to abuse, insult, and degradation, that girls are reduced to women—to wives, to whores, to mistresses, to sex slaves, to clerical workers and textile workers, to the mothers of men's children. The secondary sites of the forced female embodiment of subordination are the sites of the ritual preparations of girls and women for heterosexual intercourse, relations, or attachments. I refer to training in proper deportment and attire and decoration, all of which is training in and habituation to bodily restriction and distortion; I refer to diets and exercise and beauty regimens which habituate the individual to deprivation and punishment and to fear and suspicion of her body and its wisdom; I refer the abduction and seasoning of female sexual slaves; to clitoridectomy and other forms and sorts of physical and spiritual mutilation; all of which have no cultural or economic purpose or function if girls and women do not have to be made ready for husbands and male lovers, pimps, johns, bosses, and slavers.

Without (hetero)sexual abuse, (hetero)sexual harassment and (hetero)sexualization of every aspect of females bodies and behaviors, there would not be patriarchy, and whatever other forms or materializations of oppression might exist, they would not have the shapes, boundaries, and dynamics of the racism, nationalism, and so on that we are now familiar with.

The meanings of female heterosexuality are many, and it does not play the same political role in all social and cultural locales. But in most locales it glues each adult woman to one or more men of her caste, class, race, nation, or tribe, making her, willy nilly, a supporter of whatever politic those men adhere to, though she has little or no part in shaping or defining that politic, regardless of whether that politic is liberatory or oppressive, and regardless of whether it is liberatory for women. In the particular cases of races and classes which are politically dominant in their locale, female heterosexuality joins females in racial and/or class solidarity to dominating males and offers for their compliance the bribe of a share of the benefits their men extort from other groups. Female heterosexuality, whether literally *sexual* or not, is profoundly implicated in the racism of white women in our present time and place; the disloyalty to the civilization of white men which Adrienne Rich recommended to white women is not possible without disloyalty to the men with whom one is bonded by the institution of heterosexuality.[5] And in racial or ethnic groups which are oppressed, when a woman is not complying with the norms of female heterosexuality to the satisfaction of some man, he may bully her into line with the argument that her noncompliance or rebellion against the norms of femininity is disloyalty to her race or her community.

Lesbian feminists have noted that if the institution of female heterosexuality is what makes girls into women and is central to the continuous replication of patriarchy, then women's abandonment of that institution recommends itself as one strategy (among others) in the project of dismantling patriarchal structures. And if heterosexual encounters, relations and connections are the sites of the inscription of the patriarchal imperatives on the bodies of women, it makes sense to abandon those sites. And if female heterosexuality is central to the way sexism and racism are knit together in strange paradoxical symbiosis, it makes sense that non-participation in that institution could be part of a strategy for weakening both racism and patriarchy.

Some women speaking in other-than-lesbian feminist voices have responded by saying that withdrawal from participation in the institution of female heterosexuality is only a personal solution and only available to a few; they have said it is not a political, not a systemic strategy. I think, on the contrary, that it can be a systemic strategy, because female heterosexuality is not a given in nature, but is actively and continuously constructed. If women take the construction of ourselves and the institutions and practices which determine and govern us into our own hands, we can construct something else.

Commitment to the naturalness or inevitability of female heterosexuality is commitment to the power relations which are expressed and maintained by the institutions of female heterosexuality in patriarchal cultures around the world. (It is also, by postmodern lights, ahistorical and essentialist.) People who have power maintain that power partly by using that power to make its own historical conditions ahistorical—that is they make the prerequisites of their power into "givens." They naturalize them. A vital part of making generalized male dominance as close to inevitable as a human construction can be is the naturalization of female heterosexuality. Men have been creating ideologies and political practices which naturalize female heterosexuality continuously in every culture since the dawns of the patriarchies. (Both Freud and Lacan are naturalizers of female heterosexuality. They say that female heterosexuality is constructed, but they rescue themselves by going on to say that its construction is determined and made inevitable by the nature of civilization, or the nature of language.)

Female heterosexuality is not a biological drive or an individual woman's   20
erotic attraction or attachment to another human animal which happens to be male. Female heterosexuality is a set of social institutions and practices defined and regulated by patriarchal kinship systems, by both civil and religious law, and by strenuously enforced mores and deeply entrenched values and taboos. Those definitions, regulations, values, and taboos are about male fraternity and the oppression and exploitation of women. They are not about love, human warmth, solace, fun, pleasure, or deep knowledge between people. If any of the latter arise within the boundaries of these institutions and practices, it is because fun, solace, pleasure and acknowledgement grow like dandelions and are hard to eradicate, not because heterosexuality is natural or is naturally a site of such benefits.

So, is it possible to be a feminist without being a lesbian? My inclination is to say that feminism, which is thoroughly anti-patriarchal, is not compatible with female heterosexuality, which is thoroughly patriarchal. But I anticipate the following reply:

"You seem to suppose that all relation, connection, or encounter of any passionate or erotic or genital sort or involving any sort of personal commitment between a female and a male must belong to this patriarchal institution called "female heterosexuality," that it must be suffocated by this rubric, . . . you seem therefore to suppose that our acts and feelings and meanings are all totally formed by history, social institutions and language. That is the kind of hopeless determinism which is potentially fatal and is contradicted by your own presence here as a lesbian."

I agree that I cannot embrace any absolute historical, social determinism. The feminist lesbians' permanent project of defining ourselves and our passions and our communities is a living willful refusal of such determinism. But the free space of creation exists only when it is actively, creatively, aggressively, courageously, persistently occupied. Patriarchal histories and cultures [militate] against such space constantly, by material and conceptual coercion, by bribery, by punishment and by shaping and constraining the imagination. So long as we do not actively, perversely and obstinately create ourselves, lesbians are impossible.

In my essay, "To Be and Be Seen," following up on a tip from Sarah Hoagland, I explored at length the proposition that there are no lesbians in the universe of patriarchy. A similar and more generic point is useful here.

25   The word "virgin" did not originally mean a woman whose vagina was untouched by any penis, but a free woman, one not betrothed, not married, not bound to, not possessed by any man. It meant a female who is sexually and hence socially her own person. In any universe of patriarchy, there are no Virgins in this sense. Even female children are possessed by their male kin and are conceived of as potential wives. Hence Virgins must be unspeakable, thinkable only as negations, their existence impossible. Radically feminist lesbians have claimed positive Virginity and have been inventing ways of living it out, in creative defiance of patriarchal definitions of the real, the meaningful. The question at hand may be conceived this way: *Will* and *can* any women, many women, creatively defy patriarchal definitions of the real and the meaningful to invent and embody modes of living positive Virginity which include women's maintaining erotic, economic, homemaking, partnering connections with men? Such Virgins are no more possible *in* patriarchy than are lesbians, and if they impossibly bring themselves into existence, they will be living lives as sexually, socially, and politically outlandish and unnatural as the lives undertaken by radically feminist lesbians. What must be imagined here is females who are willing to engage in chosen connections with males who are wild, undomesticated females, creating themselves here and now.

In a way, it is not my place to imagine these wild females who have occasional and/or committed erotic, reproductive, homemaking, partnered or friendship relations with males. The work and the pleasure of that imagining belong to those who undertake to invent themselves thus. But I do have a vivid, though partial, image of them. It derives both from my own experience as an impossible being and from my intense desire for alliance and sisterhood with women of my acquaintance who engage in relations with men in the patriarchal context but who also seem to me to have a certain aptitude for Virginity. This image expresses that "perverse optimism" which I said at the beginning is one source of this writing/speaking. So I offer for your consideration a sketch of my image of these wild women: (This is not a recipe for political correctness, and I am not legislating: this is a report from my Imagination.)

These Virgins do not attire or decorate themselves in the gear which in their cultures signal female compliance with male-defined femininity and which would form their bodies to such compliance. They do not make themselves "attractive" in the conventional feminine modes of their cultures and so people who can ignore their animal beauty say they are ugly. They maintain as much economic flexibility as they possibly can to ensure that they can revert to independence any time economic partnership is binding them to an alliance less than fully chosen. They would no more have sex when they don't expect to enjoy it than they would run naked in the rain when they don't expect to enjoy it. Their sexual interactions are not sites where people with penises make themselves men and people with vaginas are made women.[6]

These Virgins who connect with men don't try to maintain the fictions that the men they favor are better than other men. When they are threatened by people who feel threatened by them, they do not point to their connections with men as soothing proof that they really aren't manhaters. They don't avail themselves of male protection. They do not pressure their daughters or their mothers, sisters, friends, or students to relate to men in the ways they do so they can feel validated by the other woman's choices. They never consider bringing any man with them to any feminist gathering that is not specifically meant to include men, and they help to create and to defend (and they enjoy) women-only spaces.

These Virgins who connect with men are not manipulable by orchestrations of male approval or disapproval, orchestrations of men's and children's needs, real or fake. They are not capable of being reduced to conformity by dread or anxiety about things lesbian, and are unafraid of their own passions for other Virgins, including those who are lesbians. They do not need to be respectable.

These Virgins refuse to enter the institution of marriage, and do not   30
support or witness the weddings of others, including the weddings of their favorite brothers. They are die-hard marriage-resisters. They come under enormous pressure to marry, but they do not give in to it. They do not consider marriage a privilege. Not even the bribe of spousal health insurance benefits lures them into marriage, not even as they and their partners get older and become more anxious about their health and their economic situations.

These Virgins have strong, reliable, creative, enduring, sustaining, ardent friendships with women. Their imagination and their politics are shaped more fundamentally by a desire to empower women and create friendship and solidarity among women than by a commitment to appease, comfort, or change men. These Virgins who connect with men do not feel that they could be themselves and be in closets; they are "out" as loose and noncompliant females, a very noticeable phenomenon on the social and political scene. They make themselves visible, audible and tangible to each other, they make community and sisterhood with each other and with lesbian Virgins, and they support each other in their wildness. They frolic and make trouble together. They create ways to have homes and warmth and companionship and intensity with or without a man included. They create value and they create meaning, so when the pressures to conform to patriarchal female heterosexuality are great, they have a context and community of resistance to sustain them and to engage their creative energies in devising new solutions to the problems conformity pretends to solve. They create music, novels, poetry, art, magazines, and newspapers, knowledge, skills and tools, political actions and programs. And in their magazines and newspapers, they articulate their imagination, their cultural and political differences, their various values; they berate each other, they support each other, they pay attention to each other.

Are these things I imagine possible? Can you fuck without losing your virginity? I think everything is against it, but *it's not my call.* I can hopefully image, but the counter-possible creation of such reality is up to those who want to live it, if anyone does.

Some women have hoped that you *do* have to be lesbian to be a real, extreme, to-the-root, troublemaking feminist, because then, since they are not lesbian and would never in the world become lesbians, they have an excuse for not thinking or acting radically feminist and not alienating men. Much of what passes for women's fear of lesbianism is really fear of men—fear of what men might do to non-compliant females. But I do not want to provide such an excuse for moderate or safe feminism.

"Do you have to be a lesbian to a feminist?" is not quite the right question. The question should be "Can a women a be heterosexual and be radically feminist?" My picture is this: you do not have to be lesbian to uncompromisingly embody and enact a radical feminism, but you also cannot be heterosexual in any standard patriarchal meaning of that word—you cannot be any version of a patriarchal wife. Lesbian or not, to embody and enact a consistent and all-the-way feminism you have to be a heretic, a deviant, an undomesticated female, an impossible being. You have to be a Virgin.

NOTES

1. This is a slightly revised version of a speech I gave, titled "Do You Have to Be A Lesbian to Be A Feminist?", at the National Women's Studies Association Annual conference in June 1990, in Akron, Ohio. I was invited to be one of two speakers in a plenary session which I was told would be on lesbianism, feminism, and homophobia, though when the program came out, there was another title given to the session, a title which did not include the word "lesbian." The original speech was published in *off our backs* in the August/September issue, 1990, and sparked a flood of very critical letters to the editor from women who thought I had answered the title question "yes."

   I am happy to acknowledge Carolyn Shafer's help in thinking through and crafting these reflections, and I am indebted also to discussion with Maria Lugones which helped me have the courage to cut through some confusions.

2. In some cultural contexts, this intimacy would not be considered *sexual.* Indeed, in my own time and place, it is difficult for some people to think of intimacy between women as really "sexual." Cf. Frye, "To Be and Be Seen," in *The Politics of Reality: Essays in Feminist Theory* (Freedom, California: The Crossing Press, 1983), 156–158.

3. In the context of European and North American cultures, it may have been a mark of women's increased status (a result of the successes of the 19th Century feminism) that

intimate relations among women have come to be taken seriously enough by patriarchal authorities to be seen as an extension of the sexual and to be rigidly forbidden.

4. Thanks to Miriam Johnson for encouraging me to be more mindful here, of the cultural specificity of the concepts of "lesbian" and "heterosexual." She suggested that the term "wife" more accurately designates what women are required to be, cross-culturally, than the term "heterosexual." But in the middle-class U.S. culture of which I am a native, at this time the legal and traditional meaning of "wife" is too narrow to designate what I am referring to. Women of my culture are not so strenuously required to marry as they are required to be heterosexual—to be sexually available to a man and not to "be sexual with" women.

5. "Disloyal to Civilization: Feminism, Racism, and Gynephobia," *On Lies, Secrets, and Silence* (NY: Norton, 1979), 275–310. . . .

6. These felicitous phrases are due to John Stoltenberg, *Refusing to Be a Man: Essays on Sex and Justice* (Portland, Oregon: Breitenbush Books, Inc.), *passim.*

16

Resistance Strategy Four: Revolution

■■■■■

TOWARD A CONSTRUCTIVE DEFINITION OF BLACK POWER

James Cone

> *If there is no struggle, there is no progress. Those who profess to favor freedom, and yet depreciate agitation, are men who want crops without plowing up the ground. They want rain without thunder and lightning. . . . This struggle may be a moral one; or it may be a physical one; or it may be both moral and physical; but there must be a struggle.*
>
> FREDERICK DOUGLASS

WHAT IS BLACK POWER?

There has been and still is much debate among the critics of Black Power regarding the precise meaning of the words. The term "Black Power" was first used in the civil rights movement in the spring of 1966 by Stokely Carmichael to designate the only appropriate response to white racism.[1] Since that time many critics have observed that there is no common agreement regarding its definition. In one sense this fact is not surprising, since every new phenomenon passes through stages of development, and the advocates of Black Power need time to define its many implications. But in another sense, this criticism is surprising, since every literate person knows that imprecision, the inability of a word to describe accurately the object of reality to which it points, is characteristic of all languages. The complexity of this problem is evident in the development of modern analytical philosophy. We are still in the process of defining such terms as "democracy," "good," "evil," and many others. In fact the ability to probe for deeper meanings of words as they relate to various manifestations of reality is what makes the intellectual pursuit interesting and worthwhile.

But if communication is not to reach an impasse, there must be agreement on the general shape of the object to which a term points. Meaningful dialogue is possible because of man's ability to use words as symbols for the real. Without this, communication ceases to exist. For example, theologians and political scientists may disagree on what they would consider "fine points" regarding the precise meaning of Christianity and democracy, but there is an underlying agreement regarding their referents.

The same is true of the words "Black Power." To what "object" does it point? What does it mean when used by its advocates? It means *complete emancipation of black people from white oppression by whatever means black people deem necessary.* The methods may include selective buying, boycotting, marching, or even rebellion. Black Power means black freedom, black self-determination, wherein black people no longer view themselves as without human dignity but as men, human beings with the ability to carve out their own destiny. In short, as Stokely Carmichael would say, Black Power means T.C.B., Take Care of Business—black folk taking care of black folks' business, not on the terms of the oppressor, but on those of the oppressed.

Black Power is analogous to Albert Camus's understanding of the rebel. The rebel says No and Yes. He says No to conditions considered intolerable, and Yes to that "something within him which 'is worthwhile'. . . and which must be taken into consideration."[2] To say No means that the oppressor has overstepped his bounds, and that "there is a limit beyond which [he] shall not go."[3] It means that oppression can be endured no longer in the style that the oppressor takes for granted. To say No is to reject categorically "the humiliating orders of the master" and by so doing to affirm that something which is placed above everything else, including life itself. To say No means that death is preferable to life, if the latter is devoid of freedom. *"Better to die on one's feet than to live on one's knees."*[4] This is what Black Power means.

It is in this light that the slogan "Freedom Now"[5] ought to be interpreted. Like Camus's phrase, "All or Nothing," Freedom Now means that the slave is willing to risk death because "he considers these rights more important than himself. Therefore he is acting in the name of certain values which . . . he considers are common to himself and to all men."[6] That is what Henry Garnet had in mind when he said "rather *die freemen, than live to be slaves.*"[7] This is what Black Power means.

A further clarification of the meaning of Black Power may be found in Paul Tillich's analysis of "the courage to be," which is "the ethical act in which man affirms his being in spite of those elements of his existence which conflict with his essential self-affirmation."[8] Black Power, then, is a humanizing force because it is the black man's attempt to affirm his being, his attempt to be recognized as "Thou," in spite of the "other,"[9] the white power which dehumanizes him. The structure of white society attempts to make "black being" into "nonbeing" or "nothingness." In existential philosophy, nonbeing is usually identified as that which threatens being; it is that ever-present possibility of the inability to affirm one's existence. The courage to be, then, is the courage to affirm one's being by striking out at the dehumanizing forces which threaten being. And, as Tillich goes on to say, "He who is not capable of a powerful self-affirmation in spite of the anxiety of non-being is forced into a weak, reduced self-affirmation."[10]

The rebellion in the cities, far from being an expression of the inhumanity of blacks, is an affirmation of their being despite the ever-present possibility of death. For the black man to accept the white society's appeal to wait or to be orderly is to affirm "something which is less than essential . . . being."[11] The black man prefers to die rather than surrender to some other value. The cry for death is, as Rollo May has noted, the "most mature form of distinctly human behavior."[12] In fact, many existentialists point out that physical life itself "is not fully satisfying and meaningful until one can consciously choose another value which he holds more dear than life itself."[13] To be human is to find something worth dying for. When the black man rebels at the risk of death, he forces white society to look at him, to recognize him, to take his being into account, to admit that he *is*. And in a structure that regulates behavior, recognition by the other is indispensable to one's being. As Franz Fanon says: "Man is human only to the extent to which he tries to impose his existence on another in order to be recognized by him."[14] And "he who is reluctant to recognize me opposes me. In a savage struggle I am willing to accept convulsions of death, invincible dissolutions, but also the possibility of the impossible."[15]

Black Power, in short, is an *attitude,* an inward affirmation of the essential worth of blackness. It means that the black man will not be poisoned by the stereotypes that others have of him, but will affirm from the depth of his soul: "Get used to me, I am not getting used to anyone."[16] And "if the white man challenges my humanity, I will impose my whole weight as a man on his life and show him that I am not that 'sho good eatin' that he persists in imagining."[17] This is Black Power, the power of the black man to say Yes to his own "black being," and to make the other accept him or be prepared for a struggle.

> I find myself suddenly in the world and I recognize that I have one right alone: That of demanding human behavior from the other. One duty alone: That of not renouncing my freedom through my choices.[18]

BLACK POWER AND EXISTENTIAL ABSURDITY

Before one can really understand the mood of Black Power, it is necessary to describe a prior mood of the black man in a white society. When he first awakens to his place in America and feels sharply the absolute contradiction between *what is* and *what ought to be* or recognizes the inconsistency between his view of himself as a man and America's description of him as a thing, his immediate reaction is a feeling of absurdity. The absurd

> is basically that which man recognizes as the disparity between what he hopes for and what seems in fact to be. He yearns for some measure of happiness in an orderly, a rational and a reasonably predictable world; when he finds misery in a disorderly, an irrational and unpredictable world, he is oppressed by the absurdity of the disparity between the universe as he wishes it to be and as he sees it.[19]

This is what the black man feels in a white world.

There is no place in America where the black man can go for escape. In every section of the country there is still the feeling expressed by Langston Hughes: *10*

> *I swear to the Lord*
> *I still can't see*
> *Why Democracy means*
> *Everybody but me.*

I can remember reading, as a child, the Declaration of Independence with a sense of identity with all men and with a sense of pride: "We hold these truths to be self-evident: that all men are created equal; that they are endowed by their creator with certain unalienable rights; that among them is life, liberty and the pursuit of happiness." But I also read in the Dred Scott decision, not with pride or identity, but with a feeling of inexplicable absurdity, that blacks are not human.

> But it is too clear for dispute, that the enslaved African race were not intended to be included, and formed no part of the people who framed and adopted this declaration; for if the language, as understood in that day, would embrace them, the conduct of the distinguished men who framed the Declaration of Independence would have been utterly and flagrantly inconsistent with the principles they asserted; and instead of the sympathy of mankind . . . they would have deserved and received universal rebuke and reprobation.

Thus the black man *"had no rights which the white man was bound to respect."*[20]

But many whites would reply: "The Negro is no longer bought and sold as chattel. We changed his status after the Civil War. Now he is free." Whatever may have been the motives of Abraham Lincoln and other white Americans for launching the war, it certainly was not on behalf of black people. Lincoln was clear on this:

> My paramount object in this struggle is to save the Union, and is not either to save or to destroy slavery. If I could save the

Union without freeing any slave, I would do it; and if I could save it by freeing some and leaving others alone, I would also do that.[21]

If that quotation still leaves his motives unclear, here is another one which should remove all doubts regarding his thoughts about black people.

I will say then that I am not, nor ever have been in favor of bringing about in any way the social and political equality of the black and white races—that I am not nor ever have been in favor of making voters or jurors of Negroes, nor of qualifying them to hold office, nor to intermarry with white people; and I will say in addition to this that there is a physical difference between the white and black races which I believe will forbid the two races living together on terms of social and political equality. And inasmuch as they cannot so live, while they do remain together, there must be the position of superior and in-ferior, and I as much as any other man am in favor of having the superior position assigned to the white race.[22]

And certainly the history of the black–white relations in this country from the Civil War to the present unmistakably shows that as a people, Americans never intended for blacks to be free. To this day, in the eyes of most white Americans, the black man remains subhuman.

15   Yet Americans continue to talk about brotherhood and equality. They say that this is "the land of the free and the home of the brave." They sing: My country 'tis of thee, sweet land of liberty." But they do not mean blacks. This is the black man's paradox, the absurdity of living in a world with "no rights which the white man [is] bound to respect."

It seems that white historians and political scientists have attempted, per-haps subconsciously, to camouflage the inhumanity of whites toward blacks.[23] But the evidence is clear for those who care to examine it. All aspects of this society have participated in the act of enslaving blacks, extinguishing In-dians, and annihilating all who question white society's right to decide who is human.

I should point out here that most existentialists do not say that "man is absurd" or "the world is absurd." Rather, the absurdity arises as man confronts the world and looks for meaning. The same is true in regard to my analysis of the black man in a white society. It is not that the black man is absurd or that the white society as such is absurd. Absurdity arises as the black man seeks to un-derstand his place in the white world. The black man does not view himself as absurd; he views himself as human. But as he meets the white world and its values, he is confronted with an almighty No and is defined as a thing. This produces the absurdity.

The crucial question, then, for the black man is, "How should I respond to a world which defines me as a nonperson?" That he is a person is beyond question, not debatable. But when he attempts to relate as a person, the world demands that he respond as a thing. In this existential absurdity, what should he do? Should he respond as he knows himself to be, or as the world defines him?

The response to this feeling of absurdity is determined by a man's ontological perspective. If one believes that this world is the extent of reality, he will either despair or rebel. According to Camus's *The Myth of Sisyphus,* suicide is the ultimate act of despair. Rebellion is epitomized in the person of Dr. Bernard Rieux in *The Plague.* Despite the overwhelming odds, Rieux fights against things as they are.

If, perchance, a man believes in God, and views this world as merely a pilgrimage to another world, he is likely to regard suffering as a necessity for entrance to the next world. Unfortunately Christianity has more often than not responded to evil in this manner.   20

From this standpoint the response of Black Power is like Camus's view of the rebel. One who embraces Black Power does not despair and take suicide as an out, nor does he appeal to another world in order to relieve the pains of this one.[24] Rather, *he fights back with the whole of his being.* Black Power believes that blacks are not really human beings in white eyes, that they never have been and never will be, until blacks recognize the unsavory behavior of whites for what it is. Once this recognition takes place, they can make whites see them as humans. The man of Black Power will not rest until the oppressor recognizes him for what he is—man. He further knows that in this campaign for human dignity, freedom is not a gift but a right worth dying for.

IS BLACK POWER A FORM OF BLACK RACISM?

One of the most serious charges leveled against the advocates of Black Power is that they are *black* racists. Many well-intentioned persons have insisted that there must be another approach, one which will not cause so much hostility, not to mention rebellion. Therefore appeal is made to the patience of black people to keep their "cool" and not get too carried away by their feelings. These men argue that if any progress is to be made, it will be through a careful, rational approach to the subject. These people are deeply offended when black people refuse to listen and place such white liberals in the same category as the most adamant segregationists. They simply do not see that such reasoned appeals merely support the perpetuation of the ravaging of the black community. Black Power, in this respect, is by nature *irrational,* i.e., does not deny the role of rational reflection, but insists that human existence cannot be mechanized or put into neat boxes according to reason. Human reason though valuable is not absolute, because moral decisions—those decisions which deal with human dignity—cannot be made by using the abstract methods of science. Human emotions must be reckoned with. Consequently, black people must say No to all do-gooders who insist that they need more time. If such persons really knew oppression—knew it existentially in their guts—

they would join black people in their fight for freedom and dignity. It is interesting that most people do understand why Jews can hate Germans. Why can they not understand why black people, who have been deliberately and systematically dehumanized or murdered by the structure of this society, hate white people? The general failure of Americans to make this connection suggests that the primary difficulty is their inability to see black men as men.

When Black Power advocates refuse to listen to their would-be liberators, they are charged with creating hatred among black people, thus making significant personal relationship between blacks and whites impossible. It should be obvious that the hate which black people feel toward whites is not due to the creation of the term "Black Power." Rather, it is a result of the deliberate and systematic ordering of society on the basis of racism, making black alienation not only possible but inevitable. For over three hundred years black people have been enslaved by the tentacles of American white power, tentacles that worm their way into the guts of their being and "invade the gray cells of their cortex." For three hundred years they have cried, waited, voted, marched, picketed, and boycotted, but whites still refuse to recognize their humanity. In light of this, attributing black anger to the call for Black Power is ridiculous, if not obscene. "To be a Negro in this country," says James Baldwin, "and to be relatively conscious is to be in rage almost all the time."

In spite of this it is misleading to suggest that hatred is essential to the definition of Black Power. As Camus says, "One envies what he does not have, while the rebel's aim is to defend what he is. He does not merely claim some good that he does not possess or of which he is deprived. His aim is to claim recognition for something which he has."[25] Therefore it is not the intention of the black man to repudiate his master's human dignity, but only his status as master.[26] The rebellion in the cities, it would seem, should not be interpreted as a few blacks who want something for nothing but as an assertion of the dignity of all black people. The black man is assuming that there is a common value which is recognizable by all as existing in all people, and he is testifying to that *something* in his rebellion. He is expressing his solidarity with the human race. With this in view, Camus's reinterpretation of the Cartesian formula, "I think, therefore I am," seems quite appropriate: "I rebel, therefore *we* exist."

25

It is important to make a further distinction here among black hatred, black racism, and Black Power. Black hatred is the black man's strong aversion to white society. No black man living in white America can escape it. Even a sensitive white man can say: "It is hard to imagine how any Negro American, no matter how well born or placed, can escape a deep sense of anger and a burning hatred of things white."[27] And another nonblack, Arnold Rose, is even more perceptive:

> Negro hatred of white people is not pathological—far from it.
> It is a healthy human reaction to oppression, insult, and terror.
> White people are often surprised at the Negro's hatred of
> them, but it should not be surprising.

The whole world knows the Nazis murdered millions of Jews and can suspect that the remaining Jews are having some emotional reaction to that fact. Negroes, on the other hand, are either ignored or thought to be so subhuman that they have no feelings when one of their number is killed because he was a Negro. Probably no week goes by in the United States that some Negro is not severely beaten, and the news is reported in the Negro press. Every week or maybe twice a week almost the entire Negro population of the United States suffers an emotional recoil from some insult coming from the voice or pen of a leading white man. The surviving Jews had one, big, soul-wracking "incident" that wrenched them back to group identification. The surviving Negroes experience constant jolts that almost never let them forget for even an hour that they are Negroes. In this situation, hatred of whites and group identification are natural reactions.[28]

And James Baldwin was certainly expressing the spirit of black hatred when he said:

The brutality with which Negroes are treated in this country simply cannot be overstated, however unwilling white men may be to hear it. In the beginning—and neither can this be overstated—a Negro just cannot *believe* that white people are treating him as they do; he does not know what he has done to merit it. And when he realizes that the treatment accorded him has nothing to do with anything he has done, that the attempt of white people to destroy him—for that is what it is—is utterly gratuitous, it is not hard for him to think of white people as devils.[29]

This feeling should not be identified as black racism. Black racism is a myth created by whites to ease their guilt feelings. As long as whites can be assured that blacks are racists, they can find reasons to justify their own oppression of black people. This tactic seems to be a favorite device of white liberals who, intrigued by their own unselfish involvement in civil rights *for* the "Negro," like to pride themselves on their liberality toward blacks. White racists who are prepared to defend the outright subjugation of blacks need no such myth. The myth is needed by those who intend to keep things as they are, while pretending that things are in fact progressing. When confronted with the fact that the so-called progress is actually nonexistent, they can easily offer an explanation by pointing to the "white backlash" caused by "black racism."

But the charge of black racism cannot be reconciled with the facts. While it is true that blacks do hate whites, black hatred is not racism. Racism, according to Webster, is "the assumption that psychocultural traits and capacities are determined by biological race and that races differ decisively from one another, which is usually coupled with a belief in the inherent superiority of a particular race and its rights to dominance over others." Where are the examples among blacks in which they sought to assert their right to dominance over other because of a belief in black superiority? The only possible example would be the Black Muslims; and even here there is no effort of Black Muslims to enslave whites. Furthermore, if we were to designate them as black racists, they certainly are not dangerous in the same sense as white racists. The existence of the Black Muslims does not entitle whites to speak of black racism as a serious threat to the American society. They should be viewed as one possible and justifiable reaction to white racism. But in regard to Black Power, it is not comparable to white racism. Stokely Carmichael, responding to the charge of black supremacy, writes:

> There is no analogy—by any stretch of definition or imagination—between the advocates of Black Power and white racists. . . . The goal of the racist is to keep black people on the bottom, arbitrarily and dictatorially as they have done in this country for over three hundred years. The goal of black self-determination and black self-identity—Black Power—is full participation in the decision making process affecting the lives of black people.[30]

Modern racism is European in origin, and America has been its vigorous offspring. It is the white man who has sought to dehumanize others because of his feelings of superiority or for his economic advantage. Racism is so embedded in this country that it is hard to imagine that any white man can escape it.

30   Black Power then is not black racism or black hatred. Simply stated, Black Power is an affirmation of the humanity of blacks in spite of white racism. It says that only blacks really know the extent of white oppression, and thus only blacks are prepared to risk all to be free. Therefore, Black Power seeks not understanding but conflict; addresses blacks and not whites; seeks to develop black support, but not white good will. Black Power believes in the utter determination of blacks to be free and not in the good intentions of white society. It says: If blacks are liberated, it will be blacks themselves who will do the liberating, not whites.

WHY INTEGRATION IS NOT THE ANSWER

Whites are not only bothered about "black racism" but also about the rejection of integration implied in Black Power. They say, "Now that we have decided to accept the Negro, he will have no part of it. You see, we knew he really preferred segregation." What, then, does Black Power say about integration?

One Black Power advocate, when a newsman asked, "What about integration?" responded, "Integration of what?" The implication is clear. If integration means accepting the white man's style, his values, or his religion, then the black man must refuse. There is nothing to integrate. The white man, in the very asking of the question, assumes that he has something which blacks want or should want, as if being close to white people enhances the humanity of blacks.[31] This question—What about integration?—also completely ignores the beastly behavior of the "devil white man" (Malcolm X's designation). Black people cannot accept relationship on this basis.

On the other hand, if integration means that each man meets the other on equal footing, with neither possessing the ability to assert the rightness of his style over the other, then mutual meaningful dialogue is possible. Biblically, this may be called the Kingdom of God. Men were not created for separation, and color is not the essence of man's humanity. But we are not living in what the New Testament called the consummated Kingdom, and even its partial manifestation is not too obvious. Therefore, black people cannot live according to what ought to be, but according to what *is*. To be sure, men ought to behave without color as the defining characteristic of their view of humanity, but they do not. Some men can verbally rise above color, but existentially they live according to it, sometimes without even being conscious of it. There are so few exceptions to this that the universal assertion is virtually untouched. Therefore, to ask blacks to act as if color does not exist, to be integrated into white society, is asking them to ignore both the history of white America and present realities. Laws may be passed, but only whites have the power to enforce them.

Instead, in order for the oppressed blacks to regain their identity, they must affirm the very characteristic which the oppressor ridicules—*blackness*. Until white America is able to accept the beauty of blackness ("Black is beautiful, baby"), there can be no peace, no integration in the higher sense. Black people must withdraw and form their own culture, their own way of life.

Integration, as commonly understood, is nothing but "'a subterfuge for white supremacy'; i.e., as always involving only a token number of Negroes integrated into 'white institutions on the white man's terms.'"[32] As Professor Poussaint shows, this means blacks accepting the white man's view of himself, blacks saying, "Yes, [we are] inferior."[33]

Any careful assessment of the place of the black man in America must conclude that black self-hatred is the worst aspect of the legacy of slavery.[34] "The worst crime the white man has committed," writes Malcolm X, "has been to teach us to hate ourselves." During slavery, black people were treated as animals, and were systematically taught that such treatment was due them because of their blackness. "When slavery was abolished, the Negro had been stripped of his culture and left with this heritage: an oppressed black man in a white man's world."[35] When blacks were rewarded, it was because they behaved according to the stereotypes devised by whites. Coupled with this was the belief that "white is right" and "black is evil." Therefore, "lighter Negroes" were given better opportunities, while "darker Negroes" had doors closed to them, giving credence to the idea that the closer you are to being white, the more nearly human you are. Unfortunately, even many of our black institutions and media promoted the idea. As Elijah Muhammad, the leader of the Black Muslims, rightly says: "The Negro wants to be a white man. He processes his hair. Acts like a white man. He wants to integrate with the white man, but he cannot integrate with himself or his own mind. The Negro wants to lose his identity because he does not know his own identity."

In the present situation, while many of the mainline civil rights workers have promoted black identity by courageously fighting against an apparent, immovable status quo, the idea of integration, at this stage, too easily lends itself to supporting the moral superiority of white society.

> Negro parents in the south never speak of sending their children to the "integrated school"; they say, "My child is going to the *white* school." No white children are "integrated" into Negro schools. Since integration is only a one-way street that Negroes travel to a white institution, then inherent in the situation itself is the implied inferiority of the black man.[36]

What is needed, then, is not "integration" but a sense of worth in being black, and only black people can teach that. Black consciousness is the key to the black man's emancipation from his distorted self-image.

As previously noted, some have called this racism in reverse. But this is merely a social myth, created by the white man to ease his guilt by accusing blacks of the same brutalities he has himself inflicted. The withdrawal of blacks is a necessary counterattack to overt, voluntary white racism. Furthermore, there is no way for blacks politically to enforce their attitudes, even if they were destructive of whites, but whites can and do enforce their attitudes upon blacks. Black identity is survival, while white racism is exploitation.

40   Black Power, then, must say No to whites who invite them to share in their inhumanity toward black people. Instead, it must affirm the beauty of blackness and by so doing free the black man for a self-affirmation of his own being as a black man. Whites cannot teach this.

IS THERE AN APPROPRIATE RESPONSE TO WHITE RACISM?

The asking of this question is inevitable. Whites want to know whether Black Power is an appropriate response to their bigotry. It is indeed interesting that they, the oppressors, should ask this question, since whatever response blacks make is nothing but a survival reaction to white oppression. It is time for whites to realize that the oppressor is in no position whatever to define the proper response to enslavement. He is not the slave, but the enslaver. And if the slave should choose to risk death rather than submit to the humiliating orders of the master, then that is his right. Bigger Thomas in Richard Wright's

Native Son demonstrates this choice when interrogated by white policemen who wanted him to confess raping a white girl:

> "Come on, now, boy. We've treated you pretty nice, but we can get tough if we have to, see? It's up to *you!* Get over there by the bed and show us how you raped and murdered that girl!"
>
> "I didn't rape her," Bigger said through stiff lips.
>
> "Aw, come on. What you got to lose now? Show us what you did."
>
> "I don't want to."
>
> "You *have* to!"
>
> "I *don't* have to."
>
> "Well, we'll *make* you."
>
> "You can't make me do nothing but die!"[37]

You can't make me do nothing but die! That is the key to an understanding of Black Power. Any advice from whites to blacks on how to deal with white oppression is automatically under suspicion as a clever device to further enslavement.

Furthermore, it is white intellectual arrogance which assumes that it has a monopoly on intelligence and moral judgment. How else can one explain the shocked indignation when the Kerner Report declared that race prejudice has shaped our history decisively. After all, Baldwin, Wright, Du Bois, and a host of other black writers had been saying for decades that racism is woven into the whole pattern of American society. Evidently the judgments of black people are not to be taken seriously (if, indeed, Whitey reads them at all).

The real menace in white intellectual arrogance is the dangerous assumption that the structure that enslaves is the structure that will also decide *when* and *how* this slavery is to be abolished. The sociological and psychological reports, made by most white scholars, assume that they know more about *my* frustration, *my* despair, *my* hatred for white society than I do. They want to supply the prescriptions to my problems, refusing to recognize that for over three hundred years blacks have listened to them and their reports and we are still degraded. The time has come for white Americans to be silent and listen to black people. Why must the white man assume that he has the intellectual ability or the moral sensitivity to know what blacks feel or to ease the pain, to smooth the hurt, to eradicate the resentment? Since he knows that he raped our women, dehumanized our men, and made it inevitable that black children should hate their blackness, he ought to understand why blacks must cease listening to him in order to be free.

Since whites do not know the extent of black suffering, they can only speak from their own perspective, which they call "reason." This probably accounts for white appeals to nonviolence and Christian love. . . . White people should not even expect blacks to love them, and to ask for it merely adds insult to injury. "For the white man," writes Malcolm X, "to ask the black man if he hates him is just like the rapist asking the *raped* . . . 'Do you hate me?' The white man is in no moral position to accuse anyone else of hate." Whatever blacks feel toward whites or whatever their response to white racism, it cannot be submitted to the judgments of white society.

When a white man asks, "Is Black Power the answer?" or says, "It takes time," "Wait, let's talk it over and solve this problem together," "I feel the same way you do, but . . . ," I must conclude that he is talking from a different perspective. There is no way in the world I can get him to see that he is the problem, not me. He has shaped my response. Bennett, then, is right when he states:

> We do not come up with the right answers to our problem be-
> cause we seldom ask ourselves the right question. *There is no*
> *Negro problem in America; there has never been a Negro problem*
> *in America—the problem of race in America is a white problem.* To
> understand that problem and to control it, we must address
> ourselves to the fears and frailties of white people. We learn
> nothing really from a study of Harlem. To understand Harlem
> we must go not to Harlem but to the conscience of "good
> white people"; we must ask not what is Harlem but what have
> you made of Harlem? Why did you create it and why do you
> need it?[38]

Therefore, when blacks are confronted by whites who want to help with the "black problem" by giving advice on the appropriate response, whites should not be surprised if blacks respond, "We wish to plead our own cause. Too long have others spoken for us."[39] I am not prepared to talk seriously with a man who essentially says, "I sit on a man's back, choking him and making him carry me, and yet assure myself and others that I am very sorry for him and wish to lighten his load by all possible means—except by getting off his back."[40] Blacks must demand that whites get off their backs.

If whites do not get off the backs of blacks, they must expect that blacks will literally throw them off by whatever means are at their disposal. This is the meaning of Black Power. Depending on the response of whites, it means that emancipation may even have to take the form of outright rebellion. No one can really say what form the oppressed must take in relieving their oppression. But if blacks are pushed to the point of unendurable pain, with no option but a violent affirmation of their own being, then violence is to be expected. "Violence is a personal necessity for the oppressed," writes John Reilly in his analysis of Richard Wright's *Native Son*. "When life in a society consists of humiliation, one's only rescue is through rebellion. It is not a strategy consciously devised. It is the deep, instinctive expression of a human being denied individuality. . . . Yet expression of the rebellion can be liberating."[41] Or again, as Bennett says: "The boundary of freedom is man's power to say 'No!' and whoever refuses to say 'No' involves himself tragically in his own degradation."[42] Black Power says No!

HOW DOES BLACK POWER RELATE
TO WHITE GUILT?

When white do-gooders are confronted with the style of Black Power, realizing that black people really place them in the same category with the George Wallaces, they react defensively, saying, "It's not my fault" or "I am not responsible." Sometimes they continue by suggesting that their town (because of their unselfish involvement in civil rights) is better or less racist than others.

There are two things to be said here. First, there are no degrees of human freedom or human dignity. Either a man respects another as a person or he does not. To be sure, there may be different manifestations of inhumanity, but that is beside the point. The major question is: Is the black man in white society a "Thou" or an "It"? Fanon puts it this way: "A given society is racist or it is not. . . . Statements, for example, that the north of France is more racist than the south, that racism is the work of underlings and hence in no way involves the ruling class, that France is one of the less racist countries in the world are the product of men incapable of straight thinking."[43] Racism, then, biologically is analogous to pregnancy, either she is or she is not, or like the Christian doctrine of sin, one is or is not in sin. There are no meaningful "in betweens" relevant to the fact itself. And it should be said that racism is so embedded in the heart of American society that few, if any, whites can free themselves from it. So it is time for whites to recognize that fact for what it is and proceed from there. Who really can take it upon himself "to try to ascertain in what ways one kind of inhuman behavior differs from another,"[44] especially if one is a direct participant? "Is there in truth any difference between one racism and another? Do not all of them show the same collapse, the same bankruptcy of man?"[45]

Second, all white men are responsible for white oppression. It is much to easy to say, "Racism is not my fault," or "I am not responsible for the country's inhumanity to the black man." *The American white man has always had an easy conscience.* But insofar as white do-gooders tolerate and sponsor racism in their educational institutions, their political, economic, and social structures, their churches, and in every other aspect of American life, they are directly responsible for racism. "It is a cold, hard fact that the many flagrant forms of racial injustice North and South could not exist without their [whites'] acquiescence,"[46] and for that, they are responsible. If whites are honest in their analysis of the moral state of this society, they know that all are responsible. Racism is possible because whites are indifferent to suffering and patient with cruelty. Karl Jaspers' description of metaphysical guilt is pertinent here.

> There exists among men, because they are men, a solidarity through which each shares responsibility for every injustice and every wrong committed in the world, and *especially for crimes that are committed in his presence or of which he cannot be ignorant.* If I do not do whatever I can to prevent them, I am an accomplice

in them. If I have not risked my life in order to prevent the
murder of other men, if I have stood silent, I feel guilty in a
sense that cannot in any adequate fashion be understood
juridically, or politically, or morally. . . . that I am still alive after
such things have been done weighs on me as a guilt that cannot be expiated.[47]

In contrast, injustice anywhere strikes a sensitive note in the souls of black
folk, because they know what it means to be treated as a thing. That is why
Fanon says, "Anti-Semitism hits me head-on: I am enraged, I am bled white
by an appalling battle, I am deprived of the possibility of being man. I cannot
dissociate myself from the future that is proposed for my brother."[48] Yes, when
blacks in Chicago hear about blacks being lynched in Mississippi, they are enraged. When they heard about Martin Luther King's death, they burned, they
looted, they got Whitey. In fact, when blacks hear about any injustice, whether
it is committed against black or white, blacks know that their existence is
being stripped of its meaning. Aimé Césaire, a black poet, put it this way:

When I turn on my radio, when I hear that Negroes have been
lynched in America, I say that we have been lied to: Hitler is
not dead; when I turn on my radio, when I learn that Jews
have been insulted, mistreated, persecuted, I say that we have
been lied to: Hitler is not dead; when, finally I turn on my
radio and hear that in Africa forced labor has been inaugurated
and legalized, I say that we have been lied to: Hitler is not
dead.[49]

White America's attempt to free itself of responsibility for the black man's
inhuman condition is nothing but a protective device to ease her guilt. Whites
have to convince themselves that they are not responsible. That is why social
scientists prefer to remain detached in their investigations of racial injustice. It
is less painful to be uninvolved. White Americans do not dare to know that
blacks are beaten at will by policemen as a means of protecting the latter's ego
superiority as well as that of the larger white middle class. For to know is to
be responsible. To know is to understand why blacks loot and riot at what
seems slight provocation. Therefore, they must have reports to explain the dis-
enchantment of blacks with white democracy, so they can be surprised. They
must believe that blacks are in poverty because they are lazy or because they
are inferior. Yes, they must believe that everything is basically all right. Black
Power punctures those fragile lies, declaring to white America the pitiless indictment of Francis Jeanson: "If you succeed in keeping yourself unsullied, it
is because others dirty themselves in your place. *You hire thugs,* and, balancing
the accounts, it is you who are the real criminals: for without you, without
your blind indifference, such men could never carry out deeds that damn you
as much as they shame those men."[50]

BLACK POWER AND THE WHITE LIBERAL

In time of war, men want to know who the enemy is. Who is for me and who is against me? That is the question. The asserting of black freedom in America has always meant war. When blacks retreat and accept their dehumanized place in white society, the conflict ceases. But when blacks rise up in freedom, whites show their racism.

In reality, then, *accommodation* or *protest* seems to be the only option open to the black man. For three hundred years he accommodated, thereby giving credence to his own enslavement. Black Power means that he will no longer accommodate; that he will no longer tolerate white excuses for enslavement; that he will no longer be guided by the oppressor's understanding of justice, liberty, freedom, or the methods to be used in attaining them. He recognizes the difference between theoretical equality and great factual inequalities. He will not sit by and wait for the white man's love to be extended to his black brother. He will protest, violently if need be, on behalf of absolute and immediate emancipation. Black Power means that black people will cease trying to articulate rationally the political advantages and moral rightness of human freedom, since the dignity of man is a self-evident religious, philosophical, and political *truth,* without which human community is impossible. When one group breaks the covenant of truth and assumes an exclusive role in defining the basis of human relationship, that group plants the seed of rebellion. Black Power means that blacks are prepared to accept the challenge and with it the necessity of distinguishing friends from enemies.

It is in this situation that the liberal white is caught. We have alluded to him earlier, but now we intend to take a closer look at his "involvement" in this war for freedom. To be sure, as Loren Miller says, "there are liberals and liberals, ranging from Left to Right." But there are certain characteristics identifiable in terms of attitudes and beliefs.

> Simply stated, [liberalism] contemplates the ultimate elimination of all racial distinctions in every phase of American life through an orderly, step-by-step process adjusted to resistance and aimed at overcoming such resistance. In the field of constitutional law, the classic liberal position, exemplified in the Supreme Court's "all deliberate speed" formula of school-segregation cases, requires and rationalizes Negro accommodation to, and acquiescence in, disabilities imposed because of race and in violation of the fundamental law.[51]

The liberal, then, is one who sees "both sides" of the issue and shies away from "extremism" in any form. He wants to change the heart of the racist without ceasing to be his friend; he wants progress without conflict. Therefore, when he sees blacks engaging in civil disobedience and demanding "Freedom Now," he is disturbed. Black people know who the enemy is, and they are forcing the liberal to take sides. But the liberal wants to be a friend, that is, enjoy the rights and privileges pertaining to whiteness and also work for the "Negro." He wants change without risk, victory without blood.

The liberal white man is a strange creature; he verbalizes the right things. He intellectualizes on the racial problem beautifully. He roundly denounces racists, conservatives, and the moderately liberal. Sometimes, in rare moments and behind closed doors, he will even defend Rap Brown or Stokely Carmichael. Or he may go so far as to make the statement: "I will let my daughter marry one," and this is supposed to be the absolute evidence that he is raceless.

But he is still white to the very core of his being. What he fails to realize is that there is no place for him in this war of survival. Blacks do not want his patronizing, condescending words of sympathy. They do not need his concern, his "love," his money. It is that which dehumanizes; it is that which enslaves. Freedom is what happens to a man on the inside; it is what happens to a man's being. It has nothing to do with voting, marching, picketing, or rioting—though all may be manifestations of it. No man can give me freedom or "help" me get it. A man is free when he can determine the style of his existence in an absurd world; a man is free when he sees himself for what he is and not as others define him. He is free when he determines the limits of his existence. And in this sense Sartre is right: "Man is freedom"; or, better yet, man "is condemned to be free." A man is free when he accepts the responsibility for his own acts and knows that they involve not merely himself but all men. No one can "give" or "help get" freedom in that sense.

60   In this picture the liberal can find no place. His favorite question when backed against the wall is "What can I do?" One is tempted to reply, as Malcolm X did to the white girl who asked the same question, "Nothing." What the liberal really means is, "What can I do and still receive the same privileges as other whites *and*—this is the key—be liked by Negroes?" Indeed the only answer is "Nothing." However, there are places in the Black Power picture for "radicals," that is, for men, white or black, who are prepared to risk life for freedom. There are places for the John Browns, men who hate evil and refuse to tolerate it anywhere.[52]

BLACK POWER: HOPE OR DESPAIR?

White racism is a disease. No excuse can be made for it; we blacks can only oppose it with every ounce of humanity we have. When black children die of rat bites, and black men suffer because meaning has been sapped from their existence, and black women weep because family stability is gone, how can anyone appeal to "reason"? Human life is at stake. In this regard black people are no different from other people. Men fight back, they grab for the last thread of hope. Black Power then is an expression of hope, not hope that whites will change the structure of oppression, but hope in the humanity of black people. If there is any expression of despair in Black Power, it is despair regarding white intentions, white promises to change the oppressive structure. Black people now know that freedom is not a gift from white society, but is, rather, the self-affirmation of one's existence as a person, a person with certain innate rights to say No and Yes, despite the consequences.

It is difficult for men who have not known suffering to understand this experience. That is why many concerned persons point out the futility of black rebellion by drawing a contrast between the present conditions of blacks in the ghetto and the circumstances of other revolutionaries in the past. The argument of these people runs like this: Revolutions depend on cohesion, discipline, stability, and the sense of a stake in society. The ghetto, by contrast, is relatively incohesive, unorganized, unstable, and numerically too small to be effective. Therefore, rebellion for the black man can only mean extermination, genocide. Moreover, fact one is that many poor blacks, being poor so long, have become accustomed to slavery, feeling any form of black rebellion is useless. And fact two, that the black bourgeoisie, having tasted the richness of white society, do not want to jeopardize their place in the structure.

This analysis is essentially correct. But to point out the futility of black rebellion is to miss the point. Black people know that they comprise less than 12 percent of the total American population and are proportionately much weaker with respect to economic, political, and military power. And black radicals know that they represent a minority within the black community. But having tasted freedom through an identification with God's intention for humanity, they will stop at nothing in expressing their distaste for white power. To be sure, they may be the minority in the black community, but truth, despite democracy, can never be measured by numbers. Truth is that which places a man in touch with the real; and once a man finds it, he is prepared to give all for it. The rebellion in the cities, then, is not a conscious organized attempt of black people to take over; it is an attempt to say Yes to truth and No to untruth even in death. The question, then, is not whether black people are prepared to die—the riots testify to that—but whether whites are prepared to kill them. Unfortunately, it seems that that answer has been given through the riots as well. But this willingness of black people to die is not despair, it is hope, not in white people, but in their own dignity grounded in God himself. This willingness to die for human dignity is not novel. Indeed, it stands at the heart of Christianity.

NOTES

1. Richard Wright used the term as early as 1954 in reference to Africa.
2. Camus, *The Rebel,* trans. Anthony Bower (New York: Random House, 1956), p. 13.
3. Ibid.
4. Ibid., p. 15. Emphasis added.
5. Most Black Power advocates have dropped the slogan because of its misuse by white liberals.
6. Camus, *The Rebel,* p. 16.

7. Quoted in Floyd B. Barbour (ed.), *The Black Power Revolt* (Boston: Porter Sargent, 1968), p. 39.

8. Tillich, *The Courage to Be* (New Haven:Yale University Press, 1952), p. 3.

9. The word "other," which designates the neighbor, occurs frequently in Franz Fanon, *Black Skins, White Masks,* trans. C. L. Markmann (New York: Grove Press, 1967).

10. Tillich, *The Courage to Be,* p. 66.

11. Ibid.

12. Rollo May, *Psychology and the Human Dilemma* (Princeton:Van Nostrand, 1967), p. 73.

13. Ibid.

14. Fanon, *Black Skins,* p. 216.

15. Ibid., p. 218.

16. Ibid., p. 131.

17. Ibid.

18. Ibid., p. 229.

19. W. R. Mueller and J. Jacobsen, "Samuel Beckett's Long Last Saturday: To Wait or Not to Wait," in Nathan Scott, Jr., *Man in Modern Theatre* (Richmond,Va.: John Knox Press, 1965), p. 77.

20. Quoted in L. H. Fishel, Jr., and Benjamin Quarles, *The Negro American* (Glenview, Ill.: Scott, Foresman and Co., 1967), pp. 204–205. Emphasis added.

21. "Reply to Horace Greeley," 1862, in *The American Tradition in Literature,* vol. 1; revised, S. Bradley, R. C. Beatty, and E. H. Long, eds. (New York: W. W. Norton, 1962), p. 1567.

22. Quoted in Charles Silberman, *Crisis in Black and White* (New York: Random House, 1964), pp. 92–93.

23. See John H. Franklin and Isidore Starr (eds.), *The Negro in Twentieth Century America* (New York: Random House, 1967), pp. 45–46. Here is an analysis by six American historians of how most scholars give a "white" twist to history.

24. It should be pointed out here that another alternative for black people is to submit to the white view of blacks. The problem of self-hatred is discussed in this chapter under the heading, "Why Integration Is Not the Answer."

25. Camus, *The Rebel,* p. 17.

26. Ibid., p. 23.

27. Silberman, *Crisis in Black and White,* p. 54.

28. Quoted in Lerone Bennett, *The Negro Mood* (New York: Ballantine Books, 1964), pp. 145–146.

29. James Baldwin, *The Fire Next Time* (New York: The Dial Press, 1963). Used with permission. Quotation is from the Dell paperback, pp. 94–95.

30. Stokely Carmichael and Charles Hamilton, *Black Power: The Politics of Liberation in America* (New York: Random House, 1967), p. 47.

31. In its crudest sense, it means black men want their women. Some psychologists have suggested that every inhuman act of white men toward black men is in part an act of sexual revenge. See Fanon, *Black Skins.*

32. Alvin Poussaint, "The Negro American: His Self-Image and Integration" in Barbour, *The Black Power Revolt,* p. 94.

33. Ibid., p. 96.

34. Fanon, Poussaint, and others agree.

35. Poussaint, in Barbour, *The Black Power Revolt,* p. 95.
36. Ibid., p. 99.
37. Wright, *Native Son* (New York: Harper & Row, 1966 ed.), pp. 311–312.
38. Lerone Bennett, *Confrontation: Black and White* (Baltimore: Penguin Books, 1966), pp. 254–255. Used with permission of Johnson Publishing Co., Chicago, the original publishers (copyright © 1965).
39. "Freedom's Journal," March, 1827, quoted in Silberman, *Crisis in Black and White,* p. 189.
40. Leo Tolstoy, quoted in ibid., p. 224.
41. Wright, *Native Son,* p. 395.
42. Bennett, *Confrontation,* p. 256.
43. Fanon, *Black Skins,* p. 85.
44. Ibid., p. 86.
45. Ibid.
46. Clark, *Dark Ghetto,* p. 229.
47. Quoted in Fanon, *Black Skins* (Copyright © 1967 by Grove Press), p. 89. Emphasis added. Used with permission.
48. Ibid., pp. 88–89.
49. Quoted in ibid., p. 90. Used with permission.
50. Quoted in ibid., pp. 91–92.
51. Quoted in Francis L. Broderick and August Meier, *Negro Protest Thought in the Twentieth Century* (New York: Bobbs-Merrill Co., 1965), p. 334.
52. For an analysis of John Brown by black writers, see W. E. B. DuBois, *John Brown* (New York: International Publishers, 1962); and Bennett, *Confrontation* and *Negro Mood.*

REVOLUTION: IT'S NOT NEAT OR PRETTY OR QUICK

Pat Parker

The following speech was given at the BASTA conference in Oakland, California, in August 1980. It represented three organizations: The Black Women's Revolutionary Council, the Eleventh Hour Battalion, and the Feminist Women's Health Center in Oakland.

I have been to many conferences: People's Constitutional convention in Washington, D.C., Women's Conference on Violence in San Francisco, Lesbian conference in Los Angeles, International Tribunal on Crimes Against Women in Belgium. I've been to more conferences than I can name and to many I would like to forget, but I have never come to a conference with as much anticipation and feeling of urgency.

We are in a critical time. Imperialist forces in the world are finding themselves backed against the wall; no longer able to control the world with the threat of force. And they are getting desperate. And they should be desperate. What we do here this weekend and what we take from this conference can be the difference, the deciding factor as to whether a group of women will ever again be able to meet not only in this country, but the entire world. We are facing the most critical time in the history of the world. The superpowers cannot afford for us to join forces and work to rid this earth of them, and we cannot afford not to.

In order to leave here prepared to be a strong force in the fight against imperialism we must have a clear understanding of what imperialism is and how it manifests itself in our lives. It is perhaps easier for us to understand the nature of imperialism when we look at how this country deals with other countries. It doesn't take a great amount of political sophistication to see how the interest of oil companies played a role in our relationship with the Shah's Iran. The people of Iran were exploited in order for Americans to drive gas guzzling monsters. And that is perhaps the difficult part of imperialism for us to understand.

The rest of the world is being exploited in order to maintain our standard of living. We who are 5 percent of the world's population use 40 percent of the world's oil.

5   As anti-imperialists we must be prepared to destroy all imperialist governments; and we must realize that by doing this we will drastically alter the standard of living that we now enjoy. We cannot talk on one hand about making revolution in this country, yet be unwilling to give up our video tape records and recreational vehicles. An anti-imperialist understands the exploita-

tion of the working class, understands that in order for capitalism to function, there must be a certain percentage that is unemployed. We must also define our friends and enemies based on their stand on imperialism.

At this time, the super powers are in a state of decline. The Iranians rose up and said no to U.S. imperialism; the Afghanis and Eritreans are saying no to Soviet-social imperialism. The situation has become critical and the only resource left is world war between the U.S. and the Soviet Union. We are daily being given warning that war is imminent. To some people, this is no significant change, just escalation. The Blacks, poor whites, Chicanos, and other oppressed people of this country already know we're at war.

And the rest of the country's people are being prepared. The media is bombarding us with patriotic declarations about "our" hostages and "our" embassy in Iran. This government is constantly reminding us of our commitment to our allies in Israel. Ads inviting us to become the few, the chosen, the marine or fly with the air force, etc. are filling our television screens.

And it doesn't stop there. This system is insidious in its machinations. It's no coincidence that the "right wing" of this country is being mobilized. Media sources are bombarding us with the news of KKK and Nazi party activity. But we who were involved in the civil rights movement are very familiar with these tactics. We remember the revelations of FBI agents, not only infiltrating the Klan but participating in and leading their activities. And we are not for one moment fooled by these manipulations.

The Klan and the Nazis are our enemies and must be stopped, but to simply mobilize around stopping them is not enough. They are functionaries, tools of this governmental system. They serve in the same way as our armed forces and police. To end Klan or Nazi activity doesn't end imperialism. It doesn't end institutional racism; it doesn't end sexism; it does not bring this monster down, and we must not forget what our goals are and who our enemies are. To simply label these people as lunatic fringes and not accurately assess their roles as part of this system is a dangerous error. These people do the dirty work. They are the arms and legs of the congressmen, the businessmen, the Tri-lateral Commission.

And the message they bring is coming clear. Be a good American—Support registration for the draft. The equation is being laid out in front of us. Good American = Support imperialism and war.

To this, I must declare—I am not a good American. I do not wish to have the world colonized, bombarded and plundered in order to eat steak.

Each time a national liberation victory is won I applaud and support it. It means we are one step closer to ending the madness that we live under. It means we weaken the chains that are binding the world.

Yet to support national liberation struggles alone is not enough. We must actively fight within the confines of this country to bring it down. I am not prepared to let other nationalities do my dirty work for me. I want the people of Iran to be free. I want the people of Puerto Rico to be free, but I am a revolutionary feminist because I want me to be free. And it is critically important

10

to me that you who are here, that your commitment to revolution is based on the fact that you want revolution for yourself.

In order for revolution to be possible, and revolution *is* possible, it must be led by the poor and working class people of this country. Our interest does not lie with being a part of this system, and our tendencies to be co-opted and diverted are lessened by the realization of our oppression. We know and understand that our oppression is not simply a question of nationality but that poor and working class people are oppressed throughout the world by the imperialist powers.

15   We as women face a particular oppression, not in a vacuum but as a part of this corrupt system. The issues of women are the issues of the working class as well. By not having this understanding, the women's movement has allowed itself to be co-opted and mis-directed.

It is unthinkable to me as a revolutionary feminist that some women's liberationist would entertain the notion that women should be drafted in exchange for passage of the ERA. This is a clear example of not understanding imperialism and not basing one's political line on its destruction. If the passage of the ERA means that I am going to become an equal participant in the exploitation of the world; that I am going to bear arms against other Third World people who are fighting to reclaim what is rightfully theirs—then I say Fuck the ERA.

One of the difficult questions for us to understand is just "what is revolution?" Perhaps we have had too many years of media madness with "revolutionary eye make-up and revolutionary tampons." Perhaps we have had too many years of Hollywood fantasy where the revolutionary man kills his enemies and walks off into the sunset with his revolutionary woman who has been waiting for his return. And that's the end of the tale.

The reality is that revolution is not a one step process: you fight—you win—it's over. It takes years. Long after the smoke of the last gun has faded away the struggle to build a society that is classless, that has no traces of sexism and racism in it, will still be going on. We have many examples of societies in our life time that have had successful armed revolution. And we have no examples of any country that has completed the revolutionary process. Is Russia now the society that Marx and Lenin dreamed? Is China the society that Mao dreamed? Before and after armed revolution there must be education, and analysis, and struggle. If not, and even if so, one will be faced with coups, counterrevolution and revision.

The other illusion is that revolution is neat. It's not neat or pretty or quick. It is a long dirty process. We will be faced with decisions that are not easy. We will have to consider the deaths of friends and family. We will be faced with the decisions of killing members of our own race.

20   Another illusion that we suffer under in this country is that a single facet of the population can make revolution. Black people alone cannot make a revolution in this country. Native American people alone cannot make revolution in this country. Chicanos alone cannot make revolution in this country.

Asians alone cannot make revolution in this country. White people alone cannot make revolution in this country. Women alone cannot make revolution in this country. Gay people alone cannot make revolution in this country. And anyone who tries it will not be successful.

Yet it is critically important for women to take a leadership role in this struggle. And I do not mean leading the way to the coffee machine.

A part of the task charged to us this week-end is deciding the direction we must take. First I say let us reclaim our movement. For too long I have watched the white-middle class be represented as my leaders in the women's movement. I have often heard that the women's movement is a white middle class movement.

I am a feminist. I am neither white nor middle class. And the women that I've worked with were like me. Yet I am told that we don't exist, and that we didn't exist. Now I understand that the racism and classism of some women in the movement prevented them from seeing me and people like me. But I also understand that with the aid of the media many middle class women were made more visible. And this gave them an opportunity to use their skills gained through their privilege to lead the movement into at first reformist and now counterrevolutionary bullshit.

These women allowed themselves to be red-baited and dyke-baited into isolating and ignoring the progressive elements of the women's movement. And I, for one, am no longer willing to watch a group of self-serving reformist idiots continue to abort the demands of revolutionary thinking women. You and I are the women's movement. Its leadership and direction should come from us.

We are charged with the task of rebuilding and revitalizing the dreams of the 60's and turning it into the reality of the 80's. And it will not be easy. At the same time that we must weed reformist elements out of our movement we will have to fight tooth and nail with our brothers and sisters of the left. For in reality, we are "all products of a decadent capitalist society."

At the same time that we must understand and support the men and women of national liberation struggles—the left must give up its undying loyalty to the nuclear family. In the same way it is difficult for upper and middle class women to give up their commitment to the nuclear family, but the nuclear family is the basic unit of capitalism and in order for us to move to revolution it has to be destroyed. And I mean destroyed. The male left has duped too many women with cries of genocide into believing it is revolutionary to be bound to babies. As to the question of abortion, I am appalled at the presumptions of men. The question is whether or not we have control of our bodies which in turn means control of our community and its growth. I believe that Black women are as intelligent as white women and we know when to have babies or not. And I want no man regardless of color to tell me when and where to bear children. As long as women are bound by the nuclear family structure we cannot effectively move toward revolution. And if women don't move, it will not happen.

25

We do not have an easy task before us. At this conference we will disagree; we will get angry; we will fight. This is good and should be welcomed. Here is where we should air our differences but here is also where we should build. In order to survive in this world we must make a commitment to change it; not reform it—revolutionize it. Here is where we begin to build a new women's movement, not one easily co-opted and mis-directed by media pigs and agents of this insidious imperialist system. Here is where we begin to build a revolutionary force of women. Judy Grahn in the "She Who" poem says, "When she who moves, the earth will turn over." You and I are the she who and if we dare to struggle, dare to win, this earth will turn over.

FEMINIST REVOLUTION: DEVELOPMENT THROUGH STRUGGLE

bell hooks

Today hardly anyone speaks of feminist revolution. Thinking that revolution would happen simply and quickly, militant feminist activists felt that the great surges of activity—protest, organizing, and consciousness-raising—which characterized the early contemporary feminist movement were all it would take to establish a new social order. Although feminist radicals have always recognized that society must be transformed if sexist oppression is to be eliminated, feminist successes have been mainly in the area of reforms (this is due primarily to the efforts and visions of radical groups like Bread and Roses and the Combahee River Collective, etc.). Such reforms have helped many women make significant strides towards social equality with men in a number of areas within the present white supremacist, patriarchal system but these reforms have not corresponded with decreased sexist exploitation and/or oppression. Prevailing sexist values and assumptions remain intact and it has been easy for politically conservative anti-feminists to undermine feminist reforms. Many politically progressive critics of feminist movement see the impulse towards reforms as counter-productive. Arguing in favor of reforms as a stage in revolutionary process in her essay "Feminism: Reform or Revolution," Sandra Harding writes:

> . . . it could well be that the reformers have in mind a long-range goal, which is something like a picture of a new society. The reforms fill in that picture bit by bit. Some pieces can be filled in with comparatively little trouble (e.g., equal pay for equal work), other pieces are filled in only with great difficulty (e.g., equal access to every job). But whether the difficulty is great or small, there is always a precedent in the society—somewhere—for each kind of change, and the only changes demanded are those which fill in the picture of the desired new society. Thus at the end of a long series of small quantitative changes, everything would have changed gradually so that the whole system was completely different. . . . On this alternative model a series of reforms might constitute a revolution.

Reforms can be a vital part of the movement towards revolution but what is important is the types of reforms that are initiated. Feminist focus on reforms to improve the social status of women within the existing social structure allowed women and men to lose sight of the need for total transformation of society. The ERA campaign, for example, diverted a great deal of money and human resources towards a reform effort that should have been a massive political campaign to build a feminist constituency. This constituency would have guaranteed the success of the ERA. Unfortunately, revolutionary reforms focused first and foremost on educating masses of women and men about feminist movement, showing them ways it would transform their lives for the better, were not initiated. Instead women involved with feminist reforms were inclined to think less about transforming society and more about fighting for equality and equal rights with men.

Many radical activists in the women's movement who were not interested in obtaining social equality with men in the existing social structure chose to attack exploitative and oppressive sexist behavior. Identifying men as the villains, the "enemy," they concentrated their attention on exposing male "evil." One example of this has been the critique and attack on pornography. It is obvious that pornography promotes degradation of women, sexism, and sexualized violence. It is also obvious that endless denunciations of pornography are fruitless if there is not greater emphasis on transforming society and by implication sexuality. This more significant struggle has not been seriously attended to by feminist movement. The focus on "men" and "male behavior" has overshadowed emphasis on women developing themselves politically so that we can begin making the cultural transformations that would pave the way for the establishment of a new social order. Much feminist consciousness-raising has centered on helping women to understand the nature of sexism in personal life, especially as it relates to male dominance. While this is a necessary task, it is not the only task for consciousness-raising.

Feminist consciousness-raising has not significantly pushed women in the direction of revolutionary politics. For the most part, it has not helped women understand capitalism: how it works, as a system that exploits female labor and its inter-connections with sexist oppression. It has not urged women to learn about different political systems like socialism or encouraged women to invent and envision new political systems. It has not attacked materialism and our society's addiction to over-consumption. It has not shown women how we benefit from the exploitation and oppression of women and men globally or shown us ways to oppose imperialism. Most importantly, it has not continually confronted women with the understanding that feminist movement to end sexist oppression can be successful only if we are committed to revolution, to the establishment of a new social order.

New social orders are established gradually. This is hard for individuals in the United States to accept. We have either been socialized to believe revolutions are always characterized by extreme violence between the oppressed and their oppressors or that revolutions happen quickly. We have also been taught to crave immediate gratification of our desires and swift responses to our demands. Like every other liberation movement in this society, feminism has suffered because these attitudes keep participants from forming the kind of commitment to protracted struggle that makes revolution possible. As a consequence, feminist movement has not sustained its revolutionary momentum. It has been a successful rebellion. Differentiating between rebellion and revolution Grace and James Boggs emphasize:

> Rebellion is a stage in the development of revolution, but it is not revolution. It is an important stage because it represents the "standing up," the assertion of their humanity on the part of the oppressed. Rebellion informs both the oppressed and everybody else that a situation has become intolerable. They establish a form of communication among the oppressed themselves and at the same time open the eyes and ears of people who have been blind and deaf to the fate of their fellow citizens. Rebellions break the threads that have been holding the system together and throw into question the legitimacy and the supposed permanence of existing institutions. They shake up old values so that relations between individuals and between groups within the society are unlikely ever to be the same again. The inertia of the society has been interrupted. Only by understanding what a rebellion accomplishes can we see its limitations. A rebellion disrupts the society, but it does not provide what is necessary to establish a new social order.

Although feminist rebellion has been a success it is not leading to further   5
revolutionary development. Internally its progress is retarded by those feminist activists who do not feel that the movement exists for the advancement of all women and men, who seem to think it exists to advance individual participants, who are threatened by opinions and ideas that differ from the dominant feminist ideology, who seek to suppress and silence dissenting voices, who do not acknowledge the necessity for continued effort to create a liberatory ideology. These women resist efforts to critically examine prevailing feminist ideology and refuse to acknowledge its limitations. Externally the progress of feminist movement is retarded by organized anti-feminist activity and by the political indifference of masses of women and men who are not well enough acquainted with either side of the issue to take a stand.

To move beyond the stage of feminist rebellion, to move past the impasse that characterizes contemporary feminist movement, women must recognize the need for reorganization. Without dismissing the positive dimensions of feminist movement up to this point, we need to accept that there was never a strategy on the part of feminist organizers and participants to build mass awareness of the need for feminist movement through political education. Such a strategy is needed if feminism is to be a political movement impacting on society as a whole in a revolutionary and transformative way. We also need to face the fact that many of the dilemmas facing feminist movement today were created by bourgeois women who shaped the movement in ways that served their opportunistic class interests. We must now work to change its direction so that women of all classes can see that their interest in ending sexist oppression is served by feminist movement. Recognizing that bourgeois opportunists have exploited feminist movement should not be seen as an attack upon all bourgeois women. There are individual bourgeois women who are repudiating class privilege, who are politically progressive, who have given, are giving, or are willing to give of themselves in a revolutionary way to advance feminist movement. Reshaping the class politics of feminist movement is strategy that will lead women from all classes to join feminist struggle.

To build a mass-based feminist movement, we need to have a liberatory ideology that can be shared with everyone. That revolutionary ideology can be created only if the experiences of people on the margin who suffer sexist oppression and other forms of group oppression are understood, addressed, and incorporated. They must participate in feminist movement as makers of theory and as leaders of action. In past feminist practice, we have been satisfied with relying on self-appointed individuals, some of whom are more concerned about exercising authority and power than with communicating with people from various backgrounds and political perspectives. Such individuals do not choose to learn about collective female experience, but impose their own ideas and values. Leaders are needed, and should be individuals who acknowledge their relationship to the group and who are accountable to it. They should have the ability to show love and compassion, show this love through their actions, and be able to engage in successful dialogue. Such love, Paulo Freire suggests, acts to transform domination:

> Dialogue cannot exist, however, in the absence of profound
> love for the world and for women and men. The naming of the
> world, which is an act of creation and re-creation, is not possi-
> ble if it is not infused with love. Love is at the same time the
> foundation of dialogue and dialogue itself. It is thus necessarily
> the task of responsible subjects and cannot exist in a relation of
> domination. Domination reveals the pathology of love: sadism
> in the dominator and masochism in the dominated. Because
> love is an act of courage, not of fear, love is commitment to
> others. No matter where the oppressed are found, the act of
> love is commitment to their cause—the cause of liberation.
> And this commitment, because it is loving, is dialogical. . . .

Women must begin the work of feminist reorganization with the understanding that we have all (irrespective of our race, sex, or class) acted in complicity with the existing oppressive system. We all need to make a conscious break with the system. Some of us make this break sooner than others. The compassion we extend to ourselves, the recognition that our change in consciousness and acting has been a process, must characterize our approach to those individuals who are politically unconscious. We cannot motivate them to join feminist struggle by asserting a political superiority that makes the movement just another oppressive hierarchy.

Before we can address the masses, we must recapture the attention, the support, the participation of the many women who were once active in feminist movement and who left disillusioned. Too many women have abandoned feminist movement because they cannot support the ideas of a small minority of women who have hegemonic control over feminist discourse the development of the theory that informs practice. Too many women who have caring bonds with men have drifted away from feminist movement because they feel that identification of "man as enemy" is an unconstructive paradigm. Too many women have ceased to support feminist struggle because the ideology has been too dogmatic, too absolutist, too closed. Too many women have left feminist movement because they were identified as the "enemy." Feminist activists would do well to heed the words of Susan Griffin when she reminds us in her essay "The Way of All Ideology":

> For a deeply political knowledge of the world does not lead to a creation of an enemy. Indeed, to create monsters unexplained by circumstances is to forget the political vision which above all explains behavior as emanating from circumstance, a vision which believes in a capacity born to all human beings for creation, joys, and kindness, in a human nature which, under the right circumstances, can bloom.
>
> When a movement for liberation inspires itself chiefly by a hatred for an enemy rather than from this vision of possibility, it begins to defeat itself. Its very notions cease to be healing. Despite the fact that it declares itself in favor of liberation, its language is no longer liberatory. It begins to require a censorship within itself. Its ideas of truth become more and more narrow. And the movement that began with a moving evocation of truth begins to appear fraudulent from the outside, begins to mirror all that it says it opposes, for now it, too, is an oppressor of certain truths, and speakers, and begins, like the old oppressors, to hide from itself.

To restore the revolutionary life force to feminist movement, women and men must begin to re-think and re-shape its direction. While we must recognize, acknowledge, and appreciate the significance of feminist rebellion and the women (and men) who made it happen, we must be willing to criticize, re-examine, and begin feminist work anew, a challenging task because we lack historical precedents. There are many ways to make revolution. Revolutions can be and usually are initiated by violent overthrow of an existing political structure. In the United States, women and men committed to feminist struggle know that we are far outpowered by our opponents, that they not only have access to every type of weaponry known to humankind, but they have both the learned consciousness to do and accept violence as well as the skill to perpetuate it. Therefore, this cannot be the basis for feminist revolution in this society. Our emphasis must be on cultural transformation: destroying dualism, eradicating systems of domination. Our struggle will be gradual and protracted. Any effort to make feminist revolution here can be aided by the example of liberation struggles led by oppressed peoples globally who resist formidable powers.

The formation of an oppositional world view is necessary for feminist struggle. This means that the world we have most intimately known, the world in which we feel "safe" (even if such feelings are based on illusions), must be radically changed. Perhaps it is the knowledge that everyone must change, not just those we label enemies or oppressors, that has so far served to check our revolutionary impulses. Those revolutionary impulses must freely inform our theory and practice if feminist movement to end existing oppression is to progress, if we are to transform our present reality.

TOWARD THE NEW FRONTIERS OF FAIRY VISION . . . subject-SUBJECT CONSCIOUSNESS

Harry Hay

This last summer [1979] that wonderful Gay brother Don Kilhefner, together with John Burnside, Mitch Walker, and I, evoked a Spiritual Conference for Radical Fairies to be held in the Arizona Desert over the Labor Day weekend. At the opening of that Gathering, we called upon Gay Brothers to tear off the ugly green frog-skin of Hetero-male imitation in which we had wrapped ourselves in order to get through school with a full set of teeth to reveal the beautiful Fairy Prince hidden beneath.

Perhaps—before I go any further—I should explain what I mean by Fairy Spirituality. To me the term "spiritual" represents the accumulation of all experiential consciousness from the division of the first cells in the primeval slime, down through all biological-political-social evolution to your and to my latest insights through Gay Consciousness just a moment ago. What else can we call this overwhelmingly magnificent inheritance—other than spiritual?

The pathways we explored, during our Desert Retreat, to transform ourselves from Hetero-imitating Gays into Radical Fairies were many. Because the old ways of fairy transformation were obliterated during the nightmarish centuries of Judeo-Christian oppression, we felt ourselves free to invent new ones. So . . . to begin with . . .

- We reached out to reunite ourselves with the cornered, frightened, rejected little Sissy-kids we all once were;

- We reached out to recapture and restore in full honors that magick of "being a different species perceiving a different reality" (so beautifully projected almost a century ago by J. M. Barrie's *Peter Pan*) which may have encapsulated our boyhood and adolescence;

- We told that *different* boy that he was remembered . . . loved . . . and deeply respected;

- We told him we now recognized that he, in true paradox, had always been the real source of our Dream, of our strength to resist, of our stubborn endurance—a strength, again in true paradox, that few Hetero Males can even begin to approach, let alone match;

- We told that beloved little Sissy that we had experienced a full paradigm shift and that he could now come home at last to be himself in full appreciation.

Carl Jung, in this respect, proved to be absolutely right. When the Fairies reached out to make reunion with that long-ago-cast-out shadow-self so long suppressed and denied, the explosive energies released by the jubilations of those reunions were ecstatic beyond belief. When we caught up that lonely little Sissy-boy in an ecstatic hug of reuniting, we were recapturing also the suddenly remembered sense of awe and wonder of Marvelous Mother Nature who in those years so powerfully surrounded him. We were—yes—even re-capturing the glowing innocence of that Sissy-boy's Dream. And in that Dream, the glowing non-verbal dream of young Gayhood, may lie the key to the enormous and particular contribution that Gay people may have to make to our beloved Humankind—a key known as *subject-SUBJECT Consciousness.*

5   How to infect other Fairies with the same excitement we bubbled with in the Desert, and have soared and circled with ever since? One way would be to share the steps by which *we* made the breakthroughs to riveting percep-tions hereinafter to be known as subject-SUBJECT Consciousness. And then, beyond that, to share some of the gleaming insights these new dimensions to the Gay Vision lend to problems that heretofore have locked us in.

To begin: How old were you when you first began to be aware that you held a sense of beauty, an excitement, within you that was different from what other boys felt? I must have been about four when one night I inadvertently beheld my father's genitals. I thought they were the most beautiful things I'd ever seen. And—equally—in that flashing instant I knew I could never tell this *to anybody!* I was nine when my Father attempted to *unmake* the Sissy in me by teaching me to use a pair of boxing gloves—and I simply *couldn't* under-stand why he wanted me to hit somebody else (sixty years later I can still feel the stifling paralysis of that bewilderment). I didn't want to hurt the other boys, I wanted to be tender to them in the same way I wanted them to be ten-der to me—*even as I also knew,* in that very same moment, that here again I couldn't share such heresies WITH ANYONE. All this time I would pretend that I had a friend who felt the same was as I did, *and who understood everything.* But of course I knew there was really no such person. I knew that I was the only one like this in the whole world!

And then came that wonderful day—that shattering day, full of glitter and glisten and fireworks in my head and tumult of thunder and trumpets in my blood—when I discovered a *word,* a name, even though it was not yet in or-dinary dictionaries, for me—FOR US! I wasn't the *only* one after all. I wasn't a wicked genie. I wasn't possessed by Evil or, maybe, crazy. There had been *others*—maybe even now others—maybe even one whom someday I could meet. Another—*just like me*—who would understand *everything.* And he would reach for my hand and we would run to the top of the hill to see the sunrise . . . and we'd never be lonely again! My source, of course, was a book by Edward Carpenter, in the locked glass cabinet behind the Lady Librarian's desk. There was another book in the case—about grass—by a man named Whitman, which I would discover on another day when the Librarian had to step out on an errand.

I suppose I was about eleven when I began first thinking about, and then fantasizing about, *him*! And, of course, I perceived him *as subject*. I knew that all the other kids around me thought of girls as SEX-OBJECTS to be manipulated, to be lied to in order to get them to "give in," and to be otherwise (when the boys were together without them) treated with contempt. And strangely, the girls seemed to think of the boys as objects, too. But HE whom I would *love* would be another ME. We wouldn't manipulate each other—*we would share*—and we'd always understand each other completely *and forever*!

Then came that second shattering day in my life, when I first met that other. And suddenly, between us, that socially invisible Arc flashed out and zapped into both our eagerly ready bodies *total systems of knowledge*; perhaps one of those inheritable consciousnesses which Dr. Ralph Sperry of Cal Tech has recently been rewarded for discovering—a system of knowledge which our flesh and brains had always been capable of but never, until that moment of imprinting, had actually contained. Like two new-hatched chicks whose incubator-attendant has now sharply tapped on their tray so that their feet, registering the vibrations, suddenly trigger body-mechanisms by which the chicks can know to peck at the ground around their feet thereby triggering further, in turn, how to feed an drink—so we two young Fairies knew, through that flashing Arc of Love, the tumult of Gay Consciousness in our vibrant young bodies in ways that we, in the moments before, never could have imagined and now would never again forget for as long as we lived. And this, *in ourselves and, simultaneously, in each other,* we also knew—subject-to-SUBJECT!

We must not suppose that we share subject-SUBJECT vision *only* in the spheres of Love and personal relations. Actually, almost at once, we also begin to become aware that we have been accumulating bits and pieces of subject-SUBJECT perceptions and insights all our lives—talking to trees and birds and rocks and Teddy Bears, and remembering what all we had shared by putting it down in poetry, storing it all up for that wonderful day when we finally would flash on to what it all meant. The personal collecting and storing up of these secret treasures, these beautiful beckoning not-as-yet comprehensible secret sacra, is part of the hidden misery-cum-exaltation of growing up Gay. For the world we inherit, the total Hetero-Male-oriented-and-dominated world of Tradition and of daily environment, the *summum bonum* of our history, our philosophy, our psychology, our culture, and very languages of communication—*all* are totally subject-OBJECT in concept, in definition, in evolution, in self-serving orientation. Men and Women are—sexually, emotionally, and spiritually—*objects* to one another.

Under the "fair-play-without-which-there-ain't-no-game" rules of Hetero-Male aggressive territoriality, even the Hetero-Males—precisely because they conceive of themselves as in lifelong competition each with the others—engage themselves endlessly in tug-of-war games of Domination and Submission. The most lofty system of governance the Hetero-Male has devised—Democracy—must be seen as a domination of Minorities by a Majority, a tyranny of the Majority if you will. Domination-submission, subject-OBJECT.

Fair play, the Golden Rule, Equality, Political Persuasion, give-and-take—all of these are conditions of subject-OBJECT thinking. In each case, a given person is the *object* of another person's perceptions, to be influenced, persuaded, cajoled, jaw-boned, manipulated and therefore, in the last analysis, *controlled*. In the parliaments of government, the game of administration is to persuade Minorities to make of themselves *objects of approval* instead of objects of *disapproval*—but *objects* nonetheless.

To all of this we fairies should be, essentially, alien. Because those *others* with whom we seek to link, to engage, to slip into, to merge with are others *like me,* are SUBJECTS . . . like *ME*! I say "we fairies *should be* alien" to as many aspects of our Hetero-Male-dominated surroundings as we can be sensitive to, because we also know, all too glumly, just how easily and how often we fall prey to self-invited oppressions. How often do we allow ourselves, through fuzzy thinking, to accept or to identify with Hetero-originating definitions or misinterpretations of ourselves? The Hetero-male, incapable of conceiving that there could possibly be a window on the world other than his own, is equally incapable of perceiving that we Gay People might no fit in *either* of his Man/Woman categories, that we might turn out to belong to quite other classifications. He might not be able to handle perceiving that the notion of all persons being only varying combinations of male and female is simply a Hetero-male-derived notion suitable only to Heteros and *holding nothing of validity insofar as Gay people are concerned.*

Yet we fairies allow Bully-boy to persuade us to search out the "feminine" in ourselves—didn't good old Bully-boy used to tell us we threw balls like a girl? Wow, that surely is pretty sexist thinking we've internalized right there. Did you ever ask the girls back then if they thought you threw a ball like them? *They'd* have straightened you out in nothing flat! *They'd* have told you that you didn't throw a ball like a girl, but like something *other.* You were *not* a feminine boy, like the boys said, you were OTHER!

What *other*? Let us enter this brave new world of subject-SUBJECT consciousness, this new planet of Fairy-vision, and find out. All kinds of our friends would like to hear what we see. For instance, the Women of Women's Liberation would give their eyeteeth to know how to develop some measure of subject-to-SUBJECT relations with their men. And we who have known the jubilation of subject-to-SUBJECT visions and visitations *all our lives* have neither shared nor even spoken!

15   Of course, we haven't as yet spoken because we haven't as yet learned how to communicate subject-SUBJECT realities. Subject-SUBJECT is a multidimensional consciousness which may never be readily conveyable in the Hetero-male-evolved two-dimensional, or Binary, language to which we are presently confined. And we need more than mere words and phrases. We need what Scientists invent out of whole cloth when they attempt to describe and communicate new concepts. We need working models, a whole new mathematics, perhaps a new poetry—allegories—metaphors—a music—a new way of dancing. *We must re-examine every system of thought heretofore developed,* every

Hetero-male-evolved subject-OBJECT philosophy, science, religion, mythology, political system, language—divesting them every one of their binary subject-OBJECT base and re-inserting a subject-SUBJECT relation. Confronted with the loving-sharing Consensus of subject-SUBJECT relationships *all Authoritarianism must vanish.* The Fairy Family Circle, co-joined in the shared vision of *non-possessive love*—which is the granting to any other and all others that total space wherein each may grow and soar to his own freely selected, full potential—reaching out to one another subject-to-SUBJECT, *becomes for the first time in history the true working model of a Sharing Consensus!*

To even begin to prepare ourselves for a fuller participation in our Gay subject-SUBJECT inheritance, we must, both daily and hourly, practice throwing off all those Hetero-imitating habits, compulsions, and ways of misperceiving which we constantly breathe in from our environmental surround. For this practice we need the constant company of our Fairy Families. We need the spiritual and emotional support of that non-verbal empathy which Sociologists assure us comprises almost seven-eighths of communication in any culture, that empathy we now refer to as Body Language. We need the marvelous input of each other's minute-by-minute new discoveries, as each of us begins to explore this vast new universe, this subject-SUBJECT frontier of human consciousness. As ours are the first deliberate feet upon this pristine shore, there are no guide-posts as yet erected, nor maps to be found in bottles, nor even the prospectuses of ancient visionary seers.

Well . . . not *quite* right. Sufi, for instance, is a philosophical discipline capable of bringing its students to subject-SUBJECT ways of relating and perceiving the landscapes of earth and heaven around them. It was invented and developed by Gay Persian mystic poets and kindred Islamic scholars, such as the great philosopher-poet Omar Khayyám, during the eleventh and twelfth centuries A.D.[1] It has long been generally recognized that Sufi vision was a capacity open only to a few—though the theory never went on to say *why.* For those capable of cultivating subject-to-SUBJECT vision, explanations were not necessary. For the Heteros, who were incapable of subject-to-SUBJECT perceptions, explanations could only have been incomprehensible.

In the last decade, Hetero Flower Children have revived some of Sufi's trance-inducing rituals *without,* however, comprehending the spiritual prerequisite that the participants be capable of relating *to each other,* as well as to the landscape and skyscape around, subject-to-SUBJECT, physically as well as emotionally and intellectually. Now it is time for Fairies to reclaim these penetrating exercises and restore to Sufi its liberating and transcendent capacities for subject-to-SUBJECT thought and perception.

Re-working all previously developed systems of Hetero thought will mean, of course, that all the data we previously have gathered concerning Shamanism and Magick must also be *re-*examined, *re-*worked, and *re-*organized along subject-SUBJECT evaluations—which is just as well because, for instance, failing to perceive the *lethal* subject-OBJECT character of most traditionally evolved Berdache ritualism and priestcraft, Gay scholars have tragically *misled* brothers and sisters of vulnerable minorities and thereby, in consequence, toxi-fied themselves at precisely those moments when we desperately needed their crystalline clarifications.[2]

20
It is time, therefore, that we Fairies faced the reality that *no* Hetero-dominated culture, geared as each of them is to subject-OBJECT conformi-ties, is ever about to discover acceptable Gay-Consciousness-tolerances with themselves if left to their own devices. *Only* when we Fairies begin to vali-date the contributions Gay Consciousness is capable of developing and deliv-ering are the Heteros going to begin to sit up and take notice. Only when we begin to manifest the new dimensions of subject-SUBJECT relationships su-perimposed over the now-obsolete Hetero subject-OBJECT traditions—*and the Heteros begin to perceive the value of that superimposition*—will they begin to see a value in altering their priorities. Only when they begin to become aware of their need for our contributions to their world-visions (and when they equally discover *that their laws are in our way,* impeding our further output in their favor) will they find themselves sufficiently challenged to restructure their perceptions of essential human variations.

In the meantime, Fairies everywhere must begin to stand tall and beauti-ful in the sun. Fairies must begin to throw off the filthy green frog-skin of Hetero-Imitation and discover the lovely Gay-Conscious not-MAN (*anandros,* as the discerning early Greeks called us) shining underneath. Fairies must begin creating their new world through fashioning for themselves supportive Families of Conscious Choice within which they can explore, in the loving security of shared consensus, the endless depths and diversities of the newly revealed subject-SUBJECT inheritances of the Gay Vision!

Let us gather therefore—
   in secure and consecrated places . . .
To re-invoke from ancient ashes our Fairy Circle . . .
To dance . . .
To meditate—not in the singular isolation of Hetero subject-OBJECT praxis,
   but rather in Fairy Circles reaching out to one another in subject-SUBJECT
   evocation . . .
To find new ways to cherish one another . . .
To invent new rhyme and reason and ritual
   replacing those obliterated in the long nightmare of our
   Oppression—and so, in fact, re-invent ourselves . . .
To break through to ever more spiritually encompassing and emotionally resurrec-
   tive Gay Families and Fairy Family Collectives, who by the very mutuality of
   their subject-SUBJECT sharing are strengthened to reach out contributively to
   the Hetero community around them . . .
And so finally—
To penetrate ever more comprehensively the essential nature of
   covenants needed to lay the groundwork of a new worldwide subject-
   SUBJECT consciousness SHARABLE BY ALL!

NOTES

1. Jalāl al-Din-Rūmī (1207–1273 C.E.) is another Sufi whose poetry exudes homoerotic sentiment. See Will Roscoe, *Queer Spirits: A Gay Men's Myth Book* (Boston: Beacon, 1995), pp. 202–7.

2. Hay means that Berdaches were involved in the spiritual belief systems of their tribes, which reflected a predominantly heterosexual orientation. Blind imitation of Two-Spirit roles or romantic idealization of their social status misses a crucial distinction. Only in recent history have those individuals who now identify as Gay had the opportunity to form genuinely subject-SUBJECT relationships and to develop a self-conscious "Gay window."

17

Resistance Strategy Five: Coalition

■ ■ ■ ■

BREAKING A CYCLE

Elly Bulkin

The pitting of anti-Semitism and racism against each other, the pressure to see opposing them in either/or terms, arguments about the degrees of oppression, degrees of opposition—all are part of a cycle of competition which is oiled by the powers that be, and is often played into by those of us with relatively little power. The tension lurks at or just below the surface, ready to break out when some balance is not achieved, when some full acknowledgment is not granted to one group or the other. Sometimes the comparisons, the contrasts, the weighings are unavoidable. Sometimes they are done in ways that reflect one person's racism, another's anti-Semitism.

The cycle is fueled, in part, by what Melanie Kaye/Kantrowitz has called "the 'scarcity' theory of political struggle,"[1] the false assumption that ultimately one must choose which of the two oppressions to confront, that one cannot choose to oppose both. A Black woman ends an article on racism with a footnote that gratuitously explains why, in contrast to Blacks, Jews cannot properly be called an oppressed group.[2] Some Jewish women resent the visibility thus far of Third World women in the movement, the attention they see given to racism as opposed to Jewish oppression. Women Against Imperialism, a group of non-Jewish and Jewish white women, argues against "putting more energy into the issue of Jewish oppression than into the much more basic issue of support for [Third World] liberation struggles."[3]

Despite these arguments, despite the tangle of issues and the tensions within and between groups, feminists—Jewish and non-Jewish, Third World and white—have in the last few years increasingly acknowledged the ways that Jewish oppression and racism intersect; how, together and individually, they anger, hurt, endanger, divide us. In the process, strong feminist statements have been made which have refused the divisions.

Writing about being fired from a large Southwestern state university, Melanie Kaye/Kantrowitz has described how the anti-Jewish attitudes in the women's studies program merged with the specific "assumption, that to be a strongly identified Jew *meant* being less anti-racist, as though the struggles were mutually exclusive or, worse, antagonistic. . . ."[4] The subsequent dismissal by the white Christian coordinator of Kaye/Kantrowitz, "the only identified Jew in the program—and the only out dyke,"[5] left her clear about the various strains of bias—including classism—which had combined to get her fired. It also left her clear about her own belief that "there is no contradiction between being a proud Jew and a fighter against racism. I fight against racism because I am a Jew; because my Jewish parents taught me to hate injustice and cruelty; and because I know danger when I smell it."[6]

A similar argument is asserted by the lesbians from the Necessary Bread Affinity Group, "northern Black and southern white; Anglo, Jewish, daughters of engineers and domestic workers . . . first- and tenth-generation Americans, Cuban immigrants, transplanted Chicanas." In a statement prepared for the massive June 12, 1982 disarmament demonstration in New York City, Necessary Bread said:

> We know the fear of violence, not just from the Klan and the American Nazi Party, but from the less readily visible, the more "respectable," those who share the anti-Semitism and racism and queer-loathing of these groups, and could find in us "appropriate" targets for hatreds supported by every Establishment institution in this society.
>
> We know too that these threats, these acts of violence are meant to divide us, to make us see each other as the enemy. We refuse to accede to such pressure, regardless of its source.[7]

And the Jewish lesbian group Di Vilde Chayes has written:

> We do not accept the idea that our fight against anti-Semitism robs political energy from our fight against racism. To maintain that all our energy must be devoted to only one of these oppressions is divisive and strategically unsound.[8]

For all of us, Jew and non-Jew, white women and women of color, statements are, naturally, a lot easier to make than to act on. Words on the page are inevitably clearer than the words we must come up with when we have only seconds for a response and probably no time for rethinking or revisions, for putting the emphasis on *this* part of the sentence rather than on *that* one so that our intent is as precise as we can make it. Surely, statements are far clearer than the plans we make for outreach; the rap we prepare for streetcorner leafletting; the proposals we first make for political action and then reconsider, revise, perhaps defend, probably compromise on at a meeting at which everyone shares neither our individual identity nor our specific political perspective and priorities. And, in any event, we do not yet know how to raise the issues of Jewish oppression *and* racism in the best possible way, or, given the history and complexity of both, in ways that will assure us not only that we have done it well, but that we are likely to be heard.

Certainly, *I* do not know how to do it, especially when the issues intersect: when, for example, my stomach knots up as I pace back and forth, phone in hand, as I struggle for the words that will explain to a woman of color that I am not being "obstinate," as she charges, when I insist that I want to know what work on Jewish oppression another woman of color has done before I agree that she would be a good addition to a racism and anti-Semitism panel; when I struggle for the words that will, at the same time, acknowledge that our discussion is necessarily affected by my being white, by her history of dealing with white women who want simply to exercise power in such a situation. Or when, at a meeting between a Jewish and Black community group, I search for the language that will respond adequately to a Black man who wonders whether I am not asking an awful lot when I insist that, although he suffers frequently from the racism of people who are white and Jewish, he direct his anger at the whiteness that can allow us certain privileges, not at our Jewishness.

I do not think I am alone among Jewish women in the uncertainty of my reactions, in my frustration at being unable to pull out the exact words at the precise time I need them; in my anger at prejudices that render ineffective the most cogent argument; in my desire to do a better job of fighting Jewish oppression, of confronting racism; in my tendency to play and re-play interactions to try to figure out what I could have done better. Too often the dynamic is so complex that I am lucky to be able to pull apart the strands and look at them in the clear light before I am called upon for a response. Too often the strands will simply not be parted.

While ideally, we should all be actively opposed to every oppression, the reality is that it's exceedingly hard, sometimes near impossible, to work against the oppression of someone whose foot we feel on the back of our neck. The optimum political goal is, I think, quite clear. It is exemplified by the Combahee River Collective statement: "We struggle together with Black men against racism, while we also struggle with Black men about sexism."[9] Achieving a concrete political realization of that formulation is more complicated. The reality is that the racism of many white Jewish women discourages many non-Jewish women of color from strongly confronting Jewish oppression; the anti-Semitism of many non-Jewish women of color discourages many white Jewish women from being strongly anti-racist. The prejudice of each group is often affected by the other's actions. But it is not caused by these actions. Each has a life of its own. Each is the inevitable by-product of the society in which we live. And if a non-Jewish woman of color responds with anti-Semitism to my racism, she is no less responsible for her words and actions than I am for my own; if I counter her anti-Semitism with my own racism, I too play into a cycle that must, at some point, at every point, be broken.

The tendency for feminists to fall into this trap does not single out our movement from the rest of society as any less able to deal politically with these issues. Rather, it marks the women's movement as an extension of the larger society in which the same conflicts get raised with depressing regularity. A Black man objects that when a handful of Jews are killed the news gets front-page coverage in the daily papers, whereas when hundreds of Africans are murdered, the item gets tucked away in fifteen lines on page five; he focuses his anger on the Jews whose suffering has, for the moment, been recognized, rather than on a media that responds to Western political priorities, values the lives of those in the West over those in the Third World, and should be pressured into seeing as equally deplorable, equally newsworthy, deaths anywhere on the globe. A Jewish man objects to affirmative action quotas on the grounds that his Hungarian-born parents managed to pull themselves out of poverty without any such assistance; he focuses his anger on the people of color who benefit from such efforts, rather than on the institutional racism that has kept them from more than token representation in many jobs and professional schools.

For white Jewish feminists, breaking this cycle of competition involves, in part, how we perceive the racism *and* the anti-racism of the women's movement. From a white perspective, it is not all that difficult to overstate the commitment to fighting racism within the movement, and, as a consequence, to skew our expectation of what we can expect from it in opposition to Jewish oppression. Much of it is a question of our angle of vision. For over a decade, many parts of the women's movement have, after all, at least acknowledged racism as a critical issue; in some instances, the opposition to it by white women has gone well beyond acknowledgement. Yet this is a far cry from a movement that is fully dedicated to fighting racism.

The belief that a staunchly anti-racism women's movement exists does not take into account the *major* limitations of the anti-racist work done thus far by those of us who are white. Too often the steps we take are positive, but ultimately or potentially only cosmetic: the inclusion of racism on a list of organizational concerns; the Third World keynote speaker at a largely white feminist conference; the mailings of announcements by a white to a Third World group. Too often we magnify the mostly superficial gains made by women of color within a predominantly white women's movement, and forget their day-to-day encounters with racism.

One example from the 1981 National Women's Studies Conference on racism at the University of Connecticut: Going off campus with a half dozen women, I entered the local ice cream parlor immediately behind a dark-skinned Black woman. As she reached forward to open the restaurant door, she said quietly, but loud enough for me to hear, "Here I come, white folks!" I was momentarily startled, muttered something inane and hardly supportive, and realized that I was quite unprepared for this particular venture into white America. The moment I walked through the door, *my* skin-color did not grab the attention of the white person sitting over a sundae in the booth furthest away from where we entered. A few hours after I had been on a panel on racism in the lesbian community, I could imagine going out for an ice cream as a simple and uncomplicated act.

The world out there brings me up short, reminds me not just of what I have failed to accomplish, but of *why* I am even trying to do anti-racist work. It raises for me too the broader question as to why *anyone* who does not share the most immediate impact of some oppression makes a commitment to combat it. I find one answer in the link between ethics and self-interest. The most effective work by white Jews against racism, for instance, emerges, I think, from some combination of the two, the belief that racism is simply wrong *and* the belief that struggling against it will benefit us personally and politically, that such work, as Black feminist Alice Walker has said about opposition to any oppression, "lightens the load on all of us."[10]

15   Anti-racist activism by those of us who are white and Jewish in ways that make us visible *as Jews* who are also strongly committed to fighting anti-Semitism has the potential for *supporting* Jewish survival and Jewish concerns through our involvement in coalitions in which anti-Semitism can become integrated into political action and analysis. Such work can make non-Jews look at assumptions in ways that may lead them to rethink stereotypes and reconsider the impression that racism and Jewish oppression are at loggerheads, that one must select one or the other as a political priority.

Although ethics and enlightened self-interest together form an effective motivation for political work, separately they are sorely wanting. Done purely for others without a strong sense of its general benefits, such work can subsequently lead to the expectation of "repayment": "I'll focus on anti-racism in organizing this demonstration, so that later on I can get you to work against Jewish oppression." A consequence can be a surface commitment to the issues, so that they function as bargaining chips in a larger political game. Done solely as a means of raising consciousness, of assuaging guilt, of sharing feelings, the work is dead-ended, a form of political self-improvement quite alien to the kind of activist political perspective described by Mab Segrest when she writes, "whatever consciousness I arrive at through language must also find its expression in activity in the world."[11]

An analogous situation occurs when a non-Jewish woman of color includes anti-Semitism in a list of oppressions and sees Jews as a useful group with whom to work in anti-racist coalitions, but, perhaps talking about *other* women's anti-Jewish attitudes, does not consider her own, and, perhaps accepting without question references to historical and current anti-Semitism, does no work to attain more than a surface knowledge of it. In both cases, the issues remain abstract, picked up in an attempt to be "politically correct," to avoid criticism, to be politically expedient. In both cases, the question is deferred as to how doing such work will change not just the individual, but her relationship with everyone with whom she comes into contact, Jewish and non-Jewish, Third World and white.

Whatever our motivation, we need to begin with a clear sense that the two oppressions operate in the women's movement in different ways, that these differences will affect both analysis and strategy. Historically, as now, women of color in the movement have been excluded, tokenized, placed on a pedestal, and, when they work in autonomous Third World feminist groups, ignored by many white feminists. Frequently inclusion comes late: white women with the economic resources and institutional access to start a project seek Third World feminists to participate only when things are well under way; an issue is defined by white women who then ask women of color to provide input within already established parameters. In these kinds of situations, the women of color function more as political symbols than as individuals: when the participation of one or two or more women of color is used by white women to "prove" to themselves or others that Third World women *as a group* have "endorsed" a particular project or political stance; when white women apply a "dancing dog" double standard to women of color, the wonder being not that they are doing their work well, but that they are doing it all.[12]

Anti-Semitism in the movement operates differently. Jewish women in the U.S. have been central in the women's movement since its inception, though often not as identifiable Jews. The fact of centrality is difficult even to acknowledge because the standard anti-Jewish response is to see more than token Jewish visibility as a bid for "Jewish control": at the 1981 Women in Print Conference, all of the Jewish women were asked to stand. About a third of the women rose. But the pleasure those of us felt was dashed some time later when a report on the conference cited it as a place where the writer "learned that feminist publishing is controlled by JEWISH-WORKING-CLASS-LESBIANS and the 4-H,"[13] an attempt at humor that simply recalls the stereotype of Jews as in control of the media. For white Jewish women, unlike for women of color, the initial question is not presence but visibility.[14] "The question is," as Evelyn Torton Beck has said, "can Jewish women have a voice as Jewish women? Or is the price of being active and respected to be white but not Jewish?"[15]

While the Women in Print example illustrates an external pressure for Jewish women to be silent as Jews, Jewish oppression also manifests itself in what Letty Cottin Pogrebin has described as the "self-hatred and denial of a part of oneself or one's origins [that] is a kind of *invisibility imposed from within*."[16] Pogrebin's discussion places this invisibility squarely within a societal context of anti-Semitism that actively fosters self-hatred, rewards assimilation, and defines any visible Jewish presence as "too much." The relative silence among Jewish feminists about Jewish oppression must, I think, be seen within this framework.

It is essential not to fall into the trap of "blaming the victim." However, the responsibility for any silence regarding anti-Semitism has to be shared by those of us who did not *ourselves* raise it. This point is critical because one way

20

in which white Jewish women have seen women of color in competitive terms has to do with the fact that racism is now acknowledged in many parts of the women's movement where Jewish oppression is not. Going from competition to strategizing involves some historically-based understanding of the role of the oppressed in crying out against her oppression, in insisting that it be confronted. While it would be terrific for women to take the initiative to learn about oppressions that do not affect each of us most directly and to be active in opposing them, the unfortunate political reality is that the impetus has almost always come from those groups—lesbians, the disabled, older women, poor women—who suffer the oppression immediately and *demand* that other women pay attention.

Whereas white Jewish women usually have had the option of being in the movement as white women, not as *visible* Jewish women, women of color, except for those relatively few whose skin color, features, and accent allow them to "pass" for white, have *had* to be there as who they were. Certainly whatever attention has been paid to racism by white feminists has resulted from over a decade's worth of women of color consistently and loudly raising that issue inside and outside the women's movement. Although I have long held the idea, for instance, that racism, like other oppressions, was wrong, I have no illusion that I would have even begun to *act* on that anti-racist belief in the absence of the work of women of color. Only later did I develop some sense of how often they spoke, and in how many different ways, before I was able to hear. Repeatedly I notice how often I continue to get caught looking over my left shoulder when the racism is clear as day over my right one.

So, while I want the responsibility for dealing with Jewish oppression to be taken up by non-Jews, I do not expect a whole lot to happen quickly. Anti-Semitism is too deeply ingrained for that. Additionally, I have no reason to believe that non-Jewish women—white women and women of color—learn any faster than I or any of the white women I know. Nothing I have read, nothing in my personal experience, has taught me that anything more than the most superficial acknowledgment of an oppression's presence—and sometimes not even that—will occur without years of groundwork by those on whom it weighs most heavily.[17] As a lesbian, for instance, I have been in many settings—feminist academic, community activist, progressive Jewish—where it remained for the dykes among us to remind people that we were there, that recognizing our existence and concerns in some serious way was not a divergence from the "real" issues. Eventually, where we have stood up often enough over the years, we have not always had to be the ones to remind, to prod, to object.

From this perspective, I am a lot more concerned about the willingness of non-Jewish women to identify and confront Jewish oppression now that it is being raised with considerable consistency within the feminist community by Jewish women. Women need to deal with both racism and anti-Semitism on a day-to-day basis regardless of the actual presence of women of color and/or Jewish women. This is especially critical in the many places in this country where non-Jewish women have little or no contact with Jews and white women have little or no contact with women of color. Although the attendance of only two Jewish women at the 1982 Womanwrites: Southeast Lesbian Writers Conference, for instance, resulted in an extremely small Jewish women's caucus, the non-Jewish women had no less responsibility for addressing the issue of anti-Semitism than if many Jewish women had attended; the responsibility was taken, in part, by a Black woman who, at the conference's closing session, offered an impromptu overview of Black-Jewish relations in the South.

How those of us who are Jewish and white perceive the women's movement—who is definitely in it and who is not, whose presence we experience most immediately—has major implications for the political work we do. We create obstacles to such work when, in the course of arguing for strenuous opposition to anti-Semitism, we do not accurately describe both the degree of the movement's anti-racist commitment and the steps which remain to be taken. One facet of this problem can be illustrated in a 1982 interview with Evelyn Torton Beck. Beginning with the observation about racism that ". . . we have taken a stand as a movement against it, although I don't think we've eradicated it by a long shot," Beck adds:

> I've thought a lot about why our movement has been able and willing to dedicate itself so fully to fighting racism and so unwilling to cover Jewish issues. I think it has partially to do with the fact that Jews have not been so segregated. You can dedicate yourself to fighting racism, because there are groups that have been left out. But Jews *are* very much in the movement; so, if you're going to commit yourself to fighting anti-Semitism, you have to deal with it immediately, on a daily basis—in a way that most white feminists still don't have to deal with women of color because there is still not that much working together. Immediately taking this into your life appears to be somewhat more threatening.[18]

Beck builds on her assumption of full anti-racism dedication by white women a competitive argument that itself illustrates how limited this anti-racism is. The fact that the women's movement is still at the point at which inclusion of women of color is a vital issue is itself a measure of the inadequacy thus far of any movement-wide dedication to anti-racism. From this perspective, Beck's failure to describe as "very much in the movement" the many women of color who are active as feminists, *regardless* of whether she or other white women are doing political work *with them,* reflects this larger problem. Such a political view perceives the "movement" as white and defines women of color as, at best, on its periphery, at the same time that it presents in overstated terms the movement-wide dedication to anti-racism.

From an activist perspective, bringing in "groups that have been left out" is only an initial step in a complicated process. Beck's contention that "you can dedicate yourself to fighting racism, because there are groups that have been left out" implies that one can be seriously committed to anti-racism while doing far less than one has to do to be equally committed to opposing anti-Semitism; that, in some ways, it is *easier* to be anti-racist because that involves most white women only with women who are out there, clearly Other, rather than with women who are a daily part of our lives. Some non-Jewish feminists are, indeed, reluctant to deal with Jewish oppression out of the fear that doing so will negatively affect their personal relationships with Jewish women; that fear can override the awareness that their refusal to deal with it can itself badly hurt such relationships and thereby prevent them from doing necessary work not just on a political but on a personal level. But others might find it far more pressing to deal with anti-Semitism *because* of their personal commitment to specific Jewish women. Similarly, a significant motivation for white women to confront racism is the interaction with women of color that, among other things, allows for an understanding of their identity and oppression which simply cannot be gained without personal contact.

Clarifying one's motivation for opposing either oppression involves pulling back from one's anger at the other group to look at the larger political picture, the larger stakes. For non-Jewish women of color, it means questioning the kinds of assumptions that led one woman of color at a workshop for Jewish women and women of color to state "that she would not deal with Jewish women until we 'dealt with' Zionism."[19] For Jewish women, it means avoiding the kind of tit-for-tat mode of thinking that contends that the anti-racist work done by white Jewish women obligates women of color to reciprocate. Writing in this vein, Letty Pogrebin says:

> many Jewish women specifically resent that, for years, they have
> talked openly about "confronting" their racism, while with a
> few noteworthy exceptions black women's anti-Semitism has
> been largely unmentionable.[20]

Although Pogrebin does not depict white Jewish women as having gone beyond the level of "talk," her message to those women is clear: if we have done this, we have done enough. And her message to Black women is: because we have done this, you owe us something which you have not paid.

Ignoring in her discussion of "Black-Jewish Relations" responsibility on the part of Jewish women for the breach in relations, Pogrebin appears to accept without question the appropriateness of some Jewish women's years of resentment. In doing so, she casts doubt on the political motivations of Jewish women who do—or have done—anti-racist work. As Alice Walker has written in a published response to Pogrebin's article:

> It depressed me that Pogrebin imagines Jewish women's work
> for "civil rights, welfare rights, Appalachian relief was work that
> did not necessarily affect [their] own lives." Meaning, logically,
> that this work was charity, dispensed to the backward, the poor,
> and the benighted, and that Jewish feminists should now be

able to expect "payment" in the form of support. Fortunately, I have worked with too many Jewish women in social move- ments to believe that many of them think this—rather than that any struggle against oppression lightens the load on all of us—but if they do, we are worse off than I thought.[21]

We are just as badly off when, having overstated the extent of white anti- racism, those of us who are Jewish and white fall into the trap of overstating the extent and intransigence of anti-Semitism among non-Jewish people of color. Doing so contributes to the competitive cycle: while white Jewish women have taken racism seriously, non-Jewish women of color do not take anti-Semitism seriously. Thus the cycle moves on apace, political strategizing gets done in far greater isolation than is either necessary or desirable, the pos- sibilities of coalition seem increasingly remote, and the people who benefit certainly don't come from any of *our* communities.

For me the issue is not whether to confront Jewish oppression, but how   *30* to do so. With comparatively few exceptions, non-Jewish women of color— like non-Jewish white women—have neither sufficiently explored their own anti-Semitism nor actively opposed it. In terms of non-Jewish women of color, no less than of non-Jewish white women, personal and political inter- actions must be based on the belief that, as Irena Klepfisz has written, "anti- Semitism, *like any other ideology of oppression,* must *never* be tolerated, must *never* be hushed up, must *never* be ignored, and that, instead, it must *always* be ex- posed and resisted."[22]

For Jewish women, the rage at the anti-Semitism of non-Jewish women of color sometimes seems far greater than at the anti-Semitism of the non- Jewish whites who have immeasurably more power. For white Jews who were raised with a belief in some "special relationship" between Jews and Blacks, the recurrence of anti-Semitism among Blacks can seem a final sundering of that perceived link, more painful than the anti-Semitism of whites and thereby drawing on a deeper level of anger. For Jews of color, the pain of such anti- Semitism is especially sharp, coming as it does from within their own group, perhaps even from non-Jews within their own immediate family.

Perhaps the intensified anger stems from *their* failure to meet *our* expecta- tions, our assumptions that their gut-level experience of their own oppression will provide them with a ready store of empathy for others. When, for in- stance, I am dyke-baited on my block by teenagers, white and Black, I am, in total defiance of logic, angrier at the Black kids than at the white ones: *they,* I mutter to myself, should know better! Sometimes rewarded, more often not, these expectations are put into perspective by Cherríe Moraga's comment: "Oppression does not make for hearts as big as all outdoors. Oppression makes us big and small. Expressive and silenced. Deep and dead."[23] On every side, it makes us deep and dead.

Unrealistic expectations can skew how Jewish women define the issues, at- tribute responsibility. Pogrebin's article, for example, left me with the impression that I would be hard put to find more than four or five Black people *in the entire country* who thought Jewish oppression a serious issue. What does it mean that she chooses to end an article on anti-Semitism in the women's movement with "Problem 5: Black-Jewish Relations," a litany of examples of anti-Jewish statements by Black people, including several women who would probably not identify as feminists but who *do* have anti-Jewish things to say?[24] What does it mean to single out Black people in this way, as no other racial/ethnic group is singled out? What is the impression left on the reader? Reversing this situation can put it in useful perspective. How might Pogrebin, or another Jewish woman, respond to an article by a non-Jewish woman of color on racism in the women's movement that concluded with a section on "Black-Jewish Relations," placed responsibility for the breach on white Jewish women, and rattled off a series of racist statements made by white Jews?[25] Would this not illustrate Pogrebin's statement: "That this game of blacks versus Jews is continued in the Women's Movement is one of the gravest failures of feminism"?[26]

The fact of Third World anti-Semitism—like the fact of white anti-Semitism—is undeniable. A problem is how to acknowledge it, deplore it, oppose it, *and* place it in some kind of context. How to hear Barbara Smith say, "I have seen some Black women be blatantly anti-Semitic with a self-righteousness they would probably not exhibit in any other case,"[27] *and* know that this statement presents only part of the picture. How to read Gloria Z. Greenfield's description of the 1981 New England Women's Studies Association workshop for Jewish women and women of color at which the presence of working-class Jews "was ignored with remarks that 'all Jews are rich' and 'there's no such thing as a poor Jew',"[28] *and* know that the women who made these anti-Jewish remarks were not representative of all the women of color present, that four Third World women, Cherríe Moraga, Julia Perez, Barbara Smith, and Beverly Smith wrote in response to the confrontation at that conference:

> We are not trying to side-step the pervasive fact of color oppression in this country and are committed to confronting white racism, whether practiced by Jews or non-Jews. However, we feel it is critical for women of color not to fall into the trap of countering racism on the part of Jews with anti-Semitism.
>
> The issue is not a simple one and as women of color who have struggled for nearly a decade in a white-dominated feminist movement, we understand and empathize with the tendency to react to racism with despair. We feel that this is not a time for viewing this one event as an impasse, but rather as a moment of harsh enlightenment—reckoning with the extent and depth to which we are separated from each other.
>
> We don't have to be the same to have a movement, but we *do* have to admit our fear and pain and be accountable for our

ignorance. In the end, finally, we must refuse to give up on
each other.[29]

35

Within and outside the women's community, we are faced with the question of whether we *will,* in fact, give up on each other, whether we will generalize from our worst experiences and proceed in a climate smoggy with a distrust so thick that effective political work cannot take place. Examples of anti-Semitism among people of color—as among non-Jewish whites—are depressingly easy to locate. The 1981–1982 issue of *Jazz Spotlite News,* a Black publication, includes, "as a public service by The Third World Institute," an "excerpt from the 'Protocols of The Learned Elders of Zion',," on Jewish "control of the press."[30] Jewish protests of a fall, 1982 program on Israel on *Like It Is,* a Black WABC weekly show, gave WABC an excuse to try to crack down on its independence, and led Reverend Calvin Butts, head of the Organization of African American Clergy, to characterize the "affair as 'a pound of flesh' . . . extracted from our community"; when Black protests succeeded in quashing WABC's attack, host Gil Noble "said nothing about the anti-Semitic undercurrents of that protest . . . [and] repeated the infamous 'pound of flesh' line from *The Merchant of Venice,* adding that the Blacks, in response, had 'extracted eight pounds of flesh!' "[31]

Without doubt, non-Jewish people of color—like non-Jewish whites—exist for whom no amount of Jewish history and information on Jew-hating will be enough for them to rethink their anti-Semitism. When challenged about the "Protocols" excerpt, for instance, one Black woman denied that they were a tsarist forgery and, indifferent to this information about their actual history, supported her argument with such sources as *The Black American,* a New York City newspaper which has supported the 1980 presidential candidacy of the notoriously anti-Jewish Lyndon Larouche and has printed articles maintaining that the Holocaust did not happen.[32]

Such resistance, however, is not uniform. When asked about the anti-Jewish "pound of flesh" reference, for example, a Black woman first defended Butts on the grounds that he "didn't know" that the reference was anti-Jewish and then, after some discussion, admitted that, even if Butts and Noble had acted out of ignorance, they were, in fact, perpetuating anti-Semitism. For this woman, information and political dialogue did make a difference. Neither of these examples cancels out the other. Nor are they affected by the existence of other Blacks, by other non-Jewish people of color, who would have *immediately* identified as anti-Jewish both the "Protocols" reprint and the "pound of flesh" quote from *The Merchant of Venice.* They do, however, illustrate a diversity that needs to be acknowledged.

The goal of acknowledging opposition to anti-Semitism is definitely not to express gratitude or to single out a few individuals as "good" representatives of their group. Opposition to anti-Semitism, as to racism and other oppressions, is not a favor that merits thanks, nor is it a means to establish a token few who are "politically right-on," while everyone else lies mired hopelessly in "political incorrectness." Such an acknowledgement is, however, part of a political strategy, a means to break a cycle in which silence begets more silence. It will help make clear to white Jewish women that interactions and alliances with non-Jewish women of color are not by definition a dead end, though, like other work that crosses lines of significant difference, they are bound at times to seem overwhelmingly difficult. It will help provide non-Jewish women of color with the sense that they are not necessarily alone in their opposition to Jewish oppression, that other women like them have begun to take public and private stands against it. Without exaggeration, without minimizing the extent of Jewish oppression or racism, each of us benefits, as we oppose one or both, from knowing that we are not working in isolation. The greater the sense of isolation, the more formidable the task appears and the more likely we might be to wait until someone takes it on first.

On all sides, the barriers seem, at times, insurmountable, the cycles of competition seem impossible to break. The way out of the impasse involves challenging our own assumptions, checking them for accuracy, scrutinizing them for political implications. It certainly involves examining those areas where, practically before we know it and often against our desires, Jewish women and non-Jewish women of color become embroiled in competition, shut out the world beyond the women's movement, and view each other with enmity. Without such examination, non-Jewish women of color and Jewish women will not break fully out of our current situation. Like Jews and the Polish Underground in the Warsaw of 1943, we will remain, as Irena Klepfisz has written, "two oppressed groups facing a common enemy unable to overcome ancient hatreds, struggling separately."[33]

NOTES

1. Melanie Kaye/Kantrowitz, "Anti-Semitism, Homophobia, and the Good White Knight," *off our backs* (May 1982), p. 30.
2. Hope Landrine, "Culture, Feminist Racism & Feminist Classism: Blaming the Victim," *off our backs* (November 1979), p. 3. Several letters from Jewish women about the article appeared in the January 1980 issue: by Helene Rosenbluth, Paula Tobin, Sylvia Kohan, Simone Wallace, and Ellen Ledley; Chaya Gusfield, Elia Sheva Dreyfuss, Zimma, Nora Krauss, and Madeline Poplin; and Lynne S. Brandon (p. 28).
3. Women Against Imperialism, "Taking Our Stand Against White Supremacy," *off our backs* (July 1982), p. 20.
4. Kaye/Kantrowitz, p. 30.
5. Kaye/Kantrowitz, p. 31.
6. Kaye/Kantrowitz, p. 31.
7. Necessary Bread Affinity Group, "Necessary Bread Disarmament Statement," *Feminist Studies,* vol. 8, no. 3 (Fall 1982). Necessary Bread consisted of Dorothy Allison, Elly Bulkin, Cheryl Clarke, Jan Clausen, Jewelle Gomez, Barbara Kerr, Cherríe Moraga, Carroll Oliver, Mirtha Quintanales, and Barbara Smith.

8. Di Vilde Chayes, "An Open Letter to the Women's Movement," *off our backs* (July 1982), p. 21.

9. Combahee River Collective, "A Black Feminist Statement," *Capitalist Patriarchy and the Case for Socialist Feminism,* ed. Zillah R. Eisenstein (New York: Monthly Review Press, 1979), p. 366.

10. Alice Walker, letter of May 9, 1982, *Ms.* (February 1983), p. 16; reprinted in Walker, *In Search of Our Mothers' Gardens: Womanist Prose* (New York: Harcourt Brace Jovanovich, 1983), p. 354.

11. Mab Segrest, "Mama, Granny, Carrie Bell: Race and Class, A Personal Accounting," *Conditions Ten* (1984).

12. My wording here draws on Samuel Johnson's statement: "Sir, a woman preaching is like a dog's walking on his hind legs. It is not done well; but you are surprised to find it done at all" (*Boswell's Life of Johnson,* vol. 1, p. 287). In "Black Women on Black Women Writers: Conversations and Questions," Linda C. Powell says: ". . . it's been my experience that what's been operating in the women's community is that whole thing that if a black woman speaks the language and is nice around white folk, 'the dancing dog' is in operation. She can speak at conferences. She can write reviews. And even if she's mediocre, it's not bad for a negro. Occasionally, they hit pay dirt" (*Conditions: Nine,* 1983, p. 101).

13. "Medea Media's Hotterline . . . ," *Feminist Bookstores Newsletter* (November 1981), p. 15.

14. For a discussion of an earlier period in which a problem for Jewish feminists was "not presence but visibility," see Elinor Lerner, "American Feminism and the Jewish Question, 1890–1940," in *Ambiguous Encounter: Anti-Semitism and Jewish-Gentile Relations in American History,* ed. David Gerber (Urbana: University of Illinois Press, 1985). An earlier version of this paper was presented at the 1983 National Women's Studies Association Conference.

15. "A Nice Jewish Girl: Evi Beck," interview by Fran Moira, *off our backs* (August–September 1982), p. 10.

16. Letty Cottin Pogrebin, "Anti-Semitism in the Women's Movement," *Ms.* (July 1982), p. 69.

17. In her article "Anti-Semitism in the Women's Movement," Annette Daum finds a "note of despair" in Pogrebin's closing statement: "It is for decent persons to come forward and sound that note of hope, either through self-repair or through declarations of abhorrence of anti-Semitism. We Jews can't get rid of anti-Semitism by ourselves." "Taken to its logical conclusion," Daum writes, "no action should have been required regarding equality for women except to wait for decent men to repair themselves. The same principles of consciousness-raising used so successfully in the women's movement can and should be applied to the problem of anti-Semitism within the movement" ("Anti-Semitism in the Women's Movement," *Pioneer Women,* September–October 1983, p. 22).

18. Beck, pp. 9, 10.

19. Gloria Z. Greenfield, "Shedding," *Nice Jewish Girls: A Lesbian Anthology* ed. Evelyn Torton Beck (Watertown, MA: Persephone Press, 1982; reprinted and distributed by The Crossing Press, 1984), p. 8.

20. Pogrebin, p. 70.
21. Walker, p. 16.
22. Irena Klepfisz, "Anti-Semitism in the Lesbian/Feminist Movement," *Nice Jewish Girls,* p. 50.
23. Cherríe Moraga, "A Long Line of Vendidas," *Loving in the War Years/lo que nunca pasó por sus labios* (Boston: South End Press, 1983), p. 135.
24. I disagree with the inclusion of Carole Clemmons Gregory's "Love Letter" in Pogrebin's list of anti-Jewish examples. In the poem, Gregory is transferring Black identity to Old Testament characters, a common Afro-American literary device, rather than commenting on interactions between Black and Jews.
25. For another instance of focusing on people of color in such a way as to imply greater responsibility on their part for anti-Semitism, see Selma Miriam, "Anti-Semitism in the Lesbian Community: A Collage of Mostly Bad News by One Jewish Dyke," *Sinister Wisdom 19* (1982), pp. 50–60; my response, *Sinister Wisdom 21,* pp. 108–113; and Selma Miriam's reply in the same issue, pp. 115–118.
26. Pogrebin, p. 70.
27. Barbara Smith, "Introduction," *Home Girls: A Black Feminist Anthology,* ed. Barbara Smith (New York: Kitchen Table: Women of Color Press, 1983), p. xliv.
28. Greenfield, p. 8.
29. Cherríe Moraga, Julia Perez, Barbara Smith, Beverly Smith, "Racism and Anti-Semitism" (letter), *Gay Community News,* March 7, 1981, p. 4. See also Rosario Morales' article on the workshop, "Double Allegiance: Jewish Women and Women of Color," *A Working Conference on Women and Racism: New England Women's Studies Association Newsletter* (May 1981).
30. *Jazz Spotlite News* (1981–1982), p. 133.
31. Lawrence Bush, "WABC, Blacks and Jews," *Jewish Currents* (February 1983), p. 7.
32. *The Black American* has published such articles as George Nicholas' "Jewish 'Hit Squad' Targets Dissidents," which refers to the Institute of Historical Review, a white organization dedicated to proving that the Holocaust didn't happen, as "a small, serious center of scholarship" (vol. 20, no. 20, pp. 28, 38); and Keith Stimely's "Zionists Duck Chance to Prove 'Holocaust'," which outlines the Institute for Historical Review's "inability" to find someone to claim its $50,000 reward by demonstrating that "gas chambers for the purpose of killing human beings existed at or in the Auschwitz Concentration Camp during World War II" (vol. 21, no. 57). Both articles appear to be reprints. Although my copies of these articles don't have dates on them, these articles appeared between 1981 and 1983.
33. Klepfisz, p. 49.

BEYOND RACIAL IDENTITY POLITICS: TOWARD A LIBERATION THEORY FOR MULTICULTURAL DEMOCRACY

Manning Marable

Americans are arguably the most "race-conscious" people on earth. Even in South Africa, the masters of apartheid recognized the necessity to distinguish between "Coloureds" and "black Africans." Under the bizarre regulations of apartheid, a visiting delegation of Japanese corporate executives, or the diplomatic corps of a client African regime such as Malawi, could be classified as "honorary whites." But in the USA, "nationality" has been closely linked historically to the categories and hierarchy of national racial identity. Despite the orthodox cultural ideology of the so-called "melting pot," power, privilege and the ownership of productive resources and property have always been unequally allocated in a social hierarchy stratified by class, gender and race. Those who benefit directly from these institutional arrangements have historically been defined as "white," overwhelmingly upper class and male. And it is precisely here within this structure of power and privilege that "national identity" in the context of mass political culture is located. To be an "all-American" is by definition *not* to be an Asian American, Pacific American, American Indian, Latino, Arab American or African-American. Or viewed another way, the hegemonic ideology of "whiteness" is absolutely central in rationalizing and justifying the gross inequalities of race, gender and class, experienced by millions of Americans relegated to the politically peripheral status of "Others." As Marxist cultural critic E. San Juan has observed, "whenever the question of the national identity is at stake, boundaries in space and time are drawn. . . . A decision is made to represent the Others—people of color—as missing, absent, or supplement." "Whiteness" becomes the very "center" of the dominant criteria for national prestige, decision-making authority and intellectual leadership.

Ironically, because of the centrality of "whiteness" within the dominant national identity, Americans generally make few distinctions between "ethnicity" and "race," and the two concepts are usually used interchangeably. Both the oppressors and those who are oppressed are therefore imprisoned by the closed dialectic of race. "Black" and "white" are usually viewed as fixed, permanent and often antagonistic social categories. Yet, in reality, "race" should be understood not as an entity within the histories of all human societies, or grounded in some inescapable or permanent biological or genetic difference between human beings. "Race" is first and foremost an unequal relationship between social aggregates, characterized by dominant and subordinate forms of social interaction, and reinforced by the intricate patterns of public discourse, power, ownership and privilege within the economic, social and political institutions of social.

Race only becomes "real" as a social force when individuals or groups behave toward each other in ways which either reflect or perpetuate the hegemonic ideology of subordination and the patterns of inequality in daily life. These are, in turn, justified and explained by assumed differences in physical and biological characteristics, or in theories of cultural deprivation or intellectual inferiority. Thus, far from being static or fixed, race as an oppressive concept within social relations is fluid and ever-changing. An oppressed "racial group" changes over time, geographical space and historical conjuncture. That which is termed "black," "Hispanic" or "Oriental" by those in power to describe one human being's "racial background" in a particular setting can have little historical or practical meaning within another social formation which is also racially stratified, but in a different manner.

Since so many Americans view the world through the prism of permanent racial categories, it is difficult to convey the idea that radically different ethnic groups may have roughly the same "racial identity" imposed on them. For example, although native-born African-Americans, Trinidadians, Haitians, Nigerians and Afro-Brazilians would all be termed "black" on the streets of New York City, they have remarkably little in common in terms of language, culture, ethnic traditions, rituals, and religious affiliations. Yet they are all "black" racially, in the sense that they will share many of the pitfalls and prejudices built into the institutional arrangements of the established social order for those defined as "black." Similarly, an even wider spectrum of divergent ethnic groups—from Japanese Americans, Chinese Americans, Filipino Americans, and Korean Americans to Hawaiians, Pakistanis, Vietnamese, Arabs and Uzbekis—are described and defined by the dominant society as "Asians" or, worse still, as "Orientals." In the rigid, racially stratified American social order, the specific nationality, ethnicity and culture of a person of color has traditionally been secondary to an individual's "racial category," a label of inequality which is imposed from without rather than constructed by the group from within. Yet as Michael Omi, Asian American Studies professor at the University of California at Berkeley has observed, we are also "in a period in which our conception of racial categories is being radically transformed." The waves of recent immigrants create new concepts of what the older ethnic communities have been. The observations and generalizations we imparted "to racial identities" in the past no longer make that much sense.

5   In the United States, "race" for the oppressed has also come to mean an identity of survival, victimization and opposition to those racial groups or elites which exercise power and privilege. What we are looking at here is *not* an *ethnic* identification or culture, but an awareness of shared experience, suffering and struggles against the barriers of racial division. These collective experiences, survival tales and grievances form the basis of a historical conscious-

ness—a group's recognition of what it has witnessed and what it can anticipate in the near future. This second distinct sense of racial identity is imposed on the oppressed and yet represents a reconstructed critical memory of the character of the group's collective ordeals. Both definitions of "race" and "racial identity" give character and substance to the movements for power and influence among people of color.

In the African-American experience, the politics of racial identity have been expressed by two great traditions of racial ideology and social protest: integrationism and black nationalism. The integrationist tradition was initiated in the antebellum political activism of the free Negro community of the North, articulated by the great abolitionist orator Frederick Douglass. The black nationalist tradition was a product of the same social classes, but influenced by the pessimism generated by the Compromise of 1850, the Fugitive Slave Act, the Dred Scott decision, and the failure of the slave uprisings and revolts such as Nat Turner's to end the tyranny and inhumanity of the slave regime. The integrationist perspective was anchored in a firm belief in American democracy, and in the struggle to outlaw all legal barriers which restricted equal access and opportunities to racial minorities. It was linked to the politics of building coalitions with sympathetic white constituencies, aimed at achieving reforms within the context of the system. The integrationist version of racial politics sought the deracialization of the hierarchies of power within society and the economic system. By contrast, the black nationalist approach to racial politics was profoundly skeptical of America's ability to live up to its democratic ideals. It assumed that "racial categories" were real and fundamentally significant, and that efforts to accumulate power had to be structured along the boundaries of race for centuries to come. The nationalist tradition emphasized the cultural kinship of black Americans to Africa, and emphasized the need to establish all-black-owned institutions to provide goods and services to the African-American community.

Although the integrationists and nationalists seemed to hold radically divergent points of view, there was a subterranean symmetry between the two ideologies. Both were based on the idea that the essential dilemma or problem confronting black people was the omnipresent reality of race. The integrationists sought power to dismantle the barriers of race, to outlaw legal restriction on blacks' access to the institutions of authority and ownership, and to assimilate into the cultural "mainstream" without regard to race. The black nationalists favored a separatist path toward empowerment, believing that even the most liberal-minded whites could not be trusted to destroy the elaborate network of privileges from which they benefited, called "white supremacy." But along the assimilationist-separatist axis of racial-identity politics is the common perception that "race," however it is defined, is the most critical organizing variable within society. Race mattered so much more than other factors or variables that, to a considerable degree, the concept of race was perpetuated by the types of political interventions and tactical assumptions by activists and leaders on both sides of the assimilationist/separatist axis.

Both schools of racial identity espoused what can be termed the politics of "symbolic representation." Both the nationalists and integrationists believed that they were speaking to "white power brokers" on behalf of their "constituents"—that is, black Americans. They believed that the real measure of racial power a group wielded within any society could be calibrated according to the institutions it dominated or the numbers of positions it controlled which influenced others. For the integrationists, it was a relatively simple matter of counting noses. If the number of African-Americans in elective offices nationwide increased from 103 in 1964 to over 8,000 in 1993, for example, one could argue that African-Americans as a *group* had increased their political power. Any increase in the number of blacks as mayors, members of federal courts, and on boards of education, was championed as a victory for *all* black people. The black nationalists tended to be far more skeptical about the promise or viability of an electoral route to group empowerment. However, they often shared the same notions of symbolic representation when it came to the construction of social and economic institutions based on private-ownership models. The development of a black-owned shopping plaza, supermarket or private school was widely interpreted as black social and economic empowerment for the group as a whole.

The problem with "symbolic representation" is that it presumes structures of accountability and allegiance between those blacks who are elevated into powerful positions of authority in the capitalist state and the millions of African-Americans clinging to the margins of economic and social existence. The unifying discourse of race obscures the growing class stratification within the African-American community. According to the Census Bureau, for example, back in 1967 about 85 per cent of all African-American families earned between $5,000 and $50,000 annually, measured in inflation-adjusted 1990 dollars. Some 41 per cent earned between $10,000 and $25,000. In short, the number of extremely poor and destitute families was relatively small. The Census Bureau's statistics on African-American households as of 1990 were strikingly different. The size of the black working class and the number of moderate-income people had declined significantly, and the two extremes of poverty and affluence had grown sharply. By 1990, about 12 percent of all black households earned less than $5,000 annually. One-third of all blacks lived below the federal government's poverty level.

10   Conversely, a strong African-American petty bourgeoisie, representing the growth of thousands of white-collar professionals, executives and managers created by affirmative-action requirements, has been established. The average median income of African-American families in which both the wife and husband were employed rose from about $28,700 in 1967 to over $40,000 in 1990, an increase of 40 per cent. More than 15 per cent of all African-American households earn above $50,000 annually, and thousands of black professional families have incomes exceeding $100,000 annually. Many of these newly affluent blacks have moved far from the problems of the main cities into the comfortable white enclaves of suburbia. Nevertheless, many of the strongest

advocates of racial-identity politics since the demise of Black Power and the black freedom movement come from the most privileged, elitist sectors of the black upper middle class. The dogmatic idea that "race" alone explains virtually everything that occurs within society has a special appeal to some African-American suburban elites who have little personal connection with the vast human crisis of ghetto unemployment, black-on-black crime, a rampant drugs trade, gang violence, and deteriorating schools. Moreover, for black entrepreneurs, traditional race categories could be employed as a tool to promote petty capital accumulation, by urging black consumers to "buy black." Racial-identity politics in this context is contradictory and conceptually limited in other critical respects. As noted, it tends to minimize greatly any awareness or analysis of class stratification and concentrations of poverty or affluence among the members of the defined "racial minority groups."

Issues of poverty, hunger, unemployment and homelessness are viewed and interpreted within a narrowly racial context—that is, as a by-product of the large racist contradiction within the society as a whole. Conversely, concentrations of wealth or social privilege within sectors of the racial group are projected as "success stories"—see, for example, issue after issue of *Ebony, Black Enterprise* and *Jet*. In the context of racial-identity politics, the idea of "social change" is usually expressed in utilitarian and pragmatic terms, if change is expressed at all. The integrationists generally favor working within the established structures of authority, influencing those in power to dole out new favors of additional privileges to minorities. Their argument is that "democracy" works best when it is truly pluralistic and inclusive, with the viewpoints of all "racial groups" taken into account. But such a strategy rarely if ever gets to the root of the real problem of the persuasiveness of racism—social inequality. It articulates an eclectic, opportunistic approach to change, rather than a comprehensive or systemic critique, informed by social theory. In the case of the racial separatists, the general belief that "race" is a relatively permanent social category in all multiethnic societies, and that virtually all whites are immutably racist, either for genetic, biological or psychological reasons, compromises the very concept of meaningful social change. If allies are nonexistent or at best untrustworthy, or if dialogues with progressive whites must await the construction of broad-based unity among virtually all blacks, then even tactical alliances with social forces outside the black community become difficult to sustain.

But perhaps the greatest single weakness in the politics of racial identity is that it is rooted implicitly in a competitive model of group empowerment. If the purpose of politics is the realization of a group or constituency's specific objective interest, then racial-identity politics utilizes racial consciousness or the group's collective memory and experiences as the essential framework for interpreting the actions and interests of all other social groups. This approach is not unlike a model of political competition based on a "zero-sum" game such as poker, in which a player can be a "winner" only if one or more other players are "losers." The prism of a group's racial experiences tends to diffuse the parallels, continuities and common interests which might exist between oppressed racial groups; this serves to highlight and emphasize areas of dissension and antagonism.

The black-nationalist-oriented intelligentsia, tied to elements of the new African-American upper middle class by income, social position, and cultural outlook, began to search for ways of expressing itself through the "permanent" prism of race, while rationalizing its relatively privileged class position. One expression of this research for a social theory was found in the writings of Afrocentric theorist Molefi Asante. Born Arthur Lee Smith in 1942, Asante emerged as the founding editor of the *Journal of Black Studies* in 1969. Asante became a leading force in the National Council of Black Studies, the African Heritage Studies Association, and, after 1980, occupied the chair of the African-American Studies Department at Temple University. Asante's basic thesis, the cultural philosophy of "Afrocentrism," began with the insight that people of European descent or cultures have a radically different understanding of the human condition from people of African and/or non-Western cultures and societies. "Human beings tend to recognize three fundamental existential postures one can take with respect to the human condition: feeling, knowing, and acting," Asante observed in 1983. Europeans utilize these concepts separately in order to understand them objectively. Thus "Eurocentrists" tend to understand their subjects "apart from the emotions, attitudes, and cultural definitions of a given context." Scholars with a "Eurocentric" perspective—those who view the entire history of human development from the vantage point of European civilization—are also primarily concerned with a "subject/object duality" which exists in a linear environment. European cultures and people are viewed as the central subjects of history, the creative forces which dominate and transform the world over time. Asante states that this "Euro-linear" viewpoint helps to explain the construction of institutional racism, apartheid and imperialism across the nonwhite world.

By contrast, the Afrocentric framework for comprehending society and human development is radically different, according to Asante. Afrocentrism "understands that the interrelationship of knowledge with cosmology, society, religion, medicine, and traditions stands alongside the interactive metaphors of discourse as principle means of achieving a measure of knowledge about experience." Unlike a linear view of the world, the Afrocentric approach is a "circular view" of human interaction which "seeks to interpret and understand." In theoretical terms, this means that the study of African and African-American phenomena should be within their original cultural contexts, and not within the paradigmatic frameworks of Eurocentrism. Drawing upon African cultural themes, values and concepts, Afrocentrism seeks therefore the creation of a harmonious environment in which all divergent cultures could coexist and learn from each other. Rather than seeking the illusion of the melting pot, Asante calls for the construction of "parallel frames of reference" within the context of a multicultural, pluralistic environment. "Universality,"

Asante warns, "can only be dreamed about when we have slept on truth based on specific cultural experience."

The practical impact of the theory of Afrocentrism was found among black educators. After all, if people of African descent had a radically different cultural heritage, cosmology and philosophy of being than whites, it made sense to devise an alternate curriculum which was "Afrocentric." Such an alternative approach to education would be completely comprehensive, Asante insisted, expressing the necessity for "every topic, economics, law communication, science, religion, history, literature, and sociology to be reviewed through Afrocentric eyes." No African-American child should "attend classes as they are currently being taught or read books as they are currently being written without raising questions about our capability as a people. . . . All children must be centered in a historical place, or their self-esteem suffers." By 1991, approximately 350 "Afrocentric academies" and private schools were educating more than 50,000 African-American students throughout the country. Many large public-school districts adopted Afrocentric supplementary and required textbooks, or brought in Afrocentric-oriented educators for curriculum-development workshops. Several public-school systems, notably in Detroit, Baltimore, and Milwaukee, established entire "Afrocentric schools" for hundreds of school-aged children, transforming all aspects of their learning experience. On college campuses, many Black Studies programs began to restructure their courses to reflect Asante's Afrocentric philosophy.

There is no doubt that Afrocentrism established a vital and coherent cultural philosophy which encouraged African-Americans to react favorably towards black nationalism. Some Afrocentric scholars in the area of psychology, notably Linda James Myers, established innovative and effective measures for promoting the development of positive self-conception among African-Americans. Asante used his position at Temple to create a scholastic tradition which represented a sharp critique and challenge to Eurocentrism. The difficulty was that this scholarly version of Afrocentrism tended to be far more sophisticated than the more popular version of the philosophy embraced by elements of the dogmatically separatist, culturally nationalist community. One such Afrocentric popularizer was Professor Len Jeffries, the chair of the Black Studies program at the City College of New York. Jeffries claimed that white Americans were "ice people" due to environmental, psychological and culture factors inherent in their evolution in Europe; African-Americans by contrast were defined as "sun people," characteristically warm, open, and charitable. At the level of popular history, the vulgar Afrocentrists glorified in an oversimplistic manner the African heritage of black Americans. In their writings, they rarely related the actual complexities of the local cultures, divergence of languages, religions, and political institutions, and tended to homogenize the sharply different social structures found within the African diaspora. They pointed with pride to the dynasties of Egypt as the classical foundation of African civilization, without also examining with equal vigor or detail

15

Egypt's slave structure. At times, the racial separatists of vulgar Afrocentrism embraced elements of a black chauvinism and intolerance towards others, and espoused public positions which were blatantly anti-Semitic. Jeffries' public statements attacking Jews, and the countercharge that he espoused anti-Semitic viewpoints, made it easier for white conservatives to denigrate all African-American Studies, and to undermine efforts to require multicultural curricula within public schools.

Scholarly Afrocentrism coexisted uneasily with its populist variety. When Jeffries was deposed as chair of City College's Black Studies Department in the controversy following his anti-Semitic remarks, Asante wisely stayed outside the debate. Nevertheless, there remained theoretical problems inherent in the more scholarly paradigm. Afrocentric intellectuals gave eloquent lip service to the insights of black scholars such as W.E.B. Du Bois as "pillars" of their own perspective, without also acknowledging that Du Bois's philosophy of culture and history conflicted sharply with their own. Du Bois's major cultural and philosophical observation, expressed nearly a century ago in *The Souls of Black Folk,* claimed that the African-American expresses a "double consciousness." The black American was "an American, a Negro; two souls, two thoughts, two unreconciled strivings; two warring ideals in one dark body, whose dogged strength alone keeps it from being torn asunder." Africa in effect represents only half of the dialectical consciousness of African-American people. Blacks are also legitimately Americans, and by our suffering, struggle and culture we have a destiny within this geographical and political space equal to or stronger than any white American. This realization that the essence of the inner spirit of African-American people was reflected in this core duality was fundamentally ignored by the Afrocentrists.

Vulgar Afrocentrists deliberately ignored or obscured the historical reality of social class stratification within the African diaspora. They essentially argued that the interests of all black people—from Joint Chiefs of Staff chairman General Colin Powell to conservative Supreme Court Associate Justice Clarence Thomas, to the black unemployed, homeless, and hungry of America's decaying urban ghettoes—were philosophically, culturally and racially the same. Even the scholarly Afrocentric approach elevated a neo-Kantian idealism above even a dialectical idealist analysis, much less speaking to historical materialism except to attack it as such. Populist Afrocentrism was the perfect social theory for the upwardly mobile black petty bourgeoisie. It gave them a vague sense of ethnic superiority and cultural originality, without requiring the hard, critical study of historical realities. It provided a philosophical blueprint to avoid concrete struggle within the real world, since potential white "allies" certainly were nonexistent and all cultural change began from within. It was, in short, only the latest theoretical construct of a politics of racial identity, a world-view designed to discuss the world but never really to change it.

How do we transcend the theoretical limitations and social contradictions of the politics of racial identity? The challenge begins by constructing new cultural and political "identities," based on the realities of America's changing multicultural, democratic milieu. The task of constructing a tradition of unity between various groups of color in America is a far more complex and contradictory process than progressive activists or scholars have admitted, precisely because of divergent cultural traditions, languages and conflicting politics of racial identity—on the part of Latinos, African-Americans, Asian Americans, Pacific Island Americans, Arab Americans, American Indians and others. Highlighting the current dilemma in the 1990s, is the collapsing myth of "brown–black solidarity."

Back in the 1960s and early 1970s, with the explosion of the civil-rights   20 and black power movements in the African-American community, activist formations with similar objectives also emerged among Latinos. The Black Panther Party and the League of Revolutionary Black Workers, for example, found their counterparts among Chicano militants in La Raza Unida Party in Texas, and the Crusade for Justice in Colorado. The Council of La Raza and the Mexican American Legal Defense Fund began to push for civil-rights reforms within government, and for expanding influence for Latinos within the Democratic Party, paralleling the same strategies of Jesse Jackson's Operation PUSH and the NAACP Legal Defense Fund.

With the growth of a more class-conscious black and Latino petty bourgeoisie—ironically, a social product of affirmative action and civil-rights gains—tensions between these two large communities of people of color began to deteriorate. The representatives of the African-American middle class consolidated their electoral control of the city councils and mayoral posts of major cities throughout the country. Black entrepreneurship increased, as the black American consumer market reached a gross sales figure of $270 billion by 1991, an amount equal to the gross domestic product of the fourteenth wealthiest nation on earth. The really important "symbolic triumphs" of this privileged strata of the African-American community were not the dynamic 1984 and 1988 presidential campaigns of Jesse Jackson; they were instead the electoral victory of Democratic "moderate" Doug Wilder as Virginia governor in 1990, and the appointment of former-Jackson-lieutenant-turned-moderate Ron Brown as head of the Democratic National Committee. Despite the defeats represented by Reaganism and the absence of affirmative-action enforcement, there was a sense that the strategy of "symbolic representation" had cemented this stratum's hegemony over the bulk of the black population. Black politicians like Doug Wilder and television celebrity journalists such as black-nationalist-turned-Republican Tony Brown weren't interested in pursuing coalitions between blacks and other people of color. Multiracial, multiclass alliances raised too many questions about the absence of political accountability between middle-class "leaders" and their working-class and low-income "followers." Even Jesse Jackson shied away from addressing a black–Latino alliance except in the most superficial terms.

By the late 1980s and early 1990s, however, the long-delayed brown–black dialogue at the national level began crystallizing into tensions around at least four critical issues. First, after the census of 1990, scores of congressional districts were reapportioned with African-American or Latino pluralities or majorities, guaranteeing greater minority-group representation in Congress. However, in cities and districts where Latinos and blacks were roughly divided, and especially in those districts which blacks had controlled in previous years but in which Latinos were now in the majority, disagreements often led to fractious ethnic conflicts. Latinos claimed that they were grossly underrepresented within the political process. African-American middle-class leaders argued that "Latinos" actually represented four distinct groups with little to no shared history or common culture: Mexican Americans, concentrated overwhelmingly in the southwestern states; Hispanics from the Caribbean, chiefly Puerto Ricans and Dominicans, most of whom had migrated to New York City and the northeast since 1945; Cuban Americans, mostly middle- to upper-class exiles of Castro's Cuba, and who voted heavily Republican; and the most recent Spanish-speaking emigrants from Central and South America. Blacks insisted that Cuban Americans were definitely not an "underprivileged minority," and as such did not merit minority set-aside economic programs, affirmative-action and equal-opportunity programs. The cultural politics of Afrocentrism made it difficult for many African-Americans to recognize that they might share any common interest with Latinos.

Second, immigration issues are also at the center of recent Latino–black conflicts. Over one-third of the Latino population of more than 24 million in the USA consists of undocumented workers. Some middle-class African-American leaders have taken the politically conservative viewpoint that undocumented Latino workers deprive poor blacks of jobs within the low-wage sectors of the economy. Third, bilingual education and efforts to impose linguistic and cultural conformity upon all sectors of society (such as "English-only" referenda) have also been issues of contention. Finally, the key element that drives these topics of debate is the rapid transformation of America's non-white demography. Because of relatively higher birth rates than the general population and substantial immigration, within less than two decades Latinos as a group will outnumber Africa-Americans as the largest minority group in the USA. Even by 1990, about one out of nine US households spoke a non-English language at home, predominantly Spanish.

Black middle-class leaders who were accustomed to advocating the interests of their constituents in simplistic racial terms were increasingly confronted by Latinos who felt alienated from the system and largely ignored and under-represented by the political process. Thus in May 1991, Latinos took to the streets in Washington DC, hurling bottles and rocks and looting over a dozen stores, in response to the shooting by the local police of a Salvadorian man whom they claimed had wielded a knife. African-American mayor Sharon Pratt Dixon ordered over one thousand police officers to patrol the city's Latino neighborhoods, and used tear gas to quell the public disturbances. In effect, a black administration in Washington DC used the power of the police and courts to suppress the grievances of Latinos—just as the white administration had done against black protesters during the urban uprisings of 1968.

The tragedy here is that too little is done by either African-American or   *25*
Latino "mainstream" leaders, who practice racial-identity politics to transcend
their parochialism and to redefine their agendas on common ground. Latinos
and blacks alike can agree on an overwhelming list of issues—such as the inclusion of multicultural curricula in public schools, improvements in public
health care, job training initiative, the expansion of public transportation and
housing for low- to moderate-income people; and greater fairness and legal
rights within the criminal justice system. Despite the image that Latinos as a
group are more "economically privileged" than African-Americans, Mexican
American families earn only slightly more than black households, and Puerto
Rican families earn less than black Americans on average. Economically, Latinos and African-Americans have both experienced the greatest declines in real
incomes and some of the greatest increases in poverty rates within the USA.
From 1973 to 1990, for example, the incomes for families headed by a parent
under thirty years of age declined by 28 per cent for Latino families and by 48
per cent for African-American families. The poverty rates for young families
in these same years rose 44 per cent for Latinos and 58 per cent for blacks.

There is also substantial evidence that Latinos continue to experience discrimination in elementary, secondary and higher education which is in many
respects more severe than that experienced by African-Americans. Although
high-school graduation rates for the entire population have steadily improved,
the rates for Latinos have declined consistently since the mid 1980s. In 1989,
for instance, 76 per cent of all African-Americans and 82 per cent of all whites
aged between eighteen and twenty-four had graduated from high school. By
contrast, the graduation rate for Latinos in 1989 was 56 per cent. By 1992, the
high-school completion rate for Latino males dropped to its lowest level, 47.8
per cent, since 1972—the year such figures began to be compiled by the
American Council on Education. In colleges and universities, the pattern of
Latino inequality was the same. In 1991, 34 per cent of all whites and 24 per
cent of all African-Americans aged between eighteen and twenty-four were
enrolled in college. Latino college enrollment for the same age group was
barely 18 per cent. As of 1992, approximately 22 per cent of the non-Latino
adult population in the USA possessed at least a four-year college degree. College graduation rates for Latino adults were just 10 per cent. Thus, on a series
of public policy issues—access to quality education, economic opportunity,
the availability of human services, and civil rights—Latinos and African-
Americans share a core set of common concerns and long-term interests.
What is missing is the dynamic vision and political leadership necessary to
build something more permanent than temporary electoral coalitions between these groups.

A parallel situation exists between Asian Americans, Pacific Americans
and the black American community. Two generations ago, the Asian American population was comparatively small, except in states such as California,
Washington, and New York. With the end of discriminatory immigration restrictions on Asians in 1965, however, the Asian American population began

to soar dramatically, changing the ethnic and racial character of urban America. For example, in the years 1970 to 1990 the Korean population increased from 70,000 to 820,000. Since 1980, about 33,000 Koreans have entered the USA each year, a rate of immigration exceeded only by Latinos and Filipinos. According to the 1990 census, the Asian American and Pacific Islander population in the USA exceeds 7.3 million.

Some of the newer Asian immigrants in the 1970s and 1980s were of middle-class origin with backgrounds in entrepreneurship, small manufacturing and the white-collar professions. Thousands of Asian American small-scale, family-owned businesses began to develop in black and Latino neighborhoods, in many instances taking the place of the Jewish merchants in the ghettoes a generation before. It did not take long before Latino and black petty hostilities and grievances against this new ethnic entrepreneurial group crystallized into deep racial hatred. When African-American rapper Ice Cube expressed his anger against Los Angeles's Korean American business community in the 1991 song "Black Korea," he was also voicing the popular sentiments of many younger blacks:

> So don't follow me up and down your market, or your little
> chop-suey ass will be a target of the nationwide boycott.
> Choose with the people, that's what the boy got. So pay respect
> to the black fist, or we'll burn down your store, right down to a
> crisp, and then we'll see you, 'cause you can't turn the ghetto
> into Black Korea.

Simmering ethnic tensions boiled into open outrage in Los Angeles when a black teenage girl was killed by Korean American merchant Soon Ja Du. Although convicted of voluntary manslaughter, Du was sentenced to probation and community service only. Similarly, in the early 1990s African-Americans launched economic boycotts of, and political confrontations with, Korean American small merchants in New York. Thus, in the aftermath of the blatant miscarriage of justice in Los Angeles last year—the acquittal of four white police officers for the violent beating of Rodney King—the anger and outrage within the African-American community was channeled not against the state and the corporations, but against small Korean American merchants. Throughout Los Angeles, over 1,500 Korean-American-owned stores were destroyed, burned or looted. Following the urban uprising, a fiercely anti-Asian sentiment continued to permeate sections of Los Angeles. In 1992–93 there have been a series of incidents of Asian Americans being harassed or beaten in southern California. After the rail-system contract was awarded to a Japanese company, a chauvinistic movement was launched to "buy American." Asian Americans are still popularly projected to other nonwhites as American's successful "model minorities," fostering resentment, misunderstandings and hostilities among people of color. Yet black leaders have consistently failed to explain to African-Americans that Asian-Americans as a group do not own the major corporations or banks which control access to capital. They do not own massive amounts of real estate, control the courts or city governments, have ownership of the mainstream media, dominate police forces, or set urban policies.

While African-Americans, Latinos and Asian-Americans scramble over which group should control the mom-and-pop grocery store in their neighborhood, almost no one questions the racist "redlining" policies of large banks which restrict access to capital to nearly all people of color. Black and Latino working people usually are not told by their race-conscious leaders and middle-class "symbolic representatives" that institutional racism has also frequently targeted Asian Americans throughout US history—from the recruitment and exploitation of Asian laborers, to a series of lynchings and violent assaults culminating in the mass incarceration of Japanese Americans during World War II, to the slaying of Vincent Chin in Detroit and the violence and harassment of other Asian Americans. A central ideological pillar of "whiteness" is the consistent scapegoating of the "oriental menace." As legal scholar Mari Matsuda observes.

> There is an unbroken line of poor and working Americans
> turning their anger and frustration into hatred of Asian Ameri-
> cans. Every time this happens, the real villains—the corpora-
> tions and politicians who put profits before human needs—are
> allowed to go about their business free from public scrutiny,
> and the anger that could go to organizing for positive social
> change goes instead to Asian-bashing.

What is required is a radical break from the narrow, race-based politics of the past, which characterized the core assumptions about black empowerment since the mid nineteenth century. We need to recognize that the two perspectives of racial-identity politics that are frequently juxtaposed, integration/assimilation and nationalist/separatism, are actually two sides of the same ideological and strategic axis. To move into the future will require that we bury the racial barriers of the past, for good. The essential point of departure is the deconstruction of the idea of "whiteness," the ideology of white power, privilege and elitism which remains heavily embedded within the dominant culture, social institutions and economic arrangements of the society. But we must do more than critique the white pillars of race, gender and class domination. We must rethink and restructure the central social categories of collective struggle by which we conceive and understand our own political reality. We must redefine "blackness" and other traditional racial categories to be more inclusive of contemporary ethnic realities.

To be truly liberating, a social theory must reflect the actual problems of a historical conjuncture with a commitment to rigor and scholastic truth. "Afrocentrism" fails on all counts to provide that clarity of insight into the contemporary African-American urban experience. It looks to a romantic, mythical reconstruction of yesterday to find some understanding of the cultural basis of today's racial and class challenges. Yet that critical understanding

30

of reality cannot begin with an examination of the lives of Egyptian Pharaohs. It must begin by critiquing the vast structure of power and privilege which characterizes the political economy of post-industrial capitalist America. According to the Center on Budget and Policy Priorities, during the Reagan–Bush era of the 1980s the poorest one-fifth of all Americans earned about $7,725 annually, and experienced a decline in before-tax household incomes of 3.8 per cent over the decade. The middle fifth of all US households earned about $31,000 annually, with an income gain of 3.1 per cent during the 1980s. Yet the top fifth of household incomes reached over $105,200 annually by 1990, with before-tax incomes growing by 29.8 per cent over the 1980s. The richest 5 per cent of all American households exceeded $206,000 annually, improving their incomes by 44.9 per cent under Reagan and Bush. The wealthiest 1 per cent of all US households reached nearly $550,000 per year, with average before-tax incomes increasing by 75.3 per cent. In effect, since 1980 the income gap between America's wealthiest 1 per cent and the middle class *nearly doubled.* As the Center of Budget and Policy Priorities relates, the wealthiest 1 per cent of all Americans—roughly 2.5 million people—receive "nearly as much income after taxes as the bottom 40 per cent, about 100 million people. While wealthy households are taking a larger share of the national income, the tax burden has been shifted down the income pyramid. "A social theory of a reconstructed, multicultural democracy must advance the reorganization and ownership of capital resources, the expansion of production in minority areas, and provision of guarantees for social welfare—such as a single-payer, national health-care system.

The factor of "race" by itself does not and cannot explain the massive transformation of the structure of capitalism in its post-industrial phase, or the destructive redefinition of "work" itself, as we enter the twenty-first century. Increasingly in Western Europe and America, the new division between "haves" and "have nots" is characterized by a new segmentation of the labor force. The division is between those workers who have maintained basis economic security and benefits—such as full health insurance, term life insurance, pensions, educational stipends or subsidies for the employee's children, paid vacations, and so forth—and those marginal workers who are either unemployed, or part-time employees, or who labor but have few if any benefits. Since 1982, "temporary employment" or part-time hirings without benefits have increased 250 per cent across the USA, while all employment has grown by less than 20 per cent. Today, the largest private employer in the USA is Manpower, Inc., the world's largest temporary employment agency, with 560,000 workers. By the year 2000, half of all American workers will be classified as part-time employees, or, as they are termed within IBM, "the peripherals." The reason for this massive restructuring of labor relations is capital's search for surplus value or profits.

Increasingly, disproportionately high percentages of Latino and African-American workers will be trapped within this second-tier of the labor market. Black, Latino, Asian-American, and low-income white workers all share a stake in fighting for a new social contract relating to work and social benefits: the right to a good job should be guaranteed in the same way as the human right to vote; the right to free high-quality health care should be as secure as the freedom of speech. The radical changes within the domestic economy require that black leadership reaches out to other oppressed sectors of the society, creating a common program for economic and social justice. Vulgar Afrocentrism looks inward; the new black liberation of the twenty-first century must look outward, embracing those people of color and oppressed people of divergent ethnic backgrounds who share our democratic vision.

The multicultural democratic critique must consider the changing demographic, cultural and class realities of modern post-industrial America. By the year 2000, one-third of the total US population will consist of people of color. Within seventy years, roughly half of America's entire population will be Latino, American Indian, Pacific American, Arab American and African-American. The ability to create a framework for multicultural democracy, inter-group dialogue, and interaction within and between the most progressive leaders, grassroots activists, intellectuals and working people of these communities will determine the future of American society itself. Our ability to transcend racial chauvinism and inter-ethnic hatred and the old definitions of "race," to recognize the class commonalities and joint social-justice interests of all groups in the restructuring of this nation's economy and social order, will be the key to constructing a nonracist democracy, transcending ancient walls of white violence, corporate power and class privilege. By dismantling the narrow politics of racial identity and selective self-interest, by going beyond "black" and "white," we may construct new values, new institutions and new visions of an America beyond traditional racial categories and racial oppression.

STANDING BESIDE MY SISTER, FACING THE ENEMY

LEGAL THEORY OUT OF COALITION

Mari J. Matsuda

In 1990, a group of students in my feminist legal theory class at Stanford Law School organized the Third National Conference on Women of Color and the Law. Planning the conference was their research project, undertaken in lieu of the final exam. The work, conflict, elation, and pain that constitute political organizing became a part of these students' lives. Their multicultural alliance inspired me to put into words a political theory emerging from activist coalitions: a theory of the interconnection of all forms of subordination. This theory has many origins—from the 100-year-old multiracial labor movement exemplified by the IWW's "one big union" slogan, to the student movements of the 1960s to 1970s, to the work of lesbian/feminist organizers like Suzanne Pharr who link homophobia with race, gender, and class oppression. It seems that anyone who sits down to think long and hard about the circumstances of her own oppression inevitably looks up to see others with whom to form common cause. This common cause is more than a simple alliance. It is also theory: a means of understanding and moving the world. The following piece was written as a foreword to a collection of papers delivered at the conference, which were published in the Stanford Law Review.[1]

INTRODUCTION

The Stanford Conference on Women of Color and the Law was coalition: individuals from different social positions coming together to work toward a common goal.

The conference possessed the physicality of coalition. From all corners of the country, hundreds of women, and dozens of men, came. They were law students, but their divergences in size, shape, hair, color, speech, and attire were so wondrously dramatic that no outsider who wandered into the large auditorium where they gathered would have thought, "Ah, a meeting of law students." No, it looked more like a gathering of proud tribes. As the participants sat in the sun on perfect Stanford lawns, sipping freshly brewed coffee, they laughed and talked theory as though they did this every weekend. White with Black, native with immigrant, lesbian with straight, teacher with student, women with men—as though the joy of communing across difference was their birthright.

Conference organizers buzzed about busily in their official T-shirts, arranging rides, watching the clock, shepherding speakers, and smoothing over misunderstandings. The organizers and volunteers were as diverse as the audience. White men who looked like they had just wandered over from fraternity row worked alongside their African-Asian-Latina colleagues. Watching these students work so easily with one another made me almost forget that a year of struggle, anger, tears, fears, and consciousness raising had brought them to their day in the sun. Each one had asked, at some point during that long year of working toward the conference, "Is it worth it?" Bernice Johnson Reagon, in her well-known essay on coalition, said, "You don't go into coalition because you just like it." She goes on to state, "And you shouldn't look for comfort. Some people will come to a coalition, and they rate the success of the coalition on whether or not they feel good when they get there. They're not looking for a coalition: they're looking for a home!"[2]

Through our sometimes painful work in coalition, we are beginning to form a theory of subordination. A theory that describes it, explains it, and gives us the tools to end it. As lawyers working in coalition, we develop a theory of law taking sides rather than law as value neutral. We imagine law to uplift and protect the sixteen-year-old single mother on crack rather than law to criminalize her.[3] We imagine law to celebrate and protect women's bodies; law to sanctify love between human beings, whether women to women, men to men, or women to men, as lovers may choose to love; law to respect the bones of our ancestors;[4] law to feed the children; law to shut down the sweat-sweat-shops; and law to save the planet.

This is the revolutionary theory of law that we are developing in coalition, and I submit that this is the theory of law we can develop *only* in coalition and that it is the *only* theory of law we can develop in coalition.

Looking at Subordination from Inside Coalition

When we work in coalition, we compare our struggles and challenge one another's assumptions. We learn a few tentative, starting truths—the building blocks of a theory of subordination.

We learn that all forms of oppression are not the same.[5] We learn about our ignorances and of the gaps and absences in our knowledge. We learn that although all forms of oppression are not the same, certain predictable patterns emerge:

- All forms of oppression involve taking a trait, *x,* often with attached cultural meaning,[6] and using *x* to make some group the other, reducing their entitlements and powers.

- All forms of oppression benefit someone, and sometimes both sides of a relationship of domination have some stake in its maintenance.[7]

- All forms of oppression have both material and ideological dimensions. Subordination leaves marks on the body. It is real. It is material; it is health, economy, and violence. Subordination is also ideology: language—including the language of science and law, rights, necessity, the market, neutrality, and objectivity—can serve to make domination seem natural and inevitable.

- In coalition we learn as well that there is a psychology to subordination, involving elements of sexual fear, need for control, self-hate, and other-hate.

- Finally, and most important, we learn in coalition that all forms of subordination are interlocking and mutually reinforcing, even as they are different and incommensurable.

Ask the Other Question: The Interconnection of All Forms of Subordination

The way I try to understand the interconnection of all forms of subordination is through a method I call "ask the other question." When I see something that looks racist, I ask, "Where is the patriarchy in this?" When I see something that looks sexist, I ask, "Where is the heterosexism in this?" When I see something that looks homophobic, I ask, "Where are the class interests in this?" Working in coalition forces us to look for both the obvious and the nonobvious relationships of domination, and, as we have done this, we have come to see that no form of subordination ever stands alone.[8]

If this is true, we have asked each other, then is it not also true that dismantling any one is impossible without dismantling every other? More and more, particularly in the women-of-color movement, the answer is, "No person is free until the last and the least of us is free."

In trying to explain this in my own community, I sometimes try to shake 10 people up by suggesting that patriarchy killed Vincent Chin. Most people think racism killed Vincent Chin.[9] When white men with baseball bats, hurling racist hate speech, beat a man to death, it is obvious that racism is a cause. It is only slightly less obvious, however, when you walk down the aisles of Toys-R-Us, that little boys grow up in this culture with toys that teach dominance and aggression, while little girls grow up with toys that teach about being pretty, baking, and changing a diaper. The little boy who is interested in learning how to nurture and play house is called a sissy. And when he is a little older he is called f_g.[10] He learns that acceptance for men in this society is premised on rejecting the girl culture and taking on the boy culture, and I believe that this, as much as racism, killed Vincent Chin. I have come to see that homophobia is the disciplinary system that teaches men that they had better talk like 2 Live Crew or else someone will think they "aren't real men," and I believe that this homophobia is a cause of rape and violence against women. I have come to see how that same homophobia makes women scared to choose women and sends them into the arms of men who beat them. I have come to see that class oppression has the same effect, cutting off the chance of economic independence that could free women from dependency on abusive men.

I have come to see all this from working in coalition; from my lesbian colleagues who have pointed out homophobia in places where I failed to see it; from my Native American colleagues who have said, "But remember that we were here first," when I worked for the rights of immigrant women; and from men of color who have risked my wrath to say, "But racism *is* what is killing us, why can't I put that first on my agenda?" The women-of-color movement has, of necessity, been a movement about intersecting structures of subordination. This movement suggests that antipatriarchal struggle is linked to struggle against all forms for subordination.

Beyond Race Alone

What does this mean? In coalition, we develop several levels of understanding that the phenomenon that Professor Crenshaw has called "intersectionality."[11] The women-of-color movement has demanded that the civil rights struggle move beyond race alone, suggesting several reasons why our coalitions must include more than antiracism. These reasons include the following:

1. In unity there is strength. No subordinated group is strong enough to fight the power alone; thus coalitions are formed out of necessity.[12]

2. Some of us have overlapping identity. Separating out and ranking oppression excludes some of these identities and denies the necessary concerns of significant numbers of our constituency. To say that antiracist struggle precedes all other struggle denies the existence and needs of the multiply oppressed: women-of-color, gays and lesbians of color, poor people of color, and *most* people of color experience subordination in more than one dimension.

3. Perhaps the most progressive reason for moving beyond race alone is that racism is best understood and struggled against with knowledge gained through comparative study. Even if one wanted to live as the old prototype "race man," it is simply not possible to struggle against racism alone and ever hope to end racism.

This is a threatening suggestion for many of us who have worked primarily in organizations forged in the struggle for racial justice. Our political strength and our cultural self-worth is often grounded in racial pride. Our multiracial coalitions have, in the past, succeeded because of a unifying commitment to end racist attacks on people of color. Moving beyond race, to include discussion of other forms of subordination, risks breaking coalition. Because I believe that the most progressive elements of any liberation movement are those who see the intersections and that the most regressive are those who insist on only one axis, I am willing to risk breaking coalition by pushing intersectional analysis.

An additional and more serious risk, I think, is that an intersectional analysis done from on high, that is, from outside rather than inside a structure of subordination, risks misunderstanding the particularity of that structure. Feminists have spent years talking about, experiencing, and building theory around gender. Native Americans have spent years developing an understanding of colonialism and its effect on culture. That kind of situated, ground-up knowledge is irreplaceable, and a casual effort to say, "OK, I'll add gender to my analysis," without immersion in feminist practice is likely to miss something. Adding on gender must involve active feminists, just as adding on considerations of indigenous peoples must include activists from Native communities. Coalition is the way to achieve this inclusion.

15   It is no accident that women-of-color, grounded as they are in both feminist and antiracist struggle, are doing the most exciting theoretical work on race–gender intersections. It is no accident that gay and lesbian scholars are advancing the analysis of sexuality in subordination. In raising this I do not mean that we cannot speak of subordination from the second hand. I mean to encourage us to do this and to suggest we can do this most intelligently in coalition, listening with special care to those who are actively involved in knowing and ending the systems of domination that touch their lives.[13]

CONCLUSION

This essay has suggested a theory of subordination that comes out of work in coalition. The Women-of-Color and the Law Conference is a place for this work. The women and men of many races who worked on the conference can tell us that making this place is not easy. The false efficiencies of law schools, where we edit facts out of cases and cabin concepts such as "crime" and "property" into semester-sized courses, ill-prepare us for the long, slow, open-ended efficiencies of coalition. Planning the conference involved more than inviting speakers and sending out registration forms. It took literally a thousand human hours talking long into the night, telling stories of self and culture and history, before the Stanford Women of Color and the Law Conference could happen. To lay the foundation of trust on which people could teach, challenge, listen, learn, and form theory out of coalition took time and patience. As often happens in the slow-cooking school of theory building, the organizers wondered whether all that talk was getting anywhere. Cutting off discussion and avoiding conflict would have saved hours early on, but coalition at its best never works that way. The slow and difficult early work gives us efficiencies when we need them: when the real challenges come, when justice requires action, and when there is no time to argue over how to proceed. The organizers of the conference have forged bonds and created theory that will sustain them in the contentious closing days of this century. When called on, they will answer with a courage and wisdom born in their place of coalition.

NOTES

1. Papers presented at the conference are compiled in *Stanford Law Review* 43, no. 6 (July 1991). Included are Mari J. Matsuda, "Beside My Sister, Facing the Enemy: Legal Theory Out of Coalition"; Evelyn Nakano Glenn, "Cleaning up/Kept down: A Historical Perpsective on Racial Inequality in 'women's work'"; Haunani-Kay Trask, "Coalition-Building between Natives and non-Natives"; Angela Y. Davis, Keynote address; Kimberlé Crenshaw, "Mapping the Margins: Intersectionality, Identity Politics, and Violence against Women of Color"; Nilda Rimonte, "A Question of Culture: Cultural Approval of Violence against Women in the Pacific-Asian Community and the Cultural Defense"; Patricia Williams, "Reordering Western Civ."; Sharon Parker, "Understanding Coalition"; Chezia Carraway, "Violence against Women of Color"; Judy Scales-Trent, "Women of Color and Health"; and June K. Inuzuka, "Women of Color and Public Policy: A Case Study of the Women's Business Ownership Act."

2. Bernice Johnson Reagon, "Coalition Politics: Turning the Century," in Barbara Smith, *Home Girls, A Black Feminist Anthology* (New York: Kitchen Table—Women of Color Press, 1983), 356. As Professor Kimberlé Crenshaw pointed out, on reading this essay, "Comfort means perfect peace or perfect oppression."

3. See Roberts, "Punishing Drug Addicts Who Have Babies: Women of Color, Equality, and the Right of Privacy," *Harvard Law Review* 104 (1991): 1419.

4. See a conference workshop on burial/remains discussed this issue.

5. See Trina Grillo and Stephanie Wildman, "Obscuring the Importance of Race: The Implication of Making Comparisons between Racism and Sexism (or other isms)," *Duke Law Journal* (1991): 397.

6. See Charles Lawrence, "The Id, the Ego, and Equal Protection: Reckoning with Unconscious Racism," *Stanford Law Review* 39 (1987): 317.

7. For a related discussion of Hegel's theory of the master and slave relationship, see Kendall Thomas, "A House Divided against Itself: A Comment on Mastery, Slavery, and Emancipation," *Cardozo Law Review* 10 (1989): 1481.

8. For an analysis of the relationship between sexism and heterosexism, see, e.g., Suzanne Pharr, *Homophobia: A Weapon of Sexism* (Inverness, Calif.: Chardon Press, 1988).

9. In April of 1989, mine workers in Virginia, West Virginia, and eastern Kentucky went on strike to protest Pittston Coal Company's unfair labor practices regarding health-care benefits for employees. They used Dr. King's technique of non-violent civil disobedience. For a history of the Vincent Chin murder and other cases of anti-Asian violence, see National Asian Pacific American Legal Consortium, *Audit of Violence against Asian Pacific Americans* (1994), which cited 452 reported incidents of anti-Asian violence in 1994 and noted a severe increase in anti-immigrant sentiment and widespread underreporting of anti-Asian incidents.

10. Throughout this book, homophobic, racist, and misogynist assault words are altered to omit the vowels. This is an awkward usage that attempts to recognize that these words carry significant social power in our culture and can assault even when used as examples and without intent to harm.

11. See Kimberlé Crenshaw, "Demarginalizing the Intersection of Race and Sex: A Black Feminist Critique of Antidsicrimination Doctrine," *Chicago Legal Forum* (1989): 159.
12. In addition to the political power that comes from unity, there is also joy and empowerment that comes from finding connections to others. One participant in the Stanford conference noted "the energy that comes from comparing experiences and connecting with others; the nods of 'uh-huh' when one person's story of oppression at one axis triggers another person to remember subordination at a different axis; the making of new friends, the renewal of old friendships; the knowledge that we are not alone in our struggles" are all benefits of coalition work (memo from Tony West, 19 April 1991)
13. See Mari Matsuda, "Pragmatism Modified and the False Consciousness Problem," *Southern California Law Review* 63 (1990): 1763. This piece argues for expanding pragmatic method to account for the intuitions of subordinated people. It responds to false consciousness and essentialism critiques by explaining why the charge to consider the experience of the subordinated is not the equivalent of claiming that all subordinated people are the same or that subordinated status is a necessary prerequisite to understanding subordinated status. That this kind of explanation is necessary in the present world of legal theory is itself evidence of the need for theory building in coalition.

18

Resistance Strategy Six: Neither/Nor

■■■■

LA CONCIENCIA DE LA MESTIZA: TOWARDS A NEW CONSCIOUSNESS

Gloria Anzaldúa

> *Por la mujer de mi raza*
> *hablará el espíritu.*[1]

Jose Vascocelos, Mexican philosopher, envisaged *una raza mestiza, una mezcla de razas afines, una raza de color—la primera raza síntesis del globo.* He called it a cosmic race, *la raza cósmica,* a fifth race embracing the four major races of the world.[2] Opposite to the theory of the pure Aryan, and to the policy of racial purity that white America practices, his theory is one of inclusivity. At the confluence of two or more genetic streams, with chromosomes constantly "crossing over," this mixture of races, rather than resulting in an inferior being, provides hybrid progeny, a mutable, more malleable species with a rich gene pool. From this racial, ideological, cultural and biological cross-pollinization, an "alien" consciousness is presently in the making—a new *mestiza* consciousness, *una conciencia de mujer.* It is a consciousness of the Borderlands.

UNA LUCHA DE FRONTERAS / A STRUGGLE OF BORDERS

> Because I, a *mestiza,*
> continually walk out of one culture
> and into another,
> because I am in all cultures at the same time,

alma entre dos mundos, tres, cuatro,
me zumba la cabeza con lo contradictorio.
Estoy norteada por todas las voces que me hablan
simultáneamente.

The ambivalence from the clash of voices results in mental and emotional states of perplexity. Internal strife results in insecurity and indecisiveness. The mestiza's dual or multiple personality plagued by psychic restlessness.

5   In a constant state of mental nepantilism, an Aztec word meaning torn between ways, *la mestiza* is a product of the transfer of the cultural and spiritual values of one group to another. Being tricultural, monolingual, bilingual, or multilingual, speaking a patois, and in a state of perpetual transition, the *mestiza* faces the dilemma of the mixed breed: which collectivity does the daughter of a darkskinned mother listen to?

El choque de un alma atrapado entre el mundo del espíritu y el mundo de la técnica a veces la deja entullada. Cradled in one culture, sandwiched between two cultures, straddling all three cultures and their value systems, *la mestiza* undergoes a struggle of flesh, a struggle of borders, an inner war. Like all people, we perceive the version of reality that our culture communicates. Like others having or living in more than one culture, we get multiple, often opposing messages. The coming together of two self-consistent but habitually incompatible frames of reference[3] causes *un choque,* a cultural collision.

Within us and within *la cultura chicana,* commonly held beliefs of the white culture attack commonly held beliefs of the Mexican culture, and both attack commonly held beliefs of the indigenous culture. Subconsciously, we see an attack on ourselves and our beliefs as a threat and we attempt to block with a counterstance.

But it is not enough to stand on the opposite river bank, shouting questions, challenging patriarchal, white conventions. A counterstance locks one into a duel of oppressor and oppressed; locked in mortal combat, like the cop and the criminal, both are reduced to a common denominator of violence. The counterstance refutes the dominant culture's views and beliefs, and, for this, it is proudly defiant. All reaction is limited by, and dependent on, what it is reacting against. Because the counterstance stems from a problem with authority—outer as well as inner—it's a step towards liberation from cultural domination. But it is not a way of life. At some point, on our way to a new consciousness, we will have to leave the opposite bank, the split between the two mortal combatants somehow healed so that we are on both shores at once and, at once, see through serpent and eagle eyes. Or perhaps we will decide to disengage from the dominant culture, write it off altogether as a lost cause, and cross the border into a wholly new and separate territory. Or we might go another route. The possibilities are numerous once we decide to act and not react.

A TOLERANCE FOR AMBIGUITY

These numerous possibilities leave *la mestiza* floundering in uncharted seas. In perceiving conflicting information and points of view, she is subjected to a swamping of her psychological borders. She has discovered that she can't hold concepts or ideas in rigid boundaries. The borders and walls that are supposed to keep the undesirable ideas out are entrenched habits and patterns of behavior; these habits and patterns are the enemy within. Rigidity means death. Only by remaining flexible is she able to stretch the psyche horizontally and vertically. *La mestiza* constantly has to shift out of habitual formations; from convergent thinking, analytical reasoning that tends to use rationality to move toward a single goal (a Western mode), to divergent thinking,[4] characterized by movement away from set patterns and goals and toward a more whole perspective, one that includes rather than excludes.

The new *mestiza* copes by developing a tolerance for contradictions, a tolerance for ambiguity. She learns to be an Indian in Mexican culture, to be Mexican from an Anglo point of view. She learns to juggle cultures. She has a plural personality, she operates in a pluralistic mode—nothing is thrust out, the good the bad and the ugly, nothing rejected, nothing abandoned. Not only does she sustain contradictions, she turns the ambivalence into something else. `10`

She can be jarred out of ambivalence by an intense, and often painful, emotional event which inverts or resolves the ambivalence. I'm not sure exactly how. The work takes place underground—subconsciously. It is work that the soul performs. That focal point or fulcrum, that juncture where the mestiza stands, is where phenomena tend to collide. It is where the possibility of uniting all that is separate occurs. This assembly is not one where severed or separated pieces merely come together. Nor is it a balancing of opposing powers. In attempting to work out a synthesis, the self has added a third element which is greater than the sum of its severed parts. That third element is a new consciousness—a mestiza consciousness—and though it is a source of intense pain, its energy comes from continual creative motion that keeps breaking down the unitary aspect of each new paradigm.

En unas pocas centurias, the future will belong to the mestiza. Because the future depends on the breaking down of paradigms, it depends on the straddling of two or more cultures. By creating a new mythos—that is, a change in the way we perceive reality, the way we see ourselves, and the ways we behave—*la mestiza* creates a new consciousness.

The work of *mestiza* consciousness is to break down the subject-object duality that keeps her a prisoner and to show in the flesh and through the images in her work how duality is transcended. The answer to the problem between the white race and the colored, between males and females, lies in healing the split that originates in the very foundation of our lives, our culture, our languages, our thoughts. A massive uprooting of dualistic thinking in the individual and collective consciousness is the beginning of a long struggle, but one that could, in our best hopes, bring us to the end of rape, of violence, of war.

LA ENCRUCIJADA / THE CROSSROADS

A chicken is being sacrificed
    at a crossroads, a simple mound of earth
a mud shrine for *Eshu,*
    Yoruba god of indeterminacy,
who blesses her choice of path.
    She begins her journey.

15   *Su cuerpo es una bocacalle. La mestiza* has gone from being the sacrificial goat to becoming the officiating priestess at the crossroads.

As a *mestiza* I have no country, my homeland cast me out; yet all countries are mine because I am every woman's sister or potential lover. (As a lesbian I have no race, my own people disclaim me; but I am all races because there is the queer of me in all races.) I am cultureless because, as a feminist, I challenge the collective cultural/religious male-derived beliefs of Indo-Hispanics and Anglos; yet I am cultured because I am participating in the creation of yet another culture, a new story to explain the world and our participation in it, a new value system with images and symbols that connect us to each other and to the planet. *Soy un amasamiento,* I am an act of kneading, of uniting and joining that not only has produced both a creature of darkness and a creature of light, but also a creature that questions the definitions of light and dark and gives them new meanings.

We are the people who leap in the dark, we are the people on the knees of the gods. In our very flesh, (r)evolution works out the clash of cultures. It makes us crazy constantly, but if the center holds, we've made some kind of evolutionary step forward. *Nuestra alma el trabajo,* the opus, the great alchemical work; spiritual *mestizaje,* a "morphogenesis,"[5] an inevitable unfolding. We have become the quickening serpent movement.

Indigenous like corn, like corn, the *mestiza* is a product of crossbreeding, designed for preservation under a variety of conditions. Like an ear of corn—a female seed-bearing organ—the *mestiza* is tenacious, tightly wrapped in the husks of her culture. Like kernels she clings to the cob; with thick stalks and strong brace roots, she holds tight to the earth—she will survive the crossroads.

Lavando y remojando el maíz en agua de cal, despojando el pellejo. Moliendo, mixteando, amasando, haciendo tortillas de masa.[6] She steeps the corn in lime, it swells, softens. With stone roller on *metate,* she grinds the corn, then grinds again. She kneads and moulds the dough, pats the round balls into *tortillas.*

We are the porous rock in the stone *metate*   *20*
squatting on the ground.
We are the rolling pin, *el maíz y agua,*
la masa harina. Somos el amasijo.
Somos lo molido en el metate.
We are the *comal* sizzling hot,
the hot *tortilla,* the hungry mouth.
We are the coarse rock.
We are the grinding motion,
the mixed potion, *somos el molcajete.*
We are the pestle, the *comino, ajo, pimienta,*
We are the *chile colorado,*
the green shoot that cracks the rock.
We will abide.

EL CAMINO DE LA MESTIZA /
THE MESTIZA WAY

Caught between the sudden contraction, the breath sucked
in and the endless space, the brown woman stands still, looks at
the sky. She decides to go down, digging her way along the
roots of trees. Sifting through the bones, she shakes them to see
if there is any marrow in them. Then, touching the dirt to her
forehead, to her tongue, she takes a few bones, leaves the rest in
their burial place.

She goes through her backpack, keeps her journal and address book, throws away the muni-bart metromaps. The coins
are heavy and they go next, then the greenbacks flutter
through the air. She keeps her knife, can opener and eyebrow
pencil. She puts bones, pieces of bark, *hierbas,* eagle feather,
snakeskin, tape recorder, the rattle and drum in her pack and
she sets out to become the complete *tolteca.*

Her first step is to take inventory. *Despojando, desgranando, quitando paja.*
Just what did she inherit from her ancestors? This weight on her back—which
is the baggage from the Indian mother, which the baggage from the Spanish
father, which the baggage from the Anglo?

Pero es difícil differentiating between *lo heredado, lo adquirido, lo impuesto.* She
puts history through a sieve, winnows out the lies, looks at the forces that we
as a race, as women, have been a part of. *Luego bota lo que no vale, los desmientos,*
los desencuentros, el embrutecimiento. Aguarda el juicio, hondo y enraízado, de la gente
Antigua. This step is a conscious rupture with all oppressive traditions of all cultures and religions. She communicates that rupture, documents the struggle.
She reinterprets history and, using new symbols, she shapes new myths. She

adopts new perspectives toward the darkskinned, women and queers. She strengthens her tolerance (and intolerance) for ambiguity. She is willing to share, to make herself vulnerable to foreign ways of seeing and thinking. She surrenders all notions of safety, of the familiar. Deconstruct, construct. She becomes a *nahual,* able to transform herself into a tree, a coyote, into another person. She learns to transform the small "I" into the total Self. *Se hace moldeadora de su alma. Según la concepción que tiene de sí misma, así sera.*

QUE NO SE NOS OLVIDE LOS HOMBRES

25   *"Tú no sirves pa' nada—*
you're good for nothing.
Eres pura vieja."

"You're nothing but a woman" means you are defective. Its opposite is to be *un macho.* The modern meaning of the word "machismo," as well as the concept, is actually an Anglo invention. For men like my father, being "macho" meant being strong enough to protect and support my mother and us, yet being able to show love. Today's macho has doubts about his ability to feed and protect his family. His "machismo" is an adaptation to oppression and poverty and low self-esteem. It is the result of hierarchical male dominance. The Anglo, feeling inadequate and inferior and powerless, displaces or transfers these feelings to the Chicano by shaming him. In the Gringo world, the Chicano suffers from excessive humility and self-effacement, shame of self and self-deprecation. Around Latinos he suffers from a sense of language inadequacy and its accompanying discomfort; with Native Americans he suffers from a racial amnesia which ignores our common blood, and from guilt because the Spanish part of him took their land and oppressed them. He has an excessive compensatory hubris when around Mexicans from the other side. It overlays a deep sense of racial shame.

The loss of a sense of dignity and respect in the macho breeds a false machismo which leads him to put down women and even to brutalize them. Coexisting with his sexist behavior is a love for the mother which takes precedence over that of all others. Devoted son, macho pig. To wash down the shame of his acts, of his very being, and to handle the brute in the mirror, he takes to the bottle, the snort, the needle, and the fist.

Though we "understand" the root causes of male hatred and fear, and the subsequent wounding of women, we do not excuse, we do not condone, and we will no longer put up with it. From the men of our race, we demand the admission/acknowledgment/disclosure/testimony that they wound us, violate us, are afraid of us and of our power. We need them to say they will begin to eliminate their hurtful put-down ways. But more than the words, we demand acts. We say to them: We will develop equal power with you and those who have shamed us.

It is imperative that mestizas support each other in changing the sexist elements in the Mexican-Indian culture. As long as woman is put down, the Indian and the Black in all of us is put down. The struggle of the mestiza is above all a feminist one. As long as *los hombres* think they have to *chingar mujeres* and each other to be men, as long as men are taught that they are superior and therefore culturally favored over *la mujer,* as long as to be a *vieja* is a thing of derision, there can be no real healing of our psyches. We're halfway there—we have such love of the Mother, the good mother. The first step is to unlearn the *puta/virgen* dichotomy and to see *Coatlapopeuh-Coatlicue* in the Mother, *Guadalupe.*

Tenderness, a sign of vulnerability, is so feared that it is showered on women with verbal abuse and blows. Men, even more than women, are fettered to gender roles. Women at least have had the guts to break out of bondage. Only gay men have had the courage to expose themselves to the woman inside them and to challenge the current masculinity. I've encountered a few scattered and isolated gentle straight men, the beginnings of a new breed, but they are confused, and entangled with sexist behaviors that they have not been able to eradicate. We need a new masculinity and the new man needs a movement.

Lumping the males who deviate from the general norm with man, the oppressor, is a gross injustice. *Asombra pensar que nos hemos quedado en ese pozo oscuro donde el mundo encierra a las lesbianas. Asombra pensar que hemos, como femenistas y lesbianas, cerrado nuestros corazónes a los hombres, a nuestros hermanos los jotos, desheredados y marginales como nosotros.* Being the supreme crossers of cultures, homosexuals have strong bonds with the queer white, Black, Asian, Native American, Latino, and with the queer in Italy, Australia and the rest of the planet. We come from all colors, all classes, all races, all time periods. Our role is to link people with each other—the Blacks with Jews with Indians with Asians with whites with extraterrestrials. It is to transfer ideas and information from one culture to another. Colored homosexuals have more knowledge of other cultures; have always been at the forefront (although sometimes in the closet) of all liberation struggles in this country; have suffered more injustices and have survived them despite all odds. Chicanos need to acknowledge the political and artistic contributions of their queer. People, listen to what your *jotería* is saying.

The mestizo and the queer exist at this time and point on the evolutionary continuum for a purpose. We are a blending that proves that all blood is intricately woven together, and that we are spawned out of similar souls.

SOMOS UNA GENTE

Hay tantísimas fronteras
que dividen a la gente,
pero por cada frontera
existe también un puente.
　　　　—Gina Valdés [7]

DIVIDED LOYALTIES   Many women and men of color do not want to have any dealings with white people. It takes too much time and energy to explain to the downwardly mobile, white middle-class women that it's okay for us to want to own "possessions," never having had any nice furniture on our dirt floors or "luxuries" like washing machines. Many feel that whites should help their own people rid themselves of race hatred and fear first. I, for one, choose to use some of my energy to serve as mediator. I think we need to allow whites to be our allies. Through our literature, art, *corridos,* and folktales we must share our history with them so when they set up committees to help Big Mountain Navajos or the Chicano farmworkers or *los Nicaragüenses* they won't turn people away because of their racial fears and ignorances. They will come to see that they are not helping us but following our lead.

35   Individually, but also as a racial entity, we need to voice our needs. We need to say to white society: We need you to accept the fact that Chicanos are different, to acknowledge your rejection and negation of us. We need you to own the fact that you looked upon us as less than human, that you stole our lands, our personhood, our self-respect. We need you to make public restitution: to say that, to compensate for your own sense of defectiveness, you strive for power over us, you erase our history and our experience because it makes you feel guilty—you'd rather forget your brutish acts. To say you've split yourself from minority groups, that you disown us, that your dual consciousness splits off parts of yourself, transferring the "negative" parts onto us. (Where there is persecution of minorities, there is shadow projection. Where there is violence and war, there is repression of shadow.) To say that you are afraid of us, that to put distance between us, you wear the mask of contempt. Admit that Mexico is your double, that she exists in the shadow of this country, that we are irrevocably tied to her. Gringo, accept the doppelganger in your psyche. By taking back your collective shadow the intracultural split will heal. And finally, tell us what you need from us.

BY YOUR TRUE FACES WE WILL KNOW YOU

I am visible—see this Indian face—yet I am invisible. I both blind them with my beak nose and am their blind spot. But I exist, we exist. They'd like to think I have melted in the pot. But I haven't, we haven't.

The dominant white culture is killing us slowly with its ignorance. By taking away our self-determination, it has made us weak and empty. As a people we have resisted and we have taken expedient positions, but we have never been allowed to develop unencumbered—we have never been allowed to be fully ourselves. The whites in power want us people of color to barricade ourselves behind our separate tribal walls so they can pick us off one at a time with their hidden weapons; so they can whitewash and distort history. Ignorance splits people, creates prejudices. A misinformed people is a subjugated people.

Before the Chicano and the undocumented worker and the Mexican from the other side can come together, before the Chicano can have unity with Native Americans and other groups, we need to know the history of their struggle and they need to know ours. Our mothers, our sisters and brothers, the guys who hang out on street corners, the children in the playgrounds, each of us must know our Indian lineage, our afro-*mestisaje,* our history of resistance.

To the immigrant *mexicano* and the recent arrivals we must teach our history. The 80 million *mexicanos* and the Latinos from Central and South America must know of our struggles. Each one of us must know basic facts about Nicaragua, Chile and the rest of Latin America. The Latinoist movement (Chicanos, Puerto Ricans, Cubans and other Spanish-speaking people working together to combat racial discrimination in the market place) is good but it is not enough. Other than a common culture we will have nothing to hold us together. We need to meet on a broader communal ground.

The struggle is inner: Chicano, *indio,* American Indian, *mojada, mexicano,* 40
immigrant Latino, Anglo in power, working class Anglo, Black, Asian—our psyches resemble the bordertowns and are populated by the same people. The struggle has always been inner, and is played out in the outer terrains. Awareness of our situation must come before inner changes, which in turn come before changes in society. Nothing happens in the "real" world unless it first happens in the images in our heads.

EL DÍA DE LA CHICANA

I will not be shamed again
Nor will I shame myself.

I am possessed by a vision: that we Chicanas and Chicanos have taken back or uncovered our true faces, our dignity and self-respect. It's a validation vision.

Seeing the Chicana anew in light of her history. I seek an exoneration, a seeing through the fictions of white supremacy, a seeing of ourselves in our true guises and not as the false racial personality that has been given to us and that we have given to ourselves. I seek our woman's face, our true features, the positive and the negative seen clearly, free of the tainted biases of male dominance. I seek new images of identity, new beliefs about ourselves, our humanity and worth no longer in question.

Estamos viviendo en la noche de la Raza, un tiempo cuando el trabajo se hace a lo quieto, en el oscuro. El día cuando aceptamos tal y como somos y para en donde vamos y porque—ese día sera el día de la Raza. Yo tengo el conpromiso de expresar mi visión, mi sensibilidad, mi percepción de la revalidación de la gente mexicana, su mérito, estimación, honra, aprecio, y validez.

45   On December 2nd when my sun goes into my first house, I celebrate *el día de la Chicana y el Chicano.* On that day I clean my altars, light my *Coatlalopeuh* candle, burn sage and copal, take *el baño para espantar basura,* sweep my house. On that day I bare my soul, make myself vulnerable to friends and family by expressing my feelings. On that day I affirm who we are.

On that day I look inside our conflicts and our basic introverted racial temperament. I identify our needs, voice them. I acknowledge that the self and the race have been wounded. I recognize the need to take care of our personhood, of our racial self. On that day I gather the splintered and disowned parts of *la gente mexicana* and hold them in my arms. *Todas las partes de nosotros valen.*

On that day I say, "Yes, all you people wound us when you reject us. Rejection strips us of self-worth; our vulnerability exposes us to shame. It is our innate identity you find wanting. We are ashamed that we need your good opinion, that we need your acceptance. We can no longer camouflage our needs, can no longer let defenses and fences sprout around us. We can no longer withdraw. To rage and look upon you with contempt is to rage and be contemptuous of ourselves. We can no longer blame you, nor disown the white parts, the male parts, the pathological parts, the queer parts, the vulnerable parts. Here we are weaponless with open arms, with only our magic. Let's try it our way, the mestiza way, the Chicana way, the woman way.

On that day, I search for our essential dignity as a people, a people with a sense of purpose—to belong and contribute to something greater than our *pueblo.* On that day I seek to recover and reshape my spiritual identity. *¡Anímate! Raza, a celebrar el día de la Chicana.*

EL RETORNO

> All movements are accomplished in six stages,
> and the seventh brings return.
>   —I Ching[8]

50   *Tanto tempo sin verte casa mía,*
mi cuna, mi hondo nido de la huerta.
    — *"Soledad"*[9]

I stand at the river, watch the curving, twisting serpent, a serpent nailed to the fence where the mouth of the Rio Grande empties into the Gulf.

I have come back. *Tanto dolor me costó el alejamiento.* I shade my eyes and look up. The bone beak of a hawk slowly circling over me, checking me out as potential carrion. In its wake a little bird flickering its wings, swimming sporadically like a fish. In the distance the expressway and the slough of traffic like an irritated sow. The sudden pull in my gut, *la tierra, los aguaceros.* My land, *el viento soplando la arena, el lagartijo debajo de un nopalito. Me acuerdo como era antes. Una region desértica de vasta llanuras, costeras de baja altura, de escasa lluvia, de chaparrals formados por mesquites y huizaches.* If I look real hard I can almost see the Spanish fathers who were called "the cavalry of Christ" enter this valley riding their burros, see the clash of cultures commence.

Tierra natal. This is home, the small towns in the Valley, *los pueblitos* with chicken pens and goats picketed to mesquite shrubs. *En las colonias* on the other side of the tracks, junk cars line the front yards of hot pink and lavender-trimmed houses—Chicano architecture we call it, self-consciously. I have missed the TV shows where hosts speak in half and half, and where awards are given in the category of Tex-Mex music. I have missed the Mexican cemeteries blooming with artificial flowers, the fields of aloe vera and red pepper, rows of sugar cane, of corn hanging on the stalks, the cloud of *polvareda* in the dirt roads behind a speeding pickup truck, *el sabor de tamales de rez y venado.* I have missed *la yegua colorada* gnawing the wooden gate of her stall, the smell of horse flesh from Carito's corrals. *He hecho menos las noches calientes sin aire, noches de linternas y lechuzas* making holes in the night.

I still feel the old despair when I look at the unpainted, dilapidated, scrap lumber houses consisting mostly of corrugated aluminum. Some of the poorest people in the U.S. live in the Lower Rio Grande Valley, an arid and semi-arid land of irrigated farming, intense sunlight and heat, citrus groves next to chaparral and cactus. I walk through the elementary school I attended so long ago, that remained segregated until recently. I remember how the white teachers used to punish us for being Mexican.

How I love this tragic valley of South Texas, as Ricardo Sánchez calls it; this borderland between the Nueces and the Rio Grande. This land has survived possession and ill-use by five countries: Spain, Mexico, the Republic of Texas, the U.S., the Confederacy, and the U.S. again. It has survived Anglo-Mexican blood feuds, lynchings, burnings, rapes, pillage.

Today I see the Valley still struggling to survive. Whether it does or not, it will never be as I remember it. The borderlands depression that was set off by the 1982 peso devaluation in Mexico resulted in the closure of hundreds of Valley businesses. Many people lost their homes, cars, land. Prior to 1982, U.S. store owners thrived on retail sales to Mexicans who came across the border for groceries and clothes and appliances. While goods on the U.S. side have become 10, 100, 1000 times more expensive for Mexican buyers, goods on the Mexican side have become 10, 100, 1000 times cheaper for Americans. Because the Valley is heavily dependent on agriculture and Mexican retail trade, it has the highest unemployment rates along the entire border region; it is the Valley that has been hardest hit.[10]

"It's been a bad year for corn," my brother, Nune, says. As he talks, I re-member my father scanning the sky for a rain that would end the drought, looking up into the sky, day after day, while the corn withered on its stalk. My father has been dead for 29 years, having worked himself to death. The life span of a Mexican farm laborer is 56—he lived to be 38. It shocks me that I am older than he. I, too, search the sky for rain. Like the ancients, I worship the rain god and the maize goddess, but unlike my father I have recovered their names. Now for rain (irrigation) one offers not a sacrifice of blood, but of money.

"Farming is in a bad way," my brother says. "Two to three thousand small and big farmers went bankrupt in this country last year. Six years ago the price of corn was $8.00 per hundred pounds," he goes on. "This year it is $3.90 per hundred pounds." And, I think to myself, after taking inflation into account, not planting anything puts you ahead.

I walk out to the back yard, stare at *los rosales de mamá.* She wants me to help her prune the rose bushes, dig out the carpet grass that is choking them. *Mamagrande Ramona también tenía rosales.* Here every Mexican grows flowers. If they don't have a piece of dirt, they use car tires, jars, cans, shoe boxes. Roses are the Mexican's favorite flower. I think, how symbolic—thorns and all.

60   Yes, the Chicano and Chicana have always taken care of growing things and the land. Again I see the four of us kids getting off the school bus, changing into our work clothes, walking into the field with Papí and Mamí, all six of us bending to the ground. Below our feet, under the earth lie the watermelon seeds. We cover them with paper plates, putting *terremotes* on top of the plates to keep them from being blown away by the wind. The paper plates keep the freeze away. Next day or the next, we remove the plates, bare the tiny green shoots to the elements. They survive and grow, give fruit hundreds of times the size of the seed. We water them and hoe them. We harvest them. The vines dry, rot, are plowed under. Growth, death, decay, birth. The soil prepared again and again, impregnated, worked on. A constant changing of forms, *renacimientos de la tierra madre.*

> This land was Mexican once
>   was Indian always
>   and is.
>   And will be again.

NOTES

1. This is my own "take off" on Jose Vasconcelos' idea. Jose Vasconcelos, *La Raza Cósmica: Misión de la Raza Ibero-Americana* (México: Aguilar S.A. de Ediciones, 1961).

2. Vasconcelos.

3. Arthur Koestler termed this "bisociation." Albert Rothenberg, *The Creative Process in Art, Science, and Other Fields* (Chicago, IL: University of Chicago Press, 1979), 12.

4. In part, I derive my definitions for "convergent" and "divergent" thinking from Rothenberg, 12–13.

5. To borrow chemist Ilya Prigogine's theory of "dissipative structures." Prigogine discovered that substances interact not in predictable ways as it was taught in science, but

in different and fluctuating ways to produce new and more complex structures, a kind of birth he called "morphogenesis," which created unpredictable innovations. Harold Gilliam, "Searching for a New World View," *This World* (January 1981), 23.

6. *Tortillas de masa harina:* Corn tortillas are of two types, the smooth uniform ones made in a tortilla press and usually bought at a tortilla factory or supermarket, and *gorditas,* made by mixing *masa* with lard or shortening or butter (my mother sometimes puts in bits of bacon or *chicharrones*).

7. Gina Valdés, *Puentes y Fronteras: Coplas Chicanas* (Los Angeles, CA: Castle Lithograph, 1982), 2.

8. Richard Wilhelm, *The I Ching or Book of Changes,* trans. Cary F. Baynes (Princeton, NJ: Princeton University Press, 1950), 98.

9. *"Soledad"* is sung by the group Haciendo Punto en Otro Son.

10. Out of the twenty-two border counties in the four border states, Hidalgo County (named for Father Hidalgo who was shot in 1810 after instigating Mexico's revolt against Spanish rule under the banner of *la Virgen de Guadalupe*) is the most poverty-stricken county in the nation as well as the largest home base (along with Imperial in California) for migrant farmworkers. It was here that I was born and raised. I am amazed that both it and I have survived.

OUR THIRD GENDER RESPONSIBILITIES

Harry Hay

Whereas previously Hay had employed the phrase "We are a separate people" to reinforce Lesbian/Gay identity, in these remarks he adopts a new formula for describing Gay difference. We are, he claims, a separate *gender*—a distinct *third* gender that is neither male nor female. Hay argues that such a conceptualization, based on the example of the Native American Two-Spirit, is a more affirmative and accurate description than that provided by the term homosexual, which narrows our difference to a single, sexual dimension. "Gender" evokes a constellation of social roles and traits, a psychological pattern and temperament, and a set of complex symbols and contested meanings. In Marxist terms, one might say that "sexual preference" and "sexual orientation" are inherently idealist concepts, while "gender" refers back to the material world, the world of productive roles, social functions, and identities.

Hay has often been misinterpreted as calling on Lesbians and Gay men to revive ancient "magical roles." As he recently wrote, those "laboring under prejudicial racist comparisons, not uncommon in contemporary Gay WASP Society, totally fail to appreciate that such 'magical roles' in co-conscious Tribal Societies translate, in our current perceptions, as *community services.* Community Services, inspired by our rather different Third Gender outlook on the World specific to our Gay Window's view, *are precisely what we Third Gender folk should be about.*"[1]

REMARKS ON THIRD GENDER

. . . It is time for us to reject the *lie* by which Organized Religions have attempted to obliterate us for two millennia. Sexual Orientation isn't the *only* difference between Us and the Heteros. As a result of the way we had been malignantly demeaned and diminished over the centuries, *it is the only difference LEFT* between us and the Heteros. It's time we took a leaf from the lessons Third Gender Brothers in other cultures have to teach us in how to re-earn the respect and gratitude of our Hetero Communities for the *different people that we are*—as well as for the talents and gifts we bring to share. In other parts of Earth, in the Third and Fourth Worlds, sedentary village cultures and quasi-civilized tribes—some of which rose to City-State status and then subsided again, some whose traditions still pertain today—noticed that though most men seemed naturally inclined to be competitive, to be Warriors, Hunters, and Fathers, always there were those some who seemed to be *men not for killing and men not for War.* These ones were gentler types—they seemed to want to celebrate their Brothers rather than to compete with them. These ones seemed to have particular powers of insight—they could distinguish between the Seen and the Unseen; they could sense the anguish in someone's heart and so act out stories or songs that magically dispelled the torment. In later centuries this would be called Theatre. They could mediate between the Known and the Unknown, and seemed not always so awed or terrified of the dread Supernaturals that they couldn't talk to them, or send messages to the shadowy Powers beyond the sky. In later centuries, this would be called prayer, and the agency bringing not only rain but many other needed changes of circumstances would be known as Temple.

Because these Brothers' contributions were essential to the cultural and spiritual well-being of the People, these different gentle ones were treasured—they would be seen as men of a different Gender. If Warriors and Husbandmen were men of a First Gender, then these Differents would be men of a Third Gender—and so they are still perceived, *and loved and treasured,* by the largest tribe of Native Americans in the American Southwest today, the Diné, whom the whitemen call Navajo. The Diné say, "When all the *nádleehé* [third-gender men and women] are gone, that will be the end of the Navaho."[2] And, equally, such different gentle men are seen among the largest Tribe in West Africa, the Hausa, as spirit mediators, while in Hawaii, contemporary inheritors of the traditional *mahu* role are playing a role in reviving the ancient art of hula dancing.[3] In smaller, more compact Native American Communities such as Zuni, in western New Mexico, the supernatural counterpart of the *lhamana,* Kolhamana, traditionally represented the balancing of men and women.[4]

We Third Gender men of Indo-European stock equally have similar talents and treasures to share. Living in the cracks of Hetero Western World sidewalks for a millennium, we actually have learned a great deal, should we finally begin to put it to use. Because we Queers need nothing from either Hetero men or Hetero women, we have learned to see them as *they would like to be seen*—in make-up, in hairdress, in design, and in tailoring, for instance. Because we Queers need nothing from either Hetero men or Hetero women that we couldn't just as easily supply one another, we have learned over the centuries *to listen to them non-judgmentally.* And this talent, now, can stand us in very good stead for its many modern uses and applications.

Over the centuries, listening to and observing Western World parliaments, we may have learned that for any self-loving, self-respecting Minority, the so-called Democratic process is never more than a Tyranny of the Majority. In the twenty-first-century world, when most urban areas in America will be aggregates of plural Societies, it would be unconscionable for Minorities to be always *competing with* one another and even more infuriating to have them always *voting against* one another. The only possible form of governance shall have to be an advance of political consciousness, in the electorate, to the recognition that, henceforth, they must learn to function and govern by means of the consensus process. The key to functioning by consensus is learning *to listen to one another non-judgmentally!* Radical Faeries have discovered that, by learning to slip the non-essential Hetero-male ego, we can really listen to one another with our inner ears. Listening with inner ears to discern principles held in common, community councils or coalitions might be enabled to collectively develop mutually respectful agreements on issues. To facilitate governing by the process of mutually respectful sharing consensus, Radical Faeries and, if they were of a mind, all Gay Brothers and Sisters, exercising their innate inclinations to process in subject-SUBJECT consciousness, might make a major contribution to Society by helping to create the most politically healthy of all possible communities. If Third Gender men and women could become Facilitator-Specialists in such governing processes, we might discover a loving appreciative need for us.

We need to make the leap in consciousness for a second reason, as well—to reclaim our own sense of an ancient and historical legitimacy, parallels to which are continually being held open for us to duplicate by our Brothers of the Third and Fourth Worlds. We made a wrong assessment of the strength we would garner as a result of claiming Minority status. When our Gay Liberationist Zappers hit the bricks in the 1970s shouting "We're a Minority—and we got rights just like every other Minority," we hadn't re-read our history books very carefully. When "the huddled masses yearning to be free" emigrated to the United States in the nineteenth century to earn a place for themselves in the bright and beckoning American Dream, they all, naturally, brought gifts to trade—gifts the United States was hungry for—huge quantities of raw labor power. What had *our* Gang brought?

Well, as a matter of fact they hadn't, consciously, brought anything—just their noisy deviant sexuality, which three-quarters of the country took one look at and said, "We don't like it, and it's *wrong* anyway." Of all the Minorities who came petitioning for the privileges of first-class citizenship, *we* alone hadn't thought to bring anything to share *or* trade. (As a matter of fact, we had, innately, brought tons of talent and treasures to share. But, liberated young Gays pouring out of our closets, we just hadn't thought about anything further than getting *out*. Truth to tell, in our Middle-class arrogance we just *hadn't thought!*)

But the notion of developing Third Gender is ready and willing to pay off. I spoke to a very politically involved Black Hetero friend in recent times and mentioned that I felt it might be time for us Gays to reclaim our Third Gender responsibilities, and he said, "Third Gender responsibilities? You've never said that before. That makes good political sense—that socially communicates something. Third Gender men are respected as valuable persons in a number of tribal societies."

10   At this point in time, I don't suppose we can expect the "bottom-line-driven" Western World Heteros, still mired in their almost obsolete and quite lethal subject-OBJECT consciousness, to be panting to discover how we Queers are necessary to *their* survival. But, to an ever-growing number of them, it is now becoming recognized that we who belong to the Third Gender carry a capacity for being able to leap to and develop a new and vitally

needed social consciousness—what Radical Faeries know as subject-SUBJECT consciousness—within which the collective functioning by sharing consensus is *the natural way to go.* It could be that we are expecting too much for the Heteros to comprehend how much they need to learn to survive themselves!

So it is now that I am proposing that we take a hand-up example from our potential allies in the Third and Fourth Worlds, whose cultures may well be overtaking, and even out-numbering, our Hetero Western so-called Free World sensibilities in the not-too-far distant first decades of the twenty-first century. I propose that we Gay Men *of all colors* prepare to present ourselves as the gentle non-competitive Third Gender men *of the Western World* with whole wardrobes and garages crammed with cultural and spiritual contributions to share.

In the November 8, 1992, "Opinion" section of the *Los Angeles Times,* columnist Richard Rodriguez said, "There is a great moan in the American heart. Something is wrong with the way we live. We have lost the knack, or the gift, of intimacy. We do not know how to love one another." I would submit that the American Gay/Lesbian Community, having shouldered almost entirely by itself the mobilizing of American cities to confront and contain the pandemic of AIDS—*with little help from criminally insensitive Congresses and three Administrations*—has rekindled vast surges of community groups reaching out with love to one another on a scale not seen in decades.

Equally would I submit that Third Gender Faerie men, in addition to forming superlative support groups for their own ailing Brothers and lovers, are developing through their many Gatherings across both the United States and Canada (not to slight "far Australia") whole new dimensions in the perceptions and sharings of intimacy. It is time for us Third Gender folk, actually, *to rejoice in the gifts we bring!* And, so saying, in such an endeavor—as my hetero Black Friend and well-wisher suggested earlier—we even might, in collective Gala, discover new Faerie ways to make such contributions both substantive and politically creative.

NOTES

1. Letter to Richard Schneider, March 5, 1995.
2. Quoted in Willard W. Hill, "The Status of the Hermaphrodite and Transvestite in Navaho Culture," *American Anthropologist* 37 (1935): 274.
3. See Carol E. Robertson, "The Māhū of Hawai'i," *Feminist Studies* 15(2) (1989): 313–26.
4. See Will Roscoe, *The Zuni Man-Woman* (Albuquerque: University of New Mexico Press, 1991).

BISEXUAL FEMINIST POLITICS: BECAUSE BISEXUALITY IS NOT ENOUGH

Karin Baker

I was one of hundreds of people who attended the now historic March 15, 1990 meeting of the Northampton Massachusetts queer community, called to create a public forum to discuss the controversial exclusion of bisexuals from the name and organizing committee of our pride march. All the fears I initially felt were confirmed as the meeting progressed and person after person expressed ignorant and hostile attitudes toward bisexuals and bisexuality.

Soon after coming out as bisexual I experienced the rejecting attitudes of lesbians and gay men. I was slow to understand why gay men and lesbians felt this way, since to me my bisexuality was not just a trendy image, a phase or a compromise with compulsory heterosexuality. On the contrary, I was proud of my bisexual identity. I considered it personally right for me and politically revolutionary.

The move to exclude bisexuals from the Northampton march (except in the role of "allies, along with straight supporters," as they had the gall to say) was initiated by a group of local lesbian feminists who had gained control of the march committee. Among the first steps they took was to close the committee to bisexuals; it included no gay men, and to my knowledge, all the lesbian members agreed with the policy of exclusion of bisexuals. This composition of the committee, as a result, did not reflect the community as a whole; at the meeting, for example, there were large numbers of lesbians and gay men who thought bisexuals should be included in all aspects of the march.

Still, I was not particularly surprised by the position of the march committee, which represented a strong trend in the local "women's" community. What did surprise me was the discovery that although some statements made at the meeting by the pro-exclusion people offended and hurt me, there were many times when I agreed with more of what they said than with the arguments of those who supported bisexual inclusion.

5   Don't mistake me, my sympathies were with my bisexual counterparts as we demanded validation within the community where so many of us have long participated as de facto members. The problem I had lay with the apolitical nature of the arguments for inclusion, from the bisexuals who spoke. The lesbian feminists who spoke, on the other hand, had a political vision and, specifically, a feminist analysis.

POLITICAL BISEXUALITY

This started me thinking about exactly how bisexuals fit into a feminist vision. As with the march committee, I believe that the struggles for queer liberation and women's liberation are intimately connected. Unlike the march committee, I believe that bisexuals have a particular role to play in these struggles, a role that both overlaps and diverges from that of lesbians and gay men. I believe that, as a group, bisexuals need to focus more attention on examining what this role might be.

For example, bisexuals clearly challenge compulsory heterosexuality, as do lesbians and gay men, to the degree to which they relate sexually to the same sex. At the same time, bisexuals are not limited in their sexuality to a specific sex, and thus bisexuality challenges the gender system, which we associate with biological sex, in a way that lesbians and gay men do not. Gender is as much, if not more, a tool of women's and queer oppression as compulsory heterosexuality. Thus, the role that bisexuals can potentially play in subverting the gender system is indispensable to a radical social transformation. However, this potential can only come from a bisexuality that is consciously feminist.

THE SOCIAL CONSTRUCTION
OF SEXUALITY AND GENDER

Systems of oppression are often justified by an oppressor as being rooted in biology, as based in something biologically inherent to human nature. Feminists confront the deeply held cultural belief that women are inherently (biologically) inferior to men. The institution of compulsory heterosexuality rests on the concept that only heterosexual sex is "natural," leading to queer oppression.

In fact, it is clear that the traditional ideas described above, and others like them, are not biologically based, but rather are socially constructed, and any claims as to their biological basis are attempts to demonstrate their legitimacy.

Not only the concept of women's inferiority but our very category of 10 gender itself is a social construction. Gender is a dual category system in which certain human traits are assigned to one biological sex, and certain traits to the other. Women and men are actually more alike than different, and most of our differences are social creations. The concept of the social construction of sexuality and gender plays a central role in the ideas I put forward here. By deconstructing these socially held attitudes, we can get at the basis of women's oppression and lesbian, bisexual and gay oppression, and work out a strategy for challenging them.

SCIENTIFICALLY PROVEN OR SOCIALLY IMPOSED CONCEPTS?

Gender is the social construct applied to biological sex. Even where gender is recognized as socially variable, biological sex is often assumed to be a fixed and entirely definable category. This is not the case. One way to show this is to demonstrate how rigid the framework of this dual category system is compared to the biological realities. Women, for example, are recognized as physically smaller and weaker than men, and exceptions to this, cases in which women are larger and stronger, are ignored. Our system of categorization is not able to encompass the breadth of variation here.

Even chromosomes and hormones, seen as the basis for gendered behavior, can be demonstrated to have less to do with gender than social upbringing does. For example, individuals with male chromosomes will display social traits associated with females if they are raised to belong to that gender. Furthermore, it has been shown that perhaps as much as hormones govern behavior, behavior may influence hormone production. As one author on the subject has concluded, "no matter how detailed an investigation science has thus far made, it is still not possible to draw a clear dividing line between male and female."[1]

My point is not that there are not differences between groups our culture presently divides according to gender. Rather, these differences have been fetishized and made to fit into categories that are not as easily delineable as our usual culture framework makes them appear. Men are aggressive, it is said, so an aggressive woman is "mannish," because the categories must be maintained in spite of apparent contradictions.

I am not saying it is possible, or desirable, to go beyond any recognition of difference. My object is rather to point out that there are other ways of viewing difference, and an alternative I would advocate is a more flexible *continuum,* rather than forcing human traits into one or two opposing and inflexible categories.

15   Where does this all lead? Just as class oppression did not exist before human communities had divided into classes, women's separation and subordination make them appear inferior and this perception becomes a justification for their subordination, or economically, once women lose access to economic power they do not have the means to be economically powerful. Thus, the perception of women and men as belonging to separate and opposing genders is both a tool and a product of women's oppression.

TOOLS OF OPPRESSION: GENDER AND COMPULSORY HETEROSEXUALITY

My position contrasts with much of lesbian feminist analysis which views *compulsory heterosexuality* as the basis for women's oppression. Heterosexual pairing is seen as a mechanism for the domination of women because it forces individual women into dependence on individual men while isolating women from each other. Given such a premise, the belief of some lesbian feminists is that lesbians are the true revolutionaries in the struggle for women's liberation. Lesbianism confronts the coercion of heterosexuality, avoids the domination within heterosexual pairing and, at the same time, brings women together.

There is no doubt that compulsory heterosexuality serves all the functions described above, and lesbianism most directly challenges this institution. My resistance is not to the conclusions of this analysis, but to what it leaves out.

Compulsory heterosexuality is composed of its own component building block, gender, and thus is an inadequate basis for women's oppression. Its very name reflects its basis in the gender system: compulsory "hetero" sexuality, "hetero" referring to "other" gender. Heterosexuality couldn't exist without the gender system.

True, compulsory heterosexuality is clearly the particular mechanism by which the gendering of the sexes is perpetuated and enforced. However, as a tool for analysis, gender has broader relevance. Basing feminist analysis on a gender framework is more revealing because many aspects of women's oppression go beyond the realm of intimate relationship, without, granted, ever being totally unconnected from these.

For example, women's economic oppression takes place inside, and outside, the bedroom and family. Gender is more directly relevant than compulsory heterosexuality when considering why the boss is more likely to be male than female. Thus, I would substitute gender for compulsory heterosexuality as the basic building block of women's oppression. 20

BISEXUALITY, GENDER AND WOMEN'S OPPRESSION

Lesbianism *is* a challenge to compulsory heterosexuality. Bisexuality, however, has the potential to challenge the dual gender system, which oppresses women and queer people insofar as it is a foundation of compulsory heterosexuality.

Bisexuality fits in here in two ways, but the principle in both cases is the same: bisexuals blur the lines between categories often regarded as fixed and definable. First the strict dichotomy between homosexuality and heterosexuality gets blown. Bisexuals don't even fit into a clear-cut category because of the obvious variety of bisexual experience. Thus, bisexuality blurs the supposed duality of sexuality in a manner that is itself a challenge to other dual category systems, such as that of gender.[2]

In addition to this, bisexuality is not based on gender. Compulsory heterosexuality assumes a strictly defined gender system. Lesbian and gay relationships challenge gender by avoiding traditional gender roles. However, lesbian and gay sexuality is based on attraction to a specific gender to the same degree that heterosexuality is. By definition, both heterosexuality and homo-sexuality rely equally on a strictly defined gender system. Thus both uphold the present gender system, although compulsory heterosexuality has more to do with its perpetuation.

I believe that bisexuality has the potential to go beyond gender. True, there are bisexuals whose experience contradicts this to some extent. I have known some bis to say that they are attracted to women for the qualities cul-turally associated with this gender and to men for qualities identified as mas-culine. Even in such cases, however, sexual connections are possible with either gender and thus, to this degree, the gender system is challenged.

25 However, in many cases, including my own, bisexual people recognize that most, if not all, of which they find attractive in another has little to do with gender. In my case, I am attracted to people whose gender it is impossi-ble for me to ignore, but my attraction for them involves many factors, none of which break down simply according to gender. I am attracted to people around whom I feel safe, individuals who seem to understand me better than most, who are straightforward, who can be supportive and nurturing, who are physically active and who "have some flesh on them." A few of these charac-teristics are more common with one gender, but they certainly aren't limited to that gender.

GENDER AND SEXISM:
THE CURRENT REALITIES

If one of the lesbian feminists from the Northampton march committee were reading this article, and were still with us at this point, she would undoubt-edly have at least one very valid critique. Gender exists, sexism is a reality, and any political analysis or sexual lifestyle that does not take those facts into ac-count perpetuates these institutions. A bisexual politics that does not acknowl-edge the inevitable differences between the social and personal consequences of relationships with women and relationships with men, that is, one that pre-tends it is presently possible to "go beyond gender," is misguided.

When I was first exploring these types of questions, I was hoping for insight from other bisexual women, particularly older women, who I believed would be likely to have thought about and discussed these things. During this time I at-tended a panel in which three or four bisexual people told their coming-out stories. I posed the question to the two women panelists: what do you think it means for bisexual women to remain open to relationships with women and men, the latter being members of a group that oppresses us as women?

I didn't want my question to lead the whole room into a discussion of feminism and sexuality, but I had expected to hear a bit of background on the debate and the opinions of the panelists. Instead, the woman who answered looked uncomfortable and avoided the question by reassuring me that I shouldn't let politics interfere with my personal feelings and should allow myself to do what felt good without guilt. I agreed with her as far as it went, but I thought the question was of fundamental importance to bisexuals.

It is the case that gender-blind bisexuality, if it lacks a feminist political analysis, is not a direct challenge to women's oppression. Bisexuality attacks sexism by subverting gender, but since the very manner in which it subverts gender is by ignoring it, it also ignores sexism. Unfortunately, sexism will continue in our present society, with the institutions that support it in place, even if we ignore it—more so in fact.

That means two things. On a personal level, any bisexual woman who *30* chooses to be with a man faces sexism. From the outside, her relationship will be perceived as heterosexual relationships are seen—she becomes "his" woman. Within the relationship, with sexism as deeply embedded in our society as it is, there will be times when she will experience sexist dynamics with her lover. There are few men who will never fall back on male privilege when they feel threatened—for example, they may dismiss their lover's criticism as "nagging" or wait for her to do the emotional processing necessary to smooth out a snag in the relationship.

On the level of broad social change, without lesbians women's options would be heterosexuality and bisexuality. In our social system based on the concept that women need men, neither of these orientations allows for the option that women can create lives without men. Thus, that aspect of compulsory heterosexuality that says that women need men is not challenged.

But we need to challenge this. We cannot leap from our present system to a nongendered, polysexual system of sexuality. It is necessary to confront sexism in all its institutionalized forms before we can go past it. Thus bisexuality itself is not enough. With compulsory heterosexuality still in place, even bisexual women will face strong social influences to be in relationships with men, and their power to avoid domination within these relationships will be relatively weak. Both gender and compulsory heterosexuality must be fought at the same time.

THE CENTRAL ROLE OF LESBIANS IN WOMEN'S LIBERATION

We will not be able to say any woman has freely chosen to be with a man until all women are free not to be with men. For this reason, lesbianism must be an option. More directly than bisexuality, lesbianism is a challenge to compulsory heterosexuality. Thus, lesbians play a central role in the struggle for women's liberation and must remain a visible and distinct segment of this movement.

Lesbian identity and community challenge the notion that women "need" men and create a space in which women can focus exclusively on women. In the words of a lesbian quoted in an *Outweek* article on bisexuality: ". . . to not ever seek approval of men or turn your energy to men. There's tremendous power in being a lesbian."[3] Flourishing lesbian communities and sexual politics that promote this choice are necessary if women are to overcome this oppression.

35   Clearly, lesbians and gay men also challenge gender. Heterosexual relationships are one of the main areas for playing out gender roles. In contrast, within a relationship between lesbians, or gay men, traditional gender roles cannot be played out. Even cases in which gay men or lesbians take on approximations of traditional roles can never be the same in same-sex relationships as they are in opposite-sex relationships. In general, societal perceptions of lesbians and gay men indicate that their existence is a challenge to the system of gender. Men who are gay are seen as "effeminate," whereas lesbians are "mannish."

It follows then that, aside from avoiding gender-specific sexuality, bisexuals also challenge gender in their same-sex relationships by avoiding traditional gender roles, as lesbians and gay men do. They also confront compulsory heterosexuality in their same-sex relationships, as lesbians and gay men do. Lesbians and gay men, however, are a more outright and complete challenge to compulsory heterosexuality at least insofar as they confront that aspect of the institution that compels opposite-sex relations.

To summarize the above: lesbians and gay men directly challenge compulsory heterosexuality through their same-sex relationships and indirectly challenge gender through avoiding traditional gender roles within their relationships. Lesbians, specifically, confront the male supremacist belief that all women need men. Bisexuals directly challenge gender by avoiding gender-specific attraction and indirectly challenge compulsory heterosexuality and the acting out of gender roles through their openness to same-sex relationships. All of the above are necessary elements in the struggle for women's liberation and queer liberation.

THE CHOICES WE MAKE

I don't believe, as some bisexuals do, that all people are bisexual, except on the most abstract of levels. Clearly some women are not attracted to men. Other lesbians may have some attraction to men, but their personal and political beliefs about sexism make it impossible for them to be comfortable in a relationship with a man. Sexism is intolerable for such women, even in the relatively minimal levels in which it is present in some men. Furthermore, the fact that a relationship with a man will be perceived as just another heterosexual relationship by most of society may be too repulsive an experience for some women.

I am open to being with men despite this because, to begin with, I am attracted to men. But this in itself would not necessarily be enough. The most important reason I am open to relationships with men is that I have had rewarding relationships with them. From my experience, relationships between women and men are workable, if sometimes difficult, depending to a great degree on the individual man. As a bisexual woman within mixed-gender relationship, it also helps my position within the relationship that my male partner knows I have the option to end it in favor of a relationship with a woman.

Furthermore, I believe that there *are* men who have overcome their own sexism as much as is possible under present social conditions. My current lover is an example. His awareness of sexism is such that I don't have to do the work of challenging him; he rarely slips, and if he does he catches it himself. If it weren't for my experiences with him and other men like him, I would be much more tempted to identify as a lesbian. ₄₀

QUEER MEN

Gay and bisexual men have a potential role in the struggle for women's liberation. I don't believe it's an accident that my current lover, who has confronted so much of his own sexism, is himself bisexual. Queer men are in a unique position in several ways. For one thing, they often experience social contempt for displaying traits perceived as feminine. The form of oppression they face gives them a particular interest in the abolition of the gender system and sexism, and specific insight into these institutions.

Also, gay and bisexual men are also more likely than heterosexual men to be emotionally intimate with other men and, along with this, to give and receive emotional support from each other. This challenges a major aspect of compulsory heterosexuality under which women are supposed to be the nurturers, mediators, ego-builders and support-systems for men, who are not expected to return in kind. The capacity of some bisexual and gay men to turn to other men for emotional support takes the burden off women, who traditionally "exist to do men's feeling for them," as Audre Lorde has put it.[4] Our brothers are learning to do it for themselves.

BISEXUAL COMMUNITY

Where anything approaching a "bisexual community" exists, it is incomplete and tenuous. It is not surprising that lesbian and gay communities are more cohesive and visible. Because sexuality is seen in our culture as an either/or concept, lesbian and gay sex and culture are more identifiable, making it relatively easy for lesbians and gay men to recognize each other.

Clearly, the existence of lesbian and gay communities and the gains of their respective social movements and of the women's liberation movement have all been beneficial for bisexuals. (Of course, we have participated in all of the above, as well, and not simply been the beneficiaries.) The achievements of lesbian and gay struggles and feminist organizing are part of the reason so many people are now coming out as bisexual. At the same time, the present context, which has in part been created by these movements, is a challenge to bisexuals.

45   The existence of lesbian and gay communities has led to a situation in which we bisexuals often find ourselves asking to be accepted into these communities. Upon coming out, most bisexuals feel they have more in common with lesbians and gay men because we experience the most overt social rejection around our own same-sex relationships. Thus we find ourselves in contexts with lesbians and gay men where it is impossible to be fully recognized for "who we are."

To the degree that we have attempted to form our own communities, we have had mixed success. Perhaps this is because we are coming together because of a growing realization that we don't belong in either monosexual community—straight or lesbian and gay, rather than out of some common sense of our own identity drawing us together.

OUR UNIQUENESS AS BISEXUAL PEOPLE

What is missing in such attempts at community is an understanding of why we belong together, of what gives us an identity as ourselves, as opposed to a negative identity of not x, not y. This is difficult to realize because, as mentioned, our most obvious divergence from the "norm" is our same-sex relationships. However, as long as our self-definition ends there, we will always tend to fall back on asking to be received among lesbian and gay men, instead of coalescing our own community.

In fact, as someone who is bisexual, I do see myself as a member of the queer community, if not the lesbian and gay community. A major hindrance to the recognition of our place there, however, is our own inability to define how we fit it. For this reason, among others, we need to work toward defining a bisexual politic, one based on our capacity as bisexuals to blur categories of sexuality and gender, on our role in the struggle for queer liberation and women's liberation and so on.

Returning to the Northampton, Massachusetts, pride march, the question of the uniqueness of the bisexual experience came up for me in a debate with a lesbian acquaintance as we discussed the march title. In her opinion, bisexuals need not be identified in the march title because we are oppressed only to the degree that we are perceived as lesbian or gay. This led me to question whether I believed that we are oppressed as *bisexuals,* and if so, how is that oppression experienced.

BISEXUALS AND COMPULSORY HETEROMONOSEXUALITY

50 I eventually concluded that bisexuals are oppressed as bisexuals. One aspect of oppression, in my understanding, is when a specific group is denied legitimacy by a socially upheld institution.[5] The very invisibility of bisexual experience, which led my lesbian acquaintance to see bisexuals as sometimes a subset of the category "lesbian and gay," and sometimes part of the straight world, is the basis for bisexual oppression.

In the process of exploring this idea, I developed a new perspective on the institution of compulsory heterosexuality, which I had previously conceived of as oppressive *in its compulsion to other-sex relations and prohibition of same-sex relations.* Thus far in this paper I have written as though that were my underlying assumption. In fact, compulsory heterosexuality has two components (to do my own dichotomizing): "hetero," and hidden within that, "mono." Bisexuals are sometimes affected by the first, and always by the latter. Without compulsory heterosexuality there would be no such thing as straight or queer. It is responsible for our current framework, which leaves no room for a sexuality that is not monosexual, no room for bisexuality.

If bisexuals are not bi-bashed, denied housing as bisexuals or subjected to overt forms of oppression, this is in fact a result of our invisibility, and that invisibility is, for the present, how we experience oppression. As we become more visible, our experiences of oppression will become more overt. A recent example of this is the scapegoating of bis in the AIDS crisis, which resulted from the fear of this murky category of people who blur the lines between "them" and "us," those who are innocent. This dynamic is clearly different from the type of stigma experienced by gay men as a result of AIDS.

BISEXUAL LIBERATION

A bisexual politic as foundation for a bisexual liberation movement can confront the social framework that only allows for either/or. If explicitly feminist, it has a role to play in challenging gender, the basis for women's oppression. In a general sense, bisexuality challenges our system of categorization, which provides the basis for other forms of oppression: the division between "of color" and "white," as well as "woman" and "man," "queer" and "straight" and so on.

In the shorter term a bisexual feminist politic can form the basis for a group identity upon which a bisexual community can be formed. Such a politic would create a framework for our common individual experiences. For the present, that which we have in common is harder to recognize than the shared experiences within each monosexual community. But, in fact, there are common threads within the bisexual experience. The achievement of a vibrant bisexual community would pose a significant and unique challenge to the dual gender system and the limitations inherent in compulsory heteromonosexuality. Our contribution might even go beyond this to challenge our entire oppressive social system, helping to break down the categories of identity on which much of it is based.

NOTES

1. Holly Devor, *Gender Blending: Confronting the Limits of Duality* (Bloomington, Indiana: Indiana University Press, 1989), p. 1.

2. One problem with the label "bisexual" is that the prefix "bi" assumes a dual gender system.

3. Carrie Wofford, "The Bisexual Revolution: Deluded Closet Cases or Vanguards of the Movement?" *OutWeek,* Feb. 6, 1990, p. 3.

4. Audre Lorde, *Sister Outsider: Essays and Speeches* by Audre Lorde (Trumansburg, NY: The Crossing Press, 1984).

5. Economic oppression, where present, is something other than this, but it is not unrelated.

THIS QUIET REVOLUTION

Kate Bornstein

It's one thing to play around with gender in the privacy of our own homes, or within the safe confines of "playgrounds," surrounded by others like us. As soon as we step outside the door, however, we run smack into social and legal restrictions, exclusion, and oppression.

What most of us don't run into are the children thrown into the streets by their families by reason of the child's transgender nature. Most of us don't run into savage beatings, rape, and murder at the hands of outraged people, not to mention the same or similar treatment at the hands of the very police whose job it is to protect us. Some of us run into job discrimination; but we forget that most of us never had jobs to begin with. We'll cry about losing our lovers and our community, but we don't get a chance to look into the eyes of a bone-lonely homeless transgendered person. We need to know these obscenities exist, and we need to dedicate some part of our lives to being of service to the less-privileged members of our tribe.

Over the couple of years since the publication of *Gender Outlaw,* I've had the opportunity to talk and write with quite a few folks, sharing our experiences outside the world of gender binaryism. What I found was that most folks agree that political action on behalf of gender transgressors is necessary, but not too many people know exactly what kind of political action to take.

I think of personal politics as the sum total of skills necessary to navigate a situation in which my values, standards, or boundaries are in conflict with another's or others'. When the others in question have more power, and there's no relief to the conflict in sight (assuming our own motives to be harmless and inclusive), that's when a revolution is necessary. That's when I need to look beyond my own personal politics and assume a position within a political movement, part of which is lending a hand to the rest of us at every moment of the day. So it's a dance . . . moving back and forth between taking care of myself and taking care of my family. There are quite a few transgender activist groups out there these days. Some are dedicated to social reform; some to community building; some focus on legislative representation; others make education their priority. It's a political smorgasbord out there, a place for virtually every kind of activism you can think of. And if you can't find an existing group that would serve your political aims, start one up yourself and you'll have members within a month's time.

The point of this section is not to tell you what to do. That's no one's call but your own. The point of this section is to provide some more universal guidelines for whatever it is you *do* choose to do. 5

The way you do anything is the way you do everything. That's a good concept to keep in mind when it comes to politics and political activism. It resonates with the concept of integrity.

FIRST THERE IS A GENDER, THEN THERE IS NO GENDER, THEN THERE IS

> Every day I go to work in Miami and all the kids under 8 think I am a man. As they get older they ask are you a man or are you a lady. I say you figure it out. If they tell me I'm a man, I tell them to look more closely.
>
> —Jacky Jack

I've been saying for some years now that I don't have a gender; that gender is a trap, a chimera. And it's all well and good to say there's no such thing as gender. I think it's even all well and good to believe that. The sad fact is that despite all our wonderful spiritual or philosophical takes on identity and the nature of gender, gender is here in the world and people are oppressing other people for no other reason than gender itself. The "first there is a gender . . ." reference above is from a koan used to illustrate a student's progress through Zen:

A beginning student exclaims to the elder, "Look, what a beautiful mountain!" The elder smiles and replies, "Mountain? There's no mountain there." The student, baffled, goes off to study and contemplate the elder's words. Ten years later, the student returns, a broad smile on hir face, saying "Elder! I understand! There is no mountain! We are all one! I am everywhere and everything, as are we all. What I saw before was only an illusion, created by my need to be separate!" To which, the elder responds, "Oh really? Well, all I can say is you're missing a splendid view of this mountain I'm looking at."

Gender *is.* Oppression *is.* We need to forge a politic that deals effectively and finally with gender oppression as it impacts each one of us, gender transgressors and gender defenders alike.

COHESIVENESS AND COMMUNITY

10

> I have labeled myself "female-to-femme transgender" first and foremost as a sign of my solidarity to a group of feared, harshly misunderstood people who don't have enough allies. Because I am a white, decent-looking woman who wears skirts, it would be very easy for me to shut up and go along. But I don't.

I'm still up in the air about this idea of a "transgendered community." I think defining any community by the identity of its members is ultimately a dead-end, because despite their more or less common identities, the values of its members are inevitably going to be in conflict. For example, look at the Log Cabin Republicans or the North American Man/Boy Love Association and their relationships to the larger gay and lesbian community.

I think that if we're going to put some kind of community together (one that I'd like to be a member of anyway) it's going to have to be based less on some notion of a transgender identity, and more on the idea of a transgender value. What that agreed-upon "transgender value" might be is a matter to be hashed out by all of us. Who's "all of us?" The community that I'd want to belong to would include anyone who wants to overcome gender oppression in any shape or form. That would be a meaning or mission I could get behind.

It would include the young woman who stands up to her male boss and says "No."

It would include every lesbian, gay man, or bisexual person.

It would include sex workers and S/M players.

It would include the housewife who refuses to be barefoot and pregnant in her husband's kitchen.

The transgender community I'd like to see would also include transsexuals, transvestites, cross-dressers, drag kings, drag queens, he-shes, she-males, and male and female impersonators.

It would include hermaphrodites, intersexed people, and anyone whose physiology casts them as "not men" or "not women."

This larger community would include men and women of races other than "white" who are constantly seen by many whites as "not really men and women" by reason of their race.

It would include working-class and homeless men and women who are seen by many of those in the middle class as "not really men and women" by reason of their class.

All seniors and children would be included in this community, because they're so commonly perceived as either "beyond their manhood and womanhood" or "not yet having attained it."

I was born female, and raised as expected/accepted. I cooperated, unquestioning, until I came out as a feminist in high school and looked hard at the way I had been presenting myself. Trans people cross rigid sex/gender lines, allowing themselves to project an individual expression that feels comfortable. Usually, though, the change occurs from one gender to another. See, I can't even pass for androgynous. I tentatively approached that line between masculine/feminine and came running back. I do enjoy being a girlie. This doesn't make me less queer—it only makes me less visible. [15]

I have realized that this—being skirted and lipsticked—is how I'm most comfortable. And that I can acknowledge my socialization and still be me. I crossed from one gender to an "acceptance" of that gender expression. I am not simply female; my self-awareness has made me femme. [20]

—Hanna Bordas

Membership in this community would be dependent not only on the common struggle to dismantle an oppressive system, but also every member's willingness to acknowledge each other's unique gender oppression. Until that's reached, I don't think there's much hope for a community that's anything more than a temporary bulwark against the system that would eventually wipe us all out.

The focus for each of us needs, I think, to be on our own spirit of inclusiveness. We need to get over the idea of "We're the only ones who are oppressed by the gender system." If we get over *that,* we'll have the basis for a community that thrives and supports not only its members, but its valued allies and friends. So here're some interesting questions for you:

EXERCISE

Do you choose your friends solely on the basis of their identities?

_____ yes _____ no _____ somewhat

Which is *more* important to you:

_____ your identity

_____ your principles?

Exactly how have you determined the principles of those around you? What criteria do you use?

What qualities or values do you look for in a friend?

Now measure your political affiliations by the same standards you choose your friends. Note the similarities and the differences.

The cohesiveness of any successful transgender movement will depend on basing the movement in values rather than identity.

WHERE DO WE LOOK FOR DIRECTION?

25   I bristle at the term "equal rights" when it comes to gender. I prefer the term "universal rights." It's not that I disagree with the concept of equal rights, it's just that by stating the concept of universal rights in terms of equality, we're setting up and keeping in place some us–and–them situation, if only by using the word *equal,* which is usually taken in gendered circles as implying equality *between men and women.* That doesn't work for a movement that has the potential for universal inclusivity of many genders.

  I think we need, each of us, to hammer out our own goals and purposes. We need to name what's blocking us from achieving those goals and purposes. Then we can phrase for ourselves the specific rights we need to overcome whatever's blocking us, taking into account the goals, purposes, and rights of others who are in search of freedom of gender expression.

EXERCISE

Okay, let's suppose it's a long way off in the future, and you've come to the end of your life. You're lying there on your deathbed, and you're content with the life you've lived. You're happy with your life, and you're ready to move on to whatever might lie beyond your death. Looking back on your life:

1. What did you achieve that's making you content?
2. What specific rights did you personally need in order to achieve that?
3. When you got those rights for yourself, and achieved what you achieved, what did that make you?
4. If you had a wish you could utter at this moment of your death and it would come true for future generations, what would you wish for?
5. Bonus Questions: Suppose there were some wonderful afterlife. It's as good as you'd want it to be. And suppose you were given the option of staying there after you die, or returning to this earthly existence for yet another life so that you could help make your dying wish for future generations come true. What would you do?

■ ■ ■

For a true gender revolution to occur, each individual needs to name hir own needs, rights, and only then to set about achieving those needs and rights in harmony with others who have done the same work.

WHERE'S OUR MOTIVATION?

Quite often, we're motivated to political action by either the idea or the reality of an enemy: someone who's doing us in or who we think has nefarious plans for us. A great deal can be accomplished by pointing fingers at an oppressor. That oppressor can indeed be toppled. There's a drawback to this tactic, however, when it comes to a transgender movement: Who's the oppressor?

We can't say it's "the patriarchy." We can't say it's "all traditionally gen-   *30* dered people." As the transgender movement includes anyone who is transgressing gender, we're opening the door to every single human being on the face of the planet to be a member of this movement; that means everyone is a potential ally and member of the group. So, whose face do we use for the enemy?

While it might be politically expedient in the short run to paint a face on our oppression, say the face of Senator Jesse Helms from North Carolina, that wouldn't help us if we were to learn that the good senator wears his wife's underwear when she's away at her bridge club meeting. All of a sudden, Jesse would be family!

Besides, if we think that gender oppression is only going to come from the distinguished senator and his ilk, we'll be caught unaware when some form of that oppression spills from the mouths of our next-door neighbor, our friends, family, lovers, or children. And that's where it's going to come from. Our gender oppression can come from anyone who's more highly placed, or even, differently placed, on the gender/identity/power pyramid than ourselves. So I don't think we can afford to under- or overestimate our oppression by naming it as an identity, any more than we can afford to shorthand our movement by naming it as an identity. Gender oppression is like a particularly nasty computer virus that spreads throughout an entire system, leaving bits and pieces of itself everywhere on our hard drive. We need to name the acts of oppression and exclusion. We need to name the values that precede those acts, because our politics *can* hope to change values.

EXERCISE

1. Name three incidents in which you were, or believe you might have been, oppressed or excluded by reason of your gender expression.
2. Now climb inside the head of the person or persons oppressing you for those three incidents, and name the *value* (e.g., greed, prestige, laziness, etc.) you suppose might have preceded that oppressive or exclusive act.

Those *values* are the enemy, and they can and do show up in anyone, including ourselves. If we're going to truly crusade against oppression, we need to start right here at home. So-o-o-o . . .

35

3. Name three incidents in which you may have oppressed or excluded someone else by reason of hir gender expression.
4. Now climb inside your head, and name the *value* (e.g., greed, prestige, laziness, etc.) you suppose might have preceded your oppressive or exclusive act.

▪▪▪

The enemy to true freedom of gender expression is nameless.
The enemy to true freedom of gender expression is a value system, the expression of which needs to be dealt with on a person-to-person basis.

WHAT KIND OF POLITICAL ATTENTION DO WE WANT?

Movements need to attract attention to themselves. Well, gender outlaws get attention. Period. We're strange, we're attractive, and we're dangerous. That gets us plenty of attention. I've had to tell more than one squeamish publicist to use my freak status to promote my theater work. Why not? But what about the *unwanted* attention we garner? For example, when a gender outlaw uses a public (gendered) bathroom, that's often an act that not only gets us unwanted attention, it calls for political ingenuity and/or action. What action can we take, when it seems that every move we make in this culture not only attracts attention, but also flies into the teeth of some law or social convention? I don't know. I don't know what action to take. I just know that we're entitled to live a rich life free from harm or harming others. In that context, and keeping in mind the principle that the way you do anything is the way you do everything, I think we can come up with some political guidelines that draw on the strengths we've developed as gender outlaws.

The master's tools will never dismantle the master's house.
    —*Audre Lorde*

How about putting the book down just now and contemplating the implications of Ms. Lorde's statement in light of what you've been studying here.

IF NOT THE MASTER'S TOOLS, WHICH TOOLS *CAN* WE USE?

Here are some of the tools I've become familiar with over the course of my own gender journey, tools that are available to most gender outlaws for use in any of our political actions.   40

Compassion

I've spoken a great deal about compassion in this book so far. Compassion is the foundation of a transgender politic, beginning with compassion for ourselves and extending outward to compassion toward other outlaws, friends, allies, family, and ultimately compassion even for those who recoil from us in horror.

Patient Persistence

At this writing, the appearance of gender outlaws on the streets of the wide wide world is a startling one. We need to keep on appearing on the streets, in the workplace, at the bars, in the clubs, and on the very doorsteps of those who would brand us freaks. We need to do this despite the initial pain, shame, and humiliation it might bring us. We need to appear over and over again in public, and we need to do it with honor.

One strength we possess as gender outlaws is our ability to take baby steps on any journey, persistently moving forward no matter the opposition. We never wanted to be pushed, rushed, or beaten into questioning gender. Those of us who've transitioned from one gender to another never wanted to be browbeaten into doing it. We wanted to be treated kindly with understanding, and we wanted to proceed at whatever speed was comfortable for us at the time, which for many of us meant that our transitions took a little longer than we would have liked. Most of us learned patience and all of us learned persistence.

So one principle of a transgender politic might be to use the smallest, most compassionate means possible to bring about a reconciliation of conflicting ideas and values that keep all parties concerned from living a rich life free from harm or harming others, and to patiently yet persistently up the volume or intensity of our actions until we reach that reconciliation.

45   When I experience an instance of exclusion or oppression now, I try to identify with the person excluding or oppressing me. Their hatred or fear of me is no greater than the hatred or fear I had for myself back before I came to a point of self-acceptance. How can I rage at them when they're only expressing to me what I'd expressed to myself for nearly all my life? Sure, there are going to be times to write Congress. There will be times to march in the streets. There are going to be times when we're oppressed by something so insidiously institutional that in order to even get the attention of those we need to negotiate with, we need to make some noise. But I don't think this needs to be the *first* action we take. The first action might be simply taking a fellow student aside and explaining to them why, when they've known us to be a woman, we've suddenly grown a mustache.

EXERCISE

Write down some instance of exclusion or oppression you've either experienced or might experience as a result of your messing around with gender.

What is the gentlest, most compassionate action you can take in response to that?

And if that doesn't work, what's the next most gentle, compassionate action you can take?

And if that doesn't work, what's the next most gentle, compassionate action you can take?

And if that doesn't work, what's the next most gentle, compassionate action you can take?

And if that doesn't work, what's the next most gentle, compassionate action you can take?

■■■

I think that's the way we need to proceed. Of course, there are going to be rough decisions to make. Faced with a knife at our throats, or to the throats of our loved ones, we need to act swiftly to prevent harmfulness. We need to become adept at assessing what kind of oppression calls for what kind of political response.

As to persistence, I have this Woodrow Wilson quote hanging on the wall in my house. It was given to me nearly thirty years ago by my friend, Gail Harris, who found it excerpted in an ad for McDonald's hamburgers:

Press On! Nothing in the world can take the place of persistence. Talent will not; nothing is more common than unsuccessful men with talent. Genius will not; unrewarded genius is almost a proverb. Education alone will not; the world is full of educated derelicts. Persistence and determination alone are omnipotent.

Well, I don't believe that persistence and determination *alone* are omnipotent, but I do believe they're necessary components to a successful politic.

Flexibility and Fluidity

Gaining recognition and acknowledgment from those who would defend the gender binary isn't going to be easy. The very act of questioning gender has the potential to change the face of the gender system forever. And the fun news is that there's no defense against our honest questioning, because an honest question is never an attack. What's more, there is no methodology by which a person can prove the gender binary is either basic or essential to humanity. Wary self-proclaimed opponents to this idea of shattering the binary have not come up with a single effective defense against non-linear reasoning, save brute force. And I think that on some level they know that. These gender defenders have their own code of honor; they have their own faces to save. yes, we're in the right by saying we simply want to live our harmless lives free from harm. However, there's an old old principle at work here, one it would be well to keep in mind while making allies from within the ranks of those higher up on the pyramid:

When surrounding an enemy, make sure you leave them a way to escape.
—*Sun Tzu*

When we confront a gender defender with our genderfree selves, we're backing them up against a wall, because a gender defender really believes in binaries and, well, we tend to *break* binaries. We color our identities outside the lines, and we're great at doing it. It's who we are, it's our value to this culture. But we're not going to get anywhere by backing a snarling, powerful opponent into some corner without a way for that person to save face.

We know how to be flexible. Given the exercises in this book, we've got the skills we need to adapt our identities to whatever situation we're dealing with. We're fluid in that we can use that flexibility to shift our identities as rapidly or as often as we please. In short, the nature of our gender journeys depends not one bit on *any* binary, linear construct. If we're living our lives like that, then maybe it's against our nature to use a linear, binary politic.

For me, gender has always been a social thing, not so much a biological thing or even a psychological thing. When I'm by myself my gender goes away, especially if I'm immersed in something like work or a book or household chores. But put us together, be you the closest of friends or the most anonymous and silent of passing strangers, and my gender engulfs me. It's Who I Am in the world, it's an expectant look in your eyes and all your assumptions, it's my need to satisfy those expectations.

—Sharon Minsuk

Maybe it's *important* that our revolution not rely on binary, linear methods, lest by relying upon them in one area of our lives, we fall back into relying upon binaries in all or many things that we do. Again, please remember the principle, the way you do anything is the way you do everything.

55

EXERCISE

Let's put your flexibility and fluidity to a little test. Here are some common binaries at work in our culture. Cross out the ones you honestly don't subscribe to, and circle the ones that still are operating in your life.

Male/Female	Student/Teacher	Sad/Happy
Man/Woman	Silence/Confrontation	On/Off
Young/Old	Up/Down	Homosexual/Heterosexual
Rich/Poor	Manic/Depressive	
Deserving/Undeserving	Capitalism/Socialism	Diseased/Healthy
	Female/Male	Them/Us
Civilized/Uncivilized	Sadist/Masochist	Open/Closed
Nice/Not Nice	Closeted/Out	Girl/Boy
Good/Evil	Masculine/Feminine	Lucky/Unlucky
Right/Wrong	Light/Dark	Radical/Assimilationist
Good/Bad	Powerful/Powerless	Win/Lose
Beautiful/Ugly	Legal/Illegal	Humans/Other Life Forms
Active/Passive	Faith/Fear	
Normal/Weird	Male-to-Female/Female-to-Male	Popular/Academic
White/Colored		Mind/Body
Dying/Living	Transgendered/Gendered	Pain/Pleasure
Acceptable/Embarrassing	Birth/Death	In/Out
Bravery/Cowardice	Plants/Animals	Workers/Bosses
God(dess)/The Devil	Peaceful/Violent	Angels/Demons
Kinky Sex/Vanilla Sex	Patriarchal/Feminist	Sameness/Difference
Fat/Thin	Enough/Too Much	Public/Private
Me/You	Fight/Flee	Consensual/Non-consensual
Able-bodied/Disabled	Everything/Nothing	War/Peace

Acceptance/Denial	Exclusion/Inclusion	Work/Play
Material/Spiritual	Healthy/Dysfunctional	Goddess/Slut
Penis/Vagina	Full/Empty	Macho/Wimp

Are there any other binaries that you either subscribe to or *don't* follow? List them . . . and circle the ones you subscribe to.

EXERCISE

Take a sheet of paper for each binary you circled, and divide the page in half vertically. For each binary, use the right-hand side of the page to list out all the ways the binary is true. On the left-hand side, list out all the ways it's not true.
Now look at the page as a whole, without using the true/not-true binary.
Now write down your thoughts about that binary.

If we're truly going to develop a politic that's going to dismantle the gender binary, we need to rid ourselves of binary thinking as our sole way of thinking and our own binary methodology as our sole way of doing things.

A Note on Exclusivity

Bernice Johnson Reagon has made what I think is the simplest statement about the foolishness of exclusivity:

> We've pretty much come to the end of a time when you can have a space that is "yours only"—just for the people you want to be there. Even when we have our "women-only" festivals, there is no such thing. The fault is not necessarily with the organizers of the gathering. To a large extent it's because we have just finished with that kind of isolating. There is no hiding

place. There is nowhere you can go and only be with people who are like you. It's over. Give it up.

—West Coast Women's Music Festival, 1981
Yosemite National Forest, California

Any outlaw, any Other, knows the pain associated with being excluded, locked out, or forbidden some form of freedom of expression. Most outlaws, gender or otherwise, are also familiar with the phenomenon of one oppressed or excluded group oppressing or excluding others. *Some* group, *someone,* has to stop the self-devouring hierarchy of under-represented groups that prey on less-strong under-represented groups. It's our turn to try to stop that miserable buck.

60
- Do you belong to some group that wants to exclude others by reason of their identity?
- Are there some gender outlaws whom you would see as not really transgressing gender?
- Do you believe that the way you're transgressing gender is better than the way someone else is?
- Do you believe that the way someone else is transgressing gender is better than the way you are transgressing gender?

EXERCISE

Here's a list of some identities. Let's say you were going to hold a meeting to discuss the politics of gender. All the following people arrive at the meeting. Be real honest now (this isn't a test to see how politically correct you can be), and circle the identities of people you would rather *not* attend the meeting.

Pre-operative male-to-female transsexuals	Homosexual male-to-female transvestites	Pre-operative female-to-male transsexuals
Post-operative male-to-female transsexuals	Bisexual male-to-female transvestites	Democrats
Non-operative male-to-female transsexuals	Muslims	Post-operative female-to-male transsexuals
Mormons	People who don't speak English well	Pre-teens
Drag queens	Transsexual lesbians	Men who wear their wives' underwear
Jews	Cross-dressers	Non-operative female-to-male transsexuals
Drag kings	Republicans	Libertarians
Drag queen prostitutes	Transsexual gay men	African Americans
Born-again Christians	Transsexual young urban professionals	Heterosexual female-to-male transvestites
Heterosexual male-to-female transvestites		

Homosexual female-to-male transvestites	Straight white fraternity guys	Witches
Men who wear draw string pants	Sadists	Homeless people
Bisexual female-to-male transvestites	White people	Heterosexual women
Anorexics or Bulemics	Masochists	Butches
Beautiful men and women	Lesbians	Femmes
	Police officers	Women who wear Birkenstocks
	Gay men	Ugly men and women
	Heterosexual men	

Are there any other kinds of people you would not want at the meeting? List them here.

Now, get some extra sheets of paper, one for each type of person you circled above. On each page, write the name of one type of person. Divide the sheet in half vertically, and on the left-hand side write down the reasons this person should be excluded. On the right-hand side, write down the benefits of including this person.

Now, look at the page as a whole. Could you find it within yourself to include that person? Under what conditions?

■ ■ ■

The buck has to stop somewhere, and since we gender outlaws are new at this politics game, I'm hoping we refuse to build exclusion into the way we deal with others. I'm hoping we can include even those who would exclude us. One way of doing that is to keep in mind the metaphor of the "perfect identity" at the top of that pyramid: is there really anyone who isn't an outcast of some sort or another? It still gets back down to compassion, no?

GENDER ANARCHY

Anarchy is natural to most of us. We're all anarchists in one or more areas of our lives. In my life, I refuse to obey the rules of gender. In your life, it may be the rules of the workplace, or the rules of sexuality. All of us disobey something, and disobedience requires a great deal of responsibility. We look at some rule, whether it be "Men don't wear dresses," or "You're not allowed to pirate cable television," or "It's against the law now to provide social services for illegal immigrants in the United States," and we ask ourselves, which of these can I responsibly obey

I'm gender-indifferent in a bunch of ways, but one I have the most fun with is probably my purse. It's been called a bag, a pack, a pouch, a . . . er, wallet-thing; it's none of these: it's a cute little Fiorelli purse, just big enough for my keys, my identification, and some money. For some liberal urban areas, I suppose it wouldn't be such a big deal, but for the conservative haven of mid-Michigan, a male of my size and appearance carrying a purse usually affords a second glance. Never a jeer, though, and never a stare: are "you" going to tell a six-foot 215-pound man with three earrings and two tattoos that he can't carry a purse?

—Brighn

and still maintain my integrity? Which laws have I been dealt which I must responsibly *disobey* in order to maintain my integrity?

> This is one of the paradoxes of the democratic movement—that it loves a crowd and fears the individuals who compose it.
> —*Walter Lippmann*

The laws of the land in which I'm living now are derived democratically. That means they're made by other people who are supposed to have my best interests at heart. Well, the fact is that I cannot marry a woman in this country. The fact is that a transgendered child on the street is not going to be cared for by the social machinery created by the people who are supposed to have hir best interests at heart. Exactly why that's the way things are is beyond the scope of this book, but it boils down to this: democracy and outlaws of any stripe don't mix it up very well together.

65   Democracy, in fact most *any* centralized government or politics, doesn't include me for the simple reason that I keep trying to change who and what I am every day of my life, and Democracy seeks to govern by the representation of some clearly (to them) defined "average identity." Both Democracy and twentieth-century capitalism need people with fixed identities whom they can govern and sell to. I don't have a fixed identity, and I don't want one. The demographic surveys that try, with all good intentions I'm sure, to pinpoint me as a consumer are valid the day I answer them, but not necessarily that evening. I don't *want* to be a legal, recognized entity within a system that would expect me to remain statically identified for longer than, say, twenty-four hours.

I used to think I was politically apathetic. Now I'm seeing that I hadn't located a politic out there that actively embraces and encourages my individual growth, change, fluidity, and whimsy. The closest thing I can find is anarchy. I'm not talking about the cartoon version of the Russian anarchist holding up some home-made bomb. I'm not talking about bombs at all. I'm talking about measured, personal anarchy: something we can live.

65   *Gender outlaws are outlaws because we live outside the laws of gender. We broke the rules, we found some personal freedom, a way to fully express ourselves. ::softly:: Why stop there?*

I'm a lipstick lesbian with fat hair and spike heels . . . but does power tools and work boots. So there.

—Carole Taylor

No, I don't know exactly *what* it looks like. I only know what it *doesn't* look like. It doesn't look like rules, regulations, laws, by-laws, constitutions, or being silenced for being out of order. The political organization or activist group I want to support doesn't use fear tactics, intimidation, peer pressure, categories, or the expectation that I sacrifice my integrity or honor for "the good of the many." All those tactics are what the gender system used to keep me being a man or a woman. None of those methods got me this far, and I don't suspect they would get me any further; and further is exactly where I want to go.

EXERCISE

What social taboos, if any, have you broken without harming anyone?

What company or organizational rules or regulations, if any, have you broken without harming anyone?

What spoken or unspoken codes of your family, tribe, or community, if any, have you broken without harming anyone?

What laws, if any, have you broken without harming anyone?

Did breaking any of those rules end up being beneficial to both you and others? If so, how?

■■■

Anarchy As Responsible Power Play

I'm a sadomasochist. I play with power, and the more I do, the less I find that power is able to play with me. I'm more and more aware when people try to either exert power over me, or conversely, when people manipulate me into exerting power over them. As a top in an S/M relationship, I choose to honor and respect the gift my bottom gives me: the gift of hir relinquished power. As a bottom, I'm very picky about who I choose to give my power to.

That's how I look at the gender system. I don't choose to give my powers to it, not in the least. I'm going to disobey its laws, written or assumed. Why would I want to support a political system or even an activist group that would employ the same kind of abuse of power? I've said no to gender, and I'm going to keep saying no to systems that would reign me in, classify me, pin me down, or keep me in my place. Nope. Not gonna play that game any more. What's the worse thing that could happen to me? People are gonna call me names? I'm embracing most names that people call me these days anyway . . . it's a hoot.

I am a transsexual in Bavaria. Yes, I am. For the moment I'm working very hard on my permission to become transgendered, from female to male. Please excuse my English, but I'll try to answer your questions as good as possible.

To live without gender is impossible without breaking gender conventions. Therefore you'd better learn to be good on the subject. For me, it became a sport. It's by the way the only sport never disturbed by your tits!

Of course I break rules. Doing this is easy: just ignoring. My favorite broken conventions concern clothing. The way I speak and behave is only unusual for female standards, of course.

70

But people always identify me as a man, even without hormones yet, though I have no problems with it. The problem is practicing sexuality. I am a gay man with no own body to have fun with. The much I love and need physical contact, the much I fear it to be touched. For the moment I live as a kind of asexual, but I'm not born for this state of being. My way to overcome all those shit is, to work on my transgendering procedure. I think the worst is behind me. To look forward helps.

Chris Summer

Moderation in All Things, Including Moderation

I'm not saying we all need to embrace anarchy. I'm not saying you shouldn't pay your taxes, or obey the speed limits. I'll probably go to my grave having paid most of my taxes and having obeyed most of the speed limits. The point is, I've been learning to disobey some pretty heavy cultural rules by going through my various gender transitions, and I've been finding a great deal of integrity and satisfaction on the other side of those rules.

What I'm recommending is that we as gender outlaws continue to break the rules and laws that are necessary to break in order to achieve personal integrity and the personal integrity of those whom we love and care for. And this is not some new idea. It's the old "Render unto Caesar . . ." thang.

Enough lofty political talk of anarchy and power. Please take out some sheets of paper, and let's bring this down to something tangible.

75

EXERCISE

On your own gender journey *thus far*:

- What rules have you followed?
- What laws have you obeyed?
- What conventions have you conformed with?
- What sanctions have you accepted?

EXERCISE

To get to the point at which you'd like to arrive in your gender journey:

- What rules do you think you might need to ignore?
- What laws might you have to disobey?
- With what conventions would you need to break?
- Which sanctions might you need to refuse to accept?

Gettin' angry? Oh, good!

ANGER

I was angry with my friend:
I told my wrath, my wrath did end.
I was angry with my foe:
I told it not, my wrath did grow.
   —William Blake

Anger is real. It's not going to go away. So, how can we use it? Well, we can start by naming the source of our anger, and I think the source of our transgendered orneriness isn't so much gender *per se,* but the heretofore inaccessibility to freedom of identity apart from socially mandated acceptable roles.

Roles provide the averagely gendered person on the street with an "off the rack" monogendered identity allowing them to spend their time thinking about the things that interest them. Gender outlaws don't have that luxury; we've got no place to conveniently hang our identities while we get on with the business of living life. Unless we claim membership in one of the two socially-sanctioned genders, we spend most of our time wondering how to navigate a gendered world.

Returning to the pyramid metaphor: no matter what face of the pyramid most concerns us, be it gender, race, age, class, or whatever, we're still attempting to overcome oppression in the name of what's become a "perfect identity" perched at the top of each of our struggles. We're each to some degree oppressed, held in check, violated, silenced, or shamed by one or more aspects of that perfect identity, and that's enough to make anyone angry. When that oppression is nearly universal, as in the case of gender oppression, race oppression, or class oppression, then our anger in the face of overwhelming opposition can become an underlying rage that impacts both our perception and our consequent response to the world around us.

- What about another's self-expression has made you angry?
- Can you think of a time when you were angry at someone for a good reason, and you got them to see why? If so, how did you do that?
- What about your self-expression gets others angry at you?
- Can you think of a time when someone was angry at you for a good reason, and they got you to see why? If so, how did they do that?
- What's your response to a verbal threat?
- What's your response to some symbol of a threat?

Anger feeds the strength of our passion, which in turn is guided by our reason and our honor, and the result is moderated by our compassion: that's anger's place in our new politic.

A "Gender" Liberation Front could campaign for an end to sex designation not just on TS birth certificates, but on Marriage—enabling lesbian marriages etc—we can move the focus away from places like Rape Crisis Centres to places like Smedley Hydro—the Birth Registry—We can set a profoundly radical pluralist agenda for this group—what sort of actions would be most effective—why they shouldn't bomb buildings with people in—those sorts of ideas. Can you imagine the costs of providing security for every registry office in the UK!?
—posted on the Internet

NONVIOLENCE

The way I define violence is the nonconsensual constraint of, intrusion into, occupation of, or damage to another or others' body, bodies, possessions, or space. Violence can also be the nonconsensual exclusion of a person from a public space, or the barring of access to basic human rights. There are all kinds of degrees of violence. Violence can be as ostensibly harmless as taking up to much room on public transportation. Violence can manifest as wholesale genocide. It's a form of violence to force people against their will to be something they don't feel they are. That's what's done to us by the gender/identity/power system, and while we're in the process of throwing off those constraints, none of us can afford to forward the practice of constraining others, intruding into or occupying their personal space, or wreaking any damage. In the ages-old "Battle of the Sexes," we must be the conscientious objectors.

85

One of my favourite near-daily occurrences is the ol' triple-take. That's when someone will see me somewhere in matter-life (doesn't matter where ::grin::) and do a double take at the happy "babe" with the long curly hair to try to catch which gender I am. (Like there are only two!) And then, they'll look again, (third take) sometimes staring right at me, peering to try to figure out if I'm male or female. I've even had people get right in my face, look me up an down and still not know if I am boy or girl. ::lol:: I like to flash them my best sexy grin and dance away, leaving them wondering.
::happy boy/grrl doing the Snoopy dance::
—Jos

ANY POLITICS HAS GOTTA BE FUN, AND THE LAUGH'S GOTTA BE ON US

Gender outlaws go to a lot of trouble to remake ourselves into the objects and/or subjects of our desire. Desire and the fulfillment of our desire comprise a substantial and valid reason for our gender transgressions. Let's face it: we're cute. We're more than cute, we're damned good-looking and sexy to boot. People have lots of fantasies about gender outlaws like us. We're the forbidden fruit: sweet or tart, juicy or firm, enticing or scary-looking, the fact is we rev up peoples' libidos.

Well, it's time to cash in on that. We can be as visible with our gender-blended sexuality as any traditionally gendered person is with hirs. Hey . . . drag kings and drag queens have been doing it for hundreds of years!

Emma Goldman is credited with having said, "If I can't dance, I don't want to be part of your revolution." Well, if I can't flirt, I don't want to be part of your revolution.

This Is Foolishness

In *Gender Outlaw*, I wrote briefly that the role of transgendered people in the culture might in effect be the role of the trickster or the fool: that we by our very presence hold up a mirror to the culture so that it might better see its own foolishness when it comes to its blind obedience on the subject of gender. And I still think that's the deal. That's how we're going to do it. We're seen for the most part as a joke; well, it's not that far a leap from joke to jokester, and jokester has an honorable tradition.

> I break gender rules all the time by alternating between my femme persona and my butch persona. It gives me twice the wardrobe . . . and it is so much fun to confuse everyone!
> —Puppylove

> *"Congratulate me! shouted Nazrudin to a neighbour. "I am a father."*
> *"Congratulations! Is it a boy or a girl?"*
> *"Yes! But how did you know?"*
> —Idres Shah

Whether ze's referred to as Coyote, Nazrudin, Tortoise, Lucifer, Legba, Trickster, Shaman, Wounded God, or simply as fool . . . that's the position open to each of us who teeters along any border set by the culture. We hold up to each side of that border the foolishness of *both* sides; and we're not gonna be loved or revered by the folks who live comfortably on either side. We do what we do with a sense of humor, sure, but is there anyone who as a child saw some circus clown and wasn't frightened?

> *We frighten you because we walk through walls,*
> *Like ghosts, like saints, contagion;*
> *Everywhere is borderless to us,*
> *There are no borders to our nation.*
> *You cannot raise an army to defend,*
> *You cannot make a mirror that repels,*
> *You may expect that we will pay a toll,*
> *But do not waste your intake breath with spells.*
> *The only way for sure to kill the fear*
> *That we may walk right through the walls of you*
> *Is to knock them down,*
> *And then the fear is gone.*
> —Dragon Xcalibur, Ferryman

We scare people, plain and simple. For lots of reasons, we scare them. Well, that can be sexy too under the right circumstances, but in terms of political action we need to soften that fear with a sense of humor.

As part of a movement, we can educate, reform, succor, lobby, and protest. But who's got the energy to be part of a movement twenty-four hours a day, seven days a week, for all their lives? And when we're not being "politically active" as part of some group, it's gonna come down to one-on-one politics.

In *that* arena, we as fools can only shock into awareness, or seduce and recruit. As members of a political movement, yeah, we need to address gender. As individual fools, I don't think we should be shackled to any identity . . . not even transgender.

> *Sometimes I feel like a stranger.*
> *Sometimes I tell lies.*
> *Sometimes I act like a monkey.*
> *Here comes the night.*
> —Laurie Anderson

WHY HAVE YOU BEEN STUDYING AND PRACTICING ALL THIS

95 So, now you're near the end of this book. You know what gender can mean. You know how gender can connect with desire, fear, identity, power, and even spirituality. You have some tools to work with this stuff when you want to or need to. You have some tools to help form an integral politic around gender freedom. Are you done with gender? Is it something where you can put this book down with a sigh and say, "Wow, I got through it"? I don't think so.

Unfortunately or fortunately, depending on your point of view, the only way out of this gender trap seems to lie directly through the thick of it. We won't, I think, be able to fully abandon this system until a vast majority of people (starting with me and you) first choose to push its borders, experience its possibilities, and take responsibility for its impact on the condition of humanity. We may accomplish this and scare people as in the poem by Dragon Xcalibur excerpted above. Or we may choose another route: delight.

Here's a fun exercise for you: Take another read of M. Xcalibur's poem, only this time replace the word frighten *in the first line with the word* delight. *The piece works both ways.*

We *do* naturally frighten people. I think we need to take responsibility for that entirely predictable phenomenon. We need to consciously disarm and delight, and *delight* transcends politics. Delight is what we get, and get to give others as a result of putting all this work together and living it, if only a little bit every day.

It takes a great deal of courage to be delightful in this world. Whole religious systems have risen up, joined by governments, to outlaw delightful people. But who, more than delightful people, do we like to hang out with? I think our job now is to find out for ourselves exactly how we can best express our delight in this world, and how to best acknowledge others that are doing that. . . .

Text Credits

Rodolfo Acuña, "Occupied America" from *Occupied America: A History of Chicanos,* 4th ed. by Rodolfo Acuña. Copyright © 2000 by Rodolfo Acuña. Reprinted by permission of Addison-Wesley Educational Publishers, Inc.

Gloria Anzaldúa, "La conciencia de la Mestiza: Towards a New Consciousness" from *Borderlands/La Frontera: The New Mestiza.* Copyright 1987, 1999 by Gloria Anzaldúa. Reprinted by permission of Aunt Lute Books.

Alison Bailey, "Privilege" from *Journal of Social Philosophy* (Winter 1998), pp. 104–19. Reprinted by permission of Blackwell Publishing.

Karin Baker, "Bisexual Feminist Politics: Because Bisexuality Is Not Enough" from *Closer to Home,* edited by Elizabeth Reba Weise. Copyright © 1992 by Elizabeth Reba Weise. Reprinted by permission of the publisher, Seal Press.

Sandra Bartky, "On Psychological Oppression" from *Femininity and Domination* by Sandra Bartky. Copyright © 1990 by Routledge Press. Reprinted with permission of Routledge Press, a member of the Taylor-Francis Group.

Timothy Beneke, "Gay Sexism" and "Homophobia" from *Proving Manhood,* Timothy Beneke. Copyright © 1997 by University of California Press, Berkeley. Reprinted with permission of University of California Press, Berkeley.

Lawrence Blum, "Antiracism, Multiculturalism, and Interracial Community," reprinted with permission, Office of Graduate Studies and Research, University of Massachusetts, Boston, and Lawerence A. Blum. Copyright © Lawrence A. Blum.

James Boggs, "Black Power: A Scientific Concept Whose Time Has Come" from *Racism and the Class Struggle,* James Boggs and Grace Lee. Copyright © 1970 by Monthly Review Press. Reprinted with permission of Monthly Review Press.

Edna Bonacich, "Inequality in America." Copyright © 1989 from *Sociological Spectrum* 9:1 by Edna Bonacich. Reproduced by permission of Taylor and Francis, Inc., http://www.routledge-ny.com.

Kate Bornstein, "This Quiet Revolution" from *My Gender Workbook* by Kate Bornstein. Copyright © 1998 by Routledge Press. Reprinted with permission of Routledge Press, a member of the Taylor-Francis Group.

Elly Bulkin, "Breaking a Cycle," originally published in Elly Bulkin, Minnie Bruce Pratt and Barbara Smith, *Three Feminist Perspectives on Anti-Semitism and Racism.* Brooklyn, NY: Long Han 1 Press, 1984.

Charlotte Bunch, "Not for Lesbians Only" from *Materialist Feminism and the Politics of Discourse,* edited by Rosemary Hennessy and Chrys Ingraham. Reproduced by permission of Routledge/Taylor Francis Books, Inc.

Paulo Friere, from *Pedegogy of the Oppressed* by Paulo Freire, copyright © 1988 by Continuum International Publishing Group. Reprinted with permission of The Continuum International Publishing Group.

Marilyn Frye, "Oppression," reprinted with permission from *The Politics of Reality* by Marilyn Frye. Copyright 1983 by Marilyn Frye. The Crossing Press, a division of Ten Speed Press, Berkeley, CA 94707, www.tenspeed.com.

Marilyn Frye, "Willful Virgin or Do You Have to Be a Lesbian to Be a Feminist?" reprinted with permission from *Willfull Virgin* by Marilyn Frye. Copyright 1990 by Marilyn Frye. The Crossing Press, a division of Ten Speed Press, Berkeley, CA 94707, www.tenspeed.com.

Lewis R. Gordon, "Race, Biraciality and Mixed Race-in Theory" from *Her Majesty's Other Children*. Lanham, MD: Rowman & Littlefied, 1997. Reprinted by permission of Rowman & Littlefield.

Heidi Hartmann, "Towards a Definition of Patriarchy" from "The Unhappy Marriage of Marxism and Feminism," in *Women and Revolution,* edited by Lydia Sargent (Boston, MA: South End Press, 1981). Used by permission of South End Press.

Harry Hay, "Our Third Gender Responsibilities" and "Toward the New Frontiers of Fairy Vision" from *Radically Gay* by Will Roscoe. Copyright © 1996 by Harry Hay and Will Roscoe. Reprinted by permission of Beacon Press.

bell hooks, "Feminist Revolution: Development Through Struggle" from *Feminist Theory from Margin to Center* by bell hooks. Copyright © 1984 by South End Press. Reprinted by permission of South End Press.

bell hooks, "Overcoming White Supremacy" from *Talking Back: Thinking Feminist, Thinking Black* by bell hooks. Copyright © 1989 by South End Press. Reprinted by permission of South End Press.

Patrick D. Hopkins, "Gender Treachery" from *Rethinking Masculinity,* Patrick D. Hopkins. Copyright © 1992 by Rowman & Littlefield Publishers, Inc. Reprinted with permission of Rowman & Littlefield Publishers, Inc.

Paul Carlo Hornacek, "Anti-Sexist Consciousness-Raising Groups," originally published in *For Men Against Sexism*, ed. Jon Snodgrass. Times Change Press, 1977.

Noel Ignatiev, "Treason to Whiteness Is Loyalty to Humanity," used by permission of Noel Ignatiev, who is a founding editor of *Race Traitor.*

June Jordan, "Report from the Bahamas," reprinted by permission of the Estate of June Jordan and the Watkins/Loomis Agency.

Michael S. Kimmel, "Inequality and Difference" from *The Gendered Society* by Michael Kimmel, copyright 2000 by Michael Kimmel. Used by permission of Oxford University Press Inc.

Audre Lorde, "Age, Race, Class, and Sex: Women Redefining Difference," reprinted with permission from *Sister Outsider* by Audre Lorde. Copyright 1984 by Audre

Leonard Schein, "Dangers with Men's Consciousness-Raising Groups," originally published in *For Men Against Sexism*, ed. Jon Snodgrass. Times Change Press, 1977.

Carole J. Sheffield, from "Sexual Terrorism: The Social Control of Women" by Carole Sheffield. Copyright © 1988 by Sage Press. Reprinted with permission of Sage Press.

Elizabeth V. Spelman, "Gender & Race: The Ampersand Problem in Feminist Thought" from *Inessential Women* by Elizabeth V. Spelman. Copyright © 1988 by Elizabeth V. Spelman. Reprinted by permission of Beacon Press, Boston.

John Stoltenberg, "How Men Have (a) Sex" from *Refusing to be a Man* by John Stoltenberg. Copyright © Routledge Press. Reprinted with permission of Routledge Press, a member of the Taylor-Francis Group.

Lisa Tessman and Bat-Ami Bar On, "The Other Colors of Whiteness: A Travelogue" from *The Other Colors of Whiteness: A Travelogue,* edited by Chris J. Cuomo and Kim Q. Hall. Lanham, MD: Rowman & Littlefield, 1999. Reprinted by permission of Rowman & Littlefield.

Francisco Valdes, "Notes on the Conflation of Sex, Gender, and Sexual Orientation." Copyright © 1995 by the California Law Review. Reprinted from California Law Review Vol. 83, no. 1, by permission of the University of California, Berkeley.

Alice Walker, "Coming Apart" from *You Can't Keep a Good Woman Down*. Copyright © 1980 by Alice Walker. Reprinted by permission of Harcourt, Inc.

Gloria Yamato, "Something about the Subject Makes it Hard to Name" from *Making Face, Making Soul: Creative and Critical Perspectives by Women of Color,* edited by Gloria Andalzúa. Copyright © 1990 by Gloria Andalzúa.

Iris Young, "Five Faces of Oppression" from *Justice and the Politics of Difference*. Copyright © 1990 by Princeton University Press. Reprinted by permission of Princeton University Press.